CATALOGUE OF BOOKS

ADDED TO THE

LIBRARY OF CONGRESS,

FROM

DECEMBER 1, 1867, TO DECEMBER 1, 1868.

WASHINGTON:
GOVERNMENT PRINTING OFFICE.
1869.

LIST OF ABBREVIATIONS EMPLOYED.

anon. Anonymous.
b. l. Black letter.
ed. Edition.
fol. Folio. 4°. Quarto. 8°. Octavo. 12°. Duodecimo, etc.
l. Leaves.
n. p. No place of publication.
obl. Oblong.
pl. Plates.
p. l. Preliminary leaves.
pp. Pages.
pseudon. Pseudonymous.
sm. Small.
sq. Square.
unp. Unpaged.

The books are described as folio, quarto, octavo, duodecimo, etc., according to the apparent size of the volume, and not according to the printer's designations derived from the fold of the sheets.

In the alphabetical arrangement, the prefix *Mc, M'*, or *Mac*, is treated uniformly as a component part of the word, as if spelled *Mac*. Thus, *McLeod* or *M'Leod* precedes *Maclure*. In like manner, the prefixes *New, La, Du*, etc., are treated as component parts of the words to which they belong. Thus *New England* follows *Newell* instead of preceding it, as it would do if the prefix *New* were treated as a separate word.

It is one of the aims of the present catalogue to furnish with the titles a sufficiently full collation of each work. Thus it is made a part of the description to give the number of pages in the case of all works not exceeding two volumes, together with the number of maps and plates, if any, and the name of the publisher. The information thus conveyed will, it is believed, be found of practical value to readers, as conveying at a glance some idea of the extent of each work, while the addition of publishers' names is useful as supplying a guide to the identification of editions. In the case of books printed without date, the actual or approximate date is uniformly supplied, in brackets.

Brackets in any part of a title indicate that the words included in them are not found in the title, but are inserted.

The letter S, affixed to any title, denotes that the work belongs to the library of the Smithsonian Institution, now deposited with the Library of Congress.

CATALOGUE.

Abailard, Abaelard, Abeilard, *or* Abélard, (Pierre.) Lettres et épitres amoureuses d'Heloise et d'Abeilard. [Avec les épitres imitées et mises en vers, d'après la lettre de Pope, par Colardeau, Dorat, etc]. Nouv. éd. 2 v. xxiv, 178 pp.; viii, 194 pp. 2 pl. 32°. *Genève*, 1777.

Abano (Pietro d'). Heptameron or magical elements. By R. Turner. 16°. *London, J. Harrison*, 1783.

[*In* AGRIPPA von Nettesheim (H. C.) Occult philosophy. 1783. pp. 126–172].

Abbadie (Jacques, *D. D.*) Chemical change in the eucharist. In four letters, shewing the relations of faith to sense, from the French by J. W. Hamersley. 164 pp. 8°. *London, Low, Son, and Marston*, 1867.

Abbey (Henry L). Ralph, and other poems. 64 pp. sm. 4°. *Rondout, H. Fowks*, 1866.

Abbey (*Rev.* Richard). Diuturnity; or, the comparative age of the world, showing that the human race is in the infancy of its being, and demonstrating a reasonable and rational world, and its immense future duration. 360 pp. 12°. *Cincinnati, Applegate & Co.* 1866.

Abbot (*Bvt. Brig. Gen.* Henry Livermore). Siege artillery in the campaigns against Richmond, with notes on the 15-inch gun, including an algebraic analysis of the trajectory of a shot in its ricochets upon smooth waters. 183 pp. 6 pl. 8°. *Washington, gov't printing office*, 1867.

[UNITED STATES. (*War Department*). Professional papers corps of engineers. No. 14.]

Abbot (*Rev.* Hull). Jehovah's character as a man of war, illustrated and applied. A sermon preached at the desire of the hon. artillery company in Boston, June 2, 1735. 2 p. l. 35 pp. 8°. *Boston, D. Henchman*, 1735.

Abbott (*Rev.* Jacob). Mary Gay; or, work for girls. 4 v. 18°. *New York, Hurd & Houghton*, 1865.

CONTENTS.

v. 1. Work for spring. v. 2. Work for summer. v. 3. Work for autumn. v. 4. Work for winter.

——— The Rollo books. Rollo at work. [*anon.*] New ed. 159 pp. 4 pl. 18°. *New York, Sheldon & Co.* 1865.

——— ——— Rollo at play. [*anon.*] New ed. 191 pp. 4 pl. 18°. *New York, Sheldon & Co.* 1865.

——— ——— Rollo's museum. New ed. 187 pp. 5 pl. 16°. *New York, Sheldon & Co.* 1867.

——— ——— Rollo's travels. New ed. 189 pp. 4 pl. 16°. *New York, Sheldon & Co.* 1867.

——— ——— Rollo in Paris. 226 pp. 1 pl. 16°. *Boston, W. J. Reynolds & Co.* 1854. s.

Abbott (John Stevens Cabot). The child at home; or, the principles of filial duty familiarly illustrated. 318 pp. 16°. *New York, Harpers*, 1852.

——— The empire of Austria: its rise and present power. 520 pp. 1 pl. 12°. *New York, Mason brothers*, 1859.

——— The empire of Russia, from the remotest periods to the present time. 528 pp. 1 pl. 12°. *New York, Mason brothers*, 1860.

——— The history of Napoleon iii, emperor of the French. 690 pp. 9 pl. 8°. *Boston, B. B. Russell*, 1868.

——— Italy, from the earliest period to the present day. 587 pp. 1 pl. 12°. *New York, Mason brothers*, 1860.

——— The life of general Ulysses S. Grant. 309 pp. 3 pl. 8 maps. 12° *Boston, B. B. Russell*, 1868.

Abbott (*Mrs.* Rosa). *See* **Parker** (*Mrs.* Rosa Abbott).

Abd-er-rahman ben Mohammed El-Ishbílí El-Hadhremí, *known as* Ibn Khaldún. Ibn Khalduni narratio de expeditionibus Francorum in terras islamismo subjectas. E codicibus bodleianis edidit et latine vertit C. J. Tornberg. (Ex actis reg. soc. scient. Ups. tom vii.) 1 p. l. 154 pp. 4°. *Upsaliæ, Leffler & Sebell,* 1840. s.

Abel (Niels Henrik). Œuvres complètes; avec des notes et développements, rédigées par B. Holmboe. 2 v. xvi, 479 pp; 3 pl. 294 pp. 4°. *Christiania, C. Gröndahl,* 1839. s.

Abélard (Pierre). *See* **Abailard.**

Aben Hamin. *See* **Perez de Hita** (Ginez).

Abert (J. W.) Natural history [of California, New Mexico, etc.] 8°. *Washington, Wendell & Van Benthuysen,* 1848.

[*With* EMORY (W. H.) Notes of a military reconnoisance, etc.]

——— Report of his examination of New Mexico, 1846–47. 8°. *Washington, Wendell & Van Benthuysen,* 1848.

[*With* EMORY (W. H.) Notes of a military reconnoissance, etc]

Abich (Wilhelm Hermann). Vues illustratives de phénomènes géologiques, observés sur le Vesuve et l'Etna, 1833–34. (French and German). 16 pp. 10 pl. fol. *Berlin, J. Kuhr,* 1837. s.

Abolition a sedition. By a northern man. [*anon.*] viii, 187 pp. 18°. *Philadelphia, G. W. Donohue,* 1839.

Abraham Page, Esq. A novel. [*anon.*] 354 pp. 12°. *Philadelphia, J. B. Lippincott & Co,* 1868.

Abú Ali Hosein ben Abdallah Ibn Síná. *See* **Avicenna.**

Académie des sciences, *and* Académie française. *See* **Institut** impérial de France.

Académie royale de Belgique. Bibliothèque de m. le baron de Stassart, léguée à l'académie royale de Belgique. xiv, 1336 pp. 8°. *Bruxelles, M. Hayez,* 1863. s.

Accomplish'd (The) female instructor. [By R. G. *anon.*] 4 p. l. 182 pp. 18°. *London, J. Knapton,* 1704.

Account of the interment of the remains of American patriots who perished on board the British prison ships during the American revolution. [*anon.*] With notes and an appendix, by H. R. Stiles, M. D. 246 pp. 1 pl. 8°. *New York, privately printed,* 1865.

[WALLABOUT prison ship series, No. 2].

Account (An) of Louisiana, laid before Congress by direction of the President of the United States. [*anon.*] 72 pp. 18°. *Providence, Heaton and Williams,* (1804?)

Account (An) of the New York hospital. [*anon.*] 65 pp. 1 pl. 8°. *New York, Collins & Co.* 1811.

——— The same. [*anon.*] 62 pp. 2 pl. 8°. *New York, Mahlon Day,* 1820.

Acheta *and* **Acheta** domestica. [*pseudon.*] *See* **Budgen** (Miss L. M.)

Ackerman (Abraham). First book of natural history. 9th ed. 286 pp. 12°. *New York, Cady & Burgess,* 1846. s.

Across the Atlantic. By the author of "Sketches of Cantabs." [*anon.*] x, 274 pp. 16°. *London, G. Earle,* 1851.

Actæa. [*pseudon.*] *See* **Agassiz** (E. C.)

Adams (Andrew Leith, *M. D.*) Wanderings of a naturalist in India, the western Himalayas, and Cashmere. xi, 333 pp. 1 pl. 8°. *Edinburgh, Edmonston & Douglas,* 1867.

Adams (Arthur), *and* **White** (Adam). The zoology of the voyage of H. M. S. Samarang, 1843–46. Crustacea. viii, 66 pp. 13 pl. 4°. *London, Reeve, Bentham & Reeve,* 1848.

Adams (Charles, *D. D.*) Life of Oliver Cromwell. 268 pp. 4 pl. 16°. *New York, Carleton & Porter,* 1867.

Adams (Charles Baker). Catalogue of shells collected at Panama, with notes on their synonymy, station, and geographical distribution, (Extract.) viii, 5, 335 pp. 4°. *New York, Lyceum of natural history,* 1852. s.

Adams (Daniel, *M. D.*) Arithmetic, in which the principles of numbers are analytically explained and synthetically applied; [etc.] 261 pp. 12°. *Keene, N. H., J. W. Prentiss & Co.* 1854. s.

——— The same. New arithmetic; revised ed. 306 pp. 12°. *Keene, N. H., J. W. Prentiss & Co.* 1848.

——— Book-keeping; containing a lucid explanation of the common method of book-keeping by single entry; [etc.] 141 pp. 8° *Keene, N. H., J. W. Prentiss & Co.* 1849. s.

——— Geography; or, a description of the world. 11th ed. 324 pp. 5 pl. 16°. *Boston, Lincoln & Edmands,* 1828.

——— Key to Adams' new arithmetic. Revised ed. 88 pp. 12°. *Keene, N. H., J. W. Prentiss & Co.* 1848. s.

Adams (George, *jr. instrument maker*). Essays on the microscope; containing a practical description of the most improved microscopes; a general history of insects, [etc.] 2d ed. with additions, etc. by Frederick Kanmacher. xxiii, 724 pp. 1 pl. 4°. Atlas. 32 pl. obl. fol. *London, editor*, 1798.

Adams (H. G.) Nests and eggs of familiar British birds, described and illustrated; etc. iv, 79 pp. 8 col. pl. 16°. *London, Groombridge*, 1854. S.

Adams (John G.) Vestry harmonies: a collection of hymns and tunes for all occasions of social worship. 144 pp. 16°. *Boston, universalist publ. house*, 1868.

Adams (*Mrs.* J. S.) Branches of palm. 192 pp. 16°. *Boston, Adams & Co.* 1866.

Adams (*Rev.* William, *of Oxford*). The cherry stones; or, Charlton school. A tale for youth. Edited by the Rev. H. C. Adams. 243 pp. 4 pl. 16°. *New York, gen. prot. episcopal sunday school union*, 1851. S.

——— Les messagers du roi. Allegorie. 125 pp. 5 pl. 12°. *New York, union générale des écoles du dimanche*, 1855. S.

Adams (William, *D. D.*) Thanksgiving: memories of the day; helps to the habit. 372 pp. 12°. *New York, C. Scribner & Co.* 1867.

——— The three gardens: Eden, Gethsemane, and Paradise; or, man's ruin, redemption, and restoration. 284 pp. 12°. *New York, C. Scribner & Co.* 1868.

Adams (William T.) Breaking away; or, the fortunes of a student. By Oliver Optic. [*pseudon.*] 300 pp. 8 pl. 16°. *Boston, Lee & Shepard*, 1868.

——— Dikes and ditches; or, young America in Holland and Belgium. A story of travel and adventure. By Oliver Optic. [*pseudon.*] 346 pp. 3 pl. 16°. *Boston, Lee & Shepard*, 1868.

[Young America abroad series. v. 4].

——— Down the river; or, Buck Bradford and his tyrants. By Oliver Optic. [*pseudon.*] 303 pp. 7 pl. 16°. *Boston, Lee & Shepard*, 1868.

——— Freaks of fortune; or, half round the world. By Oliver Optic. [*pseudon.*] 303 pp. 8 pl. 16° *Boston, Lee & Shepard*, 1868.

——— Make or break; or, the rich man's daughter. By Oliver Optic. [*pseudon.*] 328 pp. 6 pl. 16° *Boston, Lee & Shepard*, 1869.

Adams (William T.) Our standard bearer; or, the life of general Ulysses S. Grant. As seen and related by captain Bernard Galligasken. And written out by Oliver Optic. [*pseudon.*] 348 pp. 6 pl. 16°. *Boston, Lee & Shepard*, 1868.

——— The red cross; or, young America in England and Wales. A story of travel and adventure. By Oliver Optic. [*pseudon.*] 336 pp. 4 pl. 16°. *Boston, Lee & Shepard*, 1868.

[Young America abroad series. v. 3].

——— Seek and find; or, the adventures of a smart boy. By Oliver Optic. [*pseudon.*] 304 pp. 5 pl. 16°. *Boston, Lee & Shepard*, 1868.

——— Shamrock and thistle; or, young America in Ireland and Scotland. A story of travel and adventure. By Oliver Optic. [*pseudon.*] 343 pp. 4 pl. 16°. *Boston, Lee & Shepard*, 1868.

[Young America abroad series. v. 2].

——— The way of the world. A novel. 464 pp. 12°. *Boston, Lee & Shepard*, 1867.

Addington (Richard D.) History of the courtship and marriage and subsequent married life of Dr. R. D. Addington and Mrs Hannah E. Weed, at Richmond, Va. [etc.] 140 pp. 8°. *Richmond, author*, 1857. S.

Addison (Joseph). The free-holder; or, political essays. 4 p. l. 316 pp. 4 l. 16°. *London, J. & R. Tonson*, 1761.

——— The whig examiner. 59 pp. 18°. *London, John Darby*, 1712.

[*With* MEDLEYS (The). *London*, 1712].

Address (An) to lord Byron, with an opinion of some of his writings. By F. H. B. [*anon.*] 16 pp. 8°. *London, Wetton & Jarvis*, 1817.

[MISCELLANEOUS pamphlets, v. 56].

Address (An) to the people of the state of New York, on the subject of the constitution, agreed upon at Philadelphia, September 17, 1787. [*anon.*] 19 pp. 4°. *New York, S. & J. Loudon*, [1787].

Adelung (Johann Christoph). Three philological essays, chiefly translated from the German. cxxxii pp. 8°. [*London, T. N. Longman*, 1798].

[*With* KANT'S elements of critical philosophy].

CONTENTS:

I. History of the English language, its changes and gradual improvement.
II. Philosophical view of the English language.
III. On the relative merits and demerits of Johnson's English dictionary.

Adolphus (John). The history of England, from the accession of king George iii. to the conclusion of peace in 1783. 4th ed. revised. 3 v. 8°. *London, Cadell & Davies*, 1817.

Adriano de' Castelli (*Cardinal S. Chrysogoni*). De sermone latino et de modis latine loquendi. Eiusdem uenatio ad Ascanium cardinalem. Item iter Julij ii, pontificis romani. 8 p. l. 429 pp. 16°. *Coloniæ Agrippinæ, apud J. Gymnicum*, 1578. s.

Adventure (The) of hunch-back. *See* **Arabian** nights' entertainments.

Adye (Stephen Payne). A treatise on courts martial. Also, an essay on military punishments and rewards. 4th ed. viii, 284 pp. 12°. *London, J. Murray*, 1797.

Ægidius (*Columna or Romanus*). *See* **Colonna** (Egidio).

Ælianus. De instruendis aciebus opvs, [etc.]
[*With* VEGETIUS (F.) De re militari, 1585].

Æschines. Oration against Ctesiphon. With notes. By J. T. Champlin. New ed. xii, 178 pp. 12°. *Boston, W. H. Dennet*, 1868.

——— Quæ supersunt.
[ORATORVM græcorvm, etc. Ed. Reiske, v. 3–4].

——— *See* **Demosthenes** *and* **Æschines.**

Æschylus. Persæ. Ad fidem librorum manuscriptorum et editionum antiquarum emendarunt, [etc.] E. R. Langeus et G. Pinggerus. xvi, 307 pp. 8°. *Berolini, Duncker & Humblot*, 1825. s.

Æsopus. Fabellæ aliqvot æsopicæ, in usum puerorum selectæ. 92 pp. 32°. *Antverpiæ, C. Plantin*, 1586.
[*With* JUNIUS (A.) Emblemata, 1596].

——— The same. Esop's fables, written in Chinese by the learned Mun Mooy Seen-Shang, and compiled in their present form (with a free and literal translation) by his pupil Sloth, [Robert Thom]. 4 p. l. xxix, 104 pp. 4°. *Canton, Press office*, 1840. s.

——— The same. Fables, with illustrations by H. L. Stephens. Lithographed by J. Bien. x, 76 pp. 56 pl. 4°. *New York, Scribner*, 1868.

Æsop at court; or, the labyrinth of Versailles delineated in French and English. [*anon.*] From the Paris ed. [Illustrated] by G. Bickham. pp. 209–260. 44 pl. 4°. *London*, 1768.
[*In* BELLAMY (D.) Ethic amusements. 4°. *London*, 1761].

African (The) repository, Jan. to Dec. 1867. v. 43. 8°. *Washington, Am. col. soc.* 1867.

Agardh (Jacob Georg). Theoria systematis plantarum; accedit familiarum phanerogamarum in series naturales dispositio, secundum structuræ normas et evolutionis gradus instituta. 3 p. l. xcvi, 404 pp. 2 l. Atlas. 32 l. 28 pl. 8°. *Lundæ, C. W. K. Gleerup*, 1858. s.

Agassiz (*Mrs.* Elizabeth Carey). A first lesson in natural history. [Sea-anemones and corals; coral reefs; hydroids and jelly-fishes; star-fishes and sea-urchins]. By Actæa. [*pseudon.*] 82 pp. 12°. *Boston, Little, Brown & Co.* 1859. s.

Agassiz (Louis Jean Rudolf). An essay on classification. viii, 381 pp. 8°. *London, Longmans*, 1859. s.

——— Memoir of Hugh Miller.
[*In* MILLER (H.) Foot-prints of the Creator].

——— *and* (*Mrs.* Elizabeth Carey). A journey in Brazil. xix, 540 pp. 8 pl. 8°. *Boston, Ticknor & Fields*, 1868.

Age (L') de papier, études financières et autres. [*anon.*] 312 pp. 16°. *Paris, librairie des assurances*, 1866.

Agnes Morris; or, the heroine of domestic life. [*anon.*] 143 pp. 12°. *New York, Harpers*, 1849. s.

Ago (Felix, *pseudon.*) *See* **Rhymes** of the poets.

Agoult (Marie de Flavigny, *comtesse d'*). Nélida, por Daniel Stern. [*pseudon.*] Traduccion de M. Urrabieta. 240 pp. 8°. *Burgos, P. Polo*, 1847. s.

Agreement (The) of the customs of the East Indians with those of the Jews and other ancient people. [*anon.*] xiv, 159 pp. 6 pl. 8°. *London, W. Davis*, 1705.

Agriculture anatomiz'd; or, a new treatise of husbandry, containing a plain and practical method of improving all sorts of land. With an account how the tillage of Ireland may be improved by a cheap manure. [*anon.*] iv, 102 pp. 8°. *Dublin, J. Hoey*, 1746.

Agrippa von Nettesheim (Heinrich Cornelius). Fourth book of occult philosophy and geomancy. First translated by R. Turner. 319 pp. 2 l. 16°. [*London*, 1783].

Aguilar (Grace). Home influence; a tale for mothers and daughters. [With memoir of the author]. New ed. xvii, 386 pp. 12°. *New York, Appleton*, 1866.

——— The spirit of Judaism. Edited by I. Leeser. 2d ed. 216 pp. 18°. *Philadelphia, Jewish publ. soc.* 5609 [1849].
[JEWISH miscellany, no. xiii].

——— Woman's friendship; a story of domestic life. 357 pp. 1 pl. 12°. *New York, Appleton*, 1867.

Ahmad bin Abubeker bin Wahshih. Ancient alphabets and hieroglyphic characters explained; with an account of the Egyptian priests, their classes, initiation and sacrifices,

Ahmad—continued.
in the Arabic language. And in English by Joseph Hammer. xxi, 190 pp. 4°. *London, W. Bulmer & Co.* 1806. s.

Ahn (Friedrich). Praktischer lehrgang zur schnellen und leichten erlernung der englischensprache. Nebst angabe der aussprache mit deutschen tönen, von J. C. Oehlschläger. 2er. cursus. 122 pp. 12°. *Philadelphia, J. Weit & Co.* 1858. s.

Aigner (Hans von). Tabellen für den kubikinhalt runder Stammhölzer, [etc.] iv, 38 pp. 12°. *Breslau, T. U. Kern*, 1863. s.

Aiken (William, *M. D.*) The science and practice of medicine. 2d American, from 5th London ed. Revised and enlarged; with large additions, by Meredith Clymer, M. D. 2 v. 927 pp. 1 pl; 1079 pp. 1 map. 8°. *Philadelphia, Lindsay & Blakiston*, 1868.

Aimwell (Walter, *pseudon.*) *See* **Simonds** (W.)

Ainslie (Whitelaw, *M. D.*) Materia indica; or, some account of those articles which are employed by the Hindoos and other eastern nations in their medicine, arts, and agriculture, [etc.] 2 v. xxiv, 654 pp; xxxix, 604 pp. 8°. *London, Longman*, 1826 s.

——— Medical observations.
[*With* MURRAY (H.) Historical account of British India, v. 3].

Ainsworth (William Harrison). Rookwood; a romance. From the 2d London ed. 2 v. in 1. 204 pp; 208 pp. 12°. *Philadelphia, Carey, Lea & Blanchard*, 1836.
[Imperfect. Title v. 1 wanting].

Airy (George Biddell). On the laws of the tides on the coasts of Ireland. [Extract]. 124 pp. 1 map. 4°. *London, Royal society*, 1845. s.

——— Mathematical tracts on the lunar and planetary theories, the figure of the earth, precession and mutation, the calculus of variations, and the undulatory theory of optics. 4th ed. vi, 400 pp. 2 pl. 8°. *Cambridge, Macmillan & Co.* 1858. s.

——— Tides and waves. [Extract]. 156 pp. 6 pl. 4°. [*London, Encyclopædia britannica*, 1845]. s.

Akademische monatsschrift. Centralorgan für die gesammtinteressen deutscher universitäten. Herausgegeben under der mitwirkung der herren professoren dr. Bluhme in Bonn, dr. Bülau, dr. Erdmann in Leipzig, dr. Hoffmann in Würzburg, hofrath dr. Oppolzer in Wien, geheimrath dr. V. Vangerow in Heidelberg, und anderer akademischer lehrer von dr. J. L. Lang und dr. H. Th. Schletter. Der "Deutschen universitäts-zeitung." 3r — 6r jahrg. 4 v. 8°. *Leipzig, H. Bethmann*, 1851–54. s.
[Jahrg. 1853, pp. 113–128; 1854, heft 4 wanting].

Aken (Herrmann von). Verzeichniss sämmtlicher thiere, welche sich in [seiner] menagerie befinden. 26 pp. 1 pl. 8°. *Hamburg, F. W. C. Menck*, 1830. s.

Alabama (*State of*). Official journal of the constitutional convention, held in Montgomery, commencing Nov. 5th, 1867. iii, 291 pp. 8°. *Montgomery, Barrett & Brown*, 1868.

Alamanni (Luigi). La coltivatione di Luigi Alamanni, e le api di Giovanni Rucellai. Con annotazione del dottor Giuseppe Bianchini da Prato, sopra la coltivazione, e di Roberto Titti sopra le api. 88, 323 pp. 8°. *Milano, Societá tipografica de classici italiani*, 1804.

Alarcón (Felix de). Loa para la coronacion de Fernando el vi. 21 l. 8°. [*Lima?*] 1748. s.
[*With* MANSO DE VELASCO (J.) El dia de Lima, 1748].

Alauzet (François Isidore). Des sociétés dites de coopération. 15 pp. 8°. *Paris, Cosse, Marchal & Cie.* 1866.

Albany (*City of*). Albany directory and city register for 1851–52. 2 v. 12°. *Albany, J. Munsell*, 1851–52. s.

Albert (J. F. M.) Recherches sur les principes fondamentaux de la classification bibliographique. vii, 63 pp. 8°. *Paris, auteur*, 1847. s.

Albertano da Brescia. De doctrina dicendi et tacendi. 7 l. 4°. *Nurnberge, fratres ordinis Augustini*, 1479.
[*With* GEWS (J.) Tractatus de viciis lingue. *Nurnberge*, 1479].

Alberti (Leandro). Descrittione della decimanona regione della Italia. [Corografie dell' Istria, n. 4.] s.
[*In* ROSSETTI (D. de). Archeografo triestino, v. 2].

Albertus Magnus. De mineralibus, libri i–v. 28 l. fol. *Papie, per Christophorum de canibus*, 1491.
[*With* ARISTOTELES. Questiones Johannis Versoris super libros ethicorum. *Coloniæ*, 1491].

——— Libellus aureus de adhærendo Deo. 51 pp. 24°. *Coloniæ, J. M. Heberle & Co.* 1851.

——— Liber de laudibus gloriosissime Dei genitricis Marie. 189 l. fol. [*Basiliæ, Wensler, about* 1470?]. s.

——— Tractatus de virtutibus, [etc.]; scd'm alios vocatus paradisus anime. 34 l. 8°. *Meming*, [*about* 1475?]. s.

Albinus (Flaccus). *See* **Alcuinus** (Flaccus).

Albrecht (Heinrich Christoph). Materielen zu einer kritischen geschichte der freymaurerey. Erste sammlung. x, 199 pp. 18°. *Hamburg, F. Bachman,* 1792.

CONTENTS:

I. G. E. Lessing's Meinung über den ursprung und zweck der freymaurerey.
II. Die constitutionen der englischen freymaurer.

NOTE.—No more published.

Album der natuur. Een werk ter verspreiding van natuurkennis onder beschaafde lezers van allerlei stand. 1852–56. 5 v. 8°. *Haarlem, A. C. Kruseman,* 1852–56. s.

——— The same. Onder redactie van P. Harting, D. Lubach, en W. M. Logeman. Nieuwe reeks. 1857–62. 6 v. 8°. *Haarlem, A. C. Kruseman,* 1857–62. s.

Alcedo y Bexarano (Antonio de). Atlas to Thompson's Alcedo; or, dictionary of America and the West Indies. By Aaron Arrowsmith. 1 p. l. 5 maps in 19 sheets. fol. *London, G. Smeeton,* 1816.

Alciati (Andrea). Libellvs de magistratib. ciuilibusq; ac militaribus officijs. s.

[*With* Notitia vtraqve cvm orientis tvm occidentis, 1552].

——— Omnia emblemata. Adiecta ad calcem notæ posteriores, per C. Minoem. 18 p. l. 818 pp. 11 l. 16°. *Parisiis, Iohannes Richerius,* 1589.

Alcidama. Quæ supersunt.

[ORATORVM græcorvm, etc. Ed. Reiske. v. viii.]

Alcott (Louisa M.) Aunt Kipp. "Children and fools speak the truth." 16 pp. 8°. *Boston, Loring,* [1868].

——— Kitty's class day. "A stitch in time saves nine." 12 pp. 8°. *Boston, Loring,* 1868.

——— Little women; or, Meg, Jo, Beth, and May. 341 pp. 4 pl. 16°. *Boston, Roberts brothers,* 1868.

——— Morning glories, and other stories. 195 pp. 4 pl. 16°. *Boston, H. B. Fuller,* 1868.

——— Psyche's art. "Handsome is that handsome does." 16 pp. 8°. *Boston, Loring,* 1868.

Alcott (William A. *M. D.*) The life of Robert Morrison, the first protestant missionary to China. 132 pp. 2 pl. 16°. *New York, Carlton & Phillips,* 1856. s.

——— Tall oaks from little acorns; or, sketches of distinguished persons of humble origin. 369 pp. 6 pl. 16°. *New York, Carlton & Phillips,* 1856. s.

Alcuinus (Flaccus). De pontificibus et sanctis ecclesiæ eboracensis, poema. fol. *Oxoniæ,* 1691.

[GALE (T.) and FELL (J.) Rerum anglicarum scriptores veteres. *Oxoniæ,* 1684–91. v. 3.]

Alden (Henry M.) Harpers' pictorial history of the rebellion. *See* **Guernsey** (A. H.) *and* **Alden.**

Alden (Joseph, *D. D.*) Alice Gordon; or, the uses of orphanage. 198 pp. 16°. *New York, Harpers,* [1847]. s.

——— The lawyer's daughter. 186 pp. 1 pl. 16°. *New York, Harpers,* [1847]. s.

——— Our father; or, considerations relating to the Lord's prayer. 107 pp. 18°. *Philadelphia, presbyterian board of publication,* [1846]. s.

——— A text book of ethics for union schools and bible classes. 92 pp. 16°. *New York, A. S. Barnes & Co.,* 1869.

Aler (Paul). Gradus ad Parnassum; sive novus synonymorum, epithetorum, versuum ac phrasium poeticarum thesaurus, [etc.] Ab uno e societate Jesu. [*anon.*] Ed. à Thoma Morell. 667 pp. 8°. *Londini, soc. stationariorum,* 1802. s.

Alexander (Alexander, *claiming to be 9th Earl of Stirling*). Narrative of the oppressive law proceedings resorted to by the British government and numerous private individuals to overpower the earl of Stirling. Also, a genealogical account of the family of Alexander, earls of Sterling, etc. Followed by an historical view of their possessions in Nova Scotia, Canada, etc. vi, 259. 4°. *Edinburgh, J. Walker,* 1836.

Alexander (Archibald, *D. D.*) Biographical sketches of the founder, and principal alumni of the Log college. [With] an account of the revivals of religion, under their ministry. 369 pp. 12°. *Princeton, (N. J.), J. T. Robinson,* 1845.

——— A brief compend of bible truth. 207 pp. 1 pl. 8°. *Philadelphia, presbyterian board of publication,* 1846. s.

——— Outlines of moral science. 272 pp. 12°. *New York, C. Scribner,* 1852. s.

——— Thoughts on religious experiences. [With] an appendix containing letters to the aged. 1 p. l. 397 pp. 12°. *Philadelphia, presbyterian board of publication,* 1868.

Alexander (James Waddell). The American sunday-school and its adjuncts. 342 pp. 12°. *Philadelphia, American sunday-school union,* 1856. s.

——— Thoughts on family-worship. 2 p. l. 260 pp. 1 pl. 12°. *Philadelphia, presbyterian board of publication,* [1847]. s.

Alexander (John Henry). Reports on the standards of weight and measure for the state of Maryland, and on the construction of the yard measures. iv, 213 pp. 8°. *Baltimore,* [1845]. s.

Alexander (William). The eight beatitudes, St. Matthew, chap. v. With the Lord's Prayer. 11 pl. obl. 8°. *London, W. Jackson,* [*about* 1850].

Alexander (William, *of Texas*). Elements of discord in secessia, etc. 16 pp. 8°. *New York, W. C. Bryant & Co.* 1863.

[LOYAL publication society. No. 15.]

Alexandria (*Va.*) library. Catalogue. 61 pp. 8°. *Washington, G. S. Gideon,* 1856.

Alford (*Rev.* L. A.) The great atonement illustrated. A poem. 123 pp. 16°. *Cincinnati, J. Sherer,* 1868.

——— Masonic gem; consisting of odes, poem and dirge. Being a miniature sketch of esoteric and exoteric masonry. 48 pp. 12°. *Cincinnati, Homan, Abraham & Co.* 1867.

Alfriend (Frank H.) The life of Jefferson Davis. xvii, 645 pp. 1 portrait. 8°. *Cincinnati, Caxton publishing house,* 1868.

Alger (Horatio, *jr.*) Ragged Dick; or, street life in New York with the boot-blacks. 296 pp. 4 pl. 16°. *Boston, Loring,* 1868.

Alger (William Rounseville). The friendships of women. xvi, 416 pp. 12°. *Boston, Roberts bros.* 1868.

Algerine (The) slaves: a poem. By a citizen of Newburyport. [*anon.*] 16°. *Newburyport,* 1798.

[*With* FOSS (John). Journal of captivity. 1798].

Alhoy (Philadelphe-Maurice). Physiologie du voyageur. Vignettes de Daumier et Janet-Lange. 126 pp. 16°. *Paris, Aubert & Cie. and Lavigne,* [1841].

——— Physiologie du créancier et du debiteur. 116 pp. 16°. *Paris, Aubert & Lavigne,* [1841].

[*With* HUART (Louis). Physiologie du garde national].

Alibert (Jean Louis, *baron*). Physiologie des passions, ou nouvelle doctrine des sentimens moraux. 2 v. 2 p. l. lxxv, 372 pp; 2 p. l. 472 pp. 8°. *Paris, Bechet jeune,* 1825. s.

Alibert (J. P. *editor*). La mine de graphite de Sibérie découverte en 1847 par J. P. Alibert. Comtes-rendus des académies, des societés savantes et des journaux. [*anon.*] 134 pp. 7 pl. 8°. *Paris, imprimèrie Poitevin,* 1865. s.

Alison (William Pulteney, *M. D.*) Observations on the management of the poor in Scotland, and its effects on the health of the great towns. xv, 123 pp. 12°. *Edinburgh, Blackwood,* 1840.

All the year round. A weekly journal. Conducted by Charles Dickens. June, 1867—June, 1868. v. 18–19. 8°. *London, Chapman & Hall,* 1867–68.

Allan Cameron; or, the three birthdays. By the author of "Ilverton rectory," etc. [*anon.*] 184 pp. 3 pl. 18°. *New York, Am. tract soc.* [1864].

Alleghania; or, praises of American heroes. By Christopher Laomedon Pindar. [*pseudon.*] 148 pp. 16°. *Philadelphia, Lippincott & Co.* 1868.

Allen (Ann H.) The young lady's new oracle. 311 pp. 1 pl. 12°. *Cincinnati, E. Mendenhall,* 1857. s.

Allen (Carl Ferdinand, *editor*). Breve og aktstykker til oplysning af Christiern den andens, og Frederik den forstes historie. v. 1. xxxviiii, 715 pp. 8°. *Kjöbenhavn, C. A. Reitzel,* 1854. s.

[Wanting, v. 2, etc].

Allen (*Miss* Elizabeth). The silent harp; or, fugitive poems. 120 pp. 16°. *Burlington,* (*Vt.*) *E. Smith,* 1832.

Allen (Ethan, *D. D.*) Clergy in Maryland of the protestant episcopal church since 1783. 106 pp. 8°. *Baltimore, J. S. Waters,* 1860.

Allen (Lewis F.) American cattle: their history, breeding, and management. 528 pp. 1 pl. 12°. *New York, Taintor bros. & Co.* 1868.

——— The American herd book, containing pedigrees of short-horn cattle. v. 7. 597 pp. 53 pl. 8°. *Buffalo, Franklin printing house,* 1866.

Allen (*Rev.* L. L.) Pencillings of scenes upon the Rio Grande [during the war with Mexico]. 48 pp. 16°. *New York,* 1848.

Allen (Martha). Day-dreams. 154 pp. 12°. *Philadelphia, Lippincott & Co.* 1852. s.

Allen (William, *D. D.*) Account of Arnold's expedition against Quebec in 1775. 8°. *Portland, Day, Fraser & Co.* 1831.

[MAINE historical society. Collections, v. 1].

Allen (William H.) Eulogy on the character and services of the late Daniel Webster, [etc.] 51 pp. 8°. *Philadelphia, Crissy & Markley,* 1853. s.

Allen Prescott; or, the fortunes of a New England boy. By the author of "The young emigrants." [*anon.*] 2 v. 212 pp; 222 pp. 12°. *New York, Harpers,* 1834.

Alletz (Pierre Édouard). Harmonies de l'intelligence humaine. 2 v. xix, 367 pp; 2 p. l. 406 pp. 8°. *Paris, Parent-Desbarres,* 1846. s.

Allgemeine historie der reisen zu wasser und lande; oder sammlung aller reisebeschreibungen, welche in verschiedenen sprachen von allen völkern herausgegeben worden; ins deutsche ubersetzet [von A. C. Kästner, J. J. Schwabe, und andern]. v. 1–18. 4°. *Leipzig, Arkstee & Merkus*, 1747–64. s.

[*Note.*—Volumes 19–21 wanting].

CONTENTS.

v. 1. Einleitung. Von dem ursprunge und fortgange der schiffahrt und handlung.
Die ersten reisen der Portugiesen nach Ostindien.
Die ersten reisen der Engländer nach Guinea und Ostindien.
v. 2. Reisen nach verschiedenen theilen von Africa und den angränzenden eylanden.
v. 2–3. Die reisen langst der westlichen küste von Africa, von Capo Blanco bis nach Sierra Leona.
v. 3. Reisen nach Guinea und Benin.
v. 3–4. Beschreibung von Guinea.
v. 4. Beschreibung der küsten von Rio da Volta bis an das vorgebirge Lope Gonsalvo.
Schiffahrten und reisen nach Guinea und Benin, Kongo und Angola.
v. 4–5. Beschreibung der königreiche Loango, Kongo, Angola, Benzuela und den angränzenden ländern.
v. 5. Beschreibung der länder längst der ostlichen küste von Africa, vom vorgebirge der Guten Hoffnung nach capo Guarda Fuy.
Reisen nach dem reiche China.
v. 6. Beschreibung von China.
v. 6–7. Beschreibung von Korea, der westlichen Tartarey und Tibet.
v. 7. Reisen durch die Tartarey, Tibet and Bucharey, nach und von China.
v. 8. Reisen der Hollander nach Ostindien.
Reisen der Franzosen nach Ostindien.
v. 9. George Juan und Antonio de Ulloa reise nach Süd-America.
v. 10–11. Reisen der Franzosen und anderer nach Ostindien.
v. 12. Reisen nach Ostindien durch Südwest.
Reisen nach den Südländern.
Irrende reisen, oder solche, die kein gewisses vorgesetztes ziel haben.
v. 13. Erste reisen, entdeckungen und niederlassungen der Europäer in America.
v. 14. Geschichte und beschreibung von Neu-Frankreich, durch Charlevoix.
v. 15. Fortsetzung der reisen, entdeckungen und niederlassungen in America.
v. 16. Fortsetzung der reisen, entdeckungen und niederlassungen in dem Südlichen America.
v. 17. Fortsetzung der reisen, entdeckungen und niederlassungen in Nordamerica.
Reisen und niederlassungen auf den Antillen.
v. 18. Zusätze zu dem viii–xii bandes aus dem x bande der hollandischen ausgabe.

All-round (The) route guide. [New York, Canada, and New England]. 86 pp. 18°. *Montreal, Montreal publ. co.* 1868.

Allyn (William G.) Allyn's exchange tables, [etc.] for computing profit and loss, interest and exchange, [etc.] Also discount and advance tables. 2 p. l. 180 pp. 8°. *Buffalo, Faxon & Read*, 1841. s.

Almanac and congressional directory for 1834. *See* **United** States congressional directory.

Almanach et directorium français des États-Unis, pour 1868. 21e année. 124 pp. 12°. *New York, J. D. Zender*, [1868].

Almanach de Gotha. *See* **Gothaischer** hof kalender.

Almaraz (Ramon, *director*). Memoria de los trabajos ejecutados por la comision cientifica de Pachuca en el año de 1863, [etc.] Mandada publicar de orden de S. M. J. por el ministerio de fomento. 358 pp. 3 maps. 6 pl. 5 tab. 8°. *Mexico, Andrade y Escalante*, 1865. s.

Almon (John). Parliamentary register. *See* **Great Britain**.

Almonte (Juan Nepomuceno). Guia de forasteros y repertorio de conocimientos utiles. viii. 638 pp. 3 maps. 1 pl. 1 tab. 16°. *Mexico, J. Cumplido*, 1852. s.

Alpino (Prospero). De plantis Aegypti liber, [etc]. Accessit etiam liber de balsamo alias editus. 4 p. l. 88 l. 4°. *Venetiis, apud Franciscum de Franciscis Senensem*, 1592.

——— The presages of life and and death in diseases. In which the whole Hippocratic method of predicting the terminations and events of diseases is illustrated and confirmed. Translated by R. James. 2 v. xi, 386 pp. 12 l.; 2 p. l. 359 pp. 18 l. 8°. *London, G. Strahan*, 1746.

Alsop (Samuel). An elementary treatise on Algebra. 288 pp. 12°. *Philadelphia, E. C. & J. Biddle*, 1846. s.

——— The same. A treatise on algebra. 3d ed. 323 pp. 12°. *Philadelphia, E. C. & J. Biddle*, 1855. s.

——— First lessons in algebra. 116 pp. 12°. *Philadelphia, E. C. & J. Biddle*, 1849 s.

——— Key to first lessons in algebra. 73 pp. 12°. *Philadelphia, E. C. & J. Biddle*, 1850. s.

——— The same. New ed. 88 pp. 12°. *Philadelphia, E. C. & J. Biddle*, 1853. s.

Alton (Johann Samuel Eduard d'). De monstrorum duplicium origine atque evolutione commentatio. 49 pp. 4°. *Halis, formis plœtzianis*, 1848. s.

Alvarez (Alónso). Progress and intelligence of Americans, founded upon the normal and absolute servitude of inferior animates to mankind, as indicated by the order of nature and by the acts of creation, as laid down in the bible: progress of that servitude South and Southwest, as new territory may be acquired. Translated by the author. 595, xvii pp. 8°. [*New York*] ? *author*, 1865.

Alvarez (Francisco). Noticia del establecimiento y poblacion de las colonias inglesas en la America Septentrional. 196 pp. 8°. *Madrid, A. Fernandez*, 1778.

Alvarez de Velasco (Gabriel). Epitoma de legis hvmanæ, mvndiqve fictione, veritatis divinæ, æterni, temporalisque differentia. 56 pp. 8 l. 416 pp. 36 l. 4°. *Lvgdvni, H. Boissat & G. Remevs*, 1662. s.

Alvensleben (Maximilian von). With Maximilian in Mexico. From the note-book of a Mexican officer. x, 289 pp. 12°. *London, Longmans*, 1867.

Amadis de Gaule. Le thrésor des dovze livres d'Amadis de Gaule: assauoir, les harangues, concions, epistres, complaintes, et autres choses les plus excellentes et dignes du lecteur françois. 12 p. l. 192 l. 12°. *Paris, I. Longis & R. le Mangnier*, 1560.

Amati (Amato). Il risorgimento del comune di Milano. 2 p. l. 349 pp. 12°. *Milano, A. Lombardi*, 1865. s.

Amberg (Hans Christian). Fuldstændig dansk og tydsk ordbog. 2 v. in 1. 598 pp; 614 pp. 8°. *Kjöbenhavn, Gyldendal*, 1810. s.

[*Companion to* BADEN (I.) Fuldstændig tydsk og dansk ordbog].

Ambition. By Kate Willis. [*pseudon. for* Sarah E. Coolidge]? 318 pp. 12°. *Boston, J. French & Co.* 1856. s.

Ambrosius (*Saint, bishop of Milan*). Libri tres de officiis. 115 l. Sm. 4°. [*Coloniae, Vdalricus Zell, about* 1470].

Ambrosoli (Carlo). Su le funziono del nervo gran simpatico. *See* **Lussana** (F. *and* P), *and* **Ambrosoli.**

American (The) advertiser; designed for the cards and advertisements of the leading business establishments of the United States. 180 pp. 16°. *New York, J. P. Hall*, 1849.

[*With* BELDEN (E. P.) New York; past, present, and future. 1850].

American (The) advertising directory for manufacturers and dealers in American goods, 1831. 395 pp. 16°. *New York, Jocelyn, Darling & Co.* 1831.

American agricultural annual. 1868. 152 pp. 12°. *New York, O. Judd & Co.* 1868.

American (The) agriculturist; designed to improve the farmer, the stockbreeder, and the horticulturist. A. B. Allen, R. L. Allen, and Solon Robinson, editors. April 1842 to Dec. 1851. v. 1–10. 8°. *New York, C. M. Saxton*, 1845–51.

——— The same. A. B. Allen and O. Judd, editors. Sept. 1853 to Dec. 1867. v. 11–26. 4°. *New York, Allen & Co. and O. Judd*, 1853–67.

American (The) anti-slavery society. Annual report for 1860. 337 pp. 8°. *New York, Amer. anti-slav. soc.* 1861.

American bee journal. Edited by Samuel Wagner. v. 1. 1861. 2 p. l. 484 pp. 8°. *Philadelphia, A. M. Spangler*, [1861.]

American board of commissioners for foreign missions. First ten annual reports. 321 pp. 8°. *Boston, Crocker & Brewster*, 1834.

American (The) cyclops, the hero of New Orleans, and spoiler of silver spoons, dubbed LL. D. By Pasquino. [*pseudon.*] 27 pp. 12 pl. sm. 4°. *Baltimore, Kelly & Piet*, 1868.

American (The) eclectic medical review. Editors, R. S. Newton and P. A. Morrow. June, 1866, to June, 1868. v. 1–3 in 2 v. 8°. *New York, J. F. Trow & Co.* 1866–68.

American ephemeris and nautical almanac. *See* **United States** (Navy Department).

American (The) farmer: a monthly journal devoted to agriculture and horticulture, domestic and rural economy. [1867]. v. 2. 384 pp. 8 pl. 8°. *Rochester, N. Y, J. Turner*, 1867.

American (The) gazette: a collection of all the authentic addresses, memorials, etc. which relate to the disputes between Great Britain and the colonies. Nos. 1–5. in 1 v. 3d ed. 320 pp. 8°. *London, G. Kearsly*, 1768–69.

American gazette (The). By several gentlemen from America. No. 2–4. Feb. 20—Mar. 5, 1776. 20 pp. *London, T. W. Shaw*, 1776.

[*With* CRISIS (The). No. 17–64. 1775–76. NOTE.—No. 4, imperfect].

American homœopathic observer: a monthly journal devoted to the interests of homœopathic physicians. Jan. 1866 to Dec. 1868. v 3–5. 8°. *Detroit, Dr. E. A. Lodge*, 1866–68.

American (The) Hoyle; or gentleman's handbook of games: containing all the games played in the United States. With a treatise on the doctrine of chances. By "Trumps." [*pseudon.*] 5th ed. vii, 518 pp. 12°. *New York, Dick & Fitzgerald*, 1868.

American husbandry. Containing an account of the soil, climate, production, and agriculture of the British colonies in North America and the West Indies. By an American. [*anon.*] 2 v. 472 pp; 8 l. 319 pp. 8°. *London, J. Bew*, 1775.

American and Italian cantatrici; or, a year at the singing schools of Milan. By Lucien. [*pseudon.*] 344 pp. 12°. *London, T. C. Newby*, 1867.

American (The) journal of horticulture, and florist's companion. July, 1867–June, 1868. v. 2-3. 8°. *Boston, J. E. Tilton & Co.* 1867-68.

American (The) journal of the medical sciences. Edited by Isaac Hays. Jan. to Oct. 1868. New series. v. 55–56. 8°. *Philadelphia, H. C. Lea*, 1868.

American (The) journal of science and the arts. Conducted by B. Silliman, J. D. Dana, [and others]. Jan. to Nov. 1868. 2d series. v. 45–46. [Complete series, v. 95–96]. 8°. *New Haven, editors*, 1868.

American literary gazette and publisher's circular, Nov. 1867 to Oct. 1868. v. 10–11. 8°. *Philadelphia, G. W. Childs*, [1868].

American Lloyd's register of American and foreign shipping. Published by R. Hartshorne and J. F. H. King. xxxiv, 746 pp. 5 pl. obl. 8°. *New York, J. W. Pratt & Co.* 1868.

American medical association. First report of the committee on public hygiene of the American medical association, with sketches of the sanitary condition of Concord, Portland, New York, Philadelphia, Boston, Lowell, Baltimore, Charleston, New Orleans, Louisville, and Cincinnati. (Extract.) 226 pp. 1 tab. 8°. *Philadelphia, Am. medical association*, 1849. s.

——— Report of the standing committee on medical literature, Alfred Stillé, chairman, F. G. Smith, T. H. Yardley, P. C. Gaillard, A. Morris, T. Fithian, T. B. Johnson, presented to the American medical association. 37 pp. 8°. *Philadelphia, Am. med. assoc.* 1850. s.

——— Transactions. v. 1–14, 1848–1863. 8°. *Philadelphia, Am. med. assoc.* 1848–64.
[V. 3 and 4, 1850-51, wanting].

American naval battles. *See* **Kimball** (Horace).

American Nepos. Collection of the lives of the most remarkable men who have contributed to the discovery, the settlement, and the independence of America. 2d ed. 408 pp. 16°. *Baltimore, John Vance & Co*, 1805.

American philosophical society. Catalogue of the library. Parts 1-2. 634 pp. 8°. *Philadelphia, Amer. philos. society*, 1863–66. s.
[No more published].

American (The) quarterly church review, and ecclesiastical register. N. S. Richardson, editor. April, 1848, to Jan 1868. v. 1–19. 8°. *New Haven and New York*, [1849]-1868.

American silk society. Journal and rural economist. Gideon P. Smith, editor. v. 1–2, 1839–40. 406 pp; 357 pp. 8°. *Baltimore, Amer. silk society*, 1839–40.

American (The) stock journal, devoted to the improvement of our domestic animals throughout the United States. D. C. Linsley, editor. Jan. 1859, to Dec. 1862. v. 1–4. sm. fol. *New York, D. C. Linsley*, 1859–62.

Americanischer jugendfreund. ii. Lesebuch für mittelklassen. Nach der ein und dreissigsten auflage der lebensbilder, ii, herausgegeben von Verthelt, Jäkel, Petermann und Thomas. 12°. *New York*, 1867.

Amerika dargestellt durch sich selbst, 1818, 1819, und 1820. 3 v. 4°. *Leipzig, G. I. Göschen*, 1818–20.
[Imperfect: v. 1, pp. 21-25, and v. 3, pp. 31-33, 131-135, and 391–394 wanting.]

Amice (J. F.) Manuel de philosophie expérimentale; ou, recueil de dissertations sur les questions fondamentales de la métaphysique, extraites de Locke, [etc.] 2 p. l. ii, 476 pp. 18°. *Paris, Roret*, 1829. s.

Amiens. Catalogue méthodique de la bibliothèque communale de la ville. Médecine. xiv, 576 pp. 8°. *Amiens, Duval & Herment*, 1853. s.

Ammann (August). Die pflanzenkrankheiten. Für land- und fortswirthe, lehrer, gärtner, etc. bearbeitet. xii, 96 pp. 8°. *Stuttgart, Verfasser*, 1867. s.

Ammianus (Marcellinus). Rerum gestarum libri [quae supersunt]. 16°. [*Geneva*,] 1568.
[*In* VARII hist. rom. scriptores, v. 4].

Among the crags; or, legends of the covenanters. [*anon.*] 182 pp. 18°. *New York, American tract society*, 1868.

Ampère (André Marie). Essai sur la philosophie des sciences; ou, exposition analytique d'une classification naturelle de toutes les connaissances humaines. 2 v. lxviii, 284 pp. 2 tab; x, xcvi, 180 pp. 2 tab. *Paris, Bachelier*, 1838–43. s.

Amsterdam. Catalogus van de bibliotheek der vereeniging ter bevordering van de belangen des boekhandels. Opgemaakt door F. Muller. xv, 144 pp. 8°. *Amsterdam*, 1855. s.

Anchored. By the author of "The climbers." [*anon.*] 271 pp. 4 pl. 12°. *New York, American tract society*, 1868.

Ancient and modern Michilimackinac, including an account of the controversy between Mackinac and the Mormons. [*anon.*] 48 pp. 8°. [*n. p.*] 1854. s.

Andersen (Hans Christian). Fairy tales. A new translation, by Mrs. H. B. Paull. For young people. viii, 671 pp. 12 pl. 12°. *London, F. Warne & Co.* 1868.

Anderson (*Col.* Charles). The cause of the war: who brought it on, and for what purpose. 16 pp. 8°. *New York, W. C. Bryant & Co.* 1863.

[LOYAL publication society, no. 17].

——— Letter [on the war] addressed to the opera house meeting, Cincinnati. 15 pp. 8°. *New York, W. C. Bryant & Co.* 1863.

[LOYAL publication society, no. 21].

Anderson (Christopher). The annals of the English bible. Abridged and continued by S. I. Prime. 549 pp. 8°. *New York, R. Carter & brothers,* 1852. s.

Anderson (James, *of Stonehaven, Scotland*). The black book of Kincardineshire; containing lists of the covenanters confined in Dunnottar castle, in 1685; with an account of the persecution of episcopacy; and other miscellaneous papers connected with the county. 202 pp. 12°. *Stonehaven, W. Johnston,* 1843.

Anderson (James, *A. M*). The constitutions of the freemasons; containing the charges, regulations, etc. of that most ancient fraternity. [Reprinted from London ed. of 1723]. 12°. *Cincinnati,* 1859.

[*In* MOORE (Cornelius). The craftsman and freemason's guide. pp. 317–354. ed. 1859].

Anderson (Johann). Histoire naturelle de l'Islande, du Groenland, et d'autres pays. Traduite de l'Allemand par [M. Sellius]. 2 v. xl, 314 pp. 1 map, 3 pl; iv, 391 pp. 4 pl. 12°. *Paris, S. Jorry,* 1750.

Anderson (John T.) Exercises in the fundamental rules of arithmetic. 139 pp. 12°. *New York, L. H. Embree,* 1854. s.

Anderson (Robert, *Gen. U. S. A.*) Instruction for field artillery, horse and foot. Translated from the French, and arranged for the service of the United States. 191 pp. 58 pl. 16°. *Philadelphia, R. P. Desilver,* 1839.

Andersson (Nicolaus Johannes). Gramineæ [von Mossambique]. fol. *Berlin,* 1862.

[*In* PETERS (W. C. H.) Nat. reise nach Mossambique. Botanik.]

Andover, (*Mass.*) theological seminary. Memorial of the semi-centennial celebration of its founding. 8°. *Andover,* 1859. s.

Andræ (C. G. *editor*). Den danske gradmaaling. 1e bind, indeholdende hovedtrianglerne paa sjælland og deres forbindelser med svenske og preussiscke triangebrækker. xxviii, 579 pp. 4 pl. 4°. *Kjöbenhavn, F. S. Muhle,* 1867. s.

Andreæ, *or* Andreas (Anton). [Scriptum super logica Aristotelis]. Scriptum super tota arte veteri Aristotelis. 104 pp. fol. *Venetiis, per O. Scotem,* 1480. s.

Andres (Antonio). Sermones panegiricos. 2 v. 32 p. l. 412 pp; 8 p. l. 424 pp. 8°. *Valencia, B. Montfort,* 1771. s.

Andrews (Christopher C. *brevet major general*). History of the campaign of Mobile. 276 pp. 5 maps. 6 pl. *New York, D. Van Nostrand,* 1867.

Andrews (*Rev.* H. P.) Six steps to honor; or, great truths illustrated. 299 pp. 16°. *New York, Carlton & Porter,* 1856. s.

——— The sure anchor; or, the young christian admonished, exhorted, and encouraged. 216 pp. 12°. *Boston, J. French & Co.* 1855. s.

——— Voices from the old elm; or, uncle Henry's talks with the little folks. 277 pp. 16°. *New York, Carlton & Porter,* [1857]. s.

Andrews (Stephen Pearl), *and* **Boyle** (Augustus F.) The phonographic reporter's first book. 291 pp. 12°. *New York, Andrews & Boyle,* 1848. s.

Ange (L') conducteur des ames dévotes dans la voie de la perfection chrétienne; contenant l'ordinaire de la messe, les vêpres du dimanche; [etc]. 1 p. l. 384 pp. 1 pl. 24°. *New York, E. Dunigan & frère,* 1852. s.

Angel-voices; or words of counsel for overcoming the world. After the mode of Richter's "Best hours." 3d ed. [*anon.*] 117 pp. 16°. *Boston, Ticknor, Reed & Fields,* 1851.

Angelis (Pedro de). Memoria historica sobre los derechos de soberania y dominio de la Confederacion argentina a la parte austral del continente americano, [etc]. 54, lviii pp. 8°. *Buenos-Aires,* 1852. s.

——— De la navegacion del Amazonas. Respuesta a una memoria de M. Maury. 103 pp. 8°. *Caracas, T. Antero,* 1857. s.

Angell (Oliver). Fifth reader, [etc]. New ed. 2 p. l. 296 pp. 12°. *Philadelphia, E. H. Butler & Co.* 1849. s.

Anleitung zur ausführung der einfachsten pionnier-arbeiten im felde für schanzzeugträger und zimmerleute der k. k. linieninfanterie. [*anon.*] iv, 70 pp. 7 pl. 8°. *Lemberg, E. Winiarz,* 1856. s.

Annales de littérature médicale étrangère, rédigées par J. F. Kluyskens. 18 v. 8°. *Gand, P. F. de Goesin-Verhaeghe,* [1805–14]. s.

Annales des ponts et chaussées. Mémoires et documents relatifs à l'art des constructions et au service de l'ingénieur; lois, etc. concernant l'administration des ponts et chaussées. 4e série. 1866. 4 v. 8°. *Paris, Dunod,* [1867].

CONTENTS.

4e sér. Mémoires et documents. v. 1—2. 1866.
Lois, décrets, etc. v. 6.
Personnel.

Annales de la propagation de la foi. *See* **Association** de la propagation de la foi.

Annales télégraphiques, publiées par un comité composé de fonctionnaires de l'administration des lignes télégraphiques. v. 1–8. 8°. *Paris, Dalmont & Dunod,* 1858–65.

[Imperfect: v. 1, no. 2, wanting; v. 2, no. 6, wanting].

Annales des voyages. *See* **Malte-Brun** (V. A.)

Annals (the) of king George the first: containing not only the affairs of Great Britain, but the general history of Europe. [1714–20.] With an introduction in defence of his majesty's title. [*anon.*] 6 v. 8°. *London, A. Bell,* 1716–21.

Annals (The) of king George, year the second: a faithful history of the affairs of Great Britain for 1716, with a full and compleat history of the rebellion. [*anon.*] iv, 352, 99 pp. 4 l. 12°. *London, A. Bell, and others,* 1717.

Annals (The) and magazine of natural history, including zoology, botany, and geology. 1867. 3d series, v. 20. 8°. *London, Taylor & Francis,* 1867.

——— The same. 1868. 4th series, v. 1. 8°. *London, Taylor & Francis,* 1868.

Annan (*Rev.* Robert). Exposition and defence of the Westminster assembly's confession of faith: being the draught of an "overture" prepared by a committee of the associate reformed synod, in 1783. A new edition; with an introduction and notes by Rev. David McDill. 286 pp. 12°. *Cincinnati, Moore, Wilstach, Keys & Co.* 1855. S.

Annapolis (*Maryland*). *See* **United States** naval academy.

Annuaire de l'administration française, par M. Block, faisant suite au dictionnaire de l'administration française, 1867. viii, 384, 164 pp. 16°. *Paris, Berger Levrault,* 1867.

Annuaire encyclopédique. Publié par les directeurs de l'encyclopédie du xixe siècle, 1866–67. 1800 col. in 900 pp. 8°. *Paris, bureau de l'encyclopédie,* 1867.

Annuaire de l'instruction publique pour l' année 1867, publié par J. Delalain. 487 pp. 1 map. 16°. *Paris, Delalain et fils,* 1867.

Annuaire de la librairie, de l'imprimerie, de la papeterie, du commerce de la musique et des estampes, et des professions qui concourent à la publication des œuvres de la littérature des sciences et des arts. lix, 511 pp. 16°. *Paris, cercle de la librairie, etc.* 1867.

Annuaire du ministère de l'agriculture, du commerce, et des travaux publics pour l' année 1866.

[ANNALES des ponts et chaussées, 1866].

Annuaire de thérapeutique. *See* **Bouchardat.**

Annual (The) register: a review of public events, at home and abroad, for 1867. New series. viii, 353, 288 pp. 8°. *London, Rivingtons,* 1868.

Annual (The) of scientific discovery; or, year-book of facts in science and art for 1868. Edited by S. Kneeland. 16°. *Boston, Gould & Lincoln,* 1868.

Another Cain: a poem. [*anon.*] 15 pp. 8°. *London, Hatchard & Son,* 1822.

[MISCELLANEOUS pamphlets, v. 56].

Anquetil (Louis Pierre). L'esprit de la ligue, ou histoire politique des troubles de France pendant les 16e et 17e siècles. [*anon.*] 3 v. 16°. *Paris, J. T. Herissant fils,* 1767. S.

Anson (George, *baron Anson, of Soberton*). A voyage round the world. *See* **Walter** (*Rev.* Richard).

Anstaing. *See* **Le Maistre** d'Anstaing.

Ansted (David Thomas). Physical geography. 8°. *London,* 1852.

[*In* MANUAL of geographical science, v. 1].

Anstey (Christopher). The new Bath guide; or, memoirs of the B[lu]n[de] r[hea]d family. In a series of poetical epistles. [*anon.*] 10th ed. viii, 175 pp. 1 pl. 8°. *London, J. Dodsley,* 1776. S.

Anstey (Thomas Chisholm). Notes upon "the representation of the people act, 1867." With appendices. xi, 172, cxliv pp. 8°. *London, W. Ridgway,* 1867.

Anthon (Charles). Key to Anthon's Latin prose composition. 94 pp. 12°. *New York, Harper & brothers,* 1849. S.

Antoninus (Marcus Aurelius). The meditations, with the manual of Epictetus, and a summary of christian morality. Freely translated from the Greek, by Henry McCormac, M. D. 126 pp. 12°. *London, Longmans,* 1844. S.

Antonio (Nicolas). Bibliotheca hispana, sive hispanorum notitia, qvi post annum secularem MD, usque ad præsentem diem floruere. 2 v. 41 p. l. 633 pp; 1 p. l. 690 pp. fol. *Rome, N. A. Tinassi,* 1672.

Antrim (Benajah J.) Pantography, or universal drawings, [etc.] with the nature and importance of pasigraphy as the science of letters. 161 pp. 12°. *Philadelphia, author,* 1843. S.

Aparicio (José, *painter*). Descripcion sencilla y breve del cuadro que representa el feliz arribo y desembarco de ss. mm. y aa. en el puerto de Santa Maria, [etc.,] 1823. 15 pp. 1 pl. 8°. *Madrid, Ibarra,* 1827. s.

Aphthonius. Aphthonii sophistae progymnasmata, partim a Rodolpho Agricola, partim a Iohanne Maria Catanæo, latinitate donata. 4ª ed. 383 pp. 6 l. *Amstelodami, L. & C. Elzevir,* 1655.

Apocalypse. *See* **Bible.**

Apocrypha. *See* **Bible.**

Apollonius *Pergaeus.* Conicorum libri octo; et Sereni Antissensis de sectione cylindri et coni libri duo. 3 v. in 1. fol. *Oxoniæ; Sheldon,* 1710. s.

——— De sectione rationis libri duo ex arabico ms^to latine versi. Accedunt ejusdem de sectione spatii libri duo restituti, [etc.] Præmittitur Pappi Alexandrini præfatio ad vii^mum collectionis mathematicæ nunc primum græce edita; cum lemmatibus, ejusdem Pappi ad hos Apollonii libros. Opera [etc.] Edmundi Halley. 5 p. l. liii; 168 pp. 8°. *Oxonii, Sheldon,* 1706. s.

Apollonius *Rhodius.* Argonautica. Scholia avcta et emendata indicesque locupletissimos addidit Augustus Wellauer. 2 v. in 1. xiv, 293 pp; 318 pp. 8°. *Lipsiae, B. G. Teubner,* 1828. s.

Apollonius *Tyaneus.* Epistolæ. *Lipsiae,* 1709. *See* **Philostratus.** Quae supersvnt omnia.

Apologie pour l'ordre des francs-maçons. Par Mr. N. [*anon.*] 7 p. l. 126, 3 pp. 1 pl. 16°. *La Haye, P. F. Gosse,* 1785.

Appeal (An) to the public on behalf of Cameria, [America] a young lady who was almost ruined by the barbarous treatment of her own mother. [*anon.*] London, 1781. 30 pp. 8°. *Cincinnati, re-printed, R. Clarke & Co.* 1868.

Apperly (Charles James). Nimrod abroad. 2 v. ix, 285 pp; viii, 306 pp. 12°. *London, H. Colburn,* 1842.

Appleton (D.) and Co. [Catalogue of their] own publications. 234 pp. 3 l. 12°. *New York, Appletons,* 1859. s.

Appleton (William S.) Memorials of the Cranes of Chilton, with a pedigree of the family, and the life of the last representative. 89 pp. 4 pl. 8°. *Cambridge, J. Wilson & Son,* 1868.

Apuleius *Madaurensis* (Lucius). Opera, quæ extant, omnia. [v. 1. Asinus aureus]. Cum Philippi Beroaldi in Asinum aureum eruditissimis commentariis: recensque Godiscalci Stevvechi in L. Apuleij opera omnia quæstionibus et coniecturis, [etc]. Noua ed. v. 1. 8 p. l. 1115 pp. 16°. *Lvgdvni, vidua A. De Harsy,* 1614.

——— The same. [Opera omnia]. 4 p. l. 384 pp. 24°. *Amsterdam, Guil. Cossius?* 1624.

CONTENTS:

Vita Apvleii.
Metamorphoseon. Lib. xi.
Oratio de magia.
De mvndo, liber.
De dogmate Platonis, sive de philosophia. Libri tres.
De deo Socratis, liber.
Florida: itemqve alia fragmenta, et titvli librorvm.

Apuleius *Minor* (Lucius Caecilius Minutianus). De orthographia fragmenta et Apvleii minoris de nota aspirationis et de dipthongis libri duo. Edidit [etc.] Fredericvs Osann. xxxiv, 157 pp. 8°. *Darmstadii, C. W. Leske,* 1826. s.

Aquino (*Saint* Tommaso Niccolo). *See* **Thomas** Aquinas (*Saint*).

Arabian (The) night's entertainments. New ed. with notes by Rev. G. F. Townsend. viii, 632 pp. 16 pl. 12°. *London, F. Warne & Co.* 1866.

——— The same. The adventure of hunch-back, and the stories connected with it. With prints, engraved by W. Daniell, from pictures painted by R. Smirke. 99 pp. 17 pl. fol. *London, W. Daniell,* 1814.

Arago (Dominique François). Traité de météorologie, ou explication des phénomènes de l'atmosphère. Par M. A. [*anon.*] 120 pp. 18°. *Paris, Prinard,* 1832.

[BIBLIOTHÈQUE populaire. 5e livr].

Aratus Solensis. Phænomena et diosemeia, graece. 42 pp. 4°. *Lugduni Batavorum,* 1600.

[*With* GROOT (H. de). Syntagma arateorum, 1600].

Arbatel. Of the magic of the ancients, the greatest study of wisdom. [*anon.*]

[*With* AGRIPPA VON NETTESHEIM (Henry Cornelius). Fourth book of occult philosophy, translated by R. Turner. Sm. 4°. *London, Harrison,* 1655.]

Archambault (*Prof.* P. J). Précis élémentaire de physique. 2 v. in 1. 200 pp; 269 pp. 12°. *Paris, A. Durand,* 1855. s.

Archer (*Major* E. C.) Tours in upper India, and the Himalaya mountains, etc. 8°. *Philadelphia, F. K. Greenbank,* 1823.

[GREENBANK'S periodical library. v. 1. pp. 397-514.]

Archer (William Henry). The progress of Victoria; a statistical essay. iv, 100 pp. 8°. *Melbourne, Blundell & Co.* 1867. s.

——— Statistical notes on the progress of Victoria in agriculture, etc. 1861–66. *See* **Victoria.** Statistical notes.

Archer (William Henry). Statistical notes on the progress of Victoria, from the foundation the colonies, 1835–60. First series. Parts of 1–2. 2 v. in 1. 1 p. l. 103 pp; 56 pp. 4°. *Melbourne, J. Ferres,* [1861?] s.

—— The statistical register of Victoria, from the foundation of the colony; with an astronomical calendar for 1855. iv, 447 pp. 8°. *Melbourne, J. Ferres,* 1854. s.

Archibald (*Rev.* G. D.) Book of chants: consisting of selections from the psalms, [etc.] Adapted to appropriate music, [etc.] by D. H. Baldwin and L. W. Mason. 64 pp. 8°. *Cincinnati, Moore, Wilstach, Keys, & Co.* 1857. s.

Archie at the seaside, and other stories. [*anon.*] 209 pp. 12 pl. 18°. *Philadelphia, Am. S. S. union,* [1866.]

Architectonicæ civilis et militaris elementa. [*anon.*] 1 p. l. 50 pp. [*Vratislaviæ*], *typis universitatis,* 1777.

[*With* ELEMENTA mathesis, 1777.]

Architectural (The) magazine and journal of improvement in architecture, building, and furnishing. Conducted by J. C. Loudon. v. 1–5. 8°. *London, Longmans,* 1834–38. s.

Archiv für anatomie und physiologie. In verbindung mit mehreren gelehrten herausgegeben von J. F. Meckel. 6 v. 8°. *Leipzig, L. Voss,* 1826–32. s.

Archiv für die gesammte naturlehre, in verbindung mit [anderen], herausgegeben vom dr. K. W. G. Kastner. v. 1-18. 8°. *Nürnberg, J. L. Schrag etc.* 1824-29. s.

—— The same. v. 19–27. Archiv für chemie und meteorologie, in verbindung mit [anderen], herausgegeben vom dr. K. W. G. Kastner. v. 1–9. 8°. *Nürnberg, J. A. Stein,* 1830-35. s.

[No more published.]

Archiv für die neuesten entdeckungen aus der urwelt. Ein journal in zwanglosen heften, in gesellschaft von mehreren gelehrten herausgegeben von J. G. J. Ballenstedt, und J. F. Krüger. 6 v. 8°. *Quedlinburg & Leipzig, G. Basse,* 1819-24. s.

[No more published].

Archiv für die physiologie, von J. C. Reil (und J. H. J. Autenreith). 12 v. 8°. *Halle, Curt,* 1796-1815. s.

Archiv für die sächsische geschichte. [Vierteljahrsschrift] herausgegeben von Wilhelm Wachsmuth und Carl von Weber. v. 1-6. 8°. *Leipzig, B. Tauchnitz,* 1863-67. s.

Archiv für den thierischen magnetismus. In verbindung mit mehreren naturforschen herausgegeben von C. A. von Eschenmayer, D. G. Kieser, [und] Fr. Nasse. 10 v. 8°. *Altenburg und Leipzig, F. A. Brockhaus, etc.* 1817-21.

Archivio storico italiano. Serie 3ª. v. 5-6. 8°. *Firenze, Celini e C.* 1867.

Arenstein (Joseph). Oesterreich auf der internationalen ausstellung, 1862. xlviii, x, 128 pp. 8°. *Wien, K. hof swaller und staatsdruckerei,* 1862. s.

Aretino (Leonardo Bruni, *surnamed*). *See* **Bruni,** (Leonardo).

Arey (Henry W.) The Girard college and its founder. 85 pp. 2 pl. 12°. *Philadelphia, C. Sherman,* 1852. s.

Argensola (Bartolomé Leonardo de). The discovery and conquest of the Molucco and Philippine islands. Containing their history, description, etc. Translated [from the Spanish, by J. Stevens]. 3 p. l. 260 pp. 4 l. 1 map. sm. 4°. *London,* 1708.

Argosy (The). Edited by Mrs. Henry Wood. Dec. 1867, to Nov. 1868. v. 5-6. 8°. *London, C. W. Wood,* [1868].

Argyle (Anna, *pseudon*). *See* **Cecilias** (The.)

Argyle (Archie, *pseudon*). *See* **Cupid's** album.

Argyll (G. D. Campbell, *duke of*). *See* **Campbell** (G. D.)

Arias (Didaco Ximenez). Lexicon ecclesiasticum latino-hispanicum, ex sacris bibliis, conciliis, pontificum decretis, ac theologorum placitis [etc.] concinnatum, servata ubique vera etymologiæ, ortographiæ, et accentus ratione. Ed. ultima. 4 p. l. 438, 24 pp. fol. *Bancinone, ex typographiæ M. A. Marti viduæ,* 1763. s.

Arispe. *See* **Ramos de Arispe.**

Aristeas. Tractatulus de xxii interpretibus et de eorūdem maxima sapientia ac nominibus. 31 l. sm. 4°. *Erfordiæ,* 1483.

Aristoteles. Opera omnia quæ extant, græcè et latinè. Vetervm ac recentiorvm interpretvm, vt Adriani Turnebi, Isaaci Casauboni, Iulij Pacij studio emendatissima. Cvm Kyriaci Strozæ libris dvobus græcolatinis de republicâ. Accessit in omnes Aristotelis libros commentarius. Authore Gvillelmo Dv Val. 2 v. 16 p. l. 1251 pp. 18 l; 1104 pp. 16 l. fol. *Lutetiæ Parisiorum, typis regiis,* 1619.

—— Questiones Johannis Versoris super libros ethicarum Aristotelis et textus eiusdem. cxxii, 2 l. fol. *Coloniæ, H. Quentell,* 1491.

Aristoteles. Politiqves, or discourses of government. Translated out of Greek into French, with expositions, by Loys le Roy, called Regivs. Translated out of French into English [by J. D. 2d ed.] 15 p. l. 393 pp. 3 l. sm. fol. *London, A. Islip*, 1598.

Arizona (*Territory of*). Journals of the fourth legislative assembly, 1867. 263 pp. 8°. *Prescott, office Arizona miner*, 1868.

Arkansas (*Territory of*). Journals of the general assembly of the territory. 7th session, Oct.-Nov. 1831. 8°. *Little Rock, C. P. Bertrand*, 1832.

——— (*State of*). Journals of the general assembly, special session, Nov. 1837–March, 1838. 8°.

[Imperfect: title-page wanting].

——— The same. 2d–3d sessions, Nov. 1838–Dec. 1840. 2 v. 8°.

[Imperfect: title-page wanting].

——— Journal of the house of representatives. 4th–13th session, Nov. 1842–Jan. 1861. 10 v. 8°. *Little Rock and Arkadelphia*, 1843–61.

——— Journal of the senate. 4th–13th sessions, Nov. 1842–Jan. 1861. 10 v. 8°. *Little Rock and Arkadelphia*, 1843–61.

Arlington (Henry Bennet, 1*st earl of*). *See* **Bennet** (Henry).

Armstrong (*Gen.* John). Hints to young generals. By an old soldier. [*anon.*] 71 pp. 18°. *Kingston, J. Buel*, 1812.

Army (*British*). *See* **Great Britain.** *War department.*

Army and navy journal. *See* **United States** army and navy journal.

Army and navy prayer-book. [Diocesan miss. soc. of Virginia]. 96 pp. 24°. *Richmond, C. H. Wynne*, 1864.

Arnaldi (Enea, *conte*). Descrizione delle architetture, pitture, e scolture di Vicenzia, [etc.] Parte 2ª. Degli edifici pubblici e privati. 140 pp. 16 pl. 8°. *Vicenza, Mosca*, 1779. s.

Arnaud (François Thomas Marie Baculard d'). Épreuves du sentiment. [25 nouvelles en 5 volumes]. 24 pl. 8°. *Paris, Le Jay*, 1772.

Arnauld (Antoine), and **Nicole** (Pierre). Logic; or, the art of thinking. Translated from the French. [*anon.*] 3d ed. 6 p. l. 444 pp. 18°. *London, J. Taylor*, 1696.

Arneth (Joseph). Monumento des k. k. münz- und antiken cabinettes in Wien. Die antiken cameen, etc. xvi, 48 pp. 25 pl. fol. *Wien, k. akad. der wissenschaften*, 1849. s.

Arnhem (Openbare bibliotheek te). Catalogus, [etc.] xx, 289 pp. 8°. *Arnhem, J. A. Nijhoff & zoon*, 1858. s.

Arnim (L. Achim von), *and* **Brentano** (Clemens), *editors*. Des knaben wunderhorn. Alte deutsche lieder gesammelt. 3 v. 8°. *Heidelberg, Mohr & Winter*, 1808. s.

[v. 1, 2e aufl. 1819].

Arnold (Benedict). Letters written while on an expedition across the state of Maine, to attack Quebec, in 1775. 8°. *Portland, Day, Fraser & Co.* 1831.

[MAINE historical society. Collections, v. 1].

Arnold (Edwin). Arithmetical questions on a new plan, [etc.] 163 pp. 12°. *New York, D. Burgess & Co.* 1853. s.

——— The same. Éléments d'arithmétique sur un plan nouveau, [etc.] Traduit de l'anglais, [etc.] par A. N. Girault. 171 pp. 12°. *New York, Cady & Burgess*, 1852. s.

Arnold (Harriet N. K.) The poets and poetry of Minnesota. 336 pp. 16°. *Chicago, S. P. Rounds*, 1864.

Arnold (John L.) Lectures on anatomy, physiology, and hygiene; and disease, its cause, prevention, and cure, [etc. With] synopsis of anatomy, [etc.] 2 v. in 1. 165, 167 pp. 12°. *Cincinnati, H. M. Rulison*, 1856. s.

Arnold (Matthew). On the study of Celtic literature. xviii, 181 pp. 8°. *London, Smith, Elder & Co.* 1867.

Arnold (Thomas, *D. D.*) The history of Rome. 3 v. in 2. 536 pp; 509 pp. 8°. *New York, Appleton*, 1846.

Arnold (Thomas Kerchever). Greek reading book, [etc.] Also, a copious selection from Greek authors, with notes, [etc.] 12°. *New York, D. Appleton & Co.* 1848. s.

Arnold (W. *M. D.*) A practical treatise on the bilious remittent fever: its causes and effects. [Also], medical topography of the different military stations in [Jamaica.] xi, 320 pp. 8°. *London, J. Churchill*, 1840. s.

Arrianus. History of the expedition of Alexander the Great, and conquest of Persia. Translated from the Greek by [John] Rooke. 2d ed. 264 pp. 8°. *London, J. Davis*, 1813.

Arrom (Cecilia Bohl de). Elia; or, Spain fifty years ago. From the Spanish of Fernan Caballero. [*pseudon.*] 12°. *New York, D. Appleton & Co.* 1868.

Art journal (The). [London.] 1867. [v. 29.] New series. v. 6. 4°. *London, Virtue & Co.* 1867.

Art de voyager utilement. [*anon.*] 2 p. l. 51 pp. 16°. *Amsterdam, J. Louis de Lorme*, 1698.

[*With* LAS CASAS, (B. de.) Relation des voyages dans les Indes occidentales. *Amsterdam*, 1698].

——— The same. Art of travelling to advantage. [*anon.*] 40 pp. 8°. *London*, 1699.

[Imperfect: title wanting. *With* LAS CASAS, (Bartolomé de.) Account of the first voyages and discoveries made by the Spaniards in America. *London*, 1699].

Artedi (Peter). Descriptiones specierum piscium quos vivos præsertim dissecuit et examinavit, inter quos primario pisces regni Sueciæ facile omnes accuratissime describuntur, cum non paucis aliis exoticis. Ichthyologiæ pars v. Ed. 2a. 2 p. l. 112 pp. 8°. *Grypeswaldiæ, A. F. Röse*, 1793. s.

[*With his* Synonymia. Ed. 2a].

——— Genera piscium, [etc.] Emendata et aucta a Iohanne Iulio Walbaum. 4 p. l. 723 pp. 3 pl. 8°. *Grypeswaldiæ, A. F. Röse*, 1792. s.

[The above forms part iii of the author's "Ichthyologia"].

——— Synonymia nominum piscium fere omnium; in qua recensio fit nominum piscium, omnium facile authorum qui umquam de piscibus scripsere, [etc.] Ichthyologiæ pars iv. ed. 2a. 2 p. l. 140 pp. 8°. *Grypeswaldiæ, A. F. Röse*, 1793. s.

Arthur (R. *M. D.*) Treatment of dental caries, complicated with disorders of the pulp. 121 pp. 8°. *Philadelphia, Jones, White & M'Curdy*, 1853. s.

Arthur (Timothy Shay). After a shadow, and other stories. 248 pp. 4 pl. 16°. *New York, Sheldon & Co.* 1869.

——— Blind Nellie's boy, and other stories. 192 pp. 4 pl. 16°. *Philadelphia, Perkinpine & Higgins*, 1867.

——— The children's hour. v. 1–3. sm. 4°. *Philadelphia, T. S. Arthur & son*, 1866–68.

——— Growler's income tax. 4 pp. 8°. *New York*, 1864.

[LOYAL publication society, No. 57].

——— The heiress. 141 pp. 18°. *Philadelphia, J. W. Bradley*, 1855. s.

——— The home mission. 213 pp. 16°. *Philadelphia, J. W. Bradley*, 1853. s.

——— Juvenile library. The lost children and other stories. 154 pp. sq. 16°. *Philadelphia, Lippincott, Grambo & Co.* 1852. s.

——— The same. Who is greatest? and other stories. 153 pp. sq. 16°. *Philadelphia, Lippincott, Grambo & Co.* 1852. s.

——— The same. The wounded boy, and other stories. 154 pp. sq. 16°. *Philadelphia, Lippincott, Grambo & Co.* 1852. s.

——— Maggy's baby, and other stories. 153 pp. 16°. *Philadelphia, Lippincott, Grambo & Co.* 1852. s.

——— The maiden: a story for my young countrywomen. 162 pp. 18°. *Philadelphia, J. W. Bradley*, 1855. s.

——— Not anything for peace, and other stories. 240 pp. 4 pl. 16°. *New York, Sheldon & Co.* 1869.

——— The old man's bride. 347 pp. 1 pl. 12°. *New York, C. Scribner & Co.* 1853. s.

——— The peacemaker, and other stories. 239 pp. 4 pl. 16°. *New York, Sheldon & Co.* 1869.

——— Riches have wings; or, a tale for the rich and poor. 192 pp. 18°. *New York, Baker & Scribner*, 1847. s.

——— True riches; or, wealth without wings. 210 pp. 1 pl. 16°. *Philadelphia, J. W. Bradley*, 1852. s.

——— Uncle Ben's new year's gift, and other stories. 154 pp. 18°. *Philadelphia, Lippincott, Grambo & Co.* 1852. s.

Arti (Le) che vanno per via nella citta di Venezia. [*anon.*] 1 p. l. 60 pl. fol. [*London*,] *Lackington, Allen & Co.* 1803.

Artiga, *or* Artieda (Francisco Joseph). Epitome de la eloquencia española. Arte de discurrir, y hablar con agudeza, y elegancia en todo genero de assumptos, [etc.] xi, 511 pp. 16°. *Barcel, M. Marti*, 1750. s.

Artis (Edmund Tyrell). Antediluvian phytology. Illustrated by a collection of the fossil remains of plants peculiar to the coal formations of Great Britain, [etc.] xv, 24 l. 24 pl. 4°. *London, author*, 18[illegible]8. s.

Arundell (F. V. J.) Discoveries in Asia Minor; [with] a description of the ruins of several ancient cities. 2 v. xxiii, 358 pp; 439 pp. 1 map. 10 pl. 8°. *London, R. Bentley*, 1834.

Arwidsson (Adolph Iwar). Handlingar till upplysning af Finlands häfder. v. 4–5. 8°. *Stockholm, P. A. Norstedt & Söner*, 1851–52. s.

[Wanting, v. 1–3].

Ashcroft (John). Ashcroft's railway directory, for 1868, containing an official list of the officers and directors of the railroads in the United States and Canadas, with their financial condition and amount of rolling stock. xxxii, 367 pp. 8°. *New York, J. Ashcroft*, [1868].

Asher (Georg M. *of Heidelberg*). Sketch of Henry Hudson, the navigator. 23 pp. 8°. *Brooklyn, reprinted for private distribution*, 1857. s.

Asmodeus in New York. [*anon.*] 378 pp. 12°. *New York, Longchamp & Co.* 1868.

Asmuss (Hermann Martin). Monstrositates coleopterorum. Commentationem pathologico-entomologicam scripsit. 2 p. l. 86 pp. 10 pl. 8°. *Rigae, E. Frantzenius,* 1835. s.

Asser (John). Chronicon fani sancti Neoti, sive annales. Fol. *Oxoniæ,* 1691.

[GALE (Thomas) *and* FELL (John). Rerum anglicarum scriptores veteres. *Oxoniæ,* 1684–91. v. 3].

Associate-reformed church in North America. Constitution and standards. 612 pp. 1 l. 8°. *New York, T. & J. Swords,* 1799.

Association de la propagation de la foi. Annales de la propagation de la foi. Recueil périodique des lettres des évêques et des missionaires des missions des deux mondes, et de tous les documents relatifs aux missions et à l'œuvre de la propagation de la foi. Collection faisant suite aux lettres édifiantes. 14 v. 8°. *Lyon, editeur des annales,* [1823]-42. s.

Ast (Friedrich). Platon's leben und schriften, [etc.] 530 pp. 8°. *Leipzig, Weidmann,* 1816. s.

Astrand (J. J.) Regnebog for skoleungdommen. 2^{en} udgave. 228 pp. 12°. *Bergen, E. B. Giertsen,* 1861. s.

Atharva-veda prâtiçâkhya (The), or, caunakîyâ caturâdhyâyikâ; text, translation, and notes. By William D. Whitney. [Extract]. 285 pp. 8°. *New Haven, Am. oriental soc,* 1862. s.

Athenaeum club (New York city). Commemorative proceedings of the Athenaeum club, on the death of Abraham Lincoln. 36 pp. 1 pl. 8°. *New York, C. S. Westcott,* 1865.

Athenæus. Banquet des savans. Traduit par Lefebvre de Villebrune. 5 v. 4°. *Paris, Lamey,* 1789–91.

Athern (Anna, *pseudon?*) Step by step; or, Delia Arlington. A fireside story. 3 p. l. 448 pp. *Boston, J. Munroe & Co.* 1857. s.

Athir (Izz ed-din Abu'l-Hasan Ali ben Mohammed, *known as* Ibn-el). Chronicon quod perfectissimum inscribitur. (v. 7-12). Annos H. (228-628) continens, [etc.] Edidit C. J. Tornberg. 6 v. 8°. *Upsaliæ, C. A. Leffler,* 1851–53. (v. 11–12); *Lugduni Batavorum, E. J. Brill,* 1862–65. (v. 7–10). s.

[V. 1-6 wanting; not published in 1865].

——— The same. Chrönika. Elfte delen ifrän arabiskan öfversatt af C. J. Tornberg. Häftet 1-2. 2 v. xiv, 231 pp; 1 p. l. 355 pp. 1 l. 8°. *Lund, Berlingska bogtryckeriet,* 1851–53. s.

Atkins (Charles G.) Report [etc.] on fisheries. *See* **Foster** (N. W.) *and* **Atkins.**

Atkinson (*Rev.* J. C.) British birds' eggs and nests, popularly described. viii, 182 pp. 12 col. pl. 16°. *London, Routledge,* 1861. s.

Atlante dell' America, contenente le migliori carte geografiche, e topografiche delle principali citta, laghi, fiumi, e fortezze del nuovo mondo. [*anon.*] *Livorno, G. F. Masi & ca.* 1777.

Atlantic (The) almanac, 1868-69. Edited by O. W. Holmes and Donald G. Mitchell. 2 v. 64 pp. 4 col. pl; 80 pp. 4 pl. 8°. *Boston, Ticknor & Fields,* [1867].

Atlantic city. Its early and modern history. By Carnesworthe. [*pseudon.*] 96 pp. 16°. *Philadelphia, W. C. Harris & Co.* 1868.

Atlantic (The) monthly. A magazine of literature, science, art, and politics. Jan. to Dec. 1868. v. 21–22. 8°. *Boston, Ticknor & Fields,* 1868.

Atlantic telegraph: its history, from the commencement of the undertaking in 1854, to the sailing of the "Great Eastern" in 1866. Illustrated. By G. W. Bacon. [*anon.*] 116 pp. 1 map. 12°. *London,* 1866.

Atterbom (P. D. A.) Svenska siare och skalder. 3 v. 12°. *Upsala, N. W. Lundequist,* 1841-44.

Atuagagdliutit. Nalinginarnik tusarumināsassunik univkât. Nos. 25–68. Aug. 26, 1864—Fipruâre 26, 1866. 2 v. 4°. *Núngme nunap nálagata nakiteriviane nakitat, L. Moller-mit,* 1864-66. s.

[v. 1 wanting].

Atwater (Caleb). A history of the state of Ohio, natural and civil. 2d ed. 407 pp. 8°. *Cincinnati, Glezen & Shepard,* 1838.

Atwood (George). A description of the experiments intended to illustrate a course of lectures on the principles of natural philosophy, read in the observatory at Trinity college, Cambridge. 128 pp. 8°. [*London, author,* 1776]. s.

Aubé (Charles). Monographia pselaphiorum, cum synonymia extricata, [etc.] (Extract). 72 pp. 17 pl. 8°. *Paris, magasin de zoologie,* 1834. s.

Aubert (Michael Conrad Sophus Emil). Om mundtlig rettergang og edsvarne. Indberetning i anledning af en efter offentlig foranstaltning foretagen reise i England, Skotland, Frankrig, Belgien og de preussiske Rhinprovinser, [etc.] vii, 688 pp. 8°. *Christiania, P. T. Malling,* 1849. s.

Aubigné. *See* **Merle d'Aubigné.**

Auckland. (William Eden, 1*st baron*). *See* **Eden** (William).

Aucher-Éloy (R.) Relations de voyages en Orient, 1830-38. Revues et annotées par le comte Jaubert. 2 v. xxxix, 354 pp; 365-775 pp. 1 map. 8°. *Paris, Roret,* 1843. s.

Audiffret (G. d'). Le budget. xi, 234 pp. 8°. *Paris, A. Allouard,* 1841.

Audran (Gérard). The proportions of the human body, measured from the most beautiful antique statues. From the French. 2 p. l. 29 pl. fol. *London, John Sturt,* 1718.

Audubon (John James). The birds of America, from drawings made in the United States and their territories. 7 v. 8°. *New York, J. J. Audubon,* 1840-44.

——— A synopsis of the birds of North America. xii, 359 pp. 8°. *Edinburgh, A. & C. Black,* 1839.

Auerbach (Berthold). Barfüssele. 2er abdruck. 2 p. l. 255 pp. 16°. *Stuttgart, J. G. Cotta,* 1857.

——— The same. The little barefoot. A tale. Translated by Eliza B. Lee. 275 pp. 4 pl. 16°. *Boston, H. B. Fuller & Co.* 1867.

——— On the heights. Translated [from the German] by F. E. Bunnett. Authorized ed. 3 v. 18°. *Leipzig, B. Tauchnitz,* 1867.

Auerbach (J.) *and* **Trautschold** (H.) Ueber die kohlen von Central-Russland. (Extract). 1 p. l. 58 pp. 3 pl. 4°. *Moskau, société imp. des naturalistes,* 1860.

Auguez (Paul). Les manifestations des esprits. Réponse à M. Viennet. 173 pp. 8°. *Paris, E. Dentu,* 1857.

Augustini (Agostino). Le belle faccendiere. 8, 135 pp. 18°. *Ravenna, Pietro de Paoli,* 1655.

Augustinus (Aurelius, *saint*). De ciuitate Dei, libri [xxii.] 291 l. fol. *Rome, C. Suueynheym & A. Pannartz,* 1470.

[Imperfect: wanting pp. 7, 8, 14, 272-291].

——— Liber de conflictu viciorum et virtutum. 8 l. 4°. *Argentorati, Georgius Husner, about* 1473].

——— Questio de numerorū et per digitos et per articulos finita progressione. 4°. [n. p. 1517].

[*In* FABER (Jacques). Introductio in arithmecam Seuerini Boetij].

——— Soliloquium deuotum̄. 7 l. sm. 4°. [*Coloniæ, Johannes Valdener? about* 1474].

——— Les soliloques, les meditations, et le manuel de S. Augustin. Traduction nouvelle, [etc.] avec des notes. Nouv. éd. [etc.] 8 p. l. 414 pp. 18°. *Lyon, B. Martin,* [*about* 1709]. s.

Aunt Zelpeth's baby. By the author of "The adventures of a German toy." [*anon.*] 132 pp. 4 pl. sq. 16°. *Boston, W. V. Spencer,* 1867.

Auntie's christmas-trees. The child's gift-book for the christmas holidays. By M. A. C. [*anon.*] 308 pp. 5 pl. 18°. *New York, gen'l. prot. epis. s. s. union,* 1867.

Aurelius Victor (Sextus.) *See* **Victor.**

Aus der heimath. Ein naturwissenschaftliches volksblatt, herausgegeben von E. A. Rossmässler. Jahrgange 1862-64. 3 v. 8°. *Leipzig, E. Keil,* 1862-64. s.

Aus der natur. Die neuesten entdeckungen auf dem gebiete der naturwissenschaften. 12 v. 12°. *Leipzig, A. Abel,* 1852-58. s.

[v. 12 wanting. 2 copies of v. 7-8].

——— The same. v. 13-42, oder neue folge, v. 1-30. 30 v. in 8. 8°. *Leipzig, Gebhart & Reisland,* 1860-67. s.

[v. 13, 15, 17-23, 26, 28 wanting].

Ausonius (Decimus Magnus). Opera. Interpretatione et notis illustravit Julianus Floridus. Recensuit, etc. Joannes Baptista Souchay. [With appendix:] Obscœna e textu Ausoniano resecta. 16 pp. lxviii, 684 pp. 72 l. 1 pl. 4°. *Parisiis, J. Guerin,* 1730. s.

Austin (Samuel). Avstin's Vrania; or, the heavenly mvse: being a true story of man's fall and redemption. By S. A. 10 p. l. 136 pp. 18°. *London, R. Allot,* 1629.

Austin (William). Haec homo; wherein the excellency of the creation of woman is described. 5 p. l. 189 pp. 2 pl. 24°. *London, H. Blunden,* 1638.

Austria. *K. k. direction der administrativen statistick.* *See* **K. k.** statistische central-commission, *below.*

——— *K. k. general-direction der communications anstalten* (*Cours bureau der*). Oesterreichisches post-cours buch, [etc.] 601 pp. 1 map. sq. 12°. *Wien, k. k. hof-und staatsdruckerei,* 1864. s.

——— ——— Topographisches post-lexikon. ii abtheilung. Der kronländer Böhmen, Mähren und Schlesien umfassend. 2 p. l. 802 pp. 24 l. 4°. *Wien, k. k. hof-und staatsdruckerei,* 1852-55.

[Heft 2 wanting]. s.

——— ——— The same. Topographisches post-lexicon umfassend die Kronländer, Oesterreich ob der Enns, Salzburg, Tirol mit Vorarlberg, Steiermark, Kärnthen, Krain, dann das fürstenthum Liechtenstein. xvi, 533 pp. 4°. *k. k. druckerei,* 1861. s.

Austria. *K. k. handels-ministerium. See* **K. k.** statistische central-commission, *below.*

——— *K. k. kriegs-archive.* Anhang zu dem cataloge der im k. k. kriegs-archive befindlichen gestochenen karten. viii, 172 pp 12°. *Wien, k. k. hof- u. staats-aerarial druckerey,* 1825. s.

——— *K. k. marine (Hydrographische anstalt der).*

[*See* WÜLLERSTORF-URBAIR (B. von). Reise der öst. fregatte Novara].

——— *K. k. ministerium des innerns.* Abbildungen österreichischer rindvieh-racen. Herausgegeben im auftrage des k. k. ministeriums des innern. xii, 24 pp. 27 col. pl. obl. fol. *Wien, k. k. hof-und staatsdruckerei,* 1859. s.

——— ——— Statistische übersichten über die bevölkerung und den viehstand von Österreich. 1857. xxi, 417, 79 pp. fol. *Wien, K. k. hof- und staatsdruckerei,* 1859. s.

——— *K. k. statistische central-commission; or, direction der administrativen statistik im k. k. ministerium für handel, gewerbe und offentliche bauten (or k. k. handels-ministerium),*—1858; *or Rechnungs departement des k. k. finanz-ministeriums* (1859–60) *or K. k. direction der administrativen statistik* (1859–61).

——— ——— Ausweise über den handel von Oesterreich, [etc]. 8r.—13r jahrgange. 7 v. fol. *Wien, k. k. hof- und staatsdruckerei,* 1850-55. s.

——— ——— The same. Ausweise über den auswärtigen handel Österreich's, [etc.] xiv–xxvi jahrgang. 14 v. fol. *Wien, k. k. hof-und staatsdruckerei,* 1856–66. s.

——— ——— Mittheilungen aus dem gebiete der statistik, 1r, 3r–13r jahrgange 49 heft. in 12 v. 8°. *Wien, k. k. hof-und staatsdruckerei,* 1852–67. s.

[2r jahrgang wanting].

——— ——— Mittheilungen über handel, gewerbe und verkehrsmittel, so wie aus dem gebiete der statistik überhaupt, nach berichten an das k. k. handels-ministerium. 1r–2r jahrgang. 2 v. 8°. *Wien, C. Gerold,* 1850–51. s.

——— ——— Statistisches jahrbuch der oesterreichischen monarchie, für 1863–65. 3 v. 8°. *Wien, k. k. hof- und staatsdruckerei,* 1864–67. s.

——— ———Tafeln zur statistik der österrichischen monarchie für die jahre 1841–48. 14er–21er jahrgang. 8 v. fol. *Wien, k. k. hof-und staatsdruckerei,* 1844–53. s.

——— ——— The same. Tafeln zur statistik der österreichischen monarchie. Neue folge. v. 1-3. fol. *Wien, k. k. hof-und staatsdruckerei,* 1856–61. s.

CONTENTS:

v. 1. Das jahr 1851 mit übersichtlicher einbeziehung der jahre 1849–50 darstellend. 9 v. in 1. 1856–58.
v. 2. Die jahre 1852–54 umfassend. 9 v. in 1. 1859–60.
v. 3. Die jahre 1855–57 umfassend. 9 v. in 1. 1861.
v. 4. Die jahre 1858–59 umfassend. 8 v. in 1. 1862.

——— ——— *See, also,* **Czörnig** (C. von). Ethnographie der oesterreichischen monarchie. 1857.

——— Die benützung der berge und fliessenden wässer in Nieder-Oesterreich für die landwirthschaft und industrie. Statistisch topographisches bericht der handels-und gewerbekammer für Oesterrreich unter der Enns. v. 1. Kreis unter dem Wiener-walde. viii, 579 pp. 8°. *Wien, L. Sommer,* 1857. s.

——— Statistische uebersicht der wichtigsten productionszweige in Oesterreich unter der Enns, [etc]. Als einleitung zu ihren statistischen special-berichten herausgegeben von der n. ö. handels-und gewerbekammer. viii, clx, 607 pp. 8°. *Wien, L. Sommer,* 1855. s.

——— Movimento di navigazione in porti austriaci, e della navigazione austriaca in porti esteri negli anni solari 1856–58. 189 pp. 8°. *Trieste, Weis,* 1860. s.

Autenreith (Johann Hermann Ferdinand, *editor*). *See* **Archiv** für die physiologie, 1807–15.

Authentic (An) account of the laying of the corner stone of Washington monument, Baltimore, July 4th, 1815. 12°. 44 pp. *Baltimore, John H. Pratt,* 1815.

Autumn (An) in Silesia, Austria-proper, and the ober Enns. By the author of travels in Bohemia. [*anon.*] vii, 391 pp. 12°. *London, T. C. Newby,* 1859.

Avesta. *See* **Zoroaster.**

Avicenna *or* **Ibn Sina.** (**Abu Ali** Hosein ben' Abdallah Ibn-Sina). Liber canonis, de medicinis cordialibvs, et cantica, a Gerardo carmonensi ex arabico sermone in latinum conuersa. Postea uerò ab Andrea Alpago decorata, nunc autem demum à Benedicto Rinio illustrata, [etc.] His accesserunt Auicennæ libellus de remouendis nocumentis, etc. 22 p. l. 2004 pp. 19 l. fol. *Basileæ, Io. Heruagios,* 1556. s.

——— Canon medicinæ. Ex Gerardi cremonensis uersione, et Andreæ Alpagi bellunensis castigatione. A Ioanne Costæo, et Ioanne Paulo Mongro annotationibus iampridem illustratus. Nunc vero ab eodem Costæo recognitus, &c. Additis tabulis, etc.

Avicenna *or* **Ibn Sina**—continued. per Fabium Paulinum. 2 v. 26 p. l. 982 pp; 6 p. l. 437 pp; Indices, 15 l. fol. *Venetiis, apud Juntas,* 1695. s.

Avrigny (Hyacinthe Robillard d'). Mémoires chronologiques et dogmatiques, pour servir à l'histoire ecclésiastique depuis 1600, jusqu'en 1716, avec des réflexions et des remarques critiques. [*anon.* Revus par J. P. Lallemant]. 4 v. 16°. [*Paris, Guérin*], 1739.

Aydelott (B. P. *D. D.*) Incidental benefits of denominational division: an argument for christian union. 135 pp. 16°. *Cincinnati, C. G. Jones,* 1846.

Ayrer (Jacob). Comedy of the beautiful Sidea. 75 pp. 4°. *London, Asher & Co.* 1865.

[*With* COHN (Albert). Shakespeare in Germany. *London,* 1865].

——— Comedy of the beautiful Phaenicia, 18 pp. 4°. *London, Asher & Co.* 1865.

[*With* COHN (Albert). Shakespeare in Germany. *London,* 1865.]

Ayres (J. A.) The legends of Montauk. With an historical appendix. 127 pp. 8°. *New York, G. P. Putnam,* 1849.

Azúa. *See* **Real de Azúa.**

Baart de la Faille (Jacob). Catalogus der uitgebreide bibliotheek nagelaten, [etc.] 2 v. 8 pl. 212, 3 l; 7 p. l. 304 pp. 8°. *Groningen, R. J. Schierbeek,* 1868. s.

Babbage (Charles). The ninth Bridgewater treatise. A fragment. viii, 270 pp. 8°. *London, J. Murray,* 1838. s.

Babington (Gervase, *D. D. bishop of Worcester and Landaff*). A sermon concerning the doctrine of election. 10 pp. 8°. *Cadell & Davies,* 1798.

[*With* HILL (*Sir* Richard). Apology for brotherly love. *London* 1798].

Bach (Heinrich). Geognostische übersichtskarte von Deutschland, der Schweiz. und den angrenzenden ländertheilen, mit begleitworte, etc. 9 maps. obl. fol. text. 15 pp. 8°. *Gotha, J. Perthes,* 1855–6. s.

Bach (J. A. *M. D. professor at Strasbourg*). Des eaux gazeuses alcalines de Soultzmatt (Haut-Rhin). Histoire et topographie des bains de Soultzmatt et de ses environs, etc. Suivi d'une nouvelle analyse des eaux de Soultzmatt, par Béchamp, et de la flore des environs de Soultzmatt, par [F.] Kirschleger. viii, 275 pp. 1 pl. 8°. *Paris, J. B. Baillière,* 1853. s.

Bache (Alexander Dallas). Defence of doctor Gould. *See* **Dudley** observatory.

Bache (Richard). *See* **Jenkins** (T. A.) *and* **Bache** (R.) Report on light-houses, etc.

Bachiller y Morales (Antonio). Elementos de la filosofia del derecho ó curso de derecho natural. xv, 166 pp. 8°. *Habana, imprenta del Tiempo,* 1857. s.

Backer(George de). Dictionnaire des proverbes françois, [etc.] Par G. D. B. [*anon.*] 160 l. 16°. *Brusselles, G. de Backer,* 1710.

Backus (*Rev.* Isaac). Church history of New England, from 1690 to 1796, with a particular history of the Baptist churches in New England. 3 v. 8°. *Boston and Providence,*1777–96.

Bacon (David Francis). Memoirs of eminently pious women of Britain and America. 608 pp. 3 pl. 8°. *New Haven, D. McLeod,* 1833.

Bacon (Edward, *colonel 6th Mich. volunteers.*) Among the cotton thieves. 299 pp. 8°. *Detroit, Freepress,* 1867.

Bacon (Francis, *viscount St. Albans, lord high chancellor of England*). Works. Collected and edited by J. Spedding, R. L. Leslie, and D. D. Heath. v. 11–13. Being v. 1–3 of the literary and professional works. 8°. *Boston, Brown & Taggard,* 1860. s.

——— Essays; with annotations by R. Whately, and notes and a glossarial index by F. F. Heard. xlix, 641 pp. 8°. *Boston, Lee & Shepard,* 1868.

——— De sapientia vetervm liber. 11 p. l. 129 pp. 24°. *Londini, R. Barkervs,* 1609.

Bacon (Nathaniel). An historical and political discourse of the laws and government of England from the first times to the end of the reign of queen Elizabeth. Collected from some manuscript notes of John Selden. 4th ed. 2 v. in 1. xix, 203 pp.; xii, 178 pp. 4 l. fol. *London, D. Brown,* 1739.

NOTE.—"It was well known to the late lord chief justice Vaughan, that the groundwork was his, [Selden's], upon which Mr. Bacon raised this superstructure." Advertisement to ed. 1688–9. This work is identical with his "Discourse of the uniformity of the government of England."

Badeau (*Col.* Adam). Military history of Ulysses S. Grant, from April, 1861, to April, 1865. v. 1. xv, 683 pp. 17 maps. Portrait. 8°. *New York, Appletons,* 1868.

Bädeker (Friedrich W. J.) Die eier der europäischen voegel nach der natur gemalt. Mit einer beschreibung des nestbaues gemeinschaftlich bearbeitet mit L Brehm und W. Paessler. 2 v. 8 p. l. 40 l. 40 col. pl.; 40 l. 40 col. pl. 4°. *Leipzig, J. Bädeker,* [1855–63] s.

Baden. Hof und staatshandbuch des grossherzogthums Baden, 1857. xvi, 428 pp. 8°. *Carlsruhe, G. Braun,* [1857]. s.

Baden. Uebersicht der strafrechtspflege im grossherzogthum Baden während 1835–46. 12 v. in 3. 4°. *Carlsruhe, C. Braun'schen Hofbuchdruckerei*, 1837–48. s.

Badger (*Mrs.* C. M.) Floral belles from the green-house and garden. Painted from nature. 67 pp. 16 pl. fol. *New York, Scribner*, 1867.

Baedeker. *See* **Bädeker.**

Baer (Carl Ernst von). Anatomische und zoologische untersuchungen über das wallross (*trichechus rosmarus*), und vergleichung dieses thiers mit andern seesäugethieren. (Extract). 1 p. l. 140 pp. 1 map. 4°. *St. Petersburg, k. akademie der wissenchaften*, [1838]. s.

——— Berichte über die anmeldung eines mit der haut gefundenen mammuths, [etc.] (Extract). 127 pp. 2 pl. 8°. *St. Petersburg, k. akademie der wissenschaften*, 1866. s.

——— Crania selecta ex thesauris anthropologicis academiae imperialis petropolitanae. 28 pp. 16 pl. 4°. *Petropoli, Acad. imp. scient* 1859. s.

——— Kaspische studien. viii. Ueber ein allgemeines gesetz in der gestaltung der flussbetten. (Extract). 157 pp. 1 pl. 8°. *St. Petersburg, k. akad. der wissenschaften*, 1860. s.

——— Über das klima des Taimyrlandes.

[*With* Middendorff (A. T. von). Reise, etc. v. 1. theil 1].

——— Über Papuas und Alfuren. Ein commentar zu den beiden ersten abschnitten der abhandlung crania selecta, etc. 78 pp. 4°. *St. Petersburg, k. akad. der wissensch.* 1859. s.

——— Fragments relating to philosophical zoology. 8°. *London*, 1853.

[*With* Henfrey (A.) *and* Huxley. Scientific memoirs].

Baer (Joseph, *bookseller*). Verzeichniss der von Dr. Röth, Dr. Beil, und Dr. Bachmann dahier nachgelassen bibliotheken, sowie eines theils der bibliothek des Dr. G. Friedrich, welche den 27 Juni, 1859, versteigert werden sollen. 411 pp. 8°. *Frankfurt-am-Main, J. Baer*, 1859. s.

Baerle (Caspar van). *See* **Van Baerle.**

Baers (Jan). Olinda, ghelegen int landt van Brasil, inde capitania van Phernambuco, met mannelijcke dapperheyt ende groote couragie inghenomen, ende geluckelijck verovert op den 16 Februarij A° 1630. Onder het beleydt van den heere Henrick Lonck. 2 p. l. 38 pp. sm. 4°. *Amsterdam, H. Laurentsz*, 1630.

Baeyer. *See* **Bäyer.**

Bagatelles; [or, poetical trifles]. [*anon.*] viii, 203 pp. 18°. *London, Walkingame*, 1767.

Baggesen (Jens). Philosophischer nachlass. Herausgegeben von Carl A. R. Baggesen. 2 v. xii, 469 pp; viii, 400 pp. 8°. *Zürich, etc, F. Schulthess, et al.* 1858–63.

Bagwell (James). A thrilling narrative of the life, adventures, and terrible crimes of J. Bagwell; who was tried at Somerset, Pa. [1848], for the murder of Solomon Jones. 42 pp. 3 pl. 8°. [*Cincinnati*], *Rev. W. Miller*, [1851].

Bailey (*Rev.* B.) A dictionary of high and colloquial Malayalim and English, [etc.] viii, 852, iv. pp. 4°. *Cottayam, church mission press*, 1846. s.

Bailey (John). General view of the agriculture of the county of Durham, [etc.] xv, 412 pp. 1 col. map. 2 pl. 8°. *London*, 1810.

[Great Britain. Board of agriculture].

Bailey (J. T.) An historical sketch of the city of Brooklyn, and the surrounding neighborhood. [With] an account of the battle of Long Island. 72 pp. 1 pl. 16°. *Brooklyn, author*, 1840.

Bailey (J. W.) Notes concerning the minerals and fossils collected by Lieut. J. W. Abert in New Mexico. 8°. *Washington*, 1848.

[*With* Emory (W. H.) Military reconnoissance, etc.]

Bailey (Nathan). An universal etymological English dictionary, etc. 560 l. 8°. *London, J. Darby and others, about* 1720. s.

[Imperfect; title page and several prel. leaves wanting].

——— The same. 3d ed. 512 l. 8°. *London, J. Darby and others*, 1726.

——— The same. Dictionarium britannicum; or, a more compleat universal etymological English dictionary than any extant. 351 l. unp. fol. *London, T. Cox*, 1730.

Bailey (Rufus W.) Daughters at school instructed in a series of letters. 252 pp. 16°. *Philadelphia, presbyterian board of publication*, 1857. s.

Baillie (*Rev.* John). A memoir of Capt. W. Thornton Bate, R. N. xvi, 255 pp. 5 pl. 16°. *London, Longmans*, 1859.

Bailly (Charles François). Nouveau manuel complet de physique; ou, élémens abrégés de cette science, [etc.] Nouv. éd. [etc.] 411 pp. 8 pl. 24°. *Paris, Roret*, 1841. s.

Bain (Alexander). Mental science; a compendium of psychology and the history of philosophy. Designed as a text book for high schools and colleges 10, xxix, 428, 99 pp. 12°. *New York, D. Appleton & Co.* 1868.

Baird (James S. S.) The classical manual: an epitome of ancient geography, Greek and Roman mythology, antiquities, and chronology. xi, 179 pp. 12°. *London, Whittaker & Co.* 1852. s.

Baird (Robert, *D. D.*) The christian retrospect and register; a summary of the scientific, moral, and religious progress of the first half of the xixth century. 420 pp. 12°. *New York, M. W. Dodd*, 1851. s.

——— The progress and prospects of christianity in the United States of America; with remarks on the subject of slavery, and on the intercourse between British and American churches. 72 pp. 8°. *London, Partridge & Oakey*, [1851]. s.

Baird (Samuel J. *D. D.*) A history of the new school, and of the questions involved in the disruption of the presbyterian church in 1838. xii, 564 pp. 12°. *Philadelphia, Claxton, Remsen & Haffelfinger*, 1868.

Baker (B. F.) *and* **Fargo** (J. P.) Songs of the temple: a new collection of hymn tunes, chants, sentences, motets, and anthems. Composed and arranged for the use of christian churches of all denominations. 352 pp. obl. 16°. *Boston, Lee & Shepard*, 1868.

Baker (Daniel, *D. D.*) A plain and scriptural view of baptism. 134 pp. 16°. *Philadelphia, Presbyterian board of publication*, 1863. s.

Baker (George M.) The mimic stage. A series of dramas, comedies, burlesques, and farces, for public exhibitions and private theatricals. 290 pp. 3 pl. 16°. *Boston, Lee & Shepard*, 1869.

Baker (*Sir* Richard). A chronicle of the kings of England, from the time of the Romans unto the death of king James. [With] the reign of Charles i. and Charles ii. [and a catalogue of the nobility]. 9th ed. 38 p. l. 796 pp. 22 l. fol. *London, B. Tooke*, 1696.

Baker (*Sir* Samuel White). The Nile tributaries of Abyssinia, and the sword hunters of the Hamran Arabs. xxii, 596 pp. 2 maps. 24 pl. 8°. *London, Macmillan*, 1867.

Baker (T. *civil engineer*). Formulæ, rules, and examples for candidates for the military, naval, and civil service examinations, [etc.] Iron work, [etc]. By C. H. Dowling. 2 p. l. 191 pp; 2 p. l. 31 pp. 12°. *London, J. Weale*, 1862. s.

Baker (*Rev.* William M.) Oak-mot. [The prairie home]. 226 pp. 4 pl. 16°. *Philadelphia, Presbyterian board of publication*, 1868.

Bal (Jenny C. White del). Letters. *See* **White** (Rhoda E.)

Balbi (Adriano). Allgemeine erdbeschreibung, oder: hausbuch des geographischen wissens. Bearbeitet von H. Berghaus. 4e aufl. 2 v. lxxiv, 946 pp; vi, 734 pp. *Wien, C. A. Hartleben*, 1857.

Balch (Thomas). Letters and papers [Shippen mss. etc.] relating chiefly to the provincial history of Pennsylvania, with some notices of the writers. cxxxviii, 312 pp. 12°. *Philadelphia, Crissy & Markly*, 1855.

Balch (T. B.) A miniature poem. "Our town." 20 pp. 12°. *Georgetown, E. Hughes*, 1849. s.

Baldi (Bernardino). La nautica.

[*In* RACCOLTA di poemi didascalici. Ed. 2a. 1825].

Baldwin's (H. A.) **& Co.** consolidated business directory, 1867–68. *New York, Boston, and Philadelphia*, [*H. A. Baldwin & Co.* 1868].

Baldwin (Joseph G.) The flush times of Alabama and Mississippi. 2d ed. x, 330 pp. 4 pl. 12°. *New York, Appleton*, 1854.

Baldwin (Thomas, *aëronaut*). Airopaidia: an introduction to ærial navigation. viii, 361 pp. 8°. *Chester, author*, 1786.

Ballantyne (Robert Michael). Snowflakes and sunbeams; or, the young fur traders. A tale of the far north. vi, 429 pp. 8 pl. 12°. *London, Nelson & Sons*, 1854.

Ballenstedt (Johann Georg Just, *editor*).

[*See* ARCHIV für die neuesten entdeckungen aus der urwelt, 1819–24].

Ballou's monthly magazine. Jan. to Dec. 1868. v. 27–28. 8°. *Boston, office American union*, etc. [1868].

Baltimore clipper. [Daily]. Jan. 2, 1843, to July 8, 1851. 8 v. fol. *Baltimore*, 1843–51.

——— The same. May 8, 1861, to Jan. 6, 1863. 2 v. fol. *Baltimore*, 1861–63.

Baltimore plenary council. Concilii plenarii baltimorensis ii, in ecclesia metropolitana baltimorensi, a die 7-21 Octobris, 1866, habiti, et a sede apostolica recogniti, acta et decreta. Præside M. T. Spaulding. cliv, 410 pp. 8°. *Baltimoræ, J. Murphy*, 1868.

Baltimore sun. *See* **Sun** (The).

Bancroft (George). History of the United States, from the discovery of the American continent. 20th ed. v. 3. viii, 477 pp. 2 maps. 8°. *Boston, Little, Brown, & Co.* 1868.

Bandello (Vincenz). Narratiua disputatiōis facte de materia cōceptiōis beate virginis Marie. 117 l. sm. 4°. *Bonoñ, per Ugonem de Rugeriis de Regio*, 1481.

Banister (John). A synopsis of husbandry; being cursory observations in the several branches of rural economy, [etc.] xvi, 471 pp. 8°. *London, G. G. & J. Robinson*, 1799.

Banker's (The) magazine, journal of the money market and commercial digest. 1867-68. v. 27-28. 8°. *London, Groombridge*, 1867.

Bankers' (The) magazine, and statistical register. Edited by J. S. Homans. July, 1867, to June, 1868. 3d series. v. 2. Complete series, v. 22. 8°. *New York, J. S. Homans, jr.* 1867-68.

Banks (Edward). Report on the practicability and expence of a navigable canal, proposed to be made between the grand southern canal near Copthorne common, and Merstham. 8 pp. 1 map. 4°. *London, E. Blackader*, 1810.

[*With* RENNIE (John). Report of grand southern canal].

Banks (J.) A dictionary of the English and Russian languages. 4 v. 8°. *Moscow, Semen*, 1840. s.

Banks (John). A short critical review of the political life of Oliver Cromwell. [*anon.*] 3d ed. 359 pp. 8 l. 8°. *London, C. Davis*, [*about* 1747].

[Imperfect: wants 2 last leaves of index].

——— The same. [1st or 2d ed.] 8°. *London*, 1739.

[Imperfect: wants title page, prel. leaves, and 1 page of index. pp. 165-169 imperfect].

Banks (*Sir* Thomas Christopher). An analytical statement of the case of Alexander, earl of Sterling and Dovan, containing an explanation of his official dignities and peculiar territorial rights and privileges in the British colonies of Nova Scotia and Canada, [etc.] xlix, 123 pp. 4 tab. 8°. *London, J. Cochrane & Co.* 1832.

Banning (E. P. *M. D.*) A rational treatise on the trunkal muscles, elucidating the mechanical cause of chronic, spinal, pelvic, abdominal, and thoracic affections; with the rationale of their cure by mechanical support. xvi, 352 pp. portrait. 8°. *New York, Townsend & Adams*, 1868.

Baptist (The) hymn and tune book. *See* **Plymouth** collection.

Baptist (The) system examined, the church vindicated, and sectarianism rebuked. A review of "Fuller on baptism, [etc.]" [*anon.*] 376 pp. 18°. *Baltimore, T. N. Kurtz*, 1854. s.

Baptista *Mantuanus*. *See* **Spagnuoli** (Giovanni Battista.)

Barbaroux (Charles Jean Marie). Documents inédits. Mémoires. pp. 255-490. 8°. *Paris, Plon*, 1866.

[MÉMOIRES inédits de Pétion, etc. 1866].

Barbee (William J. *M. D.*) The first principles of geology: presenting the science in its physical and moral aspects. With a geological map of the U. S. 2d ed. 523 pp. 16°. *Louisville, (Ky.) Morton & Co.* 1868.

Barber (Edward C.) The crack shot; or, young rifleman's complete guide; being a treatise on the use of the rifle, etc. [Illustrated]. 342 pp. 16°. *New York, Townsend & Adams*, 1868.

Barber (John Warner). Connecticut historical collections, containing a general collection of facts, etc. relating to the history and antiquities of every town in Connecticut. 2d ed. 560 pp. 1 map. 6 pl. 8°. *New Haven, Durrie & Peck*, 1837.

——— *and* **Barber** (Elizabeth C.) American scenes: being a selection of the most interesting incidents in American history, [with] a historical sketch of each of the United States; also, a chronological table of the events in the late war. 408 pp. 1 pl. 16°. *Springfield, (Mass.) D. E. Fisk & Co.* 1868.

Barber (John W.) *and* **Howe** (Henry). Historical collections of the state of New Jersey. 512 pp. 13 pl. 8°. *New York, S. Tuttle*, 1844.

——— The same. [Revised ed.] 544 pp. 2 maps. 12 pl. 8°. *New Haven, J. W. Barber*, 1868.

——— Historical collections of the state of New York. 608 pp. 1 map. 12 pl. 8°. *New York, authors*, 1841.

Barber (Jonathan). Analysis of some principal phenomena of oral language. iv, x, 62 pp. 8°. *Washington, William Cooper*, 1824.

Barber (M. A. S.) Earning a living; or, from hand to mouth. 259 pp. 6 pl. 16°. *London, J. Nisbet & Co.* 1861.

——— Missionary tales for little listeners. 180 pp. 4 pl. 16°. *Philadelphia, Presbyterian board of publication*, [1848].

Barbier (Henri Auguste). Iambes. [Satires]. 12°. *Bruxelles, A. Peeters*, 1832.

[*With* HUGO (V.) Les feuilles d'automne. 1832].

Barbosa (Duarte). Description of the coasts of east Africa and Malabar in the beginning of the 16th century. Translated out of the Spanish manuscript, with notes and a preface, by H. E. J. Stanley. xi, 236 pp. 8°. *London*, 1866.

[HAKLUYT society publications. v. 35].

Barbosa du Bocage (José Vicente). Instrucções praticas sobre o modo de colligir, preparar e remetter productos zoologicos para o museo de Lisboa. 1 p. l. ii, 96 pp. 8°. *Lisboa, imprensa nacional,* 1862. s.

Barcia (Andres Gonzalez). Ensayo cronologico, para la historia general de la Florida. Por Gabriel de Cardenas y Cano. [*pseudon.*] 20 p. l. 366 pp. 28 l. 1 tab. *Madrid, N. R. Franco,* 1723.

Barclay (Jean). Argenis. Ed. novissima cum clave, hoc est, nominum propriorum elucidatione hactenus nondum edita. 576 pp. 24°. *Amstelodami, ex officiana Elzeviriana,* 1671. s.

Barclay (*Rev.* John, *pastor of the Berean assembly, Edinburgh*). Without faith, without God; or, an appeal to God concerning his own existence, [etc.] An essay proving that the knowledge of God comes only by revelation. With a preface by the Rev. David Thom. xxiv. 128 pp. 12°. *London, etc. Simpkin & Marshall,* 1836. s.

Barclay (Robert). Anarchy of the ranters and other libertines; the hierarchy of the romanists and other pretended churches refuted, in an apology for the quakers. viii, 111 pp. 12°. *Wilmington, James Adams,* 1783.

[*With* PENN (William). Brief account of the rise and progress of the people called quakers. *Wilmington,* 1783].

——— An apology for the true christian divinity; being an explanation and vindication of the principles and doctrines of the people called quakers. 548 pp. 8°. *Philadelphia, Friends' book store,* 1848. s.

Baring-Gould (Sabine). Curious myths of the middle ages. 2d series. 2 p. l. 374 pp. 1 pl. 12°. *London, Rivingtons,* 1868.

Barker (Joseph). The gospel triumphant; or, a defence of christianity against the attacks of the socialists; and an exposure of the social system of R. Owen. 448 pp. 12°. *Newcastle, J. Blackwell & Co.* 1839.

Barker-Webb (P.) *See* **Webb** (Philip Barker).

Barkow (Hans Carl Leopold). Das leben der walle in seiner beziehung zum athmen und zum blutlauf. Nebst bemerkungen über die benennung der finnwalle. 40 pp. fol. *Breslau, F. Hirt,* 1862. s.

Barlaams ok Josaphats saga. En religös romantisk fortælling om Barlaam og Josaphat, oprindelig forfattet paa Græsk i det 8de aarhundrede, senere oversat paa Latin, og herfra igjen i fri bearbeidelse ved aar 1200 overfört paa Norsk af kong Haakon Sverressön. Udgivet af R. Keyser og C. R. Unger. xxiv, 262 pp. 1 pl. 8°. *Christiania, Feilberg & Landmark,* 1851. s.

Barlaeus (Caspar). *See* **Van Baerle.**

Barlow (Joel). Political writings. New ed. 258 pp. 16°. *New York, Mott & Lyon,* 1796.

CONTENTS.

Advice to the privileged orders.
Letter to the national convention.
Letter to the people of Piedmont.
The conspiracy of kings.

——— The vision of Columbus; a poem in nine books. 258 pp. 6 l. 8°. *Hartford, Hudson & Goodwin,* 1787.

Barlow (Warren Sumner). Three voices. [Poems]. 184 pp. 12°. *Boston, White & Co.* 1868.

Barnard (Henry). Reports and documents relating to the public schools of Rhode Island, for 1848. *See* **Rhode Island.**

——— *See, also,* **United States.** (*Department of Education*).

Barnard (*Rev.* John). Sermons on several subjects. 190 pp. 8°. *London, for S. Gerrish, Boston, N. E.* 1727.

Barnes (Albert). Lectures on the evidences of christianity in the nineteenth century. 451 pp. 12°. *New York, Harper & bros.* 1868.

——— Notes on psalms. *See* **Bible,** *English.*

——— *See, also,* **Davies,** (*Rev.* Samuel). Sermons on important subjects. *New York,* 1845.

Barnes (Joseph). Remarks on mr. John Fitch's reply to mr. James Rumsey's pamphlet. xvi, 16 pp. 8°. *Philadelphia, J. James,* 1788.

Barnes (*Rev.* Joshua). Gerania: a new discovery of a little sort of people anciently discoursed of, called pygmies. 3 p. l. 110 pp. 1 pl. 18°. *London, O. Blagrave,* 1675.

Barnes (William H.) History of the thirty-ninth congress of the United States. 613 pp. portrait. 8°. *Indianapolis, Macauley & Co.* 1867.

——— The same. 2d ed. 636 pp. 18 portraits. 8°. *New York, Harpers,* 1868.

Barni (Jules Romain). Histoire des idées morales et politiques en France au dix-huitième siècle. v. 1–2. 16°. *Paris, G. Baillière,* 1865.

CONTENTS:

v. 1. L'abbé de Saint Pierre. Montesquieu. Voltaire.
v. 2. Rousseau. Diderot. D'Alembert.

Barnum (H. L.) The farmer's own book; or, family receipts for the husband and housewife. Stereotype ed. 165 pp. 16°. *Boston, Carter & Hendee,* 1832.

Barr (*Rev.* J. T.) Sunday-school facts; comprising incidents illustrative of the value and importance of the sunday-school institution. 205 pp. 18°. *New York, Carlton & Porter*, 1857. s.

Barrantes (Vicente). Catalogo razonado y critico de los libros, memorias y manuscritos, que tratan de las provincias de Extremadura, [etc.] Obra premiada por la biblioteca nacional, [etc.] viii, 320 pp. 8°. *Madrid, impresa de real orden*, 1865. s.

[SPAIN. Biblioteca nacional].

Barratt (Joseph, *M. D.*) The Indian of New England, and the northeastern provinces; with vocabularies in the Indian and English. 24 pp. 12°. *Middleton, Conn. C. H. Pelton*, 1857. s.

——— Key to the Indian language of New England, in the Etchemin, or Passamaquoddy language. No. 1. 8 pp. 12°. *Middleton, Conn. C. H. Pelton*, 1850. s.

[*With* the preceding].

——— Salices americanæ. North American willows, disposed in sections, or natural groups, with notes showing the kinds best adapted for the useful arts and ornamental culture. 8 l. 4°. *Middletown, Conn. C. H. Pelton*, 1840. s.

Barrera. *See* **La Barrera y Leirado.**

Barrett (*Mrs.* Angelica Bishop). The linden-tree cottage, and the accepted sacrifice. iv, 58 pp. 12°. *New York, Hurd & Houghton*, 1868.

Barrett (J. O.) The spiritual harp. *See* **Peebles** (J. M.) *and* **Barrett.**

Barrett (Mary). Steps in the upward way; the story of Fanny Bell. 279 pp. 3 pl. 16°. *Boston, Am. tract soc.* 1866.

Barrett (Solomon). Principles of grammar, a compendious treatise on English, Latin, Greek, German, Spanish, and French, founded on the principle of relations. 312 pp. 12°. *Philadelphia, King and Baird*, 1851.

Barrington (Shute, *bishop of Durham*). The political life of William Wildman, viscount Barrington. ii, 207 pp. 2 l. 1 pl. fol. *London, Bulmer & Co.* 1814.

Barron (William, *prof. in the university of St. Andrews*). Elements of logic; on the basis of lectures by W. Barron, with large supplementary additions, [etc.] Edited and compiled by James R. Boyd. 243 pp. 12°. *New York, A. S. Barnes & Co.* 1856. s.

Barrow (John Henry). The mirror of parliament. *See* **Great Britain.**

Barrows (*Rev.* E. P. *D. D.*) Companion to the bible. Part 1. Evidences of revealed religion. 139 pp. 12°. *New York, Amer. tract society*, 1868.

Barruel-Beauvert (Philip Auguste de). Lettre du délégué de la population française de Greytown, Amérique centrale, au commerce générale de l'empire française, etc. 39 pp. 8°. *Paris, A. Lebon*, 1856.

Barry (*Rev.* Alfred). The life and works of sir Charles Barry, R. A., F. R. S. etc. xiii, 407 pp. 34 pl. 1 chart. 8°. *London, John Murray*, 1867.

Barry (George, *D. D.*) History of the Orkney islands. With additions, by Rev. J. Headrick. xvi, 513 pp. 1 map. 10 pl. 4°. *London, Longman*, 1808.

Barry (*Rev.* James). Reviving cordial for a sin sick despairing soul in the time of temptation, from the author's own experience. 5th ed. ix, 96 pp. *Boston, J. Boyle*, 1774.

Barry (P.) The fruit garden, etc. xv, 398 pp. 1 pl. 12°. *New York, C. Scribner*, 1851. s.

Barstow (William, *M. D.*) Sulphurets; what they are, how concentrated, how assayed, and how worked. With a chapter on the blowpipe assay of minerals. 114 pp. 16°. *San Francisco, A. Roman & Co*, 1867.

Barthold (Friedrich Wilhelm). Geschichte der deutschen hansa. 3 v. in 2. 16°. *Leipzig, T. D. Weigel*, 1854.

[DEUTSCHE (Das) volk dargestellt in vergangenheit und gegenwart, etc. v. 11-13].

——— Geschichte der deutschen städte und des deutschen bürgerthums. 4 v. in 2. 16°. *Leipzig, T. D. Wiegel*, 1850.

——— Geschichte des grossen deutschen krieges vom tode Gustav Adolfs ab. 2 v. in 1. xiv, 400 pp; xv, 696 pp. 8°. *Stuttgart, S. G. Liesching*, 1842–43.

Bartholomæus *Anglicus*. *See* **Glanvil** (Bartholomew).

Bartholomæus *Pisanus*. *See* **Bartolomeo** *da Pisa*.

Bartlett (David W.) What I saw in London; or, men and things in the great metropolis. 327 pp. 1 pl. 12°. *New York, Saxton, Barker & Co.* 1860.

Bartlett (John). Familiar quotations; being an attempt to trace to their source passages and phrases in common use. 5th ed. xii, 778 pp. 12°. *Boston, Little, Brown & Co.* 1868.

Bartlett (John Russell). The progress of ethnology: an account of recent archæological, philological, and geographical researches in various parts of the globe, tending to elucidate the physical history of man. 151 pp. 8°. *New York, Am. ethnological soc.* 1847. s.

Bartlett (Joseph). Physiognomy; poem delivered at the anniversary of Φ β. κ. Harvard university, on the day of their anniversary, 1799. 16 pp. 4°. *Boston, J. Russell*, 1799.

Bartlett (William H. C.) Elements of natural philosophy. 1. Mechanics. 632 pp. 8°. *New York, A. S. Barnes & Co.* 1850. s.

Bartoli (Daniello, *soc. Jesu*). Dell' hvomo di lettere difeso et emendato. 4 p. l. 464 pp. 4 l. 18°. *Venetia, Giunti & Baba*, 1646.

——— The same. El hombre de letras, escrito en italiano, y aoro nuevamente en castellano, por G. Sanz. 18 p. l. 288 pp. 4°. *Barcelona, J. Jolis*, 1744. s.

Bartoli (Pietro Sante, *and* Francesco). Le pitture antiche delle grotte di Roma. *See* **Bellori** (G. P.) *and* **La Chausse** (M. A. de).

Bartolomeo *da Pisa, or da S. Concordio.* Sūma de casibus cōsciencie. 492 l. fol. *Coloniæ, per Arnoldum Therhuernen*, 1474. s.

Barton (Benjamin Smith, *M. D.*) Fragments of the natural history of Pennsylvania. Part i. [Birds of Philadelphia and suburbs]. xviii, 24 pp. fol. *Philadelphia, author*, 1799. s.

[No more published].

——— Memoir concerning the disease of goitre, as it prevails in different parts of North America. 94 pp. 8°. *Philadelphia*, 1800. s.

——— New views of the origin of the tribes and nations of America. [With comparative vocabularies]. cix, 133, 32 pp. 8°. *Philadelphia, author*, 1798. s.

Barton (Jerome). Comic recitations and humorous dialogues, in prose and poetry, burlesque scenes, etc. 180 pp. 16°. *New York, Dick & Fitzgerald*, 1868.

Bartos (Bartolomej, *pisar*). Kronika Prazská od léta páne 1524 az do kónce léta 1530. Dle dvou rukopisu cís, verejné knihovny Prazské k vydáni upravil K. J. Erben. 24 p. l. 376 pp. 8°. *Praze, J. G. Kalve*, 1851. s.

Bartram (John, *botanist*). A journal kept for the Floridas. 4°. *London*, 1769.

[*With* STORK (W.) A description of East Florida, 1769].

Bartram (William). Reisen durch Nord- und Süd Karolina, Georgien, Ost- und West-Florida, das gebiet der Tscherokesen, Krichks, und Tschaktahs, nebst umständlichen nachrichten von den einwohnern, dem boden und den naturprodukten, etc. Aus dem Englischen, mit erläuternden anmerkungen von E. A. W. Zimmermann. xxvi, 469 pp. 8°. *Berlin, Voss*, 1793.

[MAGAZIN von reisebeschreibungen, v. 10, 1793].

Basselin (Olivier), *and* **Le Houx** (Jean). Les vaux-de-vire édités et inédits; avec discours préliminaire, [etc.] publiés par Julien Travers. 252 pp. 18°. *Paris, Lance*, 1833. s.

Bassini (Carlo). The education of the voice, on an improved plan: being musical instructions, exercises, and recreations. 96 pp. obl. 12°. *New York, Huntington & Co.* 1868.

Batchelder (Eugene). A romance of the sea-serpent, or the ichthyosaurus. [By Wave]. Also, a collection of the ancient and modern authorities, with letters from distinguished merchants and men of science. [*pseudon.*] 2 p. l. 172 pp. 12°. *Cambridge, J. Bartlett*, 1849. s.

Batchelor (Thomas). General view of the agriculture of the county of Bedford, [etc]. xvi, 636 pp. 1 col. map. 8 pl. 8°. *London*, 1808.

[GREAT BRITAIN. Board of agriculture].

Bate (John). Mysteries of nature and art, in foure severall parts: 1. Of water works. 2. Of fire works. 3. Of drawing, washing, limning, painting, and engraving. 4. Of sundry experiments. [With separate title-page: the booke of extravagants]. 2d ed. 6 p. l. 288 pp. 8 l. 1 pl. portrait. *London, printed by Thomas Harper, for Ralph Mab*, 1635. s.

[Title page and portrait wanting].

Bates (Walter). Companion for Caraboo. A narrative of the conduct and adventures of Henry Frederic Moon, alias Henry Frederic More Smith, alias Newman, etc. now under sentence in Connecticut. xvi, 84 pp. 1 portrait. 8°. *London, Allman & Co.* 1817.

Bath and west of England society for the encouragement of agriculture, arts, manufactures, and commerce. Letters and papers on agriculture, planting, etc. selected from the correspondence of the society. v. 1–14. 15 v. 8°. *Bath, society*, 1792—1814.

[No more published of this series].

EDITIONS.

v. 1.	4th ed.	1792.	v. 8.	1796.
v. 2.	5th ed.	1792.	v. 9.	1799.
v. 3.	3d ed.	1791.	v. 10.	1805.
v. 4.	2d ed.	1792.	v. 11.	1807.
v. 5.	2d ed.	1792.	v. 12.	1810.
v. 6.	[1st ed.]	1792.	v. 13.	1814.
v. 6.	[new ed.]	1795.	v. 14.	1816.
v. 7.		1795.		

——— The same. Originally published in nine volumes, abridged in two. 2 v. 8°. *Bath, [society]*, 1802.

[v. 1 wanting].

——— Memoirs of agriculture and other œconomical arts. By Robert Dossie. 2 v. xxxii, 455 pp. 8 l; xx, 482 pp. 4 l. 8°. *London, J. Nourse*, 1768–71.

Batilly (Denis Lebey de). *See* **Lebey de Batilly.**

Battista *Mantovano.* *See* **Spagnuoli** (Giovanni Battista).

Battle (The) of Brooklyn, a farce; as it was performed on Long-Island, 27th of August, 1776. By the representatives of the tyrants of America, assembled at Philadelphia. [*anon.*] 27 pp. 12°. *New York, J. Rivington, in the year of the rebellion.* 1776.

Baudot (A. de). Églises de bourgs et villages. 2 v. 55 pp. 70 pl; 40 pp. 80 pl. 4°. *Paris, A. Morel,* 1867.

Baudot de Juilly (Nicolas). Histoire et règne de Louis XI. 6 v. 16°. *Paris, Pissot,* 1755.

Note.—This book was published under the name of Marguerite de Lussan.

Baudrillart (Jacques Joseph). Traité général des eaux et forêts, chasses et pêches. 2e partie. Dictionnaire général raisonné et historique des eaux et forêts. 2 v. 816 pp; 1006 pp. Atlas. 48 pl. 4°. *Paris, Huzard,* 1823–25.

Bauerman (H.) A treatise on the metallurgy of iron; containing outlines of the history of iron manufacture, processes of manufacture of iron and steel, etc. Illustrated by J. B. Jordan. viii, 399 pp. 12°. *London, Virtue, & Co.* 1868.

——— The same. With appendix on the Martin process of making steel, from the report of A. S. Hewitt, United States commissioner to the exposition at Paris, 1867. Illustrated. viii, 406 pp. 12°. *New York, Virtue & Yorston,* 1868.

Baumann (Ludwig Adolph). Abrisz der staatsverfassung der vornehmsten länder in Amerika, nebst nördlichen polarländern. 4 p. l. 700 pp. 8°. *Brandenburg, gebrüder Halle,* 1776.

Baumer (Johann Wilhelm). Naturgeschichte des mineralreichs, mit besonderer anwendung auf Thüringen herausgegeben. 4 p. l. 520 pp. 7 l. 11 pl. 16°. *Gotha, J. C. Dieterich,* 1763. s.

Baumstark (Eduard). Zur einkommenssteuer frage. Besonderer abdruck aus den Elden, jahrbüchern. 2 p. l. 84 pp. 8°. *Greifswald, C. A. Coch's verlagshandlung,* 1850. s.

Baur (Ferdinand Christian). Das Christenthum und diechristliche kirche der drei ersten jahrhunderte. 2[e] ausg. xxiv, 535 pp. 8°. *Tübingen, L. F. Fues,* 1860.

——— Die christliche kirche vom anfang des 4[en] bis zum ende des sechtsen jahrhunderts. x, 326 pp. 8°. *Tübingen, L. F. Fues,* 1859.

Bäyer (J. J) Gradmessung in Ostpreussen. Ausgefuhrt von F. W. Bessel, [und] Baeyer. *See* **Prussia.**

——— Nivellement zwischen Swinemünde und Berlin. Auf dienstliche veranlassung ausgeführt. x, 122 pp. 1 map. 4°. *Berlin, Dümmler,* 1840. s.

——— Die verbindungen der preussischen und russischen dreieckskettten. *See* **Prussia.**

——— Ueber die grösse und figur der erde. viii, 111 pp. 1 map. 8°. *Berlin, G. Reimer,* 1861. s.

Bayne (Peter). The christian life, social and individual. 528 pp. 12°. *Boston, Gould & Lincoln,* 1856. s.

——— Essays in biography and criticism. First series. 426 pp. 12°. *Boston, Gould & Lincoln,* 1857. s.

CONTENTS.

De Quincey; Tennyson; Mrs. Browning; Glimpses of recent British art; John Ruskin; Hugh Miller; The modern novel; Dickens; Bulwer; Thackeray; Currer Bell;-Ellis-Acton-Currer.

Baynes (Thomas Spencer). Sir William Hamilton. [A biography]. 8°. *Edinburgh, A. & C. Black,* 1857.

[*In* EDINBURGH essays, pp. 241–300. 1857].

Beadle's monthly, a magazine of to-day. January, 1866, to June, 1867. 3 v. 8°. *New York, Beadle & Co.* 1866–67.

[No more published].

Beames (*Rev.* Thomas). The rookeries of London: past, present, and prospective. 2d ed. xi, 309 pp. 2 pl. 1 tab. 8°. *London, T. Bosworth,* 1852.

Beard (George M. *M. D.*) The history and art of laryngoscopy and rhinoscopy, rhinitis, inhalations, and electrization, applied to diseases of the air-passages.

[*In* TOBOLD (Adelbert). Chronic diseases of the larynx. pp. 1–71. 8°. *N. Y.* 1868].

Beardsley (J. Edwards, *D. D.*) The history of the episcopal church in Connecticut, from the death of bishop Seabury to the present time. v. 2. xxix, 465 pp. 1 pl. 8°. *New York, Hurd & Houghton,* 1868.

Beaten tracks; or, pen and pencil sketches in Italy. [*anon.*] viii, 278 pp. 42 pl. 8°. *London, Longmans,* 1866.

Beattie (James). An essay on the nature and immutability of truth, in opposition to sophistry and scepticism. iv, 354 pp. 16°. *Philadelphia, Solomon Wieatt,* 1809.

Beattie (*Rev.* R. H.) What is faith? 102 pp. 18°. *Philadelphia, presbyterian board of publication,* 1857. s.

Beaujour (Louis Félix, *baron* de). A view of the commerce of Greece, 1787–97. From the French, by T. H. Horne. xvi, 463 pp. 8°. *London, J. Wallis,* 1800.

Beaumont (Élie de). *See* **Élie de Beaumont.**

Beaumont (*Rev.* G.) The warrior's looking-glass: wherein is shewn the trivial causes, cruel nature, and antichristian spirit of war. 204 pp. 16°. *Sheffield, J. Crome,* 1808.

Beaumont (William, *M. D.*) Physiology of digestion, with experiments on the gastric juice. 2d ed. corrected by Samuel Beaumont. 304 pp. 12°. *Burlington,* [*Vt.*] *C. Goodrich,* 1847. s.

Beausobre (Isaac de). *See* **Bible** (*English, Matthew*).

Béchamp. Analyse des eaux de Soultzmatt. 8°. *Paris, J. B. Baillière,* 1853. s.
[*In* BACH (J. A.) Des eaux de Soultzmatt, 1853].

Beck (*Dr.* August). Johann Friedrich der Mittlere, herzog zu Sachsen. Ein beitrag zur geschichte des 16ten jahrhunderts. v. 1. xv, 600 pp. 8°. *Weimar, H. Böhlau,* 1858. s.
[V. 2 wanting].

Beck (Lewis C.) Reports on mineralogy and chemistry. *Albany,* 1837–41.
[NEW YORK. Geological survey, annual reports, v. 1–5].

Becke (Franz Arnold von der). Von staatsämtern und staatsdienern. xiv, 182 pp. 1 l. 8°. *Heilbronn, J. D. Class,* 1797.

Becker (George J.) Becker's book-keeping. Blanks for the fourth series of Becker's book-keeping by double entry, [etc.] 43 l. 4°. *Philadelphia, E. H. Butler & Co.* 1851. s.

Becker (Wilhelm Adolph). Charikles, bilder altgriechischer sitte. Zur genaueren kenntniss des griechischen privatlebens. 2 v. xx, 518 pp. 5 pl. 8°. *Leipzig, F. Fleischer,* 1840.

——— Gallus, oder römische scenen aus der zeit Augusts. Zur genaueren kenntniss des römischen privatlebens. 2e ausg. 3 v. 8°. *Leipzig, F. Fleischer,* 1849.

Beckmann (Johann, *editor*). *See* **Physikalisch-ökonomische** bibliothek, 1770–98.

Becquerel (Antoine César) *and* **Lawes** (J. B.) The action of salt upon vegetation, and its use in agriculture. 8°. *New York,* 1848.
[FARMER'S library, v. 3].

Bede (Cuthbert, *pseudon.*) *See* **Bradley** (*Rev.* Edward).

Beebe (*Rev.* Gilbert). A compilation of editorial articles, copied from the "Signs of the times," in which is reflected the doctrine and order of the old school, or primitive baptists. v. 1. 768 pp. portrait. 12°. *Middletown, N. Y. B. L. Beebe,* 1868.

Beecher (Catherine E.) Domestic receipt book; designed as a supplement to her treatise on domestic economy. xiii, 293, 24 pp. 8°. *New York, Harper & bros.* 1846.

Beecher (*Rev.* Charles). A review of the "spiritual manifestations," [etc.] 75 pp. 12°. *New York, G. P. Putnam,* 1853. s.

Beecher (*Rev.* Henry Ward). Norwood; or, village life in New England. xi, 549 pp. 12°. *New York, Scribner & Co.* 1868.

——— Prayers from Plymouth pulpit. Phonographically reported. 5th ed. viii, 332 pp. 12°. *New York, C. Scribner & Co.* 1867.

——— Sermons. Selected from published and unpublished discourses, and revised by their author. 2 v. 484 pp. portrait; 447 pp. 8°. *Harper & bros.* 1868.

Beelen (Jean Theodore). Commentarius in acta apostolorum. *See* **Bible.** *Greek and Latin.*

——— Commentarius in epistolam S. Pauli ad Philippenses, [etc]. *See* **Bible.** *Greek and Latin.*

——— Interpretatio epistolæ S. Pauli ad Philippenses. *See* **Bible.** *Greek and Latin.*

Beer (August). Introduction à la haute optique. Traduit de l'Allemand par C. Forthomme. xvi, 374 pp. 2 pl. 8°. *Paris, E. Mellier; Nancy Gremblot, etc.* 1858.

Beers (F. W.) *and others.* Atlas of Greene co., N. Y. From actual surveys. 21 maps. 1 pl. 4°. *New York, Beers, Ellis, & Soule,* 1867.

——— Atlas of New London co., Conn., from actual surveys. 4 l, 29 maps. 4 pl. 4°. *New York, Beers, Ellis, & Soule,* 1868.

——— Atlas of New York, [etc]. and vicinity, from actual surveys. 61 maps. 5 pl. 4°. *New York, Ellis, & Soule,* 1867.

——— The same. 51 maps. 9 pl. 4°. *New York, Beers, Ellis, & Soule,* 1867.

——— The same. 50 maps. 3 pl. 4°. *New York, Beers, Ellis, & Soule,* 1868.

Begas (J. Antonio D.) Nuevo estilo y formulario de escribir cartas missivas, [etc.] 4 p. l. 351 pp. 16°. *Barcelona, J. F. Piferrer, about* 1793. s.

Beger (August Hermann). Additamenta in anatomen comparatam *arvicolæ amphibii Lac et arvicolæ arvalis Lac,* [etc]. 44 pp. 2 l. 8°. *Halis, typis Lipkianis,* 1867. s.

Beil (J. A.) *and others.* Technologisches wörterbuch in deutscher, französischer und englischer sprache, gewerbe, civil-und militar-

Beil—continued.
baukunst, artillerie, maschinenbau, strassen- und wasserbau, schiffbau und schiffahrt, mathematik, physik, chemie, mineralogie, u. a. m. umfassend. v. 2–3. 8°. *Wiesbaden, C. W. Kreidel*, 1855–68. s.

CONTENTS:

v. 2. Technological dictionary, containing the technical words used in manufactures and arts, [etc]. English, German, French, by prof. dr. Franke. 3 p. l. 616 pp. 1855.
v. 3. Dictionnaire technologique français, allemand, anglais, contenant les termes techniques employés dans les arts et metiers, [etc]. par Chrétien Rumpf. viii, 588 pp. 2 l. [1863–67].

Belair (Alexandre Pierre Julienne de). Élémens de fortification. 2e éd. ix, 459 pp. 30 pl. 8°. *Paris, F. Didot*, 1793. s.

Belden (E. Porter). New York; past, present, and future. 2d ed. 125 pp. 1 map. 2 pl. 16°. *New York, Prall, Lewis & Co.* 1850.

——— New York, as it is; being the counterpart of the metropolis of America. 24 pp. 1 pl. 16°. *New York, J. P. Hall*, 1849.
[*With his* New York: past, present, and future, 1850].

Belgiojoso (Christine Trivulzio, *princesse* de). Essai sur la formation du dogme catholique. [*anon.*] 4 v. 8°. *Paris, J. Renouard*, 1842–43. s.

Belgium. Annales des universités de Belgique; ou, recueil contenant les lois, arrêtés et règlements relatifs à l'enseignement supérieur, les mémoires couronnés aux concours universitaires, et d'autres documents académiques. 2e (—11e) année. 7 v. 8°. *Bruxelles, T. Lesigne*, 1844–54. s.
[1e année wanting].

——— The same. 2e série. Annales des universités de Belgique. Recueil contenant des mémoires de professeurs et d'agrégés des universités, les mémoires couronnés aux concours universitaires, [etc]. Publié sous la direction de la commission instituée par arrêté royal du 1er Mars, 1859. Années 1858–59. v. 1. 8°. *Bruxelles, T. Lesigne*, 1861. s.

——— Inventaire des archives des chambres des comptes, précédé d'une notice historique sur ces anciennes institutions. 2 v. 2 p. l. xx, 442 pp. 1 l; 2 p. l. xix, 683 pp. fol. *Bruxelles, Hayez*, 1837–45. s.

——— Inventaires des cartes et plans, manuscrits et gravés, qui sont conservés aux archives générales du royaume. xii, 413 pp. fol. *Bruxelles, Hayez*, 1848. s.

——— Recueil des discours prononcés à la chambre des représentants et au senat, dans la discussion de la loi sur l'enseignement supérieur, [1849]. 238 pp. 8°. *Bruxelles, M. Vanderborght*, 1850. s.

——— Statistique de la Belgique. Agriculture. Recensement général, [15 Oct. 1846]. 4 v. fol. *Bruxelles, ministre de l'intérieur*, 1850. s.

CONTENTS.

v. 1. Provinces d'Anvers et de Brabant. ccxvi, 500 pp.
v. 2. Provinces des deux Flandres. 2 p. l. 566 pp.
v. 3. Provinces de Hainaut et de Liége. 2 p. l. 775 pp.
v. 4. Provinces de Limbourg, de Luxembourg et de Namur. 2 p. l. 773 pp.

——— The same. Agriculture. Résumés par arrondissement et par province. ccxvi, 56 pp. 4°. *Bruxelles, ministre de l'intérieur*, 1850. s.

——— The same. Industrie. Recensement général. [15 Oct. 1846]. xxvi, 539 pp. fol. *Bruxelles, ministre de l'intérieur*, 1851. s.

——— The same. Population. Recensement général. [15 Oct. 1846]. lxix, 550 pp. fol. *Bruxelles, ministre de l'intérieur*, 1849. s.

——— The same. Population. Mouvement de l'état civil pendant les années 1845–50. 6 v. in 3. fol. *Bruxelles, ministre de l'intérieur*, 1846–51. s.

——— The same. Mines, usines minéralurgiques, machines à vapeur. Années 1839 à 1844. Compte rendu, [etc.] c, 72 pp. fol. *Bruxelles, ministre des travaux-publics*, 1846. s.

——— *Ministère des finances.* Budget des recettes et dépenses du royaume de Belgique pour l'exercice 1839. 5 p. l. lxix, 306 pp. fol. *Bruxelles, Hayez*, 1838. s.

——— *Ministère des travaux-publics.* Canal de Charleroy. Rachat de la concession, [etc.] 2 p. l. lviii, 188 pp. fol. *Bruxelles, H. Remy*, 1839. s.

——— ——— Canalization de l'Escaut et de la Lys. Projet de loi présenté le 27 Décembre, 1837, [etc.] 2 p. l. xxxvi, 137 pp. fol. *Bruxelles, H. Remy*, [1838?] s.

——— ——— Chemin de fer. Compte-rendu des opérations effectuées à la date du [*or*, jusqu'au] 31 Décembre, 1840–42, [etc]. 3 v. fol. *Bruxelles, E. Devroye & Ce.* 1840–42. s.

——— ——— The same. Compte-rendu des opérations de l'exercice 1844[–59], etc. 8 v. fol. *Bruxelles, E. Devroye & Ce.* 1845–60. s.
[Wanting: 1843–46, 1850–54, 1856–57].

——— ——— The same. Embranchement du Limbourg. Rapports. 2 p. l. 23 pp. 1 map. fol. *Bruxelles, imprimerie du moniteur belge*, 1838. s.
[*With* Compte rendu, 1840].

——— ——— The same. Ligne du Hainaut. Enquête, [etc.] 2 p. l. 176 pp. fol. *Bruxelles, imprimerie du moniteur belge*, 1837. s.
[*With* Compte rendu, 1840].

——— ——— Chemin de fer direct de Bruxelles vers Gand, par Alost, en communication avec les stations diverses de la capitale, [etc.] 239 pp. 1 l. lxxxiii pp. 1 tab. 1 map. 2 plans. fol. *Bruxelles, E. Devroye & Ce.* 1846. s.

——— ——— Chemin de fer de l'Entre Samberet-Meuse, (etc.) 2 p. l. xcv, 193 pp. 1 tab. 1 map. fol. *Bruxelles, E. Devroye & Ce.* 1844. s.

——— ——— La Meuse. Études faites par ordre du gouvernment belge. i–iv. rapports du 1839–41. 3 parts in 1 v. fol. *Bruxelles, V^e^. H. Remy,* 1840–42. s.

——— ——— La navigation de la Belgique vers Paris. Études faites pour effectuer en Belgique la jonction des bassins de la Meuse et de l'Escaut, par un canal de Mons à la Sambre. Rapport, [etc.] 2 p. l. 330 pp. 1 tab. col. map. fol. *Bruxelles, V^e^. H. Remy,* 1840. s.

——— ——— Des voies navigables en Belgique. Considérations historiques suivies de propositions diverses ayant pour objet l'amélioration et l'extension de la navigation. 2 p. l. 497 pp. map. fol. *Bruxelles, Devroye & Ce.* 1842. s.

Belgravia. A London magazine. Conducted by M. E. Braddon. November, 1866, to October, 1868. v. 1–6. 8°. [*London,* 1867–68.]

Belhaven (John Hamilton, *2d baron*). *See* **Hamilton** (John).

Belidor (Bernard Forest de). Dictionnaire portatif de l'ingénieur et de l'artilleur. Totalement changée, refondue, et augmenté du quadruple, par Charles Antoine Jombert. Nouv. éd. vi, 740 pp. 8°. *Paris, auteur,* 1768. s.

Belknap (*Rev.* Jeremy). The history of New Hampshire. 3 v. 8°. *Boston, author,* 1791–92.

[*Note.*—The 1st ed. of v. 1 was published at Philadelphia in 1784].

——— The same. 3 v. 8°. *Dover, (N. H.) O. Crosby and J. Varney,* 1812.

Bell (Thomas, *professor in King's college*). A history of British quadrupeds, including the cetacea. xviii, 526 pp. 8°. *London, J. Van Voorst,* 1837. s.

——— A monograph of the fossil malacostracous crustacea of Great Britain. Part ii: crustacea of the gault and greensand. 40 pp. 11 l. 11 pl. 4°. *London,* 1862.

[PALÆONTOGRAPHICAL society publications].

Bellamy (Thomas). Guernsey pictorial directory and stranger's guide. v, 142 pp. 1 pl. 24°. *Guernsey, H. Brouard,* 1843.

Bellarmin (Robert, *cardinal*). De scriptoribus ecclesiasticis, liber vnvs. Cvm adivnctis indicibvs vndecim, [etc.] Ed. ultima. 12 p. l. 438 pp. 12°. *Lvgdvni, M. Mayer,* 1675. s.

——— Chronologia brevis, ab orbe condito, usque ad A. D. 1654 [1613.] Nunc demum continuata vsque ad annum 1654. 127 pp. 12°. *Lvgdvni, M. Mayer,* 1675. s.

Belleforest (François de). Les grandes annales et histoire générale de France, des la venve des Francs en Gavle, ivsqves av règne dv roy Henry iii. 2 v. 12 p. l. 817, 56 l; 3 p.l. 118–1692, 34 l. fol. *Paris, G. Buon,* 1579.

Bellenger (William A.) *and* **Witcomb** (——). Guide to French conversation. 6th Amer. ed. 202 pp. 18°. *New York, Leypoldt & Holt,* 1867.

Belli (Onorio). A description of some important theatres and other remains in Crete, from a ms. history of Candia in 1556. Being a supplement to the "Museum of classical antiquities" by E. Falkener. 32 pp. 1 map. 8 pl. 8°. *London, Trübner & Co.* 1854.

Bellin (Antoine Gaspard). L'exposition universelle, poëme didactique en quinze chants. 3 p. l. 416 pp. 8°. *Paris, Garnier frères,* 1867. s.

Bellin (Jacques-Nicolas). Remarques sur la carte de l'Amérique septentrionale, entre le 28e et le 72e dégré de latitude, avec une description géographique de ces parties. 131 pp. 4°. *Paris, Didot,* 1755.

Bellingeri (Carlo Francesco). Anatomisch-physiologische untersuchungen über das rückenmark und seine nerven. Deutsch bearbeitet von dr. Hermann Kaulla. Mit einem vorworte von dr. W. v. Ludwig. viii, 56 pp. 2 pl. 4°. *Stuttgart,* 1833.

Bellori (Giovanni Pietro), *and* **La Chausse** (Michel-Ange de). Le pitture antiche delle grotte di Roma, e del sepolcro de Nasonj. Disegnate, e intagliate da P. S. Bartoli e F. Bartoli. 6 p. l. 63 pp. 74 pl. fol. *Roma, stamparia di Gaetano de gli Zenobj,* 1706.

Bellows (Albert J. *M. D.*) The philosophy of eating. 342 pp. 12°. *New York, Hurd & Houghton,* 1867.

Bellows (Henry W. *D. D.*) The old world in its new face. Impressions of Europe in 1867–1868. v. 1. 454 pp. 12°. *New York, Harpers,* 1868.

Beltrami (Cesare). Considerazioni ematologiche. [Extract]. 32 pp. 8°. *Milano, Ann. univ. di medicino,* 1847. s.

Beltrami (Cesare). Studj sulla cotenna del sangue. [Extract]. 180 pp. 8°. *Milano, Ann. univ. di medicino*, 1853. s.

Ben Boland's garden; or, home life. [*anon.*] 228 pp. 2 pl. 16°. *Philadelphia, Amer. s. s. union*, 1868.

Beneden (Pierre Joseph Van). *See* **Van Beneden.**

Benedict (David). A general history of the baptist denomination in America and other parts of the world. 3d ed. viii, 970 pp. 1 portrait. 8°. *New York, L. Colby & Co.* 1848. s.

Benedict (Erastus C.) The hymn of Hildebert, and other mediæval hymns, with translations. x, 128 pp. 12°. *New York, A. D. F. Randolph*, 1867.

Benfey (Theodor). Handbuch der Sanskritsprache. 1ᵉ abth: grammatik. 2ᵉ abth: chrestomathie und glossar. 3 v. in 2. 8°. *Leipzig, F. A. Brockhaus*, 1852–54.

——— A practical grammar of the Sanskrit language, [etc.] xvii. 228 pp. 2 tab. 8°. *Berlin, A. Asher & Co.* 1863. s.

Bengel (John Albert). Gnomon of the New Testament. *See* **Bible,** *English.*

Benjamin (S. G. W.) The Turk and the Greek; or, creeds, races, society, and scenery in Turkey, Greece, and the isles of Greece. vii, 268 pp. 16°. *New York, Hurd & Houghton*, 1867.

Benner (Enos). Abhandlung über die rechenkunst, oder practische arithmetik, [etc.] 3ᵉ ausg. 178 pp. 12°. *Sumnytaun,* [*Pa.*] *herausgeber*, 1845. s.

Bennet (James Henry Arlington). The American system of practical bookkeeping, [etc.] 28th ed. 160 pp. 1 pl. 8°. *New York, M. H. Newman & Co.* 1848. s.

——— The same. 41st ed. 126 pp. 2 pl. 8°. [*New York, author*, 1862]. s.

——— Hell demolished; heaven gained; science triumphant; Moses, the old Jew, laid on his back, and the Almighty vindicated against the pretentions and falsehoods of men, [etc.] Thomas Chalmers, [etc.] against J. Arlington Bennet. 188 pp. 1 pl. 12°. *New York, author*, 1855. s.

——— A new revelation to mankind, drawn from axioms, or self-evident truths in nature, mathematically demonstrated. 188 pp. 1 portrait. 12°. *New York, proprietor*, 1855. s.

Bennett (Edward Turner). The gardens and menagerie of the zoological society delineated. Published under the superintendence of the secretary of the society. 2 v. xii, 308 pp; viii, 328 pp. 8°. *London, T. Tegg & Son*, 1835. s.

CONTENTS.

v. 1. Quadrupeds.
v. 2. Birds.

Bennett (Emerson). The bandits of the Osage. 121 pp. 8°. *Cincinnati, Robinson & Jones*, 1847.

——— Mike Fink; a legend of the Ohio. 102 pp. 8°. *Cincinnati, Robinson & Jones*, 1848.

——— The prairie flower; or, adventures in the far west. 128 pp. 8°. *Cincinnati, Stratton & Barnard*, 1849.

Benson (Egbert). Memoir, read before N. Y. historical society, Dec. 31, 1816, [on names of places in New York state]. 2d ed. 127 pp. 12°. *Jamaica, N. Y. Henry C. Sleight*, 1825.

Benson (Lawrence S.) Geometry: the elements of Euclid and Legendre simplified and arranged to exclude from geometrical reasoning the *reductio ad absurdum;* with the elements of plane and spherical trigonometry. 264 pp. 8°. *New York, Davies & Kent*, 1867.

Bentley (Charles, *artist*). Twelve views in the interior of Guiana. *See* **Schomburgk** (*Sir* R. H.)

Bentley (Rensselaer). Pictorial definer; containing the most important words in the English language familiarly defined. 170 pp. 16°. *New York, Shepard & Co.* 1852. s.

——— The pictorial reader, [etc.] 239 pp. 12°. *New York, G. F. Cooledge & bro.* 1847. s.

Bentley (Richard, *D. D.*) Remarks upon a late discourse of free-thinking, in a letter to F. H. 107 pp. 8°. *Oxford*, 1825.

[*In* RANDOLPH (John, *bishop of London*). Enchiridion theologicum, v. 2.]

Bentley's miscellany. July, 1867, to December, 1868. v. 62–64. 8°. *London, Chapman & Hall*, 1867–68.

Benton (Thomas H.) Thirty years' view; a history of the working of the American government from 1820 to 1850. 2 v. 8°. *New York, Appletons*, 1854. s.

Benzoni (Girolamo). Novae novi orbis historiæ, id est, rerum ab Hispanis in India Occidentali hactenus gestarum, et acerbo illorum in eas gentes dominatu, libri tres, Vrbani Calvetonis opera industriaque ex italicis latini facti, ac notis illustrati. His ab eodem adiuncta est, de Gallorum in Floridam expeditione historia. 16 p. l. 480 pp. 8 l. 16°. [*Genevæ*,] *hæredes E. Vignon*, 1600.

——— Brief discovrs et histoire d'vn voyage de quelques François en la Floride: et du massacre autant iniustement que barbarement executé sur eux, par les Hespagnols, 1565.

Benzoni—continued.
Reueuë et augmentée par Vrbain Cnavveton. 104 pp. 18°. [*Genevæ?*] 1579.
Note.—This work, though printed in most editions of Benzoni, is of doubtful authorship.

——— The same. De Gallorvm expeditione in Floridam, etc. 16°. [*Genevæ,*] *hæredes E. Vignon,* 1600.
[*With his* Novae novi orbis historiæ. pp. 427–480. ed. 1600].

——— Brevis insvlarvm Canariæ descriptio. 16°. [*Genevæ,*] *hæredes E. Vignon,* 1600.
[*With his* Novae novi orbis historiæ. pp. 416–426. ed. 1600].

Béranger (Pierre Jean de). Two hundred of his lyrical poems, done into English verse. By William Young. vii, 400 pp. 12°. *New York, G. P. Putnam,* 1850. s.

Berard (A. B.) School history of the United States. 224 pp. 1 pl. 12°. *Philadelphia, H. Cowperthwait & Co.* 1855. s.

Bérenger (Laurent P.) Le peuple instruit par ses propres vertus, ou cours complet d'instructions et anecdotes recueillies dans nos meilleurs auteurs, [etc.] 2 v. xxxvi, 443 pp; 2 p. l. 548 pp. 12°. *Paris, Nyon,* 1787. s.

Berg-und hüttenmannische zeitung, mit besonderer berücksichtigung der mineralogie und geologie. 4–5 jahrgang. 2 v. sm. 4°. *Freiberg, J. G. Engelhardt,* 1845–46. s.
[Imperfect].

——— The same. 7r–23r jahrgange. Neue folge. 2r–18r jahrgang. Redaction; Carl Hartmann, [7–17]; C. R. Bornemann, und Bruno Kerl [18 et seq.] 17 v. 4°. *Freiberg, J. G. Engelhardt et al,* 1848–64. s.
[v. 1–6, wanting.]

Berg (Joseph F.) Abaddon and Mahanaim; or, dæmons and guardian angels. 272 pp. 12°. *Philadelphia, Higgins & Perkinpine,* 1856. s.

Bergeron (Pierre). Histoire analytique et critique de la littérature romaine. 2 v. xiv, 473 pp; 578 pp. 8°. *Bruxelles, P. J. Voglet,* 1840. s.

Bergfeldt (Ole). Beretning om Oslo lazareth under cholera-epidemien i Christiania, 1853. 8°. *Christiania, C. C. Werner, & Co.* 1853-4.
[*With* NORWAY. Actstykker ang. cholera-epidemien i Norge].

Berghaus (Heinrich). Deutschland zeit hundert jahren. Geschichte der gebiets-eintheilung und der politischen verfassung des vaterlandes. 1e abth: Deutschland vor hundert jahren. 2e abth: Deutschland vor fünfzig jahren. v. 1-3. 8°. *Leipzig, Voigt & Günther,* 1859-61.

Berghaus (Heinrich). Physikalischer schulatlas. 12 pp. 25 maps. 4°. *Gotha, Perthes,* 1850. s.

——— Vorder-India, oder das Indo-British reich—sowie der volker, sprachen und dialekte. 1 map. fol. *Gotha,* 1858.
[Forms part of Berghaus' Atlas von Asien].

Bergmann (Carl, *M. D.*) Einige beobachtungen und reflexionen über die skelettsysteme der wirbelthiere, deren begrenzung und plan. [Extract.] 66 pp. 8°. *Göttingen, Göttinger studien,* 1845. s.

Bergmann (F. G.) Les Scythes, les ancêtres des peuples germaniques et slaves; leur état social, intellectuel et religieux. xvi, 80 pp. 8°. *Halle, H. W. Schmidt,* 1858.

Berkeley (Grantley F.) Anecdotes of the upper ten thousand; their legends and their lives. 2 v. viii, 416 pp; vii, 240 pp. 8°. *London, Bentley,* 1867.

Berkley (Cora, *pseudon?*) The Hamiltons; or, sunshine in storm. 216 pp. 24°. *New York, E. Dunigan & brother,* 1856. s.

Berkley (*Capt.* George). Naval history of Great Britain. *See* **Hill** (*Sir* J. *M. D.*)

Berlin (Gesellschaft für geburtshülfe in). Monatsschrift für geburtskunde und frauenkrankheiten. Im verein mit der gessellschaft, [etc.] herausgegeben von C. S. F. Credé, C. Hecker, Ed. Martin, A. von Ritgen. v. 19. 8°. *Berlin, A. Hirschwald,* 1862.

Berlin (Königliche bibliothek zu). Verzeichniss der chinesischen und mandchu-tungusichen bücher und handscriften, [etc.] Vom dr. Wilhelm Schott. 1 p. l. iv, 120 pp. 8°. *Berlin, druckerei der k. akademie der wissenschaften,* 1840. s.

Berlin (Königliche museum zu). Verzeichniss von werken der della robbia, majolica, glasmalereien, u. s. w. welche in den nebensälen der sculpturen-gallerie, [etc.] aufgestellt sind, von Friedrich Tieck. vi, 139 pp. 8°. *Berlin, druckerei der k. akademie der wissenschaften,* 1835. s.

Berlingeri (Francesco). Frammenti tratti dalla geografia. (Corografie dell' Istria, v. 7). 8°. *Trieste,* 1831.
[ROSSETTI (D. di). Archeografo Triestino, v. 3].

Bermudez (Jose Manuel). Vida de la gloriosa virgen dominicana santa Rosa de sta. Maria, natural de Lima, [etc.] 268 pp. 2 l. 8°. *Lima, imprenta de los Huèrfanos,* 1627. s.

Bernard de Morlaix (*monk of Cluny*). The heavenly land, from [his] De contemptu mundi. Rendered into English verse by S. W. Duffield. xv, 19 pp. 12°. *New York, A. D. F. Randolph,* 1867.

Bernard (Mountague). Four lectures on subjects connected with diplomacy. viii, 295 pp. 8°. *London, Macmillan & Co.* 1868.

Bernard (Nicholas, *D. D.*) The whole proceedings of the seige of Drogheda in Ireland. 10 p. l. 90 pp. sm. 4°. *London, W. Bladen,* 1642.

Bernays (A.) German poetical anthology, preceded by a concise history of German poetry, [etc.] 2d ed. [etc.] lvi, 370 pp. 8°. *London, Treuttell & Co.* 1831. s.

Bernhardy (Gottfried). Grundriss der römischen litteratur. 3e bearb. xxiv, 814 pp. 8°. *Braunschweig, C. A. Schwetschke u. Sohn,* 1857.

Bernolák (Anton). Slowár slowenski Cesko-lasinsko-ñemecko-uherski; seu lexicon slavicum-bohemico-latino-germanico-ungaricum. 6 v. 8°. *Budæ, typogr. reg. univers. hungaricæ,* 1825–27.

Berquin-Duvallon (——). Travels in Louisiana and the Floridas, 1802. From the French, with notes, by J. Davis. [*anon.*] viii, 181 pp. 12°. *New York, J. Riley & Co.* 1806.

Berr (Franz). Anfangsgründe der chemie, als lehrbuch für unter-realschulen. 4 p. l. 251 pp. 8°. *Brünn, Buschak & Irrgang,* 1853. s.

Berruguilla (Juan Garcia). Verdadera practica de las resoluciones de la geometria, sobre las tres dimensiones para un perfecto architecto, con una total resolucion para medir, y divider la planimetria para los agrimensores. 16 p. l. 136 pp. 18 pl. 4°. *Madrid, L. F. Mojados,* 1747. s.

Berry (The) pickers of Wisconsin. [*anon.*] 245 pp. 3 pl. 16°. *Philadelphia, presbyterian publication com.* 1867.

Berry (*Mrs.* Martha E.) The crook straightened. 279 pp. 3 pl. 16°. *Boston, W. V. Spencer,* 1868.

Berthelot (Sabin). Histoire naturelle des îsles Canaries. *See* **Webb** (Philip Barker) *and* **Berthelot.**

Berthold (*Bishop of Chiemsee*). Tewtsche theologey. 251 pp. fol. *München, H. Schobser,* 1528.

Berthold (Arnold Adolph). Mittheilungen über das zoologische museum zu Göttingen. [Extracts]. 3 v. 16°. *Göttingen, G. A. Universitat, etc.* 1846–55. s.

CONTENTS.

1. Verzeichniss der aufgestellten reptilien, 28 pp.
2. Verzeichniss der aufgestellten säugethiere, 28 pp.
3. Verzeichniss der aufgestellten vögel, 36 pp.

Bertoux (*l'abbé* Guillaume). Anecdotes françoises, depuis l'établissement de la monarchie jusqu' au règne de Louis xv. [*anon.*] 2e éd. 2 v. xii, 380 pp; 382 pp. 16°. *Paris, Vincent,* 1772.

Bertrand (Alexandre Jacques François). Lettres sur les révolutions du globe. 5e éd. x, 370 pp. 2 pl. 18°. *Bruxelles, H. Dumont,* 1833. s.

—— The same. Revues, [etc.] enrichies de nouvelles notes, [etc.] 6e éd. xi, 432 pp. 5 pl. 12°. *Paris, J. Tessier,* 1845. s.

Berwick (*Rev.* Edward). Memoirs of the life of the elder Scipio Africanus; with notes and illustrations. 190 pp. 16°. *London, R. Triphook,* 1817.

Berzelius (Johan Jacob.) Analisi chimica d'ogni specie di minerali da eseguirsi facilmente colla cannella dei saldatori. Tradotta primo dallo svedese in francese dal Fresnel; ora dal francese in italiano dal prof. Gazzeri. viii, 217 pp. 4 pl. 8°. *Napoli, L. Marotta,* 1823. s.

Berzsenyi (Daniel). Versei, kiadta egy kalauz ertekezéssel megtoldva barátja Helmeczi Mihály. lii, 207 pp. 1 portrait. 8°. *Pesten, J. T. Trattner,* 1816. s.

Besse (Joseph). An abstract of the sufferings of the people call'd quakers for the testimony of a good conscience, 1650–1666. [*anon.*] 2 v. xii, 575, xl pp; xxxii, 522, xlv pp. 8°. *London, assigns of J. Sowle,* 1733–38.
[Imperfect: v. 3 wanting].

—— The same. A collection of the sufferings of the people called quakers for the testimony of a good conscience, 1650–1689. 2 v. lv, 767 pp; 638 pp. 5 l. fol. *London, L. Hinde,* 1753.
[Imperfect: v. 2 wanting title].

Bessel (Freidrich Wilhelm), *and* **Bäyer** (J.J.) Gradmessung in Ostpreussen. *See* **Prussia.**

Betende (Der) Christ. Katholisches gebet-und erbauungsbuch für kirche und haus. [*anon.*] 382 pp. 24°. *New York, K. & N. Benziger,* 1868.

Bethune (George W. *D. D. editor*). The British female poets; with biographical and critical notices. 490 pp. 8°. *Philadelphia, Lindsay & Blakiston,* 1848. s.

Bettoni (Eugenio). Storia naturale degli uccelli che nidificano in Lombardia. v. 1. fasc. 1–18. 26 pl. fol. *Milano, pio instituto pei fanciulli dereletti in Parabiago,* 1866–67.

Beverly (Robert). The history and present state of Virginia. [*anon.*] 6 p. l. 311 pp. 6 pl. 12°. *London, R. Parker,* 1705.
[Imperfect: 9 pl. wanting].

—— The same. Histoire de la Virginie. Traduite de l'Anglois. [*anon.*] 4 p. l. 416 pp. 9 l. 15 pl. 1 tab. 16°. *Orleans et Paris, P. Ribou,* 1707.

Bewick (Thomas). A general history of quadrupeds. The figures copied by A. Anderson. 1st American ed. containing some American animals not hitherto described. 531 pp. 8°. *New York, G. & R. Waite*, 1804. s.
[Imperfect: wanting pp. 81–90, 95–96].

—— The same. A history of quadrupeds: embellished with upwards of 340 engravings, chiefly copied [etc.] by A. Anderson. 2d American, from the 8th London ed. [1824]. Also, an addenda, with some American animals not hitherto described. 335 pp. 12°. *New York, T. W. Strong*, [*about* 1855].

—— The Bewick collector. *See* **Hugo** (Thomas).

Bianchi Giovini (Angelo Aurelio). Biografia di frà Paolo Sarpi. 2 v. 3 p. l. 352 pp. 1 pl; 495 pp. 16°. *Zurigo, Orell, Füssli & Ca.* 1836.

Bianchi & Son, (*Paris*). Catalogue of mathematical, physical, chemical, mineralogical and other instruments made [by them]. 23 pp. 16°. *New York*, 1839. s.
[*With* WATKINS & HILL. Descriptive catalogue, etc.]

Bianconi (Giovanni Giuseppe). Se il mare abbia in tempi antichi occupato le pianure ed i colli d'Italia, di Grecia, dell'Asia Minore, ec. e de terreno marino detto marna bleu subapennina. 219 pp. 1 map. 8°. *Bologna, T. d'Aquino*, 1844. s.

Biasoletto (*Dr.* Bartolomeo). Escursioni botaniche sullo Schneeberg (monte nevoso) nella Carniola, [etc.] 96 pp. 1 map. 8°. *Trieste, J. Papsch & Ca.* 1846. s.

Biber (Eduard, *Ph. D.*) Life and trials of Henry Pestalozzi; with extracts from his works, illustrative of his plan of education. 8°. *Philadelphia, T. K. Greenbank*, 1833.
[GREENBANK's periodical library. v. 1. pp. 1–87].

Bible. *Polyglot.* Psalterium, hebreum, grecū, arabicū et chaldeū, cū tribus latinis ĩterptatõibus et glossis. [By Agostino Giustiniani]. 200 l. fol. *Genuae, Petrus Paulus Porrus*, 1516.

—— —— The book of Jonah, in Chaldee, Syriac, Æthiopic, and Arabic, with glossaries. Edited by W. Wright. viii, 148 pp. 2 l. 8°. *London, Williams & Norgate*, 1857.

—— —— [Novum testamentum syriace, hebraice, graece, latine, germanice, bohemice, italice, hispanice, gallice, anglice, danice, polonice; studio et lab. El. Hutteri. v. 2]. Novi testamenti secvndvs tomvs; continens epistolas S. Pavli xv; S. Petri ii; S. Iacobi i; S. Iohannis iii; S. Ivdæ i; et apocalypsin Iohannis. 2 p. l. 1091 pp. fol. [*Norimbergæ*,] 1599. s.
[v. 1 wanting].

Bible. *Armenian.* Nōrgdagaran dearhn merōh Isisovoi Krisdosi. [New testament, in the Armenian language]. 724 pp. 1 pl. 8°. [*Venice, Armenian convent of the island of St. Lazarus*,] 1816. s.

—— —— The same. 2 p. l. 543 pp. 8°. *Calcutta, baptist mission press*, 1844. s.

—— *Benga.* The first book of Moses, called Genesis, translated into the Benga language by rev. W. Clemens, [etc.] Ejanganangobo ya Mosĕs ya boho e tubakwĕ na Jĕnisis. 216 pp. 12°. *New York, Am. bible society*, 1863. s.

—— —— Sango iam. Ya Matiu e Lĕndĕkidi. 113 pp. 12°. *New York, mission house*, 1858. s.

—— —— Sango iam, ya Mark, Luk, [and] Jâne Lĕndĕkidi. The gospel according to Mark, Luke, and John, translated into the Benga language, by rev. Jas. L. Mackey, [etc.] 3 v. 12°. *New York, American bible society*, 1861–64. s.

—— —— Behadi bia metodu. The acts of the apostles, translated into the Benga language, by rev. J. L. Mackey, [etc.] 136 pp. 12°. *New York, Am. bible society*, 1864. s.

—— *Bengálí.* The old testament in the Bengálí language. Translated from the original Hebrew by the Calcutta baptist missionaries, with native assistants. 843 pp. 8°. *Calcutta, baptist mission press*, 1844. s.

—— —— The book of Genesis and part of Exodus in Bengálí. Tr. from the Hebrew, by the Calcutta baptist missionaries. 182 pp. 12°. *Calcutta, bible translation society*, 1842. s.

—— —— The new testament. [etc.] in the Bengálí language. Translated from the Greek, by the Calcutta baptist missionaries. 2 p. l. 648 pp. 8°. *Calcutta, American and foreign bible society*, 1837. s.

—— —— The same. 2 titles, 617 pp. 12°. *Calcutta, bible translation society*, 1841. s.

—— —— The four gospels, with the acts of the apostles, in Bengálí. 360 pp. 12°. *Calcutta, baptist mission press, for bible translation society*, 1841. s.

—— *Burmese.* The holy bible, containing the old and new testaments; translated into the Burmese, from the original tongues. 2d ed. 2 v. in 1. 880 pp; 318 pp. 4°. *Maulmain, Am. baptist mission press*, 1840. s.

—— *Choctaw.* The books of Joshua, Judges, and Ruth, translated into the Choctaw language. Choshua, Nanapesa uhleha holisso, Micha Lulh holisso [etc.] hoke. 151 pp. 12°. *New York, American bible society*, 1852. s.

Bible. *Choctaw.* The first and second books of Samuel, and first book of kings, translated into the Choctaw language. Samuel i holisso ummona, atukla itatuklo, micha miko uhleha, isht anumpa ummona [etc.] hoke. 256 pp. 12°. *New York, American bible society,* 1852. s.

——— ——— The new testament [etc.] translated into the Choctaw language. Pin chitokaka pi okchalinchi Chisus Klaist in testament himona, [etc.] 818 pp. 12°. *New York, American bible society,* 1848. s.

——— *Cree.* Oo meyo achimoowin St. Mark. The gospel according to St. Mark; translated into the language of the Cree Indians, [etc. by archdeacon Hunter.] iv, 87 pp. 12°. *London, Brit. and for. bible society,* 1855. s.

——— ——— The first epistle general of John, translated by Mrs. Hunter into the language of the Crees. 13 pp. 8°. *London,* 1855.

[*With* COMMON prayer, portions of, in the Cree].

——— *Creek.* The gospel according to John. Ωpωnvkv hera chanichωyvten, oksumkvlki irkinvkv, H. F. Buckner, [etc.] 190 pp. 16°. *Marion, Alabama, southern baptist convention,* 1860. s.

——— *Dakota.* Wicoicage wowapi, qa odowan wakan, heberi iapi etanhan kagapi, [etc.] The book of genesis, and a part of the psalms, in the Dakota language; translated from the original Hebrew, by the missionaries of the A. b. c. f. m. and Joseph Renville, sr. [With] Wootanin waxte Luka qa Jan, owapi qon hena eepi, [etc.] The gospels of Luke and John, in the Dakota language; translated by G. H. Pond and Joseph Renville, sr. 296 pp. 8°. *Cincinnati, American board of commissioners for foreign missions,* 1842–43. s.

——— ——— Jesus ohnihde wicaye cin oranyanpi qon: qa Palos wowapi kage ciqon; nakun, Jan woyake ciqon dena eepi, [etc]. The acts of the apostles, and the epistles of Paul, wifh the revelation of John, in the Dakota language; translated from the Greek, by Stephen R. Riggs. 228 pp. 8°. *Cincinnati, American bible society,* 1843. s.

[*With* Wicoicage wonapi, etc. 1842–43.]

——— *English.* The holy bible, containing the old testament and the new. [With the apocrypha]. Newly translated out of the original tongues by his majestie's special command. With annotations. 14 p. l. [1066] pp. 5 maps. fol. *London,* 1707–08.

——— ——— The same. According to the commonly received version. 2 v. in 1. 838, 252 pp. 12°. *New York, Am. and foreign bible society,* 1846. s.

Bible. *English.* The same. 409 l. 24°. *American and foreign bible society,* 1851. s.

——— ——— The same. 1100 pp. 8°. *New York, American & foreign bible society,* 1854. s.

——— ——— The holy scriptures, translated and corrected by the spirit of revelation, by Joseph Smith, jr. the seer. 917, 286 pp. 16°. *Plano, (Ill.) J. Smith, etc.* 1867.

——— ——— The comprehensive commentary on the holy bible. A digest of the best bible commentaries. Edited by William Jenks, D. D. [New ed.] 5 v. 8°. *Philadelphia, Claxton, Remsen & Haffelfinger,* 1869.

——— ——— A commentary on the holy scriptures: critical, doctrinal, and homiletical. By J. P. Lange, D. D. [and others]. Translated from the German, and edited by P. Schaff, D. D. [and others]. Old testament. v. 1. 8°. *New York, C. Scribner & Co.* 1868.

CONTENTS.

v. 1. General introduction. Genesis.

——— ——— The same. New testament. v. 1, 2, 4, 6, 8, and 9. 8°. *New York, C. Scribner & Co.* 1867–68.

CONTENTS.

v. 1. General introduction. Matthew, by J. P. Lange.
v. 2. Mark and Luke, by J. P. Lange and J. J. Van Oosterzel.
v. 4. Acts of the apostles, by G. V. Lechler and Rev. C. Gerok.
v. 6. 1st and 2d Corinthians, by C. F. Kling.
v. 8. Thessalonians, Timothy, Titus, Philemon, and Hebrews, by Drs. Auberlin, Riggenbach, Van Oosterzel, and Moll.
v. 9. James, Peter, John, and Jude, by Drs. Lange, Van Oosterzel, Fronmüller, and Braune.

——— ——— A briefe exposition of the whole book of ecclesiastes. By John Cotton. 277 pp. 16°. *London, R. Smith,* 1654.

——— ——— A briefe exposition of the whole book of canticles. By John Cotton. 264 pp. 16°. *London, P. Nevel,* 1642.

——— ——— The psalter, or psalmes of David, after the translation of the great bible, pointed as it shall be sung or said in churches. 80 l. fol. *London, R. Barker,* 1634.

[*With* BOOK of common prayer. ed. 1632].

——— ——— The book of psalms, from the original Hebrew, according to the commonly received version. 107 pp. 8°. *New York, American and foreign bible society,* 1850.

[*With* BIBLE. The new testament, 1850].

——— ——— Notes, critical, explanatory, and practical, on the book of psalms. [With the text]. By A. Barnes. v. 1. xlvi, 374 pp. 12°. *New York, Harpers,* 1868.

Bible. *English.* A concordance to the holy scriptures; [and] the books of the apocrypha. By S[amuel] N[ewman]. [*anon.*] 4th ed. 404 l. fol. *Cambridge, (Eng.) J. Hayes,* 1698.

——— ——— The new testament. The text of the common translation arranged in paragraphs. By James Nourse. 373, xxiii pp. 18°. *New York, G. & C. Carvill,* 1827.

——— ——— The same; according to the commonly received version. 407 pp. 8°. *New York, American and foreign bible society,* 1850. s.

——— ——— An exposition of [selected portions of] the new testament, [etc.] [Re-arranged] by Hezekiah Woodruff. 260 pp. 16°. *Auburn, H. Oliphant,* 1852. s.

——— ——— Gnomon of the new testament. Pointing out, from the natural force of the words, the simplicity, [etc.] of its divine thoughts. By J. A. Bengel. Translated by C. T. Lewis and M. R. Vincent. 2 v. 925 pp; 980 pp. 8°. *Philadelphia, Perkinpine & Higgins,* [1860].

——— ——— The new testament; with notes, pictorial illustrations, and references. v. 1. The four gospels; with a chronological harmony. By I. P. Warren. 10, 386 pp. 1 map. 8°. *Boston, Am. tract soc.* [1867].

——— ——— The divine library, [etc.] The gospel[s] of our Lord and saviour Jesus Christ, according to St. Matthew, St. Mark, St. Luke, St. John, [and] the acts of the apostles. Received version in paragraph form. 5 v. 16°. *Baltimore, T. H. Stockton,* 1856. s.

——— ——— A new version of the gospel according to Matthew, with a commentary, [and] an introduction to the reading of the holy scriptures by I. de Beausobre and J. Lenfant. xv, 407 pp. 8°. *London, Whittaker,* 1819.

——— ——— A suggestive commentary on the new testament; St. Luke. By Rev. W. H. Van Doren. 2 v. iv, 520 pp; 2 p. l. 558 pp. 12°. *New York, D. Appleton & Co.* 1868.

——— ——— The epistle of the apostle Paul to the Romans; with notes, [etc.] By Henry J. Ripley. 147 pp. 12°. *Boston, Gould & Lincoln,* 1857. s.

——— ——— The epistle to the Hebrews, with explanatory notes: a condensed view of the priesthood of Christ, and a translation of the epistle. By Henry J. Ripley. 213 pp. 12°. *Boston, Gould & Lincoln,* 1868.

——— ——— Notes on the Greek text of the epistle of Paul to Philemon, as the basis of a revision of the common English version; and a revised version, with notes. 90 pp. sm. 4°. *New York, Amer. bible union,* 1860.

——— ——— An exposition upon the 13th chapter of the revelation. By John Cotton. 5 p. l. 262 pp. 3 l. sm. 4°. *London, L. Chapman,* 1655.

——— ——— The parables of our Lord. 32 pp. 16°. *New York, D. Appleton & Co.* 1848.

——— *French.* La sainte bible, [version protestante, avec les livres apocryphes]. Par les soins de Samuel et Henry Des Marets. Éd. nouv. faite sur la version de Genêve. 2 v. 42 p. l. 366 l; 2 p. l. 434 l. 5 maps. fol. *Amsterdam, L. & D. Elzevier,* 1669.

——— ——— Le nouveau testament de notre seigneur Jésus Christ. Imprimé sur l'édition de Paris, de l'année 1805. Éd. stéréotype. 329 pp. 16°. *Londres, societé de la bible,* 1807.

——— ——— The same. Nouveau testament, traduction nouvelle, d'après la vulgate. Par Eugène de Genoude. 2 v. xii, 655 pp; 2 p. l. 566 pp. 24°. *Paris, etc. Méquignon,* 1821. s.

——— ——— Petite bible illustrée; ou, récits tirés de la [bible] à l'usage de la jeunesse. Traduction revue par l'abbé Bouquard. 277 pp. 2 pl. 16°. *Einsiedeln and New York, Benziger bros.* 1867.

——— *French and Latin.* Le pseautier de David, traduit en françois; avec des notes courtes tirées de saint Augustin, et des autres pères. 3e éd. 3 pl. 592 pp. 8 l. 1 pl. 8°. *Paris, H. Josset,* 1679. s.

——— ——— The same. Pseaumes de David, traduit en François. Avec des notes courtes, tirées de S. Augustin et des autres pères. Français et Latin. 14e éd. 3 p. l. 496 pp. 4 l. 1 pl. 16°. *Paris, Elie Josset,* 1709.

——— *German.* Hohe geistreiche lehren vnd erklärungen: oder die fürnembsten sprüche desz hohen lieds Salomonis, von der liebhabenden seele, das ist, der christlichen kirchen vnd jhrem gemahl Jesu Christo. In teutsche reimen verfasset. Mit figuren durch Jacob von der Heyden. Durch D[iego] S[tella]. [Jakob van den Star]. 67 pp. fol. *Franckfurt, E. Kieser,* 1622.

——— ——— Illustrirte pracht-bibel, oder die ganze heilige shrift des alten und neuen testaments, nach der deutschen uebersetzung D. Martin Luther's. Mit illustrationem von Otto Delitsch. xii, 1588 pp. 4 maps. 96 pl. 4°. *Leipzig, A. H. Payne,* 1862.

——— *Gothic.* Fragmenterna af Matthæi evangelium pä Götiska jemte ordforklaring och ordböjningslära. [Saint Matthew]. Akademisk afhandling af A. Uppström och H. H. Petré. 8°. *Upsala,* 1850.

Bible. *Grebo.* The first book of Moses, called Genesis, translated into the Grebo tongue; by rev. John Payne. 147 pp. 16°. *New York, American bible society,* 1856. s.

——— ——— Bible history. The pentateuch and Joshua. For the use of the protestant episcopal mission in western Africa. 96 pp. 16°. *New York, Amer. tract society,* [*about* 1848]. s.

——— ——— The gospel according to St. Luke, translated into the Grebo tongue; by the rev. John Payne. 103 pp. 16°. *New York, Amer. bible society,* 1848. s.

——— *Greek.* Η παλαια διαθηκη κατα τους εβδομηκοντα. 2 v. 3 p. l. 499 pp; 480–935 pp. 8°. Αθηνησι, Χ. Ν. Φιλαδελφεως, 1843–46. s.

——— ——— Codex friderico-augustanus, sive fragmenta veteris testamenti e codice graeco omnium qui in Europa supersunt facile antiquissimo in oriente detexit, in patriam attulit, ad modum codicis edidit Constantinus Tischendorf. 23 pp. 43 pl. oblong fol. *Lipsiae, sumtibus C. F. Koehleri,* 1846. s.

——— ——— Η καινη διαθηκη. Novvm testamentvm graecvm ita adoratvm vt textvs probatarvm editionvm medvllam margo variantvm lectionvm in svas classes distribvtarvm locorvmqve parallelorvm delectvm [etc.] exhibeat, inserviente Io. Alberto Bengelio. 5 p. l. 368 pp. 4°. *Tvbingae, J. G. Cotta,* 1734. s.

——— ——— The same. Novum testamentum, iuxta exemplaria R. Stephani et J. Millii accuratissime impressum. 2 p. l. 463 pp. 18°. *Londini, societ. stationariorum,* 1770.

——— ——— The same. Η νεα διαθηκη του Κυριου και Σωτηρος ημων Ιησου Χριστου, μεταφρασθεισα εις την απλην των νυν ελληνων διαλεκτον αδεια, [etc.] 376 l. 8°. Εν Λονδρα, Ι. Τιλλιγγου, 1828. s.

——— *Greek and English.* The epistle to the Hebrews, in Greek and English, with an analysis and exegetical commentary. By Samuel H. Turner. viii, 186 pp. 8°. *New York, Stanford & Swords,* 1852. s.

——— *Greek and Latin.* Novvm testamentvm, xii. tomis distinctvm, græce et latine. Textvm denvo recensvit, varias lectiones nvmqvam antea vvlgatas ex centvm codicibus mss. variarvm bibliothecarvm adiecit, et edidit Christianvs Fridericvs Matthæi. 12 v. in 7. 8°. *Rigae, J. F. Hartknock,* 1788. s.

——— ——— Η καινη διαθηκη. Novum testamentum, cum versione latina Ariæ Montani, [etc.] Auctore Johanne Leusden. viii, 699 pp. 18°. *Novi-Eboraci, G. Long,* 1821. s.

Bible. *Greek and Latin.* Joannis Theodori Beelen commentarius in acta apostolorum. Cui integri adduntur contextus græcus et latinus. 2 v. in 1. 2 p. l. xii, 272 pp; 1 p. l. 266 pp. 4°. *Lovanii, C. J. Fonteyn,* 1850–51. s.

——— ——— [Epistola et] interpretatio epistolæ S. Pauli ad Philippenses. iv, 136 pp. 4°. *Lovanii, Ickx & Geets,* 1849. s.

——— ——— The same. Joannis Theodori Beelen commentarius in epistolam S. Pauli ad Philippenses. Accedunt textus græcus atque latinus, et continua totius epistolæ paraphrasis. Ed. 2ª, [etc.] 2 p. l. 143 pp. 8°. *Lovanii, C. J. Fonteyn,* 1852. s.

——— *Hawaian.* [Exodus]. Ka puka ana i kakauia'i e Mose. 112 pp. 12°. *Oahu, mission press,* 1829. s.

——— *Hebrew and Latin.* Proverbia Salomonis. Versionem integram ad hebræum fontem expressit, atque commentarium adjecit Albertus Schultens. 4 p. l. cviii, 522 pp. 31 l. 4°. *Lugduni Batavorum, E. Lazac, jr.* 1748. s.

——— *Hindee or Hinduwee.* The new testament, in the Hindí language. Tr. from the Greek, by the Calcutta baptist missionaries, with native assistants. 3 p. l. 510 pp. 8°. *Calcutta, Baptist mission press,* 1844. s.

——— ——— The four gospels and the acts of the apostles in Hindui. 1 p. l. 296 pp. 8°. *Calcutta, Baptist mission press,* 1842. s.

——— *Hindustání.* The new testament, in the Hindustání language. Translated from the Greek by the Calcutta baptist missionaries, with native assistants. 3 p. l. 720 pp. 8°. *Calcutta, Baptist mission press,* 1844. s.

——— ——— The four gospels and the acts of the apostles, in Hindustání; translated from the Greek by the Calcutta baptist missionaries. 2d ed. 1 p. l. 412 pp. 8°. *Calcutta, Am. and for. bible society,* 1840. s.

——— ——— The gospel of Matthew, in Hindustání. 170 pp. 12°. *Lodiana, Am. presbyterian mission press,* 1846. s.

——— *Irish.* The books of the old testament, translated into Irish, by dr. William Bedel, late bishop of Kilmore. 1142 pp. 4°. *London,* 1685.

——— *Lapponese, or Quanian.* Hâerramek ja bæsstamek Jesus Kristus, odda testament. 2 p. l. 816 pp. 8°. *Kristianiaist, K. Gröndahl,* 1850. s.

——— *Latin.* Biblia sacra, sive libri canonici, testamenti veteris, latini recens ex hebræis facti, brevibusque scholiis illustrati ab I. Tremellis et F. Junio. Accesserunt libri qui vulgo

Bible—continued.
dicuntur apocryphi, latine redditi. Quibus etiam adjunximus novi testamenti, libros ex sermone syro ab eodem Tremellio, et ex græco a Beza in latinum versos, etc. Secunda cura Francisci Junii. 767 l. fol. *Londini, excudebant G. B. R. N. & R. B.* 1593.

——— ——— The same. Biblia sacra vulgatæ editionis Sixti v. et Clementi viii. pont. max. auctoritate recognita [etc.] Juxta editionem parisiensem A. Vitré. Nunc jussu [etc.] Petri Josephi antverpiensium episcopi, [etc.] revisa. [With appendix;] tabulæ sacræ geographicæ, [etc.] authore Augustino Lubin, etc. 3 v. in 1. 4°. *Antverpiæ, J. B. Verdussen,* 1715. s.

——— ——— The same. Bibliorum sacrorum vulgatæ versionis editio, clero gallicano dicata. 8 v. 8°. *Parisiis, fr. A. Didot,* 1785. s.

——— ——— Liber psalmorum. 129 l. 7 l. 18°. *Lugduni, Theobaldvs Paganvs* [*Thibault Payen*], 1541.

——— ——— [Psalms]. Ludolfi [Saxonis?] in psalteriū expositio. 32 p. l. ccxxxii l. 3 l. 4°. *Parisiis, B. Rembolt,* 1514.

——— ——— Tetrateuchus, sive commentarius in sancta Jesu Christi evangelia. Ed. nova, cui accessit in margine sacer textus. 5 p. l. 854 pp. 18 l. 4°. *Lovanii, Stryckwant,* 1699. s.

——— ——— Rvperti abbatis monasterii tvitiensis, commentariorum, in euangelium Iohannis libri xiv. 8 p. l. 367 pp. fol. *Colonia, F. Birckman,* 1526.

——— ——— Rvperti abbatis monasterii tvitiensis, commentariorum, in apocalypsim Iohannis, libri xii. 6 p. l. 235 pp. fol. *Colonia, F. Birckman,* 1526.

[*With* BIBLE (*Latin*), Rvperti abbatis commentar. in euangelium Iohannis, 1526].

——— *Maori. See New Zealandic.*

——— *Marathi.* The old testament, in the Marathi language. Translated out of the original tongues. Published by the Bombay auxiliary bible society. 2 p. l. 942 pp. 4°. *Bombay, mission press,* 1853. s.

——— *New Zealandic, or Maori.* Ko te kawenata hou o to tatou ariki te kai wakaora a Ihu Karaiti, [or new testament]. 356 pp. 8°. *Paihia, Mihanere,* 1837. s.

——— *Ottawa.* The gospel according to John. Translated into the Ottawa language, by Jotham Meeker, [etc.] revised, [etc.] by rev. Francis Barker, [etc.] 98 pp. 16°. *Shawanoe, press of Am. baptist board of for. missions,* 1844. s.

Bible. *Persian.* The new testament, translated from the original Greek into Persian, at Sheeraz, by the rev. Henry Martyn, [etc.] with the assistance of Meerza Sueyid Alee, [etc.] 2 title pages. 584 pp. 8°. *Calcutta, American and foreign bible society,* 1841. s.

——— ——— The four gospels and the acts of the apostles, in Persian. 1 p. l. 342 pp. 8°. *Calcutta, bible translation society,* 1841. s.

——— *Quanian. See* **Bible.** *Lapponese.*

——— *Sanscrit.* The psalms of David, faithfully rendered from the original Hebrew into Sanscrit verse; by the Calcutta baptist missionaries, with native assistants. 1 p. l. 7 pp. 1 l. 263 pp. 16°. *Calcutta, baptist mission press,* 1839. s.

——— ——— The four gospels, with the acts of the apostles, in Sanscrit. 1 p. l. 335 pp. 8°. *Calcutta, baptist mission press,* 1844. s.

——— *Shawanoe.* The gospel according to Saint Matthew. Translated into the Shawanoe language, by Johnston Lykins, aided [etc.] by James Andrew Chute. 116 pp. 16°. *Shawanoe, baptist mission press,* 1842. s.

——— *Siamese.* The new testament. Translated from the Greek. By J. T. Jones. viii, 591 pp. 8°. *Bangkok, American and foreign bible society,* 1850. s.

——— *Spanish.* Assumptos apostolicos predicables, literales, tropologicos, alegoricos, y analogicos, sobre los tres capitulos primeros del evangelio de S. Matheo. Correspondiendo uno por verso, [etc.] Trabajados, por los rr. pp. predicadores missionarios apostolicos de la regular observancia de N. S. P. S. Francisco, [etc.] y coordenados por Francisco Romeu. 2 v. 13 p. l. 556 pp. 16 l; 6 p. l. 600 pp. 15 l. 8°. *Barcelona, J. Piferrer,* 1736. s.

——— *Syriac.* Novum testamentum syriacum cum lexico et institutionibus l. syriacæ, etc. Authore Aegidio Gutbirio. 17 p. l. 606 pp. 16°. *Hamburgi, auctor,* 1663.

[*With* GUTBIER (Aegidius). Lexicon syriacum. *Hamburg,* 1667].

——— Figures de la bible. 211 pl. fol. *La Haye, P. de Hond,* 1728.

Bible (The) christian's pocket diary for 1857. (Issued quarterly). No. 1. 92 pp. 16°. *Philadelphia, T. H. Stockton,* 1857. s.

Bibliographisches jahrbuch, [etc.] *See* **Messkatalog.**

Bibliopolisches jahrbuch. 3r (— 4r) jahrbuch. 2 v. 8°. *Leipzig, J. J. Weber,* 1839–40. s.

[v. 1, 2, 5, 6, wanting].

Biblioteca de autores españoles, desde la formacion del lenguaje hasta nuestros dias. v. 53–59. 8°. *Madrid, M. Rivadeneyra,* 1861–67.

CONTENTS.

Feijoo y Montenegro (Benito Jerónimo). Obras. v. 56.
Monino (José, *conde* de Floridablanca). Obras. v. 59.
Pedroso (Eduardo Gonzales). Autos sacramentales. v. 58.
Poetas castellanos anteriores al siglo xv. v. 57.
Rojas Zorrilla (Francisco de). Comedias. v. 53.
Teresa (Saint). Escritos. v. 54–55.

Bibliotheca (The) sacra. Edited by E. A. Parks and S. H. Taylor. Jan. to Oct. 1868. v. 25. 8°. *Andover, W. F. Draper,* 1868.

Bibliothèque américaine. Contenant des mémoires sur l'agriculture, le commerce, les manufactures, les moeurs et les usages de l'Amérique; l'analyse des ouvrages scientifiques de ce pays; et des extraits des journaux publiés en Amérique. Par une société de savans et d'hommes de lettres. [*anon.*] Six premières livraisons. 3 v. 12°. *Paris, H. Caritat,* 1807.

Bibra (Ernst, *freiherr* von). Chemische untersuchungen über die knochen und zähne des menschen und der wirbelthiere. xii, 435 pp. 5 pl. 8°. *Schweinfurt, Kunstverlage,* 1844. S.

Bibron (Gabriel). *See* **Duméril** (A. M. C.) *and* **Bibron.**

Bichat (Marie François Xavier). Anatomie générale, appliquée à la physiologie et à la medicine. Nouv. éd. avec des notes et additions par P. A. Béclard. 4 v. 8°. *Paris, J. A. Brosson & J. S. Chaudé,* 1821.

——— Recherches physiologiques sur la vie et la mort. 3e éd. xx, 347 pp. 8°. *Paris, Brosson,* 1805.

——— Traité d'anatomie descriptive. Nouv. éd. 5 v. 8°. *Paris, J. A. Brosson & Chaudé,* 1823.

CONTENTS.

v. 1–3. Appareils de la vie animal; (locomotion, voix, sensations, sens internes, conducteurs du sentiment et du mouvement). Appareils de la vie organique, (digestion).
v. 4. The same, (respiration, circulation, absorption), par F. R. Buisson.
v. 5. The same, (secretions). Appareils de la génération, par Ph. Jos. Roux.

See, also, **Desault** (P. J.)

Bickersteth (*Rev.* Edward). Questions illustrating the thirty-nine articles of the church of England, [etc.] 182 pp. 12°. *Philadelphia, H. Hooker,* 1845. S.

Biddle (Horace P.) Poems. xvi, 341 pp. 16°. *New York, Hurd & Houghton,* 1868.

Biddle (John B. *M. D.*) Materia medica, for the use of students. 3d ed. 384 pp. 8°. *Philadelphia, Lindsay & Blakiston,* 1868.

Biddle (Richard). A memoir of Sebastian Cabot; with a review of the history of maritime discovery. [*anon.*] viii, 327 pp. 8°. *Philadelphia, Carey & Lea,* 1831.

——— The same. [With full ms. notes by Peter Force].

——— The same. 2d ed. viii, 333 pp. 8°. *London, Sherwood, Gilbert, & Piper,* 1832.

Bidloo (Godfried). Anatomia humani corporis, 105 tabulis, per G. de Lairesse ad vivum delineatis, demonstrata. 5 p. l. 107 l. 107 pl. fol. *Amstelodami, à Someren, etc.* 1688. S.

Bidon (Pierre). Nouveau manuel universel et raisonné du canotier. ii, 212 pp. 1 pl. 18°. *Paris, Roret,* [1852]? S.

Bidpai. Calila und Dimna, eine reihe moralischer und politischer fabeln, des philosophen Bidpai, aus dem Arabischen übersetzt von C. A. Holmboe. 4 p. l. xi, 170 pp. 8°. *Christiania, C. L. Roshauw,* 1832. S.

Bidwell (Charles Toll). The isthmus of Panama. vii, 418 pp. 1 pl. 8°. *London, Chapman & Hall,* 1865.

Biedermann (Carl). Deutschland im achtzehnten jahrhundert. 2 v. xxi, 428 pp; xxiv, 560 pp. 8°. *Leipzig, J. J. Weber,* 1854-58.

Biermer (Anton, *M. D.*) Die lehre vom auswurf. Ein beitrag zur medicinischen klinik. viii, 138 pp. 2 pl. 8°. *Würzburg, Stahel,* 1855. S.

Bigelow (Harriet Hamline). The curse entailed. v, 545 pp. 1 pl. 12°. *Boston, Wentworth & Co.* 1857. S.

Bigelow (John). Memoir of the life and public services of John Charles Frémont. 480 pp. 8 pl. 1 portrait. 12°. *New York, Derby & Jackson,* 1856.

Bigelow (John Reynolds). The American's own book; or, the constitutions of the several states in the Union. xi, 536 pp. 1 map. 2 pl. 8°. *New York, Gates, Stedman, & Co.* 1849.

Biggs (James). The history of don Francisco de Miranda's attempt to effect a revolution in South America. In a series of letters. [With] sketches of the life of Miranda, and geographical notices of Caraccas. [*anon.*] 3d ed. xi, 312 pp. 16°. *Boston, E. Oliver,* 1811.

Bigler (David). The orphan twins; or the adventures of a brother and sister. A poem. 100 pp. 16°. *New York, Stanford & Swords,* 1849. S.

Bigot (Jacques, *le père*). Relation de ce qvi s'est passé de plvs remarqvable dans la mission Abnaquise de Sainct Joseph de Sillery, et dans l'establissement de la nouuelle mission de Sainct François de Sales, 1684. 61 pp. sm. 4°. *Manate, J. M. Shea,* 1857. S.

Bigot (*Jacque, le pére*). Relation de ce qvi s 'est passé de plvs remarqvable dans la mission Abnaquise de Sainct Joseph de Sillery et de Sainct François de Sales, 1685. 32 pp. sm. 4°. *Manate, J. M. Shea*, 1858. s.

——— Relation de la mission Abnaquise de St. François des Sales, 1702. 26 pp. 8°. *Nouvelle York, J. M. Shea*, 1865.
[*With* RELATION des affaires du Canada, 1696. 1865].

Bigot (Vincent). Relation de ce qvi s'est passé de plvs remarqvable dans la mission des Abnaquis à l'Acadie, 1701. 34 pp. 12°. *Manate, J. M. Shea*, 1858. s.

Billardon de Sauvigny (L. Edme.) Les amours de Pierre le Long et de Blanche Bazu. [*anon.*] 5 p. l. 124 pp. 16°. *Paris, de Ducauroy & Malvost*, 1796.

——— The same. L'innocence du premier age en France, ou histoire amoureuse de Pierre Le Long et de Blanche Bazu; suivie de la rose ou la fête de Salency. [Avec un discours sur les progrès de la langue françoise. *anon.*] 3 p. l. 276 pp. 2 pl. 8°. *Paris, Rualt*, 1778.

Billing (Archibald, *M. D.*) The science of gems, jewels, coins, and medals, ancient and modern. xi, 221 pp. 18 phot. pl. 1 pl. 8°. *London, Bell & Daldy*, 1867.

Billing (Gottfrid). Kateketikens begrepp. Ett försök i praktisk theologi. 3 p. l. 145 pp. 8°. *Lund, H. Ohlsson*, 1867. s.

Billings (Josh, *pseudon.*) *See* **Shaw** (Henry W.)

Billingsley (John). General view of the agriculture of the county of Somerset. 2d ed. xvi, 320 pp. 1 map. 2 pl. 8°. *Bath*, 1798.
[GREAT BRITAIN: Board of agriculture].

Bingham (Caleb). The young American's speaker. 228 pp. 12°. *Philadelphia, J. B. Lippincott & Co.* 1857. s.

Biographia Britannica; or, the lives of the most eminent persons who have flourished in Great Britain and Ireland, from the earliest ages to the present times. [Enlarged] by Andrew Kippis and others. 2d ed. v. 1–5. [A-Fas.] fol. *London, C. Bathurst, W. Strahan, etc.* 1778–1793.
[No more published.]

Bion. Idyllia. *See* **Theocritus**. Idyllia. 1579.

Biondelli (Bernardino, *editor and translator*). Evangeliarium, epistolarium, et lectionarium aztecum sive mexicanum, ex antiquo codice mexicano nuper reperto depromptum. xlix pp. 1 l. 574 pp. 1 l. 1 facsim. 4°. *Mediolani, J. Bernardoni*, 1858.

Biondo (Flavio). Italiae illustratae undecima regio Histria. (Corografia dell' Istria, n. 1.) 8°. *Trieste*, 1830.
[*In* ROSSETTI (D. di). Archeografo triestino, v. 2].

Biot (Jean Baptiste). Traité élémentaire d' astronomie physique. Avec des additions relatives à l'astronomie nautique, par M. de Rossel. 2e éd. 3 v. 8°. *Paris, Klostermann*, 1810–11. s.

Birch (S. B. *M. D.*) On the action, use, and value of oxygen in the treatment of various diseases otherwise incurable, or very intractable. 2d ed. ix, 149 pp. 12°. *London, J. Churchill & sons*, 1868.

Birkbeck (Morris). Notes on a journey in America, from the coast of Virginia to the territory of Illinois. iv, 144 pp. 12°. *London, Ridgway & son*, 1818.

——— Notes on a journey through France, in 1814. With appendix. 1st Amer. ed. 143, 28 pp. 16°. *Philadelphia, M. Carey*, 1815.

Birkenfeld. Voranschlag der einnahmen und ausgabe des fürstenthums Birkenfeld für 1849, 1850. 2 v. in 1. 13 pp; 13 pp. 4°. *Oldenburg, G. Stalling & Schulze*, 1849–50. s.
[*With* OLDENBURG. Voranschlag, etc. 1849–51].

Birmingham. The first [and third to fifth] annual reports of the free libraries committee of the borough. 1862–66. 4 v. 8°. *Birmingham, [borough*, 1862–66.] s.
[Wanting second report].

——— Opening of the free reference library, Oct. 26, 1866. Inaugural address by George Dawson. 24 pp. 8°. *Birmingham, [borough*, 1866]. s.

Biron (Armand Louis Gontaut, *duc de Lauzun, duc de*). *See* **Lauzun** (*duc de*).

Bishop (A. W.) Loyalty on the frontier, or sketches of union men of the south-west; with incidents and adventures in the rebellion on the border. 228 pp. 12°. *St. Louis, R. P. Studley & Co.* 1863.

Bishop (John S.) A concise history of the war. To accompany Perrine's new war map of the southern states. 218 pp. 3 l. 1 map. 18°. *Indianapolis, Ind. C. O. Perrine*, 1864.

Bishop (Nathaniel H.) The pampas and Andes. A thousand miles' walk across South America. With an introduction by Edward A. Samuels. 310 pp. 12°. *Boston, Lee & Shepard*, 1869.

Bissett (Robert, *LL. D.*) The history of George iii, [with] a view of the progressive improvement of England. Library ed. 3 v. 8°. *Philadelphia, E. Littell*, 1828.

Blachette (L. J.), *and* **Zoéga** (Frédéric). A manual of the art of making and refining sugar from beets, including the cultivation of the plant, and the various improvements in the manufacture. Translated from portions of the treatise as published, with additions by J[ulia] de Fontenelle. 153 pp. 1 pl. 16°. *Boston, Marsh, Capen & Lyon,* 1836.

Black (Archibald Pollok). A hundred days in the east; a diary of a journey to Egypt, Palestine, Turkey in Europe, etc. x, 615 pp. 2 maps. 4 pl. 16°. *London, Shaw & Co.* 1865.

Blackbird (The), being a choice collection of the most popular American, English, Irish, and Scotch songs. 1 p. l. 36 pp. 12°. *New York, D. Felt & Co.* 1834.
[*With* KING'S choice selection of English songs.]

Blackburn (*Rev.* William M.) The college days of Calvin. 156 pp. 12°. *Philadelphia, presbyterian board of pub.* 1865.

——— Ulrich Zwingli, the patriotic reformer; a history. 324 pp. 1 map. 12°. *Philadelphia, presb. board of publ.* 1868.

——— Young Calvin in Paris, and the little flock that he fed. 166 pp. 16°. *Philadelphia, presbyterian board of publication,* 1865.

Blackford (Dominique de). Précis de l'état actuel des colonies angloises dans l'Amérique septentrionale. 99 pp. 16°. *Milan, frères Reycends,* 1771.

Blackmore (*Sir* Richard). Alfred: an epick poem. 4 p. l. xlviii, 456 pp. 8°. *London, J. Knapton,* 1723.

——— Creation. A philosophical poem, demonstrating the existence and providence of a God, [etc.] 4th ed. 1 p. l. lxix, 237 pp. 18°. *London, A. Bettesworth,* 1718. s.

Blainville (Henri Marie Ducrotay de). Manuel d'actinologie, ou de zoophytologie, etc. viii, 695 pp. Atlas, 2 p. l. 100 pl. 8°. *Paris, F. G. Levrault,* 1834. s.

Blair (Hugh). Critical dissertation on the poems of Ossian. 16°. *New Haven,* 1806.
[*In* OSSIAN. Poems, v. 2. *New Haven,* 1806].

Blair (Robert, *D. D.*) The grave. A poem. [With] an elegy written in a country churchyard by [Thomas] Gray. 31 pp. 16°. *Philadelphia, R. Aitken,* 1773.

Blake (Charles). An historical account of the Providence stage. 297 pp. 12°. *Providence, (R. I.) G. H. Whitney,* 1868.

Blake (James). A short account of [Roger Clap] and his family. 16°. *Boston, D. Clapp,* 1844.
[*In the* DORCHESTER antiquarian and historical society collections, no. 1].

Blake (*Rev.* John L.) The juvenile companion and fireside reader, [etc.] 252 pp. 1 pl. 16°. *New York, Harpers,* 1846. s.

——— The wonders of art; containing an account of celebrated ancient ruins, fortifications, public edifices, monuments, [etc.] inventions, [etc.] 252 pp. 18°. *Troy, (N. Y.) Young & Hartt,* 1845. s.

Blake (Sophia Jex), *and* **Blake** (*Rev.* Thomas William Jex). *See* **Jex-Blake.**

Blake (Stephen). The compleat gardener's practice, directing the exact way of gardening. In three parts: The garden of pleasure, the physical garden, the kitchin garden. 6 p. l. 154 pp. 3 l. 30 pl. sm. 4°. *London, T. Pierrepont,* 1664.
[Imperfect: 1 p. l. wanting].

Blakeway (*Rev.* John Brickdale). An attempt to ascertain the author of the letters published under the signature of Junius. 72 pp. 8°. *Shrewsbury, W. Eddowes,* 1813.

——— Sequel of an attempt to ascertain the author of the letters of Junius, in which that secret is, it is presumed, fully disclosed. By the author of the attempt. 29 pp. 8°. *London, Longman,* 1815.
[*With* the preceding].

Blanc (Auguste Alexandre Philippe Charles). Grammaire des arts du dessin, architecture, sculpture, peinture, gravure. 720 pp. 8°. *Paris, Renouard,* 1867.

Blanc (Honoré). Mémoire important sur la fabrication des armes de guerre. 21 pp. 4°. *Paris, assemblée nationale,* 1790. s.
[*With* TALLEYRAND-PERIGORD (C. M. de). Rapport sur l'instruction publique, 1791].

Blanc (Jean Joseph Louis). Letters on England. Translated by J. Hutton and L. J. Trotter. 2d series. 2 v. vii, 288 pp; vii, 247 pp. 12°. *London, S. Low, son, & Marston,* 1867.

Blanchard (Calvin). The art of real pleasure. 148 pp. 3 pl. 16°. *New York, C. Blanchard,* 1864.

Blanchard (Émile). Catalogue des coléoptères. *See* **Edwards** (H. Milne), **Blanchard** (E.), *and* **Lucas** (H.)

——— Métamorphoses, mœurs et instincts des insectes (insectes, myriapodes, arachnides, crustacés). 2 p. l. 716 pp. 40 pl. 8°. *Paris, G. Baillière,* 1868. s.

Blanchard (Sidney Laman). Yesterday and to-day in India. 2 p. l. 355 pp. 12°. *London, W. H. Allen & Co.* 1867.

Blancicampianus. *See* **Nausea** blancicampianus.

Blanco (Lorenzo). Saggio della semiografia dei volumi ercolanesi. vi, 61 pp. 1 tab. 8°. *Napoli, Criscuolo,* 1842. s.

Blaschke (Eduard, *M.D.*) Topographia medica portus novi-archangelscensis, sedis principalis coloniarum rossicarum in septentrionali America. 2 p. l. 86 pp. 3 tab. 1 pl. 2 maps. 8°. *Petropoli, typis K. Wienhoberi et fil.* 1842.

Blatchford (John). Narrative detailing his sufferings in the revolutionary war, while a prisoner with the British; as related by himself. With an introduction and notes by C. I. Bushnell. [*New London, T. Green,* 1788]. 127 pp. 2 pl. 8°. *New York, privately* [*re*]*printed,* 1865.

Bledsoe (Albert Taylor, *LL.D.*) The philosophy of mathematics, with special reference to the elements of geometry and the infinitesimal method. 248 pp. 12°. *Philadelphia, Lippincott & Co.* 1868.

Bleeck (A. H.) A concise grammar of the Persian language; with a new plan for facilitating the study of languages, and specimens [of extracts in 14 different languages]. xvi, 206 pp. 16°. *London, B. Quaritch,* 1857.

Bleeker (Pieter). Atlas ichthyologique des Indes orientales néêrlandaises, publié sous les auspices du gouvernement colonial néêrlandais. 6 v. in 13. With 240 col. pl. fol. *Amsterdam, F. Muller,* 1862–65. s.

CONTENTS.

v. 1. Scaroïdes et labroïdes. xxi, 168 pp. 48 pl. 1862.
v. 2. Siluroïdes, chacoïdes et hétérobranchoïdes. 2 p.l. 112 pp. 53 pl. 1862[-63].
v. 3. Cyprins. 2 p. l. 150 pp. 43 pl. 1863.
v. 4. Murènes, synbranches, leptocéphales. 2 p. l. 132 pp. 49 pl. 1864.
v. 5. Les baudroies (antennarii), les ostracions, les gymnodontes, les balistes. pp. 1–96. 38 pl. 1865.
v. 6. Pleuronectoïdes. pl. 1–9. 1865.

[No more published].

Bligh (William). A narrative of the mutiny on board his majesty's ship Bounty, and the subsequent voyage in the ship's boats from Tofoa to Timor. vii, 144 pp. 8°. *Dublin, L. White,* 1790.

Bloch (Móricz). Neues vollständiges taschenwörterbuch der ungarischen und deutschen sprache, mit aufnahme aller neu gebildeten ungarischen wörter. v. 1. Deutsch-ungarischer. v. 2. Ungarisch-deutscher. 2 v. vii, 362 pp; 312 pp. 12°. *Pesth, C. Geizel,* 1843–44.

Block (Maurice, *editor*). *See* **Annuaire** de l'administration française, etc. 1867.

Blodget (Samuel). A prospective plan of the battle near lake George, on the eighth day of September, 1755; with an explanation thereof, etc. 5 pp. 4°. *Boston, R. Draper,* 1755.

[*Note.*—The "prospective plan" is wanting].

Bloede (Victor G.) The reducer's manual, and gold and silver worker's guide, being a complete hand-book on the saving and reduction of photographic wastes, and gold and silver residues. 167 pp. 16°. *New York, J. H. Ladd,* 1867.

Blome (Richard). Description de l'isle de la Jamaïque, et de toutes celles que possédent les Anglois dans l'Amérique. [Traduit de l'Anglois]. 81 pp. 1 map. 4°. *Paris, veuve A. Cellier,* 1684.

[RECUEIL de divers voyages en Afrique et en Amérique. ed. 1684.]

Blondin (Jean Noel). Grammaire française démonstrative. 8e éd. ii, 134 pp. 8°. *Paris, J. Brianchon,* 1822. s.

Bloodgood (S. DeWitt). The sexagenary; or, reminiscences of the American revolution. [*anon.*] 203 pp. 16°. *Albany, Little & Steele,* 1833.

Bloss (C. A.) Ancient history, for the use of families and schools. Revised by J. J. Anderson. 445 pp. 4 maps. 1 pl. 1 tab. 12°. *New York, Clark & Maynard,* 1867.

Blount (Thomas). Boscobel; or, the history of king Charles ii.'s most miraculous preservation after the battle of Worcester. 12°. *London, H. G. Bohn,* 1859.

[*With* HAMILTON (A. *count*). Memoirs of the court of Charles ii. pp. 479–536. 1859].

Blount (*Sir* Thomas Pope). A natural history: containing many not common observations: extracted out of the best modern writers. 8 p. l. 469 pp. 16°. *London, R. Bentley,* 1693.

Blue (The) umbrella. By Fleeta. [*pseudon.*] 226 pp. 3 pl. 18°. *Philadelphia, Presby. board of pub.* [1866].

Blum (Georg, *editor*). *See* **Weltmeer.**

Blumenbach (Johann Friedrich). Anthropological treatises. With memoirs by Marx and Flourens, and an account of his anthropological museum by R. Wagner. Translated from the originals by T. Bendyshe. xiv, 406 pp. 4 pl. 8°. *London, anthropological society,* 1865.

CONTENTS.

On the natural variety of mankind. ed. 1775 and 1795.
Contributions to natural history, parts i. and ii.
Remarks on an hippocratic macrocephalus.

Blunt (*Rev.* John James). Vestiges of ancient manners and customs, discoverable in modern Italy and Sicily. xvi, 293 pp. 8°. *London, J. Murray,* 1823.

Bocage (J. V. Barbosa du). *See* **Barbosa** du Bocage.

Bocalini. *See* **Boccalini.**

Boccaccio (Giovanni). Il decamerone di nvovo emendata secondo gli antichi essemplari con la diuersità di molti testi in margine i espositione de lvochi difficili [con la vita dell'autore scritta da Francesco Sansovino]. 6 p. l. 501 pp. 34 l. sm. 4°. *Vinegia, G. Giolito de Ferrari,* 1546.

——— The same. The decameron; containing an hundred very pleasant novels. Translated into English, [from the Italian]. 2 v. in 1. 6 p. l. 219 l; 6 pl. 183 l. 18°. *London, E. Cotes,* 1655.

[v. 2 imperfect: title page, l. 59–60, and last leaf wanting].

——— The same. Contes et nouvelles, [le Decameron]. Traduction libre, enrichie de figures en taille-douce gravées par M. Romain de Hooge. 2 v. 11 p. l. 366 pp; 427 pp. 6 l. 1 pl. 18°. *Amsterdam, G. Gallet,* 1699–1702.

——— Il Philocolo. cxxvii, 6 l. unp. fol. *Venetia, P. Pasquale da Bologna,* 1488.

[Imperfect; wanting 1 l. Last l. ms.]

Boccalini (Trajano). Discursos politicos, y avisos del Parnaso, traduxolos de la lengua toscana en la española F. Perez de Sousa, [etc.] 17 p. l. 220 l. 4°. *Madrid, Pedro Coello,* 1634. s.

——— The same. Nueva impression, [etc.] 2 v. 12 p. l. 436 pp; 12 p. l. 287 pp. 4°. *Madrid, J. G. Lanza,* 1754. s.

——— *See* **Secretaria** di Apollo.

Böck (Wilhelm). Traité de la spédalskhed. (Éléphantiasis). *See* **Danielssen** (D. C.) *and* **Böck.**

Böckeler (O.) Cypearaceæ [von Mossambique]. fol. *Berlin,* 1864.

[*With* PETERS (W. C. H.) Nat. reise nach Mossambique. Botanik].

Böckh (August). Manetho und die hundsstern periode, ein beitrag zur geschichte der Pharaonen. 1 p. l. 396 pp. 8°. *Berlin, Veit & Co.* 1845. s.

Boddaert (Pieter, *M. D.*) Natuur-beschouwer of verzameling van de nieuwste verhandelingen over de drie ryken der natuur, [etc.] 1te stuk. xvi, 160 pp. 8°. *Gravenhaage, J. Du Mée,* 1779. s.

——— *See, also,* **Linné** (C. v.) Zamenstel der natuur.

Boddington (*Mrs.* ——). Slight reminiscences of the Rhine, Switzerland, and a corner of Italy. [*anon.*] 2 v. 216 pp; 212 pp. 16°. *Philadelphia, Carey, Lea & Blanchard,* 1835.

Bodichon (Eugène). De l'humanité. [*anon.*] 148 pp. 8°. *Alger, Dubos frères.* [*about* 1854].

[Title page wanting].

Boeckeler. *See* **Böckeler.**

Boeckh. *See* **Böckh.**

Boehtlingk. *See* **Böhtlingk.**

Boemus *Aubanus* (Ioannes). *See* **Böhme** (Johann).

Boerhaave (Hermann) *and* **Ruysch** (Frederik). Opusculum anatomicum de fabrica glandularum in corpore humano. 4°. *Amstelædami,* 1733.

[RUYSCH (F.) Opera. v. 3. No. 42].

Boesnier (——). Le mexique conquis. [*anon.*] 2 v. in 1. xvi, 216 pp; 2 p. l. 249 pp. 2 l. 2 maps. 16°. *Paris, Desaint,* 1752.

Boethius (Anicius Manlius Severinus). De consolatione philosophiæ libri v. Ad optimorum librorum mss, nondum collatorum fidem recensuit et prolegomenis instruxit Theodorus Obbarius. lxiv, 160 pp. 8°. *Ienæ, C. Hochhausen,* 1843. s.

Bogaert (P.) Toegepaste spreekwoorden. 112 pp. 12°. *Gent, J. S. Van Doosselaere,* 1852. s.

Bogatzky (Carl Heinrich von). Güldenes schatz-kästlein der kinder Gottes, deren schatz im himmel ist; bestehend in auserlesenen sprüchen der heiligen schrift, sammt beygefügten erbaulichen anmerkungen und reimen. 4 p. l. 365 pp. 12 l. obl. 48°. *Philadelphia, G. W. Mentz,* 1811.

Bohl *or* **Bohlius** (Johann Christoph). Dissertatio epistolica de usu nouarum cavae propaginum in systemate chylopoeo, ut et de corticis cerebri textura. 4°. *Amstelædami,* 1727.

[RUYSCH (F.) Opera. v. 3. No. 36].

——— Tractatio anatomica, de musculo in fundi uteri observato, antehac a nemine detecto, etc. 4°. *Amstelædami,* 1726.

[RUYSCH (F.) Opera. v. 3. No. 35].

Böhme (Johann). The manners, lawes, and cvstomes of all nations. Collected out of the best writers. Translated into English. By Ed. Aston. 8 p. l. 589 pp. 2 l. sm. 4°. *London, G. Eld,* 1611.

Bohn (Casimir). Handbook of Washington. With supplement by C. Lanman. 134 pp. 1 map. 11 pl. 18°. *Washington, C. Bohn,* 1861.

Bohn (Henry George). Catalogue of the first portion of stock, including books of prints, voyages and travels, history and biography, etc. and standard authors in all classes of literature. [To] be sold, 1868. 422 pp. 8°. *London, Sotheby, Wilkinson & Hodge,* [1867].

——— General catalogue. Part 2d, section 3d, containing Greek and Latin miscellanies, including theology, fathers of the church, phil-

Bohn—continued.
ology, modern Latin poetry, facetiæ, satires, also manuscripts, Chinese drawings and books, [etc.] pp. v, 673–858. 8°. *London, H. G. Bohn*, 1866. s.

—— The same. Part 2d, section 4th, containing French, Italian, Spanish, Portuguese, German, Dutch, Danish, and Swedish books, in all classes of literature. 2 p. l. pp. 859–1164. 8°. *London, H. G. Bohn*, 1867. s.

Böhtlingk (Otto). Ueber die sprache der Jakuten. 4°. *St. Petersburg*, 1851.
[*With* MIDDENDORFF (A. Th. von). Reise, etc. v. 3].

Bohun (R. *of new coll. Oxford*). A discourse concerning the origine and properties of wind. 9 p. l. 302 pp. 16°. *Oxford, T. Bowman*, 1671.

Boinvilliers (Édouard). Des transports à prix réduits sur les chemins de fer. viii, 167 pp. 8°. *Paris, L. Hachette & Cie*. 1859. s.

Boinvilliers-Desjardin (J. E. J. F.) Cacologie, ou recueil de locutions vicieuses. 3e éd. 192 pp. 16°. *Paris, A. Delalain*, 1812.

Boissard (Jean Jacques). Emblematum liber. Ipsa emblemata ab auctore delineata: a Theodoro de Bry sculpta, et nunc recens in lucem edita. 8 p. l. 103 pp. 54 pl. sm. 4°. *Francofurti ad Moenum*, 1593.

—— Emblemata, 1596. *See* **Lebey de Batilly** (Denis).

Boitard (Pierre, *chevalier*). Nouveau manuel complet du naturaliste préparateur, ou l'art d'empailler les animaux, de conserver les végétaux et les minéraux, de préparer les pièces d'anatomie normale et pathologique, suivi d'un traité des embaumements. Nouv. éd. 510 pp. 5 pl. 18°. *Paris, Roret*, 1852. s.

Boke (The) of keruynge. [*anon.*] Edited by F. J. Furnivall. *London, Wynkyn de Worde*, 1513, *reprint*. 8°. *London*, 1867.
[*With* FURNIVALL (F. J.) Babees book, etc. pp. 261–288. Early English text society publications. No. 32].

Boker (George H.) Calaynos: a tragedy. 2d ed. 218 pp. 12°. *Philadelphia, E. H. Butler & Co.* 1848. s.

Bold (Henry). Poems, lyrique, macaronique, heroique, etc. 7 p. l. 236 pp. 24°. *London, H. Brome*, 1664.

Bolingbroke (Henry). A voyage to the Demerary; containing a statistical account of the settlements there, and of those on the Essequibo, the Berbice, and other contiguous rivers of Guyana. 260 pp. 8°. *Philadelphia, M. Carey*, 1813.

Bollaert (William). Antiquarian, ethnological, and other researches in New Granada, Equador, Peru, and Chili; with observations on the pre-incarial, incarial, and other monuments of Peruvian nations. 279 pp. 18 pl. 8°. *London, Trübner*, 1860. s.

Bollan (William). Coloniae anglicanæ illustratæ; or, the acquest of dominion, and the plantation of colonies made by the English in America, with the rights of the colonists, examined, stated, and illustrated. Part i. [*anon.*] viii, 141 pp. 4°. *London*, 1762.
[No more published. This part contains the prefatory matter only].

Bolle (*Dr.* Carl). Leguminosæ [von Mossambique]. fol. *Berlin*, 1862.
[*With* PETERS (W. C. H.) Nat. reise nach Mossambique. Botanik].

Boller (Henry A.) Among the Indians. Eight years in the far west: 1858–66. Embracing sketches of Montana and Salt Lake. 428 pp. 1 map. 12°. *Philadelphia, T. E. Zell*, 1868.

Bollioud-Mermet (Louis). De la bibliomanie. [*anon.*] 111 pp. 8°. *La Haie*, 1761.

—— The same. (2e éd. de la réimpression). 81 pp. 18°. *Paris, académie des bibliophiles*, 1866.

Bolmar (Anthony). A collection of [French] colloquial phrases, on every topic necessary to maintain conversation. New ed. ix, 208 pp. 18°. *Philadelphia, Lea & Blanchard*, 1842.

Bolnest (Edward, *M. D.*) Aurora chymica; or a rational way of preparing animals, vegetables, and minerals, for a physical use. 8 p. l. 146 pp. 1 l. 18°. *London, J. Starkey*, 1672.

Bölsche (Wilhelm). Die korallen des norddeutschen jura-und kreide-gebirges. 50 pp. 3 pl. 8°. *Berlin, J. F. Starcke*, 1867. s.

Bolten (Joachim Friedrich). Ad Carolvm à Linné [etc.] epistola de novo qvodam zoophytorvm genere. [With appendix]. Uitvoerige beschryving en naauwkeurige natuurlyk gekleurde afbeelding van een nieuwelyks ontdekt geheel onbekend plantydyr in 't licht gegeeven [Boltenia]. 11 pp. 11 p. l. 8 pp. 1 col. pl. 4°. *Amsterdam, J. C. Sepp*, 1771. s.

Bolton (Robert). History of the protestant episcopal church, in the county of Westchester, from its foundation, 1693–1853. xxiii, 749 pp. 6 pl. 8°. *New York, Stanford & Swords*, 1855.

Bommer (J. E.) Monographie de la classe des fougères. Classification. (Extrait des bulletins de la société royale botanique de Belgique). 107 pp. 6 pl. 8°. *Bruxelles, Mayolez*, 1867. s.

Bonafons (Louis Abel de, *abbé de Fontenay*). Esprit des livres défendus, ou antilogies philosophiques; ouvrage dans lequel on a recueilli les morceaux sur la religion, la philosophie, les sciences et les arts, extrait des livres philosophiques. [*anon.*] 2e éd. 4 v. 16°. *Paris, Nyon,* 1777.

Bonaparte (Charles Lucien, *prince of Canino*). Conspectus generum avium. 2 v. 2 p. l. 543 pp; 232 pp. 8°. *Lugduni-Batavorum, E. J. Brill,* 1850–57. s.
[No more published].

——— Revue critique de l'ornithologie européenne de Degland. 206 pp. 12°. *Bruxelles, Wouters,* 1850. s.

Bonaventura (Giovanni di Fidanza, *saint*). Dieta salutis a beato Bonaduentura emendatus. 152 l, (116 numbered). 16°. *Parisiis, J. Petit,* [*about* 1474]. s.

Boniface (Alexandre), Abrégé de la grammaire française. Nouv. éd. [etc.] par J. L. B. Leresche. 2 p. l. ii, 174 pp. 16°. *Lausanne, D. Martignier,* 1852. s.

Bonnange (Ferdinand). Nouveau système de catalogue au moyen de cartes. 19 pp. 2 pl. 8°. *Paris, E. Lacroix,* 1866.

Bonnell (J. M. *D. D.*) A manual of the art of prose. 359 pp. 12°. *Louisville, J. P. Morton & Co.* 1867.

Bonner (John). A child's history of Greece. 2 v. 315 pp. 1 pl; 292 pp. 1 pl. 16°. *New York, Harpers,* 1857. s.

——— A child's history of Rome. 2 v. 307 pp. 1 pl; 311 pp. 12°. *New York, Harpers,* 1856. s.

Bonney (Edward). The banditti of the prairies. A tale of the Mississippi valley, [etc.] 196 pp. 8°. *Chicago, D. P. Cooke & Co.* 1856. s.

Bonsdorff (Eberhard Julius). Finlands tvavingode insekter (diptera), förtecknade, och i korthet beskrifne. xii, 276 pp. 8°. *Helsingfors, Finska litteratur-sällskapets tryckeri,* 1861. s.

Bontemps (Gérard, *pseudon?*) La gallerie des cvrievx, contenant en diuers tableau les chefs d'œuvres des plus excellens railleurs de ce siècle. 8 p. l. 320 pp. 18°. *Paris, C. Besongne,* 1646.

——— Bovqvet recreatif, cveilly dans les parterres des bons railleurs de ce temps. 48 pp. 18°. *Paris, C. Besongne,* 1646.
[*With* the preceding.]

Booch-Arkossy (F.) Methode Robertson für das Spanische. Praktische-theoretischer lehrgang der spanischen schrift und umgangssprache nach der Robertson'schen methode, [etc.] 2e aufl. xiii, 290 pp. 8°. *Leipzig, Arnold,* 1861. s.

——— Supplement und schlüssel zum lehrgang der spanischer schrift-und umgangs-sprache. 2e aufl. iv, 196 pp. 8°. *Leipzig, Arnold,* 1861. s.
[*With* the preceding.]

Book (The) of common prayer, with the administration of the sacramentes, and other rites and ceremonies of the church of Englande. 141 l. fol. *London, R. Barker,* 1632.
[Imperfect: l. A. 1–2. wanting].

——— The same. According to the use of the church of England, with the psalter. 79 pp. fol. *London, C. Bill,* 1711.
[*With* BIBLE, *English,* 1707–08].

Book (The) of daily prayers [etc.] according to the custom of the German and Polish Jews. Edited by Isaac Leeser, [etc. Hebrew and English]. viii, 243 l. 8°. *Philadelphia, editor,* 5608. s.

Book of keruynge. *See* **Boke.**

Book of love letters. With directions how to write them, and specimens, [etc.] By Ingoldsby North, [*pseudon.*] 156 pp. 16°. *New York, Dick & Fitzgerald,* [1867].

Book (The) of rights. Edited with translation and notes by J. O'Donovan. x, lxvii, 326 pp. 12°. *Dublin,* 1847.
[CELTIC society publications, No. 1].

Book (The) of worship. Published by order of the evangelical lutheran general synod in North America. 672 pp. 24°. *Columbia, (S. C.) Duffie & Chapman,* 1867.

Booker (John). Six pennyworth of wit for a penny; or, dreams interpreted. 24°. *London,* [17—].
[*With* PROGNOSTICATION (A) forever. 24°. London. 1653]?

Boone (*Col.* Daniel). Adventures: containing a narrative of the wars in Kentucky. 8°. *London, J. Debrett,* 1767.
[*With* IMLAY (G.) Topographical description of the western territory. pp. 338–359. ed. 1797].

Booth (*Rev.* Abraham). Commerce in the human species, and the enslaving of innocent persons, inimical to the laws of Moses, and the gospel of Christ. 40 pp. 16°. *Philadelphia, (reprinted), D. Lawrence,* 1792.

Booth (Junius Brutus, *the elder*). Booth memorials. Passages, incidents, and anecdotes in his life. By his daughter. 12°. *New York,* 1866.

Bopp (Franz). Glossarium sanscritum. viii, 216 pp. 4°. *Berolini, officini academica,* 1830. s.

Bopp (Franz). Grammatica critica linguæ sanscritæ. Ed. alt. xv, 336 pp. 4°. *Berolini, F. Dümmler,* 1832. s.

Borcke (Heros von). Memoirs of the confederate war for independence. 2 v. x, 323 pp; vii, 318 pp. 1 map. 12°. *Edinburgh, W. Blackwood & Sons,* 1866.

Bordiga (Benedetto *and* Gaudenzio). Storia delle piante forastiere. *See* **Castiglioni** (Luigi), *and others.*

Boreau (Victor). Histoire générale des temps du moyen age, [476–1453]. 5e éd. 540 pp. 16°. *Paris, J. Vermot,* 1856.

Borel (Eugène). Cours de thèmes français. Progressive exercises, for translating English into French, suitable for use with all grammars. 116 pp. 12°. *New York, Leypoldt & Holt,* 1868.

——— Grammaire française à l'usage des Anglais; arrangée d'après la 12e édition des allemands. Revised by E. B. Coe. xvi, 317, 116 pp. 12°. *New York, Leypoldt & Holt,* 1868.

Borges de F. Henriques (——). A trip to the Azores or western islands. 137 pp. 16°. *Boston, Lee & Shepard,* 1867.

Bornemann (C. R. *editor*). *See* **Berg-** und hüttenmannische zeitung.

Borszczow (E. G. *and* G. G.) Musci [etc.] nec non fungi, [etc.] in expeditione sibirica, [etc.] collecti. 4°. *St. Petersbnrg,* 1856.

[*In* MIDDENDORFF (A. T. von). Reise, etc. v. 1, theil 2].

Boruwlaski (Józef). Memoirs; containing a faithful and curious account of his birth, education, marriage, travels, and voyages; written by himself; from the French by [Hérissant] des Carrières. [French and English texts]. 7 p. l. 247 pp. 1 pl. 8°. *London,* 1788.

Boschini (Marco). Le minere della pittvra. Compendiosa informazione, [etc.] non solo delle pitture publiche di Venezia; ma dell'Isole ancora circonuicine. 16 p. l. 572 pp. 6 pl. 16°. *Venezia, F. Nicolini,* 1664. s.

Bossange (Hector), *and* son, etc. Catalogue of anatomy. 97 pp. 8°. *Paris, etc. Bossange,* 1860. s.

Bossler (Carl). De præpositionum usu apud Pindarum. 2 p. l. 88 pp. 8°. *Darmstadii, C. W. Leske,* 1862. s.

Bossuet (Jacques Bénigne). Politique tirée des propres paroles de l'écriture sainte, [etc.] 3 v. 12°. *Turin, A. Alliana,* 1824. s.

Boston (*City of*). Documents, 1867. 2 v. 8°. *Boston, A. Mudge & Son,* 1868.

——— Report of the joint special committee on the census of Boston, May, 1855, including the report of the censors, with analytical and sanitary observations. By Josiah Curtis. xiv, 104 pp. 8°. *Boston, city,* 1856. s.

Boston (The) almanac, 1868. v. 33. 24°. *Boston, G. Coolidge,* 1868.

Boston (The) book. Being specimens of metropolitan literature. [4th series]. vii, 364 pp. 12°. *Boston, Ticknor, Reed & Fields,* 1850.

Boston (The) business directory, for 1868. v. 6. 16°. *Boston, Dudley & Greenough,* 1868.

Boston business street directory. 343 pp. 1 map. 18°. *Boston, George Coolidge,* 1867.

Boston (The) directory. The former city of Roxbury included. 1868. 8°. *Boston, Sampson, Davenport & Co.* 1868.

Boston gazette. [Published semi-weekly]. v. 15–19. 1803–1807. fol. *Boston,* 1803–7.

[Imperfect].

Boston type and stereotype foundry. Specimen of printing types. J. C. Rogers, agent. 164 l. 8°. *Boston, Dutton & Wentworth,* 1828.

——— The same. 194 l. 8°. *Boston, S. N. Dickinson,* 1832.

Boswell (Roger). The art of conversation. 72 pp. 18°. *London, Cassell, Petter & Galpin,* 1867.

Both (Carl, *M. D.*) A new and effective method of treating consumption (phthisis pulmonalis) through calcification. 46 pp. 2 pl. 8°. *Boston, E. P. Dutton & Co.* 1868.

Both sides of the grape question. 2d ed. 96 pp. 18°. *Philadelphia, Lippincott & Co.* 1860.

Botta (Carlo Giuseppe Guglielmo). History of the war of the independence of the United States of America. From the Italian, by G. A. Otis. 2d ed. 2 v. 414 pp; 455 pp. 2 l. 8°. *Boston, H. Gray,* 1826.

Böttger (Rudolph). Beiträge zur physik und chemie. viii, 128 pp. 1 pl. 8°. *Frankfurt-a-M, H. L. Brönner,* 1838.

[*With* NAUMANN (C. F.) Table of mineralogical species, 1833].

Bouchardat (Apollinaire). Annual abstract of therapeutics, materia medica, pharmacy and toxicology, 1867; [with] an original memoir on gout, gravel, and urinary calculi. Translated and edited by M. J. De Rosset. 315 pp. 16°. *Philadelphia, Lindsay & Blakiston,* 1868.

Boucher de Crèvecoeur de Perthes (Jacques). Les masques; biographie sans nom. Portraits de mes connaissances dédiés à mes amis. 2 v. xliv, 484 pp; 464 pp. 12°. *Paris, Jung-Treuttel,* 1861. s.

Bouchut (Eugène). On croup, [1852.] 8°. *London*, 1859.
[NEW Sydenham society, v. 3].

Bouelles *or* **Bouilles** (Charles de). Epitome rerum geometricarum. 4°. [n. p. 1519]?
[*With* FABER (J.) Introductio in arithmecam Seuerini Boetij].

Bouquet (The). [Poetical selections]. 167 pp. 32°. *New Brunswick, (N. J.) E. B. Clayton*, 1814.

Bourdaloue (Louis, *père*). Pensées sur divers sujets de religion et de morale. 2 v. viii, 552 pp; 2 p. l. 554 pp. 8°. *Louvain, société catholique de la Belgique*, 1823. s.

Bourdon (Louis Gabriel). Voyage d'Amérique. Dialogue en vers, entre l'auteur et l'abbe * * *. [*anon.*] 156 pp. 16°. *Paris, Pichard*, 1786.

Bourgeois (———, *lawyer*). Christophe Colomb, ou l'Amérique découverte; poëme. 2 v. in 1. xv, 217 pp. 1 pl; 266 pp. 2 l. 1 pl. 8°. *Paris, Moutard*, 1773.

Bourgoing (Charles Paul Amable, *baron* de). Tableau de l'état actuel et des progrès probables des chemins de fer de l'Allemagne et du continent européen, comparés avec ce qui existe et ce qui se prépare en France à cet égard; avec une carte. xx, 393 pp. 1 map. 8°. *Paris, Carilian-Goeury & V. Dalmont*, 1842. s.

Bourne (George, *editor*). The spirit of the public journals; or, beauties of the American newspapers for 1805. [*anon.*] 300 pp. 16°. *Baltimore, Dobbin & Murphy*, 1806.

Bourne (H. R. Fox). English merchants: memoirs in illustration of the progress of British commerce. 2 v. xiv, 417 pp; x, 434 pp. 10 pl. 12°. *London, Bentley*, 1866.

Bourne (William Oland). Little silverstring: or, tales and poems for the young. 256 pp. 8 pl. 16°. *New York, C. Scribner*, 1853. s.

Bourquard (*Rev.* A. L. C.) Le palmier céleste. Recueil de prières et de pratiques pieuses d'après le cœleste palmetum. 508 pp. 2 pl. 32°. *New York, C. & N. Benziger*, 1868.

Boutauld (Michel). Les conseils de la sagesse, ou le recueil des maximes de Salomon les plus nécessaires à l'homme pour se conduire sagement. Avec des réflexions sur ces maximes. [*anon.*] 16 p. l. 333 pp. 18°. *Paris, S. Mabre-Cramoisy*, 1677. s.
[NOTE.—At one time attributed to surintendant Fouquet.]

Bouvet (Francisque). La guerre et la civilisation. x, 276 pp. 16°. *Paris, E. Dentu*, 1855.

Bow (The) in the cloud; or, covenant mercy for the afflicted. [Selections]. 360 pp. 9 pl. 8°. *Philadelphia, E. H. Butler & Co.* 1854.

Bowditch (Nathaniel). The American practical navigator, [etc.] continued by his son, J. Ingersoll Bowditch. 20th ed. xx, 319, 458 pp. 14 pl. 1 map. 8°. *New York, E. & G. W. Blunt*, 1851. s.

——— The same. 21st ed. 1 p. l. xx, 319, 458 pp. 1 map. 14 pl. 8°. *New York, E. & G. W. Blunt*, 1852. s.

——— The same. 26th ed. 8, xx, 319, 460 pp. 1 map. 14 pl. 8°. *New York, E. & G. W. Blunt*, 1856. s.

——— The same. 27th ed. 8, xx, 319, 460 pp. 1 map. 14 pl. 8°. *New York, E. & G. W. Blunt*, 1857. s.

Bowen (Abel). Bowen's Boston news-letter, and city record. v. 1. Nov. 5, 1825, to June 17, 1826. 312 pp. 52 l. 8°. *Boston, A. Bowen*, 1825–26.

——— The naval monument: containing accounts of all the battles fought between the navies of the United States and Great Britain during the late war; and an account of the war with Algiers. [With] a naval register to 1836. viii, 326 pp. 23 pl. 8°. *Boston, G. Clark*, 1840.

——— Picture of Boston; or, the citizen's and stranger's guide to the metropolis of Massachusetts, and its environs. [With] the annals of Boston. 2d ed. 316 pp. 1 map. 9 pl. 18°. *Boston, Lilly, Wait & Co.* 1833.
[Imperfect: 1 map wanting].

Bowen (Charles S. C.) The 'Alabama' claims and arbitration considered from a legal point of view. 77 pp. 8°. *London, Longmans*, 1868.

Bowerbank (James Scott). A monograph of the British spongiadæ. 2 v. 1 p. l. xx, 290 pp. 37 pl; xx, 388 pp. 8°. *London*, 1864–66.
[RAY society publications].

Bowker (J.) Wreck-elections of a busy life. [Parody of Horace Greeley's autobiography in the N. Y. ledger]. 22 pl. obl. 8°. *Hartford, Kellogg & Bulkeley*, 1868.

Bowling (W. K. *M. D.*) Historical address to the graduating class of 1868, in the medical department of the university of Nashville. 31 pp. 8°. *Nashville, Tenn, W. H. F. Ligon*, 1868. s.

Bowman (Samuel M.) Sherman and his compaigns: a military biography. 512 pp. 5 maps. 8 pl. 8°. *New York, Richardson & Co.* 1868.

Bowman (*Rev.* Thomas). The principles of christianity as taught in scripture. xviii, 175 pp. 18°. *Boston, Kneeland & Adams*, 1769.

Boyd (Andrew). Business directory and gazetteer of the towns and villages on the Albany and Susquehanna railroad; and of Cooperstown, Delhi, Norwich, Oxford, Franklin, etc. 1868–9. 220 pp. 8°. *Albany, C. Van Benthuysen & sons,* 1868.

Boyd (*Rev.* Andrew Kennedy Hutchinson). The autumn holidays of a country parson. [*anon.*] vii, 418 pp. 12°. *London, Longmans,* 1864.

Boyd (*Mrs.* E. E.) The little slate picker and other stories. 152 pp. 2 pl. 18°. *Philadelphia, J. P. Skelly & Co.* 1868.

Boyd (James R. *compiler*). Elements of logic. *See* **Barron** (W.)

Boyd (Robert, *D. D.*) Young converts; or, beginning in Zion's ways. 164 pp. 16°. *Chicago, Church & Goodman,* 1867.

Boyd (William). Woman: a poem. 15 pp. sm. 4°. *Boston, J. W. Folsom,* 1796.

Boyer (Abel). The history of queen Anne. 793 pp. 8 l. 3 pl. fol. *London, T. Woodward,* 1735.

[Imperfect. Plates wanting].

Boyle (Augustus F.) Phonographic reporter's first book. *See* **Andrews** (S. P.) *and* **Boyle.**

Boyle (John). The battle-fields of Ireland, from 1688 to 1691; including Limerick and Athlone, Aughrim, and the Boyne. [*anon.*] 323 pp. 12°. *New York, R. Coddington,* 1867.

Boyle (*Hon.* Robert). Occasional reflections upon several subjects. With a discourse about such kind of thoughts. 427 pp. 16°. *Oxford, A. A. Mason,* 1848.

Boynton (Charles Brandon, *D. D.*) The history of the navy during the rebellion. v. 2. 580 pp. 3 maps. 23 pl. 8°. *New York, Appletons,* 1868.

Boys (Félix du.) *See* **Du Boys.**

Boys (John). General view of the agriculture of the county of Kent; [etc.] To which is added, a treatise on paring and burning. 2d ed. xxiv, 293 pp. 1 tab. 1 col. map. 8°. *London,* 1805. s.

[Great Britain. Board of agriculture].

Brace (Joab, *jr.*) The principles of English grammar. 144 pp. 18°. *Philadelphia, H. Perkins,* 1840.

Brachvogel (A. Emil). Beaumarchais. An historical novel. From the German by Thérèse J. Radford. 295 pp. 8 pl. 8°. *New York, Appletons,* 1868.

Brackenridge (Henry M.) History of the late war between the United States and Great Britain. 2d ed. 363 pp. 5 pl. 16°. *Baltimore, J. Cushing,* 1817.

——— The same. 296 pp. 5 pl. 12°. *Philadelphia, J. Kay & bro.* 1844.

——— The same. Histoire de la guerre entre les États-Unis d'Amérique et l'Angleterre, 1812–15. Traduite par A. de Dalmas. 2 v. 310 pp. 1 map; 317 pp. 12°. *Paris, Corbet,* 1820.

——— Speeches on the Jew bill, in the house of delegates of Maryland, [by himself and others. With] an argument on the chancery powers, an eulogy on Thomas Jefferson and John Adams, [and letters on western antiquities,] etc. 236 pp. 8°. *Philadelphia, J. Dobson,* 1829.

Brackenridge (Hugh H.) Modern chivalry: containing the adventures of a captain, and Teague O'Regan, his servant. 2 v. vi, 210, 178 pp; 175, 163 pp. 12°. *Philadelphia, J. Johnson,* 1807–8.

Brackett (George E.) Farm talk: a series of articles illustrating various common farm topics. 130 pp. 18°. *Boston, Lee & Shepard,* 1868.

Bradbury (Charles W.) First lessons in English grammar, with a new and comprehensive arrangement of the verb. 2 p. l. 123 pp. 4°. *Boston, Higgins & Bradley,* 1856. s.

Bradbury (John). Travels in the interior of America, 1809–11, including a description of upper Louisiana, the states of Ohio, Kentucky, Indiana, and Tennessee, with the Illinois and western territories. 364 pp. 8°. *Liverpool, Smith & Galway,* 1817.

Bradbury (S. H.) Edenor: a dramatic poem. And miscellaneous lyrics. 200 pp. 12°. *London, Simpkin, Marshall & Co.* 1854. s.

Bradbury (William B.) The New York glee and chorus book, [etc.] 256 pp. obl. 12°. *New York, Mason brothers,* 1858. s.

Bradbury *and* **Evans,** *publishers.* A few leaves, represented by "nature printing," [etc.] 33 pl. fol. *London, Bradbury & Evans,* 1854. s.

Braddon (Mary Elizabeth). Birds of prey. A novel. 157 pp. 1 pl. 8°. *New York, Harpers,* 1867.

——— Lady Audley's secret. 293 pp. 8°. *Mobile, A. H. Goetzel,* 1864.

Bradford (Samuel Dexter). Works. xii, 427 pp. 1 portrait. 8°. *Boston, Phillips, Sampson & Co.* 1858. s.

Bradford (*Mrs.* S. H.) Tales for little convalescents. 85 pp. 4 pl. 16°. *New York, Hurd & Houghton,* 1868.

Bradlee (Nathaniel J.) History of the introduction of pure water into the city of Boston, with a description of its Cochituate water works. xxi, 299 pp. 4 maps. 13 pl. 8°. *Boston, A. Mudge & son*, 1868.

Bradley (*Rev.* Edward). The adventures of Mr. Verdant Green, an Oxford freshman. By Cuthbert Bede. [*pseudon.*] With illustrations. 94th thousand. vi, 338 pp. portrait. 16°. *London, J. Blackwood & Co.* 1867.

——— A tour in tartan land. By Cuthbert Bede. [*pseudon.*] xv, 430 pp. 12°. *London, Richard Bentley*, 1863.

Bradman (Arthur). A narrative of the extraordinary sufferings of Mr. Robert Forbes, his wife, and five children, during a journey through the wilderness from Canada to Kennebeck river, in 1784. 16 pp. 8°. *Philadelphia, M. Carey*, 1794.

Bradstreet (J. M.) & Son. Gazetteer of the manufactures and manufacturing towns of the United States. 1866. 9 p. l. 172 pp. 4°. *New York, J. M. Bradstreet & son*, 1866.

Brady (Robert, *M. D.*) A complete history of England, from the first entrance of the Romans to the end of the reign of Henry iii. 6 p. l. [997] pp. 34 l. 1 pl. fol. *London, S. Lowndes*, 1685.

——— The same. Continuation, Edward i to Richard ii. 467 pp. 13 l. 139 pp. fol. *London, S. Lowndes*, 1700.

——— An historical treatise of cities and boroughs. 4 p. l. 88, 39 pp. fol. *London, S. Lowndes*, 1690.

[*With his* "Continuation of the complete history of England"].

Brady (William, *sailing-master U. S. N.*) The kedge-anchor; or, young sailor's assistant, [etc.] 9th ed. 400 pp. 32 pl. 8°. *New York, author*, 1857. S.

Brahm (John Gerar William de). History of the province of Georgia; with maps of original surveys. [Edited by George Wymberley Jones]. 55 pp. 8 pl. 4°. *Wormsloe, (N. C.) privately printed*, 1849. S.

[*Note.*—Impression limited to 49 copies].

Brainard (Daniel, *M. D. of Chicago, Ill.*) Mémoire sur le traitement des fractures non réunies, et des difformités des os. 72 pp. 2 pl. 8°. *Paris, J. B. Baillière*, 1854. S.

Brainerd (David). An abridgement of [his] journal detailing the rise and progress of a remarkable work of grace among the Indians. vi, 110 pp. 2 l. 18°. *London, John Oswald*, 1748.

Brainerd (Thomas, *D. D.*) Old Pine street church. Manual of the third presbyterian church, Philadelphia. 64 pp. 1 pl. 8°. *Philadelphia, W. F. Geddes*, 1859.

Braithwaite. *See* **Brathwaite.**

Braman (*Rev.* Isaac). An eulogy on the late general George Washington, who died 14th December, 1799. Delivered at Rowley, [Mass.] February 22, 1800. 24 pp. 8°. *Haverhill, S. H. Moore*, [1800].

Branagan (Thomas). Flowers of literature; an exhibition of the most interesting geographical, historical, miscellaneous, and theological subjects in miniature. 324 pp. 24°. *Philadelphia, J. Rakestraw*, 1810.

Brande (William Thomas), *and* **Cauvin** (Joseph). A dictionary of science, literature, and art. iv, 1352 pp. 8°. *New York, Harpers*, 1848.

Brandes (Karl). Der heilige Petrus in Rom und Rom ohne Petrus. 2e aufl. 168 pp. 1 port. 16°. *New York, Benziger bros.* 1867.

——— ——— The same. Rome and the popes. From the German, by Rev. W. J. Wiseman. 215 pp. 16°. *New York, Benziger bros.* 1867.

Brandis (Johann). Über den historischen gewinn aus der entzifferung der assyrischen inschriften. Nebst einer übersicht über die grundzüge des assyrisch-babylonischen keilschriftsystems. vi, 126 pp. 1 pl. 8°. *Berlin, W. Hertz*, 1856.

Brandreth (Benjamin, *M. D.*) The doctrine of purgation. Curiosities from ancient and modern literature. A collection of quotations from Hippocrates and other medical writers, proving that purgation is the corner-stone of all curatives. Compiled by B. Brandreth. 224 pp. 8°. *New York, Baker & Godwin*, 1867.

Brandt (Gerard). Het leven en bedryf van den heere Michel de Ruiter. 4e druk. 4 p. l. 1065 pp. 12 l. 7 pl. fol. *Amsterdam, B. van Gerrevink & Erve Ratelband*, 1746.

Brandt (Johann Friedrich). Krebse. 4°. *St. Petersburg*, 1851.

[*With* MIDDENDORF (A. T. von). Reise, etc. v. 2. theil 1].

Brandt (R. J.) Okalluktualiæt, nuktérsimarsut, R. J. Brandt-mit, [etc.] ark' iksòrsimorsut titârnekartisimarsudlo P. Kragh-mit, [etc.] 118 pp. 12°. *Kjöbenhavnime, F. D. Tengnagelib*, 1839. S.

Brandy (The) drops; or, Charlie's pledge. A temperance story. By aunt Julia. [*anon.*] 103 pp. 1 pl. 16°. *New York, Carlton & Porter*, 1858. S.

Brasyls schuyt-praetjen, ghehouden tusschen een officier, een domine, en een coopman, noopende den staet van Brasyl. [*anon.*] 12 l. sm. 4°. [*Amsterdam*] ? *West-Indische kamer*, 1649.

Brathwaite (Richard). Novissima tvba. Libellus, in sex dialogos apprime Christianos, digestos. [*anon.*] 2 p. l. 97 pp. 1 l. 24°. *Londini, F. Kyngston*, 1632.

[*With* BACON (Francis *lord*). De sapientia vetervm liber. 1609].

Braun (Alexander, *prof. of botany at Freiburg*). Aquaticæ [von Mossambique]. fol. *Berlin*, 1864.

[*In* PETERS (W. C. H.) Nat. reise nach Mossambique. Botanik].

——— Betrachtungen über die erscheinung der verjüngung in der natur, insbesondere in der lebens-und bildungsgeschichte der pflanze. xvi, 364 pp. 3 col. pl. 4°. *Freiburg im Breisgau, H. M. Poppen*, 1849–50. s.

Braun (Johann Baptist). Das kirchliche vermögen von der ältesten zeit bis auf Justinian i. mit besonderer rücksicht auf die verwaltung desselben gegenüber dem staate. 4 p. l. 80 pp. 8°. *Greisser, W. Keller*, 1860. s.

Braun (Johann Wilhelm Joseph), *and* **Elvenich** (Peter Joseph). Acta romana [de Georgii Hermesii libris]. xxxii, 264 pp. 8°. *Hannoveræ, Helwing, etc.* 1838. s.

——— (*editors*). Meletemata theologica. vi, 106 pp. 8°. *Hannoveræ, ex libr. aul. helwingiana, etc.* 1838. s.

Bravo (Bartolome). Compendium latino-hispanum, utriusque linguæ, veluti lumen Petri de Salas. Accedent verba sacra ex adversariis J. L. de la Cerda. [*anon.*] Ed. nov. viii, 743 pp. 8°. [*Madrid*], *ex typographia regiæ societatis*, 1829.

Brazil. Colecção de documentos officiaes, [etc.] 8°. *Rio de Janeiro*, 1861.

[*With* RIO JANEIRO. Almanak, 1861].

——— The empire of Brazil at the Paris international exhibition of 1867. [With a glance at the empire]. 139, iii, 197 pp. 1 map. 8°. *Rio de Janeiro, E. & H. Laemmert*, 1867.

Breckenridge (Robert Jefferson). Third defence against the calumnies of Robert Wickliffe. 90 pp. 8°. *Baltimore, R. J. Matchett*, 1843. s.

Breed (William P. *D.D.*) The theatre. [An essay]. 35 pp. 18°. *Philadelphia, presbyterian board of publication*, [1868].

——— Under the oak. 304 pp. 3 pl. 18°. *Philadelphia, presb. board of pub.* [1866].

Brehm (Christian Ludwig). Die eier der europæischen voegel. *See* **Bädeker** (F. W. J.)

Breitenbach (Bernhard von). [Die heyligen reysen gen Jherusalem]. 148 l. fol. *Meyntz, Erhart rewich von Uttricht*, 1486.

[Imperfect: 16 l. wanting in the body of the work].

Breithaupt (Christian). Ars decifratoria, sive scientia occvltas scriptvras solvendi et legendi. Præmissa est disqvisitio historica de variis modis occvlte scribendi tam apvd veteres qvam recentiores vsitatis. 160 pp. 6 l. 16°. *Helmstadii, C. F. Weigand*, 1737. s.

Bremen. Zur statistik des bremischen staats. xxii, 97 pp. 4°. *Bremen, H. Strack*, 1862. s.

——— Tabellarische uebersicht des bremischen handels im jahre 1849[–62], zusammengestellt durch die behörde für die handelsstatistik. 13 v. 4°. *Bremen, J. G. Heyse, H. Strack*, 1850–63. s.

Bremen. *Museum.* Erster nachtrag zum verzeichniss der vögelsammlung des museum's. 21 pp. 16°. *Bremen, F. C. Dubbers*, 1846. s.

Bremer (Fredrika). The home; or, family cares and family joys. Translated from the Swedish, by Mary Howitt. 134 pp. 8°. *New York, Harpers*, 1843. s.

——— Life, letters, and posthumous works. Edited by Charlotte Bremer. From the Swedish, by F. Milow [and] Emily Nonnen. x, 439 pp. 12°. *New York, Hurd & Houghton*, 1868.

Brentano (Clemens, *editor*). Des knaben wunderhorn. *See* **Arnim** (L. A. von), *and* **Brentano.**

Brents (*Major* John A.) The patriots and guerillas of East Tennessee and Kentucky. 171 pp. 2 pl. 12°. *New York, J. A. Brents*, 1863.

Brereton (*Rev.* C. D.) Observations on the administration of the poor laws in agricultural districts. 3d ed. 124 pp. 8°. *London, Hatchard & son*, [*about* 1825].

——— A practical inquiry into the number, means of employment, and wages of agricultural laborers. 2d ed. xxiii, 110 pp. 8°. *London, Hatchard & son*, [*about* 1826].

[*With* BRERETON, (C. D.) Observations on the poor laws, &c. 3d ed.]

Bretonneau (Pierre). On diphtherite [1826]. 8°. *London*, 1859.

[NEW SYDENHAM society, v. 3].

Breydenbach (Bernhard von). *See* **Breitenbach.**

Brewster (*Sir* David). The kaleidoscope, its history, theory, and construction, with its application to the useful arts. 2d ed. viii, 189 pp. 1 pl. 16°. *London, J. Murray*, 1858. s.

Brice (Wallace A.) History of Fort Wayne, from the earliest known accounts of this point, to the present period. Embracing an extended view of the aboriginal tribes of the northwest, more especially the Miamies. xvi, 324, 33 pp. 7 pl. 8°. *Fort Wayne, (Ind.) D. W. Jones & son*, 1868.

Bridgeman (Thomas). The American gardener's assistant. In three parts. Revised by S. E. Todd. New ed. 529 pp. 8°. *New York, W. Wood & co.* 1867.

CONTENTS.

1. Kitchen gardening.
2. Fruit gardening.
3. Flower gardening.

Bridgens (R.) Sketches illustrative of the manners and costumes of France, Switzerland, and Italy. iv pp. 46 l. 50 col. pl. 4°. *London, Baldwin, Cradock & Joy*, 1821.

Brief (A) extract, or summary of important arguments, advanced by some late distinguished writers, in support of the supremacy of the British legislature, and their right to tax the Americans. By a Liveryman. [*anon.*] 48 pp. 8°. *London, J. Wilkie*, 1775.

Brief (A) view of the conduct of Pennsylvania for the year 1755; with an account of the inhumanities committed by the Indians [and] anecdotes relating to Quakers. [*anon.*] 88 pp. 8°. *London, R. Griffiths*, 1756.

Briefe (A) treatise conteyning manie proper tables and easie rules, verye necessary and needefull, for the use and commoditie of all people, collected out of certaine learned mens workes. Newlie set forth and alowed. [*anon.*] 56 l. *b. l.* 18°. *London, J. Walley*, 1585.

[*With* BRUNFELS (O.) A very true pronosticatiō. 1536]. [*Note.*—By Wm. Rastell?]

Briefe über religionswesen und freymäurerey. An allerley leser. [*anon.*] 120 pp. 18°. *Frankfort a. M; Schäfer*, 1780.

[*With* MEINE gedanken über die zwey kleine freymaurerische schriften, 1780].

Briefless (Jeremiah, *pseudon.*) *See* **Maidenthorpe.**

Bright (Richard, *M. D.*) Clinical memoirs on abdominal tumours and intumescences. Reprinted from "Guy's hospital reports." Edited by G. H. Barlow. xviii, 326 pp. 8°. *London*, 1860.

[NEW SYDENHAM society. v. 6].

Brinton (Daniel G. *M. D.*) The myths of the new world; a treatise on the symbolisms and mythology of the red race of America. viii, 309 pp. 8°. *New York, Leypoldt & Holt*, 1868.

Brisbane (William Henry). Slaveholding examined in the light of the holy bible. viii, 222 pp. 16°. *Philadelphia, Am. and for. anti-slavery society*, 1847. s.

Briseño (Ramon). Estadistica bibliográfica de la literatura chilena. Obra compuesta en virtud de encargo especial del consejo de la universidad de Chile. xiv, 546 pp. 4°. *Santiago, imprenta chilena*, 1862. s.

Brisseau-Mirbel (Charles François). Élémens de physiologie végétale et de botanique. 2 v. 5 p. l. 1,088 pp. Atlas, 72 pl. 8°. *Paris, Magimel*, 1815.

Brisson (Mathurin Jacques). Ornithologia, sive synopsis methodica sistens avium divisionem in ordines, sectiones, genera, species, ipsarumque varietates: [*or*] Ornithologie; ou méthode contenant la division des oiseaux en ordres, sections, genres, espèces et leurs variétés. [Lat and Fr.] 6 v. 4°. *Paris, J. B. Bauche*, 1760. s.

—— The same. [In Latin only]. 2 v. 10 p. l. 500 pp; 527 pp. 8°. *Lugduni Batavorum, T. Haak*, 1763. s.

Brissot de Warville (Jean Pierre). Examen critique des voyages dans l'Amérique septentrionale, de m. le marquis de Cha[s]tellux: ou, lettre dans laquelle on réfute principalement ses opinions sur les quakers, sur les nègres, sur le peuple, et sur l'homme. 2 p. l. 143 pp. 8°. *Londres*, 1786.

—— The same. A critical examination of the marquis de Cha[s]tellux's travels in North America, intended as a refutation of his opinions concerning the quakers, the negroes, the people, and mankind. From the French, with additions and corrections. 89 pp. 8°. *Philadelphia, J. James*, 1788.

—— Oration upon the necessity of establishing at Paris a society to cooperate with those of America and London, toward the abolition of the trade and slavery of the negroes, delivered 19th February, 1788, at Paris. 25 pp. 8°. *Philadelphia, F. Bailey*, 1788.

[*With* CLARKSON (*Rev.* T.) Impolicy of the slave-trade. *Philadelphia*, 1788].

—— Reise durch die Vereinigten Staaten von Nord-America, im jahr 1788. Aus dem Französischen von T. F. Ehrmann. lxviii, 628 pp. 1 tab. 8° *Dürkheim an der Haard, F. L. Pfähler*, 1792.

—— *and* **Clavière** (Étienne). The commerce of America with Europe. Shewing the importance of the American revolution to the interests of France, and pointing out the actual position of the United States in regard to trade, manufactures, and population. From

Brissot—continued.
the French, with the life of Brissot, by the translator. xxxv, 228 pp. portrait. 18°. *New York, T. & J. Swords,* 1795.

Bristed (Charles Astor). The cowards' convention. 16 pp. 8°. *New York,* 1864.
[LOYAL publication society, no. 68].

——— The interference theory of government. 109 pp. 16°. *New York, Leypoldt & Holt,* 1867.

Bristol (T. W.) Report on the mineral region of lake Superior. *See* **Houghton** (J.) *and* **Bristol.**

Britain (Great). *See* **Great Britain.**

British almanac and companion. 1828–30, 1843–44, 1849, and 1868. 7 v. 16°. *London, C. Knight,* 1828–68.

British (The) association for the advancement of science. Report of the 36th meeting, Aug. 1866. 8°. *London, J. Murray,* 1867.

British birds. The water birds. 268 pp. 13 col. pl. 16°. *London, religious tract society,* [1865]? s.

British liberties; or, the free-born subject's inheritance: containing the laws that form the basis of those liberties, with observations thereon. [*anon.*] 6 p. l. lxxix, 396 pp. 8°. *London, E. & C. Dilly,* 1766.

British museum. Catalogue of the additions to the manuscripts, 1848–53. 2 p. l. 371, 204 pp. 8°. [*London*], *by order of the trustees,* 1868.

——— Catalogue of the fishes in the British museum. By Albert Günther. v. 7. 8°. *London, by order of the trustees,* 1868.

——— A catalogue of the manuscripts in the Cottonian library. By J. Planta. xv, 618 pp. 38 l. fol. *London, L. Hansard,* 1802.

——— Catalogue of the specimens of heteropterous hemiptera in the collection of the British museum. By Francis Walker. Part ii. Scutata. pp. 241–417. 8°. *London, trustees of the Brit. mus.* 1867.

——— A guide to the Blacas collection of antiquities. By C. T. Newton. 35 pp. 16°. [*London*], *by order of the trustees,* 1867.

——— List of the specimens of birds in the collection of the British museum. By G. R. Gray. Part iii. Sect. 3 and 4. Capitonidæ and Picidæ. 137 pp. 16°. *London, by order of the trustees,* 1868.

British (The) naturalist; or, sketches of the more interesting productions of Britain and the surrounding sea, in the scenes which they inhabit. xvi, 380 pp. 12°. *London, Whittaker, Treacher & co.* 1830. s

Brittan (Harriette G.) Scenes and incidents of every-day life in [Liberia], Africa. vi, 353 pp. 12 pl. 12°. *New York, Pudney & Russell,* 1860.

Brittan (S. B.) Man and his relations: illustrating the influence of the mind on the body, the relations of the faculties to the organs, and to the elements, objects, and phenomena of the external world. 4th ed. xiv, 578 pp. portrait. 8°. *New York, Townsend & Adams,* 1868.

——— *and* **Richmond** (B. W.) A discussion of the facts and philosophy of ancient and modern spiritualism. ix, 378 pp. 8°. *New York, Partridge & Brittan,* 1853. s.

Brix (*Dr.* P. W.) Heizversuche. 4°. *Leipzig,* 1860.
[*In* HARTIG (E.) Untersuchungen über die heizkraft der steinkohlen Sachsens. 1860].

Broadway (The) annual. A miscellany of original literature in poetry and prose. Sept. 1867, to Aug. 1868. v. i. 8°. *London, G. Routledge & sons,* [1868].

Broca (Paul). On the phenomena of hybridity in the genus homo. Edited by C. C. Blake. xiv, 119 pp. 8°. *London, anthropological society,* 1864.

Brockett (L. P. *M. D.*) Men of our day; or, biographical sketches of patriots, orators, statesmen, generals, reformers, financiers and merchants, now on the stage of action. xxiv, 653 pp. 6 pl. 8°. *Philadelphia, Zeigler, McCurdy & co.* 1868.

Brockhurst (*Rev.* Joseph Sumner). The wife; or, love and madness. A tragedy in five acts. xxxi, 213 pp. 8°. *Cambridge,* [*Eng.*] *Deighton, Bell & co.* 1856. s.

Brodhead (John Romeyn). Oration on the conquest of New Netherland, before the N. Y. hist. soc. 1864. 87 pp. 1 map. 3 pl. 8°. *New York,* 1864.

Brodhead (L. W.) The Delaware water gap: its scenery, its legends, and its early history. xii, 220 pp. 9 phot. pl. 16°. *Philadelphia, Sherman & Co.* 1867.

Brodie (*Sir* Benjamin Collins). Psychological inquiries, in a series of essays, intended to illustrate the mutual relations of the physical organization and the mental faculties. [*anon.*] viii, 264 pp. 16°. *London, Longmans,* 1854. s.

Broglie (Albert, *prince de*). L'église et l'empire romain au ive siècle. 1e partie. Règne de Constantin. 2e éd. 2 v. xv, 471 pp; 3 p. l. 448 pp. 8°. *Paris, Didier & ce.* 1857.

Broken idols. A story for girls. [*anon.*] 422 pp. 3 pl. 16°. *Boston, Mass. S. S. Soc.* 1868.

Broken (The) pitcher; or, the ways of providence. By the author of "Luke Darrell, the Chicago newsboy." [*anon.*] 282 pp. 4 pl. 16°. *Chicago, Tomlinson bros.* 1866.

Bromme (Traugott). Atlas zu Alex. v. Humboldts kosmos. 2 p. l. 136 pp. 42 maps. obl. 4°. *Stuttgart, Krais & Hoffmann,* [1851].

Bromwell (William). Off-hand sketches; a companion for the tourist and traveller over the Philadelphia, Pottsville and Reading railroad. 194 pp. 16°. *Philadelphia, J. W. Moore,* 1854.

Bronn (Heinrich Georg, *editor*). *See* **Neues** jahrbuch für mineralogie, etc.

Brontë (Charlotte). Jane Eyre. A novel. 483 pp. 1 pl. 12°. *New York, Carleton,* 1867.

Brooke (*Mr.* ——). The history of a reprobate; or, the adventures of David Doubtful. 2d Amer. ed. 71 pp. 18°. *Philadelphia, M. L. Weems,* 1795.

Brooke (Henry), *and* **Gordon** (Thomas). Essays against popery, slavery, and arbitrary power. [*anon.*] xiv, 240 pp. 18°. *Manchester, R. Whiteworth,* [1746?]

Brookes (Richard, *M. D.*) The general gazetteer; or, compendious geographical dictionary. [1st ed.] 394 l. 8 maps. 8°. *London, J. Newbery,* 1762.
[Maps imperfect].

Brooklyn (Spooner's) directory, for the year 1823. 57 pp. 16°. *Brooklyn, Alden Spooner,* 1823.

Brooklyn (The) city and business directory for the year ending May 1st, 1869. By G. T. Lain. iv, 789, 72 pp. 1 map. 8°. *Brooklyn, Lain & co.* 1868.

Brooklyn (Mercantile library of). A catalogue of the books. 2 p. l. 138 pp. 8°. *Brooklyn, Baker & Godwin,* 1858. s.

Brooks (A. *M. D.*) The thesaurus musicus. *See* **Everett** (L. C.) *and* **Brooks.**

Brooks (Charles). Some reasons for the immediate establishment of a national system of education for the United States. 22 pp. 8°. *New York,* 1865.
[Loyal publication society, no. 86].

Brooks (Edward). The normal mental arithmetic. 156 pp. 16°. *Philadelphia, H. Cowperthwait & co.* 1858. s.

Brooks (Sarah Warner). Even-songs and other poems. 103 pp. sq. 16°. *Boston, Little, Brown & co.* 1868.

Broom (W. W.) An Englishman's thoughts on the crimes of the south, and the recompence of the north. 24 pp. 8°. *New York,* 1865.
[Loyal publication society, no. 84].

—— Great and grave questions for American politicians, with a topic for America's statesmen. By Eboracus. [*pseudon.*] 122 pp. 8°. *New York, C. S. Westcott & co.* 1865. s.

Brother Mason, the circuit rider; or, ten years a methodist preacher. [*anon.*] 310 pp. 1 pl. 12°. *Cincinnati, H. M. Rulison,* 1855. s.

Brougham (John). The Bunsby papers. 2d series. Irish echoes. With designs by Mc Lenan. 298 pp. 2 pl. 12°. *New York, Derby & Jackson,* 1856.

Broughton (J. C. Hobhouse, *baron*). *See* **Hobhouse** (John Cam).

Brown (Andrew Betts). Notes on the various departments of the Paris exhibition, 1867. 12°. *London,* 1868.
[*In* Engineering facts and figures for 1867].

—— *editor.* *See* **Engineering** facts and figures.

Brown (Carrie L.) Poems. 112 pp. 16°. *Boston, C. M. Brown,* 1867.

Brown (*Rev.* Henry). Arminian inconsistencies and errors, in which it is shown that all the distinctive doctrines of the presbyterian confession of faith are taught by standard writers of the methodist episcopal church. 430 pp. 12°. *Philadelphia, W. S. & A. Martien,* 1857. s.

Brown (Ignatius). History of Indianapolis, from 1818 to 1868. 100 pp. 8°. *Indianapolis, Logan & co.* 1868.
[*With* Indianapolis directory, 1868].

Brown (*Rev.* Isaac V.) Memoirs of the rev. Robert Finley, D. D. With brief sketches of some of his cotemporaries. 370 pp. portrait. 8°. *New Brunswick, Terhune & Letson,* 1819.

Brown (James, *grammarian*). An appeal from the absurdities and contradictions which pervade and deform the old theory of English grammar, to the true constructive principles of the English language. 1 p. l. x, 209 pp. 8°. *Philadelphia, J. T. Lange,* 1850. s.

—— An English grammar, in three books. Book i–ii. 2 v. 12°. *Philadelphia, J. J. Lange,* 1849. s.
[v. 3 wanting].

Brown (*Rev.* James Baldwin). Idolatries, old and new: their cause and cure. 4 p. l. 158 pp. 12°. *London, Jackson, Walford & Hodder,* 1867.

—— The soul's exodus and pilgrimage. 2d ed. xx, 415 pp. 12°. *London, Smith, Elder & co.* 1862.

Brown (James Harris). Scenes in Scotland; with sketches and illustrations, historical, biographical, and literary. xii, 240 pp. 17 pl. 16°. *Glasgow, R. Griffin & co.* 1833.

Brown (John, *philomath*). Horologiographia: or, the art of dyalling, being the second book of the use of the trianguler quadrant. 305 pp. 3 l. 15 pl. 18°. *London, J. Wingfield,* 1671.

Brown (*Rev.* John). Divine help implored under the loss of godly and faithful men. A funeral sermon Oct. 31, 1725, after the death of the rev. Thomas Symmes. 70 pp. 12°. *Boston, printed by T. Fleet for S. Gerrish,* 1726.

Brown (*Rev.* John, *of Haddington*). Select remains. [With] address to students in divinity. 187 pp. 16°. *Pittsburgh, Cramer, Spear & Eichbaum,* 1810.

Brown (John P.) The dervishes; or, oriental spiritualism. With illustrations. viii, 415 pp. 12°. *London, Trübner & co.* 1868.

Brown (J. P. H. *dentist*). The teeth: their health, disease, and treatment. 120 pp. 16°. *Augusta, (Ga.) Chron. & Sent. off.* 1867.

Brown (Robert, *farmer*). General view of the agriculture of the West Riding of Yorkshire. 8, xiv, 293, 121 pp. 1 map. 8°. *Edinburgh,* 1799. s.

[GREAT BRITAIN. Board of agriculture].

Brown (Robert, *the botanist of the British museum*). Miscellaneous botanical works. Edited by J. G. Bennett. v. 2. 8°. *London, R. Hardwicke,* 1867.

[RAY society publications. 1867].

CONTENTS.

iii. Systematic memoirs.
iv. Contributions to systematic works.

Brown (*Rev.* Robert C. Lundin). British Columbia. An essay. 2 p. l. 64, xxxiii pp. 12°. *New Westminster, royal engineer press,* 1863. s.

Brown (*Captain* Thomas). The zoologist's text-book, embracing the characters of the classes, orders, and genera, of almost the whole animal kingdom. 2 v. 578 pp; 16 pp. 107 pl. 12°. *Glasgow, etc. A. Fullerton & co. etc.* 1832. s.

Brown-Séquard (Charles Edouard). Lectures on the diagnosis and treatment of functional nervous affections. 89 pp. 8°. *Philadelphia, J. B. Lippincott & co.* 1868.

Brown University, (*Providence, R. I.*) Catalogus senatus academici et eorum qui munera et officia gesserunt, quique alicujus gradus laurea donati sunt, in universitate brunensi, Providentiæ. 81 pp. 8°. *Providentiæ, Knowles, Anthony & co.* 1860. s.

Browne (Albert G. *jr.*) Sketch of the official life of John A. Andrew, as governor of Massachusetts, [with his] valedictory address upon retiring from office, Jan. 5, 1866. xii, 211 pp. portrait. 16°. *New York, Hurd & Houghton,* 1868.

Browne (Alexander). [Ars pictoria; or, an academy treating of drawing, painting, limning, etching. With] an appendix to the art of painting in miniture or limning. 2 p. l. 110 pp. 1 l. 2 p. l. 20 pp. sm. fol. *London, A. Tooker,* 1675.

[Imperfect: title page, etc. wanting].

Browne (James Alexander). England's artillerymen. An historical narrative of the services of the royal artillery, from the formation of the regiment to 1862. xiii, 330 pp. 6 pl. 16°. *London, Hall, Smart & Allen,* 1865.

Browne (John Ross). Etchings of a whaling cruise, with notes of a sojourn on the island of Zanzibar. To which is appended a brief history of the whale fishery, [etc.] xv, 580 pp. 12 pl. 8°. *New York, Harpers,* 1846. s.

Browne (William). Works. With a memoir, and notes, by W. C. Hazlitt. v. 1. xxxix, 201 pp. sm. 4°. *London, Roxburghe library,* 1868.

Browning (Elizabeth Barrett). Poems of childhood. With illustrations by Hennessy and Thwaites. 162 pp. portrait. 8°. *New York, J. Miller,* 1867.

Browning (W. S.) Leisure hours. [Tales and essays]. vii, 312 pp. 8°. *London, Whittaker & co.* [*printed at*] *Paris, A. & W. Galignani,* 1841. s.

Brownlow (Emma Sophia Cust, *countess*). *See* **Cust.**

Brownson (Orestes A.) The American republic: its constitution, tendencies, and destiny. xvi, 439 pp. 8°. *New York, P. O'Shea,* 1866.

Bruce (D. & G.) A specimen of printing types. 62 l. 8°. *New York,* 1820.

——— The same. 33 l. 8°. *New York,* 1818.

[*With* the preceding].

Brücker (Jacob). History of philosophy. *See* **Enfield** (William).

Brückner (G.) Amerikas geographie und naturgeschichte. 2 p. l. 200 pp. 1 l. 2 pl. 8°. *St. Louis, C. Witter,* 1858. s.

Brueys (David Augustin de), *and* **Palaprat** (Jean de). Œuvres choisies. Ed. stéréotype. 2 v. in 1. xv, 253 pp; 252 pp. 16°. *Paris, Didot,* 1812.

Brüll (A.) Comparison of the resisting properties of iron and steel. From the French by A. A. Fesquet. 12°. *Philadelphia, H. C. Baird,* 1868.

[*In* URBIN (Ed.) Guide for puddling iron and steel. ed. 1868. pp. 48-83].

Brullé (Auguste). Crustacés: insectes. 4°. *Paris,* 1836-44.

[*In* WEBB (P. B.) *and* BERTHELOT. Histoire naturelle des îles Canaries. v. 2].

Brulliot (François). Dictionaire de [des] monogrammes, chiffres, lettres initiales et marques figurées sous lesquels les plus célèbres peintres, dessinateurs, et graveurs ont designé leurs noms. 663 pp. 1 l. 4°. *Munich, J. G. Zeller,* 1817.

——— The same. Table générale des monogrammes, etc. Pour servir de suite au dictionnaire des monogrammes. xvi, 533 pp. 4°. *Munich, J. G. Zeller,* 1820.

Brun (Charles le). *See* **Le Brun.**

Brunet (Pierre Gustave). Imprimeurs imaginaires et libraires supposés; étude bibliographique, suivie de recherches sur quelques ouvrages imprimés avec des indications fictives de lieux ou avec des dates singulières. 290 pp. 8°. *Paris, Tross,* 1866.

Brunfels *or* **Brunsfeld** (Otto). A very true pronosticatiõ, with a kalender, gathered out of the moost auncyent bokes of ryght holy astronomers, for the yere of our lorde 1536. And for all yeres here after perpetuall. Translated out of latyn in to Englysshe by Johñ Ryckes preest. 31 l. *b. l.* 24°. *London, J. Byddell,* [1536].

Bruni (Leonardo, *surnamed* Aretino). Epistolarum libri viii, ad fidem codd. mss. suppleti, et castigati et plusquam xxxvi epistolis, quæ in editione quoque fabriciana deerant, locupletati recensente Laurentio Mehus qui Leonardi vitam scripsit, Manetti, et Poggii orationes præmisit, librumque nonum ac decimum in lucem protulit. v. 1. cxxviii, 142 pp. 8°. *Florentiae, B. Paperinii,* 1741. s.

[v. 2 wanting].

——— Opusculum de nobilitate. 24 l. sm. 4°. [*Romæ? about* 1470].

Brunius (C. G.) Konstanteckningar under en resa ar 1849, fran Lund om Linköping och Strengnäs till Fahlun och Ater om Upsala, Stockholm och Vexiö. 8 p. l. 782 pp. 8°. *Lund, C. W. K. Gleerup,* 1851. s.

Brunsfelsius (Otto). *See* **Brunfels.**

Brunswick (*Township of, Maine*). An answer to the remarks of the Plymouth company, or proprietors of the Kennebeck purchase, published by their vote of 31st of January last, on the plan and extracts of deeds published by the proprietors of the township of Brunswick, etc. 33 pp. 4°. *Boston,* 1753.

Brunton (Mary Balfour). Discipline: a novel. 2 v. 212 pp; 218 pp. 16°. *Philadelphia, Key & Biddle,* 1834.

Brush (George Jarvis). System of mineralogy. *See* **Dana** (James D.), *and* **Brush.**

Bruslé de Montpleinchant (*Abbé* Jean Christopher). Le festin nuptial dressé dans l'Arabie heureuse au mariage d'Ésope, de Phédre, et de Pilpai avec trois fées. Par M. de Palaidor. [*pseudon.*] 9 p. l. 384 pp. 18°. *Pirou en basse Normandi* [*Bruxelles*], *chez Florent A-Fable* [*J. B. Liener*], 1700.

Bruzen de la Martinière (Antoine Augustin). Nouveau recueil des épigrammatistes françois, anciens et modernes. Par B. L. M. [*anon.*] 2 v. xxx, 407 pp. 2 pl; 3 p. l. 354 pp. 3 l. 1 pl. 16°. *Amsterdam, frères Wetstein,* 1720.

Bry (Theodore de, *engraver*). Emblematum liber. 1593. *See* **Boissard** (Jean Jacques).

——— Emblemata. 1596. *See* **Lebey de Batilly** (Denis).

Bryan (Daniel). The appeal for suffering genius, a poetical address; and the triumph of truth, a poem. xiii, 80 pp. 8°. *Washington, Way & Gideon,* 1826.

Bryan (George J.) Life of George P. Barker, with sketches of his speeches, and the funeral sermon of J. C. Lord, D. D. 215 pp. portrait. 16°. *Buffalo, O. G. Steele,* 1849.

Bryant (Jacob). A mythological, etymological, and historical dictionary; extracted from the analysis of ancient mythology. By W. Holwell. xix, 449 pp. 14 l. 8°. *London, C. Dilly,* 1793.

Bryant (William Cullen). Poems. With illustrations by E. Leutze. 2d ed. 378 pp. 20 pl. 8°. *Philadelphia, Carey & Hart,* 1847.

Brydenbach. *See* **Breitenbach.**

Buch (Christian Leopold von). Petrifications recueillies en Amérique par mr. Alexandre de Humboldt et par mr. Charles Degenhardt. 2 p. l. 32 pp. 2 pl. fol. *Berlin, imprimerie de l' academie des sciences,* 1839.

Buchan (Alexander). Handy book of meteorology. 2d ed. xii, 371 pp. 8 col. maps. 8°. *Edinburgh, W. Blackwood & sons,* 1868.

Buchanan (George). [Paraphrasis psalmorum Davidis poetica. Cum collectanea Nathanis Chytraei]. 5 p. l. 551 pp. 24°. [*Herbornae, typis G. Coruinii,* 1637].

[Title page wanting].

Buchanan (James, *grammarian*). A regular English syntax. Wherein is exhibited the whole variety of English construction, properly exemplified. 5th Amer. ed. xxviii, 196 pp. 16°. *Philadelphia, C. Cist,* 1792.

Buchanan (*Rev.* John Laurie). A general view of the fishery of Great Britain, drawn up for the consideration of the undertakers of the North British fishing. viii, 253 pp. 8°. *London, O. Hay,* 1794.

Büchner (Alexander). Geschichte der englischen poesie. Von der 14en bis zur 19en jahrhunderts. 2 v. viii, 368 pp; 400 pp. 8°. *Darmstadt, J. P. Diehl,* 1855.

Büchner (Andreas Elias, *editor*). *See* **Miscellanea** physica-medico-mathematica, [etc.] 1727-30.

Büchner (Louis). Natur und geist. Gespräche zweier freunde über die real-philosophischen fragen der gegenwart. v. 1. Makrokosmos. xiv, 300 pp. 12°. *Frankfurt a M; Meidinger.* 1857.

Buchner (Otto). Die feuermeteore, insbesondere die meteoriten historisch, und naturwissenschaftlich betrachtet. iv, 192 pp. 8°. *Giessen, J Ricker,* 1859. s.

——— Die meteoriten in sammlungen, ihre geschichte, mineralogische und chemische beschaffenheit. xxvi, 202 pp. 8°. *Leipzig, W. Engelmann,* 1863. s.

Buchon (J. A.) *See* **Collection** de chroniques nationales françaises.

Buck (Daniel Dana). The christian virtues, personified and exhibited as a divine family. An illustrated allegory. 1 p. l. 290 pp. 2 pl. 12°. *New York and Auburn, Miller, Orton, & Mulligan,* 1856. s.

Buckeridge (B.) An essay towards an English school of painters. 8°. *London,* 1754.

[*In* PILES (Roger de). Art of painting. 3d ed. 1754].

Buckingham (Henry A.) Harry Burnham, the young continental; or, memoirs of an American officer during the revolution. 256 pp. 8°. *New York, Burgess & Garrett,* 1852.

Buckingham (*Rev.* Thomas). The private journals of the expedition against Canada, in the years 1710–11. 59 pp. 12°. *New York, Wilder & Campbell,* 1825.

[*With* KNIGHTS (*Madame* Sarah Kemble). Journal in 1704. *New York,* 1825.]

Buckle (Henry Thomas). History of civilization in England. From 2d Lond. ed. [With] alphabetical index. v. 2. xxx, 476 pp. 8°. *New York, Appletons,* 1861. s.

Buckly (J. Gillis). An epitome of phrenology and temperamental physiology. 144 pp. 12°. *Cincinnati, author,* 1857. s.

Bucknill (John Charles, *M. D.*) Unsoundness of mind in relation to criminal acts. 2d ed. lvi, 148 pp. 16°. *London, Longmans,* 1857.

Bucquet (Jean Baptiste Marie). Introduction à l'étude des corps naturels, tirés du règne mineral. 2 v. xl, 453 pp; 404 pp. 16°. *Paris, J. T. Herissant,* 1771. s.

Budgen (*Miss* L. M.) Episodes of insect life. By Acheta domestica. [*pseudon.*] 3 v. 8°. *New York, J. S. Redfield,* 1851. s.

——— March winds and April showers; being notes and notions on a few created things. By "Acheta". [*pseudon.*] xiii, 254 pp. 12°. *London, L. Reeve,* 1854. s.

Budget (The). A collection of letters in favour of public liberty, 1764–70. 3 v. xvi, 268 pp; 288 pp; 264 pp. 16°. *London, J. Walker,* 1789.

Buds, blossoms, and leaves; poems. By Eulalie, [*pseudon.*] vii, 194 pp. 12°. *Cincinnati, Moore, Wilstach & Keys,* 1854. s.

Buechner. *See* **Büchner.**

Buenos-Aires. Registro estadistico del estado de Buenos-Aires. 1857. v. i. vi, 176 pp. 4°. *Buenos-Aires, imprenta de la Tribuna,* 1858. s.

Buffalo. The commercial advertiser directory for the city of Buffalo, 1854. 482 pp. 12°. *Buffalo, Jewett, Thomas & co.* 1854. s.

Buffon (George Louis Leclerc, *comte* de). Oeuvres complètes, avec un complément, par M. Lesson. 10 v. 12°. *Paris, Didier,* 1847. s

[v. 7 wanting].

CONTENTS.

v. 1. Histoire naturelle de la théorie de la terre.
v. 2-3. Histoire des minéraux, v. 1-2.
v. 4. Histoire naturelle de l'homme et des animaux.
v. 5-7. Histoire naturelle des quadrupèdes, v. 1-3.
v. 8-10. Histoire naturelle des oiseaux, v. 1-3.

——— *and* **Bexon** (Gabriel Léopold Charles Amé). Histoire naturelle des oiseaux. Avec 1008 pl. color. dont 35 représentent des insectes et des madrépores, dessinées et gravées par Martinet. Planches. 10 v. 4°. *Paris, imprimerie royale,* 1770–86. s.

[Wanting, text and titles].

Buffon (George Louis Leclerc, *comte* de), *and* **Daubenton** (Louis Jean Marie). Histoire naturelle, générale et particulière. v. 1–15, 23–31. 24 v. 4°. *Paris, imprimerie royale,* 1749–83. s.

CONTENTS.

v. 1. Théorie de la terre.
v. 2. Histoire générale des animaux.
v. 2–15. Histoire naturelle de l'homme et des quadrupèdes.
v. 23–31. Histoire naturelle des oiseaux.

——— The same. Supplement. v. 1–5. 4°. *Paris, imprimerie royale*, 1774—78. s.
[Wanting, v. 6–7].

Builder (The); an illustrated weekly magazine, for the architect, engineer, archæologist, constructor, and art lover, conducted by Geo. Godwin. 1867. v. 25. fol. *London, office of the* [*builder*], 1867.

Builders' (The) guide. 2d ed. 98 pp. 24°. *Washington, Robert A. Waters*, 1851.

Buisson (Mathieu François Régis). Traité d'anatomie descriptive. *See* **Bichat** (M. F. X.)

Bulfinch (Maria H.) Frank Stirling's choice. 194 pp. 2 pl. 16°. *Boston, E. P. Dutton & co.* 1867.

——— Ruth and aunt Alice. A story for children, preparatory to confirmation. 219 pp. 1 pl. 18°. *New York, gen. prot. epis. s. s. union*, 1868.

Bulfinch (Thomas). Oregon and Eldorado; or, a romance of the rivers [Columbia and Amazon]. xiv, 464 pp. 12°. *Boston, J. E. Tilton & co.* 1866.

Bullard (*Rev.* Asa). The children's album of pictures and stories. 208 pp. 1 pl. 8°. *Springfield, (Mass.) W. J. Holland & co.* 1867.

——— The same, abridged. 160 pp. 1 portrait. 8°. *Springfield and Boston, W. J. Holland & co.* 1867.

Bulletin des neuesten und wissenswürdigsten aus der naturwissenschaft, sowie den künsten, manufakturen, technischen gewerben, der landwirthschaft und der bürgerlichen haushaltung. Herausgegeben von S. F. Hermbstädt. 15 v. 8°. *Berlin, C. F. Amelang*, 1809–13. s

——— *See, also*, **Museum** des neuesten und wissenswürdigsten, 1814–18.

Bulletin du bibliophile. Revue mensuelle, publiée par J. Techener. 12e série. [Années 1855–56.] 2 v. 8°. *Paris, Techener*, 1855–56.

Bullinger (*Rev.* Henry). Decades. [Fifty sermons.] Edited by Rev. Thomas Harding. 5 v. in 4. 8°. *Cambridge, (Eng.) university press*, 1849.

[**Parker** society publications].

CONTENTS.

v. 1–2. Of the four general councils; the word of God; true faith; justification by faith; the apostles' creed; the ten commandments.
v. 3. Ten commandments, continued; of the law; of christian liberty, works, etc.; of sin.
v. 4. Of the gospel; of God; of Christ; of the soul.
v. 5. Of the holy catholic church; of the ministry; of prayer; of sacraments; of the institutions of the church.

Bullions (Peter, *D. D.*) A Latin reader: adapted to Bullions and Morris' Latin grammar. With vocabulary and exercises in Latin prose composition. Revised ed. v, 380, 8 pp. 12°. *New York, Sheldon & co.* 1869.

——— The principles of English grammar. 19th ed. xii, 216 pp. 12°. *New York, Pratt, Woodford & co.* 1846. s.

——— The principles of Latin grammar. 14th ed. xii, 312 pp. 12°. *New York, Pratt, Woodford & co.* 1846. s.

——— *See, also*, **Cicero**, *and* **Jacobs** (C.F.W.)

Bullock (William). Six months residence and travels in Mexico. 2d ed. 2 v. xvi, 255 pp. 7 pl; vii, 264 pp. 1 map. 3 pl. 1 tab. 16°. *London, J. Murray*, 1825.
[Imperfect: plate 1, v. 2, wanting].

Bulwer Lytton (*Sir* Edward George Earle Lytton, *baron Lytton*). "My novel;" or, varieties in English life, by Pisistratus Caxton. [*pseudon.*] Libr. ed. 4 v. 12°. *Philadelphia, Lippincott*, 1860.

——— What will he do with it? By Pisistratus Caxton. [*pseudon.*] A novel. 311 pp. 8°. *New York, Harpers*, 1859.

Bulwer (*Sir* Henry Lytton Earle). Historical characters: Talleyrand, Cobbett, Mackintosh, Canning. 4th ed. 2 v. vi, 481 pp; 434 pp. 8°. *London, R. Bentley*, 1868.

Bunn (Alfred). Old England and New England, in a series of views taken on the spot. 315 pp. 16°. *Philadelphia, A. Hart*, 1853.

Bunsen (Christian Carl Josias, *baron* von). Die basiliken des christlicher Roms nach ihrem zusammenhange mit idee und geschichte der kirchenbaukunst. 94 pp. 1 pl. 4°. *München, Cotta*, [1847]. s.

——— God in history; or, the progress of man's faith in the moral order of the world. From the German by Susanna Winkworth. 2 v. 8°. *London, Longmans*, 1868.

Bunsen (Ernest de). The hidden wisdom of Christ and the key of knowledge; or, history of the apocrypha. 2 v. x, 479 pp; vi, 515 pp. 8°. *London, Longmans*, 1865.

Bunsen (Frances, *baroness*). A memoir of baron [Christian Carl Josias von] Bunsen. 2 v. 3 p. l. 637 pp. 4 pl; 3 p. l. 616 pp. 6 pl. 8°. *London, Longmans*, 1868.

Burchett (Josiah). A complete history of the most remarkable transactions at sea, from the earliest accounts of time to the last war with France. 28 p. l. 799 pp. 17 l. 8 maps. 1 pl. fol. *London, J. Walthoe*, 1720.

Burckhardt (*Dr.* Fritz). Die erfindung des thermometers und seine gestaltung im xvii. jahrhundert. 1 p. l. 48 pp. 1 pl. 4°. *Basel, H. Georg*, 1867. s.

Burckhardt (Jacob). Die zeit Constantin's des grossen. ix, 512 pp. 8°. *Basel, Schweighauser*, 1853.

Burdett (Charles). The gambler; or, the policeman's story. 179 pp. 16°. *New York, Baker & Scribner*, 1848. s.

Bureaud-Riofrey (A. M.) Du choléra; moyens préservatifs et curatifs, ou philosophie des grandes épidémies. 116 pp. 8°. *Paris, Germer-Baillière*, 1847. s.

Burg (Maria). Seedtime and harvest. *See* **Koch** (Rosalie), *and* **Burg.**

Burgess (J. T.) Angling: a practical guide to bottom fishing, trolling, spinning, and fly fishing. With a chapter on sea fishing. viii, 182 pp. 1 pl. 16°. *London, Warne & co.* 1867.

Burgess (*Rev.* Richard). Description of the circus on the via appia near Rome; with some account of the circensian games. viii, 111 pp. 3 pl. 1 tab. 12°. *London, J. Murray*, 1828.

Burgess (Samuel Walter). Historical illustrations of the origin and progress of the passions, and their influence on the conduct of mankind; with sketches of human nature and human life. [*anon.*] 2 v. viii, 507 pp. 1 pl; 495 pp. 8°. *London, Longmans*, 1825.

Burgoyne (*Gen.* John). Briefe des generals Lee, and des generals Burgoyne bey gelegenheit der ankunft des letztern in Boston. 8 pp. 8°. *Braunschweig*, 1777.

[*In* REMER (J. A.) Amerikanisches archiv. v. 1].

Burhans (Hezekiah). The monotonical speller, and docile reader, of the English language. 180 pp. 18°. *New York, Day, Baker & Crane*, 1845.

——— The scientific spelling book, containing the principles of English orthography and pronunciation. 252 pp. 24°. *New York, Baker & Crane*, 1845.

Burius. *See* **Bury.**

Burk (Edward). The hurricane: a poem, by an eye-witness. Also, historical notices of St. Domingo, from the seizure of Toussaint l'Ouverture to the death of Christophe. With illustrations. [*anon.*] 75 pp. 8°. *Bath*, 1844.

Burke (Edmund). An account of the European settlements in America. 2 v. 4 p. l. 312 pp. 1 map; 2 p. l. 300 pp. 10 l. 1 map. 8°. *London, R. & J. Dodsley*, 1757.

——— The same. 2[d] ed. 4 p. l. 324 pp. 5 l. 1 map; 6 p. l. 308 pp. 1 map. 12°. *London, R. & J. Dodsley*, 1758.

——— Rede womit er seinen vorschlag einer ausöhnung mit den colonien empfielet, gehalten in parlement 22 März, 1775. 111 pp. 8°. *Braunschweig, F. Waisenhaus*, 1777.

[*In* REMER (J. A.) Amerikanisches archiv. v. 1).

Burke (*Sir* John Bernard). A genealogical and heraldic dictionary of the peerage and baronetage of the British empire. 30th ed. xlvii, 1308 pp. 8°. *London, Harrison*, 1868.

Burke's weekly for boys and girls: an illustrated journal of instruction and entertainment. T. A. Burke, editor. July 6, 1867 to June 27, 1868. v. 1. 2 p. l. 416 pp. 4°. *Macon, (Ga,) J. W. Burke & co.* 1868.

Burkitt (Lemuel), *and* **Read** (Jesse). A concise history of the Kehukee baptist association, from its original rise down to 1803. Revised by H. L. Burkitt. 351 pp. 16°. *Philadelphia, Lippincott, Grambo, & co.* 1850. s.

Burlamaqui (Jean Jacques). Principles of natural and politic law. Translated by Mr. Nugent. 5th ed. 2 v. xxiv, 216 pp; — pp. 8°. *Cambridge, (Mass.) univ. press*, 1807. s.

Burleigh (Charles C.) Reception of George Thompson in Great Britain. 238 pp. 18°. *Boston, J. Knapp*, 1836.

Burnet (Gilbert, *bishop of Salisbury*). The history of the reformation of the church of England. 6 v. 18°. *London, W. Baynes & son*, 1825.

Burney (Sarah Harriet). Clarentine: a novel. 2 v. 264 pp; 250 pp. 12°. *Philadelphia, M. Carey*, 1818.

Burnham (George P.) Stray subjects, [etc.] 1848. *See* **Durivage** (F. A.) *and* **Burnham.**

Burns (Robert). The poetical works of Robert Burns, with [life, by himself]. 2 v. 216 pp; 229 pp. 24°. *Philadelphia, B. Johnson, etc.* 1804.

——— *and* **M'Lehose** (Agnes Craig). The correspondence between Burns and Clarinda. With a memoir of Mrs. M'Lehose (Clarinda). Edited by her grandson, W. C. M'Lehose. xi, 297 pp. 12°. *Edinburgh, W. Tait*, 1843.

Burroughs (*Rev.* Eden). The profession and practice of christians held up to view by way of contrast to each other. [pp. 1-70]. 16°. *Windsor, N. E. Hough & Spooner*, 1784.

[Imperfect: pp. wanting at the end].

Burton (William E.) Waggaries and vagaries. A series of sketches, humorous and descriptive. 192 pp. 8 pl. 12°. *Philadelphia, Carey & Hart*, 1848. s.

Burton. Annales monasterii burtonensis ab miv-mcclxiii. [*anon.*] fol. *Oxoniæ*, 1684.

[GALE (Thomas) *and* FELL (John). Rerum anglicarum scriptores veteres. v. 1. *Oxoniæ*, 1684].

Bury *or* **Burius** (Willem de). Romanorum pontificum brevis notitia, ritus ecclesiasticos a singulis institutos praecipue declarans. Accedit onomasticon vocum obscuriorum, quæ in missali, breviario, martyrologia romano, [etc.] continentur. 11 p. l. 610 pp. 12 l. 1 pl. 16°. *Patavii, J. Manfrè*, 1753. s.

Bush (*Rev.* George). The millennium of the apocalypse. 2d ed. xix, 206 pp. 16°. *Salem, J. P. Jewett*, 1842.

Bushnell (Horace, *D. D.*) The moral uses of dark things. 360 pp. 12°. *New York, C. Scribner & co.* 1868.

Businger (Lukas Caspar). Das fromme kind. Katholisches gebetbüchlein für die reifere jugend. 192 pp. 48°. *New York, K. & N. Benziger*, 1868.

——— Der heil. Aloysius, die lilie von Castiglione. 320 pp. 32°. *New York, K. & N. Benziger*, 1868.

Bussy-Rabutin (Roger, *comte* de). Lettres de messire Roger de Rabutin, comte de Bussy; avec les réponses. Nouv. éd. 6 v. 16°. *Amsterdam, Z. Chatelain*, 1731.

Butler (*Rev.* Alban). Vie des pères, des martyrs, et des autres principaux saints, tirées des actes originaux et des monumens les plus authentiques, avec des notes historiques et critiques; ouvrage traduit librement de l'Anglais d'Alban Butler, par l'abbé Godescard. Nouv. éd. Augmentée du Traité des fêtes mobiles, et d'un 15e volume, traduit de l'Anglais de Charles Butler. 15 v. 12°. *Lille, L. Lefort*, 1824. s.

——— The same. v. 16. Vies de plusieurs vénérables serviteurs et servantes de Dieu, à la canonisation desquels on a travaillé dans le 18e siècle, [etc.] suivies de notices sur la vie et les écrits de Bossuet et Fénélon; et du Traité de la mort des persécuteurs de l'église, par Lactance; traduit par Godescard. 2 p. l. 437 pp. 12°. *Lille, L. Lefort*, 1828. s.

Butler (Benjamin Franklin.) Character and results of the war. How to prosecute and how to end it. Speech at the Academy of music, New York, April 2, 1863. Reported by A. F. Warburton. 16 pp. 8°. *New York, W. C. Bryant & co.* 1863.

[LOYAL publication society, no. 7].

Butler (Charles). Vies des pères, des martyrs et des autres principaux saints. Supplément à l'ouvrage de mm. A. Butler et Godescard. Traduit en partie de l'Anglais, et considérablement augmenté. 12°. *Lille, L. Lefort*, 1824. s.

[*In* BUTLER (A.) Vies des pères, etc. v. 15].

Butler (D. P.) The lifting cure: an original, scientific application of the laws of motion or mechanical action to physical culture and the cure of disease. With a discussion of true and false methods of physical training. 104 pp. 8°. *Boston, D. P. Butler*, 1868.

Butler (George B.) The conscription act; a series of articles communicated to the Journal of commerce. 22 pp. 8°. *New York, W. C. Bryant & co.* 1863.

[LOYAL publication society, no. 40].

Butler (Samuel) A book of characters. *See* **Overbury** (*Sir* T.), *and others.*

Butler (*Rev.* William Archer). Sermons, doctrinal and practical. First series. Edited, with memoir, by Thomas Woodward. First Am. from the 3d Cambridge ed. 446 pp. 8°. *Philadelphia, Parry & McMillan*, 1856. s.

——— The same. Second series. Edited by J. A. Jeremie. First Am. from the third Cambridge ed. 399 pp. 8°. *Philadelphia, Parry & McMillan*, 1857. s.

Buzacott (*Rev.* Aaron, *jr.*) Mission life in the Pacific. *See* **Sunderland** (*Rev.* J. P.) *and* **Buzacott.**

Buzot (François Nicholas Louis). Mémoires. 103 pp. 8°. *Paris*, 1866.

[*In* MÉMOIRES inédits de Pétion, etc. 1866].

Byford (W. H. *M.D.*) The philosophy of domestic life. 174 pp. 16°. *Boston, Lee & Shepard*, 1869.

Byrne (*Mrs.* William Pitt) Flemish interiors. [*anon.*] xv, 359 pp. 1 pl. 16°. [*London,*] *Longman & co.* [1856].

Byron (George Gordon Noël, *lord*). The beauties of lord Byron, selected from his works. By B. F. French. 10th ed. xi, 204 pp. 3 pl. 24°. *Philadelphia*, 1828. s.

——— Hebraische gesänge. Aus dem Englischen übertragen und mit sachlichen einleitungen und bemerkungen versehen von Eduard Nickles. 112 pp. 12°. *Karlsruhe, F. Gutsch*, 1863. s.

Byron's (Lord) pilgrimage to the holy land. A poem. [With] the tempest. A fragment. [*anon.*] 1 p. l. 72 pp. 8°. *London, J. Johnston*, 1817.

[MISCELLANEOUS pamphlets, v. 56].

Bywater (John). Observations on the nature of animalcules, and principles of vegetable physiology. 8°. *Liverpool, Smith & Galway*, 1817.

[*In* BRADBURY (J.) Travels in America, 1809-11. ed. 1817].

Caballero (Fernan, *pseudon*). *See* **Arrom** (C. Bohl de).

Cabanis (Jean Louis). Saeugethiere; Voegel. 8°. *Leipzig*, 1848.

[*In* SCHOMBURGK (R.) Versuch einer fauna und flora Britisch-Guiana].

Cabasilas (Nikolaos, *archbishop of Thessalonica, the nephew*). De vita in Christo, libri septem. Ex duobus codicibus vindobonensibus tertio monacensi nunc primum graece editi. 240 pp. 8°. *Greifswald, C. A. Koch' verl.* 1849. s.

[*With* GASS (W.) Beiträge, etc. v. 2 [*or*] Die mystik des N. Cabasilas.]

Cæsar (Caius Julius). Quæ extant. Interpretatione et notis illustravit J. Godvinus, in usum delphini. ed. 9ª. vi, 490 pp. 64 l. 8°. *Londini, J. Rivington*, 1780.

——— Commentarii de bello gallico. With notes and lexicon. By G. Stuart. 336 pp. 1 map. 16°. *Philadelphia, Eldredge & bro.* 1868.

——— The same. Commentaries on the Gallic war. [Lat.] With a vocabulary and notes. By W. Bingham. 348 pp. 1 map. 12°. *Philadelphia, E. H. Butler & co.* 1868.

Cahier (Charles). Monographie de la cathédrale de Bourges. *See* **Martin** (A.) and **Cahier.**

Caille. *See* **La Caille.**

Cajetanus de Thienis. *See* **Tiene** *Gaetano.*

California (*State of*). Appendix to journals of senate and assembly of the seventeenth session of the legislature [1867–68]. 3 v. 8°. *Sacramento, D. W. Gelwichs*, 1868.

——— Journals of the senate and assembly, 17th session [1867–68]. 2 v. 8°. Sacramento, state printer, 1868.

——— Catalogue of the California state library, prepared by W. C. Stratton. 2 p. l. 409 pp. 8°. *Sacramento, state printer*, 1860. s.

California (The) state register and year book of facts; for the year 1859. 2d year. 420 pp. 12°. *San Francisco, H. G. Langley & S. A. Morison*, 1859. s.

Callender (James Thompson). The conduct of Meriwether Jones, in a series of letters to the public. 120 pp. 8°. *Richmond, H. Pace*, 1802.

Calliat (Victor) *and* **Leroux de Lincy** (Adrien Jean Victor). Hotel de ville de Paris mesuré, dessiné, gravé et publié par Victor Calliat, avec une histoire de ce monument et des recherches sur le gouvernement municipal de Paris par Le Roux de Lincy. [Avec supplément]. 2 v. in 1. 4 p. l. vi, 68 pp. 1 l; 3 p. l. ii, 5 pp. 43 pl. fol. *Paris, chez l'auteur*, 1844-56.

Calprenède (Gautier de Costes, *sieur de la*). *See* **La Calprenède.**

Calvert (George H. *editor*). Illustrations of phrenology. From the Edinburgh phrenological journal, [etc.] 192 pp. 12°. *Baltimore, W. & J. Neal*, 1832.

Calvetonus (Urbanus). *See* **Chauveton** (U.)

Calvin (Jean). Letters of John Calvin, compiled from the original manuscripts, and edited with historical notes by dr. Jules Bonnet. Translated from the original Latin and French [by David Constable]. 2 v. 483 pp. 1 pl; 454 pp. 8°. *Philadelphia, presbyterian board of publication*, [1858]. s.

——— Opuscula. De animæ immortalitate. Contra anabaptistas, libertinos, et Franciscum quendam. De vitandis superstitionibus. Cōtra pseudonicodemos [etc.] 8 p. l. 489 pp. 18 l. 16°. [*Genevæ*], *N. Barbirius & T. Courtéau*, 1563. s.

Camberlyn d'Amouquies (Jean Baptiste Guillaume). Miscellanea. [Poemata latina]. 2 p. l. 253 pp. 8°. *Gandae, P. F. de Goesin-Verhaeghe*, 1828. s.

Cambios de la Habana con Lóndres, Paris, Hamburgo, Amsterdam y Lisbon, y números fijos ó multiplicadores, para los negocios de dinero á premio desde cinco á diez y ocho por ciento al año de 365 dias. Por F. de M. [*anon.*] viii, 338 pp. 8°. *Habana, P. N. Palmer é hijo*, 1824. s.

Cambini (Andrea). Two very notable commentaries. The one of the originall of the Tvrcks and empire of the house of Ottomanno, written by Andrewe Cambine, and thother of the warres of the Turcke against George Scanderbeg, prince of Epiro, translated oute of Italian into Englishe by John Shute. 9 p. l. 70 l. marked 100. 45 l. *b. l.* sm. 4°. *London, H. Toye*, 1562.

Cambridge, *England* (*The university of*). Calendar for 1805. xiv, 180 pp. 18°. *Cambridge, J. Deighton*, 1805.

——— A catalogue of the manuscripts preserved in the library. 2 v. xvi, 552 pp; 4 p. l. 548 pp. 8°. *Cambridge, university press*, 1856–57. s.

Cambridge (The) directory. [With] an almanac and city record. By J. Ford. 112 pp. 18°. *Cambridge, (Mass.), chronicle office*, 1848.

Camden (William). Annalivm rervm anglicarvm, et hibernicarvm, regnante Elizabetha [tomus alter]: sive pars quarta. 2 p. l. 286 pp. 5 l. sm. fol. *Londini, S. Waterson*, 1627.

——— The same. The historie of the princesse Elizabeth, late queene of England. Contayning all the passages of state both at home and abroad, during her raigne. Composed by way of annals. 10 p. l. 630 pp. 8 l. portrait fol. *London, B. Fisher*, 1630.

——— The same. The history of the most renowned and victorious princess Elizabeth, queen of England; containing all the most important and remarkable passages of state, during her reign. 3[d] ed. 9 p. l. 661 pp. 20 l. fol. *London, C. Harper, and J. Amery*, 1675.

——— Gulielmi Camdeni, et illustrium virorum ad G. Camdenum epistolae. Cum appendice varii argumenti. Accesserunt annalium regni regis Jacobi i. apparatus, et commentarius de antiquitate, dignitate, et officio comitis marescalli Angliae. Praemittitur G. Camdeni vita. Scriptore Thoma Smitho. 11 p. l. 613 pp. 4°. *Londini, R. Chiswell*, 1691.

[Imperfect: portrait wanting].

Camden society publications. Nos. 94 and 95. sm. 4°. *London*, 1867.

CONTENTS.

Dingley (Thomas). History from marble. [Edited] by J. G. Nichols. [No. 94].
Levins (Peter). Manipulus vocabulorum. A dictionary of English and Latin words, arranged in the alphabetical order of the last syllables. Re-edited by H. B. Wheatley. [No. 95].

Camerarius *or* **Kammermeister** (Joachim, *senior*). Historica narratio; de fratrum orthodoxorum ecclesiis in Bohemia, Moravia, et Polonia; nunc primum edita. 18 p. l. 448 pp. 6 l. 16°. *Heidelbergæ, typis Voegelianis*, [1605].

Camerarius *or* **Kammermeister** (Joachim, *junior*). Symbolorvm et emblematvm ex re herbaria desvmtorvm centvria vna collecta. 6 p. l. 110 l. 7 l. 4°. *Norimbergæ, impensis J. Hoffmanni & H. Camoxii*, 1590. s.

Cameron (G. Poulett). Personal adventures and excursions in Georgia, Circassia, and Russia. 2 v. xvi, 349 pp; iv, 317 pp. 8°. *London, H. Colburn*, 1845.

Cammann (Henry J.), *and* **Camp** (Hugh N.) The charities of New York, Brooklyn, and Staten island. xi, 596 pp. 19 pl. 8°. *New York, Hurd & Houghton*, 1868.

Camões (Luis de). Lusiadas. 2 v. 2 p. l. xxxviii, 228 pp; 299 pp. 32°. *Coimbra, imprensa da universidade*, 1800. s.

——— The same. La Lusiade; poëme héroïque en dix chants, nouvellement traduit du Portugais, avec des notes et la vie de l'auteur. 2 v. 2 p. l. xxix, 320 pp. 5 pl; 4 p. l. 291 pp. 5 pl. 8°. *Paris, Nyon*, 1776. s.

——— The same. Die Lusiaden. Epische dichtung nach José da Fonseca's portugiesischer ausgabe im versmaase des originals übertragen von F. Booch-Arkossy. lxxxviii, 532 pp. 1 portrait. 16°. *Leipzig, Arnold*, 1854. s.

Camp (Hugh N.) Charities of New York, etc. *See* **Cammann** (Henry J.) *and* **Camp**.

Campani (Giovanni). De quadratura circuli demonstratio. *See* **Faber** (Jacques). Introductio in arithmecam Seuerini Boetij.

Campbell (Alexander). Christian baptism; with its antecedents and consequents. 444 pp. 12°. *Bethany, (Va.) A. Campbell*, 1851. s.

Campbell (A. D.) A grammar of the Teloogoo language, commonly termed the Gentoo, [etc.] 3[d] ed. xxi, 202, 18 pp. 8°. *Madras, Hindu press*, 1849. s.

Campbell (Gabriel). A new elementary course in the German language. 2d ed. 194 pp. 12°. *Chicago, Church, Goodman & Donnelly*, 1867.

Campbell (George Douglas, *duke of Argyl*). The reign of law. 5th ed. vii, 435 pp. 4 pl. 12°. *London, A. Strahan*, 1867.

Campbell (John Douglas Sutherland, *marquess of Lorn*). A trip to the tropics and home through America. xii, 355 pp. 1 pl. 8°. *London, Hurst & Blackett*, 1867.

Campbell (Thomas, *poet*). The complete poetical works; with an original biography and notes. Edited by Epes Sargent. xii, 479 pp. 2 portraits. 12°. *Boston, Phillips, Sampson & co.* 1854. s.

Campdomercus (Jan Jakob). Epistola de glandulis, fibris, cellulisque lienalibus. 4°. *Amstelœdami*, 1725.

[*In* Ruysch (F.) Opera. v. 3. no, 19].

Campe (Joachim Heinrich). Allgemeine revision des gesammten schul- und erziehungswesens, von einer gesellschaft praktischer erzieher. 16 v. 12°. *Hamburg, C. E. Bohn, etc.* 1785–92. s.

——— Wörterbuch der deutschen sprache. 5 v. 4°. *Braunschweig, in der schulbuchhandlung*, 1807–11.

——— Wörterbuch zur erklärung und verdeutschung der unserer sprache ausgedrungenen fremden ausdrücke. Ein ergänzungsband zu Adelung's und Campe's wörterbüchern. Neue ausg. xiv, 673 pp. 4°. *Braunschweig, in der schulbuchbandlung*, 1813.

——— Descubrimiento y conquista de la America, o compendio de la historia general del neuvo mundo, por el autor del nuevo Robinson: traducido del Frances, corregido y mejorado por d. Juan Corradi. 3 v. 18°. *Madrid*, 1803.

Camstrup (Nicolaas Jansz.) Rampspoedige reys-beschryving, ofte journaal van het ed: oostindische compagnies schip Blydorp. 78 pp. 8 pl. sm. 4°. *Amsterdam, B. Mourik,* [*about* 1780].

[*In* SCHOUW-TOONEL van rampspoedige reistochten].

Canada. General report of the commissioner of public works, for 1865–66. 8°. *Ottawa, Hunter, Rose & co.* 1867.

——— Journals of the legislative council and legislative assembly. v. 26. Session, 1866. 2 v. 8°. [*Ottawa,* 1866].

——— Miscellaneous statistics for 1866. Municipal returns. Part ii. 8°. *Ottawa, Hunter, Rose & co.* 1867.

——— Report of the minister of agriculture [and statistics] for 1866. 8°. *Ottawa, Hunter, Rose & co.* 1867.

——— Report of the superintendent of education for Lower Canada, for the years 1855, 1856, 1857, 1858. 4 v. 8°. *Toronto, J. Lovell,* 1856–59. s.

——— The same. Rapport du surintendant de l'education pour le Bas-Canada, pour l'année 1855. 8°. *Toronto, J. Lovell,* 1856. s.

——— Sessional papers. v. 26. Fifth session of the eighth parliament. Session, 1866. 4 v. 8°. *Ottawa, Hunter, Rose & co.* 1866.

——— *See, also,* **Quebec.**

Cannibal Jack. [*pseudon.*] *See* **Reid** (Mayne).

Capgrave (John). Noua legenda Angliæ. [*anon.*] 6 p. l. 334 l. 1 l. fol. *Impressa lōdonias, i domo Winđdi de Worde,* 1516.

Capitolinus (Julius). [Vitæ imperatorum romanarum]. Antoninvs Pivs ad Diocletianum Aug.) 16°. *Geneva,* 1568.

[*In* VARII historiæ romanae scriptores, v. 3].

Cappoch (Thomas, *rebel bishop of Carlisle*). Trial [1746], and life. [Reprint of the authentic history, etc.] 2d ed, 31 pp. 12°. *Carlisle, S. Jefferson,* 1839.

Capuron (José). Nuevos elementos de medicina, arregladas a la nosografia filosofica, para el uso de los alumnos. Traducidos de la segunda edicion latina, por d. Ramon Frau, y d. Juan Trias. 2 v. xv, 411 pp; 326 pp. sm. 4°. *Barcelona, viuda é hijos de Antonio Brusi,* 1834.

Caraccioli (Louis Antoine de). Viage de la razon por la Europa. Traducido de Francés en Castellano, por F. M. Nipho. 4ª impression. 2 v. 4 p. l. 256 pp; 4 p. l. 282 pp. 16°. *Madrid, Escribano,* 1788. s.

Caraccioli (Roberto). Opus quadragesimale perutilissimum quod de penitentia dictum est. 265 l. 4°. *Venetiis, V. de Spira,* 1472.

Caraccioli (Roberto). Sermo ī festo anūtiatōis ūginis Marie, tribus aliis sermonibus de predestinato, numero dañatorum et de cathenis. 22 l. *Venetiis, V. de Spira,* 1472.

[*With his* Opus quadragesimale perutilissimum. *Venetiis,* 1472].

Caraffa (Andrea). Elementarum physicæ mathematicæ volumen primum. vi, 336 pp. 2 l. 3 pl. 8°. *Romae, J. B. Marini & soc,* 1840. s.

[No more published]?

Cardell (William S.) The boy of principle, the man of honor; or, the story of Jack Halyard. 310 pp. 1 pl. 16°. *Philadelphia, U. Hunt & son,* 1855. s.

Cardenas y Cano (Gabriel de, *pseudon.*) *See* **Barcia** (Andres Gonzalez).

Care (Henry). English liberties; or, the freeborn subjects' inheritance. [*anon.* With additions], by William Nelson. 5th ed. 5 p.l. 288 pp. 18°. *Boston, J. Franklin, for N. Buttolph,* 1721.

——— The same. 6th ed. viii, 350 pp. 16°. *Providence, (R. I.) J. Carter,* 1774.

Career and adventures of John H. Surratt, since his flight from America, [and] his final arrest in Egypt by U. S. consul Hale. 99 pp. 8°. *Philadelphia, C. W. Alexander,* [1866].

——— The same. Leben und abentheuer von John H. Surratt, seit seiner flucht von America [und] seine endliche verhaftung in Egypten durch den Ver. Staat. consul Hale. 99 pp. 8°. *Philadelphia, C. W. Alexander,* 1866.

Carey (Mathew). Address to congress; being a view of the ruinous consequences of a dependence on foreign markets for the sale of the great staples of this nation, flour, cotton, and tobacco. 2d ed. 8°. *Philadelphia, Carey & Lea,* 1822.

[*In his* Essays on political economy. pp. 383-408. ed. 1822].

——— Address to the farmers of the United States, on the ruinous consequences to their vital interests of the existing [free-trade] policy of this country. 2d ed. 8°. *Philadelphia, Carey & Lea,* 1822.

[*In his* Essays on political economy. pp. 409-461. ed. 1822].

——— Essays on political economy; or, the most certain means of promoting the wealth, power, resources, and happiness of nations, applied particularly to the United States. 546 pp. 5 l. 8°. *Philadelphia, Carey & Lea,* 1822.

Carey—continued.

CONTENTS.

Address of the Philadelphia society for the promotion of national industry.
The new olive branch.
Address to congress.
Address to the farmers of the U. S.
The farmers' and planters' friend.
Strictures on Cambrelling's "an examination of the new tariff."

——— The new olive branch; or, an attempt to establish an identity of interests between agriculture, manufactures, and commerce. 2[d] ed. 8°. *Philadelphia, M. Carey & sons,* 1821.

[*In his* Essays on political economy. pp .253–382 ed. 1822].

Cario *or* **Carion** (Johann). The three bokes of cronicles, gathered wyth great diligence of the beste authours. [With] an appendix, contenyng notable thynges, from 1532 to 1550. Gathered by John Funcke, of Nurenborough. Translated from the German. 8 p. l. 278 l. marked 279. 12 l. *b. l.* sm. 4°. *London, G. Lynne,* 1550.

Carl (Philipp, *editor*). Repertorium für physikalische technik für mathematische und astronomische instrumentenkunde. 2 v. 1 p. l. iv, 355 pp. atlas. 2 p. l. 37 pl; iv, 320 pp. atlas. 2 p. l. 40 pl. 8°. *München, R. Oldenbourg,* 1865–67. s.

[v. 2, 1e heft wanting].

Carl the young emigrant; a memoir of schools and schoolmasters. [*anon.*] 233 pp. 1 pl. 12°. *Philadelphia, Am. s. s. union,* 1851. s.

Carleton (George W.) Our artist in Peru. [50 drawings on wood]. Leaves from the sketch-book of a traveller during the winter of 1865–66. viii, 50 pp. sq. 16°. *New York, Carleton,* 1866.

Carli (*Conte* Gianrinaldo). Delle antichità di Capodistria. 8°. *Trieste,* 1831.

[*In* ROSSETTI (D. de'). Archeografo triestino. v. 3].

Carlina (Francesco). Nuove tavole dei moti apparenti del sole pel meridiano di Milano calcolate sin piu moderni elementi. 116 pp. 8°. *Milano, regia stamperia,* 1833. s.

Carlyle (Thomas). Critical and miscellaneous essays. 4 v. 12°. *Boston, Monroe & co.* 1838–39.

——— The French revolution: a history. 3 v. 12°. *London, J. Fraser,* 1837.

——— Shooting Niagara: and after? 55 pp. 16°. *London, Chapman & Hall,* 1867.

Carmichael (*Mrs.* A. C.) Domestic manners and social condition of the white, coloured, and negro population of the West Indies. 8°. *Philadelphia, T. K. Greenbank,* 1833.

[GREENBANK'S periodical library, v. 2. pp. 488–609].

Carmichael (Richard, *M. D.*) An essay on venereal diseases, and the uses and abuses of mercury in their treatment. With notes by G. Emerson. xiii, 360 pp. 5 pl. 8°. *Philadelphia, J. Dobson,* 1825.

Carmichael (*Rev.* Robert). A treatise on the calculus of operations. xii, 170 pp. 8°. *London, Longmans,* 1855. s.

Carolina. Grant and release of one-eighth part of Carolina from his majesty to lord Carteret. 22 pp. 1 map. sm. 4°. (*n. p.*) 1744.

——— Surrender of seven-eighth parts of Carolina from lord Carteret to his majesty. 22 pp. sm. 4°. (*n.p.*) 1744.

[*With* CAROLINA. Grant and release of one-eighth part of Carolina from his majesty to lord Carteret. sm. 4°. 1744].

——— The two charters granted by Charles III to proprietors of Carolina, with the first and last fundamental constitutions of that colony. 60, viii pp. sm. 4°. *London, R. Parker,* 1704.

Carpenter (Francis B.) Six months at the white house with Abraham Lincoln. 359 pp. 16°. *New York, Hurd & Houghton,* 1866.

Carpenter (William Benjamin). Principles of human physiology. 5th Am. from 4th London ed. Edited, with additions, by Francis G. Smith. 1091 pp. 2 pl. 8°. *Philadelphia, Blanchard & Lea,* 1853. s.

Carrington (*Mrs.* M. J.) Ab-sa-ra-ka, home of the Crows; being the experience of an officer's wife on the plains. [*anon.*] 284 pp. 3 maps. 12°. *Philadelphia, J. B. Lippincott & co.* 1868.

Carroll (*Rev.* Andrew). Moral and religious sketches and collections, with incidents of ten years' itinerancy in the west. v. 1. 302 pp. 12°. *Cincinnati, author,* 1857. s.

Carruthers (William, *of Va.*) The Kentuckian in New York; or, the adventures of three southerns. By a Virginian. [*anon.*] 2 v. 223 pp; 219 pp. 12°. *New York, Harpers,* 1834.

Cartée (Cornelius S.) Elements of physical and political geography. 342 pp. 12°. *Boston, Hickling, Swan & Brown,* 1856. s.

Carter (John, *F. S. A.*) The ancient architecture of England, including the orders during the British, Roman, Saxon, and Norman eras, and under the reigns of Henry iii and Edward iii. A new and improved ed. with notes, by John Britton. viii, 74 pp. 2 l. 109 pl. fol. *London, H. G. Bohn,* 1845. s.

Carter (John). A visit to Sherwood forest. With a critical essay on the life and times of Robin Hood. New ed. iv, 100 pp. 16°. *London, Longmans,* 1860.

Carter (Matthew). Honor redivivus; or, the analysis of honor and armory. 3 p. l. 351 pp. 6 pl. 16°. *London, H. Herringman*, 1673.

Carter (*Rev.* Thomas). French mission life; or, sketches of remarkable conversions and other events among French romanists in the city of Detroit. 157 pp. 16°. *New York, Carlton & Porter*, 1857. s.

Carteromaco (Nicolò, *pseudon*). *See* **Forteguerri** (Nicolò).

Carus (Julius Victor). Jahresbericht über die im gebiete der zootomie erschienenen arbeiten. i. Bericht über die jahre 1849–52. viii, 228 pp. 8°. *Leipzig, W. Engelmann*, 1856. s.

Cary (Edward). Trip of the Oceanus. *See* **French** (*Rev.* J. C.), *and* **Cary**.

Cary (Samuel Fenton, *editor*). The national temperance offering, and sons and daughters of temperance gift. 320 pp. 16 pl. 8°. *New York, R. Vandien*, [1850]. s.

Casanova de Seingalt (Jacques). Mémoires. Écrits par lui-même. Éd. originale. 12 v. 16°. *Leipsic, Paris, and Bruxelles*, 1826-38.

Casper (Johann Ludwig). A hand-book of the practice of forensic medicine, based upon personal experience. v. 1. Thanatological division. Translated from the 3d ed. of the original by G. W. Balfour. xvi, 317 pp. 8°. *London*, 1861.

[NEW SYDENHAM society, v. 12].

Cass (Lewis). An examination of the question now in discussion, between the American and British governments, concerning the right of search. By an American. 55 pp. 12°. *Baltimore, N. Hickman*, 1842. s.

Cassagnac. *See* **Granier de Cassagnac**.

Cassani (Angelo C.) Saggio di proverbi triestini raccolti ed illustrati. x, 107 pp. 1 l. 12°. *Trieste, C. Coen*, 1860. s.

Cassels (*Rev.* Samuel J.) Christ and antichrist; or, Jesus of Nazareth proved to be the messiah, and the papacy proved to be the anti-christ predicted in the holy scriptures. 348 pp. 12°. *Philadelphia, presbyterian board of publication*, [1846]. s.

——— Liberty poems. 92 pp. 12°. [*New York, author*,] 1851.

Cassïen (Jean). De institutis cenobiorum, origĩe, causis et remedijs vitiorum collationibus patrum. 208 l. fol. *Basilee*, [*J. Amberbach*], 1485.

[Imperfect: wanting l. 2-10 & 14 other l].

Castanis (Christophorus Plato). The Greek exile; or, a narrative of the captivity and escape of C. P. C. during the massacre on the island of Scio, with adventures in Greece and America. 272 pp. 12°. *Philadelphia, Lippincott, Grambo, & co.* 1857.

Castellanos (Juan de). Primera parte de las elegias de varones illvstres de Indias. 10 p. l. 382 pp. 4°. *Madrid, A. Gomez*, 1589.

Castiglioni (Luigi), *and others*. Storia delle piante forastiere le più importanti nell 'uso medico ed economico. [*anon.*] Colle loro figure in rame incise da B. e G. Bordiga. 4 v. 4°. *Milano, G. Marrelli*, 1791-94.

Castillo Solorzano (Alfonso del). The Spanish pole-cat; or, the adventures of senora Rufina. [From the Spanish,] by Sir R. L'Estrange and [J.] Ozell. 392 pp. 1 pl. 18°. *London, E. Curll*, 1717.

Catalog over de til den internationale fiskerindstilling i Bergen 1865 indsendte gjenstande. 215 pp. 1 pl. 16°. *Bergen, C. Dahl*, 1865. s.

Catalogue of portraits of foreigners who have visited England, as noticed by Clarendon, Heath, Thurloe, etc. 24°. *London*, 1814.

[*In* FLINDALL (J. M.) Amateur's pocket companion, 1812].

Cates (William L. R.) A dictionary of general biography; with a classified and chronological index of the principal names. 4 p. l. 1300 pp. 8°. *London, Longmans*, 1867.

Catholic (The) world. A monthly magazine of general literature and science. April 1865 to Sept. 1868. v. 1—7. 8°. *New York, L. Kehoe*, 1865–68.

Catinelli (Carlo). Sulla identità dell'antico coll'odierno Timavo. 8°. *Trieste*, 1830.

[*In* ROSSETTI (D. de'). Archeografo triestino, v. 2].

Catlow (Joseph Peel, *M. D.*) On the principles of æsthetic medicine, or the natural use of sensation and desire in the maintenance of health and the treatment of disease, as demonstrated by induction from the common facts of life. 325 pp. *London, J. Churchill & sons*, 1867.

Catullus (Caius Valerius). Poems, translated into English verse. With life of the poet, excursûs, and illustrative notes. By J. Cranstoun. xii, 291 pp. 16°. *Edinburgh, W. P. Nimmo*, 1867.

Cauchois-Lemaire (Louis Augustin François). Lettres politiques, religieuses, et historiques. 2 v. xii, 463 pp; xvi, 557 pp. 2 v. 8°. *Paris, Delaforest, etc.* 1828–32. s.

CONTENTS.

v. 1. Lettres sur les cent-jours (1819); lettres politiques, morales, et religieuses.

v. 2. Réponse à un catholic romain, etc.; épitres d'un chrétien à un catholic romain, (1826); épitre maintenant Louis-Philippe aux libéraux; lettres, etc.

Caughey (*Rev.* James). Arrows from my quiver, pointed with the steel of truth, and winged by faith and love. With an introduction by rev. D. Wise. 477 pp. 12°. *New York, W. C. Palmer*, 1867.

——— Glimpses of life in soul saving; or, selections from [his] journal and other writings. With an introduction by rev. D. Wise. 477 pp. 8°. *New York, W. C. Palmer*, 1868.

Caumont (Arcisse de). Définition élémentaire de quelques termes d'architecture. 168 pp. 8°. *Paris, Derache, etc.* 1846. s.

Causei de La Chausse (Michel-Ange de). *See* **La Chausse**

Caussin (Nicolas). Polihystor symbolicvs. Electorum symbolorum, et parabolarum historicarum stromata, xii libris complectens. Quæ ad omnem emblematvm, ænigmatvm, hieroglyphicorvm cognitionem præstant. Ed. ultima. 597 pp. 21 l. 16°. *Coloniæ Agrippinae, apud J. Kinchivm*, 1654. s.

Cauvin (Joseph). Dictionary of science, literature, and art. *See* **Brande** (W. T.) *and* **Cauvin.**

Cauwenberghe. *See* **Van Cauwenberghe.**

Cavalcanti (Bartolomeo). Trattati sopra gli ottimi reggimenti delle repubbliche antiche e moderne. xii, 240 pp. 8°. *Milano, società tipografica de' classici italini*, 1805.

Cavallo (Tiberius). A complete treatise on electricity, in theory and practice. 3[d] ed. 2 v. xxiv, 362 pp. 2 pl; 313 pp. 7 l. 3 pl. 8°. *London, C. Dilly*, 1786. s.

Caux. *See* **Grimaud de Caux.**

Cavé (Marie Elizabeth). Drawing without a master. The Cavé method for learning to draw from memory. 134 pp. 12°. *New York, G. P. Putnam & son*, 1868.

Cawdray (Robert). A treasury or storehouse of similes. London, 1609. Edited, with introduction, by J. G. Pilkington. 3[d] ed. vii, 416 pp. 8°. *London, R. D. Dickinson*, 1868.

Caxton (William). Book of curtesye, 1477–8. Reprinted, with two ms. copies of the same treatise. Edited by F. J. Furnivall. xii, 57 pp. 8°. *London, Trübner & co.* 1868.

[EARLY English text society publications. Extra series, 1867. No. 3].

Caylus (Anne Claude Philippe de Tubières, de Grimoard, de Pestels, de Lévi, *comte de*). Les confidences réciproques, ou anecdotes de la société de madame la comtesse de B. [*anon.*] 2 v. vii, 147 pp; 159 pp. 18°. *Londres* [*Paris*], 1779.

——— Les étrennes de la Saint Jean. [*anon.*] 3e éd. viii, 197 pp. 24°. *Troyes, veuve Oudot*, 1751.

Cazeaux (Paulin, *M. D.*) A theoretical and practical treatise on midwifery, including the diseases of pregnancy and parturition. Revised by S. Tarnier. From the French, by W. R. Bullock, M. D. 1124 pp. 5 pl. 8°. *Philadelphia, Lindsay & Blakiston*, 1868.

Cean-Bermudez (Juan Agustin). Sumario de las antiguedades romanas que hay en España, en especial las pertinecientes á las bellas artes. 2 p. l. xxxi, 538 pp. fol. *Madrid, M. de Burgos*, 1832. s.

Cecil Castlemaine's gage, and other novelettes. By Ouida. [*pseudon.* for mad. De la Rama?] Collected and revised by the author. 491 pp. 1 pl. 12°. *London, Chapman & Hall*, 1867.

Cecilias (The); or, the force of circumstances. By Anna Argyle. [*pseudon.*] 177 pp. 8°. *New York, Am. news co.* 1866.

Celesia (Emanuele). The conspiracy of Gianluigi Fieschi; or, Genoa in the 16th century. From the Italian, by D. H. Wheeler. xxxii, 343 pp. portrait. 8°. *London, Sampson Low*, 1866.

Cellini (Benvenuto). Trattati e discorsi. xiv, 176 pp. 12°. *Lipsia, L. Voss*, 1835. s.

[Opere, v. 3].

——— Vita, scritta da lui medesimo. 2 v. xliv, 194 pp; 288 pp. 5 pl. 12°. *Lipsia, L. Voss*, 1833. s.

[Opere, v. 1–2].

Celtic society publications. The book of rights. Edited, with translation and notes, by J. O'Donovan. 12°. *Dublin*, 1847. [No. 1].

——— Cambrensis eversus. By John Lynch. Edited, with translation and notes, by rev. M. Kelly. 3 v. 12°. *Dublin*, 1848–51. [No. 2].

——— Miscellany of the Celtic society. Edited by J. O'Donovan. 8°. *Dublin*, 1849. [No. 3].

CONTENTS.

The genealogy of Corca Laidhe.
Poem on the battle of Dun, by Gilla Brighde MacConmidhe.
Docwra's tracts.
Poems, pedigrees, and extracts.

Censorinus. Ad Q. Cærillivm de die natali liber. Lvd. Carrione recensente. 7 p. l. 44 pp. 5 l; 19 pp. 3 l. 16°. *Lvgdvni, F. Le Prevx*, 1593. s.

[*With* FIOCCO (A. D.) De potestatibvs Romanorvm, 1561].

Cepari (Virgilio). *See* **Life** (The) of St. Aloysius Gonzaga.

Cerfberr de Medelsheim (Maximilien Charles Alphonse E.) Rapport à. m. le ministre de l'intérieur [de France], sur différents hôpitaux, hospices, établissements et sociétés

Cerfberr de Medelsheim—continued. de bienfaisance, et sur la mendicité, dans les états de Sardaigne, de Lombardie et de Venise, de Rome, de Parme, de Plaisance et de Modène. viii, 414 pp. 4°. *Paris, imprimerie royale,* 1840. s.

Cernuschi (Henri). Illusions des sociétés coopératives. 102 pp. 16°. *Paris, Lacroix, Verboeckhoven et Cie,* 1866.

Certain ancient tracts concerning the management of landed property reprinted. 3 p. l. 318 pp. 8°. *London, C. Bathurst,* 1767.

CONTENTS.

XENOPHON. Treatise of householde.
FITZHERBERT (*Sir* A.) Boke of husbandry.
——— Surveyinge.

Chadwick (Henry). Base ball player's book of reference. By Chad. [*pseudon.*] 76 pp. 18°. *New York,* 1866.

Chahta vba isht tahoa holisso; or, Choctaw hymn book. 4th ed. 2 p. l. 248 pp. 18°. *New York, S. W. Benedict,* 1851. s.

Chaimis *or* **Chai** (Bartolomeo). Interrogatoriū siue cōfessionale. 111 l. unp. sm. 4°. [*Venetiis*] ? 1480.

Chalklen (*Rev.* Charles William). Semiramis, an historical morality; and other poems. 2 v. clxxxiii, 171 pp; 358 pp. 16°. *London, W. Pickering,* 1847.

Challen (James). The cave of Machpelah, and other poems. 220 pp. 12°. *Philadelphia, C. Sherman,* 1854 [1856]. s.

——— The gospel and its elements. 208 pp. 18°. *Philadelphia, Challen & sons,* 1856. s.

Challoner (Richard, *D. D.*) Catholic christian instructed in the sacraments, sacrifices, ceremonies, and observances of the catholic church. 102[d] ed. 281 pp. 2 l. 18°. *St. Louis, P. Fox,* 1868.

Chambaud (Louis). A grammar of the French tongue. With an essay on the proper method for teaching and learning that language. Revised by M. des Carrières. xxxii, 463 pp. 12°. *London, A. Strahan,* 1801.

Chamberlayne (Edward, *LL. D.*) Angliæ notitia; or, the present state of England compleat. Together with divers reflections upon the ancient state thereof. 2 v. in 1. [Part 1, 14th ed. part 2, 11th ed.] 11 p. l. 358 pp; 12 p. l. 344 pp. 1 pl. 16°. *London, T. Newcomb,* 1682.

——— The same. 17th ed. 2 v. in 1. 9 p. l. 274 pp; 3 p. l. 400 pp. 1 pl. 16°. *London, R. Scot, etc.* 1691–92.

Chamberlayne (John, *son of Edward*). Magnæ Britanniæ notitia; or, the present state of Great Britain, with divers remarks upon the ancient state thereof. 4th ed. 2 v. in 1. 11 p. l. 455, 200, 56 pp. 8°. *London, T. Goodwin, etc.* 1718.

——— The same. 7th ed. 2 v. in 1. 4 p. l. 466, 263, 66 pp. 8°. *London,* 1736.

[Imperfect: title page and dedication wanting].

Chamberlen (Paul). An impartial history of the life and reign of Queen Anne. 514 pp. 10 pl. fol. *London, W. Lloyd,* 1738.

[Some plates imperfect].

Chambers (Robert *and* William). Chambers' educational course. No. 6. Elements of zoology; or, natural history of animals. Edited by D. M. Reese. 1 p. l. 535 pp. 12°. *New York, A. S. Barnes & co.* 1849. s.

——— Chambers' encyclopædia: a dictionary of universal knowledge for the people, illustrated. A–Z. 10 v. 8°. *Philadelphia, J. B. Lippincott & co.* 1866–68.

——— Chambers' journal of popular literature, science, and arts, 1867. 8°. *London, W. & R. Chambers,* 1867.

Chambre (Marin Cureau de La). *See* **La Chambre.**

Champagny (François Joseph Marie Thérèse Nompère, *comte* Franz de). Les Césars. 2e éd. 2 v. xxiii, 552 pp; 571 pp. 8°. *Paris, L. Maison,* 1853.

Champgrand (— Goury de). *See* **Goury de Champgrand.**

Champlin (J. T.) Lessons on political economy. 219 pp. 12°. *New York, A. S. Barnes & co.* 1868.

Chandler (A.) & co. Specimen of ornamental types and embellishments. 24 l. 8°. *New York,* 1820.

[*With* BRUCE (D. & G.) Specimen of printing types, 1820].

Chandler (Richard). Proceedings house of Commons. *See* **Great Britain.**

Chandler (Thomas Bradbury, *D. D.*) The appeal farther defended; in answer to the farther misrepresentations of dr. Chauncy. vi, 240 pp. 8°. *New York, H. Gaine,* 1771.

Channing (George G.) Early recollections of Newport, R. I. 1793-1831. 284 pp. 16°. *Newport, (R. I.) A. J. Ward,* 1868.

Channing (William Ellery, *D. D.*) Remarks on the character and writings of John Milton. [*anon.*] 3d ed. 116 pp. 18°. *Boston, Perkins & co.* 1828.

Chantreau (Pierre Nicolas). Arte de hablar bien Francés, ó gramatica completa dividida en tres partes. Nueva ed. revista. 468 pp. 8°. *Paris, Bossange,* 1824.

——— The same. El novissimo Chantreau, ó arte de hablar bien Francés, y ahora cuidadosamente emendado, por P. Puiggari, y en lo tocante á la parte castellana, corregida por F. M. F. P. Y. M. M. viii, 392 pp. 8°. *Perpiñan, J. B. Alzine*, 1841. s.

Chapin (Edwin Hubbell, *D. D.*) Christianity the perfection of true manliness. 213 pp. 12°. *New York, H. Lyon*, 1856. s.

——— Moral aspects of city life. A series of lectures. 191 pp. 12°. *New York, H. Lyon*, 1856. s.

Chapman (Ernest Theodore). Water analysis. *See* **Wanklyn** (J. A.) *and* **Chapman.**

Chapman (James). Travels in the interior of south Africa, comprising fifteen years' hunting and trading; with journeys across the continent from Natal to Walvisch bay, and visits to lake Ngami and Victoria falls. 2 v. xiv, 454 pp. 1 map, 4 pl; ix, 480 pp. 1 map, 4 pl. 8°. *London, Bell & Daldy*, 1868.

Chapuis (Félicien), *and* **Dewalque** (Guillaume). Description des fossiles des terrains secondaires de la province de Luxembourg. (Extract). 393 pp. 38 pl. 4°. *Bruxelles, Acad. royale de Belgique*, 1853. s.

Charant (A.) A letter in answer to divers curious questions concerning the religion, manners, and customs, of the countries of Muley Arxid, king of Tafiletta. [Mauritania]. Englished out of French. [*anon.*] 71 pp. 18°. *London, M. Pitt*, 1671.]

[*With* FRÉJUS (R. de). Relation of voyage into Mauritania, 1681].

Chardin (Jean). Travels of sir John Chardin into Persia and ye East Indies, threugh the Black sea and the country of Colchis. Also the coronation of Solyman iii. [Translated from the French]. 2 v. in 1. 6 p. l. 417 pp.; 154 pp. 1 map, 13 pl. fol. *London, M. Pitt*, 1686.

Charles i (*King of England*). The king cabinet opened; or, certain secret letters and papers written with the king's own hand, taken at Nasby-field, with annotations. Published by order of parliament. 2 p. l. 56 pp. sm. 4°. *London, Robert Bostock*, 1645.

Charles ii (*King of England*). An account of his majesty's escape from Worcester, dedicated to Mr. Pepys by the king himself. 12°. *London, H. G. Bohn*, 1859.

[*In* HAMILTON (A. *count*). Memoirs of the court of Charles ii. pp. 455–476. 1859].

Charles (*Mrs.* Elizabeth). The Draytons and the Davenants, a story of the civil wars. [*anon.*] 509 pp. 12°. *New York, M. W. Dodd*, 1867.

Charles (*Mrs.* E.) On both sides of the sea: a story of the commonwealth and the restoration. A sequel to "The Draytons and the Davenants." [*anon.*] 510 pp. 12°. *New York, M. W. Dodd*, 1867.

——— Wanderings over bible lands and seas. [*anon.*] 301 pp. 1 pl. 2 phot. pl. 1 map. 12°. *London, T. Nelson & sons*, 1866.

Charlestown (The) [*Mass.*] directory. No. 16. [For 1868]. By Sampson, Davenport & co. 294 pp. 1 map. 8°. *Charlestown, A. E. Cutter*, 1868.

Charlevoix (Pierre François Xavier de). History and general description of New France. Translated, with notes, by J. G. Shea. v. 1–3. 8°. *New York, J. G. Shea*, 1866–68. s.

——— The same. Allgemeine geschichte und beschreibung von Neu-Frankreich, was die entdeckungen und groberungen der Franzosen in dem nordlichen America betrifft. 4 p. l. 648 pp. 20 l. 18 maps. 4°. *Leipzig, Arkstee & Merkus*, 1756.

[ALLGEMEINE historie der reisen. v. 14].

——— A voyage to North America. Containing the geographical description and natural history of Canada and Louisiana. Also, a description and natural history of the West Indies. 2 v. 5 p. l. 288 pp. 2 maps; 335 pp. 10 l. 5 maps. 8°. *Dublin, J. Exshaw*, 1766.

Charlie But, and other stories for boys. [*anon.*] 170 pp. 7 pl. 18°. *Philadelphia, Am. s. s. union*, [1865].

Charma (Antoine, *prof. at Caen*). Essai sur les bases et les développemens de la moralité. [Théorie et l'histoire de la volonté.] xvi, 486, ii pp. 8°. *Paris, L. Hachette*, 1834. s.

——— Essai sur le langage. 2e éd. vii, 319 pp. 8°. *Paris, L. Hachette*, 1846. s.

——— Lanfranc: notice biographique, littéraire et philosophique. (Extrait des Mémoires de la sociéte des antiquaires de Normandie). 160 pp. 8°. *Paris, L. Hachette*, 1850. s.

——— Leçons de logique. viii, 419 pp. 8°. *Paris, L. Hachette*, 1840. s.

Charpentier (Jean Pierre). Histoire de la renaissance des lettres en Europe, au quinzième siècle. 2 v. 2 p. l. 383 pp; 2 p. l. 403 pp. 8°. *Paris, Ve. Marie Nyon*, 1843. s.

Charters (The) of Virginia, Maryland, Connecticut, Rhode Island, Pennsylvania, Massachusetts Bay, and Georgia, [with] a narrative of the proceedings of the colonies in consequence of the stamp act. 69 pp. 1 map. 4°. *London, W. Owen*, 1766.

With HORSMANDEN (D.) Journal of proceedings in negro conspiracy, 1741–42. *New York*, 1744].

Chase (A. W. *M. D.*) Dr. Chase's recipes; or, information for everybody: an invaluable collection of about eight hundred practical recipes. 42ᵈ ed. 384 pp. 16°. *Ann Arbor, (Mich.) author,* 1867.

Chase (Pliny Earle). The common school arithmetic; [with] key. 256, 31 pp. 12°. *Worcester, A. Hutchinson & co.* [1848]. s.

——— Elements of arithmetic. *See* **Mann** (H.) *and* **Chase.**

——— *See, also,* **Stone** (A. P.) Key to Chase's common school arithmetic. 1853.

Chase (Salmon Portland). Speech in the peace conference of 1861. 11 pp. 8°. *New York, W. C. Bryant & co.* 1863.
[LOYAL publication society. No. 37].

Chase (Warren). The life-line of the lone one; or, autobiography of the world's child. [*anon.*] 12°. *Boston, B. Marsh,* 1857.

Chasseneu *or* **Chasseneuz** (Barthélemy de). Catalogvs gloriæ mundi, laudes, honores, excellentias, ac præeminentias omnium fere etatuum, plurimarumque rerum illius continens. 12 parts in 1 v. 10 p. l. 375 l. fol. *Lugd. D. de Harsy,* 1529.

Chastelain (Georges). Chronique de J. de Lalain. 8°. *Paris, J. A. Buchon,* 1826.
[COLLECTION de chroniques nationales françaises, v. 41].

——— Les ducs de Bourgogne. 2 v. 8°. *Paris, J. A. Buchon,* 1827.
[COLLECTION de chroniques nationales françaises, v. 42–43].

Chateau Lescure; or, the last marquis. A story of Brittany and the Vendée. [*anon.* By James B. Kirker?] 198 pp. 16°. *New York, E. Dunigan & bro.* 1855. s.

Chateaubriand (René François Auguste de). The spirit and beauty of the christian religion; selections from Chateaubriand's Genius of christianity. Translated from the French, with an introduction, by Emma B. Stork. 213 pp. 12°. *Philadelphia, Lindsay & Blakiston,* 1858. s.

Chatrian (Alexandre). Madame Thérèse. *See* **Erckmann** (É.) *and* **Chatrian.**

Chatto (John). An account of the bibliography of diptheria. 8°. *London,* 1859.
[NEW SYDENHAM society, v. 3].

Chaucer (Geoffrey). Legende of goode women. Edited, with an introduction and notes, by H. Corson. xxxviii, 145 pp. 12°. *Philadelphia, F. Leypoldt,* 1864.

Chaudoir (Maximilien, *baron*) *and* **Hochhuth** (Johann Heinrich). Enumeration des carabiques et hydrocanthares, recueillis pendant un voyage au Caucase et dans les provinces transcaucasiennes. Carabiques, par le baron de Chaudoir. Hydrocanthares, par H. Hochhuth. 268 pp. 8°. *Kiew, J. Wallner,* 1846. s.

Chauncy (Charles, *D. D.*) An appeal to the public answered, in behalf of the non-episcopal churches in America; wherein the reasons for an American episcopate are shewn to be insufficient, [etc.] 205 pp. 12°. *Boston, Kneeland & Adams,* 1768.
[*With* CHANDLER (T. B. *D.D.*) Appeal to the public, [etc.] ed. 1767].

——— A letter to a friend, containing remarks on a sermon, by John [Ewer], bishop of Llandaff, before the society for the propagation of the gospel in foreign parts, Feb. 20, 1767. In which the highest reproach is undeservedly cast upon the American colonies. 56 pp. 12°. *Boston, Kneeland & Adams,* 1767.
[*With* CHANDLER (T. B. *D.D.*) Appeal farther defended. ed. 1771].

——— A compleat view of episcopacy, as exhibited from the fathers of the christian church, until the close of the second century: containing an impartial account of them, of their writings, and of what they say concerning bishops and presbyters. 474 pp. 2 l. 8°. *Boston, T. Leverett,* 1771.

——— A letter to rev. George Whitefield, vindicating certain passages he has excepted against in a late book entitled, Seasonable thoughts on the state of religion in New England. 39 pp. 12°. *Boston, Rogers & Fowle,* 1745.
[*With* CHANDLER (T. B. *D.D.*] Appeal farther defended. ed. 1771].

——— A letter to a friend, giving a concise but just account of the Ohio defeat, etc. [*anon.*] 15 pp. 4°. *Boston, Edes & Gill,* 1755.

——— A second letter to a friend; giving a more particular narrative of the defeat of the French army at Lake George by the New-England troops, etc. [*anon.*] 16 pp. sm. 4°. *Boston, Edes & Gill,* 1755.

——— A reply to Dr. Chandler's appeal defended. 180, x pp. 12°. *Boston, D. Kneeland,* 1770.
[*With* CHANDLER (T. B. *D.D.*) Appeal farther defended. ed. 1771].

Chauveau (A.) Traité d'anatomie comparée des animaux domestiques. [1ᵉ partie. Ostéologie, syndesmologie, myologie]. 3 p. l. v, 304 pp. 8°. *Paris, J. B. Baillière,* 1855. s.
[2e partie wanting].

Chauvenet (William). A treatise on the method of least squares; or, the application of the theory of probabilities in the combina-

Chauvenet—continued.
tion of observations. Being the appendix to the author's manual of spherical and practical astronomy. pp. 469–566. 4 l. 8°. *Philadelphia, Lippincott & co.* 1868.

Chauveton (Urbain). *See* **Benzoni** (G.) Novæ novi orbis historiæ.

Cheeseman (Lewis, *D.D.*) Ishmael and the church. 328 pp. 8°. *Philadelphia, Parry & McMillan,* 1856. s.

Cheever (Henry Theodore). Memorials of the life and trials of a young christian in pursuit of health, as developed in the biography of Nathaniel Cheever, M.D. With introduction, by rev. George B. Cheever. 2 p. l. xxiii, 355 pp. 12°. *New York, C. Scribner,* 1851. s.

——— The whale and his captors; or, the whaleman's adventures, and the whale's biography. 314 pp. 12°. *New York, Harpers,* 1850. s.

Chellis (Mary Dwinell). Deacon Sims' prayers. [*anon.*] 393 pp. 3 pl. 16°. *Boston, Mass. s. s. soc.* 1868.

——— The temperance doctor. 370 pp. 1 pl. 16°. *New York, nat. temp. soc.* 1868.

——— Old Sunapee. 439 pp. 4 pl. 16°. *Boston, H. Hoyt,* 1867.

Chelsea (The) [Mass.] directory for 1868. By J. Bent. 180 pp. 8°. *Chelsea, S. Orcutt,* 1868.

Chemnitz (Martin). Examinis concilii tridentini opus integrum; doctrinæ papisticæ refutatio. 2 v. in 1. 16 p. l. 440 pp. 15 l; 6 p. l. 456 pp. 21 l. 12°. *Francofurdi ad Mœnum,* 1590. s.

Chenavard (Aimé). Nouveau recueil de décorations intérieures, contenant des dessins de tapisseries, tapis, meubles, etc. la plupart exécutés dans les manufactures royales. 42 pl. fol. *Paris, Laconte,* 1837.

Cheney (T. Apoleon, *LL. D.*) Historical sketch of the Chemung valley. 59 pp. 6 l. 8°. *Watkins, N. Y.* 1868.

Chenu (Jean Charles). Manuel de conchyliologie et de paléontologie conchyliologique. 2 v. 2 p. l. vii, 508 pp; 3 p. l. 327 pp. 8°. *Paris, V. Masson,* 1859–62. s.

Cherbuliez (Victor). Le prince Vitale, essai et récit à propos de la folie du Tasse. 356 pp. 12°. *Paris, M. Lévy frères,* 1864.

Cherokee almanac, 1849–50. Nvtodisesdi udetiyvsadisv. 2 v. in 1. 36 pp; 36 pp. 16°. *Park Hill, mission press,* 1849–50.

Cherokee hymns. Compiled from several authors, and revised. 7th ed. 69 pp. 24°. *Park Hill, mission press,* 1844.
[*With* BIBLE (Cherokee). The gospels, etc.]

Cherokee primer. Anitsalagi tsunalenvtodi tsunadeloquasdi. 24 pp. 24°. *Park Hill, mission press,* 1840.

——— The same. *Park Hill, mission press,* 1846.

Cherry the missionary; or, the church in the wilderness. [*anon.*] 236 pp. 4 pl. 16°. *Philadelphia, American s. s. union,* 1868.

Cheseboro' (Caroline). The beautiful gate, and other tales. 233 pp. 1 pl. 16°. *Auburn, Miller, Orton, & Mulligan,* 1855. s.

Chetwood (William Rufus). A general history of the stage, from its origin in Greece down to the present time. With memoirs of the principal performers on the English and Irish stage for these last fifty years. 4 p. l. 256 pp. 16°. *London, W. Owen,* 1749.

Chevalier (Michel). Lettres à m. Wolowski, sur la question des banques.
[*In* WOLOWSKI (L. F. M. R.) La banque d'Angleterre. 1867. pp. 189–250, 391–400.]

——— On the probable fall in the value of gold; the commercial and social consequences which may ensue, and the measures which it invites. Translated from the French, with preface, by Richard Cobden. 211 pp. 8°. *New York, D. Appleton & co.* 1859. s.

Chevreul (Michel Eugène). De la loi du contraste simultané des couleurs et de l'assortiment des objets coloriés. Atlas. 1 p. l. 2 pp. 40 col. pl. 4°. *Paris, Pitois-Levrault & cie,* 1839. s.

Chevrier-Scherer (Frédéric). Description des chrysides du bassin du Léman. xvii, 134 pp. 8°. *Genève, Ramboz & Schuchardt,* 1862. s.

Chiabrera (Gabriello). Rime. 3 v. 8°. *Milano, societá tipografica de' classici italiani,* 1807.

CONTENTS:

v. 1. Canzoni eroiche, lugubri, sacre, morali. Canzoni liriche, sonetti. xlvii, 422 pp. 1 portrait.
v. 2. Canzonette amorose morale; gli scherzi, [etc.] 392 pp.
v. 3. Poemati profani e sacri. 316 pp.

Chicago academy of sciences. Transactions. v. 1. part 1. 4 p. l 129 pp. 1 map. 18 pl. 8°. *Chicago, the academy,* 1867.

Chicago (The) almanac and advertiser, 1855. Compiled by E. H. Hall. 82 pp. 18°. *Chicago, Chicago printing co.* 1855. s.

——— The same. Hall's business directory of Chicago, [1856]. xii, 94 pp. 16°. *Chicago, Hall & co.* 1856. s.

Chicago *directories.*—Hall & co's. Chicago city directory and business advertiser, for 1854-55. 3d annual ed. 8°. *Chicago, R. Fergus,* [1854]. s.

——— D. B. Cooke & co's. directory of Chicago for 1858 and 1859. 2 v. 8°. *Chicago, D. B. Cooke & co.* 1858-59.

——— Smith & Du Moulin's Chicago city directory for the year ending May 1, 1860. 8°. *Chicago, Smith & Du Moulin,* [1859].

——— Halpin & Bailey's Chicago city directory for the years 1861, 1863, and 1864 3 v. 8°. *Chicago, Halpin & Bailey,* 1861-64.

Child (*Sir* Josiah). Britannia languens; or, a discourse of trade. [*anon.*] 4 p. l. 310 pp. 4 l. 16°. *London, T. Dring,* 1680.

——— A new discourse of trade, with treatise on usury. New ed. xxxix, 224 pp. 16°. *London, Richardson & Urquhart,* 1775.

Child (Lydia Maria, *wife of David Lee Child*). Good wives. xiv, 316 pp. 1 pl. 16°. *Boston, Carter, Hendee & co.* 1833.

——— The same. Biographies of good wives. 6th ed. vi, 288 pp. 12°. *New York, C. S. Francis,* 1855.

Childe (E. V.) Edward Vernon; my cousin's story. 194 pp. 12°. *New York, Harpers,* 1848. s.

Children's hearts and hands. [*anon.*] 96 pp. 16°. *Philadelphia, American sunday school union,* 1868.

Chili. Anuario estadistico de la republica de Chile. v. 1-6. 4°. *Santiago de Chile, imprenta nacional,* 1861-64. s.

——— Apuntes hidrográficos sobre la costa de Chile, acompañados de algunos planos levantados por los oficiales de la armada de la republica. 192 pp. 8°. *Santiago, imprenta nacional,* 1866. s.

——— Documentos parlamentarios. Discursos de apertura en los sesiones del congreso i memorias ministeriales. 5 v. 8°. *Santiago, Ferrocarril,* 1858-59. s.

CONTENTS.

v. 1. Correspondientes a la administracion Prieto, 1831-51. 2 p. l. 395 pp.
v. 2-3. Correspondientes al primer [i] segundo quinquenios de la administracion Bulnes, 1842-46. 2 p. l. 467 pp; 2 p. l. 800 pp.
v. 4. En los dos primeros años del primer quinquenio de la administracion Montt, 1842-53. 2 p. l. 493 pp. 2 tab.
v. 5. En los tres ultimos años del primer quinquenio de la administracion Montt, 1854-56. 2 p. l. 658 pp. 1 l. 7 tab.

——— Estadistica comercial de la republica de Chile correspondiente al año de 1865-66. 2 v. 4°. *Valparaiso, imprenta del Mercurio,* 1866-67. s.

——— Estadistica de la republica de Chile. Provincia del Maule. v. 1. viii, 179 pp. 8°. *Santiago, imprenta de los tribunales,* 1845. s.

——— *Departamento de guerra y marina.* Memoria que el ministro de estado en los departamentos de guerra y marina presenta al congreso nacional, 1839-48. 10 v. in 1. 4°. *Santiago, imprenta del estado, etc.* 1839-48. s.

——— *Departamento de guerra.* Memoria que el ministro de estado en el departamento de guerra presenta al congreso nacional de 1865. 8°. *Santiago de Chile, imprenta nacional,* 1865. s.

——— *Departamento de justicia, culto, etc.* Memoria que el ministro de estado en el departamento de justicia, culto e instruccion publica presenta al congreso nacional de 1856-58. 3 v. 8°. *Santiago de Chile, imprenta nacional,* 1856-58. s.

——— *Departamento de marina.* Memoria que el ministro de estado en el departamento de marina presenta al congreso nacional de 1849-53. 5 v. 4°. *Santiago de Chile, J. Belin i co.* 1849-53. s.

Chinese mission. *See* **Presbyterian** church, U. S. A.

Choiseul-Gouffier (Marie Gabriel Florent Auguste, *comte* de). Voyage pittoresque de la Grèce. [*anon.*] 2 v. [v. 1, 1e tirage]. 3 p. l. xvi, 204 pp. 127 pl. and maps. 1 tab; 2 p. l. xii pp. 2 l. 518 pp. 157 pl. on 70 l. 1 portrait. fol. *Paris, Tilliard, graveur,* 1782-1820, *et J. J. Blaise,* 1824.

Chouquet (Gustave). First lessons in learning French. 8th ed. 179 pp. 18°. *New York, R. Lockwood & son,* 1853. s.

Christian (The) examiner. Jan. to June, 1868. v. 84. [New ser. v. 5]. 8°. *New York, J. Miller,* 1868.

Christian (The) orator; or, a collection of speeches delivered before religious benevolent societies. By a gentleman of Massachusetts. [*anon.*] 3d ed. 298 pp. 18°. *Charlestown, S. Etheridge,* 1819.

Christie (*Rev.* William). A review of Dr. Priestley's theological works, with observations on his character and conduct as a christian minister. 8°. *Northumberland, (Pa.) J. Binns,* 1806.

[*In* PRIESTLEY (J.) Memoirs. v. 2. pp. 482-824. *Northumberland,* 1806].

Christine de Pisan. Extraits des écrits. 2 v. 8°. *Paris,* 1786.

[ROBERT (L. F. G. de). Collection des ouvrages françois, composés par des femmes. 1786-89. v. 2-3].

Christliche (Der) sänger, eine sammlung der vornehmsten und gebräuchlichsten lieder, [etc.] vi, 440 pp. 18°. *Skippackville, (Penn.) S. K. Cassel,* 1855. s.

Christmas blossoms, and new year's wreath, for 1849, 1850, 1851, and 1854. By uncle Thomas. [*pseudon.*] 4 v. 12°. *Philadelphia, E. H. Butler & co.* 1849–54. s.

Christmas (The) gift, and other stories. [*anon.*] 176, 17 pp. 18°. *Philadelphia, Am. s. s. union,* 1868.

Christmas greens. [*anon.*] 147 pp. 1 pl. 16°. *Philadelphia, Am. s. s. union,* 1865.

Christophers (John Crowch, *M.D.*) Observations on syphilis, and on inoculation as the means of diagnosis in ulcers and discharges invading the genital organs. iv, 74 pp. 8°. *London, J. Churchill,* 1853.

Chronica regvm Manniæ et insularvm. The chronicle of Man and the Sudreys. Edited from the manuscript codex in the British museum, and with historical notes, by P. A. Munch. xxxiv, 191 pp. 1 pl. 8°. *Christiania, Brogger & Christie,* 1860. s.

——— The same. [Extra paper, with portrait of Munch]. 8°. *Christiania, Brogger & Christie,* 1860. s.

Chronica. *See* **Cronycke.**

Chronicles of Yonkers. [*anon.*] 23 pp. 8°. *Yonkers, privately printed,* 1864.

Chronicon ecclesiæ ripensis, sev annales episcoporum ripensium, qvos ex veteri codice manuscripto eruit et edidit Petrus Terpager. 43 pp. 16°. *Havniæ, ex typographeo regiæ majest.* 1708.

[*With* TORFESEN (Thormod). Historia Vinlandiae antiqvae. 1705].

Chronique de la conquête de Constantinople et de l'établissement des Français en Morée, écrite en vers politiques par un auteur anonyme. [*anon.*] Traduit par J. Buchon. xlvii, 456 pp. 1 l. 8°. *Paris, Verdière,* 1825.

[COLLECTION de chroniques nationales françaises. v. 4].

Chroniqueuse [*pseudon.*] *See* **Logan** (Olive).

Chrysostom (Joannes *Saint*). Opera. [Latin]. 8 p. l. cxii l. fol. *Basilea, J. de Psortz,* 1504.

——— The same. Tomvs 1–3 opervm. [Latin]. 3 v. in 1. fol. *Basiliæ, A. Cratander,* 1522.

CONTENTS:

v. 1. Homiliae in Matthæum.
v. 2. In Ioannis evangelia homiliae.
v. 3. De lavdibvs Pavli homiliae. In epistolam ad Titum, ad Philemon, ad Hebræos, 1–2 ad Timotheum, ad Corinthios, homiliae. Aduersus uituperatores uitæ monasticæ libri.

——— Sermo de penitencia. 6 l. sm. 4°. [*n. p. about* 1476].

Church (Albert E.) Elements of the differential and integral calculus. Improved ed. containing the elements of the calculus of variations. viii, 344 pp. 8°. *New York, G. P. Putnam,* 1850. s.

Church (Benjamin). History of Philip's war, commonly called the great Indian war, of 1675–76. Also, of the French and Indian wars at the eastward. With notes, [and] an appendix. By S. G. Drake. 2[d] ed. 360 pp. 3 pl. 16°. *Boston, J. H. A. Frost,* 1827.

Church (*Mrs.* Florence Marryat). "Too good for him." iv, 444 pp. 16°. *London, F. Warne & co.* 1868.

Church of England. Portions of the book of common prayer, in the language of the Cree Indians. [By archdeacon Hunter]. Transmitted with phonetic symbols. [By rev. R. Hunt]. 6 p. l. 52 pp. 8°. *London, church missionary house,* 1856. s.

Church review and ecclesiastical register. *See* **American** quarterly church review.

Churchill (Fleetwood, *M. D.*) On the diseases of infants and children. xii, 636 pp. 8°. *Philadelphia, Lea & Blanchard,* 1850. s.

Churchill (*Sir* Winston). Divi britannici: being a remark upon the lives of all the kings of this isle, from 2855 B. C. to 1660 A. D. 3 p. l. 362 pp. 1 l. fol. *London, T. Roycroft,* 1685.

Churchman (John). The magnetic atlas, or variation charts of the whole terraqueous globe. vii, 80 pp. 4°. *London, J. Sewell,* 1794.

Churchyard (Thomas). The mirror of man, and manners of men. London, 1594. 8 l. 4°. *Reprinted, Auchinleck press, A. Boswell,* 1816.

——— A mvsicall consort of heauenly harmonie called Chvrchyards charitie. London, 1595. 1 p. l. 23 pp. 4°. *Reprinted, Auchinleck press, A. Boswell,* 1816.

——— A pleasant discourse of court and wars: with a replication to them both. Called [Churchyards] cherrishing. 12 l. 4°. *Reprinted, Auchinleck press, A. Boswell,* 1816.

——— A praise of poetrie. London, 1595. pp. 25–43. 4°. *Reprinted, Auchinleck press,* 1816.

——— A sad and solemne funerall, of the right honorable sir Francis Knowles. London, 1596. 4 l. 4°. *Reprinted, Auchinleck press, A. Boswell,* 1816.

——— A trve discovrse historicall, of the succeeding governovrs in the Netherlands, and the ciuill warres there begunn in 1565. With the memorable services of our honorable English generals, captaines, and souldiers, espe-

Churchyard—continued.
cially under sir Iohn Norice, 1577-1598. Translated and collected by T. C. and Ric. Ro. [Richard Robinson] out of E. M[eteranus] his 15 bookes Historiæ belgicæ; and other collections added. 6 p. l. 154 pp. sm. 4°. *London, M. Lownes,* 1602.

[Imperfect: pp. 15-16 wanting].

Cicero (Marcus Tullius). Opera quæ extant omnia: ex sola fere codd. mss. fide emendata. Studio atque industria J. Gulielmii et J. Gruteri. 4 v. in 2. 9 p. l. 547 pp; 2 p. l. 765 pp. fol. *London, J. Dunmore,* 1681.

——— De natura deorum libri tres. Cum notis integris Paulli Manucii, Petri Victorii, Joachimi Camerarii, Dionys. Lombini, Fulv. Ursini, et Joannis Walkeri, recensuit Joannes Davisius. Ed. 3ª. 6 p. l. 434 pp. 12°. *Cantabrigiæ, C. Crounfield, &c,* 1733.

——— De officijs cū libris eiusdem, de amicitia, senectute, et paradoxis cum Petri Marsii, Francisci Maturancii, et Jodosi Badij ascensij explanatione. 6 p. l. ccxxxvi l. fol. *Lugduni, P. Balet,* 1516.

——— The same. De officiis libri tres. Item, Cato major, seu de senectute; Lælius, sive de amicitia; paradoxa; et somnium Scipionis. Ed. J. Olivet. 5 p. l. 258 pp. 8°. *Edinburgi, A. Kincaird & A. Donaldson,* 1758. s.

——— The same. 1 p. l. 261 pp. 5 l. 18°. *Glasguae, A. Stalker,* 1732.

——— The same. Les offices, traduits en François, sur la nouvelle édition latine de Grævius. 12 p. l. 402 pp. 23 l. 18°. *La Haye, H. van Bulderen,* 1692.

——— The same. Officia. Ein büch zü seynem sune Marco. Welchs Johansen von Schwartzenbergs etc. verteütschet, vnd volgens, durch jne, in zyerlicher Hochteütsch gebracht, mit vil figuren vnnd teütschen reymen gemeynem nutz zü güt in druck gegeben worden. 8 p. l. xci l. fol. *Augspurg, H. Steyner,* 1531.

——— Cato major, or his discourse of old-age. [Translated by James Logan]. With notes [by B. Franklin]. viii, 159 pp. sm. 4°. *Philadelphia, B. Franklin,* 1744.

——— [Epistolæ]. Los dos lìbros de las epistolas selectas; con traduccion i declaraciones en lengua castellana, hechas por Pedro Simon Abril. 23 p. l. 320 pp. 16°. *Valentiae, S. Fauli,* 1770. s.

——— Rhetorica s. de oratore comm. Omniboni Leoniceni. De perfecto oratore. Topica. Partitiones oratoriae. De claris oratoribus. De petitione consulatus. De optimo genere oratorum. Aeschinis et Demosthenis orationes contrariae per Leonardum Aretinum in lat. conversa. Epistola editoris H. Squarzafici ad Petrum Brusonum. 211 l. fol. *Venitiis, T. de Blauis,* 1488.

——— Orationum, volumen primum, a Dionysio Lambino emendatum. Ed. recens. 668 pp. 48°. *Lugduni, J. Canier,* 1679.

——— The same. Orationes quædam selectæ, notis illustratæ. [Edidit Carolus Folsom]. Ed. stereotypa. 278 pp. 12°. *Bostoniæ, Hilliard, Gray, et soc.* 1835.

——— The same. Hvict oraisons. 3 p. l. 381 pp. 18°. *Paris, A. de Sommaville,* 1653.

——— Oratio pro A. Licinio Archia. Jacobus Tollius emendavit. 7 p. l. 120 pp. 24°. *Lugd. Batav. Daniel Gaesbeeck,* 1677.

——— *Translator.* [Arati Phænomena]. Interpretatio [latinis versibus reddita]. 36 pp. 4°. [*Lugduni-Batavorum*], 1600.

[*With* GROAT (H. de). Syntagma arateorum, 1600).

Cincinnati (The) almanac, 1839-40. 2 v. 88 pp. 1 map; 82 pp. 1 map. 1 pl. 24°. *Cincinnati, Glezen & Shepard,* 1839-40.

Cincinnati (Williams') almanac, business guide, and annual advertiser, 1850. 200 pp. 1 map. 16°. *Cincinnati, C. S. Williams,* 1850. s.

Cincinnati chamber of commerce and merchants' exchange. Annual reports for 1864 to 1867. 4 v. 8°. *Cincinnati,* 1864-67.

Cincinnati (daily) commercial. July, 1867, to June, 1868. 2 v. fol. *Cincinnati, M. Halstead & co.* 1867-68.

Cincinnati directory for 1829, 1831, 1836, 1840, 1842, and 1843. 6 v. 16°. and 8°. *Cincinnati,* 1829-43.

[v. for 1831 and 1836-37 imperfect].

Cincinnati (daily) gazette. v. 2-3; Dec. 27, 1828, to Dec. 21, 1829. v. 7-9; Jan. 7, 1833, to Dec. 31, 1835. 9 v. fol. *Cincinnati,* 1828-35. *See* **Liberty Hall** and Cincinnati gazette.

Circe; or, three acts in the life of an artist. A novel. By Babington White. [*pseudon.*] 146 pp. 8°. *New York, Harpers,* 1867.

[*Note.*—Largely plagiarized from the "Dalila" of Octave Feuillet].

——— The same. 2 v. 274 pp; 279 pp. 12°. *London, Ward, Lock & Tyler,* 1867.

Cisneros (Francisco Jimenez de). *See* **Jimenez de Cisneros.**

Civil (The) engineer and architect's journal, 1867. v. 30. 4°. *London, W. Kent & co.* 1867.

Civilingenieur (Der). Zeitschrift für das ingenieurwesen. Unter besonderer mitwirkung von Julius Weisbach, herausgegeben von

Civilingenieur—continued.
Gustav Zenner, und C. R. Bornemann. Neue folge, v. 1–10. 4°. *Freiberg, J. G. Engelhardt, etc.* 1854–64. s.

——— *See, also,* **Ingenieur** (Die).

Clack (*Mrs.* Louise). General Lee and Santa Claus. Christmas gift to her little southern friends. 36 pp. 6 pl. sm. 4°. *New York, Blelock & co.* 1867.

Claims (The) of the American loyalists reviewed and maintained upon incontrovertible principles of law and justice. [*anon.*] viii, 138 pp. 8°. *London, G. & T. Wilkie,* 1787.

Clap (Roger). Memoirs, 1630. Boston, 1731. 62 pp. 1 l. 16°. *Boston, [reprinted by] D. Clap,* 1844.
[DORCHESTER antiquarian and historical society. Collections, No. 1].

Clar (Fr.) Anno 1724. Zur charakteristik der polnischen herrschaft. 2 p. l. 249 pp. 12°. *Bromberg, C. M. Roskowski,* 1862.

Clarendon (Henry Hyde, *2d earl of*). *See* **Hyde** (Henry).

Claret de Fleurieu (Charles Pierre, *comte* de). *See* **Fleurieu.**

Clark (A. N.) Excursion of the Putnam phalanx to Mount Vernon, Dec. 1860. 40 pp. 8°. *Hartford, C. G. Geer,* 1861.

Clark (*Rev.* Daniel, *jr.*) A candid discussion of christian baptism. 199 pp. 16°. *Auburn, Derby & Miller,* 1854. s.

Clark (*Rev.* D. W. *editor*). Fireside reading. Historical sketches; or, narratives of striking events in the course of human affairs. 443 pp. 16°. *Cincinnati, Swormstedt & Poe,* 1856. s.

——— The same. Traits and anecdotes of birds and fishes. 382 pp. 12°. *Cincinnati, Swormstedt & Poe,* 1856. s.

——— The same. Travel and adventure; comprising some of the most striking narratives on record. 416 pp. 16°. *Cincinnati, Swormstedt & Poe,* 1856. s.

——— Select lectures; comprising some of the more valuable lectures delivered before the young men's christian association, in Exeter Hall, London, from 1847 to 1855. 439 pp. 12°. *Cincinnati, Swormstedt & Poe,* 1856. s.

——— True tales for the spare hour; or, sketches of life and character. 415 pp. 16°. *Cincinnati, Swormstedt & Poe,* 1856. s.

Clark (John, *M.D.*) Observations on the diseases in long voyages to hot countries, and particularly on those which prevail in the East Indies. New ed. xvi, 366 pp. 8°. *London, J. Murray,* 1778.

Clark (Joshua V. H.) Lights and lines of Indian character, and scenes of pioneer life. 375 pp. 1 portrait. 12°. *Syracuse, E. H. Babcock & co.* 1854. s.

Clark (Peter H.) The black brigade of Cincinnati; being a report of its labors and a muster-roll of its members, etc. 30 pp. 8°. *Cincinnati, J. D. Boyd,* 1864.

Clark (Stephen W.) Analysis of the English language, designed as an introduction to English grammar. 168 pp. 1 chart. 12°. *New York, A. S. Barnes & co.* 1851. s.

——— First lessons in English grammar. 156 pp. 1 pl. 12°. *New York, A. S. Barnes & co.* 1857. s.

——— A practical grammar; in which words, phrases, and sentences are classified according to their offices, and their various relations to one another. 40th ed. 309 pp. 12°. *New York, A. S. Barnes & co.* 1868.

Clark (*Rev.* William George). Peloponnesus; notes of study and travel. xv, 344 pp. 5 maps. 8°. *London, J. W. Parker & son,* 1858.

Clarke (Charles). The flying scud. A sporting novel. iv, 312 pp. 16°. *London, Chapman & Hall,* 1868.

Clarke (Edward). A treatise upon the law of extradition. With the conventions upon the subject existing between England and foreign nations, and the cases decided thereon. x, 183 pp. 12°. *London, Stevens & Haynes,* 1867.

Clarke (*Rev.* Edward William). The churchyard stile; twelve sermons adapted to the mechanical and agricultural population. xxiv, 211 pp. 8°. *London, B. Fellowes,* 1835. s.

Clarke (Henry, *LL.D.*) Seaman's desiderata; or, concise, practical rules for computing the apparent time at sea. With additions and corrections by John Garnett. 48 pp. 18 l. 1 pl. sm. 4°. *New Brunswick, A. Blauvelt,* 1801.

Clarke (*Rev.* James Freeman). The hour which cometh, and now is: sermons preached in Indiana-place chapel, Boston. 6, 364 pp. 12°. *Boston, W. V. Spencer,* 1868.

Clarke (John). An introduction to the making of Latin: comprising, after an easy, compendious method, the substance of the Latin syntax, with proper English examples. xii, 276 pp. 16°. *Worcester, Isaiah Thomas,* 1786.

Clarke (*Mrs.* Stirling). The ladies' equestrian guide. vi, 216 pp. 9 pl. 4°. *London, Day & son,* 1857.

Clarke (Thomas). The two angels; or, love led: a story of either paradise; in six cantos. 194 pp. 16°. *Chicago, Clarke & Brown,* 1867.

Clarke (William). The natural history of nitre. 8 p. l. 93 pp. 18°. *London, N. Brook,* 1670.

Clarke (William H.) The American organ or organist's parlor companion. A complete system of instruction. 136 pp. obl. 4°. *Boston, S. D. & H. W. Smith,* [1868].

—— Home recreations: a collection of new songs and instrumental pieces, original and selected, arranged for the parlor organ, melodeon, or piano-forte. 144 pp. obl. 16°. *Boston, S. D. & H. W. Smith,* 1867.

Clarkson (Thomas). Water baptism and the Lord's supper, as christian rites. 16°. *Philadelphia,* 1811.

[*In* DELL (W.) *and others.* Doctrines of baptism, etc. 1811. pp. 73-148].

Clavière (Étienne). Commerce of America with Europe. *See* **Brissot de Warville** (J. P.) *and* **Clavière.**

Clay (Henry). Private correspondence. Edited by Calvin Colton. 642 pp. 2 pl. 8°. *Boston, A. S. Barnes & co.* 1855. S.

—— Speeches. [Edited] by Richard Chambers. 504 pp. 1 pl. 8°. *Cincinnati, Shepard & Stearns,* 1842.

Cleave (E.) Prominent mercantile houses and corporate bodies that have contributed to the growth and prosperity of New York city. 42 l. 6 pl. 8°. [*New York, E. Cleave,* 1868].

[*With* STONE (W. L.) History of New York city. 1868 ed.]

Clemency Franklyn. [A novel. *anon.*] 2 v. 313 pp; 333 pp. 16°. *London, Macmillan,* 1866.

Cler (Albert). Physiologie du musicien. Vignettes de Daumier, etc. 126 pp. 16°. *Paris, Aubert & cie; & Lavigne,* [1841].

[*With* ALHOY (M.) Physiologie du voyageur].

Cleveland (Charles Dexter). A compendium of English literature, chronologically arranged, from Sir John Mandeville to William Cowper. 776 pp. 8°. *Philadelphia, E. C. & J. Biddle,* 1848. S.

—— Lyra sacra americana; or gems from American sacred poetry. With notes and biographical sketches. viii, 328 pp. 18°. *New York, C. Scribner & co.* 1868.

Cleveland (Henry Russell). A selection from [his] writings. With a memoir, by George S. Hillard. li, 384 pp. 12°. *Boston, printed for private distribution,* 1844. S.

Clichtove (Josse). Ars supputādi tam per calculos quos per notas arithmeticas. 4°. n. p. [1517]?

[*In* FABER (J.) Introductio in arithmecam Seuerini Boetij].

—— Elucidatorivm ecclesiasticvm, ad officivm ecclesiae pertinentia planivs exponens. 6 p. l. 230 l. fol. *Basileæ, Io. Frobenius,* 1519.

[*With* THIERRY (Jean, *of Langres*). Homiliarius doctorum. 1516].

Clodoré (Jean de). Relation de ce qui s'est passé dans les isles et terre-ferme de l'Amérique, pendant la dernière guerre avec l'Angleterre et avec un journal du dernier voyage du Sr de la Barre en le terre-ferme, et isle de Cayenne. Par I. C. S. D. V. [*J. Clodoré, secrétaire de vaisseaux*]. 2 v. 30 p. l. 386 pp; 3 p. l. 494 pp. 18°. *Paris, G. Clovzier,* 1671.

Cloizeaux (A. Des). *See* **Des Cloizeaux.**

Clok (Henry, *V. S.*) The diseases of sheep explained and described, with the proper remedies to prevent and cure the same. With an essay on cattle epidemics. 146 pp. 5 pl. 12°. *Philadelphia, Claxton, Remsen & Haffelfinger,* 1868.

Clopper (Jonas). Fragments of the history of Bawlfredonia: containing an account of the discovery and settlement of the great southern continent, and of the formation and progress of the Bawlfredonian commonwealth. By Herman Thwackius. [*pseudon.*] 2 p. l. 164 pp. 1 pl. 8°. [*Baltimore*]? 1819.

Closset (A. de). Histoire de la langue et de la littérature provençales. 1 p. l. xviii, 112 pp. 8°. *Bruxelles, T. Lesigne,* 1845. S.

Cluny (Alexander). Le voyageur américain, ou observations sur l'état actuel, la culture, le commerce des colonies brittaniques en Amérique. Traduit de l'Anglois. Augmenté par m. Jh. M[andrillon]. [*anon.*] viii, 197, 164 pp. 1 map. 3 tab. 8°. *Amsterdam, J. Schuring,* 1782.

Cluver (Philipp). Introductio in universam geographiam tam veteram quam novam, notis, etc. olim ornata a J. Bunone; jam locupletata annotationibus, etc. J. F. Hekelii et J. Reiskii. 3 p.l. 429 pp. 22 l. 36 maps. 6 pl. 4°. *Londini, S. Nicholson,* 1711.

Coates (George). Herd book; containing the pedigrees of improved short-horned cattle. [Continued] by H. Strafford. v. 17. 8°. *London, S. & J. Brawn,* 1867.

Cobarruvias Orozco (Sebastian de). *See* **Covarrubias Horozco.**

Cobb (Howell). A scriptural examination of the institution of slavery in the United States; with its objects and purposes. 173 pp. 12°. *Georgia, author,* 1856. S.

Cobb (Sophia Dickinson). Hillsboro' farms. 423 pp. 12°. *Boston, Lee & Shepard,* 1869.

Cobbe (Frances Power). Hours of work and play. 2 p. l. 274 pp. 16°. *London, N. Trübner & co.* 1867.

Cobbett (William). The democratic judge; or, the equal liberty of the press, as exhibited, explained, and exposed, in the prosecution of William Cobbett, for a pretended libel against the king of Spain and his embassador, [etc.] By Peter Porcupine. [*pseudon.*] 102 pp. 8°. *Philadelphia, W. Cobbett,* 1798.

——— A grammar of the English language. 213 pp. 18°. *New York, J. Doyle,* 1833.

——— History of the American jacobins, commonly denominated democrats. By Peter Porcupine. [*pseudon.*] 48 pp. 8°. *Philadelphia,* 1796.

[*With* PLAYFAIR (William). History of Jacobinism. *Phila.* 1796.]

——— Letters to lord Hawkesbury and Henry Addington, on the peace with Buonaparte. 2d ed. 4 p.l. 259, xciv. pp. 8°. *London, Cobbett & Morgan,* 1802.

——— Paper against gold, and glory against prosperity. 2 v. viii, 523 pp; iv. 100, cxxvii pp. 8°. *London, J. McCreery,* 1815.

——— The rush-light. By Peter Porcupine. [*pseudon*]. v. 1. nos. 1-5. Feb. 15-April 30, 1800. 258 pp. 8°. *New York, W. Cobbett,* 1800.

[*With* COBBETT (W.) The scarecrow. *Phila.* 1796.]

——— The scare-crow; being an infamous letter sent to J. Oldden, threatening destruction to his house and violence to his tenant, W. Cobbett; with remarks on the same. By Peter Porcupine. [*pseudon.*] 23 pp. 8°. *Philadelphia, W. Cobbett,* 1796.

——— Le tuteur anglais; ou, grammaire regulière de la langue anglaise. 8, 328 pp. 8°. *Philadelphia, T. & W. Bradford,* 1805.

[Imperfect. pp. wanting at the end].

——— A year's residence in the U.S. of America. Part 1. [Description of the climate, seasons, and soil, and of ruta baga turnip culture]. 134 pp. 16°. *New York, Clayton & Kingsland,* 1818.

Cobden (Richard). Political writings. 2 v. vii, 496 pp; v, 447, vii pp. 8°. *London, Ridgway,* 1867.

CONTENTS.

v. 1. England, Ireland, and America, 1835.
Russia, 1836.
1793 and 1853, in three letters.
v. 2. Letter to Henry Ashworth.
How wars are got up in India. The origin of the Burmese war.
What next—and next? [Russian war].
The three panics; an historical episode.

Cochem (Martin von). Grosser baumgarten bepflanzt mit den schönsten morgen-abend-mess-, beicht-, communion- und vespergebeten, nebst vielen andern andachtsübungen zu Gott, etc. Neu herausgegeben von F. Willam. 510 pp. 18°. *New York, C. & N. Benziger,* 1868.

Cochran (*Rev.* Wesley). The life of human souls. 224 pp. 16°. *Philadelphia, Perkinpine & Higgins,* 1868.

Cockburn (William, *M.D.*) Profluvia ventris; or, nature and causes of loosenesses plainly discovered, [etc.] 10 p. l. 178 pp. 16°. *London, B. Barker,* 1701.

Coddington (David Smith). Speeches and addresses, with a biographical sketch. [Edited by J. Coddington]? xxxii, 177 pp. portrait. 8°. *New York, Appletons,* 1866.

Coffin (Robert Barry). Cakes and ale at Woodbine; from twelfth night to new year's day. By Barry Gray. [*pseudon.*] 229 pp. 12°. *New York, Hurd & Houghton,* 1868.

Cogadh Gaedhel re Gallaibh. The war of the Gaedhil with the Gaill; or, the invasions of Ireland by the Danes and other Norsemen. The original Irish text, edited with translation and introduction, by James Henthorn Todd. ccvii, 348 pp. 2 fac-sim. 8°. *London, Longmans,* 1867.

[GREAT BRITAIN and Ireland (Chronicles, etc. of) during the middle ages].

Coggeshall (William T.) The signs of the times: comprising a history of the spirit-rappings, in Cincinnati and other places; with notes on clairvoyant revealments. 144 pp. 16°. *Cincinnati, author,* 1851.

Coghill (J. Henry). Abroad. Journal of a tour through Great Britain and on the continent. xi, 314 pp. 12°. *New York, Sheldon & co.* 1868.

Cogolludo (Diego Lopez de). Historia de Yucathan. Sacada a lvz por Francisco de Ayeta. Engraved title. 15 p. l. 760 pp. 16 l. 1 pl. fol. *Madrid, J. Garcia,* 1688.

Cohen (Bernard). Supplement to the seventh edition of Fairman on the funds. 50 pp. 8°. *London, J. Richardson,* 1827.

[*With* FAIRMAN (William). Account of the funds. 1824].

Coke (Edward Thomas). A subaltern's furlough: descriptive of scenes in the United States, upper and lower Canada, [etc.] during 1832. 2 v. 222 pp; iv, 188 pp. 12°. *New York, Harpers,* 1833.

Colburn (Warren). Arithmetic; being a sequel to first lessons in arithmetic. 3d ed. xi, 267 pp. 16°. *Boston, Cummings, Hilliard & co.* 1826.

——— Intellectual arithmetic, upon the inductive method of instruction. 172 pp. 18°. *Hallowell, (Me.) Glazier & co.* 1828.

——— Introduction to algebra. 276 pp. 12°. *Boston, Hilliard, Gray & co.* 1841. s.

Colburn's united service magazine, and naval and military journal. Sept. 1867, to Dec. 1868. 4 v. 8°. *London, Hurst & Blackett,* [1868].

Cole (Christian). Historical and political memoirs, containing letters by sovereign princes, state ministers, admirals, and general officers, etc. from almost all the courts in Europe, 1697–1708. [2d ed.] xii, 559 pp. fol. *London, J. Millan,* 1735.

Cole (Henry). Hand-book of Hampton court. With embellishments. By Felix Summerly. [*pseudon.*] 16°. *London,* 1841.

Coleman (Lyman, *D. D.*) A church without a bishop. The apostolical and primitive church, popular in its government, and simple in its worship. With an essay by A. Neander. 432 pp. 12°. *Boston, Gould, Kendall & Lincoln,* 1844.

Coles (*Rev.* George). Incidents of my later years. 315 pp. 18°. *New York, Carlton & Phillips,* 1855. s.

Colfax (Schuyler). Speeches. 8°. *New York,* 1868.

[*In* MARTIN (E. W.) The life of Schuyler Colfax. Appendix].

Colhouer (T. H.) Republican methodism contrasted with episcopal methodism; and the policy of the methodist church, illustrated and defended. With an introductory essay by rev. W. Reeves. vii, 186 pp. 16°. *Philadelphia, Daughaday & co.* 1868.

Collection de chroniques nationales françaises, écrites en langue vulgaire du 13e au 16e siècle, avec notes, etc. par J. A. Buchon. 47 v. 8°. *Paris, Verdière,* 1824–29.

CONTENTS.

- v. 1–2. Histoire de Constantinople, par Du Fresne Du Cange.
- v. 3. La prise de Constantinople, par Geoffroy De Ville Hardoin.
- v. 4. Conquête de Constantinople, par un auteur anonyme.
- v. 5–6. Chronique de Ramon Muntaner.
- v. 7–8. Branche des royaux lignages; chronique métrique de Guillaume Guiart.
- v. 9. Chronique métrique de Godefroy de Paris.
- v. 10. Poésies de Froissart.
- v. 11–25. Chroniques de Froissart.
- v. 26–40. Chroniques de Monstrelet et continuations.
- v. 41. Chronique de J. de Lalain, par G. Chastelain.
- v. 42–43. Des ducs de Bourgogne, par G. Chastelain.
- v. 43–47. Chroniques de Jean Molinet.

Collection (A) of epigrams, [with] a critical dissertation on this species of poetry. [*anon.* By W. Oldys? 1st series]. xxiii pp. 132 l. 16°. *London, J. Walthoe,* 1727.

——— The same. 2d ed. 2 v. xii pp. 172 l; 132 l. 16°. *London, J. Walthoe,* 1735–37.

Collection (A) of hymns for the use of native christians of the Mohawk language. Ne karoronh ne teyrighwaghkwatha ne ne enyontste ne yagorihwiyoghstonh kanyengehaga niyeweantenh. Translated by A. H. Hill. 39, 68 pp. 32°. *New York,* 1829.

Collections with regard to the case of the American loyalists. [*anon.*] 7 pp. fol. [*London? about* 1783].

Collingwood (Cuthbert). Rambles of a naturalist on the shores and waters of the China sea: being observations in natural history during a voyage to China, Formosa, Borneo, Singapore, etc. 1866–67. 1 p. l. xiv, 445 pp. 3 pl. 8°. *London, J. Murray,* 1868.

Collins (Arthur). The peerage of England; or, an historical and genealogical account of the present nobility, with the coats of arms of each family. 3d ed. corrected. 2 v. in 1. 3 p. l. 486, 286, 23 pp. 8°. *London, A. Collins,* 1715.

——— The same. 2d ed. 4 v. 8°. *London, W. Innys,* 1741.

——— The same. [Supplement, (to ed. 1741,) containing succession of peers from 1740.] 2 v. viii, 398 pp. 8 l; 2 l. 399–820 pp. 8 l. 8°. *London, W. Innys,* 1750.

——— The same. 4th ed. 7 v. 8°. *London, H. Woodfall,* 1768.

Collins (Charles Allston). At the bar. A tale. 2 v. 4 p. l. 303 pp; 2 p. l. 330 pp. 12°. *London, Chapman & Hall,* 1866.

——— The bar sinister. A tale. 2 v. 2 p. l. 305 pp; 2 p. l. 336 pp. 12°. *London, Smith, Elder & co.* 1864.

Collins (William Wilkie). The moonstone. A novel. With illustrations. 223 pp. 1 pl. 8°. *New York, Harpers,* 1868.

Collyer (*Rev.* Robert). Nature and life: sermons. 6th ed. 4 p. l. 313 pp. 16°. *Boston, H. B. Fuller,* 1868.

Colman (George, *the younger*). Poetical works. 16°. *Philadelphia,* 1834.

CONTENTS.

Broad grins. viii, 81 pp.
Poetical vagaries. xii, 168 pp.
Eccentricities for Edinburgh. v, 75 pp.

Colman (Julia). The boys' and girls' illustrated bird book. 140 pp. 4 col. pl. sm. 4°. *New York, Carlton & Porter,* [1857]. s.

Colmeiro (Miguel). La botanica y los botanicos de la peninsula hispano-lusitana. Estudios bibliográficos y biográficos. Obra premiada por la biblioteca nacional. xi, 216 pp. 8°. *Madrid, gobierno,* 1858. s.

[SPAIN. Biblioteca nacional].

Colonizationist (The) and journal of freedom, [April, 1833, to April, 1834, incl.] 384 pp. 1 pl. 8°. *Boston, G. W. Laight,* 1833–34.

Colonna (Egidio). Liber de regimine principū. 134 l. fol. *Rome, Stephanus Plannck,* 1482.

Colquhoun (John Campbell). William Wilberforce, his friends and his times. vii, 448 pp. 12°. *London, Longmans,* 1866.

Colton (*Rev.* Caleb C.) Remarks, critical and moral, on the talents of Lord Byron, and the tendencies of Don Juan. By the author of Hypocrisy, a satire. [*anon.*] 48 pp. 8°. *London, G. Woodfall,* 1819.
[MISCELLANEOUS pamphlets, v. 56].

Colton (Calvin). Public economy for the United States. 536 pp. 8°. *New York, A. S. Barnes & co.* 1848. s.

——— The same. 2d ed. 536 pp. 8°. *New York, A. S. Barnes & co.* 1849.

Columbian (The) magazine, or monthly miscellany, Sept. 1786, to Dec. 1787. v. i. [With supplement]. 890 pp 27 pl. 8°. *Philadelphia, T. Seddon and others,* 1786–87.

Columbus. Amerikanische miscellen. Herausgegeben von C. N. Röding. Jan. 1827, zu März, 1832. 11 v. in 5. 8°. *Hamburg, Herold und Hoffmann & Campe,* 1827–32.
[*Note.*—Vols. for 1825–26 wanting to complete the set].

Columbus (*Ohio*) directory, 1848, containing a brief history of the city, etc. By J. Siebert. 2 p. l. 264 pp. 16°. *Columbus, S. Medary,* 1848.

——— The same. By E. Glover and W. Henderson. 1850–51. 239 pp. 16°. *Columbus, E. Glover,* 1850.

Comenius (Jan Amos). Janua linguarum trilinguis, [anglo-latino-græca]; adjunctis metaphrasi græca et anglicana versione. 6 p. l. 276 pp. 16 pl. 16°. *Londini, J. Redmayne,* 1670.

——— Janua linguarum reserata: sive omnium scientiarum et linguarum seminarium: id est compendiosa latinam et anglicam, aliasque linguas, et artium etiam fundamenta addiscendi methodus: una cum januæ latinitatis vestibulo. Translated [into English] by T. Horn. 207 l. 16°. *London, company of stationers,* 1673.

Comer (George N.) Comer's navigation simplified. A manual of instruction in navigation as practised at sea. 112, 51 pp. 3 pl. 8°. *New York, Harpers,* 1868.

Cometh up as a flower. An autobiography. [*anon.*] 2 v. 2 p. l. 327 pp; 294 pp. 12°. *London, R. Bentley,* 1867.

Comfort (Lucy Randall, *pseudon?*) Folks and fairies, stories for little children. With engravings. 259 pp. 1 pl. sq. 16°. *New York, Harpers,* 1868.

Comforts of human life; or smiles and laughter of Charles Chearful and Martin Merryfellow. By Charles Chearful. [*pseudon.*] 2d ed. 238 pp. 1 pl. 12°. *London, Oddy & co.* 1807.

Comical fights and fighting comicals, showing how the noble art is burlesqued. [*anon.* Illustrated.] 31 pp. 4°. *New York, Abraham & Needham,* 1868.

Commercial convention. Proceedings of the commercial convention, held in Detroit, July 11–14, 1865. 276 pp. 8°. *Detroit, convention,* 1865.

Commercial (The) and financial chronicle; a weekly newspaper. July, 1867, to Dec. 1868. v. 5–7. fol. *New York, W. B. Dana & co.* 1867–68.

Compagnoni (Giuseppe). Storia dell' America, in continuazione del compendio della storia universale del conte di Segur. [Con uno indice.] 29 v. in 15. 24°. *Milano, Fusi, Stella, e compagnia,* 1820–23.

Companion (The). After-dinner table talk. By Chetwood Evelyn, esq. [*pseudon.*] 192 pp. 1 portrait. 8°. *New York, G. P. Putnam,* 1850. s.

Complete course of meditations for the use of the sisters of charity. [*anon.*] 3 v. 16°. *Philadelphia, Sherman & co.* 1868.

Compton (Charles). The savings bank assistant; containing a practical and ready method of calculating interest on deposits in savings banks; with numerous tables. xi, 144 pp. 12°. *London, author,* 1829. s.

Comstock (John Lee). Natural history of quadrupeds. 73 pp. 4°. *New York, Pratt Woodford & co.* 1848.

——— The young botanist; being a treatise on the science. 3d ed. 243 pp. 1 col. pl. 24°. *New York, Pratt, Woodford & co.* 1850. s.

Conant (Helen S.) The butterfly hunters. With illustrations. vi, 167 pp. sm. 4°. *Boston, Ticknor & Fields,* 1868.

Concord (*New Hampshire*). A municipal register, containing the city charter and ordinances, [etc.] 80 pp. 8°. *Concord, city council,* 1855.

——— The Concord directory, 1867–8. 150 pp. 8°. *Boston, Dudley & Greenough,* 1867.

Condie (D. Francis, *M. D.*) A practical treatise on the diseases of children. 6th ed. 783 pp. 8°. *Philadelphia, H. C. Lea,* 1868.

Confederate States of America (*The so-called*). Compilation of the tariff act, approved May 21st, 1861, showing the rates of duties payable on imported goods, wares, and merchandise,

Confederate states, etc.—continued. from and after Sept. 1, 1861, alphabetically arranged. By P. E. Walden. vii, 282 pp. 8°. *New Orleans, Corson & Armstrong,* 1861.

Conference on missions held in 1860 at Liverpool; including the papers read, the deliberations, and the conclusions reached. Edited by the secretaries to the conference. 10th thousand. xi, 428 pp. 8°. *London, J. Nisbet & co.* 1860. s.

Configliachi (Pietro) *and* **Rusconi** (Mauro). Del proteo anguino di Laurenti monografia. 3 p. l. 119 pp. 4 pl. 4°. *Pavia, Fusi e comp.* 1819. s.

Congrès international des réformes douanières réuni à Bruxelles, 23-25 Septembre, 1856. 2 p. l. xx, 363 pp. 8°. *Bruxelles, M. Weissenbruch,* 1857. s.

Congressional (The) globe and appendix; first session, fortieth congress. Mar. 4-30, July 3-20, Nov. 21-Dec. 2, 1867. 4°. *Washington,* 1867.

Connecticut (*Colony of*). Public records from Aug. 1689, to May, 1706. Edited by C. J. Hoadly. vi, 574 pp. 8°. *Hartford, Case, Lockwood & Brainard,* 1868.

——— (*State of*). Annual report of the board of education, 1868, [with] the annual report of the secretary of the board. 8°. *New Haven, Tuttle, Morehouse & Taylor,* 1868.

——— Goodwin's annual legislative statistics, 1850-65. 2 v. in 1. 8°. *New Haven,* 1850-65,

Conradi (Andreas Christian). Cholera i Christiania og dens Omegn i aaret 1853. 8°. *Christiania,* 1854.

[*With* NORWAY. Actstykker ang. cholera-epidemien i Norge].

Constance Aylmer. A story of the 17th century. By H. F. P. [*anon.*] 347 pp. 12°. *New York, C. Scribner & co.* 1869.

Constant-Rebecque (Henri Benjamin de). Collection complète des ouvrages publiés sur le gouvernement représentatif et la constitution actuelle de la France, formant une espèce de cours de politique constitutionelle. 4 v. in 6. 8°. *Paris, etc. P. Plancher, etc.* 1817-20. s.

[v. 1-2 imperfect].

CONTENTS:

v. 1. Introduction; réflexions sur les constitutions et les garanties; esquisse de constitution; de la liberté des brochures, des pamphlets et des journaux.

v. 2. Observations sur le discours de le ministre de l'intérieur en faveur du projet de loi sur la liberté de la presse; de la responsabilité des ministres; de la doctrine politique qui peut réunir les partis en France; histoire de la session de la chambre des deputés, 1816-17; questions sur la législation actuelle de la presse en France.

v. 3. Des elections de 1817; entretien d'un électeur avec lui-même; réponse aux attaques dirigees contre lui pendant les élections; lettres et pièces relatives à Wilfred Regnault, condamné à mort; exposé de la prétendue conspiration de Lyon, en 1817; extrait du compte rendu de m. de Sainneville; lettres à m. Ch. Durand sur les protestants de Nimes; des élections de 1818; des réactions politiques; essai sur la contre-révolution d' Angleterre en 1660.

v. 4. Éloge de sir Samuel Romilly; annales de la session de 1817 à 1818; de la liberté des anciens; session des chambres de 1818 à 1819; première lettre à mm. les habitants du départment de la Sarthe; de l' opinion sur la nouvelle législation de la presse; seconde lettre à mm. les habitants du département de la Sarthe.

Constitution (The) [Washington daily]. April 13, 1859, to June 31, 1861. 4 v. fol. *Washington,* 1859-61.

——— The same. June 8, 1863, to June, 1868. 10 v. fol. *Washington, T. B. Florence,* 1863-68.

Contarini (Pietro). Frammento tratto dall' argoa voluptas. (Corografie dell' Istria, no. 8). 8°. *Trieste,* 1831.

[*In* ROSSETTI (D. de'). Archeografo triestino, v. 3].

Conversations-lexicon. (Allgemeine deutsche real-encyklopädie für die gebildeten stände). 8e original auflage. 12 v. 8°. *Leipzig, F. A. Brockhaus,* 1833-37. s.

——— The same. Universal register zur 8e aufl. des conversations-lexikon. viii, 283 pp. 8°. *Leipzig, F. A. Brockhaus,* 1839. s.

——— The same. Allgemeine deutsche real-encyklopädie für die gebildeten stände. Conversations-lexikon. 11e aufl. v. 11-14. Occu-Venedig. 8°. *Leipzig, Brockhaus,* 1867-68.

Conversations-lexikon der neuesten zeit und literatur. 4 v. 8°. *Leipzig, F. A. Brockhaus,* 1832-34. s.

Conway (James). Forays among salmon and deer. xii, 248 pp. 12°. *London, Chapman & Hall,* 1861.

Conyngham (*Capt.* David P.) Sherman's march through the south. With sketches and incidents of the campaign. 431 pp. 12°. *New York, Sheldon & co.* 1865.

Cook (James). A second voyage round the world in 1772-75. 2 p. l. 102 pp. 4°. *Lonon, J. Almon,* 1776.

——— A voyage towards the South Pole, and round the world, in 1772-75, [including] captain Furneaux's narrative of his proceedings in the adventure. 4th ed. 2 v. xl, 378 pp; 3 p. l. 396 pp. 1 map. 62 pl. 4°. *London, W. Strahan & T. Cadell,* 1784.

Cooke (*Miss* Anna B.) The home of the tulip, and other stories. 200 pp. 5 pl. 8°. *New York, gen. prot. episc. s. s. union,* 1867.

Cooke (George). Animals after the first masters, including Carl du Jardin, D. Stoop, Dietrich, Paul Potter, Berghem, Cuyp, [etc.] for examples in drawing. 1 p. l. 30 pp. obl. 4°. [*London, Moon, Boys, & Graves,* 1829]?

Cooke (John Esten). Fairfax; or, the master of Greenway court. A chronicle of the valley of the Shenandoah. 405 pp. 12°. *New York, Carleton & co.* 1868.

——— Mohun, or the last days of Lee and his paladins. Final memoirs of a staff officer serving in Virginia. From the mss. of col. Surrey of Eagles-nest. [*pseudon.*] 509 pp. 6 pl. 12°. *New York, F. J. Huntington & co.* 1869.

Cooke (M. C.) Index fungorum britannicorum. A complete list of fungi found in the British islands. 1 p. l. 58 pp. 8°. *London, R. Hardwicke,* [*about* 1864]. S.

——— A manual of botanic terms. iv, 90 pp. 27 pl. 16°. *London, R. Hardwicke,* [1862]. S.

——— A plain and easy account of British fungi; with descriptions of the esculent and poisonous species, and a tabular arrangement of orders and genera. viii, 148 pp. 24 col. pl. 16°. *London, R. Hardwicke,* 1862. S.

Cooley (Le Roy C.) A text book of natural philosophy; an accurate, modern, and systematic explanation of the elementary principles of the science. 315 pp. 12°. *New York, C. Scribner & co.* 1868.

Cooper (James Fenimore). The bravo: a tale. [*anon.*] 2 v. 240 pp; 236 pp. 12°. *Philadelphia, Carey & Lea,* 1831.

——— The headsman; or, the abbaye des vignerons: a tale. [*anon.*] 2 v. 263 pp; 261 pp. 12°. *Philadelphia, Carey, Lea & Blanchard,* 1833.

——— The heidenmauer; or, the benedictines. A legend of the Rhine. [*anon.*] 2 v. 226 pp; 248 pp. 12°. *Philadelphia, Carey & Lea,* 1832.

——— Homeward bound; or, the chase. A tale of the sea. [*anon.*] 2 v. 276 pp; 287 pp. 12°. *Philadelphia, Carey, Lea & Blanchard,* 1838.

——— The monikins. Edited by the author of The spy. [*anon.*] 2 v. 251 pp; 244 pp. 12°. *Philadelphia, Carey, Lea & Blanchard,* 1835.

——— Notions of the Americans: picked up by a travelling bachelor. [*anon.*] 2 v. 340 pp; 359 pp. 12°. *New York, Stringer & Townsend,* 1850.

——— The pathfinder; or, the inland sea. 2 v. 240 pp; 233 pp. 12°. *Philadelphia, Lea & Blanchard,* 1840.

——— The pilot: a tale of the sea. [*anon.*] 5th ed. 2 v. 295 pp; 268 pp. 12°. *Philadelphia, Carey & Lea,* 1833.

——— The pioneers; or, the sources of the Susquehanna. [*anon.*] 2 v. 284 pp; 327 pp. 12°. *Philadelphia, Carey & Lea,* 1832.

——— The red rover: a tale. 534 pp. 12°. *New York, Townsend & co.* 1859.

——— The spy: a tale of the neutral ground. [*anon.*] 2 v. v. 1. 7th ed. v. 2. 6th ed. 264 pp; 288 pp. 12°. *Philadelphia, Carey & Lea,* 1834.

——— Stories of the prairie, and other adventures of the border. Selected from the works of Cooper. 339 pp. 3 pl. 16°. *New York, Hurd & Houghton,* 1868.

——— The water-witch; or, the skimmer of the seas: a tale. [*anon.*] 2 v. 256 pp; 251 pp. 12°. *Philadelphia, Carey & Lea,* 1831.

——— The wept of Wish-ton-wish: a tale. [*anon.*] 2 v. 251 pp; 234 pp. 12°. *Philadelphia, Carey, Lea & Carey,* 1829.

Cooper (Peter). Letter on slave emancipation, [addressed to Abraham Lincoln]. 8 pp. 8°. *New York, W. C. Bryant & co.* 1863.
[LOYAL publication society, no. 23].

——— The death of slavery. Letter to gov. Seymour. [With] a letter to Abraham Lincoln. 12 pp. 8°. *New York,* 1863.
[LOYAL publication society, no. 28].

Cooper (Susan Fenimore). Mount Vernon: a letter to the children of America, [sketching the life of Washington]. 70 pp. 2 pl. 18°. *New York, Appletons,* 1859.

Cooper (Thomas, *bishop of Lincoln*). Cooper's chronicle. *See* **Lanquet** (T.)

Cooper (Thomas, *M. D. LL. D. formerly of Manchester*). [Observations on the chemical, philosophical, metaphysical, political, and miscellaneous writings and religious opinions of Joseph Priestley]. 1 v. in 2. 8°. *Northumberland, (Pa.) J. Binns,* 1806.
[*In* PRIESTLEY (J.) Memoirs. 1806. Appendices 1–5. pp. 223–481].

——— Political essays. 2d ed. 2 p. l. 88 pp. 8°. *Philadelphia, R. Campbell,* 1800.

——— Some information respecting [the United States of] America. 2d ed. 240 pp. 1 map. 8°. *London, J. Johnson,* 1795.

Cooper (*Rev.* W. D?) The history of North America. 4 p. l. 159 pp. 8 pl. 18°. *Lansingburgh, T. Spencer,* 1795.

Copeland. *See* **Copland.**

Copello (Juan, *M.D. of Lima*). Memoria sobre la profilaxis de la tisis pulmonar tuberculosa. 267 pp. 8°. *Lima, J. Enrique del Campo,* 1867. S.

——— Nuovo zoonomia, ovvero dottrina der rapporti organici. v. 2. Parte patologico ovvero filosofia della vita morbosa. 526 pp. 8°. *Lima, A. Alfaro y ca.* 1861. S.
[v. 1 wanting].

Copies and extracts of several newspapers printed in New England, in the months of September, October, and November, 1765, and referred to in the letters transmitted from Francis Bernard, esq. governor of the Massachusetts bay, to the lords commissioners for trade and plantations. 5, 108 pp. fol. [*n. p.* 1765]?

Copies of the informations and original papers relating to the proof of the horrid conspiracy against the late king, his present majesty, and the government. 1 p.l. 141 pp. fol. *London, T. Newcomb*, 1685.

[*With* SPRAT (T. *bishop*). True account and declaration of the horrid conspiracy, etc. 1685].

——— The same.

[*With* SPRAT (T. *bishop*). True account and declaration, etc. 2d ed. 1685].

——— The same. 3d ed. 207 pp. 16°. *London, T. Newcomb*, 1685.

Copland (Alexander). The existence of other worlds, peopled with living and intelligent beings, deduced from the nature of the universe. 210 pp. 12°. *London, J. G. & F. Rivington*, 1834.

——— The mummy awaked; a poetic contrast between the knowledge of the ancient Egyptians and that of modern times. 12°. *London, J. G. & F. Rivington*, 1834.

[*In* the preceding. pp. 167–210].

Coppée (Henry). Life and services of gen. U. S. Grant. [Revised ed.] 566 pp. 2 pl. 2 maps. 12°. *Chicago, western news co.* 1868.

Coppo (Pietro). Del sito dell' Istria, a Gioseffo Faustino. (Corografie dell' Istria, n. 2). 8°. *Trieste*, 1830.

[ROSETTI (D. de'). Archeografo triestino, v. 2].

Copway (George). The traditional history and characteristic sketches of the Ojibway nation. 266 pp. 2 pl. 12°. *Boston, B. B. Mussey & co.* 1851.

Cordier (Claude Simon). La vie de sainte Frémiat de Chantal, fondatrice de l'ordre de la visitation de Saint Marié. 2 p. l. 172 pp. 16°. *Orléans, Couret de Villeneuve*, 1768. s.

Cordier (Mathurin). Selecta colloquiorum centuria. Notis anglicis adspersa, a G. Willymot, usui scholarum. Ed. nova. 144 pp. 24°. *Edinburgi, Gul. Anderson*, 1783.

——— The same. [With English translation, by John Clarke]? vii, 168 pp. 24°. [*n. p. about* 1780]?

[Imperfect].

——— The same. Les colloqves, diuisez en quatre liures. Traduits de Latin en François, par Gabriel Chapuis Tour. Latin and French. 4 p. l. 598 pp. 32°. *Paris, I. Libert*, 1646.

Cordonnier (Hyacinthe). *See* **Saint Hyacinthe.**

Cordus (Euricius, *pseudon.*) *See* **Urbanus** (Henricus).

Cornelius (Peter von). Zwölf bilder zu Göthe's Faust. Gestochen von F. Ruscheweyh. 12 pl. fol. *Franckfurt am Main, J. F. Wenner*, [1816]. s.

Cornell (Sarah G.) Carl's home. 333 pp. 1 pl. 16°. *Boston, H. Hoyt*, 1867.

Corner (*Miss* Julia). The child's pictorial history of England. From the 13th London ed. 201 pp. 1 pl. 16°. *Philadelphia, H. F. Anners*, 1853. s.

Cornhill (The) magazine. July, 1867, to Dec. 1868. v. 16–18. 8°. *London, Smith, Elder & co.* 1867–68.

Cornwallis (Caroline Frances). Philosophical theories and philosophical experience. By a pariah. [*pseudon.*] 91 pp. 16°. *London, W. Pickering*, 1841.

[SMALL books on great subjects, No. 1].

——— Selections from [her] letters. Also some unpublished poems, original and translated. And "Philosophical theories and philosophical experience." xv, 482 pp. 8°. *London, Trübner & co.* 1864.

Cornwallis (Kinahan). A panorama of the new world. 2 v. viii, 430 pp; 300 pp. 12°. *London, T. C. Newby*, 1859.

Corréard (J.) Cours de dessin topographique à l'usage des officiers et sous officiers d'infanterie et du cavalerie, etc. xiii pp. 25 col. pl. obl. 4°. *Paris, J. Corréard*, 1852. s.

Cortes (Fernando). Historia de Nueva-España, aumentada con otros docvmentos, y notas por Francisco Antonio Lorenzana. 10 p. l. 400 pp. 9 l. 1 map. 32 plates. 4°. *México, Joseph Antonio de Hogal*, 177C.

——— Preclara de noua maris oceani hyspania narratio, [secunda narratio. Item de rebus, et insulis nouiter repertis]. 4 p. l. xlix, xii l. fol. *Norimberga, F. Peypus Arthimesius*, 1524.

[NOTE.—The 'tertia narratio,' which is frequently found with the above, is wanting in this copy].

Corvinus. *See* **Messala** Corvinus.

Corvinus a Belderen (Jan Arnoldus). Venatorius illustratus. *See* **Venatorius** (D.)

Costa (Christovam da). [Aromatum et medicamentorum in orientali India nascentium his toria]. Ed 2a. 4°. *Antverpiæ*, 1593.

[*In* ORTA (G. de). Aromatvm, etc. historia, 1593. pp. 241–312].

[Imperfect: title page and pp. 225–40 wanting].

Costa (Etbin Henrik, *editor*). Vodnikor spomenik, [*or*] Vodnik-album. Mit beiträgen von 86 verfassern. xii, 168 pp. 4 pl. 4°. *Laibach, I. v. Kleinmayr & F. Bamberg*, 1859. s.

Costard (J. P.) Lettre du lord Velford à milord Dirton, son oncle. Précédée d'une lettre de l'auteur. [*anon.*] 60 pp. 8°. *Paris, L'Esclapart,* 1765.

Coste (Xavier Pascal). Monuments modernes de la Perse. 3 p. l. 57 pp. 1 l. 71 pl. fol. *Paris, A. Morel,* 1867.

Costello (Dudley). Holidays with hobgoblins, and talks of strange things. 2 p. l. 332 pp. 4 pl. 16°. *London, John Camden Hotten,* 1861.

Costello (Louisa Stuart). Memoirs of Anne, duchess of Brittany, twice queen of France. xiv, 420 pp. 12°. *London, W. & F. G. Cash,* 1855.

Cotton (*Rev.* Alfred Johnson). Cotton's keepsake. Poems on various subjects, [with] autobiographical sketch, and a condensed history of the early [Indiana] settlements. 526 pp. portrait. 12°. *Cincinnati, Applegate & co.* 1858.

Cotton (Charles). Complete angler. *See* **Walton** (Izaak) *and* **Cotton.**

Cotton (*Rev.* Henry). A typographical gazetteer attempted. 2[d] series. xvi, 376 pp. 8°. *Oxford, Clarendon press,* 1866.

Cotton (*Rev.* John, *pastor at Boston, Mass.*) The bloudy tenent, washed and made white in the bloud of the lambe. Wherein the great questions of this present time are handled, viz: how farre liberty of conscience ought to be given to those that truly feare God? 195 pp. sm. 4°. *London, Hannah Allen,* 1647.

——— A briefe exposition of the whole book of Canticles. *See* **Bible,** *English.*

——— A briefe exposition of the whole book of Ecclesiastes. *See* **Bible,** *English.*

——— An exposition upon the 13th chapter of the Revelation. *See* **Bible,** *English.*

——— God's promise to his plantation. 3 p. l. 20 pp. sm. 4°. *London, John Bellamy,* 1630.

——— The keyes of the kingdom of heaven. Reprint. iv, 108 pp. 12°. *Boston, Tappan & Dennett,* 1843.

——— A modest and cleare answer to mr. Ball's discourse of set formes of prayer. 2 p. l. 49 pp. sm. 4°. *London, Henry Overton,* 1642.

——— The powring out of the seven vials: with an application to our time. 2 p. l. 156 pp. sm. 4°. *London, H. Overton,* 1645.

——— Reply to mr. [Roger] Williams, his examination. 144 pp. sm. 4°. *London, Hannah Allen,* 1647.

[*With* COTTON (John). Bloudy tenent, etc. *London,* 1647].

——— A treatise of the covenant of grace. 3[d] ed. 8 p. l. 233 pp. 16°. *London, Peter Parker,* 1671.

——— The way of the churches of Christ in New-England. 4 p. l. 116 pp. 2 l. sm. 4°. *London, Matthew Simmons,* 1645.

——— The way of congregational churches cleared. 2 p'ts in 1 v. 6 p. l. 104, 44 pp. sm. 4°. *London, M. Simmons,* 1648.

Cotton (*Rev.* John, *great grandson of preceding, pastor at Newton, Mass.*) Wisdom, knowledge, and the fear of God recommended to rulers and people. A sermon preached in Massachusetts, May 30th, 1753, being the day for the election of his majesty's council. 42 pp. 12°. *Boston, J. Draper,* 1753.

Cotton (*Sir* Robert). An exact abridgment of the records in the tower of London, from king Edward ii unto king Richard iii, of all the parliaments holden in each kings reign, and the several acts in every parliament: [with] the names and titles of all the dukes, marquesses, earls, viscounts, and barons, summoned to every of the said parliaments. Revised by William Prynne. 16 p. l. 716 pp. 71 l. fol. *London, W. Leake,* 1657.

Cottonian library. *See* **British Museum.**

Cottu (Charles). Des moyens de mettre la charte en harmonie avec la royauté. 2 p. l. 348 pp. 8°. *Paris, C. Gosselin,* 1828. s.

Country (The) gentleman. A journal for the farm, the garden, and the fireside, devoted to improvement in rural affairs, etc. Jan. 1853 to Dec. 1865. v. 1–26, in 25 v. 4°. *Albany, L. Tucker & son,* 1853–65.

Note.—After Dec. 1865, the Country gentleman was merged into the Cultivator and Country gentleman.

Courier du Bas-Rhin, Jan.–Dec. 1779. 2 v. Nos. 1–104. 838 pp. 4°. *Cleves, Sitzmann,* 1779.

[Imperfect: Nos. 72, 73, 75, and 92, wanting].

Courier de Boston. Nos. 1–26, 23 April, to 15 Oct. 1789. 206 pp. 4°. *Boston, S. Hall,* 1789.

[Imperfect: 1 l. wanting at the end.]

Courier de l'Europe, gazette anglo-françoise. July, 1778, to July, 1779. v. 4–5. 418, 7 pp; 416, 6 pp. 4°. *Londres, E. Cox,* 1778–9.

[Imperfect: vol. 4, t. p. and nos. 1-9 wanting; vol. 5, no. 17, wanting].

Cournot (Antoine Augustin). Des institutions d'instruction publique en France. viii, 575 pp. 8°. *Paris, Hachette,* 1864.

Court (The) sermon, 1674. [*anon.*] Supposed to have been written by Gilbert Burnet, bishop of Salisbury. viii, 54 pp. 1 facsimile. 8°. *Cincinnati, R. Clarke & co.* 1868.

Courtship and marriage. [*anon.*] iv, 308 pp. 12°. [*Boston, W. H. Piper & co.* 1868].

[*With* PHYSIOLOGY of marriage, etc. 1868].

Cousin (Victor). Cours de l'histoire de la philosophie. Introduction à l'histoire de la philosophie. Nouv. éd. 2 p. l. iv, 444 pp. 8°. *Paris, Didier*, 1841. s.

——— The same. Histoire de la philosophie du xviii[e] siècle. Nouv. éd. 2 v. 2 p. l. iv, 472 pp; 2 p. l. 513 pp. 8°. *Paris, Didier*, 1841. s.

Cousin Amy; or, home duties. [*anon.*] 216 pp. 18°. *Philadelphia, presby. board of pub.* 1868.

Cousin Franck's household; or, scenes in the old dominion. By Pocahontas. [*pseudon.*] 2[d] ed. vii, 259 pp. 1 pl. 12°. *Boston, Upham, Ford & Olmstead*, 1853. s.

Covarrubias Horozco (Sebastian de). Tesoro de la lengva castellana, o española. 10 p. l. 602, 79 pp. fol. *Madrid, L. Sanchez*, 1611.

Cowdery (M. F.) Elementary moral lessons. 261 pp. 12°. *Philadelphia, H. Cowperthwait & co.* 1856. s.

Cowing (John P.) & co. Catalogue of pumps, fire-engines, hydraulic rams, etc. 1867. [Illustrated]. 118 pp. 8°. *New York, Bradstreet press*, 1867.

Cowley (Charles). A history of Lowell, [Mass.] 2[d] revised ed. 235 pp. 9 pl. 12°. *Boston, Lee & Shepard*, 1868.

Cox (Edward). Companion to the sea medicine chest, and compendium of domestic medicine, etc. Revised by R. Davis. 1st Am. ed. 216 pp. 12°. *New York, S. S. & W. Wood*, 1851.

Cox (Homersham). Antient parliamentary elections. A history showing how parliaments were constituted, and representatives of the people elected in antient times. xiii, 200 pp. 8°. *London, Longmans*, 1868.

——— A history of the reform bills of 1866 and 1867. ix, 302 pp. 8°. *London, Longmans*, 1868.

Cox (Samuel Sullivan). A buckeye abroad; or, wanderings in Europe, and in the orient. 444 pp. 9 pl. 12°. *New York, G. P. Putnam*, 1852.

Cox (Sandford C.) The evangelist, and other poems. 134 pp. 18°. *Cincinnati, author*, 1867.

Coxe (*Rev.* Arthur Cleaveland). Halloween: a romaunt, with lays meditative and devotional, by the author of Christian ballads. 180 pp. 24°. *Philadelphia, J. B. Lippincott & co.* 1869.

——— Thoughts on the services: designed as an introduction to the liturgy, and an aid to its devout use. 2[d] ed. xxiv, 336 pp. 18°. *Baltimore, J. Robinson*, 1859.

Coxe (*Rev.* William). Account of the Russian discoveries between Asia and America, [with] the conquest of Siberia, and the history of the transactions and commerce between Russia and China. 4th ed. xxiv, 18, 500 pp. 5 maps. 1 pl. 8°. *London, Cadell & Davies*, 1803.

——— Travels into Poland, Russia, Sweden, and Denmark, interspersed with historical relations and political inquiries. 3 v. 8°. *Dublin, S. Price*, 1784.

Crafts (W. A.) The southern rebellion: being a history of the United States from the commencement of Buchanan's administration through the war for the suppression of the rebellion. 2 v. viii, 652 pp. 2 maps. 24 pl; 648 pp. 26 pl. 4°. *Boston, S. Walker*, 1862–67.

Craik (*Mrs.* Dinah Maria Muloch). The woman's kingdom. A love story. [*anon.*] 183 pp. 1 pl. 8°. *New York, Harpers*, 1868.

Crane (Anne Moncure). Emily Chester. 12°. *Boston, Ticknor & Fields*, 1867.

——— Opportunity. A novel. 336 pp. 12°. *Boston, Ticknor & Fields*, 1867.

Crantz *or* Cranz (David). Historie von Grönland; enthaltend die geschichte der dortigen mission der evangelischen brüder zu Neu-Herrnhut und Lichtenfels. 17 p. l. 1132 pp. 13 l. 2 maps. 4 pl. 16°. *Barby, Ebens*, 1765.

——— The same. 6 p. l. 402 pp. 2 maps. 4 pl. 16°. *Frankfurt und Leipzig*, 1779.

Crawford (Charles). An essay on the propagation of the gospel, in which there are numerous facts and arguments adduced to prove that many of the Indians in America are descended from the ten tribes. 2[d] ed. 154 pp. 12°. *Philadelphia, J. Humphreys*, 1801.

Crawford (John). Monumental designs. *See* **Schumacher** (Jacob) *and* **Crawford**.

Creamer (Hannah Gardner). Delia's doctors; or, a glance behind the scenes. 262 pp. 12°. *New York, Fowler & Wells*, 1852. s.

Creppin (J. Baptiste). Essai géologique sur le Jura suisse. 1 p. l. 152 pp. 1 col. map. 4°. *Delémont, Helg & Boéchat*, 1867. s.

Crévier (Jean Baptiste Louis). Rhétorique françoise. 2 v. xx, 304 pp; 282 pp. 16°. *Avignon, J. A. Joly*, 1812.

Cricketana. By the author of "The cricket field." [J. P. *anon.*] vi, 238 pp. 5 pl. 16°. *London, Longman*, 1865.

Crippen (William G.) Green peas, picked from the patch of Invisible Green, esq. [*pseudon.*] 311 pp. 12°. *Cincinnati, Moore, etc.* [1856]. s.

Crisis (The). [A weekly political newspaper]. No. 2–63. Jan. 28, 1775, to March 30, 1776. 7–406 pp. fol. *London, T. W. Shaw*, 1775–76.
[Imperfect: nos. 28 and 30, and extra no. Aug. 9, 1775, wanting].

Crisis (The). No. 17-64. 113-412 pp. fol. *London, T. W. Shaw*, 1775-76.
[No. 17 imperfect].

Critical and historical account of all the celebrated libraries in foreign countries, as well ancient as modern. By a gentleman of the Temple. [*anon.*] 18°. *London*, 1739.

Croffut (W. A.) *and* **Morris** (John M.) The military and civil history of Connecticut during the war of 1861-65. 892 pp. 12 pl. 8°. *New York, L. Bill*, 1868.

Croker (Thomas Crofton). Catalogue of a collection of ancient and mediæval rings and personal ornaments, formed for lady Londesborough. x, 88 pp. 2 pl. 4°. *London, printed for private reference*, 1853. s.

Croll (Oswaldus). Philosophy reformed and improved. The discovering the great and deep mysteries of nature. Made English, by H. Pinnell. 11 p. l. 226 pp. 16°. *London, L. Lloyd*, 1657.
[*With* PARACELSUS. Of chymical transmutation. 1657].

Croly (David G.) Seymour and Blair: their lives and services. With an appendix, containing a history of reconstruction. 275 pp. 3 pl. 16°. *New York, Richardson & co.* 1868.

Croly (*Rev.* George). The modern Orlando. [*anon.*] Cantos i-vii. New ed. 214 pp. 12°. *London, H. Colburn*, 1848.

——— Tales of the Great St. Bernard. [*anon.*] 3 v. 12°. *London, H. Colburn*, 1828.

——— The same. [*anon.*] 2 v. 240 pp; 242 pp. 12°. *New York, J. & J. Harper*, 1829.

Cromwell: a tragedy in five acts. [*anon.*] 124 pp. 12°. *New York, Dick & Fitzgerald*, [1868].

Cronstedt (Axel Fredrik). Essai d'une nouvelle minéralogie. Traduit du Suédois et de l'Allemand de Wiedman, par Dreux fils. 2 p. l. xxxvi, 391 pp. 16°. *Paris, P. F. Didot le jeune*, 1771. s.

Cronycke (Die) van Hollandt, Zeelandt, ende Vrieslant, beghinnende van Adams tiden tot die geboerte ons heren Jhesu, voertgaende tot den iare 1517. [*anon.*] 2 p. l. 435 l. 4. l. fol. *Leyden, Jan Seuerst*, 1517.
NOTE.—Known as "Divisie chronijk."

Crooked (The) elm; or, life by the way-side. [*anon.* By Thomas W. Higgins?] 452 pp. 1 pl. 12°. *Boston, author*, 1857. s.

Crooks (George R.) A first book in Greek. *See* **M'Clintock** (J.) *and* **Crooks.**

Cross (Maurice). Selections from the Edinburgh review; comprising the best articles in that journal, from its commencement to the present time. With dissertation and notes. 4 v. 8°. *London, Longmans*, 1833.

Crowfield (Christopher, *pseudon.*) *See* **Stowe** (*Mrs.* H. B.)

Crowquill (Alfred, *pseudon.*) *See* **Forrester** (Alfred Henry).

Croyland (*Abbey of.*) Historiæ croylandensis continuatio. [*anon.*] fol. *Oxoniæ*, 1684.
[GALE (T.) *and* FELL (J.) Rerum anglicarum scriptores veteres. v. 1. *Oxoniæ*, 1684].

Crüger (Hermann). Organographical observations on certain epigynous monocotyledons. 8°. *London*, 1853.
[*In* HENFREY (A.) *and* HUXLEY. Scientific memoirs, art. 6].

Cruikshank (J. *and* A.) Sabbath school gems of music and poetry; designed expressly for the sabbath school. 144 pp. obl. 16°. *New York, A. S. Barnes & co.* 1850. s.

Cruise (The); a poetical sketch, in eight cantos. By a naval officer. [*anon.*] xxiv, 448 pp. 8°. *London, J. Hatchard*, 1808.

Crusenstolpe (Fredrik). Koran. Öfversatt frän Arabiska. Historisk inledning, etc. 1843. *See* **Koran.**

Crusenstolpe (Magnus Jacob von). Der russische hof von Peter i. bis auf Nicolaus i. Und einer einleitung; Russland vor Peter dem ersten. [7-9 band fortgesetzt von C. Volckhausen]. 9 v. 16°. *Hamburg, Hoffmann & Campe*, 1855-60.

Cruttenden (D. H.) The objective or synthetic arithmetic, in which the science is learned from the art. First course. 396, vii pp. 12°. *New York, J. M. Bradstreet & son*, 1868.

Cudworth (Ralph, *D.D.*) The true intellectual system of the universe; wherein all the reason and philosophy of atheism is confuted, and its impossibility demonstrated. A treatise on immutable morality; with a discourse concerning the Lord's supper. With account of the author, by T. Birch. 1st Amer. ed. 2 v. 804 pp; 756 pp. 8°. *Andover, Gould & Newman*, 1837.

Cullerier (Auguste). Atlas of venereal diseases. Translated from the French, with notes and additions, by F. J. Bumstead, M.D. 328 pp. 26 pl. 4°. *Philadelphia, H. C. Lea*, 1868.

Cullum (*Bvt. maj. gen.* George W.) Biographical register of the officers and graduates of the U. S. military academy at West Point, N. Y. from its first establishment, 1802, to the army re-organization of 1866-67. 2 v. xvi, 619 pp; 665 pp. 8°. *New York, Van Nostrand*, 1868.

Culpepper (Nicholas). A guide to midwives. Enlarged. 3 p.l. [446] pp. 18°. [*London*, 1672].
[Title page wanting].

——— A physicall directory; or, a translation of the London dispensatory, made by the colledge of physicians in London. 9 p.l. 319 pp. [marked 345]. 12 l. 1 portrait. sm. 4°. *London, P. Cole*, 1649.

Cultivator (The), a monthly publication designed to improve the soil and the mind. Conducted by J. Buel, etc. v. 1-4. 1834–38. 4 v. in 2. 4°. *Albany, N. Y. state agricultural society*, 1837–38.

——— The same. v. 5-6. 1838–39. 2 v. in 1. fol. *Albany, Packard, Van Benthuysen & co.* 1838–39.

——— The same. v. 7-10. The cultivator, a consolidation of Buel's cultivator and Genesee farmer. W. Gaylord and L. Tucker, editors. (Cult. v. 7-10, 1840-43. Cult. and Farm. v. 1-4.) fol. *Albany, J. Buel & co.* 1840-43.

——— The same. [2d series.] The cultivator, a monthly journal devoted to agriculture, horticulture, etc. New series, 1844-52. 9 v. 8°. *Albany, L. Tucker, editor*, 1844-52.

——— The same. 3d series. The cultivator, a monthly journal for the farm and garden, etc. 1853-65. 13 v. 8°. *Albany, L. Tucker*, 1853-65.

——— The same. The cultivator and country gentleman. Devoted to the practice and science of agriculture and horticulture, etc. Jan. 1866, to June, 1868. v. 27-31. 4°. *Albany, L. Tucker & son*, 1866-68.

——— *See, also,* **Country** (The) gentleman. 1853–65. v. 1–26.

Culver (Richard). The practical reader. 502 pp. 12°. *Philadelphia, J. B. Lippincott & co.* 1855. S.

Cumberland (Richard, *LL. D.*) Memoirs. Written by himself. Containing an account of his life and writings, with anecdotes and characters of distinguished persons of his time. 356 pp. 8°. *New York, Brisban & Brannan*, 1806.

Cumings (Samuel). The western navigator; containing directions for the navigation of the Ohio and Mississippi. With charts. v. 2. 4, 238 pp. 8°. *Philadelphia, E. Littell*, 1822.

Cummings (Jacob A.) An introduction to ancient and modern geography. 3d ed. xx, 322 pp. 1 pl. 16°. *Boston, Cummings & Hilliard*, 1815.

Cummings (M. F.) *and* **Miller** (C. C.) Modern American architecture. Designs and plans for villas, farm-houses, city residences, etc. 19 l. 55 pl. fol. *Toledo, (O.) S. Baily & co.* 1868.

Cummins (Maria S.) Haunted hearts. A tale of New Jersey. New ed. viii, 342 pp. 18°. *London, Sampson Low, son, & Marston*, 1868.

Cupid's album. By Archie Argyle. [*pseudon.*] 332 pp. 12°. *New York, Doolady*, 1866.

Cureau de la Chambre (Marin). *See* **La Chambre.**

Currier (*Mrs.* Sophronia). Alice Tracy; or, faint, yet pursuing. 299 pp. 16°. *Boston, E. P. Dutton & co.* 1868.

Curson (Henry). A compendium of the laws and government, ecclesiastical, civil, and military, of Great Britain, and the plantations, with the maritime power thereof, and jurisdiction of courts therein. 2d ed. 7 p. l. 642 pp. 7 l. 16°. *London, J. Walthoe*, 1716.

Curtis (Newton M.) The prairie guide; or the rose of the Rio Grande. 100 pp. 8°. *New York, Garrett & co.* [1850]?

Curtis's botanical magazine. [Edited] by J. D. Hooker. 3d series. v. 23. [*or* v. 93]. 8°. *London, Reeve & co.* 1867.

Curtman (W. J. G.) Lehrbuch der erziehung und des unterrichts. i. Die erziehungslehre. ii. Die unterrichtslehre. 7e aufl. 2 v. xxviii, 420 pp; viii, 673 pp. 8°. *Leipzig, C. F. Winter*, 1866.

Cust (Emma Sophia, *countess Brownlow*). Slight reminiscence of a septuagenarian from 1802 to 1815. 2d ed. viii, 199 pp. 12°. *London, J. Murray*, 1867.

Cuvier (Georges Léopold Chrétien Frédéric Dagobert, *baron*). La ménagerie du muséum national. *See* **Lacépède** (B. G. E. de) *and* **Cuvier.**

——— Rapport historique sur les progrès des sciences naturelles depuis 1789, et sur leur état actuel, [etc.] xvi, 299 pp. 4°. *Paris, imprimerie imperiale*, 1810. S.

——— Recherches sur les ossemens fossiles, etc. 3e éd. 5 v. in 7. 4°. *G. Dufour & E. d'Ocagne*, 1825–26. S.

——— La règne animal distribué d'après son organisation, pour servir de base à l'histoire naturelle des animaux et d'introduction à l'anatomie comparée. Nouv. éd. publiée par une réunion de disciples de G. Cuvier. [With appendix]. Table alphabétique des auteurs cités. 10 v. in 20. 8°. *Paris, Fortin, Masson & cie*, [1836–46]. S.

Cuvier—continued.

CONTENTS.

v. 1. Mammifères et races humaines, avec un atlas, par Laurillard, Milne-Edwards, et Roulin. 1 v. in 2. xxxvi, 350 pp. 21 pl.
v. 2. Oiseaux, avec un atlas, par A. d'Orbigny.
v. 3. Reptiles, avec un atlas, par Duvernoy. 1 v. in 2. 169 pp. 46 col. pl.
v. 4. Poissons, avec un atlas, par Valenciennes. 1 v. in 2. 392 pp. 122 col. pl.
v. 5. Mollusques, avec un atlas, par Deshayes.
v. 6. Insectes, avec un atlas, par Audouin, Blanchard, Doyère, et Milne-Edwards. 1 v. in 4. xii, 557 pp; 443 pp. 202 col. pl.
v. 7. Arachnides, avec un atlas, par Dugès et Milne-Edwards. 106 pp. 31 col. pl.
v. 8. Crustacés, avec un atlas, par Milne-Edwards. 1 v. in 2. 278 pp. 80 col. pl.
v. 9. Annélides, avec un atlas, par Milne-Edwards. 54 pp. 30 col. pl.
v. 10. Zoophytes, avec un atlas, par Milne-Edwards, Blanchard, et de Quatrefages. 160 pp. 100 col. pl.

[v. 2 and v. 5 wanting].

Czermak (Johann N.) On the laryngoscope, and its employment in physiology and medicine. Translated from the French by G. D. Gibb; with additions, and appendix on rhinoscopy, by the author. 8°. *London*, 1861.

[NEW SYDENHAM society, v. 11].

Czörnig (Carl, *freiherr* von). Ethnographie der oesterreichischen monarchie. Herausgegeben durch die k. k. direction der administrativen statistik. 3 v. 4°. *Wien, k. k. hof- und staatsdruckerei*, 1857. S.

[*Note.*—A large map in 4 sections is wanting; a reduced colored copy is, however, bound with v. 1].

D'Abano (Pietro). *See* **Abano.**

Dabney (Robert L. *D.D.*) A defence of Virginia, [and, through her, of the South], in recent and pending contests against the sectional party. 356 pp. 8°. *New York, Hale & son*, 1867.

Dagg (John L. *D.D.*) The elements of moral science. 374 pp. 12°. *New York, Sheldon & co.* 1860. S.

Dagnall (John M.) The Mexican; or, love and land. Founded on the invasion of Maximilian. 228 pp. 1 pl. 18°. *New York, American news co.* 1868.

Dahl (Johann Christian Wilhelm). Versuch einer kirchlichen staatistik der Mecklenburg-Schwerin-Güstrowschen und Mecklenburg-Strelitzschenländer. 200 pp. 16°. *Rostock, Stiller*, 1809. S.

Daillé (Jean). A treatise on the right use of the fathers in the decision of controversies existing at this day in religion. From the French, by T. Smith. Re-edited and amended by G. Jekyll. 2[d] ed. xxiv, 359 pp. 8°. *London, H. G. Bohn*, 1843.

Daily (M. H.) The farmer's, liverres' and teamsters' guide, for handling, riding, and driving wild and vicious horses, with valuable receipts for curing various diseases of the horse. 62 pp. 8°. *Indianapolis, Downey & Brouse*, 1867.

Daily constitutional union. *See* **Constitutional** union (Washington daily).

Daily evening dispatch. [Washington]. April 30 to May 6, 1867. fol. *Washington, T. Z. Hoover & co.* 1867.

[No more published. *With* EVENING leader].

Daily (The) madisonian. *See* **Madisonian.**

Daily morning chronicle. [Washington]. J. W. Forney, editor. March 31, 1861, to June 30, 1868. 12 v. fol. *Washington, D. C. Forney*, 1861–68.

Daily national intelligencer. July, 1867, to June, 1868. 2 v. fol. *Washington, Snow, Coyle & co.* 1867–68.

Daily (The) times. [Washington]. March 15, 1864, to December 30, 1865. v. 1–4. 2 v. fol. *Washington, W. D. Hughes*, 1864–65.

Daily (The) true delta. [New Orleans]. Nov. 1860, to May, 1862. 3 v. fol. *New Orleans, J. Maginnis*, 1860–62.

Daily (The) union. [Washington]. May 1, 1845, to April 10, 1858. 25 v. fol. *Washington*, 1845–59.

Dalechamps (Jacques). De l'histoire genéralé des plantes, tome second: avqvel sont representées et descriptés plusieurs sortes de plantes par mesme ordre qu'au premier. Avec vn ample index contenant les vertvs des simple médicaments. Faite français par Jean Des Moulins. [*anon.*] 60 p. l. 758 pp. 15 l. fol. *Lyon, héritiers Guil. Rouille*, 1615. S.

[v. 1 wanting.]

Dalgairns (John Bernard). The devotion to the heart of Jesus. With an introduction on the history of Jansenism. 1st American from 2[d] London ed. 284 pp. 1 pl. 18°. *Baltimore, J. Murphy & co.* 1855. S.

Dallas (William Sweetland). Zoology. 8°. *London*, 1855.

[*In* ORR (W. S.) Circle of the sciences; organic nature. v. 2].

Dalrymple (Alexander). Letter to dr. [John] Hawkesworth, [concerning the existence of a southern continent]. 18 l. 4°. [*London*, 1773]?

[*With* COOK (James). Second voyage round the world. 4°. *London*, 1776].

Dalrymple (*Sir* John). Memoirs of Great Britain and Ireland; from the dissolution of the last parliament of Charles ii, till the capture of the French and Spanish fleets at Vigo. New ed. 3 v. 8°. *London, Strahan*, 1790.

Dalton (John Call). A treatise on physiology and hygiene. 399 pp. 12°. *New York, Harpers,* 1868.

Daly (Augustin). A legend of "Norwood;" or, village life in New England. An original dramatic comedy of American life. Founded on a novel by rev. H. W. Beecher. 79 l. 8°. *New York, author,* 1867.

Dalyell (*Sir* John Graham). The powers of the creator displayed in the creation; or, observations on life amidst the various forms of the humbler tribes of animated nature [etc.] 2 v. 1 p. l. vi, 286 pp. 70 col. pl; xiii, 359 pp. 46 [47] col. pl. 4°. *London, J. Van Voorst,* 1851–53.

——— The same. v. 3. To which is prefixed a memoir of the author. (Supplemental volume). li, 113 pp. 1 portrait. 28 pl. 4°. *London, J. Van Voorst,* 1858.

Dalzell (James M). John Gray, of Mount Vernon; the last soldier of the revolution. Born 1764; died 1868. 64 pp. 8°. *Washington, Gibson brothers,* 1868.

Dana (Charles A.) *and* **Wilson** (J. H.) The life of Ulysses S. Grant, general of the armies of the United States. xvi, 424 pp. 4 maps. 1 portrait. 8°. *Springfield, Gurdon Bill & co.* 1868.

Dana (*Mrs.* Eliza A.) The broken fold: poems of memory and consolation. 124 pp. 16°. *New York, A. D. F. Randolph,* 1868.

Dana (James Dwight). Manual of mineralogy With illustrations. 2[d] ed. 432 pp. 16°. *New Haven, Durrie & Peck,* 1849.

——— *and* **Brush** (George Jarvis). A system of mineralogy. Descriptive mineralogy, comprising the most recent discoveries. 5th ed. xlviii, 827 pp. 8°. *New York, J. Wiley & son,* 1868.

Daniel (*Rev.* Ch.) Des études classiques dans la société chrétienne. 445 pp. 8°. *Paris, Julian Lanier & cie.* 1853. S.

Daniel (Samuel). The collection of the history of England. [To Edward iii, inclusive]. 4 p. l. 262 pp. sm. fol. *London, S. Waterson,* 1634.

Danielssen (Daniel Cornelius). Fauna littoralis Norvegiae. fol. 1856. *See* **Sars** (M.), **Koren** (J.) *and* **Danielssen.**

——— *and* **Boeck** (Wilhelm). Traité de la spédalskhed ou éléphantiasis des Grecs. Tradit du Norwégien sous les yeux de mr. D. Danielssen, par L. A. Casson (de Nogaret). xxiii, 535 pp. 8°. Atlas. 24 col. pl. 4°. *Paris, J. B. Baillière,* 1848.
[Atlas wanting].

Dante Alighieri. Göttliche comödie. Metrisch übertragen und mit kritischen und historischen erläuterungen versehen von Philalethes. [*pseudon.* der könig Johann von Sachsen.] Neue ausg. nebst einem portraite Dantes, einer karte und zwei grundrissen der hölle. 3 v. 8°. *Leipzig, B. G. Teubner,* 1865-66. S.

Darby (William). A geographical description of the state of Louisiana. 270 pp. 9 l. xvii pp. 1 map. 8°. *Philadelphia, J. Melish,* 1816.

——— View of the United States, historical, geographical, and statistical. 654 pp. 11 maps. 18°. *Philadelphia, H. S. Tanner,* 1828.

Darley (Felix O. C.) Illustrations of Rip Van Winkle; etched. 11 pp. 6 pl. obl. fol. [*New York, American art union,* 1849].

——— Sketches abroad with pen and pencil. vii, 191 pp. 14 pl. 12°. *New York, Hurd & Houghton,* 1868.

Darras (J. E.) A general history of the catholic church; from the commencement of the christian era until the present time. 1st Am. from the last Fr. ed. With an introduction and notes, by M. J. Spalding. v. 4. 8°. *New York, P. O'Shea,* 1866.

Dartmouth (*Massachusetts*). Centennial celebration. Proceedings in connection with the celebration at New Bedford, Sept. 14, 1864, of the two hundredth anniversary of the incorporation of the town of Dartmouth. 129 pp. 8°. *New Bedford, (Mass.) city council,* 1865. S.

Darwin (Charles). The variation of animals and plants under domestication. 2 v. viii, 411 pp; viii, 486 pp. 8°. *London, J. Murray,* 1868.

——— The same. With a preface, by Asa Gray. With illustrations. 2 v. 494 pp; 568 pp. 12°. *New York, O. Judd & co.* 1868.

Dassié (F.) Le routier des Indes orientales et occidentales. Avec vingt-six différentes navigations. 1 p. l. 202 pp. 4°. *Paris, J. de la Caille,* 1677.

Dauban (C. A.) *See* **Mémoires** inédits de Pétion, etc.

Daubenton (Louis Jean Marie). Instruction pour les bergers et pour les propriétaires de troupeaux; avec d'autres ouvrages sur les moutons et sur les laines. [Avec un] discours sur la vie et les ouvrages de Daubenton. 3e éd. avec des notes. lxiv, 536 pp. 8°. *Paris, l'imprimerie de la république,* 1803.

——— Histoire naturelle. *See* **Buffon** (G. L. L. *comte* de), and **Daubenton.**

Daubrée (Gabriel Auguste). Description géologique et minéralogique du departement du Bas-Rhin. xvi, 500 pp. 1 col. map, 5 col. pl. 8°. *Strasbourg, E. Simon,* 1852. S.

Daughters of the cross; or, the cottage and the palace. [*anon.*] 228 pp. 16°. *New York, American tract society*, 1868.

Davenant (Charles, *LL. D.*) A discourse upon grants and resumptions. Shewing how our ancestors have proceeded with such ministers as have procured grants to themselves of the crown revenue. [With observations on the Roman revenues. *anon.*] 3[d] ed. 12 p. l. 448 pp. 12°. *London, J. Knapton*, 1704.

——— Discourses on the public revenues, and on the trade of England. [*anon.*] 2 v. 7 p. l. 280 pp; 4 p. l. 434 pp. 12°. *London, J. Knapton*, 1698.

——— An essay on the East India trade. [*anon.*] 64 pp. 12°. *London, J. Knapton*, 1698.

[*With* DAVENANT (C.) Essay upon the ballance of trade. 1700].

——— An essay upon the probable methods of making a people gainers in the ballance of trade. [*anon.*] 8 p. l. 204 pp. 12°. *London, J. Knapton*, 1700.

——— Essays upon the ballance of power. The right of making war, peace, and alliances. Universal monarchy. [With] appendix. [*anon.*] 288, 125 pp. 16°. *London, J. Knapton*, 1701.

——— Essays upon peace at home, and war abroad. 2[d] ed. v. 1. 12 p. l. 425 pp. 16°. *London, J. Knapton*, 1704.

——— A report to the commissioners of publick accounts of the kingdom. 2 parts in 1 v. 78 pp; 75 pp. 12°. *London*, 1712.

Davidson (Samuel, *D. D.*) An introduction to the study of the new testament, critical, exegetical, and theological. 2 v. xx, 520 pp; vi, 547 pp. 8°. *London, Longmans*, 1868.

Davies (Charles, *LL.D.*) Arithmetic. 340 pp. 12°. *Philadelphia, A. S. Barnes & co.* 1843. s.

——— The same. School arithmetic. Revised ed. 336 pp. 12°. *Philadelphia, A. S. Barnes & co.* 1855. s.

——— Elementary geometry, with applications in mensuration. 216 pp. 12° *Philadelphia, A. S. Barnes & co.* 1842. s.

——— Elements of analytical geometry. Revised ed. 352 pp. 8°. *New York, A. S. Barnes & co.* 1849.

——— Elements of descriptive geometry. 174 pp. 34 pl. 8°. *New York, A. S. Barnes & co.* 1859.

——— Key to Davies' Bourdon, with many additional examples, illustrating the algebraic analysis, [etc.] 205 pp. 8°. *New York, A. S. Barnes & co.* 1856. s.

——— Key to Davies' elementary algebra, [etc.] 99 pp. 12°. *Philadelphia, A. S. Barnes & co.* 1842. s.

Davies (Hugh). Faunula indica. *See* **Latham** (John) *and* **Davies.**

Davies (Walter). General view of the agriculture and domestic economy of North Wales; containing the counties of Anglesey, Caernarvon, Denbigh, Flint, Meirionydd, Montgomery. xvi, 510 pp. 1 col. map. 2 pl. 8°. *London*, 1810.

[GREAT BRITAIN. Board of agriculture].

——— General view of the agriculture and domestic economy of South Wales; containing the counties of Brecon, Caermarthen, Cardigan, Glamorgan, Pembroke, Radnor. 2 v. xvii, 613 pp. 1 col. map. 1 col. pl.; vi, 536 pp. 1 map. 8°. *London*, 1815.

[GREAT BRITAIN. Board of agriculture].

Davila Padilla (Agustin). Historia de la fvndacion y discvrso de la provincia, de Santiago de Mexico, de la orden de predicadores por las vidas de sus varones insignes y casos notables de Nueua España. Ed. 2[a]. 4 p. l. 654 pp. 3 l. fol. *Brvsselas, Ivan de Meerbeqve*, 1625.

Daviot (D. Z.) On diphtherite. [1845]. 8°. *London*, 1859.

[NEW SYDENHAM society. v. 3].

Davis (Andrew Jackson). Memoranda of persons, places, and events, embracing authentic facts, visions, impressions, discoveries, in magnetism, clairvoyance, spiritualism. Also quotations from the opposition. With appendix. 488 pp. 12°. *Boston, W. White & co.* 1868.

——— The penetralia; being harmonial answers to important questions. 328 pp. 8°. *Boston, B. Marsh*, 1856. s.

——— The present age and inner life; ancient and modern spirit mysteries classified and explained. A sequel to spiritual intercourse. 424 pp. 3 pl. 12°. *Boston, W. White & co.* 1869.

——— A stellar key to the summer land. Illustrated with diagrams and engravings of celestial scenery. Part i. viii, 202 pp. 12°. *Boston, W. White & co.* 1867.

Davis (Caroline E. Kelley). The upward path. 330 pp. 1 pl. 12°. *Boston, H. Hoyt*, 1868.

Davis (Eliza B.) Edith; or, the light of home. 282 pp. 12°. *Boston, Crosby, Nichols & co.* 1856. s.

Davis (James J. *M.D.*) A guide to health. Containing a short and concise mode of treatment for most forms of disease to which man is liable, with sanative agents. 190 pp. 16°. *New York, Oakley & Mason,* 1868.

Davis (John). The first settlers of Virginia; an historical novel. xii, 284 pp. 12°. *New York, J. Riley & co.* 1805.

Davis (*Rev.* John). Elements of astronomy. 343 pp. 19 pl. 12°. *Philadelphia, Lippincott & co.* 1868.

——— An introduction to astronomy. 205, 333–343 pp. 16 pl. 12°. *Philadelphia, Lippincott & co.* 1868.

[NOTE.—The same as part 1 of his Elements of astronomy].

Davis (Mary F.) History of the introduction of the harmonial philosophy into Germany. 12°. *Boston, W. White & co.* 1868.

[*In* DAVIS (A. J.) Memoranda of persons, etc. pp. 465–488. 12°. 1868].

Davis (Thomas, *of Longleat*). General view of the agriculture of Wiltshire. xix, 268 pp. 1 col. map. 2 pl. 8°. *London,* 1811.

[GREAT BRITAIN: Board of agriculture].

Davis (W. W. H.) History of the Hart family, of Warminster, Bucks county, Pennsylvania. [With] the genealogy of the family, from its first settlement in America. Printed privately. 139, 20 pp. 1 pl. 8°. *Doylestown, (Pa.) W. W. H. Davis,* 1867.

Davis (Z. A.) The freemason's monitor; containing a delineation of the fundamental principles of freemasonry. With explanations and plates of all the emblems of the degrees; also, constitutions, regulations. New ed. 380 pp. 28 pl. 12°. *Philadelphia, J. B. Lippincott & co.* 1856. S.

Davison (G. M.) The traveller's guide through the middle and northern states. 8th ed. 395 pp. 1 map. 18°. *Saratoga Springs, G. M. Davison,* 1840.

Dawn. [A novel. *anon.*] 404 pp. 12°. *Boston, Adams & co.* 1868.

Dawson (C. C.) Saratoga; its mineral waters, and their use in preventing and eradicating disease, and as a refreshing beverage. [Illustrated]. 34 l. 1 map. 32°. *New York, Russell bros.* 1868.

Dawson (Henry B.) The sons of liberty in New York. Read before the New York historical society, May 3d, 1859. 118 pp. 8°. *New York,* 1859.

Dawson (Thomas, *D.D.*) Memoirs of St. George, the English patron, and of the most noble order of the garter. 9 p. l. 336 pp. 1 pl. 12°. *London, Henry Clements,* 1714.

Day (Horace). The opium habit, with suggestions as to the remedy. [*anon.*] 335 pp. 12°. *New York, Harpers,* 1868.

Dean (Amos, *LL.D.*) The history of civilization. In seven volumes. v. 1. xxiv, 695 pp. 1 portrait. 8°. *Albany, J. Munsell,* 1868.

Deane (Charles). Bibliographical tracts. No. 1. Spurious reprints of early books. ["Salem witchcraft; Calef's More wonders of the invisible world; and Mather's Wonders of the invisible world." *anon.*] 19 pp. 8°. *Boston, Cambridge university press,* 1865.

——— Communication [to the Mass. hist. soc. 1866–67], respecting the seal of the "council for New England." 4 pp. 8°. [*Cambridge, Mass.* 1867].

——— Remarks on Sebastian Cabot's mappemonde. From the proceedings of the Amer. antiq. soc. April, 1867. 8 pp. 8°. *Cambridge,* [*Mass.*] *J. Wilson & sons,* 1867.

Dearborn (Benjamin). The columbian grammar. With notes critical and explanatory. 2 p. l. 140 pp. 16°. *Boston, S. Hall,* 1795.

De Beck (William L.) Murder will out. The first step in crime leads to the gallows. The horrors of the queen city. By an old citizen. [*anon.*] 128 pp. 8°. *Cincinnati,* 1867.

Debrett (John). Correct peerage of the united kingdom of Great Britain and Ireland. 7th ed. 2 v. lxviii, 1073, 18 pp. 89 pl. 18°. *London, J. D. Dewick,* 1809.

——— Parliamentary papers. *See* **Great Britain.**

——— Parliamentary register. *See* **Great Britain.**

Debrett's illustrated baronetage, with the knightage, of Great Britain and Ireland, 1868. xvi, 644, 55 pp. 16°. *London, Dean & son,* 1868.

——— Illustrated peerage of Great Britain and Ireland, 1868. xxxi, 650, 55 pp. 16°. *London, Dean & son,* 1868.

De Bry (Theodore). *See* **Bry** (T. de).

De Burgh (William). The elements of maritime international law, with a preface on some unsettled questions of public law. xlix, 238 pp. 8°. *London, Longmans,* 1868.

Decker (Thomas). The gull's hornbook: imprinted at London for R. S. 1609. [Reprint]. vi, 44 pp. 16°. *London, W. McMullen,* 1862.

De Costa (B. F.) Lake George: its scenes and characteristics, with glimpses of the olden times. [With] some account of Ticonderoga, with a description of the route to Schroon lake and the Adirondacks. With notes of lake Champlain. 181, xiv pp. 1 map. 8 pl. 18°. *New York, A. D. F. Randolph,* 1868.

Deems (Charles, *D. D.*) Annals of southern methodism for 1855. [With historical sketches]. 385 pp. 12°. *New York*, 1856.

Defoe (Daniel). A true collection of the writings of the author of the true born English-man. 2d ed. corrected and enlarged by himself. 12 p. l. 470 pp. 1 pl. 8°. *London*, 1705.

CONTENTS.

Argument [in favor of a] standing army.
Character of dr. Samuel Annesley.
Danger of the protestant religion.
Enquiry into occasional conformity.
Enquiry into the occasional conformity of dissenters.
Freeholders plea against stock-jobbing elections.
Letter to mr. How.
Mock-mourners, a satyr.
New test of the church of England's loyalty.
Original paper of the collective body of the people of England, examined and arrested.
Poor man's plea.
Reasons against a war with France.
Six distinguishing characters of a parliament man.
Shortest way with the dissenters.
Spanish descent, a poem.
True born English-man, a satyr.
Two great [political Spanish succession] questions considered.

——— Jure divino, a satyr. By the author of the true born Englishman. [*anon.*] xliv, v, 278 pp. 1 pl. 12°. *London*, 1706.

——— The life and strange surprising adventures of Robinson Crusoe, of York, mariner. 356 pp. 8 pl. 12°. *New York, Hurd & Houghton*, 1868.

——— Memoirs of capt. George Carleton, who served in the two last wars against France and Spain, [with] an account of the conduct of the earl of Peterborough. [*anon.*] 4 p. l. 352 pp. 12°. *London, T. Astley*, 1743.

——— A plan of the English commerce. 3 p. l. xvi, 368 pp. 12°. *London, C. Rivington*, 1727.

——— A treatise concerning the use and abuse of the marriage bed. [*anon.*] 4 p. l. 406 pp. 12°. *London, T. Warner*, 1727.

——— A true relation of the apparition of one Mrs. Veal, to one Mrs. Bargrave, at Canterbury, 1705. [*anon.*] 13th ed. 2 p. l. 12 pp. 12°. [*London, D. Midwinter*, 1732].

[*With* DRELINCOURT (C.) Christian's defence against the fears of death, 1732].

De Kroyft (S. Helen). A place in thy memory. 191 pp. 1 pl. 12°. *New York, J. F. Trow*, 1850. S.

De la Borde (*Le sieur*). *See* **La Borde**.

Delacour (Alfred Charlemagne Lartigue, *known as*). La cagnotte. *See* **Labiche** (E. M.) *and* **Delacour**.

Delafosse (Gabriel, *de l'institut*). Nouveau cours de minéralogie, comprenant la description de toutes les espèces minérales, avec leur applications directes aux arts. 3 v. Atlas. 24 pp. 40 pl. 8°. *Paris, Roret*, 1858–62. S.

Delbée (—— *Sieur*). Journal dv voyage aux isles dans la Guinée. 18°. *Paris*, 1671.

[*In* CLODORÉ (J. de). Relation de ce qui s'est passé, etc. v. 2. pp. 345–394].

Delepierre (Joseph Octave). Historical difficulties and contested events. [With a bibliographical index]. 179 pp. 12°. *London, J. Murray*, 1868.

De Lesdernier (Emily Pierpont). Headland home; or, a soul's pilgrimage. 346 pp. 12°. *New York, J. Miller*, 1868.

——— Hortense. The last of a noble name. A romance of real life. 362 pp. 12°. *New York, W. Maxwell & co.* 1867.

Deleuze (Joseph Philippe François). Practical instruction in animal magnetism. Translated [with an appendix] by T. C. Hartshorn. Revised ed. 12°. *New York, Appleton & co.* 1846.

Deliciae lvsitano-hispanicæ: in quibus continentur de magnitudine hispanici imperii relatio: noui orbis regionum à Lusitanis subactarum breuis descriptio. De Lusitania ceteræ Hispaniæ adiuncta historia. [*anon.*] 48 pp. 18°. *Coloniæ Agrippinæ, Greuenbruch*, 1613.

Delille (C. J.) Condensed French instruction, consisting of grammar and exercises with cross references. 2d American ed. 143 pp. 18°. *New York, Leypoldt & Holt*, 1868.

——— Elements of French grammar. 57 pp. 16°. *New York, Leypoldt & Holt*, 1867.

[*With* BELLENGER (W. A.) *and* WITCOMB. Guide to French conversation. Am. ed. 1867].

——— The same. 57 pp. 16°. *New York, Leypoldt & Holt*, 1868.

[*With* FISHER (E. T.) Easy French reading. 1868].

Deli (William) *and others*. The doctrines of baptism, and the Lord's supper. 148 pp. 16°. *Philadelphia, Kimber & Conrad*, 1811.

Del Rio (Andres, *professor of mineralogy at Mexico*). Elementos de orictognosia, ó del conocimiento de los fosiles, segun el sistema de Bercelio, y segun los principios de A. G. Werner. Con la sinonimia inglesa, alemana y francesa. Parte práctica. 2a ed. vii, 682 pp. 8°. *Filadelfia, J. F. Hurtel*, 1832. S.

[Last leaf of index wanting].

Democratic (National) convention. Official proceedings of the national democratic convention, held in Cincinnati. June 2–6, 1856. 78 pp. 8°. *Cincinnati, Enquirer co.* 1856.

Democratic (The) speaker's hand-book. Compiled by Matthew Carey, jr. [*pseudon?*] 395 pp. 8°. *Cincinnati, Miami print*, 1868.

Democritus: or, the laughing philosopher. [*anon.*] x, 192 pp. 16°. *London, J. Hornton*, [*about* 1784].

Demogeot (Jacques Claude). Histoire de la littérature française depuis ses origines jusqu'en 1830. iv, 668 pp. 12°. *Paris, J. Hachette & cie.* 1852.

—— The same. 3e ed. viii, 678 pp. 16°. *Paris, J. Hachette & cie.* 1857.

Demorest's monthly magazine and mme. Demorest's mirror of fashions. Jan. 1866, to Dec. 1868. v. 2–4. 4°. *New York, W. J. Demorest,* 1866–68.

Demorest's parlor annual and illustrated ladies' almanac. 48 pp. 4°. *New York, office of "Demorest's Monthly,"* 1869.

Demorest's young America. A boys' and girls' monthly magazine. Nov. 1866, to Oct. 1868. v. 1–2. sq. 16°. *New York, W. J. Demorest,* 1866–68.

Demosthenes *and* **Æschines.** [Orations for the crown, translated into English by Thomas Dawson]. 25 p. l. 318 pp. 8°. [*London,* 1732].

[Imperfect: title-page, etc. wanting].

Denison (*Rev.* Charles Wheeler). Winfield [S. Hancock], the lawyer's son, and how he became a major general. 323 pp. 4 pl. 12°. *Philadelphia, Ashmead & Evans,* 1865.

Denison (Edmund Beckett, *LL. D.*) A rudimentary treatise on clocks, and watches and bells. With illustrations. 5th ed. viii, 424 pp. 1 pl. 16°. *London, Virtue & co.* 1868.

Denison (John L. *editor*). An illustrated history of the new world: containing a general history of all the various nations, states, and republics of the western continent, comprising a complete history of the United States to the present time. 868 pp. 33 pl. 8°. *Norwich, (Conn.) H. Bill,* 1868.

Denison (*Mrs.* Mary Andrews). Among the squirrels. iv, 327 pp. 8 pl. 12°. *New York, G. Routledge & sons,* 1868.

—— Carrie Hamilton; or, the beauty of true religion. 296 pp. 1 pl. 12°. *Philadelphia, Am. baptist pub. society,* 1855. s.

—— Led to the light. A sequel to "Opposite the jail." 352 pp. 3 pl. 16°. *Philadelphia, J. S. Claxton,* 1867.

—— Orange leaves. [Sketches and essays]. 384 pp. 7 pl. 12°. *Philadelphia, J. B. Lippincott & co.* 1856. s.

Denmark. Valdemar den andens jydske lov, efter den flensborgske codex-tilligemed den 1590 foranstaltede ny udgave af loven, og den af Ekenberger 1593 besörgede plattydske oversættelse af samme, udgivne ved P. G. Thorsen. 307 pp. 1 pl. 12°. *Kjöbenhavn, Berlingske bogtrykkeri,* 1853. s.

Denton (William). The past and future of our planet; or, lectures on geology. 343 pp. 12°. *Boston, W. Denton,* 1868.

De Palaidor. [*pseudon.*] *See* **Puslé de Montpleinchant** (J. C.)

De Peyster (J. Watts). The decisive conflicts of the late civil war, or slaveholders' rebellion. Battles morally, territorially, and militarily decisive. [No. 3. The Pennsylvania-Maryland campaign of June–July, 1863]. 163 pp. 8°. *New York, Macdonald & co.* 1867.

Depping (Georges Bernard). Merveilles et beautés de la nature en France, ou description de tout ce que la France offre de curieux et d'intéressant, [etc.] 2e éd. 535 pp. 1 map. 4 pl. 12°. *Paris, A. Eymery,* 1812.

De Quincey (Thomas). Letters to a young man whose education has been neglected. 162 pp. 16°. *Philadelphia, J. Penington,* 1843. s.

Derby (George, *M. D.*) An inquiry into the influence upon health of anthracite coal, when used as fuel for warming dwelling-houses; with some remarks upon special evaporating apparatus. 46 pp. 18°. *Boston, A. Williams & co.* 1868.

Derheims (Jean Lambert). Histoire naturelle et médicale des sangsues. 168 pp. 6 pl. 8°. *Paris, J. B. Baillière,* 1825. s.

Dernier (Le) des protocoles, ou quelques chapitres de l'histoire de la Belgique, 1830–38. Par un ancien diplomate français. [*anon.*] viii, 210 pp. 8°. *Paris, Ledoyen,* 1838. s.

Desault (Pierre Joseph). Œuvres chirurgicales, ou exposé de la doctrine et de la pratique de P. J. Desault, par Xav. Bichat. 3e éd. 3 v. 8°. *Paris, Méquignon,* 1813.

CONTENTS.

v. 1. Maladies des parties dures.
v. 2. Maladies des parties molles.
v. 3. Maladies des voies urinaires.

Desbordes Valmore (Marceline Josèphe Félicité Desbordes, *madame*). L'atelier d'un peintre. Scènes de la vie privée. 2 v. viii, 370 pp; 2 p. l. 314 pp. 12°. *Paris, Charpentier,* 1823.

Des Cloizeaux (A.) Manuel de minéralogie. v. 1. 2 p. l. 1, 572 pp. 22, 52 pl. 8°. *Paris, Dunod,* 1862. s.

[v. 2 not yet published, 1868].

Description of the city of Canton, with an appendix, containing an account of the Chinese empire, Chinese weights and measures, and the imports and exports of Canton. [*anon.*] 2d ed. 1 p. l. v, 188 pp. 1 map. 8°. *Canton,* 1839. s.

Desessarts (Toussaint Nicolas Lemoyne, *known as*). Précis historique de la vie, des crimes et de supplice de Robespierre, et de ses principaux complices. 247 pp. 1 portrait. 16°. *Paris, A. Stapleaux, etc.* 1797.

Desfontaines (*Abbé* Pierre François Guyot). Histoire des ducs de Bretagne, [etc.] v. 5-6. *See* **Galet** (J.) Dissertation historique sur l'origine des Bretons, etc.

Deshoulières (Antoinette du Ligier de Lagarde, *and* Antoinette Thérèsa). Œuvres de madame et de mademoiselle Deshoulières. 2e éd. 3 v. in 2. 18°. *Paris, Lemarchand,* 1802.

Desmarets (Jean, *seigneur de St. Sorlin*). Ariana. [A romance]. In two parts. Translated out of the French. [*anon.*] 2 p. l. 328 pp. sm. fol. *London, T. Walkley,* 1636.

——— Les ievx de cartes des roys de France, des reines renommées, de la géographie et des fables. Par I. D. M. 5 p. l. 60 pp. 52 pl. 24°. *Paris, F. Lambert,* 1664.

Des Marets (Samuel *and* Henry). *See* **Bible,** (*French, protestant*). fol. 1669.

De Smet (Peter J.) Letters and sketches, with a narrative of a year's residence among the Indian tribes of the Rocky mountains. 244, 12 pp. 12°. *Philadelphia, M. Fithian,* 1843.

——— Missions de l'Orégon, et voyages aux Montagnes-Rocheuses, aux sources de la Colombie, de l'Athabasca et du Sascatshawin, en 1845-46. ix, 589 pp. 12°. *Gand, Van der Schelden,* 1848.

Des Moulins (Charles). Le bassin hydrographique du Couzeau dans ses rapports avec la vallée de la Dordogne, la question diluviale et les silex ouvrés. [Extract]. 180 pp. 8°. *Bordeaux, société linnéenne,* 1864. s.

——— Études sur les échinides. 1e partie, (études générales), etc. [Extracts]. 520 pp. 8°. *Bordeaux, société linnéenne,* 1835-37. s.
[No more published].

CONTENTS:

1e. mémoire. Prodrome d'une nouvelle classification de ces animaux.
2e. mémoire. Généralites; étude analytique des parties solides de ces animaux.
3e. mémoire. Synonymie générale.

Des Mousseaux (Gougenot). Les médiateurs et les moyens de la magie; les hallucinations et les savants, le fantome humain et le principe vital. xv, 447 pp. 8°. *Paris, Plon,* 1863.

Desormeaux (A. J. *M.D.*) The endoscope, and its application to the diagnosis and treatment of affections of the genito-urinary passages. Translated by R. P. Hunt. 2 p. l. 108 pp. 8°. *Chicago, R. Fergus' sons,* 1867.

Destrilhes (——). Confidences sur la Turquie 2e éd. xli, 253 pp. 8°. *Paris, E. Dentu,* 1855.

Detroit (*City of*). Sixteenth annual report of the board of water commissioners. 8°. *Detroit, Free press printing house,* 1868. s.

Detroit young men's society. Catalogue of the library, with a historical sketch. 169 pp. 8°. *Detroit, O. S. Gulley,* 1865. s.

Detune (——). Catalogue des livres rares et précieux de la bibiothèque de feu M. D... [*anon.*] 167 pp. 3 l. 8°. *Paris, A. A. Renouard,* 1806.

Deuerling (*Dr.* A.) Cicero's bedeutung für die römische literatur. 2 p. l. 104 pp. 8°. *Augsburg, K. Kollmann,* 1866. s.

Deutsches archiv für die physiologie. In verbindung mit den hernn Albers, Autenreith, [et al.] herausgegeben von J. F. Meckel. 8 v. 8°. *Halle, buchhandlung des waisenhauses,* 1815–23. s.

De Veaux (S.) The travellers own book, to Saratoga springs, Niagara falls, and Canada. 258 pp. 2 maps. 4 pl. 18°. *Buffalo, Faxon & Read,* 1841.

Deventer. (*Holland*). Openbare bibliotheek. Catalogus bibliothecæ publicæ daventriensis. 2 v. viii, 320 pp; xii, 352 pp. 8°. *Daventriae, J. de Lange,* 1832–64. s.

Dew (Thomas R.) Review of the debate in the Virginia legislature of 1831–32, [on the abolition of slavery]. 133 pp. 8°. *Richmond, T. W. White,* 1832.
[*With* VIRGINIA and Kentucky resolutions of 1798-99. ed. 1832].

Dewees (William Potts, *M. D.*) An essay on the means of lessening pain, and facilitating certain cases of difficult parturition. 2d ed. 156 pp. 8°. *Philadelphia, T. Dobson & son,* 1819.

Dewey (*Rev.* Chester). Report on the herbaceous flowering plants of Massachusetts. ix, 277 pp. 8°. *Boston,* 1840.
[MASSACHUSETTS. Zoological and botanical survey].

Deyeux (Théophile). Physiologie du chasseur. Vignettes d'Eugène Forest. 122 pp. 16°. *Paris, Aubert & Lavigne,* [1841].
[*With* ALHOY (M.) Physiologie du voyageur].

Diary (The) of Martha Bethune Baliol, from 1753 to 1754. [*anon.*] 317 pp. 12°. *London, Chapman & Hall,* 1853.

Diary of a southern refugee, during the war. By a lady of Virginia. [*anon.*] 360 pp. 18°. *New York, Hale & son,* 1867.

Diaz (José Francisco). Historia del senado romano. Con un prologo de Victor Gebhardt. xliii, 359 pp. 2 l. 8°. *Barcelona, L. Tasso,* 1867. s.

Diaz del Castillo (Bernal). The true history of the conquest of America. From the Spanish, by M. Keatinge. viii, 333 pp. 1 map; iv, 440 pp. 8°. *Salem, (Mass.) Cushing & Appleton*, 1803.

Dibbits (Johannes Elbertus). Herder beschouwd als theoloog, inzonderheid als verklaarder van den bijbel. xii, 298 pp. 8°. *Utrecht, T. DeBruyn*, 1863. s.

Diccionario de la lengua castellana por la academia española. Novena ed. 3 p. l. 761 pp. 2 l. fol. *Madrid, F. M. Fernandez & ca.* 1834.

Dicey (Edward). A month in Russia during the marriage of the czarevitch. viii, 248 pp. 2 phot. pl. 8°. *London, Macmillan & co.* 1867.

Dickens (Charles). Bleak house. With illustrations by H. K. Browne. xvi, 624 pp. 39 pl. 8°. *London, Chapman & Hall*, [1862].

——— The same. Riverside ed. 4 v. in 2. 633 pp. 23 pl; 628 pp. 21 pl. 12°. *New York, Hurd & Houghton*, 1868.

——— Characters introduced and principal incidents in the works of C. Dickens. [Diamond ed.] sq. 18°. *Boston*, 1867.

[*In his* Uncommercial traveller. Diamond ed. pp. 299–382].

——— Child-pictures from Dickens. Illustrations by S. Eytinge, jr. 4 p. l. 241 pp. 8 pl. sq. 16°. *Boston, Ticknor & Fields*, 1868.

——— Christmas books. [Diamond ed.] vii, 225 pp. 8 pl. 18°. *Boston, Ticknor & Fields*, 1867.

——— The same. Additional christmas stories. [Diamond ed.] sq. 18°. *Boston*, 1867.

[*In his* Uncommercial traveller. Diamond ed. pp. 169–298].

——— A christmas carol in prose. Being a ghost story of christmas. Für den schulgebrauch erklärt von dr. L. Riechelmann. vii, 96 pp. 8°. *Leipzig, B. G. Teubner*, 1864. s.

——— The same. 111 pp. 20 pl. 8°. *Boston, Ticknor & Fields*, 1869.

——— [David Copperfield]. The personal history of David Copperfield. With illustrations by H. K. Browne. xiv, 624 pp. 39 pl. 8°. *London, Chapman & Hall*, [1862].

——— The same. Riverside ed. 4 v. in 2. 12°. *New York, Hurd & Houghton*, 1868.

——— Dombey and son. With illustrations by H. K. Browne. xvi, 624 pp. 39 pl. 8°. *London, Chapman & Hall*, [1862].

——— The same. Riverside ed. 4 v. in 2. 12°. *New York, Hurd & Houghton*, 1867.

——— Great expectations. Riverside ed. 2 v. in 1. 336 pp. 5 pl; 334 pp. 5 pl. 12°. *New York, Hurd & Houghton*, 1869.

——— Hard times for these times. Riverside ed. 2 v. in 1. 333 pp. 4 pl; 338 pp. 5 pl. 12°. *New York, Hurd & Houghton*, 1868.

——— Little Dorrit. With illustrations by H. K. Browne. xiv, 625 pp. 39 pl. 8°. *London, Chapman & Hall*, [1862].

——— The same. Riverside ed. 4 v. in 2. 325 pp. 24 pl; 294 pp. 20 pl. 12°. *New York, Hurd & Houghton*, 1868.

——— Our mutual friend. Riverside ed. Illustrated by Darley, Gilbert, Cruikshank, Phiz, etc. 4 v. in 2. 12°. *New York, Hurd & Houghton*, 1868.

——— Pictures from Italy. American notes. Riverside ed. 2 v. in 1. 285 pp. 6 pl; 320 pp. 4 pl. 12°. *New York, Hurd & Houghton*, 1868.

——— The posthumous papers of the Pickwick club. [Original issue]. 20 nos. in 19 parts. With 43 illustrations, by R. Seymour and Phiz [H. K. Browne]. xiv, 609 pp. 43 pl. 8°. *London, Chapman & Hall*, 1837.

——— The same. [Diamond ed.] With illustrations by S. Eytinge. 464 pp. 17 pl. 18°. *Boston, Ticknor & Fields*, 1867.

——— The same. Globe ed. Illustrated by Darley and Gilbert. 4 v. in 1. 18°. *New York, Hurd & Houghton*, 1867.

——— The same. The Pickwick papers. Riverside ed. 4 v. in 2. 12°. *New York, Hurd & Houghton*, 1868.

——— The readings, as condensed by himself. 10 v. in 1. 16°. *Boston, Ticknor & Fields*, 1868.

CONTENTS.

A christmas carol, As condensed by himself, for his readings. 53 pp. 1 pl.
Bardell and Pickwick. 23 pp. 1 pl.
David Copperfield. 59 pp. 1 pl.
Mr. Bob. Sawyer's party. 21 pp. 1 pl.
The story of little Dombey. 45 pp. 1 pl.
Nicholas Nickleby at the Yorkshire school. 45 pp.
Boots at the Holly-tree inn. 18 pp.
Doctor Marigold. 37 pp. 1 pl.
Nicholas Nickleby at the Yorkshire school. (Short reading). 29 pp. 1 pl.
Mrs. Gamp. 18 pp. 1 pl.

——— Sketches by Boz, illustrative of every-day life and every-day people. [Diamond ed.] pp. 227–500. 8 pl. 18°. *Boston, Ticknor & Fields*, 1867.

[*With his* Christmas books. Diamond ed. *Boston*, 1868].

——— A tale of two cities. Riverside ed. 2 v. in 1. 259 pp; 256 pp. 18 pl. 12°. *New York, Hurd & Houghton*, 1868.

——— The uncommercial traveller, and additional christmas stories. [Diamond ed.] Illustrations by S. Eytinge, jr. 382 pp. 12 pl. sq. 18°. *Boston, Ticknor & Fields*, 1867.

Dickinson (*Rev.* A.) Sermon. [In Cherokee]. [With] the story of David Rouge. 24 pp. 24°. [*Cherokee, about* 1845]?

Dickinson (Anna E.) What answer? [A story of the war]. 301 pp. 12°. *Boston, Ticknor & Fields*, 1868.

Dickinson (Daniel Stevens). Speeches, correspondence, etc. Edited, with a biography, by J. R. Dickinson. xi, 743 pp; xvi, 719 pp. 8°. *New York, Putnam & son*, 1867.

Dickinson (John). Letters from a farmer in Pennsylvania to the inhabitants of the British colonies. [*anon.*] 136 pp. 8°. *London, J. Almon*, 1774.

Dickinson (Samuel N.) A help to printers and publishers; being a series of calculations, showing the quantity of paper required for a given number of signatures in book-work, and the number of tokens contained therein. Also an extensive table for job work. 8, viii pp. 6 l. 219 pp. 6 l. 12°. *Boston, author*, 1835.

Dickson (*Rev.* A. F.) Plantation sermons, or plain and familiar discourses for the instruction of the unlearned. 170 pp. 12°. *Philadelphia, presbyterian board of publication*, 1856. s.

Dickson (R. W.) General view of the agriculture of Lancashire. Revised and prepared for the press, by W. Stevenson. xii, 653 pp. 3 l. 1 col. map. 8°. *London*, 1815.
[GREAT BRITAIN: Board of agriculture].

Dickson (Samuel Henry, *M. D.*) Studies in pathology and therapeutics. 201 pp. 12°. *New York, W. Wood & co.* 1867.

Dictionary of the Panjabi language, prepared by a committee of the Lodiana mission. vi, 438 pp. 4°. *Lodiana, mission press*, 1854. s.

Dictionnaire du commerce et de l' industrie, par mm. Blanque ainé, Brongniart, Ch. Dupin, J. Laffitte, Pance, Parisot, E. Pereyre, H. Say, etc. Revu et augmenté d' un grand nombre d' articles sur le commerce en Belgique. 4 v. in 1. 8°. *Bruxelles, société typographique belge*, 1837–40. s.

Dictionnaire des sciences médicales, composé des meilleurs articles puisés dans tous les dictionnaires et traités spéciaux qui ont paru jusqu'à ce jour. 13 v. 8°. *Bruxelles, A. Wahlen, J. Denaet*, 1828-30.
[v. 1, also entitled Encyclopédie du xix. siècle].

Diday (P.) A treatise on syphilis in new-born children and infants at the breast. Translated by G. Whitley. xii, 272 pp. 8°. *London*, 1859.
[NEW SYDENHAM society, v. 1.]

Diefenbach (Lorenz). Celtica. 2 v. in 1. 349 pp; 479 pp. 8°. *Stuttgart, A. Liesching & co.* 1840.

CONTENTS.

v. 1. Sprachliche documente zur geschichte der Kelten.
v. 2. Versuch einer genealogischen geschichte der Kelten.

——— Origines europaeae. Die alten völker Europas mit ihren sippen und nachbarn. [Nebst eines lexikon der von den alten aufbewahrten sprachreste der Kelten und ihrer nachbarn]. 2 p. l. 451 pp. 8°. *Frankfort am Main, J. Baer*, 1861.

Dilletanti society. *See* **Society** (The) of dilletanti.

Dillon (John B.) A history of Indiana, from its earliest exploration by Europeans to 1816; comprehending a history of the discovery, etc. of the territory northwest of the river Ohio, and a view of the progress of public affairs in Indiana, 1816–56. xii, 637 pp. 2 maps. 6 pl. 8°. *Indianapolis, Bingham & Doughty*, 1859.

Dilworth (Thomas). The schoolmaster's assistant: being a compendium of arithmetic, practical and theoretical. 220 pp. 1 portrait. 18°. *Philadelphia, R. Aitkin*, 1781.

Dineley (Thomas). *See* **Dingley.**

Dingelstedt (Franz). The Amazon. Translated from the German, by J. M. Hart. 315 pp. 12°. *New York, G. P. Putnam & son*, 1868.

——— Iean Gvtenberg, premier maitre imprimevr, ses faits et discours les plus dignes d'admiration, et sa mort. De l'Allemand, par Gustave Revilliod. 69 pp. 6 pl. fol. *Genève, J. G. Fick*, 1858.

Dingley (Thomas). History from marble. Compiled in the reign of Charles ii. Printed in photolithography by V. Brooks, from the original [ms.] With an introduction and descriptive table of contents by J. G. Nichols. 92, ccxl pp. sm. 4°. *London*, 1867.
[CAMDEN society publications. No. 94].

Diogenes *sinopensis or cynicus.* [Epistolæ, interprete Francisco Aretino *or* Francesco d'Arezzo]. 20 l. 4°. *Nurmberge, F. Creussner*, [*about* 1475]. s.

Dippel (Joseph). Versuch einer systematischen darstellung der philosophie des Carolus Bovillus, nebst einem kurzen lebensabrisse. xviii, 256 pp. 8°. *Würzburg, F. E. Thein*, 1865. s.

Dircks (H.) Worcesteriana; a collection of literary authorities, affording historical, biographical, and other notices relating to Edward Somerset, sixth earl and second marquis of Worcester, [etc.] xvi, 271 pp. 8°. *London, author*, 1866. s.
[*Note.*—Only 100 copies printed].

Dirix (M. E. *M.D.*) Woman's complete guide to health. 342 pp. 12°. *New York, Townsend & Adams*, 1869.

Disosway (Gabriel P.) The earliest churches of New York and its vicinity. 416 pp. 11 pl. 8°. *New York, J. C. Gregory*, 1865.

Dissertation (A) concerning the pre-existency of souls. Originally written in the Latine tongue by C. P. and now made English by D. F. [and] D. P. [*anon.*] 5 p. l. 131 pp. 24°. *London, J. Wickins*, 1684.

Disturnell (John). The eastern tourist; being a guide through the states of Connecticut, Rhode Island, Massachusetts, Vermont, New Hampshire, and Maine. Also, a dash into Canada. 144 pp. 1 pl. 16°. *New York, J. Disturnell*, 1848. s.

——— The great lakes, or inland seas of America; embracing a full description, [with their] commerce. 192 pp. 1 map. 6 pl. sq. 16°. *New York, C. Scribner*, 1863.

——— The same. With a guide to the upper Mississippi river. 218 pp. 2 maps. 10 pl. sq. 16°. *New York, American news co.* 1868.

——— Influence of climate, in a commercial, social, sanitary, and humanizing point of view. Also, a paper on the influence of climate in the equatorial regions, [etc. 2d ed.] 32 pp. 1 tab. 1 col. map. 4°. *New York, [J. Disturnell]*, 1866. s.

——— Railroad, steamboat, and telegraph book; being a guide through the middle, northern, and eastern states, and Canada, [etc.] 108 pp. 1 col. map. 18°. *New York, J. Disturnell*, 1850. s.

——— The traveller's guide to the Hudson river, etc; forming the northern tour through the United States and Canada. 324 pp. 1 map. 4 pl. 18°. *New York, American news co.* 1864.

——— United States register, or blue book for 1868. 116 pp. 12°. *New York, American news co.* 1868.

Dittmar (Siegmund Gottfried). Erinnerungen aus meinem umgange mit Garve, nebst einigen bemerkungen über dessen leben und charakter. 16°. *Breslau*, 1801. s.

[GARVE (C.) Sämmtliche werke, v. 13].

Dockquerye (*Sir* Henry). *See* **Docwra.**

Dr. Leslie's boys. By the author of "Money," etc. [*anon.*] 228 pp. 3 pl. 18°. *Philadelphia, presbyterian pub. com.* 1868.

Docwra *or* **Docquerye** (*Sir* Henry). Relation of service done in Irelande. [With] a narration of the services done by the army ymployed to Lough Foyle, written in 1614. Edited by J. O'Donovan. 12°. *Dublin*, 1849.

[*In* CELTIC society publications, no. 3, pp. 183-325].

Dod's parliamentary companion. 36th year. 32°. *London, Whittaker & co.* 1868.

Dodd (James B.) An elementary and practical arithmetic. xix, 244 pp. 12°. *New York, Pratt, Woodford & co.* 1849. s.

Dodge (Alice A.) Kate Woodman; or, the heart revealed. 229 pp. 3 pl. 16°. *Boston, American tract soc.* [1865].

——— Rebe's common sense. 320 pp. 3 pl. 18°. *Boston, American tract soc.* 1867.

Dodge (J. R.) Red men of the Ohio valley; an aboriginal history, 1650–1795; embracing thrilling incidents in the settlement of the states of Kentucky, Ohio, Indiana, and Illinois. 435 pp. 12°. *Springfield (Ohio), ruralist pub. co.* 1860.

Dodge (Mary Abigail). Woman's wrongs: a counter-irritant. By Gail Hamilton. [*pseudon.*] 212 pp. 16°. *Boston, Ticknor & Fields*, 1868.

Dodge (M. E.) A few friends, and what they did to amuse themselves. A tale in nine chapters, containing descriptions of twenty pastimes and games, and a fancy dress party. 182 pp. 12°. *Philadelphia, J. B. Lippincott & co.* 1869.

Dodington (George Bubb, *baron Melcombe*). Diary, from 1749—1761. With appendix. By H. P. Wyndham. xv, 502 pp. 8°. *Salisbury, E. Easton*, 1784.

——— The same. New ed. xv, 506 pp. 8°. *Salisbury, E. Easton*, 1784.

Dodonæus *or* **Dodoens** (Rembert). Frvmentorvm, legvminvm, palvstrivm et aqvatilivm herbarvm, ac eorvm, qvae eo pertinent, historia. Additae svnt imagines vivæ, etc. 270 pp. 16°. *Antverpiæ, C. Plantinus*, 1566.

——— Florvm, et coronariarvm odoratarvmqve nonnvllarvm herbarvm historia [Illustrata]. 307 pp. 16°. *Antverpiæ, C. Plantinus*, 1568.

[*With his* Frvmentorvm, etc. historia, 1566].

Dodsley (Robert). The chronicles of the kings of England, from William the conqueror to 1795. In imitation of the holy writings. By Nathan ben Saddi, a Jew. [*pseudon.*] 196 pp. 16°. *Worcester, J. Thomas*, 1795.

——— A collection of poems. By several hands. [*anon.*] 6 v. 16°. *London, J. Dodsley*, 1770.

Dodwell (Edward). Views and descriptions of Cyclopian, or, Pelasgic remains, in Greece and Italy; with constructions of a later period. 2 p. l. 34 pp. 131 pl. fol. *London, A. Richter & co.* 1834.

Doenniges (*Dr.* Wilhelm). Acta Henrici vii. imperatoris Romanorum et monumenta quædam alia medii aevi. 2 v. in 1. xxiv, 178 pp; lxii, 253 pp. 4°. *Berolini, Nicolai,* 1839. s.

Dolby (Anastasia). Church embroidery, ancient and modern, practically illustrated. viii, 176 pp. 20 pl. sm. 4°. *London, Chapman & Hall,* 1867.

——— Church vestments: their origin, use, and ornament, practically illustrated. viii, 203 pp. 37 pl. 4°. *London, Chapman & Hall,* 1868.

Dolly's christmas chickens. By the author of "Cosmo's visit." [*anon.*] 180 pp. 5 pl. 18°. *New York, R. Carter & bros.* 1868.

Dombay (Franz Lorenz von). Grammatica linguae persicae, accedunt dialogi, historiae, sententiae, et narrationes persicae. 4 p. l. 114 pp. 4°. *Vindobonae, A. Camesina,* 1804.

Domenech (Emmanuel). Le Mexique tel qu'il est, la vérité sur son climat, ses habitants, et son gouvernement. 2e éd. iv, 350 pp. 8°. *Paris, Dentu,* 1867.

Domestic (the) chemist, for the detection of adulteration in articles employed in domestic economy, medicine, and the arts, [with] the art of detecting poisons, and introduction to chemical analysis. [*anon.*] xvi, 340 pp. 1 pl. 18°. *London, Bumpus & Griffin,* 1831.

Domeyko (Ignacio). Araucania i sus habitantes. Recuerdos de un viaje hecho en las provincias meridionales de Chile en [1845]. 5 p. l. 121 pp. 2 maps. 8°. *Santiago, imprenta chilena,* 1845.

——— The same. 3 p. l. 106 pp. 2 maps. 8°. *Santiago, imprenta chilena,* 1846.

"Don John," or Don Juan unmasked; with review of the poem. [*anon.*] 2d ed. 40 pp. 1 pl. 8°. *London, W. Hone,* 1819.
[Miscellaneous pamphlets. v. 56].

Donck (Adriaen van der). *See* **Van der Donck.**

Doni (Antonio Francesco). Mondi celesti, terrestri, et infernali, de gli academici Pellegrini. 8 p. l. 431 pp. 7 l. 16°. *Vicenza, heredi di Perin,* 1597.
[Imperfect: pp. 219-220 wanting].

Donkersley (*Rev.* Richard). Facts for boys and girls about boys and girls. 284 pp. 6 pl. 18°. *New York, Carlton & Porter,* 1865.

Donndorff (Johann August). Zoologische beyträge zur xiii ausgabe des linneischen natursystems, v. 3. [*or,*] Amphibiologische und ichthyologische beyträge zur xiii ausgabe des linneischen natursystems. vi, 980 pp. 8°. *Leipzig, Weidmann,* 1798. s.
[v. 1 and 2, 1792-95, wanting].

Donnegan (James). A new Greek and English lexicon. Revised and enlarged, by R. B. Patton. viii, 1413 pp. 8°. *Boston, Hilliard, Gray & co.* 1836.

Donnersmarck. *See* **Henckel von Donnersmarck.**

Dora Grafton; or, "every cloud has a silver lining." 406 pp. 12°. *Boston, J. French & co.* 1856. s.

Doran (John). Saints and sinners; or, in church and about it. 2 v. 4 p. l. 336 pp; 3 p. l. 338 pp. 12°. *London, Hurst & Blackett,* 1868.

Dorchester antiquarian and historical society. Collections. 4 v. 12°. *Boston, D. Clapp,* 1844-59.

CONTENTS.

BLAKE (James). Annals of Dorchester. (no. 2).
CLAP (Roger). Memoirs. 1630. (no. 1).
HISTORY of Dorchester. (no. 4).
MATHER (Richard). Journal and life. (no. 3).

Doré (Paul Gustave). Historical cartoons; or, rough pencillings of the world's history, from the first to the nineteenth century. With descriptive text, by T. Wright. 21 l. 20 pl. obl. 8°. *London, J. C. Hotten,* [1868].

——— (*Illustrator*). *See* **Tennyson** (Alfred), Elaine. Guinevere.

Dorléans *or* **D'Orléans** (Pierre Joseph). The history of the revolutions in England under the family of the Stuarts, 1603-1690. From the French, by J. Stevens. With introduction by L. Erhard. 2d ed. 12 p. l. 328 pp. 6. l. 8°. *London, E. Curll,* 1722.

Dossie (Robert, *editor*). Memoirs of agriculture, and other œconomical arts. *See* **Bath** and West of England society.

Doten (Elizabeth). The inner mystery. An inspirational poem. 34 pp. 16°. *Boston, Adams & co.* 1868.

Dotty Dimple stories, no. 1. Dotty Dimple at her grandmother's. By Sophie May. [*pseudon.*] 190 pp. 4 pl. 18°. *Boston, Lee & Shepard,* 1868.

——— The same. no. 2. Dotty Dimple at home. By Sophie May. [*pseudon.*] 171 pp. 4 pl. 18°. *Boston, Lee & Shepard,* 1868.

——— The same. No. 3. Dottie Dimple out west. By Sophie May. [*pseudon.*] 171 pp. 4 pl. 12°. *Boston, Lee & Shepard,* 1869.

Douai (Musée de). Catalogues des collections d'histoire naturelle. *See* **Potiez** (V.)

Double (The) fault, and how it was remedied. [*anon.*] 187 pp. 3 pl. 16°. *Boston, Mass. s. s. soc.* 1867.

Dougherty (*Rev.* Peter). A Chippewa primer. [Chippewa and English]. 84 pp. 12°. *New York, board of foreign missions of the presbyterian church*, 1844. S.

—— *and* **Dodd** (D.) Short reading lessons in the Ojibwa language. 95 pp. 12°. *Grand Traverse bay, board of foreign missions of the presbyterian church*, 1847. S.

Douglas (Amanda M.) Sydnie Adriance; or, trying the world. 355 pp. 12°. *Boston, Lee & Shepard*, 1869.

Douglas (Robert, *D. D.*) General view of the agriculture of the counties of Roxburgh and Selkirk. xv, 378 pp. 2 col. maps. 2 pl. 8°. *London*, 1798. S.

[GREAT BRITAIN: Board of agriculture].

Douglas (William). Soldiering in sunshine and storm. ["From India to the Crimea and home."] viii, 322 pp. portrait. 12°. *Edinburgh, A. & C. Black*, 1865.

Douglass (William, *M. D.*) A summary, historical and political, of the first planting, progressive improvement, and present state of the British settlements in North America. 2 v. iii, 568 pp; 2 p. l. 416 pp. 8°. *Boston, Rogers & Fowle, and D. Fowle*, 1749–51.

—— The same. [With appendix "to render this work more compleat, from Salmon's Geographical and historical grammar," 1757.] v. 2. 2 p. l. 440 pp. 8°. *Boston, D. Fowle*, 1753.

—— The same. 2 v. viii, 568 pp; 3 p. l. 416 pp. 8°. *London, R. Baldwin*, 1755.

Dow (Lorenzo). Perambulations of cosmopolite; or, travels and labors in Europe and America. [With his other works. Edited] by Orrin Scofield. 421 pp. portrait. 8°. *Rochester, O. Scofield*, 1842.

CONTENTS.

Journal.
Chain of Lorenzo.
Reflections on matrimony.
Analects upon the rights of man.
Babylon to Jerusalem.
Dialogue between the curious and singular.
Fulfillment of prophecy.
Dow's lawsuit.

Dow (Peggy). Vicissitudes; or the journey of life [with supplementary reflections]. portrait. 8°. *Rochester, O. Scofield*, 1842.

[*With* DOW (L.) Perambulations of cosmopolite. Ed. 1842. pp. 423–508].

Dowler (Bennett, *M. D.*) Tableaux, geographical, commercial, geological, and sanitary, of New Orleans. 40 pp. 8°. *New Orleans, Daily Delta Office*, [1853]?

Dowling (Charles Hutton). Iron-work. Practical formulæ and general rules for finding the strain and breaking weight of wrought iron bridges, with sundry useful tables, [etc.] 2 p. l. 31 pp. 12°. *London, J. Weale*, 1862.

[*With* BAKER (T.) Formulæ, etc. 1862].

Dowling (John, *D. D.*) The conference hymn book. New ed. 304 pp. 32°. *New York, U. D. Ward*, 1868.

Downame (*Rev.* John). Fovre treatises, tending to dissuade all christians from swearing, drunkenesse, whoredome and bribery. [With] a treatise of anger. 5 p. l. 235 pp; 3 p. l. 82 pp. sm. 4°. *London, M. Baker*, 1613.

Downey (*Rev.* William Scott). Proverbs. 5th ed. 104 pp. 16°. *Boston, Hewes & co.* 1854.

Doyère (M. P. Louis N.) Insectes (lépidoptères). Atlas, etc. *See* **Cuvier** (G. L. C. F. D.) Règne animal, 1836–46. v. 6.

Doze proposições sobre a legitimidade religiosa da verdadeira tolerancia dos cultos, por Ephraim. [*pseudon.* Note signed I. de B.] ix, 195 pp. 8°. *Rio de Janeiro, Laemmert*, 1864. S.

Drake (Daniel, *M. D.*) Notices concerning Cincinnati. 60, iv pp. 8°. *Cincinnati, author*, 1810.

Draper (Edward Alured). An address to the British public on the case of brigadier general Picton, late governor of the island of Trinidad. xvi, 282, 59 pp. 8°. *London, J. Budd*, 1806.

Draper (John William). History of the American civil war. v. 2. 614 pp. 8°. *New York, Harpers*, 1868.

Drapiez (Auguste). Traité élémentaire d' ornithologie, ou histoire naturelle des oiseaux, etc. xii, 300 pp. 32°. *Paris, Mairet & Fournier*, 1842. S.

Drei spiegelbilder unserer zeit. [*anon.*] 190 pp. 16°. *Cincinnati, Benziger bros.* 1868.

CONTENTS.

i. Zuge aus dem leben Pius ix.
ii. Die engel der christlichen charitas. (Die barmberzigen schwestern).
iii. Die freimaurer, wie sie sind.

Drelincourt (*Rev.* Charles). The christian's defence against the fears of death. Translated by M. d'Assigny. 13th ed. 4 p. l. 502 pp. 8°. *London, D. Midwinter*, 1732.

Dreux du Radier (Jean François). Mémoires historiques, critiques, et anecdotiques des reines régentes de France. [*anon.*] Nouv. éd. 6 v. 16°. *Amsterdam, M. Rey*, 1776.

Driscoll (Frederick). The twelve days campaign. An impartial account of the final campaign of the late war. [With remarks on the defense of the British provinces]. 103 pp. 1 map. 8°. *Montreal, Longmoore & co.* 1866.

Drisler (Henry). A reply to the bible view of slavery, by J. H. Hopkins, D. D. 20 pp. 8°. *New York, C. S. Westcott & co.* 1863.

[LOYAL publication society, No. 39].

Drugulin (Wilhelm E.) Deutscher portrait-katalog. [Mit] anhang. Ausländer. 2 p. l. 178 pp. 1 l. 96 pp. 8°. *Leipzig, G. A. Drugulin,* [1854].

Druids' (The) magazine; a compendium of druidical proceedings. Edited by P. A. and R. A. Hunt. v. 1-4 in 2 v. 8°. *London, R. Willoughby,* 1830-33.

Duane (William). The system of infantry discipline; according to the regulation established for the army of the U. S. 19 March, 1818. viii, 284 pp. 8°. [*Philadelphia*], 1814. s.

Dubini (Angelo, *M. D.*) Entozoografia umana per servire di complemento agli studj d'anatomia patologica, seguita da un' appendice sui parassita esterni del corpo umano tanto animali che vegetabili. Ed. riveduta dall' autore. [Extracts]. 544 pp. 18 pl. 8°. *Milano, societa' degli editori degli annali universali etc,* [1849-] 1850. s.

Dublin proverbs: a collection of questions proposed to the candidates for the gold medal at the general examinations, 1816-22. 2 p. l. 202 pp. 8°. *London, G. & W. B. Whittaker,* 1823. s.

Dublin (The) review. v. 48-52. May 1860-Nov. 1862. New series. v. 1-8. July 1863-April 1867. 13 v. 8°. *London,* 1860-67.

Dublin university magazine: a literary and political journal. July, 1867, to Dec. 1868. v. 70-72. 8°. *Dublin, G. Herbert,* 1867-68.

Dubois (*l'abbé* J. A.) Description of the character, manners and customs of the people of India, and of their institutions—religious and civil. Translated from the French ms. 2 v. 390 pp; 368 pp. 8°. *Philadelphia, M. Carey & son,* 1818.

Du Bois (William E.) Pledges of history. A brief account of the collection of coins belonging to the mint of the United States, particularly of the antique specimens. 138 pp. 1 pl. 18°. *Philadelphia, C. Sherman,* 1846.

Dubourg (Matthew). Views of the remains of ancient buildings in Rome and its vicinity. 18 l. 26 pl. fol. *London, J. Taylor,* 1820.

Du Boys (Félix). Étude sur les associations coopératives, précédée d'une dissertation sur les corporations ouvrières en droit romain. 190 pp. 8°. *Grenoble, Maisonville,* 1866.

Dubroca (Louis). Éloge funèbre de Washington. 16°. *Paris,* 1835.

[*In* FONTANES (L.) *and* DUBROCA. Éloges funèbres de Washington].

Dubuque (*Iowa*). Dubuque city directory for 1868-9. With an accurate history of the city. Compiled by J. M. Wolfe. 268 pp. 8°. *Dubuque, Bames & Ryan,* 1868.

Du Cange (Charles Du Fresne, *sieur*). Histoire de l'empire de Constantinople sous les empereurs français jusqu'à la conquête des Turcs. Revue par J. A. Buchon. 2 v. 8°. *Paris, Verdière,* 1829.

[COLLECTION de chroniques nationales françaises, v. 1-2].

Du Chaillu (Paul B.) Stories of the gorilla country. Narrated for young people. Illustrated. 292 pp. incl. 9 pl. 12°. *New York, Harpers,* 1868.

——— Wild life under the equator. Narrated for young people. 231 pp. 10 pl. 12°. *New York, Harpers,* 1869.

Du Clot (Joseph François). Osservazioni preliminari, ossia introduzione all' opera intitolata la sacra bibbia vendicata. Traduzione dal Francese. 2 p. l. 235 pp, 12°. *Torino, Bianco,* 1824. s.

Dudevant (Armandine Lucile Aurore Dupin, *madame*). Œuvres. Nouv. éd. Revue par l'auteur et accompagnée de morceaux inédits. 441 pp. 16°. *Paris, Perrotin,* 1844.

CONTENTS.

André, La marquise, Lavinia, Metella, Mattea.

——— La comtesse de Rudolstadt, par George Sand. [*pseudon.*] Nouv. éd, revue et corrigeé. 2 v. 2 p. l. 423 pp; 2 p. l. 423 pp. 16°. *Paris, Charpentier,* 1845.

——— Monsieur Sylvestre. Par George Sand. [*pseudon.*] 338 pp. 16°. *Paris, Lévy,* 1866.

——— Spiridion. Par George Sand. [*pseudon.*] 472 pp. 8°. *Paris, F. Bonnaire,* 1839.

Dudley (Paul). An essay on the merchandize of slaves and souls of men, with an application thereof to the church of Rome. By a gentleman. [*anon.*] 63 pp. 4°. *Boston, B. Green,* 1731

Duer (William Alexander). A letter addressed to Cadwallader D. Colden, in answer to his strictures on the report of the select committee on steam navigation. 127 pp. 8°. *Albany, E. & E. Hosford,* 1817.

Duer (W. A.) A reply to mr. Colden's vindication of the steamboat monopoly. 184, xxvii pp. 8°. *Albany, E. & E. Hosford,* 1819.

Duffield (George, *D. D.*) The bible rule of temperance: total abstinence from all intoxicating drink. 206 pp. 18°. *New York, nat. temperance society,* 1868.

Dufour (Léon). Recherches anatomiques et physiologiques sur les hémiptères. [Extract]. 333 pp. 19 pl. 4°. *Paris, acad. des sciences,* 1833. S.

Dufrénoy (Adélaide Gillette Billet). Bibliothèque choisie pour les dames. 3 séries in 36 v. 18°. *Paris, Lefuel,* 1818–1821.

Dufrénoy (Pierre Armand) *and* **Élie de Beaumont** (Jean Baptiste). Explication de la carte géologique de la France. 2 v. 1 p. l. xxii, 825 pp. 1 l. 1 col. map; xii, 813 pp. 4°. *Paris, imprimerie nationale,* 1841–48. S.

Du Fresne du Cange. *See* **Du Cange.**

Dugès (Antoine). Arachnides. Atlas. *See* **Cuvier** (G. L. C. F. D.) Règne animal. 1836–46. v. 7.

Du Huys (Charles). The Percheron horse. Translated from the French. 100 pp. 6 pl. 12°. *New York, O. Judd & co.* 1868.

Dumas (Alexandre Davy). Paul Jones, the son of the sea. 105 pp. 8°. *New York, Garrett & co.* [1853].

——— Tales of Algeria; or, life among the Arabs, from [his Le] Véloce, by R. M. Bache. 351 pp. 5 pl. 12°. *Philadelphia, Claxton, Remsen & Haffelfinger,* 1868.

——— Tausend und ein gespenst. 3 v. 12°. *Stuttgart zu Guttenburg,* 1850. S.

Du Moncel (*Vicomte* Théodore Achille Louis). Étude du magnétisme et de l'électro-magnétisme au point de vue de la construction des électro-aimants. 2 p. l. 268 pp. 1 pl. 8°. *Paris, L. Hachette & cie.* 1858. S.

——— Exposé des applications de l'électricité. v. 1–2. 8°. *Paris, L. Hachette & cie,* 1853–54. S.

——— The same. 2e éd. v. 1–3. 8°. *Paris, L. Hachette & cie,* 1856–57. S.

[v. 2. wanting].

——— [The same. v. 4. only entitled] Revue des applications de l'électricité en 1857–58. 616 pp. 3 pl. 8°. *Paris, L. Hachette & cie,* 1859. S.

——— The same. Exposé des applications de l'électricité. v. 5. Revue des découvertes faites de 1859 à 1862. 2 p. l. vi, 560 pp. 2 pl. 8°. *Paris, L. Hachette & cie,* 1862. S.

Dumont (Jean) *and* **Rousset du Missy** (Jean). The history of John, duke of Marlborough. By the author of the history of prince Eugene. [*anon.*] 3d ed. 2 p. l. 348 pp. 4 l. 1 pl. 16°. *London, J. Hodges,* 1755.

——— Memoirs of prince Eugene of Savoy. Translated from the French by W. Mudford. [*anon.*] 256 pp. 16°. *New York, E. Sargeant,* 1811.

Dun (R. Graham) and co. The mercantile agency reference book, containing ratings of the merchants, manufacturers, and traders generally, throughout the United States. Jan. 1868. 4°. *New York, R. G. Dun & co.* 1868.

Dun, Barlow & co. The same. July, 1868. 4°. *Dun, Barlow & co.* 1868.

Dunbar (E. E.) American pioneering, an address before the travellers' club. 45 pp. 8°. [*New York, travellers' club*], 1863.

[Travellers' club paper, No. 1].

Duncker (Maximilian Wolfgang). Geschichte des alterthums. 2e aufl. 4 v. 8°. *Berlin, Duncker & Humboldt,* 1855–57.

——— Die geschichte der Griechen. 2 v. vi, 635 pp; vii, 907 pp. 8°. *Berlin, Duncker & Humboldt,* 1856–57.

[v. 3–4 of the preceding].

Duncumb (John). General view of the agriculture of the county of Hereford. viii, 173 pp. 2 maps, 3 pl. 8°. *London,* 1815.

[Great Britain: Board of agriculture].

Dundas (*Col.* David). Principles of military movements, chiefly applied to infantry. Illustrated by manœuvres of the Prussian troops, and by an outline of the British campaigns in Germany, during the war of 1757. With appendix. 2 p. l. viii, 267, 91 pp. 25 pl. 4°. *London, T. Cadell,* 1788.

Dunker (Wilhelm, *editor*). *See* **Palæontographica.**

Dunlop (John). History of Roman literature, from its earliest period to the Augustan age. 2 v. 354 pp; 286, 62 pp. 8°. *Philadelphia, E. Littell,* 1827. S.

Dunn (*Rev.* Ballard S.) Brazil, the home for southerners. iv, 272 pp. 12 l. portrait. 12°. *New York, G. B. Richardson,* 1866.

Dunod (——— *publisher*). Librairie ancienne et moderne. Catalogue. Architecture, mécanique, ponts et chaussées, mines, télégraphes, chemins-de-fer, navigation. 1 p. l. 251 pp. 8°. *Paris,* [*Dunod*], 1868. S.

Dupanloup (Félix Antoine Philippe, *évêque d'Orléans*). De l'éducation. 7e éd. 3 v. 16°. *Paris, Douniol,* 1866.

Du Petit Thouars (Abel Aubert). Voyage autour du monde sur la frégate la Vénus, pendant les années 1836–1839. 10 v. 8°. atlas. 4 v. fol. *Paris, Gide,* 1840–55. s.

CONTENTS.

v. 1—4. Relation. [Par A. Du Petit Thouars]. 4 v. 8°. 1840–43. Atlas pittoresque. 70 pl. fol.
v. 6–10. Physique. Par U. de Tessan. 5 v. 8°. 1842-44.
Zoologie. Mammifères, oiseaux, reptiles et poissons. [Par Isidore Geoffroy Saint-Hilaire, F. Prévost et O. Des Murs, Duméril, et A. Valenciennes]. 2 p. l. 351, iii pp. 8°. 1855. Atlas de zoologie. 3 p. l. 78 col. pl. fol. 1846.
Botanique. Atlas de botanique. 3 p. l. 28 pl. fol. 1846.

Du Plessis Mornay. *See* **Mornay** (Philippe de).

Duponchel (Philogène Auguste Joseph). Histoire naturelle des lépidoptères de France. v. 6–11. *See* **Godart** (J. B.)

Dupuis (A.) Les papillons: guide de l'amateur des lépidoptères. 2 p. l. 259 pp. 17 col. pl. 12°. *Paris, C. Albessard,* 1863. s.

Duran (Jean Alexandre). Code des créations universelles et de la vie des êtres. viii, 132 pp. 1 pl. 8°. *Bordeaux, Lanefranque,* 1841. s.
[*With his* Révélation, etc. 8°. 1846].

——— Nouveau système de physique générale en opposition avec les principes reçus, proclamé par la science actuelle. 70 pp. 8°. *Paris, Moquet & Hauquelin,* 1843. s.
[*With his* Révélation, etc. 8°. 1846].

——— Révélation scientifique. Dieu à J. A. Duran. 344 pp. 8°. *Bordeaux, Cruzel,* 1846. s.

Durant (Charles F.) Exposition of a new theory of animal magnetism. 225 pp. 1 pl. 12°. *New York, Wiley & Putnam,* 1837. s.

Duranti (Jean Étienne). De ritibvs ecclesiæ catholicæ libri tres. 5ª ed. 8 p. l. 680 pp. 27 l. 12°. *Lvgdvni, P. Landry,* 1606. s.

Durivage (Francis Alexander) *and* **Burnham** (George P.) Stray subjects, arrested and bound over. Being the fugitive offspring of the "old 'un" and the "young 'un." [*pseudon.*] 199 pp. 8 pl. 8°. *Philadelphia, Carey & Hart,* 1848. s.

Durret (——). Voyage de Marseille à Lima, et dans les autres lieux des Indes Occidentales. Par le sieur D. [*anon.*] 2 pts. in 1 v. xxxv, 282, 246 pp. 5 pl. 16°. *Paris, J. P. Coignard,* 1720.

Durrie (Daniel S.) A genealogical history of the Holt family in the United States. 367 pp. 8°. *Albany, J. Munsell,* 1864.

Dusch (Th. von). On thrombosis of the cerebral sinuses. Translated by G. Whittey. 8°. *London,* 1861.
[New Sydenham society, v. 11].

Dussauce (H.) A practical guide for the perfumer. Edited from notes and documents of Debay, Lunel, etc. 376 pp. 12°. *Philadelphia, H. C. Baird,* 1868.

——— Treatise on the coloring matters derived from coal tar. 196 pp. 16°. *Philadelphia, H. C. Baird,* 1863.

Dutchess county (*New York*). Transactions of the society of Dutchess county for the promotion of agriculture, with select essays on rural economy. v. 1–2 in 1. v, 90 pp; 88 pp. 12°. *Poughkeepsie, Bowman, Parsons & Potter,* 1807.

Duvallon (Berquin). *See* **Berquin-Duvallon** (——).

Duvergier de Hauranne (Ernest). Huit mois en Amérique, lettres et notes de voyage, 1864–65. 2 v. xi, 439 pp; 503 pp. 16°. *Paris, Lacroix, Verboeckhoven et cie.* 1866.

Duvernoy (George Louis). Des caractères anatomiques des grandes singes pseudo-anthropomorphes. [Extract]. 248 pp. 16 pl. 4°. *Paris, museum d'histoire naturelle,* 1855. s.

——— Cours d'anatomie comparée commencé au muséum d'histoire naturelle, 23 Avril, 1851. [Extract]. 24 pp. 4°. *Paris, muséum, etc.* 1855. s.
[*With his* Des caractères des grandes singes].

——— Mémoires sur le système nerveux des mollusques acéphales lamellibranches ou bivalves. [Extract]. 210 pp. 13 pl. 4°. *Paris, acad. des sciences,* 1853.
[Imperfect: wanting pl. 8, 9].

——— Nouvelles études sur le rhinocéros fossiles. [Extract]. 144 pp. 8 pl. 4°. *Paris, muséum d'histoire naturelle,* 1854. s.

——— Reptiles. Atlas. *See* **Cuvier** (G. L. C. F. D.) Règne animal, 1836–46. v. 3.

Dwight (M. A.) Grecian and Roman mythology. With an introductory notice by Tayler Lewis. xx, 438 pp. 17 pl. 12°. *New York, G. P. Putnam,* 1849. s.

Dwight (Sereno Edwards). Select discourses. With a memoir of his life, by William T. Dwight. lxviii, 382 pp. 12°. *Boston, Crocker & Brewster,* 1851. s.

Dwight (Theodore, *jr.*) The northern traveller; containing the routes to the springs, Niagara, Quebec, and the coal mines, etc. 6th ed. 250 pp. 17 maps. 9 pl. 18°. *New York, J. P. Haven,* 1841.

Dwight (Timothy, *D.D.*) Greenfield hill: a poem, in seven parts. 184 pp. 8°. *New York, Childs & Swaine,* 1794. s.

Dwight (Timothy). Theology; explained and defended in a series of sermons. With a memoir of the author. 9th ed. 4 v. 8°. *New Haven, T. Dwight & son,* 1836. s.

Dwight (Wilder). Life and letters. vii, 351 pp. 1 portrait. 8°. *Boston, Ticknor & Fields,* 1868.

Dyer (Thomas Henry, *LL.D.*) The history of the kings of Rome. With a prefatory dissertation on its sources and evidence. cxxxv, 440 pp. 8°. *London, Bell & Daldy,* 1868.

Eads (James B.) System of naval defences. Report to the secretary of the navy, Feb. 22, 1868. 30 pp. 10 pl. 4°. *New York, D. Van Nostrand,* 1868.

Eames (Jane A.) My mother's jewel; or, happy in life, happy in death. 3d ed. 222 pp. 3 pl. 16°. *New York, gen. prot. ep. s. s. union,* 1851. s.

Earle (John). A book of characters. *See* **Overbury** (*Sir* T.) *and others.*

Early English text society. Nos. 21, 27–28, 30–32, and extra series, nos. 1 and 3. 8°. *London, Trübner,* 1867–68.

CONTENTS.

No. 21. LA TOUR LANDRY (G. de). Book for the instruction of his daughters.
27. LEVINS (Peter). Manipulus vocabulorum: a rhyming dictionary of the English language. Edited by H. B. Wheatley.
28. LANGLAND (William). The vision of William concerning Piers Plowman. Part i. Edited by Rev. W. W. Skeat.
30. PIERCE the ploughmans crede.
31. MYRC (J.) Instructions for popish priests.
32. FURNIVALL (F. J. *Editor*). The babees book, etc.
Extra series. 1. ROMANCE (The) of William of Palerne.
Extra series. 3. CAXTON. Book of curtesye.

Eastcott (*Rev.* Richard). Sketches of the origin, progress, and effects of music, with an account of the ancient bards and minstrels. vii, 277 pp. 8°. *Bath, S. Hazard,* 1793.

East India company. A collection of treaties and engagements with the native princes and states of Asia, concluded on behalf of the E. I. co. by the British governments in India; also copies of sunnuds, or grants, of certain privileges and immunities to the company by the mogul and other princes. xx, 623 pp. 4°. *London, Cox & son,* 1812.

——— Papers respecting the negociation for a renewal of the E. I. company's exclusive privileges, with a copy of the bill as passed. xii, 566 pp. 4°. *London, E. Cox & son,* 1813.

Eastman (George W.) *See* **Fulton** (Levi S.) *and* **Eastman.**

Eastwick (Edward B.) Venezuela: or, sketches of life in a South American republic; with the history of the loan of 1864. 2d ed. xi, 418 pp. 1 map. 8°. *London, Chapman & Hall,* 1868.

Eaton (*Rev.* Samuel J. M.) History of the presbytery of Erie; with biographical sketches of all its ministers, and historical sketches of its churches. xv, 463 pp. 12°. *New York, Hurd & Houghton,* 1868.

Ebel (Johann Gottfried). Ueber den bau der erde in dem Alpen-gebirge, nebst einigen betrachtungen über die gebirge und den bau der erde überhaupt. 2 v. xxx, 408 pp; x, 428 pp. 8 l. 12°. *Zürich, O. Füssli & co.* 1808.
[Geological map wanting]. s.

Eberl (Friedrich). Die kirche und die association der arbeiter. x, 213 pp. 8°. *Passau, A. Deiter,* 1866. s.

Ecce ecclesia; an essay, showing the essential identity of the church in all ages. [*anon.*] 576 pp. 12°. *New York, Blelock & co.* 1868.

Echevelar (Manuel de). Instruccion exacta y util de las derrotas y navegaciones que se executan en todos tiempos en la America septentrional de unos puertos à otros: con las advertencias de sondas, y notas, para ponerlas en pràctica. 41 pp. sm. 4°. *Cadiz, M. Espinosa de los Monteros,* [1766]?
[*With* NODAL (B. G. de *and* G. de). Relacion del viage al descubrimiento del estrecho de San Vicente. [1776]?

Echo (The) from the army. What our soldiers say about the copperheads. 7 pp. 8°. *New York,* 1865.
[LOYAL publication society. no. 2].

Echo-bank. A temperance tale. By "Ervie." [*pseudon.*] 269 pp. 1 pl. 18°. *New York, national temperance society,* 1868.

Eckartshausen (Carl von). Aufschlüsse zur magie aus geprüften erfahrungen über die verborgene philosophische wissenschaften und verdeckte geheimnisse der natur. 4 v. 8°. *München, J. Lentner,* 1788–91. s.
[v. 4 wanting; v. 1. 2e. aufl. 1790].

Eclectic (The) magazine of foreign literature, science, and art. 1845–51. v. 4–8, 15–18, 20–24. Edited by J. H. Agnew [and] W. H. Bidwell. 14 v. 8°. *New York, Leavitt & co. W. H. Bidwell,* 1845–51.
[*Note.*—For v. 1–3, *see* ECLECTIC museum].

——— The same. W. H. Bidwell, editor. Jan. to Dec. 1868. New series. v. 7–8. 8°. *New York,* [*W. H. Bidwell*], 1868.

Eclectic medical journal. Jan. to Dec. 1868. v. 28. 8°. *Cincinnati, J. M. Scudder,* 1868.

Eclectic (The) museum of foreign literature, science, and art. Edited by J. H. Agnew. Jan. to Dec. 1843. v. 1–3. 8°. *New York, E. Littell,* 1843.
See, also, **Eclectic** magazine.

Eclectic (The) review. June, 1809, to Dec. 1850. 80 v. in 83. 8°. *London*, 1809-50.
[v. 1 to v. 5, pt. 1, Jan. 1805 to June, 1809, wanting].

——— The same. [8th series]. Jan. to Dec. 1868. v. 14-15. 8°. *London, Hodder & Stoughton*, 1868.

Economist (The), weekly commercial times, bankers' gazette, and railway monitor: a political, literary, and general newspaper. July 1867, to Dec. 1868. v. 25, part 2—v. 26. fol. *London, T. H. Meredith*, 1867-68.

Eddy (Daniel C. *D.D.*) Walter's tour in the east. Walter in Athens. 226 pp. 4 pl. 16°. *New York, Sheldon & co.* 1865.

Eddy (Zachary, *D.D.*) Immanuel; or, the life of Jesus Christ our Lord, from his incarnation to his ascension. With an introduction, by R. S. Storrs, D.D. 752 pp. 7 pl. 8°. *Springfield, (Mass.) W. J. Holland & co.* 1868.

Edelman (George W.) The bullion dealer's guide. 29 pp. 8°. *New York, G. F. Nesbitt & co.* 1868.

Eden (Lizzie Selina). A lady's glimpse of the late war in Bohemia. viii, 305 pp. 1 pl. 12°. *London, Hurst & Blackett*, 1867.

Eden (Richard). The decades of the newe worlde of West India, written by Peter Martyr. [With compilations from various writers concerning the West and East Indies]. 24 p.l. 361 l. 13 l. *b. l.* 12°. *Londini, Guil. Powell*, 1555.

——— The same. The history of trauayle in the West and East Indies, and other countries; with a discourse on the northwest passage. Gathered in parte, and done into English, by R. Eden. Augmented by R. Willes. [2d ed.] 10 p. l. 466 l. 6 l. *b. l.* 12°. *London, R. Jugge*, 1577.

Eden (William, 1st *baron Auckland*). The history of New Holland, from its first discovery in 1816, to the present time. And a discourse on banishment. 4°. *London, J. Stockdale*, 1790.
[*With* PHILLIP (A.) Voyage to Botany bay. Appendix. pp. lxxvii-clxxv. ed. 1790].

Edgar (William). Vectigalium systema; or, a complete view of that part of the revenue of Great Britain commonly called customs. 3 p. l. 330 pp. 12°. *London, J. Baskett*, 1714.

Edge (Frederick Milne). Major General McClellan and the campaign on the Yorktown peninsula. 201 pp. 8°. *New York*, 1865.
[LOYAL publication society, no. 81].

——— Whom do English tories wish elected to the presidency? 4 pp. 8°. *New York*, 1864.
[LOYAL publication society, no. 69].

Edinburgh (Royal college of physicians of). Historical sketch and laws, from its institution to Dec. 1865. 3 p. l. 170 pp. 1 pl. 8°. *Edinburgh, college*, 1867. s.

Edinburgh (Royal society of). Transactions. v. 24. 4°. *Edinburgh, Grant & son*, 1867.

Edinburgh medical journal. July, 1867-June, 1868. v. 13. in 2 v. 8°. *Edinburgh, Oliver & Boyd*, 1868.

Edinburgh (The) review, or critical journal. Jan. to Oct. 1868. v. 127-128. 8°. *London, Longmans*, 1868.

Edinburgh review (Selections from the). *See* **Cross** (M.)

Edith Hale; a village story. By Thrace Talmon. [*pseudon.*] 521 pp. 12°. *Boston, Phillips, Sampson & co.* 1856. s.

Edwards (Amelia Blandford). Archie Lovell; a novel. 8°. *New York, W. P. & F. C. Church*, 1867.

——— Barbara's history. [A novel]. 476 pp. 1 pl. 12°. *London, Hurst & Blackett*, [1864.]

Edwards (Bryan). The history, civil and commercial, of the British colonies in the West Indies. 3 v. 4°. *London, J. Stockdale*, 1793-1801.

Edwards (Charles). Pleasantries about courts and lawyers of the state of New York. 528 pp. 1 portrait. 8°. *New York, Richardson & co.* 1867.

Edwards (*Mrs.* C. M.) The itinerant; or, the rainbow side. 299 pp. 5 pl. 18°. *New York, Carlton & Porter*, 1856. s.

Edwards (Edward). A comparative table of the principal schemes which have been proposed for the classification of libraries, and of human knowledge generally. [With] a special report on a classed catalogue for the Manchester free library. vi, 22 pp. 2 pl. fol. *Manchester, C. Simms & co.* 1855. s.

——— The life of sir Walter Ralegh, based on contemporary documents; with his letters, now first published. 2 v. lvi, 723 pp. 2 pl. 2 tab; lxxxv, 530 pp. 2 pl. 8°. *London, Macmillan & co.* 1868.

Edwards (Henri Milne). Élémens de zoologie, ou leçons sur l'anatomie, la physiologie, la classification, et les moeurs des animaux. 568 pp; Atlas. 41 pl. 8°. *Bruxelles, H. Dumont*, 1837. s.

——— The same. viii, 1066 pp. 1 tab. 1 map. 8°. *Paris, Crochard*, 1834. s.

——— Mammifères, insectes, arachnides, crustacés, annelides, zoophytes. Atlas, etc. *See* **Cuvier** (G. L. C. F. D.) Règne animal. ed. 1836-48.

Edwards (Henri Milne), *and* **Haime** (Jules). Recherches sur la structure et la classification des polypiers récents et fossiles. (Extract). 7 mémoires in 1 v. 8°. *Paris, Annales des sciences naturelles,* 1848–49. s.

CONTENTS.

M. 1. Observations sur la structure et le développement des polypiers en général. [53 pp. 3 pl.]
M. 2. Monographie des turbinolides. [134 pp. 4 pl.]
M. 3. Monographie des eupsammides. [266 pp. 5 pl.]
M. 4. Monographie des astreides. [283 pp.]
M. 5. Monographie des oculinides. [58 pp. 2 pl.]
M. 6. Monographie des fungides. [72 pp.]
M. 7. Monographie des poritides. [50 pp. 1 pl.]

Edwards (Jonathan, *D. D. president of Union college, N. Y.*) The injustice and impolicy of the slave trade and of the slavery of the Africans: illustrated in a sermon before the Connecticut society for the promotion of freedom, New Haven, Sept. 15, 1791. 37 pp. 12°. *New Haven, T. & S. Green,* 1791.

Edwards (*Mrs.* L. E.) Miss Forrester. A novel. 3 v. 12°. *London, Tinsley,* 1865.

Edwards (*Rev.* Morgan). Materials for a history of the baptists in Rhode Island. 8°. *Providence, Knowles, Anthony & co.* 1867.

[*In* RHODE ISLAND historical society. Collections. v. 6].

Effie Morison; or, the family of Redbraes. A narrative of truth. By the author of "Allan Cameron." [*anon.*] 157 pp. 2 pl. 18°. *New York, Am. tract soc.* 1865.

Effinger (*Rev.* Conrad Maria). Geistlicher wegweiser für eheleute. Ein lehr und gebetbuch für christliche hausväter und hausmütter. 446 pp. 4 pl. 18°. *Einsiedeln und New York, C. & N. Benziger,* 1868.

——— Hinauf zu Gott! Katholisches gebet- und erbauungsbuch für heilsbegierige seelen. 447 pp. 24°. *New York, C. & N. Benziger,* 1868.

——— Neuer leidenskelch. Ein gebet u. erbauungsbuch besonders für leidende christen. Mit bildern. 444 pp. 24°. *New York, C. & N. Benziger,* 1868.

Egger (Augustin). Lob Gottes im munde der anschuld. Ein katholisches gebetbüchlein für die lieben kinder. 128 pp. 32°. *New York, C. & N. Benziger,* 1868.

Egger (Émile). Notions élémentaires de grammaire comparée pour servir à l'étude des trois langues classiques. viii, 179 pp. 12°. *Paris, A. Durand,* 1852. s.

Egilsson (Sveinbjörn). Lexicon poëticum antiquæ linguæ septentrionalis. lii, 934 pp. 8°. *Hafniæ, societas regia antiquariorum septentrionalium,* [1854–] 1860. s.

Egron (Adrien César). Le livre de l'ouvrier, ses devoirs envers la société, la famille et lui-même. 2 p. l. xv, 407 pp. 12°. *Paris, P. Mellier,* 1844. s.

Eguren (José Maria de). Memoria descriptiva de los códices notables conservados en las archivos ecclesiasticos de España. Obra premiada por la biblioteca nacional, [etc.] xcix, 100 pp. 2 l. 8°. *Madrid, gobierno,* 1859. s.

[SPAIN. Biblioteca nacional].

Ehlers (Ernst). Die borstenwürmer (annelida chaetopoda) nach systematischen und anatomischen untersuchungen dargestellt. Abtheil. i. 290 pp. 11 pl. 4°. *Leipzig, W. Engelmann,* 1864. s.

——— Zoologische beiträge in Neapel und Messina. *See* **Keferstein** (W.) *and* **Ehlers.**

Ehrenberg (Christian Gottfried, *editor*). Symbolae physicae, seu icones et descriptiones corporum naturalium novorum aut minus cognitorum quae ex itineribus per Libyam, Ægyptum, Nubiam, Dongalam, Syriam, Arabiam et Habessiniam F. G. Hemprich et C. G. Ehrenberg studio annis 1820–25 redierunt. Pars zoologica. 4 v. fol. *Berolini, officina academica,* 1828–32. s.

CONTENTS.

[v. 1.] Mammalia, etc. Percensuit C. G. Ehrenberg. Dec. 1–2. 81 l. 20 col. pl. 1828–30.
[v. 2.] Aves. Percensuit C. G. Ehrenberg. Dec. 1. 30 l. 10 col. pl. 1828.
[v. 3.] Insecta. Percensuit Fr. Klug. Dec. 1–5. 93 l. 50 col. pl. 1829–32.
[v. 4.] Animalia evertebrata. Percensuit C. G. Ehrenberg. 64 pp. 10 col. pl. 1828.

Ehrenberg (Hermann). Texas und seine revolution. 2 p. l. 258 pp. 8°. *Leipzig, O. Wigand,* 1843.

Eichhorn (Carl Friedrich). Deutsche staats- und rechtsgeschichte. 2^e verbesserte aufl. 4 v. 8°. *Göttingen, Vandenhöck & Ruprecht,* 1818–23.

Eichhorn (Johann Gottfried). Geschichte der litteratur. v. 6. abth. 1, [or] Geschichte der theologischen wissenschaften seit der verbreitung der alten litteratur. theil 1. 1 p. l. xiv, 532 pp. 8°. *Göttingen, Vandenhöck & Ruprecht,* 1810. s.

[Theil 2 wanting.]

Eichthal (Gustave d'). Études sur l'histoire primitive des races océaniennes et américaines. 172 pp. 8°. *Paris, Dondey-Dupré,* [1845].

Einaiut Oollah. *See* **Inajut-Ullah.**

Einarson (Halfdan). Historia literaria Islandiæ; autorum et scriptorum tum editorum tum ineditorum indicem exhibens. Ed. nova. 16 p. l. 251 pp. 9 l. 8°. *Havniae, etc. Gyldendal,* 1786. s.

Eisenhart (Hugo). Ueber den beruf des odels im staate und die natur der pärieverfassung. 3 p. l. 198 pp. 8°. *Stuttgart, J. G. Cotta*, 1852.

——— Die gegenwärtige staatenwelt. 1er band. Die morgenländische staatenwelt: buddhistisches und muhammedanisches staatensystem. vii, 302 pp. 8°. *Leipzig, F. Fleischer*, 1856.

Eldridge (Abby). Hattie Powers: or, the daughter's mission. 312 pp. 4 pl. 16°. *Boston, H. Hoyt*, 1867.

——— Lucy Clifton. [A story]. 288 pp. 3 pl. 18°. *Philadelphia, presbyterian board of publication*, 1865.

Eleanor: an autobiography. [*anon.*] 302 pp. 4 pl. 16°. *Philadelphia, Am. s. s. union*, 1866.

Elegantiarum viginti precepta. [*anon.*] 10 l. sm. 4°. *Lyptzick, per Mel chiorem Lotter*, 1519.

Elementa mathesis, ad geographiam, staticam, aerometriam, hydraulicam applicatæ. [*anon.*] 2 p. l. 140, 255 pp. 16°. [*Vratislaviae*], *typis universitatis*, 1777. s.

Elements of chess; combining theory with practice, and comprising the whole of Philidor's games. [*anon.*] 208 pp. 1 pl. 8°. *Boston, W. Pelham*, 1805.

Élie de Beaumont (Jean Baptiste Armand Louis Léonce). Explication de la carte géologique de la France. *See* **Dufrenoy** (P. A.) *and* **Élie de Beaumont**.

Eliot (Charles W.) *and* **Storer** (Frank H.) A compendious manual of qualitative chemical analysis. iv, 102, 37 pp. 12°. *Boston, authors*, 1868.

——— ——— A manual of inorganic chemistry, arranged to facilitate the experimental demonstration of the facts and principles of the science. 2d ed. xiv, 605, lix pp. 12°. *New York, Ivison, Phinney & co.* [*printed in London*], 1868.

Eliot (George, *pseudon.*) *See* **Evans** (Marian).

Eliot (*Sir* Thomas). The book named the governour. Londini, A. D. 1564. A new edition, by A. T. Eliot. xxxviii pp. 1 l. 293, vi pp. 8°. *Newcastle-upon-Tyne, J. Hernaman*, 1834.

Ella Ross, the widow's daughter; or, a story of an earnest life. [*anon.*] 198 pp. 3 pl. 16°. *New York, American tract society*, 1867.

Ellen Herbert; or, family changes. [*anon.*] 206 pp. 16°. *New York, Harpers*, [1847]. s.

Ellendt (Friedrich). Lehrbuch der allgemeinen geschichte. 4e verbesserte aufl. xvi, 568 pp. 8°. *Königsberg, gebrüder Bornträger*, 1853.

Ellet (*Mrs.* Elizabeth F.) Evenings at Woodlawn. 348 pp. 12°. *New York, Baker & Scribner*, 1849. s.

——— The queens of American society. 464 pp. 14 pl. 8°. *New York, C. Scribner & co.* 1867.

Elliot (Charles Morgan). Magnetic survey of the eastern archipelago. [Extract]. [47], clvii pp. 2 maps. 8 pl. 4°. *London, royal society*, 1851.

Elliot (Daniel Giraud). The birds of North America. Parts 1-11. fol. *New York, author*, 1867-68.

——— A monograph of the pittidae, or family of ant thrushes. 102 pp. 31 col. pl. fol. *New York, D. Appleton & co.* 1863. s.

Elliot (George T. *jr. M.D.*) Obstetric clinic; a contribution to the study of obstetrics and the diseases of women and children. xiv, 458 pp. 8°. *New York, Appletons*, 1868.

Elliott (Franklin Reuben). Popular deciduous and evergreen trees and shrubs, for planting in parks, gardens, cemeteries, etc. 125 pp. 8°. *New York, F. W. Woodward*, 1868.

Elliott (Stephen, *LL.D.*) A sketch of the botany of South Carolina and Georgia. 2 v. viii, 743 pp. 12 pl. 8°. *Charleston, (S. C.) J. R. Schenck*, 1821-24.

Elliott (William, *of Beaufort, S. C.*) Carolina sports, by land and water; including incidents of devil fishing, etc. 172 pp. 12°. *Charleston, Burges & James*, 1846. s.

Ellis (John, *M.D.*) Family homœopathy. 6th ed. 404 pp. 12°. *New York, C. T. Hulburt*, 1867.

Ellis (John F.) Musical almanac for 1868. And Washington city general advertiser. 168 pp. 8°. *Washington, J. F. Ellis*, [1868]. s.

Ellwood (Thomas). Davideis; the life of David, king of Israel. 159 pp. 16°. *Wilmington, Johnson & Preston*, 1797.

Elmira (*N. Y.*) directory and business advertiser. *See* **Galatian** (A. B.) History of Elmira.

Elton (J. F.) With the French in Mexico. x, 206 pp. 2 maps. 1 pl. 8°. *London, Chapman & Hall*, 1867.

Elvenich (Peter Joseph). Acta hermesiana quae compluribus G. Hermesii libris a Gregorio xvi. per litteras apostolicas damnatis ad doctrinam Hermesii explicandam, scripsit. Fasc. i. xiv, 232 pp. 8°. *Goettingae, Vandenhoeck & Ruprecht*, 1836. s.

——— Acta romana [de Georgii Hermesii libris]. *See* **Braun** (J. W. J.) *and* **Elvenich**.

——— Meletemata theologica. *See* **Braun** (J. W. J.) *and* **Elvenich**.

Ely (*Abbey of, England*). Historia ecclesiæ eliensis. [*anon.*] fol. *Oxoniæ*, 1691.

[GALE (T.) *and* FELL (J.) Rerum anglicarum scriptores veteres. *Oxoniæ.* v. 3.]

Emanuel (Harry). Diamonds and precious stones: their history, value, and distinguishing characteristics. With simple tests for their identification, [and a bibliography]. xvi, 266 pp. 6 pl. 12°. *London, J. C. Hotten*, 1865.

Emerald (The), an illustrated [weekly] literary journal. Feb. to Aug. 1868. v. 1. fol. *New York, D. O'Sullivan & co.* 1868.

Emerson (Ralph Waldo). Essays. [1st series]. 2 p. l. 303 pp. 16°. *Boston, J. Munroe & co.* 1841.

Eminent women of the age; being narratives of the lives and deeds of the most prominent women of the present generation. By J. Parton, H. Greeley, [and others]. 628 pp. 14 pl. 8°. *Hartford, S. M. Betts & co.* 1868.

Emmons (Ebenezer, *M.D.*) American geology, containing a statement of the principles of the science, with full illustrations of characteristic American fossils. v. 1. xvi, 194 pp. 2 pl; 251 pp. 18 pl. 8°. *Albany, Sprague & co.* 1855. s.

——— Report on the quadrupeds of Massachusetts. 1 p. l. 86 pp. 8°. *Cambridge*, 1840.

[MASSACHUSETTS. Zoological and botanical survey].

Emmons (S. Bullfinch). Philosophy of popular superstition, and the effects of credulity and imagination upon the moral, social, and intellectual condition of the human race. 288 pp. 1 pl. 12°. *Boston, Crown & co.* 1853.

Emmons (William). Authentic biography of Richard M. Johnson, of Kentucky. 92 pp. 16°. *Boston, proprietor*, 1832.

Empis (G. S.) On diphtherite, 1850. 8°. *London*, 1859.

[NEW SYDENHAM society, v. 3].

Emsmann (August Hugo). Physikalisches handwörterbuch, hilfsbuch für jedermann bei physikalischen fragen. 2 v. iv, 565 pp; 1 p. l. 714 pp. 8°. *Leipzig, O. Wigand*, 1865. s.

Énault (Louis). L'Amérique centrale et méridionale. xxxvi, 444 pp. 20 pl. sm. fol. *Paris, Mellado et cie.* 1857.

Encyclopædia americana. A popular dictionary of art, science, literature, history, politics, and biography; including original articles in American biography. Edited by F. Lieber. 13 v. 8°. *Philadelphia, Carey, Lea & Carey*, 1829–33.

Encyclopédie, ou dictionnaire raisonné des sciences, des arts et des métiers, par une société de gens de lettres. Mis en ordre et publié par Diderot; et quant à la partie mathématique, par d'Alembert. 3e ed. 36 v. Plates, 3 v. 4°. *Genève, etc. J. L. Pellet*, 1778–79. s.

——— [The same]. Table analytique et raisonnée des matières contenues dans les 39 volumes in quarto du Dictionnaire des sciences, des arts et des métiers. 6 v. (A–Z). 4°. *Lyon, A. LeRoy*, 1770–71.

Enfield (William, *LL. D.*) The history of philosophy, from the earliest periods; drawn up from Brucker's Historia critica philosophiæ. xvi, 670 pp. 8°. *London, T. Tegg*, 1839.

Engel (Heinrich, *auctioneer*). Verzeichniss der hinterlassen bibliotheken des h. K. A. Varnhagen von Ense, sowie des h. dr. Ernst H. F. Meyer, welche nebst mehreren anderen bücher-sammlungen am 3. Oct. 1859, werden sollen. 1 p. l. ii, 326 pp. 8°. *Leipzig, T. O. Weigel*, 1859. s.

Engels (Johann Adolph). Sammlung kleiner schriften über gegenstände des bürgerlichen lebens, der geschichte, der religion, und der naturkunde. vi, 252 pp. 12°. *Crefeld, J. H. Funcke*, 1827. s.

Engineering facts and figures for 1864–67. An annual register of progress in mechanical engineering and construction. Edited by A. B. Brown. 4 v. 8°. *London, A. Fullarton & co.* 1865–68.

[1863 wanting].

England (Church of). *See* **Church** of England.

England's black tribunal: containing the complete tryal of king Charles i, and a relation of the sufferings and death of the nobility, [etc.] who were sacrificed for their loyalty. [With] preface by a true churchman. [*anon.* 6th ed.] xxxii, 306 pp. 1 pl. 12°. *London, C. Rivington*, 1737.

England's vanity: or the voice of God against the monstrous sin of pride, wherein naked breasts and shoulders are condemned as unlawful. [*anon.*] 144 pp. 1 pl. 18°. *London, J. Dunton*, 1683.

English (The) catalogue of books for 1867, containing a complete list of all the books published in Great Britain and Ireland; also, of the principal books published in the United States, with an index to subjects. 84 pp. 8°. *London, Low*, 1868.

Enquiry (An) into the methods to retrieve the sugar trade. By the author of the detection of the state and situation of the present sugar planters of Barbadoes and the Leward islands. [*anon.*] 31 pp. 8°. *London, J. Wilford*, 1733.

Enquiry (An) into the principles of population, exhibiting a system of regulations for the poor. [*anon.*] xvi, 336 pp. 8°. *London, J. Duncan*, 1832.

Ephræm Syrus (*Saint*). Sermones xix secundum traductionem Ambrosii. 71 l. fol. *Brixiæ, Baptista Fargengo*, 1490.

Epictetus. Manual. 12°. *London*, 1844.
[*In* ANTONINUS (M. A.) The meditations, 1844].

Épinay (Louise Florence Pétronille Tardieu d'Esclavelles, *madame* de La Live d'). Les conversations d'Émilie. [*anon.*] Nouv. éd. 208 pp. 16°. *Paris, Pissot*, 1776.

Erasmus *or* **Gerhardt** (Desiderius). De ratione studii, ac legendi interpretandique auctores libellus aureus. Officiū discipulorum ex Quintiliano. Concio de puero Jesv. Expostulatio Jesv ad mortales. Carmina scholaria. 22 l. sm. 4°. *Argentorati, Matthias Schurerius*, 1516.

——— Epistola nvncvpatoria ad Carolvm Caesarem. Exhortatio ad studium euangelicae lectionis. Paraphrasis in euangeliū Matthaei, nunc primū nata et aedita. Epistola ad R. D. Mathæum card. sedun[ensem]. 201 l. 16°. *Basileæ, Jo. Frobenius*, 1522.

——— Paraphrasis in euangelium secundum Ioannem, ad illustrissimū principem Ferdinandvm nunc primum excusa. 199 l. 16°. *Basileae, apvd Joannem Frobenium*, 1523.
[*With his* EPISTOLA noncopatoria, etc.]

Erckman (Émile) *and* **Chatrian** (Alexandre). Histoire d'un conscrit de 1813. With English notes by F. Bôcher. 236 pp. 12°. *Boston, S. R. Urbino*, 1868.

——— Madame Thérèse; or, the volunteers of '95. [From the French by Charlotte L. Forten]. 3[d] thousand. 289 pp. 10 pl. 12°. *New York, C. Scribner & co.* 1869.

Erhardt (*Rev.* J. *missionary*). Vocabulary of the Enguduk Iloigob, as spoken by the Masai tribes in east Africa. [Edited by L. Krapp]. 111 pp. 8°. *Ludwigsburg, F. Riehm*, 1857. s.

Erichson (Wilhelm Ferdinand). Insecten. (Hymenopteren und neuropteren). 4°. *St. Petersburg*, 1851. s.
[*In* MIDDENDORFF (A. T. von). Reise, etc. v. 2, theil 1].

Erlenmeyer (Albrecht, *M. D.*) Uebersicht der öffentlichen und privaten irren- und idioten- anstalten aller europaischen staaten. 2 p. l. 145 pp. 8°. *Neuwied, J. H. Heuser*, 1863. s.

Ernst (Jacob). Illustrations of the symbols of masonry, scripturally and morally considered. 356 pp. 1 portrait. 8°. *Cincinnati, Jacob Ernst & co.* 1868.

Erpenius. *See* **Van Erpe.**

Erring, yet noble. A tale of and for women. [*anon.*] 569 pp. 12°. *New York, John Bradburn*, 1865.

Ersch (Johann Samuel), **Gruber** (J. G.) *and others, editors.* Allgemeine encyclopädie der wissenschaften und künste. 1[e] section, v. 85-86; 2[e] section, v. 7, 18, und 20. 5 v. 4°. *Leipzig, Gleditsch,* [*und*] *Brockhaus*, 1830-68. s.

Erskine (Thomas, *advocate*). An essay on faith. 3[d] ed. 155 pp. 16°. *Edinburgh, Waugh & Innes*, 1823.
[*With his* Internal evidence of revealed religion. ed. 1823.]

Erxleben (Johann Christian Polycarp). Systema regni animalis per classes, ordines, genera, species, varietates, cvm synonymia et historia animalivm. Classis 1. Mammalia. xlviii, 636 pp. 32 l. 8°. *Lipsiae, Weygand*, 1777. s.
[No more published].

Escalante Fontaneda (Hernando de). Memoir respecting Florida, written in 1575. Translated from the Spanish by Buckingham Smith, [with notes]. 57 pp. 1 map. 4°. *Washington*, 1854.
[*With* SOTO (H. de). Letters to authorities of Santiago de Cuba. 4°. *Washington*, 1854].

Eschricht (Daniel Friedrich). Das physische leben, in populären vorträgen. 1 v. in 2. xii, 513 pp. 18 pl. 8°. *Berlin, A. Hirschwald*, (*printed at Kopenhagen, Schultze*), 1852. s.

CONTENTS.

v. 1. Das leben im allgemeinen: ernährungsleben.
v. 2. Bewusztes leben: vorzüge des menschlichen organismus.

Eschscholtz (Johann Friedrich). Zoologischer atlas, enthaltend abbildungen neuer thierarten während des v. Kotzebue zweiter reise um die welt, in den jahren 1823-26 beobachtet. 5 v. in 1. fol. *Berlin, G. Reimer*, 1829-33.

Escovar (Manuel Rodriguez). Metodo gubernativo para las escuelas de primeras letras, anotado por Julian Arranz. 100 pp. 5 pl. 8°. *Madrid, V. Hernando*, 1845. s.

Esling (*Mrs.* Catherine H. Waterman). The broken bracelet, and other poems. 288 pp. 8°. *Philadelphia, Lindsay & Blakiston*, 1850. s.

Esmarch (Fr.) On the use of cold in surgery. Translated by E. Montgomery. 8°. *London*, 1861.
[NEW SYDENHAM society. v. 11].

Esquiros (Alphonse). English seamen and divers. ix, 322 pp. 12°. *London, Chapman & Hall*, 1868.

——— Religious life in England. xiv, 354 pp. 12°. *London, Chapman & Hall*, 1867.

Essays and reviews. Recent inquiries in theology, by eminent English churchmen; being "Essays and reviews." 2d American, from the 2d London ed. Edited by rev. F. H. Hedge. xiv, 498 pp. 12°. *Boston, Walker, Wise & co.* 1861. s.

Essen (C. G. von). Om bikt och aflösning. 153 pp. 8°. *Helsingfors, J. C. Frenckell & son*, 1867. s.

Estienne (Henri, *editor*). Oratorvm vetervm orationes Aeschinis, Lysiae, Andocidis, Isaei, Dinarchi, Antiphontis, Lycvrgi, Herodis, et aliorum. Cum interpretatione lat. quarundam. 594 pp. fol. [n. p.] *H. Stephanus*, 1575.

Estrada (Alvaro Florez). An impartial examination of the dispute between Spain and her American colonies. From the original [Spanish], by W. Burdon. viii, 199 pp. 8°. *London, Sherwood, Neely & Jones*, 1812.

États-Unis (Les) en 1866. [*anon.*] 22 pp. 8°. *Genève, J. Cherbuliez*, 1866.

Ettmüller (Michael Ernst). Epistola de cerebri corticali substantia, etc. 4°. *Amstelædami*, 1721. s.

[*In* RUYSCH (F.) Opera. v. 3. no. 27].

——— Epistola de ovario novo. 4°. *Amstelædami*, 1729. s.

[*In* RUYSCH (F.) Opera. v. 3. no. 40].

Etzler (J. A.) The new world, or mechanical system, to perform the labors of man and beast by inanimate powers, that cost nothing, for producing and preparing the substances of life. 86 pp. 1 pl. 8°. *Philadelphia, P. H. Stollmeyer*, 1841. s.

Euclides. Elements of geometry, from the Latin translation of Commandine. With a preface by Dr. J. Keill, 1867. Revised by S. Cunn. 9th ed. 8 l. 275 pp. 10 pl. 8°. *London, C. Hitch and L. Hawes*, 1762.

———The same. Elements of Euclid, viz., the first six books, together with the eleventh and twelfth, [etc.] Also the book of Euclid's data. Corrected by Robert Simson. Also annexed, elements of plane and spherical trigonometry. Revised by J. Wright. 11th ed. 520 pp. 3 pl. 8°. *Edinburgh, Cuthell & Martin*, 1803.

——— The same. 516 pp. 3 pl. 8°. *Philadelphia, T. & R. Desilver*, 1825. s.

Eulogies and orations on the life and death of George Washington. 304 pp. 8°. *Boston, W. P. & L. Blake, etc.* 1800. s.

Euripides. The crowned Hippolytus. Translated into English verse by M. P. Fitz-Gerald. With a selection from the pastoral and lyric poets of Greece. 237 pp. 16°. *London, Chapman & Hall*, 1867.

Eustachi (Bartolomeo). Tabulæ anatomicæ præfatione notisque illustravit Jo. Maria Lancisius. xliv, 115 pp. 6 l. 47 pl. fol. *Amstelædami, R. & G. Wetstein*, 1722. s.

Eutropius. Historiæ romanæ libri x. 16°. *Geneva*, 1568.

[*In* VARII historiæ romanæ scriptores, v. 4].

——— The same. Eutropii historiæ romanæ breviarum; with an English translation by John Clarke. 3d Am. ed. 176 pp. 2l. 16°. *New York, E. Duyckinck*, 1805.

Evangelisches gesangbuch, oder eine sammlung geistreicher lieder. 4e aufl. viii, 600 pp. 24°. *Neu Berlin, (Penn.) H. Fischer*, 1850. s.

Evans (Marian). Silas Marner, the weaver of Raveloe. 276 pp. 8°. *Mobile, S. H. Gœtzel*, 1863.

———The Spanish gypsy. A poem. By George Eliot. [*pseudon.*] 5 p. l. 287 pp. 16°. *Boston, Ticknor & Fields*, 1868.

Evans (Thomas William, *M. D.*) La commission sanitaire des États Unis, son origine, son organisation, et ses résultats. 178 pp. 5 pl. 8°. *Paris, E. Dentu*, 1865.

——— Sanitary institutions during the Austro-Prussian-Italian conflict. Conferences of the international societies of relief for wounded soldiers. An essay on ambulance wagons, [etc.] Catalogue of the author's sanitary collection. 3d ed. x, 237 pp. 8°. *Paris, S. Raçon & cie.* 1868. s.

Evelyn (Chetwood, esq. *pseudon.*) *See* **Companion** (The). 1850.

Evening (The) leader. [Washington daily. L. Hill, editor]. Feb. 14, to April 11, 1867. fol. *Washington*, 1867.

[No more published].

Evening (The) post. [New York daily]. July 1867 to Dec. 1868. 3 v. fol. *New York*, 1867–68.

Evening (The) star. [Washington daily]. July 14, 1853, to Dec. 1868. 31 v. fol. *Washington*, 1853–68.

Evening union. *See* **Constitutional** union. [Washington daily.]

Everard (Giles) *and others.* Panacea; or the universal medicine, being a discovery of the wonderfull vertues of tobacco, taken in a pipe,

Everard—continued.
with its operation and use both in physick and chyrurgery. 8 p. l. 79, 55 pp. 1 pl. 18°. *London, S. Miller*, 1659.

Everett (Edward). The Monroe doctrine. [With] a letter of J. Q. Adams, and an extract from a speech of Geo. Canning. 77 pp. 8°. *New York, W. C. Bryant & co.* 1863.
[LOYAL publication society, no. 34].

——— Orations and speeches on various occasions. v. 4. xiv, 788 pp. 8°. *Boston, Little, Brown & co.* 1868.

Everett (Lemuel C.) *and* **Brooks** (A.) The thesaurus musicus; a book of sacred music. Revised ed. 272 pp. obl. 8°. *Richmond, (Va.) authors*, [1856]. s.

Everett (William). Changing base; or, what Edward learnt at school. 282 pp. 3 pl. 16°. *Boston, Lee & Shepard*, 1868.

Evergreen (The) for 1847. A present for all seasons. 8°. *Philadelphia, Carey & Hart*, 1847. s.

Everhardi (Nicolaas). Ioannis secundi hagiensis, poetæ elegantissimi opera. 2ª ed. 172 pp. 18°. *Parisiis, Iacobus Dupuis*, 1861.

Everhart (James B.) Poems. 144 pp. 1 pl. 12°. *Philadelphia, J. B. Lippincott & co.* 1868.

Eversmann (Eduard). Fauna lepidopterologica volgo-uralensis. 1 p. l. xiv, 633 pp. 8°. *Casani, typis universitatis*, 1844. s.

Every-day wonders illustrated; or, facts in physiology which all should know. [*anon.*] 88 pp. 24°. *Philadelphia, Am. sunday school union*, [1853]. s.

Every Saturday. A journal of choice reading, selected from foreign current literature. Jan. 1866, to Dec. 1868. v. 1–6. 8°. *Boston, Ticknor & Fields*, 1866–68.

Evidences of natural and revealed religion; also the doctrines and institutions of christianity. By the author of "Reasons why I am a churchman." [*anon.*] 224 pp. 16°. *New York, general protestant episcopal sunday school union*, 1848. s.

Ewald (Alexander Charles). A reference book of English history. 3 p. l. 246 pp. 12°. *London, F. Warne & co.* 1866.

Examiner (The); containing political essays on important events, [with] public laws and official documents. Oct. 25, 1813, to July 29, 1815. Barent Gardenier, editor. 4 v. in 3. 8°. *New York, B. Gardenier*, 1812–15.

Examples of goodness, narrated for the young. Translated from the German. [*anon.*] 116 pp. 4 pl. 12°. *Philadelphia, J. K. Simon*, 1852. s.

Exercices de piété pour le soulagement des ames du purgatoire. Traduit de l'Allemand [par R. N. *anon.*] 288 pp. 3 pl. 24°. *New York, C. & N. Benziger*, 1867.

Exercise for garrison and field ordnance, [with] manœuvres of horse artillery, as altered from the manual of gen. Kosciusko. By an officer of the U. S. artillery. [*anon.*] 2 pts. 128 pp. 18 pl. 8°. *New York, Pelsue & Gould*, 1812.

Exhibition of 1867, Paris. Exposition universelle de 1867 à Paris. Catalogue général publié par la commission impériale. 2e éd. 1538 pp. 12°. *Paris, Dentu*, 1867.

Exiles (Antoine François Prévost d'). *See* **Prévost d'Exiles.**

Explanation (An) of the map which delineates that part of the federal lands between Pennsylvania west line, the rivers Ohio and Scioto, and lake Erie. [*anon.*] 24 pp. 8°. *Salem, Dabney & Cushing*, 1787.

——— The same. Description du sol, des productions, etc. de cette portion des États-Unis, située entre la Pennsylvanie, les riviéres de l'Ohio et du Scioto, et le lac Erié. Traduite. 30 pp. 8°. *Paris*, 1789.
[*With* the preceding].

Expositio himnorum cum notabili commento quod semper implicat historias, cū optimis allegationibus sacre scripture illorum sanctorū vel sanctarū de quibus tales hymni decantantur. cxxxiii, 13 l. sm. 4°. *Colonia, per H. Quentell*, 1494.
[*With* TEXTUS sequentiarum. *Colonia*, 1494].

Exposition. *See* **Exhibition.**

Eyler (Emilie, *pseudon.*) *See* **Osten** (Mary).

Eyster (Nellie, *pseudon ?*) Sunny hours; or, child life of Tom and Mary. 206 pp. 4 pl. 16°. *Philadelphia, Ashmead & Evans*, 1866.

——— The same. Illustrated by White. 206 pp. 4 pl. 16°. *Philadelphia, D. Ashmead*, 1867.

——— Sunny hour stories. Chincapin Charlie. Illustrated by White. 272 pp. 3 pl. 16°. *Philadelphia, D. Ashmead*, 1867.

——— The same. On the wing. Illustrated by White. 240 pp. 4 pl. 16°. *Philadelphia, D. Ashmead*, 1868.

Faber (Jacques). Introductio in arithmecam Seuerini Boetij pariter et Jordani. Ars supputādi tam per calculos quos per notas arithmeticas suis quidem regulis elegāter expressa Judoci Clichtouei. Questio de numerorū et per digitos et per articulos finita progressione ex Aurelio Augustino. Epitome rerum geometricarum ex geometrico introductorio Caroli Bouilli. De quadratura circuli demonstratio ex Campano. 32 l. sm. 4°. [*n. p.*] 1517.

Faber (Théodore). Sketches of the internal state of France. Translated from the French. 256 pp. 16°. *Philadelphia, J. & A. Y. Humphreys*, 1812.

Fabricius *or* **Faber** (Johann Albert) Opusculorum historico-critico-literariorum sylloge quæ sparsim viderant lucem nunc recensita denuo et partem aucta indice instruuntur. 2 p. l. 538 pp. 12 l. 4°. *Hamburgi, sumptibus viduæ Felgineriæ*, 1738. s.

Fackler (D. Parks). Agents' monetary life and valuation tables, with valuable explanations. 44, vii pp. 1 table. 1 pl. 8°. *New York, Insurance monitor office*, 1868.

Facts and arguments on the transmission of intellectual and moral qualities from parents to offspring. [*anon.*] 2d ed. 191 pp. 16°. *New York, J. Winchester*, 1844.

Faes (José Estevan). Memoria sobre un sistema de defensa para las costas y fronteras de la republica [de Chile]. 1 p. l. 14 pp. 4°. *Santiago de Chile*, 1844.
[*With* CHILE. (Min. de guerra). Memoria, 1844].

Fagrskinna. Kortfattet norsk konge-saga fra slutningen af det tolfte eller begyndelsen af det trettende aar-hundrede. Udgivet af P. A. Munch og C. R. Unger. xvi, 216 pp. 8°. *Christiania, P. T. Malling*, 1847. s.

Fairbairn (William). On the application of cast and wrought iron to building purposes. viii, 183 pp. 1 tab. 3 pl. 8°. *London, J. Weale*, 1854. s.

Fairclough (*Rev.* Joseph W.) An address delivered before the Hibernian society of Alexandria, D. C. on St. Patrick's day, 17th March, 1825. 16 pp. 16°. *Alexandria, H. Pittman*, 1825.
[*With* O'CONNOR (T.) Inquisition examined. ed. 1825].

Fairfax (Thomas, 3d *baron Fairfax of Cameron*). Short memorials [of the civil war]. Written by himself. [Edited by] Brian Fairfax. xi, 128 pp. 2 l. 18°. *London, R. Chiswell*, 1699.

Fairfield (Jane). The autobiography of Jane Fairfield, embracing a few select poems by Sumner Lincoln Fairfield. viii, 328 pp. 1 portrait. 12°. *Boston, Bazin & Ellsworth*, 1860. s.

Fairfield (Sumner Lincoln). A few select poems. 12°. *Boston, Bazin & Ellsworth*, 1860.
[*In* FAIRFIELD (Jane). Autobiography. 1860].

——— Poems and prose writings. In 2 volumes. v. 1. [Poems]. 400 pp. 8°. *Philadelphia, proprietor*, 1841. s.
[No more published].

——— The siege of Constantinople. A poem. 64 pp. 8°. *Charleston, (S. C.) W. Riley*, 1822. s.

Fairholt (Frederick W). Gog and Magog, the giants in Guildhall; their real and legendary history. With an account of other civic giants, at home and abroad. xii, 152 pp. 7 pl. 16°. *London, J. C. Hotten*, 1859.

Fairman (William). An account of the public funds transferable at the bank of England, and of the stocks of some of the principal companies in London. Also, a history of the national debt and sinking fund. Enlarged, and brought down to 1824, by B. Cohen. 7th ed. viii, 287 pp. 8°. *London, J. Richardson*, 1824.

Fairy bells, and what they tolled us. [*anon.*] From the German, by S. W. Lander. 204 pp. 4 pl. 16°. *Boston, H. B. Fuller*, 1868.

Fairy stories for children. [*anon.*] 128 pp. 16°. *Philadelphia, C. H. Davis*, 1854. s.

Faithful (The) mother's reward; a narrative of the conversion and happy death of J. B. who died in the tenth year of his age. [*anon.*] With an introduction, by Charles Hodge, D.D. xvi, 325 pp. 16°. *Philadelphia, presbyterian board of publication*, 1853. s.

Falconer (Hugh, *M.D.*) *and* **Cautley** (*Sir* Proby T.) Fauna antiqua sivalensis; being the fossil zoology of the Sewalik hills in the north of India. Pars 1a. Atlas, parts 1-9. 92 pl. fol. *London, Smith, Elder & co.* 1846–49. s.
[No more published].

CONTENTS.

Parts 1–6. Proboscidea.
Part 7. Hippopotamidæ.
Part 8. Suidæ and rhinocerotidæ.
Part 9. Equidæ, camelidæ, siratherium.

Falconer (William, *M.D.*) Remarks on the influence of climate, situation, nature of country, population, nature of food, and way of life, on mankind. xvi, 552 pp. 13 l. 4°. *London, C. Dilly*, 1781.

Falconnet (Francisco de P.) Manifestacion dirigada á la honorable cámara de diputados por el agente de los tenedores de bonos mexicanos. 23 pp. 8°. *Mexico, J. M. Lara*, 1852.

Fales (William R.) Memoir of W. Fales, the Portsmouth cripple. 151 pp. 16°. *Philadelphia, Lindsay & Blakiston*, 1851.

Falkener (Edward). A description of some important theatres and other remains in Crete. *See* **Belli** (O.)

Family (The) doctor; or, mrs. Barry and her bourbon. [*anon.*] 384 pp. 3 pl. 16°. *Boston, H. Hoyt*, 1868.

Fanfares (Les) et covrées abbadesqves des rovle bontemps de la havte et basse coqvaigne et dépendances. Par I. P. A. [*anon. Chambéry*, 1613]. Reimpression textuelle, précédée d'une introduction. [*anon.*] 8 p. l. xii, 176 pp. 18°. *Paris, J. Gay*, 1863.

Fanning (Thomas W.) The hairbreadth escapes and humorous adventures of a volunteer in the cavalry service. 200 pp. 8°. *Cincinnati, P. C. Browne*, 1865.

Farey (John, *sr.*) General view of the agriculture and minerals of Derbyshire. 3 v. 8°. *London*, 1811-17.
[GREAT BRITAIN: Board of agriculture].

Fargo (J. P.) Songs of the temple. *See* **Baker** (B. F.) *and* **Fargo**.

Faris el-Shidiac. A practical grammar of the Arabic language. With interlineal reading lessons, dialogues and vocabulary. 2d ed. by Rev. H. G. Williams. 2 p. l. 162 pp. 18°. *London, B. Quaritch*, 1866.

Farley (Frederick A. *D.D.*) Unitarianism defined. The scripture doctrine of the father, son, and holy ghost. A course of lectures. 272 pp. 12°. *Boston, Walker, Wise & co.* 1860.

Farmer (Hugh). The general prevalence of the worship of human spirits, in the antient heathen nations, asserted and proved. lv, 495 pp. 8°. *London, Galabin & Baker*, 1783.

Farmer's (The) magazine. July, 1867—June, 1868. 3d series. v. 32-33. 8°. *London, Rogerson & Tuxford*, 1867-68.

Farnham (Thomas J. *or* J. T.) The early days of California; embracing what I saw and heard there, with scenes in the Pacific. vi, 314 pp. 10 pl. 12°. *Philadelphia, J. E. Potter*, 1862.

Farquharson (Martha). Elsie Dinsmore. 288 pp. 4 pl. 16°. *New York, M. W. Dodd*, 1867.

——— Holidays at Roselands; with some after scenes in Elsie's life; being a sequel to Elsie Dinsmore. 367 pp. 3 pl. 16°. *New York, M. W. Dodd*, 1868.

——— Hugo and Franz. 288 pp. 3 pl. 18°. *Philadelphia, presb. board of pub.* [1865].

——— The Shannons; or, from darkness to light. 336 pp. 4 pl. 16°. *Philadelphia, presb. pub. com.* 1868.

Farrar (*Rev.* Frederic William). Seekers after God. [Biographies of Seneca, Epictetus, and Marcus Aurelius]. xiii, 336 pp. 3 pl. 12°. [*London*], *Macmillan & co.* [1868].
[SUNDAY library for household reading, v. 3].

——— (*editor*). Essays on a liberal education. [By various authors]. 2d ed. viii, 384 pp. 8°. *London, Macmillan & co.* 1868.

Fashion and folly. By aunt Hattie. [*pseudon.*] 287 pp. 3 pl. 16°. *Boston, Graves & Young*, 1867.
[BROOKSIDE series, no. 4].

Favre (Alphonse, *prof. of geology in academy of Geneva*). Recherches géologiques dans les parties de la Savoie, du Piémont, et de la Suisse, voisines du mont Blanc. 3 v. 8°. Atlas. 32 pl. fol. *Paris, V. Masson et fils*, 1867. s.

Favre (Eugène). Première leçons de langue allemande. 4e éd. 150 pp. 12°. *Genève, J. Kessmann*, 1853. s.

Faye (Andreas). Udtog af Norges riges historie, [etc.] 1 p. l. 60 pp. 12°. *Christiania, P. J. Hoppes*, 1834. s.

Faye (Frants Christian). Om cholera-epidemien i Norge 1853. 8°. *Christiania*, 1854.
[*In* NORWAY. Actstykker ang. cholera-epidemien i Norge].

Featley (Daniel, *D.D.*) The dippers dipt; or, the anabaptists dvck'd and plung'd over head and eares, at a disputation in Southwark. [With] a discourse of their originall, severall sorts, peculiar errours, etc. 9 p. l. 191 pp. 1 pl. sm. 4°. *London, N. Bourne*, 1645.

Fechner (Gustav Theodor). Ueber die seelenfrage. Ein gang durch die sichtbare welt, um die unsichtbare zu finden. vii, 228 pp. 12°. *Leipzig, C. F. Amelang*, 1861.

Federal (The) ready reckoner; or, trader's valuable guide, in purchasing and selling all kinds of articles. [*anon.*] 139 pp. 18°. *Worcester, (Mass.) L. Worcester*, 1795.

Feilitzsch (Fabian Carl Ottokar, *freiherr* von). Die lehre von den fernewirkungen des galvanischen stromes. Elektromagnetismus, elektrodynamik, induction und diamagnetismus. xviii, 834 pp. 1 l. 3 pl. 8°. *Leipzig, L. Voss*, 1856-65.
[KARSTEN (G.) Allgemeine encyclopädie der physik, v. 19].

Felix (Marcus Minucius). Octavius; or, a vindication of christianity against paganism. Translated by P. Lorrain [from the French of D'Ablancourt]. viii, 126 pp. 16°. *London, R. Royston*, 1682.
[*With* MURET (P.) Rites of funeral. ed. 1683].

Fell (Archie, *pseudon?*) Earthen vessels. 464 pp. 5 pl. 16°. *Boston, Henry Hoyt*, 1868.

Felton (Cornelius Conway). Familiar letters from Europe. 392 pp. 12°. *Boston, Ticknor & Fields*, 1865.

Female life in prison. By a prison matron. [*anon.*] 2d ed. revised. 2 v. ix, 298 pp; vii, 299 pp. 12°. *London, Hurst & Blackett*, 1862.

Female (The) review. Life of Deborah Sampson, the female soldier in the war of the revolution; with an introduction and notes by J. A. Vinton. 267 pp. 1 portrait. sm. 4°. *Boston, Wiggin & Lunt*, 1866.

Fenderich (Charles). Portfolio of living American statesmen. 1 p. l. 70 lith. pl. fol. *Washington, C. Fenderich*, 1837.

Fénélon (François de Salignac de La Mothe). Aventures de Télémaque, fils d'Ulysse. Édition à l'usage des élèves du lycée national; publiée par P. Y. de Séprés. 2 p. l. 436 pp. 16°. *Paris, Mansut fils*, [*about* 1840]. s.

——— Démonstration de l'existence de Dieu, tirée de l'art, de la nature, des preuves intellectuelles, et de l'idée de l'infini même. Nouv. éd. viii, 322 pp. 1 portrait. 16°. *Lyon, etc. Perisse frères*, 1827. s.

——— Lettres choisies tirées des oeuvres spirituelles. 310 pp. 12°. *Turin, Alliana & Paravia*, 1825. s.

[*With* LA MENNAIS (H. F. R. de). Mélanges, 1825].

Fenestella (L. *pseudon.*) *See* **Fiocco** (A. D.)

Fenn (Charles). Compendium of the English and foreign funds, debts, and revenues of all nations; banks, railways, mines, and the principal joint stock companies. Brought down to the present times, by R. L. Nash. 9th ed. xx, 584 pp. 1 pl. 8°. *London, E. Wilson*, 1867.

Fenn (Joseph). A new and complete system of algebra; or, specious arithmetic. 5 p. l. 306 pp. 4°. *Dublin, A. M'Culloh*, [1800]? s.

Fer (Francisco de). Cartas escritas al autor del Correo de Europa, en que le da noticias de lo que ha observado en España. 2 p. l. 107 pp. 16°. *Burdeos, L. Boudrie*, [*about* 1783]. s.

Ferguson (James, *F. R. S.*) Astronomy explained upon sir Isaac Newton's principles, and made easy to those who have not studied mathematics. 10th ed. 4 p. l. 503 pp. 8 l. 17 pl. 8°. *London, J. Johnson, etc.* 1799. s.

——— Lectures on select subjects in mechanics, hydrostatics, pneumatics, and optics. With the use of the globes, the art of dialing, etc. viii, 252 pp. 2 l. 23 pl. 4°. *London, A. Millar*, 1764. s.

Ferguson (*Rev.* Jesse B.) History of the relation of the pastor to the "christian church" at Nashville; being a discourse, [etc.] 24 pp. 8°. *Nashville, M'Kennie & Brown*, 1855. s.

[*With his* Spirit communion. 1854].

——— Relation of pastor and people: statement of belief on unitarianism, universalism, and spiritualism. 23 pp. 8°. *Nashville, Union and American steam press*, 1854. s.

[*With his* Spirit communion. 1854].

——— Spirit communion: an immovable fact in the internal consciousness and external history of man, being an address, [etc.] 96 pp. 8°. *Nashville, M. W. Wetmore*, 1855. s.

[*With his* Spirit communion. 1854].

——— Spirit communion: a record of communications from the spirit spheres, with incontestible evidence of personal identity. 276 pp. 8°. *Nashville, Union and American steam press*, 1854. s.

Fergusson (James). A history of architecture in all countries, from the earliest times to the present day. 3 v. 8°. *London, J. Murray*, 1862–67.

Fergusson (William, *prof. of surgery*). System of practical surgery. 3d Am. from last English ed. 630 pp. 8°. *Philadelphia, Lea & Blanchard*, 1848. s.

Ferland (J. B. A.) Cours d'histoire du Canada. 1re partie, 1534–1663. xi, 522 pp. 4°. *Québec, A. Coté*, 1861. s.

Fernandez de Piedrahita (Lucas). Historia general de las conqvistas del nvevo reyno de Granada. 1a parte. 8 p. l. 599 pp. 4 l. fol. *Amberes, J. B. Verdussen*, [1688].

[No more published].

Fernandez de Santa Cruz (Manuel). Regla de S. Augustin, que han de guardar las religiosas del convento del maximo doct. S. Geronimo de la Puebla de los Angeles. Con las ordenanças, y constituciones [del convento]. 46, 2 l. 8°. *Puebla, herederos J. de Villa Real*, 1701.

Ferrara (Gabriello). Sylva chirvrgiæ, in tres libros divisa: in qvorvm i. de observationibus chirurgicis, ii. de medicamentis itidem ad chirurgiam pertinentibus, iii. de medicamentis per destillationem acquisitis agitur. [P. Uffenbachio interprete]. 8 p. l. 437 pp. 34 pl. 16°. *Francofurti, J. de Tetter*, 1625. s.

Ferrario (Giulio). Storia ad analisi degli antichi romanzi di cavalleria e dei poemi romanzeschi d'Italia, con dissertazioni sull' origine, sugl' istituti, sulle cerimonie de' cavalieri. 3 v. 8°. *Milano, autore*, 1828–29. s.

Ferrario (Ottavio). Corso di chimica generale. 5 v. 8°. *Milano, L. di Giacomo Pirola*, 1837–46. s.

——— The same. v. 6–10. Parte seconda. La chimica organica applicata alle scienze mediche, alle arti, e sopratutto all'agricoltura. 8°. *Milano, L. di Giacomo Pirola*, 1842–46. s.

Fessenden (Thomas Green). The husbandman and housewife: a collection of valuable receipts and directions, relating to agriculture and domestic economy. 191 pp. 16°. *Bellow's Falls (Vt.) Bill, Blake & co.* 1820.

Fessenden (Thomas Green). Terrible tractoration, and other poems. By Christopher Caustic, M. D. [*pseudon.*] 3[d] Amer. ed. viii, 264 pp. 1 pl. 16°. *Boston, Russell, Shattuck & co.* 1836.

Festus (Sextus Pompeius). Fragmenta de verborum veterum significatione. *Venetiis,* 1517. *See* **Perotti**, (M.) etc. Cornvcopiæ.

Fetridge (W. Pembroke). Harper's phrase-book; or, hand-book of travel talk. Being a guide to conversation in English, French, German, and Italian. 309 pp. sq. 16°. *New York, Harpers,* 1868.

Feuillet (Octave). Camors; or, life under the new empire. From the French. 388 pp. 12°. *New York, Blelock & co.* 1868.

Feuerbach (Anselm von). Caspar Hauser. An account of an individual kept in a dungeon, separated from all communication with the world, from early childhood to about the age of seventeen. Translated from the German. [By H. G. Linberg]. 2[d] ed. ix, 168 pp. 18°. *Boston, Allen & Ticknor,* 1833.

Few (A) words in behalf of the loyal women of the United States. By one of themselves. [*anon.*] 23 pp. 8°. *New York, W. C. Bryant & co.* 1863.

[LOYAL publication society, no. 10].

Fichte (Immanuel Hermann). Die idee der persönlichkeit und der individuellen fortdauer. 216 pp. 8°. *Leipzig, Dyk,* 1855.

Fichte (Johann Gottlieb) *and* **Schelling** (Friedrich Wilhelm Joseph von). Fichtes und Schellings philosophischer briefwechsel aus dem nachlasse beider; herausgegeben von I. H. Fichte und K. F. A. Schelling. iv, 131 pp. 8°. *Stuttgart, etc. J. G. Cotta,* 1856. s.

Ficino (Marsilio). Opuscula. De sole: et lumine libri duo. Apologia eiusdem in librum suum de sole; et lumine. Catalogus librorum. 29 l. sm. 4°. *Venetiis, per Bernardinum Venetum de Vitalibus,* 1503.

Fidler (*Rev.* Isaac). Observations on professions, literature, manners, and emigration, in the United States and Canada, made during a residence there in 1832. 247 pp. 12°. *New York, Harpers,* 1833.

Field (*Rev.* Chester). Scripture illustrated by interesting facts, incidents, and anecdotes. With an introduction, by rev. John Todd. 203 pp. 16°. *New York, Harpers,* 1847. s.

Field (Cyrus West). Proceedings at the banquet held in honor of Cyrus W. Field, esq. of New York, in Willis's rooms, London, 1st July, 1868, ["as an acknowledgment of his devotion to the interests of Atlantic telegraphy."] 80 pp. 12°. *London, Metchim & son,* 1868. s.

Field (Henry M. *D. D.*) History of the Atlantic telegraph. 2[d] ed. 435 pp. 2 pl. 12°. *New York, Scribner & co.* 1867.

Field (J. M.) The drama in Pokerville; the bench and bar of Jurytown, and other stories. By "Everpoint." [*pseudon.*] 200 pp. 8 pl. 12°. *Philadelphia, Carey & Hart,* 1847. s.

Field (Kate). Planchette's diary. 95 pp. 16°. *New York, J. S. Redfield,* 1868.

Figuier (Guillaume Louis). The insect world; being a popular account of the orders of insects, together with a description of the habits and economy of some of the most interesting species. From the French, [by Y. D.] 3 p. l. 519 pp. 12 pl. 8°. *London, Chapman & Hall,* 1868.

Filelfo (Giovanni Mario Jacopo). Epistolare Marii Philelfi. 159 l. 4°. *Basiliae, per Ioannem de Amerbach,* 1489. s.

Fillmore (A. D.) *and* **Skene** (Robert). Christian psaltery, a collection of new and old sacred music. 400 pp. obl. 8°. *Cincinnati, R. W. Carroll & co.* 1867.

Filson (John). The discovery, settlement and present state of Kentucky. 8°. *London, J. Debrett,* 1797.

[*With* IMLAY (G.) Topographical description of the western territory. pp. 306–387. 1 map. 1797].

Finch (*Rev.* Josiah John). Sermons; with a memoir of his life. xv, 314 pp. 1 portrait. 12°. *Charleston, southern baptist publication society,* 1853. s.

Findlater (*Rev.* Charles). General view of the agriculture of the county of Peebles. xx, 413 pp. 4 tab. 1 map. 2 pl. 8°. *London,* 1814. s.

[GREAT Britain: Board of agriculture].

Finsch (Otto). Die papageien, monographisch bearbeitet. v. 1. xii, 363 pp. 1 col. map. 1 pl. 8°. *Leiden, E. J. Brill,* 1867. s.

Finx. *See* **Francisci.**

Fiocco *or* **Fiocchi** (Andrea Domenico). De potestatibvs Romanorvm, lib. ii. hactenus L. Fenestellæ, et falsò, et mutili adscripti, studio ac industria Egidii Wiitsii, [etc.] Pomponii Læti, Raphaelis Volaterrani, et Henrici Bebelii, eiusdem argumenti libelli. 8 p. l. 85, 2 l. 16°. *Antverpiæ, ex officina G. Syluii,* 1561. s.

Fischer (Christian August). Beyträge zur genauern kenntniss der spanischen besitzungen in Amerika: aus dem Spanischen übersetzt von C. A. Fischer. xvi, 276 pp. 12°. *Dresden, H. Gerlach,* 1802.

Fischer (Johann Baptist). Synopsis mammalium. xlii, 752 pp. 8°. *Stuttgardtiae, J. G. Cotta*, 1829-30. s.

Fischer (Johann Gustav). Anatomische abhandlungen über die perennibranchiaten und derotremen. 1[es] heft. Die visceralbogen und deren muskeln; die gehirnnerven. 172 pp. 6 pl. 4°. *Hamburg, O. Meissner*, 1864. s.

——— Die familie der seeschlangen systematisch beschrieben. 2[e] ausg. 2 p. l. 78 pp. 3 col. pl. 4°. *Hamburg, naturw. vereins*, 1856. s.

——— Neue schlangen des naturhistorischen museums zu Hamburg. (Extract). 38 pp. 3 pl. 4°. *Hamburg, naturw. vereins*, 1856. s.

Fischer (Nicolaus Wolfgang). Systematischer lehrbegriff der chemie in tabellen dargestellt. 4 p. l. 249 pp. 4°. *Berlin, Veit & co.* 1838. s.

Fischer (Sebastian). Branchiopoden und entomostracen. 4°. *St. Petersburg*, 1851.

[*In* MIDDENDORF (A. T. von). Reise, etc. v 2. theil 1].

Fish (Henry C. *D.D.*) The agent's manual of life assurance. 165 pp. 16°. *New York, Wynkoop & Hallenbeck*, 1868.

——— History and repository of pulpit eloquence, (deceased divines), containing [their] masterpieces. [With] historical sketches of preaching in different countries represented, and biographical and critical notices of the several preachers and their discourses. 2 v. xiii, 613 pp. 1 pl; vi, 622 pp. 8°. *New York, M. W. Dodd*, 1856.

——— Insurance guide and hand-book. *See* **Walford** (Cornelius).

Fisher (Edward T.) Easy French reading: being selections of historical tales and anecdotes, with notes. 175 pp. 16°. *New York, Leypoldt & Holt*, 1868.

Fisk (Wilbur, *D. D.*) Travels on the continent of Europe, viz: in England, France, Italy, [etc.] 1st ed. xv, 688 pp. 8 pl. 8°. *New York, Harpers*, 1838.

Fiske (John). Tobacco and alcohol. i. It does pay to smoke. ii. The coming man will drink wine. [With the bibliography of tobacco]. 163 pp. 16°. *New York, Leypoldt & Holt*, 1869.

Fitch (John). Chickamauga, the price of Chattanooga. A description of the strategic plans, marches, and battles of the campaign of Chattanooga. [*anon.*] pp. 451-482. 1 map. 8°. *Philadelphia, J. B. Lippincott & co.* 1864.

Fitzgeffrey (Charles). Life and death of sir Francis Drake. xxiii, 101 pp. 12°. *Kent, (Eng.) private press of Lee priory, J. Warwick*, 1819.

[*Note*—A reprint of "Sir Francis Drake, his honorable life's commendacion, and his tragical death's lamentation"].

Fitzgerald (Percy). Charles Lamb; his friends, his haunts, and his books. vii, 229 pp. 2 pl. sq. 16°. *London, R. Bentley*, 1866.

——— The dear girl. 3 v. 12°. *London, Tinsley bros.* 1868.

——— The life of David Garrick. xvii, 492 pp. 2 pl. 1 tab. 8°. *London, Tinsley bros.* 1868.

Fitzgerald (Rosa). The half-sisters, a romance of the southside. 147 pp. 8°. *Washington, Intelligencer*, 1867.

Fitzgibbon (William). The mine of wealth and guide for the million: containing instructions for the manufacture of wines, liquors, etc; cookery [and] miscellaneous receipts, and a family medical department. 240 pp. 8°. *Philadelphia, Barclay & co.* 1868.

Fitzherbert (*Sir* Anthony). The boke of husbandry. viii, 120 pp. 8°. *London, C. Bathurst*, 1767.

[*In* CERTAIN ancient tracts concerning landed property. ed. 1767].

——— The boke of surveyinge and of improuements. viii, 100 pp. 8°. *London, C. Bathurst*, 1767.

[*In* CERTAIN ancient tracts concerning landed property. ed. 1767].

Five black arts. A popular account of printing, pottery, gaslight, glass, iron. Condensed from the Encyclopædia Britannica. vii, 392 pp. 32 pl. 8°. *Columbus, (O.) Follett, Foster & co.* 1861.

Five lessons for young men. [The theatre. The circus. The race-ground. Intemperance. Of bad example]. By a man of sixty. [*anon.*] 198 pp. 16°. *Albany, A. Southwick*, 1837.

Fix (W.) Amerikanischer kinderfreund. Zweites lesebuch für schule und haus, mit einem anhang von August Schnabel. vi, 230 pp. 12°. *Philadelphia, Schäfer & Koradi*, 1868.

Flachat (Eugène). Navigation à vapeur transocéanienne. 2 v. 444 pp; 462 pp. atlas. 48 pl. 8°. *Paris, Baudry*, 1866.

CONTENTS.

[v. 1.] Études scientifiques.
[v. 2.] Études économiques et de statistique.

Flachat (Jules). Notes sur le fleuve du Darien, et sur les différents projets de canaux interocéaniques du centre Amérique. Extrait des mémoires de la Société des ingénieurs civils. 133 pp. 3 maps. 8°. *Paris, Lacroix*, 1866.

Fleetwood (John, *D. D.*) The life of Jesus Christ: and the lives and sufferings of his apostles and evangelists, [etc. And] a history of the Jews. With notes by J. N. Brown, D. D. New ed. 750 pp. 1 map. 16 pl. 8°. *Philadelphia, Bradley & co.* 1868.

Fleming (*Rev.* John). Short sermon: also hymns, in the Muskokee or Creek language. 35 pp. 24°. *Boston, American board of foreign missions,* 1835.

Fleming (William *and* Elizabeth). A narrative of the sufferings and surprising deliverances of William and Elizabeth Fleming, who were taken captive by captain Jacob, commander of the Indians, etc. [*anon.*] 20 pp. 8°. *Boston, Green & Russell,* 1756.

[The last two leaves *ms.*]

Fleurs de la piété chrétienne. Recueil complet de prières, extraites en grande partie des plus belles prières de l'église, et des écrits des saints pères. Traduites par l' abbé Gobat. 448 pp. 32°. *New York, C. & N. Benziger,* 1868.

Flint (Austin, *M. D.*) A treatise on the principles and practice of medicine. 3^d ed. xvi, 1002 pp. 8°. *Philadelphia, H. C. Lea,* 1868.

Flint (Henry M.) The railroads of the United States: their history and statistics. With a synopsis of the railroad laws, and an article on iron and steel rails. 452 pp. 12°. *Philadelphia, J. E. Potter & co.* 1868.

Flint (Timothy). The life and adventures of Daniel Boone, the first settler of Kentucky, interspersed with incidents in the early annals of the country. New ed. 256 pp. 1 map. 3 pl. 12°. *Cincinnati, U. P. James,* 1868.

Flinter (George Dawson). A view of the present condition of the slave population of Puerto Rico. Showing the impolicy and danger of prematurely emancipating the West India slaves. 117 pp. 8°. *Philadelphia, A. Waldie,* 1832.

Floccus. *See* **Fiocco.**

Flores. *See* **Roxo de Flores.**

Floridablanca (José Monino, *conde de*). *See* **Monino.**

Florus (Lucius Annæus). De gestis Romanorvm libri iv. a mendis accvratissime repurgati, unà cū adnotationibus Io. Camertis. Ad haec, Sexti Rvffi de historia Ro. epitome. Item, Messalae Corvini de progenie Avgvsti Caes. libellus, nunc primū excusus. 10 p. l. 128 pp. fol. *Basiliae, apvd Io. Hervagivm,* 1532. s.

Flourens (Marie Jean Pierre). Recueil des éloges historiques lus dans les séances publiques de l'académie des sciences. 2e série. 436 pp. 12°. *Paris, Garnier,* 1867. s.

CONTENTS.

De la méthode naturelle et des Jussieu. Éloge de B. L. Desfontaines. Éloge de J. J. de Labillardière. Éloge de P. de Candolle. Éloge d' A. Du Petit Thouars. Éloge de B. Delessert. De Peyssonel et des prétendues plantes marines.

——— The same. 3e série. 3 p. l. 366 pp. 12°. *Paris, Garnier,* 1862. s.

CONTENTS.

Éloge de F. Magendie. De la découverte des fonctions distinctes des racines des nerfs. Analyse des travaux de Charles Bell sur le système nerveux. Éloge de J. A. Chaptal. Éloge de L. J. Thenard. Éloge de F. Tiedemann. Discours prononcés aux funérailles de Arago et Dufrénoy. Notices sur Daubenton, Guéneau de Montebeillard, et Bexon.

Flower (William Henry, *editor*). Recent memoirs on the cetacea, by professors Eschricht, Reinhardt, and Lilljeborg. xi, 312 pp. 6 pl. 4°. *London,* 1866.

CONTENTS.

1. On the Greenland whale. By D. F. Eschricht and J. Reinhardt.
2. On the species of orca inhabiting the northern seas. By D. F. Eschricht.
3. Pseudorca crassidens. By J. Reinhardt.
4. Synopsis of the cetaceous mammalia of Scandinavia. By W. Lilljeborg.

[RAY society].

Foley (L. E.) Histoire statistique de la colonisation algérienne. *See* **Martin** (A. E. V.) *and* **Foley.**

Folies (Les) du spiritisme. [*anon.*] 72 pp. 8°. *Paris, libr. du petit journal,* [1866].

Follen (Charles, *prof. of German in Harvard university*). A practical grammar of the German language. 14th ed. xxiv, 283 pp. 12°. *Boston, Phillips, Sampson & co.* 1849. s.

——— The same. 21st ed. xxiv, 283 pp. 8°. *Boston, J. Munroe & co.* 1859. s.

Follen (Eliza Lee). The well-spent hour. 203 pp. 4 pl. 16°. *Boston, H. B. Fuller,* 1868.

Fonblanque (Edward Barrington de). Niphon and Pe-che-li; or, two years in Japan and Northern China. 2^d ed. 286 pp. 1 map. 9 pl. 8°. *London, Saunders, Otley & co.* 1863.

Fontaine (Pierre François Léonard). Description de le mariage de l'empereur Napoléon avec Marie-Louise d'Autriche. *See* **Percier** (Charles) *and* **Fontaine.**

Fontaneda. *See* **Escalante Fontaneda** (Hernando de).

Fontanes (Louis, *marquis* de) *and* **Dubroca** (Louis). Éloges funèbres de Washington. [Avec une préface par Isaiah Townsend, jr. d'Albany, N. Y.] 72 pp. 12°. *Paris, Casimir,* 1835. s.

Fontenay (Louis Abel de Bonafons, *abbé* de). *See* **Bonafons.**

Forbes (Charles, *M.D.*) Vancouver island; its resources and capabilities as a colony. 2 p. l. 63, 18 pp. 1 l. 8°. [*Victoria*], *colonial government*, 1862. s.

Forbes (James David). A general view of the progress of mathematical and physical science, principally from 1775 to 1850. 4°. *Boston, Little, Brown & co.* 1860.
[ENCYCLOPÆDIA britannica, v. 1. dissert. 6].

Forbin (Louis Nicolas Philippe Auguste, *comte* de). Charles Barimore, suivi des œuvres inédites. [Le quaker de Philadelphie; romances en verse; réflexions detachées]. xv, 298 pp. 8°. *Paris, Challamel*, 1843. s.

Forestus. *See* **Forreest.**

Forme (The) and manner of making and consecrating bishops, priestes, and deacons. 14 l. fol. *London, R. Barker*, 1634.
[*With* BOOK of common prayer. ed. 1632].

Formey (Jean Henri Samuel). A concise history of philosophy and philosophers. 7 p. l. 283 pp. 18°. *London, F. Newbery*, 1766.

Forreest *or* **Forestus** (Petrus). Observationvm et curationum medicalinium libri 25. 9 v. in 6. 16°. *Lvgdvni-Batavorvm, F. Raphelengius*, 1589–97. s.
[Lib. 8–10 wanting].

Forrester (Alfred Henry). Goodnatured hint about California. By Alfred Crowquill. [*pseudon.*] 9 pl. obl. 24°. *London*, [*about* 1849].

Forster (Carl) *and* **Bellenger** (William A.) Nowy przewodnik w rozmowach nowoczesnych w jezyku polskim i francuskim, [etc.] Nouveau guide de conversations modernes en polonais et en français, [etc.] Nouv éd. 236 pp. 18°. *Berlin, B. Behr*, 1865.

Forster (Carl) *and* **Boltz** (A.) Nowy przewodnik w rozmowach nowoczesnych w jezyku polskim i ruskim. 236 pp. 18°. *Berlin, B. Behr*, 1855.

Forster (Johann Reinhold). Descriptiones animalium quae, in itinere ad maris australis terras per annos 1772–74 suscepto, collegit, observavit et delineavit. Nunc demum editæ auctoritate et impensis academiae litterarum regiae Berolinae, curante H. Lichtenstein. xv, 424 pp. 8°. *Berolini, officina academica*, 1844. s.

Forteguerri (Nicolò). Ricciardetto di Niccolò Carteromaco. [*pseudon.*] 3 v. 8°. *Milano, societá tipografica de' classici italiani*, 1813.

Fortnightly (The) review. Edited by John Morley. Jan. to Dec. 1868. New series. v. 3–4. (Complete series. v. 9-10). 8°. *London, Chapman & Hall*, 1868.

Fortune (E. F. T.) A concise and authentic history of the bank of England. With dissertations on metals and coin, bank notes and bills of exchange. 3[d] ed. 6 p. l. 134 pp. 18°. *London, T. Boosey*, 1802.

Fosgate (Blanchard, *M. D.*) Sleep psychologically considered with reference to sensation and memory. 188 pp. 12°. *New York, G. P. Putnam & co.* 1850. s.

Fossati (Gaspardo). Aya Sofia, Constantinople, as recently restored by order of h. m. the sultan Abdul-Medjid. From the original drawing by Fossati. Lithographed by L. Haghe. 6 pp. 25 pl. fol. [*London*], *Colnaghi & co.* 1852. s.

Foster (G. G.) Fifteen minutes around New York. 111 pp. 8°. *New York, De Witt & Davenport*, [*about* 1850].

Foster (*Rev.* John, *of Bristol, Eng.*) Essays in a series of letters. 10th ed. xx, 456 pp. 8°. *London, Holdsworth & Ball*, 1833.

CONTENTS.

1. On a man's writing memoirs of himself.
2. On decision of character.
3. On the application of the epithet romantic.
4. On the aversion of men of taste to evangelical religion.

Foster (John Y.) New Jersey and the rebellion: a history of the services of the troops and people of New Jersey in aid of the union cause. 872 pp. 4 maps. 1 portrait. 8°. *Newark, (N. J.) M. R. Dennis & co.* 1868.

Foster (Nathan W.) *and* **Atkins** (Charles G.) Report of commission on fisheries, [on the restoration of sea fish to the rivers and inland waters of Maine]. Senate doc. no. 7. 128 pp. 8°. [*Augusta*], *Stevens & Sayward*, 1868. s.

Foster (*Rev.* Randolph S.) Nature and blessedness of christian purity. With an introduction, by Edmund S. Janes. 226 pp. 1 pl. 12°. *New York, Harpers*, 1851. s.

Foster (Sarah Haven). Watchwords for little soldiers; or, stories on bible texts. 184 pp. 4 pl. 16°. *Boston, sunday school society*, 1868.

Foster (The) brothers; or, pleasing better than teasing. [*anon.*] 173 pp. 3 pl. 16°. *Boston, W. V. Spencer*, 1868.

Fouqué (Friedrich Heinrich Carl de la Motte). Undine. Eine erzählung. 133 pp. 16°. *London, Simpkin, Marshall & co.* 1851.
[*With* LEBAHN (F.) German language. ed. 1851].

Fournel (Henri). Richesse minérale de l'Algérie, accompagnée d'éclaircissements historiques et géographiques sur cette partie de l'Afrique septentrionale. Publié par ordre du gouvernment. v. 1. Texte. [Province de Constantiné]. xvii, 476 pp. 4°. *Paris, imprimerie nationale*, 1849. s.
[No more published].

Fournier (Pierre Simon). De l'origine et des productions de l'imprimerie primitive en taille de bois; avec une réfutation des préjugés plus ou moins accrédités sur cet art. 263 pp. 12°. *Paris, J. Barbou,* 1759.

Fowle (William Bentley). A key to Fowle's diagrams, for the illustration of human physiology. 180 pp. 12°. *Boston, Fitz, Hobbs & co.* 1850. s.

——— The mind and heart; or, school and fireside reading for children. 159 pp. 12°. *Boston, M. Cotton,* 1856. s.

Fowle (William F.) Catalogue of [his] very choice collection of books, sold at Boston, Dec. 1864. viii, 147 pp. 8°. *Cambridge, (Mass.) Riverside press,* 1864.
[With the prices].

Fowler (J.) The history of the troubles of Suethland and Poland, which occasioned the expulsion of Sigismundus the third, with a continuation of those troubles until the truce, 1629; the treaty of pacification between those two kingdomes, concluded at Stumbsdorff, 1635; with the life and death of s[r]. George Dvglas, ambassadour from Great Brittaine. 3 p. l. 254 pp. 8 portraits. sm. fol. *London, T. Roycroft for H. Twyford,* 1656.

Fowler (Orrin S.) A home for all; or, the gravel wall and octagon mode of building. 192 pp. 1 pl. 12°. *New York, Fowler & Wells,* 1856.

Fowler (William Chauncey, *LL. D.*) History of Durham, Connecticut, from the first grant of land in 1662, to 1866. 460 pp. 8°. *Hartford, Wiley, Waterman & Eaton,* 1866.

——— Memorials of the Chaunceys, including president Chauncey, his ancestors and descendants, [with appendix]. vii, 336 pp. portrait. 4 tab. 8°. *Boston, H. W. Dutton & son,* 1858.

Fowles (*Rev.* James Henry). Sermons preached in the church of the Epiphany, Philadelphia. [With a biographical sketch]. xli, 479 pp. portrait. 8°. *Philadelphia, congregation,* 1855. s.

Fownes (George, *Ph. D.*) Chemistry, as exemplifying the wisdom and beneficence of God. 158 pp. 12°. *New York, Wiley & Putnam,* 1844. s.

Fox (Charles James). A history of the early part of the reign of James ii. with appendix. xxxii, 201, cci pp. 8°. *Philadelphia, A. Small,* 1808.

Fox *or* **Foxe** (John). Acts and monuments of matters most special and memorable, happening in the church; with an universal history of the same. 9th ed. 3 v. fol. *London, company of stationers,* 1684.

Fracastoro (Girolamo). Della siffilide, ovvero del morbo gallico. 105 pp. portrait. 8°. *Milano,* 1825.
[Raccolta di poemi didascalici. ed 2a. v. 2].

France. Annuaire militaire de l'empire français, 1867. lxxi, 760 pp. 12°. *Paris, Berger-Levrault,* 1867.

——— Appendice au compte rendu sur le service du recrutement de l'armée. Statistique médicale de l'armée pendant l'année 1865. 304 pp. 4°. *Paris, imprimerie impériale,* 1867.

——— Exploration scientifique de l'Algérie pendant les années 1840–42, publiée par ordre du gouvernement et avec le concours d'une commission académique. Physique générale. ii. Observations sur le magnétisme terrestre, par G. Aimé. 3 p. l. iv, 229 pp. 24 pl. 4°. *Paris, imprimerie royale,* 1846. s.

——— Legislation relative à la banque de France, et règlements intérieurs. [Lois et statuts. An. viii à 1841]. 4°. *Paris, banque de France,* 1830–41. s.

——— A memorial containing a summary view of facts, [with special reference to America], with their authorities, in answer to the observations sent by the English ministry to the courts of Europe. Translated from the French. [*anon.*] 190 pp. 8°. *New York, H. Gaine,* 1757.

——— Rapport et discussion d'une pétition relative à la banque de France et à la banque de Savoie. Séances du sénat des 20 et 30 Mai, 1864. (Extrait du Moniteur universel). 205 pp. 8°. *Paris, E. Panckoucke & cie.* 1864. s.

——— Recueil des dispositions législatives actuellement en vigueur, sur les élections politiques, départementales et municipales. 132 pp. 4°. *Paris, imprimerie royale,* 1838. s.

——— Règlement concernant l'exercice et les manoeuvres de l'infanterie. Du premier Août, 1791. Nouv. éd. accompagnée de notes par mm. B. et L. [*anon.*] 2 p. l. 368 pp. 1 pl. 12°. *Paris, Magimel, Anselin & Pochard,* 1816. s.
[Plate 1 wanting].

——— Règlement provisoire sur le service intérieur des troupes à cheval. xliv, 338 pp. 8°. *Paris, Magimel, Anselin & Pochard,* 1816. s.

——— *Bibliothèque nationale* [*or*] *impériale.* Catalogue de l'histoire de France. Publié par ordre de l'empéreur. v. 1-6. 4°. *Paris, Didot,* 1855–59. s.

——— *Chambre des députés.* Enquête sur les tabacs. [Questions relatives à la culture, au commerce, à la fabrication, et à la vente]. xv, 645 pp. 8 l. 1 map. 4°. *Paris, A. Henry,* 1837. s.

France. *Ministère de l'agriculture, commerce et des travaux publics.* Compte rendu des travaux des ingénieurs des mines pendant l'année 1839. 2 p. l. 187 pp. 1 col. map. 4°. *Paris, imprimerie royale,* 1840. s.

——— ——— Enquête relative à diverses prohibitions etablies à l'entrée des produits étrangers, commencée la 8 Oct. 1834, [etc.] 3 v. 4°. *Paris, imprimerie royale,* 1835. s.

CONTENTS.

v. 1. Documents généraux, [etc.]
v. 2. Poteries. Plaqués. Verreries.
v. 3. Fils et tissus de laine et de coton.

——— ——— Enquête sur les fils et tissus de lin et de chanvre. xviii, 326 pp. 4°. *Paris, imprimerie royale,* 1838. s.

——— ——— Enquête sur le régime des sucres. xxiii, 742 pp. 4°. *Paris, imprimerie impériale,* 1863. s.

——— ——— Exposition des produits de l'industrie française en 1839. Rapport du jury central. 3 v. 8°. *Paris, L. Bouchard-Huzard,* 1839. s.

——— ——— Rapport fait à la commission sur le tracé du chemin de fer de Paris à Chalons-sur-Saone; par m. le comte Daru, [etc.] au nom d'une sous-commission, composée de mm. Févre, Daullé, Le Masson, comte Daru. 248 pp. 2 tab. 4 maps, etc. 4°. *Paris, imprimerie royale,* 1853. s.

——— ——— Situation des travaux [publics] au 31 Décembre, 1839. iv, 485 pp. 4°. *Paris, imprimerie royale,* 1840. s.

——— *Ministère des finances.* Éclaircissements sur le rapport et la déclaration générale de la cour des comptes concernant les comptes de 1833–39. 5 v. 4°. *Paris, imprimerie royale,* 1835-41. s.
[Wanting 1836 and 1838].

——— ——— The same. Éclaircissements en réponse aux observations faites par la cour des comptes dans le rapport au roi et la déclaration générale sur les comptes de 1840–41. 2 v. 4°. *Paris, imprimerie royale,* 1842. s.

——— ——— *Cour des comptes.* Rapport au roi sur les comptes de 1830. 1 p. l. 134 pp. 4°. *Paris, imprimerie royale,* 1832. s.

——— ——— The same. Rapport au roi et déclarations générales de la cour des comptes de l'année 1831–41. 8 v. 4°. *Paris, imprimerie royale,* 1833–43. s.

——— ——— Tableau général du commerce de la France avec ses colonies et les puissances étrangères pendant l'années 1844 [et] 1848. 2 v. 4°. *Paris, imprimerie nationale,* 1845–48. s.

——— *Ministère de la guerre.* Procès verbaux et rapports de la commission nommée par le roi, le 7 Juillet 1833, pour aller recueillir en Afrique tous les faits propres à éclairer le gouvernement sur l'état du pays et sur les mesures que réclame son avenir. 476 pp. 4°. *Paris, imprimerie royale,* 1834. s.

——— ——— Procès-verbaux et rapports de la commission d'Afrique, institutée par ordonnance du roi, du 12 Déc. 1833, [et] supplement. 2 v. in 1. 539 pp; 41 pp. 4°. *Paris, imprimerie royale,* 1834. s.

——— ——— Tableau dè la situation des établissements français dans l'Algérie en 1839 [et] 1842-49. 5 v. 4°. *Paris, imprimerie nationale [et] royale,* 1840–51. s.

——— *Ministère de l'intérieur.* Analyse des réponses des directeurs [des maisons centrales de force, et de correction], à une circulaire ministérielle du 10 Mars, 1834, sur les effets du régime de ces maisons [etc.] 2 p. l. vii, 141 pp. 4°. *Paris, imprimerie royale,* 1836. s.

——— ——— Analyse des voeux des conseils généraux de département sur divers objets d'administration et d'utilité publique; sessions de 1842–43. Supplément au bulletin officiel du ministère de l'intérieur. 2 v. xi, 361 pp; x, 283 pp. 8°. *Paris, imprimerie royale,* 1843–44. s.

——— ——— Compte rendu au roi sur les élections municipales de 1837. 75 pp. 4°. *Paris, imprimerie royale,* 1839. s.

——— ——— Instruction et programme pour la construction des maisons d'arrêt et de justice. Atlas de plans de prisons cellulaires. 65 pp. 25 pl. fol. *Paris,* 1841. s.

——— ——— Projet de loi sur les prisons présenté à la chambre des pairs le 10 Juin, 1844. Observations de la cour de cassation et des cours royales. viii, 674 pp. 4°. *Paris, imprimerie royale,* 1845. s.

——— ——— The same. Observations de les préfets sur ce projet de loi. 2 p. l. viii, 124 pp. 4°. *Paris, imprimerie royale,* 1846.

——— ——— Rapport au roi sur l'exécution, pendant l'années 1838–1841, de la loi du 21 Mai 1836, relative aux chemins vicinaux. 4 v. 4°. *Paris, imprimerie royale,* 1839–43. s.

——— ——— Rapport au roi sur les hôpitaux, les hospices et les services de bienfaisance. 160 pp. 4°. *Paris, imprimerie royale,* 1837. s.

——— ——— Recensement de la population du royaume opéré in 1841. 2 p. l. 100 pp. 4°. [*Paris, imprimerie royale,* 1842]? s.

France. *Ministère de la marine et des colonies.* Notices sur les colonies françaises, [etc.] 3 p. l. 767 pp. 8°. Atlas. 1 p. l. 14 maps. fol. *Paris, Challamel aîné,* 1866. s.

——— ——— Règlement général sur l'administration des quartiers, sous-quartiers, et syndicats maritimes; l'inscription maritime; le recrutement de la flotte; la police de la navigation; les pêches maritimes. xlviii, 274 pp. 8°. *Paris, imprimerie impériale,* 1867. s.

Francis (George W.) Chemical experiments; illustrating the theory, practice, and application of the science of chemistry. 5th ed. 2 p. l. 252 pp. 8°. *London, D. Francis,* 1849. s.

Francis (James B.) Lowell hydraulic experiments. Being a selection from experiments on hydraulic motors, on the flow of water over weirs, in open canals, and through submerged orifices and diverging tubes. 2d ed. xi, 251 pp. 23 pl. 4°. *New York, D. Van Nostrand,* 1868.

——— On the strength of cast-iron pillars, with tables. Extracted from the proceedings of the Amer. acad. of arts and sciences. 71 pp. 8°. *New York, D. Van Nostrand,* 1865. s.

Francis (John). History of the bank of England, its times and traditions, from 1694 to 1844. With appendix to the close of 1861, by J. S. Homans. 1st Am. ed. 476 pp. 1 pl. 8°. *New York, office of the banker's magazine,* 1862.

Francis (Valentine Mott, *M. D.*) A thesis on hospital hygiene. 217 pp. 3 portraits. 8°. *New York, J. F. Trow,* 1859.

Francis de Sales (*Saint*). The mind: a book on religious life. From the original French by mrs. North Peat. 274 pp. 12°. *New York, gen. prot. episc. book society,* 1868.

——— A treatise on the love of God. [Translated from the French]. New ed. 624 pp. 12°. *Dublin, J. Duffy,* 1860.

Francisci, *born* **Finx** (Erasmus). Der hohe traur-saal, oder steigen und fallen grosser herren. 4 v. 18°. *Nürnberg, M. & J. F. Endtern,* 1669–81.

Franck (A. *bookseller*). Catalogue général des livres anciens et modernes en vente aux prix marqués. 1e partie. 2 p. l. 436 pp. 8°. *Paris,* 1859. s.

Franck (Richard). Northern memoirs, calculated for the meridian of Scotland, [with] the contemplative and practical angler. xxxix, 304 pp. 16°. *London, H. Mortlock,* 1694.

Francklin (*Lieut. col.* William). Researches on the tenets and doctrines of the Jeynes and Boodhists; conjectured to be the brachmanes of ancient India. [With] a discussion on the worship of the serpent. viii, 213 pp. 6 pl. 4°. *London, author,* 1827.

François de Sales (*Saint*). *See* **Francis de Sales.**

Frank Grover, the blacksmith's boy. [*anon.*] 275 pp. 2 pl. 18°. *Boston, Mass. s. s. soc.* 1867.

Frank Leslie's pictorial papers. *See* **Leslie** (Frank).

Franke (Traugott). Technological dictionary, English, German, French. *See* **Beil** (J. A.) Technologisches wörterbuch, v. 2.

Frankland (Edward). Lecture notes for clinical students; embracing mineral and organic chemistry. xx, 422 pp. 12°. *London, J. Van Voorst,* 1866.

Franklin (Benjamin). Memoirs of the life and writings of B. Franklin, written by himself to a late period, and continued to the time of his death, by his grandson, William Temple Franklin, [etc.] New ed. 6 v. 8°. *London, H. Colburn,* 1833. s.

CONTENTS.

v. 1-2. Life.
v. 3-4. Correspondence.
v. 5-6. Posthumous and other writings.

——— Autobiography. Edited from his manuscript, with notes, and an introduction, by J. Bigelow. 409 pp. portrait. 8°. *Philadelphia, Lippincott & co.* 1868.

——— The same. Der weg zum glück, oder [sein] leben und meynungen. Von ihm selbst geschrieben. 128 pp. 24°. *Reading, (Pa.) H. B. Sage,* 1820.

——— Private correspondence. Comprising a series of letters on miscellaneous, literary, and political subjects, written between 1753 and 1790. Published from the originals, by W. T. Franklin. 2d ed. with additions. 2 v. xxiv, 486 pp. 1 pl; xi, 475 pp. 8°. *London, H. Colburn,* 1817.

——— La science du bonhomme Richard. [Précédée de l'histoire typographique de l'auteur]. xvi, 16 pp. fol. *Paris, C. L. F. Pankoucke,* 1827. s.

Franklin (Josephine). The Martin and Nelly stories. Martin and the miller. 178 pp. 4 pl. 16°. *Boston, Taggard & Thompson,* 1865.

——— The same. Martin on the mountain. 158 pp. 4 pl. 16°. *Boston, Taggard & Thompson,* 1865.

——— The same. Trouting; or, gypsying in the woods. 187 pp. 4 pl. 16°. *Boston, Taggard & Thompson,* 1865.

Franklin (William, *of Connecticut*). The building associations of Connecticut and other states examined, with a review of the New York and Massachusetts systems. Also, a model plan. 225, iv pp. 4°. *New Haven, W. Franklin,* 1856.

Franklin. *See, also,* **Francklin.**

Fransioli (*Rev.* Joseph). Patriotism, a christian virtue. A sermon preached at St. Peter's (catholic) church, Brooklyn, July 26th, 1863. 8 pp. 8°. *New York, W. C. Bryant & co.* 1863.
[LOYAL publication society, no. 24].

Fraser (*Rev.* Robert W.) The sea-side naturalist. Out-door studies in marine zoology and botany, and maritime geology. 292 pp. 8 pl. 12°. *London, Virtue & co.* 1868.

Frazer's magazine, for town and country. Jan. to Dec. 1868. v. 77–78. 8°. *London, Longmans,* [1868].

Frauenfeld (Georg, *ritter* von). Mollusken. 16 pp. 2 l. 2 col. pl. 4°. *Wien,* 1868. s.
[*In* WÜLLERSTORF-URBAIR (B. von). Reise der Novara. Zoologischer theil. v. 2. abth. 3].

Frauenstädt (Julius). Der materialismus. Seine wahrheit und sein irrthum. Eine erwiderung auf L. Büchner's "Kraft und stoff." xv, 208 pp. 16°. *Leipzig, F. A. Brockhaus,* 1856.

Fred Freedland; or, the chain of circumstances. By Willis Loveyouth. [*pseudon.*] 288 pp. 1 pl. 12°. *Boston, E. O. Libby & co.* 1859. s.

Fred and Maria and me. By the author of "The flower of the family." Illustrated by W. Magrath. [*anon.*] 71 pp. 4 pl. sq. 16°. *New York, C. Scribner & co.* 1868.

Frederick ii (*king of Prussia*). Oeuvres complètes. 17 v. 8°. [*n. p.*] 1790.

CONTENTS.

v. 1. Mémoires pour servir à l'histoire de la maison de Brandebourg.
v. 2–4. Mémoires sur le règne de Frédéric ii. écrits par lui-même. v. 1–3.
v. 2. Histoire de mon temps.
v. 3–4. Histoire de la guerre de sept ans.
v. 4. Mémoires de 1763 jusqu'à 1775.
Mémoires de la guerre de 1778.
Correspondance de l'empereur avec le roi, au sujet de la succession de la Bavière.
v. 5–9. Melanges en vers et en prose. v. 1–5.
v. 5. Considérations sur l'état présent du corps politique de l'Europe.
Essai sur les formes de gouvernement, et sur les devoirs des souverains.
Dialogues des morts.
Examen critique du systême de la nature.
Avant-propos sur la Henriade de M. de Voltaire.
Dissertation sur l'innocence des erreurs de l'esprit.
Poésies.
v. 6. Le palladion, poëme grave.
Pensées sur la religion.
Épitres.
L'école du monde, comédie.
v. 7. Éloges.
Dissertation sur les raisons d'établir ou d'abroger les lois.
Discours sur les satiriques.
Discours sur les libelles.
Discours sur la guerre.
Essai sur l'amour propre, envisagé comme principe de morale.
Examen de l'essai sur les préjugés.
Sur l'éducation.
Dialogue de morale à l'usage de la jeune noblesse.
De l'utilité des sciences et des arts dans un état.
Lettres sur l'amour de la patrie.
De la littérature allemande.
Commentaire théologique de don Calmet sur barbe-bleue.
v. 8. Anti-Machiavel, ou examen du prince de Machiavel.
Instructions militaires.
Instruction militaire du roi de Prusse pour ses généraux.
Des marches des armées.
Instruction pour la direction de l'académie des nobles à Berlin.
L'art de la guerre. Poëme.
La guerre des confédérés, poëme.
v. 9. Épitres, odes, poésies diverses.
v. 10–17. Correspondance.
v. 10–12. Lettres du prince royal de Prusse et de Voltaire.
v. 12. Lettres du roi de Prusse et de M. Darget.
Tantale en procés. Comédie.
v. 13–14. Lettres du roi et de m. d'Alembert.
v. 15. Lettres du roi et du marquis d'Argens.
v. 16. Lettres du roi et de m. Jordan.
Lettres du roi et de la marquise du Châtelet.
Lettres du roi et de m. de Fontenelle.
Lettres du roi et de m. Rollin.
Lettres du roi et de m. de Condorcet.
Lettres à m. Grimm.
Lettres à m. Algarotti.
v. 17. Vie d'Henri-Auguste baron de la Motte Fouqué.
Lettres du roi et du général Fouqué.
Réflexions sur le caractere et les talens militaires de Charles xii.

——— The same. Oeuvres de Frédéric le grand. 32 v. in 18. 8°. Atlas. 4°. *Berlin, R. Decker,* 1846–57.

CONTENTS:

v. 1–7. Oeuvres historiques de Frédéric ii. roi de Prusse. 7 v. 1846–47.
v. 8–9. Oeuvres philosophiques de Frédéric ii. 2 v. 1848.
v. 10–15. Oeuvres poétiques de Frédéric ii. 6 v. 1849–50.
v. 16–27. Correspondance de Frédéric ii. 12 v. in 13 parts. 1850–56.
v. 28–30. Oeuvres militaires de Frédéric ii. [etc.] 3 v. 8°. Atlas. 4°. 1856.
Table chronologique générale des ouvrages de Frédéric le grand et catalogue raisonné des écrits qui lui sont attribués. 4 p. l. 165 pp. 1857.

Frederick de Algeroy, the hero of Camden plains. A revolutionary tale. By Giles Gazer. [*pseudon.*] 235 pp. 12°. *New York, Collins & Hannay,* 1825.

Freedley (Edwin T.) Philadelphia and its manufactures; a hand-book of the great manufactories and representative mercantile houses of Philadelphia in 1867. 634 pp. 6 pl. 8°. *Philadelphia, E. Young & co.* [1867].

Freeman (Charles). An account of Limerick, [Maine]. 8°. *Portland, Day, Fraser & co.* 1831.
[MAINE historical society. Collections. v. 1].

Freeman (Edward Augustus). The history of the Norman conquest of England, its causes and its results. v. 1–2. [449–1066]. 8°. *Oxford, Clarendon press,* 1867–68.

Freeman (*Mrs.* Theresa J.) Silver lake; or, the belle of Bayou Luie. A tale of the south. 344 pp. 12°. *Saint Louis, P. M. Pinckard,* 1867.

Free masonry: its pretensions exposed in faithful extracts of its standard authors; with a review of Town's speculative masonry; its dangerous tendency exhibited in extracts from the abbé Barruel and prof. Robison, etc. By a master mason. [*anon.*] xvi, 399 pp. 8°. *New York,* 1828. s.

Freiesleben (Johann Carl). Magazin für die oryktographie von Sachsen. Ein beytrag zur mineralogischen kenntniss dieses landes und zur geschichte seiner mineralien. v. 1–7 in 3 v. 8°. *Freyberg, Craz & Gerlach, etc.* 1828–36. s.

——— The same. v. 8–9. [*or,*] Vom vorkommen des apatit, flus, gips, schwerpath und strontian in Sachsen, [etc.] 1 p. l. 342 pp. 8°. *Freyberg, J. G. Engelhardt,* 1837. s.

——— The same. v. 10. [*or,*] Vom vorkommen der salzigen fossilien sowie der salz- und mineral quellen in Sachsen. 2 p. l. 204 pp. 8°. *Freyberg, J. G. Engelhardt,* 1839. s.

[*With* v. 8–9].

——— The same. v. 11. [*or,*] Vom vorkommen der brennbaren fossilien in Sachsen. x, 198 pp. 8°. *Freyberg, J. G. Engelhardt,* 1845. s.

——— The same. v. 12. [*or,*] Vom vorkommen der gold- und quecksilbererze in Sachsen. 2 p. l. 123 pp. 8°. *Freyberg, J. G. Engelhardt,* 1846. s.

[*With* v. 11].

——— The same. v. 13–14. [*or,*] Vom vorkommen der silbererze in Sachsen. 2 v. 4 p. l. 200 pp; 2 p. l. 215 pp. 8°. *Freyberg, J. G. Engelhardt,* 1847. s.

[*With* v. 11–12].

——— The same. v. 15. [*or,*] Vom vorkommen der kupfererze in Sachsen. 2 p. l. 283 pp. 8°. *Freiberg, J. G. Engelhardt,* 1848. s.

[*With* v. 14].

——— (The same. 1[es] extraheft). Die sächsischen erzgänge in einer vorläufigen aufstellung ihrer formationen. x, 108 pp. 8°. *Freiberg, J. G. Engelhardt,* 1843. s.

——— (The same. 2[es]—3[es] extraheft.) Die sächsischen erzgänge in localer folge nach ihren formationen zusammengestellt. 2 v. xi, 187 pp; vi, 213 pp. 8°. *Freiberg, J. G. Engelhardt,* 1844–45. s.

[*With* extraheft 1].

——— (The same. 4[es] extraheft). Beiträge zur geschichte, statistik und litteratur des sächsischen erzbergbaues. Aus dessen nachlasse herausgegeben von C. H. Müller. viii, 139 pp. 8°. *Freiberg, J. G. Engelhardt,* 1848. s.

[*With* extraheft 1].

Freind (John, *M.D.*) The history of physick, from the time of Galen to the beginning of the sixteenth century. 2 v. 2 p. l. 312 pp; 2 p. l. 415, 72 pp. 12°. *London, J. Walthoe,* 1727. s.

[v. 1, 3d ed: v. 2. 2d ed.]

French (Benjamin Franklin, *editor*). The beauties of sir Walter Scott and Thomas Moore; selected from their works; with historical and explanatory notes. 10th ed. xi, 204 pp. 1 pl. 18°. *Philadelphia,* 1828.

French (*Rev.* J. Clement) *and* **Cary** (Edward). The trip of the steamer Oceanus to Fort Sumter and Charleston, (S. C.) 1865. [*anon.*] 174 pp. 6 pl. 8°. *Brooklyn, "The Union" printing house,* 1865.

Freng (Lars Hansen). Beretning om Sorgenfri lazareth under cholera-epidemien i Christiania 1853. 8°. *Christiania,* 1854.

[*In* NORWAY. Actstykker ang. cholera-epidemien i Norge].

Frentz (Gerard). Epistola de vasis sanguiferis periostii tibiæ, ut et viis, per quas vesicula fellea sarcinam acquirit. 4°. *Amstelædami,* 1725. s.

[RUYSCH (F.) Opera, v. 3, no. 20].

Frere (M.) Old Deccan days; or, Hindoo fairy legends, current in southern India. Collected from oral tradition. With an introduction and notes by sir B. Frere. The illustrations by C. F. Frere. xxxv, 331 pp. 5 col. pl. 12°. *London, J. Murray,* 1868.

Frerichs (Friedrich Theodor). A clinical treatise on diseases of the liver. Translated by Charles Murchison. v. 1. xxvii, 402 pp. 1 col. pl. 8°. *London,* 1860.

[NEW SYDENHAM society, v. 7].

Freycinet (Louis de). Voyage autour du monde, exécuté sur les corvettes de s. m. l'Uranie et la Physicienne, pendant les années 1817–20. [v. 4]. Observations du pendule. 3 p. l. 292 pp. 4°. *Paris, Pillet aîné,* 1826. s.

Friederichs (Carl, *prof. in the university of Berlin*). Pindarische studien. 106 pp. 8°. *Berlin, E. S. Mittler & sohn,* 1863. s.

Friend (The); an independent monthly. Jan. to Dec. 1867. v. 2. 8°. *New York, Friend assoc.* 1867.

Friendship's offering; a christmas, new year, and birthday present, for 1848 and 1851. 2 v. 12°. *Boston, Phillips & Sampson,* 1848-51. s.

Friendship's offering; for 1852, 1854, and 1855. 3 v. 12°. *Philadelphia, E. H. Butler & co.* 1852–55. s.

Fries (Elias Magnus). Monographia hymenomycetum Sueciae. v. 1. Sistens agaricos, coprinos, bolbitios. xi, 484 pp. 8°. *Upsaliae, C. A. Leffler,* 1857. s.

Frink (*Rev.* Thomas). A king reigning in righteousness, and princes ruling in judgment. A sermon preached before the governor, etc. being the anniversary for the election of his majesty's council, Massachusetts bay, May 31, 1758. 93 pp. 8°. *Boston, S. Kneeland,* 1758.

Friswell (James Hain). Varia: readings from rare books. viii, 341 pp. 1 pl. 16°. *London, S. Low, son & Marston,* 1866.

Frithjiof *or* **Fridjof**. Frithiof's saga. From the Swedish of Esaias Tegnér, by W. L. Blackley. 1st Amer. ed. By Bayard Taylor. xxviii, 201 pp. 16°. *New York, Leypoldt & Holt,* 1867.

Frivaldsky von Friwald (Emmerich). Monographia serpentum Hungariae. 4 p. l. 62 pp. 8°. *Pestini, Trattner de Petróza,* 1823. s.

Froissart (Jehan). Chroniques. 15 v. 8°. *Paris, J. A. Buchon,* 1824–26.

[COLLECTION de chroniques nationales françaises, v. 11–25].

——— Poésies. Publiées par J. A. Buchon. 2 p. l. 512 pp. 1 l. 8°. *Paris, Verdière,* 1829.

[COLLECTION de chroniques nationales françaises, v. 10].

Frontinus (Sextus Julius). De aqvae dvctibus vrbis Romae commentarivs, adspersis Ioannis Poleni aliorvmque notis, vna cvm svis editvs a Georgio Christiano Adler. 3 p. l. 209 pp. 3 pl. 8°. *Altonae, J. H. Kaven,* 1792. s.

——— Strategematicon libri quatuor. 4°. *Antverpiæ,* 1585. s.

[*In* VEGETIUS (F.) De re militari].

Frost (John). Beauties of English history. 252 pp. 16°. *New York, Harpers,* 1846. s.

——— The book of the navy; comprising a general history of the American marine. With appendix. 344 pp. 12 pl. 12°. *New York, Appletons,* 1843.

——— Easy exercises in composition. 6th ed. 120 pp. 12°. *Philadelphia, Marshall, Williams & Butler,* 1841. s.

——— An illustrated history of Washington and his times: embracing a history of the seven years' war, the revolutionary war, the formation of the federal constitution, and the administrations of Washington. Edited by Rev. W. Hutchison. 626 pp. 23 pl. 8°. *Norwich, (Conn.) H. Bill,* 1868.

——— Thrilling adventures among the Indians. 448 pp. 46 pl. 8°. *Philadelphia, J. W. Bradley,* 1849.

Frost (*Miss* S. A.) Amateur theatricals and fairy-tale dramas. Original plays, expressly for the drawing-room performance. 180 pp. 16°. *New York, Dick & Fitzgerald,* 1868.

——— Dialogues for young folks; moral and humorous, adapted to school and church exhibitions, family gatherings, etc. 170 pp. 16°. *New York, Dick & Fitzgerald,* 1867.

——— Original letter-writer. A collection of letters and notes upon every subject of everyday life, etc. [With] a table of synonyms. 202 pp. 16°. *New York, Dick & Fitzgerald,* [1867].

Frothingham (Ephraim L.) A statement of the trinitarian principle, or law of tri-personality. [*anon.*] 123 pp. 8°. *Boston, J. P. Jewett & co.* 1853. s.

Fuchs (Conrad Heinrich). Beobachtungen und bemerkungen über gehirnerweichung. viii, 246 pp. 8°. *Leipzig, L. Gebhardt,* 1838. s.

Fuchs (C. W. C.) Der granit des Harzes und seine nebengesteine (hornfels, gneiss, diorit, syenit, etc.) [Extract]. 126 pp. 1 col. map. 8°. *Stuttgart, neue jahrbuch für mineralogie,* 1862. s.

Fuchs (Georg Friedrich Christian). Geschichte des zinks in absicht seines verhaltens gegen andere körper, und seiner anwendung auf arzneiwissenschaft und künste. 8 p. l. 498 pp. 16°. *Erfurt, G. A. Keyser,* 1788. s.

Fuchs (Leonhard). De humani corporis fabrica epitomes pars prima, duos, unum de ossibus, alterum de musculis, libros complectens. 16°. *Lvgdvni, apud A. Vincentium,* 1551. s.

[Imperfect: pp. 337 et seq. wanting].

Fuckel (Leopold). Nassaus flora. Phanerogamen. lxiv, 384, xiii pp. 1 geol. map. 11 pl. 12°. *Wiesbaden, Kreidel & Niedner,* 1856. s.

Fuente (de la). *See* **La Fuente**.

Fuller (Frances A.) *and* **Victor** (Metta Victoria Fuller). Poems of sentiment and imagination, with dramatic and descriptive pieces. 264 pp. 8°. *New York, A. S. Barnes & co.* 1851. s.

Fuller (J. G.) The Brownings: a tale of the great rebellion. [With] Lucy Lee; or all things for Christ. 310 pp. 3 pl. 16°. *New York, M. W. Dodd,* 1867.

Fuller (Richard, *D. D.*) Baptism, and the terms of communion; an argument. 4th ed. 251 pp. 12°. *Charleston, southern baptist publication society,* 1854. s.

Fuller (S. E. *of New York*). A manual of instruction in the art of wood engraving. With illustrations by the author. 48 pp. 12°. *Boston, J. Watson,* 1867.

Fuller (Thomas, *D. D.*) Good thoughts in bad times. 2 p. l. 66 pp. 24°. *London, J. Williams,* 1649.

——— Good thoughts in worse times. 3 p. l. 112 pp. 24°. *London, J. Williams,* 1649.

[*With his* Good thoughts in bad times, ed. 1649.]

Fulton (Levi S.) *and* Eastman (George W.) A practical system of book-keeping by single and double entry, etc. 5th ed. 296 pp. 12°. *New York, A. S. Barnes & co.* 1851. s.

Funck (Carl Wilhelm Ferdinand von). Geschichte kaiser Friedrichs des zweiten. [*anon.*] 9 p. l. 400 pp. 8°. *Züllichau, etc. Frommann,* 1792. s.

Fur, fin and feather: containing the game laws of the principal states of the United States and Canada. [*anon.*] 206 pp. 8°. *New York, M. B. Brown & co.* 1868.

Furber (George C.) History of Mexico: continued from the capture of Vera Cruz to the termination of the war with the United States. Being a continuation of Young's history of Mexico. 8°. *Cincinnati, J. A. & U. P. James.* 1850.

[*In* YOUNG (P.) History of Mexico. 1850 ed. pp. 471–656].

Furlong (*Capt.* Lawrence). The American coast pilot. Edited by E. M. Blunt. 3d ed. 251 pp. 8°. *Newburyport (Mass.) E. M. Blunt,* 1800.

Furness (*Rev.* William H.) The unconscious truth of the four gospels. [Essays on the life and character of Jesus]. 144 pp. 12°. *Philadelphia, J. B. Lippincott & co.* 1868.

Furnivall (Frederick J. *editor*). The babees book, Aristotle's A B C, [etc.] Part I. Early English poems and treatises on manners and meals in olden time. Part II. French and Latin poems on [the same subjects]. 4 p. l. cxxxvi, 405, 132 pp. 8°. *London, Trübner & co.* 1868.

[EARLY English text society publications. no. 32].

Gaceta del gobierno de Mexico. Del 2 de enero—30 de diciembre 1816. 2 v. 2095 pp. sm. 4°. *Mexico, J. M. de Benevento,* 1816.

Gaddis (*Rev.* Maxwell Pierson). The sacred hour; [or, religious biography of miss Sallie K. Caldwell]. 364 pp. 1 portrait. 16°. *Cincinnati, author,* 1856. s.

Gaetzschmann. *See* **Gätzschmann.**

Gaffarel (Jacques). Unheard-of curiosities: concerning the talismanical sculpture of the Persians; the horoscope of the patriarkes, and the reading of the stars. Englished by E. Chilmead. 20 p. l. 433 pp. 2 pl. 16°. *London, H. Moseley,* 1650.

Gage (*Rev.* Thomas). The English-American, his travail by sea and land; or, a new svrvey of the West-India's. 5 p. l. 220 pp. 6 l. fol. *London, R. Cotes,* 1648.

——— The same. A new survey of the West Indies; or, his voyage from Spain to Mexico; likewise his journey from Mexico through the provinces of Guaxaca, Guatemala, etc; as also his return through Nicaragua and Costa Rica to Havana. With a grammar of the Indian tongue, called Poconchi, or Pocoman. 3d ed. 4 p. l. 477 pp. 9 l. 1 map. 8°. *London, A. Clark,* 1677.

Gage (*Rev.* William Leonard). The life of Carl Ritter. viii, 243 pp. 12°. *New York, Scribner & co.* 1867.

Gaguin (Robert). De puritate conceptionis beate Marie virginis. 12 l. sm. 4°. [*Moguntiae, about* 1496].

Gaietanus de Thienis. *See* **Tiene Gaetano** (Vincenzio).

Gail (Jean Baptiste). Lettres inédites de Henri ii, Diane de Poitiers, Marie Stuart, François, roi dauphin, etc. Adressées au connétable Anne de Montmorency; et extraites du Philologue, ouvrage périodique. 2 p. l. 68 pp. 10 pl. 8°. *Paris, C. Gail,* 1818.

Gailhabaud (Jules). L'architecture du vme au xviime siècle, et les arts qui en dépendent. Publiés d'apres les travaux inédits des principaux architectes français et étrangers. 4 v. 4°. atlas fol. *Paris, Gide,* 1858.

Gaimard (Joseph Paul, *président de la commission*). Voyages de la commission scientifique du nord en Scandinavie, en Laponie, au Spitzberg et aux Feröe, pendant les années 1838–40, sur la corvette la Recherche, [etc.] 4 v. 8°. *Paris, A. Bertrand,* [1843–49]. s.

CONTENTS.

2e div. Météorologie; par mm. V. Lottin, A. Bravais, C. B. Lilliehöök, P. A. Siljeström, Ch. Martins, J. de Laroche-Poncié, L. L. Læstadius, et E. Pottier. v. 1. 2 p. l. 495 pp.

3e div. Magnétisme terrestre; par mm. V. Lottin, A. Bravais, C. B. Lilliehöök, P. A. Siljeström, E. G. Meyer, J. de Laroche-Poncié, et par mm. le capitaine Fabvre et les officiers de la corvette la Recherche. v. 1. 2 p. l. 565 pp; v. 2. 1e partie 2 p. l. pp. 1–248.

4e div. Aurores boréale; par mm. V. Lottin, A. Bravais, C. B. Lilliehöök, et P. A. Siljeström. 2 p. l. 566 pp.

Galatian (A. B.) History of Elmira, Horseheads, and the Chemung valley, with sketches of the churches, schools, societies, railroads, etc. Also, directory and business advertiser for 1868. 4 p. l. 280, 33 pp. 8°. *Elmira, (N. Y.) Wheeler & Watts*, 1868.

Galavis y Nidos (Jacinto Bejarano). Sentimentos patrióticos, ó conversaciones christianas, que un cura de Aldea inspira à sus feligreses. 2 v. xxviii, 408 pp; 2 p. l. 515 pp. 16°. *Madrid, imprenta real*, 1791. s.

Galaxy (The). An illustrated magazine of entertaining reading. May to Dec. 1867. v. 4. 8°. *New York, W. C. & F. P. Church*, 1868.

—— The same. Jan. to Dec. 1868. v. 5–6. 8°. *New York, Sheldon & co.* 1868.

Gale (George). Upper Mississippi; or, historical sketches of the mound-builders, the Indian tribes, and the progress of civilization in the northwest, from A. D. 1600 to the present time. 460 pp. 1 portrait. 12°. *Chicago, Clarke & co.* 1867.

Galerie (La) agréable du monde, où l'on voit en un grand nombre de cartes et de tailles-douces, les principaux empires, roïaumes, républiques, [etc.] dans les quatres parties de l'univers; avec une courte description. 66 v. in 27. fol. *Leide, P. Van der Aa*, [*about* 1720].

Galesburg (*city of, Illinois*). Directory. *See* **Knox county** (*Illinois*).

Galet *or* **Gallet** (*Abbé* Jacques). Dissertation historique sur l'origine des Bretons, sur leur établissement dans l'Armorique, et sur leurs premiers rois. [*anon.*] [*or*, Histoire des ducs de Bretagne, etc. par P. F. G. Desfontaines. v. 5–6]. 2 v. xlvi, 324 pp; 1 p. l. xii, 388 pp. 3 l. 16°. *Paris, Rollin*, 1739. s.

Galfridus *monemutensis*. *See* **Jeffrey** of Monmouth.

Galland (Antoine). Paroles remarquables et maximes des orientaux. fol. *Mæstricht*, 1780.

[*In* HERBELOT (B. d'). Bibliothèque orientale. Supplement. pp. 202-254].

Gallaudet (Thomas H.) *and* **Hooker** (Horace). The school and family dictionary. 221 pp. 16°. *New York, Pratt, Woodford & co.* 1847. s.

Gallicanus (Vulcatius). Avidivs Cassivs. 16°. [*Geneva*], 1568.

[*In* VARII historiæ romanæ scriptores, v. 3].

Gallois (Julien Jean César le). *See* **Le Gallois**.

Galloway (Joseph). Cool thoughts on the consequences to Great Britain of American independence, etc. [*anon.*] 70 pp. 8°. *London, J. Wilkie*, 1780.

Galt (John). The bachelor's wife; a selection of curious and interesting extracts, with cursory observations. vii, 444 pp. 12°. *Edinburgh, Oliver & Boyd*, 1824.

—— The entail; or, the lairds of Grippy. [*anon.*] v. 1. 240 pp. 12°. *Philadelphia, E. Littell*, 1823.

—— The same. [*anon.*] v. 2. 216 pp. 12°. *New York, Harpers*, 1823.

Gand. *See* **Ghent.**

Ganilh (Charles). La théorie de l'économie politique, fondée sur les faits résultans des statisques de la France et de l'Angleterre, etc. 2 v. 2 p.l. xxxii, 531 pp; 2 p.l. 466 pp. 1 l. 8°. *Paris, Deterville*, 1815. s.

Ganot (A.) Elementary treatise on physics, experimental and applied. Translated and edited from Ganot's Élémens de physique. By E. Atkinson. 3d ed. xii, 861 pp. 1 col. pl. 8°. *London, Longmans*, 1868.

Gantt (E. W.) Prophecy and fulfillment. Address in favor of reunion in 1863. 8°. *New York*, 1865.

[LOYAL publication society, pp. 23-45. In no. 36].

Ganz neue entdeckungen von der freimäuerey und deren geheimnisse. Nebst denen theses metaphysic oder solomonische physic. [*anon.*] 134 pp. 12°. *Stockholm*, 1782.

Garcia y Cubas (Antonio). Atlas geográfico é historico de la republica mexicana. 3 p. l. 31 col. maps. 2 pl. 5 l. 18 pp. fol. *Mexico, J. M. F. de Lara*, 1858. s.

—— Compendio de geografia de la republica mexicana. 210 pp. 1 map. 16°. *Mexico, M. Castro*, 1861. s.

Garcia y Garcia (Aurelio, *capt. in Peruvian navy*). Peruvian coast pilot. 1 p.l. 112 pp. 1 map. 8°. *New York, E. & G. W. Blunt*, 1866. s.

Garcias Lasso de la Vega. *See* **Garcilaso** de la Vega.

Garcilaso (José Antonio). Tablas historigraphicas y cronologicas sacro-prophanas, desde el nacimiento de Jesu-Christo. 8 p. l. 280 pp. 16°. *Madrid, J. de Sierra*, 1742. s.

Garcilaso de la Vega (*the inca*). La Florida del Inca. Historia del adelantado, Hernando de Soto. Y de otros heroicos caballeros, Españoles, e Indios. Van enmendadas en esta impression, muchas erratas de la primera. 16 p.l. 268 pp. 6 l. fol. *Madrid, N. R. Franco*, 1723.

—— The same. Histoire de la conquête de la Floride; ou relation de ce qui s'est passé dans la découverte de ce pays par Ferdinand de Soto. Traduit en François, par P. Richelet. 2 v. in 1. 9 p. l. 281 pp; 1 p. l. 249 pp. 5 l. 16°. *Paris, G. Nyon*, 1711.

Garcilaso de la Vega (*the inca*). Histoire des gverres civiles des Espagnols dans les Indes. Mise en François, par I. Bavdoin. 16 p. l. 631 pp. 8 l. 4°. *Paris, S. Piget*, 1658.

——— The same. Svite des gverres civiles des Espagnols dans le Perv. Traduction de l'Espagnol, par I. Bavdoin. 555 pp. 11 l. 4°. *Paris, S. Piget*, 1658.
[*With* the preceding].

Garcke (*Dr.* August). Columniferae [etc. von Mossambique]. fol. *Berlin*, 1862.
[*In* PETERS (W. C. H.) Nat. reise nach Mossambique. Botanik].

Garden (*Le comte* de). Traité complet de diplomatie, ou théorie générale des relations extérieures des puissances de l'Europe, [etc.] Par un ancien ministre. [*anon.*] 3 v. 8°. *Paris, Treuttel & Würtz*, 1833. S.

Gardeners' (The) chronicle and agricultural gazette, 1867–68. 2 v. fol. *London, J. Matthews*, 1867–68.

Gardette (Charles D.) Johnnie Dodge; or, the freaks and fortunes of an idle boy. 274 pp. 12 pl. 16°. *Philadelphia, J. W. Daughaday & co.* 1868.

Gardiner (Stephen, *bishop of Winchester, lord high chancellor of England*). A declaration of svche true articles as George Ioye hath gone about to confute as false. 180 l. *b. l.* 18°. *London, R. Toye*, 1546.
[Imperfect: l. 22 wanting].

Gardner (Alexander, *photographer*). Photographic sketch-book of the war, [1861–65]. 2 v. 53 l. 50 photog; 53 l. 50 photog. obl. 4°. *Washington, Philp & Solomons*, [1865].

Gardner (D. Pereira). Medical chemistry: being a manual of the science, with its applications to toxicology, physiology, therapeutics, hygiene, etc. 396 pp. 12°. *Philadelphia, Lea & Blanchard*, 1848. S.

——— A new medical dictionary, on the basis of Hooper and Grant. *See* **Hooper** (R.)

Gardner (*Mrs.* H. C.) Miss Carrol's school. 174 pp. 4 pl. 16°. *New York, Carlton & Porter*, 1868.

Gardner *vs.* **Jadis**, *alias* **Gardner**. The medical evidence relative to the duration of human pregnancy, given in the Gardner peerage cause before the committee for privileges of the house of lords, in 1825–6. With remarks and notes by R. Lyall, M. D. 2[d] ed. xxix, 122 pp. 8°. *London, Burgess & Hill*, 1827.

Garin (R. P. *missionary*). Catechisme recueil de prières et de cantiques à l'usage des sauvages d'Albany, (Baie d'Hudson). 1 p. l. 94 pp. 12°. *Montreal, L. Perrault*, 1854. S.

Garland (A) of christmas carols, ancient and modern, including some never before given in any collection. Edited, with notes, by Joshua Sylvester. xvi, 210 pp. 16°. *London, John Camden Hotten*, 1861.

Garnett (James Mercer). Constitutional charts; or, comparative views of the legislative, executive, and judiciary departments in the constitutions of all the states in the union. 6 pp. 6 tab. pp. 49–64. 4°. *Richmond, T. W. White*, 1829.

Garrett (Phineas). Excelsior dialogues: comprising new and original first-class school dramas, colloquies, etc. 382 pp. 12°. *Philadelphia, P. Garrett & co.* 1867.

Gartenbeobachter (Der). Eine zeitschrift des neuesten und interessantesten im gebiete der blumistik und horticultur, herausgegeben von C. Gerstenberg. 6 v. 8°. *Nürnberg, E. H. Zeh'sche b.* 1837–42. S.
[No more published].

Garve (Christian). Sämmtliche werke. 18 v. 16°. *Breslau*, 1801–04. S.

CONTENTS.

v. 1–4, 14. Versuche über verschiedene gegenstände aus der moral, der litteratur, und dem gesellchaftlichen leben.
v. 5–6. Vermischte aufsätze welche einzeln oder in zeitschriften erschienen sind.
v. 7, 15. Sammlung einiger abhandlungen.
v. 8. Ubersicht der vornehmsten principien der sittenlehre.
v. 9. Eigene betrachtungen über die allgemeinsten grundsätze der sittenlehre.
v. 10–11. Fragmente zur schilderung des geistes, des charakters, und der regierung Friedrichs des zweyten.
v. 12. Vertraute briefe an eine freundin.
v. 13. Erinnerungen aus meinem umgange mit Garve, nebst einigen bemerkungen über dessen leben und charakter, von S. G. Dittmar: Allgemeines register über C. Garve's sämmtliche werke.
v. 16–17. Briefe an Christian Felix Weisse und einige andere freunde.
v. 18. Briefwechsel zwischen C. Garve und Georg Joachim Zollikofer, nebst einigen briefen des erstern an andere freunde.

Gaskell (Elizabeth Cleghorn). Round the sofa. [*anon.*] 2[d] ed. 2 v. 2 p. l. 340 pp; 2 p. l. 297 pp. 12°. *London, S. Low, son & co.* 1859.

Gasparin (Agénor Étienne, *comte* de). America before Europe. Principles and interests. Translated by Mary L. Booth. 3[d] ed. xi, 419 pp. 12°. *New York, C. Scribner*, 1862.

——— Reconstruction. A letter to president Johnson. Translated by Mary L. Booth. 2[d] ed. 70 pp. 8°. *New York*, 1865.
[LOYAL publication society. no. 87].

——— *and others.* Réponse de mm. de Gasparin, Laboulaye, Martin et Cochin, à la ligue loyale et nationale de New York, 1863. 20 pp. 8°. *New York, W. C. Bryant & co.* 1864.
[LOYAL publication society. no. 41].

Gasparin (Agénor Étienne, *comte* de). The same. Reply to the loyal national league of New York, together with the address of the league, etc. 30 pp. 8°. *New York, W. C. Bryant & co.* 1864.

[LOYAL publication society. no. 42].

——— The same. Antwort an die loyal national league zu New York. From the French, by F. Schutz. 11 pp. 8°. *New York,* 1864.

[LOYAL publication society. no. 43].

Gass (W.) Beiträge zur kirklichen literatur und dogmengeschichte des griechischen mittelalters. v. 2, [*or*] Die mystik des Nikolaus Cabasilas vom leben in Christo. 3 p. l. xii, 224, 240 pp. 8°. *Greisswald, C. A. Koch,* 1849.

[v. 1, *or* Gennadius und Pletho, 1844, wanting].

——— Geschichte der protestantischen dogmatik in ihrem zusammenhange mit der theologie überhaupt. v. 1. xvi, 488 pp. 8°. *Berlin, G. Reimer,* 1854. S.

[v. 2, 1857, wanting].

Gätzschmann (Moriz Ferdinand). Vollständige anleitung zur bergbaukunst; [*or*], Die auf- und untersuchung von lagerstätten nutzbarer mineralien. 1er theil. viii, 480 pp. 8°. *Freiberg, J. G. Engelhardt,* 1856. S.

Gaub *or* **Gaubius** (Jan). Epistola de pilis, pinguedine, septoque scroto; necnon de papillis piramidalibus, ut et de corpore reticulari, sub cuticulo sito, etc. 4°. *Amstelædami,* 1824. S.

[RUYSCH (F.) Opera. v. 2. no. 18].

Gaupp (Ernst Theodor). Die germanischen ansiedlungen und landtheilungen in den provinzen des römischen westreiches. xiv, 612 pp. 8°. *Breslau, J. Max & cie.* 1844.

Gauss (Carl Friedrich) *and* **Weber** (Wilhelm). Atlas des erdmagnetismus nach den elementen der theorie entworfen. iv, 36 pp. 18 maps. 4 tab. 4°. *Leipzig, Weidmann,* 1840. S.

Gaussen (L.) The wonders of the Abendberg. And the [institution for the cure of cretins]. New ed. 35 pp. 1 pl. 8°. *Berne,* 1857. S.

Gazer (Giles, *pseudon.*) *See* **Frederick** de Algeroy.

Gedenkwurdige (De) voyagie van Ferdinand de Soto. *See* **Relaçáõ** verdadéira, etc.

Geheime (De) brieven-schryver, aangetoond met verscheydene voorbeelden, [etc. *anon.*] xvi, 176 pp. 16°. *Amsterdam, B. Mourik,* [*about* 1760]. S.

Gelli (Giovanni Battista). Opere. 3 v. 8°. *Milano, societá tipografica,* 1804-07.

Gelli—continued.

CONTENTS.

v. 1. La circe. xxvi, 225 pp. 1 portrait. 1804.
v. 2. Capricci del bottaio. x, 272 pp. 1805.
v. 3. La sporta. Commedia. xxvi, 103 pp. 1807.
Lo errore di Gio. Battista Gelli, fiorentino. 73 pp.

Gellius (Aulus). Noctivm atticarvm commentarii. 192 l. fol. *Brixiæ, par Boninū de Boninis de Ragusia,* 1485.

Gem (The) annual: a christmas, new year, and birthday present, for 1854-55. 2 v. 12°. *Philadelphia, E. H. Butler & co.* 1854-55. S.

Gems from sacred mines. [*anon.*] 195 pp. 12°. *New York, A. D. F. Randolph & co.* 1868.

General (The) stud book; containing pedigrees of race horses, etc. from the earliest accounts to 1826. 3 v. 8°. *London, J. & C. Weatherby,* 1827-32. S.

[NOTE. v. i. 3d ed. 1827; v. ii, iii, 2d ed. 1832].

General theological seminary of the protestant episcopal church in the U. S. A. Proceedings relating to the organization of the general theological seminary from its inception to its final establishment in the city of New York; together with the regular proceedings of the board of trustees, 1821–38. Compiled by a member of the board. x, 668 pp. 8°. *New York, D. Dana, jr.* 1854. S.

——— The same. v. 2. Proceedings of the board of trustees. 1838-54. 1 p. l. viii, 207-211, 8, 213-900 pp. 8°. *New York, D. Dana, jr.* 1854. S.

Generibvs (De) ebriosorvm, et ebrietate vitanda. [*anon.*] 45 l. 18°. [*n. p.*] 1557.

Genesee (The) farmer and gardener's journal. A weekly paper, devoted to agriculture, horticulture, and rural economy. N. Goodsell, editor. Jan. 1831, to Dec. 1832. v. 1-2. 4°. *Rochester, L. Tucker & co.* 1831–32.

——— The same. L. Tucker, editor. Jan. 1834, to Dec. 1836. v. 4-7. 4°. *Rochester, L. Tucker,* 1834-36.

——— The same. Jan. to Dec. 1839. v. 9. 4°. *Rochester, L. Tucker,* 1839.

——— The same. A monthly journal devoted to agriculture and horticulture, domestic and rural economy. Jan. 1840, to Dec. 1865. Second series, v. 1-26 in 24 v. 4°. *Rochester, J. Harris, etc.* 1840-65.

[NOTE. Vols. 1-5, second series, are known as the New Genesee farmer].

See, also, **Cultivator** (The): *and* **Goodsell's** (N.) Genesee farmer.

Genet (Edmond Charles). Growth and manufacture of silk. [With] letter from the secretary of the treasury in relation to the growth and manufacture of silk, adapted to the different parts of the union. 8, 220 pp. 1 tab. 5 pl. 8°. *Washington, Gales & Seaton,* 1828. S.

Geneva (*Switzerland*). Catalogue de la bibliothèque publique de Genève, rédigé par Louis Vaucher. 2 v. xliv, 948, 133 pp. 8°. *Genève*, 1834. s.

Genius (The) of America, 1778. *See* **Watch** (The), an ode.

Gentleman's (The) magazine and historical review. By Sylvanus Urban, gent. Jan. to May, 1868. New series, v. 5. Complete series, v. 224. 8°. *London, Bradbury, Evans & co.* 1868.

[No title page or index published].

——— The same. June to Nov. 1868. Entirely new series. v. 1. Complete series, v. 225. 8°. *London, Bradbury, Evans & co.* 1868.

Gentz (Friedrich) *and* **Müller** (Adam Heinrich). Briefwechsel zwischen F. Gentz und A. H. Müller. 1800-29. vi, 411 pp. 8°. *Stuttgart, J. G. Cotta*, 1857. s.

Geoffrey of Monmouth. *See* **Jeffrey** of Monmouth.

Georg (*Dr.* L.) Elementar-grammatik der französischen sprache, nebst eingeflochtenen conversations-uebungen. 3e ausg. 294 pp. 8°. *Genf, J. Kessmann*, 1854. s.

George Melville. An American novel. [*anon.*] 386 pp. 1 pl. 12°. *New York, W. R. C. Clark & co.* 1858. s.

Georgetown advocate. [Tri-weekly]. June 26, 1845, to June 18, 1846. fol. *Georgetown, D.C.* 1845–46.

——— The same. Feb. 6, 1847, to March 29, 1853. 6 v. fol. *Georgetown, D. C.* 1847–53.

Georgia (*Colony of*). Account shewing the progress of the colony of Georgia in America from its first establishment. 1 p. l. 71 pp. fol. *London, [published by order of the trustees of the colony]*, 1741.

——— The same. 1 p. l. iii, 68 pp. fol. *Annapolis, J. Green*, 1742.

Gerhard (Eduard). Griechische und etruskische trinkschalen des königlichen museums zu Berlin. vi, 34 pp. 19 col. pl. fol. *Berlin, A. W. Schade*, 1840. s.

——— Etruskische und kampanische vasenbilder des königlichen museums zu Berlin. 48 pp. 30 col. pl. 5 pl. fol. *Berlin, G. Reimer*, 1843. s.

Gersdorf (E. G. *editor*). Codex diplomaticus Saxoniæ regiæ. *See* **Saxony.**

——— *See, also,* **Leipziger** repertorium.

Gerstäcker (Carl Eduard Adolph). Coleoptera (fortsetzung), und hymenoptera [von Mossambique]. fol. *Berlin*, 1862.

[*In* PETERS (W. C. H.) Nat. reise nach Mossambique. Zoologie, v. 5].

Gerstel (Adolf Heinrich). Die witwen-societät der medicinischen facultät zu Wien von 1758 bis 1858, etc. vii, 238 pp. 8°. *Wien, Mechitharisten-buchdruckerei*, 1858. s.

Gerstenberg (Carl, *editor*). *See* **Gartenbeobachter** (Der).

Gerstner (Clara von). Beschreibung einer reise durch die Vereinigten Staaten von Nordamerica, in den jahren 1838 bis 1840. In gesellschaft des ritters F. A. von Gerstner unternommen. xii, 456 pp. 16°. *Leipzig, J. C. Hinrich*, 1842.

Gerstner (Franz Anton, *ritter* von). Die innern communicationen der Vereinigten Staaten von Nordamerica. 2 v. iv, 376 pp. 15 pl. 1 map; 2 p. l. 339 pp. 19 pl. 4°. *Wien, L. Klein*, 1843.

Geruzez (Nicolas Eugène). Études littéraires sur les ouvrages français prescrits pour l'examen du baccalauréat ès lettres. viii, 228 pp. 8°. *Paris, J. Delalain*, 1849. s.

Gervais (Paul). Reptiles, etc. 4°. *Paris*, 1836–44.

[*In* WEBB (P. B.) *and* BERTHELOT. Histoire naturelle des îles Canaries, v. 2].

Gesäng (Das) der einsamen und verlassener turtel-taube nemlich der christlichen kirche. Und nun zum gebrauch der einsamen und verlassenen zu Zion gesammlet, etc. 11 p. l. 359 pp. 5 l. 4°. *Ephrata, drucks der brüderschaft*, 1747. s.

Gesangbuch für die sonntagschulen der evangelisch-lutherischen und deutsch-reformirten kirchen in den Vereinigten Staaten. 2e aufl. xvi, 271 pp. 32°. *Allentown, (Pa.) S. K. Probst*, 1856. s.

Gesner (Conrad). Thierbuch, das ist ein kurtze beschreybung aller vierfüssigen thieren. Durch Cünrat Forer in das Teütsch gebracht. 4 p. l. 202 l. fol. *Zürych, C. Froschower*, 1563.

Getchell (Frank H. *M. D.*) The maternal management of infancy. 67 pp. 16°. *Philadelphia, Lippincott & co.* 1868.

Gews (Johann). Tractatus de peccatis oris, siue vicijs lingue. 93 l. 4°. *Nurnberge, fratres ordinis Augustini*, 1479.

Geyelin (George Kennedy). Geyelin's poultry breeding, in a commercial point of view. Natural and artificial hatching, rearing and fattening, on entirely new and scientific principles. With a preface by C. L. Flint. With illustrations. 127 pp. 12°. *Boston, A. Williams & co.* 1867.

Geyer (Carl). Zuträge zur sammlung exotischer schmetterlinge. *See* **Hubner** (Jacob).

Geyer (Charles A.) Notes on the vegetation and general character of the Missouri and Oregon territories, 1843–44. [From Hooker's London journal of botany, v. 4–5]. 92 pp. 8°. [*London*, 1845–46]. s.

Gförer (August Friedrich). Geschichte der ost-und westfränkischen Carolinger, vom tode Ludwigs des frommen bis zum ende Conrads i. [840–918]. 2 v. iv, 504 pp; viii, 496 pp. 8°. *Freiburg im Breisgau, Herder*, 1848.

——— Kritische geschichte des urchristenthums. 1r theil. Philo und die jüdisch-alexandrinische theosophie. 2e unveränderte aufl. 1 v. in 2. lxxvi, 534 pp. 1 l; 2 p. l. 406 pp. 8°. *Stuttgart, E. Schweizerbart*, 1835.

Ghent (*Belgium*). Recueil des règlemens de police de la ville de Gand, etc. v. 2–3. 8°. *Gand, imprimeur de la régence*, 1819–33. s. [v. 1 wanting].

Ghillany (Friedrich Wilhelm). Diplomatisches handbuch. Sammlung der wichtigsten europaeischen friedensschluesse, congressacten und sonstigen staatsurkunden, vom westphaelischen frieden bis auf die neueste zeit. Mit [einem bibliographie und] kurzen geschichtlichen einleitungen. 3 pts. in 2 v. xxx, 414 pp; 813 pp. 8°. *Noerdlingen, C. H. Beck*, 1855.

Ghislandi (Eliseo). Sulla istruzione dei sordomuti. 108 pp. 4°. *Milano, A. Lamperti*, 1865. s.

Giannetasio (Niccolò Partenio). Vniversalis geographiæ elementa exposita. 7 p. l. 512 pp. 2 l. 2 pl. 18°. *Neapoli, J. Raillard*, 1692.

Gibbs (Josiah Willard). A Latin analyst on modern philological principles. viii, 150 pp. 12°. *Haven, Peck, White & Peck*, 1858. s.

Gibson (Edmund, *bishop of London*). Two letters: the first to the masters and mistresses of families in the English plantations abroad; exhorting them to encourage the instruction of their negroes in the christian faith. The second, to the missionaries there. [With] an address to the serious christians among ourselves. 31 pp. 16°. *London, J. Downing*, 1727.

Gibson (*Mrs.* Elizabeth Bordley). Biographical sketches of the Bordley family, of Maryland, for their descendants. Edited by Elizabeth Mifflin. 2 pts. in 1 v. 159 pp. 16°. *Philadelphia, H. B. Ashmead*, 1865.

Giebel (Christoph Gottfried Andreas). Odontographie. Vergleichende darstellung des zahnsystemes der lebenden und fossilen wirbelthiere. xx, 129 pp. 52 pl. 4°. *Leipzig, A. Abel*, 1855. s.

Giebel (C. G. A.) Die säugethiere in zoologischer, anatomischer und palæontologischer beziehung umfassend dargestellt. xii, 1108 pp. 8°. *Leipzig, A. Abel*, 1855. s.

Giesebrecht (Wilhelm). Geschichte der deutschen kaiserzeit [900–1056]. 2 v. xxxvi, 826 pp; xxi, 620 pp. 8°. *Braunschweig, C. A. Schwetschke & sohn*, 1855.

Gildersleeve (Basil L.) A Latin grammar. 284 pp. 12°. *New York, Richardson & co.* 1867.

Giles (Chauncey). The magic spectacles. 180 pp. 1 pl. 18°. *New York, J. R. Putnam*, 1868.

——— The wonderful pocket, chestnutting, and other stories. Illustrated by F. A. Chapman. 163 pp. 6 pl. sq. 18°. *New York, J. R. Putnam*, 1868.

Giles (Henry). Human life in Shakespeare. 286 pp. 16°. *Boston, Lee & Shepard*, 1868.

Gilibert (Johann Emmanuel, *editor*). Caroli Linnæi systema plantarum Europæ, exhibens characteres naturales generum, characteres essentiales generum et specierum, necnon floras tres novas, lugdunæam, delphinalem, lithuanicam. 7 v. 8°. *Coloniæ-Allobrogum, Piestre & Delamolliere*, 1785–87.

Gill (John, *D. D.*) A reply to a defence of the divine right of infant baptism, by Peter Clark, [with] some strictures on a late treatise, by David Bostwick. 112 pp. 12°. *New York, reprinted by F. Van Dyke & T. Pringle*, 1766.

Gill (Theodore Nicholas). Catalogue of the fishes of the eastern coast of North America, from Greenland to Georgia. 63 pp. 8°. *Philadelphia, [academy of natural sciences*, 1861]. s.

——— Review of Holbrook's ichthyology of South Carolina. (From the Am. jour. of science and arts. v. 36, pp. 89–94). [*anon.*] 8°. *New Haven*, 1864. s.

[*With* HOLBROOK (J. E.) Ichthyology of South Carolina. 4°. 1855].

——— Synopsis of the fishes of the gulf of St. Lawrence and the bay of Fundy. (Extract). 24 pp. 8°. *Montreal, Canadian naturalist*, 1865. s.

——— Synopsis of the fresh water fishes of the western portion of the island of Trinidad, (W. I.) Reprinted from the annals of the lyceum of nat. history, New York. v. 6. 70 pp. 8°. *New York, H. Baillière*, 1858. s.

Gilleland (J. C.) History of the late war between the United States and Great Britain. 3d ed. 175 pp. 18°. *Baltimore, Schaeffer & Maund*, 1818.

Gillet (Ransom H.) Democracy in the United States. What it has done, what it is doing, and what it will do. xiv, 414 pp. 2 pl. 12°. *New York, Appletons*, 1868.

Ginella (Franz Gustav Stephan). De authentia epistolarum s. Pauli apostoli pastoralium, etc. 2 p. l. 180 pp. 8°. *Vratislaviæ, G. O. Aderholz*, 1865. s.

Gioberti (Vicenzio). Introduction à l'étude de la philosophie. Ouvrage traduit de l'Italien, par L. J. Alary. 3 v. 8°. *Moulins, M. Place*, 1845–47. s.

Giovanetti (Jacopo). Du régime des eaux et particulièrement de celles qui servent aux irrigations. 2 p. l. iii, 208 pp. 8°. *Paris, imprimerie royale*, 1844. s.

Giovio (Paolo). La prima parte dell'historie del svo tempo. Tradotto [del Latino] per m. Lodouico Domenichi. 632 pp. 16 l. 8°. *Fiorenza, L. Torrentino*, 1558.

Giraldus *cambrensis* (Silvester Gerald de Barri, *commonly called*). Opera. v. 6. Itinerarivm Kambriæ, et descriptio Kambriæ. Edited by J. F. Dimock. lxxi, 286 pp. 8°. *London, Longmans*, 1868.

[Great Britain and Ireland. Chronicles and memorials during the middle ages].

Girardin (Émile de). Émile. Fragmens. 2e éd. 4 p. l. 283 pp. 8°. *Paris, A. Desrez*, 1827–39. s.

Girding on the armor. By the author of the "Win and wear" series. [*anon.*] 362 pp. 4 pl. 16°. *New York, Carters*, 1868.

Giseke (Bernhard). Thrakisch-pelasgische stämme der Balkanhalbinsel, und ihre wanderungen in mythischer zeit. v, 143 pp. 8°. *Leipzig, B. G. Teubner*, 1858.

Gistel (Johannes). Lexicon der entomologischen welt, der carcinologischen und arachnologischen. Adressenbuch der lebenden entomologen und entomophilen, etc. der carcinologen und arachnologen sammt ihren schriften, [etc.] mit doppelten registern und einer aufzählung aller entomologischen, carcinologischen und arachnologischen schriftsteller von Aristoteles an bis zur gegenwart. 328 pp. 8° *Stuttgart, E. Schweizerbart*, 1846. s.

Giuliani (Giuseppe). Il forestiere instrutto nelle cose piu rare di architettura e di alcune pitture della citta' di Vicenza, [etc.] 2a ed. 106 pp. 29 pl. 8°. *Vicenza, G. Giuliani*, 1804. s.

[Wanting v. 1].

Giustiniani (Agostino). *See* **Bible** (*Polyglot*). Psalterium hebreum, grecū, etc.

Giustiniani (Michele). Gli scrittori ligvri. Parte i. 10 p. l. 496 pp. 6 l. 4°. *Roma, N. A. Tinassi*, 1667. s.

[No more published].

Glad tidings; or walks with the wonderful. By a lover of the word. [*anon.* By Harvey A. Ingham?] With introduction by rev. W. L. Parsons. 94 pp. 18°. *Rochester, Darrow & Kempshall*, 1868.

Gladden (Washington). Plain thoughts on the art of living; designed for young men and women. 2 p. l. 236 pp. 16°. *Boston, Ticknor & Fields*, 1868.

Gladstone (William Ewart). "Ecce homo." [A criticism]. 201 pp. 16°. *London, Strahan & co.* 1868.

Gladwin (Francis). A compendious vocabulary, English and Persian, including all the oriental simples in the materia medica, etc. 1 p. l. 178 pp. 4°. *Malda, in Bengal*, 1780.

Glanvil, Glanvilla, *or* **Glantville** (Bartholomew). Van den proprieteyten der dinghen. 452 l. 11 pl. 4°. *Haerlem, J. Bellaert*, 1485.

Gleig (*Rev.* George Robert). A subaltern in America; comprising his narrative of the campaigns of the British army, at Baltimore, Washington, etc. [*anon.*] 266 pp. 12°. *Philadelphia, Carey & Hart*, 1833.

Glenn (Jessie, *pseudon?*) Cousin Paul. [A novel]. 332 pp. 12°. *New York, Carleton & co.* 1868.

Gloag (*Rev.* Paton J.) The primeval world: a treatise on the relations of geology to theology. 194 pp. 12°. *Edinburgh, F. & T. Clark*, 1859.

Gloucester *and* **Rockport** (Massachusetts). The Gloucester and Rockport directory, for 1869. By Sampson, Davenport & co. 206 pp. 8°. *Gloucester, Proctor bros.* 1868.

Glyndon (Howard, *pseudon.*) *See* **Redden** (Laura C.)

Gobineau (Arthur de). Essai sur l'inégalité des races humaines. 4 v. 8°. *Paris, Didot*, 1853–55.

Godart (Jean Baptiste). Histoire naturelle des lépidoptères ou papillons de France [etc.] Continuée par P. A. J. Duponchel. v. 5e et v. 7e, 1e partie. (Nocturnes. v. 2e et v. 4, 1e partie). 8°. *Paris, Crevot*, 1827. s.

Gödart (Johann). Metamorphoses naturelles, ou histoire des insectes, observée tres-exactement suivant leur nature et leurs proprietez. 3 v. 16°. *Amsterdami, G. Gallet*, 1700. s.

[v. 3 wanting].

Godefroy de Paris. Chronique métrique, suivie de la taille de Paris, au 1313. Publiée par J. A. Buchon. vii, 304, x, 200 pp. 8°. *Paris, Verdière*, 1827.

[Collection de chroniques nationale françaises, v. 9].

Godey's lady's book. Edited by mrs. S. J. Hale and L. A. Godey. July, 1867, to Dec. 1868. v. 75–77. 8°. *Philadelphia, L. A. Godey*, 1867–68.

Godin (A. L. J.) Vie et aventures de Joachim Murat. Par m. L. [*anon.*] viii, 231 pp. 16°. *Paris, Ménard & Desenne*, 1816.

Godoy (Manuel de, *principe de la Paz y Bassano*). Memorias de don M. Godoy, principe de la Paz, ò sea cuenta de su vida politica; para servir a la historia del reinado del señor don Carlos iv. de Borbon. Reimpresa sobre la edicion original, publicada en Paris por el mismo principe. 6 v. 12°. *Gerona, Vicente Oliva*, 1839.

Goedart. *See* **Gödart.**

Goelicke. *See* **Gölicke.**

Goeppert. *See* **Göppert.**

Goerres. *See* **Görres.**

Goethe. *See* **Göthe.**

Goina (Giovanni Battista). De situ Istriæ libellum. (Corografie dell' Istria, n. 3). 8°. *Trieste*, 1830.

[*In* ROSSETTI (D. de). Archeografo triestino, v. 2.]

Golden (The) coast: or, a description of Guinney. [*anon.*] 3 p. l. 88 pp. sm. 4°. *London, S. Speed*, 1665.

[Imperfect: title and last leaf in fac simile].

Golden links; or, thoughts for the hours. [*anon.* By M. Maria Shoemaker?] 144 pp. 24°. *Philadelphia, Claxton, Remsen & Haffelfinger*, 1869.

Golden truths. [Selections in prose and verse from religious authors]. viii, 243 pp. 16°. *Boston, Lee & Shepard*, 1868.

Goldingham (John) *and* **Taylor** (Thomas Glanville). Meteorological register kept at the East India company's observatory, at Madras, for the years 1822–43. clvii pp. fol. *Madras, Madras gov't*, 1844. S.

Goldoni (Carlo). Mémoires de m. Goldoni, pour servir à l'histoire de sa vie, et à celle de son théatre. 3 v. 8°. *Paris, veuve Duchesne*, 1787.

——— Scelta di alcune commedie. 6ª ed. Corretta da L. Pio. xxii, 490 pp. 16°. *Parigi, L. Fayalle, etc.* 1818. S.

Goldsmith (Oliver). The citizen of the world; or, letters from a Chinese philosopher, residing in London, to his friends in the east. 2 v. v, 286 pp; 238 pp. 8 l. 16°. *London, author*, 1762.

——— Essays. 330 pp. 16°. *New York*, 1809.

——— The Grecian history, from the earliest state to the death of Alexander the great. 5th Am. ed. 2 v. in 1. 335 pp. 16°. *Philadelphia, A. Small*, 1817.

——— History of Rome, improved by W. Grimshaw. 2d ed. 235 pp. 16°. *Philadelphia, J. Grigg*, 1826.

[Imperfect: title-page wanting].

——— The vicar of Wakefield. 146 pp. 18°. *Washington, Davis & Force*, 1823.

——— The same. With memoirs. 252 pp. 32°. [*n. p. n. d.*]

[Imperfect: title and pp. 251–2 wanting].

Gölicke (Andreas Ottomar). Epistola de cursu arteriarum per piam matrem, etc. 4°. *Amstelædami*, 1724. S.

[RUYSCH (F.) Opera. v. 3, no. 24].

Gomard (———). Manual of bayonet exercise: [Translated from the French, and] prepared for the use of the army of the United States, by G. B. McClellan. xii, 106 pp. 24 pl. 12°. *Philadelphia, Lippincott*, 1852.

Gonzalez de Mendoza (Juan). The historie of the great and mightie kingdome of China, and the situation thereof. Out of Spanish by R. Parke. 4 p. l. 410 pp. b. l. sm. 4°. *London, E. White*, 1588.

Gooch (Robert). On some of the most important diseases peculiar to women; with other papers. Prefatory essay by Robert Ferguson, M. D. lvi, 235 pp. 8°. *London*, 1859.

[NEW SYDENHAM society. v. 2].

Gooch (*Rev.* William). General view of the agriculture of the county of Cambridge. xv, 303 pp. 1 tab. 2 maps. 8°. *London*, 1811. S.

[GREAT BRITAIN. Board of agriculture].

Good stories. Part 3. 172 pp. 4 pl. sq. 16°. *Boston, Ticknor & Fields*, 1868.

CONTENTS.

Christmas with the baron.
Stephen Yarrow.
A family christmas in Germany.
The christmas banquet. By N. Hawthorne.
Three of a trade; or, red little Kriss Kringle. By Fitz-James O'Brien.
Adventures of a new year's eve. By H. Zschökke.

——— The same. Part 4. 262 pp. 3 pl. sq. 16°. *Boston, Ticknor & Fields*, 1868.

CONTENTS.

From hand to mouth. By Fitz-James O'Brien.
Count Ernest's home. By Paul Heyse.
Little Peg O'Shaughnessy.
A shabby genteel story. By W. M. Thackeray.

Good words. Edited by N. Macleod, D. D. 1860–68. v. 1–9. 8°. *London, Strahan & co.* 1860–68.

Goodison (John). Drawing from objects. A manual for teachers and pupils. 54 pp. sm. 4°. *New York, Ivison, Phinney & co.* 1866.

Goodrich (Chauncey A. *D. D.*) Elements of Greek grammar. 4th ed. iv, 247 pp. 16°. *Hartford, O. D. Cooke & co.* 1827.

Goodrich (C. A.) Lessons in Greek parsing. 2d ed. 138 pp. 18°. *New Haven, Durrie & Peck,* 1842.

Goodrich (Frank Boott). Women of beauty and heroism, from Semiramis to Eugénie. 400 pp. 19 pl. sm. fol. *New York, Derby & Jackson,* 1859.

Goodrich (Samuel Griswold). The balloon travels of Robert Merry and his young friends over various countries in Europe. Edited by Peter Parley. [*pseudon.*] 312 pp. 8 pl. 12°. *J. C. Derby & co.* 1855. s.

——— Common school history. By Peter Parley. [*pseudon.*] Revised and adapted to the use of the pupils of the blind department of the Virginia institution for the education of the deaf and dumb, and of the blind. [In raised characters]. v. 1. [Ancient history]. 4°. *Staunton,* [*Va.*] *blind department of Virginia institute,* 1849. s.

——— Géographie élémentaire à l'usage des écoles et des familles, [etc.] Par Peter Parley. [*pseudon.*] 80 pp. 8°. *Philadelphie, E. H. Butler & cie.* 1854. s.

——— The first book of history. By the author of Peter Parley's tales. [*pseudon.*] 5th ed. 240 pp. 16 col. maps. sq. 12°. *Boston, Jenks, Hickling & Swan,* 1852. s.

——— The second book of history, combined with geography; containing the modern history of Europe, Asia, and Africa. Revised ed. 336 pp. 1 pl. 14 col. maps. sq. 12°. *Boston, Jenks, Hickling & Swan,* 1854. s.

——— The third book of history, containing ancient history in connection with ancient geography. Improved ed. 189 pp. 9 maps. sq. 12°. *Boston, Jenks, Palmer & co.* 1850. s.

——— Peter Parley's kaleidoscope, or parlor pleasure book; consisting of gleanings from many fields of the curious, the beautiful, and the wonderful. 512 pp. 8°. *New York, J. S. Brown & co.* 1858. s.

Goodsell's Genesee farmer. July, 1833, to Aug. 1834. v. 1. 4°. *Rochester, N. Goodsell,* 1834.

Goodwin (Harvey, *D. D.*) Memoir of bishop [W. F.] Mackenzie. viii, 439 pp. 3 maps. 4 pl. 12°. *Cambridge, Deighton, Bell & co.* 1864.

Goodwin (*Mrs.* H. B.) Dr. Howell's family. 361 pp. 12°. *Boston, Lee & Shephard,* 1869.

Goodwin (William). Goodwin's annual legislative statistics of state officers, senate, and house of representatives, of Connecticut, May session, 1868. 8, 4 pp. 8°. *New Haven, by the compiler,* 1868.

Göppert (Heinrich Robert). Beiträge zur kenntniss der dracäneen. 19 pp. 3 pl. 4°. *Breslau, universität,* 1854. s.

——— Die fossile flora des uebergangsgebirges. x, 299 pp. 44 pl. 4°. *Breslau und Bonn, k. Leop. Carol. akad. der naturforscher,* 1852. s.

——— Fossile hölzer. 4°. *St. Petersburg,* 1848. s.

[*In* MIDDENDORF (A. T. von). Reise, etc. v. 1 theil 1].

——— Die tertiärflora auf der insel Java, etc. 169 pp. 14 col. pl. 4°. *Gravenhage, ministerium der koloniën,* 1854. s.

Gordon (S. T.) Short voluntaries for the organ, harmonium, or melodeon. Selected and arranged from the best authors. 64 pp. obl. 12°. *New York, S. T. Gordon,* 1868.

Gordon (Thomas). Essays against popery, etc. *See* **Brooks** (H.) *and* **Gordon** (T.)

Gordon (William R.) The supreme godhead of Christ the corner-stone of christianity. 2d ed. 188 pp. 12°. *New York, ref. prot. Dutch church,* 1855. s.

Gore (*Mrs.* Catherine Grace Frances). Heckington. A novel. 2d ed. 358 pp. 16°. *London, Chapman & Hall,* 1864.

Gorgias. Quæ supersunt. 8°. *Lipsiæ,* 1770.

[*In* ORATORUM graecorum quæ supersunt. Ed. Reiske. v. 5 and 8].

Görres (Jacob Joseph). Athanasius. 4e ausg. 8°. *Regensburg, Manz,* 1838. s.

——— Altteutsche volks-und meisterlieder aus den handscriften der heidelberger bibliothek. lxvii, 336 pp. 1 pl. 8°. *Frankfurt a M: Wilmans,* 1817. s.

Gorton (John). A general biographical dictionary. A new ed. 4 v. 8°. *London, H. G. Bohn,* 1851. s.

Gory (Hippolyte Louis). Histoire naturelle et iconographie des coléoptères. v. 2–4. *See* **Laporte** (F. L. de, *comte* de Castelnau) *and* **Gory.**

Gothaischer hof kalender. 1776–1866. 90 v. 32°. *Gotha,* 1776–1866.

——— The same. Almanach de Gotha, pour 1844, 1848, 1850–51, 1853, 1855–66. 17 v. 32°. *Gotha,* 1844–66.

Göthe (Johann Wolfgang von). Faust, traduction complète, précédée d'un essai sur Goethe, accompagnée de notes et de commentaires, et suivie d'une étude sur la mystique du poëme, par H. Blaze. cxxi, 556 pp. 16°. *Paris, Charpentier,* 1840.

——— Poésies, [etc.] Traduites pour la première fois de l'Allemand, par mme. E. Panckoucke. xlviii, 155 pp. 32°. *Paris, C. L. F. Panckoucke,* 1825. s.

Gott mein heil. Volkständiges gebet- und erbauungsbuch für katholische christen. 381 pp. 3 pl. 18°. *Einsiedeln & New York, C. & N. Benziger,* 1866.

Goudar (Ange). The Chinese spy; or, emissary from the court of Pekin, commissioned to examine into the present state of Europe. [*anon.* Translated from the French]. 6 v. 16°. *London, S. Bladon,* 1765.

Gouffé (Jules). The royal cookery book (le livre de cuisine). Translated from the French by Alphonse Gouffé. xviii, 793 pp. 16 pl. 8°. *London, Low, son & Marston,* 1868.

Goulburn (Edward Meyrick, *D.D.*) Thoughts on personal religion, being a treatise on the christian life in its two chief elements, devotion and practice. New ed. xxxii, 360 pp. 16°. *London, Rivingtons,* 1868.

Gould (Augustus Addison, *M.D.*) Lamarck's genera of shells. *See* **Lamarck** (J. B. P. A. de M. de).

——— Report on the invertebrata of Massachusetts, comprising the mollusca, crustacea, annelida, and radiata. 8°. *Cambridge, Folsom, Wells & Thurston,* 1841. s.

[MASSACHUSETTS. Zoological and botanical survey].

Gould (John, *F. R. S.*) The birds of Australia. Supplement. Part iv. 16 l. 16 col. pl. fol. *London, author,* 1867.

——— Birds. 4°. *London,* 1844.

[*In* HINDS (R. B.) The zoology of H. M. S. Sulphur. v. 1].

——— A prospectus of [his] works on ornithology, etc. (with a list of subscribers to, or possessors of, the works). 26 pp. 4°. [*London, author*], 1868. s.

Gould (J. E.) Amphion: a collection of four, five, and six-part songs, for male voices, in five books—first bass, second bass, first tenor, second tenor, and piano score. Words chiefly by H. A. Clarke. 5 v. 16°. *Boston, O. Ditson & co.* 1868.

Gould (Roland F.) The life of Gould, an ex-man-of-war's-man, with incidents of sea and shore, including the three years' cruise of the battle-ship Ohio, under commodore Hull. 240 pp. 1 portrait. 16°. *Claremont, (N. H.) manuf. co.* 1867.

Gould (S. Baring). *See* **Baring-Gould** (S.)

Goury de Champgrand (———). Traité de venerie, et de chasses. xii, 208 pp. 39 pl. 4°. *Paris, C. J. B. Herissant,* 1769.

Gove (Mary S.) *See* **Nichols** (*Mrs.* M. S. Gove).

Government (The) of the tongue. By the author of the whole duty of man. [*anon.* By lady Dorothy Pakington?] 4th ed. 7 p. l. 224 pp. 1 pl. 8°. *Oxford,* 1675.

Gowans (William, *bookseller*). A catalogue of books of proverbs, sayings, maxims, apophthegms, adages, and similitudes, etc. [*anon.*] 16 pp. 8°. *New York, W. Gowans,* 1851. s.

Gracey (*Rev.* Samuel L.) Annals of the sixth Pennsylvania cavalry. 372 pp. 1 map. 8°. [*Philadelphia*], *E. H. Butler & co.* 1868.

Gracian (Baltasar). L'homme de cour. De l'Espagnol, par le sieur Amelot de la Houssaie. Avec des notes. 32 p. l. 326 pp. 9 l. 1 pl. 4°. *Paris, veuve Martin, etc.* 1684.

Gradus ad Parnassum. *See* **Aler** (P.)

Graetz. *See* **Grätz.**

Gräfe (Alfred von). Three memoirs on iridectomy in certain forms of iritis, choroiditis, and glaucoma. Translated by Thomas Windsor. 8°. *London,* 1859.

[NEW SYDENHAM society, v. 5].

Graham (Patrick, *D.D.*) General view of the agriculture of Stirlingshire. viii, 415 pp. 1 tab. 1 col. map. 8°. *Edinburgh,* 1812. s.

[GREAT BRITAIN: Board of agriculture].

Graham (Samuel). Memoir, with notices of the campaigns in which he was engaged from 1779 to 1801. Edited by J. J. Graham. xvii, 318 pp. 2 maps. 4 pl. 12°. *Edinburgh, R. & R. Clark,* 1862.

Grahame (James, *LL.D.*) The history of the United States of North America, from the plantation of the British colonies till their assumption of national independence. 2d ed. 4 v. 8°. *Boston, Little & Brown,* 1845.

Grahame (Nellie, *pseudon?*) The beginning and the end. [A story]. 288 pp. 4 pl. 18°. *Philadelphia, presby. board of publication,* 1864.

Grammont (*Count*). *See* **Hamilton** (Anthony, *count*).

Granier de Cassagnac (Bernard Adolphe). Histoire des classes nobles et des classes anoblies. v. 1. 580 pp. 8°. *Paris, H. L. Delloye,* 1840.

[No more published].

Granville de Vigne. *See* **Held** in bondage, 1864.

Grashof (F.) Angewandte mechanik. 8°. *Leipzig,* 1856–65.

[KARSTEN (G.) Allgemeine encyclopädie der physik. v. 5].

Grässe (Johann Georg Theodor). Leitfaden der allgemeinen literatur-geschichte. 3e ausg. ix, 357 pp. 8°. *Leipzig, G. Gräbner,* 1861. s.

Grateloup (Jean Pierre Sylvestre de). Mémoire de géo-zoologie sur les oursins fossiles (Échinides), qui se rencontrent dans les terrains calcaires des environs de Dax, (département des Landes). [Extract]. 89 pp. 2 pl. 8°. *Bordeaux, société linnéenne*, 1836. s.
[*With* DES MOULINS (C.) Études sur les échinides].

Grattan (Thomas Colley). High-ways and by-ways; or, tales of the roadside, picked up in the French provinces. 2d series. [*anon.*] 2 v. 264 pp; 264 pp. 12°. *Philadelphia, Carey & Lea*, 1825.

Grätz (Albrecht Heinrich). Epistola de vasorum sanguineorum extremitatibus, placentæ uterinæ, mammarumque structura, etc. 4°. *Amstelædami*, 1722. s.
[RUYSCH (F.) Opera. [no. 30]. v. 3].

Grätz (Jan Henrik). Epistola de arteria et vena bronchiali, etc. 11 pp. 1 pl. 4°. *Amstelædami*, 1731. s.
[RUYSCH (F.) Opera. [no. 22]. v. 3].

——— Epistola de pia matre, ejùsque processibus. 8 pp. 1 pl. 4°. *Amstelædami*, 1724. s.
[RUYSCH (F.) Opera. [no. 23]. v. 3].

——— Epistola de structura nasi cartiliginea, vasis sanguiferis arteriosis membranæ et cavitatis tympani et ossiculorum auditus eorumque periostio. 11 pp. 1 pl. 4°. *Amstelædami*, 1724. s.
[RUYSCH (F.) Opera. [no. 24]. v. 3].

Graves (William). Two letters respecting the conduct of rear admiral [Thomas] Graves on the coast of the United States, July to November, 1781. [Fac-simile reprint of the 1782 ed.] 2 p. l. 39 pp. 4°. *Morrisania, N. Y.* [*J. M. Bradstreet*], 1865.

Gray (Alice). Jolly and Katy in the country. 360 pp. 4 pl. 18°. *New York, Carters*, 1866.

——— Nellie's stumbling block. 246 pp. 2 pl. 16°. *New York, Carters*, 1866.

Gray (Asa, *M.D.*) Botany for young people and common schools. How plants grow, a simple introduction to structural botany. With a popular flora. 233 pp. sm. 4°. *New York, Ivison, Phinney & co.* 1868.

——— Manual of the botany of the northern United States, including the district east of the Mississippi and north of North Carolina and Tennessee. 5th ed. 701 pp. 20 pl. 8°. *New York, Ivison, Phinney & co.* 1867.

Gray (Barry, *pseudon.*) *See* **Coffin** (Robert Barry).

Gray (Henry, *F. R. S.*) Anatomy, descriptive and surgical. The drawings by H. V. Carter, M.D. The dissections jointly by the author and dr. Carter. 4th ed. by T. Holmes. xxxiv, 788 pp. 8°. *London, Longmans*, 1866.

Gray (James, *D.D.*) A dissertation on the coincidence between the priesthoods of Jesus Christ and Melchisedec, [etc.] Together with a sketch of the life of Jesus Christ. 158 pp. 12°. *Hagerstown, (Md.) J. M. Campbell*, 1845. s.

Gray (John Edward). Hand-book of British water-weeds, or algae. The diatomaceæ, by William Caruthers. iv, 123 pp. 12°. *London, R. Hardwicke*, 1864. s.

——— Mammalia. 4°. *London*, 1840.
[*In* HINDS (R. B.) The zoology of H. M. S. Sulphur. v. 1].

——— Synopsis of the species of starfish in the British museum. iv, 18 pp. 16 pl. 4°. *London, J. Van Voorst*, 1866. s.

Gray (Thomas). Letters to Horace Walpole. 4°. *London, Robinson*, 1798.
[*With* WALPOLE (H.) Works, v. 5, 1798].

Graydon (Alexander). Memoirs of his own times. With reminiscences of the men and events of the revolution. Edited by J. S. Littell. xxiv, 504 pp. 8°. *Philadelphia, Lindsay & Blakiston*, 1846.

Greyjackets (The), and how they lived, fought and died for Dixie. With incidents and sketches of life in the confederacy. By a confederate. [*anon.*] 574 pp. 11 maps. 5 pl. 8°. *Philadelphia, Jones, bros. & co.* 1867.

Great Britain. *Board of agriculture and internal improvements.* General view of the agriculture of the counties, [etc. named below]. Drawn up for the consideration of the board of agriculture and internal improvements. 73 v. 8°. *London, etc.* 1795–1820. s.

CONTENTS.

BAILEY (John). Durham. 1810.
BATCHELOR (Thomas). Bedford. 1808.
BILLINGSLEY (John). Somerset. 2d ed. 1798.
BROWN (Robert). West riding of Yorkshire. 1799.
DAVIES (Walter). North Wales. 1810.
——— South Wales. 2 v. 1815.
DAVIS (Thomas). Wiltshire. 1811.
DICKSON (R. W.) Lancashire. 1815.
DOUGLAS (Robert, *D.D.*) Roxburgh and Selkirk. 1798.
DUNCOMB (John). Hereford. 1815.
FAREY (John, *sr.*) Derbyshire. 3 v. 1811–17.
FINDLATER (*Rev.* Charles). Peebles. 1814.
GOOCH (*Rev.* William). Cambridge. 1811.
GRAHAM (Patrick, *D. D.*) Sterlingshire. 1812.
HASSALL (Charles). Monmouth. 1812.
HEADRICK (*Rev.* James). Angus, or Forfarshire. 1813.
HENDERSON (*Capt.* John). Caithness. 1812.
——— Sutherland. 1812.
HOLLAND (Henry). Cheshire. 1812.
HOLT (John). Lancaster. 1795.
KEITH (George Skene). Aberdeenshire. 1811.
KENT (Nathaniel). Norfolk. 1796.
KERR (Robert). Berwick. 1809.
LESLIE (William). Nairn and Moray. 1811.
LOWE (Robert). Nottingham. 1798.
MACDONALD (James). Hebrides. 1811.
MACFARLAN (Duncan). *See* WHYTE.
MACKENZIE (*Sir* George Stuart). Ross and Cromarty. 1810.
MAVOR (William). Berkshire. 1809.
MIDDLETON (John). Middlesex. 2d ed. 1809.
MURRAY (Adam). Warwick. 1813.

Great Britain—continued.

NAISMITH (John). Clydesdale. 1806.
PARKINSON (Richard). Huntingdon. 1811.
——— Rutland. 1808.
PITT (William). Leicester. 1809.
——— Northampton. 1809.
——— Stafford. 1808.
——— Worcester. 1810.
PLYMLEY (Joseph). Shropshire. 1813.
PRIEST (St. John). Buckinghamshire. With an appendix, by mr. [Richard] Parkinson. 1810.
QUAYLE (Thomas). Isle of Man. 1812.
——— Islands on the coast of Normandy, subject to the crown of Great Britain. 1815.
ROBERTSON (George). Inverness. 1808.
——— Kincardineshire. 1810.
——— Mid-Lothian. 1795.
——— Perth. 1799.
RUDGE (Thomas). Gloucester. 1807.
SHIRREFF (John). Orkney islands. 1814.
——— Shetland islands. 1814. [With the preceding].
SINGER (William). Dumfries. 1812.
SMITH (John, *D. D.*) Argyle. 1805.
SMITH (Samuel). Galloway. 1810.
SOMERVILLE (Robert). East-Lothian. 1805.
STEVENSON (William). Dorset. 1820.
——— Surrey. 1809.
STRICKLAND (Hugh Edwin). East riding of Yorkshire. 1812.
THOMSON (John). Fife. 1800.
TROTTER (James). West-Lothian. 1811.
TUKE (John). North riding of Yorkshire. 1800.
VANCOUVER (Charles). Devon. 1808.
——— Hampshire, including the isle of Wight. 1810.
WHYTE (Andrew) *and* MACFARLAN (Duncan). Dumbarton. 1811.
WILSON (John). Renfrewshire. 1812.
WORGAN (G. B.) Cornwall. 1811.
YOUNG (Arthur). Essex. 1807.
——— Hertfordshire. 1804.
——— Lincoln. 1799.
——— Norfolk. 1804.
——— Oxfordshire. 1809.
——— Suffolk. 1804.
——— Sussex. 1808.

——— *Navy department.* The navy list for Jan. 1852, Jan. 1853, Jan. 1854, and Jan. 1855. 4 v. 12°. *London, J. Murray,* 1852–55. s.

——— ——— The same. Dec. 1867, March, June, and Sept. 1868. 4 v. 12°. *London, J. Murray,* 1867–68.

——— *Parliamentary papers.* Appendix to report of the committee of the hon. house of commons on East-India patronage. Minutes of evidence. 463 pp. 4°. [*London, public printer,* 1809].

——— ——— Extracts from papers, printed by order of the house of commons, 1839, relative to the West Indies. xxiii, 678 pp. 8°. *London, W. Clowes & sons,* 1840.

——— ——— Hansard's parliamentary debates. 3d series. v. 188–192 [to June 25, 1868]. 5 v. 8°. *London, C. Buck,* 1868.

——— ——— The history and proceedings of the house of commons, from the death of queen Anne [to 1734. Edited by R. Chandler]. 3 v. 8°. *London,* 1741.

NOTE.—The same as v. 6–8 of the 14 v. ed. of 1742–44.

——— ——— The history, debates, and proceedings of both houses of parliament, 1743–74. 7 v. 8°. *London, J. Debrett,* 1792.

——— ——— The mirror of parliament. 1828–37. Edited by J. H. Barrow. 36 v. fol. *London, proprietors,* 1828–37.

——— ——— The same. 2nd series. 1837-41. 24 v. 8°. *London, Longman,* 1837–41.

——— ——— Parliamentary papers; consisting of a complete collection of kings' speeches, messages to parliament, etc. 1660–1796. A collection of the lords' protests, 1242–1796. Standing orders of the houses of lords and commons, etc. 3 v. 8°. *London, J. Debrett,* 1797.

——— ——— The parliamentary register; or, history of the proceedings and debates of the house of commons. [1774–80]. 17 v. 8°. *London, J. Almon,* 1775–1780.

——— ——— The same. Lords and commons. [1780–96]. 45 v. 8°. *London, J. Debrett,* 1781–96.

——— ——— The same. Lords and commons. [1797–1801]. v. 1–6. 8°. *London, J. Debrett,* 1797–98.

[Imperfect: 1799–1801 wanting].

——— ——— [Parliamentary reports and papers]: session of 1867. 76 v. in 77. fol. *London,* 1867.

[V. 60 wanting].

——— ——— Report of the commissioners [*sir* W. Jardine, W. J. Ffennell, and G. K. Richards] appointed to inquire into salmon fisheries (England and Wales); together with the minutes of evidence. xliv, 545 pp. fol. *London, stationery office,* 1861.

——— ——— Report from the select committee of the house of commons on public libraries, 1849 and 1850. 2 v. fol. [*London, stationery office*], 1849–50.

——— ——— The senator; or, parliamentary chronicle. Containing a weekly register, [of] the proceedings and debates of the lords and commons. [1790–1801]. v. 1–26. 8°. *London, C. Cooke and W. Stratford,* 1790–1800.

[Imperfect. v. 27–28 wanting.]

——— ——— Thirteenth report of her majesty's civil service commissioners, with appendix. xx, 569 pp. 8°. *London, Eyre & Spottiswoode,* 1868.

——— *Record office publications.* Calendar of the Carew manuscripts preserved in the archiepiscopal library at Lambeth. 1575-1588. Edited by J. S. Brewer and W. Butler. cx, 580 pp. 8°. *London, Longmans,* 1868.

——— ——— Calendar of state papers, domestic series, of the reign of Elizabeth, 1591-94, preserved in her majesty's public record office. Edited by Mary A. E. Green. xii, 699 pp. 8°. *London, Longmans,* 1867.

Great Britain. Calendar of state papers. Domestic series, of the reign of Charles i, 1637. Edited by J. Bruce. xiii, 675 pp. 8°. *London, Longmans*, 1868.

——— ——— Calendar of state papers and manuscripts, relating to English affairs, existing in the archives and collections of Venice, and in other libraries of northern Italy. v. 2. 1509-19. Edited by R. Brown. lxxiv, 643 pp. 1 pl. 8°. *London, Longmans*, 1867.

——— ——— Letters and papers, foreign and domestic, of the reign of Henry viii. Arranged and catalogued by J. S. Brewer. v. iii. parts 1-2. 2 v. 8°. *London, Longmans*, 1867.

——— *Royal observatory, Greenwich.* Astronomical and magnetical and meteorological observations, 1848. Under the direction of G. B. Airy. 682 pp. 4 l. 4°. *London, J. Murray*, 1850.

——— *War department.* The army list for Jan. 1852, Jan. 1853, and Jan. 1857. 3 v. 16°. *London, Parker, etc.* 1852–57. s.

Great (The) mass meeting of loyal citizens at Cooper institute, [N. Y.] March 6, 1863. Speeches of Brady, Van Buren, etc. 16 pp. 8°. *New York*, 1865.

[Loyal publication society, no. 3].

Greeley (Horace). Abraham Lincoln. A lecture delivered during the winter of 1867-68. 22 l. 16°. [1868].

[Newspaper cuttings].

——— An address on success in business, delivered at the Cooper union, Nov. 11, 1867. 38 pp. 2 pl. 8°. *New York, S. S. Packard*, 1868.

——— Recollections of a busy life, including reminiscences of American politics and politicians, from the opening of the Missouri contest to the downfall of slavery; to which are added miscellanies. 624 pp. 1 portrait. 8°. *New York, J. B. Ford & co.* 1868.

Green (Ashbel, *D. D.*) Discourses delivered in the college of New Jersey; with a historical sketch of the college, from its origin to the accession of president Witherspoon. xi, 419 pp. 8°. *Philadelphia, E. Littell*, 1822.

Green (*Rev.* Thomas Sheldon). A treatise on the grammar of the new testament; embracing observations on the literal interpretation of numerous passages. New ed. xiv, 244 pp. 12°. *London, S. Bagster & sons*, 1862.

Greenbank's periodical library; a republication of voyages, travels, history, biography, science, tales, and poems. [In 3 v.] v. 1–2. 622 pp; 622 pp. 8°. *Philadelphia, T. K. Greenbank*, 1833.

Greenbank's—continued.

PRINCIPAL CONTENTS.

Archer (E. C.) Tours in India. v. 1.
Biber (E.) Life of Pestalozzi. v. 1.
Carmichael (A. C.) Domestic manners, etc. of the West Indies. v. 2.
Hazlitt (W.) Journey through France and Italy. v. 1.
Journal of an officer, on the western coast of Africa. v. 2.
Körner (C. T.) Life and writings. v. 1.
Lamb (C.) Last essays of Elia. v. 1.
Moir (D. M.) The wounded spirit. v. 1.
Ritchie (L.) The game of life. v. 1.
Ségur (P. P. de). History of Peter the great. v. 1.
Service afloat. v. 2.
Sherer (M). [Tales of the wars of our times]. The rival. v. 1.
——— ——— The Tyroler. v. 2.
Upham (E.) History of the Ottoman empire. v. 2.

Greene (George Washington). The life of Nathanael Greene, major-general in the army of the revolution. v. 1. xxiv, 583 pp. portrait. 8°. *New York, G. P. Putnam & son*, 1867.

Greene (Jerome B.) The world's progress, and other poems. 112 pp. 16°. *Worcester, (Mass.) author*, 1856. s.

Greene (Richard Henry). The Todd genealogy; or, register of the descendants of Adam Todd. 143, xvii pp. 8°. *New York, Wilbur & Hastings*, 1867.

Greene (Samuel S.) Analysis. A treatise on the structure of the English language. 258 pp. 12°. *Philadelphia, Thomas, Cowperthwait & co.* 1848. s.

——— An introduction to the study of English grammar. 224 pp. 16°. *Philadelphia, Cowperthwait & co.* 1868.

Greenleaf (Jonathan). Account of Wells, [Maine]. *See* **Hubbard** (Jeremiah), *and* **Greenleaf.**

Greenleaf (*Rev.* Jonathan). Thoughts on prayer, [etc]. 156 pp. 12°. *Philadelphia, presbyterian board of publication*, [1857]. s.

Greenleaf (Lawrence N.) King Sham, and other atrocities in verse; including a humorous history of the Pike's peak excitement. 139 pp. 16°. *New York, Hurd & Houghton*, 1868.

Greenwald (E. *D.D.*) The foreign mission work of pastor Louis Hanns, and the church at Hermansburg. 51 pp. 18°. *Philadelphia, lutheran board of publication*, 1867.

——— An order of family prayer. 180 pp. 12°. *Lancaster, (Pa.) St. Andrew's society*, 1867.

——— Dr. Parrot's ascent of mount Ararat. Collated from his printed report. 76 pp. 1 pl. 18°. *Philadelphia, lutheran board of publication*, 1807.

Greenwich (*Royal observatory*). *See* **Great Britain.** *Royal observatory.*

Greenwood (Francis W. P. *D.D.*) Lives of the twelve apostles, [with] a life of John the Baptist. [4th ed.] viii, 232 pp. 16°. *Boston, American unitarian association,* 1868.

—— Sermons to children. New ed. viii, 134 pp. 16°. *Boston, American unitarian association,* 1868.

Greenwood (Grace, *pseudon.*) *See* **Lippincott** (*Mrs.* Sara Jane).

Gregg (Josiah). Commerce of the prairies; or, the journal of a Santa Fé trader, during eight expeditions across the great western prairies, and a residence of nearly nine years in northern Mexico. 4th ed. 2 v. 320 pp; 318 pp. 1 map. 6 pl. 12°. *Philadelphia, J. W. Moore,* 1850.

Gregorius *turonensis.* *See* **Gregory** (*Saint*).

Gregorovius (Ferdinand). Geschichte der stadt Rom in mittelalter. Vom fünften jahrhundert bis zum sechszehnten jahrhundert. v. 1-6. 8°. *Stuttgart, J. G. Cotta,* 1859-67. s.

Gregory *or* **Grégoire** (George Florent, *saint, called bishop of Tours*). Historiæ ecclesiasticæ Francorum libri decem, cura Leglay et Teulet, collatis. Emendaverunt et animadversionibus Theod. Ruinart, D. Bouquet aliorumque doctorum virorum, et suis illustraverunt J. Guadet et Collotis. N. R. Taranne. [Texte latin]. 2 v. 3 p. l. xv, 516 pp. 1 pl; 2 p. l. 554 pp. 8°. *Paris, société de l'histoire de France,* 1836-38. s.

Gregory (John, *M.D.*) Lectures on the duties and qualifications of a physician. New ed. 4 p. l. 238 pp. 8°. *London, W. Strahan,* 1772.

Gretsch (Nicolaus). Examen de l'ouvrage de m. le marquis de Custine intitulé La Russie en 1839. Trad. du Russe, par Alexandre Kouznetzoff. 4 p. l. 107 pp. 8°. *Paris, comptoir des imprimeurs-unis,* 1844. s.

Grey (*Mrs.* E. C.) Mary Seaham. A novel. 3d ed. ii, 415 pp. 16°. *London, Chapman & Hall,* [1865]?

Griesinger (Wilhelm, *M.D.*) Die pathologie und therapie der psychischen krankheiten. viii, 397 pp. 8°. *Stuttgart, A. Krabbe,* 1845. s.

Griffith (Allen Ayrault). A drill book for practice of the principles of vocal physiology, and acquiring the art of elocution and oratory. 96 pp. 1 portrait. 8°. *Chicago, Adams, Blackmer & Lyon,* 1868.

Griffith (Richard). The triumvirate; or, the authentic memoirs of A. B. and C. [*anon.*] 2 v. 296 pp; 338 pp. 16°. *London, W. Johnston,* 1764.

Griffith (*Sir* Richard, *bart.*) Localities of the Irish carboniferous fossils arranged as an appendix to the synopsis [of M'Coy]. 4°. *London,* 1862.

[*With* M'Coy (F.) A synopsis of the carboniferous fossils of Ireland. pp. 209-271]. s.

Griffith (William, *M. D.*) Posthumous papers. Palms of British India. Arranged by John McClelland. xvi, 182, xvii-xxviii pp. 123 pl. [175-242 b.] fol. *Calcutta, C. A. Serrao,* 1850. s.

Grimaud De Caux (Gabriel) *and* **Martin Saint-Ange** (Gaspard Joseph). Physiologie de l'espèce. Histoire de la génération de l'homme, précédée de l'étude comparative de cette fonction dans les divisions principales du règne animal. xiv, 440 pp. atlas. xv pp. 12 col. pl. and 12 outline copies. 4°. *Paris, V. Masson,* 1847.

Grimke (Sarah M.) Letters on the equality of the sexes, and the condition of woman. Addressed to Mary S. Parker. 128 pp. 8°. *Boston, J. Knapp,* 1838.

Grimm (Herman). Novellen. 414 pp. 12°. *Berlin, W. Hertz,* 1856.

Griscom (John H. *M. D.*) The use of tobacco, and the evils, physical, mental, moral, and social, resulting therefrom. 37 pp. 24°. *New York, G. P. Putnam & son,* 1868.

Grivel (Guillaume). L'ami des jeunes gens. [*anon.*] 2e éd. 2 v. in 1. x, 223 pp; 239 pp. 16°. *Lille, J. B. Henry,* 1766. s.

Groesbeck (John). The Crittenden commercial arithmetic and business manual. 5th ed. 348 pp. 12°. *Philadelphia, E. C. & J. Biddle,* 1868.

Groneweg (L.) Meteorological observations made in Montgomery county, southern Ohio, and a condensed treatise on meteorology in general. 29 pp. 9 tab. 8°. *Germantown, (O.)* [*author*], 1856.

Grönlands historiske mindesmærker, udgivne af det kongelige nordiske oldskrift-selskab. 3 v. 8°. *Kjöbenhavn, Brünnich & Möller,* 1838-45.

CONTENTS.

v. 1. Indledende undersögelse.
Om Gunbjörns skjær.
Om Are Marsön.
Præsten Are Thörgilssons.
Brudstykker af Landnama.
Erik den rödes saga.
Thorfinn Karlsefnes saga.
Uddragg af Eyrbyggja.
v. 2. Uddrag af Floamanna-saga.
Uddrag af Olaf Trygvessöns saga.
Uddrag af Olaf den helliges saga.
Uddrag af Fostbræda-saga.
Skjald-helge, Grönlands laugmand.
Uddrag af Gisle Sursöns saga.
Fortælling om Thrond fra Oplandene.
Om Audun den Vestfjordske.
Beretningerne om Lig-Lodin.
Fortælling om Einar Sokkesön.

Grönlands—continued.

Udtog af Rafn Sveinbjörnsons saga.
Udtog af Gudmund Aresöns saga.
Uddrag af biskop Pauls saga.
Af den hellige Thorlaks saga.
Af kong Hakon Hakonsöns saga.
Uddrag af Sturlunga saga.
Af tillæget til Landnama.
Af biskop Arne Thorlasöns saga.
v. 3. Uddrag af de islandske annaler.
Diplomer vedkommende Grönland.
Geographiske optegnelser.
Blandede optegnelser.
Brödrene Zenos reiser.
Nyere reiser til Grönland. Af C. Pingel.
Grönlands antiquariske chorographie.
Grönlands gamle geographie.
Diplomer angaeende Grönland.
Fortegnelse over Grönlands biskopper.
Chronologisk udsigt.
Historisk navneregister.
Geographisk register.
Antiquarisk sacregister.

Groot. *See* **Grotius**; *also*, **Hofstede de Groot.**

Groote (Het) tafereel der dwaasheid, vertoonende de opkomst, voortgang en ondergang der actie, bubbel en windnegotie, in Vrankryk, Engeland, en de Nederlanden, gepleegt in den jaare 1720. Als meede konstplaaten, comedien en gedigten uytgegeven. Gedruckt tot waarschouwinge voor de nakomelingen, in't noodlottige jaar, voor veel zotte en wyze. 126 pp. 74 pl. fol. [*Amsterdam, D. Onder de Linden*], 1720.

Gros (Jean Baptiste Louis, *baron*). Négociations entre la France et la Chine, en 1860. Extrait de sa correspondance et de son journal, pendant la seconde mission qu'il a remplie dans l'extrême orient. 2 p. l. 248 pp. 4°. *Paris, J. Dumaine*, 1864.

Grose (*Rev.* John). Ethics, rational and theological, with cursory reflections on the general principles of deism. 550 pp. 5 l. 8°. *London, author*, 1782.

Grosh (*Rev.* A. B.) The odd-fellow's improved manual. 378 pp. 8 pl. 12°. *Philadelphia, T. Bliss & co.* 1869.

——— The same. Des sonderbaren bruders verbessertes handbuch. Aus dem Englischen in's Deutsche übertragen von J. C. Brunner. 498 pp. 1 portrait. 24°. *Philadelphia, T. Bliss & co.* 1869.

Grotius *or* **Groot** (Hugo de). Syntagma arateorvm: opvs poeticæ et astronomiæ studiosis vtilissimvm. 6 p. l. 5 parts in 1 v. 4°. [*Lugduni Batavorum*], *apud C. Raphelengivm*, 1600. s.

CONTENTS.

Arati phænomena, etc. 42 pp.
Ciceronis interpretatio H. Grotii versibus interpolata. 36 pp.
Phænomena aratea Germanico Cæsare interprete, etc. 95 pp. including 43 pl.
Notae H. Grotii ad Aratum. 24 pp.
Notae ejusdem ad Germanici phænomena, etc. 128 pp.

Grube (Eduard). Anneliden. 46 pp. 4 l. 4 pl. 4°. *Wien*, 1868. s.

[*In* Wüllerstorf-Urbair (B. von). Reise der Novara. Zoologischer theil. v. 2. abth. 3].

——— Parisiten. 4°. *St. Petersburg*, 1851.

[*In* Middendorff (A. T. von). Reise, etc. v. 2. theil 1].

Gruber (Eberhard Ludwig). Grundforschende fragen, welche denen neuen täufern im witgensteinischen, insonderheit zu beantworten vorgelegt waren, sammt. 2e aufl. 58 pp. 24°. *Germantown*, [*Pa.*] *C. Saur*, 1774.

[*With* Mack (Alexander). Kurze vorstellung der äussern, etc. 1774].

Gruber (Johann Gottfried). Klopstock's leben. 149 pp. 8°. *Leipzig*, 1831. s.

[*With* Klopstock (F. G.) Oden. 1831. v. 1].

Grumbler (Anthony, *pseudon.*) *See* **Hoffman** (David).

Grützner (August). Die augustin'sche silberextraction in ihrer anwendung auf hüttenproducte und erze. xii, 174 pp. 4 pl. 8°. *Braunschweig, F. Vieweg & sohn*, 1851. s.

Guainerio (Antonio). Incipit tractatus de egritudinibus capitis editus per Antonium Guayneriū. In hoc volumiē aggregati sunt ōes tractat' quos clarissim' et verissim' medicīe interpres Antoni's Guaineri's ad diuersas corporis hūani egritudines edidit. 255 l. fol. *Papie, A. d' Carcano*, 1488.

CONTENTS.

De egritudinibus capitis.
De pleurisi.
De passionibus stomachi.
De fluxibus.
De matricibus.
De jūcturis siue de arthetica et calculosa passiœ.
De peste et de venenis.
De febribus.
De balneis aquae ciuitatis antiqssime.
Antidotariū.

Guards (The). A novel. [*anon.*] 2 v. 215 pp; 216 pp. 12°. *New York, Harpers*, 1827.

Guarini (Giovanni Battista). Il pastor fido. [*anon.*] 256 pp. 32°. *Parigi, T. Jolly*, 1706.

——— The same. Il pastor fido, tragicommedia. 268 pp. 18°. *Avignone, F. Seguin aîné*, 1816. s.

Güell y Renté (José). Pensamientos christianos, filosóficos y politicos. 5 p. l. 147 pp. 8°. *Valladolid, J. M. Lezcano y Roldan*, 1854. s.

——— Paralelo entre los reinas catolicas doña Isabel ia y doña Isabel iia. 2 p. l. 112 pp. 8°. *Paris, J. Claye*, 1858. s.

Guenther. *See* **Günther.**

Guépratte (Charles). Problêmes d'astronomie nautique et de navigation; suivis d'un recueil de tables nécessaire à la résolution de ces problêmes. 3e éd. v. 2. tables. 516 pp. 8°. *Brest, Lefournier & Deperiers*, 1834.

[v. 1 wanting].

Guérard (Benjamin Edme Charles). Polyptyque de l'abbé Irminon; ou, dénombrement des manses, des serfs, et des revenus, de l'abbaye de Saint Germain des Prés, sous le règne de Charlemagne, publié d'après le manuscrit de la bibliothèque du roi. Avec des prolégomènes pour servir à l'histoire de la condition des personnes et des terres depuis les invasions des barbares jusqu' à l'institution des communes. 2 v. in 3. vii, 984 pp; 3 p. l. 463 pp. 4°. *Paris, imprimerie royale,* 1844.

Guericke (Otto von). Experimenta nova magdeburgica de vacuo spatio. Accedit quædam virtutibus mundanis, et systemate mundi planetario; sicut et de stellis fixis. 6 pl. 244 pp. 2 l. fol. *Amstelodami, apud J. Janssonium à Waesberge,* 1672. s.

Guérin-Méneville (Félix Édouard). Rapport sur les progrès de la culture d'ailante, et de l'éducation du ver à soie (*bombyx cynthia*) que l'on élève en plein air sur ce végétal. 104 pp. 8°. *Paris, imprimerie impériale,* 1862. s.

——— *and* **Percheron** (Achille Remi). Genera des insectes, ou exposition détaillée de tous les caractères propres à chacun des genres de cette classe d'animaux. 3 pts. in 1 v. 50 col. pl. 8°. *Mequignon-Marvis,* 1835[-38]. s.
[Imperfect. Livraison 6 wanting. pl. 51-60].

Guernsey (Alfred H.) *and* **Alden** (Henry M.) Harpers' pictorial history of the great rebellion. Part 2. iv, 381-836 pp. fol. *New York, Harpers,* 1868.
NOTE.—Completes the work.

Guernsey (Henry N. *M. D.*) The application of the principles and practice of homœopathy to obstetrics, and the disorders peculiar to women and young children. x,752 pp. 1 pl. 8°. *Philadelphia, F. E. Boericke,* 1867.

Guernsey (Lucy Ellen). Sophie Kennedy's experience; or, the stepmother. 244 pp. 2 pl. 12°. *New York, gen. prot. episc. s. s. union,* 1856. s.

Guersant (Paul). On croup. [1835]. 8°. *London,* 1859.
[NEW SYDENHAM society, v. 3].

Gueudeville (Nicolas). Suite du voyage de l'Amérique, ou dialogues de monsieur le baron de Lahontan et d'un sauvage dans l'Amérique. Avec les voyages du même en Portugal et en Danemarc. 8 p. l. 222 pp. 2 maps. 4 pl. 16°. *Amsterdam, Boeteman,* 1704.

Guggenbühl (*Dr.* Ludwig) *and others.* Raccolta di relazioni, lettere ed articoli diversi, compilate e pubblicate da chiarissimi contemporanei alemani, francesi, inglesi, italiani e della Norvegia concernenti lo stabilimento dell' Abendberg per la cura e l'educazione dei fanciulli cretini, voltate in lingua italiana del cav. L. V. Ferrero di Ponsiglione. 5 parts in 1 v. 8°. *Genova, r. i. de' sordo-muti,* 1854. s.

Guiard. *See* **Guyard.**

Guiart (Guillaume). Branche des royaux lignages. Chronique mètrique. Publiée par J. A. Buchon. 2 v. 8°. *Paris, Verdière,* 1826.
[COLLECTION de chroniques nationales françaises. v. 7-8].

Guide (A) to the city of Chicago. [*anon.*] 196 pp. 24 pl. 18°. *Chicago, T. E. Zell & co.* 1868.

Guide (A) through the university of Cambridge: likewise a description of the town, county, and environs of Cambridge. A new ed. 7 p. l. 132 pp. 1 map. 6 pl. 12°. *Cambridge, J. Deighton & sons,* 1820. s.

Guild (Reuben Aldridge). Life, times, and correspondence of James Manning, and the early history of Brown university. 523 pp. 4 pl. 12°. *Boston, Gould & Lincoln,* 1864.

Guillermus *parisiensis.* Epistolarum et evangeliorum de tẽpore et sanctis liber. cxxv pp. 4°. *Colonia,* [*Ulricus Zell*], 1482.

——— Postilla super epistolas et euangelia de tempore et sanctis et pro defunctis. 191 l. 4°. [*n. p. about* 1480].

Guillim (John). A display of heraldry. 6th ed. 5 p. l. 3 l. ms. [index]. 20, 460 pp. 11 l. fol. *London, R. & J. Bonwicke, etc.* 1724.

Guiton de Morveau. *See* **Guyton de Morveau.**

Guitton (Eugène, *M. D.*) Nouvelle classification zoologique, basée sur les appareils et les fonctions de la reproduction. [Extract]. 147 pp. 2 tab. 8°. *Paris, Revue et magazin de zoologie,* 1854. s.

Guizot (Marguerite Andrée Élisa Dillon, *madame*). Clara; or, the discipline of affliction. Translated from the French. 147 pp. 1 pl. 18°. *Philadelphia, A. Hart,* 1850. s.

Gulf (The) stream; or, Harry Maynard's bible. By the author of "Poor Nicholas," etc. [*anon.*] 213 pp. 18°. *Philadelphia, presbyterian board of publication,* 1864.

Gumposch (Victor Philipp). Die philosophische und theologische literatur der Deutschen von 1400 bis auf unsere tage. 1er band. Die philosophische literatur. xii, 640 pp. 8°. *Regensburg, G. J. Manz,* 1851.

Gunning (*Mrs. general*). Love at first sight. A novel. From the French. With alterations and additions. 5 v. in 3. 16°. *London, H. Lowndes,* 1797.

Günther (Albert C. L. G.) The fishes of Zanzibar. *See* **Playfair** (R. L.) *and* **Günther.**

——— The reptiles of British India. xxvii, 452 pp. 26 pl. 4°. *London*, 1864.
[RAY society].

——— *editor*. *See* **Record** (The) of zoological literature.

Gurley (*Rev.* Ralph Randolph). Life of Jehudi Ashmun, late colonial agent in Liberia; with a sketch of the life of the rev. Lott Cary. 396, 160 pp. portrait. 8°. *New York, Leavitt, Lord & co.* 1835.

Guthrie (Frederick). The elements of heat and of non-metallic chemistry. viii, 210 pp. 12°. *London, J. Van Voorst*, 1868.

Guthrie (William, *of London*). A universal geography; or, a view of the present state of the known world, etc. The astronomical part by James Ferguson, F. R. S. 3d Am. ed. With extensive additions and alterations by several American editors. 2 v. 4 p. l. 514 pp; 640 pp. 8°. *Philadelphia, B. Warner*, 1820. s.
[Imperfect: one or more pages at end of v. 2 wanting].

Guthrie (*Rev.* William, *of Finnick, Scotland*). The christian's great interest. [With] some account of the author. 155 pp. 18°. *Philadelphia, W. Young*, 1789.

Guy (William Augustus). Outline of general pathology. 12°. *New York*, 1846. s.
[*With* HOOPER (R.) Physicians' vade-mecum. 1846].

Guyard *or* **Guiard** (Antoine). Dissertation sur l'honoraire des messes; où l'on traite de son origine, des illusions et autres abus qui s'en sont suivis. [*anon.*] Nouv. éd. xx, 467 pp. 16°. [*Paris*]? 1757. s.

Guyon (Jeanne Marie Bouvier de la Mothe) *and* **Cowper** (William). Poems, translated from the French, by W. Cowper. With some original poems of [William] Cowper. xii, 131 pp. 24°. *Newport-Pagnel, J. Wakefield*, 1801.

Guyton de Morveau (Louis Bernard). Tratado de la educacion pública, con la planta de un colegio. Traducido del Frances, por J. A. Porcél. 4 p. l. 382 pp. 16°. *Madrid, J. Ibarra*, 1768. s.

Haan (Willem de). Crustacea [japonica]. xvi, xxxi, 243 pp. 72 pl. fol. *Lugduni Batavorum*, 1850. s.
[SIEBOLD (P. F. von). Fauna japonica].

Hacker (William). Guide for the order of high priesthood [in masonry]. 22 pp. 12°. *Portland, J. Covell*, 1864. s.

Hackett (*Rev.* Horatio B.) Illustrations of scripture, suggested by a tour through the holy land. 340 pp. 12 pl. 12°. *Boston, Heath & Graves*, 1856. s.

Hadrianus. *See* **Adriano.**

Haeseler (Charles H. L. *M. D.*) Across the Atlantic. Letters from France, Switzerland, Germany, Italy, and England. 397 pp. 12°. *Philadelphia, T. B. Peterson & bros.* 1868.

Hagen (Carl). Deutsche geschichte von Rudolf von Habsburg bis auf die neueste zeit. 5 pts. in 3 v. 8°. *Frankfort a M; Meidinger, sohn & co.* 1854.

Hagen (Hermann August). Neuroptera [von Mossambique]. fol. *Berlin*, 1862.
[*In* PETERS (W. C. H.) Nat. reise nach Mossambique. Zoologie, v. 5].

Hagen (Johann vom, *clergyman at Steinheim*). Briefe introdvctions, both natvrall, pleasant, and delectable, vnto the art of chiromancie, or manuell diuination, and phisiognomy. [With] as well the artificial as naturall astrology, with the nature of the planets. Translated into English by F. Withers. 133 l. *b. l.* 24°. *London, T. Pvrfoot*, 1633.

Hagenbach (Carl Rudolf). Der evangelische protestantismus in seiner geschichtlichen entwickelung in einer reihe von vorlesungen dargestellt. 2e durchgesehene aufl. 2 v. xii, 532 pp; viii, 519 pp. 8°. *Leipzig, S. Hirzel*, 1854.
[v. 3-4 *of his* Vorlesungen über wesen und geschichte der reformation].

——— Lehrbuch der dogmengeschichte. 3e verb. aufl. xii, 771 pp. 8°. *Leipzig, S. Hirzel*, 1853.

Haime (Jules). Recherches sur polypiers. *See* **Edwards** (H. M.) *and* **Haime.**

Hainaut *or* **Hainault.** Inventaire analytique et chronologique des archives des chambres du clergé, de la noblesse et du tiers état du Hainaut; etc. xiv, 365 pp. 4°. *Mons, E. Hoyois*, 1852. s.

Haines (Elijah M.) Historical and statistical sketches of Lake county, state of Illinois. 112 pp. 1 pl. 16°. *Waukegan, (Ill.) E. G. Howe*, 1852. s.

Hake (L.) Enigmatical recreations; comprehending classical, historical, and biographical notorieties, illustrative of eminent characters and memorable events; etc. 2 p. l. 130 pp. 16°. *London, author*, 1837. s.

Hakluyt society. Publications.

CONTENTS.

39. MORGA (A. de). The Phillippine islands, etc. in the 16th century.

Hale (*Mrs.* C. L.) Woodland lays, legends, and charades. 282 pp. 12°. *Philadelphia, Lippincott & co. for the author*, 1868.

Hale (*Rev.* Edward E.) If, yes, and perhaps. Four possibilities and six exaggerations, with some bits of fact. 3 p. l. 296 pp. 12°. *Boston, Ticknor & Fields,* 1868.

Hale (*Rev.* John). A modest inquiry into the nature of witchcraft. 158 pp. 16°. [*Boston,* 1697]?

[Imperfect: title page and pp. 1-10 wanting].

Hale (Lucretia P.) The struggle for life; or, Board court and Langdale. A story of home. 4th ed. xiv, 311 pp. 12°. *Boston, A. Williams & co.* 1868.

Hale (*Mrs.* Sarah Josepha). Manners; or, happy homes and good society all the year round. 377 pp. 12°. *Boston, J. E. Tilton & co.* 1868.

——— (*editor*). *See* **Poet's** (The) offering, for 1850.

Hales (Stephen, *D.D.*) Some considerations on the causes of earthquakes. Read before the Royal society, April 5, 1750. 23 pp. 8°. *London, R. Manby & H. S. Cox,* 1750.

Halévy (Ludovic). La belle Hélène, grand duchess of Gerolstein. *See* **Meilhac** (H.) *and* **Halévy.**

Half-yearly (The) abstract of the medical sciences; being a digest of British and continental medicine. July–Dec. 1867. v. 46. 12°. *London, Churchill & sons,* 1868.

Haliburton (R. G.) Intercolonial trade our only safeguard against disunion. 42 pp. 8°. *Ottawa, G. E. Desbarats,* 1868.

Hall (*Rev.* Edwin). The ancient historical records of Norwalk, Conn. with a plan of the ancient settlement, and of the town in 1847. 320 pp. 1 map. 9 pl. 12°. *Norwalk, J. Mallory & co.* 1847.

Hall (Francis). Travels in Canada and the United States in 1816–17. 332 pp. 8°. *Boston, Wells & Lilly,* 1818.

Hall (Frederic, *lawyer*). Life of Maximilian i. late emperor of Mexico, with a sketch of the empress Carlotta. 317 pp. 4 pl. 12°. *New York, J. Miller,* 1868.

Hall (Hiland). History of Vermont, from its discovery to its admission into the union in 1791. xii, 522 pp. 1 map. 8°. *Albany, J. Munsell,* 1868.

Hall (*Judge* James). Legends of the west. 435 pp. 2 pl. 12°. *New York, T. L. Magagnos & co.* 1854.

Hall (*Mrs.* James, *wife of prof.* James Hall). Phantasia, and other poems. 144 pp. 3 pl. 8°. *New York, G. P. Putnam,* 1849. s.

Hall (John, *D. D. of New York*). Family prayers, for four weeks. 160 pp. 16°. *New York, A. D. F. Randolph,* 1868.

Hall (Newman, *D.D.*) A parting word. 88 pp. 18°. *New York, Sheldon & co.* 1868.

——— Sermons. With a history of Surrey chapel and its institutions. 309 pp. 1 portrait. 12°. *New York, Sheldon & co.* 1868.

Hall (Spencer). A letter to John Murray, esq. upon an æsthetic edition of the works of Shakespeare. 37 pp. 8°. *London, Chapman & Hall,* 1841. s.

Hallam (Henry). Introduction to the literature of Europe in the 15th, 16th, and 17th centuries. 4 v. 8°. *Paris, A. & W. Galignani & co.* 1837–39. s.

Haller (Albrecht von). Tagebuch der medicinisch litteratur der jahre 1745 bis 1774. Gesammelt, herausgegeben und mit verschiedenen abhandlungen aus der geschichte und litteratur der medicin begleitet von J. J. Römer und P. Usteri. v. i. theile 1–2. 2 v. 12°. *Bern,* 1789–90. s.

[Th. iii, 1791, wanting].

Hallgrimsson (Jónas). Ljóðmæli. B. Pjetursson og K. Gislason hafa sjed um prentunina. xvi, 323 pp. 16°. *Kaupmannahöfn, J. D. Kristi,* 1847. s.

Halliday (Andrew, *editor*). *See* **Savage** club-papers.

Halm (Friedrich). Griseldis. Dramatisches gedicht in fünf akten. 138 pp. 8°. *Wien, C. Gerold,* 1837. s.

Hamburg (*Free city of*). Hamburgische rath und bürgerschlüsse von jahren 1841–55. Herausgegeben von dr. Friedrich Lorenz Hoffman, etc. 14 v. 4°. *Hamburg, raths buchdrucker,* 1851–56. s.

Hamburgisches magazin, oder gesammlete schriften, zum unterricht und vergnügen, aus der naturforschung und den angenehmen wissenschaften überhaupt. 26 v. 16°. *Hamburg, etc. G. C. Grund, etc.* 1748–67. s.

——— The same. v. 27. Dreyfaches universal register und repertorium, über die 26 bände des hamburgischen magazins. 4 p. l. 488 pp. 8°. *Hamburg, etc. A. H. Hollens wittwe,* 1767. s.

——— The same. Neues hamburgisches magazin, oder fortsetzung gesammleter schriften, aus der naturforschung, der allgemeinen stadt- und landoekonomie, und den angenehmen wissenchaften überhaupt. 18 v. 16°. *Hamburg, Holle,* 1767–77. s.

Hamerton (Philip Gilbert). Etching and etchers. xxvi, 354 pp. 35 pl. 8°. *London, Macmillan & co.* 1868.

Hamilton (Andrew Jackson). Letter to the president of the United States [on the position of the colored race]. 18 pp. 8°. *New York*, 1865.
[LOYAL publication society, no. 26].

Hamilton (Anthony, *count*). Memoirs of the court of Charles ii. by count Grammont, as edited by sir W. Scott. [With] the personal history of Charles, etc. vi, 536 pp. 12°. *London, H. G. Bohn*, 1859.

Hamilton (Gail, *pseudon.*) *See* **Dodge** (Mary A.)

Hamilton (James A.) The constitution vindicated. Nationality, secession, slavery. 12 pp. 8°. *New York*, 1864.
[LOYAL publication society, no. 50].

Hamilton (John C.) Coercion completed, or treason triumphant. 25 pp. 8°. *New York*, 1864.
[LOYAL publication society, no. 66].

——— The slave power: its heresies and injuries to the American people. Speech, Nov. 1864. 23 pp. 8°. *New York*, 1864.
[LOYAL publication society, no. 74].

Hamilton (*Sir* William, *professor at Edinburgh*). Philosophy. Arranged and edited by O. W. Wight. 530 pp. 8°. *New York, Appletons*, 1853.

Hammer-Purgstall (Joseph von, *editor*). *See* **Ahmad.** Ancient alphabets.

Hammitt (Samuel A.) Piney woods tavern; or, Sam Slick in Texas. [*anon.*] 309 pp. 12°. *Philadelphia, T. B. Peterson*, [1858]. s.

Hammond (William A. *M. D.*) Insanity in its medico-legal relations. Opinion relative to the testamentary capacity of the late J. C. Johnston, of Chowan co. N. C. 72 pp. 8°. *New York, Baker, Voorhis & co.* 1866.

Hamon (*Abbé, of the congregation of St. Sulpice, Paris*). A treatise on catechism. Translated from the French, by Mary F. Snowden. x, 167 pp. 24°. *Cincinnati, John P. Walsh*, 1866.

Hamst (Olphar, *anagram*). *See* **Thomas** (Ralph).

Hancock (John, *of Lisburn, Ireland*). Reasons for withdrawing from a people called quakers; [with] a friendly expostulation; and considerations on revelation, the scriptures, etc. iv, 142 pp. 8°. *London, J. Johnson*, 1802.

——— Thoughts on the abuse of figurative language, as applied to religious subjects: with observations addressed to the quakers. 69 pp. 8°. *Belfast, J. Smith*, 1803.
[*With* the preceding].

Hanka (Waclaw, *editor*). Kralodworsky rukopis, [etc. *or*,] Königinhofer handschrift. Sammlung altböhmischer lyrisch-epischer gesänge, nebst andern altböhmischen gedichten. Verteutscht und mit einer historisch-kritischen einleitung versehen von Wenceslaw Aloys Swoboda, [etc.] xxviii, 244 pp. 1 pl. 8°. *Prag, J. G. Calve*, 1829. s.

Hankins (Marie Louise). Women of New York. 349 pp. 36 pl. 12°. *New York, M. L. Hankins & co.* 1861.

Hann (James). The elements of plane trigonometry. 2 p. l. 128 pp. 12°. *London, J. Weale*, 1849. s.

Hanna (John S.) Ready reckoner and log-book. A set of tables for the measurement of square timber, boards, planks, and scantling. 106 pp. 18°. *Lockhaven, Pa.* 1868.

Hannah (*Rev.* John) *and* **Jobson** (*Rev.* Frederick James). The method of man's reconciliation with God, [by J. H.] and the fullness of christian privilege, [by F. J. J.]; two sermons, etc. Edited by rev. D. W. Clark. 102 pp. 12°. *Cincinnati, L. Swormstedt & A. Poe*, 1857. s.

Hannay (James). Three hundred years of a Norman house; the barons of Gournay from the 10th to the 13th century. With genealogical miscellanies. 3 p. l. 288 pp. 12°. *London, Tinsley bros.* 1867.

Hanover (*Germany*). Das staatsbudget und das bedürfniss für kunst und wissenschaft im königreich Hannover. 92 pp. 4°. *Hannover, Hahn'sche hof buchhandlung*, 1866. s.

——— *Statistische bureau.* Zur statistik des königreichs Hannover. 7(8) v. in 1 v. fol. *Hannover, Hahn. F. Culemann*, 1850-60. s.

——— Königliche polytechnische schule zu Hannover. Katalog der bibliothek. xv, 483 pp. 8°. *Hannover, W. Reimschneider*, 1868. s.

Hans and his northern home. [*anon.*] 245 pp. 8 pl. 16°. *Philadelphia, American s. s. union*, 1859. s.

Hansard's parliamentary debates. *See* **Great Britain.** (*Parliamentary papers*).

Hanson (*Rev.* John H.) Poems; with a memoir, by his sister, Christian Hanson. 167 pp. 12°. *New York, Pott & Amery*, 1869.

Happy Charlie, and other stories; by the author of "Kitty's victory," etc. [*anon.*] 170 pp. 5 pl. 18°. *New York, R. Carter & bros.* 1865.
[*With* WHAT Elise loved best, etc. 1865].

Harbinger (The), devoted to social and political progress. Published by the Brook farm phalanx. v. 1-6. 6 v. 8°. and fol. *New York*, 1845-48.

Harbison (Massy). A narrative of [her] sufferings from Indian barbarity; with some account of the cruelties of the Indians on the Allegheny river, 1790-94. Communicated by herself. 98 pp. 24°. *Pittsburgh, D. & M. Maclean*, 1828.

Hardee (*Lieut. col.* William J.) Rifle and light infantry tactics. 2 v. 250 pp; 232 pp. 64 pl. 32°. *Philadelphia, Lippincott*, 1855.

Harding (Carl Ludwig, *editor*). *See* **Kleine** astronomische ephemeriden.

Hardwicke's science-gossip; an illustrated medium of interchange and gossip for students and lovers of nature. 1865-68. 4 v. 8°. *London, R. Hardwicke*, 1866-69.

Hardy (Alfred, *M. D.*) The dartrous diathesis, or eczema and its allied affections. Translated [from the French], by H. G. Piffard. xi, 94 pp. 12°. *New York, Moorhead, Simpson, & Bond*, 1868.

Harkey (Simeon W.) The character and value of an evangelical ministry, etc. 190 pp. 18°. *Baltimore, T.N. Kurtz*, 1853. s.

Harlan (Richard, *M.D. of Philadelphia*). Medical and physical researches; or, original memoirs in medicine, surgery, physiology, geology, zoology, and comparative anatomy. xxxix, 653 pp. 1 tab. 39 pl. 8°. *Philadelphia, printed by Lydia R. Bailey*, 1835. s.

Harland (Marion, *pseudon.*) *See* **Terhune** (Mary V. H.)

Harless (A. von). Das buch von den ägyptischen mysterien. Zur geschichte der selbst auflösung des heidnischen hellenenthums. vi, 132 pp. 8°. *München, J. G. Cotta*, 1858.

Harlow (Samuel R.) *and* **Hutchins** (S. C.) Life sketches of the state officers, senators, and members of the assembly of the state of New York, in 1868. 402 pp. portrait. 8°. *Albany, Weed, Parsons & co.* 1868.

Harold and other stories. By the author of "Jennie Graham," etc. [*anon.*] 240 pp. 3 pl. 18°. *Philadelphia, presbyterian board of publication*, 1866.

Harper's bazar. A repository of fashion, pleasure, and instruction. Nov. 1867, to Dec. 1868. v. 1. fol. *New York, Harpers*, 1868.

Harper's hand-book for travellers in Europe and the east. With a railroad map, corrected to 1868. Seventh year. 662 pp. 53 l. 6 pp. 12°. *New York, Harpers*, 1858.

Harper's new monthly magazine. Dec. 1867, to Nov. 1868. v. 36-37. 8°. *New York, Harpers*, 1868.

Harper's New York and Erie railroad guide-book; etc. 175 pp. 12°. *New York, Harpers*, [1851.] s.

Harper's pictorial history of the great rebellion. *See* **Guernsey** (A. H.) *and* **Alden** (H. M.)

Harper's phrase book. *See* **Fetridge** (W. P.)

Harper's weekly. A journal of civilization. Jan. to Dec. 1868. v. 12. fol. *New York, Harpers*, 1868.

Harris (John, *D.D. F.R.S.*) Navigantium atque itinerantium bibliotheca; or, a compleat collection of voyages and travels; consisting of above four hundred of the most authentick writers. 2 v. 7 p. l. lxvii, 862 pp. 7 l. 6 maps. 11 pl; 3 p.l. 928, 56 pp. 6 l. 3 maps. 12 pl. fol. *London, T. Bennet*, 1705.

——— The same. Consisting of above six hundred of the most authentic writers. Revised, with additions. 2 v. 7 p. l. xvi, 934 pp. 12 maps. 22 pl; 5 p.l. 1056 pp. 11 l. 10 maps. 17 pl. fol. *London, T. Osborne*, 1764.

Harris (Thomas L.) An epic of the starry heaven. 210 pp. 12°. *London, Partridge & Britton*, 1854. s.

Harrison (William B.) The mechanic's tool-book. With practical rules and suggestions for use of machinists, iron-workers, and others. 278 pp. 12°. *New York, D. Van Nostrand*, 1868.

Harriss (Julia Mildred). Wild shrubs of Alabama; or, rhapsodies of restless hours. By the minstrel maiden of Mobile. 180 pp. portrait. 12°. *New York. C. B. Norton*, 1852. s.

Harry Budd; or, the history of an orphan boy. [*anon.*] 235 pp. 7 pl. 16°. *New York, Carlton & Phillips*, 1856. s.

Harsha (*Rev.* William W.) Heavenly light for earthly firesides. 427 pp. 8°. *Chicago, S. M. Kennedy*, 1868.

Hart (John S. *LL.D.*) In the school room. Chapters in the philosophy of education. 276 pp. 12°. *Philadelphia, Eldredge & brother*, 1868.

Hart (John S. *editor.*) *See* **Iris** (The), for 1852.

Hartford (*City of, Connecticut*). Geer's Hartford city directory for 1868–69. 537 pp. 1 map. 16°. *Hartford, Hartford steam printing co.* 1868.

Harting (James Edmund). The birds of Middlesex. xvi, 284 pp. 1 pl. 12°. *London, J. Van Voorst*, 1866.

Hartmann (*Rev.* Anastasius). Das kreuz des weltmenschen und des wahren christen. Gebet- und erbauungsbüchlein für kranke und leidende. 2e aufl. 320 pp. 24°. *New York, C. & N. Benziger*, 1868.

Hartmann (Carl, *editor*). *See* **Berg** und hüttenmannische zeitung.

Hartmann (J. E.) Stuttgarts romantische umgebungen. Ein führer für fremde und ein gedenkbuch für Württemberger. 4 p. l. 204 pp. 6 pl. 1 map. 8°. *Stuttgart, k. hofbuchdruckerei zu Guttenburg,* 1847. s.

Hartwig (Georg, *of Heidelberg*). The harmonies of nature; or, the unity of creation. xix, 406 pp. 8 pl. 8°. *London, Longmans,* 1866.

Harvard university (*Cambridge, Mass.*) Addresses at the inauguration of C. C. Felton, as president of Harvard college, etc. 149 pp. 8°. *Cambridge, Sever & Francis,* 1860. s.

——— A catalogue of the officers and students, 1867–68. First term. 105 pp. 16°. *Cambridge, Severs & Francis,* 1867.

——— The Harvard register. [Edited by undergraduates of the University]. 1827–28. 2 p. l. 384 pp. 8°. *Cambridge, Hilliard & Brown,* 1828.

NOTE.—No more published.

Harvester (The): for gathering the ripened crops on every homestead, leaving the unripe to nature. By a merchant. [*anon.*] 150 pp. 12°. *Boston, W. White & co.* 1868.

Harvey (J. H.) Four lectures on civil liberty and expansion of intellect, as connected with human happiness; delivered at Walsall. iv, 222 pp. 12°. *London, Longmans,* 1845.

Harvey (Thomas, *teacher at Geneva*). Cours de thèmes anglais préparés sur le recueil de morceaux choisis de Favre et S. Strebinger. 214 pp. 12°. *Genève, J. Kessmann,* 1853. s.

Harvey (Thomas W.) A practical grammar of the English language, for the use of schools of every grade. 264 pp. 12°. *Cincinnati, Wilson, Hinkle & co.* [1868].

Harvey (William Henry). Phycologia australica; or, a history of Australian seaweeds; and a synopsis of all known Australian algæ. 5 v. 8°. *London, L. Reeve,* 1858–63.

Hassall (Charles). General view of the agriculture of the county of Monmouth. xi, 142 pp. 1 col. map. 1 pl. 8°. *London,* 1812. s.

[GREAT BRITAIN: Board of agriculture].

Hasskarl (Justus Carl). Enantioblastae [von Mossambique]. fol. *Berlin,* 1864.

[*In* PETERS (W. C. H.) Nat. reise nach Mossambique. Botanik].

Hatch (Israel T.) Reciprocity. Speech at the convention at Detroit, 1868. 8°. *Buffalo, Mathews & Warren,* 1865.

[*In* HAYES (J. D.) "Niagara ship canal," etc. pp. 47–58. 1865].

Hatfield (Edwin F. *D. D.*) History of Elizabeth, New Jersey; including the early history of Union co. 701 pp. 7 pl. 8°. *New York, Carlton & Lanahan,* 1868.

Hauch (John Carsten). Robert Fulton; an historical novel. Translated by Paul C. Sinding. x, 450 pp. 12°. *New York, Macdonald & Palmer,* 1868.

Hauranne (Ernest Duvergier de). *See* **Duvergier de Hauranne.**

Haus (Das) Rothschild. Seine geschichte und seine geschäfte. Aufschlüsse und enthüllungen zur geschichte des jahrhunderts, insbesondere des stattsfinanz- und börsenwesens. [*anon.*] 2 v. 320 pp; 217 pp. 12°. *Prag & Leipzig, I. L. Kober,* 1857.

Häusser (Ludwig). Deutche geschichte vom tode Friedrichs des grossen bis zur gründung des deutschen bundes. 4 v. 8°. *Leipzig & Berlin, Weidmann,* 1855–60.

Havelock (*Sir* Henry Marshman). Three main military questions of the day: i. A home reserve army. ii. The more economic military tenure of India. iii. Cavalry as affected by breechloading arms. vii, 209 pp. 2 maps. 8°. *London, Longmans,* 1867.

Haverty (Martin). The history of Ireland, from the earliest period to the present time; derived from native annals, and from the researches of dr. O'Donovan, [and others]. xxii, 838, 19 pp. 33 pl. 4 maps. 4°. *New York, T. Farrell & son,* 1867.

Hawes (J. H.) Manual of United States surveying. System of rectangular surveying employed in subdividing the public lands of the United States. [With] an appendix in regard to entering, locating, purchasing, and settling lands. 234 pp. 12°. *Philadelphia, Lippincott,* 1868.

Hawke (Michael). Killing is murder, and no murder: or an exercitation concerning a pamphlet, of one W. Allen; intituled Killing no murder. 4 p. l. 56 pp. [1 portrait inserted]. sm. 4°. *London, author,* 1657.

Hawkins (Benjamin Waterhouse). A comparative view of the human and animal frame. 27 pp. 18 pl. fol. *London, Chapman & Hall,* 1860.

Hawley (Bostwick, *D. D.*) Manual of methodism; or, the doctrines, general rules, and usages of the methodist episcopal church, with scripture proofs and explanations. 176 pp. 16°. *New York, Carlton & Lanahan,* 1868.

Hawley (*Rev.* M. L.) The psalms in meter. 267 pp. 16°. *New York, author,* 1868.

Hawley (Zerah). A journal of a tour through Connecticut, Massachusetts, New York, Pennsylvania, and Ohio, including a year's residence in the western reserve. 158 pp. 24°. *New Haven, S. Converse,* 1822.

Hawthorne (Nathaniel). Passages from the American note-books of N. Hawthorne. 2 v. 1 p. l. 222 pp; 228 pp. 12°. *Boston, Ticknor & Fields,* 1868.

Haxthausen (August von). Die landliche verfassung Russlands. Ihre entwickelungen und ihre feststellung in der gesetzgebung von 1861. xvi, 423 pp. 8°. *Leipzig, F. A. Brockhaus,* 1866.

Hay (*Rev.* Charles A.) Conversion of captain William E. Sees. Harrisburg, Pa. 49 pp. portrait. 18°. *Philadelphia, lutheran board of publication,* 1867.

Hayden (Joel), **Gere** (Collins) & co. Illustrated catalogue of brass work. [Lithographed.] 40 pp. 8°. *New York, F. Mayer & co.* 1867.

Hayden (William B.) On the phenomena of modern spiritualism. [An exposition of Swedenborgianism]. 137 pp. 12°. *Boston, O. Clapp,* 1855. s.

Hayes (Charles W. *and* Robert P.) A new parish register, with an index and summary, of parochial statistics. 43 pp. 2 l. 4°. *Buffalo, M. Taylor,* 1859. s.

Hayes (Isaac I. *M. D.*) Cast away in the cold: an old man's story of a young man's adventures, as related by captain John Hardy, mariner. vi, 263 pp. 2 pl. sm. 4°. *Boston, Ticknor & Fields,* 1869.

——— Physical observations in the arctic seas. Made on the west coast of north Greenland, the vicinity of Smith strait, and the west side of Kennedy island, during 1860 and 1861. Reduced and discussed by C. A. Schott. xi, 270 pp. 3 maps. 3 pl. 4°. *Washington, Smithsonian inst.* 1867.

[SMITHSONIAN contributions. v. 15.]

Hayes (J. D.) *and* **Hatch** (Israel T.) "The Niagara ship canal:" and "reciprocity." 58 pp. 8°. *Buffalo, Matthews & Warren,* 1865.

Hayward (George, *M. D.*) Surgical reports, and miscellaneous papers on medical subjects. 452 pp. 12°. *Boston, Phillips, Sampson & co.* 1855. s.

Hayward (John). The Columbian traveller and statistical register. Principally relating to the United States. 40 pp. 1 map. 3 pl. 8°. [*Boston*], *J. Hayward,* 1833.

Hazlitt (William). Notes of a journey through France and Italy, [including observations on the fine arts]. 8°. *Philadelphia, T. R. Greenbank,* 1833.

[*In* GREENBANK'S periodical library. v. 1. pp. 173–277].

Hazlitt (William Carew). Hand-book to the popular, poetical, and dramatic literature of Great Britain, from the invention of printing to the restoration. xii, 704 pp. 8°. *London, J. R. Smith,* 1867.

——— Memoirs of William Hazlitt. With portions of his correspondence. 2 v. xxxii, 317 pp. portrait; 312 pp. 2 pl. 12°. *London, R. Bentley,* 1867.

Headley (Joel Tyler). The life of Ulysses S. Grant, general in chief, U. S. A. 458 pp. 4 pl. 12°. *New York, E. B. Treat & co.* 1864.

——— Miscellaneous works. With a biographical sketch and portrait of the author. 2 v. 322 pp; 319 pp. 12°. *New York, J. S. Taylor,* 1849. s.

Headley (*Rev.* Phineas Camp). The court and camp of David. 368 pp. 16 pl. 8°. *Boston, H. Hoyt,* 1868.

——— Half hours in bible lands; or, stories and sketches from the scriptures and the east. 6 v. sm. 4°. *Philadelphia, J. E. Potter & co.* 1867.

CONTENTS.

v. 1. The grove, the tent, and the altar. 128 pp. 24 pl.
v. 2. Patriarchs, kings, and kingdoms. 128 pp. 24 pl.
v. 3. Prophets, apostles, and magicians. 128 pp. 24 pl.
v. 4. Spies, traitors, and assassins. 128 pp. 24 pl.
v. 5. Jesus the redeemer. 128 pp. 24 pl.
v. 6. The friends of Jesus. 128 pp. 24 pl.

Headrick (*Rev.* James). General view of the agriculture of the county of Angus, or Forfarshire. xxxi, 590, 120 pp. 3 tab. 1 col. map. 8°. *Edinburgh,* 1813. s.

[GREAT BRITAIN: Board of agriculture].

Heard (Franklin Fiske). Criminal abortion. *See* **Storer** (Horatio R.) *and* **Heard**.

Hearn (William Edward, *LL. D.*) The government of England, its structure, and its development. vii, 569 pp. 8°. *London, Longmans,* 1867.

Heath (James). A brief chronicle of the late intestine warr in the three kingdoms of England, Scotland, and Ireland. 1637–1663. 2[d] ed. 4 pts in 1 v. 13 p. l. 864 pp. 15 l. 16°. *London, W. Lee,* 1663.

Heaviside (John T. C.) American antiquities; or, the new world the old, and the old world the new. 45 pp. 8°. *London, Trübner & co.* 1868.

Heavysege (Charles). Saul: a drama in three parts. New and revised ed. 436 pp. 16°. *Boston, Fields, Osgood & co.* 1869.

Hebenstreit (Wilhelm). Dictionarium editionum tum selectarum tum optimarum auctorum classicorum et graecorum et romanorum, ad optimos bibliographorum libros collatum, emendavit, supplevit, notulisque criticis instruxit W. Hebenstreit. xxiv, 275 pp. 12°. *Vindobonae, C. Armbruster*, 1828.

Hecker (Just Friedrich Carl). The epidemics of the middle ages. Translated by B. G. Babington. 3d ed. completed by the author's treatise on child-pilgrimages. xxiv, 360 pp. 8°. *London, Trübner & co.* 1859. s.

Hedman (J. *M. A.*) The English fireside upon the banks of the Rhine. An almanack for the year 1829. Exhibiting a choice of English and German tales, etc. 4 p. l. 426 pp. 1 pl. 24°. *Heidelberg, J. Engelmann*, [1829].

Heeren (Arnold Hermann Ludwig). Handbuch der geschichte des europäischen staatensystems und seiner colonien. 3e ausg. xxxviii, 880 pp. 8°. *Göttingen, J. F. Röwer*, 1819. s.

——— *and* **Ukert** (Friedrich August) *editors*. Geschichte der europäischen staaten. Geschichte von England, von J. M. Lappenberg, [und] R. Pauli. 4 v. 8°. *Hamburg and Gotha, Perthes*, 1834–55.

——— ——— Geschichte der Teutschen, von J. F. Pfister. 5 v. 8°. *Hamburg, Perthes*, 1829–35.

Heermans (J.) War power of the president; summary imprisonment; habeas corpus. 10 pp. 8°. *New York*, 1863.
[LOYAL publication society. no. 32].

Hegel (Carl). Geschichte der städteverfassung von Italien, seit der zeit der römischen herrschaft bis zum ausgang des zwölften jahrhunderts. Mit einem anhang über die französische und deutsche städteverfassung. 2 v. xii, 499 pp. 4 l; 465 pp. 3 l. 8°. *Leipzig, Weidmann*, 1847.

Held (Adolf). Carey's socialwissenschaft und das merkantilsystem. xii, 216 pp. 8°. *Würzburg, F. E. Thein*, 1866. s.

Held in bondage, or Granville De Vigne. By Ouida. [*pseudon.*] 2 v. 443 pp; 454 pp. 12°. *Philadelphia, J. B. Lippincott & co.* 1864.

Helfenstein (Ernest, *pseudon.*) *See* **Smith** (*Mrs.* Elizabeth O.) The salamander, etc.

Heller (Camil). Crustaceen. 1 p. l. 280 pp. 25 l. 25 pl. 4°. *Wien*, 1868.
[*In* WÜLLERSTORF-URBAIR (B. von). Reise der Novara. Zoologischer theil. v. 2. abth. 3].

Helmersen (Gregor von). Geognostische beobachtungen. 4°. *St. Petersburg*, 1848.
[*In* MIDDENDORFF (A. T. von). Reise, etc. v. 1. theil 1].

Helmholtz (Hermann Ludwig Ferdinand). Handbuch der physiologischen optik. xiv, 874 pp. 11 pl. 8°. *Leipzig, L. Voss*, 1856–67. s.
[KARSTEN (G.) Allgemeine encyclopädie der physik. v. 9].

Helmont (Franciscus Mercurius van). The spirit of diseases; or, diseases from the spirit: laid open in some observations concerning man, and his diseases. 7 p. l. 215 pp. 18°. *London, S. Howkins*, 1694.

——— Two hundred querie concerning the doctrine of the revolution of humane souls, and its conformity to the truths of christianity. [*anon.*] 3 p. l. 166 pp. 24°. *London, R. Kettlewell*, 1684.

Héloïse. Lettres et épitres amoureuses d'Héloïse et d'Abeilard. *See* **Abailard** (Pierre).

Helps (Arthur). Fruits of leisure: essays written in the intervals of business. [*anon.*] 3d American from the 5th English ed. 133 pp. 16°. *New York, A. D. F. Randolph*, 1853. s.

——— The life of Las Casas, "the apostle of the Indies." 2d ed. 292 pp. 1 map. 12°. *London, Bell & Daldy*, 1868.

Hemans (*Mrs.* Felicia Dorothea). Poems. xi, 356 pp. 18°. *London, W. Blackwood & sons*, 1867.

Hemsterhuis (Franciscus). Oeuvres philosophiques. Nouv. éd. augmentée de plusieurs pièces inédites, de notes et d'une étude sur l'auteur et sa philosophie, par L. S. P. Meyboom. 3 v. in 1. 8°. *Leuwarde, W. Eekhoff*, 1846–50. s.

Henderson (*Capt.* John). General view of the agriculture of the county of Caithness, etc. With an appendix, including an account of improvements carried on by sir William Sinclair, on his estates in Scotland. xii, 371, 222 pp. 1 col. map. 12 pl. 8°. *London*, 1812. s.
[GREAT BRITAIN: Board of agriculture].

——— General view of the agriculture of the county of Sutherland. xii, 238 pp. 1 col. map. 9 pl. 8°. *London*, 1812. s.
[GREAT BRITAIN: Board of agriculture].

Henfrey (Arthur), *and* **Huxley** (Thomas Henry). Scientific memoirs, selected from the transactions of foreign academies of science, and from foreign journals. Natural history. iv, 354 pp. 12 pl. 8°. *London, Taylor & Francis*, 1853. s.

CONTENTS.

BAER (Carl Ernst von). Fragments relating to philosophical zoology. (art. 7.)
CRUGER (Hermann). Organographical observations on certain epigynous monocotyledons. (art. 6.)
HOFFMANN (Hermann). On the circulation of sap in plants. (art. 1.)

Henfrey—continued.

HOFFMEISTER (W. W.) On the development of zostera. (art. 8.)

KOREN (J.) and DANIELSSEN (Dan. C.) Observations on the development of the pectinibranchiata. (art. 11.)

KROHN (August). On the development of the ascidians. (art. 10.)

MOHL (Hugo von). Investigation of the question: Does cellulose form the basis of all vegetable membranes? (art. 4.)

MÜLLER (Heinrich). Upon the male of argonauta argo and the hectocotyli. (art. 2.)

SIEBOLD (Carl Theodor Ernst von). A few remarks upon the hectocotyli. (art. 3.)

VERANY (Giovanni Battista) and VOGT (Carl). Memoir upon the hectocotyli and the males of certain cephalopods. (art. 5.)

WICHURA. On the winding of leaves. (art. 9.)

Henry (James, *M. D.*) A half year's poems. [With appendix: a dialogue between a stethoscopist and an unborn child]. 154, 14 pp. 1 pl. 8°. *Dresden, C. C. Meinhold,* 1854. s.

——— Poems, chiefly philosophical, in continuation of my book, and a half year's poems. [With appendix: Cain, a soliloquy]. 286, 15 pp. 8°. *Dresden, C. C. Meinhold & sons,* 1856. s.

Henry (Joseph, *LL. D.*) Defence of doctor Gould. *See* **Dudley** observatory.

Henry's birthday; or, beginning to be a missionary. [*anon.*] 159 pp. 16°. *New York, Carlton & Phillips,* 1856. s.

Henshaw (*Mrs.* Sarah Edwards). Our branch and its tributaries: being a history of the work of the northwestern sanitary commission, and its auxiliaries, during the war of the rebellion. 432 pp. 2 maps. 1 pl. 8°. *Chicago, A. L. Sewell,* 1868.

Hentz (Caroline Lee Whiting). The flowers of elocution: a class book. 322 pp. 12°. *Philadelphia, C. Desilver,* 1855. s.

Herald (The) of health, and journal of physical culture, devoted to hygienic medication, bodily development, and laws of life. M. L. Holbrook, M. D. editor. Jan. to Dec. 1867. New series, v. 9–10; (complete series, v. 43–44). 8°. *New York, Miller, Wood & co.* [1867].

Herbelot (Barthélemy d'). Bibliothèque orientale, ou dictionnaire universel, contenant tout ce qui regarde la connoissance des peuples de l'orient. Leurs histoires, traditions, religions, sectes, sciences, arts, etc. 26, 954 pp. 1 tab. fol. *Maestricht, J. E. Dufour & P. Roux,* 1776.

——— The same. Supplément. Par C. Visdelou et A. Galland. 284 pp. fol. *Maestricht, J. E. Dufour,* 1780.

[*With* the preceding].

Herbert (*Lady* ———). Impressions of Spain in 1866. 4 p. l. 280 pp. 15 pl. 8°. *London, R. Bentley,* 1867.

Herbert (*Mrs.* ———). Weakness and strength; or, out of the deep. 295 pp. 4 pl. 18°. *Philadelphia, presbyterian publishing committee,* 1867.

Herbst (Johann Friedrich Wilhelm). Natursystem aller bekannten in- und auslandischen insekten. *See* **Jablonsky** (C. G.) *and* **Herbst.**

Herckmans (Elias). Der zee-vaert lof. In vi boecken. 10 p. l. 235 pp. 4 l. fol. *Amsterdam, J. Pietersz,* 1634.

Herculano de Carvalho e Araujo (Alexandre). Historia de Portugal. v. 2. 8°. *Lisboa, Bertrand e filhos,* 1847.

Herder (Ferdinand von). Enumeratio plantarum in regionibus cis- et transiliensibus, etc. *See* **Regel** (E.) *and* **Herder.**

Hermann (Carl Friedrich). Culturgeschichte der Griechen und Römer. Aus dem nachlasse des verstorbenen herausgegeben von C. G. Schmidt. 2 v. in 1. iv, 244 pp; 203 pp. 8°. *Göttingen, Vandenhoek & Ruprecht,* 1857–58.

——— Lehrbuch der griechischen antiquitäten. 3 v. 8°. *Heidelberg, J. C. B. Mohr,* 1841–52.

CONTENTS.

v. 1. Lehrbuch der griechischen staatsalterthümer, aus dem standpuncte der geschichte. 3e aufl.

v. 2. Lehrbuch der gottesdienstlichen alterthümer der Griechen.

v. 3. Lehrbuch der griechischen privatalterthümer, mit einschluss der rechtsalterthümer.

Hermbstädt (Sigismund Friedrich, *editor*). *See* **Bulletin** des neuesten und wissenswürdigsten, 1809–13; *also,* **Museum** des neuesten und wissenswürdigsten, 1814–18.

Hernandez (José de la Luz). Memoir on the salubrity of the isle of Pines. 56 pp. 8°. *Habana,* [*author*], 1857. s.

Herndon (*Mrs.* Mary E.) Louise Elton; or, things seen and heard. A novel. 407 pp. 12°. *Philadelphia, Lippincott, Grambo & co.* 1853. s.

Herodianus. Historiæ de imperio post Marcum, liber primus (Gr. and Lat.) Angelo Politiano interprete. 16°. [*Geneva*], 1568.

[*In* VARII historiæ romanæ scriptores, v. 2].

Herodotus. Historiarum libri ix. Accedit libellus de vita Homeri et index historicus. Curavit F. Palm. Nova ed. stereotypa. 3 v. 24°. *Lipsiæ, C. Tauchnitz,* 1839.

Heroine (The) of a week. [*anon.*] 133 pp. 8 pl. 18°. *Philadelphia, American s. s. union,* 1850. s.

Herr, lehre uns beten! Katholisches gebet- und erbauungsbuch für kirche und haus. 446 pp. 4 pl. 18°. *Einsiedeln & New York, C. & N. Benziger,* 1867.

Herrich-Schäffer (G. A. W.) *See* **Schäffer** (G. A. W. H.)

Herschel (*Sir* John Frederick William, *editor*). A manual of scientific enquiry; prepared for the use of officers in her majesty's navy, and travellers in general. xi, 488 pp. 1 map. 2 pl. 8°. *London, J. Murray*, 1849. s.

——— The same. 2d ed. xi, 503 pp. 1 map. 2 pl. 8°. *London, J. Murray*, 1851. s.

——— The same. Originally edited by sir J. F. W. Herschel, bart. 3d ed. superintended by the rev. Robert Main. xvii, 429 pp. 2 maps. 8°. *London, J. Murray*, 1859.

Hesse (C. E.) Recherches sur les bdellodes, etc. *See* **Van Beneden** (P. J.) *and* **Hesse.**

Heston (*Rev.* Newton). The anniversary speaker; or, young folks on the sunday school platform; being a collection of addresses, dialogues, recitations, hymns, etc. 2d series. 215 pp. 18°. *Philadelphia, Perkenpine & Higgins*, 1865.

Hetty Porter; or, God knows best. [*anon.*] 167 pp. 4 pl. 16°. *New York, Carlton & Porter*, [1867].

Heuschling (Philippe François Xavier Théodose). Statistique internationale. *See* **Quételet** (L. A. J.) *and* **Heuschling.**

Hewitt (Abram S.) Paris universal exposition, 1867. The production of iron and steel in its economic and social relations. iv, 104 pp. 8°. *Washington, gov't printing office*, 1868.

Hewitt (Mary Elizabeth). Poems: sacred, passionate, and legendary. 196 pp. 12°. *New York, Lamport, Blakeman & Law*, 1854. s.

Heydenreich (*Rev.* L. W.) The life of Gustavus-Adolphus. 130 pp. 4 pl. 16°. *Philadelphia, lutheran board of publication*, 1868.

Heywood (John). Proverbs and epigrams. Reprinted from the original (1562) ed. and collated with the second (1566) edition; with an appendix of variations. 2 p. l. 223 pp. portrait. 8°. *Manchester*, 1867.
[SPENSER society publications, no. 1].

Heywood (J. C.) Salome. A dramatic poem. 222 pp. 16°. *New York, Hurd & Houghton*, 1867.

Heyworth (Lawrence). Glimpses at the origin, mission and destiny of man; with miscellaneous papers on taxation, peace, war, the sabbath, intoxicants, etc. xii, 218 pp. 8°. *London, Williams & Norgate*, 1866.

Hickey (William). The constitution of the United States of America, with an alphabetical analysis: the declaration of independence; the articles of confederation; and other interesting matter. 4th ed. xlvi, 521 pp. 1 pl. 12°. *Philadelphia*, 1851.

Hicks (*Rev.* W. W.) Story of Ike Cottle, the tin-washer. 175 pp. 3 pl. 18°. *New York, board of publication of the reformed church*, 1868.

Hieronymus Sophronius (Eusebius, *known as saint* Jerome). *See* **Jerome** (*Saint*).

Higgins (Thomas W. *author?*) *See* **Crooked** (The) elm. 1857.

Highways and hedges; or, following the master. [*anon.*] 360 pp. 3 pl. 16°. *Boston, Mass. s. s. society*, 1867.

Higinus. *See* **Hyginus.**

Hildeburn (*Mrs.* Mary J.) Flora Morris' choice; or, "be not conformed to the world." 320 pp. 4 pl. 16°. *Philadelphia, presbyterian publishing committee*, 1867.

——— George Lee; or, making the best of trials. 224 pp. 3 pl. 18°. *Philadelphia, presbyterian publishing committee*, 1867.

Hill (George). The ruins of Athens; Titania's banquet, a mask; and other poems. 160 pp. 8°. *Boston, Otis, Broaders & co.* 1839.

Hill (George, *editor*). Selections from Pope, Dryden, and various other British catholic poets who preceded the nineteenth century; with biographical and literary notices of those and other British catholic poets, etc. 319 pp. 12°. *New York, Trow & Smith*, 1868.

Hill (*Sir* John, *M. D.*) The naval history of Britain, from the earliest periods to the year 1756. Compiled from the papers of captain Geo. Berkley. iv pp. 3 p. l. 706 pp. 5 maps. 9 pl. fol. *London, Osborne & Shipton*, 1756.

Hill (*Rev.* Pascoe Grenfell). Fifty days on board a slave-vessel in the Mozambique channel, in April and May, 1843. 115 pp. 1 map. 16°. *London, J. Murray*, 1844.

Hill (Richard, *of Jamaica*). A week at Port-Royal [Jamaica]. 2 p. l. 109 pp. 12°. *Montego-bay* [*Jam.*] *Cornwall chronicle office*, 1855. s.

Hill (Thomas). A most briefe and pleasaunt treatyse, teachynge howe to dress, sowe, and set a garden, [etc.] gathered out of the principallest authors in this art. [1st ed.] 68 l. *b. l.* 18°. *London, T. Marshe*, 1563.

Hillard (George Stillman). A memoir [of Henry R. Cleveland]. 12°. *Boston*, 1844. s.
[*In* CLEVELAND (H. R.) A selection from [his] writings].

Hillary (William, *M.D.*) Observations on the changes of the air, and the concomitant epidemical diseases in the island of Barbadoes. [With] a treatise on the yellow fever, and such other diseases as are indigenous or endemial, in the West India islands. 2d ed. 4 p. l. 360 pp. 2 l. 8°. *London, L. Hawes*, 1766.

Hillebrand (Joseph). Die deutsche nationallitteratur seit dem anfange des achtzehnten jahrhunderts, besonders seit Lessing, bis auf die gegenwart, etc. 3 v. 8°. *Hamburg, F. & A. Perthes,* 1845–46. s.

Hiller (*Rev.* O. Prescott). The pleasures of religion, a poem: etc. vii, 136 pp. 12°. *London, W. White,* 1856. s.

——— Sermons on the ten commandments. 161 pp. 16°. *Boston, T. H. Carter & sons,* 1868.

Hillhouse (John). The annunciation. A poem. 64 pp. 6 pl. 16°. *New York, Pott & Amery,* 1868.

Hillman (Joseph). The revivalist: a collection of choice revival hymns and tunes, original and selected. Rev. L. Hartsough, musical editor. 240 pp. 16°. *Troy, (N.Y.) J. Hillman,* 1868.

Hill-side flowers. [*anon.*] With an introduction by the rev. bishop Simpson. 246 pp. 1 pl. 8°. *New York, author,* 1856. s.

Hillyard (Clark). Practical farming and grazing: with observations on the breeding and feeding of sheep and cattle, etc. 4th ed. vii, 352 pp. 8°. *London, J. Murray,* 1844.

Himes (Charles F.) Leaf prints; or, glimpses at photography. 38 pp. 1 pl. 4°. *Philadelphia, Benerman & Wilson,* 1868.

Hind (Henry Youle). Reports of progress, together with a preliminary and general report, on the Assinniboine and Saskatchewan exploring expedition; made under instructions from the provincial secretary, Canada. 219 pp. 5 col. maps. fol. *London, stationery office,* 1860. s.

Hinds (Richard Brinsley, *editor*). The zoology of h. m. s. Sulphur, under the command of capt. sir Edward Belcher, [etc.] 1836–42. 2 v. 1 p. l. 150 pp. 64 pl; 1 p. l. 72, v pp. 21 col. pl. 4°. *London, Smith, Elder & co.* 1844, [1843–45].

CONTENTS.

v. 1. Mammalia, by J. E. Gray. Birds, by J. Gould. Fish, by J. Richardson.
v. 2. Mollusca, by R. B. Hinds.

Hines (*Rev.* Gustavus). Oregon and its institutions; comprising a full history of Willamette university, the first established on the Pacific coast. 326 pp. 4 pl. 12°. *New York, Carlton & Porter,* [1868].

Hinman (Royal Ralph). A catalogue of the names of the early puritan settlers of the colony of Connecticut; with the time of their arrival in the country and colony, their standing in society, etc. Nos. 1, 2, and 4. 348, 493–684 pp. 3 portraits. 8°. *Hartford, Case, Tiffany & co.* 1852–54.

[Nos. 3, 5, and 6 wanting].

Hinton (John Howard, *editor*). The history and topography of the United States of North America, from the earliest period to the present time. New ed. by S. L. Knapp. 2 v. xvi, 427 pp. 1 map. 11 pl; 507 pp. 29 pl. 4°. *Boston, S. Walker,* 1834.

Hippocrates. Libellus de medicorū astrologia a Petro de Abbano in Latinū traductus. 4 l. sm. 4°. *Venetiis, Erhardus Ratdolt de Augusta,* 1485.

[*With* OPUSCULŪ repertorii pronosticon in mutationes aeris. *Venetiis,* 1485].

Histoire de la dernière guerre, commencée l'an 1756, et finie par la paix d'Hubertsbourg, le 15 Février, 1763. [*anon.*] Nouv. éd. 192 pp. 2 maps. 1 pl. 16°. *Cologne,* 1769. s.

Histoire populaire de Napoléon 1er, suivie des anecdotes impériales. Par un ancien officier de la garde. [*anon.*] 320 pp. 6 pl. 8°. *Paris, Bernardin-Béchet,* [*about* 1841].

Historia de Bruce y Emilia, ó el Quixote de la amistad. Obra inglesa. [*anon.*] Traducida al Frances por el p. Chanin, y extractada libremente al Castellano por d. F. E. y C. 2 v. 6 p. l. 190 pp; 2 p. l. 216 pp. 16°. *Madrid, Repullés,* 1808. s.

[Translation of The amicable Quixote. *London,* 1789].

Historiæ romanæ scriptores (Varii). *See* **Varii** historiæ romanæ scriptores.

Historical (The) and local new Bath guide, containing an accurate description of the public buildings, institutions, and amusements of the city, [etc. *anon.*] 176 pp. 1 map. 1 pl. 12°. *Bath,* [*Eng.*] 1823. s.

Historischer verein für Niedersachsen. Katalog der bibliothek. xii, 287 pp. 8°. *Hannover, P. C. Göhmann,* 1866. s.

Historisches taschenbuch. Herausgegeben von Friedrich von Raumer. 10 v. 12°. *Leipzig, F. A. Brockhaus,* 1830–39. s.

——— The same. Neue folge. 10 v. 12°. *Leipzig, F. A. Brockhaus,* 1840–49. s.

——— The same. 3e folge. 10 v. 12°. *Leipzig, F. A. Brockhaus,* 1850–59. s.

——— The same. 4e folge. v. 1–7. 12°. *Leipzig, F. A. Brockhaus,* 1860–66. s.

History of the American revolution. [*anon.*] 64, 8 pp. 8°. [*London, about* 1825].

History (The) of Bacon's and Ingram's rebellion in Virginia, in 1675 and 1676. [*anon.* Edited by C. Deane]. 50 pp. 8°. *Cambridge, (Mass.) J. Wilson & son,* 1867.

[100 copies printed].

History (The) of the campaigns in 1796–99 in Germany, Italy, Switzerland, etc. [*anon.*] 2d ed. 4 v. 12 maps. 4 pl. 8°. *London, T. Gardiner and others,* 1812.

[Map 4 in vol. 1 wanting].

History of the Delaware and Iroquois Indians formerly inhabiting the middle states. With anecdotes, illustrating their manners and customs. [*anon.*] 153 pp. 1 pl. 18°. *Philadelphia, American s. s. union,* 1832.

History (The) of father La Chaise, jesuite, and confessor to Lewis xiv. Made English from the French original. [*anon.*] 6 p. l. 376 pp. 18°. *London, H. Rhodes,* 1693.

[Imperfect: pp. 193-240 wanting].

History (The) of our national debts and taxes, 1688–1751. [*anon.*] 2d ed. 4 pts. in 2 v. 254 pp; 329 pp. 8°. *London, M. Cooper,* 1753.

Hita (Ginez Perez de). *See* **Perez de Hita.**

Hitchcock (Edward, *D. D.*) Elementary geology. 8th ed. 361 pp. 2 maps. 1 tab. 12°. *New York, M. H. Newman & co.* 1847.

——— History of a zoological temperance convention. Held in Central Africa in 1847. 160 pp. 16°. *Boston, N. Noyes,* 1855. s.

——— The religious bearings of man's creation. A discourse delivered August 24, 1856. 52 pp. 8°. *Albany, Van Benthuysen,* 1856. s.

——— Supplement to the Ichnology of New England. A report to the government of Massachusetts, in 1863. x, 96 pp. 20 pl. 4°. *Boston, Wright & Potter, state printers,* 1865. s.

Hittell (John S.) Yosemite: its wonders and its beauties. 59 pp. 1 map. 20 phot. pl. 12°. *San Francisco, H. H. Bancroft & co.* 1868.

Hjort (Peder). Om det engelske konjugationssystem. Med et tillæg om forholdet imellem Dansk og Engelsk. 1 p. l. 121 pp. 4°. *Kjöbenhavn, J. C. Scharling,* 1843. s.

Hobart (*Rev.* Noah). Civil government the foundation of social happiness. A sermon preached before the assembly of Connecticut, the day of election, May 10th, 1750. 52 pp. 18°. *New London, T. Green,* 1751.

——— A serious address to the members of the episcopal separation in New England, occasioned by mr. Wetmore's vindication of the professors of the church of England in Connecticut. 139 pp. 16°. *Boston, J. Bushell & J. Green, for D. Henchman,* 1748.

——— The same. A second address to the members of the episcopal separation in New England, [with] a letter from mr. Dickinson in answer to mr. Wetmore. 172 pp. 12°. *Boston, D. Fowle,* 1751.

[Title-page imperfect].

Hobhouse (John Cam, *baron* Broughton). Historical illustrations of the fourth canto of Childe Harold; containing dissertations on the ruins of Rome; and an essay on Italian literature. 384 pp. 8°. *New York, Kirk & Mercein,* 1818. s.

Hochhuth (Johann Heinrich). Hydrocanthares. *See* **Chaudoir** (M.) *and* **Hochhuth.** Enumération des carabiques et hydrocanthares, etc. 1846. s.

Hochstetter (*Dr.* Ferdinand von). Geologie von Neu-Seeland. 4°. *Wien,* 1864.

[*In* WÜLLERSTORF-URBAIR (B. von). Reise der öst. fregatte Novara. Geologischer theil].

——— New Zealand: its physical geography, geology, and natural history, with special reference to the results of government expeditions in the provinces of Auckland and Nelson. Translated from the German original, published in 1863, by Edward Sauter, with additions to 1866 by the author. xvi, 515 pp. 2 maps. 17 pl. (10 col.) 8°. *Stuttgart, J. G. Cotta,* 1867. s.

Hodge (Archibald Alexander, *D. D.*) The atonement. 440 pp. 12°. *Philadelphia, presb. board of pub.* [1867].

Hodges (John F.) First steps in practical chemistry. 4th ed. viii, 103 pp. 12°. *London, Longmans,* 1859. s.

Hodgins (J. George). Sketches and anecdotes of her majesty the queen, the late prince consort, and other members of the royal family. Chiefly for young people. 309 pp. 8 pl. 16°. *London, Sampson, Low, son & Marston,* 1868.

Hodgson (Adam). Remarks during a journey through North America, 1819–21. With an account of the [Creeks, Chocktaws, Chickasaws, and Cherokees]. Also, a letter to J. B. Say, on the comparative expense of free and slave labour. 335 pp. 8°. *New York, S. Whiting,* 1823.

Hodgson (B. H.) [On the aborigines of India]. Essay the first: on the Kocch, Bódo, and Dhimál tribes, in three parts. 200 pp. 2 l. 2 pl. 8°. *Calcutta, J. Thomas,* 1847.

CONTENTS.

Part 1. Vocabulary.
Part 2. Grammar.
Part 3. Location, numbers, creed, customs, condition, etc. of the people.

Hoefer. *See* **Höfer.**

Hoerbye. *See* **Hörbye.**

Höfer (Jean Chrétien Ferdinand, *M. D.*) Nomenclature et classifications chimiques, suivies d'un lexique historique et synonymique, etc. vii, 184 pp. 12°. *Paris, J. B. Baillière,* 1845. s.

Hoffer (Isaac). Genealogy of Mathias Hoffer and his descendants in the United States. 2 p. l. 31 pp. 16°. *Mount Joy, (Pa.) J. R. Hoffer,* 1868.

Hoffer (Jacob R.) Andrew Hofer, the Tyrolean patriot. 16°. *Mount Joy, (Pa.) J. R. Hoffer,* 1868.

[*With* HOFFER (Isaac). Genealogy of M. Hoffer, etc. pp. 31–34. ed. 1868].

Hoffman (Charles Fenno). Grey-slayer: a romance of the Mohawk. 4th ed. 540 pp. 12°. *New York, Baker & Scribner,* 1849. s.

Hoffman (David). Miscellaneous thoughts on men, manners, and things. By Anthony Grumbler. [*pseudon.*] 2d ed. 374 pp. 12°. *Baltimore, Plaskitt & Cugle,* 1841. s.

——— Viator; or, a peep into my note-book. 355 pp. 12°. *Baltimore, Plaskitt & Cugle,* 1841. s.

Hoffmann (Friedrich Wilhelm, *editor*). Blüthen spanischer poesie. Metrisch übertragen. 3e aufl. xix, 472 pp. 16°. *Leipzig, G. Gräbner,* [1857]. s.

Hoffmann (*Dr.* Hermann). On the circulation of sap in plants. 8°. *London,* 1853.

[*In* HENFREY (A.) *and* HUXLEY. Scientific memoirs. art. 1].

Hoffmann (J. J.) A Japanese grammar. [Translated from the Dutch]. Printed with the government Chinese and Japanese types. 6 p. l. 348 pp. 1 l. 8°. *Leiden, minister for colonial affairs,* 1868.

Hofmeister (W.) On the development of zostera. 8°. *London,* 1853.

[*In* HENFREY (A.) *and* HUXLEY. Scientific memoirs. art. 8].

Hofstede de Groot (P.) Lineamenta historiæ ecclesiæ christianæ. Alt. ed. [etc.] xv, 251 pp. 8°. *Groningæ, J. Oomkens & fil.* 1852. s.

——— Series compendiorum theologicorum, etc. *See* **Pareau** (L. G.) *and* **Hofstede de Groot.**

Hogg (Jabez). The microscope; its history, construction, and applications. 2d ed. xvi, 457 pp. 8°. *London, H. Ingram & co.* 1856. s.

Holbach (Paul Thiry, *baron* de). The system of nature; or, the laws of the moral and physical world. Translated from the French of Mirabaud. [*pseudon.*] 3 v. 8°. *London, G. Kearsley,* 1797. s.

Holbrook (John Edwards). Ichthyology of South Carolina. 1 p. l. 182 pp. 27 col. pl. 4°. *Charleston, (S. C.) J. Russell,* 1855. s.

[No more of this edition published].

——— North American herpetology; or, a description of the reptiles inhabiting the United States. [1st ed.] v. 1–3. 4°. *Philadelphia, J. Dobson,* 1836–38. s.

[No more of this edition published].

——— Southern ichthyology: or, a description of the fishes inhabiting the waters of South Carolina, Georgia, and Florida. No. 2. 32 pp. 4 col. pl. 4°. *New York, Wiley & Putnam,* 1847. s.

[*With* his Ichthyology of South Carolina, 1855]. [No more published].

Holbrook (Nelson M.) The progressive readers. *See* **Town** (S.) *and* **Holbrook.**

Holcombe (*Rev.* Hosea). A history of the rise and progress of the baptists in Alabama. With a miniature history of the denomination from the apostolic age down to the present time. 375 pp. 16°. *Philadelphia, King & Baird,* 1840.

——— Our children in heaven. 318 pp. 12°. *Philadelphia, Lippincott & co.* 1868.

Holden (Luther, *M. D.*) A manual of the dissection of the human body. With notes and additions by E. Mason, M. D. iv, 588 pp. 8°. *New York, R. M. De Witt,* 1868.

Holden (Oliver). The union harmony, or universal collection of sacred music. 2 v. in 1. 120 pp; 185 pp. 53 pp. *ms.* obl. 8°. *Boston, Isaiah Thomas & E. T. Andrews,* 1793.

Holderness (Mary). Notes relating to the manners and customs of the Crim Tatars; written during four years' residence among that people. viii, 168 pp. 3 pl. 16°. *London, J. Warren,* 1821.

Holiday hours improved. [*anon.*] 1 p. l. 224 pp. 12°. *Philadelphia, American s. s. union,* [1850]. s.

Holinshed (Ralph). Chronicles of England, Scotland, and Ireland. [Shakespeare ed.] 2 v. 7 p. l. 126 l. 289 pp. (4 p. l. 540 pp. 14 l. 2 p. l. 28 l. 115 pp. 4 l); 2 p. l. pp. 291–1868 marked 1876. 52 l. fol. *London, J. Harrison & J. Hunne,* 1577.

[Imperfect: v. 1. title in facsimile, 2 p. l. wanting; Hist. Scot. pp. 437–38 wanting; Hist. Ireland, pp. 71–74 wanting: v. 2. 1 pl. wanting].

Holland (Henry). General view of the agriculture of Cheshire. xii, 375 pp. 1 l. 2 maps. 6 pl. 8°. *London,* 1808. s.

[GREAT BRITAIN: Board of agriculture].

Holland (John). Poems. 108 pp. 12°. *Boston, Williams & co.* 1858.

Holland (Josiah G.) Kathrina, her life and mine, in a poem. Illustrations by W. J. Hennessy and C. C. Griswold. xii, 281 pp. 8°. *New York, C. Scribner & co.* 1869.

Holland. *See* **Netherlands.**

Holmes (John). A new grammar of the Latin tongue. 12th ed. enlarged by E. Harwood. 2 p. l. xii, 80, 24 pp. 16°. *London, J. F. & C. Rivington,* 1782.

Holmes (*Mrs.* Mary J.) The christmas font. A story for young folks. 67 pp. 12 pl. 18°. *New York, G. W. Carleton,* 1868.

——— Rose Mather: a tale of the war. 407 pp. 12°. *New York, G. W. Carleton & co.* 1868.

——— Tempest and sunshine; or, life in Kentucky. 381 pp. 12°. *New York, Appletons,* 1857.

Holst (Axel). Beretning om Pipervigens lazareth under cholera epidemien i Christiania, 1853. 8°. *Christiania,* 1854.

[*In* NORWAY. Actstykker ang. cholera epidemien i Norge].

Holt (John, *of Walton, Eng.*) General view of the agriculture of the county of Lancaster. 2 p. l. xii, 242 pp. 1 map. 5 pl. 8°. *London,* 1795. s.

[GREAT BRITAIN: Board of agriculture].

Holwell (*Rev.* William). A mythological dictionary. *See* **Bryant** (Jacob).

Home to Christmas. By Fan Fan. [*pseudon.*] 213 pp. 1 pl. 16°. *New York, Broughton & Wyman,* 1868.

Home evangelization: a view of the wants and prospects of our country, based on the facts and relations of colportage. By one of the secretaries of the American tract society. 171 pp. 18°. *New York, American tract society,* [1849]. s.

Home life in Africa; or, a new glimpse into an old corner of the world. [*anon.* With an introduction by F. D. Huntington]. 184 pp. 16°. *Boston, A. Williams & co.* 1868.

Home twilight stories. Briery wood, and other stories. [*anon.*] 226 pp. 7 pl. 18°. *Boston, Gould & Lincoln,* 1867.

——— The same. The hero without courage, and other stories. [*anon.*] 244 pp. 10 pl. 18°. *Boston, Gould & Lincoln,* 1867.

——— The same. Much ado about nothing, and other stories. [*anon.*] 246 pp. 8 pl. 18°. *Boston, Gould & Lincoln,* 1867.

——— The same. The young fortune seekers, and other stories. [*anon.*] 239 pp. 9 pl. 18°. *Boston, Gould & Lincoln,* 1867.

Homerus. Werke. Prosaisch übersetzt von J. St. Zauper. 3e verb. aufl. 4 v. in 2. 16°. *Prag, J. G. Calve,* 1852–53.

Homerus—continued.

CONTENTS.

v. 1–2. Ilias. v. 3–4. Odyssee.

——— Homer and the Iliad. By J. S. Blackie. 4 v. 8°. *Edinburgh, Edmonston & Douglas,* 1866.

CONTENTS.

v. 1. Homeric dissertations.
v. 2–4. The Iliad in English verse [with] notes.

——— Iliad. Translated into English verse in the Spenserian stanza, by Philip Stanhope Worsley. v. 2. Books xiii–xxiv. Translated by John Conington. xxviii, 322 pp. 8°. *Edinburgh, W. Blackwood & sons,* 1868.

Hood (Edwin Paxton). The age and its architects: ten chapters on the English people in relation to the times. 2d ed. iv, 456 pp. 16°. *London, Partridge & Oakey,* 1852.

Hood (Thomas). The comic annual for 1842. 2d ed. x, 326 pp. 12 pl. 16°. *London, H. Colburn,* 1842.

——— The plea of the midsummer fairies, Hero and Leander, Lycus the centaur, and other poems. viii, 222 pp. 8°. *London, Longmans,* 1827. s.

Hook (Walter Farquhar, *D. D.*) Lives of the archbishops of Canterbury. New series. Reformation period. v. 1–2. 8°. *London, R. Bentley,* 1868.

[v. 6–7 of the entire series].

Hooker (Horace). The school and family dictionary. *See* **Gallaudet** (T. H.) *and* **Hooker.**

Hooper (Richard, *D. D.*) Certayne divine tractates, and other godly sermons. 128 pp. fol. *London, H. Fetherstone,* 1618.

[*With his* LAWES of ecclesiastical politie. ed. 1617].

——— Of the laws of ecclesiastical politie. Eight [five] books. [4th ed.] 29 p. l. 453 pp. fol. *London, W. Stansby,* 1617.

Hooper (Robert, *M. D.*) A new medical dictionary; containing an explanation of the terms in anatomy, etc. with the formulas of the principal pharmocopœias, etc. On the basis of Hooper and Grant. Adapted to the present state of science, etc. By D. Pereira Gardner. 686 pp. 8°. *New York, Harpers,* 1847. s.

——— Physicians' vade-mecum; or, a manual of the principles and practice of physic, with an outline of general pathology and therapeutics, by Wm. Augustus Guy. With additions by James Stewart. x, 541 pp. 12°. *New York, Harpers,* 1846. s.

Hoopes (Josiah). The book of evergreens. A practical treatise on the coniferæ, or cone-bearing plants. 435 pp. 12°. *New York, O. Judd & co.* [1868].

Hope (A. R.) A book about boys. xii, 247 pp. 16°. *Boston, Roberts bros.* 1869.

Hope Douglass: By F. S. A. author of "The silver lining." [*anon.*] 347 pp. 2 pl. 16°. *Boston, Mass. s. s. soc.* [1867].

Hopffer (Heinrich Carl). Lepidoptera [von Mossambique]. fol. *Berlin*, 1862.

[*In* PETERS (W. C. H.) Nat. reise nach Mossambique. Zoologie. v. 5].

Hopkins (John). Psalms in metre. *See* **Sternhold** (Thomas). *and* **Hopkins.**

Hopkins (John Baker). The English revolution. viii, 176 pp. 12°. *London, W. Freeman,* 1868.

Hopkins (Mark, *D. D.*) Lectures on moral science. Delivered before the Lowell institute, Boston. 304 pp. 12°. *Boston, Gould & Lincoln,* 1862.

Hopkins (Samuel, *D. D.*) A dialogue containing the slavery of the Africans; showing it to be the duty and interest of the American states to emancipate all their African slaves. With an address to the owners of slaves, [and with] the institution of the society, in New York, for promoting the manumission of slaves. [*anon.*] 72 pp. 16°. *New York, reprinted, R. Hodge,* 1785.

[*With* BOOTH (*Rev.* A.) Commerce in the human species].

——— Memoirs of the life of mrs. Sarah Osborn. 380 pp. 16°. *Worcester, (Mass.) L. Worcester,* 1799.

Hopkins (Thomas). On winds and storms; with an essay on weather and its varieties. vii, 260 pp. 8°. *London, Longman, etc.* 1860. s.

Horatius *christianvs.* *See* **Maianus** (Ioannes Otho).

Horatius Flaccus (Quintus). Poemata omnia. Quibus resp. index Th. Treteri nuper excusus. 1 p. l. 294 pp. 16°. *Antverpiæ, ex officina C. Plantini,* [1576]? s.

[Wanting first 2 leaves].

——— Odes, epodes, and carmen seculare. Translated into English verse. By W. Boscawen. xli, 531 pp. 8°. *London, J. Stockdale,* 1793.

Hörbye (Christian Lorents Ragnholdus). Beretning om Ankerlökkens lazareth under cholera epidemien i Christiania. 853 pp. 8°. *Christiania,* 1854.

[*With* NORWAY. Actstykker ang. cholera epidemien i Norge].

Horlock (———). The country gentleman. By Scrutator. [*pseudon.*] 5th ed. 358 pp. 16°. *London, Chapman & Hall,* 1868.

——— The master of the hounds. By Scrutator. [*pseudon.*] 7th ed. 416 pp. 16°. *London, Chapman & Hall,* 1867.

Hornor (S. S.) The medical student's guide in extracting teeth, [etc.] With illustrations. 76 pp. 8°. *Philadelphia, Lindsay & Blakiston,* 1856. s.

Hornstein (Ferdinand Friedrich). Ueber die basaltgesteine des unteren Mainthales. [From Zeitschrift der d. geol. gesellsch. 1867. pp. 297–372]. 2 p. l. 76 pp. 1 map. 1 pl. 8°. *Berlin, J. F. Starcke,* 1867. s.

Hort (*Mrs.* Alfred). Hena; or, life in Tahiti. [A novel]. 2 v. 288 pp; 272 pp. 12°. *London, Saunders, Otley, & co.* 1866.

Horta (Garcia da). *See* **Orta** (Garcia de).

Horticulturist (The) and journal of rural art and rural taste. Edited by A. J. Downing, etc. Jan. 1846, to Dec. 1868. v. 1–23. 8°. *Albany, Philadelphia, and New York,* 1846-68.

[Wanting: v. 8, for 1853; v. 12-16, for 1857-61; v. 19, for 1864].

Horton (Rushmore G.) The life and public services of James Buchanan. Including the most important of his state papers. 428 pp. portrait. 12°. *New York, Derby & Jackson,* 1856.

Hosmer (Burr Griswold). Poems. vi, 171 pp. 16°. *Cambridge, Riverside press,* 1868.

Hosmer (*Mrs.* Margaret). A story of domestic life. 382 pp. 8°. *Philadelphia, T. B. Peterson & bros.* 1868.

Hotten (John Camden, *editor*). Abyssinia and its people; or, life in the land of Prester John. vi, 384 pp. 1 map. 8 pl. 12°. *London, J. C. Hotten,* 1868.

Hottinger (Johann Heinrich). Promtuarium sive bibliotheca orientalis: exhibens catalogum, sive, centurias aliquot, tam authorum, quam librorum hebraicorum, syriacorum, arabicorum, ægyptiacorum, æthiopicorum, etc. 4 p. l. 332, 46 pp. 4°. *Heidelbergæ, Wyngaerden,* 1658.

Hough (Franklin Benjamin, *editor*). *See* **New York** (*State*). Census, 1865: *also,* **New York** (*State*). Civil list, 1855: *and,* **Proceedings** of a convention. Boston, 1780.

Hourier (Évariste) *and* **Malepeyre** (François). Nouveau manuel complet de la fabrication de l'eau-de-vie de pommes de terre, de betterave, etc. 136 pp. 1 pl. 18°. *Paris, Roret,* 1855.

Hours at home: a popular monthly, of instruction and recreation. Edited by J. M. Sherwood. v. 5-7. May, 1867, to Oct. 1868. 8°. *New York, C. Scribner & co.* 1867-68.

Hours with my picture book. [*anon.*] 90 pp. 11 pl. sm. 4°. *Philadelphia, American s. s. union,* [1865].

Housekeeper (M. R. *pseudon.*) *See* **My** husband's crime.

Houseworth (Thomas) and co. California scenery. A series of stereoscopic views of most of the points of interest on the Pacific coast [of the United States]. 67 photographs. 4°. *San Francisco, T. Houseworth & co.* [1868].

Houttuyn (Martin). Natuurlyke historie of uitvoerige beschryving der dieren, planten, en mineraalen, volgens het samenstel van den heer Linnæus. Met [296] naauwkeurige afbeeldingen. 37 v. 8°. *Amsterdam, F. Houttuyn,* 1761–85. s.

CONTENTS.

(I. Deel. Ryk der dieren).
v. 1-3. Zoogende dieren. De menschen.
v. 4-5. Vogelen.
v. 6. Dieren van beiderley leven.
v. 7-8. Visschen.
v. 9-13. Insekten.
v. 14. Wormen en slakken.
v. 15. Schulpdieren.
v. 16. Horeens.
v. 17. Zee gewassen.
v. 18. Plaant-dieren.
(II. Deel. Ryk der planten).
v. 19. Palmboomen.
v. 20-21. Boomen.
v. 22-24. Heesters.
v. 25-29. Kruiden.
v. 30. Bolplanten.
v. 31. Grasplanten.
v. 32. Varens, mossen, enz.
(III. Deel. Ryk der mineralien).
v. 33. Versteeningen.
v. 34. Delfstoffen.
v. 35. Steenen.
v. 36-37. Mynstoffen.

Hoveden (Roger of). Chronica magistri Rogeri de Houedene. Edited by W. Stubbs. v. 1. cix, 282 pp. 8°. *London, Longmans,* 1868.

[GREAT BRITAIN and Ireland. Chronicles and memorials of the middle ages].

Hovey (Alvah, *D.D.*) A memoir of the life and times of the rev. Isaac Backus. 369 pp. 12°. *Boston, Gould & Lincoln,* 1859.

How the south rejected compromise in the peace conference of 1861. [With] the speech of S. P. Chase, of Ohio. 11 pp. 8°. *New York, W. C. Bryant & co.* 1863.

[LOYAL publication society, no. 37].

How the war was commenced. An appeal to the documents. Southern documents especially quoted. From the Cincinnati daily commercial. 16 pp. 8°. *New York,* 1864.

[LOYAL publication society, no. 46].

——— The same. Wie der krieg angefangen wurde. [Übersetzt von F. Schütz]. 15 pp. 8°. *New York,* 1864.

[LOYAL publication society, no. 53].

Howard (Caroline). Poetry and prose for the young. The first and last oath; with other stories. 2 p. l. 131 pp. 16°. *Charleston, southern baptist publication society,* 1856. s.

Howard (Edward). Rattlin, the reefer. Edited by captain Marryat. [*anon.*] 284 pp. 8°. *London, Routledge & co.* 1856.

Howard (*Rev.* Luke, *of Dover, Kent*). Love and truth in plainness manifested; being a collection of [his] several writings. With an account of his convincement, labours and sufferings for the truth. 6 p. l. 316 pp. 1 l. 16°. *London, T. Sowle,* 1704.

Howard Grey; a story for boys. By a young lady of Philadelphia. [*anon.*] 231 pp. 16°. *Philadelphia, Parry & McMillan,* 1855. s.

Howe (Henry). Historical collections of New Jersey. *See* **Barber** (J. W.) *and* **Howe.**

Howe (Julia Ward). From the oak to the olive. A plain record of a pleasant journey. vi, 304 pp. 12°. *Boston, Lee & Shepard,* 1868.

Howe (Samuel G.) The Cretan refugees and their American helpers. A statement addressed to the contributors for the relief of Cretan refugees. 64 pp. 1 map. 1 pl. sm. 4°. *Boston, Lee & Shepard,* 1868.

Howe (*Lieut. gen. sir* William). The narrative of lieut. gen. sir William Howe, in a committee of the house of commons, on the 29th of April, 1779, relative to his conduct in North America. 2d ed. 110 pp. 4°. *London, H. Baldwin,* 1780.

Howell (James). A survay of the signorie of Venice, of her admired policy, and method of government, etc. 3 p. l. 210 [233] pp. 4 l. 2 pl. fol. *London, R. Lowndes,* 1651.

Howell (John Edward). Poems. 2 v. 362 pp; 514 pp. 12°. *New York, author,* 1867.

Howell (*Rev.* Robert Boyte C.) The covenants. 2 p. l. 135 pp. 12°. *Charleston, Southern baptist publication society,* 1855. s.

——— The cross. xi, 226 pp. 12°. *Charleston, Southern baptist publication society,* 1854. s.

——— The evils of infant baptism. 6th ed. 310 pp. 16°. *Charleston, Southern baptist publication society,* 1854. s.

Howison (John). Sketches of Upper Canada, domestic, local, and characteristic, [with] some recollections of the United States of America. 2d ed. 353 pp. 8°. *Edinburgh, Oliver & Boyd,* 1822.

Howitt (William). The student life of Germany. From the unpublished ms. of dr. Cornelius. [*pseudon.*] Containing nearly forty of the most famous student songs. 467 pp. 8°. *Philadelphia, Carey & Hart,* 1842. s.

Howland (Edward). Grant as a soldier and statesman: being a succinct history of his military and civil career. 631 pp. 9 pl. 8°. *Hartford, J. B. Burr & co.* 1868.

Hows (John W. S.) The practical elocutionist, and academical reader and speaker. 430 pp. 12°. *New York, G. P. Putnam*, 1849. s.

Hozier (H. M.) The seven weeks' war. Its antecedents and its incidents. 2 v. xi, 390 pp. 5 maps; vi, 324 pp. 8 maps. 8°. *London, Macmillan & co.* 1867.

Huart (Louis). Physiologie du garde national. Vignettes de mm. Maurisset et Trimolet. 3e éd. 128 pp. 16°. *Paris, Aubert & Lavigne*, [1841].

—— Physiologie de l'étudiant. Vignettes de mm. Alophe et Maurisset. 126 pp. 16°. *Paris, Aubert & Lavigne*, [1841].
[*With his* Physiologie du garde national].

—— Physiologie du tailleur. Vignettes par Gavarni. 121 pp. 16°. *Paris, Aubert & Lavigne*, [1841.]
[*With his* Physiologie du garde national].

Hubbard (Jeremiah) *and* **Greenleaf** (Jonathan). An account of Wells, [Maine]. 8°. *Portland, Day, Fraser & co.* 1831.
[MAINE historical collections. v. 1].

Hubbard (*Rev.* William). The history of the Indian wars in New England from the first settlement to 1677. Revised, with a life of the author, and notes, by S. G. Drake. 2 v. xxxi, 292 pp; 303 pp. 1 map. sm. 4°. *Roxbury, (Mass.) W. E. Woodward*, 1865.

Hubbell (*Rev.* George A.) The chapel hymn book: containing hymns with the first strain of the melody prefixed. 336 pp. 32°. *New York, N. Tibbals & co.* 1868.

Hübner (Jacob). Zuträge zur sammlung exotischer schmett[er]linge, bestehend in bekundigung einzelner fliegmuster neuer oder rarer nichteuropäischer gattungen. 1tes–3tes hunderts. 3 v. in 1. 4°. *Augsburg, verfasser, C. Geyer*, 1818–25. s.

—— The same. (Fortsetzung des hübner'schenwerkes). Von Carl Geyer. 4tes–5tes hunderts. 2 v. 4°. *Augsburg, C. Geyer*, 1832–37. s.
[*With* preceding. Plates wanting. 2 copies].

Hübner (Johann). The historical companion: being a new introduction to the political history of all nations. iv, 309 pp. 1 l. 16°. *London, G. Smith*, 1842.

Hübner (Otto). Oesterreichs finanzlage und seine hilfsquellen. v, 228 pp. 7 tab. 8°. *Wien, Jasper, Hügel & Manz*, 1849. s.

Huc (*Abbé* Évariste Régis). L'empire chinois; faisant suite à l'ouvrage intitulé Souvenirs d'un voyage dans la Tartarie et le Thibet. 3e éd. 2 v. xxviii, 463 pp. 1 map; 479 pp. 16°. *Paris, Gaume frères*, 1857.

—— Souvenirs d'un voyage dans la Tartarie et le Thibet, 1844–46. 4e éd. 2 v. xv, 430 pp. 1 map; 524 pp. 16°. *Paris, Gaume frères & J. Duprey*, 1860.

Hudson (Henry). An abstract of [his] iournall, for the discouerie of the north-west passage, begunne 17th Aprill, 1610, ended with his end, being treacherously exposed by some of the companie. 8°. *New York, J. Riley*, 1811.
[*In* NEW YORK historical society. Collections. v. 1. 1st series].

—— A second voyage or employment, for finding a passage to the East Indies by the north-east. 1608. 8°. *New York, J. Riley*, 1811.
[*In* NEW YORK historical society. Collections. v. 1. 1st series].

Huë (J. F.) Les ports de France. *See* **Vernet** (C. J.) *and* **Huë**.

Huebner. *See* **Hübner**.

Huet (Pierre Daniel). Histoire du commerce et de la navigation des anciens. xxiv, 496 pp. 8°. *Lyon, B. Duplain*, 1763. s.

Hufeland (Christoph Wilhelm). Die kunst das menschliche leben zu verlängern. 2 v. xxviii, 336 pp; 448, xxx pp. 1 pl. 8°. *Jena*, 1778.

Hughes (*Rev.* Thomas Smart). An essay on the political system of Europe; its connection with the government of Great Britain, and the general policy of the European states. xviii, 156 pp. 1 portrait. 16°. *London, G. Bell*, 1855.

Hughs (*Mrs.* Mary). Buds and blossoms for the young. 205 pp. 10 pl. sq. 16°. *Philadelphia, Lindsay & Blakiston*, 1848. s.

—— The ivy wreath. [Tales for the young]. 175 pp. 5 pl. sq. 16°. *Philadelphia, Lindsay & Blakiston*, 1849. s.

Hugo (Thomas). The Bewick collector. A descriptive catalogue of the works of Thomas and John Bewick. The whole described from the originals. xxiii, 562 pp. 8°. *London, Lovell, Reeve & co.* 1866.

Hugo (Victor Marie). Les feuilles d'automne. Suivi de plusieurs pièces nouvelles et des iambes, par Auguste Barbier. 1 p. l. 214 pp. 12°. *Bruxelles, A. Peeters*, 1832. s.

—— The Rhine: from the French. By D. M. Aird. 3 p. l. 218 pp. 7 pl. 16°. *London, D. Aird*, 1843.

—— Toilers of the sea. Authorized English translation by W. M. Thomas. Illustrations by G. Doré. xii, 370 pp. 2 pl. 16°. *London, Low, son, & Marston*, 1867.

Hugo Blanc, the artist. A tale of practical and ideal life. By an artist. [*anon.* Lester A. Roberts]? 411 pp. 12°. *New York, Hilton & co.* 1867.

Huidekoper (*Rev.* Frederic). The belief of the first three centuries concerning Christ's mission to the underworld. xii, 187 pp. 12°. *Boston, Crosby, Nichols & co.* 1854. s.

Humboldt (Carl Wilhelm von). Gesammelte werke. 7 v. 8°. *Berlin, G. Reimer*, 1841–48. s.
[v. 7 wanting].

Humboldt (Friedrich Heinrich Alexander von). Atlas zu [seine] kosmos. *See* **Bromme** (T.)

Hume (David). The history of England, from the invasion of Julius Cæsar to the revolution in 1688. 5 v. in 10. 190 pl. fol. *London, R. Bowyer*, 1806.

Hume (Hamilton). The life of Edward John Eyre, late governor of Jamaica. xvi, 320 pp. portrait. 12°. *London, R. Bentley*, 1867.

Humphry (George Murray, *M.D.*) The human foot and the human hand. viii, 215 pp. 16°. *Cambridge, (Eng.) Macmillan & co.* 1861.

——— (*editor*). *See* **Journal** of anatomy, etc. 1867–68.

Hunt (Robert, *F. R. S.*) Popular romances of the west of England; or, the drolls, traditions, and superstitions of old Cornwall. 1st and 2d series. 2 v. xxiv, 319 pp; viii, 292 pp. 2 pl. 12°. *London, J. C. Hotten*, 1865.

Hunt's merchant's magazine. *See* **Merchant's** magazine.

Hunten (——). Enlarged edition of [his] celebrated piano forte school. 112 pp. 4°. *Philadelphia, Lee & Walker*, 1868.

Hunter (John, *surgeon, F. R. S.*) Inaugural dissertation on the varieties of man. From the Latin by T. Bendyshe. 8°. *London, anthropological society*, 1865.
[*In* BLUMENBACH (J. F.) Anthropological treatises. pp. 357–394. 1865].

Hunter (John Dunn). Manners and customs of several Indian tribes located west of the Mississippi; including some account of the Indian materia medica: [and] the history of the author's life during a residence of several years among them. 402 pp. 8°. *Philadelphia, author*, 1823.

Hunter (William). An oration delivered in Newport, on the 4th July, 1801. 32 pp. 12°. *Newport (R. I.), office of the Newport Mercury*, 1801.
[DUANE pamphlets, v. 37].

Huntington (*Rev.* Elijah B.) History of Stamford, Connecticut, from its settlement in 1641, to the present time, including Darien, which was one of its parishes until 1820. 3 p. l. 492 pp. 18 pl. 8°. *Stamford, author*, 1868.

Huntington (Frederic Dan, *D.D.*) Graham lectures. Human society; its providential structure, relations, and offices, etc. 4 p. l. 307 pp. 8°. *New York, R. Carter & brothers, [for the Brooklyn institute]*, 1860. s.

Hupfeld (Hermann). Die quellen der Genesis, und die art ihrer zusammensetzung. xiv, 224 pp. 8°. *Berlin, Wiegand & Grieben*, 1853.

Husband hunting; or, the mother and daughters. A tale of fashionable life. By S. J. [*anon.*] 2 v. 276 pp; 282 pp. 16°. *Boston, Wells & Lilly*, 1825.

Huss (Magnus). Ueber die endemischen krankheiten Schwedens, etc. Aus dem Schwedischen übersetzt, etc. von G. von dem Busch. xv, 162 pp. 8°. *Bremen, C. Schünemann*, 1851. s.

Hutchins (Stephen C.) Life sketches of state officers, etc. of New York, in 1868. *See* **Harlow** (S. R.) *and* **Hutchins.**

Hutchins (Thomas). An historical narrative and topographical description of Louisiana, and West Florida, comprehending the Mississippi, with its branches and settlements. 8°. *London, J. Debrett*, 1797.
[*In* IMLAY (G.) Topographical description of the western territory. Ed. 1797. pp. 388–458].

——— A topographical description of Virginia, Pennsylvania, Maryland, and North Carolina. 8°. *London, J. Debrett*, 1797.
[*In* IMLAY (G.) Topographical description of the western territory. Ed. 1797. pp. 485–511].

Hutchinson (Thomas). The history of Massachusetts, 1628–1750. 3d ed. 2 v. 478 pp. 5 l; 447 pp. 2 l. 8°. *Salem, T. C. Cushing; Boston, Thomas & Andrews*, 1795.

Hutchinson (Thomas J.) The Parana; with incidents of the Paraguayan war, and South American recollections, 1861–68. xxvii, 404 pp. 1 map. 8 pl. 8°. *London, E. Stanford*, 1868.

Hutchison (*Rev.* William). Illustrated history of Washington and his times. *See* **Frost** (John, *LL.D.*)

Hutton (Charles, *LL.D.*) A course of book-keeping, according to single entry. Adapted to the currency of the United States, by a citizen of Philadelphia. 2d improved ed. 55 l. sm. 4°. *Philadelphia, Bennett & Walton*, 1815.

Huxley (Thomas Henry). The origin of species; or, the causes of the phenomena of organic nature, [etc.] 150 pp. 12°. *New York, D. Appleton & co.* 1863. s.

——— (*editor*). Scientific memoirs. *See* **Henfrey** (A.) *and* **Huxley.**

——— *and* **Youmans** (William Jay, *M. D.*) The elements of physiology and hygiene; a text-book for educational institutions. 420 pp. 12°. *New York, Appletons,* 1868.

Huys (Charles du). *See* **Du Huys.**

Hyde (Catherine, *marchioness* Broglio Solari). Letters containing a sketch of her life, and recollections of celebrated characters, with notes. xii, 142 pp. 16°. *London, W. Pickering,* 1845.

Hyde (Henry, *second earl of Clarendon*). State letters [from Ireland] during the reign of James the second, and diary 1687–90. With an appendix from archbishop Sancroft's manuscripts in the Bodleian library [concerning the petition of the seven bishops to James ii.] 2 v. xxxvi, 476 pp; 154, 337 pp. 10 l. 4°. *Oxford, Clarendon press,* 1763.

——— ——— The same. 2 v. xxxii, 407 pp; 480 pp. 10 l. 8°. *Dublin, Eliz. Watts,* 1765.

Hyginus *or* **Higinus** (Caius Julius). Fabvlarvm liber. Eivsdem poeticon astronomicon libri quatuor. Quibus accesserunt similis argumenti, Palæphati, F. Fulgentii, Phornati, Albrici, Arati, Procli, Apollodori, Lilii, [etc. libri]. Index rerum sententiarum. 8 p. l. 317, 60 l. 16°. *Parisiis, J. Parant,* 1578. s.

Hyll. *See* **Hill.**

Hymn and tune book, for the church and the home. xxxvi, 329 pp. sm. 4°. *Boston, American unitarian association,* 1868.

Hymns for youth. 320 pp. 32°. *Philadelphia, presbyterian board of publication,* [1848]. s.

Ibn' Jemin (*Emir* Mahmúd Ben Jemin-eddin Ferjumendi, *known as*). Bruchstücke. Aus dem Persischen von Ottokar Maria freiherrn von Schlechta-Wssehrd. 191 pp. 8°. *Wien, k. k. hof-und staatsdruckerei,* 1852. s.

Ibn-el-Athir. *See* **Athir.**

Ibn Khaldun. *See* **'Abd-er-rahmann.**

Ida. [A poem. *anon.* 2d ed.] 1 p. l. 69 pp. 12°. *Philadelphia, E. S. Morris,* 1857. s.

Illiger (Johann Carl Wilhelm, *editor*). *See* **Magazin** für insectenkunde, 1801–07.

Illinois (*Stat of*). Journals of the senate and house of representatives of the 25th general assembly, 1867. 1st, 2nd, and 3rd sessions. 4 v. 8°. *Springfield, Baker, Bailhache, & co.* 1867.

——— Reports made to the 25th general assembly, 1867. 2 v. in 1. 8°. *Springfield, Baker, Bailhache, & co.* 1867.

——— Report of the auditor of public accounts to the 25th general assembly. [1867]. 99 pp. 8°. *Springfield, Baker, Bailhache & co.* 1867.

——— Report of the adjutant general. 1861–66. 8 v. 8°. *Springfield, Baker, Bailhache & co.* 1867.

Illinois state agricultural society. Transactions, with reports from county agricultural societies, and kindred associations. v. 6. 1865–6. 8°. *Springfield, Baker, Bailhache & co.* 1868.

Illustracion americana de Frank Leslie. *See* **Leslie** (F.)

Illustrated London news. July, 1867, to June, 1868. v. 51–52. fol. *London, G. C. Leighton,* 1867–68.

Illustrirte landwirthschaftliche dorfzeitung. Herausgegeben unter mitwirkung einer gesellschaft praktischer land- haus- und forstwirthe, von William Löbe. 16er–21er jahrgang. 1855–60. 6 v. 4°. *Leipzig, E. Keil,* 1855–60. s.

Illustrirte zeitung. Wöchentliche nachrichten über alle ereignisse, zustände und persönlichkeiten der gegenwart. v. 1–12. fol. *Leipzig, J. J. Weber,* 1843–53. s.

——— The same. v. 13–23, 25. Neue folge. v. 1–11, 13. 12 v. fol. *Leipzig, J. J. Weber,* 1852–55. s.
[Imperfect].

Ilverton rectory; or, the non-conformists in the 17th century. Founded on fact. By the author of "Allan Cameron", etc. [*anon.*] 188 pp. 4 pl. 18°. *New York, American tract society,* 1864.

Imlay (Gilbert). A topographical description of the western territory of North America: [with additions]. 3d ed. xii, 598 pp. 14 l. 3 maps. 1 pl. 8°. *London, J. Debrett,* 1797.

Impartial (An) account of lieut. col. Bradstreet's expedition to fort Frontenac, etc. By a volunteer on the expedition. [*anon.*] 60 pp. 8°. *London, T. Wilcox, etc.* 1859.

Impartial (An) inquiry into the management of the war in Spain, by the ministry at home, and into the conduct of [the] generals abroad. [*anon.*] 4 p. l. 265, 139 pp. 12°. *London, J. Morphew,* 1712.

Inajut-Ullah *or* **Inatulla.** Bahar-danush; or, garden of knowledge. An oriental romance. Translated from the Persic of Einaiut Oollah. By Jonathan Scott. 3 v. 8°. *Shrewsbury, J. & W. Eddowes,* 1799.

Indagine (Joannes de). *See* **Hagen** (Johann vom).

Indépendance (L') absolue des Américains des États-Unis. Prouvée par l'état de leur commerce avec les nations européennes. [*anon.*] 149 pp. 8°. *Paris, Laran,* [1798].

Index librorvm prohibitorvm cum regvlis confectis per patres à tridentina synodo delectos. Instructione adiecta de exequendæ prohibitionis ratione. 77 l. 24°. *Coloniae, apud G. Cholinum,* 1598. s.
[*With* TRENT (Council of). Canones et decreta, 1597].

Indiana (*State of*). First to eleventh annual report[s] of the trustees of the Indiana asylum for the education of the deaf and dumb, [etc.] For the years 1844–54. 11 v. in 3. 8°. *Indianapolis, state printer, etc.* 1845–55. s.

——— Circular of the trustees of the Indiana asylum for the education of the deaf and dumb, and the rules of internal economy. 8 pp. 8°. *Indianapolis, institution,* 1855. s.
[*With their* Annual reports].

Indianapolis (*City of, Indiana*). Logan's Indianapolis directory for 1868. xiv, 280 pp. 8°. *Indianapolis, Logan & co.* 1868.

Ingenieur (Der). Zeitschrift für das gesammte ingenieurwesen. Herausgegeben von C. R. Bornemann, C. R. Brückmann, G. E. Röting [und] C. Hartmann. 2 v. 4°. *Freiberg, J. G. Engelhardt,* 1848–50.
See, also, **Civilingenieur** (Der). s.

Ingersoll (Charles M.) Conversations on English grammar. 3^d ed. xix, 296 pp. 16°. *Philadelphia, Carey & Lea,* 1822.

Inglenook. A story for children. By Carrie Carleton. [*pseudon.*] 239 pp. 1 pl. 16°. *New York, A. Roman & co.* 1868.

Ingraham (Edward D.) Catalogue of [his] library, sold at public sale, at [Philadelphia], March 20, 1855. 184 pp. 8°. *Philadelphia, M. Thomas & sons,* 1855.
[With prices].

Innstädten. *See* **Sonklar** edler von Innstädten.

Inquiry (An) into the history of the originals of king James' bible: when were they written; where were they written; who wrote them; and how they have been preserved and handed down? [*anon.* By Oliver White]? viii, 568 pp. 8°. *New York, Eckler,* 1868.

Institut de France. (*Académie des sciences*). Mémoires présentés par divers savants à l'académie des sciences. v. 18. 4°. *Paris, imprimerie impériale,* 1868.

——— ——— The measure of the earth: being an account of several observations made for that purpose by divers members of the royal academy of science at Paris. Translated by R. Waller, etc. 40 pp. 5 pl. fol. *London, R. Roberts, T. Basset, etc.* 1688.
[*With* MEMOIRS for a natural history of animals. 1688].

Instructive and curious epistles. *See* **Lettres** édifiantes et curieuses.

Interesting tracts relating to the island of Jamaica, from its conquest [by the English, 1655], down to 1702. vi, 300 pp. 4°. *St. Jago de la Vega,* [*Jamaica*], *Lewis, Lunan & Jones,* 1800.

Internal (The) revenue record and customs journal. July, 1867, to Dec. 1868. v. 6–8. 4°. *New York, P. Vr. Van Wyck,* [1867–68].

International coinage. 1. Report of senator Sherman. 2. Report of senator Morgan. 3. Bill to establish a uniform coinage. 4. Report of S. B. Ruggles. 42 pp. 8°. [*Washington, gov't printing office,* 1868].

International copyright association. Meeting of authors and publishers at the rooms of the N. Y. historical society, April 9, 1868, and organization of the international copyright association. 46 pp. 8°. *New York, international copyright assoc.* 1868.

International exhibitions. *See* **Exhibition.**

International statistical congress. Compte-rendu des travaux de la session du congrès international de statistique réuni à Florence, 1867, publié par l'ordre de S. E. M. de Blasiis, ministre de l'agriculture, de l'industrie et du commerce, sous la direction du Pierre Maestri, chef du bureau de la statistique générale d' Italie. vii, 651 pp. 4°. *Florence, G. Barbèra,* 1868. s.

Into the light; or, the Jewess. By C. A. O. [*anon.*] 322 pp. 12°. *Boston, Loring,* 1868.

Investor's (The) monthly manual, in connection with The economist, a newspaper for investors in stocks. Jan. to Dec. 1868. v. 4. fol. *London,* [*D. Aird,* 1868].

Iowa (*State of*). The census, as returned in 1867. 250 pp. 8°. *Des Moines, F. W. Palmer,* 1867.

——— Legislative documents, submitted to the 12th general assembly, Jan. 1868. 2 v. 8°. *Des Moines, F. W. Palmer,* 1868.

——— Report of the adjutant general, Jan. 1868. 8°. *Des Moines, F. W. Palmer,* 1868.

Iowa grand lodge. Proceedings of the grand lodge of Iowa of ancient, free, and accepted masons, at its twenty-fifth grand annual communication, held at Des Moines, Tuesday, June 2, A. S. 5868, A. D. 1868. 608, cccxxx, lx pp. 8°. *Davenport, Luse & Griggs,* 1868.

Iowa grand lodge. The same. June, 1864, to June, 1868. v. 4. ix pp. 1 l. 847 pp. 1 pl. cccxxxvi, x pp. 8°. *Iowa city*, 1868.

——— Transactions of the grand chapter of the state of Iowa, from its organization, June 8, 1854, to its thirteenth grand annual convocation, October 17, 1867, inclusive. xxxi, 613, v, 27 pp. 8°. *Davenport, Luse & Griggs*, 1868.

Iowa state agricultural society. Report of the secretary [J. M. Shaffer] for the year 1867. 534, 124 pp. 8°. *Des Moines, F. W. Palmer*, 1868.

Iris (The): an illuminated souvenir for 1851 to 53. Edited by John S. Hart. 3 v. 8°. *Philadelphia, Lippincott, Grambo & co.* 1851–53. s.

Irminon (*Abbé de Saint-Germain des Prés*). Polyptychum. *See* **Guérard** (B. E. C.) Polyptyque de l'abbé Irminon. v. 2.

Irving (C. *LL. D.*) Irving's series of catechisms, improved by Kerney. Catechism of astronomy. 5th Am. ed. revised by M. J. Kerney. 82 pp. 24°. *Baltimore, J. Murphy & co.* 1854. s.

——— The same. Catechism of Grecian antiquities, etc. 5th Am. ed. viii, 91 pp. 1 pl. 24°. *Baltimore, J. Murphy & co.* 1854. s.

——— The same. Catechism of Jewish antiquities, etc. 6th Am. ed. 90 pp. 1 pl. 24°. *Baltimore, J. Murphy & co.* 1850. s.

——— The same. Catechism of Roman antiquities, etc. 5th Am. ed. revised by M. J. Kerney. 104 pp. 1 pl. 24°. *Baltimore, J. Murphy & co.* 1851. s.

——— The same. Catechism of Roman history, etc. 5th Am. ed. revised by M. J. Kerney. 89 pp. 1 pl. 24°. *Baltimore, J. Murphy & co.* 1851. s.

Irving (Washington). Works. Author's revised ed. v. 1–13. 12°. *New York, Putnam*, 1849–50.

CONTENTS.

Astoria. v. 8.
Bonneville's adventures. v. 10.
Bracebridge Hall. v. 6.
Crayon miscellany. v. 9.
Knickerbocker's N. York. v. 1.
Life of Columbus. v. 3-5.
Life of Goldsmith. v. 11.
Mahomet and his successors. v. 12-13.
Sketch-book. v. 2.
Tales of a traveller. v. 7.

——— *and* **Paulding** (James K.) Salmagundi; or, the whim-whams and opinions of Launcelot Langstaff, and others. 2 v. 400 pp. portrait. 18°. *New York, D. Longworth*, 1807-08.

——— The same. With an essay and notes by J. Lambert. 2 v. in 1. 2 l. liv, 211 pp; 2 l. 230 pp. 16°. *London, J. M. Richardson*, 1811.

——— The same. 2d series. no. 1. 58 pp. 18°. *Philadelphia, M. Thomas*, 1819.

Isa Greame's world. [*anon.*] 360 pp. 4 pl. 16°. *Philadelphia, American s. s. union*, [1865].

Iselin (Isaac). Über die geschichte der menschheit. 2 v. xxiv, 440 pp; 1 p. l. 500 pp. 16°. *Carlsruhe, C. G. Schmieder*, 1784. s.

Isert (Paul Erdmann). Voyages en Guinée et dans les îles Caraïbes en Amérique. De l'Allemand. viii, 390 pp. 2 p. l. 8°. *Paris, Maradan*, 1793.

"**It isn't right**;" or, Frank Johnson's reason. [*anon.*] 280 pp. 3 pl. 16°. *Philadelphia, American s. s. union*, 1867.

Italy. Statistica del regno d'Italia. Censimento generale. (31 Dicembre 1861). Popolazione. Per cura del ministro d'agricoltura, industria e commercio. 3 v. 4°. *Torino, tipografia litteraria*, 1864–66. s.

——— ——— The same Censimento generale, 31 Dicembre 1861. Popolazione di diritto. xvi, 327 pp. 8°. *Firenze, tipografia litteraria*, 1865. s.

——— The same. Popolazione. Movimento dello stato civile nell' anno 1864-[66]. Pubblicato per cura del ministro d'agricoltura, industria e commercio. 2 v. 4°. *Firenze, Tofani*, 1866–68. s.

——— The same. Istruzione pubblica e privata anno scolastico 1862–3. [Per cura del ministro dell'istruzione pubblica]. 2 v. in 1. xxvi; 131 pp; xxxii, 246 pp. 4°. *Firenze, Tofani*, 1866. s.

CONTENTS.

Parte i. Istruzione primaria.
Parte ii–iii. Ginnasi, licei e scuole tecniche. 1862–63. Istituti superiori. 1863–64.

——— The same. Movimento della navigazione italiana all' estero. 1864. [Per cura del ministro della marina]. xiii, 283 pp. 4°. *Firenze, G. Civelli*, 1866. s.

——— The same. Movimento della navigazione nei porti del regno. Pesca del pesce, del corallo e delle spugne. Marineria mercantile. Costruzione novali. Infortuni maritimi. 1864. [Per cura del ministro della marina]. xviii, 319 pp. 4°. *Firenze, tipografia litteraria*, 1866. s.

'Izz ed-din Abú'l'hasan 'Ali Ben Mohammed. *See* **Athir** (Ibn-el).

Jablonsky (Carl Gustav) *and* **Herbst** (Johann Friedrich Wilhelm). Natursystem aller bekannten in- und ausländischen insekten, als eine fortsetzung der von Büffonschen naturgeschichte. Nach dem system des ritter C. von Linné bearbeitet. v. 1–2. Der käfer. xxiv, 310 pp. 1 pl; xvi, lxiv, 330 pp. 3 l. 8°. *Berlin, J. Pauli*, 1785. s.
[2 copies; one wanting plates].

Jablonsky—continued.
——— The same. Fortgesetzt von J. F. W. Herbst. v. 2-9. 8°. *Berlin, J. Pauli,* 1789-1801. s.
[Imperfect: wanting plates].

Jackson (*Col.* J. R.) Chartography. 8°. *London,* 1852.
[*In* MANUAL of geographical science. v. 1].

Jackson (J. W.) Elements of conic sections. 2 p. l. 87 pp. 6 pl. 12°. *Albany, O. Steele,* 1838. s.

Jacobs (Christian Friedrich Wilhelm). A Greek reader, selected chiefly from Jacob's Greek reader, adapted to Bullion's Greek grammar, etc. By rev. Peter Bullion. 2[d] ed. 539 pp. 12°. *New York, Pratt, Woodford & co.* 1846. s.
——— The same. 15th ed. 539 pp. 12°. *New York, Pratt, Woodford & co.* 1853. s.

Jacquin (Joseph Franz, *edler* von). Beyträge zur geschichte der vögel. 5 p. l. 45 pp. 19 col. pl. 4°. *Wien, C. F. Wappler,* 1784. s.
[*With* SCHÄFFER (J. C.) Elementa ornithologica].

Jahrbuch für 1836-44. Herausgegeben von [J.] H. C. [E.] Schumacher, etc. 8 v. 12°. *Stuttgart und Tubingen, J. G. Cotta,* 1836-44. s.
[No volume for 1842 was published].

Jahrbuch der chemie und physik. *See* **Journal** für chemie und physik.

Jahrbuch für freimaurer auf das jahr 1867. [Von] C. Van Dalen. 7er jahrgang. 3 p. l. 218 pp. 24°. *Leipzig, Förster & Findel,* 1867.

Jahrbuch für kinder-heilkunde und physische erziehung. Dr. Fr. Mayr, haupt-redacteur. v. 1-3. 8°. *Wien, typogr. liter. art. anstalt,* 1858-60. s.

Jais (Aegidius). Guter samen auf ein gutes erdreich. Ein lehr- und gebetbuch für katholische christen. Neu bearbeitet von G. Hürsemann. 384 pp. 24°. *New York, C. & N. Benziger,* 1868.

Jamaica (*Island of*). Laws, confirmed by the crown. [Edited by] William Wood. [With] Francis Hanson's account of the island and government of Jamaica, wrote in 1682. xxx, 457 pp. 8°. *London, W. Wilkins,* 1716.

Jamblichus *chalcidensis.* Περι μυστηριων λογος. De mysteriis liber. Praemittitur epistola Porphyrii ad Anebonem Aegyptium, eodem argumento. Thomas Gale, Anglus, Græce nunc primum edidit, Latine vertit, et notas adjecit. 20 p. l. 316 pp. 4 l. fol. *Oxonii, e theatro sheldoniano,* 1678. s.

James (Constantin). Toilette d'une Romaine au temps d'Auguste, et cosmétiques d'une Parisienne au xixe siècle. iv, 300, 8 pp. 12°. *Paris,* 1865.

James (John). History of the worsted manufacture in England, from the earliest times; with introductory notices of the manufacture among the ancient nations, and during the middle ages. xvi, 640, 40 pp. 8 pl. 8°. *London, Longmans,* 1857.

James (*Rev.* John Angell). Christian progress: a sequel to the anxious enquirer after salvation. 2[d] ed. 180 pp. 16°. *Charleston, (S. C.) southern baptist publication society,* 1855. s.

James (Robert, *M. D.*) A medicinal dictionary; including physic, surgery, anatomy, chymistry, and botany, in all their branches relative to medicine. Together with a history of drugs, etc. 3 v. fol. *London, T. Osborne,* 1743-45. s.
[v. 3. N-Z, wanting].

Jamin (Nicolas). Pensées relatives aux erreurs du tems. D'après l'éd. de Turin de 1823, etc. 3 p. l. 386 pp. 8°. *Louvain, bibliothèque catholique de la Belgique,* 1824. s.

Janes (*Rev.* E. L. *and others*). Perfect love; or, the speeches in the New York preachers' meeting, 1867, upon the subject of sanctification. With bishop Janes' sermon, on sin and salvation, at Morristown, [N. J.] Aug. 1867. Edited by H. Mattison. 129 pp. 16°. *New York, N. Tibbals & co.* 1868.

Janeway (J. J.) The communicant's manual; or, a series of meditations designed to assist communicants in making preparation for the Lord's supper. 264 pp. 16°. *Philadelphia, presbyterian board of publication,* 1848. s.

Janin (Jules). Les amours du chevalier de Fosseuse. 113 pp. 16°. *Paris, J. Miard,* 1867.

Jansen *or* **Jansenius** (Cornelius, *bishop of Yprés*). Tetrateuchus, sive commentarius in sancta Jesu Christi evangelia. *See* **Bible** (*Latin*).

Jardine (Alexander). Practical geometry. 8°. *London,* 1854.
[*In* ORR (W. S.) Circle of the sciences. Mathematical sciences].

Jarry (*General, of the British army*). Instruction concerning the duties of light infantry in the field. 2[d] ed. viii, 219 pp. 24°. *London, A. Dulau & co.* 1803.

Jay (Cyrus). The law: what I have seen, what I have heard, and what I have known. xii, 351 pp. 12°. *London, Tinsley bros.* 1868.

Jay (John). The great issue. An address. 32 pp. 8°. *New York,* 1864.
[LOYAL publication society. no. 75].
——— Report [to the governor of New York] on Antietam cemetery. With a communication in reply to a letter written gov. Fenton by hon. John Covode. 48 pp. 8°. [*Albany*], 1868.

Jeaffreson (John Cordy). A book about lawyers. 2 v. in 1. 432 pp. 12°. *New York, Carleton & co.* 1867.

——— The life of Robert Stephenson. With chapters on his important professional works, by W. Pole. 2 v. xv, 362 pp. 1 pl; ix, 335 pp. 6 pl. 8°. *London, Longmans,* 1864.

Jean *or* **Jehan d' Arras.** Romans of Partenay, or of Lusignen: otherwise known as the tale of Melusine. Translated from the French of La Coudrette, (about 1500–1520 A. D.) Edited by rev. W. W. Skeat. xx, 299 pp. 8°. *London, N. Trübner & co.* 1866.

[EARLY English text society, no. 22].

Jefferson (Thomas). Notes on the state of Virginia. 2 p. l. 280 pp. 18°. *Boston, Lilly & Wait,* 1832.

Jefferys (Thomas). The American atlas: or, a geographical description of the continent of America; and chiefly the British colonies. 2 p. l. 30 maps. fol. *London, R. Sayer & J. Bennett,* 1782.

Jeffrey of Monmouth. The British history of Geoffrey of Monmouth. From the Latin by A. Thompson. New edition, revised by J. A. Giles. xxvii, 282 pp. 8°. *London, J. Bohn,* 1842.

Jemál-ed-dín Abú'lmehásin Yúsuf Ibn Taghrí Berdi, *called* Etz-Tzáhirí (*El-emír el-kébir*). Maured allatafet, seu rerum ægyptiacarum annales, ab anno Christi 971, usque ad annum 1453. E codice ms. Bibl. acad. Cantab. textum arab. primus edidit, Latine vertit, notisque illust. J. D. Carlyle. 2 p. l. 327 pp. 4°. *Cantabrigiæ, typis academicis,* 1792.

Jenkin (*Mrs.* C.) Madame de Beaupré. 278 pp. 16°. *New York, Leypoldt & Holt,* 1869.

Jenks (*Rev.* William, *D. D.*) Comprehensive commentary on the holy bible. *See* **Bible.** (*English*).

Jennings (Louis J.) Eighty years of republican government in the United States. 1st Am. from 2d Lond. ed. xv, 288 pp. 12°. *New York, C. Scribner,* 1868.

Jerningham (Edward). An essay on the eloquence of the pulpit in England. 18°. *Boston, B. & J. Homans,* 1805.

[*In* KNOX (T.) Principles of eloquence. pp. 55-123].

Jerome (Chauncey). History of the American clock business for the past sixty years. 144 pp. 1 pl. 16°. *New Haven, F. C. Dayton, jr.* 1860.

Jerome (*Saint*). Aureola ex suauissimis salutiferisque floribus Joronimi contexta. [Cum prefatione Thomae Dorniberg]. 42 l. 4°. [*Spira, about* 1493].

Jeronymo (*Father*). *See* **Lobo** (Jeronymo).

Jerrey (William). A treatise on the cause and cure of the "milk sickness." 21 pp. 2 phot. pl. 16°. *Belleville, (Ill.) Advocate printing house,* 1868.

Jerrold (William Blanchard). On the boulevards; or, memorable men and things drawn on the spot, 1853-66. [With] trips to Normandy and Brittany. 2 v. iv, 332 pp; iv, 322 pp. 12°. *London, W. H. Allen & co.* 1867.

Jervis (Swynfen). A dictionary of the language of Shakspeare. [Edited by Alexander Dyce]. 2 p. l. 374 pp. 4°. *London, J. R. Smith,* 1868.

Jessen-Schardeböl (Erik Johan). Afhandling om de norske Finners og Lappers hedenske religion. 1 p. l. 82 pp. 1 l. 1 pl. 4°. [*Kiöbenhavn, G. G. Salikath,* 1767].

[*With* LEEM (Knud). Beskrivelse over Finmarkens Lapper. etc.]

Jésus l'ami des enfants. Petites heures à l'usage de la jeunesse catholique. [*anon.*] 254 pp. 2 pl. 48°. *New York, C. & N. Benziger,* 1867.

Jeter (Jeremiah B. *D.D.*) "How then can man be justified with God." 22 pp. 16°. *Charleston, (S. C.)* 1853. S.

[SOUTHERN baptist publication society. Tracts on important subjects. 1854].

——— Popular charges against the baptists refuted. 25 pp. 16°. *Charleston, (S.C.)* 1853. S.

[SOUTHERN baptist publication society. Tracts on important subjects. 1854].

——— The mirror; or, a delineation of different classes of christians, [etc.] With an introduction, by A. M. Poindexter. 246 pp. 16°. *Charleston, (S. C.) southern baptist publication society,* 1855. S.

Jewell (Frederick S.) Aids to the study of the English language. 14 pp. 12°. [*New York,* 1851].

[*With* CLARK (S. W.) Analysis of the English language. 1851].

Jewett (*Mrs.* Susan W.) The old corner cupboard; or, the every-day life of every-day people. [*anon.*] 304 pp. 12°. *Cincinnati, Truman & Spofford,* 1856.

Jewsbury (Geraldine Endsor). The half-sisters. 8th ed. 305 pp. 16°. *London, Chapman & Hall,* 1866.

——— The sorrows of gentility. 2d ed. 347 pp. 16°. *London, Chapman & Hall,* 1864.

Jex-Blake (Sophia). A visit to some American schools and colleges. xii, 250 pp. 12°. *London, Macmillan,* 1867.

Jex-Blake (*Rev.* Thomas William). A long vacation in continental picture galleries. viii, 224 pp. 18°. *London, Parker,* 1858.

Jimenez (Francisco). Memoria sobre la determinacion astronómica de San Juan Teotihuacan. 8°. *Mexico,* 1865.

[*In* ALMARAZ (R.) Memoria por la comision cientifica de Pachuca].

Jimenez de Cisneros (Francisco). Cartas, dirigadas á Diego Lopez de Ayala, publicadas por P. Gayangos y Vicente de la Fuente. xlii, 271 pp. 3 pl. 8°. *Madrid, colegio de sordomudos,* 1867.

Joannes Secundus. *See* **Everhardi** (Nicolaas).

Jobard (Jean Baptiste Ambroise Marcellin). Industrie française. Rapport sur l'exposition de 1839. 2 v. 2 p. l. xvi, xliii, 429 pp; 2 p. l. 484 pp. 8°. *Bruxelles, etc. auteur,* 1841–42. s.

Jobert (Antoine Claude Gabriel). Ideas; or, outlines of a new system of philosophy. 2 essays in 1 v. 338 pp. 16°. *London, Simpkin, Marshall & co.* 1848–49. s.

Jobson (*Rev.* Frederick James). The fullness of christian privilege. *See* **Hannah** (J.) *and* **Jobson.**

John (*Saint*). Gospel. *See* **Bible.**

——— Revelation. *See* **Bible.**

Johns (*Rev.* Bennet George). Blind people: their works and way; with sketches of the lives of some famous blind men. ix, 196 pp. 3 pl. 16°. *London, J. Murray,* 1867.

Johns (J. *D.D.*) A memoir of the life of the rev. William Meade, D. D. bishop of Virginia. vi, 537 pp. 2 portraits. 12°. *Baltimore, Innes & co.* 1867.

Johnsen *or* **Jonas** (Arngrim). Specimen Islandiæ historicum, et magna ex-parte chorographicum. 7 p. l. 174 pp. 4°. *Amstelodami,* 1643.

Johnson (Alvin J.) New illustrated family atlas of the world, with physical geography, and with descriptions, geographical, statistical, etc. 136 pp. 1 pl. 110 maps. fol. *New York, A. J. Johnson,* 1868.

Johnson (*Miss* Anna C.) The myrtle wreath; or, stray leaves recalled. By Minnie Myrtle. [*pseudon.*] 380 pp. 12°. *New York, C. Scribner,* 1854. s.

Johnson (A. G.) Special report on the present state of education in the United States and other countries, and on compulsory instruction. By V. M. Rice. 253 pp. 8°. *Albany, Van Benthuysen & sons,* 1867.

[NOTE.—The preface states distinctly that Johnson is the compiler of the report].

Johnson (Cuthbert W.) The farmer's and planter's encyclopædia of rural affairs; embracing all the most recent discoveries in agricultural chemistry, suited to the comprehension of unscientific readers. With additions by G. Emerson, M. D. Rev. ed. of 1868. vii, 1179 pp. 17 pl. 8°. *Philadelphia, J. B. Lippincott & co.* 1868.

Johnson (*Lieut. col.* John). A journey from India to England, through Persia, Georgia, Russia, Poland, and Prussia, in 1817. x, 376 pp. 13 pl. 4°. *London, Longman & co.* 1818.

Johnson (Lorenzo D.) Memoir of mrs. Thomazin Johnson, of Braintree, Mass. with an account of her pious lineage, from J. Alden, the first pilgrim father who placed foot on Plymouth rock. 117 pp. 24°. *Boston, J. Loring,* 1835.

Johnson (R. G.) An historical account of the first settlement of Salem, in West Jersey, by John Fenwick, with events down to the present generation. 173 pp. 18°. *Philadelphia, O. Rogers,* 1839.

Johnson (Samuel, *LL.D. the lexicographer*). A dictionary of the English language, with a history of the language, and an English grammar. With corrections and additions by Rev. H. J. Todd. 4 v. 4°. *London, Longmans,* 1818.

——— The prince of Abissinia. [Rasselas]. A tale. [*anon.* 1st ed.] 2 v. viii, 159 pp; viii, 165 pp. 18°. *London, R. & J. Dodsley,* 1759.

Johnson (Samuel W.) How crops grow. A treatise on the chemical composition, structure, and life of the plant. 394 pp. 12°. *New York, O. Judd & co.* 1868.

Johnson (Walter R.) System of natural philosophy. *See* **Moffat** (J. M.)

Johnston (Alexander Keith). Handy royal atlas of modern geography. 4 p. l. 90 pp. 45 maps. fol. *Edinburgh, W. Blackwood & sons,* 1868.

Johnston (John). A manual of chemistry on the basis of dr. Turner's elements of chemistry. *See* **Turner** (E.)

Jonas (Arngrim). *See* **Johnsen** *or* **Jonas** (Arngrim).

Jones (Andrew A.) Jones' digest. Being a particular and detailed account of the duties performed by the officers [of] the customhouse departments of the United States, especially of those of the district of New York. [With] a tariff of duties on merchandise. 370 pp. 8°. *New York,* 1835.

Jones (Charles Colcock, *D. D.*) The history of the church of God during the period of revelation. [Old testament period]. 8, 558 pp. 8°. *New York, C. Scribner & co.* 1867.

Jones (Charles Henry). Memoir of William Rodman. 42 pp. 1 phot. portrait. 8°. *Privately printed,* 1867.

Jones (*Rev.* George). Life-scenes from the old testament. 496 pp. 2 maps. 9 pl. 12°. *Philadelphia, J. C. Garrigues & co.* 1868.

Jones (H. Longueville). The universities. Le Keux's memorials of Cambridge. *See* **Wright** (T.) *and* **Jones.**

Jones (John, *M. D. of Jesus college, Oxford*). The mysteries of opium reveal'd. 4 p. l. 371 pp. 8°. *London, R. Smith,* 1700.

Jones (Joseph, *M. D. of Nashville*). Researches upon "spurious vaccination," or the abnormal phenomena accompanying and following vaccination in the confederate army, 1861-1865. [From the Nashville journal of medicine and surgery]. 164 pp. 8°. *Nashville, (Tenn.)* 1867. S.

Jones (Owen). One thousand and one initial letters. 28 pl. fol. *London, Day & son,* 1864.

Jones (Samuel). Communications [to the N. Y. historical society, containing remarks on Clinton's historical discourse, the last edition of the revised laws, Smith's history of New York, etc.] 8°. *New York, Bliss & White,* 1821.

[*In* NEW YORK historical society. Collections. 1st series. v. 3].

Jones (Thomas, *accountant*). Book-keeping and accountantship, elementary and practical. In two parts. With a key for teachers. 205 pp. 8°. *New York, J. Wiley,* 1849. S.

Jones (*Rev.* Tiberius Gracchus). Duties of a pastor to his church. 104 pp. 18°. *Charleston, (S.C.) southern baptist publication society,* 1853. S.

Jones (William Alfred). Essays upon authors and books. 236 pp. 12°. *New York, Stanford & Swords,* 1849. S.

Jonston (Johann). Theatrum universale omnium animalium, piscium, avium, quadrupedum, exanguium, aquaticorum, insectorum, et angium, cclx tabulis ornatum, ac plus quam trecentis piscibus et animalibus nuperrime ex Indiis Orientalibus allatis locupletatum. 6 v. in 2. fol. *Amstelædami, R. & G. Westen,* 1718. S.

Jordan (J. P.) Die slavischen sprachdialekte in kurzer grammatik, chrestomathie und dem nöthigen wörterverzeichniss. 2 v. 2 p. l. 172 pp; 116 pp. 8°. *Leipzig, W. Engelmann,* 1845.

CONTENTS.

v. 1. Die polnische sprache.
v. 2. Die polnische sprache für Böhmen.

Jordan (Thomas) *and* **Pryor** (J. P.) The campaigns of lieut. gen. N. B. Forrest, and of Forrest's cavalry. 704 pp. 7 maps. 5 pl. 8°. *New York, Blelock & co.* 1868.

Josefa de la Providencia (*Madre*). Relacion del origen y fundacion del monasterio del señor San Joaquin de religiosas nazarenas carmelitas descalzas de esta ciudad de Lima, contenida en algunos apuntes de la vida y virtudes de la venerable madre Antonia Lucia del Espiritu Santo, fundadora del instituto nazareno. 21 p. 176 l. 15 l. 4°. *Lima, imprenta real de los niños expósitos,* 1793. S.

Journal (The) of agriculture. 3d series. July, 1867, to June, 1868. v. 3-4. 8°. *Edinburgh,* 1867-68.

Journal (The) of anatomy and physiology, conducted by G. M. Humphrey, Wm. Turner, [etc.] v. 1. iv. 378 pp. 15 pl. 8°. *London and Cambridge, Macmillan & co.* 1867.

——— The same. v. 2. 2d series. v. 1. iv, 452 pp. 9 pl. 8°. *Cambridge and London, Macmillan & co.* 1868.

Journal (The) of applied chemistry. 1868. v. 3. fol. *New York, Dexter & co.* 1868.

Journal für chemie und physik, in verbindung mit mehreren gelehrten herausgegeben. v. 43-57: [*or*], Jahrbuch der chemie und physik. v. 13-27. Unter besonderer mitwirkung der [anderen] herausgegeben vom dr. J. S. C. Schweigger und dr. Fr. W. Schweigger-Seidel. 15 v. 8°. *Halle, E. Anton,* 1825-29. S.

[v. 1-32 wanting].

Journal of discourses by Brigham Young, president of the church of latter-day saints, his two counsellors, the twelve apostles, and others. Reported by G. D. Watt. Nov. 1, 1853, to Dec. 1, 1859. v. 1-6. 8°. *Liverpool,* 1854-59.

Journal (The) of education for Upper Canada. Edited under the direction of rev. Egerton Ryerson, chief superintendent of education, by J. G. Hodgins. Jan. to Dec, 1848. v. 1. 8°. *Toronto, J. H. Lawrence,* 1848.

——— The same. Jan. 1849, to Dec. 1853. v. 2-7. 4°. *Toronto, T. H. Bentley and Lovell & Gibson,* 1849-54.

——— The same. Jan. 1856, to Dec. 1868. v. 9-22. 4°. *Toronto, Lovell & Gibson,* 1856-68.

Journal für freimaurerei. Als manuscript gedruckt für brüder. 2 v. x, 642, vi pp; 652 pp. 8°. *Altenburg,* 1804-5.

Journal of an officer employed in the expedition under the command of captain Owen, on the western coast of Africa. [*anon.*] 8°. *Philadelphia, T. K. Greenbank,* 1833.

[*In* GREENBANK'S periodical library. v. 2. pp. 16-59].

Journal (The) of speculative philosophy. Edited by Wm. T. Harris, 1867. v. 1. 256 pp. 8°. *St. Louis, G. Knapp & co.* 1867.

Journal (The) of the telegraph. J. D. Reid, editor. Dec. 1867, to Nov. 1868. v. 1. 4°. *New York,* 1867-68.

Jovius (Paulus). *See* **Giovio** (Paolo).

Joyce (P. W.) Hand-book of school management and methods of teaching. viii, 180 pp. 16°. *Dublin, McGlashan & Gill,* 1863.

Joyce (Robert Dwyer, *M. D.*) Legends of the wars in Ireland. 352 pp. 16°. *Boston, J. Campbell,* 1868.

Juan y Santacilia (Jorge) *and* **Ulloa** (Antonio de). A voyage to South America; describing at large the Spanish cities, towns, provinces, etc. on that extensive continent. From the Spanish; with notes, and an account of the Brazils. By J. Adams. 5th ed. 2 v. xxvii, 479 pp. 1 map. 5 pl; iv, 419 pp. 7 l. 2 pl. 8°. *London, J. Stockdale,* 1807.

—— The same. Reise nach Süd-America. 10 p. l. 656 pp. 14 l. 17 maps. 21 pl. 4°. *Leipzig, Arkstee & Merkus,* 1751.

[ALLGEMEINE histoire der reisen. v. 9].

Judd (*Rev.* Willard). Memoirs and remains, embracing a review of professor Stuart [on christian baptism], miscellanies, and a biographical sketch, by O. B. Judd, with an introductory essay by S. H. Cone. xxviii, 452 pp. 12°. *New York, L. Colby,* 1845.

Juet (Robert). The third voyage of Henry Hvdson toward Noua Zembla, and at his returne, to New-found Land, and Cape Cod. and so to thirtie three degrees; and along the coast to the northward, and up the riuer neere to fortie three degrees. 8°. *New York, J. Riley,* 1811.

[*In* NEW YORK historical society. Collections. v. 1. 1st series].

Julia de Fontenelle (Jean Sebastien Eugène). Nouveau manuel complet du blanchiment, du blanchissage, nettoyage et dégraissage des fils et étoffes de coton, chanvre, lin, laine, soie, abaca, agave, china-grass, jute, etc. Nouv. éd. entièrement refondue, [etc.] par Rouget de Lisle. 2 v. xii, 291 pp. 6 pl; 2 p. l. 322 pp. 6 pl. 18°. *Paris, Roret,* 1855. s.

—— *and* **Malepeyre** (F.) The arts of tanning, currying, and leather dressing; theoretically considered in all their details. Edited from the French, with numerous emendations and additions, by Campbell Morfit. 557 pp. 1 portrait. 8°. *Philadelphia, H. C. Baird,* 1833.

Jullien (Marc Antoine). Essai sur l' emploi du tems, ou méthode qui a pour objet de bien régler sa vie, premier moyen d'être heureux; etc. 3e éd. viii, 568 pp. 1 pl. 8°. *Paris, Dondey-Dupré,* 1824. s.

Junghans (Wilhelm). Die geschichte der fränkischen könige Childerich und Chlodovech, kritisch untersucht. 152 pp. 8°. *Göttingen, Vandenhoeck & Ruprecht,* 1857.

Junghuhn (Frans Willem). Java, seine gestalt, pflanzdecke und innere bauart. Nach der 2en verb. aufl. des holländischen originals in's Deutsche übertragen von J. K. Hasskarl. Atlas [*or*] Java album. Landschafts-ansichten von Java nach der natur gezeichnet. 11 col. pl. fol. *Leipzig, Arnold,* 1852-54. s.

[Title page wanting].

Junker (E.) Lucy; or, married from pique. A story from real life. From the German. By J. A. Sigmund. 52 pp. 8°. *Boston, Loring,* 1868.

Jurami (Antonio Miguel). Testimonia ex catholicæ ecclesiæ, et summorum pontificum oraculis, atque sapientissimorum et probatissimorum virorum scriptis pro commendatione doctrinæ angelici doctoris S. Thomæ Aquinatis undique decerpta, atque in unum collecta. 266 pp. 16°. *Matriti, vidua J. Ibarra,* 1789. s.

Justinus. Ivstino clarissimo abreviador de la historia general del famoso y excellente historiador Trogo Pompeyo. Traduzido en lengua castellana [por Jorge Bustamente. ed. 3a]. 2 p. l. 208 l. 16°. *Anvers, M. Nutio,* 1586.

[NOTE. l. 207-208 imperfect].

Juvenalis (Decimus Junius) *and* **Persius** Flaccus (Aulus). Satiræ. Interpretatione ac notis illustravit Ludovicus Prateus, in usum delphini. 428 pp. 8°. *Philadelphia, M. Carey,* 1814.

Kaemtz. *See* **Kämtz.**

Kaldenberg & son. [Illustrated catalogue of] meerschaum pipes, cigar holders, amber work, etc. 17 pl. obl. 8°. *New York,* 1868.

Kalisch (*Dr.* M.) Die kunstfehler der ärzte. xxxii, 315 pp. 8°. *Leipzig, Veit & co.* 1860. s.

Kalm (Peter). Reis door Noord Amerika. 2 v. viii, 223 pp. 1 map. 3 pl; 6 p. l. 240 pp. 4 l. 1 pl. 8°. *Utrecht, J. van Schoonhooven en comp.* 1772.

—— The same. Travels into North America; containing its natural history, and [an] account of its plantations and agriculture, with the civil, ecclesiastical and commercial

Kalm—continued. state of the country. Translated by J. R. Forster. 3 v. 8°. *Warrington and London, W. Eyres and T. Lowndes*, 1770–71.

Kammermeister. *See* **Camerarius.**

Kämtz (Ludwig Friedrich). Vorlesungen über meteorologie. xvi, 591 pp. 6 pl. 8°. *Halle, Gebauer*, 1840.
[Plates wanting].

Kandler (Pietro). Corografie dell' Istria. Introduzione. 8°. *Trieste*, 1830.
[*In* ROSSETTI (D. de). Archeografo triestino. v. 2].

——— Il duomo di Trieste, con appendice delle sue inscrizioni. 8°. *Trieste*, 1829.
[*In* ROSSETTI (D. de). Archeografo triestino. v. 1].

——— Indicazione per scoperte archeologiche. 8°. *Trieste*, 1829.
[*In* ROSSETTI (D. de). Archeografo triestino. v. 1].

Kant (Immanuel). Critik der reinen vernunft. 2e aufl. xliv, 884 pp. 8°. *Riga, J. F. Hartknoch*, 1787. s.

Kapp (Friedrich). Leben des amerikanischen generals Johann Kalb. xiv, 306 pp. 1 portrait. 8°. *Stuttgart, Cotta*, 1862.

Karsten (Gustav, *professor at Kiel, editor*). Allgemeine encyclopädie der physik. Bearbeitet von P. W. Brix, G. Decker, F. C. O. von Feilitzsch, F. Grashof, F. Harms, H. Helmoltz, G. Karsten, H. Karsten, C. Kuhn, J. Lamont, J. Pfeiffer, E. E. Schmid, F. Schulz, L. Seidel, G. Weyer, W. Wundt. 1e–19e lieferung. 8°. *Liepzig, L. Voss*, 1856–67. s.
[Lief. 9 wanting].

CONTENTS.

v. 1. Einleitung in die physik. Von G. Karsten. 1856–65.
v. 2. Lehrbuch der krystallographie. Von dr. Hermann Karsten. 1856–61.
v. 5. Angewandte mechanik. Von F. Grashof. 1856–63.
v. 9. Handbuch der physiologischen optik. Bearbeitet von H. Helmholtz. 1856–67.
v. 15. Handbuch des magnetismus. Bearbeitet von dr. J. Lamont. 1863–67.
v. 19. Die lehre von den fernewirkungen des galvanischen stromes. Elektromagnetismus, elektrodynamik, induction und diamagnetismus. Bearbeitet von dr. frh. v. Feilitzsch. 1856–65.
v. 20. Handbuch der angewandten elektricitätslehre, mit besonderer berücksichtigung der theoretischen grundlagen. Bearbeitet von Carl Kuhn. 1859–66.
v. 21. Lehrbuch der meteorologie. Bearbeitet von dr. Ernst Erhard Schmid. 8°. atlas. 21 pl. oblong 4°. 1857–60.

Karsten (Hermann, *professor at Rostock*). Lehrbuch der krystallographie. viii, 169 pp. 8°. *Leipzig*, 1856–61.
[KARSTEN (G.) Allgemeine encyclopädie der physik. v. 2].

Karsten (H. T. *of Amsterdam*). Commentatio critica de Platonis quae feruntur epistolis, praecipue tertia, septima et octava. viii, 248 pp. 8°. *Trajecti-ad Rhenum, Kemink et fil.* 1864. s.

Kastner (Carl Wilhelm Gottlob, *editor*). *See* **Archiv** für die gesammte naturlehre. 1824–35.

Kavanagh (Julia). Daisy Burns: a tale. 9th ed. 3 v. in 1. 472 pp. 12°. *New York, Appletons*, 1866.

——— Sybil's second love. 3 v. in 1. 432 pp. 12°. *New York, Appletons*, 1867.

Keate (George). An account of the Pelew islands. Composed from the journals of capt. H. Wilson and his officers, who, in 1783, were there shipwrecked. [*anon.*] 131, viii pp. 24°. *New York, Duyckinck & co.* 1796.

Keckley (Elizabeth). Behind the scenes; or, thirty years a slave, and four years in the white-house. 371 pp. portrait. 12°. *New York, G. W. Carleton & co.* 1868.

Keeler (Ralph). Gloverson and his silent partners. 372 pp. 12°. *Boston, Lee & Shepard*, 1869.

Keene (*Mrs.* Sarah F. Prince). Grace Irving's vacation, with its sunbeams. [*anon.*] 308 pp. 2 pl. 16°. *Boston, Mass. s. s. society*, 1867.

Keepsake (The). Edited by F. M. Reynolds [and others]. 1829–39, 1841–45, 1847–48. 18 v. 16°. *and* 8°. *London*, 1829–48.

Keerwolff (Bartel). Epistola de auricularum cordis, etc. structura. 4°. *Amstelœdami*, 1725.
[RUYSCH (F.) Opera, v. 3, no. 25].

Keferstein (Wilhelm). Untersuchungen ueber niedere seethiere. (Extract). viii, 136 pp. 11 pl. 8°. *Leipzig, Zeitschrift für wissenschaftliche zoologie*, 1862. s.

——— *and* **Ehlers** (Ernst). Zoologische beiträge gesammelt im winter 1859–60, in Neapel und Messina. iv, 112 pp. 15 pl. 4°. *Leipzig, W. Engelmann*, 1861. s.
[2 copies].

Keill (John, *M. D.*) The elements of plane and spherical trigonometry. [With] a short treatise of the nature and arithmetic of logarithms. 8°. *London, C. Hitch and L. Hawes*, 1762.
[*In* EUCLIDES. Geometry. *London*, 1762. pp. 277–399. 3 pl.]

Keith (*Rev.* George). A further discovery of the spirit of falshood and persecution in Sam. Jennings, and his party that joyned with him in Pensilvania. 52 pp. sm. 4°. *London, R. Levis*, 1694.

——— Immediate revelation (or, Jesus Christ, the eternal son of God, revealed in man, revealing the knowledge of God, and the things of his kingdom, immediately) not ceased, but remaining a standing and perpetual ordinance in the church of Christ, etc. 2d ed. 3 p. l. 259 pp. 2 l. 16°. [*London*] ? 1676.

Keith (G.) A journal of travels from New Hampshire to Caratuck. 2 p. l. 92 pp. sm. 4°. *London, Brab. Aylmer,* 1706.

Keith (George Skene). A general view of the agriculture of Aberdeenshire. 2 p. l. 16, 672 pp. 1 col. map. 6 pl. 8°. *Aberdeen,* 1811. s.
[GREAT BRITAIN: Board of agriculture].

Keith (*Sir* William). The history of the British plantations in America. Part 1, containing the history of Virginia; with remarks on the trade and commerce of that colony. 4 p. l. 187 pp. 2 maps. 4°. *London, society for the encouragement of learning,* 1738.

Kelley (Caroline E.) Gerty Harding's mission. 260 pp. 4 pl. 16°. *Boston, H. Hoyt,* 1867.

——— Ruth Chenery. [A story]. 323 pp. 4 pl. 16°. *Boston, H. Hoyt,* [1867].

Kelley (William D.) The practice of justice our only security for the future. Remarks in support of his proposed amendment to the bill "to guarantee to certain States a republican form of government;" delivered in the house of representatives, Jan. 1865. 61 pp. 8°. *New York,* 1865.
[LOYAL publication society, no. 82].

Kellogg (Edward). A new monetary system: the only means of securing the respective rights of labor and property, and of protecting the public from financial revulsions. Edited by his daughter, M. K. Putnam. 3^d ed. 366 pp. 12°. *New York, Kiggins, Tooker & co.* 1868.

Kellogg (*Rev.* Elijah). Charlie Bell, the waif of Elm island. 325 pp. 4 pl. 16°. *Boston, Lee & Shepard,* 1869.
[ELM island stories, no. 2].

——— Lion Ben of Elm island. 265 pp. 4 pl. 16°. *Boston, Lee & Shepard,* 1869.
[ELM island stories, no. 1].

Kelly (T. W.) Menana; a romance of the red Indians; [with] the death robe, and two other poems of the American woods. 3 p. l. 298 pp. 8°. *London, author,* 1861.

Kelso (Isaac). Light, more light; or, danger in the dark. [*anon.*] 300 pp. 1 pl. 12°. *Cincinnati, E. Hampson,* 1855. s.

Kemble (*Miss* Adelaide). *See* **Sartoris** (*Mrs.* A. K.)

Kempis (Thomas à). De imitatione Christi. Hie vahet an das erst tail vonn der nachuolgunge Cristi vñ von verschmehung der welt. [*anon.*] cxxvii l. sm. 4°. *Augspurg, E. Öglin & J. Nadler,* 1508.

Kendall (George Wilkins) *and* **Nebel** (Carl). The war between the United States and Mexico illustrated, embracing pictorial drawings of all the principal conflicts, with a description of each battle. iv, 52 pp. 12 col. pl. fol. *New York, Appletons,* 1851.

Kennedy (Grace). Father Clement, a romantic catholic story. ix, 155 pp. 12°. *New York, Stanford & Swords,* 1848.

Kennedy (Patrick). Journal of an expedition in 1773, from Kaskaskias village, to the head waters of the Illinois river. 8°. *London, J. Debrett,* 1797.
[*In* IMLAY (G.) Topographical description of the western territory. Ed. 1797. pp. 506–511].

Kenney (James). Raising the wind. A farce in two acts. 40 pp. 16°. *New York, M. Doolady,* 1868.
[*With* SENTER (A. E.) The diddler. 1868].

Kennion (John W.) The architects' and builders' guide. An elaborate description of all the [noteworthy] buildings already constructed, and about to be erected in New York and its environs. 3 parts in 1 v. xxxi, 318, vii pp. 5 pl. 8°. *New York, Fitzpatrick & Hunter,* 1868.

Kent (Nathaniel). General view of the agriculture of the county of Norfolk. xvi, 236 pp. 1 l. 1 map. 3 pl. 8°. *London,* 1796. s.
[GREAT BRITAIN: Board of agriculture].

Kentucky (*State of*). Annual report of the auditor of public accounts, 1857. 493 pp. 8°. *Frankfort, A. G. Hodges,* 1857. s.

——— Annual report of the superintendent of public instruction, 1865. 236 pp. 8°. *Frankfort, (Ky.) state printer,* 1866. s.

Kepler (Johann). Opera omnia. Edidit dr. Ch. Frisch. v. 7. 8°. *Francofurti-a-M; Heyder & Zimmer,* 1868. s.

Kératry (Émile, *comte* de). The rise and fall of the emperor Maximilian. A narrative of the Mexican empire, 1861–67: from authentic documents, with the imperial correspondence. Translated by G. H. Venables. viii, 312 pp. 1 pl. 12°. *London, Low, son & Marston,* 1868.

Kerhallet (Charles Philippe). Manuel de la navigation à la cote occidentale d'Afrique. 2e éd. v. 3. xv, 333 pp. 8°. *Paris, dépôt des cartes et plans de la marine,* 1858. s.

Kerl (Bruno, *editor*). *See* **Berg** und hüttenmannische zeitung.

Kerl (Simon). The Alamo, and other poems original and collected. 359 pp. 12°. *New York, for the author,* 1868.

Kernwood; or, after many days. A historical romance, founded on the events of the late war, from the manuscript of a confederate spy. By L'innconnue. [*pseudon.*] 390 pp. 12°. *Louisville, author,* 1867.

Kerr (Robert, *farmer*). General view of the agriculture of the county of Berwick. xxxii, 504,73 pp. 1 map. 3 pl. 8°. *London*, 1809. s.
[GREAT Britain: Board of agriculture].

Kerr (Robert, *surgeon*). A general history and collection of voyages and travels; forming a complete history of the origin and progress of navigation, discovery, and commerce, by sea and land, from the earliest ages to the present time. 18 v. 8°. *Edinburgh, W. Blackwood*, 1811–17.
[v. 18 wanting].

Ketchum (William). An authentic and comprehensive history of Buffalo, with some account of its early inhabitants, both savage and civilized, and historic notices of the six nations or Iroquois Indians. 2 v. xvi, 432 pp; vii, 443 pp. 2 maps. 8°. *Buffalo, Rockwell, Baker & Hill*, 1864–65.

Keyser (Jacob Rudolf, *prof. at Christiania*). Den norske kirkes historie under katholicismen. 2 v. 3 p. l. iv, 462 pp; 3 p. l. 910 pp. 1 portrait. 8°. *Christiania, C. Tonsberg*, 1856–58. s.

——— The private life of the old Northmen. Translated from the [Norwegian] by rev. M. R. Barnard. 2 p. l. 177 pp. 12°. *London, Chapman & Hall*, 1868.

Keyserling (Alexander, *graf* von). Fossile mollusken. 4°. *St. Petersburg*, 1848. s.
[*With* MIDDENDORFF (A. T. von). Reise, etc. v. 1. theil 1].

Khaldun (Ibn). *See* **Abd-er-rahman.**

Kiddle (Henry). A new manual of the elements of astronomy, descriptive and mathematical. 284 pp. 12°. *New York, Ivison, Phinney & co.* 1868.

Kilbourne (Payne Kenyon). A biographical history of the county of Litchfield, Connecticut: comprising biographical sketches of distinguished natives and residents of the county; with a list of judges, sheriffs, senators, etc. from the organization of the county to the present time. 413 pp. 4 pl. 12°. *New York, Clark, Austin & co.* 1851.

Kimball (Horace). American naval battles; being a complete history of the battles fought by the navy of the United States, from its establishment in 1794 to the present time. With engravings. [*anon.*] 278 pp. 12°. *Boston, J. J. Smith*, 1836.

Kimball (James William). Heaven. 281 pp. 12°. *Boston, Gould & Lincoln*, 1857. s.

Kimball (Richard B.) Henry Powers, banker. 12°. *Carleton*, 1868.

Kimber (Emmor). Arithmetic made easy to children. 6th ed. 120 pp. 18°. *Philadelphia, Kimber & Sharpless*, 1816.

King's choice selection of English songs. 36 pp. 1 pl. 12°. *New York, D. Felt & co.* 1834.

Kinglake (Alexander William). The invasion of the Crimea: its origin, and an account of its progress down to the death of Lord Raglan. v. 3–4. 8°. *London, W. Blackwood & sons*, 1868.

——— The same. v. 2. [Containing v. 3–4 of the London ed.] 632 pp. 5 maps. 1 pl. 12°. *New York, Harpers*, 1868.

Kingsley (*Rev.* Charles). The hermits. 3 p.l. 335 pp. 3 pl. 12°. [*London*], *Macmillan & co.* [1868].
[SUNDAY library for household reading. v. 2].

——— Phaethon; or, loose thoughts [upon religion] for loose thinkers. 91 pp. 12°. *Philadelphia, H. Hooker*, 1824. s.

——— Three lectures delivered at the royal institution on the ancien regime as it existed on the continent before the French revolution. xxiv, 136 pp. 16°. *London, Macmillan & co.* 1867.

Kingston (William H. G.) Adventures of Dick Onslow among the red skins. A book for boys, with illustrations. vii, 336 pp. 16°. *Boston, J. E. Tilton & co.* 1864.

Kip (William Ingraham, *D.D.*) The christmas holydays in Rome. xii, 304 pp. 12°. *Boston, E. P. Dutton & co.* 1869.

——— The unnoticed things of scripture. 280 pp. 12°. *New York, A. Roman & co.* 1868.

Kircher (Athanasius). Iter exstaticum coeleste, quo mundi opificium, id est, coelestis expansi, siderumque tam errantium, quàm fixorum natura, vires, proprietates singulorumque compositio et structura, novâ hypothesi exponitur ad veritatem, etc. Hâc 2a ed. prælusionibus et scholiis illustratum; ipso auctore annuente a Gaspare Schotto, etc. Accessit ejusdem auctoris Iter exstaticum terrestre, et synopsis mundi subterranei. 12 p. l. 704 pp. 12 pl. 4°. *Herbipoli, J. A. Endter, etc.* 1671.

Kirk (*Rev.* Edward Norris). Sermons on different subjects. With introduction by S. H. Cox, D. D. viii, 316 pp. 12°. *New York, J. F. Trow*, 1840.

Kirk (John Foster). History of Charles the bold, duke of Burgundy. v. 3. viii, 555 pp. 3 maps. 8°. *Philadelphia, Lippincott*, 1868.

Kirschleger (Friedrich, *M. D.*) Flore de Soultzmatt. 8°. *Paris*, 1853. s.
[*In* BACH (J. A.) Des eaux de Soultzmatt. 1853].

Kitto (John, *D. D.*) An illustrated history of the holy bible: being a connected account of the remarkable events, and distinguished characters contained, in the old and new testaments, and in Jewish history, during the four hundred years intervening between the time of Malachi and the birth of Christ, etc. 735 pp. 18 pl. 4 maps. 8°. *Norwich (Conn.) H. Bill,* 1868.

Klatt (F. W.) Ensatae (von Mossambique). fol. *Berlin,* 1864.

[*In* PETERS (W. C. H.) Nat. reise nach Mossambique. Botanik].

Kleine astronomische ephemeriden für das jahr 1831–35. Herausgegeben von C. L. Harding und G. Weisen. 5 v. 12°. *Göttingen, Vandenhoeck & Ruprecht,* 1830–34. s.

Kleine (Das) römische missal und vesperal zum gebrauche der layene, enthaltend die mess- und vesper-liturgie der sonntage und feste des jahrs. 3e vermehrte aufl. 530 pp. 18°. *Mainz, Kirchheim, Schott & Thielmann,* 1844.

Kling (*Rev.* Christian Friedrich). Epistles of Paul to the Corinthians. *See* **Bible,** (*English*). Commentary. By J. P. Lange. New testament. v. 6.

Klipstein (Louis F.) Analecta anglo-saxonica. Selections, in prose and verse, from the Anglo-Saxon literature; with an introductory ethnological essay, etc. 2 v. 430 pp; 444 pp. 12°. *New York, G. P. Putnam,* 1849. s.

Klob (Julius M., *M. D.*) Pathological anatomy of the female sexual organs. From the German by J. Kammerer, and B. F. Dawson. xvii, 299 pp. 8°. *New York, Moorhead, Simpson & Bond,* 1868.

Klopstock (Friedrich Gottlieb). Oden. Mit erläuternden anmerkungen und einer biographie des dichters von J. G. Gruber. 2 v. xvi, 149, 334 pp; 1 p. l. 389 pp. 8°. *Leipzig, G. J. Göschen,* 1831. s.

Klotzsch (*Dr.* Friedrich). Papilionacea [etc. von Mossambique]. fol. *Berlin,* 1862.

[*In* PETERS (C. W. H.) Nat. reise nach Mossambique. Botanik].

Klug (Johann Christoph Friedrich). Coleoptera [von Mossambique]. fol. *Berlin,* 1862.

[*In* PETERS (W. C. H.) Nat. reise nach Mossambique. Zoologie, v. 5].

——— Symbolae physicae, seu icones et descriptiones insectorum, quae ex itinere per Africam borealem et Asiam occidentalem F. G. Hemprich et C. G. Ehrenberg redierunt. fol. *Berlin,* 1829–32. s.

[EHRENBERG (C. G.) Symbolae physicae. v. 3].

Klupfel (Carl). Nachtrag zu dem wegweiser durch die literatur der Deutschen. Nachträge i–vii. 7 v. 8°. *Leipzig, G. Mayer,* 1853–67.

Kluyskens (Jean François, *editor*). *See* **Annales** de littérature médicale étrangère. 1805–14.

Knapp (*Rev.* Jacob). Autobiography. [Also, views on various subjects, and five sermons]. With an introductory essay by R. Jeffery. xxvi, 341 pp. portrait. 12°. *New York, Sheldon & co.* 1868.

Kneschke (Emil). Das deutsche lustspielen vergangenheit und gegenwart. Kritische beiträge zur literaturgeschichte unseres volkes. vi, 469 pp. 8°. *Leipzig, Veit & co.* 1861. s.

Knight (Charles). Popular history of England. With illustrations. 8°. *London, Bradbury, Evans & co.* [1867–68].

Knight (E. Cordelia). Dinarbas; a tale: being a continuation of Rasselas, prince of Abissinia. [*anon.*] xii, 336 pp. 16°. *London, C. Dilly,* 1790.

Knight (James, *M. D.*) The improvement of the health of enfeebled children and adults by natural means, including a history of food. 496 pp. 5 pl. 12°. *New York, Sackett & Mackay,* 1868.

Knötel (August). System der ägyptischen chronologie, nebst einem kurzen abrisse der ältesten ägyptischen geschichte. vii, 123 pp. 8°. *Leipzig, Dyk,* [1857].

Knox (T. *M. A.*) The principles of eloquence. containing hints to public speakers. 53 pp. 18°. *Boston, B. & J. Homans,* 1805.

Knox (William). The controversy between Great Britain and her colonies reviewed, etc. [*anon.*] 207, liv. pp. 8°. *London, J. Almon,* 1769.

——— The same. 100 pp. 8°. *Boston, Mein & Fleming,* 1769.

Knox county (*Illinois*). Dewey's county directory. [With] an historical sketch of the townships. By J. L. Dewey. 257 pp. 1 map. 4 pl. 8°. *Galesburg (Ill.) Liberal book and job office,* 1868.

Koberstein (Carl August). Grundriss der geschichte der deutschen national-litteratur. 4e aufl. 1–2 abth. 1 hälfte. 2 p. l. 835 pp. 8°. *Leipzig, J. E. W. Vogel,* 1845–47. s.

Koch (C. L.) Deutschlands crustaceen, myriapoden und arachniden. Ein beitrag zur deutschen fauna. Herausgegeben von dr. Herrich—Schäffer. 40 heft. [each with 24 l. of text and 24 col. pl.] 16°. *Regensburg, F. Pustel,* [1835–41]. s.

Koch (Gabriel). Die geographische verbreitung der europäischen schmetterlinge in anderen welttheilen. 2e ausg. 2 p. l. 154 pp. 8°. *Leipzig, H. Costenoble,* 1857. s.

Koch (Rosalie) *and* **Burg** (Maria). Seedtime and harvest. Tales translated from the German by Trauermantel. 299 pp. 6 col. pl. 16°. *New York, P. O'Shea,* 1867.

Koehler. *See* **Köhler.**

Koelle. *See* **Kölle.**

Koenig. *See* **König.**

Koeppen. *See* **Köppen.**

Koerber. *See* **Körber.**

Kohen *or* **Cohen** (Joel). Dell' origine di Trieste, etc. 8°. *Trieste,* 1829.
[*In* ROSSETTI (D. de') Archeografo triestino. v. 1].

Köhler (Fr.) *and* **Witter** (Conrad). Pocket dictionary of the German and English languages, with the pronunciation of every German word in English characters. Part i. German and English. Part ii. English and German. xiv, 447, 366 pp. 18°. *St. Louis, C. Witter,* 1867.

——— The same. Neues taschen-wörterbuch der englischen und deutschen sprache. Mit angabe der englischen aussprache in deutschen buchstaben. Theil i. Englisch-deutsch. Theil ii. Deutsch-englisch. viii, 444, 386 pp. 18°. *St. Louis, C. Witter,* 1867.

Kok (Jacobus). Vaderlandsch woordenboek. 35 v. 8°. *Amsteldam, J. Allart,* 1785–96.
[NOTE.—v. 1–12, 2d ed].

——— The same. Byvoegsels. 3 v. 8°. *Amsteldam, J. Allart,* 1797–99.

Kolk. *See* **Schröder van der Kolk.**

Kölle (Fr. Ludwig). Englisches sprachbuch. Naturgemässe anleitung zur vollständigen erlernung des Englischen. xviii, 346 pp. 8°. *Stuttgart, hof buchdrukerei zu Guttenberg,* 1850. s.

Kölliker (Albert, *editor*). *See* **Zeitschrift** für wissenschaftliche zoologie.

Kollonitz (Paula). The court of Mexico. Translated by J. E. Ollivant. 3d ed. xix, 303 pp. 8°. *London, Saunders, Otley & co.* 1868.

Kongelige nordiske oldskrift-selskab. Aarbögen for nordisk oldkynghied og historie. 1866–67. 2 v. 8°. *Kjöbenhavn, Gyldendal,* [1867–68].

See, also, **Grönlands** historiske mindesmærker.

König (E.) La science der vrai, philosophie théorique et pratique, spéculative et expérimentale; traduite de l'Allemand et développée par ——. 2 p. l. iv, 445 pp. 8°. *Paris, Ladrange,* 1844. s.

König (Urban). *See* **Regius** (Urban).

Königsberger naturwissenschaftliche unterhaltungen. 3 v. 8°. *Königsberg, gebrüder Bornträger,* 1844–56. s.
[v. 3, heft 3, 1858, wanting].

Koninck (Laurent Guillaume de) *and* **Le Hon** (H.) Recherches sur les crinoïdes du terrain carbonifère de la Belgique, suivies d'une notice sur le genre Woodocrinus. [Extract]. 1 p. l. 217 pp. 8 l. 8 pl. 4°. *Bruxelles, académie royale,* 1854. s.

Kopp (Hermann). Einleitung in die krystallographie, und in die krystallographische kenntniss der wichtigeren substanzen. xii, 346 pp. 8°. *Braunschweig, F. Vieweg & sohn,* 1849. s.
[Wanting atlas. 4°. 28 pl].

Kopp (Ulrich Friedrich). Bilder und schriften der vorzeit. 2 v. viii, 296 pp. 32 pl; x, 422 pp. 13 pl. 8°. *Mannheim,* [*Frankfort, Varrentrapp*], 1819.

CONTENTS.

v. 1. Ueber den geburts-adel.
Gemählde des sachsen-rechts.
Reise-bemerkungen.
Phönicische unschriften.
Paläographische kritik.
v. 2. Gemählde des sachsen-rechts. Fortsetzung.
Ueber eine noch nicht erklärte messingene taufschüssel.
Schrift aus bild.
Entwickelung der semitischen schriften.

Kopp (—, *teacher at Stargard, Prussia*). Römische literaturgeschichte und alterthümer, für hohere lehranstalten bearbeitet. 4 pts. in 1 v. 16°. *Berlin, J. Springer,* 1858.

CONTENTS.

Part 1. Römische literaturgeschichte.
Part 2. Römische staatsalterthümer.
Part 3. Römische kriegsalterthümer.
Part 4. Römische privatalterthümer.

Köppen (Adolphus Louis). The world in the middle ages: an historical geography, with accounts of the origin and development, the institutions and literature, the manners and customs of the nations in Europe, western Asia, and northern Africa, from the 4th to the 15th century. 3 p. l. 232 pp. 6 maps. fol. *New York, Appletons,* 1854.

——— The same. 2 v. xviii, 851 pp. 12°. *New York, Appletons,* 1856.

Koran (The): commonly called the Alcoran of Mohammed; translated into English immediately from the original Arabic; with explanatory notes [and] a preliminary discourse, by George Sale. New ed. xvi, 132, 516 pp. 4 pl. 1 map. 8°. *London, W. Tegg & co.* 1850. s.

——— The same. Koran, öfversatt från arabiska originalet, jemte en historisk inledning af Fredrik Crusenstolpe. v, 158, 783, 27 pp. 8°. *Stockholm, P. A. Norstedt & söner,* 1843. s.

Körber (Johann). S. Irenæus de gratia sanctificante. vi, 250 pp. 8°. *Wirceburgi, F. E. Thein,* 1865. s.

Koren (Johan). Fauna littoralis Norvegiæ. fol. 1856. *See* **Sars** (M.) **Koren** *and* **Danielssen.**

——— *and* **Danielssen** (Daniel Cornelius). Observations on the development of the pectinibranchiata. 8°. *London,* 1853.

[*In* HENFREY (A) *and* HUXLEY (T. H.) Scientific memoirs. art. 11].

Koristka (Carl, *professor at Prague*). Studien über die methoden und die benützung hypsometrischer arbeiten, nachgewiesen an den niveauverhältnissen der umgebungen von Prag. x, 107 pp. 2 col. maps. 4°. *Gotha, J. Perthes,* 1858. s.

Körner (Carl Theodor). Briefwechsel. *See* **Schiller** (J. C. F. von).

——— Life and writings (written by his father), [C. G. Körner], with selections from his poems, tales, etc. From the German, by G. F. Richardson. [v. 1]. 8°. *Philadelphia, T. K. Greenbank,* 1833.

[GREENBANK'S periodical library. v. 1. pp. 354-396].

Krabbe (Otto, *Ph. D.*) Ecclesiae evangelicae Hamburgi instauratae historiam exposuit. 1 p. l. 111 pp. 4°. *Hamburgi, J. A. Meissner,* 1840. s.

Krafft (Ulrich). Das ist die arch Noe: leret wie Gott Noe gebotten hatt die arch zü bauwen. Geprediget zü Ulm Jmiar mdix. 46 l. sm. 4°. *Straszburg, C. Kerner,* 1517.

Krakas maal eller kvad om kong Ragnar Lodbroks krigsbedrifter og heltedöd, med dansk, latinsk, og fransk oversættelse, etc. udgivet af C. C. Rafn. 4 p. l. 152 pp. 2 pl. 8°. *Kjöbenhavn, J. H. Schultz,* 1826. s.

Krause (*Prof.* W. *of Gottingen*). Die anatomie des kaninchens. In topographischer und operativer rücksicht bearbeitet. xvi, 271 pp. 8°. *Leipzig, W. Engelmann,* 1868. s.

Krauss (E. C. F.) Elements of German grammar. 104 pp. 12°. *Boston, author,* 1867.

Kraut (Wilhelm Theodor). Grundriss zu vorlesungen über das deutsche privatrecht, mit einschluss des lehn- und handelsrechts, nebst beigefügten quellen. 4e verm. ausg. xxxix, 546 pp. 8°. *Göttingen, Dieterich,* 1856.

Krey (Johann Bernhard). Die rostock'schen theologen seit 1523. Ein historischer versuch. 68 pp. 8°. *Rostock, Adler's erben,* 1817. s.

——— Die rostock'schen humanisten. Ein historischer versuch. 120 pp. 8°. *Rostock, Adler's erben,* 1817-13. s.

[*With* the preceding].

Krohn (August). On the development of the Ascidians. 8°. *London,* 1853.

[*In* HENFREY (A.) *and* HUXLEY (T. H.) Scientific memoirs. art. 10].

Kröyer (Henrik Nikolaj). De danske östersbanker, et bidrag til kundskab om Danmarks fiskerier. 4 p. l. 168 pp. 1 col. map. 1 pl. 8°. *Kjöbenhavn, S. Trier,* 1837. s.

Krüger (J. F. *editor*). *See* **Archiv** für die neuesten entdeckungen aus der urwelt. 1820-24.

Kuhn (Adalbert), **Schleicher** (August) *and others.* Beiträge zur vergleichenden sprachforschung auf dem gebiete der arischen, celtischen und slawischen sprachen. Herausgegeben von A. Kuhn und A. Schleicher. v. 1-4. v. 5, parts 1-3. 8°. *Berlin, F. Dümmler,* 1858-67.

Kuhn (Carl, *prof. at Munich*). Handbuch der angewandten elektricitätslehre, mit besonderer berücksichtigung der theoretischen grundlagen. xxviii, 1396 pp. 1 l. 2 pl. 8°. *Leipzig,* 1859-67.

[KARSTEN (G.) Allgemeine encyclopädie der physik. v. 20].

Kuhn (J. A.) Der philosophische und theologische rationalismus in seinem einflusse auf wissenschaft und leben. viii, 104 pp. 12°. *Schaffhausen, T. Hurter,* 1857. s.

Kühner (Raphael). Latin grammar; with exercises, Latin reader and vocabularies. Translated and remodelled by J. T. Champlin. 435 pp. 12°. *Boston, Phillips, Sampson & co.* 1850. s.

Kumpfmüller (Johann Baptist). De Anastasio sinaïta. vi, 178 pp. 8°. *Wirceburgi, F. E. Thein,* 1865. s.

Kupffer (A. Th.) Recherches expérimentales sur l'élasticité des métaux, faites à l'observatoire physique centrale de Russie. v. i. xxxii, 431 pp. 9 pl. 4°. *St. Petersbourg, administration des mines,* 1860. s.

Kurtz (B. *D. D.*) Why are you a lutheran? or, a series of dissertations explanatory of the doctrines, government, discipline, liturgical economy, and distinctive traits of the evangelical lutheran church in the United States. With an introduction by John G. Morris. 2 p. l. 227 pp. 16°. *Baltimore, T. N. Kurtz,* 1853. s.

Kurz (Heinrich). Geschichte der deutschen literatur, mit ausgewählten stücken aus den werken der vorzüglichsten schriftsteller. 2e aufl. 3 v. 8°. *Leipzig, B. G. Teubner,* 1857-59.

Kussmaul (Adolf) *and* **Tenner** (Adolf). On the nature and origin of epileptiform convulsions caused by profuse bleeding, and also of those of true epilepsy. Translated by Eduard Bronner. 8°. *London*, 1859.

[NEW SYDENDAM society, v. 5].

Kustel (Guido). A treatise on concentration of all kinds of ores; including the chlorination process for gold and silver ores generally. 259 pp. 7 pl. 8°. *San Francisco, Truesdell, Dewey & co.* 1868.

La Barrera y Leirado (Cayetano Alberto de). Catálogo bibliográfico y biografico del teatro antiguo español, [etc.] Obra premiada por la biblioteca nacional, [etc]. xiii, 274 pp. 2 l. 8°. *Madrid, gobierno*, 1860. s.

[SPAIN: Biblioteca nacional].

Labarte (Jules). Histoire des arts industriels au moyen age et à l'époque de la renaissance. v. 4. 8°. *Paris, A. Morel*, 1867.

[Completes the work].

Labiche (Eugène Marin) *and* **Delacour** (Alfred Charlemagne Lartique, *known as*). La cagnotte, comédie-vaudeville en cinq actes. 119 pp. 12°. *Paris, E. Dentu*, 1864.

Labor (The) question. Extracts, magazine articles, and observations relating to social science and political economy as bearing upon the subjects of labor, trades unions, co-operative societies, and model houses and cottages. 144 pp. 12°. *Chicago, Merchants and farmers and mechanic's savings bank, for the use of its depositors*, 1867.

La Borde (*Le sieur* de). Relation de l'origine, moeurs, coustumes, religion, guerres et voyages des Caraibés, sauvages des isles Antilles. 40 pp. 4°. *Paris, veuve A. Cellier*, 1684.

[*In* RECUEIL de divers voyages en Afrique et en l'Amerique. ed. 1684].

Laboulaye (Édouard René Lefebvre). Abdallah; or, the four-leaved shamrock. Translated by Mary L. Booth. ix, 181 pp. 18°. *London, Sampson Low, son & Marston*, 1868.

——— Separation: war without end. Translated by J. McKaye. 19 pp. 8°. *New York*, 1864.

[LOYAL publication society. no. 8].

Labus (Giovanni). Iscrizione greca illustrata. 8°. *Trieste*, 1829.

[*In* ROSSETI (D. de'). Archeografo triestino. v. 1].

La Caille (Nicolas Louis de). Leçons élémentaires de mathématiques. Nouv. éd. augmentée, par l' abbé Marie. xv, 404 pp. 8°. *Paris, Desaint*, 1770. s.

La Calprenède (Gautier de Costes, *sieur* de). Hymen's præludia; or, loves master-piece. Being [the] romance intituled Cleopatra. Rendered into English by R. Loveday. [*anon.*] 4 p. l. 536, 572 pp. fol. *London, P. Parker*, 1674.

[NOTE. This edition is not mentioned by Lowndes].

Lacépède (Bernard Germain Étienne de La Ville, *comte de*) *and* **Cuvier** (Georges Léopold Chrétien Frédéric Dagobert, *baron*). La ménagerie du muséum national, d' histoire naturelle, ou les animaux vivants, peints d' après nature, sur vélin, par le citoyen Maréchal, peintre du muséum, avec une note descriptive et historique pour chaque animal. 1 p. l. 9 pp. 85 l. 41 pl. fol. *Paris, Miger, etc.* 1801. s.

La Chambre (Marin Cureau de). A discovrse of the knowledg of beasts, wherein all that hath been said for and against their ratiocination is examined. 4 p. l. 304 pp. 16°. *London, H. Mosely*, 1657.

La Chausse (Michael-Ange de). Le pitture antiche delle grotte di Roma. *See* **Bellori** (G. P.) *and* **La Chausse.**

La Condamine (Charles Marie). Lettre a madame * * * sur l' émeute populaire excitée en la ville de Cuenca au Pérou, le 29 d' août 1739. Contre les académiciens des sciences, envoyés pour la mesure de la terre. [Avec] pièces justificatives extraites du procès criminel de la mort du sieur Jean Seniergues. [*anon.*] 108 pp. 1 pl. 12°. [*Paris*], 1746.

Laconia; or, legends of the White mountains. By an old mountaineer, [*anon.* J. P. Scribner?] 489 pp. 12°. *Boston, Lilly & bro.* 1856.

Lacroix (Eugène). Bibliographie des ingénieurs, des architectes, des chefs d' usines industrielles des élèves des écoles polytechniques et professionelles et des agriculteurs. 2e série. 1857-61. 3e éd. x, 186 pp. 8°. *Paris, E. Lacroix*, 1863. s.

Lactantius *Firmianus*. Traité de la mort des persécuteurs de l'église. 8°. *Lille*, 1828. s.

[*With* BUTLER (A.) Vie des pères, etc. v. 16].

[Sometimes attributed to Lucius Caecilius].

Lacy (Rophino). Fra Diavolo; or, the inn of Terracina. A comic opera, in three acts. Music by Auber. 48 pp. 12°. *Philadelphia, Ledger job printing office*, 1867.

Lady Byron's responsive, "Fare thee well." [*anon.*] 2d ed. 16 pp. 8°. *London, R. Edwards*, 1816.

[MISCELLANEOUS pamphlets. v. 56].

Lady [Selina] Huntingdon portrayed; including brief sketches of some of her friends and co-laborers. [*anon.*] 319 pp. 1 portrait. 12°. *New York, Carlton & Porter*, [1857]. s.

Lady's (The) almanac, 1868. 128 pp. 32°. *Boston, G. Coolidge,* 1868.

Laet (Johannes de). Beschrijvinghe van West-Indien. 2e druck. 14 p.l. 622 pp. 9 l. 13 maps. fol. *Leyden, Elzeviers,* 1630.

Laetus (Pomponius). *See* **Leto** (Giulio Pomponio).

La Farelle (F. Felix de). Du progrès social au profit des classes populaires non indigentes, ou études philosophiques et économiques sur l'amélioration matérielle et morale. 2 v. xii, 421 pp. 1 l; 2 p.l. 402 pp. 1 l. 8°. *Paris, Maison,* 1839. s.

La Fayette (Marie Madeleine Pioche de la Vergne, *comtesse* de). The princess of Cleves. [*anon.*] 410 pp. 16°. *London, J. Watts,* 1720.
[CROXALL'S collection of novels, v. 2].

——— Zayde. A Spanish history. By monsieur Segrais. [A borrowed name]. 211 pp. 16°. *London, J. Watts,* 1729.
[CROXALL'S collection of novels, v. 1].

Lafont (J. B. Angelvy). Treatise on French pronunciation and genders. 101 pp. 16°. *Chicago, printer's co-operative association,* 1868.

La Fuente (P. G. de, *editor*). Oratoria sagrada, o coleccion escojida de sermones de oradores sagrados americanos. v. 1. 1 p.l. 573 pp. 1 portrait. 8°. *Santiago, imprenta del independente,* 1866. s.

La Harpe (Jean François de). Abrégé de l'histoire générale des voyages. Nouv. éd. 24 v. 8°. *Paris, E. Ledoux,* 1820.

La Hontan (N. *baron* de). Voyages du baron de Lahontan en Portugal, et en Danemarc. [Written by N. Gueudeville]? 1 p.l. pp. 107-222. 2 maps. 3 pl. 16°. *Amsterdam, Boeteman,* 1704.
[*In* GUEDEVILLE (N.) Suite du voyage, etc. *Amsterdam,* 1704].

Laidlaw (G.) Reports and letters on light narrow guage railways. By sir Charles Fox and [others]. With remarks on the advantages to be derived by the counties of Bruce, Grey, Ontario, etc. from direct railway communication with Toronto. 69 pp. 1 map. 8°. *Toronto, Globe print. co.* 1867.

Lairtullier (E.) Les femmes célèbres de 1789 à 1795, et leur influence dans la révolution. 2 v. 393 pp; 415 pp. 8°. *Paris, Dondey-Dupré,* 1840.

Lalaisse (Hippolite) *and* **Benoist** (——). Gallerie armoricaine. Costumes et vues pittoresques de la Bretagne. 2 v. 109 pl; 125 pl. sm. fol. *Nantes, Le Charpentier,* [*about* 1820].

Lamarck (Jean Baptiste Pierre Antoine de Monnet, *chevalier* de). Histoire naturelle des animaux sans vertèbres, [etc.] v. 5-7. 8°. *Paris, Deterville, etc.* 1818-22. s.
[v. 1-4 wanting].

——— Lamarck's genera of shells, with a catalogue of species. Translated from the French, by Augustus A. Gould. xv, 110 pp. 1 pl. 16°. *Boston, Allen & Ticknor,* 1833. s.

——— *and* **Poiret** (Jean Louis Marie). Encyclopédie méthodique. Botanique, par m. de Lamarck, [v. 1-4]. Continuée par J. L. M. Poiret, [v. 5-8]. 8 v. 4°. *Paris, Panckoucke & H. Agasse,* 1783-1808. s.

——— The same. Supplement. 5 v. 4°. *Paris, Agasse,* 1810-17. s.

——— The same. Tableau encyclopédique et méthodique des trois règnes de la nature. Botanique. Par m. de Lamarck [v. 1-2]: continuée par J. L. M. Poiret. [v. 3]. Illustrations des genres. Texte, 3 v. Atlas. 1000 pl. in 4 v. 4°. *Paris, Panckoucke & Agasse,* 1791-1823. s.

Lamartine (Alphonse Marie Louis Prat de). Joan of Arc. A biography. From the French, by Sarah M. Grimké. 108 pp. portrait. 16°. *Boston, Adams & co.* 1867.

——— Raphael. Blätter aus dem zwanzigsten jahre. Deutsch von Friedrich Müller. 280 pp. 12 pl. 12°. *Stuttgart, k. hofbuchdruckerei zu Guttenberg,* 1849. s.

La Martinière (Antoine Augustin Bruzen de). *See* **Bruzen de la Martinière.**

Lamb (*Lady* Caroline). Graham Hamilton. [*anon.*] 2 v. in 1. 112 pp; 86 pp. 12°. *Philadelphia, Carey & Lea,* 1822.

Lamb (Charles). Eliana: being the hitherto uncollected writings of C. Lamb. xiii, 437 pp. 12°. *New York, Hurd & Houghton,* 1864.

——— The last essays of Elia; being a sequel to essays published under that name. 8°. *Philadelphia, T. K. Greenbank,* 1833.
[GREENBANK'S periodical library. v. 1. pp. 279-328].

Lambert (John). Travels through Canada and the United States, 1806-08. [With] biographical notices and anecdotes of leading characters in the U. S. 3d ed. 2 v. xxxiv, 544 pp. 1 map. 15 pl; viii, 532 pp. 2 pl. 8°. *London, Baldwin, Cradock & Joy,* 1816.

La Mennais (Hugues Félicité Robert de). Mélanges religieux et philosophiques. 2 v. in 1. 264 pp; 150 pp. 12°. *Turin, Alliana & Paravia,* 1825. s.

Lamenther. [*pseudon.*] *See* **Life** of Lamenther.

Lamont (Johann). Handbuch des magnetismus. 1863-67. 8°. *Leipzig,* 1863-67.
[KARSTEN (G.) Allgemeine encyclopädie der physik. v. 15].

La Mont (——— de, *town-major of Toulon*). The art of war; duties of military officers. 143 pp. 12°. *Philadelphia, R. Bell,* 1776.

[*In* VALLIÈRE (J. F. *marquis* de). Art of war. 12°. *Philadelphia,* 1776].

La Mothe Le Vayer (François de). Oeuvres. Nouv. éd. 7 v. in 14. 8°. *Dresde, M. Groell,* 1756–59.

CONTENTS.

v. 1. La vie de mr. Le Vayer. De l'instruction de monseigneur le dauphin. Avec portrait.
v. 2. Sciences dont la connoissance peut devenir utile à un prince. La geographie, la rhétorique, la morale, l'oeconomique, la politique, la logique.
v. 3. ——— The same. La physique, l'éloquence françoise, observations diverses svr la composition des livres.
v. 4. Opuscules ou petits traitéz. De la lecture de Platon et de son éloquence. Du sommeil et des songes. De la patrie et des étrangers. De bon et du mauvais usage des récitations. Des voiages, et de la découverte de nouveaux païs. Des habits, et de leur modes differentes. Du secret et de la fidelité. De la vie et de la mort. De la prosperité. Des adversitéz. De la noblesse. Des offenses, et injures. De la bonne chère. De la lecture des livres, et de leur composition.
v. 5. De la hardiesse, et de la crainte. De l'ingratitude. Du mensonge. Des monstres. De la liberté et de la servitude. Prose chagrine. Discours chrétien de l'immortalité de l'ame, avec le corollaire.
v. 6. Discours ou homilies académiques.
v. 7. La promenade, en 9 dialogues. Discours de l'histoire, où est examinée celle de la vie de Charles v, [etc.] Discours sur la bataille de Lützen en 1632. Discours sur la proposition de trêve au Païs-bas, en 1633.
v. 8. Jugement sur les anciens et principaux historiens grecs et latins, dont il nous reste quelques ouvrages. Discours de la contrarieté d'humeurs qui se trouve entre certaines nations, [etc.] En quoi la pieté des François diffère de celle des Espagnols.
v. 9. De la vertu des payens.
v. 10. Discours pour montrer, que les doutes de la philosophie sceptique sont de grand usage dans les sciences. Du peu de certitude qu'il y a dans l'histoire.
v. 11–13. Petits traités en forme de lettres écrites à diverses personnes.
v. 14. Derniers petits traités en forme de lettres écrites à divers personnes, Table des matières.

La Motte Fouqué (F. H. C. de). *See* **Fouqué.**

Lampridius (Aelius). [Vitæ imperatorum romanorum]. Commodvs Ant. ad Diocletianum Aug. 16°. [*Geneva*], 1568.

[*In* VARII historiæ romanæ scriptores. v. 3].

Lamy (Bernard). Apparatus biblicus, sive manuductio ad sacram scripturam. Nova ed. 16 p. l. 586 pp. 36 l. 11 p. l. 12°. *Lugduni, J. Certe,* 1696. s.

Lancaster (*Pennsylvania*). Bryson's Lancaster directory for 1843. 60 pp. 8°. *Lancaster, J. H. Bryson,* 1843.

Lancet (The). A journal of British and foreign medicine, physiology, surgery, chemistry, etc. 1867, v. 2; 1868, v. 1. 8°. *London, G. Fall,* 1867–68.

Lancewood (Lawrence, *pseudon?*) Louis Sinclair; or, the silver prize medals. The story of a boy who escaped from the hands of a real enchanter. 241 pp. 5 pl. 16°. *Boston, Graves & Young,* 1867.

[LINDENDALE stories. No. 3].

Lander (Sarah W). Spectacles for young eyes. Berlin. 192 pp. 7 pl. 16°. *Boston, Walker, Fuller & co.* 1865.

——— The same. New York. 203 pp. 10 pp. 16°. *New York, Sheldon & co.* 1869.

Landis (Robert W.) Liberty's triumph. A poem. xvii, 544 pp. 12°. *New York, J. Wiley,* 1849. s.

Landrin (M. H. C. *jr.*) A treatise on steel: comprising its theory, metallurgy, properties, practical working, and use. From the French, with notes, by A. A. Fesquet. 352 pp. 12°. *Philadelphia, H. C. Baird,* 1868.

Landry (Geoffroi de La Tour). *See* **La Tour Landry.**

Landwirthschaftliche congress. Verhandlungen [der 1en sitzung] des landwirthschaftlichen congresses gehalten zu Wien im monate März 1849. 405 pp. 8°. *Wien, k. k. hof-und staatsdruckerei,* 1849. s.

Lane (*Rev.* Benjamin I.) Sabbath evening lectures: being a series of thirteen lectures on the doctrine of future punishment. 331 pp. 12°. *Troy, (N.Y.) Young & Hartt,* 1844. s.

Lang (August). Abbildungen von turnübungen. 20 pl. obl. fol. [*Chicago*], *A. Lang,* 1868.

Lang (*Rev.* J.) Results of the serf emancipation in Russia. 8 pp. 8°. *New York,* 1864.

[LOYAL publication society. No. 47].

Lang (J. J. *editor*). *See* **Akademische** monatsschrift.

Lange (Johann Peter, *D.D.*) *and others.* Commentary on the holy scriptures. *See* **Bible** (*English*).

Langeac (*Chevalier* N. de l'Espinasse de). Colomb dans les fers; précédée d'un précis historique sur Colomb. 2 p. l. 150 pp. 1 pl. 12°. *Paris, A. Jombert jeune,* 1782.

Langham (William, *M. D.*) The garden of health: containing the sundry rare and hidden vertues and properties of all kinds of simples and plants. 2d ed. 4 p. l. 688 pp. sm. 4°. *London, T. Harper,* 1633.

[Imperfect: wanting all after p. 688].

Langhorne (John, *D. D.*) Letters supposed to have passed between m. de St. Evremond and mr. Waller, [etc.] 216 pp. 16°. *Baltimore, Coale & Thomas,* 1809. s.

Langille (*Rev.* J. H.) Save the erring; or, the gospel purpose. 164 pp. 3 pl. 18°. *New York, American tract society,* 1865.

Langtoft (Peter). The chronicle of Pierre de Langtoft, in French verse, from the earliest period to the death of king Edward i. Edited by T. Wright. v. 2. xvi, 487 pp. *London, Longmans*, 1868.

[GREAT BRITAIN and Ireland: Chronicles and memorials during the middle ages].

Lanier (Sidney). Tiger-lilies. A novel. v, 252 pp. 16°. *New York, Hurd & Houghton*, 1867.

Lanman (Charles). Dictionary of the United States congress, and the general government. 5th ed. 628 pp. 8°. *Hartford, T. Belknap & H. E. Goodwin*, 1868.

——— Essays for summer hours. 3d ed. 266 pp. 16°. *New York, M. W. Dodd*, 1853.

——— Letters from the Alleghany mountains. 198 pp. 12°. *New York, Geo. P. Putnam*, 1849.

Lanquet (Thomas). Cooper's chronicle, contenynge the whole discourse of the histories as well of thys realme, as all other countries. To the vii yere of the raigne of quene Elizabeth. 30 p. l. 384 l. sm. 4°. [*London*], 1565.

[Continuation, at the end, for 100 years, 1564–1664, *in ms.*]

La Perrière (Guillaume de). La morosophie, contenant cent emblêmes moraux, illustrez de cent tetrastiques latins, reduitz en autant de quatrains françoys. 13 p. l. 100 l. 16°. *Lyon, Macé Bonhomme*, 1553.

Lapide (Joannes de, *or* **Johann von Stein**). Premonitio circa sermões de cōceptōne gloriose virginis Marie per quendam Meffreth nuncupatū collectos. 5 l. fol. *In urbe Basilea*, 1488.

La Placette (Jean). Traité des jeux-de-hazard, défendu contre les objections de mr. de Joncourt et de quelques autres. 18 p. l. 287 pp. 16°. *La Haye, H. Scheurleer*, 1714.

——— Nouvelles réflexions sur la prémotion physique, et sur les jeux de hazard, [etc.] 4 p. l. 134 pp. 16°. *La Haye, H. Scheurleer*, 1714.

[*With his* Traité des jeux-de-hazard].

La Platiére (M. J. Phlipon, *madame* Roland de la). *See* **Roland de la Platiére.**

Laporte (François L. de, *comte de* Castelnau) *and* **Gory** (Hippolyte Louis). Histoire naturelle et iconographie des coléoptères, publiée par monographies séparées. 4 v. 8°. *Paris, P. Duménil*, [1835–41]. s.

[Imperfect].

Lappenberg (Johann Martin). Geschichte von England. 8°. *Hamburg, F. Perthes*, 1834–37.

[HEEREN (A. H. L.) *and* UKERT (F. A.) Geschichte der europäischen staaten. Geschichte von England. v. 1–2].

La Puente (Pedro de). Reflexiones sobre el bando de 25. de Junio ultimo, contraidas a lo que dispone para con los eclesiasticos rebeldes. 4 p. l. 243 pp. 8°. *Mexico, Maria F. Jauregui*, 1812.

LaQuintinye (Jean de). The compleat gard'ner; or, directions for cultivating and right ordering of fruit-gardens and kitchen-gardens; with divers reflections on several parts of husbandry. [With a] treatise of orange-trees, [and] the raising of melons. Made English by John Evelyn. [2 v. in 1]. 22 p. l. 468 pp. 12 pl. fol. *London, M. Gillyflower*, 1693.

Larcom (Lucy). Poems. x, 275 pp. 12°. *Boston, Fields, Osgood & co.* 1869.

La Rochefoucauld (François vi, 2e *duc de*). Moral reflections, sentences, and maxims. Newly translated from the French. With an introduction and notes. To which are added moral sentences and maxims of Stanislaus, king of Poland. xxxii, 189 pp. 1 pl. 8°. *New York, W. Gowans*, 1851. s.

Laroche-Héron (C. de). Les servantes de Dieu en Canada. Essai sur l'histoire des communautés religieuses de femmes de la province. Éd. revue. 158 pp. 1 l. 8°. *Montreal, J. Lovell*, 1855. s.

La Roquette (Jean Baptiste Marie Alexandre Dezos de). Notice sur la vie et les travaux de m. le baron A. de Humboldt. 88 pp. 4°. *Paris, L. Martinet*, 1860. s.

Larrey (Dominique Jean, *baron*). Mémoires de chirurgie militaire et campagnes. 4 v. 8°. *Paris, J. Smith*, 1812–17.

La Sagra (Ramon de). Informe sobre el estado actual de la industria belga, con aplication a España [etc.] 312 pp. 8°. *Madrid, imprenta nacional*, 1842. s.

——— Notes sur les produits espagnols envoyés à l'exposition de Londres, suivies de quelques considérations sur l'état présent et l'avenir de l'industrie espagnole. 88 pp. 8°. *London, H. Baillière*, 1851. s.

Las Cases (Emmanuel Augustin Dieudonne Joseph, etc. *marquis* de). Letters from the Cape of Good Hope, in reply to mr. [William] Warden; with extracts from the great work now compiling for publication under the inspection of Napoleon. By C—. [*anon.*] 186 pp. 12°. *New York, Wiley & Co.* 1817.

[*Note.*—"The author is a Frenchman, and, we are satisfied, the notorious count de Las Cases." Quarterly review. v. xvii. p. 507].

Lascelles. *See* **Lassels.**

Lasius (Georg Sigismund Otto). Beobachtungen über die Harzgebirge, nebst einem profilrisse, als ein beytrag zur mineralogischen naturkunde. 2 v. 3 p. l. x, iv, 296 pp. 1 tab. 1 col. map; 2 p. l. iv, 297–559 pp. 8°. *Hannover, Helwing*, 1789. s.

[A map, published separately, wanting].

La Solle (Henri Frédéric de). Amusemens des eaux de Passy. 3 v. 16°. *Paris, Poinçot*, 1787.

Lassels (Richard). The voyage of Italy; or, a compleat journey through Italy. 2 v. in 1. 18 p. l. 160 pp; 1 p. l. 272 pp. 2 l. 16°. *London, C. Shortgrave*, 1685–86.

Lasset uns beten! Volkständiges gebet- und andachtsbuch für katholische christen. 286 pp. 2 pl. 24° *Einsiedeln & New York, C. & N. Benziger*, 1867.

Last (the) shilling: or, the selfish child. [*anon.*] 211 pp. 6 pl. 18°. *Philadelphia, American s. s. union*, 1867.

Latham (Henry). Black and white. A journal of a three months' tour in the United States. xii, 304 pp. 8°. *London, Macmillan & co.* 1867.

Latham (John) *and* **Davies** (Hugh). Faunula indica, i. e. catalogus animalium Indiæ Orientalis quæ hactenus naturæ curiosis innotuerunt. Secundis curis editus, etc. a Joanne Reinholdo Forster. 2 p. l. 38 pp. fol. *Halæ ad Salam, J. J. Gebauer*, 1795. s.

Latham (Robert Gordon). On the varieties of the human species. 12°. *London*, 1854.

[*In* ORR (W. E.) Circle of the sciences. Organic nature. v. 1. 1854].

Latourette (Marc Antoine Louis Claret de). Chloris lugdunensis. viii, 44 pp. 8°. *Coloniæ-Allobrogum*, 1785.

[*In* GILIBERT (J. C.) C. Linnæi systema plantarum Europæ, etc. v. 1].

La Tour Landry (Geoffroi de). The book of the knight of La Tour Landry, compiled for the instruction of his daughters. Translated from the French in the reign of Henry vi. and edited from the ms. by T. Wright. xv, 227 pp. 8°. *London, Trübner & co.* 1868.

[EARLY English text society publications. no. 33].

Latta (*Rev.* S. A.) Chain of sacred wonders. vi, viii, 212 pp. 1 portrait. 12°. *Cincinnati, author*, 1849. s.

[No more published].

Laurenti (Joseph Nicolaus). Specimen medicum, exhibens synopsin reptilium emendatum, cum experimentis circa venena et antidota reptilium austriacorum. 215 pp. 5 pl. 12°. *Vienna, J. T. de Trattnern*, 1768. s.

Laurentie (Pierre Sebastien). De l'étude et de l'enseignement des lettres. xii, 484 pp. 8°. *Paris, Méquignon jeune*, 1828. s.

——— Histoire, morale, et littérature. Fragments. 4 p. l. 459 pp. 8°. *Paris, Lagny frères*, 1838. s.

——— The same. Études sur les historiens latins. 2e éd. 4 p. l. 488 pp. 8°. *Paris, Lagny frères*, 1838. s.

——— Introduction à la philosophie, ou traité de l'origine et de la certitude des connoissances humaines. 2e éd. xiii, 510 pp. 8°. *Paris, Méquignon jeune*, 1829. s.

Laurie (Thomas, *D. D.*) Glimpses of Christ in holy scripture. 264 pp. 12°. *Boston, Gould & Lincoln*, 1869.

Laurillard (Charles Léopold). Atlas, etc. *See* **Cuvier** (G. L. C. F. D). Règne animal. 1836–46. v. 1. Mammifères.

Lauzun (Armand Louis de Gontaut, *duc de Biron, duc de*). Lettres sur les états généraux de 1789, ou détail des séances de l'assemblée de la noblesse et des trois ordres, du 4 Mai au 15 Novembre. Précédées d'une notice historique sur Biron par maistre de Roger de la Lande. xxiii, 68 pp. portrait. 12°. *Paris, mme. Bachelin-Deflorenne*, 1865.

Lavater (Johann Caspar). The pocket Lavater, or the science of physiognomy, to which is added an inquiry into the analogy existing between the brute and human physiognomy, from the Italian of Porta. 3d ed. 144 pp. 44 pl. 48°. *New Haven, Baldwin & Treadway*, 1829.

——— The same. [New ed.] 116 pp. 44 pl. 24°. *Hartford, Andrus & Judd*, [*about* 1840]?

La Vega (Garcilaso de). *See* **Garcilaso** de la Vega (*the inca*).

Law (*Rev.* William). An introduction to theosophy, or the science of the "mystery of Christ," [etc. *or*, Selections from the works of Law, by Christopher Walton]. xx, 512 pp. 16°. *London, J. Kendrick*, [1854]. s.

Law (The) list, [for 1868]. By W.W. Dalbiac. xx, 1043 pp. 16°. *London, Stevens & sons*, [1868].

Lawes (J. B.) Action of salt on vegetables. *See* **Becquerel** (A. C.) *and* **Lawes.**

Lawrence (*Massachusetts*). The Lawrence directory, [etc.] A business directory, general events of the years 1856–57, and an almanac for 1859. By Adams, Sampson & co. 184 pp. 18°. *Lawrence, (Mass.) J. C. Dow*, 1859. s.

Lawrence, (*Mass.*) The Lawrence directory, for 1868–69. By Sampson, Davenport & co. 268 pp. 8°. *Lawrence, J. C. Dow & co.* 1868.

Lawson (William). A new orchard and garden: or, the best way for planting, grafting, and to make any ground good, for a rich orchard. With the country hous-wifes garden for herbs of common use. As also the husbandry of bees. [7th ed?] 3 p. l. 112 pp. sm. 4°. *London, W. Sawbridge*, 1660.

[*With* MARKHAM (G.) A way to get wealth. 10th ed.]

——— The same. [4th ed.] 1 p. l. 39 pp. 8°. London, 1626. *Reprinted, Philadelphia, R. P. Smith*, 1858.

[NOTE.—Imperfect reprint. The title-page is given in full, but the country housewife's garden, and all after, is excluded from the body of the work].

Layard (Edgar Leopold). The birds of South Africa. A descriptive catalogue of all the known species occurring south of the 28th parallel of south latitude. xvi, 382, xxi pp. 1 pl. 8°. *Capetown, J. C. Juta*, 1867. s.

Leach (Daniel) *and* **Swan** (Robert). An elementary intellectual arithmetic, etc. 160 pp. 16°. *Boston, Jenks, Hickling & Swan*, 1853. s.

Leadbetter (Charles). Astronomy; or, the true system of the planets demonstrated. 2 p. l. viii, 120 pp. 1 pl. 4°. *London, J. Wilcox*, 1727.

Leader (The). A weekly journal of news, literature, politics, economy, and art. Apr. 18, to Oct. 10, 1868. v. 1. fol. *Baltimore*, 1868.

Leaflets of memory: an illuminated annual for 1849, 1850, 1851, 1854, and 1855. Edited by Reynell Coates, etc. 5 v. 8°. *Philadelphia, E. H. Butler & co.* 1849–55. s.

League (The) [and free trader]. Organ of the American free-trade league. R. Pell, editor. June, 1867, to May, 1868. v. i. 4°. *New York, J. Sarell*, 1868.

Leavitt (*Rev.* John M.) Afranius, and the Idumean, tragedies. With the Roman martyrs and other poems. iv, 255 pp. 16°. *New York*, [*author*], 1869.

——— Faith: a poem, in three parts. 118 pp. 12°. *Cincinnati, author*, 1856. s.

Lebeau (Jean). Chronique de Richard ii. xii pp. 1 l. 79 pp. 8°. *Paris, Verdière*, 1826.

[COLLECTION de chroniques nationales françaises, v. 25].

Leben und abentheuer von Surratt. *See* **Career** and adventures of J. H. Surratt.

Lebey de Batilly *or* **Lebeus Batillius** (Denis). Emblemata, a Iano Iac. Boisardo delineata, et a Theodoro de Bry sculpta, et nunc recens in lucem edita. 71 l. 65 pl. sm. 4°. *Francofurti ad Moenum*, 1596.

[*With* BOISSARD (Jean Jacques). Emblematum liber. 1593].

Le Boys de Guays (J. F. E.) The true system of religious philosophy, in letters to a man of the world disposed to believe. Translated from the French by John Murdock. 3d ed. revised and corrected by George Bush. 1st and 2d series. 259 pp. 12°. *Boston, O. Clapp*, 1857. s.

Le Brun (Charles). Dissertation sur un traité de C. Le Brun concernant le rapport de la physionomie humaine avec celle des animaux. 7 pp. 38 pl. fol. *Londres, J. Carpenter & fils*, 1827.

Leckie (Gould Francis). An historical research into the nature of the balance of power in Europe. ix, 371 pp. 8°. *London, Taylor & Hessey*, 1817.

Le Courtier (*Abbé* François Joseph). Le dimanche. xxxix, 419 pp. 8°. *Paris, auteur*, 1838. s.

Le Duc (A. L. Léouzon). *See* **Léouzon Le Duc**.

Lee (Benjamin, *M. D.*) Contributions to the pathology, diagnosis, and treatment of angular curvature of the spine. xii, 129 pp. 12°. *Philadelphia, Lippincott & co.* 1867.

Lee (Daisy, *pseudon?*) In self and out of self. 202 pp. 4 pl. 16°. *New York, Carlton & Porter*, 1867.

Lee (Edwin, *M. D.*) The effect of climate on tuberculous disease, etc. viii, 223 pp. 12°. *London, J. Churchill*, 1858. s.

Lee (*Mrs.* Eliza Buckminster). Naomi; or, Boston, two hundred years ago. vii, 448 pp. 16°. *Boston, Crosby & Nichols*, 1848.

Lee (Frances). False shame. 215 pp. 4 pl. 16°. *New York, Carlton & Porter*, [1866].

Lee (Henry W.) Cornelia [A. Lathrop]: or, the deaf mute. 72 pp. 1 portrait. 18°. *Rochester, D. Hoyt*, 1853. s.

Lee (Holme, *pseudon.*) *See* **Parr** (*Miss* Harriet).

Lee (*Mrs.* Jarena, *colored methodist*). Religious experience and journal, etc. 97 pp. 1 portrait. 8°. *Philadelphia, author*, 1849. s.

Lee (*Rev.* Samuel). Eschatology; or, the scripture doctrine of the coming of the Lord, the judgment, and the resurrection. xii, 267 pp. 12°. *Boston, J. E. Tilton*, 1859.

Lee (*Capt.* Thomas J.) A collection of tables and formulæ useful in surveying, geodesy, and practical astronomy, including elements for the projection of maps. 2d ed. xviii, 242 pp. 8°. *Washington, Taylor & Maury*, 1853.

Lee (*Miss* ——, *of Brooklyn*). Redesdale. By the author of "Grace Houghton's story." 147 pp. 1 pl. 16°. *Boston, E. P. Dutton & co.* 1869.

Leeds (Lewis W.) Lectures on ventilation; delivered in the Franklin institute, Philadelphia, 1866-67. 2 p. l. 60 pp. 8°. *New York, J. Wiley & son,* 1868.

Leem *or* **Leemius** (Knud). Beskrivelse over Finmarkens Lapper, deres tungemaal, levemaade, etc. med J. E. Gunneri anmaerkninger, og E. J. Jessen-s afhandling om de norske Finners og Lappers hedenske religion. 7 p. l. 20, 544 pp. 101 pl. 4°. *Kiöbenhavn, G. G. Salikath,* 1767.

Le Fanu (J. Sheridan). All in the dark. 2 v. vi, 299 pp; iv, 290 pp. 12°. *London, R. Bentley,* 1866.

Lefèbvre Laboulaye (Édouard René). *See* **Laboulaye.**

Lefèvre d'Étaples (Jacques). *See* **Faber.**

Le Gallois (Julien Jean César). Experiments on the principle of life, and particularly on the principle of the motions of the heart, and on the seat of this principle. Translated by N. C. and J. G. Nancrede. viii, 328 pp. 1 pl. 8°. *Philadelphia, M. Thomas,* 1813.

Legion; or, feigned excuses. [*anon.*]. 109 pp. 12°. *New York, Dana & co.* 1856. s.

Le Guay (G. *or* Claude). Alliances dv roy avec le Tvrc, et avtres: justifiées contre les calomnies des Espagnols et de leurs partisans. 8 p. l. 275 pp. 16°. *Paris, Tovssainct dv Bray,* 1526.

Le Hon (H.) Recherches sur les crinoïdes du terrain carbonifère de la Belgique. *See* **Koninck** (L. G. de) *and* **Le Hon.**

Le Houx (Jean). Les vaux-de-vire. *See* **Basselin** (Olivier) *and* **Le Houx.**

Leib (Charles). Nine months in the quartermaster's department; or, the chances for making a million. 200 pp. 12 pl. 12°. *Cincinnati, Moore, Wilstach, Keys & co.* 1862.

Leiden. *See* **Leyden.**

Leipziger repertorium der deutschen und ausländischen literatur. Unter mitwirkung der universität Leipzig herausgegeben von E. G. Gersdorf. 7er–13er jahrgang. v. 25–52. 28 v. 8°. *Leipzig, T. O. Weigel,* 1849–55. s.

[v. 1–24; v. 35, heft 5; and v. 39 wanting].

Leirado. *See* **La Barrera y Leirado.**

Le Keux (John, *engraver*). Memorials of Cambridge. *See* **Wright** (Thomas) *and* **Jones** (H. L.)

Le Maistre d'Anstaing (J.) Recherches sur l'histoire et l'architecture de l'église cathédrale de Notre-dame de Tournai. v. 2. 376 pp. 8°. *Tournai, Massart & Janssens,* 1843. s.

Lemmens *or* **Lemnius** (Levin). The secret miracles of nature. 398 pp. fol. *London,* 1658. s.

[Imperfect: title and p. l. wanting].

Lemniscvs historiarvm, narrationum, fabularum, ex Cicerone, Aulo Gellio, et aliis probatis auctoribus collectus. [*anon.*] 6 p. l. 204 pp. 24°. *Hardervici, E. Arnold,* 1645.

[*With* APHTHONIUS. Progymnasmata, etc. 1655].

Lemnius (Levin). *See* **Lemmens.**

Lemon (Mark). Up and down the London streets. 348 pp. [Illustrated]. 8°. *London, Chapman & Hall,* 1867.

Lemoyne (Toussaint Nicolas). *See* **Desessarts** (T. N. L.)

Lenfant (Jacques). New version of Matthew. *London,* 1819. *See* **Bible** (*English*).

Lennox (Mary). Ante bellum. Southern life as it was. [A novel]. 322 pp. 12°. *Philadelphia, Lippincott & co.* 1868.

Lenoir (Alexander). La franche-maçonnerie rendue à sa véritable origine, ou l'antiquité de la franche-maçonnerie prouvée par l'explication des mystères anciens et modernes. 302 pp. 9 pl. 4°. *Paris, Fournier,* 1814.

Lenz (Heinrich Friedrich Emil, *M.D.*) Magnetische beobachtungen. 4°. *St. Petersburg,* 1848.

[*In* MIDDENDORFF (A. T. von). Reise, etc. v. 1. theil 1].

Leo (Heinrich). Ferienschriften. Vermischte abhandlungen zur geschichte der deutschen und keltischen sprache. 2 pts. in 1 v. 251 pp; vi, 325 pp. 8°. *Halle, E. Anton,* 1847–52.

CONTENTS.

Th 1. Ueber das verhältniss der deutschen sprache zu den keltischen sprache.
Einige bemerkungen zu altdeutsch eigennamen.
Grammatik des manxischen dialectes.
Th 2. Grammatik der irischen sprache.

—— Die malbergische glosse, ein rest altkeltischer sprache und rechtsauffaszung. Beitrag zu den deutschen rechtsalterthümern. 2 pts. in 1 v. xii, 156 pp; 164 pp. 8°. *Halle, E. Anton,* 1842–45.

Leonard (Agnes). Vanquished. A novel. 392 pp. 12°. *New York, G. W. Carleton & co.* 1867.

Leonhard (Carl Cäsar von, *editor*). *See* **Neues** jahrbuch für mineralogie, etc.

Léouzon Le Duc (Louis Antoine). La Russie contemporaine. 2e éd. xiv, 440 pp. 16°. *Paris, L. Hachette & cie.* 1854.

Lepage du Pratz (——). The history of Louisiana; or, of the western parts of Virginia and Carolina. Translated from the French, with some notes. A new ed. 4 p. l. xxxvi, 387 pp. 2 maps. 8°. *London, T. Becket,* 1774.

Lepsius (Carl Richard). Das allgemeine linguistische alphabet. Grundsätze der übertragung fremder schriftsysteme und bisher noch ungeschriebener sprachen in europäische buchstaben. iv, 64 pp. 8°. *Berlin, W. Hertz,* 1855. s.

——— The same. Standard alphabet for reducing unwritten languages and foreign graphic systems to a uniform orthography in European letters. ix, 73 pp. 8°. *London, Seeleys,* 1855. s.

——— Inscriptiones umbricae et oscae quotquot adhuc repertae sunt omnes. Ad ectypa monumentorum a se confecta edidit. Commentationes. xv, 208 pp. 8°. *Lipsiæ, G. Wigand,* 1841. s.

——— Letters from Egypt, Ethiopia, and the peninsula of Sinai. With extracts from his chronology of the Egyptians, with reference to the exodus of the Israelites. Revised by the author. Translated by Leonora and Joanna B. Horner. 578 pp. 2 maps. 1 pl. 12°. *London, H. G. Bohn,* 1853.

Lerchenfeld (Gustav, *freiherr* von). Geschichte Bayerns unter könig Maximilian Joseph i. Mit besonder beziehung auf die entstehung der verfassungs-urkunde. xii, 416 pp. 1 l. 1 tab. 8°. *Berlin, Veit & co.* 1854. s.

Lerebours (Nicolas Marie Paymal). Excursions daguerriennes. Vues et monuments les plus remarquables du globe. 1 p. l. 9 pl. obl. 4°. *Paris, Lerebours, etc.* 1842. s.

Leroux de Lincy (Adrien Jean Victor). Hotel de Paris. *See* **Calliat** (Victor) *and* **Leroux de Lincy.**

Le Roy (Julien David). Rapport fait à l' académie royale des sciences, 1791, d' un mémoire important, de m. Blanc, sur la fabrication des armes de guerre, etc. 11 pp. 4°. *Paris, académie de sciences,* 1791. s.
[*With* TALLEYRAND-PERIGORD (C. M. de). Rapport sur l'instruction publique, 1791].

Lesbonax. Lesbonactes quæ supersunt. 8°. *Lipsiæ,* 1770.
[ORATORUM græcorum quæ supersunt. Ed. Reiske. v. 5. 8].

Lescure (P. de). Eux et elles. Histoire d'un scandale. 2e éd. vii, 137 pp. 12°. *Paris, Poulet-Malassis & De Broise,* 1860.

Lesdernier (Emily Pierpont de). *See* **De Lesdernier.**

Lesley (Joseph Peter). Man's origin and destiny, sketched from the platform of the sciences, in a course of lectures. Boston, 1865–66. iv, 381 pp. 8°. *Philadelphia, Lippincott & co.* 1868.

Leslie (*Rev.* Charles). A reply to a book entitul'd, Anguis flagellatus; or, a switch for the snake, [by J. Wyeth]: being a second defence; or, the third and last part of the snake in the grass—shewing that the quakers are plainly self-condemn'd in this their last answer. [*anon.*] 4 p. l. 381 pp. 12°. *London, C. Brome,* 1702.

——— A short and easy method with the deists: wherein the certainty of the christian religion is demonstrated by infallible proofs, etc. With a letter to a deist, etc. To which is prefixed a preface by the rev. W. Jones. 64 pp. 12°. *London, F. C. & J. Rivington,* 1819. s.

Leslie's (Frank) chimney corner. June, 1865, to Nov. 1868. v. 1–7. fol. *New York, F. Leslie,* 1865–68.

Leslie's (Frank) illustrated newspaper. March, 1865, to Sept. 1868. v. 20–26. fol. [*New York, F. Leslie,* 1865–68].

——— The same. Ilustracion americana de Frank Leslie. Oct. 1867, to Oct. 1868. v. 3–4. fol. *New York, F. Leslie,* 1867–68.

Leslie's (Frank) lady's magazine. Jan. 1866, to Dec. 1868. v. 18–23. sm. fol. *New York, F. Leslie,* 1866–68.

Leslie's (Frank) pleasant hours. Devoted to light and entertaining literature. Aug. 1866, to Jan. 1869. v. 1–5. 8°. *New York, F. Leslie,* 1866–69.

Leslie (*Mrs.* Madeline). Live and learn. 285 pp. 3 pl. 16°. *Boston, A. F. Graves,* 1868.
[WOODBINE series].

Leslie (*Rev.* William). General view of the agriculture in the counties of Nairn and Moray. viii, 526 pp. 1 tab. 1 col. map. 1 pl. 8°. *London,* 1811. s.
[GREAT BRITAIN: Board of agriculture].

Lesquereux (Léo). Catalogue des mousses de la Suisse. (Extract). 54 pp. 4°. *Neuchâtel, société des sciences nat.* 1844. s.

——— Quelques recherches sur les marais tourbeaux en général. 140 pp. 4°. *Neuchâtel, société des sciences nat.* 1844. s.

Lessing (Gotthold Ephraim, *editor*). Fragmente des Wolfenbüttelschen ungenannten. *See* **Reimarus** (H. S.)

Leto (Giulio Pomponio). [Grammaticæ compendium]. 40 l. 4°. *Venetiis, per Baptistam de Tortis,* 1484.
[*With* FILELFO (M.) Epistolare. 1489].

——— Romanæ historiæ compendium ab interitu Gordiani junioris vsque ad Iustinum iii. 16°. [*Geneva*], 1568.
[*In* VARII historiæ romanæ scriptores. v. 3].

Lette (Adolph). Ueber die verfassungszustände in Preussen. 2 p. l. 124 pp. 8°. *Berlin, F. Duncker*, 1857.

Letters to a school-boy. By his father. [*anon.*] 208 pp. 1 pl. 16°. *New York, Carlton & Porter*, 1867.

Lettres édifiantes et curieuses, écrites des missions étrangères par quelques missionaires de la compagnie de Jésus. [Recueilli par P. le Gobien]. Recueil 1—26 in 24 v. 16°. *Paris*, 1707-43.

[Recueil 27-34 wanting to complete this edition].

——— The same. De l'Amérique Septentrionale. 4 p. l. 152 pp. 16°. *Bruxelles, G. Pauwels*, 1771.

——— The same. Instructive and curious epistles from catholic clergymen of the society of Jesus, in China, India, Persia, the Levant, and either America; being selections [from] the "Lettres édifiantes." With appendix. Translated by rev. T. A. Power. xi, 373 pp. 16°. *Dublin, T. O'Gorman*, 1839.

——— *See, also,* **Association** de la propagation de la foi. Annales.

Lettsom (John Coakley). The naturalist's and traveller's companion, containing instructions for collecting and preserving objects of natural history, etc. 1 p. l. xvi, 89 pp. 4 l. 1 col. pl. 8°. *London, E. & C. Dilly*, 1774.

Letus (Pomponius). *See* **Leto** (Giulio Pomponio).

Le Vayer (François de la Mothe). *See* **La Mothe Le Vayer** (François de).

Leven ('t) van den waereld-beruchten kapitein der moordenaaren, Louis Dominique de Cartouche. Uit het Fransch vertaald. [*anon.*] 4 p. l. 116 pp. 8 pl. 18°. *Amsteldam, B. Koene*, 1773.

Lever (Charles). Maurice Tiernay, the soldier of fortune. 11th ed. 495 pp. 16°. *London, Chapman & Hall*, 1868.

——— Roland Cashel. 2 v. iv, 312 pp; 300 pp. 1 pl. 16°. *London, Chapman & Hall*, [1862].

——— Sir Jasper Carew, his life and experiences. 10th ed. 480 pp. 16°. *London, Chapman & Hall*, 1868.

Lévizac (Jean Pons Victor Lecoutz de). A theoretical and practical grammar of the French tongue. Revised and corrected by S. Pasquier. 7th Am. ed. x, 444 pp. 16°. *New York, Collins & co.* 1829.

Lewald (Fanny). Lake-house. Translated from the German, by Nathaniel Greene. 304, 16 pp. 12°. *Boston, Ticknor & Fields*, 1861.

Lewes (George Henry). The history of philosophy from Thales to Comte. 3d ed. 2 v. cxv, 407 pp; x, 663 pp. 8°. *London, Longmans*, 1867.

CONTENTS.

v. 1. Ancient philosophy. v. 2. Modern philosophy.

Lewins (William). A history of banks for savings in Great Britain and Ireland, including a full account of Gladstone's financial measures for post office banks, government annuities, and government life insurance. xvi, 445 pp. 8°. *London, S. Low, son & Marston*, [1866].

Lewis (Alonzo). The history of Lynn. 260 pp. 8°. *Boston, J. H. Eastburn*, 1829.

Lewis (*Rev.* David). Recollections of a superannuate; or, sketches of life, labor, and experience in the methodist itinerancy. Edited by rev. S. M. Merrill. 311 pp. 12°. *Cincinnati, author*, 1857. s.

Lewis (Dio, *M. D.*) The new gymnastics for men, women, and children. 10th ed. xi, 286 pp. 12°. *Boston, Ticknor & Fields*, 1868.

Lewis (*Mrs.* Estelle Anna). Child of the sea, and other poems. 179 pp. 12°. *New York, G. P. Putnam*, 1848. s.

Lewis (William H. *D. D.*) The interleaved book of family prayers. v, 39 pp. 18°. *Waterbury, (Conn.) Abbott & bros.* 1868.

Leyden (*Holland*). Mvsevm anatomicvm academiæ Lvgdvni-Batavae, descriptvm ab Edvardo Sandifort (t. 1-2; et) Gerardo Sandifort. 4 v. fol. *Lvgdvni-Batavorvm, S. & J. Lvchtmans*, 1793-1835. s.

Leydig (Franz). Anatomisch-histologische untersuchungen über fische und reptilien. vi, 120 pp. 4 pl. 4°. *Berlin, G. Reimer*, 1853. s.

——— Ueber die molche (salamandrina) der württembergischen fauna. [Extract]. iv, 120 pp. 3 pl. 8°. *Berlin, Nicolaische b.* 1868. s.

Lhomond (Charles François). Epitome historiæ sacræ, ad usum tyronum linguæ latinæ. Ed. 2a amer. 142 pp. 24°. *Philadelphia, J. F. Watson*, 1812.

——— The same. Epitome historiæ sacræ. Quam prosodiæ signis, novaque vocum omnium interpretatione, adornavit G. Ironside. Ed. 20. 156 pp. 24°. *Novi-Eboraci, G. Long*, 1842.

——— Viri illustres urbis Romæ, a Romulo ad Augustum. [With] a dictionary of all the words which occur in the book. By J. Hardie. vii, 136 pp. 66 l. 18°. *New York, G. Long*, 1835.

Libellus de modo cōfitendi et penitēdi. [*anon.*] 24 l. sm. 4°. *Antverpiae, G. Leeu*, 1486.

Liberty hall and Cincinnati gazette. [Weekly]. v. 14. June 9, 1818, to Mar. 2, 1819. New series. [Semi-weekly]. v. 1. Mar. 9, 1819, to Mar. 3, 1820. fol. *Cincinnati,* 1819–20.

——— The same. New series. v. 7–8. Jan. 3, 1826, to Feb. 23, 1827. fol. *Cincinnati,* 1826–27.

Libri-Carrucci (Guglielmo Bruto Icilio Timoleonte). Monuments inédits ou peu connus, faisant partie du cabinet de G. Libri, et qui se rapportent à l'histoire des arts de l'ornementation chez différents peuples. [French and English]. 2e éd. 2 p. l. 14 pp. 1 l. 65 pl. (a–e; 1–60). fol. *Londres,* 1864.

Lieber (Francis, *LL. D,*) An address on secession, delivered in South Carolina in 1851. 12 pp. 8°. *New York,* 1865.
[LOYAL publication society. No. 77].

——— Amendments of the constitution, submitted to the consideration of the American people. 39 pp. 8°. *New York,* 1865.
[LOYAL publication society. No. 83].

——— The arguments of secessionists. 7 pp. 8°. *New York, Holman,* 1863.
[LOYAL publication society. No. 35].

——— Letter to hon. E. D. Morgan, on the amendment of the constitution abolishing slavery. [With the] resolutions passed by the N. Y. union league club, concerning conditions of peace with the insurgents. 4 pp. 8°. *New York,* 1865.
[LOYAL publication society. No. 79].

——— Lincoln oder McClellan? 4 pp. 8°. *New York, H. Ludwig,* 1864.
[LOYAL publication society. No. 59].

——— The same. Lincoln of McClellan. [Dutch]. 4 pp. 8°. *New York,* 1865.
[LOYAL publication society. No. 71].

——— The same. Lincoln or McClellan. From the German, by T. C. 8 pp. 8°. *New York,* 1865.
[LOYAL publication society. No. 67].

——— No party now, but all for our country. 8 pp. 8°. *New York,* 1864.
[LOYAL publication society. No. 16].

——— Slavery, plantations, and the yeomanry. 8 pp. 8°. *New York,* 1863.
[LOYAL publication society. No. 29].

Life and its aims; in two parts. Ideal life, Actual life. [*anon.*] 362 pp. 12°. *Philadelphia, Lippincott, Grambo & co.* 1854. s.

Life among the Mormons, and a march to their Zion: [with] a chapter on the Indians of the west. By an officer of the U. S. army. [*anon.*] xv, 219 pp. 4 pl. 12°. *New York, Moorhead, Simpson & Bond,* 1868.

Life below. In seven poems. [*anon.*] 286 pp. 16°. *New York, Hurd & Houghton,* 1868.

Life (The), campaigns, and battles of general Ulysses S. Grant. With introduction by B. J. Lossing. [*anon.*] 502 pp. 5 pl. 8°. *New York, L. Bill,* 1868.

Life (The) of Hannah More. With a critical review of her writings. By the rev. sir Archibald Mac Sarcasm, bart. [*pseudon.*] viii, 208 pp. 8°. *London, T. Hurst,* 1802.

Life in the itinerancy, in its relations to the circuit and station, and to the minister's home and family. [*anon.*] 335 pp. 12°. *New York and Auburn, Miller, Orton & Mulligan,* 1856. s.

Life (The) of Lamenther: a true history. Written by herself. [*pseudon.*] vii, 221 pp. 8°. *London, for the proprietor,* 1771.

Life in New York, in doors and out of doors. With 40 engravings, by W. Burns. [*anon.*] 48 l. 8°. *New York, Bruce & bro.* 1851.

Life (The) of St. Aloysius Gonzaga. [Based on the work of Virgilio Cepari. [*anon.*] 393 pp. portrait. 12°. *Philadelphia, P. F. Cunningham,* 1867.

Life (The) and times of hon. Schuyler Colfax, comprising an authentic account of the life and public services of this distinguished orator, patriot, and statesman. [*anon.*] 50 pp. 1 pl. 12°. *New York, E. B. Treat & co.* [1868].

Life (The) and travels of Thomas Thumb, [Charles S. Stratton], in the United States, England, France, and Belgium. [*anon.*] 144 pp. 7 pl. sq. 16°. *Philadelphia, Lindsay & Blakiston,* 1849. s.

Life (The) of William iii, late king of England, and prince of Orange. [*anon.*] 3 p. l. 701 pp. 12°. *London, S. & J. Sprint,* 1703.
[Title-page imperfect].

Life (The), writings, opinions, and times of lord Byron. [With] copious recollections of the lately destroyed ms, originally intended for posthumous publication, and entitled Memoirs of my own life and times, by lord Byron. By an English gentlemen, in the Greek military service, and comrade of his lordship. [*anon.*] 3 v. 8°. *London, M. Iley,* 1825.

Life's changes, By E. L. A. [*anon.*] 174 pp. 1 pl. 18° *Boston, Mass, s. s. society,* [1867].

Life's lottery; or, life and its aims. 362 pp. 12°. *Philadelphia, Claxton, Remsen, & Haffelfinger,* 1869.

Liggins (*Rev.* John, *editor*). The oriental picture gallery; or, illustrations from India, China, and Japan. With explanatory remarks, and missionary information. 32 pp. 4°. *New York, Hurd & Houghton,* 1867.

Lights and shadows of domestic life, and other stories. [*anon.*] 2 p. l. 267 pp. 12°. *Boston, Ticknor, Reed & Fields*, 1850. s.

Ligon (Richard). Histoire de l'isle des Barbades. Traduit de l'Anglois. 4 p. l. 204 pp. 2 maps. 12 pl. 4°. *Paris, veuve A. Cellier*, 1684.

[*In* RECUEIL de divers voyages en Afrique et en l'Amérique. éd. 1684].

Liguori (Alfonso). Die herrlichkeiten Maria's. Aus dem Italianischen übersetzt. Herausgegeben von der versammlung der allerheiligsten erlösers. 1e Am. ausg. 754 pp. 1 pl. 16°. *Baltimore, J. Murphy & co.* 1852. s.

Lilljeborg (Wilhelm). Synopsis of the cetaceous mammalia of Scandinavia (Sweden and Norway). Translated from the Swedish, with additions and corrections, by the author. 4°. *London*, 1866.

[RAY society: *In* FLOWER (W. H.) Recent memoirs on the cetacea. pp. 219-309].

Lily. A novel. By the author of "The busy moments of an idle woman". [*anon.*] 330 pp. 12°. *New York, Harpers*, 1855.

Lincoln (Enoch). Remarks on the Indian languages [of Maine]. 8°. *Portland, Day, Fraser & co.* 1831.

[*In* MAINE historical society. Collections. v. 1].

——— Some account of the catholic missions in Maine. 8°. *Portland, Day, Fraser & co.* 1831.

[*In* MAINE historical society. Collections. v. 1].

Lincoln's anecdotes. A complete collection of the anecdotes, stories, and pithy sayings of the late Abraham Lincoln, 16th president of the U. S. 63 pp. sm. 4°. *New York*, 1868.

L'inconnue. [*pseudon*]. *See* **Kernwood.**

Lincy (Leroux de). *See* **Leroux de Lincy.**

Linda (Luca da). Estratto delle relazioni e descrizioni universali e particolari del mondo. (Corografie dell' Istria, n. 6). 8°. *Trieste*, 1830.

[*In* ROSSETTI (D. de) Archeografo triestino. v. 2].

Lindley (Thomas). Narrative of a voyage to Brazil. With general sketches of the country, its productions, inhabitants, [etc.] xvi, 297 pp. 8°. *London, J. Johnson*, 1805.

Link, and other stories. By cousin Zilpha. [*pseudon.* C. A. G.] 136 pp. 4 pl. 18°. *Boston, American tract society*, 1868.

Linné (Carl von). Fundamentorum botanicorum pars prima [et] pars secunda. 3 v. 8°. *Coloniæ Allobrogum, Piestre & Delamolliere*, 1786-87.

[*In* GILIBERT (J. E.) C. Linnæi systema plantarum Europæ, etc. v. 5-7].

Linné—continued.

CONTENTS.

v. 1-2. Fundamentorum botanicorum pars i, exhibens omnes dissertationes academicas, quæ varios aphorismos philosophiæ botanicæ illustrare possunt. 2 p. l. lxxvi, 604 pp. 2 l. 1 tab. 3 pl; 2 p. l. 732 pp. 2 pl.

v. 3. Fundamentorum pars ii, exhibens 1°. Dissertationem de vita et meritis Linnæi in re herbaria. 2°. Philosophiam botanicam. 3°. Criticam botanicam. 2 p. l. xxxii pp. 2 l. 594 pp. 2 l.

[v. 1 imperfect, wanting pp. 49-64].

——— Genera plantarum Europæ. 8°. *Coloniæ Allobrogum*, 1786.

[*In* GILIBERT (J. E.) C. Linnaei systema plantarum Europæ, etc. v. 2].

——— Kortbegrip van het zamenstel der natuur, met zeer veele zoorten vermeerdert door P. Boddaert. (Mammalia, Aves). c, 439 pp. 8°. *Amsterdam, D. Schuurman*, 1783. s.

——— Species plantarum Europæ. 8°. *Coloniæ Allobrogum*, 1786.

[*In* GILIBERT (J. E.) C. Linnaei systema plantarum Europæ, etc. v. 3-4].

——— [Systema naturæ]. Des vollständiges natursystem nach der zwölften lateinischen ausgabe, und nach anleitung des holländischen houttuynischen werks, mit einer ausführlichen erklärung, ausgefertiget von Philipp Ludwig Statius Müller. 6 v. in 8. 8°. Atlas. obl. 4°. *Nürnberg, G. N. Raspe*, 1773-76. s.

CONTENTS.

1r theil. Von den säugenden thieren. 12 p. l. 508 pp. 7 l. 32 pl. 1773.

2r theil. Von den vögeln. 8 p. l. 638 pp. 16 l. 28 pl. 1773.

3r theil. Von den amphibien. 350 pp. 8 l. 1774.

4r theil. Von den fischen. 8 p. l. 400 pp. 8 l. 11 pl. 1774.

5r theil. Von den insecten. 1 v. in 2. 7 p. l. 758 pp; 7 p. l. pp. 761-1166. 51 l. 36 p. l. 1774-75.

6r theil. Von den würmern. 1 v. in 2. 8 p. l. 638 pp; 8 p. l. pp. 641-960. 55 l. 37 pl. 1775.

——— The same. Des vollständigen natursystems supplements- und registerband über alle sechs theile oder classen des thierreichs, [etc.] Von P. L. S. Müller. 8 p. l. 384 pp; 20 p. l. 536 pp. 8°. 3 pl. 4°. *Nürnberg, G. N. Raspe*, 1776. s.

——— The same. Des vollständigen natursystems fortsetzung, nach der dreizehnten lateinischen ausgabe, mit ausführlicher erklärung, [etc.] Von dr. Johann Wolf. 1r-2r theil. Saugethiere. 2 v. xvi, 352 pp. 18 pl; xii, 627 pp. 20 pl. 8°. *Nürnberg, Raspe*, 1796-1808. s.

——— Systema plantarum Europæ. *See* **Gilibert (J. E.)**

Linné (Carl von, *the son*). Supplementum plantarum europæarum, [etc.] 8°. *Coloniæ Allobrogum*, 1786.

[*In* GILIBERT (J. E.) C. Linnæi systema plantarum Europæ, etc. v. 4].

Linton (W. J.) The flower and the star, and other stories for children. Illustrated. 120 pp. 12°. *Boston, Ticknor & Fields,* 1868.

Lippincott (*Mrs.* Sara Jane). Haps and mishaps of a tour in Europe. By Grace Greenwood. [*pseudon.*] xii, 437 pp. 12°. *Boston, Ticknor, Reed & Fields,* 1854.

——— Stories and legends of travel and history, for children. By Grace Greenwood. [*pseudon.*] 290 pp. 12°. *Boston, Ticknor & Fields,* 1857. s.

Lippincott's magazine of literature, science and education. Jan. to Dec. 1868. v. 1–2. 8°. *Philadelphia, J. B. Lippincott & co.* 1868.

Lippitt (Francis J.) The special operations of war. iv, 126 pp. 12°. *Providence, S. S. Rider & bro.* 1868.

Literary (The) souvenir; or, a cabinet of poetry and romance. 1825–37. Edited by A. A. Watts. [Illustrated]. 12°. *London, Whittaker & co. etc.* 1825–37.

Lithgow (William). The totall discourse of the rare adventures, and painful peregrinations of long nineteene yeares trauayles, from Scotland, to the most famous kingdomes in Europe, Asia, and Affrica. [3[d] ed.] 7 p. l. 507 pp. 2 l. 1 pl. 4°. *London, N. Okes,* 1632.
[Imperfect: pp. 363–366 wanting].

Little (Otis). The state of trade in the northern colonies; with a description of Nova Scotia. 84 pp. 8°. *London, G. Woodfall,* 1748.

Little Lou's sayings and doings. [*anon.*] 287 pp. 8 pl. sm. 4°. *New York, Hurd & Houghton,* 1868.

Little sheaves. By Christie Pearl. [*pseudon.*] 254 pp. 3 pl. 18°. *Boston, American tract society,* 1867.

Little (The) Spaniard; or, old José's grandson. By May Mannering. [*pseudon.*] 221 pp. 4 pl. 12°. *Boston, Lee & Shepard,* 1869.
[HELPING-HAND series].

Livermore (Harriet). A narration of religious experience. In twelve letters. v. 1. 282 pp. 18°. *Concord, J. B. Moore,* 1826.

Livingston (Edward). An answer to mr. Jefferson's justification of his conduct in the case of the New Orleans batture. xi, 187 pp. 2 pl. 8°. *Philadelphia, W. Fry,* 1813.

Livingston (John, *lawyer*). The United States lawyer's directory and official bulletin for 1850; together with the manual of the American legal association. vii, 144, 31 pp. 8°. *New York, J. Livingston,* 1850. s.

——— The same. The law register, state record, [and] official directory for the United States. 1038 pp. 8°. *New York, merchants' union law co.* [1868].

Livingston (*Mrs.* O. M.) Poems. viii, 242 pp. 16°. *Cambridge, Riverside press,* 1868.

——— The same. viii, 242 pp. 12°. *New York, Hurd & Houghton,* 1868.

Lizars (John, *M. D.*) Anatomy of the brain, from the celebrated dissections of John Lizars, comprising 15 engravings (colored) after nature, with accompanying explanations. Edited by Landon Rives. 16 l. 15 col. pl. fol. *Cincinnati, H. W. Derby,* 1854. s.

Llewellyn (E. L.) The deserted mill; or, the reward of industry. 246 pp. 2 pl. 16°. *Philadelphia, J. Hamilton,* 1867.

Lloyd (Thomas). Congressional register. *See* **United States.**

Löbe (William, *editor*). *See* **Illustrirte** landwirthschaftliche dorfzeitung. 1855–60.

Löbell (Johann Wilhelm). Gregor von Tours und seine zeit, vornehmlich aus seinen werken geschildert. Ein beiträg zur geschichte der entstehung und ersten entwickelung romanisch-germanischer verhältnisse. x, 568 pp. 1 tab. 8°. *Leipzig, F. A. Brockhaus,* 1839.

Lobo (Jeronymo). Relation de la rivière du Nil, de sa source et de son cours. [*anon.* Traduite de la Portugaise en l'Anglois par P. Wyche]. 4°. *Paris, veuve A. Cellier,* 1864.
[*In* RECUEIL de divers voyages en Afrique et en l'Amérique. ed. 1684. pp. 205–252].

——— Voyage historique d'Abissinie. Traduite du Portugais, et augmentée par Le Grand. 4°. *Paris,* 1728.

Locke (D. R.) Ekkoes from Kentucky. By Petroleum V. Nasby. [*pseudon.*] Illustrated by T. Nast. 324 pp. 8 pl. 12°. *Boston, Lee & Shepard,* 1868.

——— The impendin crisis uv the dimocracy, bein a breef and concise statement uv the past experience, etc. uv the dimokratic party. By Petroleum V. Nasby. [*pseudon.*] 23 pp. 12°. *Toledo, (Ohio), Miller, Locke & co.* 1868.

Locker (Frederic, *editor*). *See* **Lyra** elegantiarum.

Locmán. *See* **Lokmán.**

Lodbrok. *See* **Krakas** maal, etc.

Loebe. *See* **Löbe.**

Loebell. *See* **Löbell.**

Loehr. *See* **Löhr.**

Loew. *See* **Löw.**

Lofft (Capel). Laura; or, an anthology of sonnets, (on the Petrarcan model), and elegaic quatuorzains; English, Italian, Spanish, Portuguese, French and German; original and translated. With a preface, critical and biographic, notes and index. 5 v. 16°. *London, B. R. Crosby & co.* 1813–14.

Logan (Eliza). The Italian bride. A play, in five acts. 132 pp. 12°. *Savannah, J.M. Cooper & co. (for private distribution)*, 1856. s.

Logan (*Capt.* John). Analogia honorum; or, a treatise of honour and nobility according to the laws and customs of England. fol. *London*, 1724.

[*In* GUILLIM (J.) Display of heraldry. ed. 1724. pp. 57-275. 63 pl].

——— The same. Second part of honour civil; treating of the customs, government, privileges, armorial ensigns of honour of the city of London, [and other cities of England]. 30 pp. fol. *London*, 1724.

[*In* GUILLIM (J.) Display of heraldry. ed. 1724].

——— Dictionary explaining the several terms used by heralds, in English, Latin and French, with their etymologies, derivations, etc. fol. *London*, 1724.

[*In* GUILLIM (J.) Display of heraldry. ed. 1724].

Logan (Olive). Chateau Frissac; or, home scenes in France. By Chroniqueuse. [*pseudon.*] viii, 327 pp. 12°. *London, Tinsley bros.* 1862.

——— The same. viii, 329 pp. 12°. *New York, Appletons*, 1865.

——— Photographs of Paris life; being a record of the politics, art, fashion, and anecdote of Paris, during the past eighteen months. By Chroniqueuse. [*pseudon.*] 2[d] ed. xv, 344 pp. 16°. *London, Tinsley bros.* 1862.

Löhr (Matthias Joseph). Enumeratio der flora von Deutschland und der angrenzenden länder im ganzen umfange von Reichenbach's Flora germanica excursoria, vom Mittelländischen meere bis zur Nord- und Ost-see. Geordnet nach dem natürlichen systeme von De Candolle und der reihenfolge von Koch's Synopsis, mit allen synonymen, varietäten und fundorten, unter besonderer berücksichtigung der gegenden am Rheine. xxi, 820 pp. 16°. *Braunschweig, F. Vieweg & sohn*, 1852. s.

Lokmán. Fables. Édition arabe, avec une traduction française et accompagnée de remarques et d'un vocabulaire arabe-français. Par C. Schier. 57, 16 pp. 8°. *Dresde, Arnold*, 1831.

——— The same. Fabvlæ et adagia quædam Arabvm, ab Erpenio cum latina versione pridem edita; at nunc notis, etc. illustrata. 126 pp. sm. 4°. *Amstelodami, I. Ianson*, 1636.

[*With* VAN ERPE (T.) Grammatica arabica. *Amstelodami*, 1636].

London (Thomas Sherlock, *bishop of*). *See* **Sherlock**.

London (Royal geographical society of). Proceedings. Session 1866-67. Edited by H. W. Bates. v. ii. nos. i-vi. 8°. *London*, 1867.

——— Journal. v. 37. 1867. 8°. *London, J. Murray*, 1868.

London (Royal society of). Catalogue of scientific papers. (1800–1863). Compiled and published by the Royal society of London. v. 1. A.—Clu. 4°. *London, stationery office*, 1867.

London (University college). Calendar. Sessions 1867–68 [and] 1868–69. 2 v. 8°. *London, J. Walton*, [1867–68]. s.

London (The), Edinburgh, and Dublin philosophical magazine and journal of science. July, 1867—June, 1868. 4th series. v. 24–26. 8°. *London, Taylor & Francis*, 1867–68.

London (The) encyclopædia, or universal dictionary of science, art, literature, and practical mechanics, comprising a popular view of the present state of knowledge. [Edited by rev. E. Smedley]? 22 v. 8°. *London, T. Tegg*, 1845.

London (The) geological journal, and record of discoveries in British and foreign palæontology. Nos. 1–3. Sept. 1846, Feb. and May, 1847. 132 pp. 23 pl. 8°. *London, J. Churchill*, 1846–47. s.

London (The) magazine: or, gentlemans' monthly intelligencer. April, 1732, to June, 1785. 54 v. in 53. 8°. *London, R. Baldwin*, 1732–85.

——— The same. The general index to twenty-seven volumes; 1732–58 inclusive. 280 l. 8°. *London, R. Baldwin*, 1760.

London orphan asylum for the reception of destitute orphans, etc. List of life and annual subscribers. 37–221 pp. 12°. *London*, 1840. s.

London times. *See* **Times** (The).

Longchamp (—, *M. D.*) La révolution du Paraguay. *See* **Rengger** (A.) *and* **Longchamp**.

Longfellow (Henry Wadsworth). The New England tragedies. i. John Endicott. ii. Giles Corey of the Salem farms. 179 pp. 16°. *Boston, Ticknor & Fields*, 1868.

Long Island (*New York*). Curtin's directory. With a business directory of patrons. 1868-69. 411 pp. 8°. *New York, D. Curtin*, 1868.

Longley (Elias). Furst fōnetic redur. [*anon.*] Furst ed. 72 pp. 16°. *Sinsinati, Lonjli & brudur*, 1850. s.

Loomis (Alfred L. *M. D.*) Lessons in physical diagnosis. [Illustrated]. 159 pp. 8°. *New York, R. M. De Witt*, 1868.

Loomis (Elias, *LL. D.*) A treatise on algebra. Revised ed. 384 pp. 8°. *New York, Harpers*, 1868.

Loomis (E.) A treatise on meteorology. With a collection of meteorological tables. 305 pp. 3 pl. 8°. *New York, Harpers,* 1868.

Loomis (William Isaacs). Incidents and facts in my life. 36 pp. 8°. *New York, Holman,* 1867. s.

Loosjes Petruszoon (Adriaan). Gedenzuil ter gelegenheid der vry-verklaaring van Noord-America. [Met eene] beknopte historie van de Vereenigde Staaten, [en] bylaagen. 6 p. l. 64, 176 pp. 8°. *Amsterdam, W. Holtrop,* 1782.

Lopez de Mendoza (Iñigo). Memorial de cosas notables. 10 p. l. 454 pp. 17 l. 4°. *Guadalajara, F. de Corruellas & P. de Robles,* 1564.

[NOTE.—Title supplied in ms.]

Loqmán. *See* **Lokmán.**

Lord (John, *LL. D.*) The old Roman world, the grandeur and failure of its civilization. 2d ed. 605 pp. 8°. *New York, C. Scribner & co.* 1868.

Lorenzana (Francisco Antonio, *editor*). *See* **Cortés** (F.) Historia de Nueva-España. *Mexico,* 1770.

Lorenzo (Corvini). Dell' innesto nella peripneumonia o pulmonera de' bovini memoria. xxxii, 198 pp. 8°. *Milano, i. r. istituto lombardo, etc.* 1856. s.

Lorn (John Douglas Sutherland Campbell, *marquess of*). *See* **Campbell** (John D. S.)

Lorrain (Alfred M.) The square-rigged cruiser; or, Lorrain's sea sermons, [etc.] 252 pp. 16°. *Cincinnati, author,* 1851. s.

Lorris (Guillaume de), *and* **Meun** *or* **Meung** (Jean de, *dit* Clopinel). Le roman de la rose. Accompagné de plusieurs autres ouvrages, [etc.] 4 v. 16°. *Amsterdam, J. F. Bernard,* 1735. s.

Lossing (Benson J.) The home of Washington and its associations, historical, biographical, and pictorial. [2d ed.] 376 pp. 8°. *New York, W. A. Townsend,* 1866.

——— Pictorial history of the civil war in the United States of America. v. 2–3. 8°. *Hartford, T. Belknap,* 1868.

——— A pictorial history of the United States. Illustrated by Lossing and Barritt. 778 pp. 31 pl. 8°. *Hartford, T. Belknap,* 1867.

Lost but found; or, the Jewish home. [By] Aunt Hattie. [*pseudon.*] 279 pp. 3 pl. 16°. *Boston, Graves & Young,* 1868.

Lott (Emmeline). The mohaddetyn in the palace. Nights in the harem; or the mohaddetyn in the palace of Ghezire. 2 v. 3 p. l. 308 pp; 350 pp. 12°. *London, Chapman & Hall,* 1867.

Loudon (*Mrs.* Margracia). The light of mental science; being an essay on moral training. viii, 127 pp. 12°. *London, Smith, Elder & co.* 1845.

Louisiana (*State of*). Documents of the third legislature of the state, session of 1856. 8°. *Baton Rouge, Advocate steam press print,* 1856. s.

Louvre (Musée nationale du). *See* **Musée** nationale de Louvre.

Lovejoy (*Rev.* James C.) Memoir of rev. Charles T. Torrey, who died in the penitentiary of Maryland, where he was confined for showing mercy to the poor. viii, 364 pp. 1 portrait. 12°. *Boston, J. P. Jewett & co.* 1847.

Lovers' (The) dictionary: a poetical treasury of lovers' thoughts, fancies, addresses, and dilemmas. By J. H. [*anon.*] xxxvi, 789 pp. 2 pl. 12°. *New York, Harpers,* 1867.

Löw (Hermann). Diptera [von Mossambique]. fol. *Berlin,* 1862.

[*In* PETERS (W. C. H.) Nat. reise nach Mossambique. v. 5].

——— Die dipteren-fauna Süd-Afrika's. 1e abtheilung. (Aus abhandl. des nat. vereins für Sachsen und Thüringen in Halle). xi, 330 pp. 2 pl. 4°. *Berlin, G Bosselmann,* 1860. s.

Lowe (Robert). General view of the agriculture of the county of Nottingham. xii, 192 pp. 1 col. map. 8°. *London,* 1798. s.

[GREAT BRITAIN: Board of agriculture].

Lowe (Robert, *M. P.*) Primary and classical education. An address delivered before the philosophical institution of Edinburgh, Nov. 1, 1867. Revised. 32 pp. 8°. *Edinburgh, Edmonston & Douglas,* 1867.

Lowell (James Russell). Fireside travels. 4 p. l. 324 pp. 12°. *Boston, Ticknor & Fields,* 1864.

——— Under the willows, and other poems. 286 pp. 12°. *Boston, Fields, Osgood & co.* 1869.

Lowell (*Massachusetts*) city library. Catalogue. 412 pp. 8°. *Lowell, Stone & Huse,* 1861. s.

——— ——— Annual report of the directors for the year 1861. 7 pp. 8°. *Lowell, city,* [1861]. s.

[*With their* Catalogue. 1861].

Lowell (The) directory for 1851. By George Adams. 240 pp. 18°. *Lowell, O. March,* 1851. s.

——— The same. The Lowell directory, 1868. By Sampson, Davenport & co. 420 pp. 8°. *Lowell, J. Merrill & son,* 1868.

Lowrie (John M. *D. D.*) The translated prophet. [A biography of Elijah]. 320 pp. portrait. 12°. *Philadelphia, presbyterian board of publication,* 1868.

Lowry (*Rev.* Robert). Chapel melodies. *See* **Vail** (S. J.) *and* **Lowry.**

Lowth (Robert, *bishop of Oxford*). A short introduction to English grammar. With critical notes. xii, 132 pp. 18°. *Philadelphia, R. Aitken,* 1775.

Loyal national league of New York. Address to A. Gasparin, E. Laboulaye, etc. friends of America in France. By Jas. McKaye. 8°. *New York,* 1863.

[LOYAL publication society. No. 42. pp. 17-26].

——— Address to the people of the State of New York. Convention at Utica, Oct. 20, 1863. 4 pp. 8°. *New York,* 1863.

[LOYAL publication society. No. 31].

Loyal publication society. Publications. 89 nos. in 3 v. 8°. *New York,* 1863-66.

CONTENTS.

ALEXANDER (William). Elements of discord in secessia. No. 15.
ANDERSON (*Col.* Charles). The cause of the war. No. 17.
——— Letter to the opera-house meeting, Cincinnati. No. 21.
ARTHUR (Timothy S.) Growler's income tax. No. 57.
BRISTED (Charles A.) The cowards' convention. No. 68.
BROOKS (Charles). Reasons for a national system of education. No. 86.
BROOM (W. W.) Crimes of the South. No. 84.
BUTLER (B. F.) Character and results of the war. Speech, 1863. No. 7.
BUTLER (Geo. B.) The conscription act. No. 40.
CHASE (S. P.) Speech in the peace conference, 1861. No. 37.
COOPER (Peter). The death of slavery. Letter to gov. Seymour. No. 28.
——— Letter on slave emancipation. To president Lincoln. No. 23.
DRISLER (Henry). Reply to the bible view of slavery, by bishop Hopkins. No. 39.
ECHO from the army. What our soldiers say about the copperheads. No. 2.
EDGE (Frederick M.) McClellan and the campaign on the peninsula. No. 81.
——— Whom do English tories wish elected to the presidency? No. 69.
EVERETT (Edward). The Monroe doctrine. No. 34.
FEW (A) words in behalf of the loyal women of the United States. No. 10.
FRANSIOLI (*Rev.* Jos.) Patriotism, a christian virtue. A sermon. No. 24.
GANTT (E. W.) Address in favor of reunion, in 1863. No. 36, part 2.
GASPARIN (A E. *comte* de). Reconstruction. No. 87.
——— *and others.* Réponse à la ligue loyale et nationale de New York. No. 41.
——— The same. English translation. No. 42.
——— The same. German translation. No. 43.
GREAT (The) mass-meeting of loyal citizens, New York, March 6, 1863. Speeches of Brady, Van Buren, etc. No. 3.
HAMILTON (A. J.) Letter to the president on the colored race. No. 26.
HAMILTON (J. A.) The constitution vindicated. No. 50.
HAMILTON (J. C.) Coercion completed; or, treason triumphant. No. 66.
——— The slave power, its heresies and injuries to the American people. No. 74.
HEERMANS (J.) War power of the president. No. 32.
HOW the South rejected compromise in the peace conference of 1861. No. 37.

Loyal—continued.

HOW the war was commenc'd. An appeal to the documents. No. 46.
——— The same. German translation. No. 53.
JAY (John). The great issue. An address. No. 75.
KELLEY (W. D.) The practice of justice our only security for the future. No. 82.
LABOULAYE (Édouard R. L.) Separation: war without end. No. 8.
LANG (*Rev.* J.) Results of the serf emancipation in Russia. No. 47.
LIEBER (F. *LL. D.*) An address on secession in S. C. in 1851. No. 77.
——— Amendments of the constitution. No. 83.
——— The arguments of secessionists. No. 35.
——— Letter to E. D. Morgan, on the amendment of the constitution abolishing slavery. No. 79.
——— Lincoln oder McClellan. No. 59.
——— The same. Dutch translation. No. 71.
——— The same. English translation. No. 67.
——— No party now, but all for our country. No. 16.
——— Slavery, plantations, and the yeomanry. No. 29.
LOYAL national league of N. Y. Address to A. de Gasparin, etc. No. 42.
——— Address to the people of the state, 1863. No. 31.
LOYAL publication society. Proceedings. First anniversary meeting, 1864. No. 44.
——— The same. Second anniversary, 1865. No. 78.
——— The same. Third anniversary, 1866. No. 89.
MCKAYE (James). The mastership and its fruits. No. 58.
——— The same. German translation. No. 55.
MEAGHER (Thos. F.) Letters on our national struggle, to Ireland. No. 38.
MILITARY despotism. Suspension of the habeas corpus, etc. No. 20.
NARRATIVE of privations and sufferings of United States officers and soldiers, while prisoners of war in the hands of rebel authorities. No. 76.
NEWMAN (L. C.) The bible view of slavery reconsidered. No. 39.
NORDHOFF (Charles). America for free working men. No. 80.
NORTHERN true men and southern traitors. No. 6.
OPINIONS of the early presidents, and of the fathers of the republic, upon slavery, and upon negroes as men and soldiers. No. 18.
OWEN (Robert Dale). The conditions of reconstruction. No. 25.
——— Emancipation is peace. No. 22.
——— The future of the north-west. No. 1.
PELLETAN (Eugène). An address to king cotton. No. 12.
PRESERVATION (The) of the union a national economic necessity. No. 14.
PUTNAM (G. P.) Letters from Europe touching the American contest. No. 70.
——— Soldiers' and sailors' patriotic songs. No. 49.
RAFTER (Hermann). Einheit und freiheit. No. 19.
REBEL conditions of peace, and the mechanics of the South. No. 30.
RUGGLES (S. B.) Resources of the U. S. No. 48.
SCHÜTZ (F.) and WEIL VON GERNSBACH (——). Für die freiheit aller! Für die einheit des vaterlandes. Reden in Phila. 1864. No. 72.
SMITH (Gerrit). McClellan's nomination and acceptance. No. 63.
STEBBINS (H. G.) Finances and resources of the United States. A speech. No. 45.
STEPHENS (A. H.) Speech in opposition to secession in 1860. No. 36, part 1.
——— Speeches in Georgia, Nov. 1860, Jan. 1861. No. 56.
STEVENS (J. A.) Letters of loyal soldiers. No. 64.
——— Sherman vs. Hood, etc. No. 61.
——— The submissionists and their record. No. 65.
STILLÉ (Chas. J.) How a free people conduct a long war. No. 13.
SUMNER (Charles). No property in man. A speech. No. 51.
SWINTON (William). The war for the union. No. 62.
TAYLOR (N. G.) Relief for East Tennessee. An address. No. 73.
THOMPSON (J. P. *D. D.*) Abraham Lincoln: his life and its lessons. No. 85.
——— Memorial service for three hundred thousand soldiers. No. 88.
——— Peace through victory. No. 60.

Loyal—continued.

THREE (The) voices: the soldier, farmer, and poet, to the copperheads. No. 4.
TWO (The) ways of treason. No. 33.
UPHAM (N. G.) Rebellion, slavery, and peace. An address. No. 52.
VENOM (The) and the antidote. Copperhead declarations: soldiers' letters. No. 9.
VOICES from the army. The soldiers open their batteries on the copperheads. No. 5.
WAYLAND (F. *jr.*) No failure for the North. No. 11.
WELLS (D. A.) Our burden and our strength. No. 54.
WILLIAMS (J. M.) Nullification and compromise: a retrospective view. No. 27.

——— Proceedings at the first anniversary meeting, Feb. 13, 1864, with the annual reports. 24 pp. 8°. *New York*, 1864.
[LOYAL publication society. no. 44].

——— The same. Second anniversary, Feb. 11, 1865. 30 pp. 8°. *New York*, 1868.
[LOYAL publication society. no. 78].

——— The same. Third anniversary, Feb. 27, 1866. Final report and address of the president. 13 pp. 8°. *New York*, 1866.
[LOYAL publication society. no. 89].

Lubbock (*Sir* John, *bart.*) Prehistoric times, as illustrated by ancient remains, and the manners and customs of modern savages. xxiii, 512 pp. 4 pl. 8°. *London, Williams & Norgate*, 1865.

Lubin (Augustin). Tabulæ sacræ geographicæ, etc. 4°. *Antverpiæ, J. B. Verdussen*, 1715. s.
[*With* BIBLE. (*Latin*). Biblia sacra vulgatæ editionis. 4°. *Antverpiæ*, 1715].

Lübke (Wilhelm). History of art. Translated [from the German] by F. E. Bunnett. 2 v. xvi, 466 pp; xi, 473 pp. 8°. *London, Smith, Elder & co.* 1868.

Luby (M. D. C.) New American epic poem on the discovery of America by Christopher Columbus. vii, 253 pp. 18°. *Saint Paul, (Minn.) Daily Minnesota volksblatt print*, 1868.

Lucanus (Marcus Annæus). Pharsalia; or, the civil wars of Rome, between Pompey the great and Julius Cæsar. The whole ten books Englished by Thomas May. 154 l. [12 pl. *inserted*]. 18°. *London, P. Parker*, 1679.

——— The same. La Pharsalie de Lucain, traduite en François par M. Marmontel. 2 v. 1 p. l. lxxix, 304 pp. 6 p. l; 1 p. l. 416 pp. 5 pl. 8°. *Paris, Merlin*, 1766. s.

Lucas (Hippolyte). Arachnides; myriapodes, etc. 4°. *Paris*, 1836-44.
[*In* WEBB (Philip B.) *and* BERTHELOT. Histoire naturelle des îsles Canaries. v. 2].

Lucas (Newton Ivory). A dictionary of the English and German and German and English languages, [etc; *or*,] englisch-deutsches und deutsch-englisches wörterbuch. 2 v. in 4. 8°. *Bremen, C. Schünemann*, 1854-68. s.

Lucianus *samosatensis*. Sämtliche werke. Aus dem Griechischen übersetzt und mit anmerkungen und erläuterungen versehen von C. M. Wieland. 6 v. 8°. *Leipzig, Weidmann*, 1788-89. s.

——— Piscator, sev reuiuiscentes, Bilibaldo Pirckheymero interprete. Eiusdem epistola apologetica: [Contra theologos colonienses pro Joanne Reuchlino defensio]. 26 l. sm. 4°. *Nurenbergæ, F. Peypus*, 1517.

Lucius (Friedrich Salomo). Alte und neue bundesgrüsse. xiv, 168 pp. 8°. *Leipzig, C. W. Vollrath*, 1855.

Lucy Gelding; a tale of land and sea: showing the evil effects of gambling, as it is practiced upon the Atlantic coast. By Willa West. [*pseudon.* By Mary S. F. Slocum?] 285 pp. 12°. *Chicago, E. B. Myers*, 1862. s.

Ludlow (Fitz Hugh). What shall they do to be saved? Outlines of the opium cure. 12°. *New York, Harpers*, 1868.
[*In* DAY (Horace). The opium habit. pp. 251-335].

Ludolphus *de Saxonia*. In psalteriū expositio. *Parisiis*, 1514. *See* **Bible.** (*Latin*).

Ludvigh (Samuel). Alt und neu. Uebungen für geistiges turnen. 218 pp. 3 l. 8°. *Cincinnati, S. Ludvigh*, 1868.

Lugnani (Giuseppe). Golfo di Trieste. [Elementi per la statistica di Trieste, n. 3]. 8°. *Trieste*, 1829.
[*In* ROSSETTI (D. de). Archeografo triestino. v. 1].

——— Posizioni geografiche. [Elementi per la statistica di Trieste, n. 1]. 8°. *Trieste*, 1829.
[*In* ROSSETTI (D. de). Archeografo triestino. v. 1].

——— Serate di Minerva discorsi sette letti all' adunanza del gabinetto di Minerva in Trieste. 192 pp. 8°. [*Trieste*], *Weis*, [1842]. s.

Lupton (Donald). Emblems of rarities; or, choyce observations out of worthy histories of many remarkable passages and renowned actions of divers princes and severall nations. With exquisite variety and speciall collections of the natures of most sorts of creatures. Collected by D. L. 10 p. l. 478 pp. 18°. *London, N. Okes*, 1636.

Lupton (Thomas). A thousand notable things of sundrie sorts. 3 p. l. 336 pp. 13 l. 18°. *London, R. Bird*, 1631.

Lussan (Marguerite de). Annales galantes de la cour de Henri second. 2 v. 358 pp; 377 pp. 16°. *Amsterdam, J. Desbordes*, 1799.

——— Histoire de Louis xi. *See* **Baudot de Juilly.**

Lussana (Filippo *and* Pietro) *and* **Ambrosoli** (Carlo). Su le funzioni del nervo gran simpatico e su la calorificazione animale ricerche sperimentali. [Extract]. 120 pp. 8°. *Milano,* [*Gazetta medica italiana-lombardia*], *G. Chiusi,* 1857.

Lütke (J. P.) Kurtze und gründliche anweisung, zur teutsch-jüdischen sprache, von Philoglotto. [*pseudon.*] 8 p. l. 63 pp. 16°. *Freyberg, C. Matthäi,* 1733. s.

[*With* BREITHAUPT (C.) Ars decifratoria, 1737].

Lütken (Christian Friedrik). Bidrag til kundsdab om lernæer, etc. *See* **Steenstrup** (Johan J. S.) *and* **Lütken.**

Luyken (Jan). Icones biblicæ veteris et n. testamenti. Figures du vieux et du nouveaux testament. [Sans texte]. Print verbeeldingen der historien des ouden en nieuwen testaments. 62 pl. fol. *Amsterdam, F. Houttuyn,* 1747. s.

Lycurgus. Quae supersunt. 8°. *Lipsiae,* 1770.

[ORATORVM graecorvm quæ supersunt. Ed. Reiske. v. 4 and 8].

Lyell (*Sir* Charles). Principles of geology; or, the modern changes of the earth and its inhabitants considered as illustrative of geology. 10th ed. 2 v. xvi, 671 pp. 1 map. 4 pl; xvi, 649 pp. 3 pl. 8°. *London, J. Murray,* 1867–68.

——— A second visit to the United States of North America. 2 v. 273 pp; 287 pp. 12°. *New York, Harpers,* 1849.

Lyman (Joseph B.) Cotton culture, with an additional chapter on cotton seed and its uses. By J. R. Sypher. 190 pp. 1 map. 12°. *New York, O. Judd & co.* [1868].

Lynd (James). The first book of etymology, etc. 215 pp. 12°. *Philadelphia, E. C. & J. Biddle,* 1847. s.

——— The same. The first book of etymology: [etc.] On the basis of "the first book of etymology," by James Lynd. By Joseph Thomas. 261 pp. 12°. *E. C. & J. Biddle,* 1852. s.

Lyne (*Rev.* Richard). The Latin primer: in three parts. 6th ed. xii, 256 pp. 1 tab. 12°. *London, Law & Whittaker,* 1817. s.

Lyon (Patrick). The narrative of Patrick Lyon, who suffered three month's severe imprisonment on merely a vague suspicion of being concerned in the robbery of the bank of Pennsylvania. 76 pp. portrait. 8°. *Philadelphia, F. & R. Bailey,* 1799.

Lyra elegantiarum: a collection of some of the best specimens of *vers de société and vers d'occasion* in the English language, by deceased authors. Edited by Frederick Locker. New and revised ed. xx, 345 pp. 18°. *London, E. Mixon & co.* 1867.

Lyra germanica: second series; the christian life. From the German by C. Winkworth. 6th ed. xii, 239 pp. 16°. *London, Longmans,* 1865.

Lyre maçonne; ou recueil choisi des plus jolies chansons. [*anon.*] 226 pp. 7 l. 16°. *Jerusalem,* [*Paris*]? *Raphael,* 1768.

Lysias. Quae supersunt. 8°. *Lipsiae,* 1770.

[ORATORVM graecorum quae supersunt. Ed. Reiske. v. 5–6].

Lytton (*Sir* Edward George Earle Lytton Bulwer Lytton, *baron*). *See* **Bulwer Lytton.**

Lytton (Edward Robert Bulwer). The apple of life. By Owen Meredith. [*pseudon.*] 35 pp. 18°. *Boston, Ticknor & Fields,* 1865.

Mabie (Chester W.) The royal melodia; a collection of music, original and selected, for the use of chapters and councils. 72 pp. 12°. *New York, D. B. Howell & C. W. Matre,* 1868.

Macaulay (Thomas Babington, *baron Macaulay*). Works complete. Edited by his sister, lady Trevelyan. 8 v. 8°. *London, Longmans,* 1866.

CONTENTS.

v. 1–4. History of England.
v. 5–7. Critical and historical essays.
v. 7. Biographies.
Indian penal code.
Contributions to Knight's quarterly magazine.
v. 8. Speeches and poems.

McCall (*Gen.* George Archibald). Letters from the frontiers. Written during a period of thirty years' service in the army of the U. S. 539 pp. 8°. *Philadelphia, Lippincott & co.* 1868.

McCalla (Mary). In doors and out of doors; or, life among the children. 183 pp. 4 col. pl. 16°. *Philadelphia, presbyterian board of publication,* [1857].

MacCann (William). Two thousand miles' ride through the Argentine provinces; being an account of the natural products of the country, and habits of the people; with a historical retrospect of the Rio de la Plata, Monte Video, and Corrientes. 2 v. xvi, 295 pp. 3 pl. 1 map; xi, 324 pp. 3 pl. 12°. *London, Smith, Elder & co.* 1853.

M'Causland (Dominick, *LL. D.*) Adam and the adamite; or, the harmony of scripture and ethnology. xii, 312 pp. 2 maps. 2 pl. 8°. *London, R. Bentley,* 1864.

M'Cheyne (*Rev.* Robert Murray). A basket of fragments: being the substance of sermons. 6th ed. 376, 8 pp. 16°. *Aberdeen, G. & R. King,* [*about* 1860].

M'Clintock (John, *D. D.*) *and* **Crooks** (George R). A first book in Greek, etc. xi, 315 pp. 12°. *New York, Harpers,* 1848. s.

M'Clintock (John, *D. D.*) *and* **Strong** (James *S. T. D.*) Cyclopædia of biblical, theological, and ecclesiastical literature. v. 2. C—D. viii, 933 pp. 8°. *New York, Harpers,* 1868.

M'Clure (*Sir* Robert John Le Mesurier). The north-west passage. Capt. M'Clure's despatches from h. m. s. Investigator, off Point Warren and Cape Bathurst. 45 pp. 1 map. 8°. *London, J. Betts,* 1853.

McConaughy (*Mrs.* J. E.) Clarence; or, self-will and principle. 174 pp. 2 pl. 18°. *Philadelphia, Perkinpine & Higgins,* 1866.

——— The hard master. A temperance story. 278 pp. 1 pl. 18°. *New York, national temperance society,* 1868.

——— One hundred gold dollars. 255 pp. 1 pl. 18°. *Philadelphia, J. C. Garrigues & co.* 1867.

M'Connel (J. L.) The Glenns; a family history. 280 pp. 12°. *New York, C. Scribner,* 1851. s.

McConnell (*Rev.* J. S. J.) Where is he? or, the doctrine of an intermediate place, carefully considered. 104 pp. 16°. *Philadelphia, Perkinpine & Higgins,* 1868.

M'Connell (*Rev.* N. A.) Debate on trine immersion, etc. *See* **Quinter** (*Rev.* James) *and* **M'Connell.**

McCord (Louisa S.) Caius Gracchus. A tragedy in five acts. 128 pp. 12°. *New York, H. Kernot,* 1851. s.

McCord (*Rev.* William J.) Our passover; or, the great things of the law. 120 pp. 16°. *Philadelphia, presbyterian board of publication,* 1865.

M'Cormac (Henry, *M. D.*) Summary of christian morality. 12°. *London,* 1844.
[*In* ANTONINUS (M. A.) The meditations. 1844].

McCormick (Richard C. *jr.*) A visit to the camp before Sevastopol. 212 pp. 8 pl. 12°. *New York, Appletons,* 1855.

M'Coy (*Prof.* Frederick). A synopsis of the characters of the carboniferous limestone fossils of Ireland. Prepared by F. M'Coy, for sir Richard Griffith, by whom is now appended a list of the fossil localities, etc. viii, 274 pp. 29 pl. 4°. *London, Williams & Norgate,* 1862. s.

McCready (Francis). The art of English grammar, in verse, question and answer. 2[d] ed. 249 pp. 16°. *Philadelphia, author,* 1820.

McCulloch (J.) Distillation, brewing, and malting. 81 pp. 16°. *San Francisco, A. Roman & co.* 1867.

McCurdy (J.) The American spelling book, etc. 152 pp. 16°. *Philadelphia, J. B. Lippincott & co.* 1855. s.

Macdonald (George). Alec Forbes of Howglen. 440 pp. 1 pl. 12°. *London, Hurst & Blackett,* 1867.

Macdonald (James). General view of the agriculture of the Hebrides, or western isles of Scotland. xii, 824 pp. 5 maps. 1 pl. 8°. *Edinburgh,* 1811. s.
[GREAT BRITAIN. Board of agriculture].

Macé (Jean). Histoire d'une bouchée de pain: l'homme. With a French and English vocabulary, and a list of idiomatic expressions. 260 pp. 12°. *New York, Leypoldt & Holt,* 1868.

——— The same. Die geschichte von einem bissen brod: über das leben des menschen. 225 pp. 16°. *New York, W. Radde,* 1868.

——— The servants of the stomach. [Translated from the French]. 311 pp. 12°. *New York, Harpers,* 1868.

Macfarlan (Duncan, *D. D.*) General view of the agriculture of the county of Dumbarton. *See* **Whyte** (A.) *and* **Macfarlan.**

Macfarlane (Charles). The Chinese revolution, with details of the habits, manners, and customs of China and the Chinese. vii, 243 pp. 1 map. 16°. *London, Routledge & co.* 1853.

Macgregor (Annie L.) John Ward's governess. A novel. 303 pp. 12°. *Philadelphia, J. B. Lippincott & co.* 1868.

Macgregor (John). The Rob Roy on the Baltic: a canoe cruise through Norway, Sweden, Denmark, Sleswig, Holstein, the North sea, and the Baltic. viii, 312 pp. 2 maps. 1 pl. 16°. *London, S. Low, son & Marston,* 1867.

McIlvaine (Charles Pettit, *D. D.*) The work of preaching Christ. A charge: delivered to the clergy of Ohio. Akron, June, 1863. 2[d] ed. 72 pp. 18°. *New York, A. D. F. Randolph,* 1864.

McIntosh (Maria J.) Charms and countercharms. 8th ed. 400 pp. 12°. *New York, Appletons,* 1864.

——— The lofty and the lowly; or, good in all, and none all good. 11th ed. 2 v. 299 pp; 323 pp. 12°. *New York, Appletons,* 1865.

——— Two lives; or, to seem and to be. 8th thousand. 262 pp. 2 pl. 12°. *New York, Appletons,* 1865.

——— Two pictures; or, what we think of ourselves, and what the world thinks of us. 476 pp. 12°. *New York, Appletons,* 1864.

M'Jilton (*Rev.* John N.) Report of the delegate to the educational conventions of Buffalo and Boston, to the commissioners of public schools of Baltimore, and address on the teacher's calling, nationally considered. 126 pp. 8°. *Baltimore, Bull & Tuttle,* 1860. s.

Mack (Alexander). Kurze und einfältige vorstellung der äussern, aber doch heiligen rechten und ordnungen des hauses Gottes. 2e aufl. 11 p. l. 133 pp. 24°. *Germantown,* [*Pa.*] *C. Saur,* 1774.

Mackarness (*Mrs.* Matilda Planché). Sunbeam stories. 395 pp. 12°. *Boston, etc. J. Munroe & co.* 1856. s.

McKaye (James). Address of the loyal national league to A. de Gasparin, etc. *See* **Loyal** national league.

——— The mastership and its fruits: the emancipated slave face to face with his old master. A supplemental report to E. M. Stanton, sec. of war. 38 pp. 8°. *New York,* 1864.
[LOYAL publication society. No. 58].

——— The same. Das herrenthum und seine früchte: der emancipirte sklave und sein früherer herr. Übersetzt von F. Schutz. 31 pp. 8°. *New York, H. Ludwig,* 1864.
[LOYAL publication society. No. 55].

M'Keever (Harriet B.) Children with the poets. 360 pp. 12°. *Philadelphia, Claxton, Remsen & Haffelfinger,* 1868.

——— Edith's ministry. 432 pp. 12°. *Philadelphia, Lindsay & Blakiston,* 1864. s.

——— Heavenward—earthward. 369 pp. 4 pl. 16°. *Philadelphia, J. C. Garrigues & co.* 1867.

——— Jesus on earth. 74 pp. 8 col. pl. sm. 4°. *Philadelphia, presbyterian publication committee,* 1866.

——— "Nothing but leaves." 288 pp. 3 pl. 16°. *Philadelphia, J. P. Skelly & co.* 1868.

——— Silver threads. 376 pp. 1 pl. 12°. *Philadelphia, Claxton, Remsen and Haffelfinger,* 1868.

Mackenna (Benjamin Vicuña). *See* **Vicuña Mackenna.**

M'Kenna (Theobald). Thoughts on the civil condition and relations of the roman catholic clergy, religion, and people, in Ireland. 1 p. l. 193 pp. 8°. *London, J. Budd,* 1805. s.

Mackenzie (*Sir* Alexander). Voyages from Montreal, on the river St. Laurence, through the continent of N. America, to the frozen and Pacific oceans; 1789–93. With [an] account of the fur trade of that country. 2 v. in 1. xiv, 290 pp; 332 pp. 8°. *London, T. Cadell & W. Davies,* 1802.

Mackenzie (*Sir* George). Observations upon the laws and customs of nations, as to precedency. 56 pp. fol. *London,* 1724.
[*In* GUILLIM (John). Display of heraldry. ed. 1724].

Mackenzie (*Sir* George Steuart). A general view of the agriculture of the counties of Ross and Cromarty. xi, 353 pp. 1 map. 8°. *London,* 1810. s.
[GREAT BRITAIN. Board of agriculture].

M'Laughlin (Edward A.) The lovers of the deep: with miscellaneous poems. x, 312 pp. portrait. 16°. *Cincinnati, E. Lucas.* 1841.

M'Lehose (Agnes Craig). Correspondence. *See* **Burns** (Robert) *and* **M'Lehose.**

M'Lennan (John F.) Primitive marriage. An inquiry into the origin of the form of capture in marriage ceremonies. xii, 326 pp. 12°. *Edinburgh, A. & C. Black,* 1865.

McLeod (Donald). Gloomy memories in the highlands of Scotland: *vs.* Mrs. H. B. Stowe's Sunny memories in [England] a foreign land: or a faithful picture of the extirpation of the Celtic race from the highlands of Scotland. xvi, 212 pp. 8°. *Toronto, author,* 1857.

Macleod (Henry Dunning). The elements of political economy. xliv, 573 pp. 8°. *London, Longmans,* 1858.

——— The theory and practice of banking. 2d ed. 2 v. xxxiv, 406 pp; xxiii, 340 pp. 8°. *London, Longmans,* 1866.

McMasters (Julia Russell). Silver pictures. [Poems]. 64 pp. 12°. *Philadelphia, H. Cowperthwait & co.* 1856. s.

Macmillan's magazine. Edited by D. Masson. Nov. 1867, to Oct. 1868. v. 17–18. 8°. *London, Macmillan & co.* 1868.

McPherson (Edward). A hand book of politics for 1868. 7, 307 pp. 8°. *Washington, Philp & Solomons,* 1868.

——— A political manual for 1868. 2 p. l. 124 pp. [Part iii of A hand-book of politics for 1868]. 8°. *Washington, Philp & Solomons,* 1868.

Macquart (Jean). Insectes diptères du nord de la France. [Extracts]. 5 v. 8°. *Lille, sociéte des sciences, etc.* 1823–33. s.

CONTENTS.

[v. 1.] Tipulaires. 175 pp. 4 pl. 1823.
[v. 2.] Asiliques, bombyliers, xylotomes, leptides, vesiculeux, stratiomydes, xylophagites, tabaniens. 178 pp. 3 pl. 1826. (With autograph letter).
[v. 4.] Syrphies. 2 p. l. 223 pp. 4 pl. 1829.
[v. 5.] Athéricères: créophiles, oestrides, myopaires, conopsaires, scénopiniens, céphalopsides. 2 p. l. 232 pp. 6 pl. 1833.
[v. 3 (Platypézines-hybotides) wanting].

——— Insectes diptères. 4°. *Paris,* 1836–44.
[*In* WEBB (P. B.) *and* BERTHELOT. Histoire naturelle des îles Canaries. v. 2.]

Macray (*Rev.* William Dunn). Annals of the Bodleian library, Oxford, 1598–1867. With a notice of the earlier library founded in the fourteenth century. v, 369 pp. 1 pl. 8°. *London, Rivingtons,* 1868.

McSherry (James). History of Maryland; from its first settlement in 1634, to 1848. 405 pp. 6 pl. 8°. *Baltimore, J. Murphy,* 1849.

McVicar (Malcom). The metric system of weights and measures; combining many improvements in arrangement, notation, and applications. 47 pp. 16°. *New York, Ivison, Phinney & co.* 1868.

McVickar (*Rev.* William A.) City missions. 2d ed. 96 pp. 16°. *New York, Pott & Amery,* 1868.

MacWhorter (Alexander). Yahveh Christ, or, the memorial name. With introductory letter, by Nathaniel W. Taylor. 179 pp. 12°. *Boston, Gould & Lincoln,* 1857. S.

Madden (*Sir* Frederic). Introduction to the old English versions of the Gesta Romanorum. Edited for the Roxburghe club. 21 pp. 2 l. 4°. *London, W. Nicol,* 1838.

Madden (Richard Robert). The history of Irish periodical literature, from the end of the 17th to the middle of the 19th century; with notices of remarkable persons connected with the press in Ireland. 2 v. vii, 82, 338 pp; 531 pp. 8°. *London, T. C. Newby,* 1867.

Madisonian (The). [Washington weekly]. Dec. 1, 1840, to Dec. 14, 1841. fol. *Washington,* 1840–41.

——— The same. The daily Madisonian. Dec. 15, 1841, to April 28, 1845. 5 v. fol. *Washington,* 1841–45.
[No more published].

Madrid. (Biblioteca nacional). *See* **Spain.**

Maffei (A. *conte*). Brigand life in Italy: a history of Bourbonist reaction. 2 v. xii, 313 pp; vii, 326 pp. 8°. *London, Hurst & Blackett,* 1865.

Maffei (Francisco Scipione). Istoria diplomatica che serve d'introduzione all' arte critica in tal materia. Con raccolta de' documenti non ancor divulgati, che rimangono in papiro egizio, ragionamento sopra gl' Itali primitivi. xxii, 338 pp. 4 pl. 4°. *Mantova, A. Tumermani,* 1727. S.

Maffei (Giuseppe). Storia della letteratura italiana dall' origine della lingua sino a' nostri giorni. 3a ed. v. 1 in 2 parts. vii, 1040 pp. 8°. *Italia, [Firenze, Speranza]?* 1834. S.

Magalotti (Lorenzo, *conte*). Opere. 2 v. xii, 396 pp. 1 portrait; 282 pp. 5 pl. 8°. *Milano, societá tipografica,* 1806.

Magalotti—continued.

CONTENTS.

v. i. Lettere scientifiche ed erudite sopre un effetto della neve.
v. ii. Saggi di naturali esperienze fatte nell' accademia del cimento.

Magazin für insectenkunde, herausgegeben von Karl Illiger. 6 v. 8°. *Braunschweig, K. Reichard,* 1801–07. S.
[v. 1 wanting pp. 261–492; v. 2–5 wanting titles].

Maggie and the sparrows. By the author of "Cosmo's visit," etc. [*anon.*] 180 pp. 6 pl. 18°. *New York, R. Carter & bros.* 1868.

Magic (The) oracle; or, the black art made easy. By a professor of magic. [*anon.*] 94 pp. 24°. *Boston, "Yankee Blade" office,* 1868.

Magic (The) word. [Poems]. By Alton. [*pseudon.*] 4 p. l. 183 pp. 12°. *Boston, J. Munroe & co.* 1855. S.

Maginess (James). A new, copious, and complete system of arithmetic, for the use of schools and counting-houses. 372 pp. 16°. *Harrisburg, for the author, by W. Greer,* 1821.

Maguire (John Francis). The Irish in America. xvii, 653 pp. 8°. *London, Longmans,* 1868.

Mahabharata. Βαλαβαρατα, *η συντομη της* Μαχαβαρατας, *ποιηθεισα υπο του* Αμαρα, *η* Αμαραςανδρα, *μαθητου του σοφου* Ζηναδατα, *και μεταγλωττισθεισα απο του βραχμανικου παρα* Δημητριου Γαλανου. Νυν *δε το πρωτον εκδοθεισα φιλομουσωι μεν δαπανηι* Ιωαννου Δουμα, *σπουδηι δε και επιμελειαι* Γ. Κ. Τυπαλδου, [*κ. τ. λ.*] *ξθ,* 867 pp. 8°. Αθηναις, Ν. Αγγελις, 1847. S.

Mahan (Dennis H.) An elementary course of civil engineering. New ed. 8, 428 pp. 8°. *New York, J. Wiley & son,* 1868.

——— An elementary treatise on advanced-guard, outpost, and detachment service of troops, and the manner of posting and handling them in presence of an enemy. 168 pp. 18°. *New York, J. Wiley,* 1861.

Mahony (Dennis A.) The four acts of despotism: comprising the tax bill, the finance bill, the conscription act, [and] the indemnity bill. 160 pp. 8°. *New York, Van Evrie, Horton & co.* 1863.

Maianus (Ioannes Otho). Horativs christianvs. Qvincti Horatii Flacci venvsini poetæ lyrici. Plerisque ab impudica libertate vindicatis, [etc.] 3 p. l. 226 pp. 1 l. 18°. *Avgvstæ Vindelicorvm, typis C. Mangi,* 1609.

Maidenthorpe; or, interesting events about the year 1825. By Jeremiah Briefless. [*pseudon.*] 2 v. 2 p. l. 322 pp; 2 p. l. 320 pp. 12°. *London, R. Bentley,* 1861.

Maier (I.) Israelitisches gebet- und andachtsbuch, zum gebrauche bei der häuslichen und öffentlichen Gottesverehrung. x, 460 pp. 8°. *Stuttgart, k. hofbuchdruckerei zu Guttenberg*, 1848. s.

Maine (*State of*). Annual report of the adjutant general for 1866. 8°. *Augusta, Stevens & Sayward*, 1867.

——— Documents published by order of the legislature, 1865. 8°. *Augusta, Stevens & Sayward*, 1865.

——— Public documents: being the annual reports of various public officers and institutions for 1867–68. 8°. *Augusta, Owen & Nash*, 1868.

——— Report of commission on fisheries, 1868. *See* **Foster** (N. W.) *and* **Atkins** (C. G.)

——— The water-power of Maine. Reports of the commissioners and secretary of the hydrographic survey of 1867. 8°. *Augusta, Owen & Nash*, 1868.

Mair (John *M.D.*) Nephaleia; or, total abstinence from intoxicating liquors in man's normal state of health, the doctrine of the bible. [With] diagrams of the stomach as affected by alcohol, by Dr. Sewall. 300 pp. 1 l. 1 pl. 12°. *New York, Sheldon & co.* 1861.

Makemie (*Rev.* Francis). A good conversation. A sermon preached at the city of New York, January 19, 1706–7. 2 p. l. 36 pp. 16°. *Boston, B. Green, for B. Eliot*, 1707.

Malcom (Howard, *D.D. LL.D.*) Theological index. Reference to the principal works in every department of religious literature. 478 pp. 8°. *Boston, Gould & Lincoln*, 1868.

Malepeyre (François). The arts of tanning, currying, and leather dressing. *See* **Julia de Fontenelle** (J. S. E.) *and* **Malepeyre.**

——— Nouveau manuel complet de la fabrication de l'eau-de vie, etc. *See* **Hourier** (E.) *and* **Malepeyre.**

Mallary (*Mrs.* M. Jeanie). Horace Wilde. 295 pp. 16°. *Philadelphia, J. B. Lippincott & co.* 1868.

Mallet (Paul Henri). Histoire de Dannemarc. 3e éd. 9 v. 16°. *Genève, Barde, Manget & co.* 1787.

Mallet (Robert, *civil engineer*). Great Neapolitan earthquake of 1857. The first principles of observational seismology, as developed in the report of the Royal society of London, of the expedition made by command of the society into the interior of the kingdom of Naples, to investigate the circumstances of the great earthquake of December, 1857. 2 v. xxiv, 431 pp. 35 pl; viii, 399 pp. 5 maps. 23 pl. 8°. *London, Chapman & Hall*, 1862.

Malte-Brun (Malthe Conrad Bruun, *called*). Universal geography: being a description of all parts of the world. With additions and corrections by James G. Percival. New ed. Illustrated with engravings and maps. 3 v. 4°. *Boston, S. Walker & co.* 1865.

Mamma's budget; or, daily reading for children. [*anon.*] 1st Am. from 3d English ed. 185 l. 37 pl. 16°. *Philadelphia, Hayes & Zell*, 1857. s.

Man (Thomas). Picture of a factory village: [with] remarks on lotteries. 144 pp. 12°. *Providence, for the author*, 1833.

Manchester (*City of, N. H.*) The Manchester directory, for 1869. By Sampson, Davenport & co. 280 pp. 8°. *Manchester, W. H. Fisk*, 1868.

Mandeville (*Sir* John). Tractato bellissimo delle piu marauigliose cose e piu notabile che si truouino nelle parte del mondo, scripte et racolte dallo strenuissimo caualiere asperondoro Giouanni Mandauilla frazese, che visito quasi tutti le parti del mondo habitabili, ridocto in lingua thoscana. 80 l. 1 pl. *Goth.* sm. 4°. *Firenze, L. de Morgiani & G. da Maganza*, 1492.

Mandrillon (Joseph H.) Précis sur l'Amérique Septentrional et la république des treize-États-Unis. Par M. Jh. M. [*anon.*] 164 pp. 8°. *Amsterdam, J. Schuring*, 1782.

[*With* CLUNY (A.) Le voyageur américain. éd. 1782].

Manin (Daniele). Documents et pièces authentiques. Traduits sur les originaux et annotés par F. Planat de la Faye. 2 v. xii, 487 pp. 1 l; 435 pp. 1 l. 8°. *Paris, Furne & cie.* 1860.

Manley (John). Cattaraugus county: embracing its agricultural society, newspapers, civil list, etc. biographies of the old pioneers, etc. with the statistics of each town. 140 pp. 8°. *Little Valley, (N. Y.) J. Manley*, 1858. s.

Mann (Horace). Thoughts selected from [his] writings. 240 pp. 18°. *Boston, H. B. Fuller & co.* [1868].

——— *and* **Chase** (Pliny Earle). Elements of arithmetic, part 1st. The primary-school arithmetic, etc. 160 pp. 16°. *Philadelphia, E. H. Butler & co.* 1851.

——— ——— The same. Part 2. The grammar school arithmetic, etc. 256 pp. 12°. *Philadelphia, E. H. Butler & co.* 1851. s.

Mann (Horace, *jr.*) Enumeration of Hawaiian plants. (Extract). 95 pp. 8°. *Cambridge, American academy of arts and science*, 1867. s.

Mann (Mary, *widow of Horace*). A biographical sketch of D. F. Sarmiento. 12°. *New York, Hurd & Houghton,* 1868.
[*In* SARMIENTO (D. F.) Life in the Argentine republic. ed. 1868. pp. 276–396].

Mannering (May, *pseudon?*) Billy Grimes' favorite; or, Johnny Greenleaf's talent. 191 pp. 4 pl. 16°. *Boston, Lee & Shepard,* 1868.
[HELPING-HAND series. v. 2].

——— The cruise of the Dashaway; or, Katie Putnam's voyage. 221 pp. 4 pl. 16°. *Boston, Lee & Shepard,* 1868.
[HELPING-HAND series. v. 3].

Manning (*Miss* Anne). The Lincolnshire tragedy. Passages in the life of the faire gospeller, mistress Anne Askew. [*anon.*] vii, 296 pp. 12°. *London, R. Bentley,* 1866.

Mansfield (Lewis W.) The morning watch: a narrative. [*anon.*] 175 pp. 12°. *New York, author,* 1850. s.

Manso de Velasco (Joseph). El dia de Lima. Proclamacion real que de el nombre augusto de el supremo señor d. Fernando vi, etc. hizo la muy noble, y muy leal ciudad de los reyes Lima, etc. Con la relacion de la solemne pompa de tan fausto felice aplauso, y de las reales fiestas, con que se celebró. [*With appendix.*] Loa que para la coronacion de Fernando el vi, [etc.] compuso Felix de Alarcón. 2 p. l. 268 pp. 21 l. 1 pl. 8°. [*Lima*]? 1748. s.

Mantell (Gideon Algernon). The medals of creation; or, first lessons in geology, and the study of organic remains. 2 v. xxxii, 446 pp. 5 pl; xi, 447-930 pp. 1 pl. 12°. *London, H. G. Bohn,* 1854. s.

Manual (The) of catholic prayers; with the epistles and gospels for all sundays and holidays in the year. 288, 192 pp. 2 pl. 48°. *New York, P. J. Kennedy,* 1868.

Manual (A) of devotion for soldiers and sailors, etc. 4 v. in 1. 8°. *Philadelphia, presbyterian board of publication,* 1847. s.

Manual (A) of geographical science, mathematical, physical, historical, and descriptive. [Edited by C. G. Nicolay]. 2 v. xvi, 445 pp; xii, 615 pp. Atlas, 4°. 8°. *London, J. W. Parker & son,* 1852–59.

CONTENTS.

Ansted (D. T.) Physical geography. v. 1.
Bevan (W. L.) Ancient geography. v. 2.
Jackson (J. R.) Chartography. v. 1.
Nicolay (C. G.) Maritime discovery and modern geography. v. 2.
——— Theory of description and geographical terminology. v. 1.
O'Brien (Matthew). Mathematical geography. v. 1.

Manual of piety, for the use of seminaries. 359 pp. 32°. *Baltimore, J. Murphy & co.* 1856. s.

Manuel (Louis Pierre). La police de Paris dévoilée. 2 v. 11, 402 pp. 2 l. 1 pl; 330 pp. 8°. *Paris, J. B. Garnery,* 1794.

Manuzio (Aldo, *the younger son of* Paolo). Epitome orthographiae, etc. 8 p. l. 196 pp. 16°. *Taurini, sumptibus societatis,* 1730. s.

Manzoli (Pietro Angelo). Marcelli Palingenii Stellati, zodiacvs vitæ. 315 pp. 17 l. 32°. *Amstelodami, I. Iansonius,* 1628.
[NOTE. A satire against the pope, cardinals, and church of Rome. The initials of the first 27 verses give the authors' assumed names].

Manzoni (Alessandro). I promessi sposi; storia milanese del secolo xvii, scoperta e rifatta. Ed. diligentemente eseguita. 2 v. xxv, 287 pp; 4 p. l. 300 pp. 24°. *Parma, P. Fiaccadori,* 1832. s.

Manzuoli (Nicolo). Nuova descrizione dell' Istria. (Corografie dell' Istria, n. 9.) 8°. *Trieste,* 1831.
[*In* ROSSETTI (D. de). Archeografo triestino, v. 3].

Marco Polo. *See* **Polo.**

Maréchal (——, *painter*). La ménagerie du muséum national. *See* **Lacépède** (B. G. E. de), *and* **Cuvier** (G. L. C. F. D. *baron*).

Marets (Des). *See* **Des Marets.**

Margaret; a story of life in a prairie home. By Lyndon. [*pseudon.*] 360 pp. 12°. *New York, C. Scribner,* 1868.

Margaret Claire; or, sowing beside all waters. A story for youthful laborers. [*anon.*] 217 pp. 3 pl. 18°. *Boston, Mass. s. s. society,* 1867.

Margaret Russel's school. By the author of "Squire Downing's heirs. [*anon.*] 389 pp. 4 pl. 8°. *New York, R. Carter & bros.* 1869.

Marguerite de France (*Reine de Navarre*). L'heptameron, ou histoires des amans fortunez. Des nouvelles de trés-illustre et trés excellente princesse Marguerite de Valois, royne de Navarre. Remis en son vrai ordre, par Claude Gruget 2 v. 17 p. l. 528 pp. 2 l. 1 pl; 480 pp. 3 l. 1 pl. 18°. *Paris, J. Bessin,* 1698.

Marian Elwood; or, how girls live. By one of themselves. [*anon.*] 360 pp. 12°. *New York, E. Dunigan & bro.* 1859.

Marin (Michel Ange). Le baron Van Hesden; ou, la république des incrédules. 5 v. 18°. *Toulouse, A. Birosse,* 1762. s.

Marini (Francisco Martinez). Teoria de las cortes ó grandes juntas nacionales de los reinos de Leon y Castilla. Monumentos de su constitucion politica y de la soberania del pueblo, etc. 3 v. 4°. *Madrid, F. Villalpando,* 1813. s.

Marini *or* **Marino** (Giambattista). L'adone, poema heroico, con gli argomenti del Sanvitale, o l'allegorie di L. Scoto. 4 v. 32°. *Amsterdam, D. Elsevier,* 1678.

Marion Harvie; a tale of persecution in the seventeenth century. [*anon.*] 279 pp. 1 pl. 16°. *Philadelphia, presbyterian board of publication,* 1857. s.

Marjoribanks (Alexander). Travels in South and North America. 5th ed. 480 pp. 1 pl. 12°. *London, Simpkin, Marshall & co.* 1854.

Markham (Gervase, Jarvis, *or* Jervis). The English husbandman. The first part containing the knowledge of husbandly duties, [etc.] The second part containing the art of planting, grafting, and gardening. Newlie reviewed and inlarged, by G. M. [3d ed?] 2 v. in 1. 7 p. l. 227 pp; 7 p. l. 96 pp. sm. 4°. *London, H. Taunton,* 1635.

——— The pleasures of princes, or good men's recreations. Contayning a discourse of fishing. [With] the choyce, ordring, breeding, and dyeting of the fighting cock. 1 p. l. 54 pp. sm. 4°. *London, H. Tavnton,* 1635.

[*With his* English husbandman. 1635].

——— A way to get wealth, containing sixe principall vocations, for callings, in which every good husband or huswife may lawfully imploy themselves. The first five books gathered by W. L. [William Lawson]. 10th ed. sm. 4°. *London, G. Sawbridge,* 1660–64.

CONTENTS.

Cheape and good husbandry for the well ordering of all beast and fowles. 146 pp.
Country contentments: or, the husbandman's recreations. 92 pp.
The English housewife. 188 pp.
Inrichment of the weald of Kent; or, a direction for the true ordering, manuring, and inriching of the wealds of Kent and Sussex. 20 pp.
Markham's farewell to husbandry; or the enriching of all sorts of barren and sterile grounds. 126 pp.
A new orchard and garden: with the country houswife's garden. By W. Lawson. 112 pp.

Marlitt (E.) Gold Elsie. From the German by mrs. A. L. Wister. 344 pp. 12°. *Philadelphia, J. B. Lippincott & co.* 1868.

——— The old mam'selle's secret. After the German by mrs. A. L. Wister. 297 pp. 12°. *Philadelphia, J. B. Lippincott & co.* 1868.

Maroncelli (Piero). Alle Mie prigioni di Silvio Pellico addizioni. Seguite dalle due tragedie Francesca da Rimini ed Eufemio da Messina. 2 p. l. xlvii, 179 pp. 12°. *Parigi, Baudry,* 1833. s.

Marquart (John, *jr.*) *and* **Schreiner** (Henry). Gaging simplified; or, every merchant his own gager. 44 pp. 12°. *Philadelphia, W. S. Young,* 1849. s.

Marquiset (Armand). Statistique historique de l'arrondissement de Dole. 2 v. xi, 518 pp. 15 pl; 2 p. l. 532 pp. 2 l. 3 tab. 12 pl. 8°. *Besançon, C. Deis,* 1841–42. s.

Marre (Jan de) *and* **Keulen** (Johannes van). De nieuwe groote lichtende zee-fakkel, het sesde deel, vertoonende de zeekusten, eylanden en havens van Oost-Indiën. Beginnende aan Caab de Goede Hoop, etc. 3 p. l. 76 pp. 1 l. 78 col. maps. fol. *Amsterdam, J. Van Keulen,* 1753. s.

[v. 1–5 wanting].

Marrow (S. L.) National synthesis of the elements of the English language; or, phonic manual. 44 pp. 24°. *Indianapolis, A. Q. Goodwin.* 1868.

Marryat (Florence). *See* **Church** (*Mrs.* Ross).

Marryat (Frederick). Masterman Ready; or, the wreck of the Pacific. Written for young people. New ed. 2 p. l. viii, 476 pp. 2 pl. 16°. *London, H. G. Bohn,* 1863.

Marsh (Christopher C.) The science of double-entry book-keeping, simplified by the application of an infallible rule for journalizing, etc. Rewritten from the 20th ed. 218 pp. 8°. *Philadelphia, Hogan & Thompson,* 1851. s.

——— The same. La ciencia de teneduria de libros, etc. Traducido de la 20ma ed. inglesa. Par A. G. Beck. 195 pp. 8°. *New York, J. C. Riker,* 1849. s.

Marshall (John, *surgeon, F. R. S.*) Outlines of physiology, human and comparative. 1026 pp. 8°. *Philadelphia, H. C. Lea,* 1868.

Marshall (*Rev.* Walter). The gospel mystery of sanctification. With the doctrine of justification opened and applied. xix, 378 pp. 1 l. 12°. [*London, J. Rivington,* 1756]?

[Imperfect. Title-page and leaves at the end wanting].

Marteilhe (Jean). Autobiography of a French protestant, condemned to the galleys for the sake of his religion. Translated from the French. xii, 266 pp. 16°. *London, religious tract society,* [1866].

Martens (Carl von). Guide diplomatique, etc. 2 v. xxiii, 455 pp; ix, 591 pp. 8°. *Leipsic, F. A. Brockhaus,* 1832. s.

Martens (Georg von). Die farben der pflanzen. [Extract]. 2 p. l. 150 pp. 8°. *Stuttgart, verein für vaterländische naturkunde, E. Greiner,* 1862. s.

Martha's gift. A story for the freed children. By a teacher. [*anon.*] 142 pp. 2 pl. 18°. *Philadelphia, American s. s. union,* 1868.

Martialis (Marcus Valerius). Epigrammata. Ex museo Petri Scriverii. Ab omni rerum obscœnitate verborumque turpitudine vindicata. 276 pp. 18°. *Venetiis, typis I. Zini,* 1680.

Martin (Arthur) *and* **Cahier** (Charles). Monographie de la cathédrale de Bourges. 1re partie. Vitraux du xiii siècle. 1 p. l. xii, 304 pp. 1 l; atlas. 33, 40 pl. on 71 l. fol. *Paris, Poussielgue-Rusand,* 1841–44. S.

Martin (A. E. Victor) *and* **Foley** (L. E.) Histoire statistique de la colonisation algérienne, au point de vue du peuplement et de l'hygiène. 4 p. l. 356 pp. 11 tab. 8°. *Paris, etc. Germer-Baillière,* 1851. S.

Martin (Benjamin, *the optician*). Biographia philosophica. Being an account of the lives, writings, and inventions of the most eminent [natural] philosophers and mathematicians, from the earliest ages to the present time. 2 p. l. 565 pp. 1 l. 8°. *London, W. Owen,* 1764.

Martin (Benjamin, *of Ohio*). The wandering pilgrim: composed of hymns and spiritual songs. xv, 251 pp. 24°. *Columbus, (O.) Ohio state journal rooms,* 1868.

Martin (Edward Winslow). The life and public services of Schuyler Colfax, together with his most important speeches. 512 pp. 1 pl. 8°. *New York, United States publishing co.* 1868.

Martin (Louis Aimé). Recueil de contes, historiettes morales, en vers et en prose, suivi d'un extrait de Pascal. Pour la jeunesse. 2e éd. 280 pp. 4 pl. 18°. *Paris, Demonville,* [1812].

——— Recueil de contes, historiettes morales, en vers et en prose, suivie d'un extrait de Montaigne. Pour la jeunesse. iv, 276 pp. 4 pl. 18°. *Paris, Demonville,* [1812].

Martin (Louis Auguste). Histoire morale de la Gaule, depuis les temps les plus reculès jusqu'à la chute de l'empire romain. xx, 315 pp. 8°. *Paris, Comon & cie.* 1847.

Martin (Theodore). Memoir of William Edmondstonne Aytoun, D. C. L. With an appendix. vii, 363 pp. 1 portrait. 8°. *Edinburgh, W. Blackwood & sons,* 1867.

Martin Saint-Ange (Gaspard Joseph). Physiologie de l'espèce. *See* **Grimaud de Caux** (G.) *and* **Martin Saint-Ange.**

Martineau (Harriet). The Crofton boys. New ed. 192 pp. 1 pl. 18°. *London, Routledges,* 1865.

——— Feats on the fiord. New ed. 221 pp. 1 pl. 18°. *London, Routledges,* 1865.

——— The settlers at home. 192 pp. 1 pl. 18°. *London, Routledges,* 1864.

Martinet (Jan Florentz). The catechism of nature; for the use of children. Translated from the Dutch. 136 pp. 24°. *Philadelphia, T. Lang,* 1791.

Martinius (Martin). *See* **Martinsohn.**

Martinsohn (Martin). Bellum tartaricum; or, the conquest of the empire of China, by the invasion of the Tartars. fol. *London, J. Crook,* 1655.

[*In* SEMMEDO (A.) History of China. 1655. pp. 250–307. 1 map. 1 pl.]

Martire d'Anghiera (Pietro). *See* **Eden** (Richard).

Martius (Carl Friedrich Philipp von). Akademische denkreden. 6 p. l. 619 pp. 8°. *Leipzig, F. Fleischer,* 1866. S.

Marx (C.) Zur charakteristik des struvits. *See* **Ulez** (G. L.) *and others.* Controverse, etc.

Maryland (*Province of*). A collection of the governor's several speeches, and the addresses of each house, at a convention of an assembly begun the first of May, 1739. 80 pp. fol. [*n. p.* 1739]?

——— ——— Extracts from the records, relative to the dispute between the government of New Netherlands, (now New York), and the lord proprietary of Maryland, concerning the title of the Dutch to the territories on the Delaware. 8°. *New York, Bliss & White,* 1821.

[NEW YORK historical society. v. 3. 1st series].

——— (*State of*). The constitution of the State. Formed, adopted, and ratified, 1867. With marginal notes, references, and an index, by E. O. Hinkley. 156 pp. 8°. *Baltimore, J. Murphy & co.* 1867.

——— ——— Journals of proceedings of the senate and house of delegates. Jan. session, 1868. 2 v. 8°. *Annapolis, W. Thompson,* 1867.

——— ——— Public documents. Jan. session, 1868. 8°. *Annapolis, W. Thompson,* 1868.

——— ——— Votes and proceedings of the senate, February session, 1777, [and] of the senate and house of delegates, June session, 1777. 81, 109–133 pp. fol. [*Annapolis, F. Green,* 1777]?

[Imperfect: wanting title-page, and proceedings ho. of deleg. Feb. session, *i. e.* pp. 83-108].

Maryland (The) educational journal, a school and family monthly. Devoted to popular instruction and literature. E. S. Zevely, editor. v. 1. May, 1867, to April, 1868. 376 pp. 1 map. 8°. *Baltimore, E. S. Zevely,* 1867–68.

[No more published].

Mascal (Leonard). The gouernment of cattell. Diuided into three books. 1. Oxen, kine, and calues. 2. Horses. 3. Sheepe, goats, hogges, and dogges. 3 p. l. 307 pp. 2 l. sm. 4°. *London, T. Harper, for I. Harison,* 1633.

Mascall (Edward James). Recopilacion de aduanas y sisas que pagan los articulos extrangeros que se introducen y extraen en la Gran Bretaña, etc. 11ª ed. Publicala D. F. A. D. B. 3 p. l. xii, 271 pp. 8°. *Madrid, J. del Collado,* 1817. s.

Mason (Lowell). The hallelujah; a book for the service of song in the house of the Lord; to which is prefixed the singing school, etc. 368 pp. obl. 8°. *New York, Mason bros.* [1854]. s.

——— The new carmina sacra; or, Boston collection of church music. 384 pp. obl. 8°. *Boston, Wilkins, Carter & co.* 1850. s.

Masonic funeral service, and order of exercises for a sorrow lodge. Arranged by W. L. Cunningham. 24 pp. 16°. *Philadelphia, Moss & co.* 1865.

Masonic (The) monthly. S. Evans, editor. Nov. 1865, to Oct. 1867. v. 3–4. 8°. *Boston, E. L. Mitchell & C. C. Roberts,* [1866–67].

Massachusetts (*Colony of*). A conference between the commissaries of Massachusetts-bay, and the commissaries of New-York, [appointed to settle the boundary-line], at New-Haven, Connecticut, 1767. 26 pp. 1 l. 4°. *Boston, R. Draper, printer to the governor,* 1768.

——— Journals of the house of representatives of the colony of the Massachusetts-Bay, July, 1775—Feb. 1776. 2 v. in 1. 271 pp; 332 pp. fol. *Watertown, (New England), B. Edes,* 1775–76.

——— Speeches of the governors of Massachusetts, from 1765 to 1775; and the answers of the house of representatives to the same; with their resolutions and addresses during that period. And other public papers relating to the dispute between this country and Great Britain. 421 pp. 8°. *Boston, Russell & Gardner,* 1818.

Massachusetts (*State of*). Abstract of the Massachusetts school returns for 1839–40. x, 482 pp. 8°. *Boston, Dutton & Wentworth,* 1840. s.

——— Documents relating to the northeastern boundary of the state of Maine. 275 pp. 8°. *Boston, Dutton & Wentworth,* 1828.

——— Journals of the house of representatives. May, 1777, to Oct. 1778. 2 v. in 1. 155 pp; 84 pp. fol. *Boston, T. & J. Fleet,* 1777–78.

[*With* MASSACHUSETTS (*Colony*). Journals house of representatives, July 1775–Feb. 1776. Imperfect: v. for 1777, pp. 55–66, 71–74, 79–82, 103–122, 144–150, and leaves at the end, wanting].

——— The same. Journals of the house of representatives. May, 1777, to May, 1779. 2 v. 248 pp; 208 pp. fol. *Boston, B. Edes,* 1776–77.

——— Public documents: being the annual reports of various public officers and institutions, 1866–67. 8 v. 8°. *Boston, Wright & Potter,* 1867–68.

——— *Zoological and botanical survey.* Reports on the fishes, reptiles, and birds of Massachusetts. xii pp. 2 l. 426 pp. 4 pl. 8°. *Boston, Dutton & Wentworth,* 1839. s.

CONTENTS.

Ichthyology and herpetology. By D. Humphreys Storer.
Ornithology. By William B. O. Peabody.

——— ——— Reports on the herbaceous plants and on the quadrupeds of Massachusetts. 2 v. in 1. ix, 277 pp; 1 p. l. 86 pp. 8°. *Cambridge, Folsom, Wells & Thurston,* 1840. s.

CONTENTS.

[v. 1]. Report on the herbaceous flowering plants of Massachusetts, [etc.] By Chester Dewey.
[v. 2]. Report on the quadrupeds of Massachusetts. By Ebenezer Emmons.

——— ——— A report on the insects of Massachusetts, injurious to vegetation. [By Thaddeus William Harris]. viii, 459 pp. 8°. *Cambridge, Folsom, Wells & Thurston,* 1841. s.

——— ——— Report on the invertebrata of Massachusetts, comprising the mollusca, crustacea, annelida, and radiata. [By Augustus A. Gould]. xiii, 373 pp. 15 pl. 8°. *Cambridge, Folsom, Wells & Thurston,* 1841. s.

Massachusetts (The) family almanac; or, the merchants' and farmers' calendar. 1836–37. 2 v. 27 l; 29 l. 16°. *Boston, Allen & co.* 1836–37.

Massachusetts historical society. Collections. 4th series. v. 8. [The Mather papers]. 714 pp. 8°. *Boston, Wiggin & Lunt,* 1868.

Massachusetts homœopathic medical society. Publications, 1861–66. v. 2. ix, 571 pp. 8°. *Cambridge, J. Wilson & son,* 1867.

Massmann (Heinrich Friedrich). Die baseler todtentänze in getreuen abbildungen. Nebst geschichtlicher untersuchung, sowie vergleichung mit den übrigen deutschen todtentänzen, [etc.] Sammt einem anhange; todtentanz in holzschnitten des 15ten jahrhunderts. 127 pp. 15 l. 1 tab. 6 l. 16°. Atlas, 49 pl. 4°. *Stuttgardt, etc. J. Scheible, etc.* 1847. s.

Masson (Charles François Phillibert). Mémoires secrets sur la Russie, et particulièrement sur la fin du règne de Catherine ii. et le commencement de celui de Paul i. [*anon.*] 2 v. xiii, 355 pp; 2 p. l. 295 pp. 12°. *Paris, C. Pougens,* 1800.

Masury (John W.) How shall we paint our houses? A popular treatise on the art of house-painting; plain and decorative, etc. viii, 216 pp. 8°. *New York, Appletons*, 1868.

Mather (Cotton, *D.D.*) Christodulus. A good reward of a good servant, etc. with some commemoration of mr. Thomas Walter. 33 pp. 16°. *Boston, printed by T. Fleet, for S. Gerrish*, 1725.

——— The palm-bearers. A brief relation of patient and joyful sufferings in the history of the church of Scotland, from the year 1660 to the year 1688. 58 pp. 12°. *Boston, printed by T. Fleet for S. Gerrish*, 1725.

——— The vial poured out upon the sea. A remarkable relation of certain pirates brought unto a tragical and untimely end. 51 pp. 12°. *Boston, printed by T. Fleet, for N. Belknap*, 1726.

Mather (Increase, *D. D.*) Elijah's mantle. A faithful testimony to the cause and work of God in the churches of New England, by four servants of God, [Mitchell, Higginson, Stoughton, and Mather]. 19 pp. 12°. *Boston, printed by S. Kneeland, for S. Gerrish*, 1722.

——— The life and death of Mr. Richard Mather, teacher of the church in Dorchester, New England. Cambridge, 1670. 12°. *Boston, reprinted by D. Clapp*, 1850.

[*In* DORCHESTER antiquarian and historical society. Collections. No. 3. pp. 37-108].

Mather (*Rev.* Richard). Journal. 1635. His life and death. 1670. 108 pp. 12°. *Boston, D. Clapp*, 1850.

[*In* DORCHESTER antiquarian and historical society. Collections. No. 3].

Mather (Samuel, *D. D*). The departure and character of Elijah considered and improved. A sermon after the decease of rev. Cotton Mather. 20 pp. 12°. *Boston, printed by G. Rogers, for S. Gerrish*, 1728.

——— Vita B. Augusti Hermanni Franckii; cui adjecta est narratio rerum memorabilium in ecclesiis evangelicis per Germaniam, etc. 42 pp. 12°. *Boston, T. Hancock*, 1723.

Mathews (Cornelius). Chanticleer: a thanksgiving story of the Peabody family. 130 pp. 2 pl. 16°. *New York, Brown, Loomis & co.* 1856. s.

——— The same. 130 pp. 2 pl. 16°. *New York, American news company*, [1868].

Mathews (*Rev.* J. M'D.) Letters to school girls. 247 pp. 16°. *Cincinnati, Swormstedt & Poe*, 1853. s.

Mathews (Joanna H.) Bessie and her friends. 366 pp. 4 pl. 16°. *New York, R. Carter & bros.* 1869.

Mathews (Joanna H.) Bessie at the sea-side. 357 pp. 4 pl. 16°. *New York, R. Carter & bros.* 1868.

——— Bessie in the city. 395 pp. 4 pl. 16°. *New York, R. Carter & bros.* 1868.

Matteson (*Mrs.* Frances F.) The fragment; or, letters and poems. 144 pp. 1 portrait. 16°. *Rome (N. Y.) A. Sandford*, 1855. s.

Matteucci (*Prof.* Carlo). Corso di elettrofisiologia in sei lezioni date in Torino. 1 p. l. v, 142 pp. 8°. *Torino, Castellazzo & Vercellino*, 1861. s.

Matthaei (Christian Friedrich, *editor and commentator*). *See* **Bible** (*Greek and Latin*). Novvm testamentvm. 1788.

Matthæucci (Agostino). Opus dogmaticum adversus heterodoxos, tum antiquos, tum recentes, complectens controversias fidei, etc. 8 p. l. 526 pp. 17 l. 4°. *Venetiis, N. Pezzan*, 1755. s.

Matthisson (Friedrich von). Gedichte. Ausg. letzter hand. viii, 288 pp. 16°. *Zürich, Orell, Füssli & co.* 1821. s.

Mattison (Hiram, *D. D.*) The bible doctrine of immortality. 96 pp. 18°. *New York, Carlton & Porter*, 1868.

——— Ministers' pocket ritual; a hand-book of scripture lessons and forms of service for marriages, baptisms, etc. Adapted to all denominations. 192 pp. 16°. *Philadelphia, Perkinpine & Higgins*, 1864.

Mattoon (Charles H.) Common arithmetic, upon the analytic method of instruction, [etc.] xix, 388 pp. 12°. *Columbus, (O.) S. Medary*, 1850. s.

Maturin (Charles Robert). The Albigenses, a romance. [*anon.*] 3 v. 12°. *Philadelphia, S. F. Bradford*, 1824.

Maundeville (*Sir* John). *See* **Mandeville.**

Mauritius (*Colony of*). Inundation papers. 5 v. in 1. fol. *Port Louis, gov't printers*, 1865. s.

Maury (Louis Ferdinand Alfred). Essai sur les légendes pieuses du moyen age, etc. 4 p. l. xxiv, 305 pp. 1 l. 8°. *Paris, Ladrange*, 1843. s.

——— Les fées du moyen-age, recherches sur leur origine, leur histoire et leur attributs, pour servir à la connaissance de la mythologie gauloise. ix, 101 pp. 12°. *Paris, Ladrange*, 1843. s.

Mavor (William). General view of the agriculture of Berkshire. xii, 548 pp. 3 maps. 34 pl. 8°. *London*, 1809. s.

[GREAT BRITAIN: Board of agriculture].

Maximilian Alexander Philipp, *prinz* zu Wied-Neuwied. Brésil. Quelques corrections indispensables à la traduction française de la description d' un voyage au Brésil par le prince Maximilian de Wied. 109 pp. 8°. *Francfort sur le M: H. L. Brönner*, 1853. s.

Maximilien, empereur du Mexique. Sa vie, sa mort, son procès: détails intimes et inédits. [*anon.*] 1 p. l. 157 pp. 1 portrait. 18°. *Paris, Lebigre-Duquesne*, [1867].

Maximowicz (Carl Johann). Primitiae florea amurensis. Versuch einer flora des Amurlandes. (Extract). 1 p. l. 504 pp. 1 map. 10 pl. 4°. *St. Petersburg, k. akademie der wissenchaften*, 1859. s.

May (Caroline, *editor*). *See* **Woodbine** (The).

May (*Mrs.* Carrie L.) Brownie Sandford; or, the recovered pearl. 301 pp. 4 pl. 16°. *Boston, W. H. Hill, jr. & co.* 1866.

——— Nellie Milton's housekeeping; or, sweet clover. 280 pp. 4 pl. 16°. *Boston, W. H. Hill, jr. & co.* 1867.

——— Sweet clover stories. Ruth Lovell; or, holidays at home. 304 pp. 3 pl. 16°. *Boston, W. H. Hill, jr. & co.* 1868.

——— The same. Sylvia's burden. 290 pp. 4 pl. 16°. *Boston, W. H. Hill, jr. & co.* 1867.

May (Sophie, *pseudon.*) *See* **Dotty** Dimple stories.

Mayer (J. F. *M. D.*) Die kindes-pflege wie auch die erkenntniss und behandlung der kinder-krankheiten mit wasser, im geiste der neuen wasserheillehre, etc. xv, 368 pp. 8°. *Gera & Leipzig, J. M. C. Ambruster*, 1847. s.

Mayer (Luigi). Views in Egypt, from the original drawings in the possession of Sir R. Ainslie: with historical observations, and incidental illustrations of the manners and customs of the natives of that country. 2 p. l. 102 pp. 1 l. 48 col. pl. fol. *London, R. Bowyer*, 1804.

——— Views in the Ottoman empire, chiefly in Caramania. From the original drawings in the possession of sir R. Ainslie. With historical observations, etc. [French and English texts]. 2 p. l. 40 pp. 24 col. pl. fol. *London, R. Bowyer*, 1803.

[*With his* Views in Egypt].

——— The same. Views in the Ottoman dominions in Europe, Asia, etc. from original drawings taken for sir Robert Ainslie, with descriptions. 16 pp. 35 l. 35 pl. fol. *London, R. Bowyer*, 1810.

——— Views in Palestine, from the original drawings, with an historical and descriptive account of the country and its remarkable places. [French and English texts]. 1 p. l. 47 pp. 1 l. 24 col. pl. fol. *London, R. Bowyer*, 1804.

[*With his* Views in Egypt].

Mayfield (Cora, *pseudon?*) Elmwood; or, Helen and Emma. 2 p. l. 350 pp. 12°. *Boston, etc. J. Munroe & co.* 1856. s.

Mayhew (*Rev.* Experience). Grace defended in a modest plea for an important truth. 208 pp. sm. 4°. *Boston, B. Green & co. for D. Henchman*, 1744.

Mayhew (Ira). University book-keeping, a treatise on business and accounts. 318 pp. 8°. *Boston, S. F. Nichols*, 1868.

——— University book-keeping key. 115 pp. 8°. *Boston, S. F. Nichols*, 1868.

Mayhew (Jonathan, *D. D.*) A discourse concerning unlimited submission and non-resistance to the higher powers; with reflections on the resistance made to Charles i. etc. 55 pp. 12°. *Boston, D. Fowle*, 1750.

——— A discourse occasioned by the death of Stephen Sewall, esq. chief justice of Massachusetts. 66 pp. 12°. *Boston, R. Draper*, 1760.

——— A sermon preach'd in the audience of the captain general, the council, and house of representatives of the province of Massachusetts, May 29th, 1754. 52 pp. 8°. *Boston, S. Kneeland*, 1754.

——— Two discourses delivered October 25th, 1759, the day of thanksgiving for the reduction of Quebec, with an appendix containing a brief account of two former expeditions. 67 pp. 6 l. 8°. *Boston, R. Draper*, 1759.

Maynard (*Abbé* U. *canon of Poitiers*). Des études et de l'enseignement des Jésuites à l'époque de leur suppression (1750–1773), suivi de l' examen général de l' histoire du pontificat de Clément xiv du p. [A.] Theiner. 2 p. l. 296 pp. 8°. *Paris, veuve Poussielgue-Rusand*, 1853. s.

Mayo (Elizabeth). Lessons on common things, etc. On the basis of dr. Mayo's lessons on objects. Edited by John Frost. 204 pp. 16°. *Philadelphia, J. B. Lippincott & co.* 1857. s.

Mayr (Fr. *editor*). *See* **Jahrbuch** für kinderheilkunde. 1858–60.

Mayr (Gustav L.) Formicidae. 119 pp. 4 l. 4 pl. 4°. *Wien*, 1868. s.

[*In* WÜLLERSTORF-URBAIR (B. von). Reise der Novara. Zoologischer theil. v. 2. abth. 1. A].

——— Hemiptera. 204 pp. 5 l. 5 pl. 4°. *Wien*, 1868. s.

[*In* WÜLLERSTORF-URBAIR (B. von). Reise der Novara. Zoologischer theil. v. 2. abth. 1. B].

Mazzinelli (*Abbate* Alessandro). The office of holy week, with the ordinary rubrics, summaries of the psalms, explanation of the ceremonies and mysteries, etc. Translated from the Italian. 572 pp. 24°. *Baltimore, Kelly & Piet*, 1865.

Mazzini (Giuseppe). Royalty and republicanism in Italy; or, notes and documents relating to the Lombard insurrection, and to the royal war of 1848. xxi, 237 pp. 12°. *London, C. Gilpin*, 1850. s.

Mazzuchelli (Frederigo). Scuola equestre. Elementi di cavallerizza: lezioni equestri: il cavallo ammalato, catechismo: ed avvertimenti sulle razze de'cavalli, etc. Nuova ed. 362 pp. 9 pl. 1 tab. 4°. *Milano, G. P. Giegler*, 1805.

Mead (———). The construction of maps and globes. [With] a seasonable inquiry into maps, books of geography and travel. 16 p. l. 216 pp. 18 pl. 12°. *London, T. Horne*, 1717.

Meade (William, *M. D.*) An experimental enquiry into the chemical properties and medicinal qualities of the principal mineral waters of Ballston and Saratoga, New York. With directions for [their] use. [Also] a chemical analysis of the Lebanon spring. xv, 195 pp. 2 pl. 8°. *Philadelphia, H. Hall*, 1817.

Meagher (Thomas Francis). Letters on our national struggle, addressed to the editors of the Dublin "Irishman" and "Citizen." 15 pp. 8°. *New York*, 1863.
[LOYAL publication society, no. 38].

Mease (James, *M. D.*) Description of some of the medals, struck in relation to important events in North America, before and since the declaration of independence by the United States. 8°. *New York, Bliss & White*, 1821.
[*In* NEW YORK historical society. Collections. v. 3. 1st series].

Meat-eaters [or carnivora], with some accounts of their haunts and habits. [*anon.*] 468 pp. 19 pl. 16°. *Philadelphia, American s. s. union*, [1858]. s.

Meckel (Johann Friedrich, *editor*). *See* **Archiv** für anatomie und physiologie, 1826–32.

——— *See, also,* **Deutsches** archiv für die physiologie. 1815–23.

Medical (The) record. A semi-monthly journal of medicine and surgery. Edited by G. F. Shrady, *M. D.* March, 1866, to February, 1868. v. 1–2. 8°. *New York, W. Wood & co.* [1867–68.]

Meeker (N. C.) Life in the west; or, stories of the Mississippi valley. 360 pp. 12°. *New York, S. R. Wells*, 1868.

Meerman (*Baron* Gerard). Origines typographicæ. 2 v. xi, 260 pp. 2 pl. 1 tab; viii, 312 pp. 4°. *Hagae Comitum, N. van Daalen*, 1765.

Meigs (Charles D.) Females and their diseases, etc. 670 pp. 8°. *Philadelphia, Lea & Blanchard*, 1848. s.

——— Observations on certain of the diseases of young children. 215 pp. 8°. *Philadelphia, Lea & Blanchard*, 1850. s.

Meilhac (Henri) *and* **Halévy** (Ludovic). La belle Hélène. Opera bouffe in three acts. Music composed by J. Offenbach. Libretto. [French and English]. 40 pp. 8°. *New York, J. A. Gray & Green*, 1868.

——— The grand duchess of Gerolstein. A comic opera in three acts, by J. Offenbach. [Libretto]. Translated from the French. 48 pp. 8°. *New York, J. A. Gray & Green*, 1867.

Mein (John). A state of the importations from Great Britain into the port of Boston, from the beginning of January to August 17, 1769, with the advertisements of "all the well disposed merchants," etc. [*anon.*] 130 pp. 4°. *Boston, Mein & Fleming*, 1769.

Mein spielen ist lernen. My play is study: a book for children. [*anon.*] Translated from the German, by L. Lermont. 111 pp. 4 pl. sq. 12°. *Philadelphia, J. K. Simon*, 1852. s.

Meine gedanken über die zwey kleine freymäurerische schriften: an meine brüder und an unsere brüder. [*anon.*] 63 pp. 18°. *Berlin, G. J. Decker*, 1780.

Meiners (Christoph). Geschichte des verfalls der sitten der wissenschaften, und sprache der Römer. Als enleitung zur Gibbons geschichte. 2 p. l. 316 pp. 8°. *Wien, etc. J. Stahel*, 1791. s.

Mela (Pomponius). De situ orbis libri tres. sm. 4°. *Venetiis, F. Renner de Halibrun*, 1478.
[NOTE.—The second book is misplaced, after A. Becharia's preface to the translation of Dionysius De situ orbis habitabilis, which follows the third book].

Melford (H. M.) Spanische bühnenstucke der besten dichter neuerer zeit. v. 1. *See* **Moratin** (Leändro F. de). El si de las niñas. 1839.

Melik (M. A.) L'orient devant l'occident. [Histoire de Turquie, 1826–52]. xix, 250 pp. 8°. *Paris, chez tous les libraires*, 1856.

Melish (John). A geographical description of the United States, with the contiguous British and Spanish possessions. 2d ed. 166 pp. 4 maps. 8°. *Philadelphia, author*, 1816.

——— The same. 3d ed. 175 pp. 4 maps. 8°. *Philadelphia, author*, 1818.

Melish (John). Travels through the United States of America, 1806–11, [with] travels through various parts of Britain, Ireland, and Canada. 2 v. xxii, 444 pp. 2 maps; ix, 492 pp. 6 maps. 8°. *Philadelphia, J. Melish,* 1815.

Mell (*Rev.* P. H.) Baptism in its modes and subjects. 2d ed. xii, 304 pp. 16°. *Charleston, southern baptist publication society,* 1854. s.

Mellet (Jullien). Voyages dans l'intérieur de de l'Amérique méridionale. 2e éd. 295 pp. 2 l. 8°. *Paris, Masson,* 1824.

Melville (George John Whyte). "Bones and I;" or, the skeleton at home. v, 287 pp. 12°. *London, Chapman & Hall,* 1868.

Mémoires inédits de Pétion, et mémoires de Buzot et Barbaroux. Précédés d'une introduction par C. A. Dauban. lxxvi, 544 pp. 1 pl. 8°. *Paris, Plon,* 1866.

Memoirs of monkeys, etc. [*anon.*] 2 p. l. 152 pp. 16°. *London, G. B. Whittaker,* 1825.

Memoirs of the principal transactions of the last war between the English and French in North America, from 1744 to 1748, [with] an account of the importance of Nova Scotia and Cape Breton to both nations. [*anon.*] 102 pp. 8°. *London, J. Dodsley,* 1757.

Memorials of Margaret Elizabeth, only daughter of rev. Albert Des Brisay, of the province of New Brunswick. By a friend. [*anon.*] 236 pp. 6 pl. 18°. *New York, Carlton & Phillips,* 1856. s.

Memorias historicas sobre la revolucion de Valencia, 1808, y sobre la causa criminal formada contra F. Juan Rico, V. G. Moreno, Narciso Rubio y otros. 4°. *Cadiz,* 1811.

Men of history. By eminent writers. 319 pp. 16°. *Edinburgh, W. P. Nimmo,* 1866.

Mencken (Johann Burckhard). De charlataneria eruditorum declamationes duæ, cum notis variorum. Accessit epistola Sebastiani Stadelii, etc. de circumforanea literatorum vanitate. Ed. 5a. 5 p. l. 268 pp. 1 pp. 12°. *Amstelodami, U. C. Saalbachius,* 1747. s.

Mendez Silva (Rodrigo). Catalogo real y genealogico de España, ascendencias y descendencias de nuestros catolicos principes, y monarcas supremos. Reformado, y añadido en esta vltima impression. 4 p. l. 164 l. sm. 4°. *Madrid, A. del Ribero Rodriguez,* 1656.

Mendez de Vasconzelos y Cabido (Gonçalo). De Eborensi mvnicipio commentarius. 18°. *Coloniæ Agrippinæ,* 1613.

[*In* DELICIÆ lvsitano-hispanicæ. 1613].

Mendoza (Juan Gonzalez de). *See* **Gonzalez de Mendoza.**

Menestrier (Claude François). Traité des tovrnois, iovstes, carrovsels, et avtres spectacles pvblics. 6 p. l. 399 pp. 4°. *Lyon, J. Mvgvet,* 1669.

Ménétriés (E. *of St. Petersburg*). Insecten. 4°. *St. Petersburg,* 1851.

[*In* MIDDENDORFF (A. T. von). Reise, etc. v. 2. theil 1].

——— Lépidoptères de la Sibérie orientale et en particulier des rives de l'Amour. 4°. *St. Petersbourg,* 1859.

[SCHRENCK (L. von). Reisen, [etc.] im Amur-lande. v. 2. 1e lief.]

Menge (Johann Joseph). Jesus, meine liebe! ein lehr- und gebetbuch für katholische christen. 608 pp. 1 pl. 24°. *Cincinnati, J. P. Walsh,* 1866.

Menges (Philipp). Abendskunden eines handwerkers. 95 pp. 32°. *Saratoga Springs, Potter & Judson,* 1868.

Mengin-Fondragon (Pierre Charles Joseph, *baron* de). Les soirées d'un observateur, ou mélanges politiques, critiques, et littéraires. 323 pp. 8°. *Paris, Méquignon-Havard & cie.* 1827. s.

Menken (Adah Isaacs). Infelicia. [A collection of poems]. v, 141 pp. 2 pl. 24°. *New York, H. L. Williams,* 1868.

Mennonite church. Christian spiritual conversation on saving faith, for the young, in questions and answers, and a confession of faith of the Mennonites. With appendix. 309 pp. 16°. *Lancaster, Pa: J. Baer & sons,* 1857. s.

Menzies (Sutherland). Royal favourites. 2 v. xxix, 486 pp; 2 p. l. 539 pp. 8°. *London, J. Maxwell & co.* 1865.

Merchant's (The) magazine and commercial review. Edited by W. B. Dana. Jan. to Dec. 1868. v. 58–59. 8°. *New York, W. B. Dana & co.* 1868.

Merchants' (The) and bankers' almanac for 1868. 8°. *New York, office of the bankers' magazine,* 1868.

Mercurius elencticus. Communicating the unparallell'd proceedings at Westminster, [etc. No. 11, Feb. 2, 1647, and no. 21, April 19, 1648]. 8 l. sm. 4°. [*Westminster*], 1647–48.

Mercurius melancholicus: or, newes from Westminster, and other parts. [No. 21, January 15, 1648, and No. 34, April 10, 1648]. 8 l. sm. 4°. [*Westminster*], 1648.

Mercvrivs pragmaticus. Communicating intelligence from all parts, [etc]. Nos. 19–21, Jan. 18–Feb. 1; Nos. 2 and 19, April 4, and

June 18, 1648. 19 l. sm. 4°. [*Westminster*], 1848.

Meredith (Owen, *pseudon.*) *See* **Lytton** (Edward Robert Bulwer).

Merle d'Aubigné (Jean Henri). History of the reformation in Europe in the time of Calvin. v. 1-2. xxxv, 433 pp. 1 portrait; xix, 475 pp. 12°. *New York, R. Carter & brothers*, 1863. s.

Mermet (Louis Bollioud). *See* **Bollioud Mermet.**

Merrill (*Miss* Catherine). The soldier of Indiana in the war for the Union. [*anon.*] v. 1. vi, 690 pp. 9 pl. 4 maps. 8°. *Indianapolis, Merrill & co.* 1866.

Merrill (*Rev.* Samuel H.) The campaigns of the first Maine and first District of Columbia cavalry. 436 pp. 3 pl. 12°. *Portland, Bailey & Noyes*, 1866.

Messala *or* **Messalla Corvinus** (Marcus Valerius). De progenie Avgusti Caes. fol. *Basilæ*, 1532.

[*In* FLORUS (L. A.) De gestis Romanorvm, etc. 1532.]
[NOTE. The forgery of a much later age, according to the best authorities].

Messenger (The). [A semi-weekly newspaper]. v. 1. April 17, 1816-Oct. 22, 1817. fol. *Georgetown, (D.C.) J. C. Dunn & co.* 1816-17.
[Imperfect]. s.

Messkatalog, [*or,*] bibliographisches jahrbuch für den deutschen buch- kunst- und landkarten- handel. 3r jahrgang. v. 1-2; 4r jahrgang. v. 1. 8°. *Leipzig, E. Avenarius*, 1855-56. s.

[Jhrg. 1-2; 3 (3-4); 4 (2-4), et seq. wanting].

Mestre (José Manuel). De la filosofia en la Habana: discurso. Seguido de una carta inedita del Félix Varela, y un articulo del José Z. Gonzalez del Valle. 149 pp. 12°. *Habana, imprenta "la Antillo,"* 1862. s.

Meteranus *or* **Meteren** (Emanuël Van). *See* **Van Meteren.**

Methodist (The). An advocate of lay representation. G. R. Crooks, *D.D.* editor. Jan. to Dec. 1868. v. 9. fol. *New York, H. W. Douglas*, 1868.

Methodist episcopal church. The doctrines and discipline of the methodist episcopal church. 240 pp. 32°. *New York, Carlton & Porter*, 1856. s.

Methodius *Constantinopolitanus.* [Opusculum]. Titulus in libellum continēs in se reuelationes diuinas, a sanctis angelis factas, de principio mundi et eradicatione varioru͞ regnorum atque, vltimi regis Romanorum gestis, et futuro triumpho in Turcos, atque deliberatione xpianorum, ac oppressione Sarracenorum, de restauratione ecclesie et universali pace, cū autenticis concordantiis prophetiaru͞ deque cōsumatione seculi hic annotat. 45 l. sm. 4°. *Avgvstæ Vindelicorvm, Johannes Froschauer*, 1496.

[Attributed by some to Methodius, bishop of Patara, in the 3d century].

Metropolitan (The) catholic almanac and laity's directory, for 1849, 1852, 1853, and 1855. 4 v. 12°. *Baltimore, F. Lucas, jr.* 1848-54. s.

Metropolitan (The) illustrated series. [*or*] The metropolitan first, second, third, and fourth reader; carefully arranged in prose and verse, [etc.] By a member of the order of the holy cross. [*anon.*] 4 v. 12°. *New York, D. & J. Sadlier*, 1860-63. s.

Metz (A. *M.D.*) The anatomy and histology of the human eye. 184 pp. 8°. *Philadelphia, office medical and surgical reporter*, 1868.

Metz (A.) Baron Leo von Oberg, M.D. A story of love unspoken; from the German, by Jos. A. Sigmund. 92 pp. 8°. *Boston, Loring*, 1868.

Meulman (Isaac). Catalogus van de tractaten, pamfletten, enz. over de geschiedenis van Nederland, aanwezig in de bibliotheek van Isaac Meulman. Bewerkt door J. K. Vanderwulp. v. 1-2. 4 p.l. 431 pp; 2 p.l. 383 pp. 4°. *Amsterdam, erven H. Van Munsten & zoon*, 1866-67. s.

CONTENTS.

v. 1. 1500-1644.
v. 2. 1649-88.

Meun *or* **Meung** (Jean de, *called* Clopinel). Le roman de la rose. *See* **Lorris** (G. de) *and* **Meun.**

Mexico. Documentos relativos a la reunion en esta capital de los gobernadores de los estados, convocados—para proveer à las exigencias del erario federal. 8°. *Mexico, J. M. Lara*, 1851.

Meyer (Carl Anton). Florula ochotensis phänogama. *See* **Trautvetter** (E. R. von) *and* **Meyer.**

Meyer (Friedrich Johann Lorenz). Voyage en Italie. [Traduit de l'Allemand]. xiv, 426 pp. 8°. *Paris, Henrichs*, 1802.

Meyer (Georg Friedrich Wilhelm). Beiträge zur chorographischen kenntniss des flussgebiets der Innerste in den fürstenthümern Grubenhagen und Hildesheim, [etc.] Eine anlage zur flora des königreichs Hannover. [*Or*], Die verheerungen der Innerste im fürstenthume Hildesheim, [etc.] 2 v. xxix, 368 pp. 1 tab; x, 368 pp. 2 pl. 8°. *Göttingen, Vandenhoeck & Ruprecht*, 1822. s.

Meyer (Hermann von, *editor*). *See* **Palaeontographica.**

Meyer (Jürgen Bona). Zum streit über leib und seele. Worte der kritik. xii, 130 pp. 8°. *Hamburg, Perthes-Besser & Mauke,* 1856.

Michaelis (Johann David). A dissertation on the influence of opinions on language, and of language on opinions, which gained the Prussian royal academy's prize. With an enquiry into the advantages and practicability of an universal learned language. vii, 92 pp. 4°. *London, W. Owen,* 1769.

Michaud (André Louis Gaspard). Galerie des mollusques, etc. *See* **Potiez** (V. L. V.) *and* **Michaud.**

Michigan (*State of*). The debates and proceedings of the constitutional convention of 1867. Official report by W. B. Lord, and D. W. Brown. 2 v. lxiv, 664 pp; 1072 pp. 4°. *Lansing, J. A. Kerr & co.* 1867.

——— Hughes' Michigan general shippers' guide, and railroad, express and steamboat agent's directory, 1868. By S. R. Hughes. 127 pp. 8°. *Detroit, free press,* 1868.

——— Joint documents, 1867. 8°. *Lansing, J. A. Kerr & co.* 1867.

——— Sixth annual report of the secretary of the state board of agriculture, for 1867. 496 pp. 8°. *Lansing, J. A. Kerr & co.* 1867.

——— Thirty-first annual report of the superintendent of public instruction, 1867. 8°. *Lansing, J. A. Kerr & co.* 1867.

Michigan (The) farmer. A monthly journal, devoted to agriculture, horticulture, domestic economy, and education. R. F. Johnstone, editor. Jan. 1853, to Dec. 1858. v. 11–16. 8°. *Detroit, Johnstone & Duncklee,* 1853–58.

——— The same. A weekly journal, etc. of the farm, the garden, and the household. R. F. Johnstone, editor. Jan. 1859, to Sept. 28, 1861. New (2d) series. v. 1–3. fol. *Detroit,* 1859–61.

——— The same. A journal devoted to the interests of farmers, fruit and stock growers, and their families. Oct. 5, 1861, to June, 1863. New (2d) series, v. 3–4, and new (3d) series, v. 1–2, in 1 v. 4°. *Detroit, W. M. Doty,* 1861[–63].

Michigan (The) teacher. A monthly journal, devoted to educational intelligence, etc. W. H. Payne, editor. Jan. to Dec. 1868. [v. 3]. 8°. *Ypsilanti, Payne, Whitney & Goodison,* 1868.

Microscopical society of London. *See* **Royal** microscopical society.

Middendorff (Alexander Theodor von). Reise in den äussersten norden und osten Siberiens während der jahre 1843 und 1844, mit allerhöchster genehmigung auf veranstaltung der k. akademie der wissenschaften zu St. Petersburg ausgeführt und in verbindung mit vielen gelehrten herausgegeben. 4 v. in 7. 4°. *St. Petersburg, k. akad. der wissenschaften,* 1847–57. s.

CONTENTS.

v. 1. theil 1. Einleitung. Meteorologische, geothermische, magnetische und geognostische beobachtungen. Fossile hölzer, mollusken und fische. Bearbeitet von K. E. von Baer, H. R. Göppert, Gr. von Helmersen, Al. graf Keyserling, E. Lenz, A. Th. v. Middendorff, W. v. Middendorff, Johannes Müller, Chr. Peters. lvi, 274 pp. 15 pl. 1848.

v. 1. theil 2. Botanik. [1e lief.] Phaenogame pflanzen aus dem hochnorden. Bearbeitet von E. R. v. Trautvetter. pp. ix, 1–190, pl. 1–8. 1847. [2e lief.] Tange des ochotskischen meeres. Bearbeitet von F. J. Ruprecht. pp. 193–435. pl. 9–18. 1851, [3e lief.] Florula ochotensis phänogama. Bearbeitet von E. R. v. Trautvetter und C. A. Meyer; Musci taimyrenses, boganidenses et ochotenses nec non fungi boganidenses et ochotenses in expeditione sibirica annis 1843–44 collecti et fratribus E. G. et G. G. Borszczow disquisiti. 148 pp. pl. 19–31. 1856.

v. 2. theil 1. Zoologie. Wirbellose thiere; annulaten; echinodermen; insecten; krebse; mollusken; parasiten. Bearbeitet von F. Brandt, W. F. Erichson, Seb. Fischer, E. Grube, E. Ménétriés, A. Th. v. Middendorff. 516 pp. 32 pl. 1851.

v. 2. theil 2. Zoologie. Wirbelthiere. [1e. lief.] Säugethiere, vögel und amphibien. Bearbeitet von A. Th. v. Middendorff. 256 pp. 26 pl. 1853.

v. 3. Ueber die sprache der Jakuten. Von Otto Böhtlingk. Theil 1. Einleitung. Jakutischer text. Jakutische grammatik. liv, 397 pp. 1851. Theil 2. Jakutische deutsche wörterbuch. 184 pp. 1851.

v. 4. Siberien in geographischer, naturhistorischer und ethnographischer beziehung. Theil 1. Uebersicht der natur nord- und ost-Sibiriens. 1e lief. Einleitung, geographie, und hydrographie. Nebst tafel ii bis xviii des kartenatlasses. Bearbeitet von A. [Th.] v. Middendorff. pp. ii, 1–200. 1859. 2e lief. Orographie und geognosie. Bearbeitet von A. [Th.] v. Middendorff. pp. ii. 201–332, 1859. 3e lief. Klima. Bearbeitet von A. [Th.] v. Middendorff. pp. ii, 333–523, 1861. 4e lief. Die gewächse Sibiriens. Bearbeitet von A. [Th.] v. Middendorff. pp. iv, 525–783, lvi. 1864.

v. 4. theil 2. Die thierwelt Sibiriens. Bearbeitet von A. [Th.] v. Middendorff. pp. iii, 785–1094, xiii. 1867.

Middendorff (W. von). Meteorologische beobachtungen. 4°. *St. Petersburg,* 1848.

[*In* MIDDENDORFF (A. T. von). Reise, etc. v. 1. theil 1].

Middleton (John, *land surveyor*). View of the agriculture of Middlesex, etc. and several essays on agriculture in general. 2d ed. xvi, 704 pp. 1 tab. 1 col. map. 8°. *London,* 1807. s.

[GREAT BRITAIN: Board of agriculture].

Middleton (Thomas Fanshaw, *of Cambridge*). The docrine of the Greek article; applied to the criticism and the illustration of the new testament. xvi, 388 pp. 8°. *New York, Eastburn, Kirk, & co.* 1813. s.

Miles (*Rev.* George D.) Memoir of Ellen May Woodward. 174 pp. 1 portrait. 16°. *Philadelphia, Lindsay & Blakiston*, 1850. s.

Military despotism! suspension of the habeas corpus! curses coming home to roost. [*anon.*] 16 pp. 8°. *New York, W. C. Bryant & co.* 1863.

[LOYAL publication society. no. 20].

Mill (John Stuart). On liberty. 2d ed. 207 pp. 8°. *London, J. W. Parker & son*, 1859. s.

——— Principles of political economy, with some of their applications to social philosophy. 4th ed. 2 v. xvi, 606 pp; xv, 582 pp. 8°. *London, J. W. Parker & son*, 1857. s.

Millard (Harrison). Selections from popular composers. Arranged for the social circle and quartette choirs. 128 pp. fol. *New York, S. T. Gordon*, 1868.

Miller (C. C.) Modern American architecture. *See* **Cummings** (M. F.) *and* **Miller**.

Miller (Hugh). The foot-prints of the creator; or, the asterolepis of Stromness. From the 3d London ed. With a memoir of the author, by L. Agassiz. 327 pp. 12°. *Boston, Gould & Lincoln*, 1850. s.

Miller (*Mrs.* Lydia, *widow of Hugh Miller*). Cats and dogs; or, notes and anecdotes of two great families of the animal kingdom. 240 pp. 1 pl. 12°. *London, T. Nelson & sons*, 1868.

Miller (Samuel, *D. D.*) A discourse, designed to commemorate the discovery of New York by Henry Hudson; delivered before the New York historical society, 1809. 8°. *New York, J. Riley*, 1811.

[*In* NEW YORK historical society. Collections. v. 1. 1st series].

——— Letters on unitarianism. 312 pp. 8°. *Trenton, G. Sherman*, 1821.

——— Thoughts on public prayer. 306 pp. 1 portrait. 12° *Philadelphia, presbyterian board of publication*, 1849. s.

Miller (*Rev.* William). A thrilling narrative of the life, adventures, and terrible crimes of James Bagwell; who was tried at Somerset (Pa.) for murder. [*anon.*] 42 pp. 8°. *Cincinnati, William Miller*, [1851].

Miller *and* **Richard**. [Type specimens]. 41 l. 4°. [*London*, 1851]?

Millien (Achille). La moisson. Poésies. Avec une préface par Thalès Bernard. 302 pp. 12°. *Paris, C. Vanier*, 1860. s.

Millingen (Frederick, *Osman-Seify-Bey*). La Turquie sous la règne d'Abdul-Aziz (1862–67). 491 pp. 1 map. 8°. *Paris, librairie internationale*, 1868.

Milliroux (J. Felix). L'abolition de l'esclavage par l'Angleterre, la France, les États-Unis. Rapprochements. 16 pp. 8°. *Paris, E. Dentu*, 1866.

Mills (Abraham). The ancient Hebrews: with an introductory essay concerning the world before the flood. 443 pp. 1 pl. 12°. *New York, A. S Barnes & co.* 1856. s.

Mills (Henry). Horæ germanicæ: a version of German hymns. 2d ed. 368 pp. 12°. *Auburn, Miller, Orton & Mulligan*, 1856. s.

Mills (John Cruger, *editor*). The Shaksperean oracle. 147 pp. 12°. *New York, Bunce & bro.* 1855. s.

Milton (John). Works. 5 p. l. 568 pp. fol. [London]? 1697.

CONTENTS.

The doctrine and discipline of divorce.
Tetrachordon: expositions upon the four chief places in scripture, which treat of marriage.
Colasterion: a reply to a nameless answer against The doctrine and discipline of divorce.
The judgment of Martin Bucer, concerning divorce.
Of reformation, touching church discipline in England.
The reason of church government urged against prelacy.
A treatise of civil power in ecclesiastical causes.
Considerations touching the likeliest means to remove hirelings out of the church.
Of prelatical episcopacy.
Animadversions upon the remonstrant's [bishop Hall] defence against Smectymnuus.
An apology against A modest confutation of the Animadversions, etc. against Smectymnuus.
The ready and easy way to establish a free commonwealth.
Areopagitica; a speech for the liberty of unlicenc'd printing.
The tenure of kings and magistrates.
Brief notes upon a sermon, tituled, The fear of God and the king. By M. Griffith. D. D.
Of true religion, heresie, schism, toleration, etc.
Eikonoclastes, in answer to Eikon basilike.
Articles of peace with the Irish rebels, Scotch Irish representation with observations.

——— [Paradise lost]. Ens enska skálds, J. Milton's Paradísar missir. Á Íslenzku snúinn af pjodskáldi íslendínga Joní Porlákssyni. xii, 408 pp. 8°. *Kaupmannahöfn, H. F. Popp*, 1828. s.

Milwaukee (*Wisconsin*). The Milwaukee city directory, for 1851 and 1856. 2v. 12°. *Milwaukee*, 1851–46. s.

——— The same. Directory, 1868–9. By J. Thickens. 300 pp. 8°. *Milwaukee, Hawks & Burdick*, 1868.

Mines (Flavel S.) A presbyterian clergyman looking for the church. By one of three hundred. xvii, 580 pp. 12°. *New York, Pudney & Russell*, 1855. s.

Ministerial (The) legacy. By a lady. [*anon.* S. A. B.] 212 pp. 3 pl. 12°. *Rochester, E. Darrow & bro.* 1858. s.

Minnesota railroad and river guide, for 1867-68. Compiled by A. Bailey. 486 pp. 1 map. 2 pl. 8°. *Saint Paul, J. M. Wolfe,* 1867.

Minot (George Richards). The history of the insurrections in Massachusetts, in 1786, and the rebellion consequent thereon. 2ᵈ ed. 192 pp. 8°. *Boston, J. W. Burditt & co.* 1810.

Minucius Felix (Marcus). *See* **Felix** (Marcus Minucius).

Minutes of the christian convention, held at Aurora, Illinois, Oct. 31 and Nov. 1, 1867. Containing the proceedings and resolutions of the convention [respecting freemasonry]. 2ᵈ ed. 108 pp. 16°. *Chicago, E. A. Cook,* 1868.

Miquel (Frederik Antonie Willem). Choix de plantes rares ou nouvelles cultivées et dessinées dans le jardin botanique de Buitenzorg. Publié avec un texte explicatif. 39 l. 26 col. pl. 8°. *La Haye, C. W. Mieling,* 1863. s.

——— Flora van nederlandsch Indië. [*Or*] Flora Indiae batavae. 3 v. in 4. 8°. *Amsterdam,* [*etc.*] *C. G. Van der Post, etc.* 1855-59. s.

CONTENTS:

v. 1. Continens dicotyledones polypetalas.
pt. 1. Dicotyledones polypetalae perigynae. 2 p. l. xxiv, 1116 pp. 1 portrait. pl. 1-14. 1855-58.
pt. 2. Dicotyledones polypetalae hypogynae. xii, 704 pp. pl. 15-30. 1859.
v. 2. Continens dicotyledones monopetalas, nec non ordines gymnospermi. ix, 1103 pp. 1 front. and pl. 31-36. 1856-59.
v. 3. Monocotyledones, et conspectus phytogeographicus. 2 p. l. x, 773 pp. 1 tab. 1 front. pl. 37-41. 2 maps. 1855.

——— The same. 1ᵗᵉ bijvoegsel. Sumatra, zijne plantenwereld en hare voortbrengselen. [*Or*] Supplementum primum. Prodromus florae sumatranae. xxiv, 656 pp. 4 pl. 8°. *Amsterdam, C. G. Van der Post, etc.* 1860. s.

Mirabaud (Jean Baptiste de). Le monde, son origine, et son antiquité. [*anon.*] 1ᵉ partie. xii, 244 pp. 16°. *Londres,* [*Paris, Briasson*], 1751.

Mirabaud. [*pseudon.*] *See* **Holbach** (Paul Thiry, *baron* de).

Mirandola (Giovanni Francesco Pico, *signore* della). *See* **Pico.**

Mirbel (Charles François Brisseau). *See* **Brisseau-Mirbel.**

Mirk (John). Instructions for popish priests. Edited from the ms. by E. Peacock. xi, 103 pp. 8°. *London, Trübner & co.* 1868.

[EARLY English text society publications. no. 31].

Miscellanea physico-medico-mathematica, oder, angenehme, curieuse und nützliche nachrichten von physical- und medicinischen auch dahin gehörigen kunst- und literaturgeschichten, welche in 1727-30, in Deutschland und andern reichen sich zugetragen haben, oder bekannt worden sind: gesammlet und herausgegeben von Andreas Elias Büchner. 4 v. 4°. *Erfurt, C. F. Jungnicol,* 1731-34. s.

Miscellaneous (A) metaphysical essay; or, an hypothesis concerning the formation and generation of spiritual and material beings. By an impartial inquirer after truth. [*anon.*] vi, 394 pp. 2 pl. 8°. *London, A. Millar,* 1748.

Miss Muff and little Hungry. [*anon.*] 40 pp. 4 col. pl. sm. 4°. *Philadelphia, presby. pub. com.* 1866.

Mission (The) school in Mill village. [*anon*]. 286 pp. 3 pl. 16°. *Boston, American tract society,* [1867].

Mississippi (*State of*). Constitution of the state as amended, with the ordinances and resolutions adopted by the constitutional convention, August, 1865. 56 pp. 8°. *Jackson,* (*Miss.*) *E. M. Yerger,* 1865.

——— Journals of the proceedings and debates in the constitutional convention, August, 1865. 198 pp. 8°. *Jackson,* (*Miss.*) *E. M. Yerger,* 1865.

Missouri (*State of*). Journal of the senate and house of representatives, at the adjourned session of the 24ᵗʰ general assembly, 1868. [With appendix]. 3 v. 8°. *Jefferson City, E. Kirby,* 1868.

Missouri grand lodge. Proceedings of the grand lodge of free and accepted masons, of the state of Missouri; convened in the city of Lexington, May, 1856. 128 pp. 8°. *Saint Louis, M. Niedner & co.* 1856. s.

Mitchel (John, *Irish agitator*). The history of Ireland, from the treaty of Limerick to the present time; being a continuation of the history of the abbé Macgeoghegan. xvi, 636 pp. 1 portrait. 8°. *New York, D. & J. Sadlier & co.* 1868.

Mitchell (John, *M. D. F. R. S.*) The contest in America between Great Britain and France, with its consequences and importance, etc. By an impartial hand. [*anon.*] xlix, 244 pp. 8°. *London, A. Miller,* 1757.

——— The present state of Great Britain and North America, with regard to agriculture, population, trade, and manufactures, impartially considered. [*anon.*] 4 p. l. xvi, 363 pp. 8°. *London, T. Becket,* 1767.

Mitchell (M. S.) A manual of elocution founded upon the philosophy of the human voice. 396 pp. 12°. *Philadelphia, Eldridge & bro.* 1868.

Mitchell (Samuel Augustus). Geographical question book. 140 pp. 16°. *Philadelphia, Thomas, Cowperthwait & co.* 1852. s.

——— Primary geography. 2d ed. 1 p. l. 176 pp. sq. 16°. *Philadelphia, Thomas, Cowperthwait & co.* 1849. s.

——— School geography. A system of modern geography, comprising a description of the present state of the world. 336 pp. 1 pl. 12°. *Philadelphia, Thomas, Cowperthwait & co.* 1849. s.

Mitchell (S. Weir, *M. D.*) The wonderful stories of Fuz-buz the fly, and mother Grabem the spider. [*anon.*] 79 pp. 9 pl. 16°. *Philadelphia, J. B. Lippincott,* 1867.

Mitchell (*Rev.* Walter). Bryan Maurice; or, the seeker. 288 pp. 12°. *Philadelphia, J. B. Lippincott & co.* 1867.

Mitchill (Samuel Latham, *M. D.*) A discourse delivered before the New York historical society, December, 1813. Embracing a comprehensive account of the writings which illustrate the botanical history of North and South America. 8°. *New York, Van Winkle & Wiley,* 1814.
[*In* NEW YORK historical society. Collections. v. 2. 1st series].

Mitscherlich (Eilhard). Lehrbuch der chemie. 2 v. in 3. 8°. *Berlin, E. F. Mittler,* 1833–40. s.
[v. 2. abth. i. wanting].

Moberly (*Rev.* George). The administration of the holy spirit in the body of Christ. xii, 344 pp. 8°. *Oxford, J. Parker & co.* 1868.
[BAMPTON lectures. 1868.]

Moberly (W.) British Columbia. Columbia river exploration, 1865. Instructions, reports, and journals, relating to the government exploration of country lying between the Shuswap and Okanagan lakes and the Rocky mountains. 2 p. l. 36 pp. fol. *New Westminster, government printing office,* 1866. s.

Möbius (Theodor, *editor*). Analecta norrœna, auswahl aus der isländischen und norwegischen litteratur des mittelalters. xiv, 319 pp. 8°. *Leipzig, J. C. Hinrichs,* 1859.

Model (The) merchant; or, memoirs of Samuel Budgett. 187 pp. 12°. *Philadelphia, presbyterian board of publication,* 1858. s.

Modern characteristics. A series of short essays. From the Saturday review. [*anon.*] viii, 295 pp. 12°. *London, Tinsley bros.* 1865.

Modern women, and what is said of them. A reprint of a series of articles in the Saturday review, with preface by Mrs. L. Gilbert Calhoun. [*anon.*] 371 pp. 12°. *New York, J. S. Redfield,* 1868.

Modestus. De vocabulis rei militaris libellus, etc. 4°. *Antverpiæ,* 1585.
[*In* VEGETIUS (F.) De re militari. 1585].

Moebius. *See* **Möbius.**

Moerch. *See* **Mörch.**

Moffat (A. S.) The secrets of angling. xi, 326 pp. 12°. *Edinburgh, A. & C. Black,* 1865.

Moffat (J. M.) A system of natural philosophy, for schools and academies. With emendations, notes, [etc.] by W. R. Johnson. 8th ed. Illustrated. 473 pp. 12°. *Philadelphia, E. C. Biddle,* 1845.

Mohammed (*called the prophet*). *See* **Koran.**

Mohl (Hugo von). Investigation of the question: does cellulose form the basis of all vegetable membranes. 8°. *London,* 1853.
[*In* HENFREY (A.) *and* HUXLEY (T. H.) Scientific memoirs, art. 4].

Moir (David Macbeth). The wounded spirit, a tale of life. 8°. *Philadelphia, T. K. Greenbank,* 1833.
[GREENBANK'S periodical library. v. 1. pp. 329–354].

Moir (Thomas). An inquiry into some curious and interesting subjects of history, antiquity, and science. 274 pp. 16°. *London, Lackington, Allen & co.* 1817.

Moithey (P. J. *of Vouziers*). Marie Antoinette d'Autriche, reine de France et de Navarre. Par M. de Vouziers. [*pseudon.*] 108 pp. 1 portrait. 8°. *Paris, Tiger,* [*about* 1816].

Molbech (Christian). Forelæsninger over den nyere danske poesie, etc. 2 v. x, 306 pp; 2 p. l. 322 pp. 8°. *Kiöbenhavn, C. A. Reitzel,* 1832. s.

Moleschott (Jacob). Lehre der nahrungsmittel. Für das volk. 3e aufl. xx, 329 pp. 8°. *Erlangen, F. Enke,* 1858.

Moletti (Giuseppe). Discorso, nel quale con uia facile e brieue, si dichiarano e insegnano tutti i termini, e tutti le regole appartenenti alla geografia. 65 pp. sm. 4°. *Venetia, G. Zilletti,* 1573.
[*With* PTOLEMÆUS (C.) Geografia. *Venetia,* 1574].

Molinet (Jean). Chroniques. Publiées par J. A. Buchon. 5 v. 8°. *Paris, Verdière,* 1827–28.
[COLLECTION de chroniques nationales françaises. v. 43–47].

Mollineux (*Mrs.* Mary). Fruits of retirement; or, miscellaneous poems, moral and divine. [With] some account of the author. 16 p. l. 182 pp. 18°. *Philadelphia, S. Keimer,* 1729.
[Imperfect].

Mommsen (Theodor). Römische geschichte. Bis zur schlacht von Thapsus. 3 v. 8°. *Berlin, Weidmann*, 1855–56.
[NOTE.—v. 1, 2d ed.]

Monardes (Nicolas). Delle cose, che vengono portate dall' Indie Occidentali pertinenti all'vso della medicina. Doue ancho tratta de' veneni, e della lor cura. Nouamente recata dalla Spagnola nella lingua italiana. 2 v. in 1. 7 p. l. 243 pp. 6 l. 16°. *Venetia, G. Ziletti*, 1582.

——— The same. Simplicivm medicamentorvm ex novo orbe delatorvm, qvorvm in medicina vsvs est, historia; Latino deinde donata, et contracta, in super annotationibus illustrata à Carolo Clvsio. 3ª ed. pp. 313–456. 16°. *Antverpiæ, ex officina Plantiniana*, 1593.
[*With* ORTA (G. de). Aromatvm et simplicivm medicamentorvm. 1593. Imperfect: wanting pp. 321–352.]

——— Della historia de i semplici, aromati, et altre cose che vengono portate dall' Indie Orientali, pertinenti alla medicina. Tradotti da A. Briganti. pp. 237–347. 16°. *Venetia, G. Ziletti*, 1582.
[*With* MONARDES (N.) Delle cose che vengono portate dall' Indie Occidentali, etc. ed. 1582].

Moncel (*Vicomte* Théodore Achille Louis du). *See* **Du Moncel**.

Monette (John W. *M. D.*) Observations on the epidemic yellow fever of Natchez and the southwest. 155 pp. 8°. *Louisville, (Ky.) Prentice & Weissinger*, 1842. s.

Monino (José, *conde de Floridablanca*). Obras originales, y escritos referentes a su persona. xlv, 532 pp. 8°. *Madrid, M. Rivadeneyra*, 1867.
[BIBLIOTECA de autores españoles. v. 59].

Monitory lessons to church members. [*anon.*] 161 pp. 12°. *Philadelphia, presbyterian board of publication*, [1855]. s.

Monnet (Jean). Anthologie françoise, ou chansons choisies, depuis le 13ᵉ siécle jusqu'à présent. [Mises en musique]. [Avec memoire sur la chanson, par Meusnier de Querlon. Illustré. *anon.*] 3 v. 8°. [*Paris, Barbou*], 1765.

Monnier (Henri). Physiologie du bourgeois. 124 pp. 16°. *Paris, Aubert et cie. & Lavigne*, [1841].
[*With* ALHOY (P. M.) Physiologie du voyageur].

Monro (*Rev.* Edward). The combatants: an allegory. 182 pp. 2 pl. 16°. *New York, gen. prot. episcopal s. s. union*, 1848. s.

Monselet (Charles). La lorgnette littéraire. Dictionnaire des grands et des petits auteurs de mon temps. xviii, 240 pp. 16°. *Paris, Poulet-Malassis & De Broise*, 1857.

Monstrelet (Enguerrand de). Chroniques. 15 v. 8°. *Paris, J. A. Buchon*, 1826–27.
[COLLECTION de chroniques nationales françaises. v. 26–40].

Montaigne (Camille). Plantes cellulaires. 4°. *Paris*, 1840.
[*In* WEBB (Philip B.) *and* BERTHELOT. Histoire naturelle des îles Canaries. v. 3].

Montaigne (*Abbé* ———). Recherches sur les connaissances intellectuelles des sourd-muets, considérés par rapport à l'administration des sacramens, [etc.] x, 220 pp. 8°. *Louvain, C. J. Fonteyn*, 1847. s.

Montalboddo (Fracanzano) *or* **Fracanzano da Montalboddo** (Antonio). Paesi nouamente ritrouati per la nauigatione di Spagna in Calicut, et da Albertutio Vesputio Fiorentino intitulato mondo nouo. Nouamente impresso. 124 l. 18°. *Venetia, Zorzo de Rusconi*, 1521.
NOTE.—Brunet, Gräesse, and Tirasboschi agree that this first collection of the voyages of Vespucius was compiled by Montalboddo, though others assert it to be the work of Alessandro Zorzi.

Montalembert (Charles Forbes, *comte* de). The monks of the west, from St. Benedict to St. Bernard. Authorized translation. v. 3–5. 8°. *Edinburgh, W. Blackwood & sons*, 1867.

Montcalm de Saint Véran (Louis Joseph, *marquis* de). Lettres à messieurs de Berryer et de la Molé, 1757–59. Avec une version angloise. 28, 28 pp. 8°. *Londres, J. Almon*, 1777.

Monteith (James). Youth's history of the United States. 2 p. l. 88 pp. 4°. *New York, A. S. Barnes & co.* 1858.

Montfort (—— de). Vasconiana; ou, recueil des bon mots, des pensées les plus plaisantes, et des rencontres les plus vives des Gascons. [*anon.*] 4 p. l. 482 pp. 1 l. 16°. *Paris, M. Brunet*, 1708.

Montjoie (Christophe Félix Louis Ventre de Latouloubre, *known as* Galart de). Histoire de la conjuration de Maximilien Robespierre. [*anon.*] 120 pp. 8°. *Paris*, [*auteur?* 1795]. s.

Montpleinchant (*Abbé* J. C. Bruslé de). *See* **Bruslé de Montpleinchant**.

Montresor (*Col.* J.) Journal of a tour from the St. Lawrence to the Kennebec, about 1760. 8°. *Portland, Day, Fraser & co.* 1831.
[*In* MAINE historical society. Collections. v. 1].

Mont-Rond (P. E. de). Histoire de la conquête de l'Algérie de 1830 à 1847. 2 v. 435 pp; 448 pp. 8°. *Paris, E. Marc-Aurel*, 1847.

Mooney (Thomas). Nine years in America: in a series of letters to his cousin, P. Mooney, a farmer in Ireland. Part 1. 2ᵈ ed. 154 pp. 18°. *Dublin, J. McGlashan*, 1850.

Moore (*Rev.* A. Y.) The life of Schuyler Colfax. 394 pp. portrait. 12°. *Philadelphia, T. B. Peterson & bros.* 1868.

Moore (*Rev.* Henry D. *editor*). The winter-bloom. [A literary annual]. 240 pp. 9 col. pl. 8°. *Philadelphia, Hogan & Thompson,* 1850. s.

Moore (J. F.) The Clifford household. 307 pp. 4 pl. 16°. *New York, M. W. Dodd,* 1867.

Moore (Nathaniel F.) Ancient mineralogy; or, an inquiry respecting mineral substances mentioned by the ancients, [etc.] 192 pp. 12°. *New York, G. & C. Carvill & co.* 1834. s.

Moore (Thomas, *English poet*). Beauties. *See* **French** (B. F.) The beauties of Scott and Moore.

Moore (Thomas, *of Maryland*). The great error of American agriculture exposed; and hints for improvement suggested. 72 pp. 8°. *Baltimore, author,* 1801. s.

Moore (T. V.) The last days of Jesus; or, the appearances of our Lord during the forty days between the resurrection and ascension. 300 pp. 12°. *Philadelphia, presbyterian board of publication,* [1858]. s.

Moos (H. M.) Hannah; or, a glimpse of paradise. A tale. 351 pp. 16 pl. 8°. *Cincinnati, literary eclectic publishing house,* 1868.

Moquin-Tandon (Horace Bénédict Alfred). Carya magalonensis; ou, noyer de Maguelonne. 2e éd. avec la traduction en regard. 3 p. l. xxiv, 171 pp. 12°. *Montpellier, etc. Boehm & cie,* 1844. s.

——— Ornithologie canarienne. 4°. *Paris,* 1836–44.

[*In* WEBB (Philip B.) *and* BERTHELOT (S.) Histoire naturelle des îsles Canaries. v. 2].

Moral heroism; or, the trials and triumphs of the great and good. [*anon.*] 344 pp. 6 pl. 16°. *Philadelphia, American sunday school union,* 1850. s.

Moratin (Leandro Fernandez de). El si de las niñas, comedia en tres actos, en prosa. Ilustrada con noticias biograficas y notas gramaticales en Aleman, por H. M. Melford. 162 pp. 16°. *Brunsvico, E. Leibrock,* 1839. s.

[MELFORD (H. M.) Spanisch bühnenstücke, etc. v. 1].

Moravia. Codex diplomaticus et epistolaris Moraviae. Studio et opera Antonii Boczek, etc. v. 1-6. 4°. *Olomuncii, etc. A. Skarnitzl, etc.* 1836-54. s.

CONTENTS.

v. 1. 396–1199.
v. 2. 1200–1240.
v. 3. 1241–1267.
v. 4. 1268–1293.
v. 5. 1294–1306.
v. 6. 1307–1333.

Morden (Robert). Geography, rectified; or a description of the world. 4th ed. [With] a complete geographical index. 5 p. l. 626 pp. 36 l. 78 maps. sm. 4°. *London, R. Morden and T. Cockerill,* 1700.

Morell (J. D.) An historical and critical view of the speculative philosophy of Europe in the nineteenth century. 752 pp. 8°. *New York, R. Carter & bro.* 1851.

Morford (Henry). Appletons' short trip to Europe. [1868.] Principally devoted to England, Scotland, Ireland, Switzerland, France, Germany, and Italy; with glimpses of Spain, etc. and a collation of traveller's phrases in French and German. 335 pp. 1 map. 16°. *New York, Appleton,* 1868.

——— Paris in '67; or, the great exposition, its side-shows and excursions. 395 pp. 1 pl. 12°. *New York, G. W. Carleton & co.* 1867.

Morga (Antonio de). The Philippine islands, Moluccas, Siam, Cambodia, Japan, and China, at the close of the sixteenth century. Translated from the Spanish, with notes and a preface; and a letter from Luis Vaez de Torres, describing his voyage through the Torres straits. xxx, 431 pp. 2 pl. 8°. *London, Hakluyt society,* 1868.

[HAKLUYT society publications, no. 39].

Morgan (Charles E. *M. D.*) Electro-physiology and therapeutics; being a study of the electrical and other physical phenomena of the muscular and other systems during health and disease, including the phenomena of the electrical fishes. Edited by W. A. Hammond. xvi, 714 pp. 8°. *New York, W. Wood & co.* 1868.

Morgan (Lewis H.) The American beaver and his works. 330 pp. 1 map. 23 pl. 8°. *Philadelphia, Lippincott,* 1868.

Mornand (Félix). La vie de Paris. 316 pp. 18°. *Paris, veuve Dondey-Dupré,* 1855.

Mornay (Philippe de, seigneur du Plessis Marly). A worke concerning the trewnesse of christian religion, against atheists, epicures, paynims, iewes, mahumetists, and other infidels. Translated [from the French], by sir P. Sidney and A. Golding. 12 p. l. 552 pp. b. l. sm. 4°. *London, R. Robinson, for J. B.* 1592.

Mornings of the recess. 1861-64. A series of biographical and literary papers. Reprinted by permission from the "Times." [*anon.*] 2 v. 347 pp; 346 pp. 12°. *London, Tinsley bros.* 1864.

Morrell (L. A.) The American shepherd: being a history of the sheep, with their breeds, management, and diseases. xxii, 437 pp. 12°. *New York, Harpers,* 1851.

Morris (Edmund). Farming for boys. What they have done, and what others may do, in the cultivation of farm and garden. How to begin, how to proceed, and what to aim at. [*anon.*] With illustrations. ix, 286 pp. sm. 4°. *Boston, Ticknor & Fields,* 1868.

Morris (Gouverneur). A discourse [on the history of New York from 1763-83] delivered before the New York historical society, Dec. 1812. 8°. *New York, Van Winkle & Wiley,* 1814.

[*In* NEW YORK historical society. Collections. v. 2. 1st series].

——— An inaugural discourse [on the uses of history], delivered before the New York historical society, Sept. 1816. 8°. *New York, Bliss & White,* 1821.

[*In* NEW YORK historical society. Collections. v. 3. 1st series].

Morris (Isaac). A narrative of the dangers and distresses which befel Isaac Morris and seven more of the crew belonging to the Wager storeship, etc. 87 pp. 12°. *London, S. Burt,* [*about* 1750].

Morris (John Gottlob). The catechumen's and communicant's companion for the use of young persons of the lutheran church. 3^{d} ed. 268 pp. 16°. *Baltimore, T. N. Kurtz,* 1854. s.

——— Catherine de Bora, [afterward Luther]; or, social and domestic scenes in the home of Luther. 127 pp. 12°. *Philadelphia, Lindsay & Blakiston,* 1856. s.

Morris (John M.) History of Connecticut during the war of 1861-65. *See* **Croffut** (W. A.) *and* **Morris.**

Morris (Thomas A. *D. D.*) A discourse on methodist church polity. 93 pp. 1 portrait. 16°. *Cincinnati, L. Swormstedt & A. Poe,* 1859. s.

Morris (William). The defence of Guenevere, and other poems. viii, 248 pp. 16°. *London, Bell & Daldy,* 1858.

Morrison (John, *M. D.*) Medicine no mystery; being a brief outline of the principles of medical science. xxxii, 165 pp. 8°. *London, Hurst, Chance, & co.* 1829.

Morse (Jedidiah, *D. D.*) Annals of the American revolution; [with] an account of the first settlement of the country, and of the principal Indian wars. [With] a biography of the principal military officers who were instrumental in achieving our independence. 2 p. l. 400, 50 pp. 8°. *Hartford, O. D. Cooke & sons,* 1824.

——— A sermon preached at Charlestown, November 29, 1798, on the anniversary thanksgiving in Massachusetts. With an appendix. 88 pp. 8°. *Worcester, D. Greenleaf,* 1799.

——— *and* **Morse** (Sidney Edwards). A new system of geography, ancient and modern. 23^{d} ed. 278, 100 pp. 16°. *Boston, Richardson & Lord,* 1822.

Morse (Sidney Edwards). A new system of geography. 1822. *See* **Morse** (Jedidiah) *and* **Morse** (S. E).

Mortimer (Charlotte B.) Marrying by lot. A tale of the primitive Moravians. 405 pp. 12°. *New York, G. P. Putnam & son,* 1868.

Mortimer (John). The whole art of husbandry; or, the way of managing and improving land. 3^{d} ed. 8 p. l. 592 pp. 12°. *London, H. & G. Mortlock,* 1712.

Morton (Samuel George, *M. D.*) An inquiry into the distinctive characteristics of the aboriginal race of America. 2^{d} ed. 48 pp. 8°. *Philadelphia, J. Penington,* 1844. s.

Morveau (Guyton de). *See* **Guyton de Morveau.**

Mosenthal (S. H.) Düweke. Drama in funf aufzügen. 140 pp. 16°. *Leipzig, Veit & co.* 1860. s.

Moser (Ludwig). Die gesetze der lebensdauer. Nebst untersuchungen über dauer, fruchtbarkeit der ehen, über todtlichkeit der krankheiten, verhältniss der geschlechter bei der geburt, über einfluss der witterung u. s. w. Und einem anhang enthaltend die berechnung der leibrenten. xxviii, 399 pp. 2 pl. 8°. *Berlin, Veit & co.* 1839. s.

Moses (Thomas P.) Leisure thoughts, in prose and verse. 192 pp. 12°. *Portsmouth, (N. H.) S. A. Badger,* 1849. s.

Moss (*Rev.* Lemuel). Annals of the United States christian commission. 752 pp. 10 pl. 8°. *Philadelphia, Lippincott & co.* 1868.

Motley (John Lothrop). History of the United Netherlands; from the death of William the silent to the twelve years' truce—1609. 4 v. 8°. *New York, Harpers,* 1868.

——— The rise of the Dutch republic. A history. 3 v. 8°. *New York, Harpers,* 1864.

Motschulsky (Victor von). Coléoptères de la Sibérie orientale et en particulier des rives de l'Amour, 1860.

[*In* SCHRENCK (L. von). Reisen im Amur-lande. v. 2. 2e lief].

Motschulsky (V. von). Die coleopterologischen verhaeltnisse und die käfer Russlands. [Extract from Bulletin de la societe imp. de Moscou]. 1 p. l. 141 pp. 8°. *Moscou, W. Gautier*, 1846. s.

——— Die käfer Russlands bearbeitet. (i. Insecta carabica). [Extract from Bulletin de la sociéte imp. de Moscou]. v, 72 pp. 9 tab. 1 col. map. 8°. *Moscou, W. Gautier*, 1850. s.
[*With* the preceding].

Moulins. *See* **Des Moulins.**

Mountain (Didymus). The gardeners labyrinth. Containing a discovrse of the gardeners life, in the yearly trauels to be bestowed on his plot of earth for the vse of a garden. Also the physick benefit of each herb, plant, and flowre. 4 p. l. 180 pp. 3 l. 3 pl. sm. 4°. *London, H. Ballard*, 1608.

Mount Royal popular tales. By eminent authors. [*polyon.*] 255 pp. 16°. *Montreal, W. B. Cordier & co.* 1866.

Mudie (Robert). Babylon the great: a dissection of men and things in the British capital. [*anon.*] 2 v. iv, 306 pp; vi, 303 pp. 12°. *Philadelphia, Carey & Lea*, 1825.

Mühlbach (Luise, *pseudon.*) *See* **Mundt** (Clara Müller).

Mühry (Adolf, *M. D.*) Supplement zur klimatographischen uebersicht der erde. Mit einem appendix enthaltend untersuchungen ueber das wind-system, [etc.] xii, 320 pp. 3 col. maps. 8°. *Leipzig, C. F. Winter.* 1865. s.

Mulder (Gerardus Johannes). Die chemie der oestrocknenden oele, ihre bereitung und ihre technische anwendung in künsten und gewerben. Nach der holländischen original-ausgabe bearbeitet von J. Müller. vii, 255 pp. 8°. *Berlin, J. Springer*, 1867. s.

Mulder (L.) Leesbock over de mestmakerij, de wijze van bemesting en vrucht-baarmaking van den grond, [etc.] viii, 139 pp. 16°. *Deventer, J. De Lange*, 1854. s.

Mullens (*Mrs. of Calcutta*). Life by the Ganges, or faith and victory. 288 pp. 3 pl. 16°. *Philadelphia, presbyterian pub. comm.* 1867.

Müller (Adam Heinrich). Briefwechsel. 1800-29. *See* **Gentz** (Friedrich) *and* **Müller.**

Müller (Carl). Musci [von Mossambique]. fol. *Berlin*, 1864.
[*In* PETERS (W. C. H.) Nat. reise nach Mossambique. Botanik].

——— (*Editor*). *See* **Natur** (Die).

Müller (Ferdinand Heinrich). Der ugrische volksstamm, oder untersuchungen über die ländergebiete am Ural und am Kaukasus, in historischer, geographischer und ethnographischer beziehung. Erster oder geographischer theil. 1[e] abth. xxxii, 516 pp. 12°. *Berlin, Duncker & Humblot*, 1837.

——— The same. 2[e] abth. Historisch-geographische darstellung des stromsystems der Wolga. xxxii, 679 pp. 8°. *Berlin, G. D. Lüderitz*, 1839.

Müller (Frederic Max). Chips from a German workshop. v. 1. Essays on the science of religion. v. 2. Essays on mythology, traditions, and customs. 2 v. xxxiii, 379 pp; 3 p. l. 356 pp. 8°. *London, Longmans*, 1867.

——— The languages of the seat of war in the east. With a survey of the three families of languages, Semitic, Arian, and Turanian. 2[d] ed. With an appendix on the missionary alphabet, and an ethnographical map, drawn by Augustus Petermann. xcvi, 150 pp. 1 tab. 1 col. map. 8°. *London, Williams & Norgate*, 1855. s.

——— On the stratification of language. Sir Robert Rede's lecture, 1868. 1 p. l. 44 pp. 8°. *London, Longmans*, 1868.

Muller (Frederik, *bookseller at Amsterdam*). Beschrijvende catalogus van 7000 portretten van Nederlanders, en van Buitenlanders, tot Nederland in betrekking staande, afkomstig uit de collectiën: de Burlett, Verstolk van Soelen, Lamberts, enz. xiv, 408 pp. 8°. *Amsterdam, F. Muller*, 1853. s.

——— Bibliothek van nederlandsche pamfletten. Eerste afdeeling. Verzameling van F. Muller. Naar tijdsorde gerangschikt en beschreven door P. A. Tiele. v. 1-3. 4°. *Amsterdam, F. Muller*, 1858-61. s.

CONTENTS.

v. 1. 1500-1648. 4 p. l. 406, 8, 19 pp.
v. 2. 1649-1672. 2 p. l. 232, 6 pp.
v. 3. 1672-1702. 4 p. l. 308 pp.

——— Catalogue of books relating to America, including a large number of rare works printed before 1700, amongst which a nearly complete collection of the Dutch publications on New Netherland, from 1612 to 1820. 104 pp. 16°. *Amsterdam, F. Muller*, [1850].

Müller (*Prof.* Heinrich, *of Würzburg*). Upon the male of argonauta argo and the hectocotyli. 8°. *London*, 1853.
[HENFREY (A.) *and* HUXLEY (T. H.) Scientific memoirs. art. 2].

Müller (Johann Gottwerth). Komische romane aus den papieren des braunen mannes, und des verfassers des Siegfried von Lindenberg. 8 v. 16°. *Göttingen, J. C. Dieterich*, 1786-91.

Müller (Johann Gottwerth)—continued.

CONTENTS.

v. 1–2. Die herren von Waldheim.
v. 3–6. Emmerich.
v. 7–8. Herr Thomas.

[NOTE.—v. 1-2 are of the 2d ed.]

Müller (Johannes). Catalog der hinterlassenen bibliothek. 2 p. l. 309 pp. 8°. *Bonn, C. Georgi*, 1858. s.

—— Fossile fische. 4°. *St. Petersburg*, 1848. s.

[*In* MIDDENDORFF (A. T. von). Reise, etc. v. 1. theil 1].

Müller (J. G.) Geschichte der amerikanischen urreligionen. viii, 706 pp. 8°. *Basel, Schweigerhauser*, 1855. s.

Müller (Max). *See* **Müller** (Frederic Max).

Müller (*Rev.* Michael). The blessed eucharist our greatest treasure. 360 pp. 12°. *Baltimore, Kelly & Piet*, 1868.

—— Prayer the key of salvation. 272 pp. 12°. *Baltimore, Kelly & Piet*, 1868.

Müller (Niclas). Mithras. Eine vergleichende uebersicht der berühmteren mithrischen denkmäler und erklärung des ursprungs und der sinndeute ihrer symbole, [etc.] xv, 152 pp. 1 pl. 8°. *Wiesbaden, L. Riedel*, 1833. s.

Müller (Philipp Ludwig Statius, *editor*). *See* **Linné** (C. von). Die vollständiges natursystem, 1773.

Müller (Robert). Geographische ortsbestimmungen. Magnetische beobachtungen. Meteorologische beobachtungen. 4°. *Wien*, 1862.

[*In* WÜLLERSTORF-URBAIR (B. von). Reise der Novara. Nautisch-physikalischer theil].

Müller (Wilhelm). Geschichte und system der altdeutschen religion. xiv, 424 pp. 8°. *Göttingen, Vandenhoeck & Ruprecht*, 1844.

Muloch (Dinah Maria). *See* **Craik** (*Mrs.* D. M. M.)

Mulsant (Étienne). Histoire naturelle des coléoptères de France. [v. 8]. Vesicants. [With appendix. Longipèdes. Supplement]. [Extract]. 3 p. l. 201 pp. 8°. [*Lyon, société linnéenne*], *Paris, Magnin, Blanchard & co.* 1857. s.

Munch (Peter Andreas). Det norske folks historie. Forste deel. 6 v. 8°. *Christiania, C. Tonsberg*, 1851-59. s.

—— The same. Anden hovedafdeling. (Unionsperioden). 2 v. 8°. *Christiania, C. Tonsberg*, 1861–63. s.

—— Das heroische zeitalter der nordisch-germanischen völker, und die wikinger-züge. Eine übersetzung aus "Det norske folks historie," von G. F. Claussen. vi, 252 pp. 1 l. 8°. *Lübeck, A. Dittmer*, 1854.

Munch (Peter Andreas). Die nordisch-germanischen völker, ihre ältesten heimath-sitze, wanderzüge und zustände. Eine übersetzung [aus] "Det norske folks historie," von G. F. Claussen. viii, 264 pp. 1 map. 8°. *Lübeck, A. Dittmer*, 1853.

—— Historical notes upon Man and the Sudreys. *See* **Chronica** regvm Mannæ, etc.

Mundt (*Mrs.* Clara Müller). Andreas Hofer. An historical novel. By Louisa Mühlbach. [*pseudon.*] From the German by F. Jordan. 261 pp. 8 pl. 8°. *New York, Appletons*, 1868.

—— Germany in storm and stress. Old Fritz and the new era. By L. Mühlbach. [*pseudon.*] From the German by P. Langley. 271 pp. 4 pl. 8°. *New York, Appletons*, 1868.

—— Gœthe and Schiller. An historical romance. 283 pp. 8 pl. 8°. *New York, D. Appleton & co.* 1868.

—— Maria Theresa and her fireman. An historical novel. By L. Mühlbach. [*pseudon.*] From the German. 8°. *New York, Appletons*, 1868.

[*In her* MERCHANT of Berlin. pp. 243–291].

—— The merchant of Berlin. An historical novel. By Louisa Mühlbach. [*pseudon.*] From the German by A. Coffin, *M. D.* 291 pp. 4 pl. 8°. *New York, Appletons*, 1868.

Mundt (Theodor). Charlotte Stieglitz, ein denkmal. [*anon.*] iv, 314 pp. 1 pl. 4°. *Berlin, Veit & co.* [1835].

—— Count Mirabeau. An historical novel. From the German, by Thérèse J. Radford. 273 pp. 4 pl. 8°. *New York, Appletons*, 1868.

Munkalif monastery. Codex diplomatarius monasterii sancti Michaelis, bergensis dioecesis, vulgo Munkalif dicti, conscriptus A. C. 1427. Ex originali libro membraneo, nunc primum in lucem editus a P. A. Munch. 2 p. l. vii, 220 pp. 3 pl. 4°. *Christianiæ, C. Gröndahl*, 1845. s.

Muñoz (Juan Bautista). The history of the new world. Translated from the Spanish, with notes by the translator. [v. 1]. xv, 544 pp. 8°. *London, G. G. & J. Robinson*, 1797.

[No more published. Imperfect: map and pl. wanting].

Muñoz y Romero (Tomas). Diccionario bibliográfico-histórico de los antiguos reinos, provincias, ciudades, villas, iglesias y cantuarios de España. Obra premiada por la biblioteca nacional, [etc]. vii, 329 pp. 8°. *Madrid, gobierno*, 1858. s.

[SPAIN. Biblioteca nacional].

Munsell (Joel). Catalogue of a bibliographical library, collected by Joel Munsell, Albany. 8°. *Albany, J. Munsell*, 1856.

Munson (James E.) New classification and arrangement of phonography, [etc.] 12 pp. 12°. *New York, J. E. Munson*, 1868.

Muntaner (Ramon). Chronique. Traduit du Catalan, avec notes, par J. A. Buchon. 2 v. 8°. *Paris, Verdière*, 1827.

[COLLECTION de chroniques nationales françaises. v. 5–6].

Muratori (Lodovico Antonio). A relation of the missions of Paraguay. Done into English from the French translation [of F. E. de Lourmel]. xvi, 294 pp. 1 l. 16°. *London, J. Marmaduke*, 1759.

Murchison (*Sir* Roderick Impey). Siluria. The history of the oldest fossiliferous rocks and their foundations; with a brief sketch of the distribution of gold over the earth. 3[d] ed. (Including "The Silurian system.") xx, 592 pp. 3 maps. 1 col. pl. 41 l. 41 pl. 8°. *London, J. Murray*, 1859. s.

Murdock (James, *D. D.*) Sketches of modern philosophy, especially among the Germans. 201 pp. 18°. *Hartford, J. C. Wells*, 1842.

Muret (Pierre). Rites of funeral, ancient and modern, in use through the known world. Translated by P. Lorrain. 6 p. l. 308 pp. 16°. *London, R. Royston*, 1683.

Murphy (Rosalie Miller). Destiny; or, life as it is. 336 pp. 12°. *New York, M. Doolady*, 1867.

Murr (Christoph Gottlieb von). Journal zur kunstgeschichte und zur allgemeinen literatur. 17 v. 16°. *Nürnberg, J. E. Zeh*, 1775–89. s.

[No more (of present series) published].

Murray (Adam). General view of the agriculture of the county of Warwick. xii, 193 pp. 1 col. map. 1 pl. 8°. *London*, 1813. s.

[GREAT BRITAIN: Board of agriculture].

Murray (Amelia Matilda). Recollections from 1803 to 1837. With a conclusion in 1868. 3 p.l. 90 pp. 12°. *London, Longmans*, 1868.

Murray (Andrew) *and others.* Catalogue of the coleoptera of Scotland. viii, 145 pp. 12°. *Edinburgh, W. Blackwood & sons*, 1853. s.

Murray (Charles B.) The Nansemond sweet potato: directions for propagation, culture, and preservation. 24 pp, 24°. *Cincinnati, C. H. Morris & co.* 1861.

Murray (*Mrs.* Elizabeth). The modern system of painting in water colours, from the living model. 22 pp. 8°. *New York, Hurd & Houghton*, 1868.

Murray (John, *publisher*). A hand-book for travellers in Berks, Bucks, and Oxfordshire. Including a particular description of the university and city of Oxford. vi, 244 pp. 1 map. 2 pl. 16°. *London, J. Murray*, 1868.

——— Hand-book for travellers in Derbyshire, Nottinghamshire, Leicestershire, and Staffordshire. lii, 176 pp. 1 map. 16°. *London, J. Murray*, 1868.

——— A hand-book for travellers in Durham and Northumberland. vi, 336 pp. 1 map. 16°. *London, J. Murray*, 1864.

——— A hand-book for travellers in Gloucestershire, Worcestershire, and Herefordshire. xxviii, 183 pp. 1 map. 3 pl. 16°. *London, J. Murray*, 1867.

——— Hand-book for travellers in Ireland. 2[d] ed. revised. lxx, 358 pp. 3 maps. 16°. *London, J. Murray*, 1866.

——— A hand-book for travellers in central Italy; including Lucca, Tuscany, and its off-lying islands, Florence, Umbria, the Marches, part of the patrimony of St. Peter, and the island of Sardinia. 7th ed. xi, 480 pp. 2 maps. 16°. *London, J. Murray*, 1867.

——— Hand-book to London as it is. New ed. revised. 57, 317 pp. 1 map. 2 pl. 18°. *London, J. Murray*, [1867].

——— A hand-book for travellers in North Wales. 3[d] ed. xxxviii, 184 pp. 1 map. 16°. *London, J. Murray*, 1868.

——— A hand-book for visitors to Paris. 3[d] ed. revised. 2 p.l. 267 pp. 4 maps. 3 pl. 16°. *London, J. Murray*, 1868.

——— A hand-book of Rome and its environs. 8th ed. lv, 487 pp. 3 maps. 16°. *London, J. Murray*, 1867.

——— Hand-book for travellers in Russia, Poland, and Finland. 2[d] revised ed. x, 400 pp. 3 maps. 16°. *London, J. Murray*, 1868.

——— Hand-book for travellers in Scotland. 2[d] revised ed. lx, 433 pp. 10 maps. 16°. *London, J. Murray*, 1868.

——— Hand-book for Westmoreland, Cumberland, and the lakes. xxxv, 126 pp. 1 map. 16°. *London, J. Murray*, 1867.

——— Hand-book for travellers in Yorkshire. lx, 506 pp. 2 maps. 16°. *London, J. Murray*, 1867.

Murray (Lindley). [English] exercises, adapted to Murray's English grammar. 171 pp. 16°. *Philadelphia, Bennett & Walton*, 1812.

——— The same. 180 pp. 16°. *New York, Collins & Hannay*, [*about* 1830].

——— English grammar, adapted to the different classes of learners. 21st ed. 348 pp. 16°. *York, (Eng.) T. Wilson & son*, 1811.

Murray (L.) Introduction to the English reader. 162 pp. 18°. *Philadelphia, R. Christy,* 1831.

Musée national de Louvre. Notice des tableaux exposés dans les galeries du musée national du Louvre. Par Frédéric Villot. 1re partie. Écoles d'Italie et d'Espagne. 2e éd. lviii, 277 pp. 12°. *Paris, Vinchon,* 1852. s.

Musée royal. Notice des tableaux exposés dans le musée royal. 3 p. l. 250 pp. 16°. *Paris, Vinchon,* 1836. s.

Museum des neuesten und wissenswürdigsten aus dem gebiete der naturwissenschaft, der künste, der fabriken, der manufakturen, der technischen gewerbe, der landwirthschaft, der produkten- waaren- und handelskunde, und der bürgerlichen haushaltung, [etc.] Herausgegeben von S. F. Hermbstädt. 14 v. 8°. *Berlin, C. F. Amelang,* 1814–18. s.

——— *See, also,* **Bulletin** des neuesten, etc. 1809–13.

Musical (The) bulletin: a monthly journal of musical events, reviews, etc. Jan. to Dec. 1867. v. 1. 4°. *Troy, (N. Y.) C. W. Harris,* 1867.

Musical (The) journal. Edited by Alice Hawthorne. Jan. to Dec. 1867. v. 1. 4°. *Philadelphia, S. Winner & co.* [1867].

Musset (Louis Charles Alfred de). La confession d'un enfant du siècle. Nouv. éd. 353 pp. 12°. *Paris, Charpentier,* 1859.

——— Comédies et proverbes. 2 v. 12°. *Paris, Charpentier,* 1856.

——— The same. Éd. complète. 2 v. 455 pp; 428 pp. 12°. *Paris,* 1859.

——— Contes. 372 pp. 12°. *Paris, Charpentier,* 1860.

——— Nouvelles. 372 pp. 12°. *Paris, Charpentier,* 1860.

——— Œuvres posthumes. 248 pp. 12°. *Paris, Charpentier,* 1860.

——— Poésies nouvelles, 1836–52. Nouv. éd. 281 pp. 12°. *Paris, Charpentier,* 1859.

——— Premières poésies, 1829–35. Nouv. éd. 356 pp. 12°. *Paris, Charpentier,* 1858.

Musset (Paul Edme de). Lui et elle. 238 pp. 12°. *Paris, Charpentier,* 1860.

Muurling (W.) Practische godgeleerdhied, of beschouwing van de evangeliebediening voornamelijk in de nederlandsche hervormde kerk. 3 v [in 1]. 8°. *Groningen, J. Oomkens, j. zoon,* 1851–57. s.

My husband's crime. [A novel]. By M. R. Housekeeper. [*pseudon.*] 115 pp. 12 pl. 8°. *New York, Harpers,* 1868.

My mother; or, recollections of maternal influence. [*anon.*] 240 pp. 1 pl. 12°. *New York, W. H. Hyde,* 1849. s.

My new home. By the author of "Win and wear." [*anon.*] 383 pp. 6 pl. 16°. *New York, R. Carter & bros.* 1865.

My play is study. [*anon.*] 12°. *Philadelphia,* 1852. *See* **Mein** spielen ist lernen.

Myer (Albert J.) A manual of signals: for the use of signal officers in the field, and for students, etc. New ed. 417 pp. 31 pl. 12°. *New York, D. Van Nostrand,* 1868.

Myers (P. Hamilton). The first of the Knickerbockers: a tale of 1673. 2d ed. 222 pp. 12°. *New York, G. P. Putnam,* 1849. s.

——— The young patroon; or, christmas in 1690. A tale of New York. [*anon.*] 1 p. l. 142 pp. 12°. *New York, G. P. Putnam,* 1849. s.

Myers (*Mrs.* S. A.) Margaret Ashton; or, work and win. 336 pp. 3 pl. 18°. *Philadelphia, presbyterian board of publication,* 1866.

Myrc (J.) *See* **Mirk.**

Myrtle (Lewis, *pseudon?*) Cap sheaf. A fresh bundle. 313 pp. 12°. *New York, Redfield,* 1853. s.

Myrtle (Minnie, *pseudon.*) *See* **Johnson** (Anna C.)

Mysie's work, and how she did it. By the author of "Try." [*anon.*] 360 pp. 4 pl. 18°. *Philadelphia, presby. board of pub.* 1864.

Mystery (The) finished. The negro has a soul. His normal relation is that of a servant of tribute to Shem and Japheth. The negro is not a citizen of the state, but a member of the church by divine appointment, etc. [*anon.*] 144 pp. 12°. *Memphis, public ledger printing establishment,* 1868.

Nachrichten von den vereinigten deutschen evangelisch-lutherischen gemeinen in Nord-Amerika, absonderlich in Pensylvanien. [*anon.*] Mit einer vorrede von Johann Ludewig Schulze. 16 parts in 2 v. 1518 pp. 10 l. 4°. *Halle, Waisenhaus,* 1787.

[Fortsetzung der kurtzen nachricht von einigen evangelischen gemeinen in America].

Naismith (John). General view of the agriculture of the county of Clydesdale. xix, 252 pp. 1 col. map. 8°. *London,* 1806. s.

[Great Britain: Board of agriculture].

Nall (Josephine). The widow's sixpence; or, go thou and do likewise. 204 pp. 1 pl. 18°. *Philadelphia, presbyterian board of publication,* 1858. s.

Nancy Blake letters to a western cousin. [*anon.* By Ruth N. Cromwell?] 36 pp. 8°. *New Yord, J. Bradburn,* 1864.

Naphegyi (Gabor, *M. D.*) The album of language. Illustrated by the Lord's prayer in one hundred languages, with historical descriptions of the principal languages, interlinear translation and pronunciation of each prayer, [etc.] 324 pp. 1 pl. 4°. *Philadelphia, J. B. Lippincott & co.* 1869.

——— Among the Arabs. A narrative of adventures in Algeria. 1 p. l. 252 pp. 8°. *Philadelphia, J. B. Lippincott & co.* 1868.

Naples. *Archivum.* Syllabus membranarum ad regiae Siclae archivum pertinentium. 3 v. in 2. 4°. *Neapoli, ex regia typographia,* 1824-45. s.

CONTENTS:

v. 1. Membranae hactenus distinctae. (1266-1285). [Auctore A. A. Scottus]. xvi, 294 pp. 1824.
v. 2. A Caroli ii ad Roberti regnum. Opera et studio A. de Aprea. Pars i. (1285-1300). vi, 238 pp. 1832. Pars ii. (1300-1309). 1 p. l. 227, 23 pp. 1845.

Napoleon i. The table talk and opinions of Napoleon Buonaparte. iii, 194 pp. 18°. *London, S. Low, son & Marston,* 1868.

Napoleon iii. History of Julius Cæsar. v. 1. 350 pp. 8°. *New York, A. Dowling,* 1865.

Narrative of privations and sufferings of U. S. officers and soldiers while prisoners of war in the hands of rebel authorities. Being a report of a commission of inquiry, appointed by the U. S. sanitary commission. With an appendix, containing the testimony. 86 pp. 5 pl. 8°. *Boston, office of "Littell's living age,"* 1864. [LOYAL publication society, no. 76].

Narrative (A) of a tour of observation, made in 1817, by James Monroe, president of the U. S. through the northeastern and northwestern departments of the union. With an appendix. [*anon.*] 228, xxxvi pp. 16°. *Philadelphia, S. A. Mitchell & H. Ames,* 1818.

Nation (The). A weekly journal, devoted to politics, literature, science, and art. July, 1867, to Dec. 1868. v. 5-7. 4°. *New York, E. L. Godkin & co.* 1867-68.

National association for the promotion of social science. Transactions. Belfast meeting, 1867. Edited by G. W. Hastings. 8°. *London, Longmans,* 1868.

National (The) hand-book of facts and figures, historical, statistical, etc. from the formation of the government to the present time. With a full chronology of the rebellion. 407 pp. 1 pl. 12°. *New York, E. B. Treat & co.* 1868.

National quarantine and sanitary association. Proceedings and debates of the third convention, held in the city of New York, April, 1859. 8°. *New York, printers to the board of councilmen,* 1859.

National (The) quarterly review. Edited by E. I. Sears, Dec. 1867, to Sept. 1868. v. 16-17. 8°. *New York, E. I. Sears,* 1867-68.

National (The) republican. [Washington daily]. Jan. to June, 1868. fol. *Washington,* 1868.

National (The) temperance advocate. The organ of the national temperance society and publication house. Jan. 1866, to Dec. 1867. v. 1-2. fol. *New York, J. N. Stearns,* 1866-67.

National union republican convention. Proceedings at Chicago, May 20-21, 1868. Reported by Ely, Burnham & Bartlett. 143 pp. 8°. *Chicago, Evening journal print,* 1868.

Natur (Die). Zeitung zur verbreitung naturwissenschaftlicher kenntniss und naturanschauung für leser aller stände. Herausgegeben von Otto Ule und Karl Müller. v. 1-10. 4°. *Halle, G. Schwetschke,* 1852-61. s.

Naudet (Joseph). Des changemens opérés dans toutes les parties de l'administration de l'empire romain, sous les règnes de Dioclétien, de Constantin, et de leurs successeurs, jusqu'à Julien. 3 pts. in 2 v. viii, 386 pp. 2 p. l. 348 pp. 8°. *Paris, Treuttel & Wurtz,* 1817.

Naumann (*Dr.* Robert, *editor*). *See* **Serapeum.**

Nausea *Blancicampianus, or* **Eckel** (Friedrich). Cōtra uniuersos catholicæ fidei aduersarios in symbolū apostolorum catholica. 18 p. l. 290 pp. 4°. *Moguntiæ, J. Schæffer,* 1529. s.

Nautical (The) almanac and astronomical ephemeris for 1870-71. With appendices. 2 v. 8°. *London, J. Murray,* 1866-67.

Nautical (The) magazine and naval chronicle for 1867-68. A journal of papers on subjects connected with maritime affairs. v. 36-37. 8°. *London, Simpkin, Marshall & co.* 1867-68.

Navy (British). *See* **Great Britain.** (*Navy department*).

Neal (John). Logan, a family history. [*anon.*] 2 v. 317 pp; 341 pp. 8°. *Philadelphia, Carey & Lea,* 1822.

——— Seventy-six. [*anon.*] 2 v. 268 pp; 260 pp. 12°. *Baltimore, J. Robinson,* 1823.

Nebel (Carl). The war between the United States and Mexico illustrated. *See* **Kendall** (G. W.) *and* **Nebel.**

Nebraska (*State of*). House journal. First, second, and third sessions, 1866-67. 8°. *Omaha, state printer,* 1867.

——— Senate journal. First, second, and third sessions, 1866-67. 8°. *Omaha, state printer,* 1867.

Nebrija *or* **Nebrixa** (Elio Antonio de). Introducciones latinas, contrapuesto el romance al latin, para que con facilidad puedan aprender todos, etc. vi, 254 pp. 1 portrait. 8°. *Madrid, B. Ulloa,* 1773. s.

Necker (Jacques). Dernières vues de politique et de finance. xii, 480 pp. 8°. [*Genève*], 1802. s.

Nederlandsch kruidkundig archief. Uitgegeven door W. H. DeVriese, F. Dozy, etc. 4 v. 8°. *Leyden, S. & J. Luchtmans,* 1846–59.

Nees von Esenbeck (Christian Gottfried). Erinnerungen aus dem riesengebirge, [*or*] Naturgeschichte der europäischen lebermoose, mit besonderer beziehung auf Schlesien und die oertlichkeiten des riesengebirgs. v. 1–2. 8°. *Berlin, A. Rücker,* 1833–36. s.
[Wanting: v. 3-4].

Neff petroleum company. Prospectus, with the geological reports of A. Winchell, J. S. Newberry, H. L. Smith, [etc.] and a map of Knox and adjoining counties. 46 pp. 1 pl. 1 map. 8°. *Gambier,* (*Ohio*), 1866. s.

Neill (Edward D. *editor*). The Fairfaxes of England and America in the 17th and 18th centuries, including letters from and to hon. W. Fairfax, and his sons, col. G. W. Fairfax and rev. Bryan, 8th lord Fairfax, the neighbors and friends of George Washington. 234 pp. 8°. *Albany, J. Munsell,* 1868.

Nelles (Annie, *pseudon?*) Annie Nelles; or, the life of a book agent. An autobiography. 385 pp. 4 pl. 8°. *Cincinnati, the author,* 1868.

Nellie Holmes; or, struggles with temper. By E. F. G. [*anon.*] 144 pp. 16°. *Cincinnati, Western tract and book society,* 1868.

Nelly; or, the best inheritance. By the author of "Irish Amy," etc. [*anon.*] 230 pp. 2 pl. 16°. *Philadelphia, American s. s. union,* 1867.

Nemeitz (Joachim Christoph). Séjour de Paris, c'est-à-dire, instructions fidèles pour les voiageurs de condition, comment ils se doivent conduire, s'ils veulent faire un bon usage de leur tems et argent durant leur séjour à Paris, [etc.] 2 v. 7 p. l. 420 pp. 1 map. 22 pl; 1 p. l. pp. 421–630. 27 l. 34 pl. 16°. *Leide, J. Van Abcoude,* 1727. s.

Netherlands (The) *or* **Holland**. Verslag aan den koning over de openbare werken, 1853 and 1855–64. 10 v. 4°. *Gravenhage, Van Weelden & Mingelen,* 1854–65. s.

——— Verslag van den staat der hooge-, middelbare, en lagere scholen in het koningrijk der Nederlanden over 1864–65, 1865–66. 2 v. fol. *Gravenhage* 1866–67. s.

Netty and her sister; or, the two paths. By the author of "Phil Kennedy." [*anon.*] 192 pp. 4 pl. 16°. *New York, American tract society,* [1867].

Neue gesellschaftliche erzählungen für die liebhaber der naturlehre, der haushaltungswissenschaft, der arztneykunst und der sitten. 4 v. 8°. *Leipzig, A. H. Holle,* 1758–62. s.

Neueren (Die) straf- und besserungssysteme. Erinnerungen aus einer reise durch bemerkenswerthe gefängnisse in Algier, Spanien, Portugal, England, Frankreich und Holland. Von Julius Rudolph von M——— ———, dr. [*anon.*] x, 364 pp. 1 l. 4 pl. 8°. *Berlin, Veit & co.* 1843. s.

Neues hamburgisches magazin. 1767–77. *See* **Hamburgisches** magazin.

Neues jahrbuch für mineralogie, geognosie, geologie und petrefactenkunde, herausgegeben von dr. K. C. von Leonhard und dr. H. G. Bronn. Jahrgang 1842. 8°. *Stuttgart, E. Schweizerbart,* 1842. s.
[Jahrg. 1833–41, 1843 *et seq.* wanting].

Nevada (*State of*). Annual report of the state mineralogist for 1866. 151 pp. 8°. *Carson City, J. E. Eckley,* 1867.

——— Annual report of the surveyor general for 1865. 83 pp. 8°. [*Carson City*]*? J. Church,* [1866].

Nève (Félix Jean Baptiste Joseph). Revue des sources nouvelles pour l'étude de l'antiquité chrétienne en Orient. 100 pp. 8°. *Louvain, C. J. Fonteyn,* 1852. s.

Nevius (Helen S. T.) Our life in China. 502 pp. 5 pl. 8°. *New York, R. Carter & bros.* 1869.

Newall (*Capt.* J. T.) The eastern hunters. [India]. xiv, 457 pp. 6 pl. 8°. *London, Tinsley bros.* 1866.

New Bedford (*Mass.*) The New Bedford directory, for 1867–68. No. 11. 306, 60 pp. 8°. *Boston, Dudley & Greenough,* 1867.

New book of two hundred pictures. [*anon.*] 1 col. pl. 208 pp. 12°. *Philadelphia, American s. s. union,* 1868.

Newburgh (*N. Y.*) General and business directory, 1868. Compiled by E. Carter. 8°. *Newburgh, E. M. Ruttenber & co.* 1867.

——— The same. Carter's Newburgh city directory, with a complete business directory attached, for the year ending May 1, 1869. Published by Carter & Minty. 8°. *Newburgh, C. Jannicky,* 1868.

Newburyport (*Mass.*) The Newburyport directory, with an almanac for 1858. By Caleb Miles Haskell. No. 9. 18°. *Newburyport, H. T. Crofoot,* 1857. s.

Newcomb (Simon). An investigation of the orbit of Neptune, with general tables of its motion. vi, 110 pp. 4°. *Washington, Smithsonian inst.* 1867.

[SMITHSONIAN contributions. v. 15].

Newell (Robert H.) Smoked glass. By Orpheus C. Kerr. [*pseudon.*] 277 pp. 6 pl. 12°. *New York, G. W. Carleton,* 1868.

New England (The council for). Records. Reprinted from the proceedings of the American antiquarian society, for April, 1867. 83 pp. 8°. *Cambridge,* [*Mass.*] *J. Wilson & sons,* 1867.

New England a degenerate plant. Who having forgot their former sufferings, and lost their ancient tenderness, are now become famous among the nations in bringing forth the fruits of cruelty, wherein they have far outstript their persecutors the bishops, as by these their ensuing laws you may plainly see. By Iohn Rous, Iohn Copeland, [etc.] [With] a copy of a letter from one who hath been a magistrate among them, to a friend of his in London. [By J. Cudworth]? 20 pp. sm. 4°. *London,* 1659.

New England (The) business directory. 1348 pp. 8°. *Boston, Sampson, Davenport & co.* 1868.

New England cities business directory. Giving a complete index to [their] mercantile, manufacturing, and professional interests. 544, 376 pp. 8°. *Boston, Briggs & co.* 1867.

New England (The) mercantile union business directory, six parts in one. A short advertising register, etc. 324, 9 pp. 7 maps. 8°. *New York, etc. Pratt & co. etc.* 1849. s.

Newes, true newes, laudable newes, citie newes, court news, countrey newes: the world is mad, or it is a mad world my masters, especially now when in the antipodes these things are come to passe. [*anon.*] 4 l. sm. 4°. *London, F. Cowles, etc.* 1642.

New (The) Genesee farmer. *See* **Genesee** farmer, 2[d] series.

New Hampshire (*Province of*). Provincial papers. Documents and records relating to the province of New Hampshire, from the earliest period of its settlement: 1623-1686. Published by authority of the legislature. Compiled and edited by N. Bouton. v. 1. xi, 629 pp. 8°. *Concord, G. E. Jenks,* 1867.

New Hampshire (*State of*). Journals of the house of representatives, June session, 1784, and Feb. session, 1786. 2 v. fol. *Portsmouth,* 1784-86.

——— The same. Session at Exeter, Sept., 1786, and at Portsmouth, Dec. 1786. pp. 81-190. 16°. [*Portsmouth, J. Melcher,* 1787].

——— Journals of the senate, June session, 1784, June and Oct. sessions, 1785, and Feb. session, 1786. 2 v. fol. *Exeter and Portsmouth,* 1784-86.

[Imperfect, title-page wanting].

——— The same. Session at Concord, June, 1786. 51 pp. 12°. *Portsmouth, J. Melcher,* 1787.

[*With* NEW HAMPSHIRE. Journal of the proceedings of the house of representatives, Exeter session, Sept. 1786, etc.]

——— Fifth, sixth, seventh, eighth, tenth, [and] nineteenth annual reports upon the common schools of New Hampshire; the same being the first, second, third, fourth, sixth, [and] fifteenth annual reports of the board of education, 1851-65. 6 v. 8°. *Concord, state printers,* 1851-65. s.

New Hampshire (The) annual register, and United States calendar, for the years 1849-53. By G. P. Lyon. No. 28-32. 5 v. in 2. 24°. *Concord, G. P. Lyon,* [1849-53]. s.

New Jersey (*State of*). Documents of the 92[d] legislature, [1868]. 8°. *Jersey City, J. H. Lyon,* 1868.

——— Journal of the 24th senate, [1868]. 8°. *Mount Holly, (N. J:) Herald office,* 1868.

——— Minutes of the votes and proceedings of the 92[d] general assembly, 1868. 8°. *Cape Island, (N. J:) C. S. Magrath,* 1868.

New Jersey (The) farmer. Editors, O. Pharo and D. Pettit, and D. Naar. Sept. 1855 to Aug. 1861. 6 v. 8°. *Freehold,* [*Pharo & Bartleson, and D. Naar,* 1855-61].

[No more published].

New Jersey (The) magazine. *See* **Northern** monthly.

New (The) life of Virginea: declaring the former svccesse and present estate of that plantation, being the second part of Noua Britannia. Published by the authoritie of his maiesties counsell of Virginia. [By R. I. *anon.*] 27 l. sm. 4°. *London, W. Welby,* 1612.

Newman (Louis C.) The bible view of slavery reconsidered. Letter to bishop Hopkins. 14 pp. 8°. *New York, C. S. Westcott & co.* 1863.

[LOYAL publication society, no. 39].

New Orleans daily true delta. *See* **Daily** true delta.

New (The) republic. A history of Liberia]. 2[d] ed. 252 pp. 16°. *Boston, Mass. sabbath school society*, 1851. s.

New South Wales. Journal of the legislative council, session 1866. v. 14. in two parts. fol. *Sydney, T. Richards*, 1867.

New Sydenham society (The). Publications. v. 1–8, 10–12. 8°. *London, society*, 1859–61.

CONTENTS.

BOUCHUT (E.) On croup. 1859. v. 3.
BRETONNEAU (P.) On diptherite. 1859. v. 3.
BRIGHT (R.) Clinical memoirs on abdominal tumours and intumescence. 1860. v. 6.
CASPER (J. L.) A handbook of the practice of forensic medicine, v. 1. 1861. v. 12.
CHATTO (J.) An account of the bibliography of diphtheria. 1859. v. 3.
CZERMAK (J. N.) On the laryngoscope, [etc.] 1861. v. 11.
DAVIOT (D. Z.) On diphtherite. 1859. v. 3.
DIDAY (P.) A treatise on syphilis in new born children, [etc.] 1859. v. 1.
DUSCH (T. v.) On thrombosis of the cerebral sinuses. 1861. v. 11.
EMPIS (G. S.) On diphtherite. 1859. v. 3.
ESMARCH (F.) On the use of cold in surgery. 1861. v. 11.
FRERICHS (F. T.) A clinical treatise on diseases of the liver. v. 1. 1860. v. 7.
GOOCH (R.) On some of the most important diseases peculiar to women, [etc.] 1859. v. 2.
GRAEFE (A. v.) Three memoirs on iridectomy, [etc.] 1859. v. 5.
GUERSANT (P.) On croup. 1859. v. 3.
KUSSMAUL (A.) *and* TENNER (A.) On the nature and origin of epileptiform convulsions, [etc.] 1859. v. 5.
RADICKE (G.) On the importance and value of arithmetic means, [etc.] 1861. v. 11.
SCHRÖDER VAN DER KOLK (J. L. C.) Case of atrophy of the left hemisphere of the brain, with coexistent atrophy of the right side of the body. 1861. v. 11.
——— On the minute structure and functions of the spinal cord and medulla oblongata. And on the cause and treatment of epilepsy. 1859. v. 4.
SEMPLE (R.) Memoirs on diphtheria. From the writings of Bretonneau, Guersant, Trousseau, Bouchut, Empis, and Daviot. 1859. v. 3.
TROUSSEAU (A.) On diphtherite. 1859. v. 3.
WAGNER (A.) On the process of repair after resection and extirpation of bones. 1859. v. 5.
YEAR-BOOK of medicine, surgery, etc. for 1859–60. v. 8 and 10.

New (The) Sydenham society's year-book of medicine, surgery, and the allied sciences, for 1859 and 1860. Edited by Harley, Handfield, Jones, etc. 2 v. 8°. *London*, 1860–61.
[NEW SYDENHAM society. v. 8 and 10].

New Testament. *See* **Bible.**

Newton (Hubert Anson). The metric system of weights and measures, prepared to accompany Eaton's common school arithmetic. pp. 311–324. 12°. *Boston, Taggard & Thompson*, 1867.

Newton (*Rev. J. missionary. Principal compiler*). *See* **Dictionary** (A) of the Panjábí [or Sikh] language.

Newton (Richard, *D.D.*) Bible jewels. 320 pp. 5 pl. 16°. *New York, Carters*, 1867.

——— The great pilot and his lessons. 309 pp. 6 pl. 16°. *New York, Carters*, 1867.

New York (*Colony of*). Journal of the votes and proceedings of the general assembly, 1769–75. 6 v. fol. *New York, H. Gaine*, 1769–75.
[Imperfect: v. for 1774, title-page wanting, and pp. 3–8 imperfect].

——— (*State of*). Annual report of the adjutant general, transmitted to the legislature, Jan. 31, 1868. 3 v. 8°. *Albany, C. Van Benthuysen & sons*, 1868.

——— The debates and proceedings of the convention of the state of New York, assembled at Poughkeepsie, on the 17th June, 1788, to decide on the form of federal government recommended by the convention at Philadelphia, 17th September, 1787. 144 pp. 8°. *New York, Francis Childs*, 1788.

——— Documents of the [constitutional] convention, 1846. 2 v. 8°. *Albany, Carroll & Cook*, 1846.

——— Journal of the [constitutional] convention, 1846. 1648 pp. 8°. *Albany, Carroll & Cook*, 1846.

——— The New York civil list, containing the names and origin of the civil divisions, and names and dates of election or appointment of the principal state and county officers, from the revolution to the present time. By Franklin B. Hough. [1st year]. 8°. *Albany, Weed, Parsons & co.* 1855. s.

——— The same. [6th year]. 8°. *Albany, Weed, Parsons & co.* 1860. s.

——— The same. Civil list, and forms of government of the colony and state of New York, containing notes on the various governmental organizations; lists of the principal colonial, state, and county officers, and the congressional delegations and presidential electors, with the votes of the electoral colleges. [14th year]. 12°. *Albany, Weed, Parsons & co.* 1868.

——— A record of the commissioned officers, non-commissioned officers, and privates of the regiments which were organized in the state of New York, to aid in suppressing the rebellion. v. 7–8. 4°. *Albany, Weed, Parsons & co.* 1868.

——— Report of the select committee of the legislature of 1849, on the publication of the Natural history of the state of New York. 179 pp. 10 tab. 8°. *Albany, Weed, Parsons & co.* 1850. s.

——— Report of the select committee [of the legislature of 1855–56] on the completion of the Natural history of the state. 16 pp. 8°. *Albany, [state printer]*, 1856. s.
[*With* the preceding].

New York (*State of*). The speeches of the different governors, to the legislature of the state of New York, commencing with those of George Clinton, and continued down to the present time. 247 pp. 8°. *Albany, J. B. Van Steenbergh*, 1825.

——— *Engineer of the state.* Annual report of the state engineer and surveyor on the canals of New York, 1867. 8°. *Albany, Van Benthuysen & sons*, 1868.

——— ——— Annual report of the state engineer and surveyor [on the railroads of New York], and of the tabulations and deductions from the reports of the railroad corporations, 1867. 8°. *Albany, Van Benthuysen & sons*, 1868.

——— *Railroad commissioners.* Annual report of the railroad commissioners and of the tabulations and deductions, from the reports of the railroad corporations, etc. 1855. Part i. 11 p. l. lxix, 890 pp. 2 maps. 41 pl. 27 profiles. 8°. *Albany, C. Van Benthuysen*, 1856. s.

——— *Regents of the University.* Annual report of the regents of the university of the state of New York. 81st report. 1867. 8°. *Albany, Van Benthuysen & sons*, 1858.

——— ——— Annual report of the regents of the university of the state of New York, on the condition of the state cabinet of natural history. 20th report. 1867. 8°. *Albany, Van Benthuysen & sons*, 1867.

——— *State department.* Census of the state of New York, for 1865, [etc.] By Franklin B. Hough. 2 p. l. cxxvi, 743 pp. fol. *Albany, C. Van Benthuysen*, 1867.

——— *State inebriate asylum*, Binghamton, N. Y. Ceremonies [of laying the corner-stone], etc. 184 pp. 2 pl. 8°. *New York, Wynkoop, Hallenbeck & Thomas*, 1859. s.

New York (*City of*). *Board of commissioners of the central park.* Eleventh annual report, for 1867. 167 pp. 4 maps. 2 pl. 8 photographs. 8°. *New York, W. C. Bryant & co.* 1868.

——— *Board of Education.* Twelfth annual report. 8°. *New York, W. C. Bryant & co.* 1854. s.

——— *Board of supervisors.* Reports of the special committee on volunteering, relative to operations under the President's calls for [volunteers, in 1864]. 5 v. 8°. *New York, printer to the county*, 1863–66.

——— *College of the city of, formerly N. Y. free academy.* Catalogue of the library. lxxxviii, 367 pp. 8°. *New York, W. C. Bryant & co.* 1860.

——— *New York hospital.* Catalogue of books belonging to the library. [*anon.*] 74 pp. 8°. *New York, Collins & co.* 1811.

[*With* ACCOUNT of the New York hospital, *New York*, 1811].

——— The merchants' directory, 1868–69, containing a list of importers, manufacturers, and wholesale dealers, in and adjoining New York. By J. Harford & co. 215 pp. 1 map. 24°. *New York*, 1868.

——— Trow's New York city directory, compiled by H. Wilson. For the year ending May 1, 1869. v. 82. 1419 pp. 1 map. 8°. *New York, J. F. Trow*, 1868.

——— Wilson's business directory of New York city. xxi, 624 pp. 18°. *New York, J. F. Trow*, 1868.

New York aristocracy; or, gems of japonicadom. By "Joseph". [*pseudon.*] 152 pp. 12 pl. 12°. *New York, C. B. Norton*, 1851. s.

New York Chamber of commerce. Tenth annual report, 1867-68. 8°. *New York, J. W. Amerman*, 1865.

New York (The) coach-maker's magazine, devoted to the literary, social, and mechanical interests of the craft. Edited by E. M. Stratton. June, 1866, to May, 1868. v. 8-9. iv, 188 pp. 46 pl. 1 portrait; iv, 188 pp. 46 pl. 1 por. 4°. *New York, E. M. Stratton*, 1867-68.

New York daily tribune. Jan. to Dec. 1868. 2 v. fol. *New York, Tribune association*, 1868.

New York (The) evening mail. Sept. 21, 1867, to Dec. 31, 1868. v. 1. fol. *New York*, 1868.

New York evening post. *See* **Evening** post (New York daily).

New York (The) gazette, and the weekly mercury. *See* **New York** (The) mercury.

New York (The) herald. [Daily]. Jan. to Dec. 1868. 2 v. fol. *New York*, 1868.

New York historical society. Catalogue of library. 139 pp. 8°. *New York, J. Seymour*, 1813.

[*In* NEW YORK historical society. Collections. 1st series. v. 2].

——— Collections, 1809–30. 5 v. 8°. *New York*, 1811–30.

[NOTE.—v. 4 of this set is the one published in 1829. The v. 4 published in 1826 contains the matter reprinted in v. 5, *i. e.* the continuation of Smith's History of N. Y.]

——— Proceedings, 1843–48. 6 v. 8°. *New York, press of the society*, 1844–48.

New York mercantile library association. Systematic catalogue of books; [with] appendix. xi, 312 pp. 8°. *New York, Harpers,* 1837.

—— —— The same. 2 p. l. 300 pp. 8°. *New York, E. O. Jenkins,* 1844.

New York (The) mercury. Containing the freshest advices, foreign and domestic. No. 323, Oct. 23, 1758—no. 847, Jan. 25, 1768. fol. *New York, H. Gaine,* 1758-68. s.
[Very imperfect].

—— The same. The New York gazette, and the weekly mercury, [etc.] No. 848, Feb. 1, 1768—no. 894, Dec. 19, 1768. fol. *New York, H. Gaine,* 1768. s.
[*With* the preceding; imperfect].

New York (The) mirror and ladies' literary gazette. Edited by G. P. Morris, and others. v. 1-20 in 19 v. 4°. *New York,* 1823-42.
[Being the 1st series, complete].

New York (The) times. [Daily]. Jan. to Dec. 1868. 2 v. fol. *New York,* 1868.

New York world. *See* **World** (The New York daily).

Nibelungenlied (Das). Uebersetzt von dr. Carl Simrock. 3e aufl. 1 p. l. 382 pp. 8°. *Stuttgart, J. G. Cotta,* 1843. s.

Nicephorus (Cyrus). Στοιχειων μαθηματικων εκ παλαιων εκ νεωτερων συνερανισθεντων, etc. 3 v. 8°. Μοσχαι, παρα Ρηδηγερωεκ Κλαυδιω, 1798-99. s.

Nichol (John, *LL. D.*) Views of the architecture of the heavens. 2d ed. 158 pp. 2 maps. 23 pl. 16°. *New York, Dayton & Newman,* 1842.

Nicholls (Benjamin Elliot). The mine explored; or, help to the reading of the bible. 382 pp. 5 maps. 12°. *Philadelphia, American s. s. union,* 1853. s.

Nichols (Beach) *and others.* Atlas of Montgomery and Fulton counties, New York, from actual surveys. 2 p. l. 28 maps. 4°. *New York, Stranahan & Nichols,* 1868.

Nichols (James R. *M. D.*) Chemistry of the farm and the sea. With other familiar chemical essays. 123 pp. 12°. *Boston, A. Williams & co.* 1867.

Nichols (John). The progresses and public processions of queen Elizabeth. [With] other solemnities, public expenditures, and remarkable events, during [her] reign. With historical notes. New ed. [Illustrated]. 3 v. 4°. *London, J. Nichols & son,* 1823.

—— The rise and progress of the gentleman's magazine, with anecdotes of the projector and his early associates. Being a prefatory introduction to the general index to that work, from 1787-1818. lxxx pp. portrait. 8°. *London, J. Nichols & son,* 1821.

Nichols (*Mrs.* Mary Gove). Lectures to women on anatomy and physiology. With an appendix on water cure. 303 pp. 12°. *New York, Harpers,* 1846. s.

Nichols (*Mrs.* Rebecca S.) Songs of the heart and the hearthstone. 319 pp. portrait. 8°. *Philadelphia, Thomas, Cowperthwait & co.* 1851.

Nicholson (John, *civil engineer*). The operative mechanic, and British machinist. xvi, 794 pp. 95 pl. 8°. *London, Knight & Lacey,* 1825.

Nicol (John). Life and adventures. viii, 215 pp. portrait. 16°. *Edinburgh, W. Blackwood,* 1822.

Nicolai (Friedrich). Einige bemerkungen über den ursprung und die geschichte der rosenkreuzer und freymaurer. Veranlasst durch die historisch-critische untersuchung des herrn Buhle über diesen gegenstand. xvi, 180 pp. 1 pl. 8°. *Berlin,* 1806.

Nicolay (*Rev.* C. G.) Maritime discovery, and modern geography. 8°. *London,* 1859.
[*In* MANUAL (A) of geographical science. v. 2. pp. 145-615].

Nicole (Pierre). Traité de la vraie et de la fausse beauté dans les ouvrages de l'esprit et particulièrement dans l'epigramme. [Traduit] par P. Richelet. [*anon.*] 16°. *Amsterdam, frères Wetstein,* 1720.
[*In* BRUZEN DE LA MARTINIÈRE (A. A.) Nouveau recueil des epigrammatistes françois. ed. 1720. v. 2. pp. 167-220].

Niemeyer (Felix). Clinical lectures on pulmonary phthisis. From the German, by J. L. Parke. 116 pp. 16°. *New York, Moorhead, Simpson & Bond,* 1868.

Nikephoros. *See* **Nicephorus.**

Niles (*Rev.* Samuel). A vindication of divers gospel doctrines, and of the teachers and professors of them, against the misrepresentations contained in the discourse of the rev. mr. Lemuel Briant, [with] remark on mr. John Bass' late narrative. 120 pp. 8°. *Boston, S. Kneeland,* 1752.

—— Tristitiæ ecclesiarum; or, a brief and sorrowful account of the present state of the churches in New England; [with] some healing measures, [and] an appendix. 21, 4 pp. 4°. *Boston, J. Draper,* 1745.

Nilsson (Sven). The primitive inhabitants of Scandinavia. Containing a description of the implements, dwellings, tombs, and mode of living of the savages in the north of Europe during the stone age. Translated from [the

Nilsson—continued.
author's] manuscript. Edited, with an introduction, by sir J. Lubbock. 3[d] ed. lxxix, 272 pp. 16 pl. 8°. *London, Longmans,* 1868.

Nimshi. The adventures of a man to obtain a solution of scriptural geology, to gauge the vast ages of planetary concretion, and to open Bab-Allah—the gate of God. [*anon.*] 2 v. 306 pp. 1 pl; 268 pp. 8°. *London, H. Cunningham,* 1845.

Nitsch (Paul Friedrich Achat). A general and introductory view of professor Kant's principles concerning man, the world, and the deity. 2 p. l. 134 pp. 8°. *London, J. Downes,* 1796.

No thoroughfare. By C—s D——s, Bellamy, Brownjohn, and Domby. [*pseudon.*] 2[d] ed. 15 pp. 8°. *Boston, Loring,* 1868.

Nobbes (Robert). The compleat troller; or, the art of trolling. Also, a brief account of most of the principal rivers in England. 10 p. l. 78 pp. 1 l. 18°. *London, T. James, for T. Helder,* 1682.

Noble (John). Fiscal legislation, 1842–65. A review of the financial changes of that period, and their effects upon revenue, trade, manufactures, and employment. xii, 199 pp. 8°. *London, Longmans,* 1867.

Nöhden (Georg Heinrich). A grammar of the German language. 5th ed. 2 p. l. 504 pp. 12°. *London, author,* 1826. S.

Nohl (Ludwig, *editor*). Letters of distinguished musicians: Gluck, Haydn, P. E. Bach, Weber, Mendelssohn. From the German, by lady Wallace. xviii, 467 pp. 3 pl. 8°. *London, Longmans,* 1867.

Nonius Marcellus. Compendiosa doctrina, ad filium, de proprie tale sermonum. *See* **Perotti** (N.) *and others.* Cornvcopiæ. *Venetiis,* 1517.

Noorden (Carl von). Symbolæ ad comparandam mythologiam vedicam cum mythologia germanica imprimis pertinentes ad pugnam. Dei æstivi cum dracone. Adiectis nonnullis Rigvedæ hymnis e libro viii, ix, et x typis nondum impressis ad Deum Indram. 2 p. l. 86 pp. 8°. *Bonnæ, formis C. Georgi,* [1855]?

Noordziek (J. J. F.) Het geschilstuk betrekkelijk de uitvinding der boekdrukkunst. viii, 112 pp. 8°. *Haarlem, A. C. Kruseman,* 1848. S.

Nordhoff (Charles). America for free working men. How slavery injures the free working man. iv, 39 pp. 8°. *New York,* 1865.

[LOYAL publication society. no. 80].

Norris (Thaddeus). American fish culture, embracing all the details of artificial breeding and rearing of trout; the culture of salmon, shad, and other fishes. 304 pp. 7 pl. 12°. *Philadelphia, Porter & Coates,* 1868.

North (Elisha, *M. D.*) Outlines of the science of life, which treats physiologically of both body and mind. [With essays on other subjects]. xix, 202 pp. 8°. *New York, Collins & co.* 1829.

North (Ingoldsby, *pseudon.*) *See* **Book** of love letters.

North American (The) and West Indian gazetteer. Containing an authentic description of the colonies and islands in that part of the globe. [*anon.*] 2[d] ed. xxiv pp. 119 l. 2 maps. 16°. *London, G. Robinson,* 1778.

North Carolina (*State of*). Constitution [adopted by the constitutional convention, 1868. With an] address by W. P. Rodman and G. W. Gahagan. 14 pp. 8°. [*Raleigh?* 1868].

——— Journals of the convention at its session[s] of 1865 and 1866. 2 v. in 1. 94, iii pp; 192, iii pp. 8°. *Raleigh, Cannon & Holden,* 1865–66.

North Carolina (Branson's) business directory, for 1867–8. 168, xcv pp. 8°. *Raleigh, Branson & Jones,* 1868.

Northcote (William, *surgeon*). Extracts from the marine practice of physic and surgery. 8°. *Boston,* 1777.

[*In* VAN SWIETEN (G. *baron*). Diseases incident to armies. pp. 132–165. *Boston,* 1777].

Northern true men and southern traitors. Address and resolutions of the Connecticut soldiers. Extracts from Richmond journals. 8 pp. 8°. *New York,* 1863.

[LOYAL publication society. no. 6].

North western farmer. A monthly magazine of agriculture, horticulture, home improvement, and family literature. T. A. Bland, editor. Jan. 1867, to Dec. 1868. v. 2–3. 4°. *Indianapolis, Downey & Brouse,* 1867.

Norton (*Hon. Mrs.* Caroline Elizabeth Sheridan). The lady of La Garaye. 115 pp. 12°. *New York, J. Bradburn,* 1864.

Norton (*Rev.* John, *of Boston*). Memoir of John Cotton. [Reprint]. With a preface and notes, by E. Pond. 108 pp. 18°. *Boston, Perkins & Marvin,* 1834.

Norton (John N. *D. D.*) Full proof of the ministry. A sequel to the boy who was trained up to be a clergyman. 245 pp. 12°. *New York, Redfield,* 1855. S.

Norton (John N. *D. D.*) Life of bishop [Geo. W.] Freeman, of Arkansas. 203 pp. 1 portrait. 18°. *New York, general protestant episcopal s. s. union*, 1867.

—— The life of the rt. rev. William White, bishop of Pennsylvania. 103 pp. 1 portrait. 18°. *New York, general protestant episcopal s. s. union*, 1856. s.

Norton (William A.) An elementary treatise on astronomy, with solar and other astronomical tables. xvi, 367, 112 pp. 1 pl. 8°. *New York, Wiley & Putnam*, 1845. s.

Norway. Actstykker angaaende cholera-epidemien i Norge i 1853. Besörgede ved medicinal-committeen. 2 parts in 1 v. 199 pp; 106 pp. 1 pl. 8°. *Christiania, C. C. Werner & co.* 1853–54. s.

CONTENTS.

1te afdeling. Cholera i Christiana og dens Omegn. Ved prof. [A. C.] Conradi. p. 1. Beretning om Grönlands lazareth. Ved E. [F. H.] Winge. p. 29. Beretning om Sorgenfri lazareth. Ved [L. H.] Freng. p. 49. Beretning om Ankerlökkens lazareth. Ved [C. L. R.] Hörbye. p. 57. Beretning om Pipervigens lazareth. Ved [A.] Holst. p. 67. Beretning om Oslo lazareth. Ved [O.] Bergfeldt. p. 77. Om cholera-epidemien i Norge, 1853. Ved [F. C.] Faye. p. 83.
2en afdeling. Forhandlinger i det medicinske selskab i Christiania om forplantelsesmaaden af cholera. p. 1. Betænkninger og indstillinger angaaende cholera. p. 74.

—— Diplomatarium norvegicum. Oldbreve til kundskab om Norges indre og ydre forholde, sprog slægter, sæder lovgivning og rettergang i middelalderen. Samlede og udgivne af Chr. C. A. Lange og Carl R. Unger. 12 parts in 6 v. 8°. *Christiania, P. T. Malling*, 1847–64. s.

[v. 3, pt. 1. wanting].

—— Kongeriget Norges attende ordentlige storthings forhandlinger, 1865–66. 10 v. sm. fol. *Christiania, trykt i flere bogtrykkerier*, [1865–67].

CONTENTS.

v. 1–5. Kongelige propositioner og meddelelser fremsatte, etc.
v. 6. Statsrevisionens antegnelser m. v. til statsregnskaberne for aarene 1860–63 samt andre regnskaber fremsendte, [etc.]
v. 7. Documenter, [etc.] 1865–66.
v. 8–9. Attende ordentlige storthings indstillinger og beslutninger, 1865–66.
v. 10. Kongeriget Norges attende ordentlige storthings forhandlings-protokoller, 1865–66.

Norwood (Joseph G. *M. D.*) Experimental exercises and problems in elementary chemistry: with tables for the conversion of common weights and measures into those of the metrical system. 48 pp. 8°. *Columbia, (Mo.) J. G. Norwood*, 1868.

Not wisely, but too well. A novel. By the author of "Cometh up as a flower." [*anon.*] 3 v. 12°. *London, Tinsley bros.* 1867.

Notes and queries: a medium of inter-communication for literary men, general readers, etc. 3d series. v. 12. July–Dec. 1867. sm. 4°. *London, notes and queries office*, 1868.

—— The same. General index to series the third. (12 v. 1862–67). iv, 156 pp. sm. 4°. *London*, 1868.

—— The same. 4th series. v. 1. Jan–June, 1868. sm. 4°. *London*, 1868.

Nott (Eliphalet, *D. D.*) Counsels to young men on the formation of character, and the principles which lead to success and happiness in life. 312 pp. 18°. *New York, Harpers*, 1856.

Nott (Henry Junius). Novellettes of a traveller; or, odds and ends from the knapsack of Thomas Singularity, journeyman printer. 2 v. 228 pp; 203 pp. 12°. *New York, Harpers*, 1834.

Nott (Josiah C. *M. D.*) Two lectures on the connection between the biblical and physical history of man. 146 pp. 1 map. 8°. *New York, Bartlett & Welford*, 1849.

Nouveau guide de conversations modernes en six langues, français, italien, anglais, allemand, russe, polonais. Par Bellenger, Fabrucci, Witcomb, Fischer, Forster et Boltz. Nouv. éd. v pp. 236 l. sq. 24°. *Berlin, B. Behr*, 1864.

Novi (Giuseppe). Confronto del materiale da ponte di varii sistemi d' Europa. [Extract]. 57 pp. 7 tab. 3 pl. 4°. *Napoli, r. istituto d'incorragiamento, etc.* 1862. s.

—— Uso del ferro e sua conservazione, tradizione, ed esperienze. [Extract]. 212 pp. 4°. *Napoli, r. istituto d'incorragiamento, etc.* 1863. s.

Noyce (Elisha). The boy's book of industrial information. Illustrated. xvi, 334 pp. 2 pl. 16°. *London, Ward & Lock*, 1863.

Nuevo estilo y formulario de escrivir cartas missivas. [*anon.*] 7a impression. 48 p. l. 222 pp. 16°. *Madrid, P. J. Alonso y Padilla*, 1743. s.

Nuevo libro de cuentas ajustadas, compuesto por G. M. y G. para el uso del commercio. [*anon.*] 295 pp. 16°. *Valencia, B. Montfort*, 1820. s.

Nugent (E. *C. E.*) A treatise on optics; with application to fine arts and industrial pursuits. xii, 235 pp. 8°. *New York, D. Van Nostrand*, 1868.

Nuñez de Haro y Peralta (Alonzo, *archbishop of Mexico*). Constituciones que [il] formo para el mejor regimen y govierno del Real colegio seminario de instruccion en el pueblo de Tepotzotlan. 4 p. l. 87 pp. 8°. *Mexico, F. de Zuñiga,* 1777.

Nursery (The). A magazine for youngest readers. By Fanny P. Seaverns. [Illustrated]. v. 1-3. 12°. *Boston, J. L. Shorey,* 1867-68.

Nut-brown (The) maids: or, the first hosier and his hosen. A family chronicle of the days of queen Elizabeth. [*anon.*] vii, 408 pp. 12°. *London, J. W. Parker & son,* 1859.

Nutting (Benjamin F.) Teachers'-aid drawing cards. Primary series, nos. 1-4. 8 l. 32 pl. obl. 18°. *Boston, B. F. Nutting,* 1866-67.

Nutting (*Rev.* J. K.) Tilman Loring; or, minister or merchant. 291 pp. 2 pl. 18°. *Philadelphia, J. C. Garrigues & co.* 1867.

Nyerup (Rasmus). Almindelig morskabslæsning i Danmark og Norge igjennem aarhundreder. xxviii, 326 pp. 8°. *Kjöbenhavn, Thiele,* 1816. s.

Nystrom (Juan Guillermo). Informe al supremo gobierno del Peru, sobre una espedicion al interior de la republica. 79 pp. 3 maps. 8°. *Lima, E. Prugue,* 1868.

O'Brien (Matthew). Mathematical geography. 8°. *London,* 1852.
[*In* MANUAL of geographical science. v. 1].

Ocean waves in lyric strains, a requiem; and other poems. By the hermit of St Eirene. [*anon.*] 88 pp. 8°. *Pittsburg, (Pa.) W. S. Haven,* 1856. s.

Öchelhäuser (Wilhelm). Vergleichende statistik der eisen-industrie aller länder, und erörterung ihrer ökonomischen lage im zollverein. x, 364 pp. 8°. *Berlin, Veit & co.* 1852. s.

O'Connor (Thomas). The inquisition examined, by an impartial reviewer. [*anon.*] 143 pp. 16°. *New York, J. Desnoues,* 1825.

O'Conor (Charles). Dissertations on the antient history of Ireland. 8 p. l. xlviii, 248 pp. 10 l. 1 map. 8°. *Dublin, J. Hoey,* 1753.

Odd Fellows' (The) minstrel. A collection of odes for the use of the fraternity on anniversary occasions, dedications, social reunions and festivals, funerals, lodge meetings, etc. Edited by J. Fletcher Williams. 153 pp. 32°. *Cincinnati, R. W. Carroll & co.* 1864.

Oechelhäuser. *See* **Öchelhäuser.**

Oersted. *See* **Örsted.**

Offenbach (Jacques). The grand duchess of Gerolstein. A comic opera in three acts. Translated from the French. [French and English texts]. 48 pp. 8°. *New York, J. A. Gray & Green,* 1867.

——— The opera bouffe: a collection of vocal and instrumental gems. 324 pp. 4°. *Boston, O. Ditson & co.* [1868].

——— *See, also,* **Meilhac** (Henri) *and* **Halévy** (Ludovic).

Officium parvum, b. Mariæ. Die kleinen tagzeiten der mutter Gottes, (lateinisch und deutsch), nebst einer kleinen sammlung täglicher gebete. [*anon.*] 382 pp. 24°. *New York, C. & N. Benziger,* 1868.

Ogilby (John). The entertainment of his majestie Charles ii, in his passage through the city of London to his coronation. [With] a brief narrative of his coronation: [and] his magnificent proceeding and royal feast in Westminster-Hall. 2 p. l. 192 pp. 1 l. 12 pl. fol. *London, R. Mariot,* 1662.

Ohio (The) annual register, for 1835. By J. A. Bryan. 128 pp. 18°. *Columbus, J. Gilbert & R. C. Bryan,* 1835.

Ohm (Georg Simon). Beiträge zur molecular physik. v. 1. [*or*] Elemente der analytischen geometrie im raume am schiefwinkligen coordinaten-systeme. xii, 590 pp. 1 l. 1 pl. 4°. *Nürnberg, J. L. Schrag,* 1849. s.

O'Kane (T. C.) Fresh leaves. For the use of sabbath schools. 128 pp. obl. 8°. *New York, Phillips & co.* 1868.

Olafs konungs ens helga. Udförligere saga om kong Olaf den hellige, efter det ældste fuldstændige pergaments haandskrift i det store kongelige bibliothek i Stockholm. Udgivet af P. A. Munch og C. R. Unger. xlviii, 321 pp. 1 pl. 8°. *Christiania, C. C. Werner & co.* 1853. s.

Old (The) brown pitcher, by the author of "Susy's six birthdays", etc; and other tales. [*anon.*] 222 pp. 12 pl. 16°. *New York, nat. temp. soc.* 1868. s.

Old (The) capitol and its inmates. By a lady who enjoyed the hospitalities of the government for a "season." [*anon.*] 236 pp. 16°. *New York, Hale & son,* 1867.

Old (The) guard: a monthly magazine, devoted to literature, science and art, and the political principles of 1776 and 1860. Jan. to Dec. 1868. v. 6. 8°. *New York, Van Evrie, Horton & co.* 1868.

Oldenburg (*Grand duchy of*). Statistische nachrichten über das grossherzogthum Oldenburg. 8 v. 4°. *Oldenburg, W. Berndt, G. Stalling,* 1857-66. s.

Oldenburg—continued.

CONTENTS.

1es heft, enthaltend rhederei, schiffsbau und schifffahrt im herzogthum Oldenburg für die jahre 1829 bis 1855, nebst einem nachtrag, enthaltend rhederei, schiffsbau und schifffahrt für das jahr 1856. 1857.
2es–3es heft. Stand der bevölkerung [etc.] nach der zählung vom 3. Dec. 1855. Mit einer einleitung, betr. die ergebnisse der volkszählung seit dem jahre 1815. 2 v. 1857.
4es heft. A. Durchschnittspreise des getreides und einiger andern nahrungsmittel in grossherzogthum Oldenburg aus den jahren 1817—1858. B. Stand der bevölkerung in grossherzogthum Oldenburg nach der zählung vom 3. December, 1858. 1860.
5es heft. A. Rhederei, schiffbau und schiffverkehr in herzogthum Oldenburg für die jahre 1856 bis 1860. B. Post- und telegraphen-verkehr im grossherzogthum Oldenburg für die jahre 1853 bis 1860. 1862.
6es heft. Zur statistik der bevölkerung, insbesondere stand der bevölkerung nach der volkszählung vom 3. December, 1861. 1863.
7es heft. Zur statistik der materiellen kultur nach der aufnahme vom 3. December, 1861. 1865.
8es heft. A. Zur statistik der bevölkerung, etc. B. Zur statistik der materiellen cultur, etc. 1866.

——— Voranschlag der central-ausgaben des grossherzogthums Oldenburg für das jahr 1849–51. 3 v. in 1. 4°. *Oldenburg, G. Stalling, Schulze,* 1849–51. s.

——— Voranschlag der einnahmen und ausgaben, [etc.] 1849–50. 2 v. in 1. 4°. *Oldenburg, G. Stalling,* 1849–50. s.
[*With* the preceding].

——— The same. Beilage i. zum voranschlag der militair ausgaben pro 1851. 15 pp. 27 l. 4°. *Oldenburg, Schulze,* 1851. s.
[*With* OLDENBURG. Voranschlag, etc. 1849–51].

Oldenburgischer staats kalender auf das jahr Christi 1815–44. 30 v. 12°. *Oldenburg, expedition der wöchenlichen [und] oldenburgischen anzeigen,* 1815–44. s.

Oliphant (Margaret O. W.) Brownlows. 3 v. 12°. *London, W. Blackwood & sons,* 1868.

——— Orphans. A chapter in a life. [*anon.*] 316 pp. 12°. *London, Hurst & Blackett,* 1858.

——— The same. The orphans and Caleb Field. 344 pp. 16°. *London, Chapman & Hall,* 1865.

Olive (Pedro Maria de). Diccionario de sinónimos de la lengua castellana. 2ª ed. 451 pp. 8°. [*Paris*], *D. J. Boix,* 1852.

Olive-branch (The); or, white oak farm. 329 pp. 12°. *Philadelphia, J. B. Lippincott & co.* 1857. s.

Oliver Optic's magazine. Our boys and girls. Oliver Optic [*pseudon.* of W. T. Adams], editor. Jan. to Dec. 1868. v. 3–4 in 1 v. 8°. *Boston, Lee & Shepard,* [1868].

Olney (J.) A practical system of modern geography. 38th ed. 286 pp. 1 pl. 12°. *New York, Robinson, Pratt & co.* 1842.

——— The same. 55th ed. 300 pp. 12°. *New York, Pratt, Woodford & co.* 1847. s.

——— The same. 63d ed. 296 pp. 12°. *New York, Pratt, Woodford & co.* 1850. s.

Once a month; a magazine of miscellaneous selections. Oct. 1867, to Feb. 1868. v. 3. 8°. *Springfield, (Mass.) W. J. Holland & co.* [1867–68].
[No more published].

Onderdonk (Henry). A history of Maryland upon the basis of McSherry, for the use of schools. 251 pp. 16°. *Baltimore, John Murphy & co.* 1868.

O'Neall (John Belton, *LL.D.*) Biographical sketches of the bench and bar of South Carolina. 2 v. xxxii, 431 pp. 1 tab. 3 facsimiles; iv, 616 pp. 8°. *Charleston, S. G. Courtnay & co.* 1859.

Oort (*Rev.* H. *pastor of Santpoort*). The worship of Baalim in Israel, [etc.] Translated from the Dutch by the rt. rev. J. W. Colenso. vi, 94 pp. 8°. *London, Longmans,* 1865.

Opinions of the early presidents, and of the fathers of the republic, upon slavery, and upon negroes as men and soldiers. 19 pp. 8°. *New York, W. C. Bryant & co.* 1863.
[LOYAL publication society. no. 18].

Optic (Oliver, *pseudon.*) *See* **Adams** (William T.)

Opusculū repertorii pronosticon in mutationes aeris tam via astrologica quam metheorologica. [*anon.*] 45 l. sm. 4°. *Venetiis, Erhardus Ratdolt de Augusta,* 1485.

Oram (Elizabeth). First lessons in English grammar and composition, etc. iv, 222 pp. 12°. *New York, D. Burgess & co.* 1855. s.

Oratorvm graecorvm, qvorvm princeps est Demosthenes, quae svpersvnt, monumenta commentariis integris Hieron. Wolfii, Io. Taylori, Ierem. Marklandi, aliorvm et svis, indicibvs denique instructa edidit J. J. Reiske. 12 v. 8°. *Lipsiae, W. G. Sommer,* 1770. s.
[Wanting v. 9–12].

CONTENTS.

Aeschines, v. 3, 4.	Deinarchus, v. 4, 8.
Alcidamas, v. 8.	Gorgias, v. 8.
Andocides, v. 4, 8.	Herodes Atticus, v. 8.
Antiphon, v. 7, 8.	Isaeus, v. 7.
Antisthenes, v. 8.	Lesbonax, v. 8.
Demades, v. 4.	Lycurgus, v. 4, 8.
Demosthenes, v. 1, 2.	Lysias, v. 5, 6.

Orbigny (Alcide Dessalines d'). Mollusques, échinodermes, foraminifères et polypiers, recueillis aux îles Canaries. 4°. *Paris,* 1836–44.
[*In* WEBB (Philip B.) *and* BERTHELOT. Histoire naturelle des îles Canaries, v. 2].

Orderly book of the northern army, at Ticonderoga and Mt. Independence, from Oct. 17th,

Orderly—continued. 1776, to Jan. 8th, 1777. With biographical and explanatory notes, and an appendix. viii, 224 pp. 1 map. 1 portrait. 4°. *Albany, J. Munsell*, 1859.

[MUNSELL'S historical series. No. 3].

Oregon (*State of*). The Oregon archives; including the journals, governors' messages, and public papers of Oregon, (1849–53). By La Fayette Grover, commissioner. 335 pp. 8°. *Salem, public printer*, 1853. S.

——— ——— Journal of the senate and house, proceedings, etc. for 1866. 2 v. in 1. 8°. *Salem, W. A. McPherson*, 1866.

——— ——— Report of the secretary of state, etc. 71 pp. 8°. *Salem, W. A. McPherson*, 1866.

[*With* Journal of the senate and house, 1866].

Orfila (Matthieu Joseph Bonaventure). Éléments de chimie. 7e éd. 2 v. xii, 591 pp. 7 pl; xiv, 694 pp. 3 pl. 8°. *Paris, Fortin, Masson & cie.* 1843. S.

Orléans (Pierre Joseph d'). *See* **D'Orléans.**

Orphans (The) of Glen Elder. [*anon.*] 232 pp. 4 pl. 16°. *Philadelphia, American s. s. union*, [1867].

Orr (William S. *editor*). Orr's circle of the sciences. A series of treatises on the principles of science, with their application to practical pursuits. Organic nature. 2 v. 8°. *London, W. S. Orr & co.* 1854–55. S.

CONTENTS.

v. 1. The principles of physiology, (by the editor); the structure of the skeleton, and of the teeth, (by prof. Owen); and the varieties of the human race, (by R. G. Latham). With an introductory treatise on the nature, connection, and uses of the great departments of knowledge. 2d ed. xvi, 393 pp. 1854.

v. 2. A system of natural history, [etc.] Organic nature. In 2 vol. v. 1: Botany and invertebrated animals. Botany, by Edward Smith. Zoology, by W. S. Dallas. xvi, 491 pp. 1855.

——— The same. The mathematical sciences, including simple arithmetic, algebra, and the elements of Euclid. By J. R. Young. Planes, spherical trigonometry, series, logarithms, and mensuration, by J. F. Twisden, and practical geometry, by Alexander Jardine. viii, 454 pp. 8°. *London, W. S. Orr & co.* 1854. S.

Örsted (Anders Sandöe). Om sygdomme hos planterne, som foraarsages af snyltesvampe, navnlig om rust og brand, og om midlerne til deres forebyggelse. 3 p. l. 146 pp. 1 l. 3 col. pl. 8°. *Kjöbenhavn, J. H. Schubothe*, 1863. S.

Orta (Garcia de). Due libri dell' historia de i semplici, aromati, et altre cose, che vengono portate dall' Indie Orientali pertinenti all' vso della medicina. Con alcune breui annotationi di C. Clvsio. Tradotti da Annibale Briganti. 12 p. l. 236 pp. 16°. *Venetia, G. Ziletti*, 1582.

[*With* MONARDES (Nicolas). Delle cose che vengono portato dall Indie Occidentali, etc. ed. 1582].

——— The same. Aromatvm, et simplicivm aliqvot medicamentorvm apvd Indos nascentivm historia: primum quidem lusitanica lingua conscripta. Nunc vero latino sermone in epitomen contracta, et annotatiunculis illustrata a Carolo Clvsio. 232 pp. 16°. *Antverpiæ, C. Plantin*, 1574.

——— The same. 4a ed. 217 pp. 4 l. 16°. *Antverpiae, ex officina Plantiniana*, 1593.

[Imperfect: wanting pp. 3–4, 79–96].

Osborn (Laughton). Dramatic works. v. 1. Tragedies. 3 p. l. 419 pp. 12°. *New York, Moorhead, Bond & co.* 1868.

CONTENTS.

Virginia. Calvary. Bianca Capello.

——— The same. v. 4. Comedies. 517 pp. 12°. *New York, J. Miller*, 1868.

CONTENTS.

The silver head. The double deceit.
The Montanini. The school for critics.

——— Bianca Capello, a tragedy. [Extract from his Dramatic works, v. 1. pp. 201–419]. 12°. *New York, Moorhead, Simpson & Bond*, 1868.

——— The Montanini. The school for critics. Comedies. Being in continuation and completion of the fourth volume of the dramatic series. 2 p. l. pp. 265–517. 12°. *New York, J. Miller*, 1868.

——— The school for critics. A comedy. Being in completion of the fourth volume of the dramatic series. 1 p. l. pp. 403–517. 12°. *New York, J. Miller*, 1868.

Öst (Niels Christian). Materialier til et dansk biographisk-literarisk lexicon, etc. 760 col. on 190 l. 1 tab. 4°. *Kjöbenhavn, B. Luro & Schneider*, 1835-36. S.

Ost und west. [Taglich journal. Eigenthümer und verantwortlicher redacteur; dr. C. J. von Tkalac]. 2 v. fol. *Wien, A. Eurich*, 1861-62. S.

CONTENTS.

v. 1. 20 Februar—31 December, 1861. nos. 1-286.
v. 2. 1 Jänuar—30 April, 1862. nos. 287-404.
[No more published in newspaper form].

——— The same. Ost und west. Wochenschrift für politik. ii. jahrgang. 3 Mai,—25 Oct. 1862. Eigenthümer herausgeber und verantwort. redacteur; dr. E. J. v. Tkalac. ix, 890 pp. 8°. *Wien, A. Eurich, etc.* 1862. S.

[Nos. 12, 20, 21, 22, 24 wanting; but having been confiscated, are not obtainable. No more was permitted to be published in weekly nos. after the 25th Oct.]

—— The same. Ost und west. Zeitschrift für politik. Herausgegeben und redigirt von Alexander Sandic. Nos. 1-3. 176 pp. 8°. *Wien, F. Fridrich & co.* 1863. s.

[*With* the preceding].

Osten (Mary). Grandmother's curiosity cabinet. From the German [of E. Eyler, *pseudon.*] by Anna B. Cooke. 255 pp. 1 pl. 16°. *Boston, E. P. Dutton & co.* 1869.

Otto (Emil). A practical and easy course of the German language. Enlarged ed. 155 pp. 12°. *Louisville, (Ky.) H. Knöfel,* 1868.

Ouida. [*pseudon.* of *mrs.* **De la Rama**] ? *See* **Held** in bondage; *also,* **Tricotrin.**

Our boys and girls. *See* **Oliver** Optic's magazine.

Our English home; its early history and progress. With notes on the introduction of domestic inventions. [*anon.*] iv, 204 pp. 12°. *Oxford, J. H. & J. Parker,* 1860.

Our little one. The little shoe, little feet, little footsteps. [*anon.*] 112 pp. 1 pl. 16°. *Boston, Gould & Lincoln,* 1867.

Our school-day visitor; an illustrated magazine for young people. Jan. 1867, to Dec. 1868. v. 11-12. 4°. *Philadelphia, Daughaday & Becker,* [1867-68].

Our young folks. An illustrated [monthly] magazine for boys and girls. Edited by J. T. Trowbridge and Lucy Larcom. Jan. to Dec. 1868. v. 4. 8°. *Boston, Ticknor & Fields,* 1868.

Ouseley (*Rev. sir* Frederick Arthur Gore). A treatise on harmony. xii, 267 pp. 1 tab. 4°. *Oxford, Clarendon press,* 1868.

Ovalle (Alonso de). Historica relatione del region di Cile e delle missioni, e mininisterii che esercita in quelle la compagnia di Giesv. 3 p. l. 378 pp. 27 pl. 4°. *Roma, F. Caulli,* 1646.

—— The same. An historical relation of the kingdom of Chille. [Translated out of Spanish, by a member of the Royal society]. 3 p. l. 164 pp. fol. *London, A. and J. Churchill,* 1703.

Overbury (*Sir* Thomas) *and others.* A book of characters: selected from the writings of Overbury, Earle, and Butler. xxvii, 291 pp. portrait. 16°. *Edinburgh, W. P. Nimmo,* 1865.

Overland (The) monthly. Devoted to the development of the country. July to Dec. 1868. v. i. 8°. *San Francisco, A. Roman & co.* 1868.

Overton (*Rev.* Charles). Christiana and her children; or, the second part of cottage lectures on Pilgrims progress, [etc]. 372 pp. 9 pl. 16°. *Philadelphia, American s. s. union,* [1850]. s.

Owen (*Rev.* Griffith). Materials for thought. Designed for young men. 250 pp. 12°. *Philadelphia, W. S. & A. Martien,* 1859. s.

Owen *or* **Audoenus** (John, *of Caernarvonshire*). Agvdezas de Ivan Oven, tradvcidas en metro castellano. Illvstradas, con adiciones y notas, por Francisco de la Torre. 12 p. l. 402 pp. 8°. *Madrid, F. Sanz,* 1674. s.

Owen (Richard). On the principal forms of the skeleton and teeth. 8°. *London,* 1854.

[*In* ORR (J. P.) Circle of the sciences. Organic nature. v. 1].

Owen (Robert Dale). The conditions of reconstruction; in a letter to the secretary of state. 24 pp. 8°. *New York, W. C. Bryant & co.* 1863.

[LOYAL publication society, no. 25].

—— Emancipation is peace. 7 pp. 8°. *New York, W. C. Bryant & co.* 1863.

[LOYAL publication society, no. 22].

—— The future of the north-west: in connection with the scheme of reconstruction without New England. 15 pp. 8°. *New York, E. O. Jenkins,* 1863.

[LOYAL publication society, no. 1].

Oxford (*University of*). Munimenta academica, or documents illustrative of academical life and studies at Oxford. 2 v. cl, 859 pp. 8°. *London, Longmans,* 1868.

[GREAT BRITAIN and Ireland: Chronicles and memorials during the middle ages].

Oxford (The) methodists: being an account of some young gentlemen in that city, in derision so called. [With] a short epistle to the rev. mr. Whitefield. [*anon.* By A. B.] 3^d ed. 22 pp. 8°. [*London, J. Hodges,* 1738].

[*With* WHITEFIELD (*Rev.* Geo.) Several discourses upon practical subjects. 1738].

Oxford (The) university and city guide, on a new plan. New ed. 220 pp. 1 map. 7 pl. 16°. *Oxford, H. Slatter,* 1825.

Ozanam (Antoine Frédéric). La civilization au cinquième siècle. Introduction à une histoire de la civilisation aux temps barbares. Suivie d'un essai sur les écoles en Italie du ve au xiii siècle. 2 v. 2 p. l. xxxiii, 395 pp. 1 l. 1 portrait; 2 p. l. 433 pp. 1 l. 8°. *Paris, J. Lecoffre & cie.* 1855.

—— The same. History of civilization in the 5th century. From the French by A. C. Glyn. 2 v. xxiv, 295 pp; xii, 275 pp. 12°. *London, W. H. Allen & co.* 1868.

Pabodie (William J.) Calidore; a legendary poem. 48 pp. 8°. *Boston, Marsh, Capen, Lyon & Webb,* 1839.

Pacheco (José Praxedes Pereira). L' histoire expliquée par la philosophie. 131 pp. 8°. *Paris, Poussielgue, Masson, & cie.* 1852. s.

Pacific medical and surgical journal. H. Gibbons, M. D. editor. June, 1867, to May, 1868. New series. v. 1. 8°. *San Francisco, Bancroft & co.* [1867–68].

Pacific railroad: reports of explorations. *See* **United States.** War department.

Packard (*Mrs.* E. P. W.) The prisoners hidden life; or, insane asylums unveiled. 346 pp. 12°. *Chicago, the author,* 1868.

——— Mrs. Olsen's narrative of her one year's imprisonment at Jacksonville insane asylum. 144 pp. 12°. *Chicago, A. B. Case,* 1868.
[*With* the preceding].

Padilla (Agustin Davila). *See* **Davila Padilla.**

Pae (David). A popular history of the discovery, progress, and present state of America; to which is added, a description of the principal states in the union and their respective merits as fields of emigration. iv, 164 pp. 18°. *Edinburgh, Thomas Grant,* 1852.

Paessler. *See* **Pässler.**

Paez (Ramon). Travels and adventures in South and Central America. First series. Life in the llanos of Venezuela. 473 pp. 1 map. 12 pl. 12°. *New York, C. Scribner & co.* 1868.

Page (Charles Grafton, *M. D.*) History of induction. The American claim to the induction coil and its electrostatic developments. 124 pp. 5 pl. 8°. *Washington, Intelligencer printing house,* 1867.

Page (David, *LL. D.*) Man: where, whence, and whither. Being a glance at man in his natural-history relations. 199 pp. 16°. *Edinburgh, Edmondston & Douglas,* 1867.

Paine (Martyn, *M. D.*) The institutes of medicine. viii, 826 pp. 8°. *New York, Harpers,* 1847. s.

——— The same. 8th ed. xvi, 1145 pp. portrait. 8°. *New York, Harpers,* 1867.

Palaeontographica. Beiträge zur naturgeschichte der vorwelt. Herausgegeben von W. Dunker und H. von Meyer. v. 1–6. 4°. *Cassel, T. Fisher,* 1851–58. s.
[v. 7 *et seq.* wanting].

Palaidor (—— de, *pseudon.*) *See* **Bruslé de Montpleinchant** (J. C.)

Palaprat (Jean de). Œuvres choisies. *See* **Brueys** (D. A. de) *and* **Palaprat.**

Palingenius Stellatus (Marcellus, *pseudon.*) *See* **Manzoli** (Pietro Angelo).

Pallas (Peter Simon). Description du Tibet, d'après la relation des Lamas Tangoutes, établis parmis les Mongols. De l'Allemand avec des notes par Jean de Reuilly. xii, 89 pp. 8°. *Paris, Bossange, etc.* 1808.
[*With* REUILLY (Jean, *baron* de). Voyage en Crimée].

Palliser (*Capt.* John). Papers relative to the exploration by capt. Palliser of that portion of British North America which lies between the northern branch of the river Saskatchewan and the frontier of the United States, and between the Red river and Rocky mountains. 64 pp. 8 maps and pl. fol. *London, stationery office,* 1859. s.

——— The same. Further papers relative to the [same expedition and region], and thence to the Pacific ocean. 73 pp. 3 maps. fol. *London, stationery office,* 1860. s.

Palmer (Henry Spencer). British Columbia. Williams lake and Cariboo. Report on portions of the Williams lake and Cariboo districts, and on the Fraser river, from fort Alexander to fort George. 2 p. l. 25 pp. 8°. *New Westminster, (British Columbia), royal engineer press,* 1863. s.

——— Reports of a journey of survey from Victoria to fort Alexander, via North Bentinck arm. 2 p. l. 33 pp. 8°. *New Westminster, royal engineer press,* 1863. s.

Palmer (James Croxall). Antarctic mariner's song. [Illustrated]. 92 pp. 8°. *New York, Van Nostrand,* 1868.

Palmer (John Williamson). The poetry of compliment and courtship. Selected by J. W. Palmer. xxiv, 219 pp. 10 pl. 12°. *Boston, Ticknor & Fields,* 1868.

Palmer (Lynde). The honorable club, and other tales. 270 pp. 3 pl. 18°. *Boston, Am. tract soc.* 1867.

——— The magnet stories. One day's weaving. 303 pp. 4 pl. 16°. *Troy, (N. Y.) Moore & Nims,* 1868.

Pander (Christian Heinrich). Ueber die fossilen fische des devonischen systems Russland. 3 v. in 1. 4°. Atlas. 3 v. in 1. fol. *St. Petersburg, buchdruckerei der k. akademie der wissenschaften,* 1857–60. s.

CONTENTS.

[v. 1.] Ueber die placodermen des devonischen systems. 1 p. l. 106 pp. 1 pl. (B.) atlas. 8 pl. 1857.
[v. 2.] Über die ctenodipterinen des devonischen systems. viii, 64 pp. 1 l. atlas. 9 pl. 1858.
[v. 3]. Über die saurodipterinen, dendrodonten, glyptolepiden und cheirolepiden des devonischen systems. ix, 90 pp. atlas. 17 pl. (i-xi; f-l). 1860.

Panvinio (Onofrio). Reipublicae romanae commentariorvm libri tres. 8 p. l. 947 pp. 5 l. 12°. *Venetiis, ex. off. erasmiana apud V. Valgrisium,* 1558. s.

Panzer (Georg Wolfgang Franz). D. Jacobi Christiani Schaefferi iconvm insectorvm circa Ratisbonam indigenorvm enumeratio systematica. 2 p. l. xvi, 260 pp. 4°. *Erlangae, J. J. Palm,* 1804. s.

Papencordt (Felix). Geschichte der stadt Rom im mittelalter. Herausgegeben und mit anmerkungen, [etc] versehen, von C. Höfler. xvi, 522 pp. 8°. *Paderborn, F. Schöningh,* 1857.

Papers for the schoolmaster. New series. v. 3. 8°. *London, Simpkin, Marshall & co.* 1867.

Pappus *Alexandrinus.* Lemmata in libros duos Apollonii de sectione determinata. 4°. *Glasguae, R. & A. Foulis,* 1776.
[*In* SIMSON (R.) Opera quaedam reliqua. pp. 1-57].

——— Præfatio, etc. 8°. *Oxonii,* 1706.
[*In* APOLLONIUS *Pergæus.* De sectione rationis, etc. 1706].

Pardoe (Julia). The romance of the harem. 2 v. 216 pp; 218 pp. 12°. *Philadelphia, Carey & Hart,* 1839.

Pareau (Ludovicus Gerlachus). Hermeneutica codicis sacra. 2 p. l. iv, 494 pp. 8°. *Groningae, I. Oomkens,* 1846. s.

——— Initia institutionis christianae moralis. xix, 406 pp. 1 l. 8°. *Groningae, I. Oomkens,* 1842. s.

——— *and* **Hofstede de Groot** (P.) Encyclopaedia theologi christiani. Ed. 3ª. 7 p. l. 150 pp. 8°. *Groningae, C. M. van Bolhuis Hoitsema,* 1851. s.

——— ——— Lineamenta theologiae christianae universae, ut disquisitionis de religione una verissima et praestantissima, sive brevis conspectus dogmatices et apologetices christianae. Ed. 3ª [etc.] xiv, 228 pp. 8°. *Groningae, C. M. van Bolhuis Hoitsema,* 1848. s.

Paris (Alexis Paulin). Les manuscrits françois de la bibliothèque du roi, leur histoire et celle des texts allemands, anglais, hollandois, italiens, espagnols, de la même collection. v. 1-5. 8°. *Paris, Techener,* 1836-42. s.
[v. 6-7 wanting].

Paris. *Académie royale des sciences.* Memoirs for a natural history of animals. Containing the anatomical descriptions of several creatures dissected by the Royal academy of sciences at Paris. Englished by A. Pitfield, [etc.] Frontispiece. 7 p. l. 281 pp. 30 pl. fol. *London, J. Streaterfa, T. Basset, etc.* 1688.

Parker (George Phillips). Catalogue of the extensive collection of books, forming [his] private library. 2 p. l. 167 pp. 8°. *New York, G. A. Leavitt & co. auctioneers,* 1859. s.

Parker (Richard Green). Questions in geography, adapted for the use of Morse's, or any other respectable collection of maps, etc. 114 pp. 12°. *New York, Harpers,* 1855. s.

Parker (*Mrs.* Rosa Abbott). Tommy Hickup; or, a pair of black eyes. By Rosa Abbott. 254 pp. 4 pl. 16°. *Boston, Lee & Shepard,* 1868.
[ROSA ABBOTT stories, v. 3].

——— Upside down; or, will and work. 252 pp. 4 pl. 16°. *Boston, Lee & Shepard,* 1868.
[ROSA Abbott stories, v. 4].

Parker (*Rev.* Samuel). Journal of an exploring tour beyond the Rocky Mountains. 5th ed. 422 pp. 1 map. 16°. *Auburn, J. C. Derby & co.* 1846.

Parker (*Rev.* Theodore). A discourse occasioned by the death of Daniel Webster, preached at the Melodeon, Oct. 31, 1852. vii, 108 pp. 8°. *Boston, B. B. Mussey & co.* 1853.

Parker (William Kitchen). A monograph on the structure and development of the shoulder-girdle and sternum in the vertebrata. xi, 237 pp. 31 l. 30 col. pl. fol. *London,* 1868.
[RAY society.]

Parkinson (Richard). General view of the agriculture of the county of Huntingdon. vii, 351 pp. 2 maps. 8°. *London,* 1811. s.
[GREAT BRITAIN. Board of agriculture].

——— General view of the agriculture of the county of Rutland. vii, 188 pp. 3 pl. 8°. *London,* 1808. s.
[GREAT BRITAIN. Board of agriculture. *With* PITT (W.) Agriculture of Leicester].

——— Survey of Buckinghamshire. 8°. *London,* 1810.
[GREAT BRITAIN. Board of agriculture. *In* PRIEST (St. John). Agriculture of Buckinghamshire].

Parlatore (Filippo). Le specie dei cotoni. Atlas. 2 p. l. 6 col. pl. fol. *Firenze, stamperia reale,* 1866. s.

Parliament, and parliamentary registers. *See* **Great Britain.**

Parmly (Eleazar). Thoughts in rhyme. xiv, 600 pp. portrait. 8°. *New York, T. Holman,* 1867.

Parr (*Miss* Harriet). In the silver age: "essays—that is, dispersed meditations." By Holme Lee. [*pseudon.*] New ed. x, 485 pp. 1 pl. 16°. *London, Smith, Elder & co.* 1866.

Parsons (William L. *editor*). Reminiscences of the life and character of col. Phineas Staunton, [*and*] A sermon on the death of miss Marietta Ingham. 94 pp. 1 phot. pl. 8°. *Rochester, E. Darrow & Kempshall,* 1867. s.

Parthenio Giannetasio (Niccolò). *See* **Giannetasio** (N. P.)

Particulars (The) and inventories of the estates of the late sub-governor, deputy-governor, and directors of the South Sea company. With the abstracts of the same. 2 v. 704 pp; 678 pp. fol. *London, J. Tonson*, 1721.

Parton (James). Life of Andrew Jackson. 3 v. 8°. *New York, Mason bros.* 1861.

——— People's book of biography; or, short lives of the most interesting persons of all ages and countries. xii, 624 pp. 12 pl. 8°. *Hartford, A. S. Hale & co.* 1868.

——— Smoking and drinking. viii, 151 pp. 16°. *Boston, Ticknor & Fields*, 1865.

Parton (Sarah Parker). Folly as it flies; hit at by Fanny Fern. [*pseudon.*] 355 pp. 12°. *New York, G. W. Carleton & co.* 1868.

Parvin (*Rev.* Robert J.) Union notes on the gospels. 241 pp. 16°. *Philadelphia, American sunday school union*, [1855]. s.

Paschal (George W.) The constitution of the United States defined and carefully annotated. xxviii, 407 pp. 12°. *Washington, W. H. & O. H. Morrison*, 1868.

Pasquier (*Baron* Étienne Denis). Discours prononcés dans les chambres législatives, [etc.] 1814–1836. 4 v. 8°. *Paris, Crapelet*, 1842. s.

Pasquin. [A political weekly]. Nov. 28, 1722 to Aug. 13, 1723. No. 1–56. 56 l. fol. *London, J. Peele*, 1722–23.

Pasquino [*pseudon.*] *See* **American Cyclops.**

Pässler (Carl Wilhelm Gottfried). *See* **Bädeker** (F. W. J.) Die eier der voegel, etc.

Past, present and future of greenbacks, including the national currency law. By a republican farmer. [*anon.* By C. Alvord]? 50 pp. 8°. *Milwaukee, Hanlon & Richardson*, 1868.

Pastoret (Amédée, *comte* de). Le duc de Guise à Naples, ou mémoires sur les révolutions de ce royaume en 1647 et 1648. [*anon.*] 2 p. l. 319 pp. 8°. *Paris, Ladvocat*, 1825. s.

Paterculus (Caius Velleius). Historiæ romanæ ad M. Vinicium cos. libri ii. 8°. [*Geneva*], 1568.

[*In* VARII historiæ romanæ scriptores, v. 1].

Paterson (Samuel, *auctioneer*). Joineriana: or the book of scraps. [*anon.*] 2 v. 2 p. l. 190 pp; 203 pp. 18°. *London, J. Johnson*, 1772.

Patmore (Coventry). The victories of love. 96 pp. 16°. *Boston, T. Burnham*, 1862.

Patria. La France ancienne et moderne, morale et matérielle, ou collection encyclopédique et statistique de tous les faits relatifs a l'histoire physique et intellectuelle de la France et de ses colonies. xliv, 2875 pp. 3 pl. 12°. *Paris, J. J. Dubochet, Le Chevalier & ce.* 1847.

Patriarchal (The) age; or, the story of Joseph. 342 pp. 2 maps. 12 pl. 12°. *Philadelphia, R. E. Peterson*, 1851. s.

Patterson (*Rev.* John Brown). An essay on the national character of the Athenians. [With] a biographical notice. xxxiv, 168 pp. 12°. *Edinburgh, W. Blackwood & sons*, 1860.

Patterson (Robert Hogarth). The economy of capital, or gold and trade. Amended ed. xv, 456 pp. 8°. *Edinburgh, W. Blackwood & sons*, 1865.

Paul (James). Violet; or, the times we live in. 247 pp. 12°. *Philadelphia, J. B. Lippincott & co.* 1858. s.

Paul (*Rev.* Robert). The great work, and how to do it. 252 pp. 12°. *Philadelphia, McCalla & Stavely*, 1867.

Paulding (James Kirke). Salmagundi. *See* **Irving** (W.) *and* **Paulding.**

Pauli (Reinhold). Geschichte von England. Mit einem vorworte von J. M. Lappenberg. 2 v. 8°. *Hamburg, Perthes*, 1853–55.

[HEEREN (A. H. L.) *and* UKERT (F. A.) Geschichte der europäischen staaten. Geschichte von England. v. 3-4].

Peabody (Andrew Preston, *D. D.*) Sermons connected with the re-opening of the church of the south parish, in Portsmouth, New Hampshire, [1858–59]. 112 pp. 12°. *Portsmouth, etc. J. F. Shore, jr. etc.* 1859. s.

——— (*compiler*). A sunday school hymn book; with devotional services. viii, 192 pp. 16° *Boston, J. Munroe & co.* 1857. s.

Peabody (William Bourne Oliver). Ornithology of Massachusetts. 8°. *Boston, Dutton & Wentworth*, 1839.

[MASSACHUSETTS. Zoological and botanical survey. *In* Reports on the fishes, etc.]

Peabody (The) institute of the city of Baltimore. The founder's letters and the papers relating to its dedication and its history, up to the 1st Jan. 1868. 146 pp. 2 pl. 8°. *Baltimore, W. K. Boyle*, 1868.

Peacock (Thomas Love). Crotchet castle. 2 p. l. 300 pp. 16°. *London, T. Hookham*, 1831.

——— Headlong hall. 3d ed. 216 pp. 16° *London, T. Hookham*, 1822.

Pearce (James). The words of anthems. 126 pp. 18°. *Philadelphia, F. E. Remont*, 1868.

Pebbles from the sea-shore; or Lizzie's first gleanings. By a father. [*anon.*] 126 pp. 4 pl. sq. 16°. *Philadelphia, G. S. Appleton*, 1851. s.

Peck (A. T.) Fortunes for workingmen; a new and sure way to accumulate property, recently discovered. 300 pp. 16°. *New York, Russell's American steam printing house,* 1867.

Peck (Jesse T. *D.D.*) The history of the great republic, considered from a christian standpoint. viii, 710 pp. 10 pl. 8°. *New York, Broughton & Wyman,* 1868.

Peck (John). A short poem, containing a descant on the universal plan. Also, lines on the happy end of the righteous. 4th ed. 52 pp. 16°. *Boston, J. P. Jewett & co.* 1858. s.

Peck (William Henry). The confederate flag on the ocean. A tale of the cruises of the Sumter and Alabama. 96 pp. 18°. *New York, Van Evrie, Horton & co.* 1868.

Peculiarities of the shakers, described in a series of letters from Lebanon springs, 1832. By a visitor. [*anon.*] 116 pp. 24°. *New York, J. K. Porter,* 1832.

Peebles (J. M.) *and* **Barrett** (J. O.) The spiritual harp; a collection of vocal music for the choir, congregation, and social circle. E. H. Bailey, musical editor. 297 pp. 8°. *Boston, W. White & co.* 1868.

Peet (Dudley, *M.D.*) Manual of inorganic chemistry. Enlarged by J. Peet. 125 pp. 18°. *New York, D. Van Nostrand,* 1865.

Peeters (Sjurd). *See* **Petri** (Suffridus).

Peignot (Étienne Gabriel). Le livre des singularités. xv, 464 pp. 8°. *Dijon, V. Lagier,* 1841.

Peirce (*Rev.* Bradford K.) The word of God opened. Its inspiration, canon, and interpretation considered and illustrated. 223 pp. 12°. *New York, Carlton & Porter,* 1868.

Peirce. *See, also,* **Pierce.**

Pelletan (Eugène). An address to king cotton. 19 pp. 8°. *New York, W. C. Bryant & co.* 1863.

[LOYAL publication society, no.12].

Pellico (Silvio). Opere. 2 v. in 1. 164 pp; 176 pp. 8°. *Padova, tipi della Minerva,* 1831. s.

CONTENTS.

v. 1. *Tragedie.* Eufemio di Messina; Francesca da Rimini; Ester d'Engaddi.
v. 2. *Tragedia.* Iginia d'Asti: *Cantiche.*

——— The same. Sämmtliche werke. Aus dem Italienischen, von dr. K. L. Kannegiekser und H. Müller. xv, 254 pp. 1 portrait. 8°. *Zwickau, Schumann,* 1835. s.

CONTENTS.

Leben: Meine haft, mit zusätze von P. Maroncelli; abhandlung über die pflichten der menschen; trauerspiele; poetische novellen.

——— Dei doveri degli uomini, discorso ad un giovane. 2 p.l. 130 pp. 12°. *Parigi, Baudry,* 1834. s.

——— Francesca da Rimini, ed Eufemio di Messina, tragedie. 138 pp. *Parigi, Baudry,* 1833. s.

[*With* PELLICO (S.) Le mie prigioni, 1833.

——— Le mie prigioni, memorie. 2 p.l. 351 pp. 12°. *Parigi, Baudry,* 1833. s.

——— The life of the marchesa Giulia Falletti di Barolo, reformer of the Turin prisons. From the original, by Georgiana Fullerton. 231 pp. 16°. *London, R. Bentley,* 1866.

——— Tommaso Moro, tragedia. 4 p.l. 85 pp. *Parigi, Baudry,* 1834. s.

Pelt (Anton Friedrich Ludwig). Theologische encyclopädie als system im zusammenhange mit der geschichte der theologischen wissenschaft und ihrer einzelnen zweige entwickelt. xvi, 688 pp. 8°. *Hamburg, etc. F. & A. Perthes,* 1843. s.

Pelton (C.) Key to Pelton's hemispheres, designed as an introduction to the key to his complete series of outline maps, etc. 176 pp. 8°. *Philadelphia, Sower & Barnes,* 1851. s.

Pemberton (Robert). The attributes of the soul from the cradle, and the philosophy of the divine mother, detecting the false basis, or fundamental error, of the schools, and developing the perfect education of man. vii, 392 pp. 8°. *London, Saunders & Otley,* 1849. s.

——— The happy colony. viii, 217 pp. 2 pl. 8°. *London, Saunders & Otley,* 1854. s.

Peñafael (Antonio) *and* **Villada** (Manuel). Estudio sobre una nueva especie del género "cantharis." 8°. *Mexico,* 1865.

[*In* ALMARAZ (R.) Memoria, por la comision cientifica de Pachuca].

Penington (Isaac). Works. 2 v. in 1. 25 p.l. 470 pp; 496 pp. fol. *London, B. Clark,* 1681.

[Imperfect: sub-title-page of v. 1, and pp. 495–6 of v. 2 wanting].

Pennant (Thomas). Allgemeine uebersicht der vierfüssigen thiere. Aus dem Englischen übersetzt von Johann Matthäus Bechstein. v. i. xxx, 318 pp. 34 pl. 4°. *Weimar, industrie comptoir's,* 1799. s.

[v. 2 wanting].

Pennington. *See* **Penington.**

Pennsylvania (*State of*). Annual report of the auditor of the state, and of the tabulations and deductions from the reports of the railroad and canal companies for 1867. lxix, 555 pp. 1 map. 8°. *Harrisburg, Singerly & Myers,* 1868.

——— The election laws of Pennsylvania: digested and arranged, with notes and judicial decisions. 152 pp. 8°. *Harrisburg, Singerly & Myers,* 1868.

Pennsylvania. Manual of rules of the general assembly, and legislative directory; with the constitution of the U. S. and of Pennsylvania. Compiled by J. A. Smull. 332 pp. 1 map. 1 pl. 18°. *Harrisburg, Singerly & Myers,* 1868.

——— Report of the superintendent of common schools, 1867. xlii, 424 pp. 8°. *Harrisburg, Singerly & Myers,* 1868.

——— Returns of the several banks and savings institutions of Pennsylvania, 1855. 185 pp. 8°. *Harrisburg, state printer,* 1855. s.

——— *State penitentiary for the eastern district.* Thirty-ninth annual report of the inspectors. 117 pp. 4 tab. 8°. *Philadelphia, McLaughlin bros.* 1868. s.

Pennsylvania hospital. Supplement to the catalogue raisonné of the medical library. By A. F. Müller. pp. 713–810. 8°. *Philadelphia, Collins,* 1867.

Pepe (Francesco). Novena de sábados en honor de la concepcion immaculada de Maria madre de Dios y señora nuestra. Tradúcela á nuestro Castellano T. A. Perez. 4 p. l. 368 pp. 8°. *Madrid, viuda de Ibarra,* 1796. s.

Pepperell (William). An accurate journal and account of the New England land forces during the expedition against the French settlements on Cape Breton, to the surrender of Louisbourg, with a computation of the French fishery. 40 pp. 12°. *Exon, A. & S. Bryce,* 1746.

Perce (Elbert). Gulliver Joi; his three voyages: being an account of his marvellous adventures in Kailoo, Hydrogenia, and Ejario. 272 pp. 16°. *New York, C. Scribner,* 1851. s.

Percheron (Achille Remy). Bibliographie entomologique, comprenant l'indication par ordre alphabétique de noms d'auteurs, 1°, des ouvrages entomologiques, [etc.] jusques et y compris l'année 1834; 2°, des monographies et mémoires contenus dans les recueils; suivie d'une tableau méthodique et chronologique des matières. 2 v. xii, 326 pp; 2 p. l. 376 pp. 8°. *Paris, J. B. Baillière,* 1837. s.

Percier (Charles) *and* **Fontaine** (Pierre François Léonard). Description des cérémonies et des fêtes qui ont eu lieu pour le mariage de l'empereur Napoléon avec madame l'archiduchesse Marie-Louise d'Autriche. 2 p. l. 45 pp. 1 l. 13 pl. fol. *Paris, P. Didot,* 1810.

Percival (Thomas, *M. D.*) Parental instructions; or, guide to wisdom and virtue, designed for young persons of either sex, selected from the writings of an eminent physician. 252 pp. 16°. *New York, Harpers,* 1846. s.

Percy (Thomas, *bishop of Dromore*). Folio manuscript [of the reliques of ancient English poetry]. Ballads and romances. Edited by J. W. Hales, and F. J. Furnivall. v. 1. pt. 2; v. 2. pt. 2; and v. 3. 8°. *London, Trübner,* 1868.
[NOTE.—Completes the work].

Percy's year of rhymes. 43 pp. 6 pl. 8°. *New York, Hurd & Houghton,* 1867.

Pereira (Antonio, *of Lisbon*). Appendix e illustraçaõ da tentativa theologica, sobre o poder dos bispos em tempo de Rotura. 381 pp. 4°. *Lisboa, A. V. da Silva,* 1768. s.

Pereira (Gomez). Antoniana margarita, opvs nempe physicis, medicis ac theologis non minvs vtile qvam necessarivm. 26 p. l. 831 cols. 4°. *Methymnæ Campi, G. de Millis,* 1554.

——— Obiectiones Michaëlis à Palacios aduerssus nõnulla ex multiplicibus paradoxis antonianae margaritae, et apologia eorundem. 18 l. 4°. *Methymnæ Campi, G. de Millis,* 1555.
[*With* the preceding].

Perez de Hita (Ginèz). The civil wars of Granada; and the history of the factions of the Zegries and Abencerrages, to the final conquest by Ferdinand and Isabella. From the Arabic of Abenhamin, by G. P. de Hita; and from the Spanish, by T. Rodd. xix, 438 pp. 8°. *London, T. Ostell,* 1803.
NOTE.—"On est généralement persuadé que Perez de Hita en est le véritable auteur."—*Brunet.*

Perkins (George R.) An elementary arithmetic, etc. 347 pp. 12°. *Hartford, H. H. Hawley & co.* 1849. s.

——— Higher arithmetic, etc. 342 pp. 12°. *Utica, etc. H. H. Hawley & co. etc.* 1848. s.

——— A treatise on algebra, [etc.] 2[d] ed. 420 pp. 8°. *Utica, H. H. Hawley & co.* 1847. s.

Perkins (*Rev.* James Handasyd). Memoir and writings. Edited by W. H. Channing. 2 v. xii, 527 pp; 502 pp. portrait. 12°. *Cincinnati, Truman & Spofford,* 1851.

Perkins (Joshua). The duties of human life; translated from a Sanscrit manuscript, written by an ancient brahmin, etc. 2 pts. in 1 v. xx pp. 1 l. 128 pp. 12°. *West Killingly, (Conn.) J. P. Chamberlin & co.* 1858. s.

Perotti (Niccolò), *and others.* Cornvcopiae, siue linguæ latinæ cõmentarii, etc. M. Terentii Varronis de lingua latina libri tres—sextus. Eiusdem de analogia libri tres. Sexti Pompeii Festi undeuigenti librorum fragmenta. Nonii Marcelli compendia, labore Jucundi. Additus est longus tractatus de generibus. 79 l. 718 pp. fol. *Venetiis, in aedibvs Aldi et Andreae soceri,* 1517.

Perrin (John). Entertaining and instructive exercises, with the rules of the French syntax. 7th ed. iv, 230 pp. 16°. *London, Law & son,* 1793.

Perrodin (*Rev.* John C.) Conversations of a catholic missionary with Americans. 345 pp. 16°. *Milwaukee, Hoffman bros.* 1868.

Perrot (Antoine Marie). Collection historique des ordres de chevalerie civils et militaires, existant chez les différents peuples du monde, suivie d'un tableau chronologique de tous les ordres éteints. xxiv, 294 pp. 40 pl. 4°. *Paris, André,* 1820.

——— Lehrbuch der kupferstecherkunst, der kunst in stahl zu stechen und in holz zu schneiden. (Chalcographie, siderographie und xylographie), etc. Frei nach dem Französischen ["Manuel du graveur"], bearbeitet von Theodor Thon. xviii, 379 pp. 16°. *Ilmenau, B. F. Voigt,* 1831. s.

——— Nouvel itinéraire portatif d'Italie, renfermant une description complète de ce pays et ses divers états, etc. vi, 339 pp. 1 map. 5 pl. 18°. *Paris, H. Langlois fils & cie.* 1827. s.

Perrot (M. E.) Revue de l'exposition des produits de l'industrie nationale en 1841. xviii, 393 pp. 8°. *Bruxelles, auteur,* 1841. s.

Perry (Charles, *M. D.*) A view of the Levant, particularly of Constantinople, Syria, Egypt, and Greece. xviii, 524 pp. 2 l. 33 pl. on 19 sheets. fol. *London, T. Woodward,* 1743.

Perry (*Mrs.* C. T.) The morning ride, and the schoolmates. 180 pp. 16°. *Boston, T. H. Carter & co.* 1866.

Persius Flaccus (Aulus). Satiræ. *See* **Juvenalis** (D. T.) *and* **Persius Flaccus** (A.)

——— Satirarvm liber. Isaacvs Casavbonvs recensuit, et commentario libro illustrauit. 8 p. l. 558 pp. 13 l. 16°. *Parisiis, Drovart,* 1615. s.

Perthes (Clemens Theodor). Der staatsdienst in Preussen, ein beitrag zum deutschen staatsrecht. 178 pp. 8°. *Hamburg, Perthes,* 1848.

Peschel (Oscar). Geschichte der erdkunde bis auf A. v. Humboldt und C. Ritter. Herausgegeben durch die hist. commission. xx, 706 pp. 8°. *München, J. G. Cotta,* 1865.

[NOTE.—v. 4 of Geschichte der wissenschaften in Deutschland].

Pestalozzi (Jean Henri). Lienhard und Gertrud. Ein buch für das volk. Die zwei ersten theile, in einem bande nach der ursprünglichen ausgabe neu gedruckt. Mit 13 federzeichnungen von H. Bendel, und einer musikbeilage. x, 266 pp. 13 pl. 4°. *Zurich, Meyer & Zeller,* 1844. s.

Pétau (Denis). The history of the world; or, an account of time. [Translated from the French]. Continued by others to 1659. [With] a geographical description of Europe, Asia, Africa, and America. [By R. P.] 4 p. l. 610 pp. 17 l. 154 pp. 3 l. 1 map. fol. *London, J. Streater,* 1659.

Petavius (Dionysius). *See* **Pétau** (Denis).

Peters (Christian). Formeln der mittleren monats- und tagestemperaturen für verschiedene tiefen. 4°. *St. Petersburg,* 1848. s.

[*In* MIDDENDORFF (A.T. von). Reise, etc. v. 1. theil 1].

Peters (Wilhelm Carl Hartwig). Naturwissenschaftliche reise nach Mossambique, auf befehl des königs Friedrich Wilhelm iv. in den jahren 1842–48 ausgeführt. Zoologie. v. 1, 4, and 5. fol. *Berlin, G. Reimer,* 1852–68. s.

CONTENTS.

v. 1. Säugethiere. xvi, 202 pp. 46 col. pl. 1852.
v. 4. Flussfische. xii, 116 pp. 20 pl. 1868.
v. 5. Insecten und myriopoden. Bearbeitet in verbindung mit Klug, Loew, Schaum, Hagen, Gerstaecker, Hopffer. xxiii, 566 pp. 35 col. pl. 1862.
[v. 2–3 not yet published].

——— The same. Botanik; bearbeitet von Andersson, Böckeler, Bolle, Braun, Garcke, Hasskarl, Klatt, Klotzsch, Kunth, Müller, Reichenbach, Steetz. 1 v. in 2. xxii, 584 pp. 61 pl. fol. *Berlin, G. Reimer,* 1862–64. s.

[No more published].

Pétion (Jérome). Mémoires. 8°. *Paris, Plon,* 1866.

[*In* MÉMOIRES inédits de Pétion, etc. 1866. pp. 105-176].

Petit (Augustin Adrien). Vie de saint Augustin. xii, 420 pp. 16°. *Lyon, Perisse,* 1836.

Petrarca (Francesco). De rimedi dell'vna, et l'altra fortvna. Libri ii, tradotti per Remigio fiorentino. 416, 3 l. 16°. *Venetia, D. Farri,* 1584. s.

Petri, Petrus, *or* **Peeters** (Sjurd *or* Suffridus). De scriptoribus Frisiæ, decades xvi. et semis: in quibus non modo peculiares Frisiæ, sed et totius Germaniæ communes antiquitates plurimæ indicantur, etc. 44 p. l. 498 pp. 24°. *Franqueræ, typis J. Horrei,* 1699. s.

Petrus von Rosenheim. *See* **Rosenheim.**

Peyerimhoff (H. de). Catalogue des lépidoptères d'Alsace, etc. 2 v. in 1. 123 pp; 80 pp. 8°. *Paris, F. Savy,* 1862–63. s.

Peyster (J. Watts de). *See* **De Peyster.**

Peyton (John Lewis). The adventures of my grandfather, [John Rowzée Peyton]. With extracts from his letters, and other family documents, with notes and biographical sketches. x, 249 pp. 8°. *London, J. Wilson,* 1867.

Pfeiffer (Ida). Journey to Iceland, and travels in Sweden and Norway, translated by Charlotte Fenimore Cooper. 273 pp. 12°. *New York, G. P. Putnam*, 1852.

——— A lady's second journey round the world: from London to the cape of Good Hope, Borneo, Java, etc. Panama, Peru, Ecuador, and the United States. xii, 500 pp. 12°. *New York, Harpers*, 1856.

Pfeil (Wilhelm). Neue vollständige anleitung zur behandlung, benutzung, und schätzung der forsten. 2 v. 8°. *Berlin, Veit & co.* 1854–55. s.

CONTENTS.

v. 1. Kritische repertorium der forstwirthschaft und ihrer hülfswissenschaften. 2e aufl. xxiii, 243 pp.
v. 2. Das forstliche verhalten der deutschen waldbäume und ihre erziehung. 3e aufl. 501 pp.

Pfister (Johann Christoph). Geschichte der Teutschen. Von den ältesten zeiten bis zur auflösung des reichs. 5 v. 8°. *Hamburg, F. Perthes*, 1829–35.

[HEEREN (A. H. L.) *and* UKERT (F. A.) Geschichte der europäischen staaten].

Pflüger (Eduard F. W.) Ueber die eierstöcke der säugethiere und des menschen. 4 p. l. 124 pp. 5 pl. 4°. *Leipzig, W. Engelmann*, 1863. s.

Phantom (The). June, 1841, to Feb. 1842. No. 1–7. 64 pp. 24°. *Cincinnati*, 1841–42.

Phelps (Almira H. Lincoln). Ida Norman; or, trials and their uses. [1st ed.] 272 pp. 12°. *Baltimore, Cushing & brother*, 1848. s.

Phelps (*Rev.* Austin). Ministerial culture. 28 pp. 24°. *Andover, W. F. Draper*, 1868.

Phelps (Charles A.) Life and public services of general Ulysses S. Grant, from his boyhood to the present time. And a biographical sketch of hon. Schuyler Colfax. xvi, 344 pp. 6 pl. 12°. *Boston, Lee & Shepard*, 1868.

Phelps (Elizabeth Stuart). The gates ajar. 248 pp. 12°. *Boston, Fields, Osgood & co.* 1869.

——— Gypsy's cousin Joy. 282 pp. 4 pl. 16°. *Boston, Graves & Young*, 1866.

[GYPSY series, No. 2].

——— Gypsy's year at the golden crescent. 261 pp. 3 pl. 16°. *Boston, Graves & Young*, 1868.

[GYPSY series, No. 4].

Phil Kennedy. [A story]. By H. N. N. [*anon.*] 128 pp. 2 pl. 16°. *New York, American tract society*, [1866].

Philadelphia (*City of*). Report of the board of health, 1867. 4 p. l. 50 pp. 8°. *Philadelphia, by order of the board*, 1868.

——— McElroy's Philadelphia directory for 1857. xvi, 936 pp. 1 map.. 8°. *Philadelphia, E. C. & J. Biddle*, 1857. s.

Philadelphia. Gopsill's Philadelphia city and business directory for 1868–9. Compiled by Isaac Costa. 1952 pp. 1 map. 8°. *Philadelphia, J. Gopsill*, 1868.

——— The Philadelphia merchants' and manufacturers' business directory for 1856–57. xvi, 402, 100 pp. 1 map. 4°. *Philadelphia, Griswold & co.* 1856. s.

——— McElroy and co.'s city business directory, [with] a co-partnership directory, 1867–68. 350 pp. 16°. *Philadelphia, McElroy & co.* 1868.

Philadelphia society for the promotion of national industry. Addresses. [Written by Mathew Carey]. 5th ed. 299 pp. 12°. *Philadelphia, J. Maxwell*, 1820.

——— The same. 6th ed. 8°. *Philadelphia, Carey & Lea*, 1822.

[*In* CAREY (M.) Essays on political economy. ed. 1822. pp. 7–251].

Philbeck (John D.) The primary union speaker: pieces for declamation and recitation in primary schools. 158 pp. 16°. *Boston, Taggart & Thompson*, 1866.

Philelphus (Marius). *See* **Filelfo** (G. M. J.)

Philippine islands. Calendario manual, y guia de forasteros de las islas Filipinas, 1839. 215 pp. 8°. *Manila, C. Lopez*, [1839]. s.

Phillip (Arthur). The voyage to Botany bay, with an account of the establishment of the colonies of Port Jackson and Norfolk island. [With appendix]. 2d ed. xxiii, 258, clxxv pp. 6 maps. 42 pl. 4°. *London, J. Stockdale*, 1790.

[Imperfect: 5 pl. wanting].

Phillips (Henry, *jr.*) Historical sketches of the paper currency of the American colonies, prior to the adoption of the federal constitution. 2 v. 233 pp; 264 pp. sm. 4°. *Roxbury, Mass. W. E. Woodward*, 1865–66.

CONTENTS.

v. 1. Pennsylvania.
New Jersey.
Rhode Island.
Virginia.
Vermont.
v. 2. Continental paper money.

Phillips (*Sir* Richard). Addisoniana. 2 v. xxiv, 242 pp. 7 fac similes; 260 pp. 7 l. 18°. *London, R. Phillips*, [1804].

Phillips (Rose). Minnie Gray; or, merit rewarded. 173 pp. 3 pl. 18°. *Philadelphia, J. S. Claxton*, 1857.

Philp (Robert Kemp). The history of progress in Great Britain. With numerous illustrations. xiv, 386 pp. 13 pl. 8°. *London, Houlston & Wright*, 1859. s.

Phipps (Constantine John, *baron Mulgrave*). Voyage towards the north pole, 1773. viii, 253 pp. 4°. *London, J. Nourse,* 1774.

[*With* COOK (James). Second voyage around the world. 4°. *London,* 1776].

Phipps (Joseph). The original and present state of man briefly considered; wherein is shown the [doctrine] held forth to the world by the people called quakers. [With] remarks on the arguments of S. Newton, of Norwich. 2 p. l. 209 pp. 8°. *Philadelphia, J. Crukshank,* 1783.

Phipson (Thomas Lambe). Meteors, aerolites, and falling stars. xiv, 240 pp. 1 col. pl. 8°. *London, L. Reeve & co.* 1867.

——— Phosphorescence; or, the emission of light by minerals, plants, and animals. xv, 210 pp. 1 col. pl. 16°. *London, L. Reeve & co.* 1862. s.

Photographic mosaics, an annual record of photographic progress. Edited by M. C. Lea and E. L. Wilson. 144 pp. 16°. *Philadelphia, Benerman & Wilson,* 1868.

Physikalisch-ökonomische bibliothek, worinn von den neuesten büchern, welche die naturgeschichte, naturlehre, und die land- und stadtwirthschaft betreffen, zuverlässige und vollständige nachrichten ertheilet werden, von Johann Beckmann. 20 v. 16°. *Göttingen, Vandenhoeck,* 1770-98. s.

Pianist's (The) album or home circle. v. 3. A collection of marches, waltzes, [etc.] 224 pp. 4°. *Boston, O. Ditson & co.* [1867].

Picard (Louis Benoit). L'exalté, ou histoire de Gabriel Désodry, sous l' ancien régime, pendant la révolution, et sous l' empire. 3e éd. 4 v. 12°. *Paris, Baudouin,* 1824. s.

Pichon (Thomas). Genuine letters and memoirs, relating to the natural, civil, and commercial history of the islands of Cape Breton and Saint John, from the first settlement to 1758. By an impartial Frenchman. Translated from the original manuscript. [*anon.*] xvi, 400 pp. 8° *London, J. Nourse,* 1760.

Pickering (Charles, *M. D.*) The races of man, and their geographical distribution. 447 pp. 1 map. 12 col. pl. 4°. *Boston, Little & Brown,* 1848. [WILKES (C.) U. S. exploring expedition. v. 9.]

Pico (Giovanni Francisco, *signore* della Mirandola). De morte Christi et propria cogitanda libri tres. Eiusdem de studio diuinæ humanæ philosophiæ libri duo. 72 l. sm. 4°. *Bononiæ, per Bn̄dictū Hectoreū,* 1497.

Pictet (A. Édouard). Synopsis des névroptères d'Espagne. 2 p. l. 123 pp. 14 col. pl. 8°. *Genève, H. Georg, etc.* 1865. s.

Pictorial (The) museum of animated nature. 2 v. 2 p. l. 400 pp. 1 col. pl; 2 p. l. 432 pp. 1 col. pl. fol. *London, C. Knight & co.* [1844]. s.

CONTENTS.

v. 1. Mammalia. Birds.
v. 2. Birds. Reptiles. Mollusca. Insects, [etc.]

Picture of Philadelphia; or, a brief account of the various institutions and public objects in this metropolis. [*anon.*] 288 pp. 19 l. 1 map. 1 pl. 18°. *Philadelphia, Carey & Hart,* 1835.

Piedrahita (Lucas Fernandez de). *See* **Fernandez de Piedrahita.**

Pierce (Thomas, *D. D.*) A correct copy of some notes concerning God's decrees, especially of reprobation. [*anon.*] 3 p. l. 74 pp. 1 l. sm. 4°. *London, R. Royston,* 1655.

Pierce the ploughmans crede; [with] God spede the plough. Edited from ms. by W. W. Skeat. [*anon.*] xix, 75 pp. 8°. *London, Trübner & co.* 1867.

[EARLY English text society, no. 30].

See, also, **Peirce.**

Pierer (Heinrich August, *editor*). Supplemente zu Pierer's universal lexikon. 3 v. 8°. *Altenburg, H. A. Pierer,* 1851-53. s.

Pierpont (John). The American first-class book; or, exercises in reading and recitation. 480 pp. 12°. *Boston, Hilliard, Gray, Little and Wilkins,* 1828. s.

Pierson (Emily Catharine). Jamie Parker, the fugitive. 192 pp. 16°. *Hartford, Brockett, Fuller & co.* 1851. s.

Pierson (Helen Wall). Gracie's mission. A tale of Norway. 255 pp. 2 pl. 16°. *Philadelphia, J. S. Claxton,* 1867. s.

Pietrasanta (D. L. F. *duca di Serradifalco*). *See* **Serradifalco.**

Pike (James S.) The restoration of the currency. From the N. Y. Tribune. 52 pp. 8°. *New York, Sun printing house,* 1868.

Pilade (Giovanni Francesco Boccardo). Vocabvlarivm. 33 l. sm. 4°. *Mediolani, per Petrum Martirem de Montegatiis,* 1505.

Pilpay. *See* **Bidpai.**

Pindar (Christopher Laomedon, *pseudon?*) *See* **Alleghania.**

Pingel (Christian). Om de vigtigste reiser, som i nyere tider ere foretagne fra Danemark og Norge, for igjen at opsöge det tabte Grönland og at undersöge det gjenfunde. 8°. *Kjöbenhavn, S. L. Möller,* 1845.

[*In* GRONLANDS historiske mindesmaerker. v. 3. pp. 625-794].

Piper (Ferdinand). Mythologie und symbolik der christlichen kunst, von der ältesten zeit bis in's sechzehnte jahrhundert. 1r band. Mythologie. 1 v. in 2. xliii, 510 pp; xxviii, 732 pp. 8°. *Weimar, Landes-industrie-comptoirs,* 1847–51.

[No more published].

Pirckheimer (Bilibaldus). Epistola apologetica. [Contra theologos colonienses pro Joanne Reuchlino defensio]. sm. 4°. *Nurenbergæ,* 1517.

[*In* LUCIANUS. Piscator. ed. 1517].

Pitrat (John Claudius). Paul and Julia; or, the political mysteries, hypocrisy, and cruelty of the leaders of the church of Rome. 319 pp. 1 pl. 12°. *Boston, E. W. Hinks & co.* 1855. s.

Pitt (William, *of Birmingham*). A general view of the agriculture of the county of Leicester. viii, 411 pp. 1 col. map. 35 pl. 8°. *London,* 1809. s.

[GREAT BRITAIN. Board of agriculture].

——— General view of the agriculture of the county of Northampton. xii, 320 pp. 1 col. map. 8°. *London,* 1809. s.

[GREAT BRITAIN. Board of agriculture].

——— General view of the agriculture of the county of Stafford. 2d ed. xii, 327 pp. 1 col. map. 15 pl. 8°. *London,* 1808. s.

[GREAT BRITAIN. Board of agriculture].

——— A general view of the agriculture of the county of Worcester. xx, 428 pp. 1 map. 6 pl. 8°. *London,* 1810. s.

[GREAT BRITAIN. Board of agriculture].

Pittenger (*Rev.* William). Oratory, sacred and secular; or, the extemporaneous speaker, with sketches of the most eminent speakers of all ages, and a "chairman's guide" for conducting public meetings. With introduction, by John A. Bingham. 220 pp. 12°. *New York, S. R. Wells,* 1868.

Pitton de Tournefort. *See* **Tournefort.**

Pittsburg landing, (Shiloh), and the investment of Corinth. [*anon.* By A. J. V.] 96 pp. 16°. *New York, Beadle & co.* [1862].

Placido (Gabriel de la Concepcion Valdés, *known as*). Poesias. xxvii, 479 pp. 16°. *Nueva York, Lockwood & son,* 1855. s.

Plake (*Mrs.* Kate). The southern husband outwitted by his union wife. 161 pp. 1 portrait. 12°. *Philadelphia, Moore & bro. for the authoress,* 1868.

Planché (*Miss* Matilda). *See* **Mackarness** (*Mrs.* M. P.)

Planck (Gottlieb Jacob). Geschichte der christlich-kirchlichen gesellschafts-verfassung 5 v. in 6. 12°. *Hannover, Hahn,* 1803-09. s.

Planck—continued.

CONTENTS.

v. 1. Geschichte der entstehung und ausbildung der christlich-kirchlichen gesellschafts-verfassung in römischen staat, [etc.] xxviii, 706 pp. 1803.
v. 2. Geschichte der christlich-kirchlichen gesellschafts-verfassung in den neuen staaten des occidents, [etc.] xx, 828 pp. 1804.
v. 3-5. Geschichte des pabstthums in den abendländischen kirchen von der mitte des neunten jahrhunderts an. v. 1-3. 1805–09.

Plat. *See* **Platt.**

Plato. Phedon; or, a dialogue of the immortality of the soul. 178 pp. 1 portrait. 12°. *London, J. Davidson,* 1777.

Platt (*Sir* Hugh). The garden of Eden; or, an accurate description of all flowers and fruits now growing in England, with particular rules how to advance their nature and growth. 2 v. in 1. 14 p.l. 148 pp; 8 p.l. 159 pp. 18°. *London, W. & J. Leake,* 1675.

Playfair (R. Lambert) *and* **Günther** (Albert C. L. G.) The fishes of Zanzibar. Acanthopterygii, by R. L. Playfair. Pharyngognathi, etc. by A. C. L. Günther. xiv, 153 pp. 21 pl. [6 col.] 4°. *London, J. Van Voorst,* 1866.

Playse *or* **Pleyce** (John). [Henry Hudson] his discouerie toward the north pole, in May, 1867. 8°. *New York, J. Riley,* 1811.

[*In* NEW YORK historical society. Collections. v. 1. 1st series].

Pleasants (Julia, *pseudon?*) Callamura. [A novel]. 454 pp. 12°. *Philadelphia, Claxton, Remsen & Haffelfinger,* 1868.

Plessing (Friedrich Victor Leberecht). Memnonium, oder versuche zur enthüllung der geheimnisse des alterthums. 2 v. x, 564 pp; xxxvi pp. 4 l. 694 pp. 8°. *Leipzig, Weygand,* 1787.

Plinius Secundus (Caius). Natvralis historiæ. 1a pars—3a pars. 3 v. 16°. *Venetiis, Aldus,* 1535-36. s.

Plunket (William Conyngham, *baron Plunket*). Life, letters, and speeches. [Edited] by D. Plunket. With preface, by lord Brougham. 2 v. xi, 410 pp. 1 portrait; vii, 380 pp. 8°. *London, Smith, Elder & co.* 1867.

Plutarchus. Qvæ exstant omnia, cvm latina interpretatione Hermanni Cruserii; Gulielmi Xylandri. Accedit nvnc primvm libellvs eivsdem de fluuiorum montiumque nominibus, cum versione Maussaci. [Gr. et Lat.] 2 v. 22 p. l. 1076, 114 pp. 16 l; 4 p. l. 164, 72, 80 pp. 17 l. fol. *Francofvrti, off. D. & D. Aubriorum & C. Schleichij,* 1620. s.

——— De his qui tarde a numine corripiuntur libellus. 26 l. sm. 4°. *Argentorati, ex aedibus Schurerianis,* 1514.

Plutarchus. Opuscula nuper traducta. Erasmo Roterodamo interprete. 27 l. 25 l. sm. 4°. *Basilæ, J. Frobenius,* 1514.

——— Paralelia in latinū cōuersa [a Guarino Veronense]. 6 l. 4°. *Brixiæ, per J. Brittanicum,* 1498.

[*With* POLYBIUS. De primo bello pvnico. *Brixiæ,* 1498].

Plymley (Joseph). General view of the agriculture of Shropshire. xxv, 366 pp. 2 maps. 5 pl. 8°. *London,* 1803. s.

[GREAT BRITAIN: Board of agriculture].

Plymouth collection. The baptist hymn and tune book: being "the Plymouth collection" enlarged, and adapted to the use of baptist churches. lii, 521 pp. 8°. *New York, Sheldon, Blakeman & co.* 1858. s.

Plymouth colony. The first Plymouth patent: granted June 1, 1621. From the original ms. Edited by Charles Deane. 16 pp. 4°. *Cambridge, privately printed,* 1854.

Pocket (The) letter writer. [With a dictionary of poetical quotations]. 256 pp. 32°. *Cincinnati, J. A. & U. P. James,* 1853. s.

Poe (Edgar Allan). The conchologist's first book: a system of testaceous malacology, etc. 2[d] ed. 166 pp. 12 pl. 12°. *Philadelphia, author,* 1840. s.

Poets (The) offering, for 1850. [Edited by Sarah Josepha Hale]. 576 pp. 14 pl. 8°. *Philadelphia, Grigg, Elliot & co.* 1850. s.

Poiret (Jean Louis Marie). Botanique. *See* **Lamarck** (J. B. P. A. de Monnet, *chevalier* de) *and* **Poiret.**

——— Voyage en Barbarie, ou lettres écrites de l'ancienne Numidie pendant les années 1785 et 1786. Avec un essai sur l'histoire naturelle de ce pays, [etc.] 2 v. xxiv, 363 pp; 315 pp. 2 l. 8°. *Paris, J. B. F. Née de la Rochelle,* 1789.

"**Poke**" and her sisters; or, a peep at the Clyse family. [*anon.*] 299 pp. 2 pl. 16°. *Philadelphia, American s. s. union,* 1868.

Pollard (Edward A.) The lost cause regained. 214 pp. 12°. *New York, Carleton & co.* 1868.

Pollington (John Horace Savile, *viscount*). *See* **Savile** (J. H.)

Pollock (Thomas C.) Ivanhoe masonic quartettes. 75 pp. 8°. *New York, Pond & co.* 1867.

Pollux (Julius). 'Ονομαστικον εν βιβλιοις δεκα. Onomastikon, hoc est, instrvctissimvm rervm ac synonymorvm dictionarivm, decem libris constans, [etc.] Cvm prefatione Simonis Grynæi ad ludimagistros. 9 p. l. 562 columns on 141 l. 39 l. 8°. *Basiliæ, per B. Lasium & T. Platterum,* 1536. s.

Polo (Marco). I viaggi di Marco Polo veneziano, tradotti per la prima volta dall' originale francese di Rusticiano di Pisa, e corredati d'illustrazioni e di documenti da Vincenzio Lazari, pubblicati per cura di Lodovico Posini. lxiv, 484 pp. 1 map. 8°. *Venezia, P. Naratovich,* 1847. s.

Polybius. De primo bello pvnico, ex græco in latinū traductus per Leonardum Aretinum. 26 l. fol. *Brixiæ, per J. Britanicum,* 1498.

Pomeroy (Martin M.) Sense; or, Saturday-night musings and thoughtful papers. By "Brick" Pomeroy. 273 pp. 6 pl. 12°. *New York, Carleton & co.* 1868.

——— Nonsense; or, hits and criticisms on the follies of the day. By "Brick" Pomeroy. 274 pp. 6 pl. 12°. *New York, Carleton & co.* 1868.

Pomponius Mela. *See* **Mela** (Pomponius).

Poncet de la Grave (Guillaume). Précis historique de la marine royale de France, depuis l'origine de la monarchie jusqu'au roi régnant. 2 v. xlviii, 330 pp; 2 p. l. 336 pp. 2 l. 16°. *Paris, E. Onfroy,* 1780.

Pontoppidan (Erik, *bishop of Bergen, Norway*). Versuch einer natürlichen historie von Norwegen. Aus dem Dänischen, von Johann Adolph Scheiben. 2 v. in 1. 367 pp. 16 pl; 536 pp. 13 pl. 12°. *Kopenhagen, F. C. Mumme,* 1753.

Poor (Henry V.) Manual of the railroads of the United States, for 1868–69. [With] appendix, containing a full analysis of the debts of the United States, and of the several states. 442 pp. 8°. *New York, H. V. & H. W. Poor,* 1868.

Porcacchi (Tommaso). L'isole piv famose del mondo. Intagliate da G. Porro. 12 p. l. 211 pp. fol. *Padova, P. & F. Galignani,* 1620.

Porcupine (Peter, *pseudon.*) *See* **Cobbett** (William).

Porphyrius. Epistola ad Anebonem ægyptium. fol. *Oxonii,* 1678.

[*In* JAMBLICHUS. Περι μυςτηριων λογος. T. Gale edidit. 1678].

Porta (Giovanni Battista). La fantesca. Comedia. 96 l. 18°. *Venetia, G. B. Bonfadino,* 1610.

——— An inquiry into the analogy existing between the brute and human physiognomy. From the Italian of Porta. 48°. *New Haven,* 1829.

[*In* LAVATER (J. C.) The pocket Lavater. 1829].

——— The same. 24°. *New Haven,* [1840]?

[*In* LAVATER (J. C.) The pocket Lavater. [1840]?

Porta (G. B.) Natural magick: in twenty books: wherein are set forth all the riches and delights of the natural sciences. 3 p. l. 409 pp. 3 l. fol. *London, T. Young & S. Speed,* 1658.

Porta (Luigi, *prof. at Pavia*). Delle alterazioni patologiche delle arterie per la legatura e la torsione esperienze ed osservazioni. x, 440 pp. 13 pl. 4°. *Milano, G. Bernardoni di Gio,* 1845. s.

——— Della litotrizia. xii, 400 pp. 9 pl. 8°. *Milano, D. Bernardoni,* 1859. s.

——— Della malattie generali interne riverberate da operazioni e malattie chirurgiche locali esterne. 86 pp. 4°. *Milano, G. Bernardoni,* 1854. s.

Porter (John A. *M. D.*) Principles of chemistry: embracing the most recent discoveries in the science, and its application to agriculture and the arts. 20th ed. 699 pp. 12°. *New York, A. S. Barnes & co.* 1868.

Porter (Noah, *D.D.*) The educational systems of the puritans and jesuits compared. 95 pp. 12°. *New York, M. W. Dodd,* 1851. s.

——— The human intellect: with an introduction upon physiology and the soul. xxvii, 673 pp. 8°. *New York, C. Scribner & co.* 1868.

Portico (The), a repository of science and literature. [Monthly]. Jan. 1816, to Dec. 1817. v. 1–4. 8°. *Baltimore, Neale, Wills & Cole,* 1816–17.

Portland, (*Maine*). The Portland business directory, and business man's guide for 1868. By Atwell & co. 275 pp. 12°. *Portland, B. Thurston & co.* 1868.

Porto-Alegre (Manoel de Araujo). Brasilianas. 359 pp. 8°. *Vienna, typographia imperial.* 1863.

——— Colombo. Poema. 2 v. 4 p. l. 428 pp; 2 p. l. 522 pp. 8°. *Rio de Janeiro, B. L. Garnier,* 1866.

Portrait (Le) et les avantures divertissantes du duc de Roquelaure. Par le sr. J. R. [*anon.*] 95 pp. 18°. *Cologne, P. Marteau,* 1781.

Ports (Les) de France. *See* **Vernet** (C. J.) *and* **Huë** (J. F.)

Portsmouth (*N. H.*) The Portsmouth directory. By D. Dudley. 132, 48 pp. 8°. *Portsmouth, J. F. Shores,* 1867.

Possenti (Carlo, *engineer*). Sulla sistemazione idraulica della Valdichiana osservazioni storicicritiche. 89 pp. 2 maps, etc. 8°. *Firenze, tipografia degl' ingegneri,* 1866. s.

Postlethwayt (James). The history of the public revenue, from the revolution in 1688 to christmas, 1753. 2 p. l. 352 pp. obl. fol. *London, J. Knapton,* 1759.

Post office department, U. S. *See* **United States.**

Potiez (Valéry Louis Victor). Musée de Douai. Catalogue des collections d'histoire naturelle. Galerie des vertébrés. 2e partie. Oiseaux. 1er fasc. pp. xi, 1–192. 8°. *Paris, J. B. Baillière et fils,* 1863. s.

——— *and* **Michaud** (André Louis Gaspard). Galerie des mollusques, ou catalogue méthodique, descriptif et raisonné, des mollusques et coquilles du muséum de Douai. 2 v. xxxvi, 560 pp. 2 l; 2 p. l. xxxvii–xliv, 307 pp. 2 l. Atlas, 56 pp. 37 pl. 8°. *Paris, J. B. Baillière,* 1838–44. s.

Potschka (Juvenalis). Thesaurus linguae sanctae, sive phraseologia hebraica. Accedit syntaxis hebraica ex cl. P. Petro Guarin. 511 pp. 12°. *Bambergae, Tobias Goebhardt,* 1780.

Pott (August Friedrich). Die ungleichheit menschlicher rassen hauptsächlich von sprachwissenschaftlichen standpunkte, unter besonderer berücksichtigung von des grafen von Gobineau gleichnamigem werke. Mit einem ueberblicke über die sprachverhältnisse der völker. Ein ethnologischer versuch. xl, 275 pp. 8°. *Lemgo & Detmold, Meyer,* 1856.

Potter (Alonzo, *bishop of Penn. editor*). Lectures on the evidences of christianity. Delivered in Philadelphia, by clergymen of the protestant episcopal church, 1853–4. With an introductory essay by A. Potter. 408 pp. 8°. *Philadelphia, E.H.Butler & co.* 1855. s.

Potter (George A.) The instrument of association; a manual of currency. xiv, 131 pp. 12°. *New York, Hurd & Houghton,* 1868.

Pouchot (*M. commandant of fort Niagara, Canada*). Mémoires sur la dernière guerre de l'Amérique septentrionale, entre la France et l'Angleterre. 3 v. 16°. *Yverdon,* 1781.

Pouget (François Aimé). Instructions générales en forme de catéchisme, ou l'on explique en abrégé l'histoire et les dogmes de la religion, de la morale, etc. [*anon.*] 2 v. in 1. xviii, 384 pp; 3 p. l. 242, xviii pp. 12°. *Paris, C. Herissant,* 1772. s.

Poujade (Eugène). Le Liban et la Syrie, 1845–60. iii, 315 pp. 16°. *Paris, A. Bourdilliat & cie.* 1860.

Poujard'hieu (G.) Les chemins de fer et le crédit en France. 2 p. l. 410 pp. 12°. *Paris, J. Hetzel,* 1862. s.

Poyntz (John). The present prospect of the famous and fertile island of Tobago: with a description of the situation, growth, fertility, etc. 2 p. l. 47 pp. sm. 4°. *London, G. Larkin,* 1683.

Pradt (Dominique Dufour de). The congress of Vienna. xv, 224 pp. 8°. *London, S. Leigh,* 1816. s.

Prater (Horatio). Letters to the American people, on christianity and the sabbath. xi, 144 pp. 12°. *London, J. Clayton & son,* 1856.

Pratt (Parley P.) A voice of warning, and instruction to all people, or an introduction to the faith and doctrine of the latter day saints. 3d Amer. ed. 284 pp. 24°. *Nauvoo, J. Taylor,* 1844.

Pratt (Samuel Jackson). Gleanings through Wales, Holland, and Westphalia, with views of peace and war, at home and abroad. [With] humanity; or the rights of nature. A poem. 2 v. xlix, 426 pp; xii, 450 pp. 8°. *Dublin, P. Wogan,* 1797.

Pratz (Lepage du). *See* **Lepage du Pratz.**

Pray (Lewis G.) Historical sketch of the twelfth congregational society in Boston. xii, 123 pp. 1 pl. 12°. *Boston, society,* 1863. s.

Preble (*Commander* George Henry, *U. S. N.*) The chase of the rebel steamer of war Oreto, into the bay of Mobile, by the U. S. steam sloop Oneida, Sept. 4, 1862. 60 pp. 8°. *Cambridge, (Mass.) printed for private circulation,* 1862.

Preisgekrönten (Die) entwürfe zur erweiterung der inneren stadt Wien. Mit sieben in der kaiserlich- königlichen hof- und staatsdruckerei in farbendruck ausgeführten plänen und einem erläuternden texte von prof. R. v. E. 37 pp. 7 col. pl. oblong fol. *Wien, k. k. hof- und staatsdruckerei,* 1859. s.

Preller (L.) Griechische mythologie. 2 v. viii, 528 pp; vi, 366 pp. 8°. *Leipzig, Weidmann,* 1854.

CONTENTS.

v. 1. Theogonie und goetter.
v. 2. Die heroen.

——— Römische mythologie. viii, 820 pp. 1 l. 8°. *Berlin, Weidmann,* 1858.

Prendergast (Thomas). The mastery series. French. 2d ed. xi, 107 pp. 12°. *London, Longmans,* 1868.

——— The same. German. 2d ed. xi, 86 pp. 3 l. 12°. *London, Longmans,* 1868.

Presbyterian church of the United States. Minutes of the general assembly, from the first, 1787 to 1862. 72 v. in 16 v. 8°. *Philadelphia,* 1788–1862.

——— Characters formed by the divisible type belonging to the Chinese missions of the presbyterian church in the U. S. A. 110 pp. Appendix. 12 pp. 4°. *Macao, presbyterian mission press,* 1844. s.

Presbyterian (The) historical almanac, and annual remembrancer of the church. For 1865. By J. M. Wilson. v. 7. 407 pp. 8 pl. 8°. *Philadelphia, J. M. Wilson,* 1865.

Presbyterian (The) magazine. Edited by C. Van Rensselaer. Jan. 1851, to Dec. 1857. v. 1–7. 8°. *Philadelphia,* 1852–57.

Prescott (T. C.) Some account of Emanuel Swedenborg and his writings. 32 pp. 12°. *Boston, O. Clapp,* 1854. s.

Preservation (The) of the Union, a national economic necessity. [*anon.*] From the German commercial gazette. 7 pp. 8°. *New York, W. C. Bryant & co.* 1863.

[LOYAL publication society, no. 14].

Pressensé (*Madame* E. de). Rosa. From the French. 366 pp. 4 pl. 18°. *Philadelphia, presbyterian board of publication,* 1868.

——— Theresa's journal. From the French. 297 pp. 3 pl. 16°. *Philadelphia, s. s. union,* 1868.

Prestel (Michael August Friedrich). Vorschule der geometrie. 3e aufl. viii, 288 pp. 8°. *Leipzig, E. Fleischer,* 1867. s.

Preston (Laura). Aldeane. A novel. 403 pp. 12°. *New York, A. Roman & co.* 1868.

——— A boy's trip across the plains. 233 pp. 1 pl. 16°. *New York, A. Roman & co.* 1868.

Preston (*Rev.* Thomas S.) Lectures on reason and revelation, delivered in St. Ann's church, New York, 1867. 266 pp. 12°. *New York, catholic pub. house,* 1868.

Prévost d'Exiles (Antoine François). Abrégé de l'histoire générale des voyages. *See* **La Harpe (J. F. de).**

——— Le philosophe anglois, ou histoire de monsieur Cleveland, fils naturel de Cromwell, écrite par lui même. Traduite de l'Anglois. [*pseudon.*] Nouv. éd. 7 v. in 4. 24°. *Amsterdam, Arkstee & Merkus,* 1744.

Price (*Rev.* T.) An essay on the physiognomy and physiology of the present inhabitants of Britain; with reference to their origin, as Goths and Celts. [With] remarks upon the physiognomical characteristics of Ireland, and of some of the neighbouring continental nations. xii, 123 pp. 8°. *London, J. Rodwell,* 1829.

Prickett (Abacuk). A larger discourse [of the voyage] of Henry Hudson, for the discouerie of the north-west passage, 1610. 8°. *New York, J. Riley,* 1811.
[*In* NEW YORK historical society. Collections. v. 1. 1st series].

Priest (Josiah). Slavery, as it relates to the negro, or African race, examined in the light of circumstances, history and the holy scriptures; with an account of the origin of the black man's color, and strictures on abolitionism. xii, 340 pp. 12°. *Albany, C. Van Benthuysen & co.* 1843.

Priest (*Rev.* St. John). General view of the agriculture of Buckinghamshire, etc. With an appendix containing extracts from a survey of the same county by mr. Richard Parkinson. viii, 412 pp. 3 tab. 1 map. 13 pl. 8°. *London,* 1810. s.
[GREAT BRITAIN: Board of agriculture].

Priesthood and clergy unknown to christianity; or, the church a community of co-equal brethren. By Campaginator. [*pseudon.*] 168 pp. 12°. *Philadelphia, J. B. Lippincott & co.* 1857. s.

Priestley (Joseph, *LL. D.*) An appeal to the public, on the subject of the riots in Birmingham. Part ii. To which is added a letter from W. Russell to the author. xxviii, 210 pp. 8°. *London, J. Johnson,* 1792. s.

——— Memoirs to 1795, written by himself: with a continuation, to the time of his decease, by his son, J. Priestley: and observations on his writings by T. Cooper, and W. Christie. 2 v. 3 p. l. v, 824 pp. 8°. *Northumberland, (Pa.) J. Binns,* 1806.

——— Observations on the increase of infidelity. [With] animadversions on the writings of several modern unbelievers, and especially the Ruins of Volney. 3d ed. xxvi, 179 pp. 8°. *Philadelphia, T. Dobson,* 1797.

Prima morum et pietatis præcepta. Quibus accessit summula catechismi ad piam juniòrem educationem apprime utilis. 32 pp. 16°. *Glasguæ, J Duncan,* 1782.
[*With* RUDDIMAN (T.) Rudiments of Latin. *Glasgow,* ed. 1781].

Prime (William Cowper). The Owl creek letters, and other correspondence. [*anon.*] 203 pp. 12°. *New York, Baker & Scribner,* 1848.

Prince (*Rev.* Thomas). Civil rulers raised up by God to feed his people. A sermon at the publick lecture in Boston, July 25, 1728. 24 pp. 12°. *Boston, Samuel Gerrish,* 1728.

——— The departure of Elijah lamented. A sermon occasioned by the decease of the rev. Cotton Mather. 26 pp. 8°. *Boston, D. Henchman,* 1728.

——— A sermon on the death of king George [i.] and the accession of George ii. Deliver'd in Boston, Aug. 24, 1727. 27 pp. 16°. *Boston, Daniel Henchman,* 1727.

Prince Edward Island. Abstract of the census of the population, and other statistical returns, etc. 1855. 56 l. 4°. [*Charlottetown*], *E. Whelan, queen's printer,* [1855]? s.

——— Journal of the house of assembly of Prince Edward island, [for 1854, 1856, 1859, and 1863]. 4 v. 4°. *Charlottetown, J. W. Hughes etc.* 1853–61. s.

——— Journal of the legislative council of Prince Edward island. 3d sess. 20th gen. assembly. [1857]. 3 p. l. 78 pp. 6 l. 4°. *Charlottetown, J. S. Bremner,* 1857. s.

——— The parliamentary reporter; containing an abstract of the debates and proceedings of the legislative council and house of assembly, for the session ending 14th April, 1856. As reported for "The examiner." 100 pp. 4°. *Charlottetown, Examiner office,* 1856. s.

Prince Edward Island (The) calendar, for the years 1853, 1855, 1857, 1858, 1861. 5 v. 8°. *Charlottetown, G. T. Haszard,* 1853–61. s.

Prior (William M.) The king's vesture: evidence from scripture and history. Comparatively applied to William Miller, the chronologist of 1843. 184 pp. 12°. *Boston, W. F. Brown & co.* 1862. s.

——— The empyrean canopy. By the author of the "King's vesture." [*anon.*] 4 p. l. 112 pp. 12°. *Boston, W. M. Prior,* 1868. s.

Pripovijetke iz staroga i novog zakona. [*anon.*] 2 p. l. 250 pp. 3 l. 16°. *u Becu, u stampariji Jermenskoga monastira,* 1850. s.

Pritchard (Andrew). Galerie microscopique, (traduction du Microscopic cabinet de m. Pritchard), augmentée de notes par N. P. Lerebours. 224 pp. 12 col. pl. 8°. *Paris, N. P. Lerebours,* 1843. s.

Pritchard (Sarah J.) Faye Mar of Storm cliff. 351 pp. 12°. *New York, Wynkoop & Sherwood,* 1868.

Pritchard (William T.) Polynesian reminiscences; or, life in the south Pacific islands. With preface by B. Seemann. xii, 428 pp. 4 pl. 8°. *London, Chapman & Hall,* 1866.

Probus (Valerius *or* Marcus Valerius). De notis Romanorum interpretandis libellus. Magnonis, Diaconi, aliorumque notarum veterum explicationes, etc. 208 pp. 16°. *Lvgdvni Batavorvm, apud A. Clouquium,* 1599. s.
[*With* FIOCCO (A. D.) De potestatibvs Romanorvm. 1561].

Proceedings of a convention of delegates from several of the New England states, held at Boston, Aug. 3-9, 1780, to advise on affairs necessary to promote the most vigorous prosecution of the war, and to provide for a generous reception of our French allies. Edited from an original ms. record in the N. Y. state library, with an introduction and notes. By F. B. Hough. 80 pp. 1 tab. 4°. *Albany, J. Munsell,* 1867.

Proceedings of the national convention of manufacturers, Cleveland, O. Dec. 1867. 32 pp. 8°. *Cleveland, Sanford & Hayward,* 1867.

Processionale pro ecclesiis ruralibus, ritibus romanæ ecclesiæ accommodatum, responsoria, hymnos, antiphonas, psalmos, complectens, etc. 4 p. l. 124, lxxxiii pp. 4°. *Antverpiæ, ex architypographia plantiniana,* 1819. s.

Procházka (Ignaz Joseph). Neue darstellung der empirischen psychologie. xviii, 242 pp. 5 l. 1 tab. 8°. *Wien, C. Ueberreuter,* 1841. s.

Procope-Couteaux (Michel Coltelli, *known as*). L'art de faire des garçons. [*anon.*] 312 pp. 18°. *Montpellier,* 1782.

Progrès et position actuelle de la Russie en Orient; ouvrage traduit de l'Anglais, [etc. *anon.*] 2 p. l. 226 pp. 1 col. pl. 8°. *Paris, Truchy, etc.* 1836. s.

Prosch (*Prof.* V.) Frederiksborg-stutteri. En historisk undersogelse. 148 pp. 8°. *Kjöbenhavn, C. A. Reitzel,* 1866. s.

Protestant episcopal church, *U. S. A.* *See* **General** theological seminary.

Providence *(R. I.)* Alphabetical lists of the names of persons deceased, born, and married, in the city of Providence, 1867. Prepared by E. M. Snow. iv, 75 pp. 8°. *Providence, Hammond, Angell & co.* 1868.

Providence (The) association of mechanics and manufacturers. Mechanics' festival. An account of the 71st anniversary, [etc.] held in Howard hall, [etc.] together with a sketch of the early history of the association. Prepared by Edwin M. Stone. 119 pp. 1 pl. 8°. *Providence, Knowles, Anthony & co.* 1860. s.

——— Lectures read at quarterly meetings, [etc.] 1798-99. 18 pp. 8°. *Providence,* 1860.

[*With* the preceding].

Prus (*Madame* ———, *widow of René*). A residence in Algeria, [1849-50. Translated from the French]. vii, 332 pp. 8°. *London, W. Pickering,* 1852.

Prussia. Der feldzug von 1866 in Deutschland. Redigirt von der kriegsgeschichtlichen abtheilung des grossen generalstabes. 2 v. vi, 729 pp. 41 l; atlas, 46 l. folded 8°. *Berlin, königliche hofbuchhandlung,* 1867. s.

——— Gradmessung in Ostpreussen und ihre verbindung mit preussischen und russischen dreiecksketten. Ausgeführt von F. W. Bessel, [und J. J.] Baeyer. xv, 452 pp. 7 pl. 8°. *Berlin, F. Dümmler,* 1838. s.

——— Die königlich preussische landes triangulation. Triangulation der umgegend von Berlin zwischen 52° 12′ und 52° 48′ breite und 30° 30′ und 31° 30′ länge. Herausgegeben von bureau der landes-triangulation. viii, 516, 36 pp. 2 l. 4 maps. 2 pl. 4°. *Berlin, im selbstverlage,* 1867. s.

——— Die verbindungen der preussischen und russischen dreiecksketten bei Thorn und Tarnowitz. Ausgeführt von der trigonometrischen abtheilung des generalstabes. Herausgegeben von J. J. Baeyer, etc. xvii, 442 pp. 4 pl. 4°. *Berlin, F. Duemmler,* 1857. s.

——— *K. statistische bureau.* Preussische statistik. Herausgegeben in zwanglosen heften, [etc.] v. 1-11. 4°. *Berlin, R. Decker, etc.* 1861-67. s.

——— ——— Tabellen und amtliche nachrichten über den preussischen staat, für das jahr 1849. 6 v. in 7. fol. *Berlin, A. W. Hayn,* 1851-55. s.

——— ——— The same, 1852, 1855, 1858. 3 v. fol. *Berlin, A. W. Hayn, etc.* 1855-60. s.

——— ——— The same. Ergebnisse der in den jahren 1848-57, angestellten beobachtungen des meteorologischen instituts. 2 p. l. xxiv, 179 pp. fol. *Berlin, buchdrucherei der k. akademie der wissenschaften,* 1858. s.

——— *Ministerium für handel, gewerbe und öffentliche arbeiten.* Preussisches handelsarchiv. Wochenschrift für handel, gewerbe und verkehrs anstalten. Herausgegeben von Moser und Jordan. Jahrgange 1861-66. 10 v. 4°. *Berlin, k. g. ober-hofbuchdruckerei,* 1861-66. s.

[J. 1865 wanting].

——— ——— The same. Beilage jahresberichte der handelskammern und haufmännischen korporationen des preussischen staats für 1860-64. 5 v. 4°. *Berlin, k. g. ober-hofbuchdruckerei,* 1861-64. s.

——— ——— Statistische nachrichten von den preussischen eisenbahnen. Bearbeitet auf anordnung, [etc.] von dem technischen eisenbahn-büreau des ministeriums. v. 1-13. 4°. *Berlin, Ernst & Korn,* 1855-66. s.

Pryor (J. P.) Campaigns of lieut. gen. Forrest. *See* **Jordan** (Thomas) *and* **Pryor.**

Psalms (*Book of*). *See* **Bible.**

Public ledger (The) building, Philadelphia; with an account of the proceedings connected with its opening, June 20, 1867. ix, 186 pp. 2 pl. 8°. *Philadelphia, G. W. Childs,* 1868. s.

Public opinion: a comprehensive summary of the press throughout the world on all important topics. Oct. 1861, to Dec. 1868. v. 1–14. fol. *London,* 1861–68.

Public (The) spirit: a monthly magazine of entertaining reading. Oct. 1867, to July, 1868. v. 2–3. 8°. *New York, Le Grand Benedict,* [1868].

[No more published].

Publick good without private interest. Or, a compendious remonstrance of the present sad state and condition of the English colonie in Virginea. [*anon.*] London, H. Marsh, 1657. [*Reprint*]. 8 p. l. 26 pp. sm. 4°. *Vienne, F. Köke,* [1866].

Puente (Pedro de la). *See* **La Puente.**

Puetter. *See* **Pütter.**

Pulte (J. H. *M.D.*) Woman's medical guide; containing essays on the physical, moral, and educational development of females, and the homœopathic treatment of their diseases, etc. 336 pp. 12°. *Cincinnati, Moore, Anderson, Wilstach & Keys,* 1853. s.

Pumpelly (Raphael). Geological researches in China, Mongolia, and Japan, 1862–65. vi, 143 pp. 9 pl. 4°. *Washington, Smithsonian inst.* 1867.

[SMITHSONIAN contributions. v. 15].

Punch; or, the London charivari. July, 1867, to June, 1868. v. 53–54. 4°. *London, at the office,* 1867–68.

Purcell (John B. *r. c. archbishop of Cincinnati*). The Vickers and Purcell controversy [in regard to religious free thought]. 205 pp. 16°. *Cincinnati, Benziger bros.* 1868.

Purnell (Thomas). Literature and its professors. xi, 292 pp. 12°. *London, Bell & Daldy,* 1867.

Purpose. A story based on facts. By the author of "Paul Venner." [*anon.*] 495 pp. 5 pl. 16°. *New York, Am. tract soc.* 1867.

Putnam (*Mrs.* E.) Mrs. Putnam's receipt book and young housekeeper's assistant. New ed. xxiii, 322 pp. 12°. *New York, Sheldon & co.* 1867.

Putnam (George P.) The world's progress; a dictionary of dates. With tabular views of general history and a historical chart. 4 p. l. 716 pp. 1 col. chart. 8°. *New York, G. P. Putnam,* 1851. s.

Putnam (G. P. *editor.*) Letters from Europe touching the American contest, and acknowledging the receipt, from citizens of New York, of presentation sets of the "Rebellion record," and "Loyal publication society" publications. 27 pp. 8°. *New York,* 1864.

[LOYAL publication society. no. 70].

——— Soldiers' and sailors' patriotic songs. A collection. 24 pp. 8°. *New York,* 1864.

[LOYAL publication society. no. 49].

Putnam's magazine. Original papers on literature, science, art, and national interests. Jan. to Dec. 1868. New series. v. 1–2. 8°. *New York, G. P. Putnam & son,* 1868.

Pütter (Johann Stephan). An historical development of the present political constitution of the Germanic empire. From the German, with notes, by J. Dornford. 3 v. 8°. *London, T. Payne & son,* 1790.

Quackenbos (George P. *LL. D.*) Elementary history of the United States; with numerous illustrations and maps. 212 pp. 12°. *New York, Appletons,* 1868.

——— An English grammar. 288 pp. 12°. *New York, Appletons,* 1862. s.

Quadragesimale de filio prodigo, et de angelo ipsius. Nouum editum a quodā fratre minore de obseruantia. 231 l. 16°. *Basilee, M. Furter,* 1497. s.

Quadruple (Le) oracle des dames et des demoiselles. Par Halbert (d'Angers). [*pseudon?*] xxiv, 156 pp. 1 pl. 18°. *Paris, Bernardin-Béchet,* 1862.

Quaglino (Antonio, *M. D.*) Sulle malattie interne dell'ochio: saggio di clinica et d'iconografia ottalmoscopia. (Extract). 384 pp. 12 col. pl. 8°. *Milano, Annali universali di medicina,* 1858. s.

Quaritch (Bernard). A general catalogue of books, arranged in classes, offered for sale. viii, 1130 pp. 8°. *London, B. Quaritch,* 1868.

Quarterly journal of microscopical science. Edited by E. Lankester and G. Busk. v. 8. New series. 8°. *London, J. Churchill & sons,* 1868.

Quarterly (The) journal of science. Edited by J. Samuelson and W. Crookes. v. 5. 8°. *London, J. Churchill & sons,* 1868.

Quarterly (The) review. Jan. to Oct. 1868. v. 124–125. 8°. *London, J. Murray,* 1868.

Quayle (Thomas). General view of the agriculture of the isle of Man. xvi, 293 pp. 1 tab. 1 col. map. 8°. *London,* 1812. s.

[GREAT BRITAIN: Board of agriculture].

Quayle (Thomas). General view of the agriculture and present state of the islands on the coast of Normandy, subject to the crown of Great Britain. xvi, 352 pp. 2 l. 8°. *London,* 1815. s.

[GREAT BRITAIN: Board of agriculture].

Quebec (*Province of, dominion of Canada*). Journals of the legislative assembly. 1st session. 1867–68. v. 1. 8°. [*Quebec*], 1868.

See, also, **Canada.**

Quebec diocese. Rapport sur les missions du diocèse de Québec [etc.] Mars, 1855. No. 11. 8°. *Quebec, A. Côté & cie.* 1855. s.

Quetelet (Lambert Adolphe Jacques) *and* **Heuschling** (Philippe François Xavier Théodose). Statistique internationale (population) publiée avec la collaboration des statisticiens officiels des différents états de l'Europe et des États-Unis d'Amérique. 2 p. l. cxv, 406 pp. 4°. *Bruxelles, Hayez,* 1865. s.

[Extrait du t. x. du Bulletin de la commission centrale de statistique de Belgique].

Quick (*Rev.* Robert Hebert). Essays on educational reformers. xxii, 328 pp. 12°. *London, Longmans,* 1868.

Quimby (E. T.) Analysis of French pronunciation. 54 pp. 18°. *Boston, Wright & Hasty,* 1854. s.

Quinter (*Rev.* James) *and* **M'Connell** (*Rev.* N. A.) A debate on trine immersion, the lord's supper, and feet-washing; held at Dry creek, Linn co. Iowa, Oct. 1867. Reported by J. L. M'Creery. 326 pp. 16°. *Cincinnati, H. S. Bosworth,* 1868.

Quintinye (Jean de La). *See* **La Quintinye.**

Raccolta di poemi didascalici. ed. 2a. 3 v. in 1. 8°. *Milano, società tipogr. de' classici italiani,* 1825.

1. La nautica. Bi Bernardino Baldi. 1 p. l. 85 pp.
2. Della sifillide, ovvero del morbo gallico. Di Girolamo Fracastoro. 105 pp. 1 portrait.
3. La coltivazione del riso. Del marchese Gianbattista Spolverini. 160 pp. 1 portrait.

Racine (Jean). Théatre complet et oeuvres diverses en vers. Nouv. éd. 4 v. in 2. 8°. *St. Petersburg, Pluchart & cie.* 1811. s.

Radde (Gustav). Reisen in den süden von Ost-Siberien, im auftrage der k. russischen geographischen gesellschaft ausgeführt in den jahren 1855–1859. Botanische abtheilung. Nachträge zur flora der gebiete des russischen reichs östlich vom Altai bis Kamtschatka und Sitka, [etc.] v. 1. vii, 447 pp. 9 pl. 8°. *Moskau, buchdruckerei der k. universität,* 1861. s.

Radical (The). A monthly magazine, devoted to religion. Conducted by S. H. Morse and J. B. Marvin. Sept. 1867, to Dec. 1868. v. 3–4. 8°. *Boston, Adams & co.* 1867–68.

Radicke (Gustav). On the importance and value of arithmetic means; with especial reference to recent physiological researches on the determination of the influence of certain agencies, upon the metamorphosis of tissue, [etc.] 8°. *London,* 1861.

[NEW SYDENHAM society. v. 11].

Radink (Jacobus, *bookseller at Amsterdam*). Catalogus van het magazijn van boeken, plaatwerken, en handschriften nogelaten, [etc.] xiv, 340 pp. 8°. *Amsterdam, E. J. Brill, etc.* 1867. s.

Raffaello Santi. *See* **Santi.**

Rafn (Carl Christian). Fornaldar sögur nordrlanda eptir gömlum handritum útgefnar. 2 v. xxviii, 533 pp. 1 pl; xiv, 559 pp. 8°. *Kaupmannahöfn,* 1829. s.

——— Memoria sobre o descobrimento da America no seculo decimo. Trad. por Manoel Ferreira Lagos. 1 p. l. pp. 152–280. 2 maps. 8°. *Rio de Janeiro, J. Cabral,* 1840. s.

Rafter (Hermann). Einheit und freiheit. 16 pp. 8°. *New York, Abend-zeitung print,* 1863.

[LOYAL publication society no. 19].

Rainey (Thomas). The improved abacus: an explanatory treatise on the theory of arithmetic and mensuration, etc. 316 pp. 16°. *Cincinnati, E. D. Truman,* 1850. s.

Ramirez (Bráulio Anton). Diccionario de bibliografia agrónomica y de toda clase de escritos relacionados con la agricultura; obra premiada por la biblioteca nacional. xix, 1015 pp. 1 l. 8°. *Madrid, gobierno,* 1865. s.

[SPAIN. Biblioteca nacional].

Ramon de la Sagra. *See* **La Sagra.**

Rampegolo (Antonio). Aurea biblia. Liber introductorius in biblie historias figurasque. [*anon.*] 14 p. l. 144 l. numbered as 138. 4°. *Vlm, J. Zeiner de Reutlingen,* 1476.

Ramsay (David, *M. D.*) History of the American revolution. New ed. 2 v. xii, 357 pp; 2 p. l. 360 pp. 8°. *London, J. Stockdale,* 1793.

——— History of the United States, 1607 to 1808. Continued to the treaty of Ghent, by S. S. Smith. 2d ed. 3 v. 8°. *Philadelphia, M. Carey & son,* 1818.

——— Military memoirs of Great Britain: or, a history of the war, 1755–1763. xii, 471 pp. 8°. *Edinburgh, author,* 1779.

[Imperfect: plates wanting].

Ramusio (Giovanni Battista, *editor*). Delle navigationi et viaggi, nel qvale si contiene la descrittione dell' Africa, [etc.] et la navigatione attorno il mondo, [etc.] v. 1. 4 p. l. 405 l. fol. *Venetia, heredi di L. Giunti,* 1550. s.

——— Secondo volume delle navigationi et viaggi, [etc.] nel qvale si contengono l'historia delle cose de Tartari, et diuersi fatti de'loro imperatori, [etc.] Nuova ed. 243 l. fol. *Venetia, Giunti,* 1583. s.

——— Terzo volume delle navigationi et viaggi nel qvale si contengogo la nauigationi al mondo nuouo, [etc.] 453 l. fol. *Venetia, Giunti,* 1556. s.

Ranby (John, *surgeon general British army*). The nature and treatment of gunshot wounds. 8°. *Boston,* 1777.

[*In* VAN SWIETEN (G. *baron*). Diseases incident to armies. *Boston,* 1777. pp. 120-131].

Randall (Gurdon P.) A handbook of designs, containing plans in perspective, of courthouses, universities, etc. and suggestions relative to their construction, heating and ventilation. 44 pp. 30 pl. 8°. *Chicago, Church, Goodman, & Donnelly,* 1868.

Randall (Henry S.) Fine wool sheep husbandry. 8°. *Albany,* 1862.

[*In* NEW YORK State agricultural society transactions. v. 21. pp. 663–774].

Randall (Samuel S.) First principles of popular education and public instruction. 256 pp. 12°. *New York, Harpers,* 1868.

Randolph (Paschal Beverly, *M. D.*) After death; or, disembodied man. The world of spirits, its location, extent, etc. 2^d ed. 260 pp. 8°. *Boston, author,* 1868.

Rankin (*Rev.* John). Letters on American slavery, addressed to Thomas Rankin. 118 pp. 18°. *Boston, Garrison & Knapp,* 1853.

Rantoul (Robert). Report relating to capital punishment in the commonwealth of Massachusetts. 96 pp. 8°. [*Boston, state printer*], 1836.

Raoul-Rochette. *See* **Rochette.**

Raphael. *See* **Santi** (Raffaello).

Rassman (Christian Friedrich). Kurtzgefasstes lexicon deutscher pseudonymer schriftsteller, von der altern bis auf die jüngste zeit aus allen fächern der wissenschaften. Mit einer vorrede von J. W. S. Lindner. viii, 248 pp. 8°. *Leipzig, W. Nauck,* 1830.

Rau (Carl Heinrich). Grundsätze der finanzwissenschaft. 2 v. in 1. xii, 393 pp; xiii, 413 pp. 8°. *Heidelberg, C. F. Winter,* 1850–51.

Rau (Heribert). Mozart; a biographical romance. From the German, by E. R. Sill. 323 pp. 12°. *New York, Leypoldt & Holt,* 1868.

Rau (Jan Jakob). Responsio ad qualemcunque defensionem Frederici Ruyschii, pro septo scroti. 4°. *Amstelædami,* 1721. s.

[RUYSCH (F.) Opera. v. 3. no. 33].

——— Epistola de inventoribus septi scroti. 4°. *Amstelædami,* 1721. s.

[RUYSCH (F.) Opera. v. 3. no. 34].

Rauch (*Rev.* Frederick A.) The inner life of the christian. Edited by rev. E. V. Gerhart. 333 pp. 12°. *Philadelphia, Lindsay & Blakiston,* 1856. s.

Rauh (*Dr.* —. *of Münich*). Anti-contrat social, order rationelle begründung des historischen rechts. viii, 226 pp. 16°. *Augsburg, Pilon & co.* 1854. s.

Raumer (Friedrich von, *editor*). *See* **Historisches** taschenbuch. 1830–66.

Rawlinson (George). The five great monarchies of the ancient eastern world; or, the history, geography, and antiquities of Chaldæa, Assyria, Babylon, Media, and Persia. v. 4. [Persia]. 8°. *London, J. Murray,* 1867.

[Completes the work].

Ray society publications, 1864–68. 8°. and fol. *London,* 1864–68.

BOWERBANK (J. S.) A monograph of the British spongiadæ. 2 v. 8°. 1864-66.
BROWN (Robert). The miscellaneous botanical works. 2 v. 8°. 1866-67.
DOUGLAS (J. W.) *and* SCOTT (J.) British hemiptera. v. 1. Hemiptera heteroptera. 8°. 1865.
FLOWER (W. H.) Recent memoirs on the cetacea, by professors Eschricht, Reinhardt, and Lilljeborg. fol. 1866.
GÜNTHER (A. C. L. G.) The reptiles of British India. fol. 1864.
NITZSCH (C. L.) Pterylography. Translated from the German. Edited by P. L. Sclater. fol. 1867.
PARKER (W. K.) A monograph on the structure and development of the shoulder-girdle and sternum in the vertebrata. fol. 1868.

Raynal (Guillaume Thomas François). Histoire du divorce de Henri viii. roi d'Angleterre, et de Catherine d' Arragon. 258 pp. 16°. *Amsterdam,* 1763.

——— Histoire philosophique et politique des établissemens et du commerce des Européens dans les deux Indes. [*anon*]. 7 v. [in 5]. 8°. *Amsterdam,* [*Gosse fils*], 1772-74. s.

——— The same. A philosophical and political history of the settlements and trade of the Europeans in the East and West Indies. From the French, by J. Justamond. 3^d ed. 4 v. 8°. *Dublin, J. Exshaw,* 1799.

——— A philosophical and political history of the British settlements and trade in North America. From the French. [With] an impartial history of the present war in America. xii, 410 pp. 16°. *Edinburgh, C. Denovan,* 1779.

Raynal (G. T. F.) Révolution de l'Amérique. xvi, 171 pp. 12°. *Londres, Lockyer Davis*, 1781.

——— The same. The revolution of America. [Translated from the French]. xvi, 181 pp. 8°. *London, L. Davis*, 1781.

——— The same. vii, 92 pp. 16°. *Salem, [Mass.] S. Hall*, 1782.

Raynouard (François Juste Marie). Les templiers, tragédie. Précédée d'un précis historique sur les templiers. lxxxii, 118 pp. 1 pl. 8°. *Paris, Giguet et Michaud*, 1805.

Read (Hollis). The hand of God in history; or, divine providence historically illustrated in the extension and establishment of christianity. 402 pp. 14 pl. 12°. *Hartford, H. E. Robins & co.* 1851. s.

Read (Thomas Buchanan, *editor*). The female poets of America. With portraits, biographical notices, and specimens of their writings. 420 pp. 7 portraits. 8°. *Philadelphia, E. H. Butler & co.* 1849. s.

——— Lays and ballads. 140 pp. 12°. *Philadelphia, etc. Appleton*, 1849. s.

——— The onward age; an anniversary poem. 22 pp. 12°. *Cincinnati, y. m. mercantile library association*, 1852. s.

Read. *See, also,* **Reed** *and* **Reid.**

Reade (Charles). Clouds and sunshine. And art: a dramatic tale. 288 pp. 12°. *Boston, Ticknor & Fields*, 1855.

Real academia española. Ortografia de la lengua castellana. 8ª ed. xix, 189 pp. 5 l. 16°. *Barcelona, Brusi*, 1823.

Real de Azúa (Gabriel Alejandro). Poesias diversas. viii, 304 pp. 16°. *Paris, V. Salvá*, 1839. s.

Real children: their sayings and doings. [*anon.*] 225 pp. 11 pl. 18°. *Philadelphia, American s. s. union*, 1865.

Real colegio seminario de instruccion, Tepotzotlan. Constituciones. *See* **Nunez de Haro y Peralta (A.)**

Reavis (L. U.) The new republic, or the transition complete, with an approaching change of national empire, based upon the commercial and industrial expansion of the great west, [etc.] 2ᵈ ed. 1 p. l. 124 pp. 8°. *St. Louis, J. F. Torrey & co.* 1867. s.

Rebel conditions of peace and the mechanics of the south. Extracts from Richmond journals. 4 pp. 8°. *New York*, 1863.

[LOYAL publication society. no. 30].

Rebellion (The) record: a diary of American events. Edited by Frank Moore. v. 11. 8°. *New York, D. Van Nostrand*, 1868.

Rebolledo (Bernardino, *conde* de). La constancia victoriosa. 2 p. l. 174 pp. sm. 4°. *Colonia Agrippina, Kinchio*, 1655.

[Wants portrait of queen Christina of Sweden].

Recent remarkable discoveries in central Africa, by the celebrated African explorer m. de Challue. [*anon.* A parody]. 124 pp. 8 pl. 8°. *Philadelphia, Barclay & co.* 1868.

Recollections of the early days of the national guard, comprising the prominent events in the history of the famous seventh regiment New York militia. By an ex-orderly sergeant. [*anon.* By John Mason]? 2 p. l. iv, 201 pp. 1 pl. fol. *New York, J. M. Bradstreet & son*, 1868.

Record (The) of zoological literature. 1864–66. v. 1–3. Edited by Albert C. L. G. Günther. 3 v. 8°. *London, J. Van Voorst*, 1865–67.

Recueil de divers voyages faits en Afrique et en l'Amérique, le [tout traduit de l'Anglois, et publié par les soins de H. Justel. 2ᵉ éd.] 8 p. l. 450 pp. 4 maps. 12 pl. 4°. *Paris, veuve A. Cellier*, 1684.

CONTENTS.

ALMEIDA (M. de) *and* MENDEZ (A.) Description de l'empire du Prete-Jean.
BLOME (R.) Description de l'isle de la Jamaïque.
LA BORDE (Sieur de). Relation de l'origine, [etc.] des Caraïbes.
LIGON (R.) Histoire de l'isle des Barbades.
LOBO (J.) Relation de la rivière du Nil.
RELATION du voyage fait sur les costes d'Afrique, par le comte d'Estrée, 1670–71.
TELLES. Extrait de l'histoire d'Éthiopie.

Recueil de prières pour tous les besoins de la vie. Par un prêtre du diocèse de Besançon. [*anon.*] 429 pp. 24°. *New York, C. & N. Benziger*, 1868.

Redden (Laura C.) Idyls of battle, and poems of the rebellion. By Howard Glyndon. [*pseudon.*] vi, 152 pp. 18°. *New York, Hurd & Houghton*, 1865.

Rede (Leman Thomas). The guide to the stage, containing instructions for obtaining theatrical engagements, [also] a list of the London theatres, their rules, etc. Ed. by F. C. Wemyss. 58 pp. 16°. *New York, S. French*, 1861.

[*In* MODERN standard drama. v. 28].

Redtenbacher (Jacob Ferdinand). Das dynamiden-system. Grundzüge einer mechanischen physik. x, 142 pp. 1 pl. 4°. *Mannheim, F. Bassermann*, 1857. s.

Redtenbacher (*Dr.* Ludwig). Coleopteren. iv, 249 pp. 5 l. 5 pl. 4°. *Wien*, 1868. s.

[*In* WÜLLERSTORF-URBAIR (B. von). Reise der Novara. Zoologischer theil. v. 2. abth. 1. A.]

Reed (Edward J.) Ship-building, in iron and steel. A practical treatise, giving full details of construction, processes of manufacture, and building arrangements; with results of experiments on iron and steel, and on the strength and watertightness of riveted work. xxvii, 540 pp. 5 pl. 1 tab. 8°. *London, J. Murray,* 1869.

Reed (Isaac, *editor*). *See* **Repository** (The) of wit and humor.

Reed (Sampson). Observations on the growth of the mind; with remarks on some other things. viii, 192 pp. 16°. *Boston, O. Clapp,* 1838.

Reed (William B.) A rejoinder to [George] Bancroft's historical essay on president Reed. 114 pp. 8°. *Philadelphia, author,* 1867.

Reed. *See, also,* **Read,** *and* **Reid.**

Reemelin (Charles). The wine-maker's manual. viii, 123 pp. 12°. *Cincinnati, R. Clarke & co.* 1868.

Rees (James, *editor*). Beauties of Webster. *See* **Webster** (Daniel).

Reeve (Clara). The old English baron; a Gothic story. 5th ed. xi, 263 pp. 16°. *London, C. Dilly,* 1794.

Reeves (Minnie). Ingemisco. [A novel]. By Fadette. [*pseudon.*] 341 pp. 12°. *New York, Blelock & co.* 1867.

——— Randolph Honor. By Fadette. [*pseudon.*] 382 pp. 12°. *New York, Richardson & co.* 1868.

Regale accademia ercolanese di archeologia. Dissertationis isagogicae ad hercvlanensivm explanationem pars prima. 3 p. l. 104 pp. 2 maps. 20 pl. fol. *Neapoli, ex regia typographia,* 1797. s.

——— Hercvlanensivm volvminvm quæ svpersvnt. 11 v. in 12. fol. *Neapoli, ex regia typographia,* 1793–1855. s.
[v. 7 wanting].

Regel (Eduard). Nachträge zur flora der gebiete des russischen reichs östlichs vom Altai bis Kamtschatka und Sitka, [etc.] v. 1. vii, 447 pp. 9 pl. 8°. *Moskau, buchdruckerei der k. universität,* 1861. s.
[Radde (G.) Reisen, etc. Botanische abtheilung].

——— *and* **Herder** (Ferdinand von). Enumeratio plantarum in regionibus cis-et transiliensibus a cl. Semenovio, anno 1857, collectarum. [Extract from Bulletin de la société imp. des naturalistes]. 1 p. l. 43 pp. 1 pl. 8°. *Mosquæ, typis universitatis cæsareæ,* 1864. s.

Regimē sanitatis metrice cōscriptū cū multis aphorismis ex diuersis mediciarum doctoribus collectis cū tractatu quodā de regimie contra morbū epidimie siue pestilētie. sm. 4°. *Colonie,* 1494.

——— The same. Regimen sanitatis Salerni; or, the schoole of Salernes regiment of health. [*anon.*] Corrected and enlarged, with a commentary, [by Philemon Holland]. With a discourse of fish. 3 p. l. 200 pp. 7 l. sm. 4°. *London, B. Alsop,* 1634.

Regnault (Henri Victor). Elements of chemistry, [etc.] Translated from the French, by T. Forrest Betton, and edited, with notes, by James C. Booth and William L. Faber. 2d ed. 2 v. xiv, 9-671 pp; 804 pp. 1 pl. 8°. *Philadelphia, J. B. Lippincott & co.* 1853. s.

——— The same. 3d ed. 2 v. xiv, 9-671 pp; 804 pp. 1 pl. 8°. *Philadelphia, J. B. Lippincott & co.* 1856. s.

Reichel (*Rev.* Levin T.) The Moravians in North Carolina. An authentic history. iv, 206 pp. 12°. *Salem, (N. C.) O. A. Keehln,* 1857.

Reichenbach (Heinrich Gottleib, *the son*). Gynandrae [von Mossambique]. fol. *Berlin,* 1864.
[*In* Peters (W. C. H.) Nat. reise nach Mossambique. Botanik].

Reid (John, *M.D.*) The philosophy of death; or, a general medical and statistical treatise on the nature and causes of human mortality. viii, 381 pp. 12°. *London, S. Highley,* 1841.

Reid (Mayne). The boy hunters; or, adventures in search of a white buffalo. 364 pp. 12 pl. 16°. *Boston, Ticknor & Fields,* 1858.

——— The boy slaves. With illustrations. v, 321 pp. 8 pl. 16°. *Boston, Ticknor & Fields,* 1865.

——— The bush boys; or, the history and adventures of a Cape farmer and his family in the wild karoos of southern Africa. 356 pp. 12 pl. 16°. *Boston, Ticknor & Fields,* 1857.

——— The child wife; a tale of the two worlds. 402 pp. 12°. *New York, Sheldon & co.* 1869.

——— The desert home; or, the adventures of a lost family in the wilderness. 411 pp. 12 pl. 16°. *Boston, Ticknor & Fields,* 1858.

——— The forest exiles; or, the adventures of a Peruvian family amid the wilds of the Amazon. 360 pp. 12 pl. 16°. *Boston, Ticknor & Fields,* 1857.

——— Lost Lenore; or, the adventures of a rolling stone. 392 pp. 8 pl. 16°. *London, C. H. Clarke,* [1865]?

——— The quadroon; or, a lover's adventures in Louisiana. 384 pp. 6 pl. 12°. *New York, R. M. Dewitt,* 1856. s.

——— Ran away from home; a life of adventure. By cannibal Jack. [*pseudon.*] iii, 322 pp. 8 pl. 16°. *London, D. Bryce,* [1866].

Reid (Mayne). Ran away to sea; an autobiography for boys. 359 pp. 6 pl. 16°. *Boston, Ticknor & Fields,* 1868.

——— The young voyageurs; or, the boy hunters in the north. 360 pp. 12 pl. 16°. *Boston, Ticknor & Fields,* 1857.

——— The young yägers; or, a narrative of hunting adventures in southern Africa. 328 pp. 12 pl. 16°. *Boston, Ticknor & Fields,* 1857.

Reid (Whitelaw). Ohio in the war: her statesmen, her generals, and soldiers. 2 v. 1050 pp. 7 maps, 19 pl; 949 pp. 12 pl. 8°. *Cincinnati, Moore, Wilstach & Baldwin,* 1868.

Reig y Garcia (Tomas). Tarifas perpetuas para hallar el importe de las sueldos, pres, salarias, haberes y abonos por años, meses, y dias, con sus descuentos y liquidos para los ajustes, [etc.] 4 p. l. 184 pp. 4°. *Valencia, Mallen y Berard,* 1834. S.

Reign (The) of humbug. A [tory] satire. [*anon.*] 2d ed. xv, 80 pp. 8°. *London, P. Richardson,* 1836.

Reil (Johann Christian, *editor*). *See* **Archiv** für die physiologie, 1796–1815.

Reilly's (C. Leslie) Pennsylvania state business directory for 1868–69. Containing names of merchants [and professional men]. A complete list of post offices in the state, etc. xxxvi, 516 pp. 8°. *Philadelphia, C. L. Reilly,* 1868.

Reimarus (Hermann Samuel). Von dem zwecke Jesu und seiner jünger. Noch ein fragment des Wolfenbüttelschen ungenannten. Herausgegeben von G. E. Lessing. Neue aufl. 6 p. l. 276 pp. 12°. *Berlin, A. Wever,* 1784. S.

——— [The same]. Fragmente des Wolfenbüttelschen ungenannten. Ein anhang zu dem fragment von zweck Jesu und seiner jünger. Bekanntgewacht von G. E. Lessing. 1 p. l. 298 pp. 12°. *Berlin, A. Wever,* 1784. S.

[*With his* Von dem zwecke Jesu. 1784].

Reinhardt (Johan T.) Pseudorca crassidens, a cetacean hitherto unknown in the Danish fauna. Translated from the [Danish]. 4°. *London,* 1866.

[RAY society. *In* FLOWER (W. H.) Recent memoirs on the cetacea. pp. 189–218].

Reinhold (Ernst). Lehrbuch der geschichte der philosophie. 2e aufl. xx, 764 pp. 8°. *Jena, F. Mauke,* 1839. S.

——— System der metaphysik. 2e bearbeitung. xiv, 640 pp. 8°. *Jena, F. Mauke,* 1842. S.

Reinwald (C.) Catalogue annuel de la librairie française, 1867. 8°. *Paris, C. Reinwald,* [1868].

Reisch (Gregorius). Margarita philosophica, totius philosophiae rationalis et moralis principia duodecim libris dialogice complectens. 320 l. 8°. *Basiliae, industria M. Furterij & J. Scoti,* 1508. S.

[Title page in ms.]

Relaçáo verdadéira, etc. De gedenkwaardige voyagie van Ferdinand de Soto na Florida, en desselfs ontdekking van de landen in dat gewest, met al wat aanmerkenswaardig op die vierjarige reyse is voorgevallen. Gedaan anno 1539 en vervolgens. Naauwkeurig beschreven door een Portugijs, die selfs dit alles heeft by gewoond. [*anon.*] 3 p. l. 86 pp. 2 l. 1 map. 7 pl. 16°. *Leyden, P. Van der Aa,* 1706.

Relation de l'ambassade de Migon de Rochefort, seigneur de la Pomarède, et de Guillaume Gaian, conseiller du duc d'Anjou, envoyés en Sardaigne par Louis 1er duc d'Anjou, à Hugues, juge d'Arborée, pour faire alliance avec ce prince contre le roi d'Arragon, au mois d'Aoust 1378. [*anon.*] x pp. 1 l. 208 pp. 8°. *Paris, Verdière,* 1826.

[COLLECTION de chroniques nationales françaises. v. 25].

Religious mystery considered. [*anon.*] 52 pp. 12°. *London, J. Chapman,* 1850.

Renan (Joseph Ernest). Studies of religious history and criticism. From the French, by O. B. Frothingham. With a biographical introduction. 394 pp. 8°. *New York, Carleton,* 1864.

Rengger (Albert, *M. D.*) *and* **Longchamp** (———. *M. D.*) Essai historique sur la révolution du Paraguay, et le gouvernement dictatorial du docteur Francia. xxxv, 300 pp. 1 map. 8°. *Paris, H. Bossange,* 1827.

Renté. *See* **Güell y Renté.**

Renzi (Angelo Maria). La signora di Monza (soeur Virginie Marie de Leyva) et son procès, 1595–1609. viii, 192 pp. 2 pl. 8°. *Paris, E. Dentu,* 1862. S.

Reporter (The). A periodical devoted to religion, law, legislation, and public events. Conducted by R. Sutton, [and others]. v. 1–4. 8°. *Philadelphia and Washington, R. Sutton,* 1865–67.

CONTENTS.

v. 1. Protestant episcopal church. The debates and proceedings of the general triennial convention. Held in Philadelphia Oct. 1865.

v. 2. Arguments in U. S. supreme court and court of claims.
Important subjects of congressional action.
Report of national union convention at Philadelphia, Aug. 1866.
Report of southern loyalists' convention at Philadelphia, Sept. 1866.

v. 3. Legislation relative to the supreme court of the U. S.
Arguments in U. S. supreme court on enforcement of military reconstruction acts.
Trial of John H. Surratt.

v. 4. Trial of John H. Surratt.

Repository (The): a collection of fugitive pieces of wit and humour, in prose and verse. By the most eminent writers. [Edited by Isaac Reed]. 4 v. 16°. *London, E. & C. Dilly,* 1777–83.

Republic (The). [Daily]. June 13, 1849, to Dec. 30, 1850. 3 v. fol. *Washington,* 1849–50.

Republican convention. *See* **National** union republican convention.

Rethel (Alfred). Ein todtentanz aus dem jahre 1848. Mit erklärendem texte von R. Reinick. 6 pl. obl. 4°. *Leipzig, G. Wigand,* [1849].

Retrospect (The) of medicine. Edited by W. and J. Braithwaite. Jan. to June, 1866, July, 1867, to June, 1868. v. 53, 56–57. 16°. *London, Simpkin, Marshall & co.* 1867–68.

Rettberg (Friedrich Wilhelm). Kirchengeschichte Deutschlands. Bis zum tode Karls des grossen. 2 v. xii, 652 pp. 1 map; x, 825 pp. 8°. *Göttingen, Vandenhoeck & Ruprecht,* 1846–48.

Reuilly (Jean, *baron* de). Voyage en Crimée et sur les bords de la Mer Noire, pendant l'année 1803. Suivi d'un mémoire sur le commerce de cette mer, etc. xix, 302 pp. 2 maps. 3 pl. 8°. *Paris, Bossange, etc.* 1806.

Reumont (Alfred). Andrea del Sarto [A. Vannucchi]. Mit einem grundriss des verhofs der servitenkirche in Florenz. xxviii, 231 pp. 1 pl. 1 tab. 16°. *Leipzig, F. A. Brockhaus,* 1835.

Reuterdahl (Henrik). Swenska kyrkans historia. 3 v. in 5. 8°. *Lund, C. W. K. Gleerup,* 1838–63. s.

CONTENTS.

v. 1–2. i. [8de seklern—1248]. 1838–63.
v. 2. ii. Swerige under konungarne af folkungaätten. 7 p. l. 672 pp. 1850.
v. 3. i–ii. Swerige under Calmar-unionen. 4 p. l. 521 pp. 2 l; 2 p. l. 594 pp. 2 l. 1863.

Revelations: a companion to the "New gospel of peace." According to Abraham. [*anon.*] 36 pp. 12°. *New York, Feeks & Bancker,* 1863.

Reverhorst. *See* **Van Reverhorst.**

Revival and camp meeting minstrel. Containing hymns and spiritual songs, original and selected. 422 pp. 24°. *Philadelphia, Perkinpine & Higgins,* 1868.

Revolution (The). Elizabeth Cady Stanton, and Parker Pillsbury, editors. Jan. to Dec. 1868. v. 1–2. 4°. *New York, Susan B. Anthony,* 1868.

Revue des deux mondes. 38e année. 2e période. Jan. to Dec. 1868. v. 73–78. 8°. *Paris,* [*J. Claye*], 1868.

Revue (La) française. v. 1–6. 8°. *New York, Hoskin & Snowden,* 1833–36.

Revue française des familles et des pensionnats, ou choix de nouvelles, historiettes, anecdotes, etc. tirées des meillures publications françaises. 384 pp. 1 l. 8°. *New York, F. G. Berteau,* 1845.

Rezende (André de). Lusitaniæ antiqvitates, et de antiqvitatibus Eboræ. [Item] Jacobi Moenetii Vasconcelli de eborensi mvnicipio commentarius. 346 pp. 2 l. 18°. *Coloniæ Agrippinæ, Greuenbruch,* 1613.
[*With* DELICIÆ Lvsitano-Hispanicæ, *Cologne,* 1613].

Rhode Island (*State of*). Records of the state of Rhode Island and Providence plantations in New England. Edited by J. R. Bartlett. v. 10. 1784–92. 8°. *Providence, Providence press co.* 1865.

——— Reports upon the registration of births, marriages, and deaths, in the state. 1863–1866. 11th to 14th reports. 4 v. 8°. *Providence, state printers,* 1865–67.

——— Reports and documents relating to the public schools of Rhode Island, for 1848. By Henry Barnard. 560 pp. 8°. *Providence, general assembly,* 1849. s.

Rhode Island historical society. Collections. v. 6. 8°. *Providence, Hammond, Angell & co.* 1867.

Rhodes (Hugh). The boke of nurture, or schoole of good maners: for men, seruants and children, with Stans puer ad mensam. Edited by F. J. Furnivall. 8°. *London, H. Jackson,* 1577, [*reprint,* 1867].
[*With* FURNIVALL (F. J.) Babees book. pp. 61–114. Early English text society publications. no. 32].

Rhodion *or* **Rösslin** (Eucharius). *See* **Rösslin.**

Rhodomann *or* **Rhodomanus** (Laurentius). Ποιησις χριστιανη. Poesis christiana. Palæstinæ, sev historiæ sacræ, libri novem. [Latin and Greek texts]. 321 pp. 8°. *Francofvrdi, apud A. Wecheli heredes,* 1589. s.

Rhymes of the poets. By Felix Ago. [*pseudon.*] 56 pp. 12°. *Philadelphia, E. H. Butler & co.* 1868.

Rhyming story-book. [*anon.*] 64 pp. 6 pl. sm. 4°. *New York, Hurd & Houghton,* 1867.

Riccio (Michele). De regibus Francorū lib. iii. De regibus Hispaniæ lib. iii. De regibus Hierosolymorum lib. i. De regibus Neapolis et Siciliæ lib. iv. De regibus Vngariæ lib. ii. 85 l. sm. 4°. *Basileæ, apud Ioannem Frobenivm,* 1517.

Rice (Victor M.) Special report on education in the U. S. and other countries. *See* **Johnson** (A. G.)

Rich (O.) and son. Part 1 of catalogue for 1848, containing near two thousand books, relating principally to America. 127 pp. 18°. *London, Rich & son*, 1848.

[With prices].

Richard (P. Charles). Moments perdus. Poésies. 173 pp. 16°. *Paris, vve. J. Renouard*, 1868.

Richards (C. French). John Guilderstring's sin. A novel. vi, 244 pp. 8 pp. 12°. *New York, Carleton*, 1864.

Richards (George H.) Memoir of Alexander Macomb, major general. 130 pp. 16°. *New York, M'Elrath, Bangs & co.* 1833.

Richardson (Albert D.) A personal history of Ulysses S. Grant. With a sketch of Schuyler Colfax. 560 pp. 34 pl. 8°. *Hartford, American publ. co.* 1868.

Richardson (*Sir* John). Fish. 4°. *London*, 1844.

[*In* HINDS (R. B.) The zoology of h. m. s. Sulphur. v. 1].

Richardson (Joseph, *M.D.*) A practical treatise on mechanical dentistry. 2d ed. enlarged, with 159 illustrations. 442 pp. 8°. *Philadelphia, Lindsay & Blakiston*, 1869.

Richardson (Robert). Memoirs of Alexander Campbell, embracing a view of the origin, progress, and principles of the religious reformation which he advocated. v. 1. 560 pp. portrait. 8°. *Philadelphia, Lippincott & co.* 1868.

Richardson (William H.) Journal of W. H. Richardson, a private soldier in col. Doniphan's command. 84 pp. 12°. *Baltimore, J. Robinson*, 1847. s.

——— The same. Journal of a private soldier in the campaign of New and old Mexico, under the command of col. Doniphan. 2d ed. 96 pp. 3 pl. 12°. *Baltimore, J. W. Woods*, 1848. s.

Richelet (César Pierre). Abregé des règles de la versification françoise. 16°. *Amsterdam, frères Wetstein*, 1720.

[*In* BRUZEN DE LA MARTINIÈRE (A. A.) Nouveau recueil des epigrammatistes françois. ed. 1720. v. 2. pp. 273–354].

Richerand (Anthelme Balthazar, *baron*). Nouveaux éléments de physiologie. 3d ed. revue et corrigée par l'auteur, et par Bérard ainé. Éd. belge, augmentée du traité de physiologie comparée par F. Tiedemann. 535 pp. 1 table. 8°. *Bruxelles, H. Dumont*, 1837. s.

Richings (*Rev.* Benjamin). A narrative of the sufferings and martyrdom of Robert Glover, of Mancetter, burnt at Coventry, 1555, and of mrs. Lewes of the same place, burnt at Lichfield, 1557. With some account of their friend, [rev.] Augustine Bernher. xvi, 142 pp. 2 pl. 16°. *London, L. B. Seeley & sons*, 1833.

Richmond (Allen, *pseudon?*) The first twenty years of my life. 268 pp. 1 pl. 12°. *Philadelphia, American s. s. union*, [1859]. s.

Richmond (B. W.) A discussion of spiritualism. *See* **Brittan** (S. B.) *and* **Richmond.**

Richthofen (Ferdinand Paul Wilhelm, *baron* von). The Comstock lode: its character, and the probable mode of its continuance in depth. 83 pp. 8°. *San Francisco, Sutro tunnel company*, 1866.

——— The same. 4°. *Baltimore, J. Murphy & co.* 1868.

[*In* SUTRO (A.) Mineral resources of the U. S. 1868. pp. 95–140].

Rickey (Anna S.) Forest flowers of the west. [Poems]. 138 pp. 1 portrait. 8°. *Philadelphia, Lindsay & Blakiston*, 1851. s.

Riddell (*Mrs.* J. H.) Too much alone. By F. G. Trafford. [*pseudon.*] New ed. iv, 371 pp. 12°. *London, C. J. Skeet*, 1862.

Riddell (Robert). The carpenter and joiner, and elements of hand-railing. 18 l. 32 pl. 4°. *Philadelphia, Claxton, Remsen & Haffelfinger*, 1868.

Riedesel (Friedrich Adolph von). Memoirs, and letters and journals during his residence in America. From the German, by W. L. Stone. 2 v. viii, 306 pp. 2 pl; 284 pp. 1 pl. 8°. *Albany, J. Munsell*, 1868.

Right (The) divine of kings to govern wrong! Dedicated to the Holy alliance. [*anon.*] 3d ed. 60 pp. 12°. *London, W. Hone*, 1821.

Rijkens (R. G.) Praktische handleiding voor kunstmatige ligchaams-oefeningen, ten dienste van huisgezinnen en verschillen de inrigtingen voor onderwijs en opvoeding. xlviii, 339 pp. 10 pl. 8°. *Groningen, J. Oomkens*, 1843. s.

Rimius (Heinrich). A candid narrative of the rise and progress of the herrnhuters, commonly called moravians, or unitas-fratrum; with a short account of their doctrines, [and] observations on their politics, etc. [Translated from the German]. 110 pp. 16°. *Philadelphia, reprinted by William Bradford*, 1753.

[Imperfect].

Ring (Max). John Milton and his times. An historical novel. From the German, by F. Jordan. 308 pp. 8 pl. 8°. *New York, Appletons*, 1868.

Rio Janeiro. Almanak administrativo, mercantil e industrial da corte e provincia do Rio de Janeiro para o anno de 1861, fundado por E. von Laemmert. Redigido por C. G. Ha-

Rio Janeiro—continued. ring. [With appendices]. Provincia de Rio de Janeiro, 1861. [And] Supplemento: Colecção de documentos officiaes, [etc.] vii, 673, 344, 347 pp. 1 portrait. 8°. *Rio de Janeiro, E. & H. Laemmert*, 1861. s.

Ripley (Ezra, *D.D.*) A history of the fight at Concord, on the 19th of April, 1775, showing that then and there the first British blood was shed by armed Americans, and the revolutionary war thus commenced. 2d ed. 40 pp. 8°. *Concord, H. Atwill*, 1832.

[*With* 49 pp. ms. notes, relating to the battle, collected by Peter Force].

Ripley (E. L.) System of map drawing. 11 pp. 9 maps. 6 pl. 4°. *New York, A. S. Barnes & co.* 1866.

Ripley (Henry Jones, *D.D. editor*). *See* **Bible** (*English*). The epistle to the Romans and to the Hebrews.

Ritchie (Leitch). The game of life. 8°. *Philadelphia, T. K. Greenbank*, 1833.

[GREENBANK'S periodical library. v. 1. pp. 515-588].

Ritter's geographisch-statistisches lexikon über die erdtheile, länder, meere, buchten, häfen, seen, flüsse, inseln, gebirge, staaten, städte, etc. 4e umgearb. aufl. Von W. Hoffmann, C. Winderlich, und C. Cramer. 4e aufl. 1 p. l. 1458 pp. 8°. *Leipzig, O. Wigand*, 1855.

Rivarol (Antoine, *comte* de) *and* **Champcenetz** (——). Le petit almanach de nos grands hommes. Année 1788. [*anon.*] 236 pp. 18°. [*Paris*, 1788].

Riverside (The) magazine, for young people. An illustrated monthly. Jan. to Dec. 1868. v. 2. 8°. *New York, Hurd & Houghton*, 1869.

Rizo *Néroulos* (Jacovaky). Cours de littérature grecque moderne donné à Genève. Publié par Jean Humbert. 2e éd. xxiv, 204 pp. 1 portrait. 8°. *Genève, A. Cherbuliez*, 1828. s.

Robbins (*Rev.* Chandler). A history of the second church, or old north, in Boston. [With] a history of the new brick church. viii, 320 pp. 5 pl. 8°. *Boston, J. Wilson & son*, 1852.

Robert (Ludwig). Die nacht der verhältnisse. Ein trauerspiel in fünf aufzügen, und zwei briefe über das antike und moderne und über das sogenannte bürgerliche trauerspiel. 148 pp. 12°. *Stuttgart, etc. J. G. Cotta*, 1819. s.

Robert Linton: and what life taught him. By the author of the "Win and wear" series. [*anon.*] 395 pp. 4 pl. 16°. *New York, R. Carter & bros.* 1868.

Roberton (John, *M. D.*) On the generative system: being an anatomical and physiological sketch of the parts of generation, and a treatise on their diseases. [With] letters by M. Baillie, M. D. 4th ed. 548 pp. 13 pl. 8°. *London, J. J. Stockdale*, 1817.

Roberts (*Capt.* A.) Never caught. Personal adventures connected with twelve successful trips in blockade-running during the American civil war, 1863–64. iv, 123 pp. 16°. *London, J. C. Hotten*, 1867.

Roberts (*Capt.* Lemuel). Memoirs: containing adventures in youth, vicissitudes experienced as a continental soldier, sufferings as prisoner, escapes from captivity, [etc.] Written by himself. 96 pp. 8°. *Bennington, (Vt.) A. Haswell*, 1809.

Robertson (Abraham, *M. D.*) A manual on extracting teeth. 2d ed. 200 pp. 12°. *Philadelphia, Lindsay & Blakiston*, 1868.

Robertson (George, *farmer*). General view of the agriculture of the county of Mid-Lothian. 223, 138 pp. 1 l. 1 col. map. 11 pl. 8°. *Edinburgh*, 1795. s.

[GREAT BRITAIN. Board of agriculture].

—— General view of Kincardineshire; or, the Mearns. 2 p. l. 12, 477, 63 pp. 1 l. 8 tab. 4 pl. 8°. *London*, 1810. s.

[GREAT BRITAIN. Board of agriculture].

Robertson (James, *D. D.*) General view of the agriculture in the county of Inverness. xiii, lxvi, 447 pp. 2 maps. 8°. *London*, 1808. s.

[GREAT BRITAIN. Board of agriculture].

—— General view of the agriculture in the county of Perth. 1 p. l. xx, 576 pp. 2 l. 1 tab. 1 map. 3 pl. 8°. *Perth*, 1799. s.

[GREAT BRITAIN. Board of agriculture].

Robertson (William, *D.D.*) The history of America. 2 v. xvii pp. 3 l. 488 pp; 535 pp. 4°. *London, W. Strahan*, 1777.

Robiano de Borsbeek (Louis François de Paule Marie Joseph). De la violation des cimetières. 82 pp. 12°. *Turin, Alliana & Paravia*, 1825. s.

[*With* LA MENNAIS (H. F. R. de). Melanges, etc. 1825].

Robin (*Abbé* Claude). New travels through North America, exhibiting the history of the campaign of general Washington and Rochambeau, in the year 1781. Also, narrations of the capture of general Burgoyne, and lord Cornwallis, with their armies. From the French. 112 pp. 8°. *Philadelphia, Robert Bell*, 1783.

Robinson (Charles S. *D. D.*) Short studies for sunday school teachers. vi, 247 pp. 16°. *New York, Wynkoop & Sherwood*, 1868.

Robinson (Horatio N.) A treatise on surveying and navigation. 230, 101 pp. 8°. *Cincinnati, J. Ernst,* 1852. s.

Robinson (Matthew). Considerations on the measures carrying on with respect to the British colonies in North America. [*anon.*] 160 pp. 8°. *London, R. Baldwin,* [1774].

——— The same. [*anon.*] 2[d] ed. With an appendix. 176, 45 pp. 8°. *London, R. Baldwin,* 1774.

——— The same. [*anon.*] 5th ed. 64 pp. 8°. *Boston, Edes & Gill,* 1774.

——— The same. [*anon.*] 63 pp. 8°. *Hartford, E. Watson,* 1774.

——— The same. [*anon.*] 60 pp. 8°. *Philadelphia, B. Towne,* 1774.

Robinson (*Rev.* Phinehas). Immortality: a poem, in ten cantos. 412 pp. 8°. *New York, Leavitt, Trow & co.* 1846. s.

Robinson (Samuel). A course of fifteen lectures on medical botany, denominated Thomson's new theory of medical practice, etc. 216 pp. 18°. *Boston, J. Howe,* 1834.

Robinson (Solon). Me-won-i-toc. A tale of frontier life and Indian character. 133 pp. 8°. *New York, N. Y. news co.* 1867.

Robinson (William, *M. D.*) On dysentery. 8°. *New York, Collins & co.* 1819.

[*In* NORTH (Elisha). Outlines of the science of life. ed. 1829. pp. 188-196].

Robinson Crusoe's farm yard: designed to accompany the game of natural history for children. [*anon.*] 228 pp. sq. 16°. *New York, G. P. Putnam,* 1849. s.

Robison (John). Proofs of a conspiracy against all the religions and governments of Europe, carried on in the secret meetings of free masons, illuminati, and reading societies. 3[d] ed. 389 pp. 8°. *Philadelphia, T. Dobson,* 1798.

Robortello (Francesco). Scholia in Æschyli tragoedias omnes ex vetvstissimis libris manuscriptis collecta, [etc.] 10 p. l. 216 pp. 16°. *Venetiis, ex officiana erasmiana Vincentii Valgrisii,* 1552.

Rochat (Alfred, *Ph. D.*) Über einen bisher unbekannten Percheval li Galois, [etc.] 180 pp. 8°. *Zürich, E. Kriesling,* 1855. s.

Rochefoucauld (François, *duc* de La). *See* **La Rochefoucauld.**

Rochette (Désiré Raoul). Lectures on ancient art. [Translated from the French]. viii, 184 pp. 2 pl. 16°. *London, Hall, Virtue & co.* 1864.

——— Peintures antiques inédites, précédées de recherches sur l'emploi de la peinture dans la décoration des édifices sacrés et publics, chez les Grecs et chez les Romains; faisant suite aux Monuments inédits. xvi, 470 pp. 15 col. pl. 4°. *Paris, imprimerie royale,* 1836. s.

Rockport (*Mass.*) directory, for 1869. 8°. *Gloucester, Procter bros.* 1868.

See **Gloucester** *and* **Rockport.**

Rockwell (*Rev.* J. E.) Sketches of the presbyterian church, giving a brief summary of arguments in favor of its primitive and apostolic character, [etc.] 282 pp. 1 pl. 18°. *Philadelphia, presbyterian board of publication,* 1854. s.

Rockwell (*Mrs.* M. E.) Tom Miller; or, after many days. 351 pp. 4 pl. 16°. *Philadelphia, J. C. Garrigues & co.* 1867.

Rocoles (Jean Baptiste). Les imposteurs insignes, ou histoires de plusieurs hommes de néant de toutes nations, qui ont usurpé la qualité' d'empereur, de roi, et de prince. 2 v. in 1. 3 p. l. 374 pp. 14 pl; 320 pp. 9 pl. 16°. *Bruxelles, J. Van Vlaenderen,* 1828.

Rodman (Ella, *pseudon?*) A grandmother's recollections. [A moral tale]. 235 pp. 12°. *New York, C. Scribner,* 1851. s.

Rogers (Charles). A collection of prints in imitation of drawings. [With] lives of their authors, with explanatory and critical notes. 2 v. 4 p. l. vi, 217 pp. 2 l. 44 pl; 2 p. l. 246 pp. 1 l. 70 pl. fol. *London, J. Nicols,* 1788.

Rogers (George). Washington, crowned by "equality, fraternity, and liberty." A democratic poem. 168 pp. 1 portrait. 12°. *New York, Leavitt, Trow & co.* 1849. s.

Rogers (*Rev.* James Edwin Thorold). A manual of political economy for schools and colleges. xvi, 313 pp. 16°. *Oxford, Clarendon press,* 1868.

Roget (Peter Mark). Thesaurus of English words and phrases: so classified and arranged as to facilitate the expression of ideas and assist in literary composition. Revised and edited by B. Sears. 468 pp. 12°. *Boston, Gould & Lincoln,* 1854.

——— The same. New Am. from 3[d] Lond. ed. 510 pp. 12°. *Boston, Gould & Lincoln,* 1855.

Rogg (J.) Bibliotheca mathematica. Handbuch der mathematischen literatur, vom anfange der buchdruckerkunst bis zum schlusse des jahrs 1830. Erste abth. welche die arithmetischen und geometrischen wissenschaften enthält. vi, 578 pp. 8°. *Tübingen, L. F. Fues,* 1830.

Rojo de Flores. *See* **Roxo de Flores.**

Roland de la Platière (Manon Jean Phlipon, *madame*). An appeal to impartial posterity; or, a collection of tracts written by her in the prisons of the Abbey, and St. Pelagie, in Paris. Translated from the French. 1st Amer. ed. 2 v. ix. 202, 164 pp; 202, 235 pp. 8°. *New York, A. Van Hook,* 1798.

Rolewinck von Laer (Werner). Fasciculus temporū. 8 p. l. 66 l. 4°. *Venetiis, E. Ratdolt,* 1485.

——— The same. 5 p. l. 90 l. fol. *Argentine, J. Pryss,* 1488.

——— Questiones duodecī notablēs valde et vtiles pro probris et studentibus ac alijs sacre doctrine insudantibus. [*anon.*] 14 l. 4°. [*Coloniæ, Arnold Therhoern, about* 1475].

Roll of honor. *See* **United States.** (*War department*).

Rolland (Charles). La Turquie contemporaine; hommes et choses. Études sur l'Orient. 426 pp. 8°. *Paris, Pagnerre,* 1854.

Rollin (Frank A.) Life and public services of Martin R. Delany, late major 104th U. S. colored troops. 367 pp. 12°. *Boston, Lee & Shepard,* 1868.

Rollins (E. B.) A brief illustration of the prophecies and promises of God's word; concerning the kingdom of God. By the White mountain pilgrim. [*anon.*] 176 pp. 16°. *Dayton, (Ohio), author,* 1857. s.

Roman de la rose. *See* **Lorris** (Guillaume de) *and* **Meun** (Jeun de).

Romance (The) of William of Palerne: (otherwise known as the romance of "William and the werwolf"), translated from the French, about 1350; [with] a fragment of the alliterative romance of Alisaunder, translated from the Latin by the same author, about 1340. Edited by W. W. Skeat. xliv, 328 pp. 8°. *London, Trübner & co.* 1867.

[EARLY English text society publications. Extra series, 1867. No. 1].

Romero (José M.) Memoria sobre el distrito de Pachuca. 8°. *Mexico,* 1865.

[*In* ALMARAZ (R.) Memoria por la comision cientifica de Pachuca].

Romeu (Francisco, *editor*). *See* **Bible.** (*Spanish*).

Root (George I.) The musical fountain, enlarged; a collection of temperance music, for public and social meetings, and the home circle. 126 pp. 12°. *Chicago, Root & Cady,* 1867.

Ropes (Joseph). Linear perspective, for the use of schools and students in drawing. 4th ed. 40 pp. 8 pl. 8°. *Philadelphia, J. B. Lippincott & co.* 1868.

Roquette. *See* **La Roquette.**

Ros celestis. Hymelsche douwe. [*anon.*] cxl, 2 l. sm. 4°. *Coelne, H. Boemgart van Retwech,* 1516.

Rosales (Vicente Perez). Ensayo sobre Chile, escrito en frances i publicado en Hamburgo, i traducido al español, por Manuel Miquel. 510 pp. 1 tab. 2 maps. 8°. *Santiago, Ferrocarril,* 1859. s.

Roscoe (William Stanley). Poems. vii, 195 pp. 16°. *London, W. Pickering,* 1834.

Rose (George). The great country; or, impressions of America. xvi, 416 pp. 8°. *London, Tinsley bros.* 1868.

——— Mrs. Brown's visit to the Paris exhibition. By Arthur Sketchley. [*pseudon.*] vi, 138 pp. 16°. *London, George Routledge & sons,* [1868]?

Rose (Heinrich). Handbuch der analytischen chemie. v. 1. Die lehre von den qualitativen chemisch-analytischen untersuchungen. 3e aufl. xiv, 657 pp. 8°. *Berlin, E. S. Mittler,* 1833. s.

Rosecrans (William Starke). Report on the Chickamauga campaign. 8°. *Philadelphia,* 1864.

[*In* FITCH (John). Chickamauga, the price of Chattanooga. ed. 1864. pp. 703–716].

Rosemary (The), a collection of sacred and religious poetry, from the English and American poets, [etc.] 248 pp. 8 pl. 8°. *Philadelphia, Lindsay & Blakiston,* 1849. s.

Rosenheim *or* **Rosenhaym** (Petrus von). Roseum memoriale diuinorum eloquiorum. 47 l. sm. 4°. [*n. p. about* 1480].

[*With* CHAIMIS *or* CHAI (B.) Interrogatoriū siue cōfessionale. *Venetiis?* 1480].

Rosinus *or* **Rossfeld** (Johann). Antiqvitatvm romanarvm syntagma absolvtissimvm concinnatvm. Avctvm deinde et exornatvm à Thoma Dempstero, [etc.] Ed. nova. 16 p. l. 600 pp. 40 l. 4°. *Coloniæ Allobrogvm, G. Cartier,* 1613. s.

Rossetti (Christina). The prince's progress, and other poems. 2 p. l. viii, 216 pp. 16°. *London, Macmillan & co.* 1866.

Rossetti (Domenico de, *editor*). L'archeografo triestino. Raccolta di opuscoli e notizie per Trieste e per l'Istria, [dei Leandro Alberti, Francesco Berlingeri, Flavio Biondo, Andrea de Bonomo-Stetner, conte Gianrinaldo Carli, Carlo Catinelli, Pietro Contarini, Pietro Coppo, Giovanni Battista Goina, Pietro Kandler, Joel Kohen, Giovanni Labus, Luca da Linda, prof. Lugnani, Nicolo Manzuoli, Domenico di Rossetti, prof. Stadler, Pietro Tommasini, e Ludovico Vergerio]. 4 v. 8°. *Trieste, G. Marenigh,* 1829–37. s.

Rossetti (William Michael). Fine art, chiefly contemporary; notices reprinted with revisions. xx, 392 pp. 12°. *Cambridge, McMillan & co.* 1867.

Rossfeld (Johann). *See* **Rosinus** *or* **Rossfeld** (Johann).

Rossi (Guglielmo). Sulle istituzioni di istruzione primaria nella Lombardia, e in particolare nel circondario di Monza-Allocuzione, [etc.] 3ª ed. 101 pp. 4°. *Milano, P. Agnelli,* 1866. s.

Rösslin (Eucharius). De partv hominis, et qvae circa ipsvm accidunt. 67 l. 24°. *Francofurti, apud C. Egenolphum,* 1544.

Rossmässler (Emil Adolph). Der mensch im spiegel der natur. Ein volksbuch. 5 v. 16°. *Leipzig, E. Keil,* 1850–55.

[v. 1 and 3. 2e aufl.]

——— (*Editor*). *See* **Aus** der heimath.

Rostan (J. C.) La lyre chrétienne, recueil de psaumes, d' hymnes, etc. 75 pp. 16°. *New York, T. Holman,* 1857. s.

Roth (Carl Ludwig). Römischen inschriften des kantons Basel. 4°. *Basel, Schneider,* 1843. s.

[MITTHEILUNGEN der Gesselschaft für vaterländische altenthümer in Basel. Pt. 1].

Röth (Eduard). Geschichte unserer abendländischen philosophie. Entwicklungsgeschichte unserer spekulativen, sowohl philosophischen als religiösen ideen von ihren ersten anfängen bis auf die gegenwart. 2 v. in 3. x, 461, 291 pp; xlix, 984, 319 pp. 8°. *Mannheim, F. Bassermann,* 1846-58.

CONTENTS.

v. 1. Die ägyptische und die zoroastrische glaubenslehre, als die ältestenquellen unserer spekulativen ideen.

v. 2. Geschichte der griechischen philosophie. Die übertragung der orientalischen ideenkreise nach Griechenland, und ihre fortbildung durch die ältesten jonischen denker und Pythagoras.

Roth (Paul). Geschichte des beneficialwesens, von den ältesten zeiten bis ins zehnte jahrhundert. xx, 484 pp. 8°. *Erlangen, J. J. Palm and E. Enke,* 1850.

Roulin (François Désiré). Mammifères. (Races humaines). Atlas. *See* **Cuvier** (G. L. C. F. D.) Règne animal. v. 1. 1836-46.

Round the block. An American novel. With illustrations. [*anon.*] 468 pp. 3 pl. 12°. *New York, D. Appleton & co.* 1864.

Round (The) table. A Saturday review of politics, literature, society, and art. Jan. to June, 1868. v. 7. sm. fol. *New York,* 1868.

Rous (John) *and others.* *See* **New England** a degenerate plant.

Rouse (E. S. S.) The bugle blast; or, spirit of the conflict. Comprising naval and military exploits, anecdotes, etc. 336 pp. 12°. *Philadelphia, J. Challen & son,* 1864.

Rousseau (Jean Jacques). A dissertation on political economy: [with] a treatise on the social compact; or, the principles of politic law. 1st Am. ed. 72, 214 pp. 1 portrait. 16°. *Albany, Barber & Southwick,* 1797.

——— Supplément à la collection des œuvres de Rousseau. 3 v. 18°. *Genève,* 1784. s.

Rousset de Missy (Jean). History of the duke of Marlborough. *See* **Dumont** (J.) *and* **Rousset de Missy.**

Roux (Philibert Joseph). Secrétions; génération. *See* **Bichat** (M. F. X.) Traité d'anatomie descriptive. v. 5.

Roux (—— *sergeant-major*). Le nouveau Missisipi; ou, les dangers d'habiter les bords du Scioto, par un patriote voyageur. [*anon.*] 44 pp. 12°. *Paris, Jacquemart,* 1790.

Roux de Rochelle (Jean Baptiste Gaspard). La byzanciade, poëme, [etc. *anon.*] xxviii, 346 pp. 8°. *Paris, F. Didot,* 1822. s.

——— Les trois ages; ou, les jeux olympiques, l'amphithéatre, et la chevalerie. [*anon.*] 3 p. l. 288 pp. 12°. *Paris, F. Didot,* 1816. s.

Row (Augustus). Masonic biography and dictionary. 365 pp. 12°. *Philadelphia, Lippincott & co.* 1868.

Rowe (Nicholas R. C. *M. D.*) A treatise on catarrh, its causes and effects. 47 pp. 24°. *New York,* [*author*], 1868.

Rowley (*Rev.* Henry). The story of the universities' mission to Central Africa, from its commencement, under bishop Mackenzie, to its withdrawal from the Zambesi. xii, 493 pp. 8 pl. 2 maps. 8°. *London, Saunders, Otley & co.* 1866.

Roxburghe library. Publications. sm. 4°. *London,* 1868.

CONTENTS.

BROWNE (William). Works. v. 1.

Roxo de Flores (Felipe). Invectiva contra el luxo, su profanidad y excesos por medio de proprias reflexiones que persuaden su inutilidad. Descripcion histórica y circumstanciada de los trages y adornos de diversas naciones, etc. 2ª ed. 8 p. l. 110 pp. 16°. *Madrid, imprenta real,* 1804. s.

Royaards (Herman Jan). Geschiedenis der invoering en vestiging van het christendom in Nederland. 3e uitg. xiv, 414 pp. 8°. *Utrecht, C. Van der Post, jr.* 1844. s.

Royal academy of Spain. *See* **Real** academia española.

Royal agricultural society of England. Journal. 2d series. v. 4. 8°. *London, J. Murray,* 1868.

Royal college of surgeons, England. Calendar. July 9, 1868. xvi, 317 pp. 8°. *London, Taylor & Francis,* 1868. s.

Royal (The) family of the Stuarts vindicated from the false imputation of illegitimacy, etc. [*anon.*] 44 pp. 8°. *London,* 1722.
[*With* DORLÉANS (P. J.) History of the revolutions in England. 1722].

Royal microscopical society. Transactions. New series. v. 1–5, 8–16. 8°. *London, J. Churchill & sons,* 1853–68.
[*With* QUARTERLY journal of microscopical science. 1853–68].

Royall (*Mrs.* Anne). The black book; or, a continuation of travels in the United States. 3 v. 12°. *Washington, author,* 1828–29.

——— The Tennessean; a novel, founded on facts. 372 pp. 16°. *New-Haven, author,* 1827.

Royce (M. S.) A series of brief historical sketches of the church of England, and of the protestant episcopal church in the United States. 198 pp. 16°. *New York, F. D. Harriman,* 1859. s.

Rucellai (Giovanni). Le api. Con annotazioni di R. Titi. 8°. *Milano,* 1804.
[*In* ALAMANNI (L.) La coltivazione. 1804].

Rückert (Heinrich). Culturgeschichte des deutschen volkes in der zeit des uebergangs aus dem heidenthum in das christenthum. 2 v. viii, 354 pp; vii, 527 pp. 8°. *Leipzig, T. O. Weigel,* 1853–54.

Ruddiman (Thomas). The rudiments of the Latin tongue; or, a plain and easy introduction to Latin grammar. viii, 104 pp. 16°. *Glasgow, J. Duncan & R. Farie,* 1781.

——— The same. With an essay on grammatical studies. 24th ed. xviii, 10–144 pp. 18°. *Glasgow, W. Smith,* 1782.

——— The same. 21st genuine ed. 112, 32 pp. 18°. *Edinburgh, Bell & Bradfute,* 1793.

Rudge (Thomas). General view of the agriculture of the county of Gloucester. viii, 408 pp. 3 maps. 3 pl. 8°. *London,* 1807. s.
[GREAT BRITAIN. Board of agriculture].

Rueckert. *See* **Rückert.**

Ruffin (Edmund). Agricultural, geological, and descriptive sketches of lower North Carolina, and the similar adjacent lands. 296 pp. 8°. *Raleigh, institution for the deaf, dumb, and blind,* 1861.

Ruge (Arnold). Acht reden über die religion "an die gebildeten unter ihren verehrern." 90 pp. 16°. *St. Louis, freien gemeinde,* 1868.

Ruggles (Samuel B.) Resources of the United States. Report to the international statistical congress, at Berlin, Sept. 1863. 30 pp. 8°. *New York,* 1864.
[LOYAL publication society. no. 48].

Rumpf (Christian). Dictionnaire technologique français, allemand, anglais, [etc.] *See* **Beil** (J. A.) Technologisches wörterbuch. v. 3].

Ruprecht (F. J.) Tange des ochotskischen meeres. 4°. *St. Petersburg,* 1851. s.
[*In* MIDDENDORFF (A. T. von). Reise, etc. v. 1. theil 2].

Rusconi (Mauro). Del proteo anguino. 4°. 1819. *See* **Configliachi** (P.) *and* **Rusconi.**

Ruskin (John, *LL. D.*) Time and tide, by weare and tyne. Twenty-five letters to a working man of Sunderland on the laws of work. 2d ed. viii, 199 pp. 18°. *London, Smith, Elder & co.* 1868.

Russell (*Rev.* David). Letters, chiefly practical and consolatory; designed to illustrate the nature and tendency of the gospel. 3d ed. 2 v. 4 p. l. 295 pp; 3 p. l. 353 pp. 12°. *Edinburgh, Waugh & Innes,* 1825.

Russell (John). The boke of nurture followyng Englondis gise. Edited from the ms. by F. J. Furnivall. 8°. *London,* 1868.
[*In* FURNIVALL (F. J.) Babees book, etc. pp. 115-228. Early English text-society publications. no. 32].

Russell (William). A letter to Joseph Priestley. 8°. *London,* 1792.
[*In* PRIESTLEY (J.) An appeal to the public, on the subject of the riots in Birmingham. part ii].

Russell (William S.) Pilgrim memorials, and guide for visitors to Plymouth village, [etc.] viii, 148 pp. 1 map. 7 pl. 12°. *Boston, author,* 1851. s.

Russia (*Imperatorskaia publitchnaiá biblioteka*). Catalogue des acquisitions de livres imprimés. Sept.–Dec. 1863. Catalogue des nouvelles acquisitions en langues étrangères. Jan.–Juin, 1864 [—] Juillet–Déc. 1865. 10 title pages. [Russian and French]. 462 pp. 8°. *St. Pétersbourg, W. Rogalski & co.* 1864–66. s.

——— ——— Catalogue des livres doubles de la bibliothèque impériale publique de St. Petersbourg. [French and Russian]. v. 1. x, 350 pp. 1 l. 8°. *St. Pétersbourg,* 1850. s.

——— ——— Wegweiser der kaiserlichen bibliothek zu St. Petersburg. iv, 52 pp. 12°. *St. Petersburg, buchdruckerei der k. akademie der wissenschaften,* 1860. s.

——— [*Imperial botanical garden*]. Catalogus systematicus bibliothecae horti imperialis botanici petropolitani. Curavit Ernestus de Berg. xvi, 514 pp. 8°. *Petropoli, typis academiae caes. scientiarum,* 1852. s.

Rusticiano *or* **Rustichiello.** I viaggi di Marco Polo. *See* **Polo** (M.)

Rüstow (Wilhelm). Heerwesen und kriegführung C. Julius Cäsars. xv, 184 pp. 4 pl. 8°. *Gotha, H. Scheube,* 1855. s.

Ruth Derwent: a story of duty and love. By C. J. G. [*anon.*] 320 pp. 3 pl. 16°. *Boston, American tract society,* [1867].

Rutherford (*Rev.* Samuel). Manna-crumbs for hungry souls. Excerpts from his letters gathered by W. P. Breed, *D. D.* 168 pp. 16°. *Philadelphia, presbyterian board,* 1865.

Ruysch (Frederik). Opera omnia anatomico-medico-chirurgica. 45 v. in 3. 4°. *Amstelodami, apud Janssonio-Waesbergias,*1720-35. s.

CONTENTS.

BOERHAAVE (Hermann) *and* RUYSCH (Frederik). Opusculum anatomicum de fabrica glandularum in corpore humano. 1733. [n. 42].

BOHL *or* BOHLIUS (Johann Christoph). Tractatio anatomica de musculo in fundi uteri observato, etc. 1726. [n. 36]. Dissertatio epistolica de usu nouarum cavae propaginum in systemate chylopoeo, ut et de corticis cerebri textura. 1727. [n. 37].

CAMPDOMERCUS (Jan Jakob). Epistola de glandulis, fibris, cellulisque lienalibus. 1725. [n. 20].

ETTMÜLLER (Michael Ernst). Epistola de cerebri corticali substantia. 1721. [n. 27]. Epistola de ovario novo. 1729. [n. 41].

FRENTZ (Gerard). Epistola de vasis sanguiferis periostii tibiæ, etc. 1725. [n. 21].

GAUB *or* GAUBIUS (Jan). Epistola de pilis, pinguedine, septoque scroti, etc. 1724. [n. 19].

GÖLICKE (Andreas Ottomar). Epistola de cursu arteriarum per piam matrem, etc. 1724. [n. 25].

GRÄTZ (Albrecht Heinrich). Epistola de vasorum sanguineorum extremitatibus, placentæ uterinæ, mammarumque structura, etc. 1722. [no. 31].

GRÄTZ (Jan Henrik). Epistola de arteria et vena bronchiali, etc. 1731. [n. 22]. Epistola de pia matre, ejusque processibus. 1724. [n. 23]. Epistola de structura nasi cartilaginea [et aure interna]. 1724. [n. 24].

HECQUET (Philippe). Epistola de rvyschiano vteri mvscvlo. 1727. [n. 39].

KEERWOLFF (Bartel). Epistola de auricularum cordis, [etc.] structura. 1725. [n. 26].

RAU (Jan Jakob). Responsio ad qualemcunque defensionem Frederici Ruyschii pro septo scroti. 1721. [n. 34]. Epistola de inventoribus septi scroti. 1721. [n. 35].

RUYSCH (Frederik). Dilucidatio valvularum in vasis lymphaticis, et lacteis. 1732. [n. 1]. Observationum anatomico-chirurgicarum centuria. Ac. catalogus rariorum in museo ruyschiano. 1721. [n. 2]. Adversariorum anatomico-medico-chirurgicorum decas i. 1729. [n. 3]; *ib.* decas ii. 1720. [n. 4]; *ib.* decas iii. 1723. [n. 5]. Thesaurus anatomicus i. 1721. [n. 6]; *ib.* ii. 1722. [n. 7]; *ib.* iii. 1724. [n. 8]; *ib.* iv. 1724. [n. 9]; *ib.* v. 1725. [n. 10]; *ib.* vi. 1724. [n. 11]; *ib.* vii. 1726. [n. 12]; *ib.* viii. 1727. [n. 13]; *ib.* ix. 1726. [n. 14]; *ib.* x. 1729. [n. 15]; curae posteriores seu thesaurus anatomicus [xi]. 1724. [n. 16]. Curæ renovatae. 1727. [n. 17]. Thesaurus animalium i. 1725. [n. 18]. Responsio ad Godefridi Bidloi libellum, etc. 1721. [n. 33]. Responsio ad dissertationem epistolicam Jo. Christoph Bohlii, etc. 1727. [n. 38].

SCHREIBER (Jan Frederik). Historia vitae Frederici Ruyschii. 1732.

VAN REVERHORST (Maurice). Epistola de nova artuum decurtandorum methodo. 1732. [n. 30].

VATER *or* VATERUS (Abram). Epistola viis absconditis pulmonum, etc. 1727. [n. 32]. Epistola gratulatoria ad Ruyschium in qua de mvscvlo orbiscvlari in fvndo vteri detecto gratvlatvr. 1727. [n. 40].

WEDEL *or* WEDELIUS (Christiaan). Epistola de oculorum tunicis. 1720. [n. 29].

WOLF (Jan Christiaan). Epistola de intestinorum tunicis, glandulis, etc. 1721. [n. 27].

Ryther (*Rev.* John). The seaman's preacher; consisting of nine discourses on Jonah's voyage. With a preface by Rev. J. Newton. xi, 111 pp. 16°. *Cambridge, (Mass.) W. Hilliard,* 1806.

[pp. 109-11 imperfect].

Saadi. *See* **Sadi.**

Saavedra Faxardo (Diego). Idea principis christiano-politici 100 symbolis expressa. 12 p. l. 800 pp. 24°. *Coloniæ, C. Munich,* 1650.

Sabas (*Bishop of Mojaisk*). Sacristie patriarcale dite synodale, de Moscou. 2e éd. revue, corrigée et augmentée, avec xv tables photographiées et gravées sur pierre des objets les plus remarquables de la sacristie. 3 p. l. 32, 2, ii, 1 l. 15 pl. 4°. *Moscou,* 1865. s.

——— Specimina palaeographica codicum graecorum et slavonicorum bibliothecæ mosquensis synodialis, saec. vi—xvii. [Russian and Latin]. 1 p. l. iv, 46 pp. 2 illum. titles. 47 13 pl. 4°. *Moskva, Goteā,* 1863. s.

Sabbath (The) at home; an illustrated religious magazine for the family. Jan. to Dec. 1868. v. 2. 8°. *Boston, American tract society,* [1868].

Sachsse (Carl Robert). Historische grundlagen des deutschen staats- und rechtslebens. Vorstudien zur deutschen staats- und rechtsgeschichte. xviii, 604 pp. 8°. *Heidelberg, C. F. Winter,* 1844.

Saco (José Antonio). Obras. [Escritos sobre las questiones mas vitales sobre la suerte de Cuba, etc.] Compiladas por primera vez, por un paisano del autor. [F. J. Vingut]. v. 1. 343 pp. 12°. *Nueva York, R. Lockwood & hijo,* 1853. s.

Sacy (Claude Louis Michel de). L'honneur françois, ou histoire des vertus et des exploits de notre nation, depuis l'établissement de la monarchie jusqu'à nos jours. 2e éd. 12 v. 16°. *Paris, Nyon,* 1783.

Saddi (Nathan Ben, *pseudon.*) *See* **Dodsley** (Robert).

Sadi, *or* Moslik-ed dín Sadí Ben Abdallah. Der fruchtgarten. Aus dem persischen auszugsweise übertragen durch O. M. freiherrn von Schlechta-Wssehrd. 233 pp. 1 pl. 8°. *Wien, k. k. hof- und staatsdruckerei,* 1852. s.

Saga. *See* **Fagrskrinna**; *also,* **Karlamagnus** saga; *also,* **Olafs** konungs ens helga.

Sage (Rufus B.) Scenes in the Rocky Mountains, and in Oregon, California, New Mexico, Texas, and the grand prairies; or, notes by the way during an excursion of three years. By a New Englander. [*anon.*] 303 pp. 12°. *Philadelphia, Carey & Hart,* 1846.

Sagra (Ramon de la). *See* **La Sagra.**

Sainte-Beuve (Charles Augustin). Portraits of celebrated women. From the French. By H. W. Preston. 11, 384 pp. portrait. 16°. *Boston, Roberts bros.* 1868.

Saint-Hyacinthe (Hyacinthe Cordonnier, *known as chevalier* de Thémiseul de). Matanasiana, ou mémoires littéraires, historiques et critiques du docteur Matanasius. [*pseudon.*] 2 v. 19 p. l. 479 pp. 2 pl. 16°. *La Haye, veuve de Charles Le Vier,* 1760.

Saintine (Joseph Xavier Boniface, *known as*). Le chemin des écoliers. Promenade de Paris à Marly-le-Roy, en suivant les bords du Rhin. Avec vignettes par G. Doré, Foster, etc. 634 pl. 8°. *Paris, Hachette & co.* 1861.

Saint John (*Mrs.* Horace Roscoe). Masaniello of Naples. The record of a nine-days revolution. viii, 304 pp. 12°. *London, Tinsley bros.* 1865.

Saint Petersburgh. *Imperatorskaia publitchnaia biblioteca. See* **Russia.**

Saint Pierre (Jacques Henri Bernardin de). Voyage to the island of Mauritius, (or, Isle of France), the Isle of Bourbon, the Cape of Good Hope, etc. By a French officer. [*anon.*] Translated from the French by J. Parish. 6 p. l. 291 pp. 8°. *London, W. Griffin,* 1775.

Saiz (Manuel Cecilio). Methodo castellano para aprender el idioma latino. 8 p. l. 429 pp. 16°. *Madrid, imprenta de la Gazeta,* [*n. d. before* 1800]. S.

Sala (George Augustus). From Waterloo to the peninsula. Four months' hard labor in Belgium, Holland, Germany, and Spain. 2 v. xiii, 339 pp; viii, 340 pp. 12°. *London, Tinsley bros.* 1867.

——— Notes and sketches of the Paris exhibition. 367 pp. 8°. *London, Tinsley bros.* 1868.

——— William Hogarth: painter, engraver, and philosopher. Essays on the man, the work, and the time. 318 pp. 6 pl. 12°. *London, Smith, Elder & co.* 1866.

Salas (Pedro de). Compendium latino-hispanum. *See* **Bravo** (B.) Compendium, etc.

Sale (George). A preliminary discourse. *See* **Koran** (The). 1850.

Salem (*Massachusetts*). The Salem directory, 1869. By Sampson, Davenport & co. 344 pp. 1 map. 8°. *Salem, Whipple & Smith,* [1868].

Salem athenæum. Catalogue of the library. xvi, 171 pp. 8°. *Salem, office of the gazette,* 1842.

Sales (*Saint* Francis de). *See* **Francis** de Sales.

Salis (Johann Gaudenz, *freiherr von Salis-Securis*). Gedichte. Neue [4e] aufl. viii, 164 pp. 1 portrait. 8°. *Zürich, Orell, Füssli & co.* 1808. S.

Salle (Jean Baptiste). L'entrée de Danton aux enfers. Poème inédit. Publié d'après le ms. original par G. Moreau-Chaslon. xi, 52 pp. 12°. *Paris, J. Miard,* 1865.

Salm-Reifferscheid-Dyck (Constance Marie de Théis, *princesse* de). Oeuvres complètes. 4 v. 8°. *Paris, F. Didot freres,* [&] *A. Bertrand,* 1842. S.

CONTENTS:

v. 1. Épitres. Discours. 2 p. l. xxiv, 312 pp. 1 portrait.
v. 2. Sapho. Cantate. Poésies diverses. 2 p. l. 331 pp. 1 pl.
v. 3. Vingt-quatre heures d'une femme sensible. Pensées. 2 p. l. 334 pp. 1 pl.
v. 4. Éloges. Rapports. Notice. Mes soixante ans. 2 p. l. 354 pp. 1 pl.

——— Mes soixante ans, ou mes souvenirs politiques et littéraires. 2 p. l. iv, 63 pp. 8°. *Paris, A. Bertrand* [&] *Didot,* 1844. S.

——— Pensées. 3e éd. 2 p. l. v, 180 pp. 1 portrait. 8°. *Paris, Didot* [&] *A. Bertrand,* 1836. S.

——— Vingt-quatre heures d'une femme sensible, ou une grande leçon. 3e éd. 2 p. l. 147 pp. 1 pl. 8°. *Paris, Didot* [&] *A. Bertrand,* 1836. S.

Salmon (Pierre). Mémoires. 1 p. l. xxix, 130 pp. 8°. *Paris, Verdière,* 1826.

[Collection de chroniques nationales françaises. v. 25].

Salmon (William, *M. D.*). Synopsis medicinæ; or, a compendium of astrological, galenical, and chymical physick. 3 v. in 2. 18°. *London, R. Jones,* 1671.

[Imperfect: wanting 1 l. at the end of v. 3].

Salvolini (François). Analyse grammaticale raisonnée de différens textes anciens égyptiens. v. 1. Texte hiéroglyphique et démotique de la pierre de Rosette. xxxii, 256 pp. 1 l. 4°. *Paris, ve. Dondey-Dupré,* 1836. S.

[Atlas wanting].

Samson (George Whitefield, *D. D.*) Elements of art criticism, comprising a treatise on the principles of man's nature as addressed by art, etc. Abridged ed. 408 pp. 9 pl. 12°. *Philadelphia, J. B. Lippincott & co.* 1868.

Sanchez *or* **Sancius** de Arevalo (Rodriguez). Speculum vite humane in quo discutiuntur cōmoda et incōmoda, dulcia et amara, solatia et miseriæ, prospera et aduersa, laudes et pericula omniū statuum. 14 p. l. xci l. fol. *Argentina, J. Prys,* 1507.

Sanders (*Dr.* Daniel). Wörterbuch der deutschen sprache. Mit belegen von Luther bis auf die gegenwart. 2 v. in 3. 1 p. l. 1065 pp; 1 p. l. pp. 1–825; viii, pp. 826–1828. 4°. *Leipzig, O. Wigand*, 1859–65. s.

Sandford (Francis). The history of the coronation of James ii, king of England, Scotland, France, and Ireland, and of his consort, queen Mary: Westminster, 23d of April, 1685. 5 p. l. 135 pp. 30 pl. fol. *London, T. Newcomb*, 1687.

Sandifort (Eduard *and* Gerard). Mvsevm anatomicvm. *See* **Leyden.**

Sanford (Henry S.) The different systems of penal codes in Europe; also, a report on the administrative changes in France, since the revolution of 1848. 404 pp. 8°. *Washington, senate printer*, 1854.

San Francisco (*City of*). Annual report of the superintendent of public schools, [etc.] 1867. John C. Pelton, superintendent. 239 pp. 8 pl. on 5 l. 8°. *San Francisco, J. Winterburn & co.* 1867. s.

——— Municipal reports, 1866–7. 530 pp. 2 maps. 2 pl. 8°. *San Francisco, Winterburn & co.* 1867.

San Francisco (The) directory for the year commencing Sept. 1862, [etc.] Compiled by Henry G. Langley. lxiv, 639 pp. 1 map. 8°. *San Francisco, Valentine & co.* 1862. s.

——— The same, for 1868–9. Compiled by H. G. Langley. cxii, 883 pp. 1 map. 8°. *San Francisco, H. G. Langley*, 1868.

Sanson (Nicolas, *of Abbeville*). L'Ameriqve, en plvsieurs cartes novvelles, et exactes, etc. en divers traitez de géographie, et d'histoire. 1 p. l. 112 pp. 15 maps. 4°. *Paris, chez l'avtevr*, [*about* 1650].

Sante Bartoli *or* **Santes da Bortola** (Pietro). *See* **Bartoli.**

Santi *or* **Sanzio da Urbino** (Raffaello). La favola di Amore e Psiche, [etc.] incisi all'aquaforte da Luigi Fabri. 1 p. l. 31 pl. obl. 8°. *Roma, presso l'Incisore*, 1811. s.

Sargant (William Lucas). Apology for sinking funds. vi, 247 pp. 8°. *London, Williams & Norgate*, 1868.

Sargent (Epes). Life of Thomas Campbell. 12°. *Boston*, 1854.

[*In* CAMPBELL (T.) Poetical works. 1854. pp. 1–101].

——— Standard series of speakers. No. 2. The intermediate standard speaker. 432 pp. 12°. *Philadelphia, C. Desilver*, 1857. s.

Sarmiento (Domingo Faustino). Life in the Argentine republic in the days of the tyrants; or, civilization and barbarism. With a biographical sketch of the author, by Mrs. Horace Mann. 400 pp. 1 portrait. 12°. *New York, Hurd & Houghton*, 1868.

——— Vida de Facundo Quiroga, i aspecto fisico, costumbres i hábitos de la república arjentina, seguida de apuntes biograficos sobre el general frai Felix Aldao. 2a ed. 2 p. l. viii, 374, xlvi pp. 8°. *Santiago, J. Belin i co.* 1851. s.

Sars (Michael). Beskrivelser og iagttagelser over nogle mærkelige eller nye i havet ved den bergenske kyst lebende dyr af polypernes, acalephernes, radiaternes, annelidernes, og molluskernes classer, [etc]. xii, 81 pp. 15 pl. 4°. *Bergen, C. Dahl*, 1835. s.

——— Om siphodentalium vitreum, en ny slægt og art af dentalidernes familie. 30 pp. 3 pl. 4°. *Christiania, Brogger & Christie*, 1861. s.

——— **Koren** (Johan) *and* **Danielssen** (Daniel Cornelius). Fauna littoralis Norvegiæ. [Danish and French]. 2t hefte [or] 2e livraison. 4 p. l. 101 pp. 12 pl. fol. *Bergen, F. B. Deyer*, 1856. s.

[v. 1, in German, by Sars, 1846, wanting].

Sartoris (*Mrs.* Adelaide Kemble). Medusa, and other tales. [*anon.*] 3 p. l. 228 pp. 1 pl. 8°. *London, Smith, Elder & co.* 1868.

Saturday (The) review of politics, literature, science, and art. Jan. to Dec. 1868. v. 25–26. fol. *London*, [*D. Jones*], 1868.

Saunders (Frederick). About woman, love, and marriage. 319 pp. 12°. *New York, G. W. Carleton*, 1868.

Saunders (William). An essay on the culture of the native and exotic grape. 18°. *Philadelphia, Lippincott & co.* 1860.

[BOTH sides of the grape question. ed. 1860. pp. 5–54].

Saussure (Henri de) *and* **Sichel** (Jules). Hymenoptera. Familien der vespiden, sphegiden, pompiliden, crabroniden und heterogynen. Bearbeitet von dr. Henri de Saussure. Hymenoptera fossoria et mellifera. Supplement von J. Sichel. 156 pp. 4 l. 4 pl. 8°. *Wien*, 1868. s.

[WÜLLERSTORF-URBAIR (B. von). Reise der Novara. Zoologischer theil. v. 2. abth. 1 A].

Sauvage (Élie). The little gypsy. Illustrated by Lorenz Frölich. Translated from the French by J. M. Luyster. 133 pp. 5 pl. sm. 4°. *Boston, Roberts brothers*, 1868.

Sauvageot (Claude). Palais, chateaux, hotels, et maisons de France du xve au xviiie siècle. [Illustrated]. 4 v. fol. *Paris, A. Morel*, 1867.

Sauvigny (L. Edme). *See* **Billardon de Sauvigny** (L. E.)

Savage (John). Fenian heroes and martyrs. With an historical introduction on the struggle for Irish nationality. 461 pp. 11 pl. 12°. *Boston, P. Donahoe,* 1868.

Savage (M. W.) My uncle the curate. A novel. [*anon.*] 5th ed. 294 pp. 16°. *London, Chapman & Hall,* 1867.

Savage (The) club papers. Edited by A. Halliday. xvi, 341 pp. 19 pl. 12°. *London, Tinsley bros.* 1867.

Savile (John Horace, *viscount Pollington*). Half round the old world. Being some account of a tour in Russia, the Caucasus, Persia, and Turkey, 1865–66. 2 p. l. 403 pp. 1 map. 8°. *London, E. Moxon & co.* 1867.

Savin (Una, *pseudon?*) The little gentleman in green: a fairy tale. 103 pp. 4 pl. 16°. *Boston, Loring,* 1865.

Savonarola (Girolamo Maria Francesco Matteo). Expositio vel meditatio in psalmum: in te Domine speravi. 9 l. sm. 4°. [*Vlma, J. Schäffeler? about* 1499].

Saxe (John Godfrey). Poems. xii, 465 pp. portrait. 16°. *Boston, Ticknor & Fields,* 1868.

Saxony. Codex diplomaticus Saxoniæ regiæ. Im auftrage der k. sächsischen staatsregierung herausgegeben von E. G. Gersdorf. 2e haupttheil. [*or*] Urkundenbuch des hochstifts Meissen, [etc.] 2 v. 4°. *Leipzig, Giesecke & Devrient,* 1864–65. s.

——— *Statistische bureau des ministeriums des innern.* Statistische mittheilungen aus dem königreich Sachsen, [etc.] 3 v. 4°. *Dresden,* 1851–54. s.

CONTENTS.

v. 1. Stand der bevölkerung, (3 Dec. 1849).
v. 2. Bewegung der bevölkerung, (1834–1850).
v. 3. Bevölkerung und industrie.

——— ——— Zeitschrift des statistischen bureaus des k. sächsischen ministeriums des innern. (Redigirt von dr. Ernst Engel, 1855–57). 1r–12r jahrgang. 11 v. 4°. *Leipzig, H. Hübner, B. G. Teubner,* 1855–66. s.
[Jahrg. 8, 1862, wanting].

Sayous (A.) Recueil de morceaux choisis pour servir à l'étude de la langue française, [etc.] 3e éd. 222 pp. 18°. *Genève, J. Kessmann,* 1853. s.

Scawen (John). New Spain; or, love in Mexico: an opera in three acts. [*anon.*] 2 p. l. 61 pp. 8°. *London, G. G. J. & J. Robinson,* 1790.

Schaeffer. *See* **Schäffer.**

Schaeffner. *See* **Schäffner.**

Schafarik (Paul Joseph). Elemente der altböhmischen grammatik. 2 p. l. 144 pp. 8°. *Leipsig,* 1847.

Schaff (Philip, *D. D.*) Christ in song. Hymns of Immanuel: selected from all ages, with notes. xxiv, 711 pp. sm. 4°. *New York, A. D. F. Randolph & co.* 1869.

Schäffer (Gottlieb August Willhelm Herrich-). Index alphabetico-synonymicus insectorum hemipterorum heteropterorum, [etc.] 1 p. l. 210 pp. 8°. *Regensburg, G. J. Manz,* 1853. s.

——— Synonymia lepidopterorum Europæ. Systematisches und synonymisches verzeichniss der europäischen schmetterlinge. Separatabdruck aus der Systematischen bearbeitung [etc.] 2 p. l. 72, 24, 64, 34, 48, 52, 48 pp. 4°. *Regensburg, G. J. Manz,* 1856. s.

——— Systematische bearbeitung der schmetterlinge von Europa, zugleich als text, revision und supplement zu Jakob Hübner's Sammlung europäischer schmetterlinge. 6 v. 4°. *Regensburg, G. J. Manz,* 1843–56. s.

CONTENTS.

v. 1. Tagfalter, etc. 164 pp.
v. 2. Die schwärmer, spinner und eulen. 165–450 pp. 1845.
v. 3. Die spanner. 1 p. l. 184 pp. 1847–48.
v. 4. Die zünsler und wickler. 1 p. l. 288 pp. 1849.
v. 5. Die schaben und federmotten. 1 p. l. 394 pp. 1853–55.
v. 6. 36 umrisstafeln mit erklärung. Nachträge. Systema lepidopterorum. Index, [etc.] 3 p. l. 178, 72, 24, 64, 34, 48, 52, 48 pp. 1843–56.
[v. 1, and plates, wanting].

Schäffner (Wilhelm). Geschichte der rechtsverfassung Frankreichs. Bis auf unsere zeit. 4 v. 8°. *Frankfurt am Main, J. D. Sauerländer,* 1845–50.

Schaub (Franz). Fluthbeobachtungen. Magnetische beobachtungen. 4°. *Wien,* 1862–65.
[*In* WÜLLERSTORF-URBAIR (B. von). Reise der öst. fregatte Novara. Nautisch-physikalischer theil].

——— Leitfaden für den unterricht in der nautischen astronomie in der kais. kön. marine. 2e aufl. viii, 229 pp. 12°. *Wien, C. Gerold's sohn,* 1860. s.

Schaum (Hermann Rudolph). Hemiptera und orthoptera [von Mossambique]. fol. *Berlin,* 1862.
[*In* PETERS (W. C. H.) Nat. reise nach Mossambique. v. 5].

Schefer (Leopold). Laienbrevier. 2e aufl. 2 v. in 1. 3 p. l. 305 pp; 1 p. l. 408 pp. 12°. *Berlin, Veit & co.* 1837. s.

——— The same. 11e aufl. xvi, 528 pp. 1 portrait. 16°. *Berlin, Veit & co.* 1856. s.

Schelekoff (Grigorij). Erste und zweyte reise von Oschotsk in Sibirien durch den ostlichen ocean nach den küsten von Amerika, 1783–89. Aus dem Russischen übersetzt von J. Z. Logan. 104 pp. 8°. *St. Petersburg, J. Z. Logan,* 1793.

Schelhorn (Johann Georg, *the first*). Amoenitates literariæ, quibus variæ observationes, scripta item quædam anecdota et rariora opuscula exhibentur. 14 v. in 7. 12°. *Francofurti et Lipsiæ, D. Bartholomæi & fil.* 1725–31. s.

Scheliha (——— von). A treatise on coast-defence: based on the experience gained by engineers of the army of the Confederate states, and compiled from official reports of officers of the navy of the U. S. 1861–65. xviii, 326 pp. 12 pl. 8°. *London, E. & F. N. Spon*, 1868.

Scherer (H.) Der sundzoll, seine geschichte, sein jetziger bestand und seine staatsrechtlich-politische lösung. Nebst einem anhang über die sundzollfreiheit der pommerschen und preussischen städte. Als beilagen die auf den sundzoll bezüglichen verträge, [etc.] viii, 332 pp. 1 map. 8°. *Berlin, Duncker & Humblot*, 1845.

Scherpf (G. A.) Entstehungsgeschichte und gegenwärtiger zustand des neuen staates Texas. vii, 154 pp. 2 maps. 8°. *Augsburg, M. Rieger*, 1841.

Scherzer (Carl). Statistisch-commercieller theil [der Reise der Novara]. 2 v. 4°. *Wien*, 1864–65. s.

[WÜLLERSTORF-URBAIR (B. von). Reise der Novara].

Scheuchzer (Johann Jacob). Kupfer-bibel, in welcher die physica sacra, oder geheiligte natur-wissenschafft derer in heil. schrifft vorkommenden natürlichen sachen, deutlich erklärt und bewährt. Anbey zur erläuterung und zierde des wercks in künstlichen kupfertafeln ausgegeben und verlegt durch J. A. Pfeffel. 4 v. in 5. fol. *Augspurg u. Ulm, C. U. Wagner*, 1731–35.

Schildener (Carl). Das gottesbewusstsein im volksrechte der Germanen, nebst einigen betrachtungen verwandter art über die neuere zeit. Bruchstücke aus [seinen] papieren. 50 pp. 8°. *Greifswald, C. A. Koch*, 1839.

Schiller (Johann Christoph Friedrich von). Briefwechsel mit Körner. Von 1784 bis zum tode Schillers. 4 v. 8°. *Berlin*, 1847. s.

——— Maria Stuart; ein trauerspiel. 5ᵉ aufl. 200 pp. 16°. *Tübingen, J. G. Cotta*, 1815. s.

——— The same. Maria Stuartka. Swobodně z nemeckého prelozil Pawel Jozef Saffarjk. 222 pp. 12°. *w Praze, M. B. Neuretter*, 1831. s.

——— Schiller's leben. *See* **Wolzogen** (Caroline von).

——— Trauerspiele. Neue original aufl. 3 v. in 1. 12°. *Mannheim, C. F. Schwan & G. C. Götz*, 1786–88. s.

Schiller—continued.

CONTENTS.

Die räuber. 166 pp. 1786.
Die verschwörung des fiesko zu Genua. 175 pp. 1788.
Kabale und liebe. 2 p. l. 167 pp. 1786.

Schiner (*Dr.* J. R.) Diptera. iii–vi, 388 pp. 4 l. 4 pl. 4°. *Wien*, 1868. s.

[WÜLLERSTORF-URBAIR (B. von). Reise der Novara. Zoologischer theil. v. 2. abth. 1 B].

Schivardi (Plinio). Manuale teorico pratico di elettroterapia. Esposizione critico-sperimentale di tutte le applicazioni elettrojatriche. 492 pp. 16°. *Milano, editori della biblioteca [medica moderna]*, 1864. s.

Schlegel (Carl Wilhelm Friedrich von). The philosophy of history, in a course of lectures. [From the German]. With a memoir of the author, by J. B. Robertson. 2 v. 319 pp; 302 pp. 16°. *New York, Appletons*, 1841.

Schlegel (Hermann). Abbildungen neuer oder unvollständig bekannter amphibien, [etc.] xiv, 141 pp. 8°. Atlas. 50 col. pl. fol. *Düsseldorf, Arnz & co.* 1837–44. s.

——— Essai sur la physionomie des serpens. 2 v. in 1. 3 p. l. xxviii, 251 pp; 2 p. l. 606, xvi pp. 8°. Atlas. 2 p. l. 2 tab. 1 col. map. 21 pl. fol. *Amsterdam, M. H. Schonekat*, 1837. s.

Schlegel (Johann F. Wilhelm von). The origin and history of the Danish sound and belt-tolls. From the Danish, by George P. Marsh. 8°. [*New York*, 1844].

[Extract from Hunt's merchant's magazine. v. 10. pp. 218–232].

[*With* SCHERER (H.) Der sundzoll. 1845].

Schleicher (August). Beiträge zur vergleichenden sprachforschung, etc. *See* **Kuhn** (Adalbert).

——— Linguistische untersuchungen. ii. Die sprachen Europas in systematischer uebersicht. x, 270 pp. 8°. *Bonn, H. B. König*, 1850.

Schleiden (Matthias Jacob). Das alter des menschengeschlechts, die entstehung der arten, und die stellung des menschen in der natur. Drei vorträge für gebildete laien. 62 pp. 8°. *Leipzig, W. Engelmann*, 1863.

Schleiden (Rudolf). L'intérêt de la France dans la question du Schleswig-Holstein, suivi d'un aperçu historique sur cette question, [etc. *anon.*] 112 pp. 8°. *Paris, F. Didot*, 1850. s.

Schleiermacher (Friedrich Ernst Daniel). Ueber die religion. Reden an die gebildeten unter ihren verächtern. 4ᵉ aufl. xiv, 322 pp. 8°. *Berlin, G. Reimer*, 1831. s.

Schletter (Hermann Theodor, *editor*). *See* **Akademische** monatsschrift.

Schlosser (Friedrich Christoph). Weltgeschichte für das deutsche volk. Unter mitwirkung des verfassers bearbeitet von G. L. Kriegk. [Mit einem register]. 19 v. in 9. 8°. *Frankfurt a M:* 1844-57.

CONTENTS.

v. 1-4. Geschichte der alten welt.
Orientalische völker. v. 1.
Völker der griechisch-römischen zeit.
Griechen. v. 1-3.
Römer. v. 3-4.
v. 5-8. Geschichte des mittelalters.
Die ersten zeiten des mittelalters. v. 5.
Die zeit von Karl dem grossen an bis zum beginn der kreuzzüge. v. 6.
Das zeitalter der kreuzzüge. v. 7.
Die letzen zeiten des mittelalters. v. 8.
v. 9-18. Neuere geschichte.
Geschichte des 15en jahrhunderts. v. 9-10.
Geschichte des 16en jahrhunderts. v. 11-12.
Ende des 16en und anfang des 17en jahrhunderts. v. 13.
Geschichte des 17en jahrhunderts. v. 14-15.
Geschichte des 18en jahrhunderts, v. 16-17.
Geschichte der ersten zeit des 19en jahrhunderts. v. 18.
v. 19. Register.

Schmarda (Ludwig Carl). Reise um die erde in den jahren 1853-57. 2 v. 8°. *Braunschweig, G. Westermann,* 1861. s.

Schmid (Christoph). The nightingale; or, a kind act is never lost. A tale of the Russian war, forty years ago. From the German. 91 pp. 16°. *New York, Dana & co.* 1856. s.

Schmid (Ernst Erhard). Lehrbuch der meteorologie. xvi, 1009 pp. 2 tab. 8°. Atlas. 21 pl. obl. fol. *Leipzig,* 1857-60. s.

[KARSTEN (G.) Allgemeine encyclopädie der physik. v. 21].

Schmidt (Carl). Geschichte der pädagogik, dargestellt in weltgeschichtlicher entwicklung und im organischen zusammenhange mit dem culturleben der völker. 2e aufl. besorgt durch W. Lange. v. 1, 3, and 4. 8°. *Cöthen, P. Schettler,* 1861-68.

[v. 3. 1e aufl.]

Schmidt (Julian). Geschichte der französischen literatur seit der revolution 1789. 2 v. iv, 476 pp; 630 pp. 8°. *Leipzig, F. L. Herbig,* 1858.

Schmidt (W. Adolf). Geschichte der preussisch-deutschen unionbestrebungen seit der zeit Friedrich's des grossen. [etc.] viii, 649 pp. 8°. *Berlin, Veit & co.* 1851. s.

Schmucker (Samuel M.) The life, speeches, and memorials of Daniel Webster. 548 pp. 2 pl. 8°. *Philadelphia, D. Rulison,* 1859. s.

Schneider (Christian Friderich). Danish grammar, adapted to the use of Englishmen. 7 p. l. 324 pp. 12°. *Copenhagen, F. Brummer,* [1803].

Schomburgk (Richard). Reisen in Britisch-Guiana in den jahren 1840-44. Im auftrag sr. majestät des königs von Preussen ausgeführt. Nebst einer fauna und flora Guiana's nach vorlagen von Johannes Müller, Ehrenberg, Erichson, Klotzsch, Troschel, Cabanis, und andern. Mit abbildungen und einer karte von Britisch-Guiana aufgenommen von sir Robert Schomburgk. v. 1-2. viii, x, 469 pp. 2 col. maps. 8 pl; xiv, 532 pp. 8 pl. 8°. *Leipzig, J. J. Weber,* 1847-48.

Schomburgk (*Sir* Robert Hermann). Abbildungen und einer karte von Britisch-Guiana. 8°. *Leipzig, J. Weber,* 1847-48.

[*In* SCHOMBURGK (Richard). Reisen in Britisch-Guiana. 1840-44. v. 1-2].

Schoolcraft (Henry Rowe). History of the Indian tribes of the United States; their present condition and prospects, and a sketch of their ancient status. Part vi. of the series. [Information respecting the history [etc.] of the Indian tribes]. 756 pp. 58 pl. 4°. *Philadelphia, J. B. Lippincott & co. (for Indian bureau),* 1857. s.

Schott (Arthur, *of Washington, D.C.*) Gedichte. viii, 296 pp. 16°. *Stuttgart, E. Hallberger,* 1850. s.

——— *and* **Schott** (Albert). Walachische mährchen, [etc.] Mit einer einleitung über das volk der Walachen, [etc.] xvi, 384 pp. 8°. *Stuttgart* [*etc.*] *J. G. Cotta,* 1845. s.

Schott (Charles A.) Physical observations in the Arctic seas. By Isaac I. Hayes, M. D. commanding expedition. Made on the west coast of North Greenland, the vicinity of Smith Strait, and the west side of Kennedy Channel, during 1860 and 1861. Reduced and discussed. xi, 270 pp. 3 maps. 3 pl. 4°. *Washington, Smithsonian inst.* 1867.

[SMITHSONIAN contributions. v. 15].

Schouler (William). A history of Massachusetts in the civil war. xiv, 670 pp. portrait. 8°. *Boston, E. P. Dutton & co.* 1868.

Schouw-tooneel van wederwaardigheden of verzameling van rampspoedige en ongelukkige reistochten, gedaan door nederlandsche en andere schepen. 2 p. l. 270 pp. 13 pl. sm. 4°. *Amsterdam, B. Mourik,* [*about* 1780].

CONTENTS.

Journaal van het schip Blydorp. Door N. J. Camstrup.
Journaal of rampspoedige reys-tocht van't oorlogschip het Huys in't Bosch.
Wederwaardige te huis-reyze, van het schip de Gerechtigheid.
Twee rampspoedige zee-reyze gedaan met het schippen le Prince ende Rustenwerk.
Verhaal van het droevig ongeluck, dat het schip Nieuw Vyver-Vreugd, etc.

Schreiber (Heinrich). Die feen in Europa. Eine historisch-archäologische monographie. iv, viii, 79 pp. 2 pl. 4°. *Freiburg im Breisgau, Albert-Ludwigs-universität,* 1842. s.

Schreiber (Jan Frederik). Historia vitae et meritorvm Frederici Rvysch. 4°. *Amstelædami,* 1732.

[RUYSCH (F.) Opera ommia. v. 1].

Schreiner (Henry). Gaging simplified. *See* **Marquart** (J.) *and* **Schreiner.**

Schrenck (Leopold von). Reisen und forschungen im Amurlande in den jahren 1854–1856, im auftrage der k. akademie der wissenschaften zu St. Petersburg ausgeführt, [etc.] v. i. 1–2 lief; ii. 4°. *St. Petersburg, k. akademie der wissenschaften,* 1858–67. s.

CONTENTS.

v. 1. 1e lief. Einleitung. Säugethiere. pp. xxxi, 1–213. 1 map. pl. 1–9. 1858.
2e lief. Vögel. pp. 215–567. pl. 10–16. 1860.
v. 2. 1e lief. Lépidoptères. Par E. Ménétriès. 1 p. l. pp. 1–75. pl. 1–5. 1859.
2e lief. Coléoptères. Par V. de Motschulsky. 1 p. l. pp. 77–257. pl. 6–11. 1 map. 1860.
3e lief. Mollusken. 2 p. l. pp. 259–976. pl. 12–30. 1867.

Schreven (J. van). *See* **Van Schreven.**

Schröder (Eric August). Hankbok i philosophiens historia. 3 v. 8°. *Upsala, Wahlström & co.* 1846–49. s.

Schröder van der Kolk (Jacobus Ludovicus Conradus). Case of atrophy of the left hemisphere of the brain, with coexistent atrophy of the right side of the body. Translated from the [Dutch], by W. D. Moore. 8°. *London,* 1861.

[NEW SYDENHAM society. v. 11].

——— On the minute structure and functions of the spinal cord and medulla oblongata. And on the proximate cause and treatment of epilepsy. Translated from the original [Dutch, etc.] by W. D. Moore. 2 memoirs in 1 v. ix pp. 1 l. pp. 1–83. 5 pl; 1 p. l. pp. 85–291. 5 pl. 8°. *London,* 1859.

[NEW SYDENHAM society. v. 4].

——— Oratio de debita cura infaustam maniacorum sortem emendandi eosque sanandi, [etc.] 85 pp. 8°. *Trajècti ad Rhenum, J. Altheer,* 1837. s.

Schübeler (Frederik Christian). Die culturpflanzen Norwegens beobachtet. Mit einem anhange über die altnorwegische landwirthschaft. Mit einem vorwort von Chr. Boeck. vii, 197 pp. 1 col. map. 24 pl. 4°. *Christiania, Brogger & Christie,* 1862. s.

Schubert (Friedrich Wilhelm). Handbuch der allgemeinen staatskunde von Europa. v. 7. 1e hälfte. [*or*] Handbuch der allgemeinen staatskunde des preussischen staats. b. 2. hälfte 1. Ackerbau, etc. viii, 248 pp. 8°. *Königsberg, Bornträger,* 1848. s.

[No subsequent volume published].

Schultens (Albert). Commentarius. *See* **Bible.** (*Hebrew and Latin*). Proverbia Solomonis. 1748.

Schumacher (Jacob) *and* **Crawford** (John). Monumental designs. [With a key]. 3 p. l. 52 pl. obl. 12°. *Buffalo, Clay, Cosack & co,* 1868.

Schumacher (Julius Heinrich Carl Eduard, *editor*). *See* **Jahrbuch** für 1836–44.

Schütz (Frederick) *and* **Weil von Gernsbach** (——). Für die freiheit aller! Für die einheit des vaterlandes! Reden in der deutschen massen-versammlung in Philadelphia, 1864. 11 pp. 8°. *New York,* 1864.

[LOYAL publication society. no. 72].

Schwaben *und* **Neuburg** (*Circle or district of, Bavaria*). Catalog der bibliothek des historischen kreis-vereins im regierungsbezirke von Schwaben und Neuburg. 2 p. l. 123 pp. 8°. *Augsburg, P. J. Pfeiffer,* 1867. s.

Schwartz (Johann Conrad). De plagio literario liber unus. 8 p. l. 208 pp. 4 l. 16°. *Lipsiæ, J. Fritsch,* 1706. s.

Schwartz (Theodor). Handbuch für den freimaurer, oder der hieroglyphen-deuter, [etc.] 2 p. l. 141 pp. 23 pl. 12°. *Louisville, Ky. Verfasser,* 1849. s.

Schwarz (Carl). Zur geschichte der neuesten theologie. 2e aufl. x, 437 pp. 12°. *Leipzig, F. A. Brockhaus,* 1856.

Schwegler (Albert). Römische geschichte. v. 1 and v. 2. 1e hälfte. 3 parts in 2 v. 8°. *Tübingen, H. Laupp,* 1853–56.

CONTENTS.

v. 1. Römische geschichte im zeitalter der könige.
v. 2. 1e hälfte. Römische geschichte im zeitalter der kampfs der stände.

Schweigger (Johann Salomo Christoph, *editor*). *See* **Journal** für chemie und physik.

Schweighäuser (Johann). Opuscula academica seorsim olim edita nunc recognita in unum volumen collegit auctor. 2 v. in 1. xvi, 198 pp; 3 p. l. 215 pp. 8°. *Argentorati, ex typographia societatis bipontinae,* 1806.

CONTENTS.

Pars i. Commentationes philosophicae.
ii. Commentationes philosophicae. (Exercitationes in Appianum; observationes in Suidam).

Schwenck (Conrad). Die mythologie der Semiten. 2e ausg. 3 p. l. 364 pp. 8°. *Frankfort am Main, J. D. Sauerländer,* 1855.

[v. 4 *of his* Mythologie der Griechen, Römer, Ägypter, Semiten, etc.]

Scientific (The) American. Jan. 1866, to Dec. 1868. New series, v. 14–19. fol. *New York, Munn & co.* 1866–68.

Scipio's reflections on Monroe's view of the conduct of the executive, connected with a mission to the French republic, in the years 1794, '95, '96. [*pseudon.*] 140 pp. 8°. *Boston, C. P. Wayne,* 1798.

[NOTE.—Sometimes ascribed to Alexander Hamilton].

Scot (Reynolde *or* Reginald). A perfite platforme of a hoppe garden, and necessarie instructions for the making and mayntenaunce thereof. Newly corrected and augmented. [2d ed.] 6 p. l. 63 pp. 6 l. sm. 4°. *London, H. Denham,* 1576.

Scotland. Facsimiles of national manuscripts of Scotland, selected under the direction of sir William Gibson Craig, and photozincographed by command of h. m. queen Victoria, by col. sir Henry James, etc. Part i. xviii, 43 pp. 78 illustrations. fol. *Southampton, ordnance survey office,* 1867. s.

Scott (John F.) Brudder Bones' book of stump speeches, and burlesque orations, etc. 188 pp. 12°. *New York, Dick & Fitzgerald,* 1868.

Scott (J. R.) The congregational psalmist: a collection of psalm tunes, [etc.] intended for congregational use in baptist churches. 119 pp. 12°. *Rochester, W. N. Sage,* 1855. s.

Scott (J. W.) A presentation of causes tending to fix the position of the future great city of the world in the central plain of North America, showing that the centre of the world's commerce, is moving westward to the best position [Toledo] on the great lakes. 28 pp. 8°. *Toledo, Blade print,* 1868.

Scott (*Rev.* Thomas). The force of truth: an authentic narrative [of my religious inquiries, and change of sentiment]. 141 pp. 18°. *Philadelphia, G. M. & W. Snider,* 1827.

Scott (*Sir* Walter). Beauties. *See* **French** (B. F.) The beauties of Scott and Moore.

——— Ivanhoe. 498 pp. 1 pl. 16°. *Edinburgh, A. & C. Black,* 1851.

——— Poetical works. Complete. 6 v. 12°. *New York, C. S. Francis,* 1849.

——— The same. Poetical works, containing The lay of the last minstrel; Marmion; The lady of the lake; Vision of Don Roderick; Rokeby; The bridal of Triermain; The lord of the isles; Ballads, songs, and lyrical pieces. Illustrated by Corbould. New ed. xii, 740 pp. 8 pl. 12°. *London, Routledge,* 1866.

——— The same. Containing Lay of the last minstrel, Marmion, Lady of the lake, Don Roderick, Rokeby, ballads, lyrics, and songs. With a life of the author. 647 pp. 9 pl. 16°. *New York, Appletons,* 1866.

——— Waverly poetry; being the poems scattered through the Waverly novels, [etc.] 268 pp. 12°. *Boston, Munroe & Francis,* 1851. s.

Scott (William B.) Half-hour lectures on the history and practice of the fine and ornamental arts. xii, 363 pp. 1 portrait. 16°. *London, Longmans,* 1861.

Scott. *See* **Scot.**

Scrutator. [*pseudon.*] *See* **Horlock.**

Scudéry (Georges de). Discours politiques des roys. 3 p. l. 530 pp. 16°. *Paris, L. Le Gras,* 1682. s.

Seager (Francis). The schoole of vertue, and booke of good nourture for chyldren and youth to learn theyr dutie by. 8°. *London, W. Seares,* 1557, [*reprint, Trübner & co.* 1868].

[*In* FURNIVALL (C. J.) Babees book, etc. pp. 333-35. Early English text society publications. no. 32].

Sealy (Henry Nicholas). A treatise on coins, currency, and banking. With observations on the bank act of 1844, and on the reports of the committees on the bank acts. Part ii. xviii, pp. 399-609 8°. *London, Longmans,* 1867.

Seaman (Ezra C.) Essays on the progress of nations in productive industry, civilization, population, and wealth, etc. viii, 456, 192 pp. 8°. *New York, Baker & Scribner,* 1846. s.

Searson (John). Poems on various subjects and different occasions, chiefly adapted to rural entertainment. 94 pp. 4 l. 8°. *Philadelphia, Snowden & McCorkle,* 1797.

Sea-shore (The). What Charley saw and did there. By uncle Jesse. [*pseudon.*] 96 pp. 1 col. pl. 18°. *Cincinnati, Western tract and book society,* 1868.

Secret (The) history of the loves of pope Gregory vii. commonly called St. Hildebrand, and of the cardinal de Richelieu. Collected from the French and Italian manuscripts written in their time. [*anon.*] vi, 115 pp. 16°. *London, T. Warner,* 1722.

Secundus (Ioannes *or* Janus). *See* **Everhardi** (Nicolaas).

Sedgwick (Adam, *D.D.*) A discourse on the studies of the university of Cambridge. The 5th ed. with additions, and a preliminary dissertation. cccxlii pp. 1 l. 324 pp. 8°. *Cambridge, J. W. Parker, etc.* 1850. s.

Segrais (Jean Renaud, *sieur de*). Zayde. A Spanish history. *See* **La Fayette** (M. M. P. de la Vergne, *comtesse* de).

Séguin (Marc, *aîné*). Mémoire sur les causes et sur les effets de la chaleur, de la lumière et de l'électricité. 113 pp. 8°. *Paris, A. Tromblay*, 1865.

Ségur (*Abbé* Gaston de). Short and familiar answers to the most common objections urged against religion. Edited by J. V. Huntington. 195 pp. 16°. *Baltimore, J. Murphy & co.* 1854. s.

Ségur (Joseph Alexandre Pierre, *vicomte* de). Les femmes, leur condition et leur influence chez différens peuples. 2 v. 474 pp. 1 pl; 445 pp. 1 pl. 8°. *Paris, Raymond*, 1820.

Ségur (Philippe Paul, *comte* de). History of Peter the Great, with a sketch of the history of Russia. 8°. *Philadelphia, T. K. Greenbank*, 1833.

[*In* GREENBANK'S periodical library. v. 1. pp. 89-171].

Ségur (*Monseigneur* —— de). Plain talk about the protestantism of to-day. From the French. 253 pp. 18°. *Boston, P. Donahoe*, 1868.

Seiss (Joseph A. *D. D.*) Ecclesia lutherana: a brief survey of the evangelical lutheran church. 276 pp. 12°. *Philadelphia, lutheran bookstore*, 1867.

——— *and others.* Psalms and canticles for evangelical lutheran churches. (From "The evangelical psalmist"). xiii pp. 4 l. 333–440 pp. 8°. *Philadelphia, book society of St. John's church*, 1867.

Selden (John). De dIs syris syntagmata ii. Adversaria nempe de numinibus commentitijs in veteri instrumento memoratis. Accedunt fere quæ sunt reliqua Syrorum. Prisca porro Arabum, Aegyptiorum, Persarum, Afrorum, Europæorum item theologia, subinde illustratur. Ed. alt. 20 p. l. 374 pp. 16°. *Lvgdvni Batavorvm, ex officina Bonaventuræ & A. Elsevir*, 1629. s.

Selecta patrum societatis Jesu carmina. xv, 174 pp. 16°. *Genuæ, J. B. Lertius*, 1747. s.

Selys-Longchamps (Michel Edmond, *baron* de). Faune belge. 1re partie; indication méthodique des mammifères, oiseaux, reptiles et poissons observés jusqu'ici en Belgique. xii, 310 pp. 2 col. tab. 8 pl. 8°. *Liége, H. Dessain*, 1842. s.

Semper (Carl, *Ph. D. of Würzburg*). Reisen im archipel der Philippinen. 2e theil. Wissenschaftliche resultate. v. 1. Holuthurien. Lief. 1–3. 2 p. l. pp. 1–100. pl. 1–25. 4°. *Leipzig, W. Engelmann*, 1867. s.

Semple (Robert Hunter, *editor*). Memoirs on diptheria. From the writings of Bretonneau, Guersant, Trousseau, Bouchut, Empis and Daviot. With bibliographical appendix, by John Chatto. 8 p. l. 407 pp. 8°. *London*, 1859.

[NEW SYDENHAM society. v. 3].

Senator (The); or, parliamentary chronicle. *See* **Great Britain.** (*Parliamentary papers.*)

Senault (Jean François). El hombre reo, ó la corrupcion de la naturaleza por el pecado, conforme a la doctrina de San Agustin. Traducido de Frances al Castellano por L. de Las Casas. 2 v. 28 p. l. 461 pp; 4 p. l. 521 pp. 16°. *Madrid, L. Mojados*, 1739. s.

Senebier (*Rev.* Jean). L'art d'observer. 2 v. xx, 244 pp; 2 p. l. 324 pp. 8°. *Genève, C. Philibert & B. Chirol*, 1775. s.

Seneca (Lucius Annæus). De quattuor virtutibus cardinalibus. 16 l. sm. 4°. *Colonie, H. Quentell*, 1500.

Senter (A. E.) The diddler. Hodge podge. Items from Joe Miller. 151 pp. 1 pl. 16°. *New York, M. Doolady*, 1868.

Sequester. *See* **Vibius Sequester.**

Serapeum. Zeitschrift für bibliothek-wissenschaft, handschriftenkunde und ältere litteratur. Im vereine mit bibliothekaren und litteraturfreunden herausgegeben von Robert Naumann. v. 1–16. 8°. *Leipzig, T. O. Weigel*, 1840–55. s.

Serenus *antissensis.* De sectione cylindri et coni libri duo. fol. *Oxoniæ*, 1710. s.

[*In* APOLLONIUS Pergaeus. Conicorum libri octo. Oxoniæ, 1710].

Sermones de sanctis per circulũ anni, thesaurus nouus nuncupatus. [*anon.*] 307 l. fol. *Argentine*, 1484.

Sermones quadrigesimales thesauri noui. [*anon.*] 102 l. fol. *Nurẽberge, A. Koberger*, 1496.

[*With* SERMONES thesauri noui de tempore. *Nurmberge*, 1496].

Sermones thesauri noui de sanctis. [*anon.*] 194 l. fol. *Nuremberge, A. Koberger*, 1496.

[*With* SERMONES thesauri noui de tempore. *Nurmberge*, 1496].

Sermones thesauri noui de tempore. [*anon.*] 242 l. fol. *Nurmberge, A. Koberger*, 1496.

[Imperfect: wanting l. 11–12].

Serradifalco (Domenico Lo Faso Pietrasanta, *duca* di). Del duomo di Monreale e di altre chiese siculo-normane ragionamenti tre. 87 pp. 28 pl. fol. *Palermo, autore*, 1838. s.

Serres (Étienne Renaud Augustin). Anatomie comparée du cerveau, dans les quatres classes des animaux vertébrés, appliquée à la physiologie et à la pathologie du système nerveux. Planches. 2 p. l. 46 pp. 16 pl. 4°. *Paris, Gabon & cie.* 1824. s.

Service afloat: comprising the personal narrative of a British naval officer. [*anon.*] 8°. *Philadelphia, T. K. Greenbank*, 1833.
[*In* GREENBANK'S periodical library. v. 2. pp. 73-174]

Services for congregational worship. *See* **Unitarian** (American) association.

Seuffert (Johann Michael von, *LL. D.*) Von dem verhältnisse des staats und der diener des staats gegen einander, im rechtlichen und politischen verstande. 5 p. l. 172 pp. 12°. *Würzburg, F. X. Rienner*, 1793.

Sewall (*Rev.* Joseph). He that would keep God's commandments must renounce the society of evil doers. A sermon preached at the publick lecture in Boston, July 18th, 1728, after a bloody and mortal duel. 28 pp. 12°. *Boston, D. Henchman*, 1728.

Sewall (*Hon.* Samuel, *chief justice of the prov. of Massachusetts bay*). Phænomena quædam apocalyptica ad aspectum novi orbis configurata. Or, some lines towards a description of the new heaven, as it makes to those who stand upon the new earth. 2d ed. 64, 24, 1 pp. 4°. *Boston, B. Green, etc.* 1727.

Seward (William). Journal of a voyage from Savannah to Philadelphia and England, 1740. 3 p. l. 88 pp. 8°. *London, J. Oswald*, 1740.
[*With* WHITEFIELD (G.) Journal, etc. 7 parts in 1 v.]

Shahmah in pursuit of freedom; or, the branded hand. Translated from the original Showiah, and edited by an American citizen. [*anon.*] 599 pp. 1 pl. 12°. *New York, Thatcher & Hutchinson*, 1858.

Shakespeare (William). Comedies, histories, and tragedies. Published according to the true originall copies. The second impression. 10 p. l. 886 pp. portrait. fol. *London, T. Cotes for R. Allot*, 1632.

——— The same. Plays and poems, with a life, glossarial notes, and 170 illustrations [in outline] from the plates in Boydell's edition. Edited by A. J. Valpy. 15 v. 16°. *London, A. J. Valpy*, 1832.

——— The same. The dramatic works; with a life of the poet, and notes. 7 v. 8°. *Boston, Hilliard, Gray & co.* 1836.
[v. 2. wanting].

——— The same. Shakspeare's dramatiska arbeten öfwersatta af C. A. Hagberg. 12 v. in 6. 8°. *Lund, C. W. K. Gleerup*, 1847-50. s.
[v. 2, 2a upplag. 1848].

——— Dictionary of Shakespearian quotations, selected from [his] writings. xii, 418 pp. 1 pl. 12°. *Philadelphia, F. Bell*, 1851.

——— King Richard the Third. A tragedy. Edited by R. H. Westley. 1 p. l. 114 pp. 8°. *Leipzig, G. Græbner*, 1861. s.
[Masterpieces of English literature. v 3].

——— The merchant of Venice. A comedy. Edited by R. H. Westley. 1 p. l. 82 pp. 8°. *Leipzig, G. Græbner*, 1861. s.
[Masterpieces of English literature. v. 4].

——— Romeo and Juliet. A tragedy. With notes, by dr. Otto Fiebig. iv, 100 pp. 8°. *Leipzig, G. Græbner*, 1859. s.
[Masterpieces of English literature. v. 1].

Shakespeare library and museum (*Stratford-upon-Avon*). A catalogue of the books, manuscripts, works of art, antiquities and relics, illustrative of the life and works of Shakespeare, and of the history of Stratford-upon-Avon. 183 pp. 8°. *London, Shakespeare fund*, 1868.

Shakespeare's romances. [King Henry iv.] Collected and arranged by Shakspeare ii. [*pseudon.*] 2 v. xiii, 215 pp; 208 pp. 12°. *London, Sherwood, Gilbert, and Piper*, 1825.

Shattuck (William B.) Columbian drawing book, no. 1. obl. 4°. *Cincinnati, H. W. Derby & co.* 1848. s.

Shaw (George, *M. D.*) Musei leveriani explicatio, anglica et latina. [*or*] Museum leverianum, containing select specimens from the museum of the late sir Ashton Lever, kt. with descriptions in Latin and English. [Vertebrata]. 2 v. 4 p. l. 248 pp. 60 col. pl; 4 p. l. pp. 1-48. 12 col. pl. 4°. [*London*], *J. Parkinson*, 1792-96.
[No more published].

——— Zoological lectures, delivered at the Royal institution [etc.] 2 v. 2 p. l. xiv, 248 pp. 86 pl; 2 p. l. 235 pp. 2 l. iv pp. 77 pl. (87-163). 8°. *London, G. Kearsley*, 1809. s.

Shaw (Henry W.) Josh Billings on ice, and other things. [*pseudon.*] 263 pp. 6 pl. 12°. *New York, Carleton & co.* 1868.

Shaw (Joshua). United States directory for the use of travellers and merchants. 156 pp. 40 l. 16°. *Philadelphia, J. Maxwell*, 1822.

Shea (John Gilmary). Library of American linguistics. v. 1-3, 9-13. 8°. and 4°. *New York, Cramoisy press*, 1860-64. s.

CONTENTS.

Bruyas (Jacques). Radices verborum iroquæorum. 4°. 1862. v. 10.
French-Onondaga (A) dictionary, from a manuscript of the seventeenth century. [*anon.*] By J. G. Shea. 8°. 1860. v. 1.
Gibbs (George). Alphabetical vocabularies of the Clallam and Lummi. 4°. 1863. v. 11.
——— Alphabetical vocabulary of the Chinook language. 4°. 1863. v. 9.
——— A dictionary of the Chinook jargon. 4°. 1863. v. 12.

Shea—continued.

CONTENTS.

Grammatical (A) sketch of the Heve language. Translated by Buckingham Smith. 8°. v. 3.
Maillard (*Abbé*). Grammaire de la langue mikmaque. 4°. 1864. v. 13.
Mengarini (*Rev.* G.) A Selish or Flat-head grammar. 8°. 1861. v. 2.

Sheldon (*Rev.* D. N.) Sin and redemption: a series of sermons, to which is added an oration on moral freedom. 332 pp. 12°. *New York, Sheldon, Lamport & Blakeman*, 1856. s.

Shepherd (C. W.) The north-west peninsula of Iceland: being the journal of a tour in Iceland in the spring and summer of 1862. xi, 162 pp. 1 map. 3 pl. 12° *London, Longmans*, 1867.

Sheppard (John H.) The life of Samuel Tucker, commodore in the American revolution. 384 pp. portrait. 8°. *Boston, A. Mudge & son*, 1868.

Sherer (Moyle). [Tales of the wars of our times]. The rival. [*anon.*] 8°. *Philadelphia, T. K. Greenbank*, 1833.

[*In* GREENBANK'S periodical library. v. 1. pp. 596–620].

——— [The same]. The Tyroler. [*anon.*] 8°. *Philadelphia, T. K. Greenbank*, 1833.

[*In* GREENBANK'S periodical library. v. 2. pp. 447–485].

Sherlock (Thomas, *bishop of London*). Several discourses preached at the temple church. 3d ed. 4 p. l. 240 pp. 16°. *London, J. Whiston*, 1755.

Sherwood (Adiel, *D. D.*) The Jewish and christian churches; or, the hebrew theocracy and christian church distinct organizations. xii, 123 pp. 16°. *St. Louis, T. W. Ustick*, 1850. s.

Sherwood (*Mrs.* Mary M.) The Indian pilgrim. Translated by Bábú John Harí, [etc. Hindustanee]. 360 pp. 12°. *Allahabad, presbyterian mission press*, 1847. s.

Shipp (Barnard). Fame: and other poems. 212 pp. 12°. *Philadelphia, E. H. Butler & co.* 1848. s.

Shipton (Anna). "Tell Jesus." Recollections of Emily Gosse. New ed. 158 pp. 18°. *Philadelphia, Jane Hamilton*, 1868.

Shirreff (John). General view of the agriculture of the Orkney islands. ix, 195, 66, 12 pp. 8°. *Edinburgh*, 1814. s.

[GREAT BRITAIN: Board of agriculture].

——— General view of the agriculture of the Shetland islands. vii, 135, 63, 8 pp. 8°. *Edinburgh*, 1814. s.

[GREAT BRITAIN: Board of agriculture. *With* the preceding].

Shore (Thomas). The merchant's and traveller's companion. vi, 258 pp. 1 map. 16°. *Petersburg, (Va.) E. Pescud*, 1819.

Short (A) description of the state of Tenasee. [*anon.*] [With] the constitution established 1796. 8°. *London, J. Debrett*, 1797.

[*In* IMLAY (G.) Topographical description of the western territory. pp. 512–543. 1 map. ed. 1797].

Short stories for spare moments. Selected from Lippincott's magazine. 146 pp. 8°. *Philadelphia, J. B. Lippincott & co.* 1869.

Shortland (Edward). Traditions and superstitions of the New Zealanders: with illustrations of their manners and customs. 2d ed. xi, 304 pp. 1 tab. 16°. *London, Longmans*, 1856.

Shrimpton (Charles). Lillian; or, woman's endurance. A narrative connected with the early history of Canada and the American revolution. 358 pp. 16°. *New York, N. Tibbals & co.* 1868.

Sichel (*Dr.* Jules). Hymenoptera fossoria et mellifera. *See* **Saussure** (H. de) *and* **Sichel**. Hymenopteren. pp. 141–156.

Siebold (Carl Theodor Ernst von). A few remarks upon hectocotylus. 8°. *London*, 1853.

[*In* HENFREY (A.) *and* HUXLEY (T. H.) Scientific memoirs. art. 3].

——— (*editor*). *See* **Zeitschrift** für wissenschaftliche zoologie.

Siebold (Philipp Franz von, *editor*). Fauna Japonica. Crustacea, elaborante W. de Haan. fol. *Lugduni-Batavorum, P. T. von Siebold, etc.* 1850. s.

Siècle (Le) chantant. Romances, chansons, couplets, rondeaux, [etc.] suivis des chants et chansons populaires de la France. Publié par F. Martinn. Juin, 1864—Mars, 1865. 2 v. in 1. 4°. *Paris, Gennequin*, 1864–65.

Sifflé (A. F.) Nieuwe gedichten. 2 v. viii, 208 pp; vi, 183 pp. 8°. *Middelburg, J. C. & W. Altorffer*, 1844. s.

Signs of the times. Editorials. *See* **Beebe** (*Rev.* Gilbert).

Sigonio (Carlo). Commentarius in fastos et triumphos romanos. 16°. [*Geneva*], 1568.

[*In* VARII historiæ romanæ scriptores. v. 1].

——— Fasti consvlares, ac triumphi acti à Romulo rege vsque ad Ti. Cæsarem. 16°. [*Geneva*], 1568.

[*In* VARII historiæ romanæ scriptores. v. 1].

——— De nominibvs Romanorvm. 16°. [*Geneva*], 1568.

[*In* VARII historiæ romanæ scriptores. v. 1].

Sigourney (*Mrs.* Lydia Huntley). Illustrated poems. With designs by Felix O. C. Darley. 408 pp. 14 pl. 8°. *Philadelphia, Carey & Hart*, 1849. s.

Sigourney (L. H.) Illustrated poems. New ed. 408 pp. 9 pl. 8°. *Philadelphia, A. Hart,* 1853. s.

——— Myrtis, with other etchings and sketchings. vii, 292 pp. 1 pl. 12°. *New York, Harpers,* 1846. s.

——— Past meridian. [Characteristics of old age]. 2d ed. 344 pp. 12°. *Hartford, F. A. Brown,* 1856. s.

——— The same. 2d ed. 344 pp. 12°. *Hartford, F. A. Brown,* 1857. s.

——— Poems for the sea. 152 pp. 12°. *Hartford, H. S. Parsons & co.* 1850. s.

Silber (William Beinhauer). A Latin reader, with notes and references to the grammars of Harkness, Andrews and Stoddard, and Bullions. 226 pp. 12°. *New York, A. S. Barnes & co.* 1867.

Silliman's American journal, etc. *See* **American** journal of science and the arts.

Silva (Rodrigo Mendez). *See* **Mendez Silva.**

Simmonds (P. L.) A supplement [on cotton manufacture]. *See* **Ure** (A.) The cotton manufacture of Great Britain, etc. 1861.

Simms (William Gilmore). The ghost of my husband. A tale of the Crescent city. 114 pp. 1 pl. 12°. *New York, Chapman & co.* 1866.

Simonde de Sismondi (Jean Charles Léonard). De la littérature du midi de l'Europe. 3e éd. 4 v. 8°. *Paris, Treuttel & Würtz,* 1829. s.

——— The same. 2 v. iv, 583 pp; 2 p. l. 709 pp. 8°. *Bruxelles, H. Dumont,* 1837.

Simonds (W.) The Aimwell stories. Jessie; or, trying to be somebody. By Walter Aimwell. [*pseudon.*] 320 pp. 12°. *Boston, Gould & Lincoln,* 1859. s.

Simpson (*Lt. col.* James H.) Report on the change of route west from Omaha, Nebraska territory, proposed by the Union Pacific railroad company, [etc.] 70 pp. 1 l. 2 maps. 8°. *Washington, gov't printing office,* 1865. s.

——— Report on the Union Pacific railroad and branches, Central Pacific railroad of California, Northern Pacific railroad, wagon roads in the territories of Idaho, Montana, Dakota, and Nebraska, and the Washington aqueduct, [etc.] With laws relating to the Pacific railroad. 2 p. l. 161 pp. 4 maps. 8°. *Washington, gov't printing office,* 1865. s.

Simpson (Richard). An introduction to the philosophy of Shakespeare's sonnets. 4 p. l. 82 pp. 12°. *London, Trübner & co.* 1868.

Simson (Robert, *M. D.*) Opera quaedam reliqua. Nunc primum edita, impensis quidem Philippi comitis Stanhope, cura vero Jacobi Clow. 3 p. l. xi, 685 pp. 4°. *Glasguae, R. & A. Foulis,* 1776.

CONTENTS.

i. Apollonius Pergaei de sectione determinata libri ii. restituti, duobus insuper libris aucti.
ii. Porismatum liber.
iii. De logarithmis liber.
iv. De limitibus quantitatum et rationum, fragmentum.
v. Appendix pauca continens problemata ad illustrandum praecipue veterum geometrarum analysin.

Sinclair (*Sir* John). An account of improvements carried on, on his estates in Scotland. 8°. *London,* 1812.

[GREAT BRITAIN. Board of agriculture. *In* HENDERSON (J.) Agriculture of Caithness].

——— The history of the public revenue of the British empire. 2 pts in 1 v. v, 470 pp. 8°. *Dublin, P. Byrne,* 1785.

——— Sketch of the improvement, now carrying on by sir John Sinclair, in the county of Caithness, North Britain. 16 pp. 4 pl. 4°. *London, W. Bulmer & co.* 1803.

Singer (William, *D. D.*) General view of the agriculture, state of property, and improvements, in the county of Dumfries. xxvi, 696 pp. 1 l. 1 col. map. 9 pl. 8°. *Edinburgh,* 1812. s.

[GREAT BRITAIN: Board of agriculture].

Sismondi (Jean Charles Léonard Simonde de). *See* **Simonde de Sismondi.**

Sister's (A) story. [*anon.*] 298 pp. 3 pl. 16°. *Boston, American tract society,* [1867].

Siti pittoreschi e prospettivi delle lagune Venete disegnati, intagliati e descritti. [*anon.*] 136 pp. 14 pl. 8°. *Venezia, Gondoliere,* 1838. s.

Six weeks at Long's. By a late resident. [*anon.*] 2d ed. 3 v. 12°. *London, author,* 1817.

Sketch (A) of the claims of sundry American citizens on the government of the United States, for indemnity for depredations committed on their property by the French, (prior to the 30th of September, 1800), [etc.] By a citizen of Baltimore. [*anon.*] 145 pp. 8°. *Baltimore, R. Geddes,* 1826.

Sketch (A) of the life of James William Wallack, (senior), late actor and manager. 63 pp. 8°. *New York, T. H. Morrell,* 1865.

Sketch-book by an American in Venice. [Costumi Triestini, by E. Bosa. *anon.*] 1 p. l. 24 pl. sm. fol. [*n. p.*] 1860.

Sketchley (Arthur, *pseudon.*) *See* **Rose** (George).

Skinner (*Rev.* Thomas H.) Discussions in theology. 3 p. l. 287 pp. 12°. *New York, A. D. F. Randolph,* 1868.

Skjöldebrand (Anders Fredrik). Voyage pittoresque au Cap Nord. 1 p. l. 61 pp. 60 pl. obl. fol. *Stockholm, C. Deleen & J. G. Forsgren,* 1801. s.

Slade (Frederic J.) The Bessemer and the Martin processes for manufacturing steel. From the report of A. S. Hewitt, U. S. commissioner to the universal exposition, Paris, 1867. 12°. *Philadelphia, H. C. Baird,* 1868.
[*In* LANDRIN (M. C. H. *jr.*) Treatise on steel. ed. 1868. pp. 299-334].

Slaveholder (The) abroad; or, Billy Buck's visit, with his master, to England. A series of letters from dr. Pleasant Jones to major Joseph Jones of Georgia. [*anon.*] 512 pp. 7 pl. 12°. *Philadelphia, Lippincott & co.* 1860.

Sleepy hollow cemetery, at Tarrytown, on the Hudson river. [A description, etc.] 29 pp. 3 pl. 8°. *New York, C. S. Westcott & co.* 1866.

Slight reminiscences of the Rhine. *See* **Boddington** (*Mrs.*)

Sloane (*Sir* Hans). Histoire de la Jamäique. Traduite de l'Anglois. Par m. [Raulin], ancien officier de dragons. [*anon.*] 2 v. 2 p. l. 285 pp; 248 pp. 6 pl. 16°. *Londres, Nourse,* 1751.

Smet (Peter J. de). *See* **De Smet.**

Smirke (R.) The adventure of hunch-back, [etc.] *See* **Arabian** nights' entertainments.

Smith (Adam). An inquiry into the nature and causes of the wealth of nations. With a life of the author. Also, a view of the doctrine of Smith, [etc.] 3 v. 8°. *London, J. Maynard,* 1811. s.

Smith (Asa, *teacher at New York*). Astronomia ilustrada, de Smith, [etc.] Trad. al Español [etc.] por D. Parédes. 63 pp. 1 pl. 4°. *Nueva York, D. Burgess & co.* 1853. s.

Smith (Charles, *of New York*). The American war, from 1775 to 1783. With plans. 183 pp. 6 maps. 2 pl. 8°. *New York, C. Smith,* 1797.

Smith (Edward, *M.D.*) Botany. 8°. *London,* 1851.
[*In* ORR (W. S.) Circle of the sciences. Organic nature. v. 2].

Smith (*Mrs.* Elizabeth Oakes). The salamander; found amongst the papers of the late Ernest Helfenstein. [*pseudon.*] Edited by E. Oakes Smith. 2d ed. 149 pp. 3 pl. 8°. *New York, G. P. Putnam,* 1849. s.

Smith (George, *F.A.S.*) The Cassiterides; an inquiry into the commercial operations of the Phœnicians in western Europe, with particular reference to the British tin trade. vii, 154 pp. 8°. *London, Longmans,* 1863.

Smith (Gerrit). McClellan's nomination and acceptance. 15 pp. 8°. *New York,* 1864.
[LOYAL publication society. No. 63].

Smith (*Captain* John, *of Virginia*). The last will and testament of John Smith, with some additional memoranda relating to him. [By Charles Deane]. From the proceedings of the Mass. hist. soc. Jan. 1867. 7 pp. sm. 4°. *Cambridge, (Mass.) J. Wilson & son,* 1867.

——— The sea-mans grammar; how to build, rigge, yard and mast any ship whatsoever. With experiments in the art of gunnery. [2d ed.] 2 p. l. 75 pp. *numbered as* 85. sm. 4°. *London, A. Kemb,* 1653.

Smith (John, *gent.*) England's improvement revived; in a treatise of all manner of husbandry and trade by land and sea. Plainly discovering the ways of improveing and enriching all earths. With the manner of planting timber trees. Also, the way of ordering cattel. 7 p. l. 270 pp. sm. 4°. *London, B. Southwood,* 1673.

Smith (John, *D.D. of Campbelton*). General view of the agriculture of the county of Argyle. xvi, 347 pp. 1 tab. 1 map. 3 pl. 8°. *London,* 1805. s.
[GREAT BRITAIN: Board of agriculture].

Smith (Joseph, *jr. the seer*). *See* **Bible.** *English.* Holy scriptures, translated and corrected. 16°. *Plano, (Ill.)* 1867.

Smith (Joseph, *quaker*). A descriptive catalogue of friends' books, or books written by members of the society of friends, commonly called quakers, from their first rise to the present time, with critical remarks and biographical notices. 2 v. v, 1027 pp; 984 pp. 8°. *London, J. Smith,* 1867.

Smith (J. Lewis, *M. D.*) A treatise on the diseases of infancy and childhood. 620 pp. 8°. *Philadelphia, H. C. Lea,* 1869.

Smith (Joshua Toulmin). The Northmen in New England, or America in the tenth century. xii, 364 pp. 2 maps. 12°. *Boston, Hilliard, Gray & co.* 1839.

Smith (M.) A geographical view of the British possessions in North America. With a concise history of the war in Canada. 288 pp. 24°. *Baltimore, author,* 1814.

Smith (*Rev.* Matthew Hale). Sunshine and shadow in New York. 712 pp. 12 pl. 8°. *Hartford, J. B. Burr & co.* 1868.

Smith (Roswell C.) Geography on the productive system. 356 pp. 12°. Atlas, 19 col. maps. 4°. *New York, D. Burgess & co.* 1850–54. s.

Smith (*Rev.* Samuel, *of Borgne*). General view of the agriculture of Galloway, comprehending two counties, viz. the stewartry of Kirkcudbright, and Wigtonshire. xiv, 388 pp. 1 tab. 4 pl. 8°. *London,* 1810. s.
[GREAT BRITAIN: Board of agriculture].

Smith (Solomon). Theatrical management in the west and south for thirty years. Interspersed with anecdotical sketches: autobiographically given. Fifteen illustrations. 275 pp. 8°. *New York, Harpers,* 1868.

Smith (*Rev.* Thomas, *D. D. of Magdalen coll. Oxford*). Miscellanea. 6 p. l. 198 pp. 16°. *Londini, S. Smith,* 1686.

CONTENTS.

Præmonitio ad lectorem de infantum communione apud Græcos.
Responsio ad objectiones authoris libri de fide et ritibus orientalium.
Narratio de vita, studiis, gestis, et martyrio Cyrilli Lucarii.
Hymnus matutinus Græcorum.
'Enotikon, sive de causis et remediis dissidiorum exercitatio theologica.

Smith (William, *D. D. provost of the university of Pennsylvania*). An examination of the Connecticut claim to lands in Pennsylvania, with an appendix. [*anon.*] 93, 32 pp. 1 map. 8°. *Philadelphia, T. Crukshank,* 1774.

Smith (William, *chief justice of the province of New York*). The history of the late province of New York, from its discovery, to the appointment of governor Colden, in 1762. 2 v. xvi, 320 pp; 2 p. l. 308 pp. 8°. *New York, N. Y. historical society,* 1829–30.
[NEW YORK historical society. Collections. v. 4–5 1st series].

Smith (William, *LL.D. M. C. from S. C.*) An address from William Smith, of South Carolina, to his constituents. [On the proposed commercial regulations]. 28 pp. 8°. *London, J. Debrett,* 1794.

——— A comparative view of the constitutions of the several states with each other, and with that of the United States, exhibiting in tables the prominent features of each constitution, etc. 34 pp. 2 p. l. 6 tab. 4°. *Philadelphia, J. Thompson,* 1796.

——— The speeches of mr. Smith, of South Carolina, delivered in the house of representatives of the United States, in Jan. 1794, on certain commercial regulations, proposed by mr. Madison. 75 pp. 1 tab. 8°. *London, reprinted, John Stockdale,* 1794.

Smith. *See, also,* **Smyth.**

Smithsonian institution. Annual report of the board of regents, showing the operations, expenditures and condition of the institution for 1867. 506 pp. 8°. *Washington, government printing office,* 1868.

——— Publications of learned societies and periodicals in the library. 2 v. in 1. 2 p. l. 35 pp; 2 p. l. 34 pp. 4°. *Washington, Smithsonian institution,* 1855–56. S.

——— Smithsonian contributions to knowledge. v. 15. 4°. *Washington, Smithsonian institution,* 1867.

CONTENTS.

NEWCOMB (S.) Investigation of the orbit of Neptune (no. 199).
PUMPELLY (R.) Geological researches in China, Mongolia, and Japan, 1862–65. (no. 202).
SCHOTT (C. A.) Physical observations in the Arctic seas. By I. I. Hayes. Reduced and discussed. (no. 196).
WHITTLESEY (C.) On the fresh-water glacial drift of the northwestern states. (no. 197).

Smucker (Samuel M.) *See* **Schmucker** (Samuel M).

Smyth (Alexander). Speeches in the [Virginia] house of delegates, and at the bar. 208 pp. portrait. 18°. *Richmond, S. Pleasants,* 1811.

Smyth (Charles Piazzi). Life and work at the great pyramid, Jan.–April, 1865; with a discussion of the facts ascertained. With illustrations. 3 v. 8°. *Edinburgh, Edmonston & Douglas,* 1867.

Smyth (*Rev.* Thomas). The well in the valley. 430 pp. 1 pl. 16°. *Philadelphia, American s. s. union,* 1857. S.

Smyth (William, *professor of modern history, Cambridge*). Memoir of [R. B.] Sheridan. ii, 74 pp. 16°. *Leeds, J. Cross,* 1840.

Smyth (William Henry, *admiral British navy*). Memoir, descriptive of the resources, inhabitants, and hydrography of Sicily and its islands, interspersed with antiquarian and other notices. xvi, 291, lxxiii pp. 9 l. 1 map. 13 pl. 4°. *London, J. Murray,* 1824.

Snarl of a cynic. By Benneville Ottomar Hoffman, a Pennsylvania teuton. [*pseudon.*] 40 pp. 24°. *Ephrata, (Pa.) P. M. Heitler,* 1868.

Snellaert (Ferdinand Augustijn). Oude en nieuwe liedjes, byeen verzameld. 2 p. l. iii, 62 pp. 1 l. xxxxiv pp. 12°. *Gent, H. Hoste,* 1852. S.

So sollt ihr beten! Vollständiges gebet und-andachts-büchlein für katholische christen. [*anon.*] 288 pp. 32°. *New York, C. & N. Benziger,* 1868.

Social influence; or, take care of the boys. By Zell, author of "Aunt Betsy's rule." [*anon.*] 396 pp. 4 pl. 18°. *Philadelphia, presbyterian board of publication,* [1864].

Society (The) of dilettanti. Specimens of antient sculpture, Aegyptian, Etruscan, Greek and Roman: selected from different collections in Great Britain. v. 1. 1 p. l. lxxxi, 128 pp. 75 pl. fol. *London, T. Payne etc.* 1809. S.
[v. 2, 1835, wanting].

Solari (Catherine Hyde, *marchioness* Broglio). *See* **Hyde** (Catherine, *marchioness* Broglio Solari).

Solis y Ribadeneyra (Antonio de). Historia de la conquista de Mexico, poblacion, y progresos de la America Septentrional, conocida por el nombre de Nueva España. 2 v. 12 p. l. 479 pp. 1 map. 5 pl; 7 p. l. 488 pp. 2 pl. 16°. *Barcelona, T. Piferrer*, 1771.

Solle (H. F. de la.) *See* **La Solle.**

Solorzano (Alfonso del Castillo). *See* **Castillo Solorzano.**

Somaize (Antoine Baudeau *or* Bodeau de). Le grand dictionnaire des prétievses, historiqve, poetiqve, [etc.] 2 v. 16 p. l. 314 pp. 2 l; 320 pp. 16°. *Paris, J. Ribov*, 1661.

——— La clef dv grand dictionnaire historiqve des pretievses. 46 pp. 16°. *Paris*, [*J. Ribov*], 1661.

[*With the* preceding. v. 2].

Somal (Placido Sukias). Quadro della storia letteraria di Armenia. xix, 240 pp. 8°. *Venezia, tipografia armena di s. Lazzaro*, 1829.

——— Quadro delle opere di vari autori anticamente tradotte in Armeno. [*anon.*] 45 pp. 8°. *Venezia, tipografia armena di s. Lazzaro*, 1825.

[*With* the preceding].

Some account of the Pennsylvania hospital; from its first rise to 1754. [*anon.*] 146 pp. 8°. *Philadelphia, office of the U. S. gazette*, 1817. s.

Some habits and customs of the working classes. By a journeyman engineer. [*anon.*] xi, 276 pp. 12°. *London, Tinsley bros.* 1867.

Some notes on America to be rewritten: suggested with respect to Charles Dickens. [*anon.*] 20 pp. 8°. *Philadelphia, Sherman & co.* 1868.

Somers (John, *lord Somers, baron of Evesham*). A collection of scarce and valuable tracts, on the most interesting and entertaining subjects: but chiefly such as relate to the history and constitution of these kingdoms. Selected from publick as well as private libraries; particularly that of the late lord Sommers. Revised by eminent hands. 4 v. 4°. *London, F. Cogan*, 1748.

——— The same. A second collection. 4 v. 4°. *London, F. Cogan*, 1750.

——— The same. A third collection. 4 v. 4°. *London, F. Cogan*, 1751.

——— The same. A fourth collection. 4 v. 4°. *London, F. Cogan*, 1751–52.

——— The same. A collection of scarce and interesting tracts, tending to elucidate parts of the history of Great Britain; selected from the Sommer's-collections, and arranged in chronological order. [By R. Edwards]. xvi, 627 pp. 4°. *London, R. Edwards*, 1795.

Somerville (Robert). General view of the agriculture of East Lothian. 2 p. l. 326 pp. 1 col. map. 8°. *London*, 1805. s.

[Great Britain: Board of agriculture].

Sommaire discovrs des cavses de tovs les trovbles de ce royavme, procedentes des impostures et coniurations des hérétiques et des rebelles. [*anon.*] 38 l. 16°. *Paris, P. L'Huillier*, 1573.

Sommer islands company. Copy of a petition from the governor and company of the Sommer islands, presented to the councel of state July 19th, 1651. Other copies of letters from captain Josias Forster, governor of the said islands, and from the said governor and councel there: with a petition from the inhabitants. 30 pp. sm. 4°. *London, E. Husband*, 1651.

Sommers. *See* **Somers.**

Songe (Le) du resveur. [*anon.*] Avec une préface du bibliophile Jacob. [Paul Lacroix]. x, 27 pp. 16°. *Genève, J. Gay & fils*, 1867.

Sonklar (Carl, *edler* von Innstädten). Die Oetzthaler gebirgsgruppe, mit besonderer rücksicht auf orographie und gletscherkunde, nach eigenen untersuchungen dargestellt. xvi, 292 pp. 1 col. pl. 8°. Atlas, 13 maps. fol. *Gotha, J. Perthes*, 1860. s.

[Atlas wanting].

Souter (David). General view of the agriculture of the county of Banff. viii, 339, 85 pp. 1 map. 3 pl. 8°. *Edinburgh*, 1812. s.

[Great Britain: Board of agriculture].

Southard (Samuel L.) Argument, in the case of Stacy Decow and Joseph Hendrickson, versus Thomas L. Shotwell, Trenton, N. J. Taken in short-hand by E. Hopper. [With appendix, illustrating the doctrines of the quakers on the trinity, the atonement, and the scriptures]. viii, 279 pp. 8°. *Philadelphia, E. Weaver*, 1834.

South Carolina (*State of*). Constitution, with the ordinances thereunto appended, adopted by the constitutional convention, Charleston, 1868. 46 pp. 8°. *Charleston, (S. C.) Denny & Perry*, 1868.

——— Speeches delivered in the convention, held in Columbia, in March, 1833. [With] the journal of proceedings. 80 pp. 8°. *Charleston, E. J. Van Brunt*, 1833.

Southern baptist publication society. Tracts on important subjects. 9 tracts in 1 v. 16°. *Charleston, s. b. p. society*, 1850–54. s.

Southern—continued.

CONTENTS.

1. The bible. By. J. L. Dagg. 32 pp.
2. Human depravity. By J. R. Kendrick. 24 pp.
3. Justification. By J. B. Jeter. 22 pp.
4. Sanctification. By C. D. Mallary. 47 pp.
5. The world's revolution. By R. T. Middleditch. 47 pp.
6. The spirit of missions. By E. T. Winkler. 33 pp.
7. Sabbath schools. By C. D. Mallary. 46 pp.
8. Infant baptism. By J. L. Dagg. 54 pp.
9. Charges against baptists. By J. B. Jeter. 25 pp.

Southern (The) literary journal, and monthly magazine. D. K. Whitaker, editor. Sept. 1835, to Aug. 1836. v. 1–2. 8°. *Charleston, J. S. Burges,* 1836.

——— The same. New series. B. R. Carroll, editor. 1836, to 1838. v. 3–4. 8°. *Charleston, J. S. Burges,* 1836–38.
[Imperfect: no. 1. v. 3, wanting].

Southern (The) review. Jan. 1867, to Oct. 1868. v. 1–4. 8°. *Baltimore, Bledsoe & Browne,* 1867–68.

Southworth (*Mrs.* Emma D. E. Nevitt). Fair play; or, the test of the lone isle. 670 pp. 12°. *Philadelphia, T. B. Peterson & bros.* [1868].

——— Fallen pride; or, the mountain girl's love. 467 pp. 12°. *Philadelphia, T. B. Peterson & bros.* [1868].

Soutsos (J. A.) Πραγματεια περι παραγωγης και διανομης του πλουτου. 4 p. l. 24, 488 pp. 8°. Αθηναις, Α. Κορομηλ, 1851. s.

Souvestre (Émile). Mathieu Ropars. Translated by W. Young. 16°. *New York, G. P. Putnam & son,* 1868.
[*In* YOUNG (William). Mathieu Ropars: et cetera. ed. 1868. pp. 8–75].

——— Pleasures of old age. From the French. xii, 344 pp. 12°. *London, G. Routledge & sons,* 1868.

Spagnuoli (Giovanni Battista). In Robertum Seuerinatem panægyricum carmen. 50 l. sm. 4°. *Bononiæ, expensis Benedicti Hectoris, librarii Platonisque impressoris,* 1489.

——— Parthenices [Marianæ] libri tres. 70 l. sm. 4°. *Bononiæ, imp. cura Caesaris de Nappis, impensa Benedicti Hectoris,* 1488.

Spain (*Kingdom of*). Diario de las sesiones del congreso de los diputados, 1853–65. 52 v. fol. *Madrid, imprenta nacional,* 1854–1866.

1853.	1 v.	1859.	5 v.	1863.	5 v.
1854–56.	15 v.	1860.	5 v.	1864.	5 v.
1857.	1 v.	1861.	6 v.	1865.	5 v.
1858.	2 v.	1862.	2 v.		

——— Guia de forasteros en Madrid, para el año de 1852. 566 pp. 16°. *Madrid, imprenta nacional,* [1852]. s.

——— *Biblioteca nacional.* Memoria remitida al ministro de fomiento, [etc.] por el director de la biblioteca nacional. 114 pp. 8°. *Madrid,* [*gobierno*], 1865. s.

——— ——— The same. Memoria leida en la biblioteca nacional en la sesion pública, (1866–68). 3 v. 8°. *Madrid,* [*gobierno*], 1866–68. s.

——— ——— Obra[s] premiada[s] por la biblioteca nacional, [etc.] 8 v. 8°. *Madrid, gobierno,* 1858–65. s.

CONTENTS.

BARRANTES (V.) Catálogo de los libros, [etc.] que tratan de las provincias de Extremadura. 1865.
COLMEIRO (M.) La botánica y botánicos de la peninsula hispano-lusitana. 1858.
EGUREN (J. M. de). Memoria descriptiva de los códices notables conservados en los archivos ecclesiasticos de España. 1859.
GALLARDO (B. J.) Ensayo de una biblioteca español de libros raros y curiosos, [etc.] v. 1–2. 1863–66.
LA BARRERA Y LEIRADO (C. A. de). Catálogo bibliografico y biográfico del teatro antiguo español, [etc.] 1860.
MUÑOZ Y ROMERO (T.) Diccionario bibliográfico-historico de los antiguos reinos, [etc.] de España. 1858.
RAMIREZ (B. A.) Diccionario de bibliografia agrónomica, [etc]. 1865.

——— ——— Apuntes para un catalogo de los objetosque comprende la coleccion del *Museo de antigüedas de la biblioteca nacional de Madrid,* con esclusion de los numismáticos, etc. por B. S. Castellanos de Losada. 212 pp. 2 l. 18°. *Madrid, Sanchiz,* 1847. s.

Sparrow (William, *D.D.*) A sermon preached in Staunton, (Va.) May, 1863, in memory of William Meade, D.D. late bishop of the diocese. 12°. *Baltimore, Innes & co.* 1867.
[*In* JOHNS (J. *D.D.*) Memoir of W. Meade. ed. 1867. pp. 521–537].

Spartianus (Aelius). [Vitae imperatorum romanorum, viz:] Adrianvs imp. ad Diocletianum Aug. 16°. [*Geneva*], 1568.
[*In* VARII historiæ romanæ scriptores. v. iii].

Spectateur (Le) militaire. Recueil de science, d'art et d'histoire militaires. 42ᵉ–43ᵉ année, Oct. 1867–Dec. 1868. 3ᵉ série. v. 10–14. 8°. *Paris, direction du spectateur militaire,* 1867-68.

Spectator (The). By Addison, Steele, Parnell, Hughes, Parker, Tickell, Budgell, Grove, Byrom, Henley, and others. 10 v. 12°. *New York, W. Durell & co.* 1809–10. s.
[v. 6 wanting].

Speculum exemplorum, ex diuersis libris in vnum laboriose collectum. [*anon.* Ab Aegidio Aurifabro? Ed. prima]. 504 l. fol. [*Daventriae*], *R. Paefroed,* 1481.

——— The same. Speculū exemplorū omnibus christicolis salubriter īspiciendū ut exemplis discant disciplinā ex diuersis libris in vnū laboriose collectum. [*anon.* Ab Aegidio Aurifabro]? 285 l. fol. *Argentina,* 1490.

Spence (Elizabeth Isabella). Sketches of the present manners, customs, and scenery of Scotland, with incidental remarks on the Scottish character. 2d ed. 2 v. xxviii, 227 pp; 4 p. l. 266 pp. 2 l. 16°. *London, Longmans,* 1811.

Spence (Thomas). The settler's guide in the United States and British North American provinces. 472 pp. 1 map. 11 pl. 12°. *New York, Davis & Kent,* 1862.

Spencer (Herbert). First principles of a new system of philosophy. viii, 508 pp. 12°. *New York, Appletons,* 1864.

Spencer (John, *librarian of Zion college*). Καινα και παλαια. Things new and old; or, a storehouse of similes, sentences, allegories, etc. With preface by Thomas Fuller, London, 1658. Edited, with an introduction, by J. G. Pilkington. 3d ed. 10 p. l. 695 pp. 8°. *London, R. D. Dickinson,* 1868.

Spenser society publications. sm. fol. *London, Spenser society,* 1867-68.
No. 1. HEYWOOD (John). Proverbs and epigrams.
No. 2-3. TAYLOR (John). Works.

Spitz (F. Ch.) Le fervent chrétien, ou recueil de prières à l'usage des fidèles de toutes les conditions. 4e éd. 606 pp. 24°. *New York, C. & N. Benziger,* 1868.

Spitzel *or* **Spizelius** (Gottlieb). Vetus academia Jesu Christi, in qua xxii priscæ sinceræ que pietatis professorum icones exhibentur, [etc.] 12 p. l. 228 pp. 22 pl. 4°. *Augustæ Vindelicorum, apud G. Goebelium,* 1671. S.

Spix (Johann Baptist von) *and* **Martius** (Carl Friedrich Phillipp von). Atlas zur reise in Brasilien. 1 ill. title. 9 maps, etc. 1 portrait (of Martius). 41 pl. fol. [*München, F. Fleischer,* 1823-31]. S.

Spizelius (Theophilus). *See* **Spitzel** (Gottlieb).

Spolverini (Gianbattista, *marchese*). La coltivazione del riso. 8°. *Milano,* 1825.
[*In* RACCOLTA di poemi didascalici. Ed. 2a. 1825].

Sprengel (Mathias Christoph). Allgemeines historisches taschenbuch, oder abriss der merkwürdigsten neuen welt-begebenheiten, enthaltend für 1784, die geschichte der revolution von Nord-America. 4 p. l. 182 pp. 1 map. 16 pl. 24°. *Berlin, Haude & Spener,* 1784.

Sprigg (*Rev.* D. F.) Aid to those who pray in private. Closet prayers for every morning, mid-day, and evening of the week, [etc.] viii, 215 pp. 24°. *Boston, E. P. Dutton & co.* 1869.

Spring (Samuel, *D.D.*) Moral disquisitions and strictures on the rev. David Tappan's letters to Philalethes. 252 pp. 12°. *Newbury-port, J. Mycall,* 1789.

Spruner (Carl von). Historisch-geographischer hand-atlas zur geschichte Asiens, Africa's, America's, und Australiens. 2e aufl. 11 pp. 4°. 18 col. maps. obl. fol. *Gotha, J. Perthes,* 1855. S.

Squier (Miles P. *D.D.*) The being of God, moral government, and theses in theology. Edited by J. R. Boyd. 247 pp. portrait. 16°. *Rochester, (N.Y.) Darrow & Kempshall,* 1868.

Squire Downing's heirs. [*anon.*] 358 pp. 4 pl. 16°. *New York, R. Carter & bros.* 1868.

Stadler (*Prof.* ——). Osservazioni meteorologiche. (Elementi per la statistica, etc. n. 2). 8°. *Trieste,* 1829.
[*In* ROSSETTI (D. de). Archeografo triestino. v. 1].

Staël-Holstein (Anne Louise Germaine Necker, *baronne* de). De l'influence des passions sur le bonheur des individus et des nations. 378 pp. 8°. *Lausanne, J. Mourer, etc.* 1796. S.

Staeudlin. *See* **Stäudlin.**

Stagg (Edward). Poems. 262 pp. 12°. *Saint Louis, Keith & Woods,* 1852.

Stancovich (Pietro). Deposito di monete ungheresi, carraresi, veneziane, scoperto nell' Istria. 8°. *Trieste,* 1831.
[*In* ROSSETTI (D. de). Archeografo triestino. v. 3].

——— Marmo di Lucio Menacio patrono di Pola, scoperto nell'Aprile, 1831. 8°. *Trieste,* 1830.
[*In* ROSSETTI (D. de). Archeografo triestino, v. 2].

Standard phonographic visitor. Edited by A. J. Graham. Aug, 1863, to April, 1868. v. 1-2. 16°. *New York, A. J. Graham,* 1865-68.

Stanislas i. Leszcynski, *king of Poland.* Maxims and reflections. 8°. *New York,* 1851.
[*In* LA ROCHEFOUCAULD (F. *duc* de). Moral reflections, etc. 1851. pp. 149-186].

Stanley (Arthur Penrhyn, *D.D. dean of Westminster*). Historical memorials of Westminster abbey. 2d and revised ed. lii, 632 pp. 1 pl. 8°. *London, J. Murray,* 1868.

Stannius (Friedrich Hermann). Beiträge zur kenntniss der amerikanischen manati's. 1 p. l. 37 pp. 2 pl. 4°. *Rostock, Adler's erben,* 1845. S.

——— Observationes de speciebus nonnullis generis mycetophila vel novis, vel minus cognitis. 30 pp. 1 col. pl. 4°. *Vratislaviæ, E. Pelz,* 1831. S.

Stansbury (Arthur J.) Elementary catechism on the constitution of the United States. 78 pp. 16°. *Boston, Hilliard, Gray, Little & Wilkins,* 1828.

Stark (Carl Bernhard). Forschungen zur geschichte und alterthumskunde des hellenistischen orients. Gaza und die philistäische küste. Eine monographie. xvi, 646 pp. 1 l. 1 pl. 1 map. 8°. *Jena, F. Mauke,* 1852.

Stassart (Goswin Joseph Augustin, *baron* de). Bibliothèque léguée à l'académie royale de Belgique. *See* **Academie** royale de Belgique.

——— Fables. [Avec des notes]. 6e éd. vii, 402 pp. 8 pl. 16°. *Bruxelles, Lacrosse,* 1837. s.

States (The). [Washington daily]. From commencement, April 17, 1857, to Dec. 31, 1859. 5 v. fol. *Washington,* 1857–59.

Statesman's (The) year book. A statistical, mercantile, and historical account of the states and sovereigns of the civilised world. For the year 1868–69. By F. Martin. 5th [and] 6th annual publication. 2 v. 12°. *London, Macmillan & co.* 1868.

Statistical (A) display of the finances, navigation, and commerce of Great Britain and Ireland, [etc.] exhibiting the revenue, [etc.] since 1793; the national debt, etc. 238, 17 pp. 2 tab. 4°. *London,* [1838]. s.

Stäudlin (Carl Friedrich). Geschichte der theologischen wissenschaften seit der verbreitung der alten literatur. 2 v. 8°. *Göttingen,* 1810. s.

[EICHHORN (J. G.) Geschichte der literatur, etc. v. 6].

Stearns (*Rev.* Jonathan F.) First church in Newark. Historical discourses relating to the first presbyterian church in Newark, etc. xiv, 320 pp. 5 pl. 1 map. 8°. *Newark, Daily advertiser office,* 1853. s.

Stearns (Samuel, *LL.D.*) The American oracle. Comprehending an account of recent discoveries in the arts and sciences, with a variety of religious, political, physical, and philosophical subjects. 4 p. l. 627, xviii pp. 8°. *London, J. Lackington,* 1791.

Stebbins (Henry G.) Finances and resources of the United States. Speech in the house of representatives, March 3, 1864. 22 pp. 8°. *New York,* 1864.

[LOYAL publication society. no. 45].

Stebbins (Henry S.) Atlas of the state of Ohio; from surveys under the direction of H. F. Walling. [With] an atlas of the United States. 19 pp. 2 l. 35 maps. 4°. *New York, H. H. Lloyd & co.* 1868.

Steele (J. Dorman). A fourteen weeks' course in descriptive astronomy. 318 pp. 1 map. 1 pl. 12°. *New York, A. S. Barnes & co.* 1868.

Steenstrup (Johan Japetus Smith) *and* **Lütken** (Christian Frederik). Bidrag til kundskab om det aabne havs snyltekrebs og lernæer samt om nogle andre nye oller hidtil kun ufuldstændigt kjendte parasitiske copepoder. [Extract]. 92 pp. 15 pl. 4°. *Kjöbenhavn, K. danske videnskabernes selskab,* 1861. s.

Steetz (Joachim). Aggregatæ [von Mossambique.] fol. *Berlin,* 1865.

[*In* PETERS (W. C. H.) Nat. reise nach Mossambique. Botanik].

Stein (Johann von). *See* **Lapide.**

Steindachner (*Dr.* Franz). Reptilien. 4°. *Wien,* 1867.

[*In* WÜLLERSTORF-URBAIR (B. von). Reise der Novara. Zoologischer theil].

Steinmetz (Andrew). The romance of duelling in all times and countries. 2 v. xii, 336 pp; viii, 384 pp. 12°. *London, Chapman & Hall,* 1868.

Stelle (J. Parish). The American watchmaker and jeweler, a full and comprehensive exposition of all the latest and most approved secrets of the trade. 62 pp. 16°. *New York, J. Haney & co.* 1868.

Stenzel (Gustav Adolf Harald). Geschichte Deutschlands unter den fränkischen kaisern. [1024–1125]. 2 v. xxv, 765 pp; vi, 346 pp. 8°. *Leipzig, C. Tauchnitz,* 1827–28.

Stephanus. *See* **Estienne.**

Stephens (Alexander Hamilton). The assertions of a secessionist. From [his] speeches, Nov. 1860, and Jan. 1861. 8 pp. 8°. *New York,* 1864.

[LOYAL publication society. no. 56].

——— A constitutional view of the late war between the states; its causes, character, conduct, and results. Presented in a series of colloquies at Liberty hall. v. 1. 654 pp. 7 pl. 8°. *Philadelphia, national pub. co.* 1868.

——— Speech in opposition to secession in 1860. 8°. *New York,* 1865.

[LOYAL publication society. no. 36. Prophecy and fulfillment. Part i. *or,* pp. 1–22.]

Stephens (*Mrs.* Ann Sophia Winterbotham). Doubly false. 556 pp. 12°. *Philadelphia, T. B. Peterson & bros.* 1868.

——— Mabel's mistake. 431 pp. 12°. *Philadelphia, T. B. Peterson & bros.* 1868.

——— The old homestead. 435 pp. 12°. *New York, Bunce & bro.* 1855. s.

Stephens (John Langdon). Incidents of travel in Central America, Chiapas, and Yucatan. 2 v. 424 pp. 1 map. 24 pl; 474 pp. 44 pl. 8°. *New York, Harpers,* 1843.

——— Incidents of travel in Yucatan. 2 v. xii, 459 pp. 1 map. 14 pl; xvi, 478 pp. 53 pl. 8°. *New York, Harpers,* 1843.

Stern (Daniel, *pseudon.*) *See* **Agoult** (Marie de Florigny, *comtesse d'*).

Sterne (*Rev.* Laurence). A collection of [his] letters to his most intimate friends. [With] fragment in the manner of Rabelais; and the history of a watch-coat. [And] memoirs of his life and family, by himself. xii, 239 pp. portrait. 18°. *London, J. Wenman*, 1790.

——— A sentimental journey through France and Italy. By Mr. Yorick. [*pseudon.*] 195 pp. 24°. *Brattleborough, (Vt.) W. Fessenden*, [1810].

Sternhold (Thomas), **Hopkins** (John) *and others.* The whole booke of psalmes collected into English meeter, with apt notes to sing them withall. 9 p. l. 151 pp. 8 l. fol. *London, companie of stationers*, 1635.
[*With* BOOK of common prayer. ed. 1632].

——— The same. 57 pp. 2 l. fol. *London, comp. of stationers*, 1679.
[*With* BIBLE. (*English*). *London*, 1707–08].

Steuart (John Robert). A description of some ancient monuments, with inscriptions, still existing in Lydia and Phrygia. 2 p. l. 14 pl. fol. *London, James Bohn*, 1842.

Stevens (Abel, *LL.D.*) A compendious history of American methodism. Abridged from the author's "History of the Methodist Episcopal Church." 608 pp. 11 pl. 8°. *New York, Carlton & Porter*, 1867.

Stevens (Henry). Bibliotheca americana. A catalogue of books relating to the history and literature of America. [Sold 1861]. vi, 273 pp. 8°. *London, Puttick & Simpson*, 1861.

——— Stevens' American bibliographer. v. 1. nos. 1–2. [A — Cure]. vii, 96 pp. 3 pl. 8°. *Chiswick, C. Whittingham, for subscribers only*, 1854. s.
[No more published].

Stevens (John Austin). Letters of loyal soldiers. 4 parts. 16 pp. 8°. *New York*, 1864.
[LOYAL publication society. no. 64].

——— Sherman vs. Hood. "A low tart, inclined to be very sweet." On the Chicago surrender, a poem. By Bayard Taylor, etc. 4 pp. 8°. *New York*, 1864.
[LOYAL publication society. no. 61].

——— The submissionists and their record. 2 parts. 8 pp. 8°. *New York*, 1864.
[LOYAL publication society. no. 65].

Stevenson (William). General view of the agriculture of the county of Dorset. xi, 487 pp. 3 l. 1 col. map. 8°. *London*, 1812. s.
[GREAT BRITAIN: Board of agriculture].

——— General view of the agriculture of the county of Surrey. viii, 616 pp. 1 col. pl. 8°. *London*, 1809. s.
[GREAT BRITAIN: Board of agriculture].

——— *See, also,* **Dickson** (R. W.) Agriculture of Lancashire.

Stewart (James). Additions to R. Hooper's physicians vade-mecum. *See* **Hooper** (R.)

Stewart (Robert Walter, *D. D.*) The tent and the khan: a journey to Sinai and Palestine. xv, 528 pp. 1 map. 1 pl. 8°. *Edinburgh, W. Oliphant & sons*, 1857.

Stewart. *See* **Steuart** *and* **Stuart.**

Stewech *or* **Stewechius** (Godeskalk *or* Godescalcus). Commentarivs ad FlavI VegetI Renati libros, de re militari. 8 p. l. 419 pp. 18 l. 1 tab. 4°. *Antverpiæ, apud C. Plantinum*, 1585. s.
[*With* VEGETIUS. De re militari. 1585].

Stieler (Adolf, *editor*). Hand-atlas über alle theile der erde nach dem neuesten zustande, und über das weltegebaude. Bericht nebst ausführlichen erlauterungen einzelner karten. 6e aufl. iv, 30 pp. 2 l. 4°. 1 pl. 83 col. maps. obl. fol. *Gotha, J. Perthes*, 1855. s.

——— Schul-atlas über alle theile der erde, nach dem neuesten zustande, und über das weltegebaude. 36e aufl. 1 p. l. 32 maps. 4°. *Gotha, J. Perthes*, 1856. s.

Stiles (Ezra, *D. D.*) The United States elevated to glory and honour. A sermon preached at Hartford, at the anniversary election, May 8th, 1783. 2d ed. 172 pp. 8°. *Worcester, I. Thomas*, 1783.

Stillé (Alfred, *M. D.*) Therapeutics and materia medica. A systematic treatise on the action and uses of medicinal agents, including their description and history. 3d ed. 2 v. 824 pp; 864 pp. 8°. *Philadelphia, H. C. Lea*, 1868.

Stillé (Charles J.) How a free people conduct a long war. 16 pp. 8°. *New York, A. D. F. Randolph*, 1863.
[LOYAL publication society. no. 13].

Stirling (Alexander, 9*th earl of*). *See* **Alexander** (Alexander, 9th *earl of Stirling*).

Stirling (James Hutchinson, *LL. D.*) Jerrold, Tennyson, and Macaulay, with other critical essays. [De Quincey and Coleridge upon Kant, and Ebenezer Elliott]. 4 p. l. 243 pp. 12°. *Edinburgh, Edmonston & Douglas*, 1868.

Stöckhardt (Ernst, *editor*). *See* **Zeitschrift** für deutsche landwirthe.

Stockholder (The). Monitor of finance and industry, mining and railway record. [A weekly journal]. Nov. 1867, to Nov. 1868. v. 6. fol. *New York, S. P. Dinsmore & co.* 1868.

Stockton (J. *A. M.*) The western calculator; or, a new and compendious system of practical arithmetic. 4th ed. 203 pp. 16°. *Pittsburgh, Eichbaum & Johnston,* 1826.

Stockwell (G. S. *compiler*). The republic of Liberia: its geography, climate, soil, and productions, with a history of its early settlement. 299 pp. 12°. *New York, A. S. Barnes & co.* 1868.

Stoddard (John F.) The American intellectual arithmetic. 16th ed. 164 pp. 18°. *New York, Nafis & Cornish,* 1850. s.

——— Stoddard's complete arithmetic: being the new practical arithmetic of the series. 456 pp. 12°. *New York, Sheldon & co.* 1868.

Stoddart (*Sir* John). Glossology; or, the historical relations of languages. First division. 3 p. l. 387 pp. 12°. *London, R. Griffin & co.* 1858.

Stolen (The) child; or, twelve years with the gypsies. [*anon.*] 180 pp. 3 pl. 18°. *New York, American tract society,* 1868.

Stolzman (Karol Bogumir). Partyzantka czyli wojna dla ludów powstajacych najwláściwsza. 4 p. l. xxiv, 239 pp. 2 pl. 8°. *Paryz i Lipsk, Brockhaus i avenarius,* 1844. s.

Stone (William Leete). History of New York city, from the discovery to the present day. 252 pp. 1 pl. 8°. *New York, E. Cleve,* 1868.

Stopping the leak. By aunt Hattie. [*pseudon.*] 294 pp. 3 pl. 16°. *Boston, Graves & Young,* 1865.

Storer (David Humphreys). A history of the fishes of Massachusetts. (Reprinted from the memoirs of the American academy of arts and sciences). 2 p. l. 287 pp. 39 pl. 4°. *Cambridge and Boston, Welch & Bigelow, etc.* [1853–1867]. s.

——— Ichthyology and herpetology of Massachusetts. 8°. *Boston,* 1839.

[MASSACHUSETTS. Zoological and botanical survey. *In* Reports on the fishes, etc.]

Storer (Frank H.) A compendious manual of qualitative chemical analysis. 1868. *See* **Eliot** (Charles W.) *and* **Storer.**

——— Manual of inorganic chemistry. *See* **Eliot** (Charles W.) *and* **Storer.**

Storer (Horatio Robinson, *M. D.*) Is it I? A book for every man. A companion to "Why not? A book for every woman." xix, 154 pp. 16°. *Boston, Lee & Shepard,* 1868.

[Tracts for the people. no. 2].

——— On nurses and nursing; with especial reference to the management of sick women. 80 pp. 16°. *Boston, Lee & Shepard,* 1868.

——— On criminal abortion in America. 107 pp. 8°. *Philadelphia, Lippincott & co.* 1860.

——— *and* **Heard** (Franklin Fiske). Criminal abortion: its nature, its evidence, and its law. viii, 215 pp. 8°. *Boston, Little, Brown & co.* 1868.

Stories from life, which the chaplain [B. K. P.] told. [*anon.*] 317 pp. 2 pl. 16°. *Boston, H. Hoyt,* 1866.

——— Sequel to stories from life, which the chaplain [B. K. P.] told. [*anon.*] 286 pp. 2 pl. 16°. *Boston, H. Hoyt,* 1867.

Stork (*Rev.* Theophilus). The home scenes of the new testament; or, Christ in the family. 296 pp. 1 pl. 12°. *Philadelphia, Lindsay & Blakiston,* 1857. s.

Story (The) of James Moran. By the author of "A sister's story," etc. [*anon.*] 280 pp. 3 pl. 16°. *Boston, American tract society,* [1867].

Stow (John). Thoughts on the gospel of Jesus Christ, the son of God, [etc.] By a lay-member of the church of England. [*anon.*] 800 pp. portrait. 8°. *Greenwich, H. S. Richardson,* 1846. s.

Stowe (Harriet Esther Beecher). The chimney-corner. By Christopher Crowfield. [*pseudon.*] 311 pp. 16°. *Boston, Ticknor & Fields,* 1868.

——— Men of our times; or, leading patriots of the day; being narratives of the lives and deeds of statesmen, generals, and orators. xiv, 575 pp. 18 pl. 8°. *Hartford, Hartford publishing co.* 1868.

CONTENTS.

Andrew (John A.)	Greeley (Horace).
Beecher (*Rev.* H. W.)	Howard (Oliver O.)
Buckingham (Wm. A.)	Lincoln (Abraham).
Chase (Salmon P.)	Phillips (Wendell).
Colfax (Schuyler).	Sheridan (Philip H.)
Douglass (Frederick).	Sherman (William T.)
Farragut (David G.)	Stanton (Edwin M.)
Garrison (William L.)	Sumner (Charles).
Grant (Ulysses S.)	Wilson (Henry).

Stowell (*Rev.* Hugh). A model for men of business; or, the christian layman contemplated among his secular occupations, [etc.] With an introduction, by rev. Daniel Curry. 322 pp. 16°. *New York, Carlton & Phillips,* 1855. s.

Strabo. Geographiæ opus, latine, Guarino veronense et Gregorio typhernate interpretibus. 318 l. fol. [*Tarvisii*], *J. Vercellensis,* 1480.

Strahl (Philipp, *LL. D.*) Das gelehrte Russland. xx, 514 pp. 8°. *Leipzig, F. Fleischer,* 1828.

Stranger (The) in the tropics: being a handbook for Havana and guide book for travellers in Cuba, Puerto Rico, and St. Thomas. With descriptions of the principal objects of interest, suggested to invalids (by a physician). Hints

Stranger—continued. for tours and general directions for travellers. Hand-book edition. 194 pp. 4 pl. 1 map. 12°. *New York, American news co.* 1868.

Straten-Ponthoz (*Comte* Auguste van der). Le budget du Brésil, ou recherches sur les ressources de cet empire dans leurs rapports avec les intérêts européens du commerce et de l'émigration. 3 v. 8°. *Bruxelles, C. Muquardt,* 1854.

Straus-Dürckheim (Hercule Eugène G.) Considérations générales sur l'anatomie comparée des animaux articulés, auxquelles on a joint l'anatomie descriptive du *melolontha vulgaris.* xix, 434 pp. atlas. 36 pp. 19 pl. 4°. *Paris, F. G. Levrault,* 1828. s.

Street (Francis S.) *and* **Smith's** (Francis S.) New York weekly. A journal of useful knowledge, romance, amusement, etc. Nov. 1866, to Nov. 1868. v. 22–23. fol. *New York, Street & Smith,* 1867–68.

——— Street and Smith's literary album. June, 1867, to Dec. 1868. v. 4–6. fol. *New York, Street & Smith,* 1867–68.

Strengleikar eda liodabok. En samling af romantiske fortællinger efter bretoniske folkesange (lais), oversat fra Fransk paa Norsk ved midten af trettende aarhundrede efter foranstaltning af kong Haakon Haakonssön. Udgivet af R. Keyser og C. R. Unger. xxiv, 140 pp. 1 pl. 8°. *Christiania, Feibberg & Landmark,* 1850. s.

[NOTE.—"Le plupart de ces pièces est tirée des oeuvres de Marie de France." *Grässe*].

Strickland (Hugh Edwin). A general view of the agriculture of the east riding of Yorkshire. viii, 332 pp. 1 col. map. 7 pl. 8°. *York,* 1812. s.

[GREAT BRITAIN: Board of agriculture].

Strinnholm (Anders Magnus). Svenska folkets historia, [etc.] v. 3. [*or*] Svenska folkets medeltids-historia. Första afdelningen. Frän medlet af xi ärhundradet till medlet af det xii: te. 8°. *Stockholm, Hörberg,* 1848. s.

Strobel (B. B. *M. D.*) An essay on the subject of the yellow fever, intended to prove its transmissibility. 224 pp. 8°. *Charleston, A. J. Muir,* 1840.

Strong (Howard). Analogies of color and sound. 30 pp. 8°. *Lockport, (N. Y.) J. A. Wolcott & co.* 1868.

Strong (James, *S. T. D.*) Cyclopædia of biblical literature, etc. *See* **M'Clintock** (John, *D. D.*) *and* **Strong.**

——— Epitome of Greek grammar. 60 pp. 8°. *New York, J. F. Trow,* 1856. s.

Strother (J. Hunt). The golden calf; or, the almighty dollar. A satire. 32 pp. 12°. *New York, G. E. Leefe,* 1854. s.

Strubberg (Johann Anton). Index theologarum evangelico-lutheranorum chronologicus, sistens a tempore reformationis ad nostra usque tempora illorum nomina, patriam, officia et annos emortuales. Præmissa est allocutio epistolica ad eruditos historiæ ecclesiæ et literariæ cultores, etc. 4 p. l. 222 pp. 12°. *Lemgoviæ, ex officina meyeriana,* 1727. s.

Struve (Gustav). Weltgeschichte in neun büchern. v. 1–4. (9e heft), and v. 7. 8°. *New York, G. Struve,* 1856–59. s.

[v. 4 imperfect; v. 5–6, and 8–9, wanting].

CONTENTS.

v. 1–3. Alte geschichte.
v. 4. Geschichte der mittelalters.
v. 7. Geschichte des neuzeit. v. 1. Vom anbeginn der reformation bis zum westphälischen frieden, (1517–1648).

Stuart (Moses, *D. D.*) Exegetical essays on several words relating to future punishment. 208 pp. 16°. *Philadelphia, presbyterian publ. com.* [1868].

Stuart. *See* **Steuart** *and* **Stewart.**

Stubbe (Henry, *M. D.*) The Indian nectar; or, a discourse concerning chocolata: wherein the nature of the cacao-nut, and the other ingredients of that composition, is examined. 8 p. l. 184 pp. 18°. *London, A. Crook,* 1662.

Stuckenberg (*Rev.* J. H. W.) The history of the Augsburg confession, from its origin till the adoption of the formula of concord. xxi, 335 pp. 12°. *Philadelphia, Lutheran board of publication,* 1869.

Studies in conduct. Short essays from the "Saturday review." [*anon.*] viii, 290 pp. 12°. *London, Chapman & Hall,* 1867.

Stukeley (*Rev.* William). The philosophy of earthquakes, natural and religious; or, an inquiry into their cause and their purpose. 2d ed. [With] part ii. on the same subject. 2 v. in 1. 61 pp; 32 pp. 8°. *London, C. Corbet,* 1750.

Sturdivant (John A.) Shippers' express guide. *See* **Waldron** (Neil A.) *and* **Sturdivant.**

Sue (Marie Joseph, *known as* Eugène). The mysteries of Paris. From the French, by Charles H. Town. 466 pp. 8°. *New York, Harpers,* 1843.

——— Paula Monti; ou, l'hotel Lambert. Histoire contemporaine. 2 v. in 1. 230 pp; 216 pp. 24°. *Paris, Paulin,* 1845.

Suetonius *Tranquillus* (Caius). xii Cæsares. 16°. [*Geneva*], 1568.
[*In* VARII historiæ romanæ scriptores. v. 3].

Summary (A) of English and of French history. For the use of schools. [*anon.*] 33 pp. 16°. *New York, Barnes & co.* 1868.

Summer islands. *See* **Sommer** islands.

Summerly (Felix, *pseudon.*) *See* **Cole** (Henry).

Sumner (Charles). No property in man. Speech on the proposed amendment of the constitution abolishing slavery. In the senate, April 8, 1864. 23 pp. 8°. *New York, Chapin, Bromell & Scott,* 1864.
[LOYAL publication society. no. 51].

Sun (The). [Baltimore daily]. Jan. 1, 1838, to Oct. 11, 1853. 12 v. fol. *Baltimore,* 1838-53.
[Wanting: v. 1. May 15 to Dec. 31, 1837, and July 2, 1843, to Oct. 16, 1846].

Sunbeam (The) stories. [*anon.*] 236 pp. 4 pl. 16°. *Philadelphia, American s. s. union,* 1866.

Sunbeams: the first and the last. A story for boys and girls. [*anon.*] 172 pp. 1 pl. 16°. *New York, Miller, Orton & Mulligan,* 1856. s.

Sunday morning chronicle. [Washington]. *See* **Daily** morning chronicle.

Sunday school (The) chant and tune book; a collection of canticles, hymns, and carols, for the sunday schools of the episcopal church. 189 pp. 16°. *Boston, E. P. Dutton & co.* 1866.

Sunday school (The) teacher. Devoted to the interests of sunday schools. [A monthly magazine]. Jan. to Dec. 1868. v. 3. 8°. *Chicago, Adams, Blackmer & Lyon,* 1868.

Sunday (The) times. [Washington]. Feb. 22, 1863, to March 6, 1864. v. 1 and v. 2, no. 7 in 1 v. fol. *Washington, W. D. Hughes,* 1863-64.

Sunderland (*Rev.* J. P.) *and* **Buzacott** (*Rev.* Aaron, *jr.*) Mission life in the islands of the Pacific. Being a narrative of the life and labours of the rev. A. Buzacott, missionary of Rarotonga. xxii, 288 pp. 7 pl. 12°. *London, J. Snow & co.* 1866.

Sun-rays from fair and cloudy skies. By cousin Carrie, author of "keep a good heart." [*anon.*] 260 pp. 6 pl. 16°. *New York, Appletons,* 1866.

Sunshine [and] starlight. [Pious thoughts for each day and night of the month. *anon.*] 96 pp. 32°. *Boston, E. P. Dutton & co.* 1868.

Suppressed (The) book about slavery. Prepared for publication in 1847, [but] never published until the present time. [*anon.*] 432 pp. 8 pl. 12°. *New York, Carleton,* 1864.

Surin (Jean Joseph). The foundations of the spiritual life; drawn from the book of the imitation of Jesus Christ. lxxii, 252 pp. 1 pl. 16°. *London, J. Burns,* 1844.

Susquehannah (The) title stated and examined, in a series of numbers first published in the Western star. [*anon.*] 115 pp. 12°. *Catskill, M. Crosswell,* 1796.

Susy's sacrifice. By the author of "Jolly and Katy in the country," etc. [*anon.*] 306 pp. 4 pl. 16°. *New York, Carters,* 1868.

Sutherland (William). The practical guide to the art of house decoration. 144 pp. 12°. *London, Simpson, Marshall & co.* [1868].

Sutro (Adolph). The mineral resources of the United States, and the importance and necessity of inaugurating a national system of mining, with special reference to the Comstock lode and the Sutro tunnel, in Nevada. 232 pp. 2 maps. 1 pl. 4°. *Baltimore, J. Murphy & co.* 1868.

Svensson (S. G.) Om inflytelsen af läran om satisfactio vicaria pa den lutherska dogmatiken. 1 p. l. 135 pp. 8°. *Lund, Berlingska boktryckeriet,* 1866. s.

Swainson (*Rev.* Charles Anthony) *and* **Wratislaw** (*Rev.* Albert Henry). Loci communes. Common places, delivered in Christ's college, Cambridge. 4 p. l. 135 pp. 16°. *London, J. W. Parker,* 1848.

Swan (Robert). An elementary intellectual arithmetic. *See* **Leach** (D.) *and* **Swan**.

Sweden. Bidrag til sveriges officiella statistik. 12 series. 4°. *Stockholm, P. A. Norstedt & soner, kongl. boktryckare,* 1857-67. s.

CONTENTS.

A. Befolkningsstatistik. Ny följd. i-vii. Statistika central-byrans underdaniga berättelse för aren 1851-66. 1857-68.

B. Rättsväsendet. Ny följd. i-ix. Justitie-statsministerns underdaniga embetsberättelse för aren 1857-66. 1860-68. The same. Ny följd. i. 3. a. Sammandrag af justitie-statsministerns underdaniga embetsberättelser för aren 1830 till och med 1856, [etc.] 1863. [*With* v. 1].

C. Bergshandtering. Commerce collegii underdaniga berättelse för aren 1858-66. 1859-67.

D. Fabriker och manufakturer. Commerce collegii underdaniga berättelse för aren 1858-62, 1864 and 1866. 1859-67. [1865 wanting].

E. Inrikes handel och sjöfart. Commerce collegii underdaniga berättelse för aren 1858-62, 1864 and 1866. 1859-67. [1863, '65 wanting].

F. Utrikes handel och sjöfart. Commerce collegii underdaniga berättelse för ar. 1858-62, 1864 and 1866. 1859-67. [1865 wanting].

G. Fangvarden. Ny följd. i-viii. Fangvards-styrelsens underdaniga berättelse för aren 1859-66. 1861-68.

H. Kongl. maj:ts befallningshafvandes femarsberättelser [Ny följd. i.] för aren 1856-60. 1863. Ny följd. ii. Jemte sammandrag for aren 1861-65. 1868.

I. Telegrafväsendet. Ny följd. 1-5. Telegraf-styrelsens underdaniga berättelse för aren 1861-67. 1862-68.

Sweden—continued.

K. Helso- och sjukvarden.
i. Sundhets-collegi underdaniga berättelse. Ny följd. 1-5. Aret 1861-65. 1864-68. [v. 2. 1862 wanting].
ii. Ofverstyrelsens öfver hospitalen underdaniga berättelse för ar. 1861-66. 1862-68.
L. Statens jernvägstrafik. 1-5. Trafik-styrelsens underdaniga berättelse för aren 1862-66. 4 v. 1864-67.
M. Posterverket. 1. Generalpoststyrelsens den 20 December, 1865, i underdanighet afgifna berättelse om postverkets förvaltning, 1864-1866. 1866-68.

—— Diplomatarium suecanum collegit et edidit. [*Or*], Svenskt diplomatarium, utgifvet af Joh. Gust. Liljegren [and] Bror Emil Hildebrand. 3 v. 4°. *Stockholm, P. A. Norstedt & söner*, 1829-52. s.

CONTENTS.

v. 1. 817—1285.
v. 2. 1286—1310.
v. 3. 1311—1326.

Swedenborg (Emanuel). Angelic wisdom concerning the divine providence. From the Latin by R. N. Foster. 340 pp. 8°. *Philadelphia, Lippincott*, 1868.

—— On the Athanasian creed and subjects connected with it. A translation. [From the Latin]. 207 pp. 12°. *New York, gen. conv. of New Jerusalem*, 1867.

Sweet (*Mrs.* Elizabeth). The future life, as described and portrayed by spirits through mrs. Elizabeth Sweet. 1 p. l. 403 pp. 12°. *Boston, W. White & co.* 1869.

Sweet (I. D. J.) Ready reckoner. 208 pp. 16°. *New York, R. M. De Witt*, 1868.

Sweet (O. P.) The showman's directory and guide, for 1867. 200 pp. 12°. *Rochester, Benton & Andrews*, 1867.

Sweetser (Charles H.) Book of summer resorts, explaining where to find them, how to find them, and their especial advantages, with details of time tables and prices. 72 pp. 1 l. 29, viii pp. 19 l. 5 maps. 18°. *New York, Evening mail*, 1868.

Swieten (Gerard, *baron* van). *See* **Van Swieten.**

Swift (*Rev.* Elisha P.) Memoir of the rev. Joseph W. Barr. New ed. 132 pp. 1 pl. 16°. *Philadelphia, presbyterian board of publication*, 1854. s.

Swift (John Franklin). Going to Jericho; or, sketches of travel in Spain and the east. 447 pp. 12°. *New York, A. Roman & co.* 1868.

Swinburne (Algernon Charles). William Blake. A critical essay. iv, 304 pp. 9 pl. 8°. *London, J. C. Hotten*, 1868.

Swinton (William). The war for the Union. The first, second, third, and fourth years of the war. 20 pp. 8°. *New York*, 1864.

[LOYAL publication society. no. 62].

Swoboda (Waclaw Aloys). Historisch-kritischer einleitung. *See* **Hanka** (Waclaw). Kralodworsky rukopis, etc. 1829.

Sybel (Heinrich Carl Ludolf von). Entstehung des deutschen königthums. ix, 268 pp. 8°. *Frankfurt am Main, F. Varrentrapp*, 1844.

—— History of the French revolution. From the German, by W. C. Perry. v. 1-2. 8°. *London, J. Murray*, 1867.

Sydow (Theodor Emil von). Hydrographischer atlas. 8 pp. 27 maps. 4°. *Gotha, Perthes*, 1847. s.

—— Hydrotopischer atlas. 2 p. l. 30 maps. 4°. *Gotha, Perthes*, 1856. s.

—— Orographischer atlas. 2 p. l. 26 maps. 4°. *Gotha, Perthes*, 1855. s.

—— Oro-hydrographischer atlas. 2 p. l. 26 maps. 4°. *Gotha, Perthes*, 1866. s.

—— Schul-atlas. 1 p. l. 42 maps. 4°. *Gotha, Perthes*, 1856. s.

Sylvester (Joshua). *See* **Garland** of christmas carols.

Syracuse (*New York*). Boyd's daily journal Syracuse directory, and Onondaga county business directory, [etc.] 1868-69. 317 pp. 1 map. 8°. *Syracuse, Truair & Smith*, 1868.

System (A) of instruction in the practical use of the blowpipe. [*anon.*] 2d ed. With appendix and index by G. W. Plympton. 288 pp. 12°. *New York, D. Van Nostrand*, 1868.

Tacitus (Caius Cornelius). Germania, sive de situ, moribus et populis Germaniae libellus. 1 p. l. 30 pp. fol. *Parisiis, C. L. F. Panckoucke*, 1827. s.

Taft (Jonathan). A practical treatise on operative dentistry. With illustrations. 2d ed. 430 pp. 8°. *Philadelphia, Lindsay & Blakiston*, 1868.

Tagebuch. [Buch der liebe. *anon.*] 1 p. l. 243 pp. 1 portrait of Göthe. 12°. *Berlin, F. Dümmler*, 1835. s.

Taine (Hippolyte Adolphe). The ideal in art. Translated by J. Durand. 186 pp. 16°. *New York, Leypoldt & Holt*, 1869.

—— Italy, Rome, and Naples. From the French, by J. Durand. 2d ed. xi, 363 pp. 8°. *New York, Leypoldt & Holt*, 1869.

Tainsh (Edward Campbell). A study of the works of Alfred Tennyson, poet laureate. 256 pp. 12°. *London, Chapman & Hall*, 1868.

Tait (Peter Guthrie). An elementary treatise on quaternions. xviii, 320 pp. 8°. *Oxford, Clarendon press,* 1867.

Take but earn; or, sunny meadows. [*anon.*] 332 pp. 3 pl. 16°. *Philadelphia, J. S. Claxton,* 1867.

Talks with a child on the beatitudes. [*anon.*] 132 pp. 18°. *Philadelphia, J. B. Lippincott & co.* 1864.

Tangled talk. An essayist's holiday. By T. Talker. [*pseudon.*] viii, 360 pp. 12°. *London, A. Strahan & co.* 1864.

Tangletown (The) letters; being the reminiscenses, observations, and opinions of Timotheus Trap, esq. including a report of the great mammothic reform convention. 300 pp. 1 pl. 12°. *Buffalo, Wanzer, McKim & co.* 1856. s.

Tappan (Eli T.) Treatise on geometry and trigonometry; for colleges, etc. 420 pp. 8°. *Cincinnati, Sargent, Wilson & Hinkle,* 1868.

Tappan (Francis W.) *and* **McKillop** (John). The commercial agency annual for 1857, [etc.] 235 pp. 12°. *New York, Latimer & Seymour,* 1857. s.

Tasso (Torquato). Jérusalem délivrée. Traduction nouvelle par C. J. Panckoucke, [et Framery. En prose. Avec le texte italien en regard]. 2e éd. 4 v. 32°. *Paris, C. L. F. Panckoucke,* 1824. s.

Tastu (Sabine Casimire Amable Voïart, *madame*). Poésies nouvelles. 4e éd. 2 p. l. 316 pp. 1 pl. 32°. *Paris, Didier,* 1839. s.

——— Voyage en France. 620 pp. 1 map. 3 pl. 8°. *Tours, A. Mame & cie.* 1846.

[NOTE. Printed at Paris by H. Fournier].

Tate (Thomas). The philosophy of education; or, the principles and practice of teaching. 2d ed. xii, 338 pp. 16°. *London, Longmans,* 1857.

Tatham (Edward, *D. D.*) The chart and scale of truth by which to find the cause of error. New ed. With memoir and notes, by E. W. Grinfield. 2 v. li, 368 pp; vii, 371 pp. 8°. *London, W. Pickering,* 1840.

Tavernier (Jean Baptiste). Nouvelle relation de l'intérieur du serrail du grand seigneur. 18°. *Paris,* 1679.

[*With his* Recueil de plusieurs relations, etc. 1679].

——— Recueil de plusieurs relations et traitez singuliers et curieux. Qui n'ont point esté mis dans ses six premiers voyages. Divisé en cinq parties. 4 p. l. 370 pp. 2 maps. 8 p. l. 18°. *Paris,* 1679.

Tavernier—continued.

CONTENTS.

1. Une relation du Japon, et de la cause de la persecution des chrestiens dans les isles.
2. Relation de ce qui s'est passé en Perse et aux Indes dans la negociation des deputez de France.
3. Observations sur le commerce des Indes Orientales.
4. Relation du royaume de Tunquin.
5. Histoire de la condüite des Hollandois en Asie.

Taylor (Alfred B.) Report on weights and measures read before the Pharmaceutical association, [etc.] 104 pp. 8°. *Boston, C. C. Rand & Avery,* 1859. s.

Taylor (Alfred Swaine). On poisons, in relation to medical jurisprudence and medicine. Edited, with notes and additions, by R. Eglesfeld Griffith. xvi, 13, 687 pp. 8°. *Philadelphia, Lea & Blanchard,* 1848.

Taylor (George, *of New York*). The indications of the creator; or, the natural evidences of final cause. 282 pp. 12°. *New York, C. Scribner,* 1851.

Taylor (Henry). Notes from life in seven essays. From the 3d London ed. vii, 197 pp. 12°. *Boston, Ticknor, Reed, and Fields,* 1853. s.

Taylor (Isaac, *of Ongar*). The family pen. Memorials, biographical and literary, of the Taylor family, of Ongar. 2 v. vii, 429 pp; vii, 415 pp. 12°. *London, Jackson, Walford & Hodder,* 1867.

——— The process of historical proof; exemplified and explained; with observations on the peculiar points of the christian evidence. viii, 338 pp. 8°. *London, J. Holdsworth,* 1828.

Taylor (John, *the water poet*). Works. Reprinted from the folio edition of 1630. Parts i–ii. 6 p. l. 148 pp. 1 l. pp. 1–298. fol. [*Manchester*], *Spenser society,* 1868.

[SPENSER society publications. nos. 2-3].

——— Mad fashions, odd fashions, and out of fashions; or, the emblems of these distracted times. 4 l. sm. 4°. *London, T. Banks,* 1642.

Taylor (Joseph). The general character of the dog: illustrated by anecdotes of that beautiful and useful animal in prose and verse. 120 pp. 16°. *Philadelphia, B. Johnson,* 1807.

Taylor (Nathaniel G.) Relief for East Tennessee. Address at Cooper Institute, N. Y. March 10, 1864. 32 pp. 8°. *New York, W. C. Bryant & co.* 1864.

[LOYAL publication society. no. 73].

Taylor (Thomas Glanville). Meteorological register at Madras. *See* **Goldingham** (John) *and* **Taylor**.

Tazewell (Littleton W.) A review of the negociations between the United States and Great Britain, respecting the commerce of the two countries, especially of the former with

Tazewell—continued. the West Indies. iv, 130 pp. 8°. *London, J. Murray,* 1829.

Tegnér (Esaias). Sämmtliche gedichte. Aus dem Schwedischen von Gottlieb Mohnike. 3 v. 8°. *Leipzig, C. Cnobloch,* 1840–42. s.

CONTENTS.

v. 1–2. Kleinere gedichte. 2 v. xvi, 209 pp; vii, 252 pp. 1 l.
v. 3. Die Frithjofs sage. 5e aufl. xlvi, 211 pp.

——— Frithiof's saga. From the Swedish of E. Tegnér, by the rev. W. L. Blackley. 1st American ed. edited by Bayard Taylor. 1 p. l. xxix, 201 pp. 16°. *New York, Leypoldt & Holt,* 1867.

Tell the truth, and other stories. Compiled for the presbyterian board of publication. 216 pp. 3 pl. 18°. *Philadelphia, presbyterian board of publication,* 1868.

Tellkampf (*Dr.* A.) Die höhere bürgerschule in Hannover, [etc.] 4 p. l. 136 pp. 8°. *Hannover, F. Culemann,* 1860. s.

Templar's (The) manual; containing a full and comprehensive system of tactics and drill, together with all ceremonies appertaining to the order of knighthood. 2d ed. 246 pp. 24°. *Chicago, E. B. Myers,* 1868.

Temple bar; a London magazine for town and country readers. Conducted by G. A. Sala. v. 1–24. Dec. 1860, to Nov. 1868. 8°. *London,* 1861–68.

Tennemann (Wilhelm Gottlieb). Geschichte der philosophie. 11 v. in 12. 8°. *Leipzig, G. A. Barth,* 1798–1819. s.

——— A manual of the history of philosophy. Translated from the German of Tennemann, by the rev. Arthur Johnson. Revised, enlarged, and continued, by J. R. Morell. xii, 532 pp. 12°. *London, H. G. Bohn,* 1852. s.

Tenner (Adolf). On epileptiform convulsions. *See* **Küssmaul** (A.) *and* **Tenner.**

Tennessee (*State of*). Senate and house. Journals of the first and extra sessions of the thirty-fifth general assembly, for 1867–68. [With] appendix. 3 v. 8°. *Nashville, S. C. Mercer,* 1868.

Tenney (Sanborn *and* Abby A.) Natural history of animals. Illustrated. xi, 261 pp. 1 pl. 12°. *New York, C. Scribner & co.* 1868.

Tennyson (Alfred). Elaine. Illustrated by Doré. 2 p. l. 84 pp. 9 pl. fol. *London, E. Moxon & co.* 1867.

——— Guinevere. Illustrated by Doré. 2 p. l. 41 pp. 9 pl. fol. *London, E. Moxon & co.* 1867.

——— Locksley hall. With illustrations by W. T. Hennessy. 75 pp. 5 pl. sm. 4°. *Boston, Ticknor & Fields,* 1869.

Terhune (*Mrs.* Mary Virginia Hawes). The christmas holly. [Nettie's prayer. A christmas talk with mothers]. By Marion Harland. [*pseudon.*] 86 pp. 4 pl. 8°. *New York, Sheldon & co.* 1867.

——— Ruby's husband. By Marion Harland. [*pseudon.*] 392 pp. 12°. *New York, Sheldon & co.* 1869.

Terrasson (*Abbé* Jean). The life of Sethos. Taken from private memoirs of the ancient Egyptians. [*anon.*] Done into English by [T.] Lediard. 2 v. xv, 450 pp. 1 map; 480 pp. 1 map. 12°. *London, J. Walthoe,* 1732.

Terre Haute (*Indiana*). Logan's Terre Haute directory, [for 1868]. vi, 217 pp. 8°. *Indianapolis, Logan & co.* 1868.

Testament (New). *See* **Bible.**

Tevet (Andrea). *See* **Thevet** (André).

Texas (*State of*). Journals of the convention, assembled at Austin, 1845, for the purpose of framing a constitution for the state. 378 pp. 8°. *Austin, Miner & Cruger,* 1845.

Texas (The) almanac for 1860, with statistics, [etc.] 228 pp. 8°. *Galveston, W. & D. Richardson,* 1860. s.

Textus sequentiarum cū optimo commento. [*anon.*] cxxxiii, 13 l. sm. 4°. *Colonia, per Henricum Quentell,* 1494.

Thacher (James, *M. D.*) History of the town of Plymouth, 1620–1832. 382 pp. 1 map. 1 pl. 16°. *Boston, Marsh, Capen & Lyon,* 1832.

Thackeray (William Makepeace). The adventures of Philip on his way through the world; [and] A shabby genteel story. v. 1. 4 p. l. 359 pp. 8 pl. 8°. *London, Smith, Elder & co.* 1868.

——— Burlesques. With illustrations by the author, and by R. Doyle. viii, 448 pp. 8 pl. 8°. *London, Smith, Elder & co.* 1869.

CONTENTS.

Novels by eminent hands.
Jeames's diary.
Adventures of major Gahagan.
A legend of the Rhine.
Rebecca and Rowena.
The history of the next French revolution.
Cox's diary.

——— The history of Henry Esmond, esq. a colonel in the service of queen Anne. Written by himself. xvi, 452 pp. 8°. *London, Smith, Elder & co.* 1868.

——— The history of Pendennis. His fortunes and misfortunes; his friends and his greatest enemy. 2 v. xii, 448 pp. 23 pl; iv, 448 pp. 23 pl. 8°. *London, Smith, Elder & co.* 1868.

Thackeray (W. M.) The memoirs of Barry Lyndon, esq. written by himself; with the history of Samuel Titmarsh and the great Hoggarty diamond. vi, 416 pp. 10 pl. 8°. *London, Smith, Elder & co.* 1868.

——— The Newcomes. Memoirs of a most respectable family. Edited by A. Pendennis, esq. With illustrations by R. Doyle. 2 v. iv, 464 pp. 23 pl; iv, 456 pp. 23 pl. 8°. *London, Smith, Elder & co.* 1868.

——— The Paris sketch-book of mr. M. A. Titmarsh, and the memoirs of mr. Charles J. Yellowplush. xii, 444 pp. 17 pl. 8°. *London, Smith, Elder & co.* 1868.

——— Vanity fair. A novel without a hero. 2 v. viii, 407 pp. 20 pl; iv, 392 pp. 19 pl. 8°. *London, Smith, Elder & co.* 1867.

——— The Virginians. A tale of the last century. 2 v. iv, 457 pp. 23 pl; vii, 451 pp. 23 pl. 8°. *London, Smith, Elder & co.* 1868.

Thackeray (*Miss* —, *daughter of the preceding*). Beauty and the beast. From "The Cornhill". 4th Am. ed. 24 pp. 8°. *Boston, Loring,* 1867.

——— Cinderella. 17 pp. 8°. *Boston, Loring,* 1867.

——— Jack, the giant-killer. 49 pp. 8°. *Boston, Loring,* 1867.

——— Little red riding-hood. 24 pp. 8°. *Boston, Loring,* 1867.

——— The sleeping beauty in the wood. 10 pp. 8°. *Boston, Loring,* 1867.

——— The story of Elizabeth. [A novel. *anon.*] 251 pp. 4 pl. 12°. *London, Smith, Elder & co.* 1867.

——— The village on the cliff. With illustrations by F. Walker. [*anon.*] 2d ed. 3 p. l. 318 pp. 6 pl. 8°. *London, Smith, Elder & co.* 1867.

Thayer (*Rev.* Ebenezer). Jerusalem instructed and warned. A sermon preached May 26, 1725, being the day for election of his majesty's council. 42 pp. 12°. *Boston, B. Green,* [1725].

Thayer (*Capt.* Simeon). Journal describing the perils and sufferings of the army under Benedict Arnold, in its march through the wilderness to Quebec; with notes and appendix. By E. M. Stone. 8°. *Providence, Knowles, Anthony & co.* 1867.

[*In* RHODE ISLAND historical society. Collections. v. 6.]

Theiner (Augustin). Examen général de l'histoire du pontificat de Clément xiv. 8°. *Paris,* 1853. S.

[*In* MAYNARD (*Abbé U.*) Des études des jésuites].

Theis (Constance Marie de). *See* **Salm-Reifferscheid-Dyck** (C. M. de Theis, *princesse* de).

Thémiseul (*Chevalier* de). *See* **Saint-Hyacinthe.**

Theobaldus (*Episcopus dervensis*). De naturis duodecim animalium. 17 l. sm. 4°. *In ciuitate Coloniensi, per Henricū Quentell,* [*about* 1492].

NOTE.—Sometimes attributed to the archbishop Hildebert de Tours.

——— The same. Phisiologus de naturis duodecim animalium. 18 l. sm. 4°. *Liptzck, per Vuolfgangum monacensem,* 1510.

Theological (The) eclectic: a repertory, chiefly of foreign theological literature. Selected from the periodical and other literature of [Europe]. Editor, G. E. Day, D. D. July, 1866, to June, 1868. v. 4–5. 8°. *New York, Moore, Wilstach & Baldwin,* [1866–68].

[Discontinued in June, 1868].

Theophilus, *called also* **Rugerus** (*German monk*). Theophili presbyteri et monachi libri iii. Seu diversarum artium schedula, [etc. *or*] Théophile prêtre et moine. Essai sur divers arts, publié par le cte Charles de l'Escalopier, et précédé d'une introduction, par J. Marie Guichard. 2 p. l. lxii, 315 pp. 1 pl. 4°. *Paris, J. A. Toulouse, et al.* 1843. S.

Theory (The) of money, in connection with some of the prominent doctrines of political economy. By a Scotch banker. [*anon.*] v, 217 pp. 16°. *Edinburgh, W. P. Nimmo,* 1868.

Theremin (Ludwig Friedrich Franz). The confessions of Adalbert. Translated from the German, by Samuel Jackson. 264 pp. 16°. *London, B. Wertheim,* 1838.

Thevet (André). Historia dell'India America: detta altramente Francia antartica. Tradotta di Francese da Giuseppe Horologgi. Di nouo ristampata. 16 p. l. 364 pp. 1 l. 18°. *Venetia, appresso i Gioliti,* 1584.

NOTE.—The colophon bears the date, 1561. This ed. is probably the 1st ed. published with a new title-page.

Thieme (Friedrich Eduard). Populäre astronomie. v, 258 pp. 8°. *Plauen, A. Schröter,* 1853. S.

Thienis (Gaietanus de). *See* **Tiene** *Gaetano.*

Thilorier (Jean Charles). Système universel; ou, de l'univers et de ses phénomènes, considéres comme les effets d'une cause unique. 4 v. 5 pl. 8°. *Paris, l'auteur,* 1815.

Thom (*Rev.* David). Divine inversion; or, a view of the character of God, as in all respects opposed to the character of man. xx, 298 pp. 8°. *London, Simpkin, Marshall & co.* 1842. S.

Thomas (*Rev.* Abel C.)? The gospel of slavery; a primer of freedom. By Iron Gray. [*pseudon.*] 28 pp. 16°. *New York, T. W. Strong,* [1864].

Thomas (Annie). Played out. A novel. 3 v. 12°. *London, Chapman & Hall,* 1866.

Thomas (Antoine Léonard). Eulogium on Marcus Aurelius. Translated from the French. [By D. B. Warden]. vii, 64 pp. 8°. *New York, B. Dornin,* 1808. s.

Thomas (*Mrs.* Cordelia). The sheaf; or, the work of God in the soul, as illustrated in the personal experience of [herself]. 155 pp. 18°. *Boston, H. V. Degen,* 1852. s.

Thomas (Edward). Early Sassanian inscriptions, seals, and coins. viii, 134 pp. 1 pl. 8°. *London, Trübner & co.* 1868.

Thomas (Joseph, *M. D.*) The first book of etymology. *See* **Lynd** (James).

Thomas (J. P. *editor*). The Carolina tribute to Calhoun. v, 411 pp. 1 portrait. 8°. *Columbia, (S. C.) R. L. Bryan,* 1857.

Thomas (Ralph). Handbook of fictitious names; being a guide to authors, chiefly in the lighter literature of the xix[th] century, who have written under assumed names, and to literary forgers, impostors, plagiarists, and imitators. By Olphar Hamst. [*anagram*]. xiv, 235 pp. 8°. *London, J. R. Smith,* 1868.

Thomas (T. Gaillard, *M. D.*) A practical treatise on the diseases of women. With 219 illustrations. 625 pp. 8°. *Philadelphia, H. C. Lea,* 1868.

Thomas (W. Cave). The holiness of beauty: or, the conformation of the material by the spiritual. Christian idealism. xxiii, 220 pp. 12°. *London, F. S. Ellis,* 1863.

——— The science of moderation; or, the quantitative theory of the good and the beautiful. Formative ethics. 175 pp. 12°. *London, Smith, Elder & co.* 1867.

Thomas (*Saint*), *or,* **Tommaso** *d'Aquino.* Delle delizie tarentine libri quattro. Dal testo latino recati in versi sciolti italiani da Filippo de Jorio. xv, 118 pp. 1 l. 8°. *Napoli, Filiatre Sebezio,* 1831. s.

——— Questiones disputate. 480 l. fol. *Colonie, J. Koelhoeff de Lubeck,* 1475.

[NOTE.—The first four leaves are, by mistake, bound at the end].

——— Tractatus an liceat vti judiciis astrorum, 1 l. sm. 4°. [*Coloniae, per Joannem Valdener, about* 1474.]

[*With* AUGUSTINE (*Saint*). Soliloquium].

——— Tractatus de periculis que cōtingunt circa sacramentū eukaristie et de remediis eorūdē. 9 l. sm. 4°. [*Coloniæ, per Arnold Therhœrnen? about* 1473].

Thomas *Magister.* Κατ' αλφαβητον ονοματων αττικων εκλογαι, ex dispositione Nicolai Blancardi, [etc.] Collegit partim, digessitque J. S. Bernard, M.D. qui et suas notas adjecit. 7 p. l. 936 pp. 24 l. 8°. *Lugduni-Batavorum, P. Van der Eyk & C. de Pecker,* 1757. s.

Thomassy (Marie Joseph Raymond). Missions et pêcheries, ou politique maritime et religieuse de la France. xxiv, 204 pp. 8°. *Paris, Lecoffre,* 1853. s.

Thomes (William H.) The gold hunter's library. The gold hunters in Europe; or, the dead alive. 384 pp. 4 pl. 12°. *Boston, Lee & Shepard,* 1869.

Thompson (Augustus C. *D. D.*) Seeds and sheaves; or, words of scripture; their history and fruits. 323 pp. 12°. *Boston, Gould & Lincoln,* 1869.

Thompson (Benjamin Franklin). History of Long Island; containing an account of the discovery and settlement; with other matters to the present time. 536 pp. 2 pl. 8°. *New York, E. French,* 1839.

Thompson (Charles). Evidences in proof of the book of Mormon being a divinely inspired record, written by the forefathers of the natives whom we call Indians. 256 pp. 18°. *Batavia, (N. Y.) D. D. Waite,* 1841.

Thompson (D'Arcy Wentworth). Ancient leaves; or, translations and paragraphs from poets of Greece and Rome. 3 p. l. 175 pp. 1 pl. 18°. *Edinburgh, Edmonston & Douglas,* 1862.

——— Day dreams of a schoolmaster. 2[d] ed. viii, 328 pp. 16°. *Edinburgh, Edmonston & Douglas,* 1864.

——— Fun and earnest: or, rhymes with reason. 3 p. l. 80 pp. 8 pl. sq. 16°. *London, Griffith & Farran,* 1865.

——— Sales attici; or, the maxims witty and wise of Athenian tragic drama; collected, arranged and paraphrased [from the Greek of Æschylus, Sophocles, and Euripides]. xxiii, 431 pp. 16°. *Edinburgh, Edmonston & Douglas,* 1867.

——— Scalæ novæ; or, a ladder to Latin. xx, 430 pp. 16°. *London, Williams & Norgate,* 1866.

——— Wayside thoughts; being a series of desultory essays on education. 4 p. l. 384 pp. 16°. *Edinburgh, W. P. Nimmo,* 1868.

Thompson (*Capt.* Erasmus). Local marine board examination, for officers in the mercan-

Thompson—continued.
tile marine service. Also, lectures on navigation and astronomical terms. 93 pp. 8°. *Boston, author,* 1868.

Thompson (George, *the English orator*). Lectures on British India, delivered in the Friends' meeting house, Manchester, England, in October, 1839. With a preface by W. L. Garrison. 206 pp. 16°. *Pawtucket, (R. I.) W. & R. Adams,* 1840.

Thompson (Joseph P. *D.D.*) Abraham Lincoln; his life and its lessons. A sermon, preached April 30, 1865. 38 pp. 8°. *New York,* 1865.
[LOYAL publication society. no. 85].

——— Memorial service for three hundred thousand soldiers, with the commemorative discourse, Dec. 10, 1865. 28 pp. 8°. *New York,* 1866.
[LOYAL publication society. No. 88].

——— Peace through victory; a thanksgiving sermon, preached in Broadway tabernacle church, N. Y. Sept. 11, 1864. 16 pp. 8°. *New York,* 1864.
[LOYAL publication society. No. 60].

Thompson (Mary W.) Sketches of the history, character and dying testimony of beneficiaries of the colored home in the city of New York. 78 pp. 12°. *New York, J. F. Trow,* 1851.

Thompson (*Rev.* Robert Anchor). Christian theism; the testimony of reason and revelation to the existence and character of the supreme being. xxii, 477 pp. 8°. *New York, Harpers,* 1855. s.

Thompson (Zadock). History of Vermont, natural, civil, and statistical. iv, 684, iv pp. 8°. *Burlington, C. Goodrich,* 1842.

Thomson (Andrew). Freight charges calculator. vi, 100 pp. 18°. *Philadelphia, H. C. Baird,* 1867.

Thomson (Carl Gustaf). Skandinaviens coleoptera, synoptiskt bearbetade. Häftet i. Carabici. 2 p. l. 64 pp. 8°. *Lund, Berlingska boktryckeriet,* 1859. s.

——— The same. v. 1. 8°. *Lund, Berlingska boktryckeriet,* 1859. s.

Thomson (Edward, *D. D.*) Essays, educational and religious. Collected and published with the consent of the author, by rev. E. D. Roe. 392 pp. 12°. *Cincinnati, publisher,* 1855. s.
[THOMSON'S works. v. 1.]

Thomson (James). The seasons. With engraved illustrations, and with the life of the author. By P. Murdock, augmented in notes by B. Corney. 2d ed. xlviii, 320 pp. 8°. *London, Longmans,* 1847. s.

Thomson (John, *D.D.*) General view of the agriculture of the county of Fife. 1 p. l. 413 pp. 1 map. 3 pl. 8°. *Edinburgh,* 1800. s.
[GREAT BRITAIN: Board of agriculture].

Thomson (John Lewis). Historical sketches of the late war between the United States and Great Britain. With anecdotes. xii, 359 pp. 9 pl. 12°. *Philadelphia, T. Desilver,* 1816.

Thomson (Samuel, *M. D.*) The Thomsonian materia medica, or botanic family physician, comprising a philosophical theory, the natural organization and assumed principles of animal and vegetable life, with the description of plants and their various compounds. 12th ed. 834 pp. 18 pl. 8°. *Albany, J. Munsell,* 1841.

Thon (Theodor). Lehrbuch der kupferstecherkunst, etc. 1831 *See* **Perrot** (Antoine Marie).

Thórarensen (Bjarn). Kvædi, gefin út af hinu Íslenzka bókmentafjelagi. viii, 232 pp. 16°. *Kaupmannahöfn, S. L. Möller,* 1847. s.

Thorburn (Grant). Laurie Todd's notes on Virginia: with a chapter on puritans, witches, and friends. 36 pp. 8°. *New York, author,* 1848.

Thoreau (Henry David). A week on the Concord and Merrimack rivers. New ed. 415 pp. 12°. *Boston, Ticknor & Fields,* 1868.

Thornton (Jessie, *pseudon?*) Gold-filings. [A story]. 215 pp. 3 pl. 18°. *Philadelphia, presbyterian board of publication,* 1865.

Thornton (J.) Anecdotes; accompanied with observations: designed for leisure hours. 2 v. vii, 275 pp; 286 pp. 16°. *London, W. Baynes & son,* 1821.

Thorsen (P. G.) Valdemar ii. Jydske lov. 1853. *See* **Denmark.** Valdemar, etc.

Thortsen (Carl Adolph). Historisk udsigt over den danske litteratur indtil aar 1814. 164 pp. 8°. *Kjöbenhavn, C. A. Reitzel,* 1839. s.

Thou (Jacques Auguste de). Historiarvm svi temporis. [Libri lxxx, 1543–1584. 1st fol. ed.] 4 v. in 3. fol. *Paris, Drovart,* 1606–09.

——— The same. [Libri lxxxi–cxxxviii. 1585–1607]. Accedunt commentariorvm de vita sva libri vi. v. 4 and 5. fol. *Genevae, P. de la Rovière,* 1620.

Thousand (A) notable things, on various subjects; disclosed from the secrets of nature and art. [*anon.*] 2 p. l. 272 pp. 18°. *London, T. French,* 1799.

Three (The) voices: the soldier, farmer, and poet, to the copperheads. Speech of senator Funk in the Illinois legislature, Feb. 1863. Letter of gen. Rosecrans to the legislatures of Indiana and Ohio. Poem, "The oath," by T. B. Read. 12 pp. 8°. *New York, W. C. Bryant & co.* 1863.
[LOYAL publication society. no. 4].

Three years among the working classes of the United States. By the author of "Autobiography of a beggar boy." [*anon.*] 12°. *London*, 1865.

Tiedemann (Dietrich). Geist der spekulativen philosophie. 7 v. in 6. 8°. *Marburg, akad. buchhandlung*, 1791–97. s.
[v. 2 wanting; register with v. 1].

Tiedemann (Friedrich). Traité de physiologie générale et comparé. 8°. *Bruxelles*, 1837.
[*In* RICHERAND (A. B.) Nouveaux éléments de physiologie. *Bruxelles*, 1837. pp. 357–535].

Tiedge (Christoph August). Urania. [Eine lyrisch-didaktisches gedicht]. 6e aufl. 4 p. l. 293 pp. 1 pl. 16°. *Halle, Renger*, 1819. s.

Tiele (P. A.) Bibliothek von nederlandsche pamfletten. *See* **Muller** (Frederik).

——— Mémoire bibliographique sur les journaux des navigateurs néerlandais réimprimés dans les collections de DeBry et de Hulsius, et dans les collections hollandaises du xviie siècle, et sur les anciennes éditions hollandaises des journaux de navigateurs étrangers, [etc.] xii, 372 pp. 1 pl. 8°. *Amsterdam, F. Muller*, 1867. s.

Tiene *Gaetano* (Vincenzio). Recollectẽ super octo libros physicorum Aristotelis, cũ annotationibus textuũ. 52 l. fol. *Venetiis, per Bonetũ Locatellũ*, 1496.
[*With* BARBO da Soncina. Qvæstiones metaphysicales].

Tilt (Edward John). On diseases of menstruation and ovarian inflammation, [etc.] 1 p. l. xxxv, 250 pp. 8°. *London, J. Churchill*, 1850. s.

Tim (The) Bunker papers; or, yankee farming. By Timothy Bunker, esq. [*pseudon.*] 314 pp. 9 pl. 12°. *New York, Judd & co.* 1868.

Timbs (John). London and Westminster: city and suburb. Strange events, characteristics, and changes, of metropolitan life. 2 v. viii, 324 pp; iv, 316 pp. 12°. *London, R. Bentley*, 1868.

——— Nooks and corners of English life, past and present. 2d ed. xii, 371 pp. 6 pl. 12°. *London, Griffith & Farran*, 1867.

——— Things not generally known familiarly explained. Curiosities of science, past and present, [etc.] viii, 248 pp. 1 pl. 16°. *London, Kent & co.* 1859. s.

——— *See, also,* **Year-book** (The) of facts in science and art.

Times (The). [London daily]. Jan. to Dec. 1868. 4 v. fol. *London*, 1868.

——— The same. Index. Oct. 1, 1867, to Oct. 1, 1868. By S. Palmer. 4 v. sm. 4°. *London, S. Palmer*, 1868.

Timperley (C. H.) The gallery of engravings. *See* **Wright** (George Newnham) *and* **Timperley.**

Tindall (P. B. *M. D.*) Observations on the mineral waters of Western Virginia. 141 pp. 18°. *Richmond, C. H. Wynne*, 1858.

Tip Lewis and his lamp. [*anon.*] 360 pp. 3 pl. 16°. *Boston, H. Hoyt*, 1867.

Tiphaigne de la Roche (Charles François). Bigarrures philosophiques. [*anon.*] 2 v. xii, 244 pp; 2 p. l. 294 pp. 16°. *Amsterdam, Arkstée & Merkus*, 1757.

Ti-ping tien-kwok; the history of the Ti-ping revolution, [with] a narrative of the author's adventures. By Lin-le. [A. F. L. *anon.*] 2 v. xvii, 842 pp. 2 maps. 19 pl. 8°. *London, Day & son*, 1866.

Tischendorf (Lobgott Friedrich Constantin). Origin of the four gospels. Translated by W. L. Gage. [From the German]. 287 pp. 16°. *Boston, American tract society*, [1867].

——— The same. 287 pp. 16°. *London, Jackson, Walford & Hodder*, 1868.

Tissot (Simon André). Avis au peuple sur sa santé. 11e éd. 2 v. xxxii, 350 pp; iv, 378 pp. 16°. *Lausanne, F. Grasset & ce.* 1792.

Tobey (Alvan). Christianity from God. 356 pp. 18°. *Boston, American tract society*, 1868.

Tobler (Titus). Planographie von Jerusalem. 24 pp. 3 pl. 4°. *Gotha, J. Perthes*, 1857. s.
[*With* VAN DE VELDE (C. W. M.) Plan of Jerusalem. 1857].

Tocqueville (Charles Alexis Henri Maurice Clérel de). [Democracy in America]. The republic of the United States of America, and its political institutions, reviewed and examined. Translated by Henry Reeve, with an original preface and notes by John C. Spencer. 2 v. in 1. xx, 471 pp; 404 pp. 1 portrait. 8°. *New York, A. S. Barnes & co.* 1858. s.

——— The same. Democracy in America. Translated by Henry Reeve. Edited, with notes, [etc.] and the additions made to the recent Paris editions now first translated, by Francis Bowen. 2 v. xxiii, 559 pp; xiv, 499 pp. 8°. *Cambridge*, [*Mass.*] *Sever & Francis*, 1862. s.

Todd (Alpheus). On parliamentary government in England: its origin, development, and practical operation. v. 1. xx, 629 pp. 8°. *London, Longmans,* 1867.

Todd (John, *D.D.*) Nuts for boys to crack. 267 pp. sq. 16°. *New York, American tract society,* [1866].

——— Serpents in the dove's nest. i. Fashionable murder. ii. The cloud with the dark lining. 25 pp. 3 l. 18°. *Boston, Lee & Shepard,* 1867.

——— Woman's rights. 27 pp. 18°. *Boston, Lee & Shepard,* 1867.

Todd (S. Edwards). The American wheat culturist. A practical treatise on the culture of wheat. 432 pp. 12°. *New York, Tainter, bros. & co.* 1868.

——— The young farmer's manual: detailing the manipulations of the farm in a plain and intelligible manner. [v. 1.] 459 pp. 1 portrait. 8°. *New York, F. W. Woodward,* 1867.

Toepffer (Rudolf). *See* **Töpffer.**

Tommasini (Giacomo Filippo, *vescovo di Cittanuovo*). Trieste ed i Triestini intorno al 1650. Con annotazione dell dott. Domenico de' Rossetti. 8°. *Trieste,* 1829.

[*In* ROSSETTI (D. de). Archeografo triestino. v. 1].

——— De' commentary storici-geografici della provincia dell' Istria libri otto. 8°. *Trieste,* 1837.

[ROSSETTI (D. de). Archeografo triestino. v. 4].

Tommaso d' Aquino. *See* **Thomas** (*Saint*).

Too true. A story of to-day. [*anon.*] 395 pp. 12°. *New York, G. P. Putnam & son,* 1868.

Töpffer (Rudolf). Collection des histoires en estampes. 6 v. in 2. obl. 16°. *Genève, J. Kessmann,* 1846.

CONTENTS.

v. 1. Histoire de mr. Jabot.
v. 2. Histoire de mr. Crépin.
v. 3. Monsieur Pencil.
v. 4. Le docteur Festus.
v. 5. Histoire de mr. Albert.
v. 6. Les amours de mr. Vieux Bois.

Toronto (*University of Canada*). Alphabetical catalogue of the library. 89 pp. sm. 4°. *Toronto, H. Rowsell,* 1857.

Tott (François, *baron* de). Mémoires sur les Turcs et les Tartares. [Avec une lettre à m. Ruffin en réponse à la critique qu'on a faite de ces mémoires.] 2 v. xliv, 500 pp. 7 pl; 380, 32 pp. 9 pl. 4°. *Amsterdam,* 1785.

Toucement (Jean Christien, *pseudon.*) *See* **Trömer** (Johann Christian).

Touchstone (The) of truth and falsehood: conversations between two Hindus, on hinduism and christianity. [English and Gujarâtî]. 121 pp. 12°. *Bombay, tract and book society,* 1852.

Tourghenief *or* **Tourguéneff** (I. S.) *See* **Turgenieff.**

Tournefort (Joseph Pitton de). Relation d'un voyage du Levant. 3 v. 12°. *Lyon, freres Bruyset,* 1727.

Tourtelle (Étienne). The principles of health; or, a treatise on the influence of physical and moral causes on man, and on the means of preserving health. From the French by G. Williamson, M. D. With notes. 2 v. 2 p. l. 422 pp; 490 pp. 8°. *Baltimore, J. D. Foy,* 1819.

Towerson (Gabriel, *D. D.*) An explication of the catechism of the church of England. 3 parts in 2 v. fol. *London, J. Playford for R. Chiswell, etc.* 1685.

CONTENTS.

Part 1. Explication of the questions and answers of it, and of the apostle's creed. 1st ed.
Part 2. Explication of the dialogue or ten commandments, with discourses concerning God's both natural and positive laws. 3d ed.
Part 3. Explication of the Lord's prayer. 2d ed. [Bound with part 1].

——— The same. Of the sacrament of baptism, in pursuance of an explication of the catechism of the church of England. 6 p. l. 135 pp. fol. *London, R. Chiswell,* 1687.

[*With his* Sacraments in general].

——— The same. Of the sacrament of the Lord's supper. 8 p. l. pp. 157-304. fol. *London, R. Chiswell,* 1688.

[*With his* Sacraments in general].

——— The same. Of the sacraments in general. 4 p. l. 64 pp. fol. *London, R. Chiswell,* 1686.

Townley (James, *D. D.*) Illustrations of biblical literature, exhibiting the history and fate of the sacred writings from the earliest period to the present century, [etc.] 2 v. 602 pp; 604 pp. 8°. *New York, Lane & Scott,* 1852. s.

Townsend (Calvin). Analysis of civil government, including a topical and tabular arrangement of the constitution of the United States. 342 pp. 12°. *New York, Ivison, Phinney, Blakeman & co.* 1869.

Townsend (Virginia F.) The breakwater series. The boy from Bramley. 199 pp. 3 pl. 16°. *Boston, Loring,* [1868].

——— The same. Joanna Darling; or, the home at Breakwater. 176 pp. 3 pl. 16°. *Boston, Loring,* [1868].

Tractatulus compendiosus per modum dyalogi timidis ac deuotis viris editus. Instruens nō plus curam de pullis et carnibus habere suillis q̄m quo modo verus Deus et homo qui in celis est digne tractetur. Ostendens insup.

Tractatulus—continued. etiam salubres manuductões quibus minus depositus magis abilitetur. [*anon.*] 10 l. sm. 4°. *Esslingae, Conrad Fyner,* [*about* 1475].

Tracy (Cyrus M.) A poem delivered at the dedication of the city hall, Lynn, Nov. 30, 1867. 36 pp. 8°. *Lynn, T. P. Nichols,* 1867.

Tracy (J. L.) The American historical reader: containing a brief outline of the history of the United States, [etc.] 456 pp. 12°. *Philadelphia, J. B. Lippincott & co.* 1857. s.

Trafford (F. G. *pseudon.*) *See* **Riddell** (*Mrs.* J. H.)

Traits of the tea party; being a memoir of George R. T. Hewes; with a history of that transaction, [etc.] By a Bostonian. [*anon.*] 265 pp. portrait. 18°. *New York, Harpers,* 1835.

Trap (Timotheus, *pseudon.*) *See* **Tangletown** (The) letters.

Trautschold (Hermann, *Ph. D.*) Ueber die kohlen von Central Russland. *See* **Auerbach** (J.) *and* **Trautschold.**

Trautvetter (Ernst Rudolph von). Grundriss einer geschichte der botanik in bezug auf Russland. 1 p. l. 145 pp. 8°. *St. Petersburg, druckerei der k. akademie der wissenchaften,* 1837. s.

——— Phaenogame pflanzen aus dem hochnorden. 4°. *St. Petersburg,* 1847. s.

[*In* MIDDENDORFF (A. T. von). Reise, etc. v. 1. theil 2].

——— *and* **Meyer** (Carl Anton). Florula ochotensis phänogama. [Extract.] 3 p. l. 133 pp. 14 pl. 4°. [*St. Petersburg*], 1855. s.

——— ——— The same. 4°. [*St. Petersburg*], 1855.

[*In* MIDDENDORF (A. T. von). Reise, etc. v. 1. theil 2].

Travels by sea and land of Alethitheras. [*pseudon.*] viii, 381 pp. 12°. *New York, Moorhead, Simpson & Bond,* 1868.

Travels through Europe. Containing a geographical, historical, and topographical description of that quarter of the globe. Extracted from the productions of celebrated modern travellers. By Neville Wyndham. [*pseudon.*] 4 v. 8°. *London, H. D. Simonds,* [*about* 1810].

Traver (*Rev.* Albert D.) A manual for sponsors. 136 pp. 18°. *New York, gen. prot. episcopal sunday school union,* 1853. s.

Travers (Julien). Discours préliminaire, etc. *See* **Basselin** (O.) *et* **Le Houx** (J.) Les vaux-de-dire.

Trebellius Pollio. [Vitæ imperatorum romanorum, viz:] Valerianvs pater et filius: Gallieni dvo: Saloninvs Galienus: Triginta tyranni: Divvs Claudivs. 16°. [*Geneva*], 1568.

[*In* VARII historiæ romanæ scriptores, v. 3].

Trench (Richard Chenevix, *D. D. archbishop of Dublin*). A household book of English poetry, selected and arranged, with notes. xii, 430 pp. 16°. *London, Macmillan & co.* 1868.

Trenchant (Jean). L'arithmétique, departie en trois liures. Ensemble vn petit discours des changes. Avec l'art de calculer aux getons. Reueüe et augmentée pour la 4e éd. 475 pp. 2 l. 16°. *Lyon, M. Iove & I. Pillehotte,* 1578.

[Imperfect: pp. 337–368 wanting].

Tribune (The) almanac and political register for 1869. 108 pp. 12°. *New York, Tribune print,* 1868.

Tricotrin. The story of a waif and a stray. By Ouida. [*pseudon.* of mrs. De la Rama]? 675 pp. portrait. 12°. *Philadelphia, J. B. Lippincott & co.* 1869.

Tricoupis (Spiridion). 'Ιστορια της 'ελληνικης 'επαναστασεως. *Εκδοσις δευτερα.* 4 v. 8°. *εν Λονδινω, Ταυλορ & Φρανκις, αωξ'-ξβ'.* s.

Trieste (*City of*). Tre antichi diplomi inediti tratti dell' archivio municipale di Trieste. 8°. *Trieste,* 1829.

[*In* ROSSETTI (D. de). Archeografo triestino. v. 1].

Trithemius, *or* **Trittenheim** (Johannes). Compēdiū siue breuiariū primi volvminis annalivm sive historiarvm de origine regvm et gentis Francorvm. 54 l. 1 pl. fol. *In urbe Moguntina, per Ioannem Schöffer,* 1515.

——— De purissima et immaculata conceptione virginis Marie. Et de festiuitate sancte Anne matris eius. 8 l. fol. [*n.p. about* 1497].

Troeltsch. *See* **Tröltsch.**

Troemer. *See* **Trömer.**

Trojan (The) sketch book. Edited by Abba A. Goddard. 180 pp. 1 pl. 12°. *Troy, Young & Hart,* 1846.

Trollope (Anthony). The Claverings. 2 v. 2 p.l. 313 pp. 8 pl; 2 p.l. 309 pp. 8 pl. 8°. *London, Smith, Elder & co.* 1867.

——— Travelling sketches. Reprinted from the Pall Mall gazette. 2 p. l. 112 pp. 12°. *London, Chapman & Hall,* 1866.

Trollope (*Mrs.* Frances). The life and adventures of a clever woman. 4th ed. 397 pp. 16°. *London, Chapman & Hall,* 1867.

——— Mrs. Mathews; or, family mysteries. 399 pp. 16°. *London, Chapman & Hall,* 1864.

Trollope (*Mrs.* Frances E. Ternan, *wife of* Thomas Adolphus). Aunt Margaret's trouble. By a new writer. [*anon.*] 292 pp. 16°. *London, Chapman & Hall,* 1866.

——— Mabel's progress. A novel. By the author of "Aunt Margaret's trouble." [*anon.*] 3 v. 16°. *London, Chapman & Hall,* 1867.

Trollope (Thomas Adolphus). Marietta. A novel. 2[d] ed. 419 pp. 12°. *London, Chapman & Hall,* 1862.

Tröltsch (Anton von). Die anatomie des ohres in ihrer anwendung auf die praxis und die krankheiten des gehörorganes. xii, 106 pp. 1 pl. 8°. *Würzburg, Stahel,* 1860. s.

——— Lehrbuch der ohrenheilkunde, mit einschluss der anatomie des ohres. 3[e] aufl. xvi, 437 pp. 8°. *Würzburg, Stahel,* 1867. s.

Trömer (Johann Christian). Die avantures von Deutsch Francoss, mit all sein scriptures, etc. Von Jean Christien Toucement. [*pseudon.*] 6 p. l. 574 pp. 10 pl. 8°. *Dress,* [*printed at*] *Leipszigh,* 1745.

Trotter (James). General view of the agriculture of the county of West-Lothian. iv, 340 pp. 1 col. map. 6 pl. 8°. *Edinburgh,* 1811. s.
[GREAT BRITAIN: Board of agriculture].

Trousseau (Armand). On diptherite. [1835]. 8°. *London,* 1859.
[NEW SYDENHAM society. v. 3].

Trowbridge (Catherine M.) The gold dollar. 119 pp. 2 pl. 18°. *Philadelphia, James S. Claxton,* 1868.

——— How to conquer; or, Allen Ware. A temperance tale. 297 pp. 3 pl. 12°. *Philadelphia, James S. Claxton,* 1868.

True (The) Briton. [By Philip Wharton, duke of Wharton]. June 3, 1723–Feb. 17, 1724. No. 1–74. 80 l. fol. *London, T. Payne,* 1723.
[*With* PASQUIN. *London,* 1756. No more published].

True (A) and impartial state of the province of Pensylvania, being a full answer to "A brief state," etc. and a "Brief view," etc. [*anon.*] 173, 34 pp. 12°. *Philadelphia,* 1759.
[Title-page wanting].

Trumbull (Truman, *pseudon?*) The new yankee doodle: being an account of the little difficulty in the family of Uncle Sam. 341 pp. 12°. *New York, W. O. Bourne,* 1868.
[By W. O. Bourne]?

Truths for children, in stories told again. 142 pp. 16°. *Boston, T. H. Carter & son,* 1867.

Tschudi (Johann Jacob von). Die kechua sprache. iii. abtheilung. Wörterbuch. viii, 508 pp. 1 l. 8°. *Wien, k. akademie der wissenschaften,* 1853. s.

Tuck (W. J. *M.D.*) Selections for sabbath reading, [etc.] 368 pp. 12°. *Philadelphia, J. B. Lippincott & co.* 1857. s.

Tucker (Abraham). The light of nature pursued. With life of the author by sir H. P. St. John Mildmay. 2[d] ed. 7 v. 8°. *London, R. Faulder,* 1865.

Tucker (E. W. *M.D.*) Pathogenetic practice of medicine: embracing chemico-pathology and the symptoms and treatment of chronic diseases by pathogenetic remedies, [etc.] 132 pp. 12°. *Sandusky, (Ohio), H. D. Cooke & co.* 1858. s.

Tucker (*Mrs.* Mary E.) Life of Mark M. Pomeroy, ["Brick" Pomeroy], a representative young man of America. 230 pp. 1 portrait. 12°. *New York, G. W. Carleton,* 1868.

Tuckey (Mary B.) Old James, the Irish pedlar. 61 pp. 7 pl. 8°. *Philadelphia, American s. s. union,* [1850].

Tudor (William, *jr.*) Miscellanies. By the author of "Letters on the eastern states." [*anon.*] v, 156 pp. 8°. *Boston, Wells & Lilly,* 1821.

Tuke (John). General view of the agriculture of the north riding of Yorkshire. xv, 356 pp. 1 col. map. 14 pl. 8°. *London,* 1800. s.
[GREAT BRITAIN: Board of agriculture].

Tune (—— de). *See* **Detune.**

Tuomey (Michael) *and* **Holmes** (Francis S.) Pleiocene fossils of South Carolina; containing descriptions and figures of the polyparia, echinodermata, and mollusca. xvi, 152 pp. 30 l. 30 pl. 4°. *New York, Charleston, (S. C.) J. Russell,* 1855–57. s.

Turell (*Rev.* Ebenezer). The life and character of the rev. Benjamin Colman, D.D. late pastor of a church in Boston. 9 p. l. 238 pp. 8°. *Boston, Rogers & Fowle,* 1749.

Turgenieff (Ivan Sergheïevitch). Mémoires d'un seigneur russe; ou, tableau de la situation actuelle des nobles et des paysans dans les provinces russes. Traduit du Russe par E. Charrière. xii, 405 pp. 16°. *Paris, L. Hachette & cie.* 1854.

Turnbull (George, *LL.D.*) A curious collection of ancient paintings, accurately engraved from drawings done after the originals. With critical, historical, and mythological observations upon them. 2 p. l. 42 pp. 55 pl. fol. *London, S. Birt & B. Dod,* 1744.

Turner (Edward). A manual of chemistry, on the basis of dr. Turner's elements of chemistry. By John Johnston, LL.D. 5th revised ed. 480 pp. 12°. *Philadelphia, Thomas, Cowperthwait & co.* 1852. s.

Turner (Joseph W.) Novel musical grammar: being an instructive and pleasing treatise of the elementary principles of music, in rhyme. 44 pp. 18°. *Boston, author*, 1867.

Turner (Samuel H. *D. D.*) The epistle to the Hebrews. With commentary. *See* **Bible.** (*Greek and English*).

Turner (William, *prof. at Edinburgh, editor*). *See* **Journal** of anatomy, etc. 1867–68.

Turney (*Rev.* Edmund). Ministerial culture; or the relation of theological education to the work of the ministry. 120 pp. 1 pl. 16°. *Cincinnati, Anderson, etc.* 1857. s.

Tustin (*Rev.* Josiah Philip). The evidences of christianity. xii, 249 pp. 16°. *Charleston, southern baptist publication society*, 1854. s.

Tuthill (*Mrs.* Louisa C.) Braggadocio; a book for boys and girls. 227 pp. 16°. *New York, C. Scribner*, 1851. s.

——— My wife. iv, 171 pp. 12°. *Boston, Crosby & Nichols*, 1846.

——— The nursery book; for young mothers. 205 pp. 12°. *New York, G. P. Putnam*, 1849. s.

——— Success in life. The merchant. 188 pp. 12°. *New York, G. P. Putnam*, 1850. s.

——— Tip-top: or, a noble aim, [etc.] 325 pp. 16°. *New York, C. Scribner*, 1853. s.

Tvethe (Maximilianus Braun). Norges statistik, fremstillet. vi, 395 pp. 8°. *Christiania, C. Tonsberg*, 1848. s.

Twin (The) roses, and how they were trained. [*anon.*] 326 pp. 4 pl. 16°. *Philadelphia, American s. s. union*, 1868.

Twisden (*Rev.* John Francis). Planes, spherical trigonometry, etc. 8°. *London*, 1854.

[*In* ORR'S (W. S.) Circle of the sciences. The mathematical sciences. 1854].

Two (The) ways of treason; or, the open traitor of the South face to face with his skulking abettor at the North. 12 pp. 8°. *New York, W. C. Bryant & co.* 1863.

[LOYAL publication society. no. 33].

Tyler (Samuel, *LL.D.*) The progress of philosophy in the past and in the future. 2[d] ed. 244 pp. 12°. *Philadelphia, Lippincott & co.* 1868.

Tyng (*Rev.* Stephen H. *jr.*) Trial of the Rev. S. H. Tyng, jr. in the chapel of St. Peter's church, New York, Feb. 1868. Reported by Warburton, Bonynge, and Devine, stenographers. 310 pp. 8°. *New York, J. A. Gray & Green*, 1868.

Tyrwhitt (*Rev.* Richard St. John). A handbook of pictorial art. With a chapter on perspective by A. Macdonald. xiii, 480 pp. 11 pl. 4 phot. pl. 8°. *Oxford, Clarendon press*, 1868.

Ubicini (Jean Henri Abdolonyme). La Turquie actuelle. xxviii, 474 pp. 16°. *Paris, L. Hachette & cie.* 1855.

Uhden (Hermann Ferdinand). The New England theocracy. A history of the congregationalists in New England to the revivals of 1740. With a preface by the late dr. Neander. Translated from the 2[d] German ed. by H. C. Conant. 303 pp. 12°. *Boston, Gould & Lincoln*, 1858. s.

Uhland (Ludwig). Gedichte. 8[e] vermehrte aufl. [etc.] xvi, 546 pp. 1 portrait. 8°. *Stuttgart, etc. J. C. Cotta*, 1834. s.

Uhlhorn (Gerhard, *D.D.*) The modern representations of the life of Jesus. Four discourses delivered before the evangelical union at Hanover, Germany. From the German, by C. E. Grinnell. x, 164 pp. 16°. *Boston, Little, Brown & co.* 1868.

Ule (Otto, *editor*). *See* **Natur** (Die).

Ulex (Georg Ludwig), **Wiebel** (C.) *and others*). Controverse über die frage: was ist mineral-species? [etc.] nebst einer charakteristik des struvits, [etc. von C. Marx und G. L. Ulex]. 57 pp. 1 pl. 4°. *Hamburg, F. H. Nestler & Melle*, 1846. s.

Ulloa (Antonio de). Reise nach Sud-America: Voyage to South America. *See* **Juan y Santacillas** (J.) *and* **Ulloa.**

Ulster (The) journal of archaeology. v. 1–4. 4°. *Belfast, Archer & sons*, 1853–57. s.

Uncle Rod's pet. [*anon.*] 135 pp. 1 pl. 16°. *Boston, E. P. Dutton & co.* 1869.

Underhill (Edward Bean). Struggles and triumphs of religious liberty. An historical survey of controversies pertaining to the rights of conscience, from the English reformation to the settlement of New England. With an introduction by Sewall S. Cutting. vii, 242 pp. 8°. *New York, L. Colby*, 1851. s.

Union (The); or, select Scotch and English poems. 3 p. l. 184 pp. 18°. [*Edinburgh*, 1753].

[*With* BAGATELLES. 1767. Imperfect: wanting title].

Union (The) bible dictionary, for the use of schools, bible classes, and families. [*anon.* preface signed F. A. P.] 691 pp. 16°. *Philadelphia, American s. s. union*, [1855]. s.

Unique (The); or, biography of many distinguished characters, [etc.] 3[d] ed. 254 pp. 18°. *Boston, C. H. Peabody*, 1830. s.

Unitarian (American) association. Services for congregational worship. viii, 215 pp. sm. 4°. *Boston, American unitarian association*, 1868.

United brethren in Christ. Origin, constitution, doctrine, and discipline. 64 pp. 32°. *Circleville, Ohio, conference office,* 1837.

United States of America. Address and recommendations to the states by the United States of America in congress assembled. 68 pp. 8°. *Philadelphia, D. C. Claypole,* 1783.
[Imperfect: all from p. 24, and paper no. viii, wanting].

——— The same. 62 pp. 8°. *Boston, reprinted,* 1783.
[*With* the preceding].

——— Manifeste du gouvernment américain, (10 Février 1815); ou, causes et caractère de la dernière guerre d'Amérique avec l'Angleterre; traduit sur la 11e édition anglaise, par l'auteur de la décadence de l'Angleterre. 136 pp. 8°. *Paris, Plancher,* 1816.

——— Sound dues upon American commerce to the Baltic. Message from the president, June 13, 1854. 61 pp. 8°. [*Washington,* 1854].
[33d cong. 1st sess. Ho. of rep. Ex. doc. no. 108].
[*With* SCHERER (H.) Der sundzoll. 1845].

——— *Congress.* Congressional directory. 2d session, 16th congress, to 2d session, 40th congress, 1820–1868. 68 v. 16°. 12°. and 8°. *Washington,* 1820–68.

——— ——— The congressional register; or, history of the proceedings and debates of the first house of representatives. Taken in short hand by T. Lloyd. 4 v. 8°. *New York, editor,* 1788–90.
[v. 4 imperfect: all after p. 152 of debates wanting].

——— ——— Debates in the senate of the U. S. on the judiciary, during the first session of the seventh congress; also, the several motions, resolutions, etc. 324 pp. 8°. *Philadelphia, E. Bronson,* 1802.

——— ——— Report of the joint committee on the conduct of the war. [37. 3. Sen. rep. 108]. 3 v. 8°. *Washington, gov't printing office,* 1863.

——— *Department of education.* Report of the commissioner of education, with circulars and documents accompanying the same; submitted to the senate and house of representatives, June 2d, 1868. lx, 856 pp. 8°. *Washington, gov't printing office,* 1868.

——— *Department of the interior.* Register of officers and agents, civil, military, and naval, in the service of the United States, on the 30th Sept. 1867. Compiled and printed under the direction of the secretary of the interior. xv, 877 pp. 8°. *Washington, gov't printing office,* 1868.

——— *Library of Congress.* Catalogue of books added to the library of congress, from Dec. 1, 1866, to Dec. 1, 1867. 4 p. l. 526 pp. 8°. *Washington, gov't printing office,* 1868.

——— *Navy department.* The American ephemeris and nautical almanac. 1869–70. 2 v. 8°. *Washington, bureau of navigation,* 1867-68.

——— ——— Astronomical and meteorological observations made at the United States observatory, 1865. xli, 550 pp. 4°. *Washington, gov't printing office,* 1867.

——— ——— Catalogue of the library of the U. S. naval academy. vi, 251 pp. 8°. *Annapolis, R. F. Bonsall,* 1860. S.

——— ——— Manual of the boat exercise at the U. S. naval academy. 92 pp. 18°. *New York, D. Van Nostrand,* 1868.

——— ——— Rules, regulations, and instructions, for the naval service of the U. S. Prepared by the board of navy commissioners. 75 pp. 13 l. 4°. *Washington, E. De Krafft,* 1818.

——— ——— The same. 150 pp. 23 l. 12°. *Washington, E. De Krafft,* 1818.

——— *Post office department.* List of the post offices and postmasters in the United States, with an appendix containing the names of post offices arranged by states and counties, distances from Washington, etc. Revised to Oct. 29, 1867. xxi, 305 pp. 8°. *New York, American news co.* [1868].

——— *State department.* Message from the president of the U. S. transmitting copies of correspondence, etc. growing out of the seizure and rescue of Martin Koszta. 92 pp. 8°. [*Washington,* 1854].
[33d cong. 1st sess. Ho. of reps. Ex. doc. no. 91].

——— ——— Messages of the president of the U. S. communicating, in compliance with resolutions of the senate, information relative to the compulsory enlistment of American citizens in the army of Prussia, etc. 237 pp. 8°. *Washington, G. W. Bowman,* 1860.
[36th cong. 1st sess. Senate. Ex. doc. no. 38].

——— *Treasury department.* Reports of the superintendent of the coast survey, showing the progress of the survey during the years 1852 to 1865. 14 v. 4°. *Washington, public printers, gov't. printing office,* 1853-66. S.

——— ——— Reports of the special commissioner of the revenue, for 1866, 1867, and 1868. 3 v. 8°. *Washington, gov't printing office,* 1867–69.

——— *War department.* Official register of the army for 1802. 15 pp. 8°. *Washington,* 1802.

——— ——— The same. Official army register for August, 1868. 12°. *Washington,* 1868.

——— ——— Report of the secretary of war on the several Pacific railroad explorations. [With reports by A. A. Humphreys and G. K. Warren, (including memoranda by G. B. McClellan), T. S. Jesup, J. J. Stevens, E. G. Beckwith, A. W. Whipple, J. Pope, J. G. Parke, and R. S. Williamson, etc.] 10 v. in 7. 8°. *Washington, [public printer]*, 1855. s.

——— ——— Reports of explorations and surveys to ascertain the most practicable and economical route for a railroad from the Mississippi river to the Pacific ocean. Made under the direction of the secretary of war, in 1853–54, [etc.] 12 v. in 13. 4°. *Washington, [public printer]*, 1855-60. s.

——— ——— *Quartermaster general's office.* Lists of distances; compiled for the information and guidance of officers doing duty in the quartermaster's department, in making payments for mileage. 132 pp. 12°. *Washington, gov't. printing office*, 1868.

——— ——— ——— Roll of honor. Alphabetical index to places of interment of deceased union soldiers in the various states and territories, as specified in rolls of honor, nos. i–xiii. 16 pp. 8°. *Washington, gov't printing office*, 1868.

——— ——— ——— The same. (No. xiv.) Names of soldiers who, in defence of the American Union, suffered martyrdom in the prison pens throughout the south. viii, 337 pp. 8°. *Washington, gov't printing office*, 1868.

——— ——— ——— The same. (No. xv.) Names of soldiers who died in defence of the American Union, interred in the national cemeteries at Antietam, (Md.) and at Arlington, Culpeper C. H., Cold Harbor, Winchester, Staunton, and various scattered localities in Virginia. 4 p. l. 367 pp. 8°. *Washington, gov't printing office*, 1868.

——— ——— ——— The same. (No. xvi.) Names of soldiers who died in defence of the American Union, interred in the national cemeteries and other burial places at Brookline, Cambridge, and Worcester, Massachusetts; Buffalo, Chautauqua, Cypress Hills, (additional,) Fort Niagara, Lockport, Lodi, Madison barracks, Plattsburg barracks, and Rochester, New York; Gettysburg, Mercersburg, Reading, Philadelphia, Tamaqua, and Upton, Pennsylvania; Brattleboro' and Montpelier, Vermont; City Point, (additional,) Danville, (additional,) Glendale, Richmond, and Yorktown, (additional,) Virginia. xii, 392 pp. 8°. *Washington, gov't printing office*, 1868.

——— ——— ——— Statement of the disposition of some of the bodies of deceased union soldiers and prisoners of war whose remains have been removed to national cemeteries in the southern and western states. v. 1–3. 29, 38, 59 pp. 8°. *Washington, gov't printing office*, 1868.

——— ——— *Surgeon general's office.* Catalogue of books in the library of the surgeon general's office. 147 pp. 8°. [*Washington*], 1868.

——— ——— ——— Circular No. 1. Report on epidemic cholera and yellow fever in the army of the U. S. during 1867. By J. J. Woodward, asst. surgeon, U. S. A. 156 pp. 4°. *Washington, gov't. printing office*, 1868.

——— ——— *U. S. military academy, West Point.* Register of the officers and cadets and report of the visitors, 1868. 47 pp. 16°. *Washington, gov't printing office*, 1868.

United States (The) army and navy journal, and gazette of the regular and volunteer forces. Aug. 1863, to Aug. 1868. v 1-5. sm. fol. *New York, [W. C. & F. P. Church]*, 1864–68.

United States blue book; a register of federal offices and salaries. 176 pp. 18°. *New York, R. A. Dimmick & co.* 1868.

United States christian commission. A memorial record of the New York branch, [etc.] compiled under the direction of the executive committee. 103 pp. 8°. *New York, J. A. Gray & Green*, 1866. s.

United States Lloyd's; register of American and foreign shipping. By R. T. Hartshorne and John F. H. King. xxxiv, 746 pp. 5 pl. obl. 8°. *New York, J. W. Pratt & co.* 1868.

United States (The) medical and surgical journal. Edited by G. E. Shipman, M.D. Oct. 1865, to July, 1868. v. 1-3. 8°. *Chicago, C. S. Halsey*, 1866-67.

United States odd-fellows guide for 1858, [etc.] 119 pp. 18°. *Philadelphia, Curtis & Towne*, [1858]. s.

United States post-office directory for 1867. Revised and corrected by J. Disturnell to Jan. 1867. 8°. *New York*, 1867.

Universal-lexicon der gegenwart und vergangenheit. *See* **Pierer** (H. A.)

Universe (The) no desert, the earth no monopoly: preceded by a scientific exposition of the unity of plan in creation. [*anon.*] 2 v. in 1. xii, 130 pp; 1 p. l. 239 pp. 12°. *Boston, J. Munroe & co.* 1855.

University college (London). *See* **London.**

Unpartheiische ansichten eines tiefeingeweihten freimaurers. Mit besonderer berücksichtigung des ohnlängst erschienenen buchs, Sarsena, etc. [*anon.*] 5 p. l. 85 pp. 16°. *Bamberg, C. F. Kunz*, 5817 [1817].

Upham (*Rev.* Charles Wentworth). Lectures on witchcraft, comprising a history of the delusion in Salem in 1692. vii, 280 pp. 16°. *Boston, Carter, Hendee & Babcock*, 1831.

——— The life of Washington, in the form of an autobiography; being to a great extent extracts and selections from his own writings. 2 v. 443 pp; 423 pp. 12°. *Boston, Marsh, Capen, Lyon & Webb*, 1840.

Upham (Edward). History of the Ottoman empire, from its establishment, till the year 1828. Preceded by the life of Mahomet. 8°. *Philadelphia, T. R. Greenbank*, 1833.
[*In* GREENBANK'S periodical library. v. 2. pp. 215–445].

Upham (N. G.) Rebellion, slavery, and peace. An address. 24 pp. 8°. *New York*, 1864.
[LOYAL publication society. No. 52].

Uppström (Anders) *and* **Petré** (Hjalmar Henric). Aivaggeljo thairh Matthaiu, eller fragmenterna af Matthæi evangelium pa Götiska jemte ordförklaring och ordböjningslära. 4 p. l. iv, 140 pp. 8°. *Upsala, Wahlström & co.* 1850.

Upshur (Abel Parker). The federal government; its true nature and character; being a review of judge Story's commentaries on the constitution of the United States. With introduction and notes by C. Chauncy Burr. 1 p. l. 242 pp. 12°. *New York, Van Evrie, Horton & co.* 1868.

Upward, not inward. [*anon.*] 166 pp. 2 pl. 18°. *Philadelphia, American s. s. union*, 1866.

Urbin (Édouard). A practical guide for puddling iron and steel. From the French by A. A. Fesquet. 45 pp. 12°. *Philadelphia, H. C. Baird*, 1868.

Ure (Andrew, *M. D.*) The cotton manufacture of Great Britain investigated and illustrated. To which is added a supplement, completing the statistical and manufacturing information to the present time. By P. L. Simmonds. 2 v. 414 pp. 3 pl; viii, 544 pp. 10 pl. 12°. *London, H. G. Bohn*, 1861. s.

Uring (Nathaniel). A relation of the late intended settlement of the islands of St. Lucia and St. Vincent, in America. In right of the duke of Montague and under his direction. [*anon.*] 135 pp. 2 maps. 1 tab. 8°. *London, J. Peele*, 1725.

Urwick (William, *editor*). Historical sketches of non-conformity in the county palatine of Chester. By various ministers and laymen. 5 p. l. lxix, 504 pp. 1 map. 8°. *London, Kent & co.* 1864. s.

Utica (*New York*). Directory, 1868–9. A. Boyd, compiler. 418 pp. 1 map. 8°. *Utica, J. Arnott*, 1868.

Uylenbroek (Peter Johann). Iracæ persicæ descriptio, quam, ex codicibus mss. arabicis bibl. Lugd. Bat. edidit, versione latina et annotatione critica instruxit. [Item, selectæ narrationes viatorum ad cognitionem Iracæ persicæ pertinentes]. Praemissa est dissertatio de Ibn Haukali geographi codice lugduno batavo. xx, 83, 84, 128 pp. 4°. *Lugduni-Batavorum, S. & J. Luchtmans*, 1822. s.

Uz (Johann Peter). Sämmtliche poetische werke. Neue aufl. 2 v. in 1. xvi, 304 pp; 1 p. l. 272 pp. 16°. *Leipzig, Dyckischen buchhandlung*, 1772. s.

Vacherot (Étienne). Histoire critique de l'école d'Alexandre. 3v. 8°. *Paris, Ladrange*, 1846–51.

Vail (S. J.) *and* **Lowry** (*Rev.* Robert). Chapel melodies: a collection of choice hymns and tunes, for the use of prayer and social meetings, and family devotion. 188 pp. 2 l. 16°. *New York, Biglow & Main*, 1868.

Valderrama (Adolfo). Bosquejo histórico de la poesia chilena. 270 pp. 8°. *Santiago, imprenta chilena*, 1866. s.

Valdés (Gabriel de la Concepcion). Poesias. *See* **Placido.**

Valdez (Manüel Antonio). Gazetas de Mexico, compendio de noticias de Nueva España, 1784–1785. 3 p. l. 474 pp. 8 l. 3 pl. 4°. *Mexico, Felipe de Zuñiga y Ontiveros*, 1784.

Valenciennes (Achille). Ichthyologie des îles Canaries. 4°. *Paris*, [1836–44].
[*In* WEBB (Philip B.) *and* BERTHELOT (S.) Histoire naturelle des îles Canaries. v. 2].

——— Atlas. *See* **Cuvier** (G. L. C. F. D.) La règne animal. v. 4. Poissons.

Valla (Giorgio). De ortographia opusculum. 11 l. sm. 4°. *Mediolani, per Petrum Martium de Mantegatiis*, 1505.
[*With* PILADE (G. F. B.) Vocabularivm].

Valla (Lorenzo). De elegantia lingue latine. 179 l. 4°. *Colonie, J. Koelhoff de Lubeck*, 1482.

——— De reciprocatione sui et suus. 10 l. 4°. *Colonie, J. Koelhoff de Bubeck*, 1482.
[*With his* De elegantia lingue latine. *Colonie*, 1482].

——— Inuectiua in errores Antonii Raudensis. 21 l. 4°. *Colonie, J. Koelhoff de Lubeck*, 1482.
[*With his* De elegantia lingue latine. *Colonie*, 1482].

Valla (L.) De libero arbitrio dialogus. 8 l. 4°. *Colonie, J. Koelhoff de Lubeck,* 1482.

[*With his* De elegantia lingue latine. *Colonie,* 1482].

Valle *or* **Vallibus** (Girolamo della). Jesuida ad Petrū Donatum. 16 l. sm. 4°. *Liptzk, J. Thanner,* 1509.

Vallette Laudun (——— de, *capitaine de vaisseau*). Journal d'un voyage à la Louisiane, fait en 1720. Par m——, capitaine de vaisseau du roi. [*anon.*] 8, 316 pp. 16°. *La Haye, Musier, fils, & Fournier,* 1768.

Valparaiso (*Chile*). Guia de comerciantes para el año de 1858. Valparaiso directory for 1858, published by H. W. Macklin. xxvii, 94 pp. 16°. *Valparaiso, commercial printing office,* 1857. s.

Vámbéry (Arminius). Sketches of central Asia. Additional chapter on my travels, adventures, and on the ethnology of central Asia. viii, 444 pp. 8°. *London, W. H. Allen & co.* 1868.

——— Travels in central Asia, being the account of a journey from Teheran to Khiva, Bokhara, and Samarcand, in 1863. xvii, 443 pp. 1 map. 12 pl. 8°. *London, J. Murray,* 1864.

Van Baerle (Caspar). [Medicea hospes, sive descriptio publicae gratulationis, qua Mariam de Medicis excepit senatus populusque amstelodamensis.] 4 p. l. 62 pp. 17 pl. fol. [*Amstelodami, Blaeu,* 1638 (1639)].

[Imperfect: wanting title].

Van Beneden (Pierre Joseph). Recherches sur la faune littorale de Belgique. (Extrait des mémoires de l'Académie royale des sciences de Belgique). Turbellariés. 56 pp. 7 col. pl. 4°. *Bruxelles,* 1860. s.

——— The same. Crustacés. 174 pp. 21 pl. 4°. *Bruxelles,* 1861. s.

——— The same. Polypes. 207 pp. 19 pl. 4°. *Bruxelles,* 1866. s.

——— Recherches sur les squalodons. (Extrait des mémoires de l'Académie royale des sciences de Belgique). 85 pp. 4 pl. 4°. *Bruxelles, Hayez,* 1865. s.

——— *and* **Hesse** (C. E.) Recherches sur les bdellodes ou hirudinées et les trématodes marins. (Extrait des mémoires de l'Académie royale des sciences de Belgique). 142 pp. 13 col. pl. 4°. *Bruxelles, l'Académie royale,* 1863. s.

Van Buren (Martin). Inquiry into the origin and course of political parties in the United States. Edited by his sons. ix, 436 pp. 1 portrait. 8°. *New York, Hurd & Houghton,* 1867.

Van Cauwenberghe (Charles J.) Des grossesses extra-utérines. 323 pp. 8°. *Bruxelles, T. Lesigne,* 1867. s.

Vancouver (Charles). General view of the agriculture of the county of Devon. xii, 479 pp. 1 col. map. 22 pl. 8°. *London,* 1808. s.

[GREAT BRITAIN: Board of agriculture].

——— General view of the agriculture of Hampshire, including the isle of Wight. viii, 520 pp. 9 tab. 1 col. map. 13 pl. 8°. *London,* 1810. s.

[GREAT BRITAIN: Board of agriculture].

Van der Aa (Pieter, *publisher*). *See* **Galerie** (La) agréable du monde.

Van der Donck (Adriaen) *and others.* Remonstrance of New Netherland, and the occurrences there. Addressed to the lords states general of the United Netherlands, 28th July, 1649. With secretary Van Tienhoven's answer. From the Dutch mss. by E. B. O'Callaghan. 2 p. l. 65 pp. 1 l. 4°. *Albany, Weed, Parsons & co.* 1856.

Van der Kolk. *See* **Schröder van der Kolk.**

Vander Maelen (Philippe). Dictionnaires géographiques spéciaux des provinces de la Belgique. [Avec aperçus géologique et minéralogique, botanique, et zoologique]. 8 v. 8°. *Bruxelles, à l'établissement géographique,* 1831–38. s.

CONTENTS.

[v. 1.] Mémorial de l'établissement géographique de Bruxelles, fondé par Ph. Vander Maelen. lxxxvii pp. Dictionnaire géographique de la province de Liége. 1 p. l. vii, 63, 242, 60, 48 pp. 10 tab. 1831.
[v. 2.] Dictionnaire géographique de la province de Namur. 2 p. l. ii, 141, 313 pp. 8 tab. 1832.
[v. 3.] Dictionnaire géographique de la province de Hainaut. 2 p. l. vii, 396, 527 pp. 1 p. l. 18 tab. 1832.
[v. 4.] Dictionnaire géographique de la province d'Anvers. 2 p. l. vii, 347, 170 pp. 1 p. l. 6 tab. 1836.
[v. 5.] Dictionnaire géographique de la Flandre orientale. 1 p. l. iv, 240, 248 pp. 1834.
[v. 6.] Dictionnaire géographique du Limbourg. 2 p. l. iv, 127, 149 pp. 1 pl. 10 tab. 1835.
[v. 7.] Dictionnaire géographique de la Flandre occidentale. 2 p. l. iv, 237, 121 pp. 1836.
[v. 8.] Dictionnaire géographique du Luxembourg. 2 p. l. 283, 288 pp. 2 tab. 1838.

[Dict. du Brabant [1859?] wanting].

Van der Wulp (J. K.) Catalogus van de tractaten, pamfletten, enz. over de geschiedenis van Nederland, aanwezig in de bibliotheek van Isaac Meulman. *See* **Meulman** (I.)

Van de Velde (C. W. M.) Plan of the town and environs of Jerusalem, constructed from the English ordnance survey and measurements of dr. T. Tobler. With memoir by dr. Titus Tobler. 1 map. 24 pp. 3 pl. folded 4°. *Gotha, J. Perthes,* 1857. s.

Van Doren (*Rev.* W. H.) Suggestive commentary on the new testament; St. Luke. *See* **Bible.** (*English*).

Van Erpe *or* **Erpenius** (Thomas). Grammatica arabica, cui accedunt Locmanni fabvlae, et adagia quædam Arabvm. 126 pp. sm. 4°. *Amstelodami, Ioannes Iansonius*, 1636.

Van Helmont (Franciscus Mercurius). *See* **Helmont** (F. M. van).

Van Meteren (Emanuël). [Extracts from his Historiæ belgicae]. *See* **Churchyard** (Thomas). A trve discovrse historicall of the svcceeding governovrs in the Netherlands. *London*, 1602.

Van Reverhorst (Maurits). Epistola de nova artuum decurtandorum methodo. 4°. *Amstelœdami*, 1732.

[Ruysch (F.) Opera. v. 3].

Van Schreven (J.) Korte handleiding tot het redekundig ontleden van voorstellen en volzinnen. 3e druk. xvi, 131 pp. 12°. *Deventer, A. J. Van den Sigtenhorst*, 1843. s.

Van Swieten (Gerardus, *baron*). The diseases incident to armies. With the method of cure. Translated from the [Latin] original. 114 pp. 8°. *Boston, J. D. M'Dougall*, 1777.

Varela (Felix). Carta sobre las cuestiones filosóficas de José de la Luz y Francisco Ruiz, con Manuel Gonzalez del Valle. 12°. *Habana*, 1862.

[*With* Mestre (J. M.) De la filosofia, etc. 1862].

Varii historiæ romanae scriptores, partim græci, partim latini, in vnum, velut corpus redacti, [etc.] 4 v. 16°. [*Geneva*], *H. Stephanus*, 1568. s.

CONTENTS.

Ammianus Marcellinus. Rerum gestarum libri [quae supersunt]. v. 3-4.
Capitolinus (Julius). Vitæ imperatorum romanorum, viz: Antoninvs Pivs ad Diocletianum Aug. v. 3.
Dion Cassius Cocceianus. Excerptæ et epitomes forma redactæ vitæ Pompeii magni et Cæsarum vsque ad Alexandrum Māmææ filium, per Joannem Xiphilinvm. [Græce et latine]. v. 2.
Egnazio (Giovanni Battista). In C. Suetonium Tranquillum annotationes. v. 3. In Aelium Spartianum, Lampridium et cæteros annotationes. v. 3. Græci versus ac dictiones in Latinum translatæ. v. 3. Romanorum principum libri i. v. 3.
Eutropius. Historiae romanae libri x. v. 4.
Gallicannus (Vulcatius). Avidivs Cassivs. v. 3.
Herodianus. Historiæ de imperio post Marcum liber primus (Gr. et lat). v. 2.
Lampridius (Aelius). [Vitæ imperatorum romanorum, viz:] Commodvs Ant. ad Diocletianum Aug. v. 3.
Leto (Giulio Pomponio). Romanae historiae compendivm ab interitu Gordiani junioris vsque ad Iustinum iii. v. 3.
Paterculus (Caius Velleius). Historiae romanae ad M. Vinicium cos. libri ii. v. 1.
Sigonio (Carlo). Fasti consulares, ac triumphi acti à Romulo rege vsque ad Ti. Cæsarem. v. 1. Commentarius in fastos et triumphos romanos. v. 1. De nominibvs Romanorum. v. 1.
Spartianus (Aelius). [Vitae imperatorum romanorum viz:] Adrianvs imp. ad Diocletianum Aug. v. 3.
Suetonius Tranquillus (Caius). xii Cæsares. v. 3.
Trebellius Pollio. [Vitae imperatorum romanorum, viz:] Valerianvs pater et filius: Gallieni duo: Saloninvs Galienvs: Triginta tyranni: Divvs Claudivs. v. 3.
Victor (Sextus Aurelius). De vita et moribvs imperatorvm à Cæsare Avgusto vsque ad Theodosiū imperatorem. v. 3.
Vopiscus (Flavius). [Vitae imperatorum romanorum, viz:] Divvs Aurelianvs: Tacitvs: Florianvs: Probvs: Firmvs: Satvrninvs: Proculus et Bonosus: Carvs: Numerianvs: Carinvs. v. 3.

Varin (A.) *and* **Varin** (E.) L'architecture pittoresque en Suisse, ou choix de constructions rustiques prises dans toutes les parties de la Suisse. iii pp. 48 pl. fol. *Paris, A. Morel & co.* 1861.

Varlo (Charles). Nature display'd, a new work. Lectures on philosophy. Tour through America. Poetry on different subjects. Also political hints offered to the legislature and freeholders of England, etc. 320 pp. 12°. *London, editor*, 1793.

——— A treatise on agriculture, intitled the Yorkshire farmer. 2 v. xv, 255 pp. 2 l. 2 pl; 2 p. l. 260 pp. 2 l. 1 pl. 12°. *Dublin, author*, 1766.

Varrentrapp (Georg). Ueber pönitentiarsysteme, insbesondere über die vorgeschlagene einführing des pennsylvanischen systems in Frankfurt. viii, 154 pp. 8°. *Frankfurt am Main, F. Varrentrapp*, 1841. s.

Varro (Marcus Terentius). De lingua latina libri tres. fol. *Venetiis*, 1517. *See* **Perotti** (Niccolò) *and others*. Cornvcopiae.

Vasconcelos (Jacob Moenutius). De Eborensi mvnicipio, commentarius. 18°. *Coloniæ Agrippinæ*, 1613.

[*In* Deliciæ lvsitano-hispanicæ. 1613. pp. 304-46].

Vassar (John Guy). Twenty years around the world. x, 598 pp. 8°. *New York, Rudd & Carleton*, 1861.

Vater *or* **Vaterus** (Abraham). Epistola de viis absconditis pulmonum, etc. 4°. *Amstelœdami*, 1727.

[Ruysch (F.) Opera. v. 3. no. 31].

——— Epistola gratulatoria ad Rvyschium in qua de mvscvlo orbicvlari in fvndo vteri detecto gratvlatvr. 4°. *Amstelœdami*, 1727.

[Ruysch (F.) Opera. v. 3. no. 40].

Vaughan (Samuel). An appeal to the public on behalf of Samuel Vaughan, esq; a narrative of his negotiation with the duke of Grafton. And an appendix. [*anon.*] 136 pp. 12°. *London, E. & C. Dilly*, 1770.

Veda. *See* **Atharva-veda.**

Vega (Garcilaso de la). *See* **Garcilaso** de la Vega (*the inca*).

Vegetius (Flavius Renatus). De re militari libri qvatvor; post omnes omnivm editiones ope veterum librorum correcti a Godescalco

Vegetius—continued. Stewechio heusdano. Accesserunt Sex. Ivli Frontini strategematicon libri quatuor, [etc.]: Aelianvs de instruendis aciebus: Modestvs de vocabulis rei militaris: Castrametatio rom. ex historiis Polybii, [etc.] 6 p. l. 276 pp. 4°. *Antverpiæ, apud C. Plantinum*, 1585. s.

Velasco (Gabriel Alvarez de). *See* **Alvarez de Velasco** (Gabriel).

Velasco (Joseph Manso de). *See* **Manso de Velasco** (Joseph).

Velde. *See* **Van de Velde.**

Velloso (José Marianno da Conceição). Floræ fluminensis, seu descriptionum plantarum præfectura fluminensi sponte nascentium liber primus ad systema sexuale concinnatus augustissimæ dominæ nostræ per manus ill^{mi} ac ex^{mi} Aloysii de Vasconcellos et Souza Brasiliæ pro-regis quarti, etc. 1790. v. 1. [To Syngenesia polygamia. 309 Sabbata]. 6 p. l. 352 pp. sm. fol. *Flumine Januario, typographia nationali*, 1825. s.

[No more published].

Venable (Charles S.) Arithmetic, pure and commercial. For the use of schools. 268 pp. 12°. *New York, Richardson & co.* 1868.

Veness (*Rev.* W. T.) El Dorado; or, British Guiana as a field for colonisation. vii, 198 pp. 2 maps. 8°. *London, Cassell, Petter, & Galpin*, 1867.

Venezuela. *Hacienda.* Memoria de hacienda. [*or*] Exposicion que dirige al congreso de Venezuela en 1833, 1835–48, 1850–54, y 1856, el secretario de hacienda. 8°. *Caracas, V. Espinal, etc.* 1833–56. s.

[Wanting: reports for 1834, '49, '55].

——— ——— The same. Memoria que dirige a la legislatura nacional de 1865, el ministro de hacienda. 179 pp. 8 tab. 8°. *Caracas, P. P. Del Castillo e hijos*, 1865. s.

——— ——— The same. Memoria de crédito público. [*or*], Exposicion que dirige al congreso de 1866 el ministro de crédito público de los Estados Unidos de Venezuela. 5 p. l. 301 pp. 3 tab. 8°. *Caracas, V. Espinal e hijos*, 1866. s.

Venom (The) and the antidote. Copperhead declarations. Soldiers' letters. 4 pp. 8°. *New York*, 1863.

[LOYAL publication society. no. 9].

Verany (Giovanni Battista) *and* **Vogt** (Carl). Memoir upon the hectocotyli and the males of certain cephalopods. 8°. *London*, 1853.

[*In* HENFREY (A.) *and* HUXLEY (T. H.) Scientific memoirs. art. 5].

Verazzani *or* **Verazzano** (Giovanni). [Relatione della terra per lui scoperta. Printed from the Magliabecchian ms. copy]. 8°. *New York*, 1841.

[*In* NEW YORK historical society. Collections. v. 1. 2d series].

——— The same. Translated from the Italian by J. G. Cogswell. 8°. *New York*, 1841.

[*In* NEW YORK historical society. Collections. v. 1. 2d series].

——— The same. The relation of the land by him discouered. Written in Dieppe, 1524. [Hakluyt's translation]. 8°. *New York, J. Riley*, 1811.

[*In* NEW YORK historical society. Collections. v. 1. 1st series].

Vergerio (Ludovico). Lettera sull' Istria. (Corografie dell'Istria, n. 5.) 8°. *Trieste*, 1830.

[*In* ROSSETTI (D. de). Archeografo triestino. v. 2].

Vermont (*State of*). Directory, rules, constitutions, and manual of parliamentary practice. By Henry Clark. 120 pp. 1 map. 2 pl. 16°. *Montpelier, Walton, [for gen. assembly]*, 1865.

——— The same. Annual directory for the use of the general assembly. 214 pp. 1 map. 18°. *Montpelier, Poland's printing establishment*, 1868.

——— Journal of the senate and house of representatives. 1867. 2 v. 8°. *Montpelier, Freeman printing establishment*, 1868.

——— Legislative documents and official reports. 1867 [and] 1868. 8°. *Montpelier*, 1867–68.

——— Reports (first, second, ninth, and tenth) to the legislature of Vermont, relating to the registry and returns of births, marriages, and deaths, for the years 1857, 1858, 1865, [and] 1866. 4 v. 8°. *Burlington, Rutland, [and] Montpelier*, 1859–68.

Vernet (Claude Joseph) *and* **Huë** (J. F.) Les ports de France, peints par Joseph Vernet et Huë. Accompagnés de notes historiques et statistiques sur chacune des villes où ils se trouvent situés. Par M. P. A. M***. xv, 126 pp. 26 pl. 4°. *Paris*, 1812.

Verplanck (Gulian Crommelin). Anniversary discourse, [containing sketches of the most noted of the early colonists of the United States], delivered before the New York historical society, Dec. 1818. 8°. *New York, Bliss & White*, 1821.

[*In* NEW YORK historical society. Collections. 1st series. v. 3].

Verrazzano (Giovanni). *See* **Verazzani.**

Versor (Johannes). Questiones super libros ethicorum Aristotelis. *See* **Aristoteles.** Ethicæ. *Coloniæ*, 1491.

Vespucci (Amerigo). Paesi nouamente ritrouati, etc. *See* **Montalboddo.**

Vetromile (Eugene, *Indian patriarch*). Of Vetromile's noble bible. Such as happened great-truths. For the benefit of the Penobscot, Micmac, and other tribes of the Abnaki Indians, [etc. *Or*], Vetromile wewessi ubibian. Elit'biklang'sa k'tchiulāmeuhānganal, [etc]. xii, 572 pp. 12 pl. 16°. *New York, Rennie, Shea & Lindsay*, 1860. s.

Via ad transmvtationem metallorvm fideliter aperta. [Scripsit] Aletophilus Sincerus. [*pseudon.*] 27 p. l. 304 pp. sm. 4°. *Norimbergae, officina Cremeriana*, 1742.

[NOTE.—This work is possibly an ed. of Clauder (Gabr.) De tinctura universalis, etc.]

Vibius Sequester. De fluminibus, fontibus, lacubus, nemoribus, paludibus, montibus, gentibus quorum apud poetas mentio fit. Lectionis varietatem et integras doctorum commentationes adjecit et suas Jer. Jac. Oberlinus. xx, 428 pp. 17 l. 8°. *Argentorati, A. König*, 1778. s.

Vickroy (T. R.) The principles of English grammar: with comprehensive outlines, and a concise and progressive system of analysis and parsing. 214 pp. 12°. *Philadelphia, J. A. Bancroft & co.* 1868.

Victor (*Mrs.* Metta Victoria Fuller). Poems of sentiment and imagination. *See* **Fuller** (Francis A.) *and* **Victor.**

Victor (Orville J.) The history, civil, political and military, of the Southern rebellion. v. 3–4. 533 pp. 9 maps. 6 pl; 565 pp. 8 maps. 6 pl. 8°. *New York, J. D. Torrey*, [1867–68].

Victor (Sextus Aurelius). De vita et moribvs imperatorvm à Cæsare Augusto vsque ad Theodosiū imperatorem. 16°. *Geneva*, 1568.

[*In* VARII historiæ romanæ scriptores. v. 3].

Victoria (*Queen of Great Britain and Ireland*). Leaves from the journal of our life in the highlands, from 1848 to 1861. [With] extracts giving an account of earlier visits to Scotland and tours in England and Ireland. Edited by Arthur Helps. 2d ed. xv, 315 pp. 2 pl. 8°. *London, Smith, Elder & co.* 1868.

Victoria (*British colony of*). Acts, orders in council, and notices relating to the gold fields, [etc.] 2 p. l. 124 pp. 8°. *Melbourne, Mason & Firth*, 1864. s.

——— Catalogue of the library of the parliament of Victoria. Part i. Alphabetical catalogue. xii, 244 pp. 8°. *Melbourne, Mason & Firth*, 1864. s.

Vicũna Mackenna (Benjamin). Bases del informe presentado al supremo gobierno sobre la immigracion estranjera por la comision especial nombrada con ese objeto, [etc.] 230 pp. 8°. *Santiago de Chile, imprenta nacional*, 1865. s.

——— Le Chili considéré sous le rapport de son agriculture et de l'émigration européenne. 144 pp. 12°. *Paris, Bouchard-Huzard*, 1855. s.

Vietz (Carl Johann). Das studium der allgemeinen geschichte nach dem gegenwärtigen stand der historischen wissenschaft und literatur. vii, 218 pp. 8°. *Prag, G. Haase sohn*, 1844. s.

Villada (Manuel). Catálogo de la coleccion de insectos y algunos otros animales. 8°. *Mexico*, 1865.

[*In* ALMARAZ (R.) Memoria por la comision cientifica de Pachuca].

——— Estudios sobre la fauna (y flora) de Pachuca, [etc.] 8°. *Mexico*, 1865.

[*In* ALMARAZ (Ramon). Memoria por la comision cientifica de Pachuca].

——— Estudio sobre una nueva especie del genero "cantharis." *See* **Peñafael** (Antonio) *and* **Villada.**

Villarino (Joaquin). Estudios sobre la colonizacion i emigracion Europea a Chile. 171 pp. 8°. *Santiago, imprenta nacional*, 1867. s.

Villars (Dominique). Flora delphinalis sive; elenchus generum et specierum plantarum indigenarum. vii, 127 pp. 8°. *Coloniæ Allobrogum*, 1785.

[GILIBERT (J. E.) C. Linnæi systema plantarum Europæ. v. 1].

Ville-Hardouin (Geoffroy de). Chronique de la prise de Constantinople par les Francs, et suivie de la continuation de Henri de Valenciennes. Avec notes, etc. par J. A. Buchon. xxiii, 305 pp. 1 l. 8°. *Paris, Verdière*, 1828.

[COLLECTION de chroniques nationales françaises. v. 3].

Villemain (Abel François). Cours de littérature au moyen age en France, en Italie, en Espagne et en Angleterre. 3e éd. 2 v. 2 p. l. iv, 432 pp; 2 p. l. 401 pp. 8°. *Paris, Didier*, 1841. s.

——— The same. Tableau de la littérature du xviiie siècle. 3e éd. 4 v. 8°. *Paris, Didier*, 1841. s.

Villot (Frédéric). Notice des tableaux de Louvre. *See* **Musée** nationale de Louvre.

Vilmar (August Friedrich Christian). Geschichte der deutschen national-literatur. 7e verm. aufl. 2 v. in 1. xii, 428 pp; viii, 336 pp. 12°. *Marburg, Elwert*, 1857.

Vingut (Francisco Javier). Joyas de la poesia española; [*or*], gems of Spanish poetry. [Spanish and English texts]. 120 l. 12°. *New York, F. J. Vingut & co.* 1855. s.

Viollet-le-Duc (Eugène Emmanuel). Dictionnaire raisonné de l'architecture française du xie au xvie siècle. v. 9–10. 8°. *Paris, A. Morel,* 1868.

[Completes the work].

Virgilius Maro (Publius). Opera, cum notis T. Farnabii. 384 pp. 18°. *Amstelædami, J. Blaev,* 1650.

—— The same. P. Virgilivs Maro varietate lectionis et perpetva adnotatione illvstratvs a Chr. Gottl. Heyne. Ed. [3tia] novis cvris emendata, etc. 6 v. 8°. *Lipsiæ, C. Fritsch,* 1800. s.

CONTENTS.

v. 1. Bvcolica et Georgica. lxii, 776 pp.
v. 2–4. Æneis.
v. 5. Carmina minora. vi, 538 pp.
v. 6. Indices. 798 pp.

—— The Æneid. With explanatory notes, by T. Chase. 415 pp. 16°. *Philadelphia, Eldredge & bro.* 1868.

—— Zehn eclogen. Mit einer einleitung über Virgil's leben und fortleben als dichter und zauberer. Von F. W. Genthe. 2e aufl. 1 p. l. 225 pp. 1 portrait. 16°. *Leipzig, G. Gräbner,* [1855]. s.

Virginia (*State of*). The constitution framed by the convention which met in Richmond, Dec. 3, 1867. Passed April, 1868. 41 pp. 8°. *Richmond, office of the New Nation,* 1868.

—— The debates and proceedings of the constitutional convention, assembled at Richmond, Dec. 3, 1867. W. H. Samuel, phonographic reporter. v. 1. 750 pp. 8°. *Richmond, office of the New Nation,* 1868.

—— Documents of the constitutional convention, [1867–68]. 310 pp. 8°. *Richmond, office of the New Nation,* 1867.

—— Journal of the constitutional convention, convened in Richmond, Dec. 3, 1867. 391 pp. 8°. *Richmond, office of the New Nation,* 1867.

—— Journal of the senate, 1783. 55 pp. 4°. *Richmond, Thomas Nicholson & W. Prentis,* 1783.

Virginia (The) and Kentucky resolutions of 1798 and '99; with Jefferson's original draught thereof. Also, Madison's report, Calhoun's address, resolutions of the several states in relation to state rights. With other documents in support of the Jeffersonian doctrines of '98. 82 pp. 8°. *Washington, J. Elliot,* 1832.

Visit (A) to the menagerie, by a father and his children. [*anon.*] viii, 160 pp. 8 pl. 16°. *Philadelphia, Lindsay & Blakiston,* 1849. s.

Visitation (The) manual; a collection of prayers and instructions. Compiled according to the spiritual directory and spirit of Saint Francis de Sales, [etc.] 672 pp. 1 pl. 16°. *Baltimore, J. Murphy & co.* 1858. s.

Vitet (Louis). Études sur les beaux arts; essais d'archéologie; et fragments littéraires. 2 v. vi, 460 pp; 2 p. l. 414 pp. 12°. *Paris, Comon & cie.* 1846. s.

CONTENTS.

v. 1. Musique. Peinture. Sculpture et gravure. Architecture. Melanges.
v. 2. Architecture.

—— La ligue, scènes historiques. 2 v. 2 p. l. 371 pp; 2 p. l. 543 pp. 12°. *Paris, C. Gosselin,* 1844. s.

CONTENTS.

v. 1. Les barricades.
v. 2. Les états de Blois, la mort de Henri iii.

Vizetelly (Henry). The story of the diamond necklace told in detail for the first time, chiefly by the aid of original letters, [etc.] Comprising a sketch of the life of the countess de la Motte, [and others]. 2 v. xvi, 318 pp. 1 pl; 2 p. l. 312 pp. 1 pl. 12°. *London, Tinsley bros.* 1867.

Vogt (Carl). Memoir upon the hectocotyli. *See* **Verany** (Giovanni Battista) *and* **Vogt** (C.)

Voices from the army! The soldiers open their batteries on the copperheads. 8 pp. 8°. *New York,* 1863.

[LOYAL publication society. No. 5].

Voigt (Michael Wenzel). Die quellen der seelenruhe, so wie sie der mensch in seinem gemüthe findet, [etc.] 5 p. l. 196 pp. 16°. *Prag, C. Barth,* 1799. s.

Volckhausen (C.) Nikolaus i. 16°. *Hamburg, Hoffman & Campe,* 1857–60.

[CRUSENSTOLPE (M. J. von). Der russische hof. v. 6–9].

Vollgraff (Carl). Erster versuch einer begründung sowohl der allgemeinen ethnologie durch die anthropologie, wie auch der staats- und rechts-philosophie durch die ethnologie, oder, nationalität der völker. 4 v. in 3. 8°. *Marburg, Elwert,* 1851–55.

CONTENTS.

v. 1. Anthropognosie; oder, zur kunde des menschen uberhaupt. [*anon.*]
v. 2. Ethnognosie und ethnologie; oder, herleitung classification und schilderung der nationen. [*anon.*]
1e abth. Die stufen und classen.
2e abth. Die ordnungen und zünfte.
v. 3. Polignosie und polilogie; oder, genetische und comparative staats-und rechts-philosophie.

Volney (Constantine François Chassebœuf de). Tableau du climat et du sol des États-Unis d'Amérique. Suivi d'éclaircissemens sur la Floride, sur la colonie française au Scioto, sur quelques colonies canadiennes, et sur les sauvages. 2 v. 4 p. l. xvi, 532 pp. 2 maps. 2 pl. 8°. *Paris, Courcier et Dentu,* 1803.

Voltaire (François Marie Arouët de). Fame and fancy; or, Voltaire improved. Containing the story of Candid—revised. By lord Hail-fair [Enos Cobb]? 2 v. 215 pp. 4 pl; 214 pp. 8 pl. 18°. *Boston,* 1826.

[NOTE.—In addition to the story of Candide, this work contains the second part of Candide, attributed to Thorel de Champigneulles, and a relation of the adventures of lord Hail-fair; the latter being a description of men and things in America, written probably by Enos Cobb].

Volz (Robert). Das spitalwesen und die spitäler des grossherzogthums Baden, [etc.] x, 500 pp. 8°. *Karlsruhe, Malsch & Vogel,* 1861. S.

Vouziers (M. de, *pseudon.*) *See* **Moithey** (P. J.)

Voyage au Kentoukey, et sur les bords du Genesée, précédé de conseils aux liberaux, [etc. *anon.*] 244 pp. 1 map. 8°. *Paris, M. Sollier,* 1821.

Vries (Simon de). Curieuse aenmerckingen der bysonderste Oost en West Indische verwonderens-waerdige dingen; nevens die van China, Africa, en andere gewesten des werlds. 4 v. 4°. *Utrecht, Ribbius,* 1682.

Vulgarisms and other errors of speech: including a chapter on taste, and one containing examples of bad taste. [*anon.*] x, 194 pp. 16°. *Philadelphia, Claxton, Remsen & Haffelfinger,* 1868.

Wachsmuth (Wilhelm, *editor*). *See* **Archiv** für die sächsische geschichte. 1863–64.

Wade (William, *major U. S. A.*) Reports of experiments on strength of iron. 4°. 1848–54. *Philadelphia,* 1856.

[*In* UNITED STATES. *War Department.* Reports of experiments, etc. 4°. *Philadelphia,* 1856].

Wagner (Albrecht). On the process of repair after resection and extirpation of bones. Translated, with an appendix of cases, by T. Holmes. 8°. *London,* 1859.

[NEW SYDENHAM society. v. 5. Selected monographs. pp. 111–245].

Wainewright (Jeremiah, *M.D.*) A mechanical account of the non-naturals: being a brief application of the changes made in humane bodies, by air, diet, etc. 16 p. l. 196 pp. 8°. *London, R Smith,* 1707.

Wainwright (Daniel Wadsworth). Wheat and chaff. A comedy in five acts. 84 pp. 12°. *New York, C. Roe,* 1858. S.

Waiting for the morning. [*anon.*] 230 pp. 2 pl. 16°. *Philadelphia, American s. s. union,* 1867.

Waitz (Georg). Deutsche verfassungsgeschichte. 2 v. xxvii, 296 pp; xxii, 668 pp. 8°. *Kiel, Schwers,* 1844–47.

CONTENTS.

v. 1. Die verfassung des deutschen volks vor der zeit der grossen wanderungen.
v. 2. Die deutsche verfassung im fränkischen reich. 1. Die merovingische zeit.

——— Uber die anfänge der vassalität. Aus dem 7[en] bde. der abhandlungen der Kön. gesell. der wissen. zu Göttingen. 1 p. l. 78 pp. 4°. *Göttingen, Dieterich,* 1856.

Wakeley (*Rev.* Joseph B.) The heroes of methodism, containing sketches of eminent methodist preachers, [etc.] viii, 470 pp. 3 portraits. 8°. *New York, Carlton & Porter,* 1856. S.

Walch (Georg Ludwig). Emendationes livianæ. vii, 291 pp. 8°. *Berolini, apud G. C. Nauckium,* 1815. S.

Waldo (S. Putnam). Memoirs of Andrew Jackson. 5th ed. 336 pp. portrait. 16°. *Hartford, J. & W. Russell,* 1819.

——— The tour of James Monroe, president of the United States, in the year 1817; [with] a sketch of his life. xii, 300 pp. portrait. 16°. *Hartford, F. D. Bolles & co.* 1818.

Waldron (Neil A.) *and* **Sturdivant** (John A.) Waldron & co's shippers' express guide, for the states of N. Y., Pa., N. J., Md., Del., and the Canadas. xi, 159 pp. 18°. *Philadelphia, King & Baird,* 1868.

Wales (Philip S. *M.D. U.S.N.*) Mechanical therapeutics. A treatise on surgical apparatus, appliances, and elementary operations. Illustrated. 685 pp. 8°. *Philadelphia, H. C. Lea,* 1867.

Walford (Cornelius). The insurance guide and hand-book on fire, life, marine, tontine, and casualty insurance. Am. ed. with revisions and additions, by [H. C. Fish]. vi, 572 pp. 8°. *New York, Wynkoop & Hallenbeck,* 1868.

Walker (Amasa, *LL.D.*) The science of wealth: a manual of political economy. Embracing the laws of trade, currency, and finance. 4th ed. xxxiv, 496 pp. 9 diag. 8°. *Boston, Little, Brown & co.* 1867.

Walker (Francis, *of the British museum*). Monographia chalciditum. 2 p. l. 333 pp. 8°. *London, H. Baillière,* 1839. S.

Walker (Jesse). Poems, written during his early professional years, with a brief notice of the author by rev. M. Schuyler. 196 pp. 12°. *Buffalo, Phinney & co.* 1854. S.

Walker (Robert James). American slavery, finances, and repudiation. 3[d] ed. with appendix. 9 v. in 1. 8°. *London, W. Ridgway,* 1863. s.

CONTENTS.

Jefferson Davis. Repudiation, recognition, and slavery. Letters 1–2. 58 pp; 12 pp. 1863.
Jefferson Davis. Repudiation of Arkansas bonds. Letter 3. 1864.
American thanksgiving dinner, [etc.] 94 pp. 1863.
American finances and resources. Letters 1–5. 1863–64.

Wallace (*Rev.* James A.) History of Williamsburg church, [S. C. etc.] 122 pp. 16°. *Salisbury, (N.C.) Herald office,* 1856. s.

Wallace (Robert). A dissertation on the true age of the world, in which is determined the chronology of the period from creation to the christian era. xx, 407 pp. 8°. *London, Smith, Elder & co.* 1844. s.

Wallis (S. Teackle). Leisure: its moral and political economy. A lecture, [etc.] 53 pp. 8°. *Baltimore, mercantile library association,* 1859. s.

Walmesley (*Rev.* Charles). The general history of the christian church, chiefly deduced from the apocalypse of St. John. By sig. Pastorini. [*pseudon.*] 2[d] Am. ed. 396 pp. 1 portrait. 12°. *New York, J. Doyle,* 1834. s.

Walrath (M. E.) History of the earth's formation. Its first inhabitance in connexion with the explanation of the bible. By a convocation of God's messengers through mediumship of M. E. Walrath. viii, 633 pp. 8°. *New York, for author,* 1868.

Walsh (John Henry). The horse, in the stable and the field: his varieties, management in health and disease, anatomy, physiology, etc. Illustrated. New ed. x, 623, 21 pp. 1 pl. 8°. *New York, G. Routledge & sons,* 1869.

——— A manual of domestic economy: suited to families spending from £100 to £1000 a year. xvi, 736 pp. 56 pl. 16°. *London, G. Routledge & co.* 1856.

Walsh (Michael). A new system of mercantile arithmetic; adapted to the commerce of the United States in its domestic and foreign relations. [With] a system of book-keeping. 4th ed. xi, 264 pp. 16°. *Salem, Cushing & Appleton,* 1824.

Walsingham (Thomas). Chronica monasterii S. Albani. Gesta abbatum monasterii S. Albani, a T. Walsingham compilata. Edited by H. T. Riley. v. 2. 1290–1349. xx, 519 pp. 8°. *London, Longmans,* 1867.

[GREAT BRITAIN and IRELAND. Chronicles and memorials during the middle ages].

Walton (Christopher, *editor*). An introduction to theosophy, [etc.] *See* **Law** (*Rev.* William).

——— Notes and materials for an adequate biography of the celebrated divine and theosopher, William Law. Comprising an elucidation of the scope and contents of the writings of Jacob Böhme, and of his great commentator, D. A. Freher; with a notice of the mystical divinity, [etc. With] A guide to the peculiar sciential and experiential knowledge of theology, needful to compose an adequate and suitable biography of William Law. xxxii, xv–xxxiv, 688 pp. 8°. *London, author,* 1854–56. s.

Walton (Elijah). Clouds: their forms and combinations. xi, 31 pp. 46 photog. pl. 4°. *London, Longmans,* 1868.

Walton (Izaak) *and* **Cotton** (Charles). The complete angler; or, contemplative man's recreation. With the lives of the authors, and notes, by sir J. Hawkins. 2 v. in 1. lxxviii, 303 pp. 12 pl; lviii, 128 pp. 4 l. 4 pl. 12°. *London, T. Hope,* 1760.

Wang Keaou Lwan pĭh nëen chang hăn; or, the lasting resentment of miss Keaou Lwan Wang, a Chinese tale: founded on fact. Translated from the original by Sloth. [Robert Thom]. viii, 66 pp. 1 pl. 8°. *Canton, press office,* 1839. s.

Wanklyn (James Alfred) *and* **Chapman** (Ernest Theodore). Water analysis: a practical treatise on the examination of potable water. xii, 103 pp. 16°. *London, Trübner & co.* 1868.

Warcupp (Edmund, *compiler*). Italy, in its original glory, ruine and revival, being an exact survey of the whole geography, and history of that famous country; with the adjacent islands of Sicily, Malta, etc. And whatever is remarkable in Rome. Translated out of the [Italian] originals. 4 p. l. 327 pp. 4 l. 3 pl. fol. *London, H. Twyford,* 1660.

Ward (*Rev.* F. DeW.) A christian gift; or, pastoral letters. 192 pp. 32°. *Rochester, E. Darrow,* 1853. s.

Ward (J.) Workmen and wages at home and abroad; or, the effects of strikes, combinations, and trades' unions. xx, 314 pp. 12°. *London, Longmans,* 1868.

Ward (James W.) The song of Higher-water. 30 pp. 8°. *New York, R. H. Johnston & co.* 1868.

Ward (Thomas). England's reformation, (from the time of k. Henry viii, to the end of Oates's plot). A poem in four cantos. 2 v. in 1. 2 p. l. 212 pp; 204 pp. 16°. *London, E. More,* 1719.

Ward (Thomas). Errata to the protestant bible; or, the truth of their English translations examined, [etc.] New ed. 4 p. l. 116 pp. 4°. *Dublin, R. Coyne*, 1807. s.

Ware (Henry, *jr.*) The life of the saviour. 6th ed. xi, 271 pp. 16°. *Boston, American unitarian association*, 1868.

Warfel (Linda). Early efforts. [Poems]. 136 pp. 1 portrait. 16°. *Philadelphia, Daughaday & co.* 1868.

Waring (George E.) The elements of agriculture: a book for young farmers. 2d ed. 254 pp. 16°. *New York, Tribune association*, 1868.

Warner (Anna B.) Three little spades. By the author of "Dollars and cents." [*anon.*] 268 pp. 16°. *New York, Harpers*, 1868.

——— The word. The star out of Jacob. [*anon.*] 391 pp. 8 pl. 16°. *New York, R. Carter & bros.* 1868.

——— *and* **Warner** (Susan). Ellen Montgomery's bookshelf. By the authors of "The wide wide world," "Dollars and cents," etc. [*anon.*] v. 2-4. 16°. *New York, G. P. Putnam & co.* 1854-56. s.

v. 2-3. Mr. Rutherford's children. [By Elizabeth Wetherell. *pseudon.*]
v. 4. Casper. By Amy Lothrop. [*pseudon.*]

Warner (Susan). Daisy. Continued from "Melbourn house." 435 pp. 12°. *Philadelphia, Lippincott & co.* 1868.

——— The wide, wide world. By Elizabeth Wetherell. [*pseudon.*] New ed. 413 pp. 4 pl. 16°. *London, G. Routledge & sons*, [1866].

Warren (*Le comte* Édouard de). L'Inde anglaise en 1843-1844. 2e éd. 3 v. 8°. *Paris, Comon & cie.* 1845.

Warren (Gouverneur K.) An account of the operations of the fifth army corps at the battle of Five Forks, and preliminary to it. 53 pp. 1 map. 8°. *New York, D. Van Nostrand*, 1866.

Warren (Samuel Edward). General problems in the linear perspective of form, shadow, and reflection; or, the scenographic projections of descriptive geometry. xvii, 197 pp. xvii pl. 8°. *New York, John Wiley & son*, 1868.

Warville (Jean Pierre Brissot de). *See* **Brissot de Warville.**

Was it a ghost? The murders in Bussey's woods. An extraordinary narrative. [*anon.*] 143 pp. 2 pl. 16°. *Boston, Loring*, 1868.

Washington (George). Letters to Arthur Young and sir John Sinclair, containing an account of his husbandry, with his opinions on various questions in agriculture; and many particulars of the rural economy of the United States. 128 pp. 12°. *Alexandria, (Va.) Cottom & Stewart*, 1803. s.

Washington (*City of*). Twenty-first [and] twenty-second annual reports of the board of trustees of the public schools, 1866-67. 2 v. 8°. *Washington, McGill & Witherow*, 1866-67.

Washington daily constitution. *See* **Constitution** (The).

Washington daily union. *See* **Daily** (The) union.

Washington evening star. *See* **Evening** (The) star.

Washington evening union. *See* **Constitutional** union.

Washington gazette. [Daily]. May 11, 1819, Jan. 10, 1821, to July 6, 1822, Jan. 1824, to Dec. 1825. 4 v. fol. *Washington*, 1819-25.

——— The same. [Tri-weekly]. May 5, 1821, to April 25, 1822. fol. *Washington*, 1821-22.

Washington and **Georgetown** (Boyd's) directory, [etc.] 1858. 8°. *Washington, H. Boyd*, 1858. s.

——— The same. Boyd's directory of Washington and Georgetown, 1868-69. 2 v. 8°. *Washington*, [*W. H. Boyd*, 1868-69].

Washington (The) republic. *See* **Republic** (The).

Washington republican and congressional examiner. [Semi-weekly]. Aug. 7, 1822, to July 10, 1824. fol. *Washington*, 1822-24.

Washington (The) states. *See* **States** (The).

Watch (The). An ode, [with] the genius of America addressed to general Carleton; an ode. [*anon.*] 22 pp. 4°. *London, J. Bew*, 1778.

Waterman (*Miss* Catharine H.) *See* **Esling** (*Mrs.* C. H. W.)

Watson (James C.) Theoretical astronomy relating to the motions of the heavenly bodies, embracing a derivation of the formulæ for the calculation of places, determination of orbits, [etc.] With numerous examples and tables. 662 pp. 8°. *Philadelphia, J. B. Lippincott & co.* 1868.

Watson (James Madison). Independent fifth reader: containing a complete treatise on elocution, etc. 336 pp. 1 pl. 12°. *New York, A. S. Barnes & co.* 1868.

Watson (John Forbes, *M.D.*) Index to the native and scientific names of Indian and other eastern economic plants and products. viii, 637 pp. 8°. *London, India museum*, 1868.

Watson (*Rev.* J. V.) Helps to the promotion of revivals. 223 pp. 12°. *New York, Carlton & Porter*, 1856.

Watson (Rachel M. *M.D.*) What every family wants. The family physician; containing simple remedies, easily obtained, for the cure of disease in all its forms. 208 pp. 12°. *Salem, (O.) J. K. Rukenbrod,* 1868.

Watson (Richard, *D.D. bishop of Landaff*). An apology for the Bible, in a series of letters, addressed to Thomas Paine. 201 pp. 16°. *New-Brunswick, A. Blauvelt,* 1796.

Watt (John James). Anatomico-chirurgical views of the male and female pelvis; with appropriate explanations and references to the parts, [etc.] 19 pp. 8 col. pl. 8 outline copies. fol. *London, author,* 1811.

[Entitled fasciculus ii. The first fasciculus is Anatomico-chirurgical views of the nose, mouth, larynx and fauces. 1809].

Wattenbach (Wilhelm). Deutschlands geschichtsquellen im mittelalter bis zur mitte des dreizehnten jahrhunderts. xvi, 477 pp. 8°. *Berlin, W. Hertz,* 1858.

Watts (Alaric A.) *See* **Literary** souvenir.

Watts (Henry) *and others.* A dictionary of chemistry and the allied branches of other sciences. 5 v. 8°. *London, Longmans,* 1866-68.

Watts (Isaac). Improvement of the mind. School ed. With Denman's questions. 301 pp. 16°. *New York, A. S. Barnes & co.* 1849. s.

Wayland (Francis, *jr.*) No failure for the North. [*anon.*] From the Atlantic monthly. 23 pp. 8°. *New York, W. C. Bryant & co.* 1864.

[LOYAL publication society. no. 11].

Weaver (*Rev.* G. S.) Hopes and helps for the young of both sexes. Relating to the formation of character, [etc.] 246 pp. 12°. *New York, Fowler & Wells,* 1853. s.

Weaver (Robert). Monumenta antiqua; or, the stone monuments of antiquity yet remaining in the British isles, particularly as illustrated by scripture. Also, a dissertation on "Stonehenge:" [with an] account of the Druids. xvi, 199 pp. 4 pl. 12°. *London, J. B. Nichols & son,* 1840.

Webb (*Rev.* Edward). Hindoo life, with pictures of the men, women, and children of India. 63 pp. 9 pl. sm. 4°. *Philadelphia, presby. pub. com.* 1866.

Webb (Maria). The Penns and Penningtons of the 17th century, in their domestic and religious life; illustrated by original family letters: also, notices of T. Ellwood, with some of his unpublished verses. xiv, 430 pp. 7 pl. 12°. *London, F. B. Kitto,* 1867.

Webb (Philip Barker) *and* **Berthelot** (Sabin). Histoire naturelle des îles Canaries. Ouvrage publié sous les auspices de m. Guizot, ministre de l'instruction publique. 11 parts in 3 v. 4°. Atlas, fol. *Paris, Béthune,* 1836–51. s.

CONTENTS:

v. 1. 1e partie. L'ethnographie et les annales de la conquête. [Par Berthelot]. 2 p. l. 338 pp. 3 pl. 1842.

v. 1. 2e partie. Les miscellanées canariennes, relations de voyage, excursions, chasses, navigationes, caravanes, notices, épisodes, remarques et observations diverses. [Par Berthelot]. 2 p. l. 251 pp. 1839.

v. 2. 1e partie. La géographie descriptive, la statistique, et la géologie. 2 p. l. 417 pp. 15 pl. fol. 1839.

v. 2. 2e partie. La zoologie. 1836–44. Introduction, [et mammifères], par P. B. Webb. 12 pp.
Ornithologie canarienne. Par P. B. Webb, S. Berthelot, et A. Moquin-Tandon. 48 pp. 4 col. pl.
Reptiles. Par P. Gervais. 5 pp. 1 l. 1 pl.
Ichthyologie. Par A. Valenciennes. 109 pp. 1 l. 26 pl.
Entomologie: animaux articulés. Par Brullé, (pour les crustacés et la plus grande partie des insectes); Lucas, (pour les arachnides et les myriapodes); Macquart, (pour les insectes diptères). 119 pp. 8 col. pl.
Mollusques, échinodermes, foraminifères et polypiers. Par A. d'Orbigny. 152 pp. [14 pl.]

v. 3. 1e partie. La géographie botanique. 2 p. l. 183 pp. 1 portrait. [20 pl. fol.] 1840.

v. 3. 2e partie. Phytographia canariensis. Sectio i. 2 p. l. 220 pp. 48 pl. 1836–40.
——— Sectio ultima. [Plantes cellulaires, par Camille Montaigne]. xv, 208 pp. 9 pl. 1840.

Webber (Charles Wilkins). Tales of the southern border. 400 pp. 8 pl. 8°. *Philadelphia, J. B. Lippincott & co.* 1868.

Weber (Carl von, *editor*). *See* **Archiv** für sächsische geschichte. 1863–67.

Weber (Georg). Die geschichte der deutschen literatur nach ihrer organischen entwickelung, [etc.] viii, 112 pp. 8°. *Leipzig, W. Engelmann,* 1847. s.

Weber (Thomas R.) Die pennsylvanische sammlung von kirchen-musik, [etc. *or*], The Pennsylvania collection of church music, [etc. German and English]. xvi, 160 pp. obl. 8°. [*Philadelphia*]? *compiler,* 1859. s.

Weber (Wilhelm Eduard). Atlas des erdmagnetismus. *See* **Gauss** (Carl F.) *and* **Weber.**

Webster (Daniel). Works. 14th ed. 6 v. 8°. *Boston, Little, Brown & co.* 1866.

——— The beauties of Daniel Webster, with a critical essay on his genius and writings. By James Rees. 95 pp. 12°. *New York, J. & H. G. Langley,* 1839.

——— Select speeches. 8°. *Philadelphia,* 1859.

[*In* SCHMUCKER (S. M.) The life of D. Webster, 1859].

Webster (Edward). The public and private business of the house of commons, considered in relation to the economization of the time of the house and of its members. 30 pp. 8°. *London, W. Ridgway,* 1868.

Webster (Noah, *LL. D.*) An American dictionary of the English language. Revised and greatly enlarged and improved by C. A. Goodrich and N. Porter. lxxii, 1768 pp. 4°. *Springfield, (Mass.) G. & C. Merriam,* 1869.
[NOTE.—The same as the copyrighted ed. of 1864].

——— A common-school dictionary of the English language, explanatory, pronouncing, and synonymous. Abridged from the American dictionary by W. G. Webster and W. A. Wheeler. 391 pp. 4 l. 18°. *Philadelphia, Lippincott & co.* 1868.

——— A dictionary of the English language: abridged from the American dictionary, [etc.] 4 p. l. 532 pp. sq. 16°. *New York, White, Gallaher & White,* 1830. s.

——— The same. Abridged by W. G. Webster and W. A. Wheeler. Academic ed. Illustrated. xxxii, 560 pp. 8°. *New York, Ivison, Phinney & co.* 1868.

——— A high-school dictionary of the English language, explanatory, pronouncing, and synonymous. Abridged from the quarto dictionary, by W. G. Webster and W. A. Wheeler. 415 pp. 16°. *New York, Ivison, Phinney & co.* 1868.

——— A primary school dictionary. Abridged by W. G. Webster and W. A. Wheeler. 352 pp. 18°. *New York, Ivison, Phinney & co.* 1868.

——— Elements of useful knowledge. v. 2. Containing a historical and geographical account of the United States. 206 pp. 16°. *New Haven, author,* 1804.

Wedel, *or* **Wedelius** (Christiaan). Epistola de oculorum tunicis. 4°. *Amstelœdami,* 1720.
[RUYSCH (F.) Opera. v. 3, No. 29].

Weekly (The) messenger. Jan. 29, 1813. v. 2, No. 15. Oct. 13, 1815. v. 4, No. 52. 3 v. in 1. fol. *Boston, J. Cutter,* 1813–15. s.
[Imperfect].

Weeks (Helen C.) The Ainslee stories. 3 p. l. 411 pp. 8 pl. 16°. *New York, Hurd & Houghton,* 1868.

Weighed in the balance. By the author of the "Win and wear" series. [*anon.*] 402 pp. 4 pl. 16°. *New York, R. Carter & bros.* 1868.

Weil von Gernsbach (———). Reden in Philadelphia, 1864. *See* **Schütz** (Frederick) *and* **Weil von Gernsbach.**

Weinhold (Carl). Altnordisches leben. Mit einer schrifttafel. 4 p. l. 512 pp. 8°. *Berlin, Weidmann,* 1856.

——— Die deutschen frauen in dem mittelalter. Ein beitrag zu dem hausalterthümern der Germanen. 1 p. l. v, 496 pp. 1 l. 8°. *Wien, C. Gerold,* 1851.

Weiss (Siegfried). Die praktische deutsche nationalökonomie in verbindung mit ihrer politik. iv, 352 pp. 1 tab. 8°. *Leipzig, L. Fernau,* 1852.

Weissbach (Julius, *Ph. D.*) Der ingenieur. Sammlung von tafeln, formeln und regeln der arithmetik, der theoretischen und praktischen geometrie sowie der mechanik und des ingenieurwesens, [etc.] 3[e] aufl. 3 parts in 1 v. viii, xxii, 862 pp. 1 l. 16°. *Braunschweig, F. Vieweg & sohn,* 1860–63. s.

Weisse (Christian Hermann). Die evangelienfrage in ihrem gegenwärtigen stadium. xi, 292 pp. 8°. *Leipzig, Breitkopf & Härtel,* 1856.

Weitenkampf (Johann Friedrich). Vernünftige trostgründe bey den traurigen schicksalen der menschen. 221 pp. 8 l. 12°. *Lancaster, J. Bär,* 1825. s.

Welcker (Friedrich Gottlieb). Das akademische kunstmuseum zu Bonn. 2[e] ausg. xii, 180 pp. 8°. *Bonn, E. Weber,* 1841. s.

——— Kleine schriften. v. 3. [*or*] Kleine schriften zu den alterthümern der heilkunde bei den Griechen, griechische inschriften, zur alten kunstgeschichte. viii, 555 pp. 2 pl. 8°. *Bonn, E. Weber,* 1850. s.

Weld (Charles Richard). Florence, the new capital of Italy. [Illustrated]. xviii, 431 pp. 12°. *London, Longmans,* 1867.

Weld (H. Hastings). The star of Bethlehem; or, stories for christmas. 242 pp. 6 pl. sq. 16°. *Philadelphia, Lindsay & Blakiston,* [1851]. s.

Wells (David Ames). Our burden and our strength; or, a comprehensive and popular examination of the debt and resources of our country, present and prospective. 39 pp. 8°. *New York,* 1864.
[LOYAL publication society. no. 54].

——— Reports of the special commissioner of the revenue, 1866–68. 3 v. *See* **United States.** (*Treasury department*).

Wells (J. G.) Illustrated hand-book, embracing a complete compendium of the political history of the United States. 285 pp. 5 l. 1 pl. 12°. *New York, B. W. Hitchcock,* 1868.

Weltmeer (Das). Redigirt von K. J. Clement und Georg Blum. 1[r] jahrgang—2[r] jahrgang, no. 1–26. 2 v. 4°. *Hamburg, Blum & Ackermann, etc.* 1860–61. s.
[v. 2 (27–52), et seq. wanting].

Welty (*Mrs.* E. A.) Self-made; or, living for those we love. 280 pp. 12°. *New York, Sheldon & co.* 1868.

Wendt (Ernst Emil). Papers on maritime legislation. With a translation of the German mercantile law relating to maritime commerce. xvi, 279 pp. 8°. *London, Longmans,* 1868.

Wentworth (May). Fairy tales from golden lands. 234 pp. 1 pl. 12°. *New York, A. Roman & co.* 1867.

—— The same. 2[d] series. 237 pp. 3 pl. 12°. *New York, A. Roman & co.* 1868.

West (John, *A. M.*) The substance of a journal during a residence at the Red River colony, British North America, 1820–23. With a journal of a mission to the Indians of New Brunswick and Nova Scotia, and the Mohawks on Grand river, Upper Canada, 1825–26. 2[d] ed. xvi, 326 pp. 1 map. 3 pl. 8°. *London, L. B. Seeley & son,* 1827.

West (Richard). The booke of demeanor and the allowance and disallowance of certaine misdemeanors in companie. 1619. 8°. *London, reprint,* 1868.

[*In* FURNIVALL (C. F.) Babees book, etc. pp. 289–296. Early English text society publications. no. 32].

West (Willa, *pseudon.*) *See* **Lucy Gelding.** 1862.

Westbrooke; or, laying the foundations. By the author of "Paul Venner," etc. [*anon.*] 256 pp. 3 pl. 18°. *Boston, American tract society,* 1867.

Western (The) farmers' annual and rural companion, for 1868. T. A. Bland, editor. 64 pp. 8°. *Indianapolis, T. A. Bland & co.* 1867.

Western (The) journal and civilian, devoted to agriculture, manufactures, mechanic arts, and polite literature. M. Tarver and H. Cobb, editors. v. 10–11. New series. v. 4–5. 8°. *St. Louis, M. Niedner,* 1853.

Western (The) messenger, devoted to religion, life, and literature. May, 1840, to April, 1841. v. 8. 2 p. l. 572 pp. 8°. *Cincinnati, J. B. Russell,* 1841.

Westminster assembly (The shorter catechism of the). 32 pp. 32°. *Philadelphia, presbyterian board of publication,* [1848] s.

[*With* HYMNS for youth. 1848].

Weston (*Rev.* David). The baptist movement of a hundred years ago, and its vindication. A discourse delivered at Middleborough, Mass. Jan. 16, 1868. 32 pp. 8°. *Boston, Gould & Lincoln,* 1868.

Weston (*Sir* Richard). A treatise concerning the husbandry and natural history of England. [With] preface by S. Hartlib. 2[d] ed. x, 111 pp. 12°. *London, T. Harris,* 1742.

Westropp (Hodder M.) Handbook of archæology. Egyptian, Greek, Etruscan, Roman. xvi, 458 pp. 10 pl. 8°. *London, Bell & Daldy,* 1867.

Wetenhall (Edward, *bishop of Cork and Ross*). A compendious system of Greek grammar: in English and Greek. Translated [with additions] by W. P. Farrand. 3[d] ed. Revised by W. Staughton. iv, 115 pp. 16°. *Philadelphia, P. H. Nicklin,* 1813.

—— The same. 5th ed. iv, 115 pp. 16°. *Philadelphia, A. Small,* 1824.

—— Rudiments of the Greek language; arranged for the students of Loyola college, Baltimore. Upon the basis of Wettenhall. 2[d] ed. 1 p. l. 113 l. 12°. *Baltimore, J. Murphy & co.* 1855. s.

Wetherell (Elizabeth, *pseudon.*) *See* **Warner** (Susan.)

Wettenhall (Edward). *See* **Wetenhall.**

Wetter. *See* **Van Wetter.**

What Elise loved best: or, the pet rabbits, and other stories. By the author of "Kitty's victory," etc. [*anon.*] 180, 170 pp. 10 pl. 18°. *New York, Carters,* 1865.

What shall we eat? A manual for housekeepers. Comprising a bill of fare for breakfast, dinner, and tea, for every day in the year. With an appendix, containing recipes for pickles and sauces. [*anon.*] 134 pp. 16°. *New York, G. P. Putnam & son,* 1868.

Whately (Richard, *archbishop of Dublin*). Easy lessons on reasoning. 3[d] Amer. ed. 180 pp. 12°. *Boston, W. H. Dennet,* 1868.

—— Introductory lectures on political economy, delivered at Oxford, in easter term, 1831. With remarks on tithes and on poor-laws, and on penal colonies. 4th ed. [etc.] xvi, 362 pp. 8°. *London, J. W. Parker & son,* 1855. s.

Wheatly (*Rev.* Charles). A rational illustration of the book of common prayer of the church of England. xii, 532 pp. 1 pl. 12°. *London, Bell & Daldy,* 1864.

Wheatley (Phillis). Letters. [With a brief account of her life. Edited by C. Deane]. 19 pp. 8°. *Boston, privately printed,* 1864.

—— Poems on various subjects, religious and moral. 89 pp. 1 l. 16°. *Albany, T. Spencer,* 1793.

Wheeler (*Rev.* C. H.) Letters from Eden; or, reminiscences of missionary life in the east. 432 pp. 3 pl. 16°. *Boston, American tract society,* 1868.

—— Ten years on the Euphrates; or, primitive missionary policy illustrated. With an introduction by rev. F. G. Clark. xx, 330 pp. 2 maps. 4 pl. 16°. *Boston, American tract society,* 1868.

Wheelock (Eleazer, *D. D.*) A continuation of the narrative of the Indian charity-school, begun in Lebanon, in Connecticut, now incorporated with Dartmouth college. 32 pp. 8°. *Hartford,* 1773.

Wheelwright (*Rev.* John). A sermon preached at Boston, in New England, upon a fast-day, the 19th of January, 1636–37. From the proceedings of the Mass. hist. soc. 1866–67. 22 pp. 8°. *Cambridge,* [*Mass.*] *J. Wilson & son,* 1867.

Where is the city? [An examination of the doctrines of the various sects of protestant christians. *anon.*] viii, 349 pp. 16°. *Boston, Roberts bros.* 1868.

Whitaker (*Rev.* Alexander). Good newes from Virginia. Wherein also is a narration of the present state of that country, and our colonies there. And a preface of some matters touching that plantation. [By W. Crashawe]. 14 p. l. 44 pp. sm. 4°. *London, W. Welby,* 1613.

Whitcombe (Samuel). Five letters to the prince regent, containing a view of the three branches of the legislature, the influence of the crown, and their respective relative situations at different periods, and at the present time; and also some observations on parliamentary reform. vii, 103 pp. 4°. *London, T. Bensley,* 1812.

White (Adam). Crustacea. *See* **Adams** (A.) *and* **White.** The zoology of the voyage of h. m. s. Samarang.

White (Babington, *pseudon.*) *See* **Circe.** A novel.

White (Henry). The massacre of St. Bartholomew: preceded by a history of the religious wars in the reign of Charles ix. xviii, 505 pp. 2 pl. 8°. *London, J. Murray,* 1868.

White (Henry Kirke). The poetical works and remains, [etc.] With a life by Robert Southey. 356 pp. 11 pl. 8°. *Philadelphia, E. H. Butler & co.* 1855. s.

White (Rhoda E.) Memoir and letters of Jenny C. White del Bal. x, 363 pp. portrait. 8°. *Boston, P. Donahoe,* 1868.

White (Samuel S.) Catalogue of dental materials, furniture, instruments, etc. for sale by Samuel S. White. 226 pp. 6 pl. 8°. *Philadelphia,* 1867.

White (*Mr.* Thom, *pseudon.*) *See* **Wind** and whirlwind.

White (Thomas). Religion and reason, mutually corresponding and assisting each other. 8 p. l. 200 pp. 18°. *Paris,* 1660.

Whitlaw (Charles). The scriptural code of health, with observations on the mosaic prohibitions, and on the principles and benefits of the medicated vapour bath. viii, 164 pp. 3 l. 16°. *London, author,* 1838.

Whitlock's horticultural advertiser. Oct. [?] 1867, to June, 1868. v. 1. 12°. *New York, L. L. Whitlock,* [1868].

——— The same. Whitlock's horticultural recorder. July to Dec. 1868. v. 2. 8°. *New York, L. L. Whitlock,* [1868].

Whitmore (William H.) The American genealogist. Being a catalogue of family histories and publications containing genealogical information, issued in the United States, arranged chronologically. 287 pp. 8°. *Albany, J. Munsell,* 1868.

[NOTE.—This is a 2d ed. of his Hand-book of American genealogy. 1862].

Whitney (William Dwight, *annotator*). *See* **Atharva-Veda** Praticakhya (The).

Whitney's musical guest. Nov. 1867, to Oct. 1868. v. 1. 4°. *Toledo,* (*Ohio*), *W. W. Whitney,* 1868.

Whiton (*Rev.* Samuel J.) Glimpses of west Africa, with sketches of missionary labor. 208 pp. 2 pl. 16°. *Boston, American tract society,* 1866.

Whittier (John Greenleaf). Among the hills, and other poems. 100 pp. 1 pl. 16°. *Boston, Fields, Osgood & co.* 1869.

Whittlesey (Charles). On the fresh-water glacial drift of the northwestern states. 3 p. l. 32 pp. 2 maps. 4°. *Washington, Smithsonian institution,* 1867.

[SMITHSONIAN contributions. v. 15].

Whittlesey (Sarah J. C.) Herbert Hamilton; or, the bas bleu. 123 pp. 12°. *Alexandria,* (*Va.*) *State journal office,* 1868.

Whitworth (*Sir* Charles). State of the trade of Great Britain in its imports and exports, 1697 [to 1773]: also of the trade to each particular country, during the above period, distinguishing each year. [With *ms.* additions to 1801, and an account of the number of vessels entered and cleared in the ports of Great Britain, 1772–1802]. 239 pp. [64 l. *ms.*] fol. *London, G. Robinson,* 1776.

Who's who in 1868. Edited by W. J. Lawson. 299 pp. 24°. *London, A. H. Baily & co.* 1868.

Whymper (Frederick). Travel and adventure in the territory of Alaska, formerly Russian America, and in various other parts of the north Pacific. xix, 331 pp. 1 map. 14 pl. 8°. *London, J. Murray,* 1868.

Whyte (*Rev.* Andrew) *and* **Macfarlan** (Duncan). General view of the agriculture of the county of Dumbarton. viii, 344 pp. 1 map. 3 pl. 8°. *London,* 1811. s.
[GREAT BRITAIN: Board of agriculture].

Wichura (M.) On the winding of leaves. 8°. *London,* 1853.
[*In* HENFREY (A.) *and* HUXLEY (T. H.) Scientific memoirs. art. 9].

Wickes (Thomas, *D. D.*) The son of man. 382 pp. 16°. *Boston, American tract society,* 1868.

Widenmann (Eduard). Die nordamerikanische revolution und ihre folgen. vi, 262 pp. 8°. *Erlangen, I. J. Palm,* 1820.
[Imperfect: pp. 251-257 wanting].

Wiebel (C.) Controverse über die frage: was ist mineral-species? *See* **Ulex** (G. L.) *and others.*

Wight (Danforth P. *M. D.*) Seaman's medical guide; with advice on the preservation of health in hot climates. viii, 172 pp. 1 pl. 16°. *Boston, Russell, Odiorne & Metcalf,* 1834.

Wight (Samuel F.) Adventures in California and Nicaragua, in rhyme. A truthful epic. 84 pp. 8°. *Boston, A. Mudge & son,* 1860.

Wilberforce (Samuel, *D. D. bishop of Oxford*). Life of William Wilberforce. Revised and condensed from the original ed. xiv, 452 pp. 12°. *London, J. Murray,* 1868.

Wilbrand (Franz Joseph Julius). Anatomie und physiologie der centralgebilde des nervensystems. viii, 195 pp. 2 pl. 8°. *Giessen, J. Ricker,* 1840. s.

Wilcocks (J. C.) The sea fisherman; comprising the chief methods of hook and line fishing in the British and other seas, and remarks on nets, boats, boating, etc. 2[d] ed. xiii, 303 pp. 12°. *London, Longmans,* 1868. s.

Wiley (Charles A.) Elocution and oratory: giving a thorough treatise on the art of reading and speaking. Containing numerous and choice selections of didactic, humorous, and dramatic styles, from the most celebrated authors. 444 pp. 12°. *New York, Clark & Maynard,* 1869.

Wilhelmus *parisiensis. See* **Guillermus.**

Wilk (Frederik Johan). Försök till framställning af Helsingforstraktens gneis- och granitformationer. 1 p. l. 51 pp. 1 map. 8°. *Helsingfors, J. C. Frenckell & son,* 1866. s.

Wilkes (Charles, *admiral U. S. N.*) Narrative of the United States exploring expedition, 1838-42. With an atlas. 6 v. 4°. *Philadelphia, Lea & Blanchard,* 1845.

Wilkes (George). Europe in a hurry. vi, 449 pp. 1 pl. 12°. *New York, H. Long & bro.* 1853.

Williams (*Sir* Charles Hanbury). Works. With notes by H. Walpole, earl of Orford. 3 v. 16°. *London, E. Jeffrey & son,* 1822.

Williams (*Rev.* D.) Composition, literary and rhetorical, simplified. 2 p. l. 147 pp. 18°. *London, W. & T. Piper,* 1850.

Williams (Folkstone *or* Robert Folkstone). The youth of Shakespeare. 254 pp. 8°. *Philadelphia, T. B. Peterson,* [1865]?

Williams (John, *A. M. of Lancaster, O.*) The readable dictionary; or, topical and synonymic lexicon: with etymologies, definitions and illustrations. v, 360, xxiv pp. 8°. *New York, A. S. Barnes & co.* 1868.

Williams (*Rev.* John, *archdeacon of Cardigan*). Essays on various subjects, connected with the prehistorical records of the civilized nations of ancient Europe, especially of that race which first occupied Great Britain. xii, 382 pp. 6 pl. 8°. *London, J. R. Smith,* 1858.

Williams (John, *bishop of Chichester*). An impartial consideration of those speeches which pass under the name of the five jesuits. Viz: Whitebread, Harcourt, [etc. *anon.*] 14 pp. fol. *London, R. Chiswill,* 1679.
[TRIALS for treason. v. 1].

Williams (John Mason). Nullification and compromise; a retrospective view. 32 pp. 8°. *New York, Francis & Loutrel,* 1863.
[LOYAL publication society. no. 27].

Williams (Monier). A practical grammar of the Sanskrit language, arranged with reference to the classical languages of Europe. 2[d] ed. xxiv, 370 pp. 1 tab. 8°. *Oxford, university press,* 1857.

Williams (Thomas, *M. C.*) Eulogium on the life and character of gen. Wm. Henry Harrison, delivered before the legislature of Pennsylvania, April 24, 1841. 43 pp. 8°. *Pittsburgh, W. S. Haven,* [1841].

——— Eulogy on the life and public services of Abraham Lincoln, delivered in Pittsburgh, June 1, 1865. 36 pp. 8°. *Pittsburgh, W. S. Haven,* 1865.

Williamson (Hugh, *LL. D.*) A discourse on the benefits of civil history, delivered before the New York historical society, Dec. 1810. 8°. *New York, Van Winkle & Wiley,* 1814.
[*In* NEW YORK historical society. Collections. v. 2. 1st series].

Williamson (Hugh, *M. D.*) A manual of problems on the globes. 91 pp. 1 pl. 16°. *New York, Harpers,* 1868.

Williamson (Peter). French and Indian cruelty; exemplified in the life of Peter Williamson, a disbanded soldier, containing, account of the savages of North America, a summary of the transactions of the several provinces, and a detail of the operations of the French and English at Oswego. 2d ed. 104 pp. 12°. *York, J. Jackson,* 1758.

Willis (Anson). Outlines of the United States government: its origin, branches, departments, institutions, officers, and modes of operation. iv, 434 pp. 12°. *New York, N. Tibbals & co.* 1868.

—— The same. Our rulers and our rights; or, outlines of the United States government, its origin, branches, departments, institutions, officers, and modes of operation. 2d ed. enlarged. 517 pp. 4 pl. 12°. *New York, N. Tibbals & co.* 1868.

Willis (Nathaniel Parker). Poems of early and after years. Illustrated by E. Leutze. 2 p. l. 410 pp. 17 pl. 8°. *Philadelphia, Carey & Hart,* 1848. s.

—— Rural letters and other records of thought at leisure, [etc.] 380 pp. 12°. *New York, Baker & Scribner,* 1849. s.

CONTENTS.

Letters from under a bridge; The four rivers; Glenmary poems; Open-air musings in the city; Invalid rambles in Germany in 1845; Letters from watering-places; A plain man's love.

Willis (Thomas, *M. D.*) Two discourses concerning the soul of brutes, which is that of the vital and sensitive of man. The first is physiological, showing the nature [etc.] of the same. The other is pathological, which unfolds the diseases which affect it and its primary seat, the brain and nervous stock. Englished [from the Latin] by S. Pordage. 4 p. l. 234 pp. 4 l. 7 pl. fol. *London, T. Dring,* 1683.

Willis (William). The history of Portland, from its first settlement: with notices of the neighboring towns, and of the changes of government in Maine. Part i. 8°. *Portland, Day, Fraser & co.* 1831.

[*In* MAINE historical society. Collections. v. 1].

Willison (*Rev.* John). A sacramental catechism: or, a familiar instructor for young communicants. 278 pp. 16°. *Glasgow, D. Niven,* 1794.

Willmott (Robert Aris). Pleasures, objects, and advantages of literature. 4th ed. xii, 171 pp. 16°. *London, G. Routledge & co.* 1855. s.

Wilmer (*Miss* Margaret A.) The nine prizes. 312 pp. 4 pl. 18°. *New York, board of publ. ref. church,* 1868.

Wilson (Floyd B.) Wilson's book of recitations and dialogues. With instructions in elocution and declamation. 186 pp. 16°. *New York, Dick & Fitzgerald,* [1868].

Wilson (Henry). History of the reconstruction measures of the 39th and 40th congresses. 1865–68. 467 pp. 1 portrait. 12°. *Hartford, Hartford pub. co.* 1868.

Wilson (Jacob). Phrasis: a treatise on the history and structure of the different languages of the world, with a comparative view of the forms of their words, and the style of their expressions. 384 pp. 1 portrait. 8°. *Albany, J. Munsell,* 1864.

Wilson (James Grant). Biographical sketches of Illinois officers engaged in the war against the rebellion of 1861. 120 pp. 28 pl. 8°. *Chicago, J. Barnet,* 1863.

—— The life and campaigns of Ulysses Simpson Grant, general-in-chief of the United States army. [With a sketch of the life of Schuyler Colfax]. 100 pp. 8°. *New York, R. M. De Witt,* 1868.

—— The life and letters of Fitz-Greene Halleck. 1 p. l. 607 pp. 2 pl. 12°. *New York, D. Appleton & co.* 1869.

Wilson (John). General view of the agriculture of Renfrewshire. xii, 370 pp. 5 l. 1 col. map, 2 pl. 8°. *Paisley,* 1812. s.

[GREAT BRITAIN: Board of agriculture].

Wilson (J. H.) Life of U. S. Grant. *See* **Dana** (Charles A.) *and* **Wilson.**

Wimpheling (Jacob). Elegantie maiores. Rhetorica eiusdem pueris vtilissima. 27 l. sm. 4°. *Argentine, M. Hupssuff,* 1515.

Winchester (Stephen Gardiner, *bishop of*). *See* **Gardiner** (Stephen).

Wind and whirlwind. A novel. By mr. Thom. White. [*pseudon.*] 307 pp. 12°. *New York, G. P. Putnam & son,* 1868.

Wines (E. C. *D.D.*) The promises of God, considered in their nature, source, certainty, freeness, preciousness, and sanctifying power. 96 pp. 18°. *Philadelphia, presbyterian board of publication,* 1868.

Winge (Emanuel Frederik Hagbarth). Beretning om Grönlands lazareth under cholera-epidemien i Christiania, 1853. 8°. *Christiania,* 1854.

[*In* NORWAY. Actstykker ang. cholera-epidemien i Norge].

Winkler (E. T. *compiler*). The sacred lute: a collection of popular hymns. 12, 286 pp. 24°. *Charleston, southern baptist publication society,* 1855. s.

Winkler (E. T.) The spirit of missions is the spirit of Christ. 33 pp. 16°. *Charleston,* 1853.

[SOUTHERN baptist publication society. Tracts on important subjects].

Winner (Septimus). Improved method for the violin. 79 pp. obl. 4°. *Philadelphia, C. H. Davis,* 1854. s.

Winstanley (W.) The hypocrite unmask'd; a comedy, in five acts. 95 pp. 8°. *New York, G. F. Hopkins,* 1801.

[*With* KOTZEBUE (A. F. F. von). Plays].

Winter (A) in Corsica; with the journey there and back. By two ladies. [*anon.*] viii, 347 pp. 1 map, 1 pl. 16°. *London, Sampson Low, son, & Marston,* 1868.

Winterbloom (The). *See* **Moore** (*Rev.* H. D.)

Winterbotham (William). An historical, geographical, commercial, and philosophical view of the United States of America, and of the European settlements in America and the West Indies. 1st Amer. ed. 4 v. 8°. *New York, J. Reid,* 1796.

Winthorpes (The); or, personal efforts. By the author of "The minister's wife." [*anon.*] 304 pp. 3 pl. 16°. *Boston, American tract society,* [1867].

Winthrop (*Rev.* Edward). Letters on the prophetic scriptures. 175 pp. 16°. *New York, F. Knight,* 1850. s.

Wirth (Johann Georg August). Die geschichte der Deutschen. 2er abd. der 2en verbess. aufl. 4 v. 8°. *Stuttgart, Hoffman,* 1853.

Wisconsin (*State of*). A manual of customs, precedents, and forms in use in the assembly of Wisconsin. With lists of members, etc. Compiled by L. H. D. Crane, [etc.] 3d annual ed. 97 pp. 1 pl. 8°. *Madison, state printers,* 1861. s.

——— The same. The legislative manual of the state of Wisconsin. 7th annual ed. 304 pp. 1 map. 2 pl. 12°. *Madison, Atwood & Rublee,* 1868.

Wisconsin historical society. Report and collections of the state historical society of Wisconsin, for the years 1867–69. v. 5. 438 pp. 8°. *Madison, Atwood & Rublee,* 1868.

Wislizenus (Adolphus, *M. D.*) Memoir of a tour to northern Mexico, connected with col. Doniphan's expedition, in 1846–47. 141 pp. 3 maps. 8°. *Washington, Tippin & Streeper,* 1848.

[*With* EMORY (W. H.) Notes of a military reconnoissance].

Wiser (William, *D. D.*) Incidents in the life of a pastor. 316 pp. 12°. *New York, C. Scribner,* 1851. s.

Witcomb (———). Guide to French conversation. *See* **Bellenger** (William A.) *and* **Witcomb.**

Witnessing for Jesus in the homes of the poor. With an introduction by the rev. J. C. Smith, D.D. 285 pp. 16°. *New York, A. D. F. Randolph,* 1868.

Witter (Conrad). Pocket dictionary of the German and English languages. *See* **Köhler** (F.) *and* **Witter.**

Wocel (Jan Erazim). Labyrint Sláwy. xiii, 266 pp. 8°. *w. Praze, J. B. Calve,* 1846. s.

Wolf (Ethel, *pseudon?*) The glad new year, and other poems. [Edited by H. C. Atwood]. 3 p. l. 67 pp. 8°. *New York, Moorhead, Simpson & Bond,* 1867.

Wolf (Jan Christiaan). Epistola de intestinorum tunicis, glandulis, etc. 4°. *Amstelædami,* 1721.

[RUYSCH (F.) Opera. v. 3. no. 27].

Wolf (J. W.) Beiträge zur deutschen mythologie. 2 v. xxvii, 267 pp. 4 pl; xi, 468 pp. 8°. *Göttingen, Dietrichsche buchhandlung,* 1852-57.

Wolff (*Dr.* M.) Die philonische philosophie. In ihren hauptmomenten dargestellt. 2e verm. ausg. x, 61 pp. 8°. *Gothenburg, D. F. Bonnier,* 1858.

Wolzogen (Caroline von). Schiller's leben. Verfasst aus erinnerungen der familie, seinen eigenen briefen, und den nachrichten seines freundes Körner. vi, 339 pp. 8°. *Stuttgart, J. G. Cotta,* 1851.

Wood (Benjamin). Fort Lafayette; or, love and secession. A novel. 300 pp. 12°. *New York, Carleton,* 1862.

Wood (Horace G.) The philosophy of creation: unfolding the laws of the progressive development of nature, and the spirit world. By Thomas Paine, through the hand of Horace G. Wood, medium. 120 pp. 8°. *Boston, B. Marsh,* 1854. s.

Wood (*Rev.* John George). Homes without hands. Being a description of the habitations of animals, classed according to their principle of construction. With designs by W. F. Keyl and E. Smith. xix, 632 pp. 21 pl. 8°. *London, Longmans,* 1868.

Wood (William). Nevv England's prospect. A true, lively, and experimentall description of that part of America: both as it stands to our new-come English planters; and to the old native inhabitants. [2d ed.] 4 p. l. 83, 5 pp. 1 map. sm. 4°. *London, Iohn Bellamie,* 1635.

Woodbine (The): a holiday gift. Edited by Caroline May. 332 pp. 8 pl. 12°. *Philadelphia, Lindsay & Blakiston,* 1851. s.

Woodbridge (*Rev.* W. C.) He Hoikehonua, he mea ia e hoakaka'i i ke ano o ka honua nei, a me na mea maluna iho. vii, 203 pp. 12°. *Oahu, a na misionari*, 1836. s.

Woodrow (G.) The biographical gallery, comprising 240 portraits of distinguished characters of all nations, with brief descriptive notices. 4 p. l. 51 pp. 49 pl. 12°. *London, Allan, Bell & co.* 1834.

Woodruff (Hiram). The trotting horse of America: how to train and drive him. With reminiscences of the trotting turf. Edited by Charles J. Foster. 412 pp. 1 portrait. 12°. *New York, J. B. Ford & co.* 1868.

Woods (Harriet F.) The blue-book stories. 203 pp. 3 pl. 16°. *Boston, American tract society*, [1866].

Woods (Leonard, *D.D.*) An essay on native depravity. 230 pp. 12°. *Boston, W. Peirce*, 1835.

Woods (Nicholas Augustus). The past campaign: a sketch of the war in the east, from the departure of lord Raglan to the capture of Sevastopol. 2 v. xv, 439 pp; xi, 402 pp. 12°. *London, Longmans*, 1855.

Woodward (George E.) Woodward's record of horticulture. No. 2. Edited by A. S. Fuller. 128 pp. 12°. *New York, F. W. Woodward*, 1868.

Woodward (Joseph Janvier, *M.D.*) Report on epidemic cholera and yellow fever in the army during 1867. *See* **United States.** (*War department: Surgeon general's office*).

Woodworth (Eliza, *editor*). Selections from the British poets. 365 pp. 12 pl. 12°. *New York, Carlton & Phillips*, 1856. s.

Woolman (John). Serious considerations on various subjects of importance. With some of his dying expressions. 137 pp. 18°. *London, Mary Hinde*, 1773.

Worcester (Noah, *D.D.*) Last thoughts, on important subjects, in three parts: i. Man's liability to sin. ii. Supplemental illustrations. iii. Man's capacity to obey. iv, 323 pp. 16°. *Cambridge, Brown, Shattuck & co.* 1833.

Worcester (*Massachusetts*). City document, no. 22. Inaugural address of hon. James B. Blake, mayor, [etc.]: with the annual reports of the several officers for the municipal year ending Jan. 6, 1868. 326 pp. 8°. *Worcester, city printers*, 1868. s.

——— *Free public library.* Catalogue of the circulating department. 186 pp. 12°. *Worcester, C. Hamilton*, [1861]. s.

Words for the people: in three parts. Part i. Civil government. Part ii. Government of the U. S. Part iii. Social duties. By Origen. [*pseudon.*] 295 pp. 18°. *Hartford, Case, Lockwood & co.* 1865.

Worgan (G. B.) General view of the agriculture of the county of Cornwall. xvi, 192 pp. 1 map. 15 pl. 8°. *London*, 1811. s.
[GREAT BRITAIN: Board of agriculture].

World (The). [New York daily]. Jan. to June, 1868. fol. *New York*, 1868.

World (The) almanac for 1869. 132 pp. 12°. *New York, World print*, 1868.

Worman (James H.) A complete grammar of the German language: with exercises, readings, conversations, paradigms, and an adequate vocabulary. 576 pp. 12°. *New York, A. S. Barnes & co.* 1868.

——— An elementary grammar of the German language: with exercises, readings, conversations, paradigms, and a vocabulary. 222 pp. 12°. *New York, A. S. Barnes & co.* 1867.

Wotton (*Sir* Henry). The state of christendom; or, a most exact and curious discovery of many secret passages, and hidden mysteries of the times. 8 p. l. 262, 32 pp. portrait. sm. fol. *London, H. Mosely*, 1657.

Wrangham (*Rev.* Francis). The pleiad. A series of abridgments from seven distinguished writers on the evidences of christianity. [Leland, Leslie, Doddridge, Watson, Butler, Paley, and Jenyns and Watts]. ix, 300 pp. 18°. *Edinburgh, Constable & co.* 1828.

Wratislaw (*Rev.* Albert Henry). Common places. *See* **Swainson** (*Rev.* Charles A.) *and* **Wratislaw.**

Wright (*Rev.* Alfred). Uba anumpa Mak a na ponaklo holisso. A book of questions on the gospel of Mark, in the Choctaw language, [etc.] 75 pp. 16°. *New York, S. W. Benedict*, 1852. s.

Wright (*Rev.* George Newnham) *and* **Timperley** (C. H.) The gallery of engravings. 3 v. 4°. *London, Fisher, son & co.* [1845–46].
[Wanting: pl. 63, v. 2].

Wright (Henry Goode, *M. D.*) Headaches, their causes and their cure. 4th ed. 160 pp. 16°. *London, J. Churchill & sons*, 1865.

Wright (*Mrs.* Julia McNair). Almost a nun. 398 pp. 6 pl. 16°. *Philadelphia, presbyterian publication committee*, 1868.

——— The corner stall, a New York story. 257 pp. 3 pl. 16°. *Boston, H. Hoyt*, 1868.

——— The golden heart. 360 pp. 4 pl. 16°. *Boston, H. Hoyt*, 1867.

——— The golden life. 379 pp. 4 pl. 16°. *Boston, H. Hoyt*, 1867.

Wright (J. M.) The golden work. By the author of "The golden heart," etc. [*anon.*] 391 pp. 5 pl. 16°. *Boston, H. Hoyt,* 1868.

——— Malcom's cottage and Malcom's friend. 320 pp. 3 pl. 16°. *Philadelphia, J. S. Claxton,* 1867.

——— The New York needle-woman; or, Elsie's stars. By the author of "Golden life," etc. [*anon.*] 254 pp. 3 pl. 16°. *Philadelphia, presbyterian publication committee,* 1868.

——— The shoe binders of New York; or, the fields white to the harvest. 237 pp. 3 pl. 16°. *Philadelphia, presbyterian publication committee,* [1867].

Wright (Lewis). The Clifton and other remarkable suspension bridges of the world. 2 p. l. 128 pp. 1 l. 11 pl. 12°. *London, J. Weale,* 1865. s.

Wright (Paul, *D. D.*) The new and complete life of Jesus Christ. With the lives of his apostles, [etc.] 512 pp. 8°. *Winchester, (Va.) J. F. Archbold,* 1816.

Wright (Thomas, *F. S. A.*) *and* **Jones** (H. Longueville). The universities. Le Keux's memorials of Cambridge. A series of views of the colleges, halls, and public buildings, engraved by J. Le Keux; with historical and descriptive accounts. 2 v. viii, [304] pp. 40 pl; viii, [268] pp. 36 pl. 8°. *London, Tilt & Bogue,* 1841–42. s.

Wright (W.) The book of Jonah, in Chaldee, Syriac, Æthiopic, and Arabic; with glossaries. 1857. *See* **Bible** (*Polyglot*).

Wright (William B.) Highland rambles: a poem. 183 pp. 12°. *Boston, Adams & co.* 1868.

Wronski (Hoëné). Le destin de la France, de l'Allemagne, et de la Russie, comme prolégomènes du messianisme. 584 pp. 8°. *Paris, F. Didot frères,* 1842.

Wudrian (Valentin). Creutz schule, in sich haltend: eine schöne christliche unterweisung von dem lieben creutz; vor alle creutz-brüder und schwestern, als durch welches mittel sie sich in allerhand zustoffendem creutz, trübsal, [etc.] trösten mögen. 5 p.l. 468 pp. 12°. *Ephrata, Bruderschaft,* 1762. s.

Wüllerstorf-Urbair (Bernhard von, *commodore*). Reise der österreichischen fregatte Novara um die erde in den jahren 1857, 1858, 1859. Anthropologischer theil. 2ᵉ abth. Körpermessungen, an individuen verschiedener menschenracen vorgenommen durch dr. Karl Scherzer und dr. Eduard Schwarz, bearbeitet von dr. A. Weisbach. 2 p. l. 271 pp. 4°. *Wien, K. k. hof- und staatsdruckerei,* 1867. s.

——— The same. Geologischer theil. v. 1-2. 4°. *Wien, K. k. hof-und staatsdruckerei,* 1865-66. s.

CONTENTS.

v. 1. 1. abth. Geologie von Neu-Seeland. Beiträge zur geologie der provinzen Auckland und Nelson. Von Ferdinand von Hochstetter. 1864.
v. 1. 2. abth. Paläontologie von Neu-Seeland. Fossile pflanzreste. Von Franz Unger; Fossile mollusken und echinodermen. Von Karl A. Zittel; Die foraminiferen-fauna des tertiären grünsandsteines der Orakei-bay bei Auckland. Von Ferdinand Stoliczka; Die foraminiferen der tertiären mergel des Whaingaroahafens (prov. Auckland). Von Guido Stache; Bericht über einen fast vollständigen schädel von palapteryx. Von Gustav Jaeger. viii 318 pp. 26 pl. 1865.
v. 2. 1. abth. Geologische beobachtungen. (Von Ferdinand von Hochstetter).
v. 2. 2. abth. Paläontologische mittheilungen. (Über fossile korallen von der insel Java. Von A. E. Reuss; Fossile foraminiferen von Kar Nikobar. Von C. Schwager). xiv, 1268 pp. 11 pl. 1866.

——— The same. Nautisch-physikalischer theil. Herausgegeben von der hydrographischen anstalt der k. k. marine. xix, 499 pp. 32 maps, etc. *Wien, K. k. hof- und staatsdruckerei,* 1862–65. s.

CONTENTS.

Geographische ortsbestimmungen, von Robert Müller.
Fluthbeobachtungen, zusammengestellt von F. Schaub.
Magnetische beobachtungen. (Von R. Müller und F. Schaub).
Meteorologische beobachtungen. Zusammengestellt von f. von Wüllerstorf und R. Müller.

——— The same. Statistisch-commercieller thiel, von dr. Karl von Scherzer. 2 v. ix, 368, 20 pp. 2 col. maps; vi, 540, 150 pp. 8 col. maps. 4°. *Wien, K. k. hof- und staatsdruckerei,* 1864–65. s.

——— The same. Zoologischer thiel. v. 1. [§ Reptilien; *and*] v. 2. 4°. *Wien, K. k. hof- und staatsdruckerei,* 1867–68. s.

CONTENTS.

v. 1. § Reptilien, bearbeitet von Franz Steindachner.
v. 2. 1. abtheil. A. 1. Coleoptera. Von dr. Ludwig Redtenbacher. 2. Hymenoptera. Von dr. Henri de Saussure. Nebst einem anhange von dr. J. Sichel. 3. Formicidæ. Von dr. Gustav L. Mayr. 4. Neuroptera. Von Friedrich Brauer. 4 v. in 1. 1868. s.
v. 2. 1. abtheil. B. 1. Diptera. Von dr. J. R. Schiner. 2. Hemiptera. Von dr. Gustav L. Mayr. 2 v. in 1. 1868. s.
v. 2. 3. abtheil. 1. Crustaceen. Von dr. Camil Heller. 2. Anneliden. Von prof. Ed. Grube. 3. Mollusken. Von Georg ritter von Frauenfeld. 3 v. in 1. 1868.

Wulp. *See* **Van der Wulp.**

Wunnamptamoe sampooaonk wussampoowontamun nashpe moeuwe[hko]munganash [ut] New Eng[land] Nas[hpee] Grindal R[avlinson]. [Confession of faith, Indian and English, translated by Grindal Rawson,

Wunnamptamoe—continued. of Mendon]. 7 p. l. 161 pp. 24°. *Mush-[auwomuk]*, [*Cambridge*]? *S. Green, for John* [*Usher*, 1699].

[Title imperfect, wanting pp. 1-3, 33-36, 159-161].

Würdtwein (Stephan Alexander). Bibliotheca moguntina libris sæculo primo typographico Moguntiæ impressis instructa, hinc inde addita inventæ typographiæ historia. 251 pp. 4°. *Augustæ Vindelicorum, C. F. Bürglen*, 1787.

Wuttke (Heinrich). Polen und deutsche. Politische betrachtungen. 112 pp. 8°. *Schkeuditz, W. v. Blomberg*, 1846. s.

Wyatt (Thomas, *editor*). The sacred tableaux: or, remarkable incidents in the old and new testaments, [etc.] The descriptions by distinguished American writers. x, 314 pp. 20 pl. 12°. *Boston, J. M. Whittemore*, 1848. s.

Wyeth (Samuel Douglass). The federal city; or, ins and abouts of Washington. 3d ed. 108 pp. 1 map, 13 pl. 8°. *Washington, Gibson bros.* 1868.

——— History of the library of Congress. Compiled from official documents. 16 l. 1 photog. pl. 8°. *Washington, Gibson bros.* 1868.

Wyndham (Neville, *pseudon.*) *See* **Travels** through Europe.

Wyss (Johann Rudolf von) *and* **Montolieu** (Isabelle Polier de Bottens, *baronne* de). The Swiss family Robinson. 2d series, [etc.] Translated from the French, by J. De Clinton Locke. 2 v. 258 pp; 237 pp. 16°. *New York, Harpers*, 1848. s.

Xenophon. Opera. Ad optimorvm librorvm fidem edidit G. H. Schaefer. 5 v. 18°. *Lipsiæ, C. Tauchnitz*, 1811-12. s.

CONTENTS.

v. 1. Cyropædia, [etc.] 2 p. l. 382 pp.
v. 2. Memorabilia Socratis, [etc.] xvi, 176 pp.
v. 3. Anabasis, [etc.] 2 p. l. 288 pp.
v. 4. Historia græca, [etc.] 2 p. l. 339 pp.
v. 5. Œconomicus, apologia Socratis, convivivm, Hiero, Agesilavs. 2 p. l. 208 pp.

——— A discourse upon improving the revenue of the state of Athens. Made English by Walter Moyle. 62 pp. 12°. *London, J. Knapton*, 1687.

[*With* DAVENANT (C.) Essay upon ballance of trade, 1700].

——— Treatise of householde. Translated out of the Greke by G. Hervet. 82 pp. 8°. *London, C. Bathurst*, 1767.

[CERTAIN ancient tracts concerning landed property reprinted. ed. 1767].

Ximinez de Cisneros. *See* **Jiminez de Cisneros.**

Yale (Elisha, *editor*). A select verse system, for the use of individuals, families, and schools. 215 pp. 8°. *Albany, C. H. Pease & co.* 1853. s.

Yale college. Catalogus senatus academici, et eorum qui munera et officia academica gesserunt, quique aliquovis gradu exornati fuerunt, in collegio yalensi. 148 pp. 8°. *in Novo Portu, E. Hayes*, 1856. s.

——— The same. 160 pp. 8°. *in Novo Portu, E. Hayes*, 1859. s.

——— The same. 204 pp. 8°. *in Novo Portu, Tuttle, Morehouse & Taylor*, 1868.

Yates (Edmund). Broken to harness. A story of English domestic life. 4th ed. 386 pp. 12°. *Boston, Loring*, 1866.

——— The business of pleasure. [A series of essays]. 2 v. viii, 302 pp; vi, 320 pp. 12°. *London, Chapman & Hall*, 1865.

——— Running the gauntlet. A novel. 385 pp. 12°. *Boston, Loring*, 1865.

Year-book (The) of facts in science and art: exhibiting the most important discoveries and improvements of the past year. By John Timbs. 288 pp. 1 portrait. 16°. *London, Lockwood & co.* 1868.

Yonge (Charlotte Mary). Cameos from English history from Rollo to Edward ii. xi, 379 pp. 16°. *London, Macmillan & co.* 1868.

——— Landmarks of history. Part iii. Modern history. From the beginning of the reformation to the accession of Napoleon iii. Edited by Edith L. Chase. viii, 465 pp. 12°. *New York, Leypoldt & Holt*, 1868.

——— The prince and the page. A story of the last crusade. [*anon.*] vii, 256 pp. 6 pl. 18°. *London, Macmillan & co.* 1866.

——— The pupils of St. John the divine. [*anon.*] xvi, 320 pp. 3 pl. 12°. [*London*], *Macmillan & co.* [1868].

[SUNDAY library for household reading. v. 1].

——— The six cushions. [A novel]. 196 pp. 16°. *London, J. & C. Mozley*, 1867.

Yorick's sentimental journey continued, by Eugenius. [*pseudon.*] 143 pp. 18°. *Brattleborough, (Vt.) W. Fessenden*, 1810.

[*With* STERNE (*Rev.* L.) Sentimental journey. 18°. *Brattleborough*, 1810. Imperfect: pp. 37-48 wanting].

York (*County of, Maine*). Extracts from [its] records. 8°. *Portland*, 1831.

[*In* MAINE historical society. Collections. v. 1].

Youatt (William). The horse; with a treatise on draught. viii, 472 pp. 8°. *London, Baldwin & Cradock*, 1830.

Youmans (William Jay, *M.D.*) Elements of physiology and hygiene. *See* **Huxley** (Thomas H.) *and* **Youmans.**

Young (Andrew W.) First book on civil government; being an introduction to the government class book. Designed for the younger classes in schools. 192 pp. 16°. *New York, Clark & Maynard*, 1867.

Young (Arthur). A course of experimental agriculture: containing an exact register of all the business transacted during five years on near three hundred acres of various soils, [etc.] 4 v. 8°. *Dublin, J. Exshaw, etc.* 1771.

——— General view of the agriculture of the county of Essex. 2 v. xv, 400 pp. 1 col. map. 44 pl; iii, 450 pp. 14 pl. 8°. *London*, 1807. s.
[GREAT BRITAIN: Board of agriculture].

——— General view of the agriculture of Hertfordshire. xix, 236 pp. 1 col. map. 9 pl. 8°. *London*, 1804. s.
[GREAT BRITAIN: Board of agriculture].

——— General view of the agriculture of the county of Lincoln. 2 p. l. vii, 455 pp. 3 col. maps. 11 pl. 8°. *London*, 1799. s.
[GREAT BRITAIN: Board of agriculture].

——— General view of the agriculture of the county of Norfolk. xx, 532 pp. 5 pl. 8°. *London*, 1804. s.
[GREAT BRITAIN: Board of agriculture].

——— General view of the agriculture of the county of Suffolk. 3d ed. xv, 432 pp. 1 col. map. 2 pl. 8°. *London*, 1804.
[GREAT BRITAIN: Board of agriculture].

——— General view of the agriculture of the county of Sussex. x, 471 pp. 1 col. map. 20 pl. 8°. *London*, 1808. s.
[GREAT BRITAIN: Board of agriculture].

——— View of the agriculture of Oxfordshire. xii, 362 pp. 28 pl. 8°. *London*, 1809. s.
[GREAT BRITAIN: Board of agriculture].

Young (Brigham). Discourses. *See* **Journal** of discourses.

Young (E. D.) The search after Livingstone. ["A diary kept during the investigation of his reported murder"]. Revised by rev. Horace Waller. 262 pp. 1 map, 6 pl. 12°. *London, Letts, son & co.* 1868.

Young (James Reynolds). An elementary treatise on algebra, theoretical and practical, [etc.] x, iv, 296 pp. 12°. *London, J. Souter*, 1834. s.

——— Simple arithmetic, algebra, etc. 8°. *London*, 1854.
[*In* ORR'S (W. S.) Circle of the sciences. The mathematical sciences].

Young (Philip, *M. D.*) History of Mexico: her civil wars, and colonial and revolutionary annals: 1520 to 1847: including an account of the war with the United States. Continued to the treaty of peace, 1848, by G. C. Furber. 656 pp. 1 map, 7 pl. 8°. *Cincinnati, J. A. & U. P. James*, 1850.

Young (William, *editor of the Albion, N. Y.*) Mathieu Ropars, et cetera. By an ex-editor. 236 pp. 16°. *New York, G. P. Putnam & son*, 1868.

Young (*Sir* William, *bart.*) The West-India common place book: compiled from parliamentary and official documents; shewing the interest of Great Britain in its sugar colonies, etc. xxi, 256 pp. 2 tab. 2 maps. 4°. *London, R. Phillips*, 1807. s.

Young (The) American's picture gallery. With 70 illustrations. [*anon.*] 150 pp. 4°. *Philadelphia, Lindsay & Blakiston*, [1856]. s.

Young (The) lady's mentor: a guide to the formation of character, [etc.] By a lady. [*anon.*] 284 pp. 12°. *Philadelphia, H. C. Peck & T. Bliss*, 1851. s.

Young (The) sportsman; or, Mel Carroll's twelve months in the woods. A down-east story. By cousin Hayward. [*pseudon.*] 319 pp. 16°. *Boston, Pratt bros.* 1865.

Zachos (J. C.) The high school speaker, [etc.] 334 pp. 12°. *Cincinnati, Rickey, Mallory & co.* 1858. s.

Zarate (Agustin de). Histoire de la découverte et de la conquête du Pérou. Traduit de l'Espagnol par S. D. C. [de Broë, seigneur de Citry et de La Guette]. 2 v. xl, 360 pp. 1 map, 14 pl; viii, 479 pp. 16°. *Paris, la compagnie des libraires*, 1742.

Zeitschrift für deutsche landwirth. Herausgegeben von Ernst Stöckhardt. Der neuen folge. Jahrgang 7–10, 12–17. 10 v. 8°. *Leipzig, G. Wigand*, 1856–66.
[Wanting: old series, and of new series v. 1–6, 11, and nos. 2 and 12 of v. 7].

Zeitschrift für wissenschaftliche zoologie, herausgegeben von C. T. v. Siebold und A. Kölliker. v. 1–7. 8°. *Leipzig, W. Engelmann*, 1849–55. s.
[v. 7, heft 4, et seq. wanting].

Zend-Avesta. *See* **Zoroaster.**

Zeno (Caterino). Brödrene Zenos reiser, med indledning og anmaerkninger, ved J. H. Bredsdorff. 8°. *Kjöbenhavn, S. L. Möller*, 1845.
[*In* GRÖNLANDS historiske mindesmærker. v. 3. pp. 529–624].

Zeuss (Caspar). Der Deutschen und die nachbarstämme. viii, 778 pp. 1 l. 8°. *München, I. J. Lentner*, 1837.

Ziegler (J. Melchior). Geographischer atlas über alle theile der erde, bearbeitet nach der ritterschen lehre, [etc. *and*] Erlauterungen. 2 p. l. 12 pp; 1 p. l. 24 col. maps. fol. *Berlin, D. Reimer,* 1851. s.

Zimmerman (*Rev.* J. A. E.) Der fromme landmann. Ein katholisches lehr- und gebetbuch für das fromme landvolk. 480 pp. 24°. *New York, C. & N. Benziger,* 1868.

Zionitischer meyrauchs hügel, oder: myrrhen berg, worinnen allerley liebliches und wohl reichendes nach apotheker-kunst zu bereitetes rauch-werck zu finden, [etc.] 6 p. l. 792 pp. 7 l. 16°. *Germantown, C. Sauer,* 1739. s.

Zoéga (Frederic). Art of making sugar from beets. *See* **Blachette** (L. J.) *and* **Zoéga**.

Zollikofer (Georg Joachim). Briefwechsel zwischen C. Garve und G. J. Zollikofer, etc. *See* **Garve** (C.) Sammtliche werke. v. 18.

Zorgdrager (Cornelius Gijsbertus). Beschreibung des grönländischen wallfischfangs und fischerey, nebst einer nachricht von dem bakkeljau- und stockfischfang bey Terreneuf, und einer abhandlung von Grönland, Island, u. a. Aus dem holländischen übersetzt. 3 p. l. 370 pp. 5 l. 6 maps. 7 pl. 4°. *Nürnberg, G. P. Monath,* 1750.

Zoroaster. Avesta, die heiligen schriften der Parsen. Aus dem grundtexte übersetzt, mit steter rücksicht auf die tradition von dr. F. Spiegel. v. 1–2. 8°. *Leipzig, W. Engelmann,* 1852–59.

CONTENTS.

v. 1. Der vendidad. viii, 295 pp. 1 pl.
v. 2. Vispered und Yaçna. cxxiv, 222 pp. 1 l. 4 pl.
[Wanting: v. 3. Khorda-Avesta].

Zschokke (Johann Heinrich Daniel). Hortensia; or, the transfigurations. Translated from the German. 12°. *Boston, W. White & co.* 1868.

[*In* DAVIS (A. J.) Memoranda of persons, etc. 12°. 1868. pp. 345–464].

Zumpt (Carl Gottlob). A school grammar of the Latin language. Translated by Leonard Schmitz. Corrected and enlarged by Charles Anthon. xi, 247 pp. 12°. *New York, Harpers,* 1847. s.

LAW BOOKS.

LAW BOOKS.

ABBOTT (Benjamin Vaughan) *and* ABBOTT (Austin). A digest of the reports of the United States courts and of the acts of congress, from the organization of the government to July, 1868. v. 3. 8°. *New York, Diossy & co.* 1868.
[Completing the work. 20 copies].

ABSTRACT of the decisions of the chancellor, [hon. Reuben H. Walworth], from 1841 to 1847. [*anon.*] 6 v. in 1. *See* BARBOUR (Oliver L.) Abstract, etc.

ADAMS (John, *jr.*) The doctrine of equity. A commentary on the law as administered by the court of chancery. 5th American edition, containing the notes to the previous editions of J. R. Ludlow, J. M. Collins, and Henry Wharton. With additional notes and references to recent English and American decisions, by G. Tucker Bispham. lxxxi, 811 pp. 8°. *Philadelphia, T. & J. W. Johnson & co.* 1868.

ALABAMA (*State of*). Revised code of Alabama, prepared by A. J. Walker. xvi, 960 pp. 8°. *Montgomery, Reid & Screws,* 1867.

ALABAMA reports. v. 20, 39–40. By J. W. Shepherd. 8°. *Montgomery, Barrett & Brown,* 1852–68.

ALLEN (Charles). Reports of cases in the supreme judiciary court of Massachusetts. v. 12–13. 8°. *Boston, Houghton & co.* 1867–68.
[2 copies of v. 13].

AMERICAN (The) law register. v. 15–16. 8°. *Philadelphia, Canfield & co.* 1867–68.

AMERICAN (The) law review. 1867–68. v. 2. 8°. *Boston, Little, Brown & co.* 1868.
[2 copies].

ANGELL (Joseph K.) A treatise on the law of carriers of goods and passengers, by land and by water, with an appendix of statutes regulating passenger vessels and steamboats, etc. 4th ed. Revised, corrected, and enlarged, by John Lathrop. xxxv, 700 pp. 8°. *Boston, Little, Brown & co.* 1868.

——— *and* DURFEE (Thomas). A treatise on the law of highways. 2d ed. with notes and references to the later cases. By George F. Choate. xxxvi, 579 pp. 8°. *Boston, Little, Brown & co.* 1868.

ANTIGUA (*Island of*). The laws of Antigua, from August 15, 1817, to April 4, 1845. v. 4. 4°. *London, J. B. Bateman,* 1846.

ARIZONA (*Territory of*). Laws, 1867. 8°. *Prescott,* 1868.
[2 copies].

ARKANSAS reports. v. 24. By L. E. Barber. 8°. *Little Rock, Woodruff & Blocher,* 1867.

ARNOLD (Benedict). Proceedings of a general court martial of the line, held at Raritan, New Jersey, for the trial of major-general Arnold, June 1, 1779. Published by order of congress. 55 pp. fol. *Philadelphia, F. Bailey,* 1780.
[NOTE.—Title page slightly imperfect].

AVERY (Edward) *and* HOBBS (George M.) The bankrupt law of the United States, approved March 2, 1867. With copious notes. xxii, 488 pp. 8°. *Boston, Little, Brown & co.* 1868.
[2 copies].

BARBOUR (Oliver L.) Abstract of the decisions of the chancellor, [hon. Reuben H. Walworth], from Feb. 1, 1841, to May 24, 1847. [*anon.*] 6 v. in 1. 8°. *Saratoga Springs, H. Wilbur, etc.* 1841–47.
[Being a supplement to Saratoga sentinel and democratic champion, etc.]

——— Reports of cases in law and equity in the supreme court of the state of New York. v. 49–50. 8°. *Albany, W. C. Little,* 1868.
[2 copies].

BARNES (William). General statute laws of the state of New York relating to fire, marine, life, and casualty insurance companies, and miscellaneous insurance laws. 3d ed. 173 pp. 8°. *Albany, Weed, Parsons & co.* 1868.

BEASLEY (Mercer). Reports of cases in the court of chancery, and, on appeal, in the court of errors and appeals of the state of New Jersey. v. 2. 8°. *Trenton, Phillips & Boswell,* 1863.

BEAWES (Wyndham). Lex mercatoria rediviva; or, the merchants' directory. A complete guide to all men in business, [etc.] containing an account of our mercantile companies; of our colonies and factories abroad; of our commercial treaties with foreign powers; of the duties of consuls, and of the laws concerning *aliens, naturalization, and denization.* To which is added, a sketch of the present state of the commerce of the whole world, [etc.] 4th ed. [etc.] by Thomas Mortimer. 5 p. l. 944 pp. 8 l. 1 tab. fol. *London, J. Rivington & son, etc.* 1783. s.

BELGIUM. *Ministère de la justice.* Compte de l'administration de la justice criminelle en Belgique, pendant les années 1831–34, [etc.] xviii, 176 pp. 4°. *Bruxelles, imprimerie du Moniteur belge,* 1835. s.

——— ——— Compte de la justice civile en Belgique pendant les années judiciaires 1839–43. Presenté, [etc.] par le ministre de la justice. xxiii, 288 pp. fol. *Bruxelles, imprimerie du Moniteur belge,* 1845. s.

BERRIAT-SAINT-PRIX (Jacques). Cours de procédure civile fait à la faculté de droit de Grenoble. 3e éd. 2 v. viii, 356 pp; 357–672 pp. 8°. *Paris, Nève,* 1813. s.

BEST (William Mawdesley) *and* SMITH (George James Philip). Reports of cases in the court of queen's bench and the court of exchequer, on appeal from the court of queen's bench. v. 7. 8°. *London, H. Sweet,* 1868.

BISHOP (Joel Prentiss). Commentaries on the criminal law. 4th ed. revised and enlarged. 2 v. xxxii, 778 pp; xii, 809 pp. 8°. *Boston, Little, Brown & co.* 1868.

——— The first book of the law: explaining the nature, sources, books, and practical applications to legal science, and methods of study and practice. xi, 466 pp. 8°. *Boston, Little, Brown & co.* 1868.
[3 copies].

BITTLESON (Adam) *and* WISE (Edward). *See* MAGISTRATES' cases.

BITTLESON (Adam) *and* PARNELL (Paul). *See* MAGISTRATES' cases.

BLATCHFORD (Samuel). Reports of cases in the circuit court of the United States for the second circuit. v. 4. 8°. *New York, Baker, Voorhis & co.* 1868.
[4 copies].

BLENKINSOP (Mary). Trial. *See* STOKES (*Dr.* W. H.) *and* BLENKINSOP.

BLUNTSCHLI (Johann Caspar). Das moderne völkerrecht der civilisirten staaten als rechtsbuch dargestellt. xiii, 520 pp. 8°. *Nördlingen, C. H. Beck,* 1868.

BONOMO-STETNER (Andrea de). Della giustizia dei diritti austrici carintiani sopra l'Istria. 8°. *Trieste,* 1831.
[*In* ROSSETTI (D. de). Archeografo triestino. v. 3].

BOYD (Walter). The law and practice of the high court of admiralty of Ireland, under the court of admiralty (Ireland) act, 1867, and the general orders of 1867; with a complete collection of the statutes relating to merchant shipping, and the decisions thereon. xix, 657 pp. 12°. *Dublin, Hodges, Smith & Foster,* 1868.

BRIGHTLEY (Frederick C.) Annual digest of the laws of Pennsylvania, for each of the years 1854 and 1855: namely, from 28 May, 1853, to 8 May, 1855. 2 p. l. pp. 1051–1196. 8°. *Philadelphia, Kay & brother,* 1855. s.

——— A digest of the decisions of the federal courts, from the organization of the government to the present time. viii, 976 pp. 8°. *Philadelphia, Kay & brother,* 1868.
[7 copies].

BRITISH SOLDIERS. The trial of the British soldiers, of the 29th regiment of foot, for the murder of Crispus Attucks, Samuel Gray, Samuel Maverick, James Caldwell, and Patrick Carr, March 5, 1770. [*anon.*] 146 pp. 16°. *Boston, William Emmons,* 1824.

BROOKE (*Sir* Robert). Liver des assises. *See* LIBER assissarum.

BROWNING (Ernest) *and* LUSHINGTON (Vernon). Reports of cases in the high court of admiralty of England, and on appeal to the privy council, 1863–65. xv, 524 pp. 8°. *London, Butterworths,* 1868.

BUDER (Christian Gottlieb, *editor*). Repertorivm reale pragmaticvm ivris pvblici et fevdalis [imperii romano-germanici]. Oder des heil. röm. reichs staats- und lehn recht sowohl überhaupt, als das besondere der geist- und weltlichen chur- und fürsten, grafen und freyherren, der reichs-städte und reichs-ritterschaft, [etc.] 9 p. l. 1276 pp. 1 pl. 4°. *Jena, C. H. Cuno,* 1751. s.

BUMP (Orlando F.) Practice in bankruptcy. The bankrupt law of the United States, with all the amendments, and the rules and forms as amended; with notes referring to all decisions under the act, reported to September 1, 1868. 205 pp. 8°. *Baker, Voorhis & co.* 1868.

BURCKHARD (Hugo). Die civilistischen präsumptionen. xx, 407 pp. 8°. *Weimar, Landes-industrie-comptoir,* 1866. s.

BURDELL (The) case. Closing argument of Charles Edwards, advocate for infant next of kin of Harvey Burdell, and in opposition to the claim of Emma Augusta Cunningham, for letters of administration. 66 pp. 1 map. 8°. *New York, J. S. Voorhies,* 1857?

BURR (Aaron). Reports of [his] trials for treason, and for a misdemeanor, in preparing the means of a military expedition against Mexico, at Richmond, in 1807. [With] an appendix. Taken in short-hand, by D. Robertson. 2 v. 4 p. l. 596 pp; 539 pp. 8°. *Philadelphia, Hopkins & Earle,* 1808.

BURRILL (Alexander M.) New law dictionary and glossary; containing full definitions of the principal terms of the common and civil law, together with translations and explanations of the various technical phrases in different languages, occurring in the ancient and modern reports, and standard treatises; embracing, also, all the principal common and civil law maxims. 2d ed. 2 v. xxv, 700 pp; 658 pp. 8°. *New York, Baker, Voorhis & co.* 1867.

CALIFORNIA (*State of*). Laws, [sessional], for the years 1867–68. 8°. *Sacramento, D. W. Gelwicks,* 1868.
[4 copies].

CALIFORNIA reports. By C. A. Tuttle. v. 32. 8°. *San Francisco, S. Whitney,* 1867.
[3 copies].

——— The same. v. 33. By J. E. Hale. 8°. *San Francisco, S. Whitney,* 1868.
[3 copies].

CHAFFEE (C. T.) Magistrate's docket for the state of Ohio. Compiled from the forms of hon. J. R. Swan. Revised ed. 126 pp. fol. *Jefferson, (Ohio), Abbott & Loomis,* 1861. S.

CHAMBAUD (Mirabel). Procédure administrative en matière de canaux, mines, usines, ateliers insalubres, chemins de fer; ou, codes des établissements industriels concédés ou autorisés. 2 v. xxxii, 431 pp; 2 p. l. 556 pp. 8°. *Paris, Delamotte,* 1843. S.

CHRISTY (Edwin P.) Surrogate's court, county of New York, in the matter of the last will and testament of Edwin P. Christy. 3 v. 8°. *New York, J. W. Bell,* 1864–65.

CLARKE (Edward). A treatise upon the law of extradition. With the conventions upon the subject existing between England and foreign nations, and the cases decided thereon. x, 183 pp. 16°. *London, Stevens & Haynes,* 1867.

CLIFT (Henry). A new book of declarations, pleadings, verdicts, judgments, and judicial writs; with the entries thereupon. Now digested and published by sir Charles Ingleby. 2 p.l. 939 pp. 8 l. fol. *London, C. Harper, etc.* 1703. S.

CLUSA (Jacobus de) *or* GUITRODE (Jacobus von). De contractibus qui fiunt cum pacto reemptionis perpetuorum censuum seu ad vitam. 16 l. sm. 4°. [*Coloniæ, about* 1490].

COFER (Martin H.) A supplemental digest of the decisions of the court of appeals of Kentucky, 1853–1867. iv, 583 pp. 8°. *Cincinnati, R. Clarke & co.* 1867.
[3 copies].

COLBY (John H.) A practical treatise upon the criminal law and practice of the state of New York, with precedents. 2 v. xiii, 764 pp; vii, 456 pp. 8°. *Albany, Weare C. Little,* 1868.

COLDWELL (Thomas H.) Reports of the supreme court of Tennessee, 1860–67. v. 1–4. 8°. *Nashville, S. C. Mercer,* 1867–68.

COLLIN (H. S.) *and* SCHLYTER (Carl Johan) *editors. See* SWEDEN. Corpus juris Sueo-Gotorum antiqui.

COLORADO (*Territory of.*) Laws, [sessional], 1861, 1862, 1864, 1865, 1866, and 1867. 6 v. 8°. *Denver, and Central City,* 1861–67.

——— The same. Leyes generales aprobadas en las sesiones 4a, 5a, y 6a de la asamblea legislativa del territorio. 207 pp. 8°. *Denver, D. Witter,* 1867. S.

COLVIN (John B.) The magistrate's guide, and citizen's counseller; adapted to the state of Maryland, and Washington co. D. C. 2d ed. 479 pp. 8°. *Georgetown, D. C; E. Weems,* 1819.

COMMON bench reports. New series. Cases in the court of common pleas, and in the courts of error, 1865. By John Scott. v. 20. 8°. *London, W. W. Gearing,* 1866.

CONDUCTOR generalis; or, the office, duty, and authority of justices of the peace, high-sheriffs, goalers, coroners, constables, etc. Collected out of books written on those subjects. [With] a collection out of sir Matthew Hale concerning the descent of lands. 4 p. l. xii, 300 pp. 4°. *Philadelphia, Andrew Bradford,* 1722.
[Imperfect: wanting pp. 35–38, 283–286].

CONKLIN (O. M.) *and* BURTON (Mary J.) Report of trial [for] "living and cohabiting together in a state of fornication." 14 pp. 8°. *Cincinnati, J. Todd,* 1855.

CONNECTICUT (*State of*). Private acts and resolutions. May sessions, 1867–68. 2 v. 8°. *Hartford and New Haven,* 1867–68.
[2 copies].

COOLEY (Thomas M.) A treatise on the constitutional limitations which rest upon the legislative power of the states of the American Union. xlvii, 720 pp. 8°. *Boston, Little, Brown & co.* 1868.
[2 copies].

COOTE (Henry Charles). The practice of the high court of admiralty of England; also, the practice of the judicial committee of her majesty's most honorable privy council in admiralty appeals. With forms and bills of costs.

2d ed. xix, 436 pp. 8°. *London, Butterworths,* 1868.

CORVINUS. *See* VENATORIUS.

CROKE (Alexander). Essay upon the theory and the history of laws relating to illegitimate children, and to the encouragement of marriage in general. 8°. *London, A. Strahan,* 1800.

[*With* HORNER *v.* LIDDIARD. Report of case. pp. 1-143. ed. 1800].

CUSHING (Luther Stearns). Lex parliamentaria americana. Elements of the law and practice of legislative assemblies of the United States of America. 2d ed. xxxvi, 1063 pp. 8°. *Boston, Little, Brown & co.* 1866.

DANIELL (Edmund Robert). Forms and precedents of pleadings and proceeding in the high court of chancery, with practical notes and observations, and references to the fourth ed. of Daniell's chancery practice; and also incorporating the forms in Braithwaite's record and writ practice. By Leonard Field and Edward Clennell Dunn, and John Biddle. Part ii. xlviii, 1069-2130, ccxi pp. 8°. *London, Stevens & sons,* 1868.

DARLING (John). A treatise on the administration of trust funds under the trustee relief act, [etc.] xvi, 140 pp. 8°. *London, V. & R. Stevens & G. S. Norton,* 1855. s.

DARNES (William P.) A full report of [his] trial, on a charge of manslaughter, for the death of Andrew J. Davis, on the first of June, 1840. By [T. S. Nelson]. 248 pp. 8°. *St. Louis,* 1840.

DAVIS (Edwin A.) A digest of the decisions of the supreme court of the state of Indiana. Comprising the cases reported in the eight volumes of Blackford, and the first sixteen volumes of Indiana reports, together with the revised statutes of the state, as embodied in the edition of Gavin and Hord. 2d ed. xix, 853 pp. 8°. *Cincinnati, R. Clarke & co.* 1866.

[2 copies].

DAVOUD-OGHLOU (Garabed Artin). Histoire de la législation des anciens Germains. 2 v. cviii, 660 pp; iv, 799 pp. 8°. *Berlin, G. Reimer,* 1845.

DE GEX (J. P.) JONES (H. Cadman) *and* SMITH (R. Horton). Reports of cases heard and determined by the lord chancellor, and the court of appeal in chancery, 1863. v. 1. viii, 722 pp. 8°. *London, Stevens, sons & Haynes,* 1865.

DELAWARE (*The government of New-castle, Kent, and Sussex, upon*). Laws. 363, xvii pp. fol. *Philadelphia, B. Franklin & D. Hall,* 1752.

DEVEREUX (John C.) Court of claims. Reports and digest of opinions delivered since the organization of the court. x, 261, 53 pp. 8°. *New York, Banks, Gould & co.* 1856.

DILLON (*Sir* John). The case of the children of his royal highness the duke of Sussex elucidated; a juridical exercitation. x, 59 pp. 4°. *London, Saunders & Benning,* 1832.

DISNEY (William). Reports of cases in the superior court of Cincinnati at special and general terms, from October, 1854, to January, 1858. viii, 626 pp. 8°. *Cincinnati, R. Clarke & co.* 1867.

[2 copies].

DISTRICT OF COLUMBIA. Compilation of the laws in force in the District of Columbia, April 1, 1868. 494 pp. 8°. *Washington, government printing office,* 1868. (3 copies).

——— Rules of practice in the supreme court of the District of Columbia, adopted by the court in general term, October 21, 1863. 119 pp. 8°. *Washington, government printing office,* 1863.

DIXON (Francis B.) A practical treatise on the adjustment of general average in the United States and other countries. Including the elements of maritime and insurance law; also, the rights and liabilities of underwriters and shipowners, and the general duties of shipmasters. xxiii, 472 pp. 26 l. 8°. *New York, H. Spear,* 1867.

DOBBLEMANN (Eduard). De crimine plagii. xii, 96 pp. 8°. *Berolini, E. S. Mittler & fil.* 1866. s.

DORN (Robert C.) Journal of the court for the trial of impeachments in the case of R. C. Dorn, a canal commissioner of the state of New York. 1181, 128 pp. 8°. *Albany, Van Benthuysen & sons,* 1868.

DREBING (Gustav L.) Das gemeine recht (common law), der Vereinigten Staaten von Amerika, nebst den statuten der einzelnen staaten und dem bankerott-gesetze. iv, 657, iv pp. 8°. *New York, E. Steiger,* 1867.

DRURY (W. B.) *and* WALSH (F. W.) Reports of cases in the high court of chancery, during the time of lord chancellor Plunket, 1837-40. 2 v. xxxiii, xx, 781 pp; xii, 726 pp. 8°. *Dublin, Milliken & son,* 1839-42.

DUNBAR (Reuben). Trial of Reuben Dunbar, for the murder of Stephen V. Lester and David L. Lester, eight and ten years of age, in the town of Westerlo, on Saturday, Sept. 28, 1850. Reported by Jacob C. Cuyler. 75 pp. 8°. *Albany, P. L. Gilbert,* 1850.

DUNPHY (Thomas) *and* CUMMINS (Thomas J.) Remarkable trials of all countries, particularly of the United States, Great Britain, Ireland, and France, with notes and speeches of counsel, containing thrilling narratives of fact from the court room, also historical reminiscences of wonderful events. vi, 464 pp. 8°. *New York, the compilers,* 1867.

DU PONCEAU (Peter Stephen). A dissertation on the nature and extent of the jurisdiction of the courts of the United States. xxxiii pp. 2 l. 254 pp. 8°. *Philadelphia, A. Small,* 1824.

DWINELLE (John W.) The colonial history of the city of San Francisco: being a narrative argument in the circuit court of the United States for the state of California, for four square leagues of land, claimed by that city under the laws of Spain, and confirmed to it by that court, and by the supreme court of the United States. 4th ed. xlv, 391 pp. 3 pl. 3 maps. 8°. *San Francisco, Towne & Bacon,* 1867.

EATON (Orsamus) *et al.* Trial. *See* WINANS (R.) *v.* EATON, *et al.*

ELDRIDGE (G. Morgan). A key to the bankrupt act. The bankrupt act, digested from the official copy, annotated, digested, and indexed, for the easy and convenient reference of the legal profession and of business men. 79 pp. 8°. *Philadelphia, John E. Potter & co.* 1867.

ENGLAND. Die gesetze der Angelsachsen. In der ursprache mit uebersetzung, erläuterungen, und einem antiquarischen glossar. [In Anglo-Saxon, German, and Latin]. Herausgegeben von Reinhold Schmid. 2e verm. aufl. lxxxiii, 680 pp. 1 l. 8°. *Leipzig, F. A. Brockhaus,* 1858.

EXAMINATION of the chancellor's [John Lansing, jr.] opinion in the case of R. R. Livingston and R. Fulton *v.* Van Ingen, Lansing and others. [*anon.*] 54 pp. 8°. *Albany,* 1812.

EYRE (Edward John). Report of the case of the Queen *v.* Eyre, on his prosecution, in the court of Queen's bench, for high crimes and misdemeanors alleged to have been committed by him in his office as governor of Jamaica; containing the evidence, [taken from the depositions], the indictment, and the charge of mr. justice Blackburn. By W. F. Finlason. xl, 111 pp. 8°. *London, Chapman & Hall,* 1868.

FISHER (Samuel S.) Reports of cases arising upon letters patent for inventions, determined in the circuit courts of the United States. v. 1–2. viii, 700 pp; ix, 723 pp. 8°. *Cincinnati, R. Clarke & co.* 1867–68.
[2 copies of v. 1].

FLORIDA reports. v. 7–8. By M. D. Papy. 8°. *Tallahassee,* 1859.

FRANCE. *Ministère des finances.* Recueil des lois des finances et des autres lois de la session de 1847. 364 pp. 8°. *Paris, imprimerie royale,* 1847. S.

——— *Ministère de la justice et des cultes.* Compte générale de l'administration de la justice civile et commerciale en France, pendant l'année 1865. 4°. *Paris, imprimerie impériale,* 1867. S.

——— ——— Compte général de l'administration de la justice criminelle en France, pendant l'année 1860[–64]. 5 v. 4°. *Paris, imprimerie impériale,* 1862–66.

FRAZIER (Thomas W. *judge, etc.*) Proceedings of the high court of impeachment in the case of the people of the state of Tennessee *vs.* T. W. Frazier. Begun and held at Nashville, May 11, 1867. 124, 8, 207 pp. 8°. *Nashville, S. C. Mercer,* 1867.

GAINES (Myra Clark) *v.* DE LA CROIX (F. D.) *et al.* Supreme court of the United States. Appeal from the circuit court of the United States for the eastern district of Louisiana. [Record] filed December 19, 1865. 2 v. xvi, 948 pp; iv, 1120 pp. 8°. *Washington, government printing office,* [1867].

GEORGIA (*State of*). Acts of the general assembly, [sessional], 1801–1810. 10 v. in 2. 8°. *Louisville, Augusta, and Milledgeville,* 1802–10.

GEORGIA reports. v. 26 and 29. By B. Y. Martin. 8°. *Columbus, Columbus Times steam press,* 1859–60.
[2 copies].

——— The same. v. 35. By Logan E. Bleckley. With an appendix containing several cases decided by the hon. John Erskine, in the circuit and district courts of the United States for Georgia. 8°. *Atlanta, Intelligencer office,* 1868.

GERARD (James W. *jr.*) Titles to real estate in the state of New York. A digested compendium of law applicable to the examination of titles to real estate in the state of New York. For the use of conveyancers and students at law. 400 pp. 8°. *New York, Baker, Voorhis & co.* 1869.

GOTHLAND laws. *See* GUTA-LAGH.

GRADY (Standish Grove). A treatise on the Hindoo law of inheritance, comprising the doctrines of the various schools, with the decisions of the high courts of the several presidencies of India, and judgments of the privy council on appeal. lxxiv, 493 pp. 8°. *London, Wildy & sons*, 1868.

GRAGNON-LACOSTE (———). Précis historique de la législation consulaire, ou introduction à l'étude du droit commercial. xvi, 404 pp. 8°. *Paris, [l'auteur]*, 1860. s.

GRAHAM (John Andrew). [Arguments]. In the courts of oyer and terminer, common pleas, and general sessions of the peace. viii, 80 pp. 8°. *New York, McGillda & co.* 1812.
[Imperfect].

GRATTAN (Peachy R.) Reports of cases in the supreme court of appeals of Virginia. v. 17-18. 8°. *Richmond, V. L. Fare, and Furgusson & Brady*, 1867-68.
[4 copies of v. 17].

GREAT BRITAIN. An act for amending the law for granting patents for inventions. 359 pp. fol. *London, Eyre & Spottiswoode*, 1852.

——— Bill for repealing several subsidies, and an impost, now payable on tobacco of the British plantations, and for granting an inland duty in lieu thereof. 59 pp. 12°. *London*, 1733.

——— A collection of the public general statutes, 1867-8. 8°. *London, queen's printing office*, 1868.

——— An ordinance of parliament for the relief of Ireland. 7 pp. sm. 4°. (n. p.) 1645.

——— *See, also*, ENGLAND.

GREEN (Charles Ewing). Reports of cases in the court of chancery, the prerogative court, also, on appeal in the court of errors and appeals, of the state of New Jersey. v. 2. 608 pp. 8°. *Trenton, Hough & Gillespy*, 1868.
[2 copies].

GREENLEAF (Simon). A treatise on the law of evidence. 12th ed. by Isaac F. Redfield. v. 1. 8°. *Boston, Little, Brown & co.* 1866.
[3 copies].

——— The same. 10th ed. by Isaac F. Redfield. v. 2. 8°. *Boston, Little, Brown & co.* 1868.
[3 copies].

——— The same. 8th ed. by Isaac F. Redfield. v. 3. 8°. *Boston, Little, Brown & co.* 1868.
[3 copies].

GRIMM (Jacob Ludwig Carl). Deutsche rechtsalterthümer. 2e ausg. xx, 970 pp. 8°. *Göttingen, Dieterich*, 1854.

GROSS (Eugene L.) A digest of the criminal laws of Illinois, from the adoption of the constitution to the end of the twenty-fifth general assembly, 1818-1866. Illustrated by references to the opinions of the supreme court, comprised in the first thirty-eight volumes of Illinois reports. xl, 285 pp. 8°. *Springfield, Illinois journal co.* 1868.

GUTA-LAGH, das ist: der insel Gothland altes rechtsbuch. In der ursprache und einer wiederaufgefundenen altdeutschen uebersetzung herausgegeben; mit einer neudeutschen uebersetzung nebst anmerkungen versehen von Carl Schildener. xlix, 275 pp. 4°. *Greifswald, E. Mauritius*, 1818.

——— The same. Codex iuris gotlandici, cum notis criticis. Gotlands-lagen. Utgifven af C. J. Schlyter. 2 p. l. xxxi, 382 pp. 2 pl. 4°. *Lund, Berlingska boktryckeriet*, 1852.
[SWEDEN. Corpus juris Sueo-Gotorum antiqui. v. 7].

HAYNES (R. W.) Catalogue of law books. *See* STEVENS (H. G.) *and* HAYNES.

HEISKELL (J. B.) A digest of the reported decisions of the state of Tennessee. xxiii, 613 pp. v. 1. 8°. *Memphis, bulletin publishing co.* 1868.
[2 copies].

HERTY (Thomas). A digest of the laws of Maryland, being an abridgment, alphabetically arranged, of all the public acts of assembly now in force, and of general use, from the first settlement of the state to the end of November session, 1797, inclusive, with references to the acts at large. With an appendix, [containing laws] passed November session, 1798. xii, 524, 55 pp. 8°. *Baltimore, editor*, 1799.

HEYL (Lewis). Statutes of the United States relating to revenue, commerce, navigation, and the currency. xviii, 960 pp. 8°. *Boston, Little, Brown & co.* 1868.

HILLIARD (Francis). The law of vendors and purchasers of real property. 2d ed. revised and greatly enlarged. 8°. *Boston, Little, Brown & co.* 1868.

HITTELL (Theodore H.) The civil practice act of the state of California. 393 pp. 12°. *San Francisco, S. Whitney*, 1868.

HOMANS (Benjamin). Laws of the United States, in relation to the navy and marine corps. xxviii, 223 pp. 8°. *Washington, J. & G. S. Gideon*, 1841.

HORNER *v.* LIDDIARD. A report of the case of Horner against Liddiard, upon the question of what consent is necessary to the marriage of illegitimate minors; determined, on the 24th May, 1799, in the consistorial court of London, by sir W. Scott. By A. Croke. viii, 189 pp. 8°. *London, A. Strahan*, 1800.

HOUCK (Lewis). A treatise on the law of navigable rivers. xix, 235 pp. 8°. *Boston, Little, Brown & co.* 1868.

HOWARD (Nathan, *jr.*) Practice reports in the supreme court of appeals of the state of New York. v. 34–35. 8°. *Albany, W. Gould & son,* 1868.
[2 copies of v. 35].

HOWE (*Maj. general* Robert). Proceedings of a general court martial, held at Philadelphia, for the trial of maj. gen. Howe, December 7, 1781. 24 pp. fol. *Philadelphia, Hall & Sellers,* 1782. [Imperfect; leaves wanting at the end].
[*With* SCHUYLER (*Maj. gen.* Philip). Trial. fol. 1778].

HURLSTONE (Edwin Tyrrell) *and* COLTMAN (Francis Joseph). Exchequer reports. Reports of cases argued and determined in courts of exchequer and exchequer chamber, 1864–66. With references to decisions in the American courts. James Parsons, editor. v. 3. 8°. *Philadelphia, T. & J. W. Johnson & co.* 1869.

—— —— The same. v. 4. 8°. *London, H. Sweet, etc.* 1868.

HUYSSEN (A.) Commentar zum preussischen allgemeinen berggesetz, nebst ergänzungen und verwaltungsvorschriften. 2e ausg. xvi, 259 pp. 16°. *Essen, G. D. Bädeker,* 1867. s.

IHERING (Rudolph). Geist des römischen rechts, auf den verschiedenen stufen seiner entwicklung. 2 v. in 3. 8°. *Leipzig, Breitkopf & Härtel,* 1852.

ILLINOIS (*State of*). Laws, [sessional], 1867, and special session, 1867. 2 v. 8°. *Springfield, Baker, Bailhache & co.* 1867.

—— Private laws, 1867. 3 v. 8°. *Springfield, Baker, Bailhache & co.* 1867.

—— School laws and common school decisions of the state of Illinois. Prepared and arranged by Newton Bateman, state superintendent. 328 pp. 8°. [*Springfield, by the state*], 1867.

ILLINOIS reports. v. 34–41. By Norman L. Freeman. 8°. *Chicago, E. B. Myers & Chandler, etc.* 1866–68.
[2 copies of v. 37, 40, and 41].

INDIANA reports. v. 26–27. By B. Harrison. 8°. *Indianapolis, Douglass & Connor,* 1868.
[2 copies of v. 27].

IOWA (*State of*). Laws, [sessional], extra session 1861, 1862, extra session, 1862, 1864, 1866. 1 v. 8°. *Des Moines, F. W. Palmer,* 1861-66.
[2 copies].

—— The same. For 1868. 8°. *Des Moines, F. W. Palmer,* 1868.
[4 copies].

IOWA reports. v. 21. By T. F. Withrow. 8°. *Chicago, Callaghan & Cutler,* 1868.

—— The same. v. 22–23. By Edward H. Stiles. 8°. *Ottumwa, by the reporter,* 1867.
[5 copies of v. 22; 3 copies of v. 23].

IRISH circuit court reports. *See* REPORTS, etc. on six circuits in Ireland.

IRISH (The) reports, published under the control of the council of law, reporting in Ireland; containing reports of cases in the superior courts in Ireland. Edited by George A. C. May. Common law series, 1867. v. 1. 8°. *Dublin, Edward Ponsonby,* 1868.

—— The same. Equity series, 1867. v. 1. 8°. *Dublin, Edward Ponsonby,* 1868.

JACOBUS von Guitrode. *See* CLUSA (Jacobus de).

JEDRE (John Baptist) BAPTIST (John *jr.*) *and others.* The trial of five persons for piracy, felony and robbery, who were found guilty and condemned, at a court of admiralty for the trial of piracies, felonies, and robberies, committed on the high seas, at the court-house in Boston, in New England, October 4, 1726. 34 pp. 4°. *Boston,* 1726.
[NOTE.—Title page imperfect].

JEWELL (Joseph). The Bowery tragedy. Trial of Joseph Jewell for the murder of Luciese Louis Leuba, with the speeches of the counsel, etc. 16 pp. sm. 4°. *New York, R. H. Elton,* 1836.

JOHNES (Arthur James). Remarks on the late report from the select committee on bankruptcy and the bankruptcy bill now pending, in a letter to lord Brougham and Vaux; with postcript. 25, 8 pp. 8°. *London, Wildy & sons,* 1866.

JOHNSON (Andrew). Proceedings in the trial of Andrew Johnson, president of the United States, before the United States senate, on articles of impeachment exhibited by the house of representatives; with an appendix. 1090, 50, xxviii pp. 8°. *Washington, Rives & Bailey,* 1868.

—— The same. Supplement to the congressional globe: containing the proceedings of the senate sitting for the trial of Andrew Johnson, president of the United States. xiv, 526 pp. 4°. *Washington, Rives & Bailey,* 1868.

—— The same. The great impeachment and trial of Andrew Johnson, president of the United States, with the whole of the preliminary proceedings in the house of representatives, and in the senate of the United States; with the eleven articles of impeachment, and the whole of the proceedings in the court of impeachment, etc. 289 pp. 8°. *Philadelphia, T. B. Peterson & bros.* 1868.

JONES (Hamilton C.) Reports of cases at law in the supreme court of North Carolina. v. 7. 8°. *Salisbury, J. J. Bruner*, 1861.

JOURNAL (The) of jurisprudence, 1862–1866. v. 6–10. 8°. *Edinburgh, T. & T. Clark*, 1862–66.

JUDICIAL opinions, delivered in the mayor's court of the city of New York, in the year 1802. [*anon.*] 105 pp. 8°. *New York, D. Longworth*, 1803.

JUSTINIANUS. Institutionum libri iv. In usum academiarum brasiliensium edidit E. Ferreira Franca. xii, 331 pp. 18°. *Lipsiæ, F. A. Brockhaus*, 1858. s.

KAINE (Thomas). In the matter of Thomas Kaine, an alleged fugitive from justice. Argument. [By] Charles Edwards, of counsel for the claimant, the British government. 16 pp. 8°. *New York, E. Barnes & co.* 1852.

KANSAS reports. Reports of cases in the supreme court of the state of Kansas. v. 1–4. 8°. *Lawrence, public printer*, 1864–66.

KATCHENOVSKY (*Professor*). Prize law: particularly with reference to the duties and obligations of belligerents and neutrals. Translated from the Russian, by Frederic Thomas Pratt. x, 189 pp. 8°. *London, Stevens & sons*, 1867.
[3 copies].

KEYSERLICH und künigliche laut- und lehenrecht nach gemeinen sittē und gebruch der rechten. [*anon.*] 5 p. l. cviii l. 4°. *Strassburgk, M. Hupsuff*, 1507.

KNAPP (Jerome W.) Reports of cases argued and determined before the committees of his majesty's most honorable privy council, 1829–36. 3 v. in 1. 8°. *London, J. & W. T. Clarke, etc.* 1831–36.

LAMIRANDE (Ernest Sureau). Return respecting the extradition of Lamirande from Canada. 164 pp. 8°. *Ottawa, Hunter, Rose & co.* 1868.

LAW (The) journal reports, for 1867. New series. v. 36. Parts 1, 2, and 3, in 3 v. 8°. *London, E. B. Ince*, 1867.

LAW (The) magazine and law review; or, quarterly journal of jurisprudence. November, 1867, to August, 1868. v. 24–25. 8°. *London, Butterworths*, 1868.

LAW (The) times: the journal and record of the law and the lawyers, from November, 1864, to April, 1868. v. 40–44. fol. *London, Law times office*, 1864–68.
[No. 1206, of v. 4, wanting].

LAW (The) times reports: containing all the cases argued and determined in parliament, the house of lords, the privy council, etc. from March, 1866, to August, 1868. New series. v. 14–18. 8°. *London, Horace Cox*, 1866–68.
[No. 340, of v. 14, and 447, of v. 18, wanting].

LAWRENCE (William Beach) *v.* DANA (R. H. *jr.*) *et al.* Circuit court of the United States, Massachusetts district. In equity. Bill, answer, and evidence. vii, 565 pp. 8°. *Boston, A. Mudge & son*, 1867.

——— The same. Brief for complainant. iii, 98, vii pp. 8°. *Boston*, 1867.
[*With the* preceding].

——— The same. Arguments of B. R. Curtis and J. J. Storrow, for the complainant, on the question of title. Reported by J. M. W. Yerrington. 1 p. l. 105 pp. 8°. *Boston*, 1868.
[*With the* preceding].

——— The same. Closing argument for the complainant on the question of piracy, [by] B. R. Curtis, [and] J. J. Storrow. viii, 255 pp. 8°. *Boston*, 1868.
[*With the* preceding].

LIBER assissarum. Le liver des assises et plees del corone, moues et dependauntz deuant les iustices, sibien en lour circuitz come aylours, en temps le roy Edward le tierce. Ore nouelment imprimee et corrigee, ouesque deux nouels tables, lun, de touts les principal cases contenus in cest liuer, laut monstrant south queux titles sir R. Brooke eux ad abridge. 36 p. l. 326, 10 l. *b. l.* fol. *Londini, R. Tottell*, 1580.
[Reprint of Rastell's edition, 1516. NOTE: Lib. ass. is Year book, part 5].

LIDDIARD. Marriage of illegitimate minors. *See* HORNER *v.* LIDDIARD.

LITTLETON (H. A.) *and* BLATCHLEY (J. S.) Digest of fire insurance decisions in the courts of Great Britain and America. 2d ed. revised and enlarged, by Stephen G. Clarke. 723 pp. 8°. *New York, Baker, Voorhis & co.* 1868.
[2 copies].

LIVER (Le) des assises. *See* LIBER assissarum.

LIVINGSTON (John). The law register; comprising the lawyers in the United States; the state record; the official directory for the United States; the collector's assistant. 1868. 8°. *New York, merchants' union law co.* 1868.

LORD (Henry W.) The highway of the seas in time of war. viii, 56 pp. 8°. *London, Macmillan & co.* 1862.
[2 copies].

LOUISIANA (*State of*). Civil code of the state of Louisiana: with the statutory amendments from 1825 to 1866 inclusive; and references to the decisions of the supreme court of Louisiana to the seventeenth volume of the annual reports, inclusive. Compiled and edited by

James O. Fuqua. xiv, 482, 72 pp. 8°. *New York, John F. Trow & co.* 1867.

——— Code of practice in civil cases for the state of Louisiana; with the statutory amendments, from 1825 to 1866, inclusive; and references to the decisions of the supreme court of Louisiana to the seventeenth volume of annual reports. Compiled and edited by James O. Fuqua. 440 pp. 8°. *New York, John F. Trow & co.* 1867.

LOUISIANA annual reports. v. 17. 1865. By S. F. Glenn. 8°. *New Orleans, Bloomfield & Steel,* 1866.

——— The same. v. 19. 1867. By J. Hawkins. 8°. *New Orleans, Bloomfield & co.* 1868.

LOWELL (*City of*). The charter and ordinances of the city of Lowell, with the acts of the legislature relating to the city. 262 pp. 8°. *Boston, J. E. Farwell & co.* 1863.

McADAM (David). The marine court of the city of New York: its organization, jurisdiction and practice, with forms. 164, xiv pp. 8°. *New York, McAdam & Vannett,* 1868.

MACAREL (Louis Antoine). Des tribunaux administratifs; ou, introduction à l'étude de la jurisprudence administrative, [etc.] xii, 581 pp. 8°. *Paris, J. P. Roret,* 1828. s.

McCARDLE (W. H. *ex parte*). Argument of Matt. H. Carpenter in the supreme court of the United States, March 3 and 4, 1868, in the matter of *ex parte* Wm. H. McCardle, *appellant.* Reported by D. F. Murphy. 83 pp. 8°. *Washington, government printing office,* 1868.

McRAE (Duncan G.) *and others.* Military commission. Proceedings in the case of the United States against Duncan G. McRae, W. J. Tolar, D. Watkins, S. Phillips, and T. Powers, for the murder of Archibald Beebee, at Fayetteville, N. C, 11th Feb. 1867, [with] the argument of E. G. Haywood, special judge advocate. Reported by C. Flowers and C. P. Young. 2 p. l. 398 pp. 8°. *Raleigh, (N.C.) R. Avery,* 1867.

MAGISTRATE'S cases. Reports of new magistrates' cases in all the courts of common law at Westminster, 1844 to 1848. By Adam Bittleson and Edward Wise. v. 1–2. xi, 640 pp; viii, 452 pp. 8°. *London, J. Crockford,* 1846–48.

——— The same. 1848 to 1850. By Adam Bittleson and Paul Parnell. v. 3–4. xix, 243 pp; xii, 168 pp. sm. fol. *London, J. Crockford,* 1850–51.

MAINE reports. v. 54. By W. W. Virgin. 8°. *Hallowell, Masters, Smith & co.* 1868.

[2 copies].

MARCH (John, *barrister*). Actions for slander and arbitrements. The first, being a collection of what words are actionable in the law, and what not; where an action *de scandalis magnatum* will lie; and of the nature of a libel: the other, a discourse, showing what arbitrements are good in law, and what not. Reviewed, with additions, by W. B. 4 p. l. 476 pp. 9 l. 16°. *London, E. Walbanck,* 1674.

MARRIOTT (James). Plan of a code of laws for the province of Quebec; reported by the advocate general. 2 p. l. 292 pp. 8°. *London,* 1774.

MARYLAND (*State of*). Laws, [sessional], 1861 and 1868. 2 v. 8°. *Annapolis,* 1861–68.

[2 copies].

——— Supplement to the Maryland code, containing the acts of 1861, 1861–62, 1864, 1865, 1866, and 1867. By Lewis Mayer. xi, 670 pp. 8°. *Baltimore, John Murphy & co.* 1868.

MARYLAND reports. v. 22–24. By Nicholas Brewer. 8°. *Baltimore and Annapolis, W. K. Boyle, etc.* 1867–68.

[2 copies].

MASSACHUSETTS (*State of*). Resolves of the general assembly, begun and held at Watertown, 29th of May, 1776. 59 pp. fol. *Boston, B. Edes,* 1776.

——— The same. Resolves of general assembly, held at Watertown, Aug. 30–Nov. 9, 1776, [and] at Boston, Nov. 12, 1776, to May 10, 1777. [With appendix]. 188 pp. fol. *Boston, B. Edes,* 1776–77.

[*With* MASSACHUSETTS (*Colony of*). Resolves, 1776. NOTE—Imperfect: all after p. 14 of appendix wanting].

——— The same. Resolves of the general assembly of the state of Massachusetts-bay, 27th of May, 1778, to Dec. 7, 1779. 2 v. 177, xi pp; 159 pp. fol. *Boston, T. & J. Fleet,* 1778–79.

——— Laws, [sessional], 1867 and 1868. 2 v. 8°. *Boston, Wright & Potter,* 1867–68.

[2 copies].

MASSACHUSETTS reports. v. 97. By Albert G. Browne, jr. 8°. *Boston, H. O. Houghton & co.* 1868.

[2 copies].

MEEK (Alexander B.) A supplement to Aikin's digest of the laws of Alabama, to 1841. 409 pp. 8°. *Tuscaloosa, White & Snow,* 1841.

MÉNANT (Joachim). Du droit de vie et de mort. viii, 316 pp. 8°. *Paris, Derache,* 1848. s.

METCALF (Theron). Principles of the law of contracts, as applied by courts of law. xxviii, 357 pp. 8°. *New York, Hurd & Houghton,* 1868.
[2 copies].

MICHELSEN (Andreas Ludwig Jacob). Ueber die genesis der jury. Eine germanistische untersuchung. vii, 190 pp. 8°. *Leipzig, O. Wigand,* 1847.

MICHIGAN reports. v. 15–16. By William Jennison. 8°. *Detroit, W. A. Troop & co.* 1867–68.
[2 copies of v. 15; 3 copies of v. 16].

MICKLETHWAITE *v.* WEISSER. Supreme court [New York]: in equity. Daniel Micklethwaite and others, against William Weisser, executor, etc. of Joseph Rhodes, E. S. Thebaud, and others. Case. 25, lix pp. 8°. *New York, W. C. Bryant & co.* 1850.

MILLIGAN (Lambdin P.) *and others.* [Arguments and decisions in the Indiana conspiracy case. U. S. supreme court, 1866]. 8°. *Washington, R. Sutton,* 1866.
[REPORTER (The). v. 2. nos. 16, 22–25, and 28].

MINNESOTA (*State of*). Laws, [sessional], 1867 and 1868. 2 v. 8°. *Saint Paul, pioneer printing co.* 1867–68.

MINNESOTA reports. v. 11–12. By William A. Spencer. 8°. *Chicago, etc. E. B. Myers & Chandler, etc.* 1867–68.
[2 copies of v. 11].

MISSOURI (*State of*). Laws, [sessional], 1868. 8°. *Jefferson city, E. Kirby,* 1868.
[3 copies].

MISSOURI reports. v. 41. By C. C. Whittelsey. 8°. *St. Louis, G. Knapp & co.* 1868.
[2 copies].

MOFFATT (George). On the bankrupt law of England. 47 pp. 8°. *London, William Ridgway,* 1865.

MONTEFIORE (Joshua). Commercial and notarial precedents: consisting of all the most approved forms, common and special, which are required in transactions of business: with principles of law relative to bills of exchange, insurance, and shipping. xvi, 350 pp. 8°. *Philadelphia, J. Humphrys,* 1863.

MONTRIOU (William Austin). Institutes of jurisprudence. vi pp. 3 l. 232 pp. 8°. *London, Macmillan & co.* 1866.

MOORE (Edmund F.) Reports of cases heard and determined by the judicial committee and the lords of her majesty's most honorable privy council. New series. v. 4. 8°. *London, Stevens & sons,* 1867.

MORDECAI (*Capt.* Alfred). A digest of the laws relating to the military establishment of the United States. vi, 134 pp. 16°. *Washington, Thompson & Homans,* 1833.

MORGAN (John). The attorney's vade mecum, and client's instructor, treating of actions, (such as are now most in use): of prosecuting and defending them: of the pleadings and law. Also of hue and cry. 3 v. 8°. *Dublin, Chamberlain, Burnet & co.* 1787–92.

MOUNT HOPE case. *See* STOKES (*Dr.* W. H.) *and* BLENKINSOP (Mary).

MYERS (E. B.) and company. Catalogue of law books, including their own publications. 120, x pp. 12°. *Chicago, E. B. Myers & co.* 1868.

NATURALIZATION laws. *See* UNITED STATES.

NEBRASKA (*Territory of*). Laws, [sessional], for 1857, December session, 1857, 1858, 1859, 1860, 1861, 1864, 1865, and 1867. 9 v. 8°. *Brownville, Omaha City, etc.* 1857–67.
[2 copies of 1858–67].

——— The revised statutes of the territory of Nebraska, in force July 1, 1866. Revised by A. Estabrook. 814 pp. 8°. *Omaha, E. B. Taylor,* 1866.
[2 copies].

——— (*State of*). Laws, [sessional], for 1st, 2d, and 3d sessions of the legislative assembly, 1867. 8°. *Omaha, Republican office,* 1867.
[*With* NEBRASKA (Territory of). Laws; 12th session, January, 1867].

NEVADA reports. v. 3. By A. Helm. 8°. *San Francisco, Towne & Bacon,* 1868.
[2 copies].

NEW BRUNSWICK (*Province of*). Copy of the report made to the lieutenant-governor by the commissioners appointed to inquire into the judicial institutions of the province. Jan. 1833. 161 pp. 4°. *Fredericton, (New Brunswick), J. Simpson,* 1833.

NEW HAMPSHIRE (*Province of*). Acts and laws. 1 p. l. iii, 60 pp. fol. *Boston, B. Green,* 1716.

NEW JERSEY (*State of*). A digest of the laws of New Jersey. By Lucius Q. C. Elmer. 4th ed. Containing all the laws of general application, now in force, from 1709 to 1868, inclusive, with the rules and decisions of the courts. By John T. Nixon. xxxii, 1152 pp. 8°. *Newark, Martin R. Dennis & co.* 1868.

——— Laws, [sessional], 1868. 8°. *New Brunswick, J. R. Speer,* 1868.

NEW magistrates' cases, *See* MAGISTRATES' cases.

NEW NETHERLANDS (*Colony of*). Laws and ordinances, 1638–74. Compiled and translated from the original Dutch records in the office of the secretary of state, Albany, N. Y. By E. B. O'Callaghan. xxxii, 602 pp. 8°. *Albany, Weed, Parsons & co.* 1868.

NEW reports (The). Containing cases decided in the courts of equity and common law. Editors, George Osborne Morgan, Charles Edward Jemmett, Henry Tindal Atkinson, and J. Morgan Howard. Nov. 1862, to Aug. 1865. 6 v. 8°. *London, William Maxwell,* 1863–65.

NEW YORK (*Colony of*). East-hampton book of laws. June ye 24th, 1665. [Established by the authority of James, duke of Yorke]. 8°. *New York, J. Riley,* 1811.

[*In* NEW YORK historical society. Collections. v. 1. 1st series].

See, also, NEW NETHERLAND (*Colony of*).

——— (*State of*). Private laws, 1808. 8°. *Albany,* 1808.

——— Supplement of Voorhies' annotated code. Additional notes from all the various New York reports, from 1864 to 1867. By John Townshend. pp. 1005–1070. 8°. *New York, Baker, Voorhies & co.* 1867.

——— The code as it is. The code of procedure of the state of New York, as amended to 1867. With the revised rules of the courts. Edited by John Townshend. 292 pp. 12°. *New York, Baker, Voorhies & co.* 1867.

——— Laws, [sessional], 1868. 2 v. 8°. *Albany, Van Benthuysen & sons,* 1868.

[2 copies].

NEW YORK reports. v. 37. By Joel Tiffany. [v. 10 of Tiffany]. 8°. *Albany, Weare C. Little,* 1868.

[2 copies].

——— The same. v. 38–40. By Emerson W. Keyes. [Being v. 1–3 of Keyes]. 8°. *Albany, Weare C. Little,* 1868.

NIDER *or* NYDER (Johannes). Tractatus de contractibus marcatorum. 29 l. 29 l. 4°. [*Coloniae, Ulricus Zell, about* 1480].

NORTH CAROLINA (*State of*). Public laws, [sessional], 1862–63; adjourned session, 1862–63; called session, 1863; adjourned session, 1862–63; [and] adjourned session, 1864. With comptroller's statement of revenue and expenditure, for 1861–62. 2 v. 8°. *Raleigh, W. W. Holden,* 1863–64.

——— Private laws, 1861–63; adjourned session, 1862–63; called session, 1863; adjourned session, 1863; and adjourned session, 1864. 8°. *Raleigh, W. W. Holden,* 1863–64.

——— Laws, and resolutions of a public nature, adjourned session, 1863; [and] laws, (public and private), adjourned session, 1864. 8°. *Raleigh, W. W. Holden,* 1864.

——— Laws, [public and private], regular session, 1865; and acts and resolutions passed in secret session, [1862–65]. 8°. *Raleigh, Cannon & Holden,* 1865.

——— Laws, [public and private], 1865; the same, [with] resolutions of a private nature, 1866; [and] public laws passed at the sessions of 1861–'62–'64, and one in 1859. 8°. *Raleigh, W. E. Pell,* 1866.

——— Ordinances [first to fourth sessions] of the state convention, published by pursuance of a resolution of the general assemply, [ratified 11th Feb. 1863. 93 pp. 4 l. 8°. *Raleigh W. W. Holden,* 1863.

NORWAY. Kong Christian den fjerdes norske lovbog af 1604. Efter foranstaltning af det akademiske kollegium ved det k. norske Frederiks universitet udgiven af Fr. Hallager og Fr. Brandt. xxvi, 200 pp. 1 portrait. 8°. *Christiania, C. C. Werner & co.* 1855. S.

——— Om forandringer i straffeproceslovgivningen med eller uden jury. Betænkning afgiven af den ved kgl. resolution af 11te Januar, 1853, nedsatte commission. 2 v. in 3. 8°. *Christiania, Steenske bogtrykkeri,* 1856-57. S.

NOTT (Charles C.) *and* HUNTINGTON (Samuel H.) Cases in the court of claims of the United States, December terms, 1866 and 1867. v. 3. 8°. *Washington, government printing office,* 1868.

NOVA SCOTIA (*Province of*). Revised statutes. Prepared by W. Young, J. W. Ritchie, J. McCully, [and] J. Whidden. xxi, 578 pp. 8°. *Halifax, R. Nugent,* 1851.

——— The statutes of Nova Scotia, passed in the fourth session of the general assembly, [etc.] 4 p.l. 124, x pp. 8°. *Halifax, public printer,* [1859]. S.

OHIO (*State of*). Laws, [sessional], 1865, 1866, 1867, and 1868. v. 62–65. 8°. *Columbus, R. Nevins and L. D. Myers & bro.* 1868.

[2 copies of 1868].

OHIO state reports. v. 17. By L. J. Critchfield. 8°. *Columbus, Nevins & Myers,* 1868.

[2 copies].

ONTARIO. Statutes of Ontario. 1867–68. 8°. *Toronto, H. J. Hartney,* 1868.

[2 copies].

OPDYKE (George). Libel case. *See* WEED (Thurlow).

OPINIONS of the United States courts for the eastern district of Missouri, and for the southern district of Illinois, involving the construction of the non-intercourse and captured property acts, and their relation to the prize acts. [*anon.*] 78 pp. 8°. *Washington*, 1866.

OREGON (*State of*). Acts and resolutions of the legislative assembly, etc. 1866. 110 pp. 8°. *Salem, W. A. McPherson*, 1866.

—— Reports of the decisions of the supreme court of the state of Oregon, [1862–66]. 118 pp. 8°. *Salem, W. A. McPherson*, 1866.
[*With* acts, etc. leg. assembly, 1866].

PANORMITANUS (Nikolaus). *See* TEDESCHI (Niccolo, *panormitano*).

PARKER (Amasa J.) Reports of decisions in criminal cases, made at chambers, and in the courts of oyer and terminer of the state of New York. v. 6. 8°. *Albany, William Gould & son*, 1868.

PARKER (Charles H.) The civil practice act of the state of California, including amendments of 1868, with notes and references to the decisions of the supreme court, general laws germain to the practice act, and standard forms applicable thereto. 617, 39, liv pp. 8°. *San Francisco, H. H. Bancroft & co.* 1868.

PARSONS (Theophilus). A treatise on the laws of marine insurance and general average. 2 v. l, 638 pp; ix, 701 pp. 8°. *Boston, Little, Brown & co.* 1868.
[3 copies].

PASCHAL (George W.) The constitution of the United States defined and carefully annotated. xxviii, 407 pp. 12°. *Washington, (D. C.) W. H. & O. H. Morrison*, 1868.
[2 copies].

PATENT OFFICE. *See* UNITED STATES. (*Patent office*).

PENNSYLVANIA (*State of*). Report of the commissioners on the penal code, with documents, 1828. 192 pp. 8°. *Harrisburg, S. C. Staumbach*, 1828.

—— Laws, [sessional], 1868. 8°. *Harrisburg, Singerly & Myers*, 1868.

PENNSYLVANIA state reports. v. 53–56. By P. Fraser Smith. 8°. *Philadelphia, Kay & bro.* 1868.
[2 copies].

PETERS (Richard). Reports of cases in the supreme court of the United States. v. 1 and 9. 8°. *Philadelphia*, 1828–35.

PETITION (Clément Adolphe Lucien). Thèse pour le doctorat. (Faculté de droit de Paris). 2 p. l. 128 pp. 8°. *Paris, H. & C. Noblet*, 1858. S.

CONTENTS.

Droit romain: de la publicienne. Droit français: des nullités de mariage.

PHILADELPHIA reports. Containing the decisions published in the Legal intelligencer, from 1860 to 1864, inclusive. By Henry E. Wallace. v. 4–5. 8°. *Philadelphia, King & Baird*, 1867.

PIGOTT (Nathaniel). A treatise of common recoveries, their nature and use. To which is added, the case of Page and Hayward more fully reported than in any other book extant; also, a case between the late earl of Derby and the coheirs of his elder brother. With precedents for amending recoveries. 3 p. l. 232 pp. 8 l. 8°. *Dublin, Sarah Cotter*, 1753.

POLAND (John S. *bvt. lieut. col. U. S. A.*) A digest of the military laws of the United States, 1860 to 1867. Relating to the army, volunteers, militia, and the rebellion and reconstruction of the southern states. 448 pp. 8°. *Boston, Little, Brown & co.* 1868.

POST OFFICE department. *See* UNITED STATES.

PRACTICAL (A) digest of the law of merchant ships and seamen, and commercial navigation, in so far as regulated by statute. With an appendix of forms. v. 1. Of the property in British ships. Of merchant seamen. 2d ed. xi, 177 pp. 16°. *London, P. Richardson*, 1847.

PRATER (Henry). Cases illustrative of the conflict between the laws of England and Scotland with regard to marriage, divorce, and legitimacy. 83 pp. 8°. *London, Saunders & Benning*, 1835.

PRINCE Edward island. The acts of the general assembly. iv, 328 pp. 8°. *Charlottetown, E. Whelan*, 1856. S.

PROBST (Antoine). The life, confession, and atrocious crimes of Antoine Probst. [*anon.*] 109 pp. 8°. *Philadelphia, Barclay & co.* [1866].

—— The Dearing tragedy, with a full history and confession of Antoine Probst, the monster. [*anon.*] 48 pp. 8°. *Philadelphia, C. W. Alexander*, [1866].

PROVIDENCE plantations. *See* RHODE ISLAND (*Colony of*).

PURPLE (N. H.) A compilation of all the general laws concerning real estate, and the title thereto, in the state of Illinois. vi, 553 pp. 8°. *Quincy, for the compiler*, 1849.

QUEEN'S bench reports. By J. L. Adolphus and T. F. Ellis. v. 4. 8°. *London, Benning & co.* 1845.

RASTELL (William). A colleccion of entrees, barres, replicacions, reioinders, issues, verdits, iudgements, executions, proces, contynuances, essoynes, and diuers others matters. 5 p. l. 627 l. fol. [*London*], *R. Tottell*, 1566.

RAWLE (William Henry). Equity in Pennsylvania. A lecture delivered before the law academy of Philadelphia, February 11, 1868. With the registrar's book of governor Keith's court of chancery. 93, 46 pp. 8°. *Philadelphia, Kay & brother*, 1868.

RECONSTRUCTION. Military reconstruction bills. Injunction cases. Arguments and decisions in the United States supreme court on the Mississippi and Georgia injunction cases, which were instituted to restrain the acts of congress of 1867, to provide for the more efficient government of the rebel states. 8°. *Washington, R. Sutton*, 1867.

[REPORTER (The). v. 3. nos. 43-46].

RENAULT (P. F.) Case of [his] heirs. *See* WHITE (Joseph M.) Argument and opinion.

REPORTS of cases argued and determined on six circuits in Ireland: taken during the assizes, in the years 1841-43. By H. Smythe, F. Brady, and others. xxii, 873, lxiv pp. 8°. *Dublin, Andrew Milliken*, 1843.

REPORTS of cases taken and adjudged in the court of chancery, in the reign of king Charles i, Charles ii, James ii, king William, and Queen Anne, 1615 to 1712. 3d ed. 3 v. in 1. fol. *London, Nutt & Gosling*, 1736.

RHODE ISLAND (*Colony of*). The proceedings of the first general assembly of "the incorporation of Providence plantations," and the code of laws adopted by that assembly in 1647. With notes, historical and explanatory, by W. R. Staples. 64 pp. 8°. *Providence, C. Burnett, jr.* 1847.

——— (*State of*). Charters and legislative documents, illustrative of Rhode-Island history. 68 pp. 8°. *Providence, Knowles & Vose*, 1844.

RICHARDSON (J. S. G.) Reports of cases at law and in equity, in the court of appeals and court of errors of South Carolina. Law vol. 13. Equity vol. 12. In 1 v. 8°. *Charleston, E. J. Dawson & co.* 1866.
[3 copies].

——— Reports of cases at law. v. 14. 8°. [*Charleston*], *E. J. Dawson & co.* 1867.
[3 copies].

ROBERTSON (Anthony L.) Reports of cases in the superior court of the city of New York. v. 3-5. 8°. *Albany, W. C. Little*, 1867-68.

ROUSSEAU (Samuel). A dictionary of Mohammedan law, Bengal revenue terms, Shanscrit, Hindoo, and other words, used in the East Indies, with full explanations. [With] appendix. lxiv, 287 pp. 16°. *London, J. Sewell*, 1802.

SALICA (Lex). Texte. *See* WAITZ (G.) Das alte recht der salischen Franken.

SAUNDERS (*Sir* Edmund). The reports of several pleadings and cases in the court of king's bench. 6th ed. By Edward Vaughan Williams. 2 v. in 3. 8°. *London, Benning & co.* 1845.

SAXONY. Gesetzsammlung für das königreich Sachsen vom jahre 1818-31. 14 v. 4°. *Dresden, Meinhold & söhne*, [1818-31]. s.

——— The same. Sammlung der gesetze und verordnungen, [etc.] vom jahre 1832-34. 3 v. 4°. *Dresden, Meinhold & söhne*, [1832-34]. s.

——— The same. Gesetz-und verordnungsblatt für das königreich Sachsen vom jahre 1835-52. 14 v. 4°. *Dresden, C. C. Meinhold & söhne*, [1832-52]. s.

SCHIEFER (John Frederic). An explanation of the practice of law: containing the elements of special pleading; also, elements of a plan for a reform. xxxi, 340 pp. 8°. *Dublin, Lynch, Byrne, etc.* 1793.

SCHLYTER (Carl Johan). Corpus juris Sueo-Gotorum antiqui. *See* SWEDEN.

SCHUYLER (*maj. general* Philip). Proceedings of a general court-martial, held at maj. general Lincoln's quarters, near Quaker Hill, New York, for the trial of maj. general Schuyler, October 1, 1778. [With *ms.* papers and letters referred to in Schuyler's defence]. 62 pp. 37 l. *ms.* fol. *Philadelphia, Hall & Sellers*, 1778.

SCOTT (William L.) *and* JARNAGIN (Milton P.) A treatise upon the law of telegraphs; with an appendix, containing the general statutory provisions of England, Canada, the United States, and the states of the Union, upon the subject of telegraphs. xvii, 535 pp. 8°. *Boston, Little, Brown & co.* 1868.

SEDGWICK (Theodore). A treatise on the measure of damages. 4th ed. revised and annotated by Henry Dwight Sedgwick. lxiii, 756 pp. 8°. *New York, Baker, Voorhis & co.* 1868.

SESSION cases. Cases in the court of session, teind court, etc. and house of lords. 3d series. v. 5. 8°. *Edinburgh, T. & T. Clark*, 1867.

SIMMONS (James). A digest of Wisconsin reports, from the earliest period to the year 1868: comprising all the published decisions of the supreme court of Wisconsin, presented in Burnett's, Chandler's, and 20 vols. Wisconsin reports. 7, 891 pp. 8°. *Albany, William Gould & son*, 1868.

SMITH (John William). The law of contracts. 5th American from the 4th London ed. By John George Malcolm. With notes and references to both English and American decisions, by William Henry Rawle, and with additional notes and references to recent American cases, by George Sharswood. xxiv, 544 pp. 8°. *Philadelphia, T. & J. W. Johnson & co.* 1869.

SNEED (John L. T.) Reports of cases at common law and in equity, in the supreme court of Tennessee. v. 5. 8°. *Nashville, E. G. Eastman & co.* 1850.

[2 copies].

SOUTH CAROLINA (*State of*) *v. the* BANK OF SOUTH CAROLINA. The bank case. A report of the proceedings in the cases of the bank of South Carolina and the bank of Charleston, upon *scire facias* to vacate their charters, for suspending specie payments, with the final argument and determination thereof, in the court for the correction of errors of South Carolina, 1842–43. v, 550 pp. 8°. *Charleston, W. Riley,* 1844.

SPECIAL and selected law cases, concerning the persons and estates of all men whatsoever. Collected and gathered out of the reports and year-books of the common law of England. 2 p. l. 303 pp. sm. 4°. *London, William Cooke,* 1641.

SPRAGUE (Peleg). Decisions in maritime, admiralty, and prize causes in the district court of the United States for the district of Massachusetts, 1854–64. v. 2. vi, 374 pp. 8°. *Boston, Little, Brown & co.* 1868.

[3 copies].

STAR-CHAMBER cases, showing what cavses properly belong to the cognizance of that court. Collected, for the most part, out of mr. Crompton, his booke, entituled, "The jurisdiction of divers courts." 55 pp. sm. 4°. *London, J. O. for John Grave,* 1641.

STEVENS (H. G.) *and* HAYNES (R. W.) A catalogue of modern law books, including all the reports in England, Scotland, and Ireland. lii, 177 pp. 18°. *London, Stevens & Haynes,* 1865.

STOKES (*Dr.* W. H.) *and* BLENKINSOP (Mary). Report of the trial of Dr. W. H. Stokes and Mary Blenkinsop, physician and sister superior of Mount Hope institution, before the circuit court for Baltimore co. Md., held at Towsontown, Tuesday, February 6, 1866. By Eugene L. Didier. 202 pp. 8°. *Baltimore, Kelly & Piet,* 1866.

STORY (Joseph). Commentaries on the law of partnership. 6th ed. by John C. Gray, jr. xxxv, 758 pp. 8°. *Boston, Little, Brown & co.* 1868.

——— Commentaries on the law of promissory notes. 6th ed. xliv, 739 pp. 8°. *Boston, Little, Brown & co.* 1868.

SURRATT (John Harrison). Trial in the criminal court for the District of Columbia, hon. George P. Fisher presiding. 2 v. iii, 1383 pp. 8°. *Washington, gov't printing office,* 1867.

——— The same. Trial of John H. Surratt, in the supreme court of the District of Columbia, on an indictment for murder of President Lincoln, commencing June 10, 1867. 8°. *Washington, R. Sutton,* 1867.

[REPORTER (The). v. 3–4. nos. 47–103].

SWEDEN. Corpus juris Sueo-Gotorum antiqui. Samling af Sveriges gamla lagar, pa kongl. maj:ts nadigste befallning utgifven af d. H. S. Collin och d. C. J. Schlyter. v. 1–11. 4°. *Stockholm, Z. Haeggström; Lund, Berlingska boktryckeriet, etc.* 1827–65. s.

CONTENTS.

v. 1. Codex juris vestrogotici, cum notis criticis. Westgöta-lagen. 3 p. l. lxxvii, 592 pp. 8 pl. 1827.

v. 2. Codex juris ostrogotici, cum notis criticis. Östgöta-lagen. 2 p. l. xxxi, 403 pp. 4 pl. 1830.

v. 3. Codex juris uplandici, cum notis criticis. Uplands-lagen. Utgifven af C. J. Schlyter. 2 p. l. lxxxiii, 456 pp. 3 pl. 1834.

v. 4. Codex juris sudermannici, cum notis criticis. Södermanna-lagen, utgifven af C. J. Schlyter. 2 p. l. lv, 338 pp. 2 pl. 1838.

v. 5. Codex juris vestmannici, cum notis criticis. Westmanna-lagen, utgifven af C. J. Schlyter. 2 p. l. xlv, 357 pp. 2 pl. 1841.

v. 6. Codex juris helsingici, codicis iuris smalandici pars de re ecclesiastica, et iuris urbici codex antiquior, cum notis criticis. Helsinge-lagen, etc. Utgifne af C. J. Schlyter. 4 p. l. xliii, 251 pp. 2 pl. 1844.

v. 7. Codex iuris gotlandici, cum notis criticis. Gotlands-lagen, utgifven af C. J. Schlyter. 2 p. l. xxxi, 382 pp. 2 pl. 1852.

v. 8. Codices iuris visbiensis urbici et maritimi, cum notis criticis. Utgifne af C. J. Schlyter. 2 p. l. cxiii, 580 pp. 2 pl. 1853.

v. 9. Codex iuris scanici, cum notis criticis, etc. Skane-lagen, utgifven af C. J. Schlyter. 2 p. l. clxxxiii, 652 pp. 2 pl. 1859.

v. 10. Codex iuris sueciae Magnæanus, cum notis criticis, etc. Konung Magnus Erikssons landslag, uitgifven af C. J. Schlyter. 4 p. l. cii, 459 pp. 2 pl. 1862.

v. 11. Codex iuris urbici Magnæanus, cum notis criticis, etc. Konung Magnus Erikssons stadslag, utgifven af C. J. Schlyter. 2 p. l. cv, 490 pp. 2 pl. 1865.

TEDESCHI (Niccolo, *panormitano*). [In ii decretales pars secundum]. 240 pp. fol. [*Venetiis*], *V. de Spira,* 1471.

——— [In ii decretales pars tertia]. 250 pp. fol. [*Venetiis, V. de Spira,* 1472].

[Imperfect].

TENNESSEE (*State of*). Laws, [sessional], 1867–68, and extra session, 1868. 2 v. 8°. *Nashville, S. C. Mercer,* 1868.

TEXAS (*State of*). The constitution as amended, and ordinances of the convention of 1866, and general and special laws, 1866. 8°. *Austin*, 1866.

TEXAS reports. v. 25. By Richard S. Walker. 8°. *Austin, J. Walker*, 1837.
[3 copies].

THOMPSON (Isaac Grant). A practical treatise on the law of highways, including ways, bridges, turnpikes, and plank roads, at common law and under the statutes. viii, 508 pp. 8°. *Albany, Weare C. Little*, 1868.

TILSLEY (Hugh). A treatise on the stamp laws in Great Britain and Ireland: being an analytical digest of the statutes and cases. 2d ed. xxiv, 896 pp. 8°. *London, Stevens & Norton*, 1840.

TOTHILL (William). The transactions of the high court of chancery, both by practice and precedent, with the fees thereunto belonging, and all special orders in extraordinary cases. Reviewed by sir R. O. Holdbourne. 2 p. l. 192, 61 pp. 12°. *London, S. Sweet*, 1820.

TOWNSHEND (John). A treatise on the wrongs called slander and libel, and on the remedy by civil action for those wrongs. li, 545 pp. 8°. *New York, Baker, Voorhis & co.* 1868.

TRANSCRIPT appeals. The file of opinions in cases argued before the court of appeals of the state of New York, during the January, March, June, and September terms, 1867, and January term, 1868. From original copies certified by Joel Tiffany, state reporter. 5 v. 8°. *New York, for the transcript association*, 1868.

TRIALS for treason, from 1678 to 1683. 6 v. fol. *London, Robert Pawlet, Thomas Dring, etc.* 1678-85.

TROUBAT (Francis J.) *and* HALY (W. W.) The practice in civil actions and proceedings in the supreme court of Pennsylvania, in the district court and court of common pleas for the city and county of Philadelphia, and in the courts of the United States. 4th ed. enlarged and rewritten, by A. I. Fish. v. 2. xlviii, 904 pp. 8°. *Philadelphia, Kay & bro.* 1868.

TURKEY. Khathy humaïoun; ou charte impériale ottomane du 18 Février 1856, en Français et en Turc; suivie de la prononciation du Turc figurée en lettres françaises, de notes et d'explications. Par T. X. Bianchi. xiv, 25 pp. obl. 8°. *Paris, veuve Dondey-Dupré*, 1856.

TURNBULL (Stephen H.) Practice of the district courts of the city of New York; the acts relative to the marine court, and an appendix, [containing rules of court]. 208 pp. 8°. *New York, John S. Voorhies*, 1864.

TYLER (Ransom H.) Commentaries on the law of infancy, including guardianship and custody of infants, and the law of coverture, embracing dower, marriage, and divorce, and the statutory policy of the several states in respect to husband and wife. xxxi, 970 pp. 8°. *Albany, W. Gould & son*, 1868.

UNITED STATES. Laws of the United States relative to naturalization. Published by authority of a resolution of congress. 72 pp. 8°. *Washington, Gales & Seaton*, 1816.

——— Laws relating to Indian affairs, passed since 1826; and treaties with Indian tribes, concluded since 1830. 98 pp. 8°. *Washington, Francis P. Blair*, 1833.

——— The statutes at large, treaties, and proclamations of the United States of America. 1865-67. v. 14. 8°. *Boston, Little, Brown & co.* 1868.
[12 copies].

——— The same, for the 2d session of the 40th Congress, 1867-68. 8°. *Boston, Little, Brown & co.* 1868.

——— *Patent office.* Rules and directions for proceedings in the patent office. 24 pp. 8°. [*Washington*, 1854].

——— *Post office department.* Laws and regulations for the government of the post office department. 1 p. l. 61, 59, 39 pp. 8°. *Washington, Alexander & Barnard*, 1843. S.

——— *Supreme court.* Rules of practice of the supreme court of the United States, and of the circuit and district courts in equity and admiralty jurisdiction. 97 pp. 8°. *Washington, Gideon & co.* 1852.

——— *Treasury department.* Acts of congress, and rules and regulations prescribed by the secretary of the treasury, in pursuance thereto, with the approval of the president, concerning commercial intercourse with and in states and parts of states declared in insurrection, captured, abandoned, and confiscable property, the care of freedmen, and the purchase of products of insurrectionary districts on government account. 8°. *Washington, government printing office*, 1868.

UNITED STATES digest. v. 24. Annual digest for 1864. By H. Farnham Smith. 8°. *Boston, Little, Brown & co.* 1869.
[4 copies].

——— The same. v. 25. Annual digest for 1865. By Henry W. Frost. 8°. *Boston, Little, Brown & co.* 1868.
[4 copies].

UTAH (*Territory of*). Laws, 1852-66. viii, 247 pp. 8°. *Salt Lake city, H. McEwan*, 1866.

VAN WETTER (Polynice, *LL.D.*) Traité de la possession en droit romain. [Dissertation inaugurale pour le doctorat en droit romain]. 3 p. l. 311 pp. 8°. *Gand, C. Annoat-Brœckman*, 1868. s.

VAN WETTER (P. A. H.) Droit d'accroissement entre colégataires. 434 pp. 8°. *Bruxelles, T. Lesigne*, 1866. s.

VAUX (Richard). Reports of some of the criminal cases on primary hearing. Together with some remarks on the writ of habeas corpus, and forms of proceeding in criminal cases. 2 p. l. 236 pp. 8°. *Philadelphia, T. & J. W. Johnson*, 1846.

VENATORIUS (Daniël). Arnoldi Corvini a Belderen, Venatorius illustratus, hoc est, D. Venatorii methodica codicis Justinianei enarratio; ita emendata ut plane nova videatur. 12 p. l. 635 pp. 18°. *Lugduni Batavorum, H. Verbiest*, 1656.

VERMONT reports. v. 40. By Wheelock G. Veazey. 8°. *Rutland, Tuttle & co.* 1868.

VILLETTE (*Rev.* John). The annals of Newgate; or, malefactor's register. Containing a particular account of the lives, transactions, and trials of the most notorious malefactors who have suffered an ignominious death for their offences, etc. 4 v. 34 pl. 8°. *London, J. Wenman*, 1776.

WAITZ (Georg). Das alte recht der salischen Franken. Eine beilage zur deutschen verfassungsgeschichte. x, 304 pp. 8°. *Kiel, Schwers'sche buchandlung*, 1846.

WALLACE (Henry E.) *See* PHILADELPHIA reports. v. 4-5.

WALLACE (John William). Cases argued and adjudged in the supreme court of the United States, December term, 1867. v. 6. 8°. *Washington, W. H. & O. H. Morrison*, 1868.
[20 copies].

WASHBURN (Emory). A treatise on the American law of real property. 3d ed. 3 v. 8°. *Boston, Little, Brown & co.* 1868.

WEBSTER (*Miss* Delia A.) Kentucky jurisprudence, a history of the trial of miss Delia A. Webster, at Lexington, Ky. Dec'r 17-21, 1844, before the hon. Richard Buckner. On a charge of aiding slaves to escape from that commonwealth, with miscellaneous remarks, including her views of American slavery. Written by herself. 84 pp. 12°. *Vergennes, E. W. Blaisdell*, 1845.

WEDGWOOD (William B.) The government and laws of the United States, comprising a complete and comprehensive view of the rise, progress, and present organization of the state and national governments. 5th ed. revised and enlarged. 485, 7, 4 pp. 8°. *New York, Banks and brothers*, 1868.

WEED (Thurlow). The great libel case of George Opdyke against Thurlow Weed. 156 pp. 8°. *New York, American news company*, 1865.

WEEKLY (The) notes: being notes of cases heard and determined by the house of lords, the superior courts of equity and common law, the courts of probate and divorce, and the admiralty court, 1866 and 1867. v. 1 and 2. 646 pp; 766 pp. 4°. *London, W. Clowes & sons*, 1866-67.
[No. 1 of v. 1. and nos. 22 and 48 of v. 2. wanting].

WEST VIRGINIA (*State of*). Laws, [sessional], 1868. 8°. *Wheeling, John Frew*, 1868.
[2 copies].

WHARTON (Francis). A treatise on the criminal law of the United States. 6th and revised ed. 2 v. lxxiii, 748 pp; lxii, 710 pp. 8°. *Philadelphia, Kay & brother*, 1868.

WETTER. *See* VAN WETTER.

WHITE (Joseph M.) Argument and opinion, with a preliminary historical exposition, [in the case of the heirs of P. F. Renault]. 51 pp. 8°. *New Orleans, Belin & co.* [*about* 1830].

WHITING (William). Argument, in the case of Ross Winans *v.* Orsamus Eaton, *et al.* *See* WINANS (Ross) *v.* EATON *et al.*

WIARDA (Tilemann Dothias). Willküren der Brockmänner, eines freyen friesischen volkes. Herausgegeben, übersetzt und erläutert. xxiv, 182 pp. 8°. *Berlin, G. Reimer*, 1820.

WILLIAM III. (*Prince of Orange, king of Great Britain*). Answer to the address of the lords and commons, 1689. 7 pp. fol. *London*, 1689.
[*With* GREAT BRITAIN. Address of the lords and commons, 1689. TRIALS for treason, v. 5].

WINANS (Ross) *v.* EATON (Orsamus), *et al.* Argument of William Whiting, for an alleged infringement of his [Winans'] patent for the eight-wheel railroad car. 170, 4 pp. 4 pl. 8°. *Boston, J. M. Hewes & co.* 1853. s.

WINSTON (———). Cases at law in the supreme court of North Carolina, June terms 1863 and 1864. v. 1. 8°. [*Raleigh*, 1865]?
[Imperfect: wanting title].

——— Cases in equity in the supreme court of North Carolina, June term, 1864. v. 1. 8°. [*Raleigh*, 1865]?
[Imperfect: wanting title].

WISCONSIN reports. v. 21. By O. M. Conover. 8°. *Madison, Atwood & Rublee*, 1868.
[2 copies].

WISEMAN (Sir Robert). The law of laws: or, the excellency of the civil law above all other humane laws whatsoever. Showing of how great use and necessity the civil law is to this nation. 6 p. l. 190 pp. 4 l. sm. 4°. *London, R. Royston*, 1657.

WOOD (Charles H.) *and* LONG (Joseph D.) A digest of the Illinois reports, from the earliest period to the year 1866. 2d and revised ed. [of v. 1]. 2 v. 689 pp; 689-990 pp. 8°. *Chicago, by the authors*, 1867.

WORCESTER (*City of, Massachusetts*). Laws and ordinances, [with] the act to incorporate the town, and other special acts relating to the town and city; also, the revised charter, with an appendix containing a chronological view of the town [and] city, etc. Collated and revised by a special committee. 373 pp. 8°. *Worcester, Tyler & Seagrave*, 1867.

YALE (Gregory). Legal titles to mining claims and water rights in California, under the mining law of congress of July, 1866. xxiii, 452 pp. 8°. *San Francisco, A. Roman & co.* 1867.

www.ingramcontent.com/pod-product-compliance
Lightning Source LLC
LaVergne TN
LVHW020220110826
845151LV00003B/776

* 9 7 8 1 4 2 5 5 3 3 2 6 7 *